ROAD
BRITAIN

34th edition June 2019

© AA Media Limited 2019

Original edition printed 1986.

Cartography: All cartography in this atlas edited, designed and produced by the Mapping Services Department of AA Publishing (A05687).

This atlas contains Ordnance Survey data © Crown copyright and database right 2019 and Royal Mail data © Royal Mail copyright and database right 2019.

Contains public sector information licensed under the Open Government Licence v3.0

Ireland mapping and Distances and journey times contains data available from openstreetmap.org © under the Open Database License found at opendatacommons.org

Publisher's Notes: Published by AA Publishing (a trading name of AA Media Limited, whose registered office is Fanum House, Basing View, Basingstoke, Hampshire RG21 4EA, UK. Registered number 06112600).

ISBN: 978 0 7495 8135 0

A CIP catalogue record for this book is available from The British Library.

Acknowledgements: AA Publishing would like to thank the following for information used in the creation of this atlas: Cadw, English Heritage, Forestry Commission, Historic Scotland, National Trust and National Trust for Scotland, RSPB, The Wildlife Trust, Scottish Natural Heritage, Natural England, The Countryside Council for Wales. Award winning beaches from 'Blue Flag' and 'Keep Scotland Beautiful' (summer 2018 data): for latest information visit *www.blueflag.org* and *www.keepscotlandbeautiful.org*. Road signs are © Crown Copyright 2019. Reproduced under the terms of the Open Government Licence. Transport for London (Central London Map), Nexus (Newcastle district map).

Ireland mapping: Republic of Ireland census 2016 © Central Statistics Office and Northern Ireland census 2016 © NISRA (population data); Irish Public Sector Data (CC BY 4.0) (Gaeltacht); Logainm.ie (placenames); Roads Service and Transport Infrastructure Ireland

Printer: Rotolito SpA, Italy

Contents

Map pages	**inside front cover**
Route planning	**II–XVII**
Route planner	II–VII
Channel hopping and the Isle of Wight	VIII–IX
Ferries to Ireland and the Isle of Man	X
Scotland and North Sea ferries	XI
Caravan and camping sites in Britain	XII–XV
Traffic signs	XVI–XVII
Motorways	**XVIII–XXV**
Restricted junctions	XVIII–XXI
M25 London Orbital motorway	XXII
M6 Toll motorway	XXIII
Smart motorways	XXIV–XXV
Map pages	**XXVI**
Road map symbols	**1**
Road maps	**2–173**
Britain 1:200,000 scale Some islands are shown at slightly smaller scales	2–169
Ireland 1:1,000,000 scale	170–173
District maps	**174–185**
Birmingham	174–175
Glasgow	176–177
London	178–181
Manchester	182–183
Tyne & Wear	184–185
Street map symbols	**186**
Towns, ports and airports	**187–237**
Town plans	188–234
Major airports	235–237
Port plans	VIII–XI
Channel Tunnel terminals	27
Central London	**238–253**
Central London street map	238–247
Central London index	248–253
Index to place names	**254–302**
County, administrative area map	254
Place name index	255–302
Distances and journey times	**inside back cover**

Scale 1:200,000
or 3.16 miles to 1 inch

REPUBLIC
OF
IRELAND

WALES

Cardigan Bay

Bristol Channel

ENGLISH

Map index page numbers

66 **68** **70**
Holyhead, Anglesey, Llandudno, Colwyn Bay, Rhyl, Birkenhead, Widnes, Warrington, Manchester
Bangor, Conwy, Abergele, Holywell, Ellesmere Port, Runcorn, Knutsford, Macclesfield
Bethesda, Denbigh, Mold, Queensferry, Northwich, Chester
Caernarfon, A5025, Ruthin, A494, Crewe, Kidsgrove, Congleton
SNOWDONIA, Betws-y-Coed, Wrexham, Nantwich, Newcastle-under-Lyme, STOKE-ON-TRENT
Pwllheli, Porthmadog, Llangollen, Whitchurch, Stone
Abersoch, Bala, Oswestry, Market Drayton, Stafford
Barmouth, Dolgellau, Welshpool, Newport, Cannock

54 **56** **58**
Machynlleth, Shrewsbury, Telford, WOLVERHAMPTON, Dudley
Newtown, Church Stretton, Bridgnorth, Stourbridge, Halesowen
Aberystwyth, Llangurig, Kidderminster
Llanidloes, Ludlow, Bromsgrove

42 **44** **46**
Aberaeron, New Quay, Tregaron, Llandrindod Wells, Leominster, Worcester, Redditch
Cardigan, Lampeter, Kington, Malvern
Newcastle Emlyn, Builth Wells, Hay-on-Wye, Hereford, Ledbury, Tewkesbury
Carmarthen, Llandovery, Brecon, Ross-on-Wye, Gloucester, Cheltenham
PEMBROKESHIRE COAST, Llandeilo, BRECON BEACONS, Abergavenny

40 **28** **30** **32**
St Davids, Fishguard, Haverfordwest, St Clears, Llanelli, Merthyr Tydfil, Monmouth, Stroud
Milford Haven, Pembroke Dock, Pembroke, Tenby, Swansea, Neath, Cwmbran, Chepstow
Port Talbot, Pontypridd, Newport, Avonmouth
Bridgend, CARDIFF, Clevedon, BRISTOL, Bath

18 **20**
Ilfracombe, Lynton, Minehead, Weston-super-Mare, Cheddar, Trowbridge
Lundy, EXMOOR, Glastonbury, Wells, Shepton Mallet, Frome, Warminster
16 Barnstaple, Bridgwater, Wincanton
Bideford, South Molton, Taunton, Yeovil, Shaftesbury

8 **10** **12**
Great Torrington, Tiverton, Ilminster, Crewkerne, Sherborne, Blandford Forum, Wimborne Minster
Bude, Hatherleigh, Crediton, Chard, Axminster, Bridport, Poole
Holsworthy, Okehampton, Exeter, Honiton, Lyme Regis, Dorchester, Bournemouth
4 Launceston, DARTMOOR, Weymouth

2 Isles of Scilly inset
Wadebridge, Bodmin, Tavistock, Exmouth, Dawlish
Cornwall Newquay, Buckfastleigh, Teignmouth, Newton Abbot, Torquay
Newquay, Liskeard, **6** Totnes, Paignton
St Austell, Saltash, PLYMOUTH, Torpoint
Redruth, Truro, Fowey, Kingsbridge, Dartmouth
Camborne, Falmouth
Penzance, Helston, Lizard
Land's End

Guernsey, Jersey, St-Malo
Channel Islands inset

Roscoff, Santander (Apr–Oct)

Rosslare

Legend

════	Motorway
════	Toll motorway
════	Primary route dual carriageway
────	Primary route single carriageway
────	Other A road
or V	Vehicle ferry
⛴	Fast vehicle ferry or catamaran
▨	National Park
16	Atlas page number

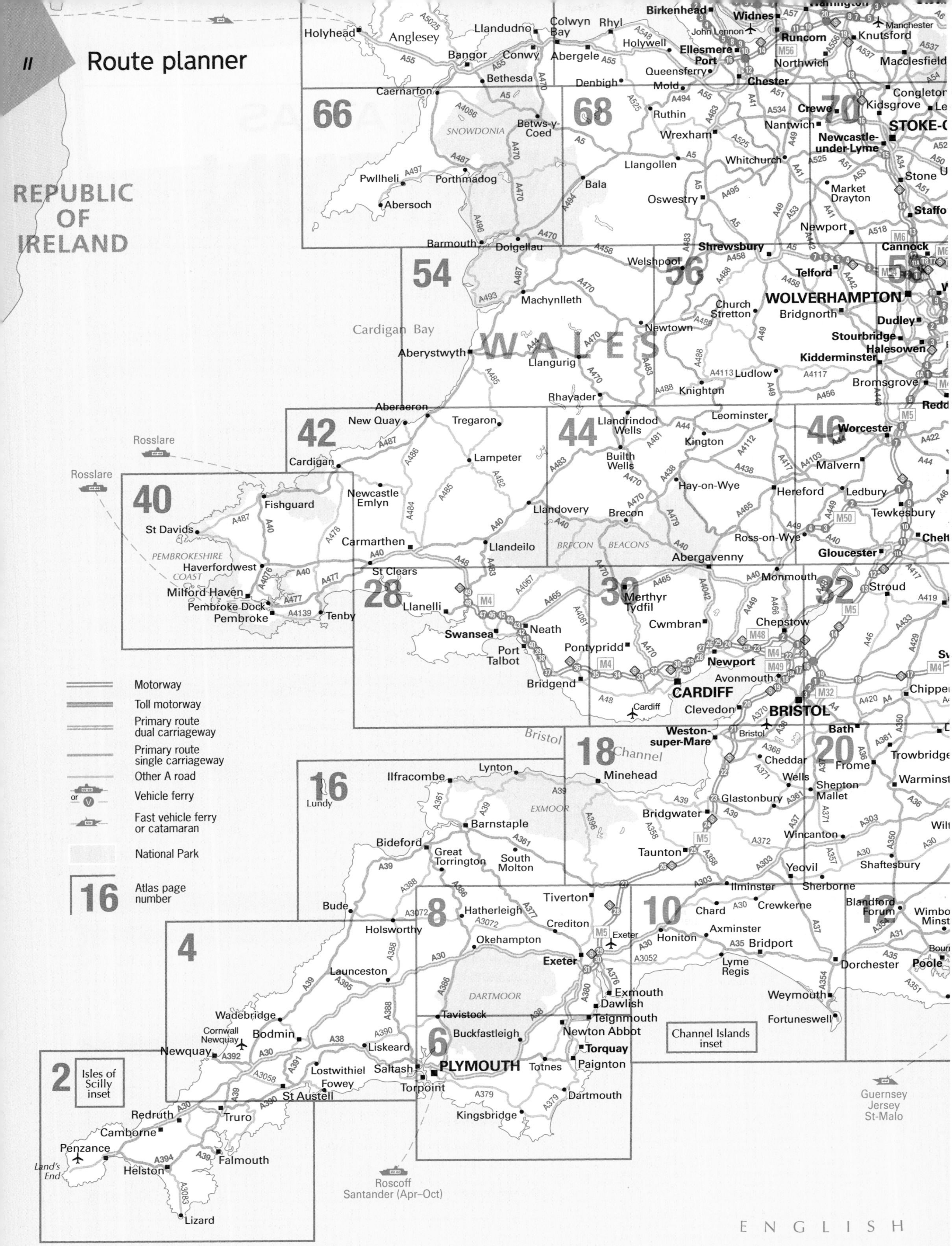

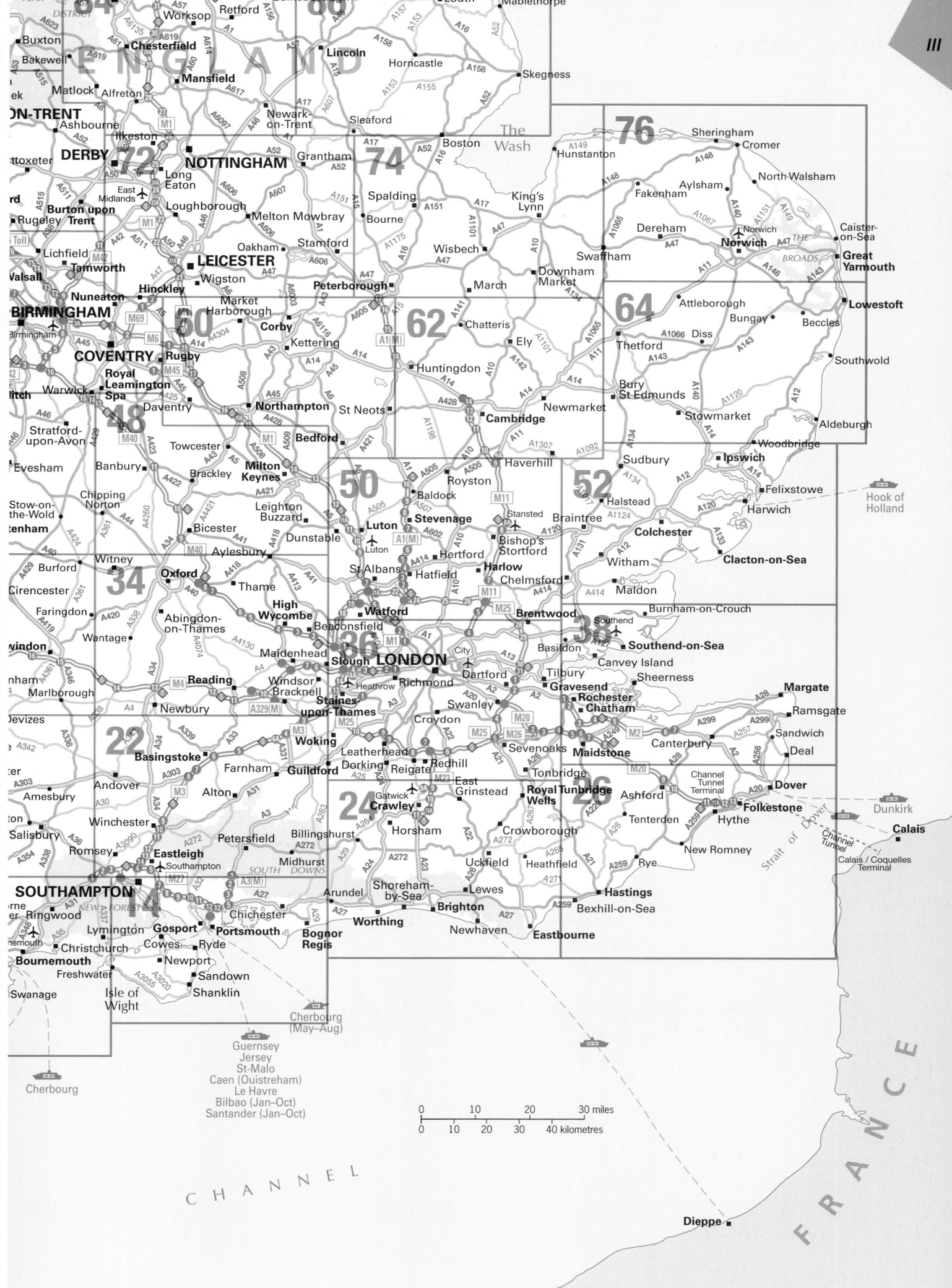

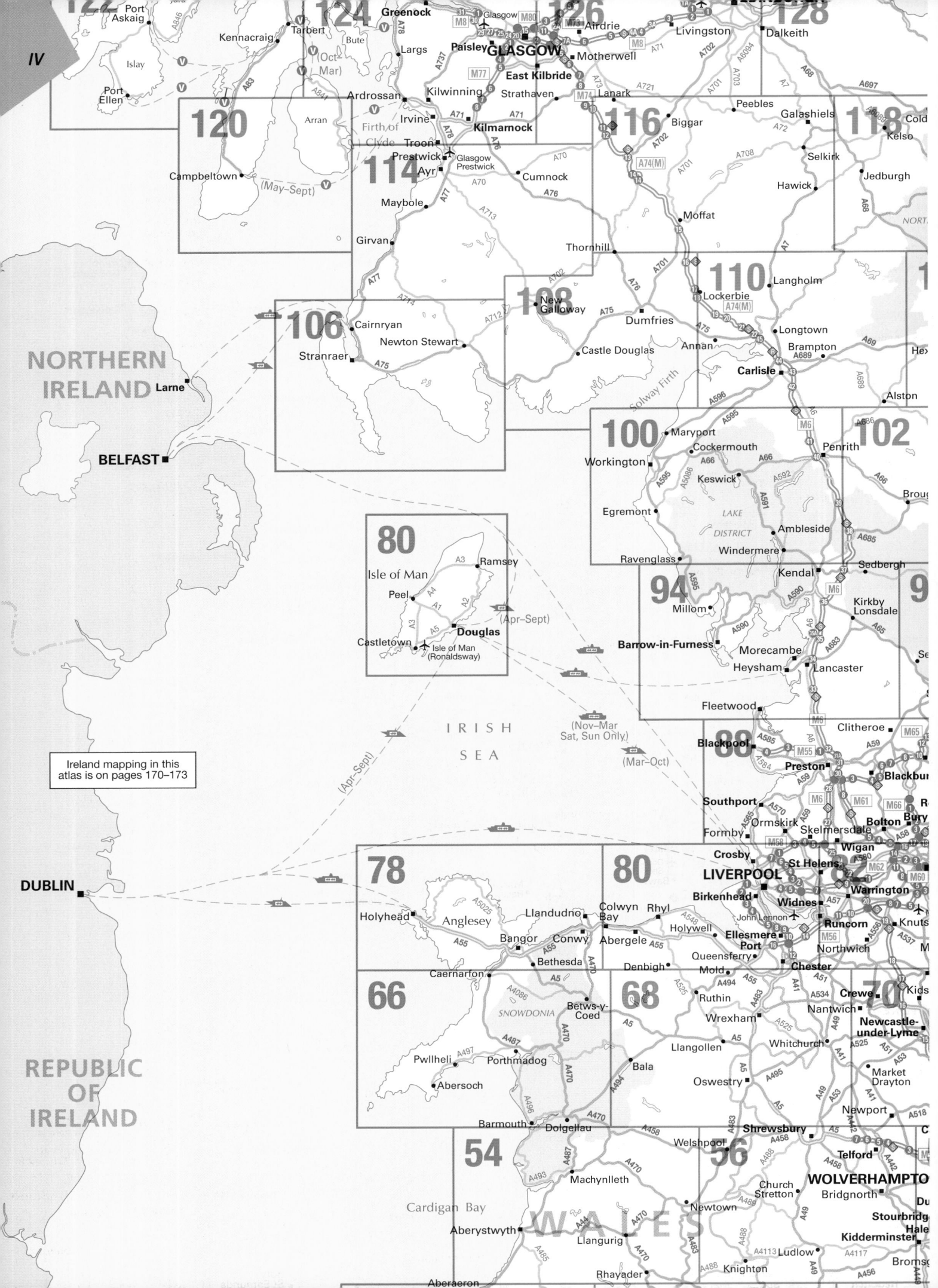

IV

122 Port Askaig
Kennacraig
Islay
Port Ellen

124 Greenock
Tarbert
Bute
Largs
Ardrossan
Irvine

126 Glasgow M80
Airdrie
Livingston
Dalkeith
M8
GLASGOW
Paisley
Motherwell
East Kilbride
Strathaven
Lanark

128
A702
Peebles
Galashiels
Biggar

120
Arran
Firth of Clyde
Kilwinning
Kilmarnock
Troon
Prestwick
Ayr

114
Glasgow Prestwick
Cumnock
Maybole
Girvan

116
M74
A74(M)
Moffat
Thornhill

118
Selkirk
Hawick
Jedburgh
Kelso
Cold
A68

NORTH

Campbeltown (May–Sept)

108 New Galloway
Dumfries
Castle Douglas

110 Langholm
Lockerbie
A74(M)
Annan
Longtown
Brampton
Carlisle

102
Alston
Hex

NORTHERN IRELAND
Larne

106 Cairnryan
Newton Stewart
Stranraer
A75

Solway Firth

100 Maryport
Cockermouth
Workington
Keswick
Egremont
LAKE DISTRICT
Ambleside
Windermere
Ravenglass

102 Penrith
A66
Broug

BELFAST

80 Isle of Man
Ramsey
Peel
Castletown
Douglas
Isle of Man (Ronaldsway)
(Apr–Sept)

94 Millom
Barrow-in-Furness
Kendal
Sedbergh
Kirkby Lonsdale
Morecambe
Heysham
Lancaster
Fleetwood

9

IRISH SEA

Ireland mapping in this atlas is on pages 170–173

(Nov–Mar Sat, Sun Only)
(Mar–Oct)

88 Clitheroe
M65
Blackpool
Preston
Blackbur
(Apr–Sept)

DUBLIN

78 Holyhead
Anglesey
Llandudno
Colwyn Bay
Rhyl
Bangor
Conwy
Abergele
Holywell
Bethesda
Denbigh
Caernarfon
Mold

80 LIVERPOOL
Crosby
St Helens
Birkenhead
Widnes
Ellesmere Port
Queensferry
Chester

82 Southport
Ormskirk
Skelmersdale
Formby
Wigan
Bolton
Bury
R
M58
M62
Runcorn
Knuts
Warrington
John Lennon
Northwich
M56

66 Snowdonia
Betws-y-Coed
Pwllheli
Porthmadog
Abersoch
Barmouth

68 Ruthin
Wrexham
Llangollen
Whitchurch
Bala
Oswestry
Llangurig

70 Crewe
Nantwich
Newcastle-under-Lyme
Kids
Market Drayton
Newport

54 Dolgellau
Machynlleth
Cardigan Bay
Aberystwyth

56 Welshpool
Shrewsbury
WALES
Newtown
Church Stretton
Bridgnorth
Llangurig
Rhayader
Knighton
Ludlow

WOLVERHAMPTON
Telford
Stourbridge
Hale
Kidderminster
Bromsgr

REPUBLIC OF IRELAND

Aberaeron

Eyemouth

Berwick-upon-Tweed

stream A1

Wooler A1

HUMBERLAND A697

Alnwick A1068

Otterburn Amble

12 A68 Morpeth Ashington

Newcastle A19 Tynemouth

A69 North Shields **South Shields**

Corbridge A69 **Gateshead** **NEWCASTLE UPON TYNE** Amsterdam (IJmuiden)

ham A695 **SUNDERLAND**

Consett A692 Chester-le-Street

Durham A1

A689 **104** **Hartlepool**

Bishop Auckland A689

Barnard A688 **Stockton-on-Tees** **Middlesbrough**

Castle A66 **Darlington**

gh A66 A66 A174 Whitby

Richmond Durham Guisborough A171

Tees Valley A172 **NORTH YORK**

A19 A172 **MOORS** A169 A171

YORKSHIRE A684 Northallerton

6 DALES A684 Leyburn A170 Scarborough

Thirsk **98** Pickering Filey

Ripon A1(M) Helmsley A170

A61 A168 Easingwold A64 Malton Bridlington

A59 A19 A166 A614 Driffield

Skipton A59 Harrogate A1079 A614 A165

A65 A65 Leeds Wetherby **York** Market A164

Keighley A658 Bradford Weighton Beverley

9 **BRADFORD** **LEEDS** A1(M) Selby **92** A1079 A164 A63 Withernsea

Burnley Halifax M1 A63 A1035 **KINGSTON**

A646 M62 Pontefract M62 Goole A15 **UPON HULL**

ochdale M62 **Wakefield** M18 Thorne **Scunthorpe** Immingham

Huddersfield A61 M1 **Barnsley** Humberside **Grimsby**

A62 A629 A635 **Doncaster** Brigg Cleethorpes Rotterdam (Europoort)

Oldham A628 Doncaster A159 A46 A18 Zeebrugge

MANCHESTER A616 Sheffield A15

Glossop Rotherham Bawtry Market A1031

Stockport **SHEFFIELD** A1(M) Rasen Louth Mablethorpe

PEAK **54** A57 A631 Gainsborough A157 A153

Manchester DISTRICT Worksop A156 Retford A16 A52

ford A537 A6135 A1 A158 Skegness

acclesfield Buxton A619 **Chesterfield** A614 **Lincoln** Horncastle A158

Bakewell **ENGLAND** A60 A15 A153 A155

Congleton A515 Matlock Alfreton A617 A607 Skegness

grove Leek **Mansfield** Newark- A17

STOKE-ON-TRENT Ashbourne M1 A6097 on-Trent Sleaford **The** **76** Sheringham Cromer

A52 Ilkeston A46 Boston **Wash** Hunstanton A149 A148

A50 **DERBY** **72** Grantham **74** A16 A148 Aylsham North Walsham

Stone Uttoxeter A52 A52 King's A148 Fakenham A140 A1151 A149

Stafford A515 Long A606 Spalding A151 Lynn A1065 Dereham Norwich Caister-

A51 Burton upon Eaton A607 Bourne A17 **Norwich** A47 THE on-Sea

annock Rugeley **Trent** M1 Loughborough A151 Wisbech A10 Swaffham BROADS **Great**

M6 Lichfield M42 Melton Mowbray A16 A47 A11 Yarmouth

M6 Toll A42 A511 Oakham Stamford Downham A146 A143

Walsall Tamworth A50 A46 **LEICESTER** A47 Market Peterborough **64** Attleborough **Lowestoft**

N Nuneaton Hinckley Wigston A6003 A47 March A1066 Bungay Beccles

dley **BIRMINGHAM** M69 **60** Market **62** Chatteris Diss

osowen Birmingham A45 M6 Harborough A605 A1(M) Ely Thetford A143

COVENTRY Rugby A14 Kettering A141 A1101 Southwold

M42 Royal M45 A508 A10 A142 Bury A140 A1120 A12

Redditch Warwick Leamington A45 A6 A14 A14 Huntingdon St Edmunds

Spa A425

	Motorway
	Toll motorway
	Primary route dual carriageway
	Primary route single carriageway
	Other A road
or V	Vehicle ferry
	Fast vehicle ferry or catamaran
	National Park
98	Atlas page number

0   10   20   30 miles
0   10   20   30   40 kilometres

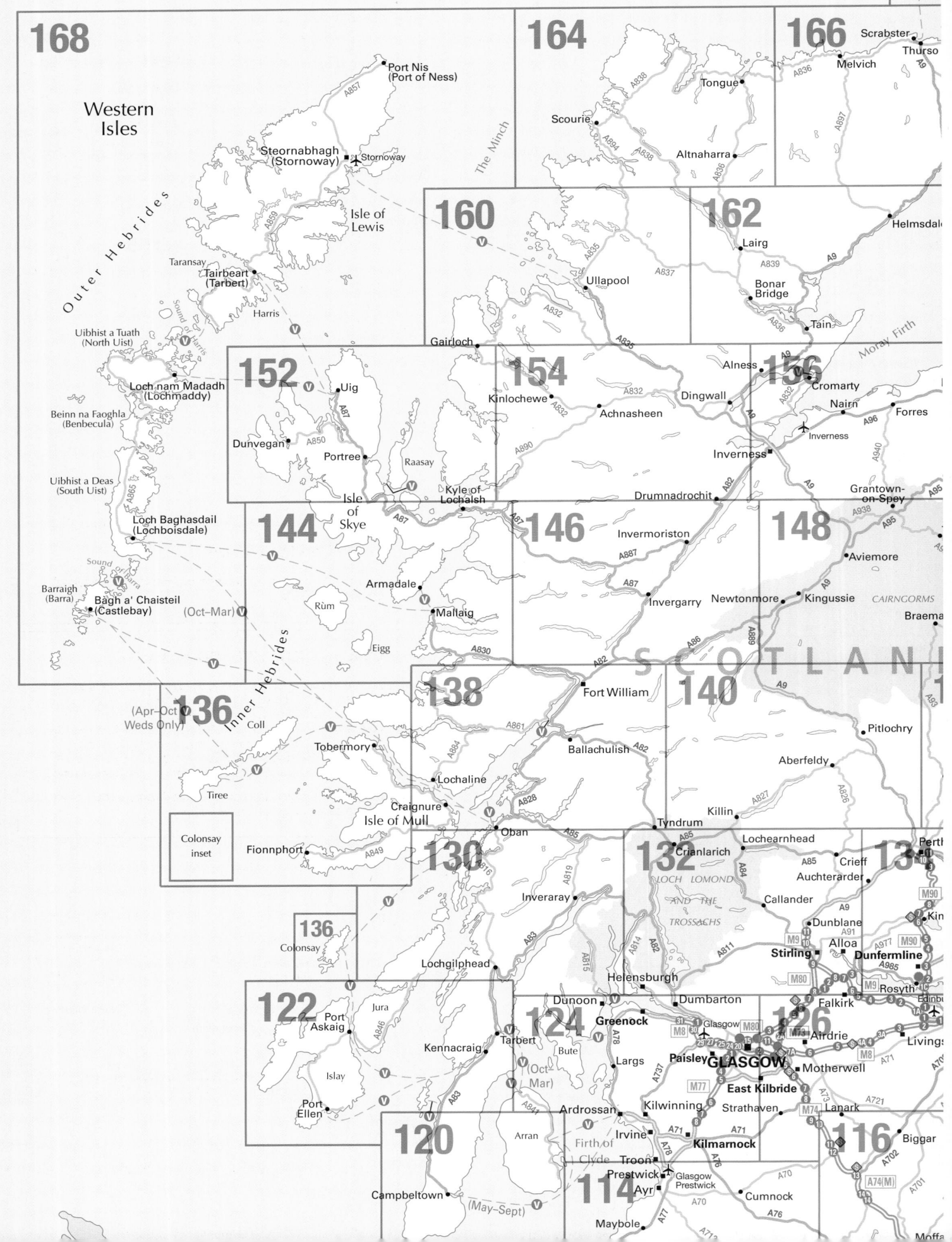

168 Western Isles

Outer Hebrides

Port Nis (Port of Ness)

Steornabhagh (Stornoway) ✈ Stornoway

Isle of Lewis

Taransay

Tairbeart (Tarbert)

Harris

Sound of Harris

Uibhist a Tuath (North Uist)

Beinn na Faoghla (Benbecula)

Loch nam Madadh (Lochmaddy)

Uibhist a Deas (South Uist)

Loch Baghasdail (Lochboisdale)

Sound of Barra

Barraigh (Barra)

Bàgh a' Chaisteil (Castlebay) (Oct–Mar)

136 (Apr–Oct Weds Only)

Inner Hebrides

Coll

Tobermory

Tiree

Colonsay inset

Fionnphort

152 Uig

Dunvegan

Portree

Raasay

Isle of Skye

Kyle of Lochalsh

144

Armadale

Rùm

Mallaig

Eigg

138 Fort William

Lochaline

Craignure

Isle of Mull

130 Oban

Inveraray

136 Colonsay

Lochgilphead

122 Port Askaig

Jura

Kennacraig

Islay

Port Ellen

120 Arran

Firth of Clyde

Campbeltown (May–Sept)

164

Scourie

Tongue

Altnaharra

The Minch

160 Ullapool

Gairloch

154 Kinlochewe

Achnasheen

146 Invermoriston

A887

Invergarry

162 Lairg

Bonar Bridge

Dingwall

Alness

Tain

Moray Firth

156 Cromarty

Nairn

Inverness ✈ Inverness

Drumnadrochit

148 Grantown-on-Spey

Aviemore

Newtonmore Kingussie

CAIRNGORMS

Braemar

S C O T L A N D

140 Pitlochry

Ballachulish

Aberfeldy

Killin

Tyndrum

132 Crianlarich

Lochearnhead

Callander

LOCH LOMOND AND THE TROSSACHS

Crieff

Auchterarder

13... Perth

Dunblane

Alloa

Dunfermline

Stirling

Rosyth

Helensburgh

Dunoon

Dumbarton

Falkirk

Edinb...

124 Greenock

Bute

Largs

126 GLASGOW

Paisley

Airdrie

Motherwell

East Kilbride

Livings...

Tarbert (Oct–Mar)

Kilwinning

Strathaven

Lanark

Ardrossan

Irvine

Kilmarnock

116 Biggar

Troon

Prestwick ✈ Glasgow Prestwick

Ayr

Cumnock

Maybole

Moffa...

166 Scrabster

Thurso

Melvich

16... Strom...

Helmsdale

114

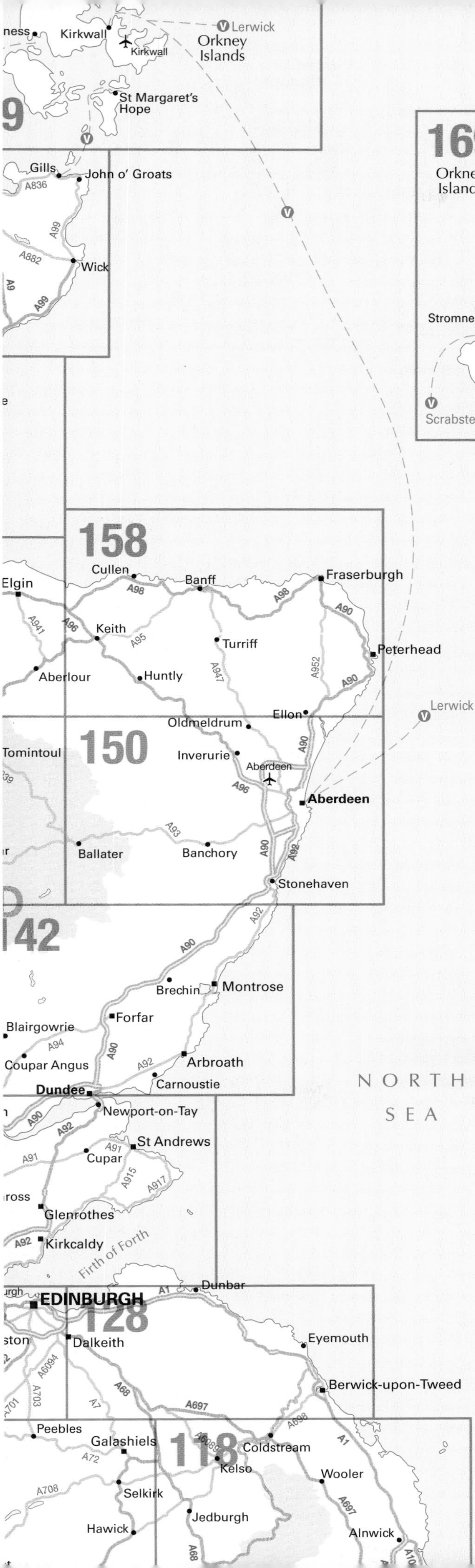

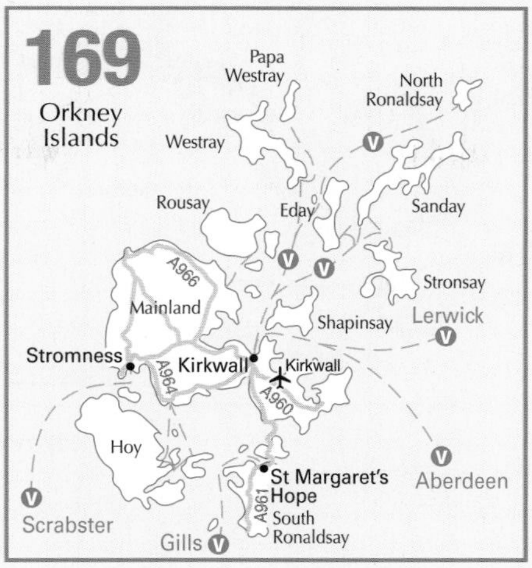

Kirkwall
Lerwick
Orkney Islands
Kirkwall
St Margaret's Hope
Gills
John o' Groats
Wick

169
Orkney Islands

Papa Westray
North Ronaldsay
Westray
Rousay
Eday
Sanday
Stronsay
Mainland
Shapinsay
Lerwick
Stromness
Kirkwall
Kirkwall
Hoy
St Margaret's Hope
South Ronaldsay
Scrabster
Gills
Aberdeen

169
Shetland Islands

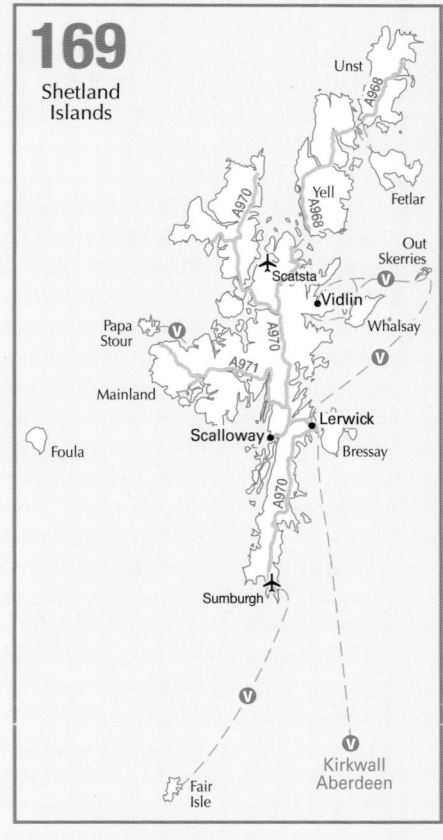

Unst
Scatsta
Yell
Fetlar
Out Skerries
Papa Stour
Vidlin
Whalsay
Mainland
Scalloway
Lerwick
Bressay
Foula
Sumburgh
Fair Isle
Kirkwall
Aberdeen

158
Cullen
Banff
Fraserburgh
Elgin
Keith
Turriff
Peterhead
Aberlour
Huntly
Ellon
Lerwick
Oldmeldrum

150
Tomintoul
Inverurie
Aberdeen
Aberdeen
Ballater
Banchory
Stonehaven

142
Brechin
Montrose
Forfar
Blairgowrie
Coupar Angus
Arbroath
Carnoustie
Dundee
Newport-on-Tay
St Andrews
Cupar
Glenrothes
Kirkcaldy
Firth of Forth

NORTH SEA

FERRY INFORMATION

Information on ferry routes and operators can be found on pages VIII–XI.

EMERGENCY DIVERSION ROUTES

In an emergency it may be necessary to close a section of motorway or other main road to traffic, so a temporary sign may advise drivers to follow a diversion route. To help drivers navigate the route, black symbols on yellow patches may be permanently displayed on existing direction signs, including motorway signs. Symbols may also be used on separate signs with yellow backgrounds.

For further information see *theaa.com/breakdown-cover/advice/emergency-diversion-routes*

EDINBURGH
Dalkeith
Eyemouth
Dunbar
Berwick-upon-Tweed
Peebles
Galashiels
Coldstream
Kelso
Selkirk
Wooler
Hawick
Jedburgh
Alnwick

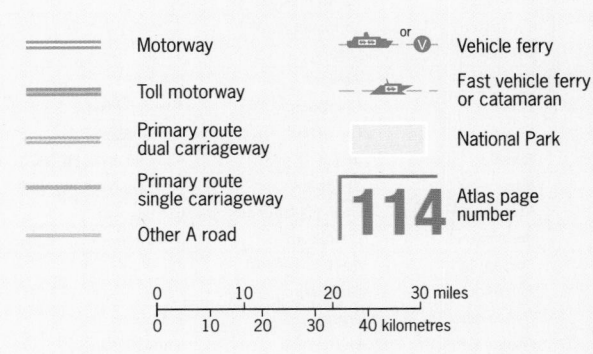

Motorway
Toll motorway
Primary route dual carriageway
Primary route single carriageway
Other A road
Vehicle ferry
Fast vehicle ferry or catamaran
National Park
114 Atlas page number

0 10 20 30 miles
0 10 20 30 40 kilometres

Channel hopping and the Isle of Wight

For business or pleasure, hopping on a ferry across to France, the Channel Islands or Isle of Wight has never been easier.

The vehicle ferry services listed in the table give you all the options, together with detailed port plans to help you navigate to and from the ferry terminals. Simply choose your preferred route, not forgetting the fast sailings (see 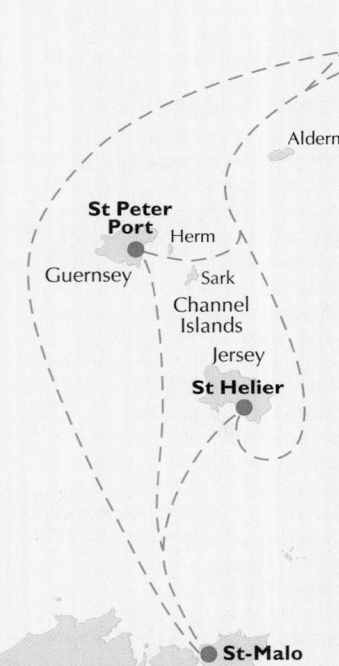).
Bon voyage!

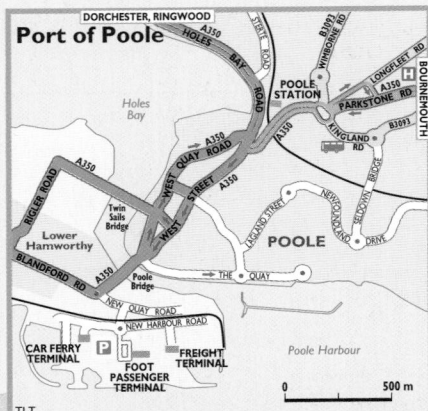

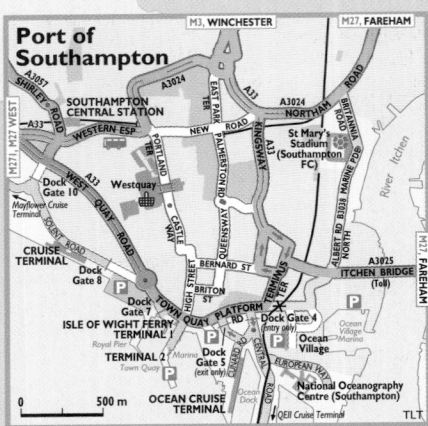

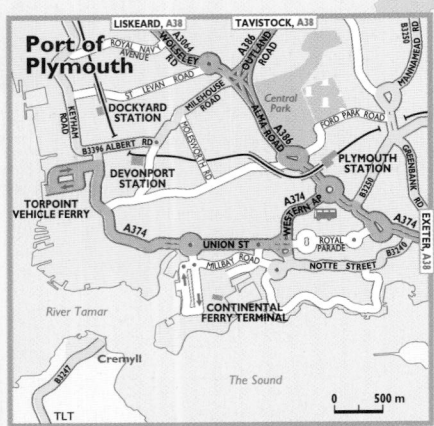

ENGLISH CHANNEL AND ISLE OF WIGHT FERRY CROSSINGS

From	To	Journey time	Operator website
Dover	Calais	1 hr 30 mins	dfdsseaways.co.uk
Dover	Calais	1 hr 30 mins	poferries.com
Dover	Dunkirk	2 hrs	dfdsseaways.co.uk
Folkestone	Calais (Coquelles)	35 mins	eurotunnel.com
Lymington	Yarmouth (IOW)	40 mins	wightlink.co.uk
Newhaven	Dieppe	4 hrs	dfdsseaways.co.uk
Plymouth	Roscoff	6–8 hrs	brittany-ferries.co.uk
Poole	Cherbourg	4 hrs 15 mins	brittany-ferries.co.uk
Poole	Guernsey	3 hrs	condorferries.co.uk
Poole	Jersey	4 hrs 30 mins	condorferries.co.uk
Poole	St-Malo	7–12 hrs (via Channel Is.)	condorferries.co.uk
Portsmouth	Caen (Ouistreham)	6–7 hrs	brittany-ferries.co.uk
Portsmouth	Cherbourg	3 hrs (May–Aug)	brittany-ferries.co.uk
Portsmouth	Fishbourne (IOW)	45 mins	wightlink.co.uk
Portsmouth	Guernsey	7 hrs	condorferries.co.uk
Portsmouth	Jersey	8–11 hrs	condorferries.co.uk
Portsmouth	Le Havre	5 hrs 30 mins	brittany-ferries.co.uk
Portsmouth	St-Malo	9–11 hrs	brittany-ferries.co.uk
Southampton	East Cowes (IOW)	1 hr	redfunnel.co.uk

The information listed is provided as a guide only, as services are liable to change at short notice. Services shown are for vehicle ferries only, operated by conventional ferry unless indicated as a fast ferry service (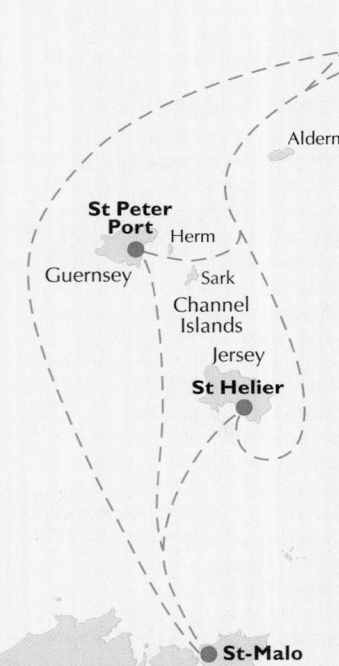). Please check sailings before planning your journey.

Travelling further afield? For ferry services to Northern Spain see brittany-ferries.co.uk.

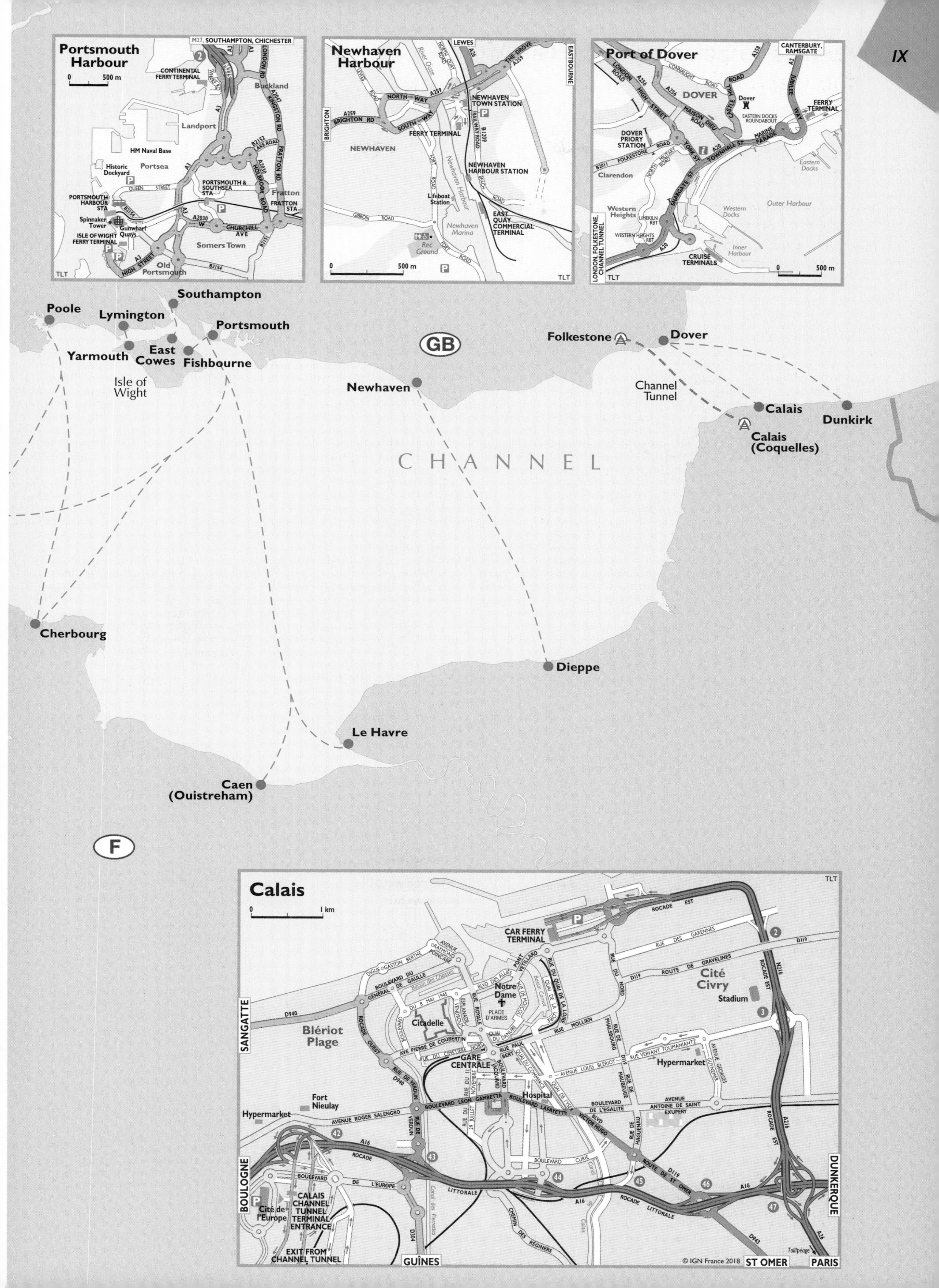

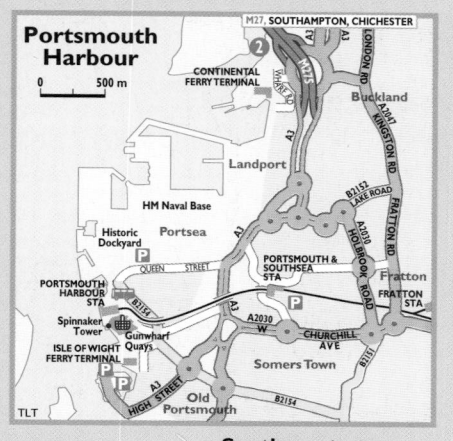

Portsmouth Harbour
0 500 m
M27, SOUTHAMPTON, CHICHESTER
CONTINENTAL FERRY TERMINAL
Buckland
Landport
HM Naval Base
Historic Dockyard
Portsea
QUEEN STREET
PORTSMOUTH & SOUTHSEA STA
Fratton
FRATTON STA
PORTSMOUTH HARBOUR STA
Spinnaker Tower
Gunwharf Quays
ISLE OF WIGHT FERRY TERMINAL
CHURCHILL AVE
Somers Town
HIGH STREET
Old Portsmouth
KINGSTON RD
FRATTON RD
LONDON RD
HOLBROOK ROAD
LAKE ROAD
TLT
Newhaven Harbour
LEWES
EASTBOURNE
BRIGHTON
BRIGHTON RD
NORTH WAY
SOUTH WAY
THE DROVE
River Ouse
NEWHAVEN TOWN STATION
FERRY TERMINAL
NEWHAVEN
RAILWAY ROAD
NEWHAVEN HARBOUR STATION
Newhaven Harbour
Lifeboat Station
GIBBON ROAD
FORT ROAD
BEACH ROAD
EAST QUAY COMMERCIAL TERMINAL
Newhaven Marina
Rec Ground
0 500 m
TLT
Port of Dover
CANTERBURY, RAMSGATE
LONDON ROAD
HIGH STREET
CONNAUGHT ROAD
CASTLE HILL ROAD
JUBILEE WAY
DOVER
Dover
MAISON DIEU ROAD
EASTERN DOCKS ROUNDABOUT
FERRY TERMINAL
DOVER PRIORY STATION
FOLKESTONE ROAD
YORK ST
TOWNWALL ST
MARINE PARADE
Clarendon
NORTH MILITARY ROAD
SNARGATE ST
Eastern Docks
Western Heights
LIMEKILN RBT
WESTERN HEIGHTS RBT
Western Docks
Outer Harbour
Inner Harbour
CRUISE TERMINALS
LONDON, FOLKESTONE, CHANNEL TUNNEL
0 500 m
TLT
Poole
Lymington
Southampton
Portsmouth
Yarmouth
East Cowes
Fishbourne
Isle of Wight
GB
Newhaven
Folkestone
Dover
Channel Tunnel
Calais
Dunkirk
Calais (Coquelles)
CHANNEL
Cherbourg
Dieppe
Le Havre
Caen (Ouistreham)
F
Calais
0 1 km
TLT
CAR FERRY TERMINAL
ROCADE EST
RUE DES GARENNES
ROUTE DE GRAVELINES
Cité Civry
Stadium
SANGATTE
DIGUE GASTON BERTHE
AVENUE RAYMOND POINCARÉ
BOULEVARD DU GÉNÉRAL DE GAULLE
Notre Dame
PLACE D'ARMES
Citadelle
Blériot Plage
ROCADE OUEST
RUE ROYALE
QUAI DU DANUBE
RUE MOLLIEN
RUE DU NORD
RUE DE PHALSBOURG
RUE VERVANT TOUMANIANTZ
Hypermarket
AVENUE LOUIS BLÉRIOT
GARE CENTRALE
Hospital
BOULEVARD LÉON GAMBETTA
BOULEVARD LAFAYETTE
BOULEVARD JACQUARD
BOULEVARD DE L'EGALITÉ
AVENUE ANTOINE DE SAINT EXUPÉRY
Fort Nieulay
Hypermarket
AVENUE ROGER SALENGRO
RUE DE VERDUN
BOULEVARD CURIE
ROUTE DE ST OMER
BOULEVARD DE L'EUROPE
ROCADE LITTORALE
BOULOGNE
Cité de l'Europe
CALAIS CHANNEL TUNNEL TERMINAL ENTRANCE
EXIT FROM CHANNEL TUNNEL
GUÎNES
CHEMIN DES RÉGINERS
ST OMER
PARIS
DUNKERQUE
Tollpéage
© IGN France 2018

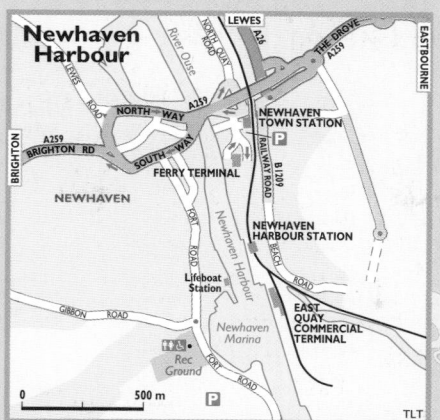

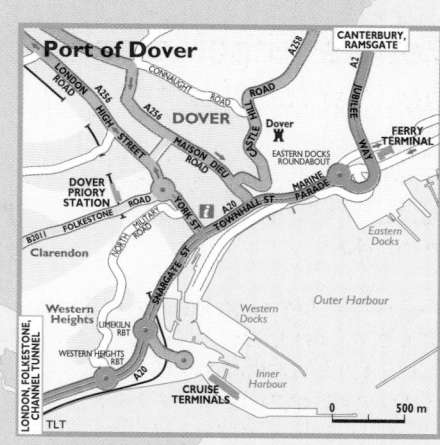

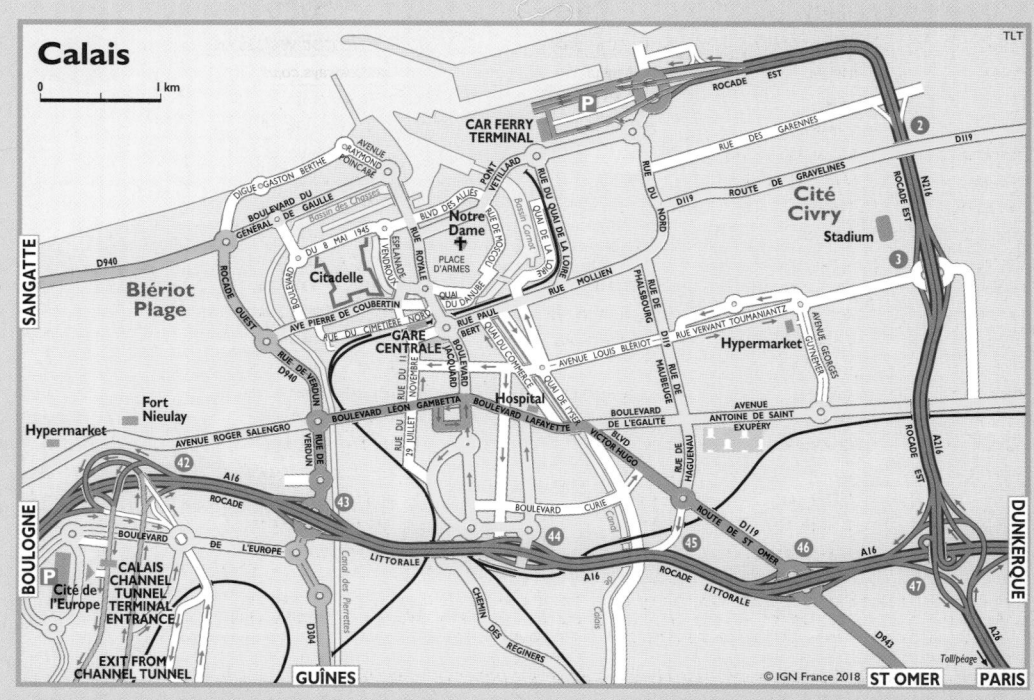

Ferries to Ireland and the Isle of Man

With so many sea crossings to Ireland and the Isle of Man the information provided in the table to the right will help you make the right choice.

IRISH SEA FERRY CROSSINGS

From	To	Journey time	Operator website
Cairnryan	Belfast	2 hrs 15 mins 🚢	stenaline.co.uk
Cairnryan	Larne	2 hrs	poferries.com
Douglas	Belfast	2 hrs 45 mins (April–Sept) 🚢	steam-packet.com
Douglas	Dublin	2 hrs 55 mins (April–Sept) 🚢	steam-packet.com
Fishguard	Rosslare	3 hrs 15 mins	stenaline.co.uk
Heysham	Douglas	3 hrs 45 mins	steam-packet.com
Holyhead	Dublin	2 hrs 🚢	irishferries.com
Holyhead	Dublin	3 hrs 15 mins	irishferries.com
Holyhead	Dublin	3 hrs 15 mins	stenaline.co.uk
Liverpool	Douglas	2 hrs 45 mins (Mar–Oct) 🚢	steam-packet.com
Liverpool	Dublin	8 hrs–8 hrs 30 mins	poferries.com
Liverpool (Birkenhead)	Belfast	8 hrs	stenaline.co.uk
Liverpool (Birkenhead)	Douglas	4 hrs 15 mins (Nov–Mar Sat, Sun only)	steam-packet.com
Pembroke Dock	Rosslare	4 hrs	irishferries.com

The information listed is provided as a guide only, as services are liable to change at short notice. Services shown are for vehicle ferries only, operated by conventional ferry unless indicated as a fast ferry service (🚢). Please check sailings before planning your journey.

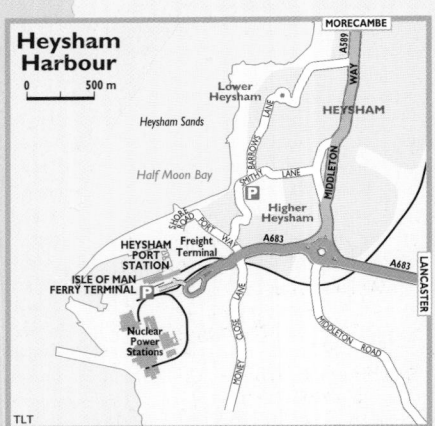
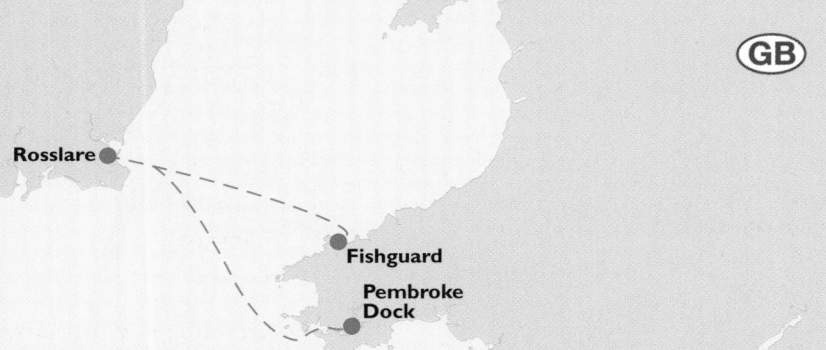
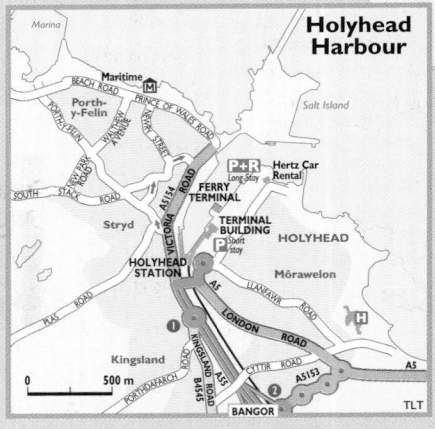
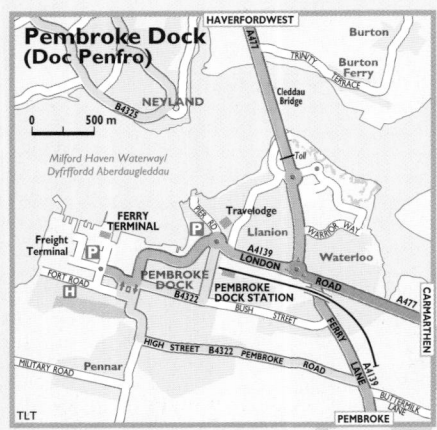
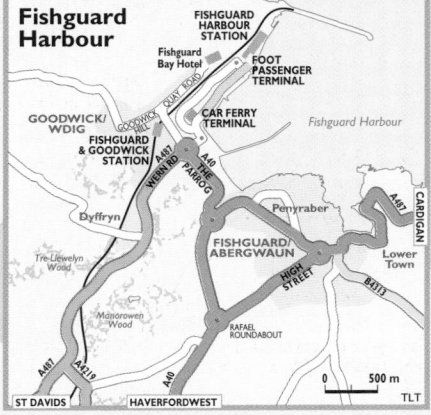

SCOTLAND FERRIES

From	To	Journey time	Operator website
Scottish Islands/west coast of Scotland			
Gourock	Dunoon	20 mins	*western-ferries.co.uk*
Glenelg	Skye	20 mins (Easter–Oct)	*skyeferry.co.uk*
Numerous and varied sailings from the west coast of Scotland to Scottish islands are provided by Caledonian MacBrayne. Please visit *calmac.co.uk* for all ferry information, including those of other operators.			
Orkney Islands			
Aberdeen	Kirkwall	6 hrs	*northlinkferries.co.uk*
Gills	St Margaret's Hope	1 hr	*pentlandferries.co.uk*
Scrabster	Stromness	1 hr 30 mins	*northlinkferries.co.uk*
Lerwick	Kirkwall	5 hrs 30 mins	*northlinkferries.co.uk*
Inter-island services are operated by Orkney Ferries. Please see *orkneyferries.co.uk* for details.			
Shetland Islands			
Aberdeen	Lerwick	12 hrs 30 mins	*northlinkferries.co.uk*
Kirkwall	Lerwick	7 hrs 45 mins	*northlinkferries.co.uk*
Inter-island services are operated by Shetland Island Council Ferries. Please see *shetland.gov.uk/ferries* for details.			

Please note that some smaller island services are day dependent and reservations are required for some routes. Book and confirm sailing schedules by contacting the operator.

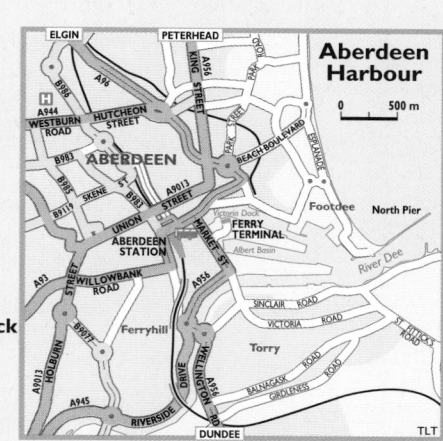

Aberdeen Harbour

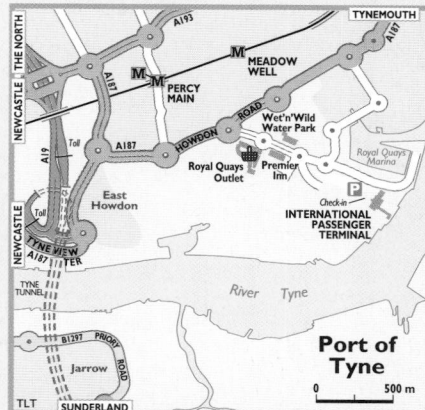

Port of Tyne

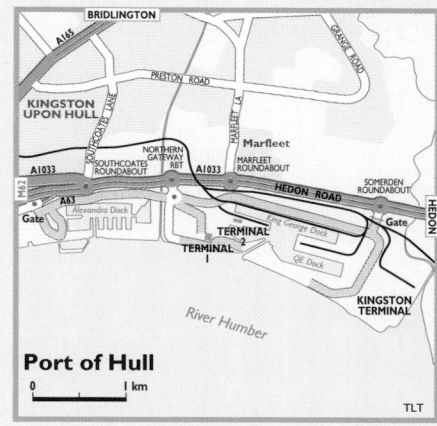

Port of Hull

For a port plan of Harwich see atlas page 53

NORTH SEA FERRY CROSSINGS

From	To	Journey time	Operator website
Harwich	Hook of Holland	7–8 hrs	*stenaline.co.uk*
Kingston upon Hull	Rotterdam (Europoort)	12 hrs	*poferries.com*
Kingston upon Hull	Zeebrugge	12 hrs	*poferries.com*
Newcastle upon Tyne	Amsterdam (IJmuiden)	15 hrs 30 mins	*dfdsseaways.co.uk*

The information listed on this page is provided as a guide only, as services are liable to change at short notice. Services shown are for vehicle ferries only, operated by conventional ferry. Please check sailings before planning your journey.

Caravan and camping sites in Britain

These pages list the top 300 AA-inspected Caravan and Camping (C & C) sites in the Pennant rating scheme. **Five Pennant Premier sites are shown in green,** Four Pennant sites are shown in blue.

Listings include addresses, telephone numbers and websites together with page and grid references to locate the sites in the atlas. The total number of touring pitches is also included for each site, together with the type of pitch available. The following abbreviations are used: **C = Caravan CV = Campervan T = Tent**
To find out more about the AA's Pennant rating scheme and other rated caravan and camping sites not included on these pages please visit **theAA.com**

ENGLAND

Alders Caravan Park
Home Farm, Alne, York
YO61 1RY
Tel: 01347 838722   **97 R7**
alderscaravanpark.co.uk
Total Pitches: 87 (C, CV & T)

Andrewshayes Holiday Park
Dalwood, Axminster
EX13 7DY
Tel: 01404 831225   **10 E5**
andrewshayes.co.uk
Total Pitches: 150 (C, CV & T)

Apple Tree Park C & C Site
A38, Claypits, Stonehouse
GL10 3AL
Tel: 01452 742362   **32 E3**
appletreepark.co.uk
Total Pitches: 65 (C, CV & T)

Atlantic Bays Holiday Park
St Merryn, Padstow
PL28 8PY
Tel: 01841 520855   **4 D7**
atlanticbaysholidaypark.co.uk
Total Pitches: 70 (C, CV & T)

Ayr Holiday Park
St Ives, Cornwall
TR26 1EJ
Tel: 01736 795855   **2 E5**
ayrholidaypark.co.uk
Total Pitches: 40 (C, CV & T)

Back of Beyond Touring Park
234 Ringwood Road,
St Leonards, Dorset
BH24 2SB
Tel: 01202 876968   **13 K4**
backofbeyondtouringpark.co.uk
Total Pitches: 80 (C, CV & T)

Bagwell Farm Touring Park
Knights in the Bottom,
Chickerell, Weymouth
DT3 4EA
Tel: 01305 782575   **11 N8**
bagwellfarm.co.uk
Total Pitches: 320 (C, CV & T)

Bardsea Leisure Park
Priory Road, Ulverston
LA12 9QE
Tel: 01229 584712   **94 F5**
bardsealeisure.co.uk
Total Pitches: 83 (C & CV)

Barn Farm Campsite
Barn Farm, Birchover, Matlock
DE4 2BL
Tel: 01629 650245   **84 B8**
barnfarmcamping.com
Total Pitches: 62 (C, CV & T)

Bath Chew Valley Caravan Park
Ham Lane,
Bishop Sutton
BS39 5TZ
Tel: 01275 332127   **19 Q3**
bathchewvalley.co.uk
Total Pitches: 45 (C, CV & T)

Bay View Holiday Park
Bolton le Sands, Carnforth
LA5 9TN
Tel: 01524 732854   **95 K7**
holgates.co.uk
Total Pitches: 100 (C, CV & T)

Beacon Cottage Farm Touring Park
Beacon Drive, St Agnes
TR5 0NU
Tel: 01872 552347   **3 J3**
beaconcottagefarmholidays.co.uk
Total Pitches: 70 (C, CV & T)

Beaconsfield Farm Caravan Park
Battlefield,
Shrewsbury
SY4 4AA
Tel: 01939 210370   **69 P11**
beaconsfieldholidaypark.co.uk
Total Pitches: 60 (C & CV)

Beech Croft Farm
Beech Croft,
Blackwell in the Peak,
Buxton
SK17 9TQ
Tel: 01298 85330   **83 P10**
beechcroftfarm.co.uk
Total Pitches: 30 (C, CV & T)

Bellingham C & C Club Site
Brown Rigg, Bellingham
NE48 2JY
Tel: 01434 220175   **112 B4**
campingandcaravanning club.co.uk/bellingham
Total Pitches: 64 (C, CV & T)

Beverley Park C & C Park
Goodrington Road, Paignton
TQ4 7JE
Tel: 01803 661961   **7 M7**
beverley-holidays.co.uk
Total Pitches: 172 (C, CV & T)

Blue Rose Caravan Country Park
Star Carr Lane, Brandesburton
YO25 8RU
Tel: 01964 543366   **99 N11**
bluerosepark.com
Total Pitches: 58 (C & CV)

Briarfields Motel & Touring Park
Gloucester Road, Cheltenham
GL51 0SX
Tel: 01242 235324   **46 H10**
briarfields.net
Total Pitches: 72 (C, CV & T)

Broadhembury C & C Park
Steeds Lane, Kingsnorth,
Ashford
TN26 1NQ
Tel: 01233 620859   **26 H4**
broadhembury.co.uk
Total Pitches: 110 (C, CV & T)

Budemeadows Touring Park
Widemouth Bay, Bude
EX23 0NA
Tel: 01288 361646   **16 C11**
budemeadows.com
Total Pitches: 145 (C, CV & T)

Burnham-on-Sea Holiday Village
Marine Drive,
Burnham-on-Sea
TA8 1LA
Tel: 01278 783391   **19 K5**
haven.com/burnhamonsea
Total Pitches: 781 (C, CV & T)

Burrowhayes Farm C & C Site & Riding Stables
West Luccombe, Porlock,
Minehead
TA24 8HT
Tel: 01643 862463   **18 A5**
burrowhayes.co.uk
Total Pitches: 120 (C, CV & T)

Burton Constable Holiday Park & Arboretum
Old Lodges, Sproatley, Hull
HU11 4LJ
Tel: 01964 562508   **93 L3**
burtonconstable.co.uk
Total Pitches: 105 (C, CV & T)

Caister-on-Sea Holiday Park
Ormesby Road, Caister-on-Sea,
Great Yarmouth
NR30 5NH
Tel: 01493 728931   **77 Q9**
haven.com/caister
Total Pitches: 949 (C &CV)

Caistor Lakes Leisure Park
99a Brigg Road,
Caistor
LN7 6RX
Tel: 01472 859626   **93 K10**
caistorlakes.co.uk
Total Pitches: 36 (C &CV)

Cakes & Ale
Abbey Lane, Theberton, Leiston
IP16 4TE
Tel: 01728 831655   **65 N9**
cakesandale.co.uk
Total Pitches: 55 (C, CV & T)

Calloose C & C Park
Leedstown, Hayle
TR27 5ET
Tel: 01736 850431   **2 F7**
calloose.co.uk
Total Pitches: 109 (C, CV & T)

Camping Caradon Touring Park
Trelawne, Looe
PL13 2NA
Tel: 01503 272388   **5 L11**
campingcaradon.co.uk
Total Pitches: 75 (C, CV & T)

Capesthorne Hall
Congleton Road, Siddington,
Macclesfield
SK11 9JY
Tel: 01625 861221   **82 H10**
capesthorne.com
Total Pitches: 50 (C & CV)

Carlyon Bay C & C Park
Bethesda, Cypress Avenue,
Carlyon Bay
PL25 3RE
Tel: 01726 812735   **3 R3**
carlyonbay.net
Total Pitches: 180 (C, CV & T)

Carnon Downs C & C Park
Carnon Downs, Truro
TR3 6JJ
Tel: 01872 862283   **3 L5**
carnon-downs-caravanpark.co.uk
Total Pitches: 150 (C, CV & T)

Cartref C & C
Cartref, Ford Heath,
Shrewsbury
SY5 9GD
Tel: 01743 821688   **56 G2**
cartrefcaravansite.co.uk
Total Pitches: 44 (C & CV & T)

Carvynick Country Club
Summercourt, Newquay
TR8 5AF
Tel: 01872 510716   **4 D10**
carvynick.co.uk
Total Pitches: 47 (C & CV)

Castlerigg Hall C & C Park
Castlerigg Hall, Keswick
CA12 4TE
Tel: 017687 74499   **101 J6**
castlerigg.co.uk
Total Pitches: 68 (C, CV & T)

Charris C & C Park
Candy's Lane, Corfe Mullen,
Wimborne
BH21 3EF
Tel: 01202 885970   **12 G5**
charris.co.uk
Total Pitches: 45 (C, CV & T)

Cheddar Mendip Heights C & C Club Site
Townsend, Priddy, Wells
BA5 3BP
Tel: 01749 870241   **19 P4**
campingandcaravanningclub. co.uk/cheddar
Total Pitches: 90 (C, CV & T)

Chy Carne Holiday Park
Kuggar, Ruan Minor,
Helston
TR12 7LX
Tel: 01326 290200   **3 J10**
chycarne.co.uk
Total Pitches: 30 (C, CV & T)

Clippesby Hall
Hall Lane, Clippesby,
Great Yarmouth
NR29 3BL
Tel: 01493 367800   **77 N9**
clippesbyhall.com
Total Pitches: 120 (C, CV & T)

Cofton Holidays
Starcross, Dawlish
EX6 8RP
Tel: 01626 890111   **9 N8**
coftonholidays.co.uk
Total Pitches: 450 (C, CV & T)

Concierge Camping
Ratham Estate, Ratham Lane,
West Ashling, Chichester
PO18 8DL
Tel: 01243 573118   **15 M5**
conciergecamping.co.uk
Total Pitches: 15 (C, CV & T)

Coombe Touring Park
Race Plain, Netherhampton,
Salisbury
SP2 8PN
Tel: 01722 328451   **21 L9**
coombecaravanpark.co.uk
Total Pitches: 50 (C, CV & T)

Corfe Castle C & C Club Site
Bucknowle, Wareham
BH20 5PQ
Tel: 01929 480280   **12 F8**
campingandcaravanning club.co.uk/corfecastle
Total Pitches: 80 (C, CV & T)

Cornish Farm Touring Park
Shoreditch, Taunton
TA3 7BS
Tel: 01823 327746   **18 H10**
cornishfarm.com
Total Pitches: 50 (C, CV & T)

Cosawes Park
Perranarworthal, Truro
TR3 7QS
Tel: 01872 863724   **3 K6**
cosawes.co.uk
Total Pitches: 59 (C, CV & T)

Cote Ghyll C & C Park
Osmotherley,
Northallerton
DL6 3AH
Tel: 01609 883425   **104 E11**
coteghyll.com
Total Pitches: 77 (C, CV & T)

Country View Holiday Park
Sand Road, Sand Bay,
Weston-super-Mare
BS22 9UJ
Tel: 01934 627595   **19 K2**
cvhp.co.uk
Total Pitches: 190 (C, CV & T)

Crealy Adventure Park and Resort
Sidmouth Road, Clyst St Mary,
Exeter
EX5 1DR
Tel: 01395 234888   **9 P6**
crealy.co.uk
Total Pitches: 120 (C, CV & T)

Crows Nest Caravan Park
Gristhorpe, Filey
YO14 9PS
Tel: 01723 582206   **99 M4**
crowsnestcaravanpark.com
Total Pitches: 49 (C, CV & T)

Deepdale Backpackers & Camping
Deepdale Farm, Burnham
Deepdale
PE31 8DD
Tel: 01485 210256   **75 R2**
deepdalebackpackers.co.uk
Total Pitches: 80 (CV & T)

Dolbeare Park C & C
St Ive Road, Landrake,
Saltash
PL12 5AF
Tel: 01752 851332   **5 P9**
dolbeare.co.uk
Total Pitches: 60 (C, CV & T)

Dornafield
Dornafield Farm, Two Mile Oak,
Newton Abbot
TQ12 6DD
Tel: 01803 812732   **7 L5**
dornafield.com
Total Pitches: 135 (C, CV & T)

East Fleet Farm Touring Park
Chickerell, Weymouth
DT3 4DW
Tel: 01305 785768   **11 N9**
eastfleet.co.uk
Total Pitches: 400 (C, CV & T)

Eden Valley Holiday Park
Lanlivery, Nr Lostwithiel
PL30 5BU
Tel: 01208 872277   **4 H10**
edenvalleyholidaypark.co.uk
Total Pitches: 56 (C, CV & T)

Exe Valley Caravan Site
Mill House, Bridgetown,
Dulverton
TA22 9JR
Tel: 01643 851432   **18 B8**
exevalleycamping.co.uk
Total Pitches: 48 (C, CV & T)

Eye Kettleby Lakes
Eye Kettleby,
Melton Mowbray
LE14 2TN
Tel: 01664 565900   **73 J7**
eyekettlebylakes.com
Total Pitches: 130 (C, CV & T)

Fields End Water Caravan Park & Fishery
Benwick Road, Doddington,
March
PE15 0TY
Tel: 01354 740199   **62 E2**
fieldsendcaravans.co.uk
Total Pitches: 52 (C, CV & T)

Flower of May Holiday Park
Lebberston Cliff, Filey,
Scarborough
YO11 3NU
Tel: 01723 584311   **99 M4**
flowerofmay.com
Total Pitches: 503 (C, CV & T)

Freshwater Beach Holiday Park
Burton Bradstock,
Bridport
DT6 4PT
Tel: 01308 897317   **11 K6**
freshwaterbeach.co.uk
Total Pitches: 750 (C, CV & T)

Glenfield Caravan Park
Blackmoor Lane, Bardsey,
Leeds
LS17 9DZ
Tel: 01937 574657   **91 J2**
glenfieldcaravanpark.co.uk
Total Pitches: 31 (C, CV & T)

Globe Vale Holiday Park
Radnor, Redruth
TR16 4BH
Tel: 01209 891183   **3 J5**
globevale.co.uk
Total Pitches: 138 (C, CV & T)

Glororum Caravan Park
Glororum Farm,
Bamburgh
NE69 7AW
Tel: 01670 860256   **119 N4**
northumbrianleisure.co.uk
Total Pitches: 213 (C & CV)

Golden Cap Holiday Park
Seatown, Chideock, Bridport
DT6 6JX
Tel: 01308 422139   **11 J6**
wdlh.co.uk
Total Pitches: 108 (C, CV & T)

Golden Coast Holiday Park
Station Road, Woolacombe
EX34 7HW
Tel: 01271 872302   **16 H3**
woolacombe.com
Total Pitches: 431 (C, CV & T)

Golden Sands Holiday Park
Quebec Road, Mablethorpe
LN12 1QJ
Tel: 01507 477871   **87 N3**
haven.com/goldensands
Total Pitches: 1672 (C, CV & T)

Golden Square C & C Park
Oswaldkirk,
Helmsley
YO62 5YQ
Tel: 01439 788269   **98 C5**
goldensquarecaravanpark.com
Total Pitches: 129 (C, CV & T)

Goosewood Holiday Park
Sutton-on-the-Forest,
York
YO61 1ET
Tel: 01347 810829   **98 B8**
flowerofmay.com
Total Pitches: 100 (C & CV)

Green Acres Caravan Park
High Knells, Houghton,
Carlisle
CA6 4JW
Tel: 01228 675418   **110 H8**
caravanpark-cumbria.com
Total Pitches: 35 (C, CV & T)

Greenhill Farm C & C Park
Greenhill Farm, New Road,
Landford, Salisbury
SP5 2AZ
Tel: 01794 324117   **21 Q11**
greenhillfarm.co.uk
Total Pitches: 160 (C, CV & T)

Greenhill Leisure Park
Greenhill Farm, Station Road,
Bletchingdon, Oxford
OX5 3BQ
Tel: 01869 351600   **48 E11**
greenhill-leisure-park.co.uk
Total Pitches: 92 (C, CV & T)

Grooby's Pit
Bridgefoot Farm, Steeping Road,
Thorpe St Peter
PE24 4QT
Tel: 07427 137463   **87 N8**
fishskegness.co.uk
Total Pitches: 18 (C & CV)

Grouse Hill Caravan Park
Flask Bungalow Farm,
Fylingdales, Robin Hood's Bay
YO22 4QH
Tel: 01947 880543 **105 P10**
grousehill.co.uk
Total Pitches: 175 (C, CV & T)

Gunvenna Holiday Park
St Minver,
Wadebridge
PL27 6QN
Tel: 01208 862405 **4 F6**
gunvenna.com
Total Pitches: 75 (C, CV & T)

**Haggerston Castle
Holiday Park**
Beal, Berwick-upon-Tweed
TD15 2PA
Tel: 01289 381333 **119 K2**
haven.com/haggerstoncastle
Total Pitches: 1340 (C & CV)

Harbury Fields
Harbury Fields Farm, Harbury,
Nr Leamington Spa
CV33 9JN
Tel: 01926 612457 **48 C2**
harburyfields.co.uk
Total Pitches: 59 (C & CV)

**Harford Bridge
Holiday Park**
Peter Tavy, Tavistock
PL19 9LS
Tel: 01822 810349 **8 D9**
harfordbridge.co.uk
Total Pitches: 198 (C, CV & T)

**Haw Wood Farm
Caravan Park**
Hinton, Saxmundham
IP17 3QT
Tel: 01502 359550 **65 N7**
hawwood.co.uk
Total Pitches: 60 (C, CV & T)

Heathfield Farm Camping
Heathfield Road, Freshwater,
Isle of Wight
PO40 9SH
Tel: 01983 407822 **13 P7**
heathfieldcamping.co.uk
Total Pitches: 75 (C, CV & T)

**Heathland Beach
Caravan Park**
London Road,
Kessingland
NR33 7PJ
Tel: 01502 740337 **65 Q4**
heathlandbeach.co.uk
Total Pitches: 63 (C, CV & T)

Hele Valley Holiday Park
Hele Bay, Ilfracombe
EX34 9RD
Tel: 01271 862460 **17 J2**
helevalley.co.uk
Total Pitches: 50 (C, CV & T)

Hendra Holiday Park
Newquay
TR8 4NY
Tel: 01637 875778 **4 C9**
hendra-holidays.com
Total Pitches: 548 (C, CV & T)

Hidden Valley Park
West Down, Braunton,
Ilfracombe
EX34 8NU
Tel: 01271 813837 **17 J3**
hiddenvalleypark.com
Total Pitches: 100 (C, CV & T)

Highfield Farm Touring Park
Long Road, Comberton,
Cambridge
CB23 7DG
Tel: 01223 262308 **62 E9**
highfieldfarmtouring.co.uk
Total Pitches: 120 (C, CV & T)

Highlands End Holiday Park
Eype, Bridport,
Dorset
DT6 6AR
Tel: 01308 422139 **11 K6**
wdlh.co.uk
Total Pitches: 195 (C, CV & T)

Hill Cottage Farm C & C Park
Sandleheath Road, Alderholt,
Fordingbridge
SP6 3EG
Tel: 01425 650513 **13 K2**
hillcottagefarm
campingandcaravanpark.co.uk
Total Pitches: 95 (C, CV & T)

Hill of Oaks & Blakeholme
Windermere
LA12 8NR
Tel: 015395 31578 **94 H3**
hillofoaks.co.uk
Total Pitches: 43 (C & CV)

Hillside Caravan Park
Canvas Farm, Moor Road,
Knayton, Thirsk
YO7 4BR
Tel: 01845 537349 **97 P3**
hillsidecaravanpark.co.uk
Total Pitches: 50 (C & CV)

Holiday Resort Unity
Coast Road, Brean Sands,
Brean
TA8 2RB
Tel: 01278 751235 **19 J4**
hru.co.uk
Total Pitches: 1114 (C, CV & T)

Hollins Farm C & C
Far Arnside, Carnforth
LA5 0SL
Tel: 01524 701767 **95 J5**
holgates.co.uk
Total Pitches: 12 (C, CV & T)

Hylton Caravan Park
Eden Street, Silloth
CA7 4AY
Tel: 016973 31707 **109 P10**
stanwix.com
Total Pitches: 90 (C, CV & T)

Island Lodge C & C Site
Stumpy Post Cross,
Kingsbridge
TQ7 4BL
Tel: 01548 852956 **7 J9**
islandlodgesite.co.uk
Total Pitches: 30 (C, CV & T)

**Isle of Avalon
Touring Caravan Park**
Godney Road, Glastonbury
BA6 9AF
Tel: 01458 833618 **19 N7**
avaloncaravanpark.co.uk
Total Pitches: 120 (C, CV & T)

Jasmine Caravan Park
Cross Lane, Snainton,
Scarborough
YO13 9BE
Tel: 01723 859240 **99 J4**
jasminepark.co.uk
Total Pitches: 68 (C, CV & T)

**Kenneggy Cove
Holiday Park**
Higher Kenneggy, Rosudgeon,
Penzance
TR20 9AU
Tel: 01736 763453 **2 F8**
kenneggycove.co.uk
Total Pitches: 40 (C, CV & T)

**Kennford International
Caravan Park**
Kennford, Exeter
EX6 7YN
Tel: 01392 833046 **9 M7**
kennfordinternational.co.uk
Total Pitches: 87 (C, CV & T)

King's Lynn C & C Park
New Road, North Runcton,
King's Lynn
PE33 0RA
Tel: 01553 840004 **75 M7**
kl-cc.co.uk
Total Pitches: 150 (C, CV & T)

Kloofs Caravan Park
Sandhurst Lane, Bexhill
TN39 4RG
Tel: 01424 842839 **26 B10**
kloofs.com
Total Pitches: 125 (C, CV & T)

**Kneps Farm
Holiday Park**
River Road, Stanah,
Thornton-Cleveleys, Blackpool
FY5 5LR
Tel: 01253 823632 **88 D2**
knepsfarm.co.uk
Total Pitches: 40 (C & CV)

**Knight Stainforth Hall
Caravan & Campsite**
Stainforth, Settle
BD24 0DP
Tel: 01729 822200 **96 B7**
knightstainforth.co.uk
Total Pitches: 100 (C, CV & T)

**Ladycross Plantation
Caravan Park**
Egton, Whitby
YO21 1UA
Tel: 01947 895502 **105 M9**
ladycrossplantation.co.uk
Total Pitches: 130 (C, CV & T)

**Lady's Mile
Holiday Park**
Dawlish, Devon
EX7 0LX
Tel: 01626 863411 **9 N9**
ladysmile.co.uk
Total Pitches: 570 (C, CV & T)

Lakeland Leisure Park
Moor Lane, Flookburgh
LA11 7LT
Tel: 01539 558556 **94 H6**
haven.com/lakeland
Total Pitches: 977 (C, CV & T)

**Lamb Cottage
Caravan Park**
Dalefords Lane, Whitegate,
Northwich
CW8 2BN
Tel: 01606 882302 **82 D11**
lambcottage.co.uk
Total Pitches: 45 (C & CV)

**Langstone Manor
C & C Park**
Moortown, Tavistock
PL19 9JZ
Tel: 01822 613371 **6 E4**
langstonemanor.co.uk
Total Pitches: 40 (C, CV & T)

Lanyon Holiday Park
Loscombe Lane,
Four Lanes, Redruth
TR16 6LP
Tel: 01209 313474 **2 H6**
lanyonholidaypark.co.uk
Total Pitches: 25 (C, CV & T)

Lebberston Touring Park
Filey Road, Lebberston,
Scarborough
YO11 3PE
Tel: 01723 585723 **99 M4**
lebberstontouring.co.uk
Total Pitches: 125 (C & CV)

Lickpenny Caravan Site
Lickpenny Lane, Tansley,
Matlock
DE4 5GF
Tel: 01629 583040 **84 D9**
lickpennycaravanpark.co.uk
Total Pitches: 80 (C & CV)

Lime Tree Park
Dukes Drive, Buxton
SK17 9RP
Tel: 01298 22988 **83 N10**
limetreeparkbuxton.com
Total Pitches: 106 (C, CV & T)

**Lincoln Farm Park
Oxfordshire**
High Street, Standlake
OX29 7RH
Tel: 01865 300239 **34 C4**
lincolnfarmpark.co.uk
Total Pitches: 90 (C, CV & T)

**Little Lakeland
Caravan Park**
Wortwell, Harleston
IP20 0EL
Tel: 01986 788646 **65 K5**
littlelakeland
caravanparkandcamping.co.uk
Total Pitches: 58 (C, CV & T)

Littlesea Holiday Park
Lynch Lane, Weymouth
DT4 9DT
Tel: 01305 774414 **11 P9**
haven.com/littlesea
Total Pitches: 861 (C, CV & T)

Long Acres Touring Park
Station Road, Old Leake,
Boston
PE22 9RF
Tel: 01205 871555 **87 L10**
long-acres.co.uk
Total Pitches: 40 (C, CV & T)

Longnor Wood Holiday Park
Newtown, Longnor,
Nr Buxton
SK17 0NG
Tel: 01298 83648 **71 K2**
longnorwood.co.uk
Total Pitches: 47 (C, CV & T)

**Lower Polladras
Touring Park**
Carleen, Breage, Helston
TR13 9NX
Tel: 01736 762220 **2 G7**
lower-polladras.co.uk
Total Pitches: 39 (C, CV & T)

Lowther Holiday Park
Eamont Bridge, Penrith
CA10 2JB
Tel: 01768 863631 **101 P5**
lowther-holidaypark.co.uk
Total Pitches: 180 (C, CV & T)

**Manor Wood Country
Caravan Park**
Manor Wood, Coddington,
Chester
CH3 9EN
Tel: 01829 782990 **69 M4**
cheshire-caravan-sites.co.uk
Total Pitches: 45 (C, CV & T)

Marton Mere Holiday Village
Mythop Road, Blackpool
FY4 4XN
Tel: 01253 767544 **88 C4**
haven.com/martonmere
Total Pitches: 782 (C & CV)

Mayfield Park
Cheltenham Road, Cirencester
GL7 7BH
Tel: 01285 831301 **33 K3**
mayfieldpark.co.uk
Total Pitches: 105 (C, CV & T)

Meadowbank Holidays
Stour Way, Christchurch
BH23 2PQ
Tel: 01202 483597 **13 K6**
meadowbank-holidays.co.uk
Total Pitches: 41 (C & CV)

**Middlewood Farm
Holiday Park**
Middlewood Lane, Fylingthorpe,
Robin Hood's Bay, Whitby
YO22 4UF
Tel: 01947 880414 **105 P10**
middlewoodfarm.com
Total Pitches: 100 (C, CV & T)

Minnows Touring Park
Holbrook Lane, Sampford
Peverell
EX16 7EN
Tel: 01884 821770 **18 D11**
minnowstouringpark.co.uk
Total Pitches: 59 (C, CV & T)

Monkey Tree Holiday Park
Hendra Croft, Scotland Road,
Newquay
TR8 5QR
Tel: 01872 572032 **3 L3**
monkeytreeholidaypark.co.uk
Total Pitches: 700 (C, CV & T)

Moon & Sixpence
Newbourn Road, Waldringfield,
Woodbridge
IP12 4PP
Tel: 01473 736650 **53 N2**
moonandsixpence.co.uk
Total Pitches: 50 (C & CV)

Moor Lodge Park
Blackmoor Lane, Bardsey, Leeds
LS17 9DZ
Tel: 01937 572424 **91 K2**
moorlodgecaravanpark.co.uk
Total Pitches: 12 (C & CV)

Moss Wood Caravan Park
Crimbles Lane, Cockerham
LA2 0ES
Tel: 01524 791041 **95 K11**
mosswood.co.uk
Total Pitches: 25 (C, CV & T)

Naburn Lock Caravan Park
Naburn
YO19 4RU
Tel: 01904 728697 **98 C11**
naburnlock.co.uk
Total Pitches: 100 (C, CV & T)

New Lodge Farm C & C Site
New Lodge Farm, Bulwick,
Corby
NN17 3DU
Tel: 01780 450493 **73 P11**
newlodgefarm.com
Total Pitches: 72 (C, CV & T)

Newberry Valley Park
Woodlands, Combe Martin
EX34 0AT
Tel: 01271 882334 **17 K2**
newberryvalleypark.co.uk
Total Pitches: 110 (C, CV & T)

Newlands Holidays
Charmouth, Bridport
DT6 6RB
Tel: 01297 560259 **10 H6**
newlandsholidays.co.uk
Total Pitches: 240 (C, CV & T)

Newperran Holiday Park
Rejerrah, Newquay
TR8 5QJ
Tel: 01872 572407 **3 K3**
newperran.co.uk
Total Pitches: 357 (C, CV & T)

Ninham Country Holidays
Ninham, Shanklin, Isle of Wight
PO37 7PL
Tel: 01983 864243 **14 G10**
ninham-holidays.co.uk
Total Pitches: 135 (C, CV & T)

North Morte Farm C & C Park
North Morte Road, Mortehoe,
Woolacombe
EX34 7EG
Tel: 01271 870381 **16 H2**
northmortefarm.co.uk
Total Pitches: 180 (C, CV & T)

**Northam Farm Caravan
& Touring Park**
Brean, Burnham-on-Sea
TA8 2SE
Tel: 01278 751244 **19 K3**
northamfarm.co.uk
Total Pitches: 350 (C, CV & T)

**Oakdown Country
Holiday Park**
Gatedown Lane, Weston,
Sidmouth
EX10 0PT
Tel: 01297 680387 **10 D6**
oakdown.co.uk
Total Pitches: 150 (C, CV & T)

Old Hall Caravan Park
Capernwray, Carnforth
LA6 1AD
Tel: 01524 733276 **95 L6**
oldhallcaravanpark.co.uk
Total Pitches: 38 (C & CV)

Ord House Country Park
East Ord,
Berwick-upon-Tweed
TD15 2NS
Tel: 01289 305288 **129 P9**
ordhouse.co.uk
Total Pitches: 79 (C, CV & T)

Oxon Hall Touring Park
Welshpool Road,
Shrewsbury
SY3 5FB
Tel: 01743 340868 **56 H2**
morris-leisure.co.uk
Total Pitches: 105 (C, CV & T)

Padstow Touring Park
Padstow
PL28 8LE
Tel: 01841 532061 **4 E7**
padstowtouringpark.co.uk
Total Pitches: 150 (C, CV & T)

Park Cliffe C & C Estate
Birks Road, Tower Wood,
Windermere
LA23 3PG
Tel: 015395 31344 **94 H2**
parkcliffe.co.uk
Total Pitches: 60 (C, CV & T)

Parkers Farm Holiday Park
Higher Mead Farm,
Ashburton, Devon
TQ13 7LJ
Tel: 01364 654869 **7 K4**
parkersfarmholidays.co.uk
Total Pitches: 100 (C, CV & T)

Park Foot C & C Park
Howtown Road,
Pooley Bridge
CA10 2NA
Tel: 017684 86309 **101 N6**
parkfootullswater.co.uk
Total Pitches: 454 (C, CV & T)

Parkland C & C Site
Sorley Green Cross,
Kingsbridge
TQ7 4AF
Tel: 01548 852723 **7 J9**
parklandsite.co.uk
Total Pitches: 50 (C, CV & T)

**Pebble Bank
Caravan Park**
Camp Road, Wyke Regis,
Weymouth
DT4 9HF
Tel: 01305 774844 **11 P9**
pebblebank.co.uk
Total Pitches: 120 (C, CV & T)

**Perran Sands
Holiday Park**
Perranporth, Truro
TR6 0AQ
Tel: 01872 573551 **4 B10**
haven.com/perransands
Total Pitches: 1012 (C, CV & T)

Petwood Caravan Park
Off Stixwould Road,
Woodhall Spa
LN10 6QH
Tel: 01526 354799 **86 G8**
petwoodcaravanpark.com
Total Pitches: 98 (C, CV & T)

Polmanter Touring Park
Halsetown, St Ives
TR26 3LX
Tel: 01736 795640 **2 E6**
polmanter.co.uk
Total Pitches: 270 (C, CV & T)

Porthtowan Tourist Park
Mile Hill, Porthtowan,
Truro
TR4 8TY
Tel: 01209 890256 **2 H4**
porthtowantouristpark.co.uk
Total Pitches: 80 (C, CV & T)

Primrose Valley Holiday Park
Filey
YO14 9RF
Tel: 01723 513771 **99 N5**
haven.com/primrosevalley
Total Pitches: 1549 (C & CV)

Quantock Orchard Caravan Park
Flaxpool, Crowcombe,
Taunton
TA4 4AW
Tel: 01984 618618 **18 F7**
quantock-orchard.co.uk
Total Pitches: 60 (C, CV & T)

Ranch Caravan Park
Station Road, Honeybourne,
Evesham
WR11 7PR
Tel: 01386 830744 **47 M6**
ranch.co.uk
Total Pitches: 120 (C & CV)

Ripley Caravan Park
Knaresborough Road, Ripley,
Harrogate
HG3 3AU
Tel: 01423 770050 **97 L8**
ripleycaravanpark.com
Total Pitches: 60 (C, CV & T)

River Dart Country Park
Holne Park, Ashburton
TQ13 7NP
Tel: 01364 652511 **7 J5**
riverdart.co.uk
Total Pitches: 170 (C, CV & T)

River Valley Holiday Park
London Apprentice,
St Austell
PL26 7AP
Tel: 01726 73533 **3 Q3**
rivervalleyholidaypark.co.uk
Total Pitches: 45 (C, CV & T)

Riverside C & C Park
Marsh Lane, North Molton Road,
South Molton
EX36 3HQ
Tel: 01769 579269 **17 N6**
exmoorriverside.co.uk
Total Pitches: 58 (C, CV & T)

Riverside Caravan Park
High Bentham, Lancaster
LA2 7FJ
Tel: 015242 61272 **95 P7**
riversidecaravanpark.co.uk
Total Pitches: 61 (C & CV)

Riverside Holiday Park
Southport New Road,
Southport
PR9 8DF
Tel: 01704 228886 **88 E7**
riversideleisurecentre.co.uk
Total Pitches: 615 (C & CV)

Riverside Meadows Country Caravan Park
Ure Bank Top,
Ripon
HG4 1JD
Tel: 01765 602964 **97 M6**
flowerofmay.com
Total Pitches: 80 (C, CV & T)

Robin Hood C & C Park
Green Dyke Lane, Slingsby
YO62 4AP
Tel: 01653 628391 **98 E6**
robinhoodcaravanpark.co.uk
Total Pitches: 32 (C, CV & T)

Rose Farm Touring & Camping Park
Stepshort, Belton,
Nr Great Yarmouth
NR31 9JS
Tel: 01493 738292 **77 P11**
rosefarmtouringpark.co.uk
Total Pitches: 145 (C, CV & T)

Rosedale Abbey C & C Park
Rosedale Abbey,
Pickering
YO18 8SA
Tel: 01751 417272 **105 K11**
rosedaleabbeycaravanpark.co.uk
Total Pitches: 100 (C, CV & T)

Ross Park
Park Hill Farm, Ipplepen,
Newton Abbot
TQ12 5TT
Tel: 01803 812983 **7 L5**
rossparkcaravanpark.co.uk
Total Pitches: 110 (C, CV & T)

Rudding Holiday Park
Follifoot, Harrogate
HG3 1JH
Tel: 01423 870439 **97 M10**
ruddingholidaypark.co.uk
Total Pitches: 86 (C, CV & T)

Run Cottage Touring Park
Alderton Road, Hollesley,
Woodbridge
IP12 3RQ
Tel: 01394 411309 **53 Q3**
runcottage.co.uk
Total Pitches: 45 (C, CV & T)

Rutland C & C
Park Lane, Greetham,
Oakham
LE15 7FN
Tel: 01572 813520 **73 N8**
rutlandcaravanandcamping.co.uk
Total Pitches: 130 (C, CV & T)

St Helens Caravan Park
Wykeham,
Scarborough
YO13 9QD
Tel: 01723 862771 **99 K4**
sthelenscaravanpark.co.uk
Total Pitches: 250 (C, CV & T)

St Ives Bay Holiday Park
73 Loggans Road,
Upton Towans, Hayle
TR27 5BH
Tel: 01736 752274 **2 F6**
stivesbay.co.uk
Total Pitches: 507 (C, CV & T)

Salcombe Regis C & C Park
Salcombe Regis,
Sidmouth
EX10 0JH
Tel: 01395 514303 **10 D7**
salcombe-regis.co.uk
Total Pitches: 110 (C, CV & T)

Sand le Mere Holiday Village
Southfield Lane,
Tunstall
HU12 0JF
Tel: 01964 670403 **93 P4**
sand-le-mere.co.uk
Total Pitches: 89 (C & CV)

Sandy Balls Holiday Village
Sandy Balls Estate Ltd,
Godshill, Fordingbridge
SP6 2JZ
Tel: 01442 508850 **13 L2**
awayresorts.co.uk
Total Pitches: 225 (C, CV & T)

Searles Leisure Resort
South Beach Road,
Hunstanton
PE36 5BB
Tel: 01485 534211 **75 N3**
searles.co.uk
Total Pitches: 413 (C, CV & T)

Seaview Holiday Park
Preston, Weymouth
DT3 6DZ
Tel: 01305 832271 **11 Q8**
haven.com/seaview
Total Pitches: 347 (C, CV & T)

Seaview International Holiday Park
Boswinger, Mevagissey
PL26 6LL
Tel: 01726 843425 **3 P5**
seaviewinternational.com
Total Pitches: 201 (C, CV & T)

Severn Gorge Park
Bridgnorth Road, Tweedale,
Telford
TF7 4JB
Tel: 01952 684789 **57 N3**
severngorgepark.co.uk
Total Pitches: 12 (C & CV)

Shamba Holidays
East Moors Lane, St Leonards,
Ringwood
BH24 2SB
Tel: 01202 873302 **13 K4**
shambaholidays.co.uk
Total Pitches: 150 (C, CV & T)

Shrubbery Touring Park
Rousdon, Lyme Regis
DT7 3XW
Tel: 01297 442227 **10 F6**
shrubberypark.co.uk
Total Pitches: 120 (C, CV & T)

Silverdale Caravan Park
Middlebarrow Plain, Cove Road,
Silverdale, Nr Carnforth
LA5 0SH
Tel: 01524 701508 **95 K5**
holgates.co.uk
Total Pitches: 80 (C, CV & T)

Skelwith Fold Caravan Park
Ambleside, Cumbria
LA22 0HX
Tel: 015394 32277 **101 L10**
skelwith.com
Total Pitches: 150 (C & CV)

Skirlington Leisure Park
Driffield, Skipsea
YO25 8SY
Tel: 01262 468213 **99 P10**
skirlington.com
Total Pitches: 930 (C & CV)

Sleningford Watermill Caravan Camping Park
North Stainley, Ripon
HG4 3HQ
Tel: 01765 635201 **97 L5**
sleningfordwatermill.co.uk
Total Pitches: 135 (C, CV & T)

Somers Wood Caravan Park
Somers Road, Meriden
CV7 7PL
Tel: 01676 522978 **59 K8**
somerswood.co.uk
Total Pitches: 48 (C & CV)

South Lytchett Manor C & C Park
Dorchester Road,
Lytchett Minster, Poole
BH16 6JB
Tel: 01202 622577 **12 G6**
southlytchettmanor.co.uk
Total Pitches: 150 (C, CV & T)

South Meadows Caravan Park
South Road, Belford
NE70 7DP
Tel: 01668 213326 **119 M4**
southmeadows.co.uk
Total Pitches: 83 (C, CV & T)

Stanmore Hall Touring Park
Stourbridge Road, Bridgnorth
WV15 6DT
Tel: 01746 761761 **57 N6**
morris-leisure.co.uk
Total Pitches: 129 (C, CV & T)

Stanwix Park Holiday Centre
Greenrow, Silloth
CA7 4HH
Tel: 016973 32666 **109 P10**
stanwix.com
Total Pitches: 337 (C, CV & T)

Stowford Farm Meadows
Berry Down, Combe Martin
EX34 0PW
Tel: 01271 882476 **17 K3**
stowford.co.uk
Total Pitches: 700 (C, CV & T)

Stroud Hill Park
Fen Road, Pidley, St Ives
PE28 3DE
Tel: 01487 741333 **62 D5**
stroudhillpark.co.uk
Total Pitches: 60 (C, CV & T)

Summer Valley Touring Park
Shortlanesend, Truro
TR4 9DW
Tel: 01872 277878 **3 L4**
summervalley.co.uk
Total Pitches: 60 (C, CV & T)

Sumners Ponds Fishery & Campsite
Chapel Road, Barns Green,
Horsham
RH13 0PR
Tel: 01403 732539 **24 D5**
sumnersponds.co.uk
Total Pitches: 86 (C, CV & T)

Swiss Farm Touring & Camping
Marlow Road, Henley-on-Thames
RG9 2HY
Tel: 01491 573419 **35 L8**
swissfarmhenley.co.uk
Total Pitches: 140 (C, CV & T)

Tanner Farm Touring C & C Park
Tanner Farm, Goudhurst Road,
Marden
TN12 9ND
Tel: 01622 832399 **26 B3**
tannerfarmpark.co.uk
Total Pitches: 120 (C, CV & T)

Tattershall Lakes Country Park
Sleaford Road, Tattershall
LN4 4LR
Tel: 01526 348800 **86 H9**
tattershall-lakes.com
Total Pitches: 186 (C, CV & T)

Tehidy Holiday Park
Harris Mill, Illogan, Portreath
TR16 4JQ
Tel: 01209 216489 **2 H5**
tehidy.co.uk
Total Pitches: 18 (C, CV & T)

Tencreek Holiday Park
Polperro Road, Looe
PL13 2JR
Tel: 01503 262447 **5 L11**
dolphinholidays.co.uk
Total Pitches: 355 (C, CV & T)

Teversal C & C Club Site
Silverhill Lane, Teversal
NG17 3JJ
Tel: 01623 551838 **84 G8**
campingandcaravanningclub.
co.uk/teversal
Total Pitches: 126 (C, CV & T)

The Laurels Holiday Park
Padstow Road, Whitecross,
Wadebridge
PL27 7JQ
Tel: 01208 813341 **4 F7**
thelaurelsholidaypark.co.uk
Total Pitches: 30 (C, CV & T)

The Old Brick Kilns
Little Barney Lane, Barney,
Fakenham
NR21 0NL
Tel: 01328 878305 **76 E5**
old-brick-kilns.co.uk
Total Pitches: 65 (C, CV & T)

The Old Oaks Touring Park
Wick Farm, Wick,
Glastonbury
BA6 8JS
Tel: 01458 831437 **19 P7**
theoldoaks.co.uk
Total Pitches: 98 (C, CV & T)

The Orchards Holiday Caravan Park
Main Road, Newbridge,
Yarmouth, Isle of Wight
PO41 0TS
Tel: 01983 531331 **14 D9**
orchards-holiday-park.co.uk
Total Pitches: 160 (C, CV & T)

The Quiet Site
Ullswater, Watermillock
CA11 0LS
Tel: 07768 727016 **101 M6**
thequietsite.co.uk
Total Pitches: 100 (C, CV & T)

Thornwick Bay Holiday Village
North Marine Road,
Flamborough
YO15 1AU
Tel: 01262 850569 **99 Q6**
haven.com/parks/yorkshire/
thornwick-bay
Total Pitches: 225 (C, CV & T)

Thorpe Park Holiday Centre
Cleethorpes
DN35 0PW
Tel: 01472 813395 **93 P9**
haven.com/thorpepark
Total Pitches: 1491 (C, CV & T)

Treago Farm Caravan Site
Crantock, Newquay
TR8 5QS
Tel: 01637 830277 **4 B9**
treagofarm.co.uk
Total Pitches: 90 (C, CV & T)

Tregoad Park
St Martin, Looe
PL13 1PB
Tel: 01503 262718 **5 M10**
tregoadpark.co.uk
Total Pitches: 200 (C, CV & T)

Treloy Touring Park
Newquay
TR8 4JN
Tel: 01637 872063 **4 D9**
treloy.co.uk
Total Pitches: 223 (C, CV & T)

Trencreek Holiday Park
Hillcrest, Higher Trencreek,
Newquay
TR8 4NS
Tel: 01637 874210 **4 C9**
trencreekholidaypark.co.uk
Total Pitches: 194 (C, CV & T)

Trethem Mill Touring Park
St Just-in-Roseland,
Nr St Mawes, Truro
TR2 5JF
Tel: 01872 580504 **3 M6**
trethem.com
Total Pitches: 84 (C, CV & T)

Trevalgan Touring Park
Trevalgan, St Ives
TR26 3BJ
Tel: 01736 791892 **2 D6**
trevalgantouringpark.co.uk
Total Pitches: 135 (C, CV & T)

Trevedra Farm C & C Site
Sennen, Penzance
TR19 7BE
Tel: 01736 871818 **2 B8**
trevedrafarm.co.uk
Total Pitches: 100 (C, CV & T)

Trevella Park
Crantock, Newquay
TR8 5EW
Tel: 01637 830308 **4 C10**
trevella.co.uk
Total Pitches: 165 (C, CV & T)

Trevornick
Holywell Bay, Newquay
TR8 5PW
Tel: 01637 830531 **4 B10**
trevornick.co.uk
Total Pitches: 688 (C, CV & T)

Truro C & C Park
Truro
TR4 8QN
Tel: 01872 560274 **3 K4**
trurocaravanandcampingpark.co.uk
Total Pitches: 51 (C, CV & T)

Tudor C & C
Shepherds Patch, Slimbridge,
Gloucester
GL2 7BP
Tel: 01453 890483 **32 D4**
tudorcaravanpark.com
Total Pitches: 75 (C, CV & T)

Twitchen House Holiday Park
Mortehoe Station Road,
Mortehoe, Woolacombe
EX34 7ES
Tel: 01271 872302 **16 H3**
woolacombe.com
Total Pitches: 569 (C, CV & T)

Two Mills Touring Park
Yarmouth Road, North Walsham
NR28 9NA
Tel: 01692 405829 **77 K6**
twomills.co.uk
Total Pitches: 81 (C, CV & T)

Ulwell Cottage Caravan Park
Ulwell Cottage, Ulwell,
Swanage
BH19 3DG
Tel: 01929 422823 **12 H8**
ulwellcottagepark.co.uk
Total Pitches: 77 (C, CV & T)

Vale of Pickering Caravan Park
Carr House Farm, Allerston,
Pickering
YO18 7PQ
Tel: 01723 859280 **98 H4**
valeofpickering.co.uk
Total Pitches: 120 (C, CV & T)

Wagtail Country Park
Cliff Lane, Marston,
Grantham
NG32 2HU
Tel: 01400 251123 **73 M2**
wagtailcountrypark.co.uk
Total Pitches: 76 (C & CV)

Waldegraves Holiday Park
Mersea Island, Colchester
CO5 8SE
Tel: 01206 382898 **52 H9**
waldegraves.co.uk
Total Pitches: 30 (C, CV & T)

Warcombe Farm C & C Park
Station Road, Mortehoe,
Woolacombe
EX34 7EJ
Tel: 01271 870690 **16 H2**
warcombefarm.co.uk
Total Pitches: 250 (C, CV & T)

Wareham Forest Tourist Park
North Trigon, Wareham
BH20 7NZ
Tel: 01929 551393 **12 E6**
warehamforest.co.uk
Total Pitches: 200 (C, CV & T)

Waren C & C Park
Waren Mill, Bamburgh
NE70 7EE
Tel: 01668 214366 **119 N4**
meadowhead.co.uk
Total Pitches: 150 (C, CV & T)

Warren Farm Holiday Centre
Brean Sands, Brean,
Burnham-on-Sea
TA8 2RP
Tel: 01278 751227 **19 J3**
warrenfarm.co.uk
Total Pitches: 975 (C, CV & T)

Watergate Bay Touring Park
Watergate Bay, Tregurrian
TR8 4AD
Tel: 01637 860387 **4 D8**
watergatebaytouringpark.co.uk
Total Pitches: 171 (C, CV & T)

Waterrow Touring Park
Wiveliscombe, Taunton
TA4 2AZ
Tel: 01984 623464 **18 E9**
waterrowpark.co.uk
Total Pitches: 44 (C, CV & T)

Wayfarers C & C Park
Relubbus Lane, St Hilary,
Penzance
TR20 9EF
Tel: 01736 763326   **2 F7**
wayfarerspark.co.uk
Total Pitches: 32 (C, CV & T)

Wells Touring Park
Haybridge, Wells
BA5 1AJ
Tel: 01749 676869   **19 P5**
wellstouringpark.co.uk
Total Pitches: 72 (C, CV & T)

Wheathill Touring Park
Wheathill, Bridgnorth
WV16 6QT
Tel: 01584 823456   **57 L8**
wheathillpark.co.uk
Total Pitches: 25 (C & CV)

Whitecliff Bay Holiday Park
Hillway Road, Bembridge,
Whitecliff Bay
PO35 5PL
Tel: 01983 872671   **14 H9**
wight-holidays.com
Total Pitches: 653 (C, CV & T)

Whitefield Forest Touring Park
Brading Road, Ryde,
Isle of Wight
PO33 1QL
Tel: 01983 617069   **14 H9**
whitefieldforest.co.uk
Total Pitches: 90 (C, CV & T)

Whitemead Caravan Park
East Burton Road, Wool
BH20 6HG
Tel: 01929 462241   **12 D7**
whitemeadcaravanpark.co.uk
Total Pitches: 105 (C, CV & T)

Widdicombe Farm Touring Park
Marldon, Paignton
TQ3 1ST
Tel: 01803 558325   **7 M6**
widdicombefarm.co.uk
Total Pitches: 180 (C, CV & T)

Wild Rose Park
Ormside,
Appleby-in-Westmorland
CA16 6EJ
Tel: 017683 51077   **102 C7**
harrisonholidayhomes.co.uk
Total Pitches: 226 (C & CV)

Wilksworth Farm Caravan Park
Cranborne Road,
Wimborne Minster
BH21 4HW
Tel: 01202 885467   **12 H4**
shorefield.co.uk/camping-
touring-holidays/our-parks/
wilksworth-caravan-park
Total Pitches: 85 (C, CV & T)

Willowbank Holiday Home & Touring Park
Coastal Road, Ainsdale,
Southport
PR8 3ST
Tel: 01704 571566   **88 C8**
willowbankcp.co.uk
Total Pitches: 87 (C & CV)

Wolds View Touring Park
115 Brigg Road, Caistor
LN7 6RX
Tel: 01472 851099   **93 K10**
woldsviewtouringpark.co.uk
Total Pitches: 60 (C, CV & T)

Wood Farm C & C Park
Axminster Road,
Charmouth
DT6 6BT
Tel: 01297 560697   **10 H6**
woodfarm.co.uk
Total Pitches: 175 (C, CV & T)

Wooda Farm Holiday Park
Poughill, Bude
EX23 9HJ
Tel: 01288 352069   **16 C10**
wooda.co.uk
Total Pitches: 200 (C, CV & T)

Woodclose Caravan Park
High Casterton, Kirkby
Lonsdale
LA6 2SE
Tel: 015242 71597   **95 N5**
woodclosepark.com
Total Pitches: 22 (C, CV & T)

Woodhall Country Park
Stixwold Road, Woodhall Spa
LN10 6UJ
Tel: 01526 353710   **86 G8**
woodhallcountrypark.co.uk
Total Pitches: 115 (C, CV & T)

Woodland Springs Adult Touring Park
Venton, Drewsteignton
EX6 6PG
Tel: 01647 231695   **8 G6**
woodlandsprings.co.uk
Total Pitches: 81 (C, CV & T)

Woodlands Grove C & C Park
Blackawton, Dartmouth
TQ9 7DQ
Tel: 01803 712598   **7 L8**
woodlandsgrove.co.uk
Total Pitches: 350 (C, CV & T)

Woodovis Park
Gulworthy, Tavistock
PL19 8NY
Tel: 01822 832968   **6 C4**
woodovis.com
Total Pitches: 50 (C, CV & T)

Yeatheridge Farm Caravan Park
East Worlington, Crediton
EX17 4TN
Tel: 01884 860330   **9 J2**
yeatheridge.co.uk
Total Pitches: 122 (C, CV & T)

SCOTLAND

Auchenlarie Holiday Park
Gatehouse of Fleet
DG7 2EX
Tel: 01556 506200   **107 P7**
swalwellholidaygroup.co.uk
Total Pitches: 451 (C, CV & T)

Beecraigs C & C Site
Beecraigs Country Park,
The Visitor Centre, Linlithgow
EH49 6PL
Tel: 01506 844516   **127 J3**
beecraigs.com
Total Pitches: 36 (C, CV & T)

Blair Castle Caravan Park
Blair Atholl, Pitlochry
PH18 5SR
Tel: 01796 481263   **141 L4**
blaircastlecaravanpark.co.uk
Total Pitches: 226 (C, CV & T)

Brighouse Bay Holiday Park
Brighouse Bay, Borgue,
Kirkcudbright
DG6 4TS
Tel: 01557 870267   **108 D11**
gillespie-leisure.co.uk
Total Pitches: 190 (C, CV & T)

Cairnsmill Holiday Park
Largo Road, St Andrews
KY16 8NN
Tel: 01334 473604   **135 M5**
cairnsmill.co.uk
Total Pitches: 62 (C, CV & T)

Craig Tara Holiday Park
Ayr
KA7 4LB
Tel: 0800 975 7579   **114 F4**
haven.com/craigtara
Total Pitches: 1144 (C & CV)

Craigtoun Meadows Holiday Park
Mount Melville, St Andrews
KY16 8PQ
Tel: 01334 475959   **135 M4**
craigtounmeadows.co.uk
Total Pitches: 56 (C, CV & T)

Faskally Caravan Park
Pitlochry
PH16 5LA
Tel: 01796 472007   **141 M6**
faskally.co.uk
Total Pitches: 430 (C, CV & T)

Glen Nevis C & C Park
Glen Nevis, Fort William
PH33 6SX
Tel: 01397 702191   **139 L3**
glen-nevis.co.uk
Total Pitches: 380 (C, CV & T)

Hoddom Castle Caravan Park
Hoddom, Lockerbie
DG11 1AS
Tel: 01576 300251   **110 C6**
hoddomcastle.co.uk
Total Pitches: 200 (C, CV & T)

Huntly Castle Caravan Park
The Meadow, Huntly
AB54 4UJ
Tel: 01466 794999   **158 D9**
huntlycastle.co.uk
Total Pitches: 90 (C, CV & T)

Invercoe C & C Park
Ballachulish, Glencoe
PH49 4HP
Tel: 01855 811210   **139 K6**
invercoe.co.uk
Total Pitches: 66 (C, CV & T)

Linwater Caravan Park
West Clifton,
East Calder
EH53 0HT
Tel: 0131 333 3326   **127 L4**
linwater.co.uk
Total Pitches: 64 (C, CV & T)

Loch Ken Holiday Park
Parton, Castle Douglas
DG7 3NE
Tel: 01644 470282   **108 E6**
lochkenholidaypark.co.uk
Total Pitches: 40 (C, CV & T)

Lomond Woods Holiday Park
Old Luss Road, Balloch,
Loch Lomond
G83 8QP
Tel: 01389 755000   **132 D11**
woodleisure.co.uk
Total Pitches: 115 (C & CV)

Milton of Fonab Caravan Park
Bridge Road,
Pitlochry
PH16 5NA
Tel: 01796 472882   **141 M6**
fonab.co.uk
Total Pitches: 154 (C, CV & T)

River Tilt Caravan Park
Blair Atholl, Pitlochry
PH18 5TE
Tel: 01796 481467   **141 L4**
rivertiltpark.co.uk
Total Pitches: 30 (C, CV & T)

Sands of Luce Holiday Park
Sands of Luce, Sandhead,
Stranraer
DG9 9JN
Tel: 01776 830456   **106 F7**
sandsofluceholidaypark.co.uk
Total Pitches: 80 (C, CV & T)

Seaward Caravan Park
Dhoon Bay,
Kirkudbright
DG6 4TJ
Tel: 01557 870267   **108 E11**
gillespie-leisure.co.uk
Total Pitches: 25 (C, CV & T)

Seton Sands Holiday Village
Longniddry
EH32 0QF
Tel: 01875 813333   **128 C4**
haven.com/setonsands
Total Pitches: 640 (C & CV)

Silver Sands Holiday Park
Covesea, West Beach,
Lossiemouth
IV31 6SP
Tel: 01343 813262   **157 N3**
silver-sands.co.uk
Total Pitches: 140 (C, CV & T)

Skye C & C Club Site
Loch Greshornish, Borve,
Arnisort, Edinbane, Isle of Skye
IV51 9PS
Tel: 01470 582230   **152 E7**
campingandcaravanning
club.co.uk/skye
Total Pitches: 105 (C, CV & T)

Thurston Manor Leisure Park
Innerwick, Dunbar
EH42 1SA
Tel: 01368 840643   **129 J5**
thurstonmanor.co.uk
Total Pitches: 120 (C & CV)

Trossachs Holiday Park
Aberfoyle
FK8 3SA
Tel: 01877 382614   **132 G8**
trossachsholidays.co.uk
Total Pitches: 66 (C, CV & T)

Witches Craig C & C Park
Blairlogie, Stirling
FK9 5PX
Tel: 01786 474947   **133 N8**
witchescraig.co.uk
Total Pitches: 60 (C, CV & T)

WALES

Bron Derw Touring Caravan Park
Llanrwst
LL26 0YT
Tel: 01492 640494   **67 P2**
bronderw-wales.co.uk
Total Pitches: 48 (C & CV)

Bron-Y-Wendon Caravan Park
Wern Road, Llanddulas,
Colwyn Bay
LL22 8HG
Tel: 01492 512903   **80 C9**
bronywendon.co.uk
Total Pitches: 130 (C & CV)

Bryn Gloch C & C Park
Betws Garmon,
Caernarfon
LL54 7YY
Tel: 01286 650216   **67 J3**
campwales.co.uk
Total Pitches: 177 (C, CV & T)

Caerfai Bay Caravan & Tent Park
Caerfai Bay, St Davids,
Haverfordwest
SA62 6QT
Tel: 01437 720274   **40 E6**
caerfaibay.co.uk
Total Pitches: 106 (C, CV & T)

Cenarth Falls Holiday Park
Cenarth, Newcastle Emlyn
SA38 9JS
Tel: 01239 710345   **41 Q2**
cenarth-holipark.co.uk
Total Pitches: 30 (C, CV & T)

Daisy Bank Caravan Park
Snead, Montgomery
SY15 6EB
Tel: 01588 620471   **56 E6**
daisy-bank.co.uk
Total Pitches: 80 (C, CV & T)

Dinlle Caravan Park
Dinas Dinlle, Caernarfon
LL54 5TW
Tel: 01286 830324   **66 G3**
thornleyleisure.co.uk
Total Pitches: 175 (C, CV & T)

Eisteddfa
Eisteddfa Lodge, Pentrefelin,
Criccieth
LL52 0PT
Tel: 01766 522696   **67 J7**
eisteddfapark.co.uk
Total Pitches: 100 (C, CV & T)

Fforest Fields C & C Park
Hundred House, Builth Wells
LD1 5RT
Tel: 01982 570406   **44 G4**
fforestfields.co.uk
Total Pitches: 120 (C, CV & T)

Fishguard Bay Resort
Garn Gelli, Fishguard
SA65 9ET
Tel: 01348 811415   **41 J3**
fishguardbay.com
Total Pitches: 102 (C, CV & T)

Greenacres Holiday Park
Black Rock Sands, Morfa
Bychan, Porthmadog
LL49 9YF
Tel: 01766 512781   **67 J7**
haven.com/greenacres
Total Pitches: 945 (C & CV)

Hafan y Môr Holiday Park
Pwllheli
LL53 6HJ
Tel: 01758 612112   **66 G7**
haven.com/hafanymor
Total Pitches: 875 (C & CV)

Hendre Mynach Touring C & C Park
Llanaber Road, Barmouth
LL42 1YR
Tel: 01341 280262   **67 L11**
hendremynach.co.uk
Total Pitches: 240 (C, CV & T)

Home Farm Caravan Park
Marian-Glas, Isle of Anglesey
LL73 8PH
Tel: 01248 410614   **78 H8**
homefarm-anglesey.co.uk
Total Pitches: 102 (C, CV & T)

Islawrffordd Caravan Park
Tal-y-bont, Barmouth
LL43 2AQ
Tel: 01341 247269   **67 K10**
islawrffordd.co.uk
Total Pitches: 105 (C, CV & T)

Kiln Park Holiday Centre
Marsh Road, Tenby
SA70 8RB
Tel: 01834 844121   **41 M10**
haven.com/kilnpark
Total Pitches: 849 (C, CV & T)

Pencelli Castle C & C Park
Pencelli, Brecon
LD3 7LX
Tel: 01874 665451   **44 F10**
pencelli-castle.com
Total Pitches: 80 (C, CV & T)

Penisar Mynydd Caravan Park
Caerwys Road, Rhuallt,
St Asaph
LL17 0TY
Tel: 01745 582227   **80 F9**
penisarmynydd.co.uk
Total Pitches: 71 (C, CV & T)

Plas Farm Caravan & Lodge Park
Betws-yn-Rhos, Abergele
LL22 8AU
Tel: 01492 680254   **80 B10**
plasfarmcaravanpark.co.uk
Total Pitches: 54 (C & CV)

Plassey Holiday Park
The Plassey, Eyton,
Wrexham
LL13 0SP
Tel: 01978 780277   **69 L5**
plassey.com
Total Pitches: 90 (C, CV & T)

Pont Kemys C & C Park
Chainbridge, Abergavenny
NP7 9DS
Tel: 01873 880688   **31 K3**
pontkemys.com
Total Pitches: 65 (C, CV & T)

Presthaven Sands Holiday Park
Gronant, Prestatyn
LL19 9TT
Tel: 01745 856471   **80 F8**
haven.com/presthavensands
Total Pitches: 1102 (C & CV)

Red Kite Touring Park
Van Road, Llanidloes
SY18 6NG
Tel: 01686 412122   **55 L7**
redkitetouringpark.co.uk
Total Pitches: 66 (C & CV)

River View Touring Park
The Dingle, Llanedi,
Pontarddulais
SA4 0FH
Tel: 01635 844876   **28 G3**
riverviewtouringpark.co.uk
Total Pitches: 60 (C, CV & T)

Riverside Camping
Seiont Nurseries, Pont Rug,
Caernarfon
LL55 2BB
Tel: 01286 678781   **67 J2**
riversidecamping.co.uk
Total Pitches: 73 (C, CV & T)

The Trotting Mare Caravan Park
Overton, Wrexham
LL13 0LE
Tel: 01978 711963   **69 L7**
thetrottingmare.co.uk
Total Pitches: 65 (C, CV & T)

Trawsdir Touring C & C Park
Llanaber, Barmouth
LL42 1RR
Tel: 01341 280999   **67 K11**
barmouthholidays.co.uk
Total Pitches: 70 (C, CV & T)

Trefalun Park
Devonshire Drive, St Florence,
Tenby
SA70 8RD
Tel: 01646 651514   **41 L10**
trefalunpark.co.uk
Total Pitches: 90 (C, CV & T)

Tyddyn Isaf Caravan Park
Lligwy Bay, Dulas,
Isle of Anglesey
LL70 9PQ
Tel: 01248 410203   **78 H7**
tyddynisaf.co.uk
Total Pitches: 80 (C, CV & T)

White Tower Caravan Park
Llandwrog, Caernarfon
LL54 5UH
Tel: 01286 830649   **66 H3**
whitetowerpark.co.uk
Total Pitches: 52 (C & CV)

CHANNEL ISLANDS

Daisy Cottage Campsite
Route de Vinchelez, St Ouen,
Jersey
JE3 2DB
Tel: 01534 481700   **11 a1**
daisycottagecampsite.com
Total Pitches: 29 (C, CV & T)

Fauxquets Valley Campsite
Castel, Guernsey
GY5 7QL
Tel: 01481 255460   **10 b2**
fauxquets.co.uk
Total Pitches: 120 (CV & T)

Rozel Camping Park
Summerville Farm, St Martin,
Jersey
JE3 6AX
Tel: 01534 855200   **11 c1**
rozelcamping.com
Total Pitches: 100 (C, CV & T)

Signs giving orders

**Signs with red circles are mostly prohibitive.
Plates below signs qualify their message**

Entry to
20mph zone

End of
20mph zone

Maximum
speed

National speed
limit applies

School crossing
patrol

Stop and
give way

Give way to
traffic on
major road

Manually operated temporary
STOP and GO signs

No entry for
vehicular traffic

No vehicles
except bicycles
being pushed

No cycling

No motor
vehicles

No buses
(over 8
passenger
seats)

No
overtaking

No
towed
caravans

No vehicles
carrying
explosives

No vehicle or
combination of
vehicles over
length shown

No vehicles
over
height shown

No vehicles
over
width shown

Give priority to
vehicles from
opposite
direction

No right turn

No left turn

No
U-turns

No goods vehicles
over maximum
gross weight
shown (in tonnes)
except for loading
and unloading

WEAK BRIDGE
No vehicles
over maximum
gross weight
shown
(in tonnes)

Parking
restricted to
permit holders

No stopping during
period indicated
except for buses

No stopping during
times shown
except for as long
as necessary to set
down or pick up
passengers

No waiting

No stopping
(Clearway)

**Signs with blue circles but no red border mostly give
positive instruction.**

Ahead only

Turn left ahead
(right if symbol
reversed)

Turn left
(right if symbol
reversed)

Keep left
(right if symbol
reversed)

Vehicles may
pass either
side to reach
same
destination

Mini-roundabout
(roundabout
circulation – give
way to vehicles
from the
immediate right)

Route to be
used by pedal
cycles only

Segregated
pedal cycle
and pedestrian
route

Minimum speed

End of minimum
speed

Buses and
cycles only

Trams only

Pedestrian
crossing
point over
tramway

One-way traffic
(note: compare
circular 'Ahead
only' sign)

With-flow bus and
cycle lane

Contraflow bus lane

With-flow pedal cycle lane

Warning signs

Mostly triangular

Distance to
'STOP' line
ahead

Dual
carriageway
ends

Road narrows on
right (left if
symbol reversed)

Road
narrows on
both sides

Distance to
'Give Way'
line ahead

Crossroads

Junction on
bend ahead

T-junction with
priority over
vehicles from
the right

Staggered
junction

Traffic merging
from left ahead

The priority through route is indicated by the broader line.

Double bend first
to left (symbol
may be reversed)

Bend to right
(or left if symbol
reversed)

Roundabout

Uneven road

Plate below
some signs

Two-way
traffic crosses
one-way road

Two-way traffic
straight ahead

Opening or
swing bridge
ahead

Low-flying aircraft
or sudden
aircraft noise

Falling or
fallen rocks

Traffic signals
not in use

Traffic signals

Slippery road

Steep hill
downwards

Steep hill
upwards

Gradients may be shown as a ratio i.e. 20% = 1:5

Tunnel ahead

Trams crossing ahead

Level crossing with barrier or gate ahead

Level crossing without barrier or gate ahead

Level crossing without barrier

Patrol

School crossing patrol ahead (some signs have amber lights which flash when crossings are in use)

Frail (or blind or disabled if shown) pedestrians likely to cross road ahead

No footway for 400 yds

Pedestrians in road ahead

Zebra crossing

Safe height 16'-6"

Overhead electric cable; plate indicates maximum height of vehicles which can pass safely

14'-6"   4.4 m

Available width of headroom indicated

Sharp deviation of route to left (or right if chevrons reversed)

STOP when lights show

Light signals ahead at level crossing, airfield or bridge

Red   STOP
Green   Clear
IF NO LIGHT - PHONE CROSSING OPERATOR

Miniature warning lights at level crossings

Cattle

Wild animals

Wild horses or ponies

Accompanied horses or ponies

Cycle route ahead

Ice

Risk of ice

Queues likely

Traffic queues likely ahead

Humps for ½ mile

Distance over which road humps extend

Hidden dip

Other danger; plate indicates nature of danger

Soft verges for 2 miles

Soft verges

Side winds

Hump bridge

Ford

Worded warning sign

Quayside or river bank

Risk of grounding

Direction signs

Mostly rectangular

Signs on motorways - blue backgrounds

Nottingham 23 M1

At a junction leading directly into a motorway (junction number may be shown on a black background)

Nottingham A52 25 ½ m

On approaches to junctions (junction number on black background)

M1 The NORTH Sheffield 32 Leeds 59

Route confirmatory sign after junction

A404 Marlow   Birmingham, Oxford M40   4 ½ m

Downward pointing arrows mean 'Get in lane'
The left-hand lane leads to a different destination from the other lanes.

A46 (M69) Leicester, Coventry (E)   2 ½ m   The NORTH WEST, Birmingham, Coventry (N) M6

The panel with the inclined arrow indicates the destinations which can be reached

Signs on primary routes - green backgrounds

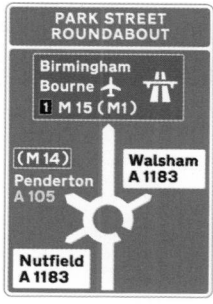
PARK STREET ROUNDABOUT
Birmingham Bourne 1 M15 (M1)
(M14) Penderton A105
Walsham A1183
Nutfield A1183

On approaches to junctions

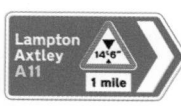
Lampton Axtley A11   14'-6"   1 mile

At the junction

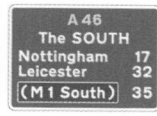
A46 The SOUTH
Nottingham 17
Leicester 32
(M1 South) 35

Route confirmatory sign after junction

TURPIN'S CROSSROADS
Biggleswick A11
Lampton (M11)
Dorfield A123
Axtley B1991
Steam railway

On approaches to junctions

Swansea Abertawe A483

On approach to a junction in Wales (bilingual)

Blue panels indicate that the motorway starts at the junction ahead.
Motorways shown in brackets can also be reached along the route indicated.
White panels indicate local or non-primary routes leading from the junction ahead.
Brown panels show the route to tourist attractions.
The name of the junction may be shown at the top of the sign.
The aircraft symbol indicates the route to an airport.
A symbol may be included to warn of a hazard or restriction along that route.

Signs on non-primary and local routes - black borders

HANGMAN'S CROSSROADS
Axtley B1234
(M11) Lampton A11
Townley A11

On approaches to junctions

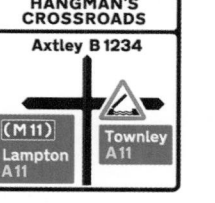
(A1(M)) 8
Barnes 10
Mackstone 2½
Elkington 1
A404 (A41)
Millington Green (A4011) 3

Market Walborough B486 7

At the junction

WC

Direction to toilets with access for the disabled

Green panels indicate that the primary route starts at the junction ahead.
Route numbers on a blue background show the direction to a motorway.
Route numbers on a green background show the direction to a primary route.

Emergency diversion routes

In an emergency it may be necessary to close a section of motorway or other main road to traffic, so a temporary sign may advise drivers to follow a diversion route. To help drivers navigate the route, black symbols on yellow patches may be permanently displayed on existing direction signs, including motorway signs. Symbols may also be used on separate signs with yellow backgrounds.

For further information visit:
theaa.com/breakdown-cover/advice/emergency-diversion-routes

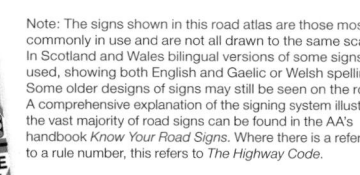

Note: The signs shown in this road atlas are those most commonly in use and are not all drawn to the same scale. In Scotland and Wales bilingual versions of some signs are used, showing both English and Gaelic or Welsh spellings. Some older designs of signs may still be seen on the roads. A comprehensive explanation of the signing system illustrating the vast majority of road signs can be found in the AA's handbook *Know Your Road Signs*. Where there is a reference to a rule number, this refers to *The Highway Code*.

Restricted junctions

Motorway and primary route junctions which have access or exit restrictions are shown on the map pages thus:

M1 London - Leeds

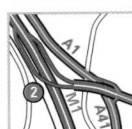
Northbound
Access only from A1 (northbound)

Southbound
Exit only to A1 (southbound)

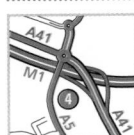
Northbound
Access only from A41 (northbound)

Southbound
Exit only to A41 (southbound)

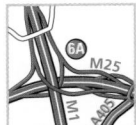
Northbound
Access only from M25 (no link from A405)

Southbound
Exit only to M25 (no link from A405)

Northbound
Access only from A414

Southbound
Exit only to A414

Northbound
Exit only to M45

Southbound
Access only from M45

Northbound
Exit only to M6 (northbound)

Southbound
Exit only to A14 (southbound)

Northbound
Exit only, no access

Southbound
Access only, no exit

Northbound
No exit, access only

Southbound
Access only from A50 (eastbound)

Northbound
Exit only, no access

Southbound
Access only, no exit

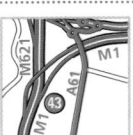
Northbound
Exit only to M621

Southbound
Access only from M621

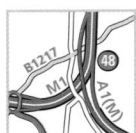
Northbound
Exit only to A1(M) (northbound)

Southbound
Access only from A1(M) (southbound)

M2 Rochester - Faversham

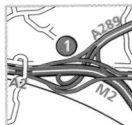
Westbound
No exit to A2 (eastbound)

Eastbound
No access from A2 (westbound)

M3 Sunbury - Southampton

Northeastbound
Access only from A303, no exit

Southwestbound
Exit only to A303, no access

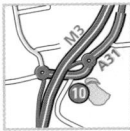
Northbound
Exit only, no access

Southbound
Access only, no exit

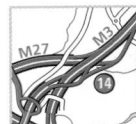
Northeastbound
Access from M27 only, no exit

Southwestbound
No access to M27 (westbound)

M4 London - South Wales

For junctions 1 & 2 see London district map on pages 178–181

Westbound
Exit only to M48

Eastbound
Access only from M48

Westbound
Access only from M48

Eastbound
Exit only to M48

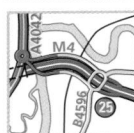
Westbound
Exit only, no access

Eastbound
Access only, no exit

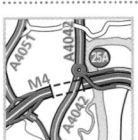
Westbound
Exit only, no access

Eastbound
Access only, no exit

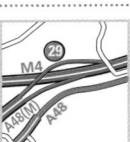
Westbound
Exit only to A48(M)

Eastbound
Access only from A48(M)

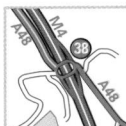
Westbound
Exit only, no access

Eastbound
No restriction

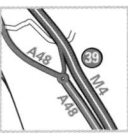
Westbound
Access only, no exit

Eastbound
No access or exit

M5 Birmingham - Exeter

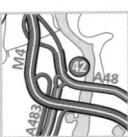
Northeastbound
Access only, no exit

Southwestbound
Exit only, no access

Northeastbound
Access only from A417 (westbound)

Southwestbound
Exit only to A417 (eastbound)

Northeastbound
Exit only to M49

Southwestbound
Access only from M49

Northeastbound
No access, exit only

Southwestbound
No exit, access only

M6 Toll Motorway

See M6 Toll motorway map on page *XXIII*

M6 Rugby - Carlisle

Northbound
Exit only to M6 Toll

Southbound
Access only from M6 Toll

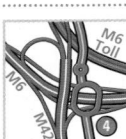
Northbound
Exit only to M42 (southbound) and A446

Southbound
Exit only to A446

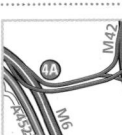
Northbound
Access only from M42 (southbound)

Southbound
Exit only to M42

Northbound
Exit only, no access

Southbound
Access only, no exit

Northbound
Exit only to M54

Southbound
Access only from M54

Northbound
Access only from M6 Toll

Southbound
Exit only to M6 Toll

(top right)

Westbound
Exit only to A483

Eastbound
Access only from A483

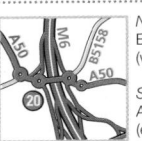
Northbound
No restriction

Southbound
Access only from M56 (eastbound)

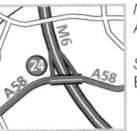
Northbound
Exit only to M56 (westbound)

Southbound
Access only from M56 (eastbound)

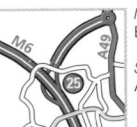
Northbound
Access only, no exit

Southbound
Exit only, no access

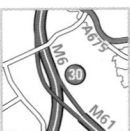
Northbound
Exit only, no access

Southbound
Access only, no exit

Northbound
Access only from M61

Southbound
Exit only to M61

Northbound
Exit only, no access

Southbound
Access only, no exit

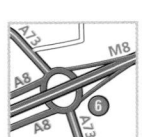
Northbound
Exit only, no access

Southbound
Access only, no exit

M8 Edinburgh - Bishopton

For junctions 7A to 29A see Glasgow district map on pages 176–177

Westbound
Exit only, no access

Eastbound
Access only, no exit

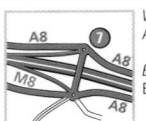
Westbound
Access only, no exit

Eastbound
Exit only, no access

Westbound
Access only, no exit

Eastbound
Exit only, no access

M9 Edinburgh - Dunblane

Northwestbound
Access only, no exit

Southeastbound
Exit only, no access

Northwestbound
Exit only, no access

Southeastbound
Access only, no exit

Northwestbound
Access only, no exit

Southeastbound
Exit only to A905

Northwestbound
Exit only to M876 (southwestbound)

Southeastbound
Access only from M876 (northeastbound)

M11 London - Cambridge

Northbound
Access only from A406 (eastbound)

Southbound
Exit only to A406

Northbound
Exit only, no access

Southbound
Access only, no exit

Northbound
Exit only, no access

Southbound
No direct access, use jct 8

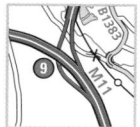
Northbound
Exit only to A11

Southbound
Access only from A11

Northbound
Exit only, no access

Southbound
Access only, no exit

Northbound
Exit only, no access

Southbound
Access only, no exit

M20 Swanley - Folkestone

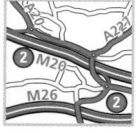
Northwestbound
Staggered junction; follow signs - access only

Southeastbound
Staggered junction; follow signs - exit only

Northwestbound
Exit only to M26 (westbound)

Southeastbound
Access only from M26 (eastbound)

Northwestbound
Access only from A20

Southeastbound
For access follow signs - exit only to A20

Northwestbound
No restriction

Southeastbound
For exit follow signs

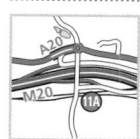
Northwestbound
Access only, no exit

Southeastbound
Exit only, no access

M23 Hooley - Crawley

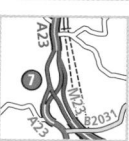
Northbound
Exit only to A23 (northbound)

Southbound
Access only from A23 (southbound)

Northbound
Access only, no exit

Southbound
Exit only, no access

M25 London Orbital Motorway

See M25 London Orbital motorway map on page XXII

M26 Sevenoaks - Wrotham

Westbound
Exit only to clockwise M25 (westbound)

Eastbound
Access only from anticlockwise M25 (eastbound)

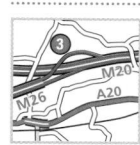
Westbound
Access only from M20 (northwestbound)

Eastbound
Exit only to M20 (southeastbound)

M27 Cadnam - Portsmouth

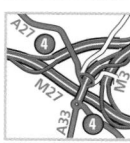
Westbound
Staggered junction; follow signs - access only from M3 (southbound). Exit only to M3 (northbound)

Eastbound
Staggered junction; follow signs - access only from M3 (southbound). Exit only to M3 (northbound)

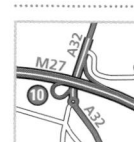
Westbound
Exit only, no access

Eastbound
Access only, no exit

Westbound
Staggered junction; follow signs - exit only to M275 (southbound)

Eastbound
Staggered junction; follow signs - access only from M275 (northbound)

M40 London - Birmingham

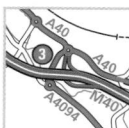
Northwestbound
Exit only, no access

Southeastbound
Access only, no exit

Northwestbound
Exit only, no access

Southeastbound
Access only, no exit

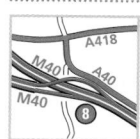
Northwestbound
Exit only to M40/A40

Southeastbound
Access only from M40/A40

Northwestbound
Exit only, no access

Southeastbound
Access only, no access

Northwestbound
Access only, no exit

Southeastbound
Exit only, no access

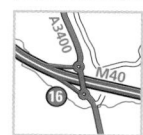
Northwestbound
Access only, no exit

Southeastbound
Exit only, no access

M42 Bromsgrove - Measham

See Birmingham district map on pages 174–175

M45 Coventry - M1

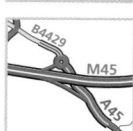
Westbound
Access only from A45 (northbound)

Eastbound
Exit only, no access

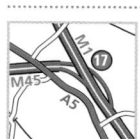
Westbound
Access only from M1 (northbound)

Eastbound
Exit only to M1 (southbound)

M48 Chepstow

Westbound
Access only from M4 (westbound)

Eastbound
Exit only to M4 (eastbound)

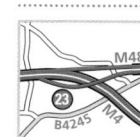
Westbound
No exit to M4 (eastbound)

Eastbound
No access from M4 (westbound)

M53 Mersey Tunnel - Chester

Northbound
Access only from M56 (westbound). Exit only to M56 (eastbound)

Southbound
Access only from M56 (westbound). Exit only to M56 (eastbound)

M54 Telford - Birmingham

Westbound
Access only from M6 (northbound)

Eastbound
Exit only to M6 (southbound)

M56 Chester - Manchester

For junctions 1,2,3,4 & 7 see Manchester district map on pages 182–183

Westbound
Access only, no exit

Eastbound
No access or exit

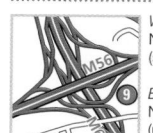
Westbound
No exit to M6 (southbound)

Eastbound
No access from M6 (northbound)

Westbound
Exit only to M53

Eastbound
Access only from M53

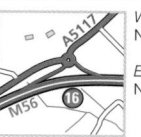
Westbound
No access or exit

Eastbound
No restriction

M57 Liverpool Outer Ring Road

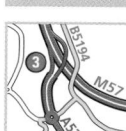
Northwestbound
Access only, no exit

Southeastbound
Exit only, no access

Northwestbound
Access only from A580 (westbound)

Southeastbound
Exit only, no access

M58 Liverpool - Wigan

Westbound
Exit only, no access

Eastbound
Access only, no exit

M60 Manchester Orbital

See Manchester district map on pages 182–183

M61 Manchester - Preston

Northwestbound
No access or exit

Southeastbound
Exit only, no access

Northwestbound
Exit only to M6 (northbound)

Southeastbound
Access only from M6 (southbound)

XX

M62 Liverpool - Kingston upon Hull

Westbound
Access only, no exit

Eastbound
Exit only, no access

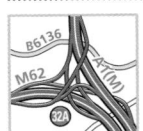

Westbound
No access to A1(M)
(southbound)

Eastbound
No restriction

M65 Preston - Colne

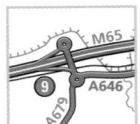

Northeastbound
Exit only, no access

Southwestbound
Access only, no exit

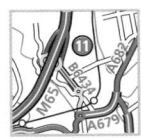

Northeastbound
Access only, no exit

Southwestbound
Exit only, no access

M66 Bury

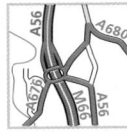

Northbound
Exit only to A56
(northbound)

Southbound
Access only from A56
(southbound)

Northbound
Exit only, no access

Southbound
Access only, no exit

M67 Hyde Bypass

Westbound
Access only, no exit

Eastbound
Exit only, no access

Westbound
Exit only, no access

Eastbound
Access only, no exit

Westbound
Exit only, no access

Eastbound
No restriction

M69 Coventry - Leicester

Northbound
Access only, no exit

Southbound
Exit only, no access

M73 East of Glasgow

Northbound
No exit to A74 and A721

Southbound
No exit to A74 and A721

Northbound
No access from or exit to A89. No access from M8 (eastbound)

Southbound
No access from or exit to A89. No exit to M8 (westbound)

M74 and A74(M) Glasgow - Gretna

Northbound
Exit only, no access

Southbound
Access only, no exit

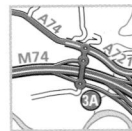

Northbound
Access only, no exit

Southbound
Exit only, no access

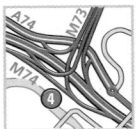

Northbound
No access from A74 and A721

Southbound
Access only, no exit to A74 and A721

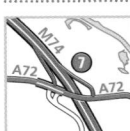

Northbound
Access only, no exit

Southbound
Exit only, no access

Northbound
No access or exit

Southbound
Exit only, no access

Northbound
No restriction

Southbound
Access only, no exit

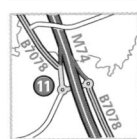

Northbound
Access only, no exit

Southbound
Exit only, no access

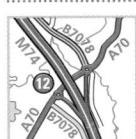

Northbound
Exit only, no access

Southbound
Access only, no exit

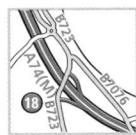

Northbound
Access only, no exit

Southbound
Access only, no exit

M77 Glasgow - Kilmarnock

Northbound
No exit to M8
(westbound)

Southbound
No access from M8
(eastbound)

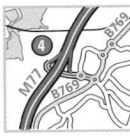

Northbound
Access only, no exit

Southbound
Exit only, no access

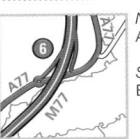

Northbound
Access only, no exit

Southbound
Exit only, no access

Northbound
Access only, no exit

Southbound
No restriction

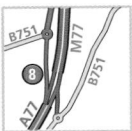

Northbound
Access only, no exit

Southbound
Exit only, no access

M80 Glasgow - Stirling

For junctions 1 & 4 see Glasgow district map on pages 176–177

Northbound
Exit only, no access

Southbound
Access only, no exit

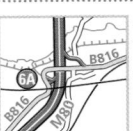

Northbound
Access only, no exit

Southbound
Exit only, no access

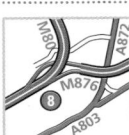

Northbound
Exit only to M876
(northeastbound)

Southbound
Access only from M876
(southwestbound)

M90 Edinburgh - Perth

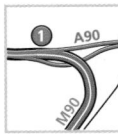

Northbound
No exit, access only

Southbound
Exit only to A90
(eastbound)

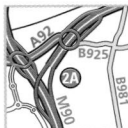

Northbound
Exit only to A92
(eastbound)

Southbound
Access only from A92
(westbound)

Northbound
Access only, no exit

Southbound
Exit only, no access

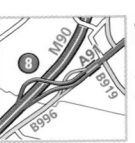

Northbound
Exit only, no access

Southbound
Access only, no exit

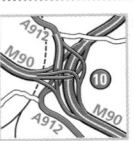

Northbound
No access from A912
No exit to A912
(southbound)

Southbound
No access from A912
(northbound).
No exit to A912

M180 Doncaster - Grimsby

Westbound
Access only, no exit

Eastbound
Exit only, no access

M606 Bradford Spur

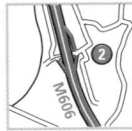

Northbound
Exit only, no access

Southbound
No restriction

M621 Leeds - M1

Clockwise
Access only, no exit

Anticlockwise
Exit only, no access

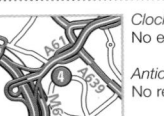

Clockwise
No exit or access

Anticlockwise
No restriction

Clockwise
Access only, no exit

Anticlockwise
Exit only, no access

Clockwise
Exit only, no access

Anticlockwise
Access only, no exit

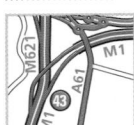

Clockwise
Exit only to M1
(southbound)

Anticlockwise
Access only from M1
(northbound)

M876 Bonnybridge - Kincardine Bridge

Northeastbound
Access only from M80
(northbound)

Southwestbound
Exit only to M80
(southbound)

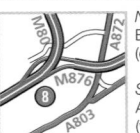

Northeastbound
Exit only to M9
(eastbound)

Southwestbound
Access only from M9
(westbound)

A1(M) South Mimms - Baldock

Northbound
Exit only, no access

Southbound
Access only, no exit

Northbound
No restriction

Southbound
Exit only, no access

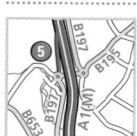

Northbound
Access only, no exit

Southbound
No access or exit

A1(M) Pontefract - Bedale

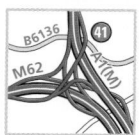

Northbound
No access to M62 (eastbound)

Southbound
No restriction

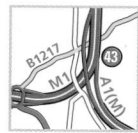

Northbound
Access only from M1 (northbound)

Southbound
Exit only to M1 (southbound)

A1(M) Scotch Corner - Newcastle upon Tyne

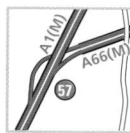

Northbound
Exit only to A66(M) (eastbound)

Southbound
Access only from A66(M) (westbound)

Northbound
No access. Exit only to A194(M) & A1 (northbound)

Southbound
No exit. Access only from A194(M) & A1 (southbound)

A3(M) Horndean - Havant

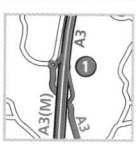

Northbound
Access only from A3

Southbound
Exit only to A3

Northbound
Exit only, no access

Southbound
Access only, no exit

A38(M) Birmingham Victoria Road (Park Circus)

Northbound
No exit

Southbound
No access

A48(M) Cardiff Spur

Westbound
Access only from M4 (westbound)

Eastbound
Exit only to M4 (eastbound)

Westbound
Exit only to A48 (westbound)

Eastbound
Access only from A48 (eastbound)

A57(M) Manchester Brook Street (A34)

Westbound
No exit

Eastbound
No access

A58(M) Leeds Park Lane and Westgate

Northbound
No restriction

Southbound
No access

A64(M) Leeds Clay Pit Lane (A58)

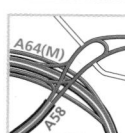

Westbound
No exit (to Clay Pit Lane)

Eastbound
No access (from Clay Pit Lane)

A66(M) Darlington Spur

Westbound
Exit only to A1(M) (southbound)

Eastbound
Access only from A1(M) (northbound)

A74(M) Gretna - Abington

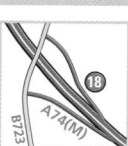

Northbound
Exit only, no access

Southbound
No exit

A194(M) Newcastle upon Tyne

Northbound
Access only from A1(M) (northbound)

Southbound
Exit only to A1(M) (southbound)

A12 M25 - Ipswich

Northeastbound
Access only, no exit

Southwestbound
No restriction

Northeastbound
Exit only, no access

Southwestbound
Access only, no exit

Northeastbound
Exit only, no access

Southwestbound
Access only, no exit

Northeastbound
Access only, no access

Southwestbound
Exit only, no access

Northeastbound
No restriction

Southwestbound
Access only, no exit

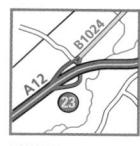

Northeastbound
Exit only, no access

Southwestbound
Access only, no exit

Northeastbound
Access only, no exit

Southwestbound
Exit only, no access

Northeastbound
Exit only, no access

Southwestbound
Access only, no exit

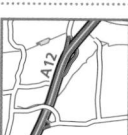

Northeastbound
Exit only, no access

Southwestbound
Access only, no exit

Northeastbound
Exit only (for Stratford St Mary and Dedham)

Southwestbound
Access only

A14 M1 - Felixstowe

Westbound
Exit only to M6 & M1 (northbound)

Eastbound
Access only from M6 & M1 (southbound)

Westbound
Exit only, no access

Eastbound
Access only, no exit

Westbound
Exit only to M11 (for London)

Eastbound
Access only, no exit

Westbound
Exit only to A14 (northbound)

Eastbound
Access only, no exit

Westbound
Access only, no exit

Eastbound
Exit only, no access

Westbound
Exit only to A11 Access only from A1303

Eastbound
Access only from A11

Westbound
Access only from A11

Eastbound
Exit only to A11

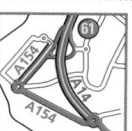

Westbound
Exit only, no access

Eastbound
Access only, no exit

Westbound
Access only, no exit

Eastbound
Exit only, no access

A55 Holyhead - Chester

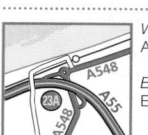

Westbound
Exit only, no access

Eastbound
Access only, no exit

Westbound
Access only, no exit

Eastbound
Exit only, no access

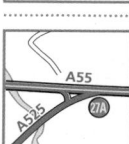

Westbound
Exit only, no access

Eastbound
No access or exit.

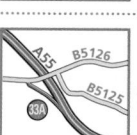

Westbound
No restriction

Eastbound
No access or exit

Westbound
Exit only, no access

Eastbound
No access or exit

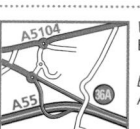

Westbound
Exit only to A5104

Eastbound
Access only from A5104

Refer also to atlas pages 36–37 and 50–51

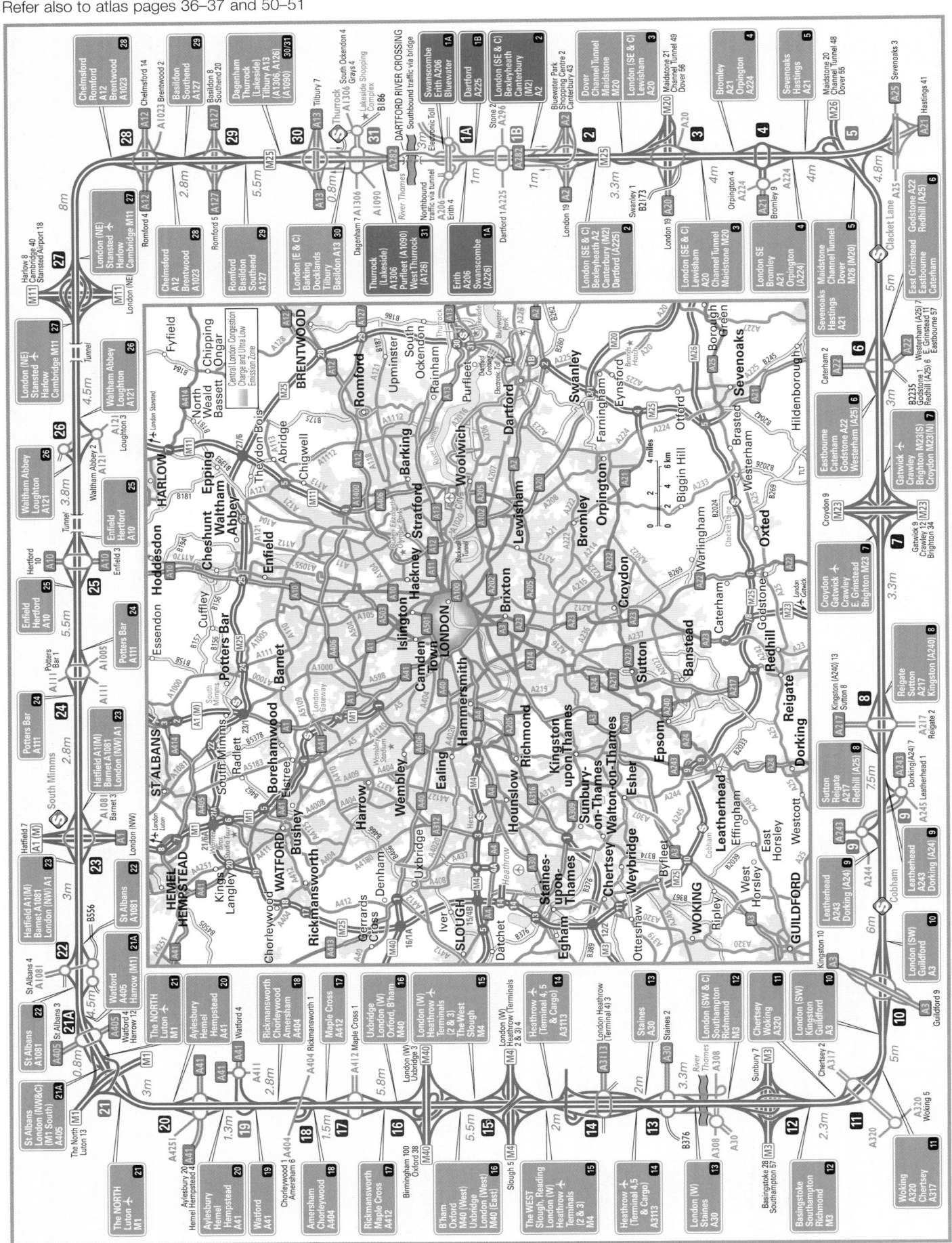

Refer also to atlas pages 58–59

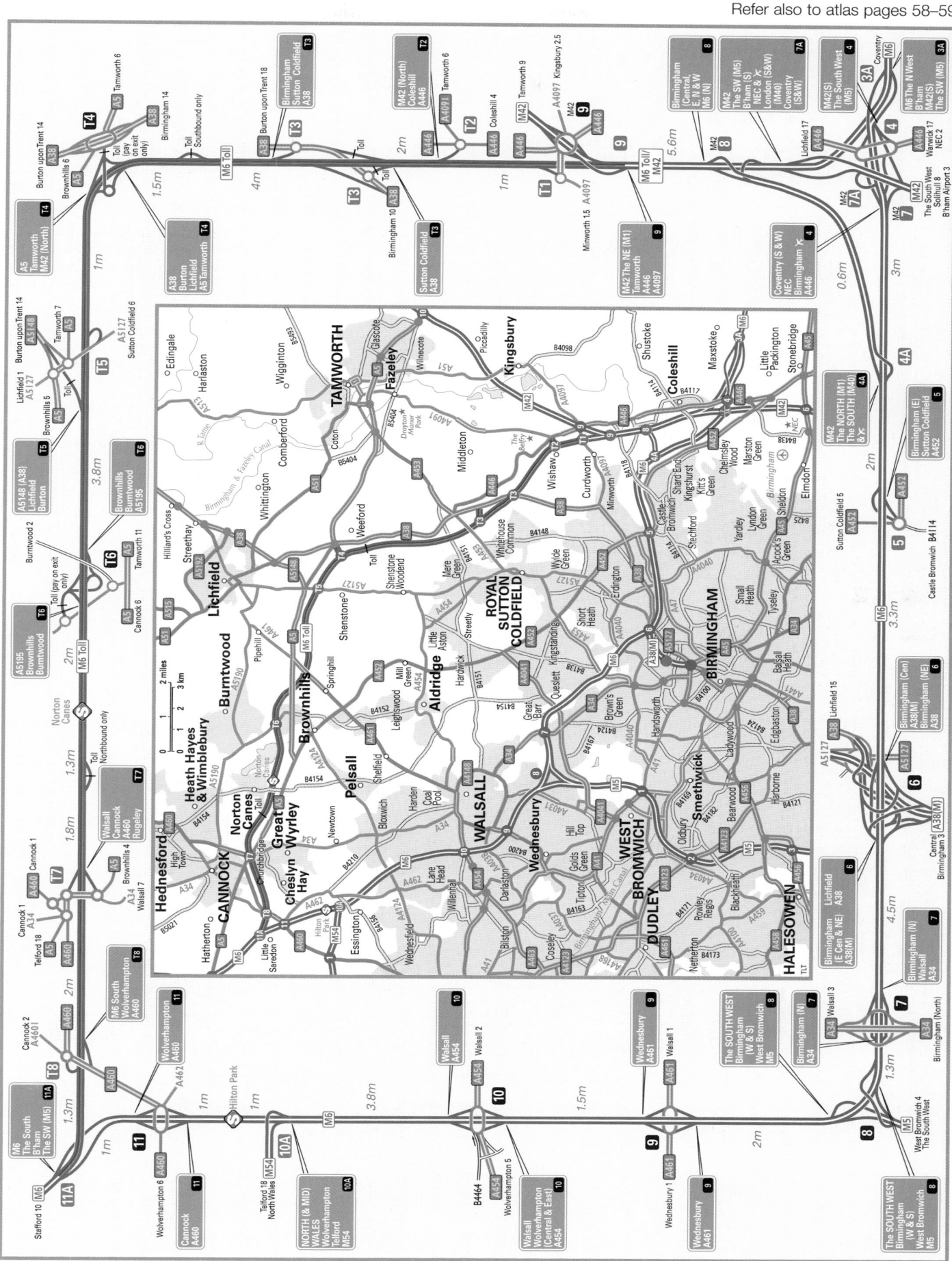

Smart motorways

Since Britain's first motorway (the Preston Bypass) opened in 1958, motorways have changed significantly. A vast increase in car journeys over the last 61 years has meant that motorways quickly filled to capacity. To combat this, the recent development of **smart motorways** uses technology to monitor and actively manage traffic flow and congestion.

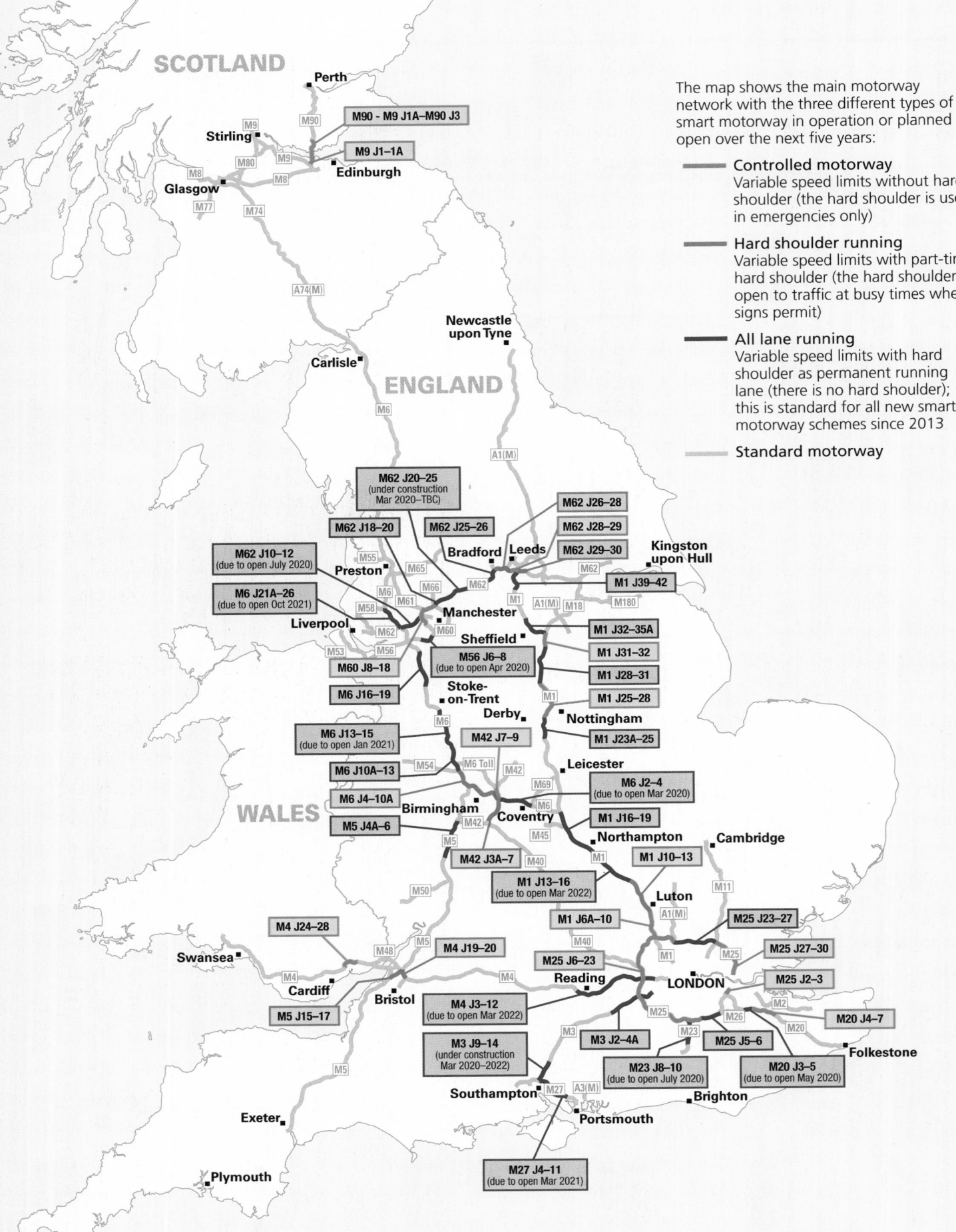

The map shows the main motorway network with the three different types of smart motorway in operation or planned to open over the next five years:

Controlled motorway
Variable speed limits without hard shoulder (the hard shoulder is used in emergencies only)

Hard shoulder running
Variable speed limits with part-time hard shoulder (the hard shoulder is open to traffic at busy times when signs permit)

All lane running
Variable speed limits with hard shoulder as permanent running lane (there is no hard shoulder); this is standard for all new smart motorway schemes since 2013

Standard motorway

Smart motorways (*Intelligent Transport Systems* in Scotland) are the responsibility of Highways England, Transport Scotland and Transport for Wales

How they work

Smart motorways utilise various active traffic management methods, monitored through a regional traffic control centre:

- Traffic flow is monitored using CCTV
- Speed limits are changed to smooth traffic flow and reduce stop-start driving
- Capacity of the motorway can be increased by either temporarily or permanently opening the hard shoulder to traffic

- Warning signs and messages alert drivers to hazards and traffic jams ahead
- Lanes can be closed in the case of an accident or emergency by displaying a red X sign
- Emergency refuge areas are located regularly along the motorway where there is no hard shoulder available

In an emergency

On a smart motorway there is often no hard shoulder so in an emergency you will need to make your way to the nearest **emergency refuge area** or motorway service area.

Emergency refuge areas are lay-bys marked with blue signs featuring an orange SOS telephone symbol. The telephone connects to the regional control centre and pinpoints your location. The control centre will advise you on what to do, send help and assist you in returning to the motorway.

If you are unable to reach an emergency refuge area or hard shoulder (if there is one) move as close to the nearside (left hand) boundary or verge as you can.

If it is not possible to get out of your vehicle safely, or there is no other place of relative safety to wait, stay in your vehicle with your seat-belt on and dial 999 if you have a mobile phone. If you don't have a phone, sit tight and wait to be rescued. Once the regional traffic control centre is aware of your situation, via the police or CCTV, they will use the smart motorway technology to set overhead signs and close the lane to keep traffic away from you. They will also send a traffic officer or the police to help you.

Sign indicating presence of emergency refuge areas ahead

This sign is located at each emergency refuge area

Signs

Motorway signals and messages advise of abnormal traffic conditions ahead and may indicate speed limits. They may apply to individual lanes when mounted overhead or, when located on the central reservation or at the side of the motorway, to the whole carriageway.

Where traffic is allowed to use the hard shoulder as a traffic lane, each lane will have overhead signals and signs. A red cross (with no signals) displayed above the hard shoulder indicates when it is closed. When the hard shoulder is in use as a traffic lane the red cross will change to a speed limit. Should it be necessary to close any lane, a red cross with red lamps flashing in vertical pairs will be shown above that lane. Prior to this, the signal will show an arrow directing traffic into the adjacent lane.

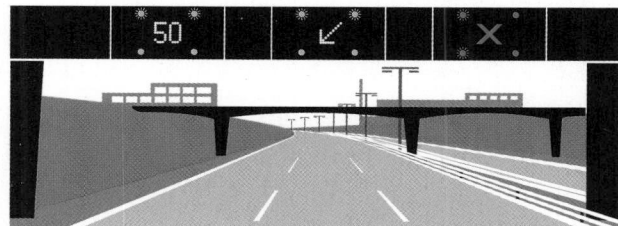

These signals are mounted above the carriageway with a signal for each traffic lane; each signal has two pairs of lamps that flash. You should obey the signal for your lane

Move to adjacent lane (arrow may point downwards to the right)

Leave motorway at next exit

Red lamps flashing from side to side in pairs, together with a red cross, mean 'do not proceed in the traffic lane directly below'. More than one lane may be closed to traffic

Where variable speed limit signs are mounted over individual lanes and the speed limit is shown in a red ring, the limit is mandatory. You will be at risk of a driving offence if you do not keep to the speed limit. Speed limits that do not include the red ring are the maximum speeds advised for the prevailing conditions.

Speed limits of 60, 50 and 40mph are used on all types of smart motorways. When no speed limit is shown the national speed limit of 70mph is in place (this is reduced to 60mph for particular vehicles such as heavy or articulated goods vehicles and vehicles towing caravans or trailers).

Quick tips

- Never drive in a lane closed by a red X
- Keep to the speed limit shown on the gantries
- A solid white line indicates the hard shoulder – do not drive in it unless directed or in the case of an emergency
- A broken white line indicates a normal running lane

- Exit the smart motorway where possible if your vehicle is in difficulty. In an emergency, move onto the hard shoulder where there is one, or the nearest emergency refuge area
- Put on your hazard lights if you break down

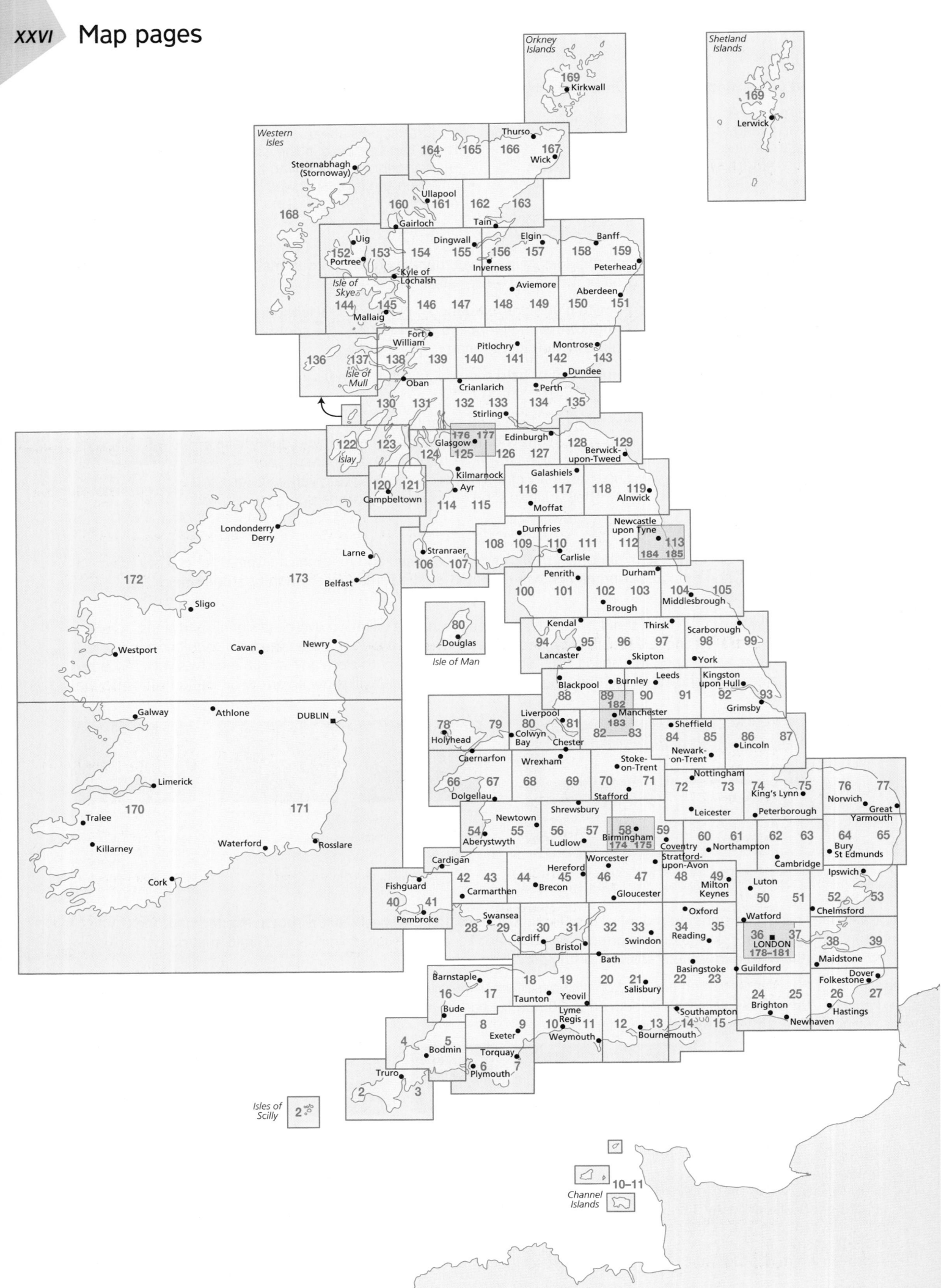

Orkney Islands 169 Kirkwall

Shetland Islands 169 Lerwick

Western Isles Steornabhagh (Stornoway)

Thurso
164 165 166 167 Wick

168

160 Ullapool 161 162 163
Gairloch Tain

Uig Dingwall Elgin Banff
152 153 154 155 156 157 158 159
Portree Inverness Peterhead
Kyle of
Lochalsh Aviemore Aberdeen
Isle of Skye 144 145 146 147 148 149 150 151
Mallaig

Fort William Pitlochry Montrose
136 137 138 139 140 141 142 143
Isle of Mull Dundee
Oban Crianlarich Perth
130 131 132 133 134 135
Stirling

122 123 176 177 Edinburgh 128 129
Islay 124 125 Glasgow 126 127 Berwick-upon-Tweed

120 121 Kilmarnock Galashiels
114 115 Ayr 116 117 118 119
Campbeltown Moffat Alnwick

Dumfries Newcastle upon Tyne
108 109 110 111 112 113
Stranraer Carlisle 184 185
106 107

Londonderry Derry Penrith Durham
Larne 100 101 102 103 104 105
Brough Middlesbrough
172 173 Belfast
Kendal Thirsk Scarborough
Sligo 94 95 96 97 98 99
Skipton York
Westport Cavan Newry Lancaster

Galway Athlone Blackpool Burnley Leeds Kingston upon Hull
DUBLIN 88 89 90 91 92 93
182
80 Liverpool 81 Manchester Grimsby
Douglas 78 79 183 Sheffield
Isle of Man Colwyn 82 83 84 85 Lincoln 86 87
170 171 Bay Chester Newark-on-Trent
Limerick Caernarfon Wrexham Stoke-on-Trent Nottingham
66 67 68 69 70 71 72 73 74 75 76 77
Tralee Dolgellau Stafford King's Lynn Norwich
Killarney Leicester Peterborough Great Yarmouth
Waterford Rosslare Newtown Shrewsbury
Cork 54 55 56 57 58 59 60 61 62 63 64 65
Aberystwyth Ludlow Birmingham Coventry Northampton Cambridge Bury St Edmunds
174 175 Stratford- Ipswich
Cardigan Worcester upon-Avon Luton
42 43 44 45 46 47 48 49 50 51 52 53
Fishguard Carmarthen Hereford Milton Chelmsford
Brecon Gloucester Keynes
40 41 Oxford Watford 36 37 38 39
Pembroke Swansea 30 31 32 33 34 35 LONDON Maidstone
28 29 Swindon Reading 178–181 Dover
Cardiff Guildford Folkestone
Bristol Bath Basingstoke 24 25 26 27
Barnstaple 18 19 20 21 22 23 Brighton Hastings
16 17 Salisbury Southampton Newhaven
Bude Taunton Yeovil
Lyme
8 9 Regis 10 11 12 13 14 15
Exeter Weymouth Bournemouth
4 5 Torquay
6 7
Truro Plymouth
2 3
Isles of Scilly 2

10–11
Channel Islands

Motoring information

M4	Motorway with number
Toll T4	Toll motorway with toll station
6	Motorway junction with and without number
5	Restricted motorway junctions
Fleet S R	Motorway service area, rest area
	Motorway and junction under construction
A3	Primary route single/dual carriageway
1	Primary route junction with and without number
3	Restricted primary route junctions

S	Primary route service area
BATH	Primary route destination
A1123	Other A road single/dual carriageway
B2070	B road single/dual carriageway
	Minor road more than 4 metres wide, less than 4 metres wide
	Roundabout
	Interchange/junction
	Narrow primary/other A/B road with passing places (Scotland)
	Road under construction

	Road tunnel
Toll	Road toll, steep gradient (arrows point downhill)
5	Distance in miles between symbols
or V	Vehicle ferry
	Fast vehicle ferry or catamaran
	Railway line, in tunnel
X	Railway/tram station, level crossing
+++++	Tourist railway
✈ H	Airport (major/minor), heliport

F	International freight terminal
H	24-hour Accident & Emergency hospital
C	Crematorium
P+R	Park and Ride (at least 6 days per week)
	City, town, village or other built-up area
628 / 637 Lecht Summit	Height in metres, mountain pass
	Snow gates (on main routes)
	National boundary
	County, administrative boundary

Touring information
To avoid disappointment, check opening times before visiting

	Scenic route
i	Tourist Information Centre
i	Tourist Information Centre (seasonal)
V	Visitor or heritage centre
	Picnic site
	Caravan site (AA inspected)
▲	Camping site (AA inspected)
	Caravan & camping site (AA inspected)
	Abbey, cathedral or priory
	Ruined abbey, cathedral or priory
	Castle
	Historic house or building
M	Museum or art gallery
	Industrial interest
	Aqueduct or viaduct
	Vineyard, brewery or distillery

	Garden
	Arboretum
	Country park
	Agricultural showground
	Theme park
	Farm or animal centre
	Zoological or wildlife collection
	Bird collection
	Aquarium
RSPB	RSPB site
	National Nature Reserve (England, Scotland, Wales)
	Local nature reserve
	Wildlife Trust reserve
	Forest drive
	National trail
	Viewpoint

	Waterfall
	Hill-fort
	Roman antiquity
	Prehistoric monument
1066	Battle site with year
	Steam railway centre
	Cave or cavern
	Windmill, monument
	Beach (award winning)
	Lighthouse
	Golf course
	Football stadium
	County cricket ground
	Rugby Union national stadium
	International athletics stadium
	Horse racing, show jumping

	Motor-racing circuit
	Air show venue
	Ski slope (natural, artificial)
	National Trust site
	National Trust for Scotland site
	English Heritage site
	Historic Scotland site
	Cadw (Welsh heritage) site
★	Other place of interest
	Boxed symbols indicate attractions within urban areas
	World Heritage Site (UNESCO)
	National Park and National Scenic Area (Scotland)
	Forest Park
	Sandy beach
	Heritage coast
	Major shopping centre

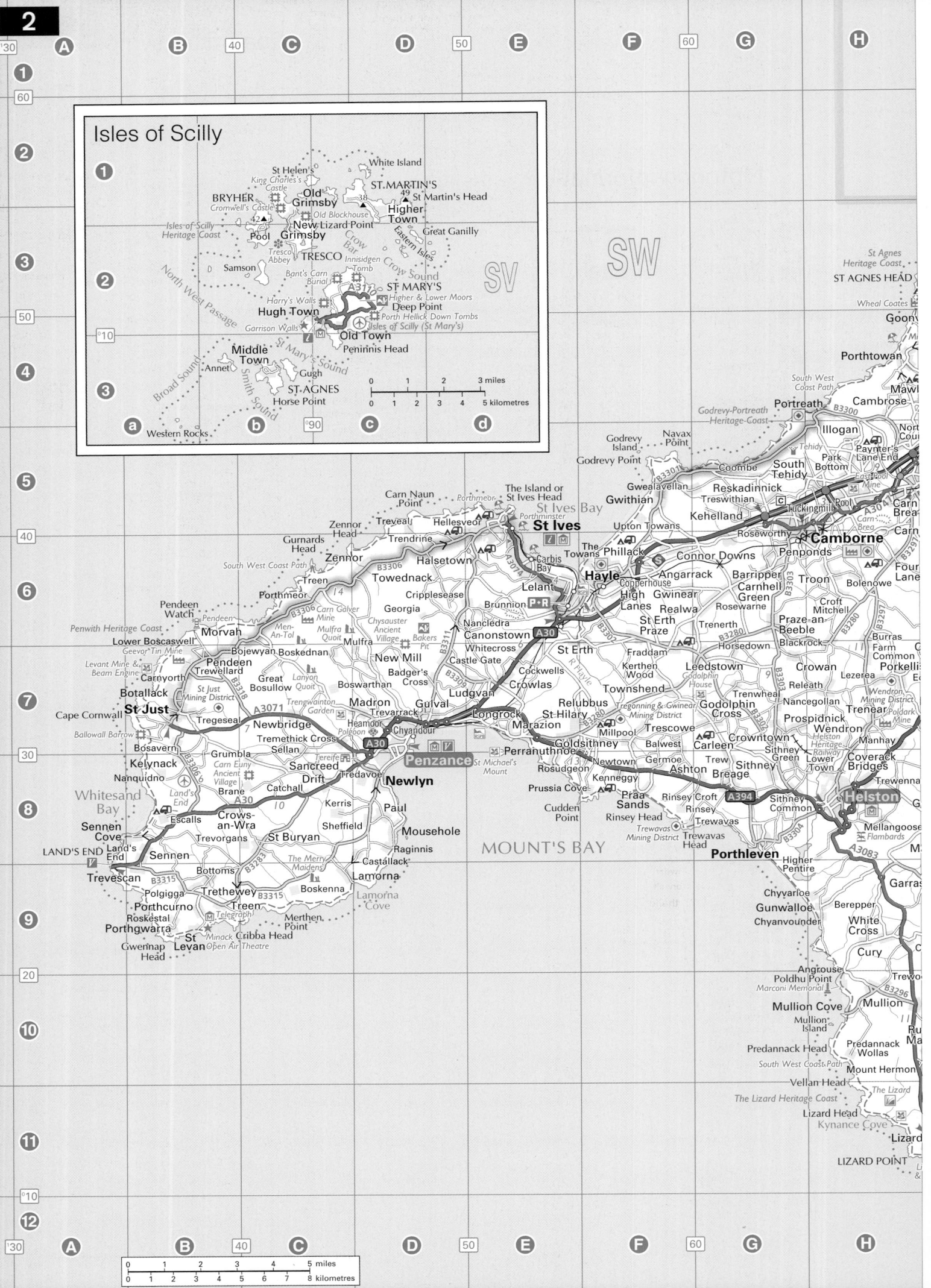

2

Isles of Scilly

White Island
St Helen's
BRYHER
King Charles's Castle
OLD GRIMSBY
Cromwell's Castle
ST. MARTIN'S
38
49 St Martin's Head
Old Blockhouse
42
Higher Town
New Lizard Point
Grimsby
Pool
TRESCO
Tresco Abbey
Crow Bar
Great Ganilly
Samson
Bant's Carn Burial
Innisidgen Tomb
Crow Sound
Eastern Isles
Isles-of-Scilly Heritage Coast
North West Passage
A3111
ST MARY'S
Higher & Lower Moors
Harry's Walls
Deep Point
Porth Hellick Down Tombs
Hugh Town
Isles of Scilly (St Mary's)
Garrison Walls
Old Town
Broad Sound
St Mary's Sound
Peninnis Head
Middle Town
Annet
Gugh
Smith Sound
ST. AGNES
Horse Point

SV

SW

0   1   2   3 miles
0   1   2   3   4   5 kilometres

Western Rocks

St Agnes Heritage Coast
ST AGNES HEAD
Wheal Coates
Goon

Porthtowan
Godrevy-Portreath Heritage-Coast
South West Coast Path
Portreath
B3300
Cambrose
Mawl
Illogan
Nor Cou

Godrevy Island
Godrevy Point
Navax Point
Coombe
Tehidy
Paynter's Lane End
East Pool Mine

South Tehidy
Park Bottom

Carn Brea

Gwealavellan
Reskadinnick
Treswithian
Tuckingmill
A304
Carn Brea

Carn Naun Point
Porthmeor
Gwithian
The Island or St Ives Head
St Ives Bay
Upton Towans
Kehelland
Roseworthy
Carn Brea
Camborne
Penponds
Four Lane

Zennor Head
Treveal
Trendrine
Hellesveor
Porthminster
St Ives
The Towans
Phillack
B3301
Connor Downs
Angarrack
Barripper
Troon
Bolenowe

Gurnards Head
Treen
Halsetown
Carbis Bay
Hayle
Copperhouse
High Gwinear
Lanes
Carnhell Green
Realwa
Rosewarne
Croft Mitchell
Burras

Zennor
B3306
Towednack
Cripplesease
Georgia
Brunnion
P+R
Nancledra
Canonstown
A30
St Erth
Praze
Fraddam
Kerthen Wood
Leedstown
Townshend
Trenerth
Praze-an-Beeble
Blackrock
Farm Common
Porkelli

Penwith Heritage Coast
Pendeen Watch
Morvah
Men-An-Tol
Carn Galver Mine
Mulfra Quoit
Chysauster Ancient Village
Bakers Pit
Whitecross
Castle Gate
Cockwells
Crowan
Horsedown
Lezerea
B3280
E

Lower Boscaswell
Geevor Tin Mine
Bojewyan
Boskednan
Mulfra
New Mill
Badger's Cross
Ludgvan
Crowlas
Godolphin House
Godolphin Cross
Nancegollan
Wendron Mining District
Trenear
Poldark

Pendeen
Trewellard
Great Bosullow
Lanyon Quoit
Boswarthan
B3309
R Hayle
Relubbus
St Hilary
Tregonning & Gwinear Mining District
Trenwheal
Crowntown
Sithney
Railway
Manhay

Carnyorth
Trewinnard Garden
Madron
Trevarrack
Gulval
Longrock
Marazion
Millpool
Trescowe
Balwest
Carleen
Sithney Green
Lower Town
Coverack Bridges

Botallack
St Just Mining District
Heamoor
Polgoon
Chyandour
RSPB
Goldsithney
Newtown
Germoe
Trew
Breage
Ashton
Helston
Trewenna

St Just
A3071
Tregeseal
Newbridge
Tremethick Cross
Sellan
Tereife
Penzance
St Michael's Mount
Perranuthnoe
Rosudgeon
Kenneggy
Praa Sands
Rinsey Croft
A394
Sithney Common
Helston

Ballowall Barrow
Bosavern
Grumbla
Carn Euny Ancient Village
Sancreed
Drift
Tredavoe
Newlyn
Prussia Cove
Rinsey
Rinsey Head
Trewavas

Kelynack
Nanquidno
Brane
Catchall
Kerris
Paul
Cudden Point
Trewavas Mining District
Trewavas Head
Porthleven
Higher Pentire

Whitesand Bay
Land's End
Sennen Cove
Escalls
Crows-an-Wra
St Buryan
Sheffield
Mousehole
Raginnis
MOUNT'S BAY
A3083
Chyvarloe
Gunwalloe
Chyanvounder
White Cross

LAND'S END
Land's End
Sennen
Trevorgans
The Merry Maidens
Castallack
Lamorna
Cury
Garras

Trevescan
B3315
Bottoms
Trethewey
Treen
Boskenna
Lamorna Cove
Angrouse
Poldhu Point
Marconi Memorial
B3296
Trewo

Polgigga
Porthcurno
Merthen Point
Mullion Cove
Mullion Island
Mullion
Ru
Ma

Roskestal
Porthgwarra
Gwennap Head
St Levan
Minack Cribba Head
Open Air Theatre
Telegraph
Predannack Head
Predannack Wollas
South West Coast Path
Mount Hermon

Vellan Head
The Lizard Heritage Coast
The Lizard
Lizard Head
Kynance Cove
Lizard

LIZARD POINT
Li
&

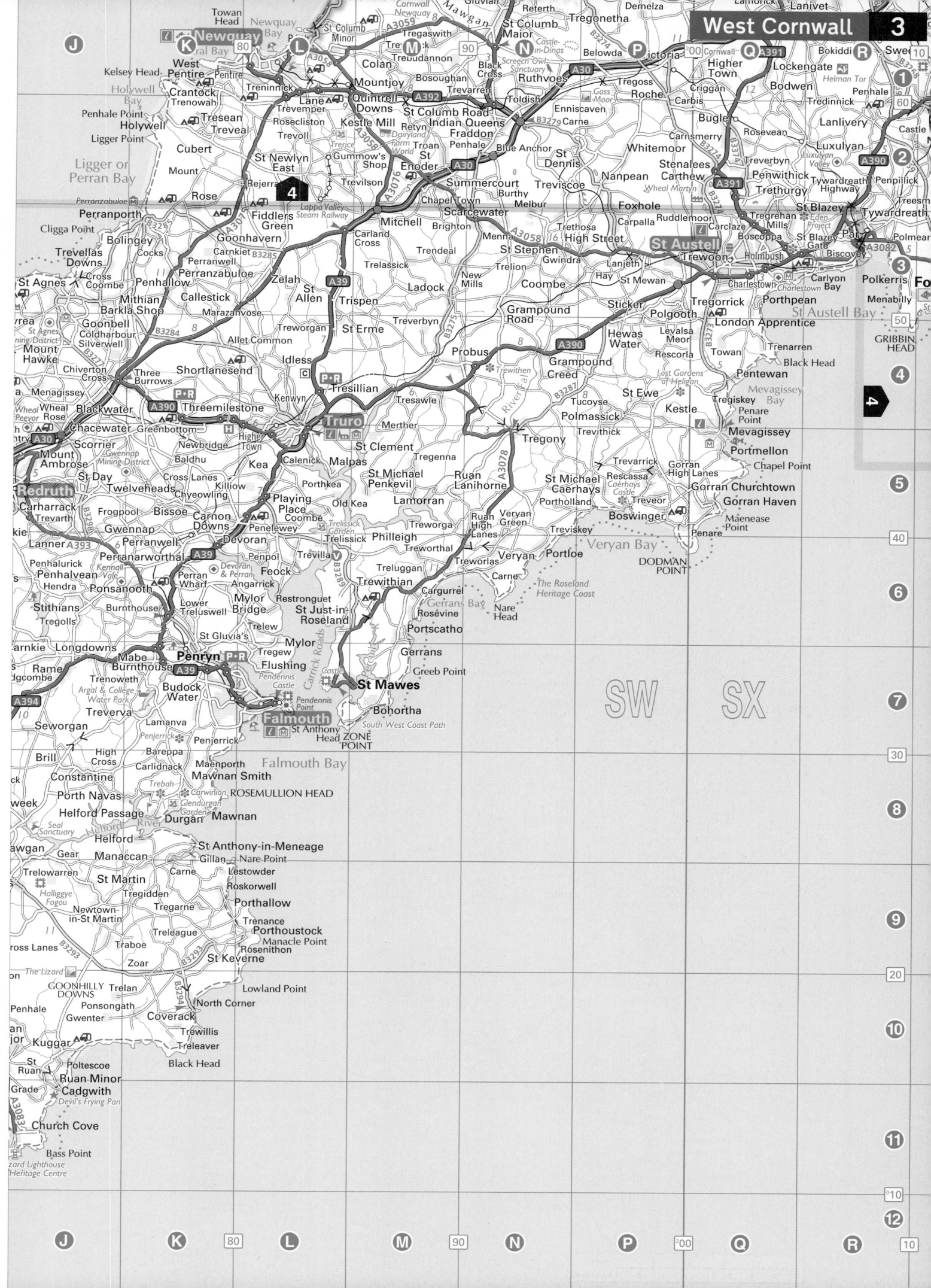

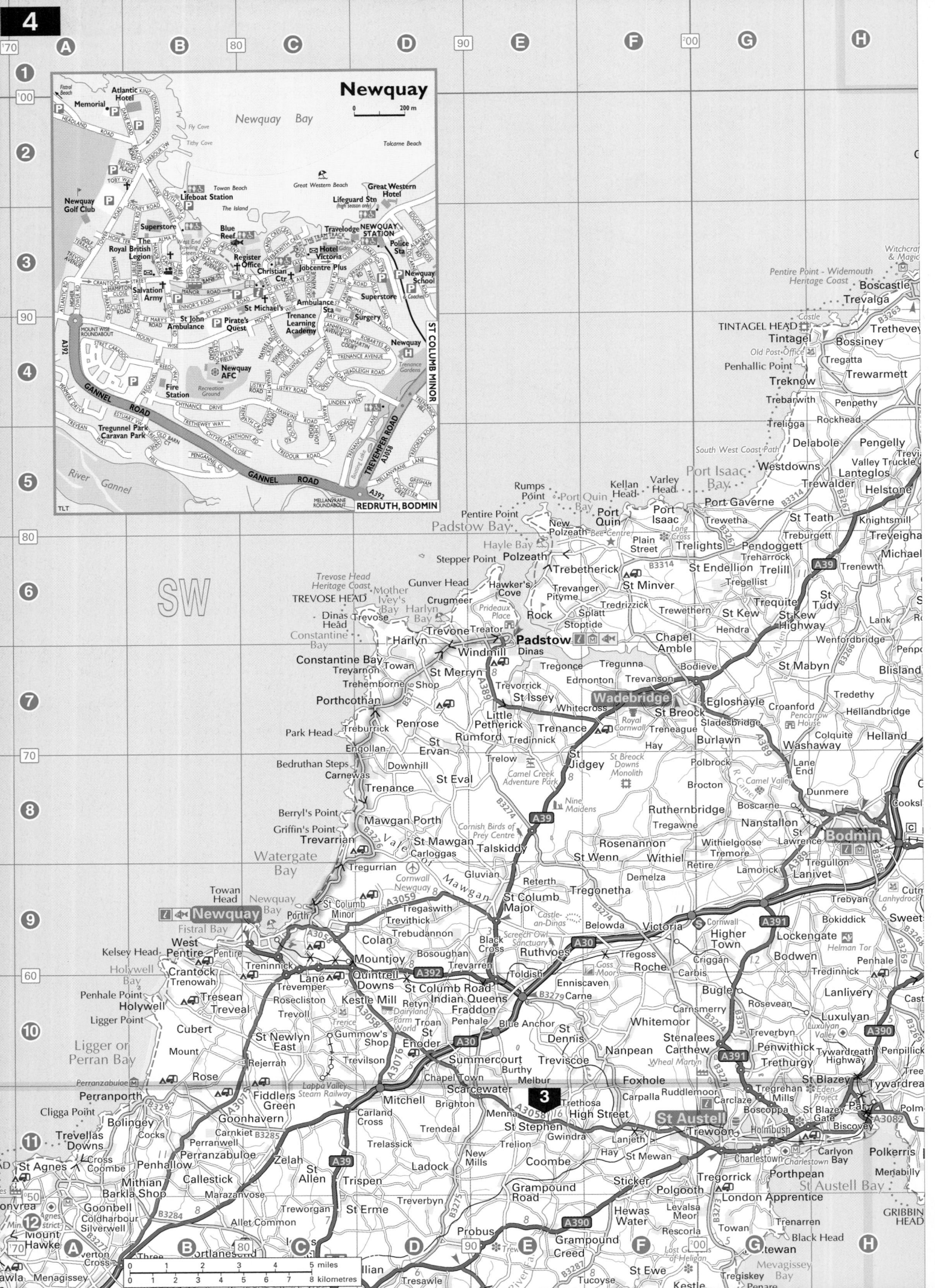

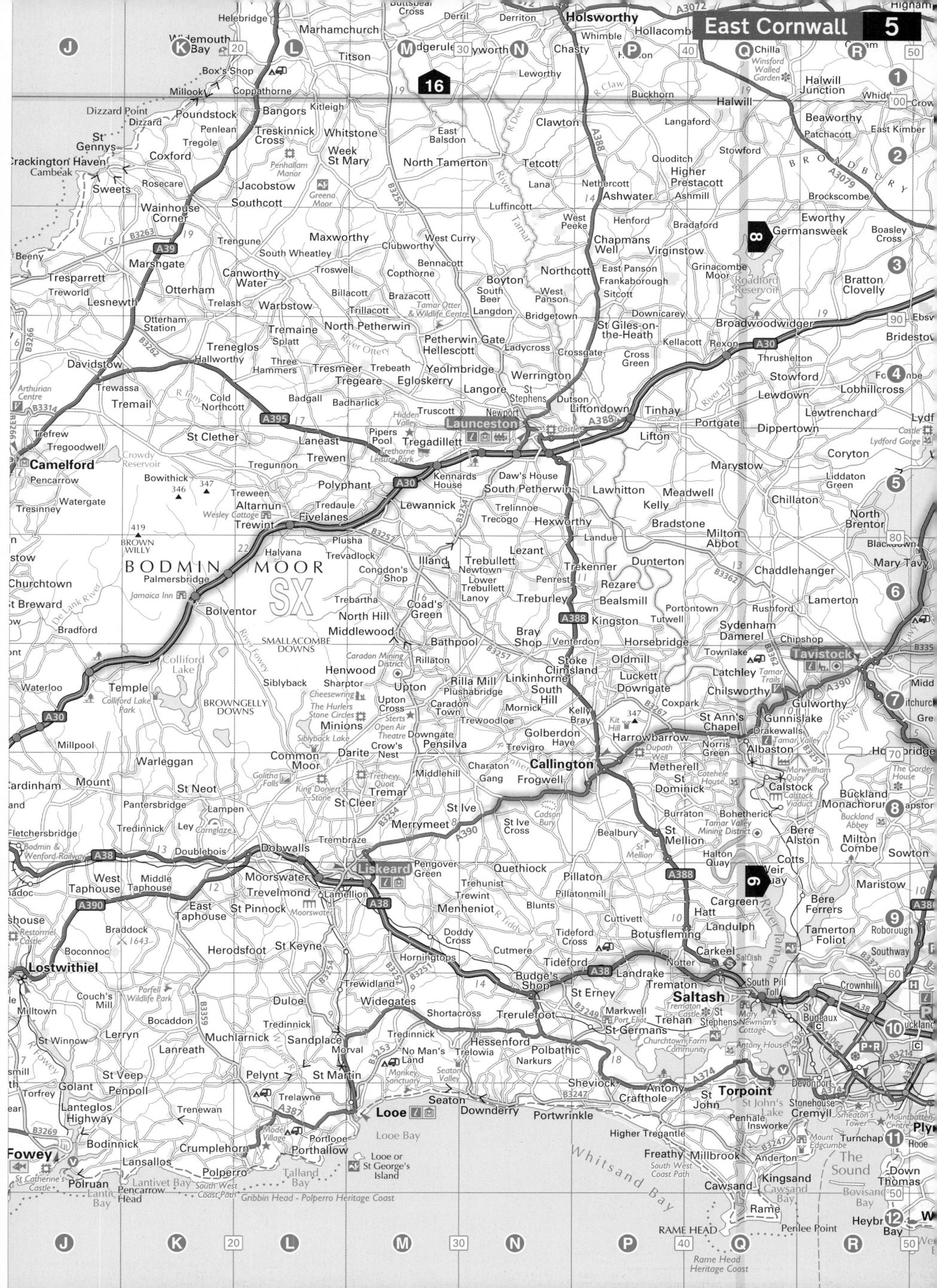

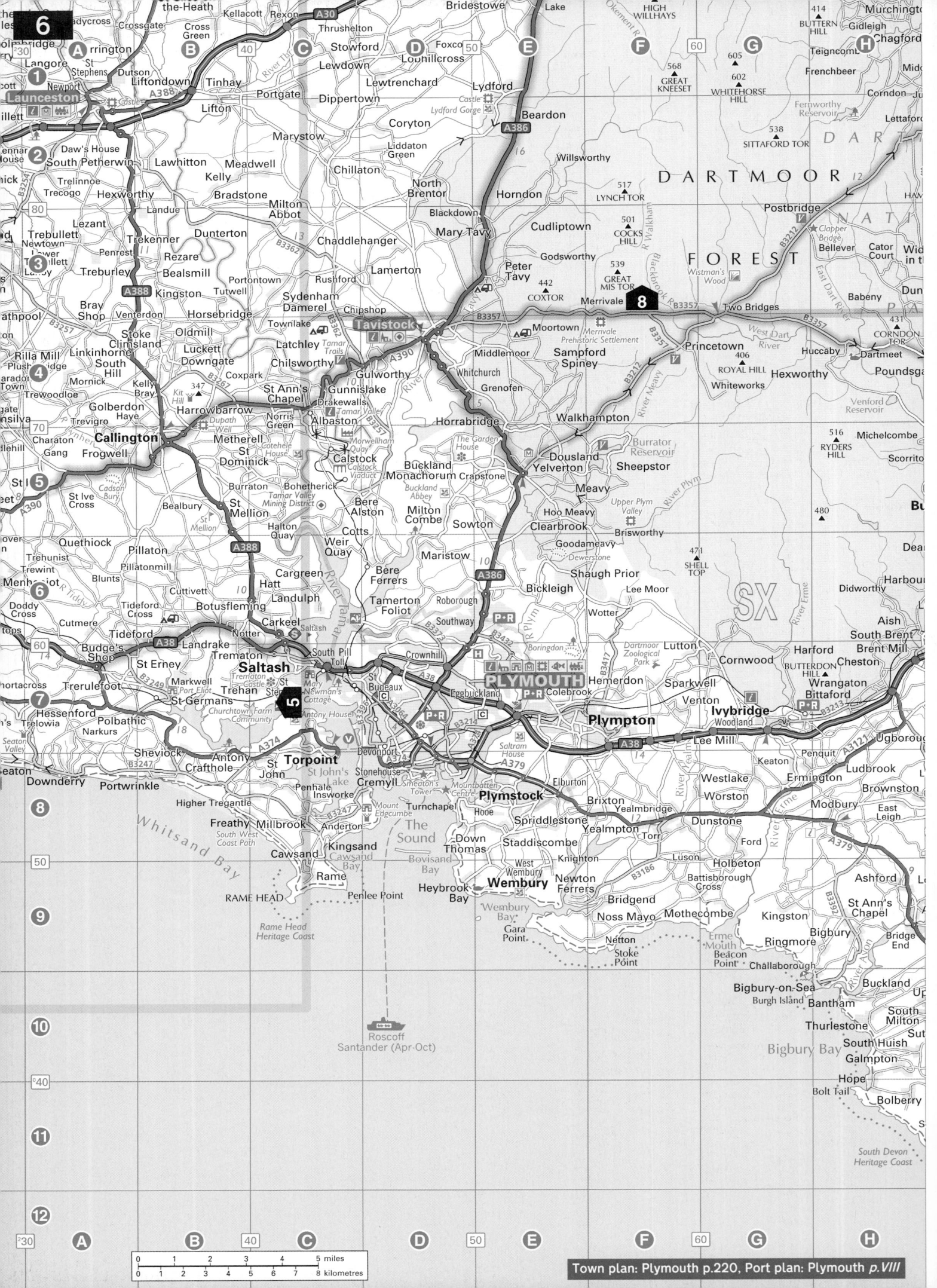

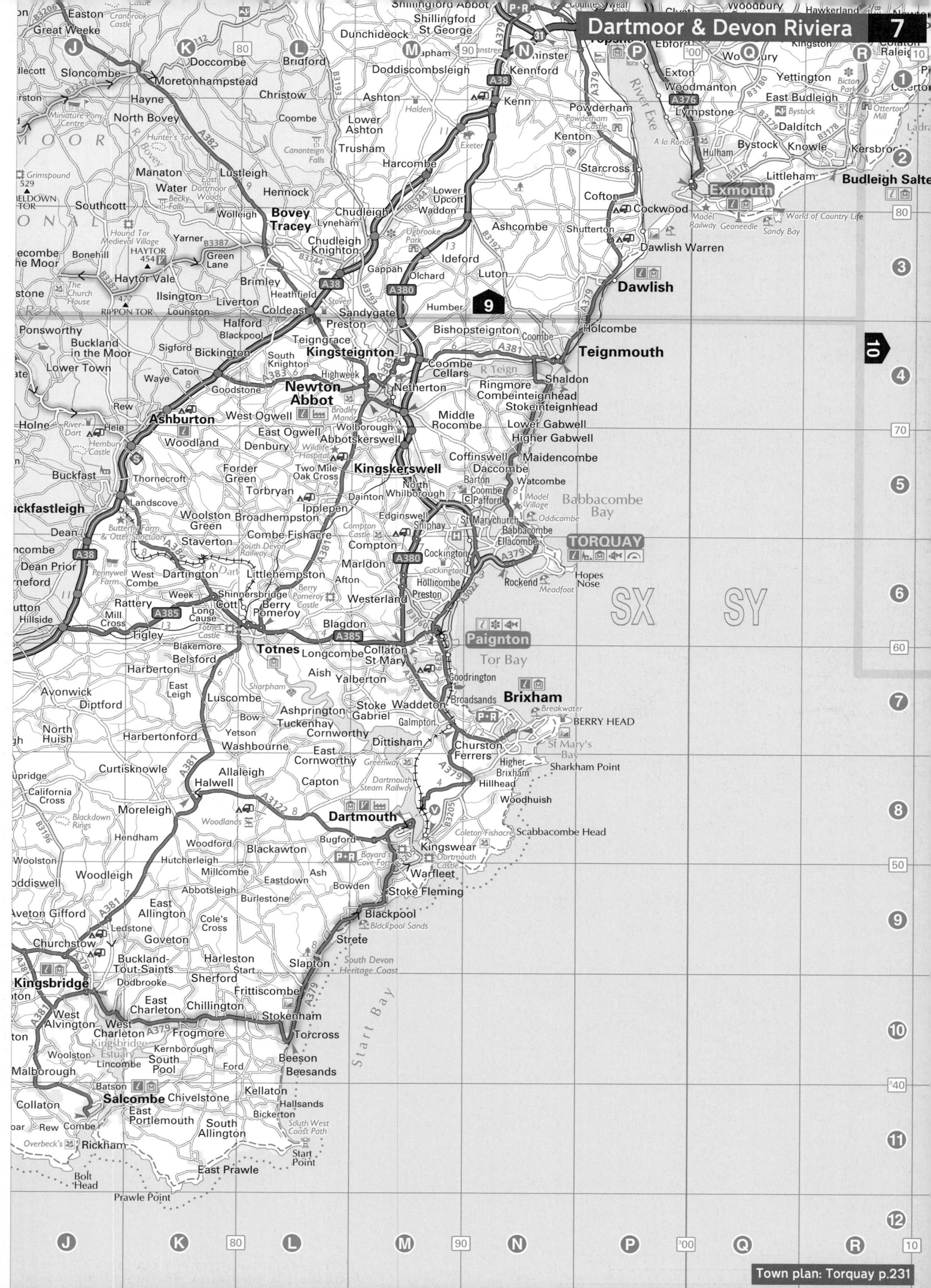

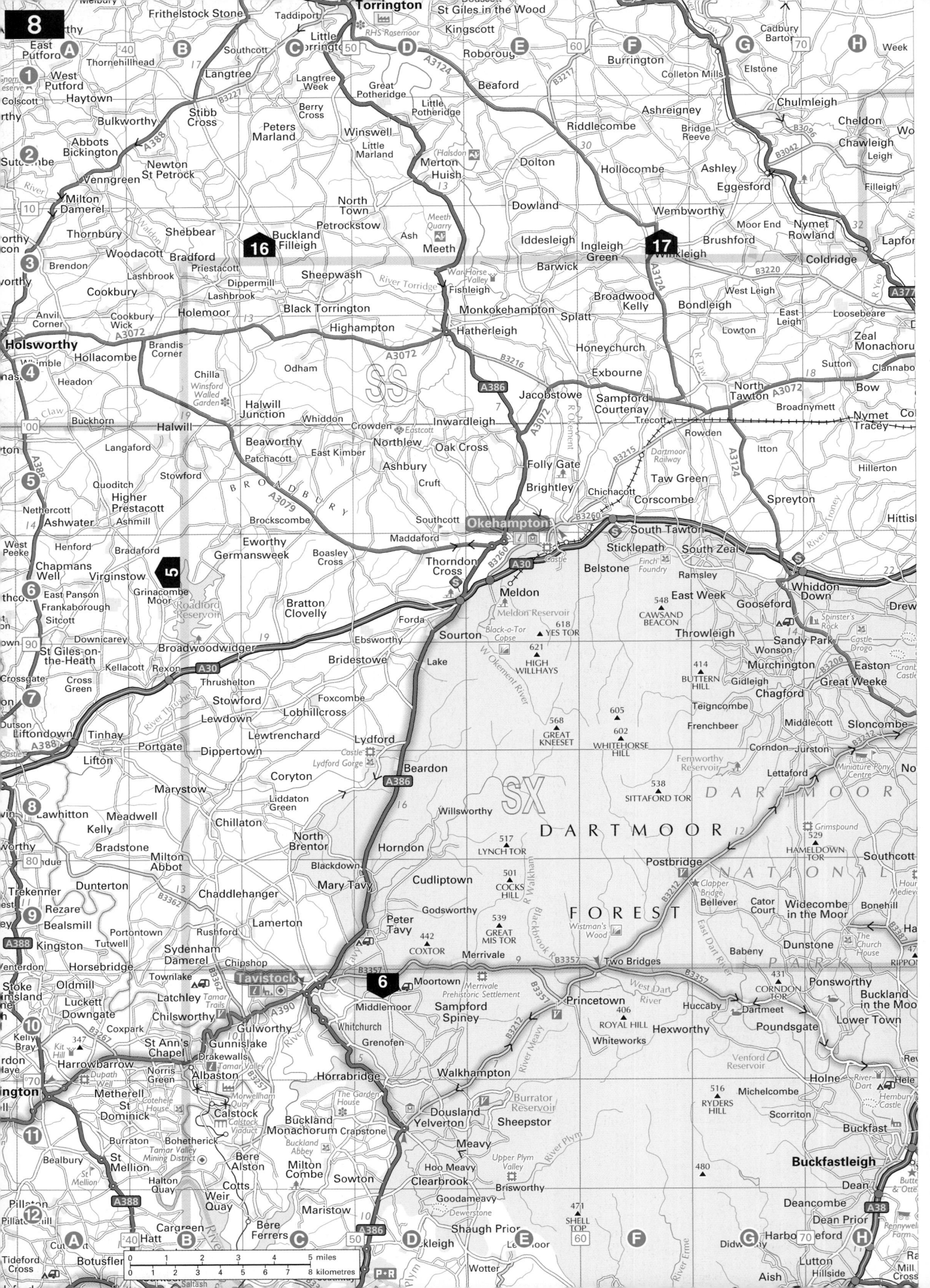

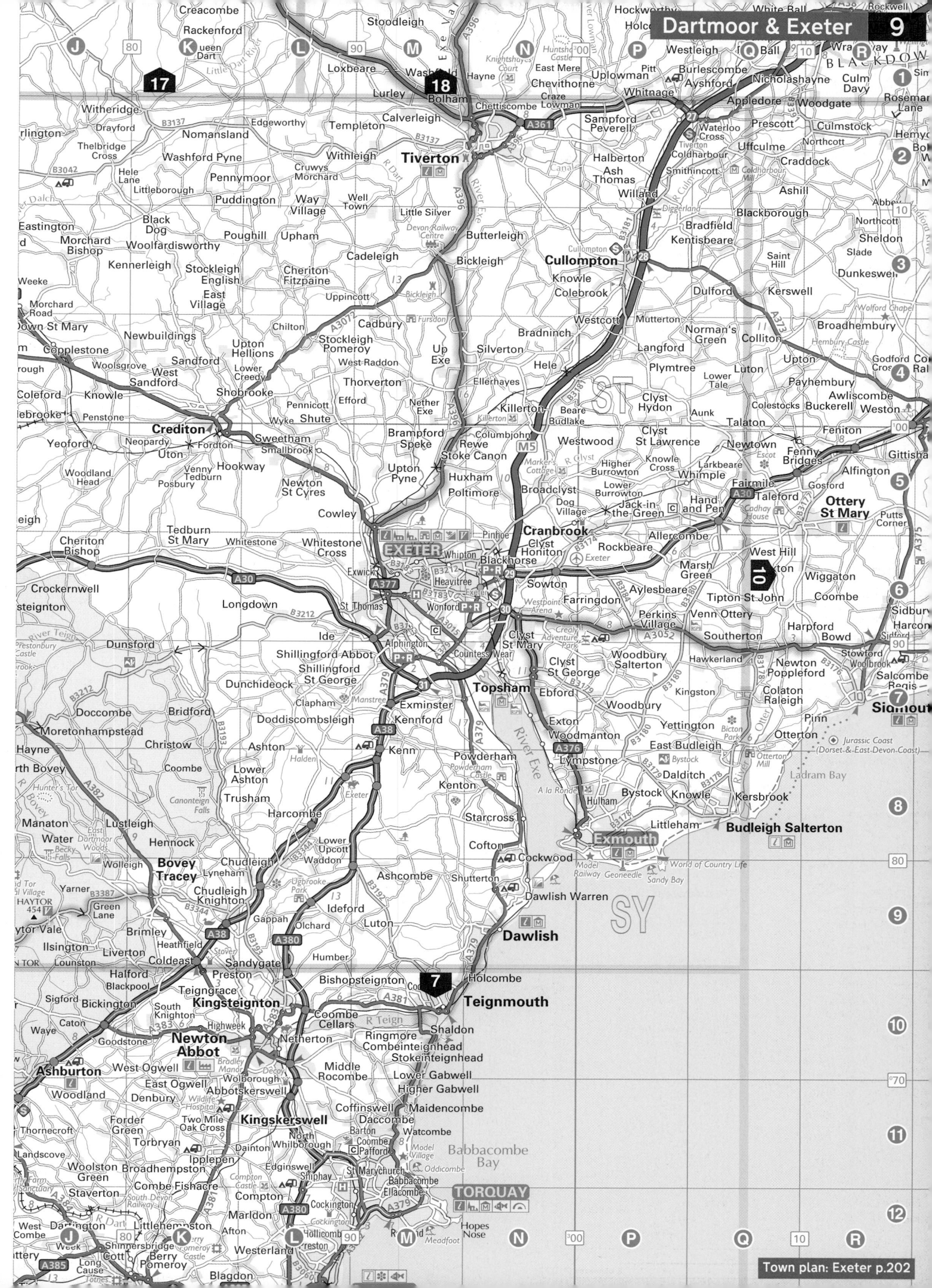

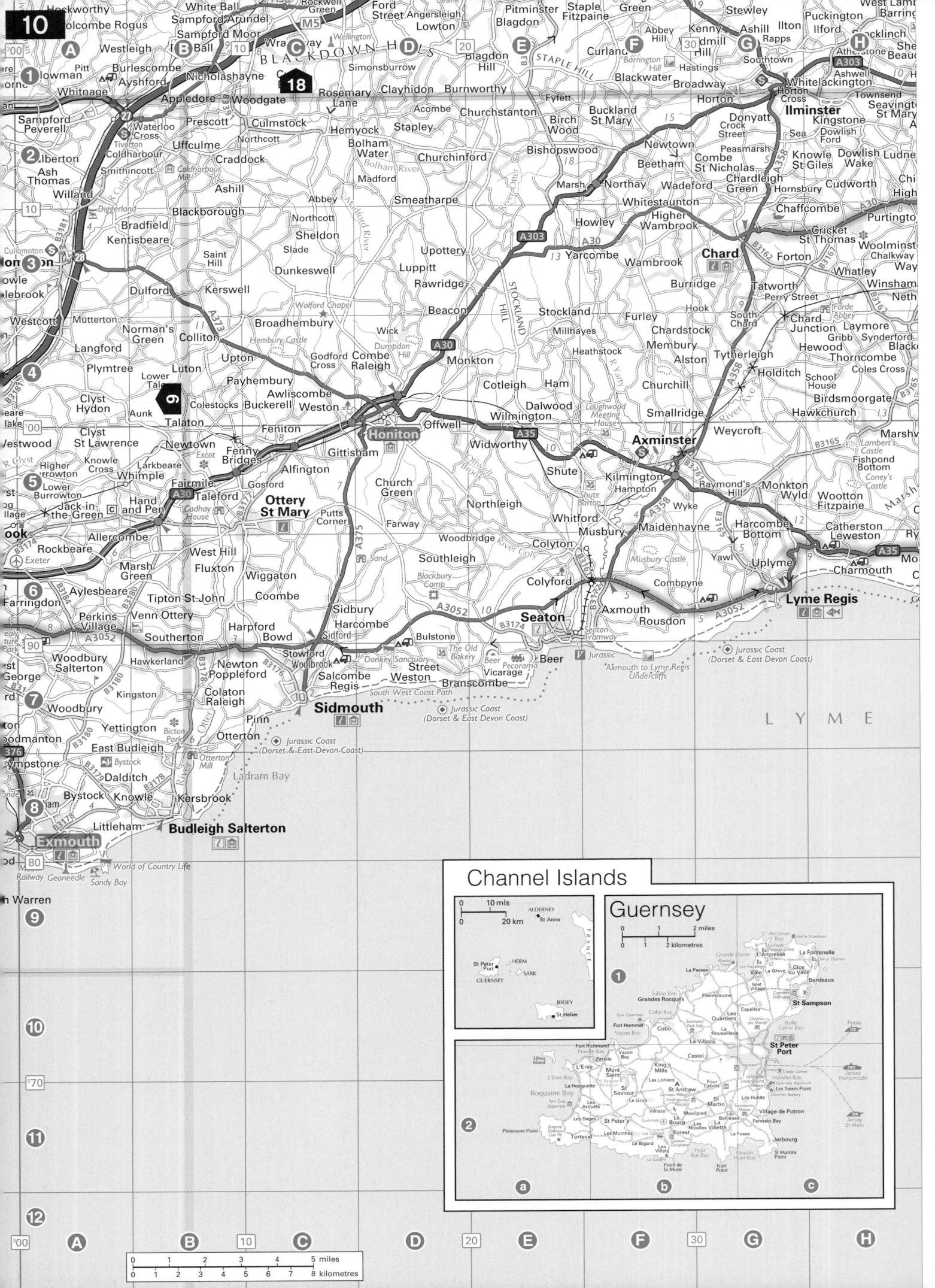

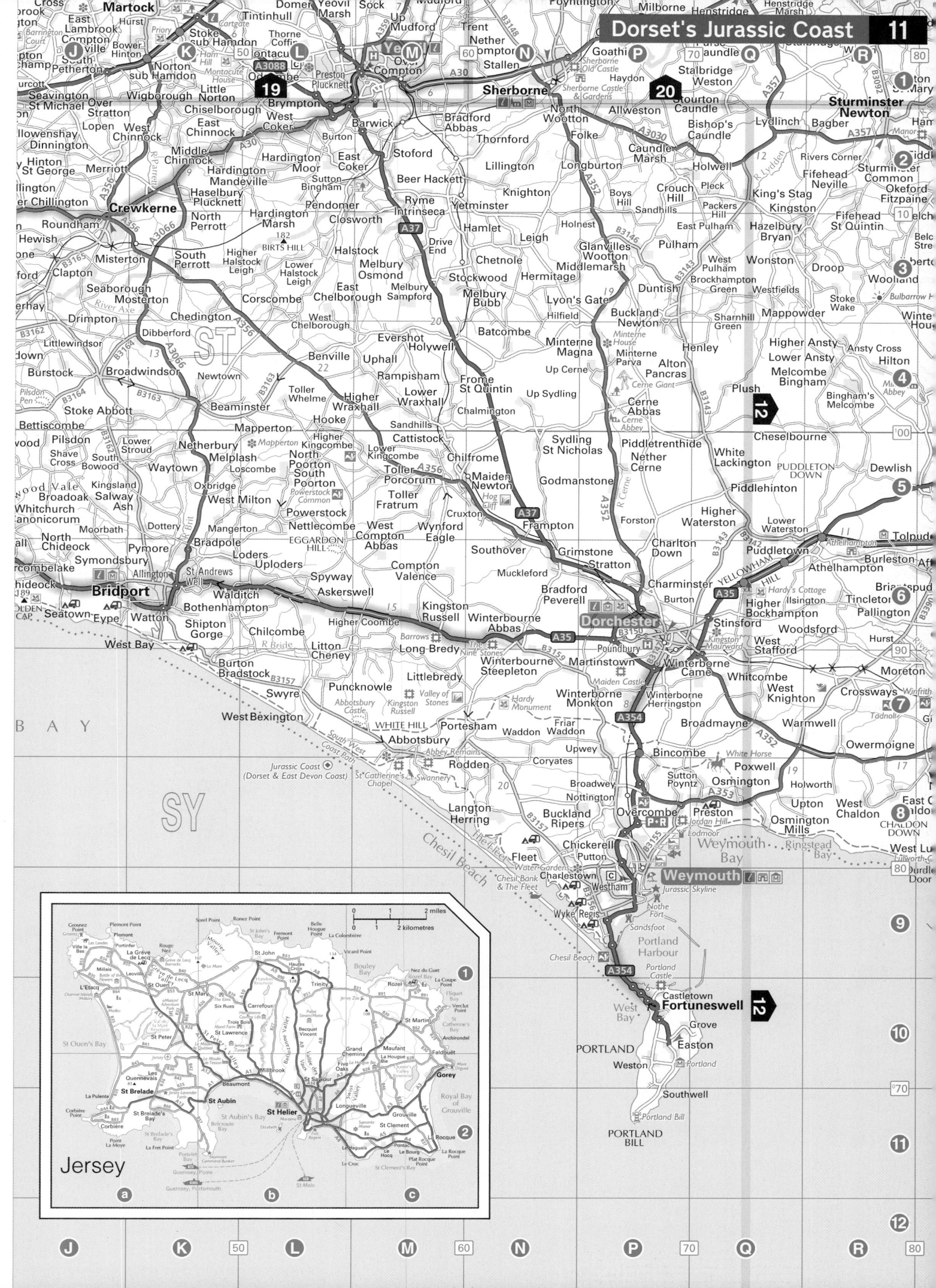

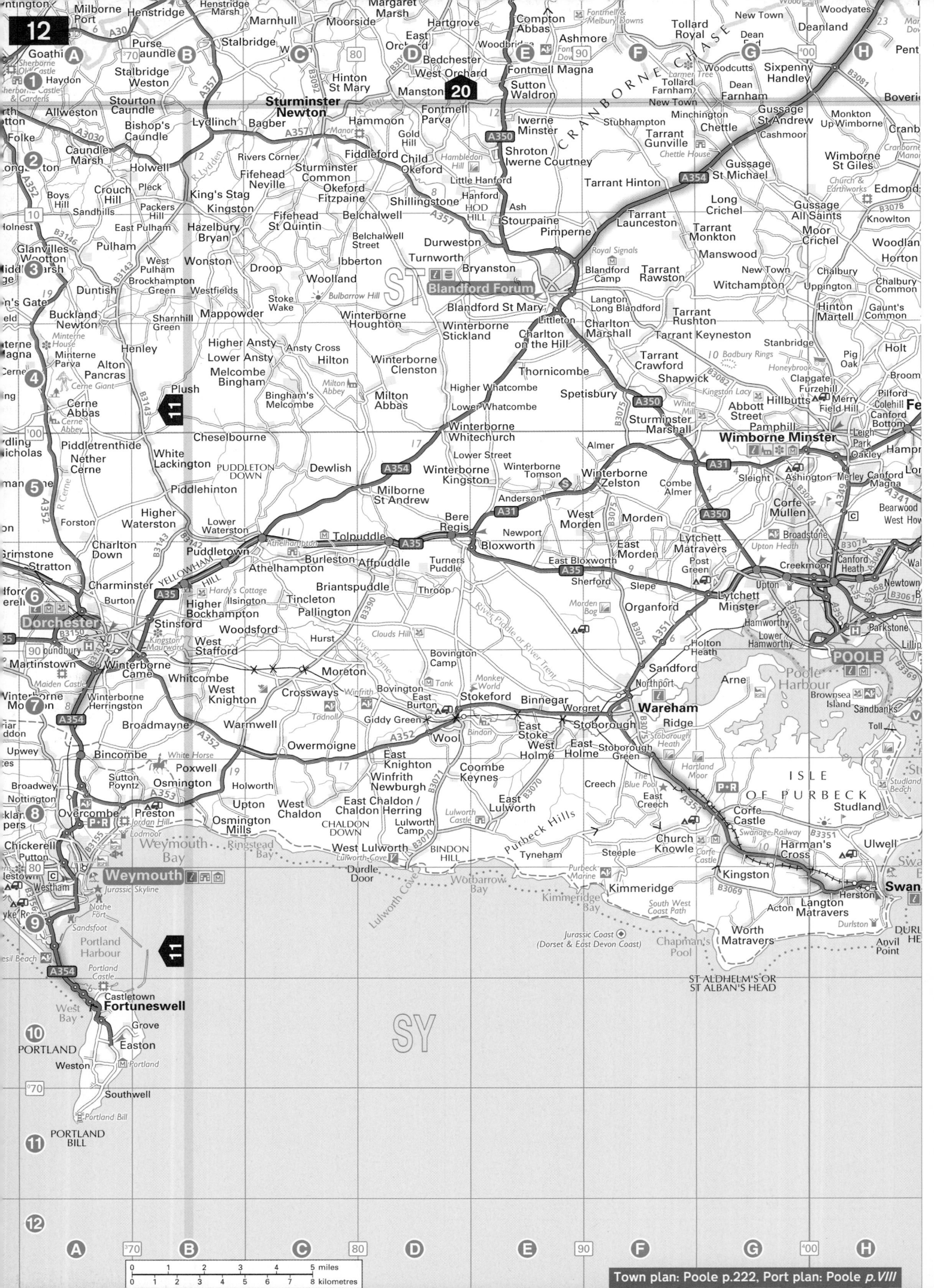

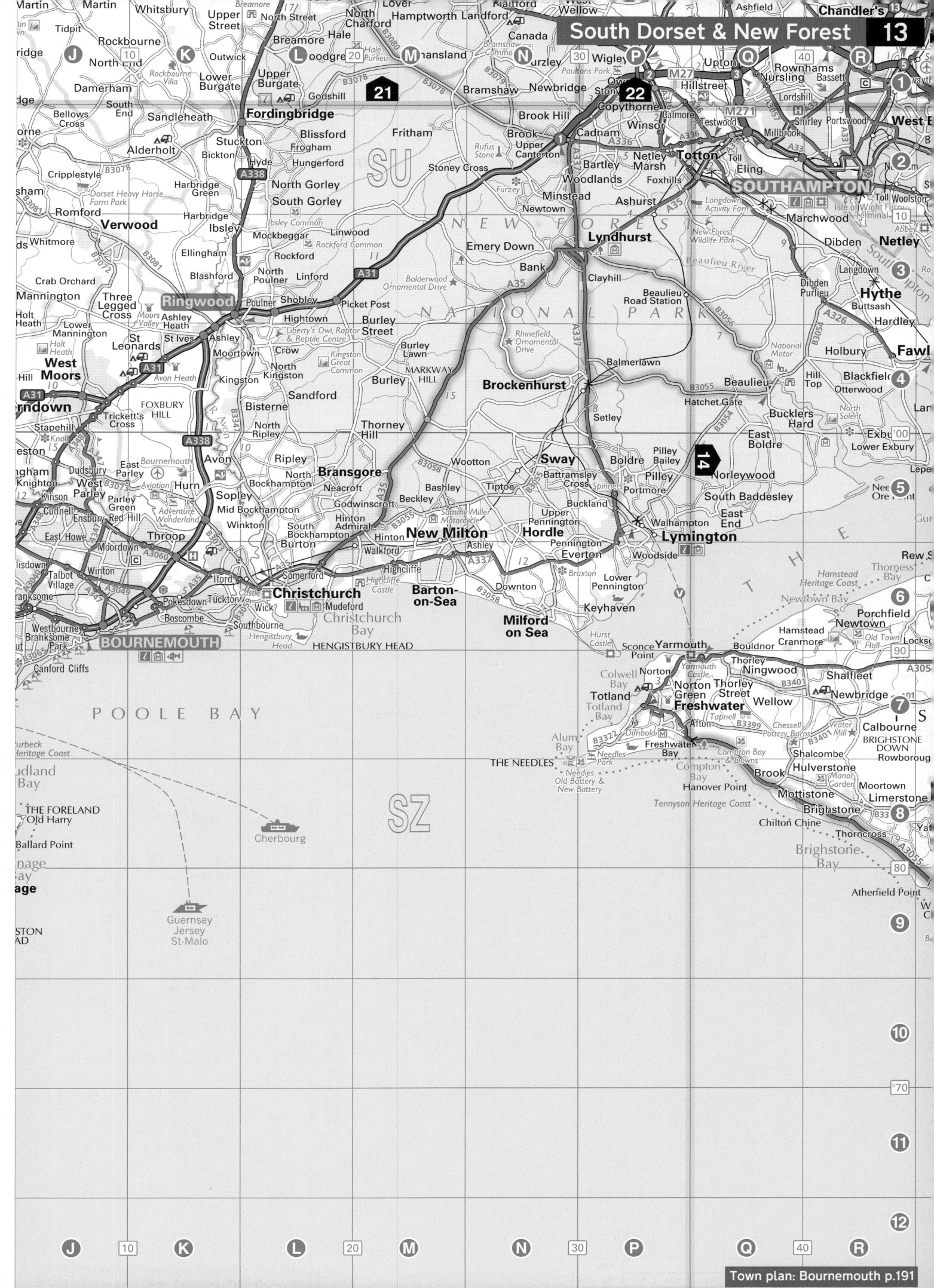

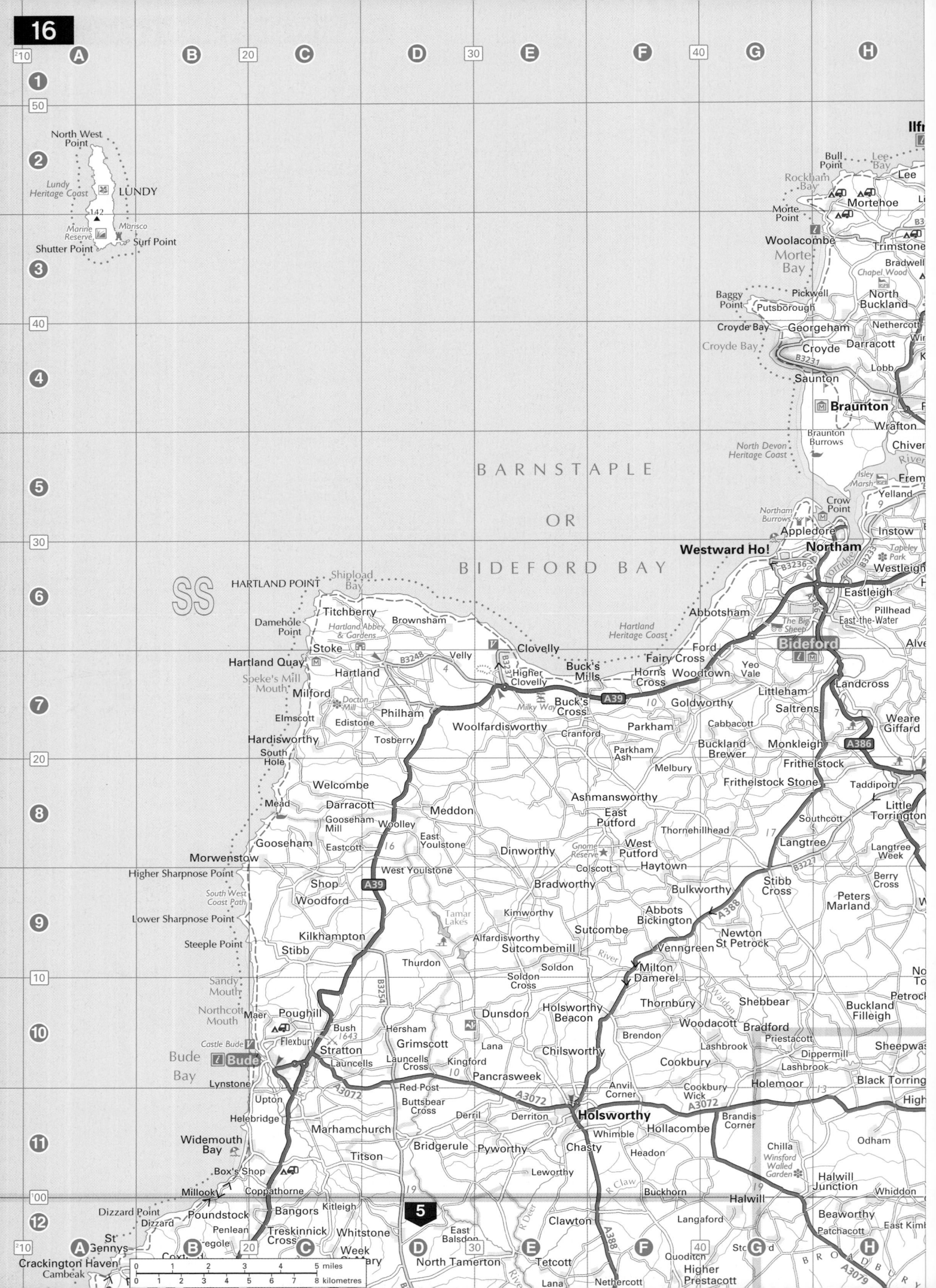

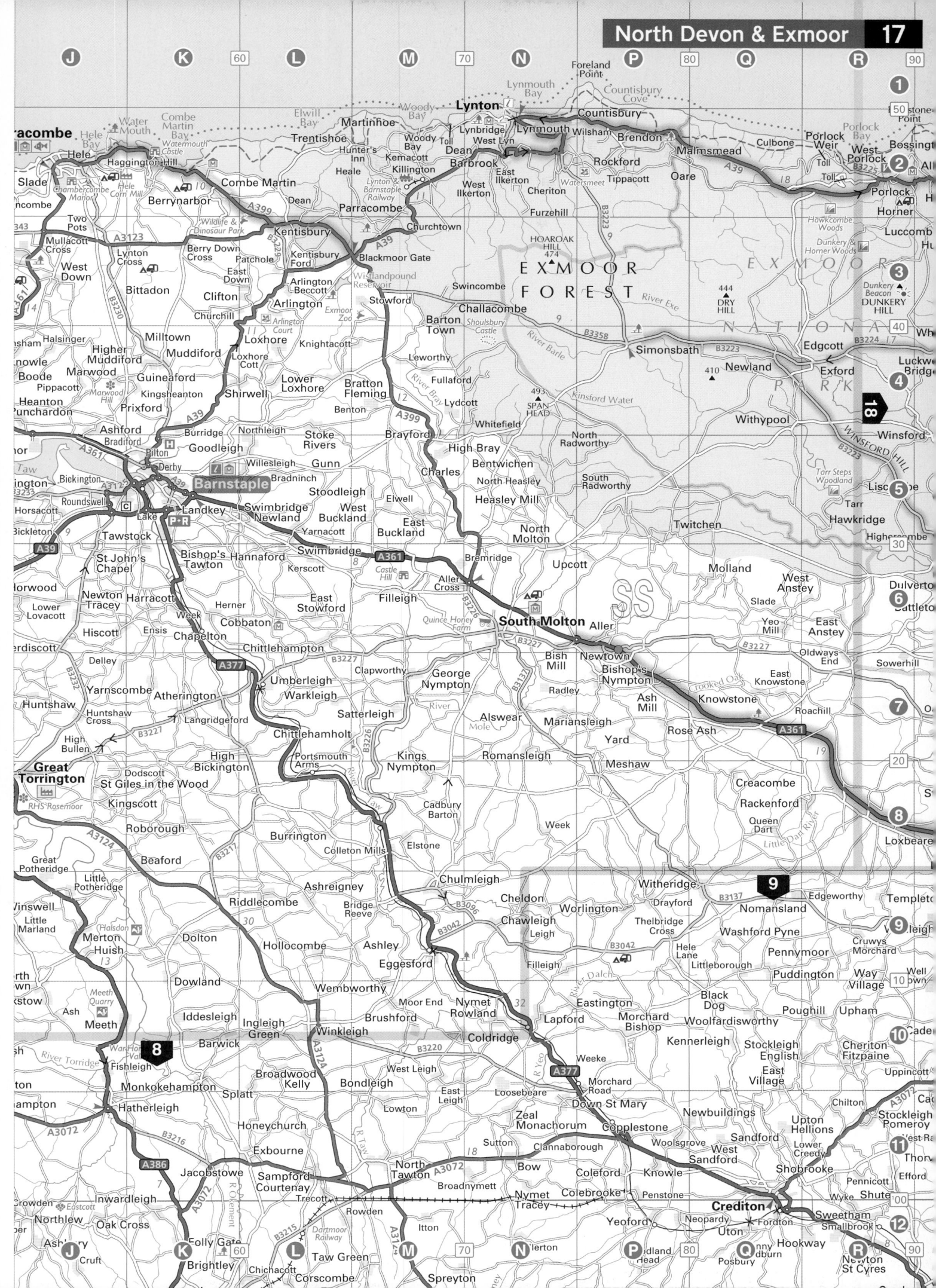

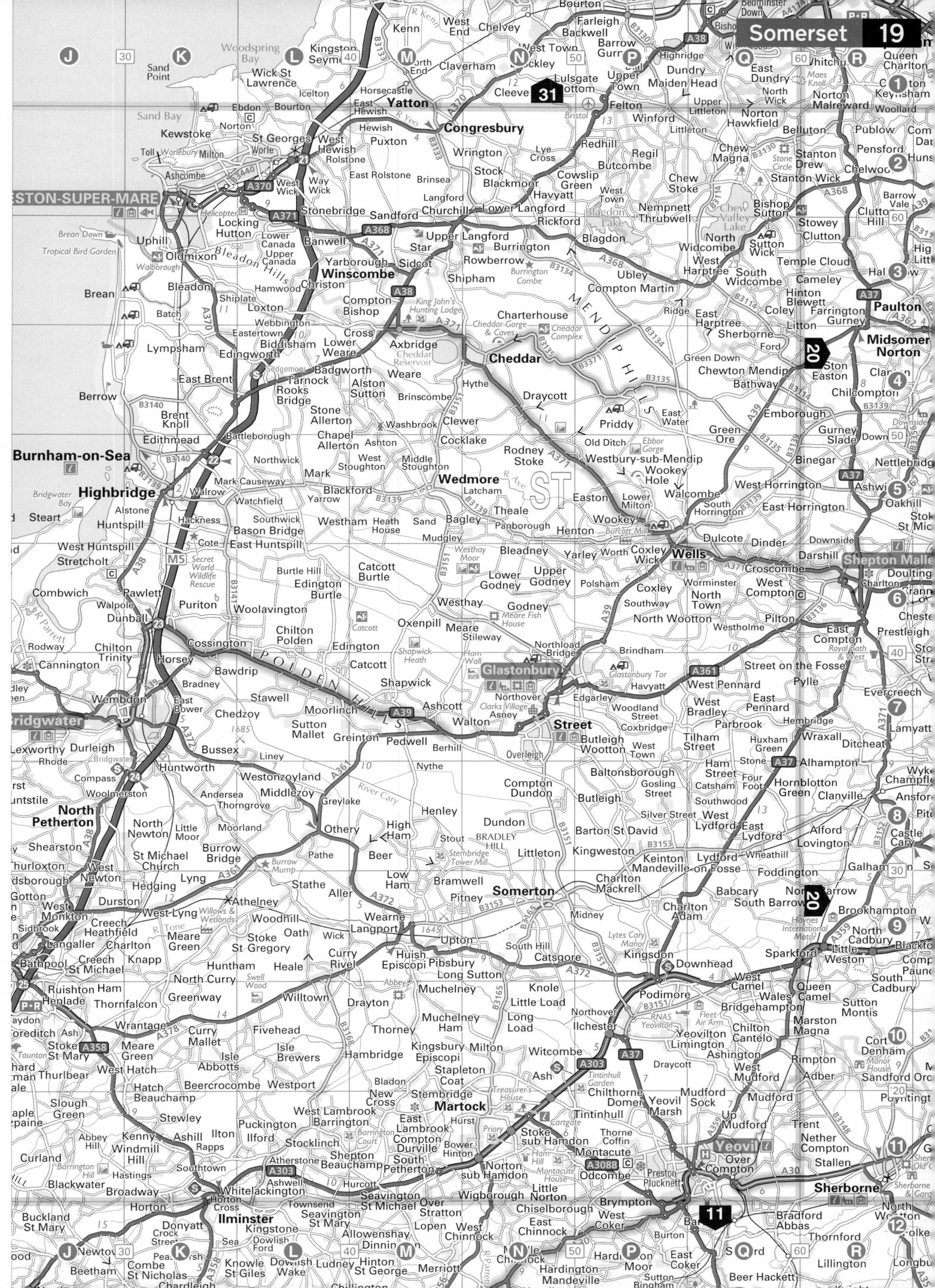

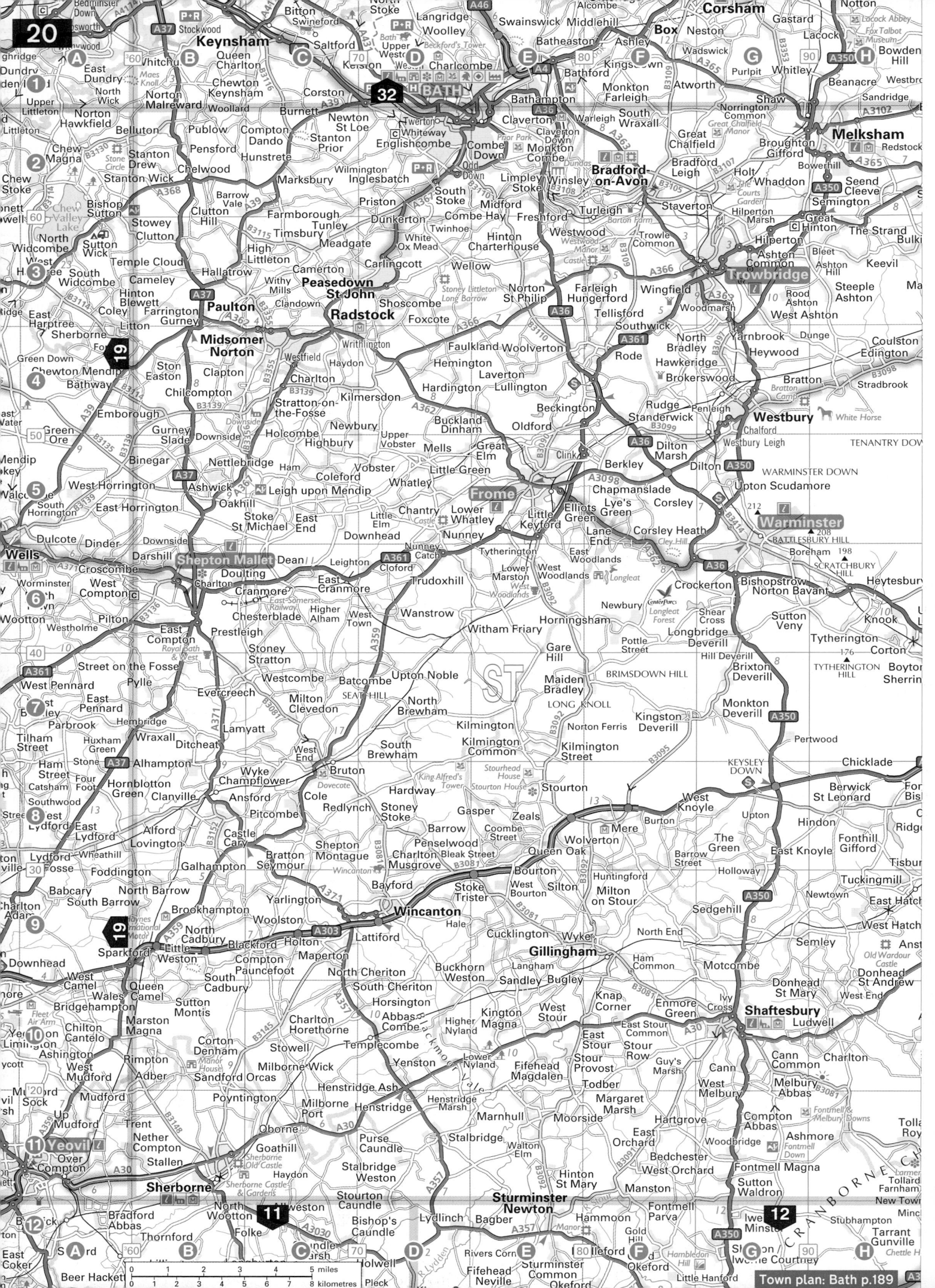

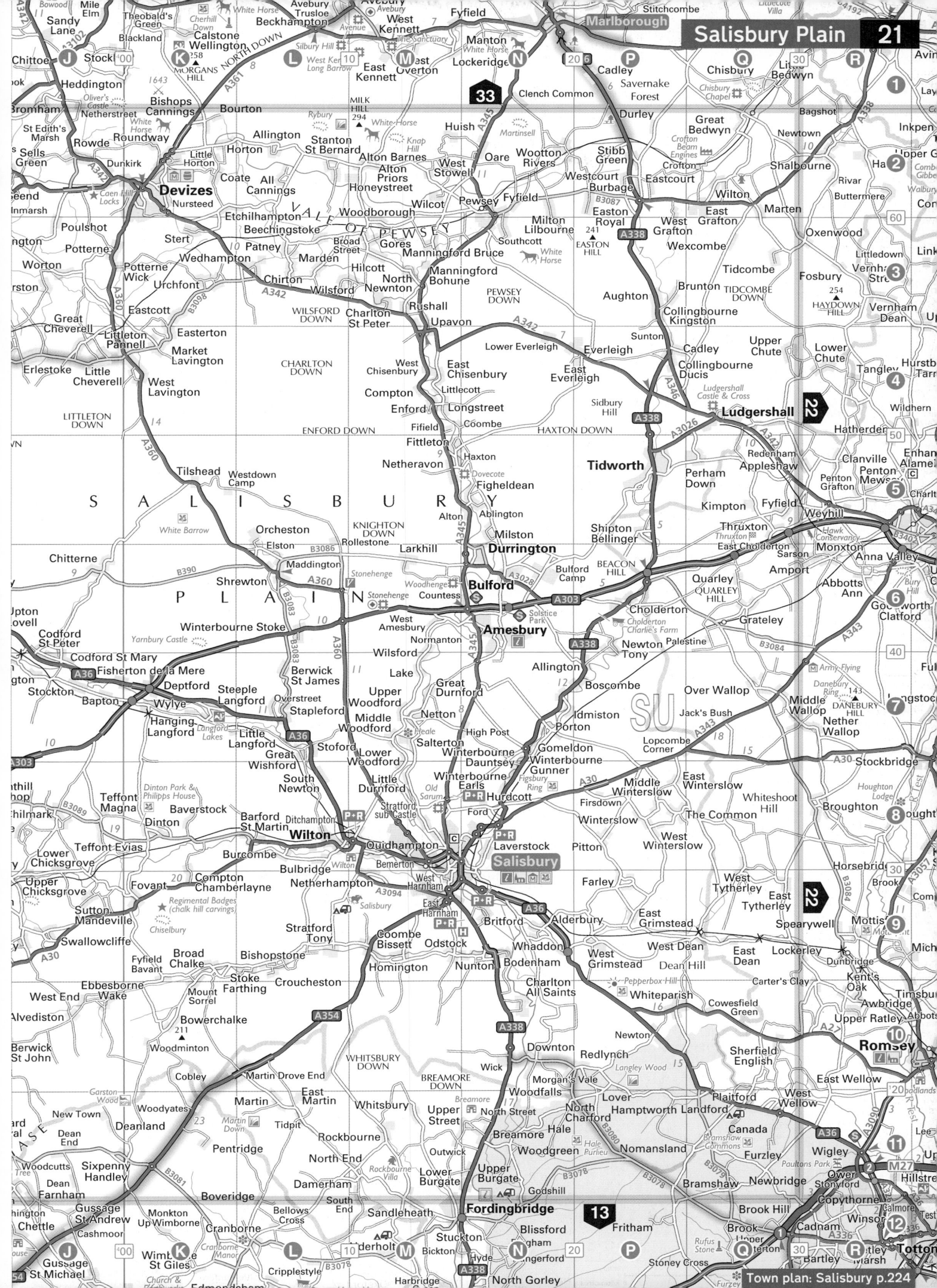

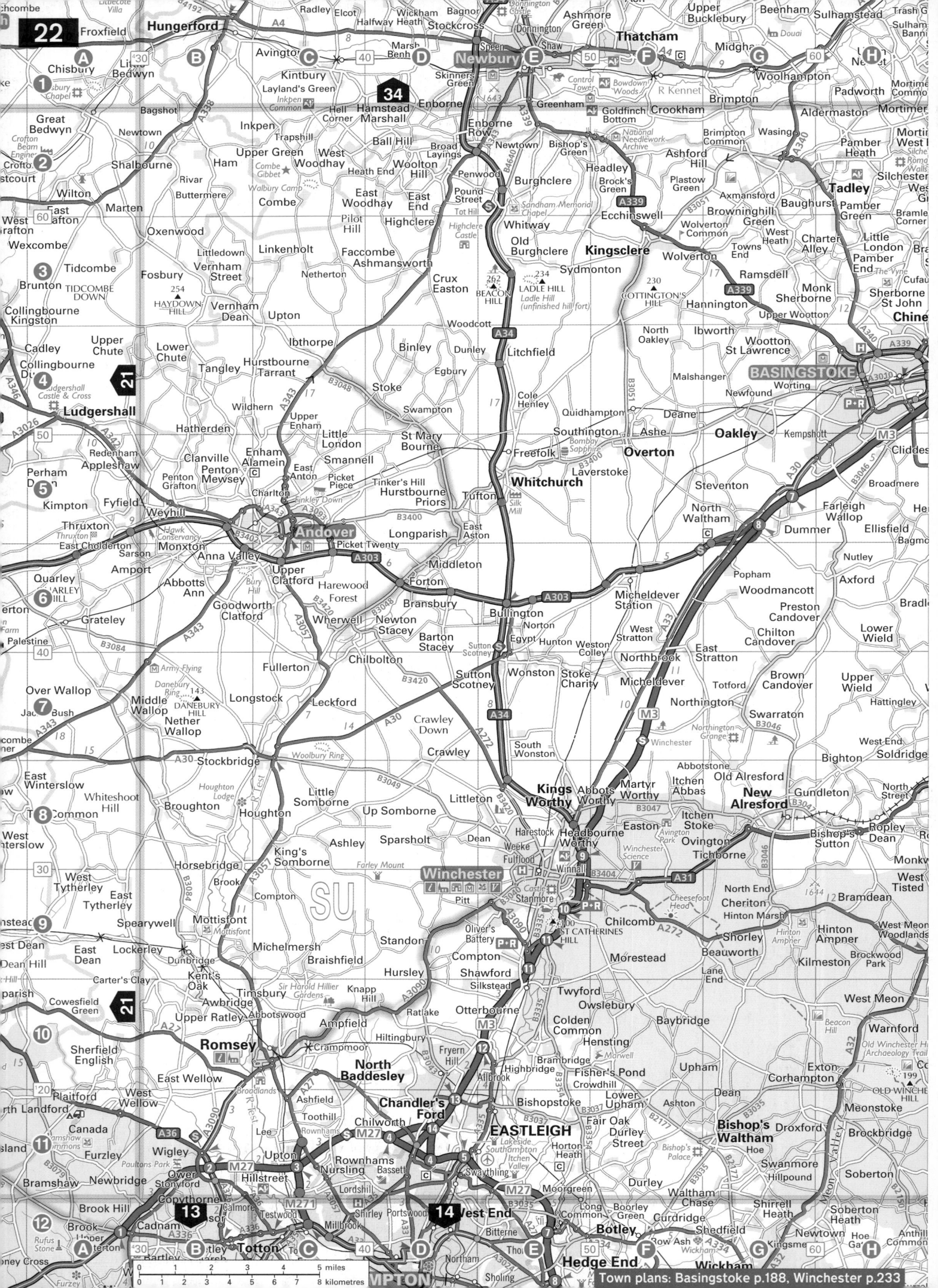

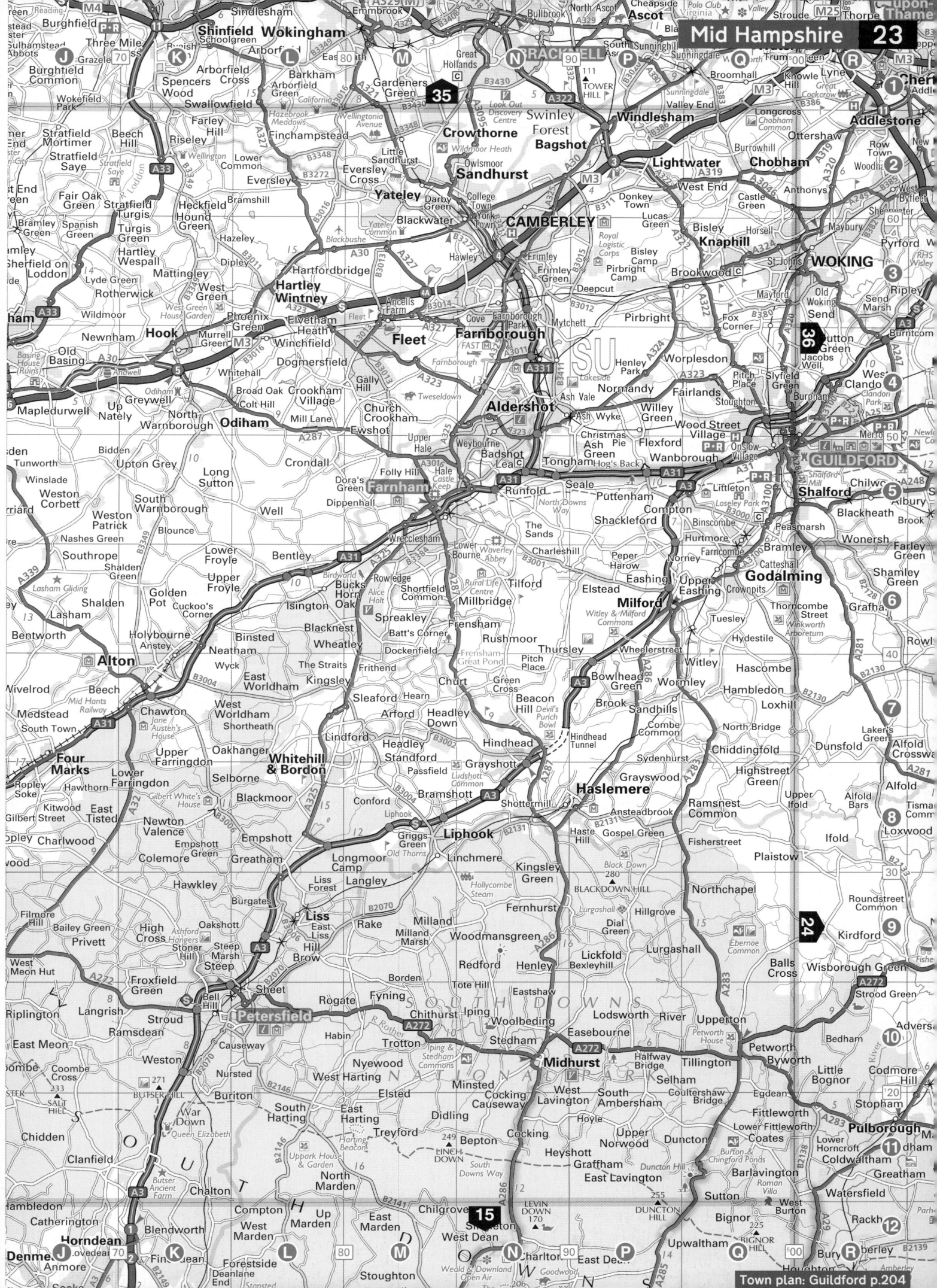

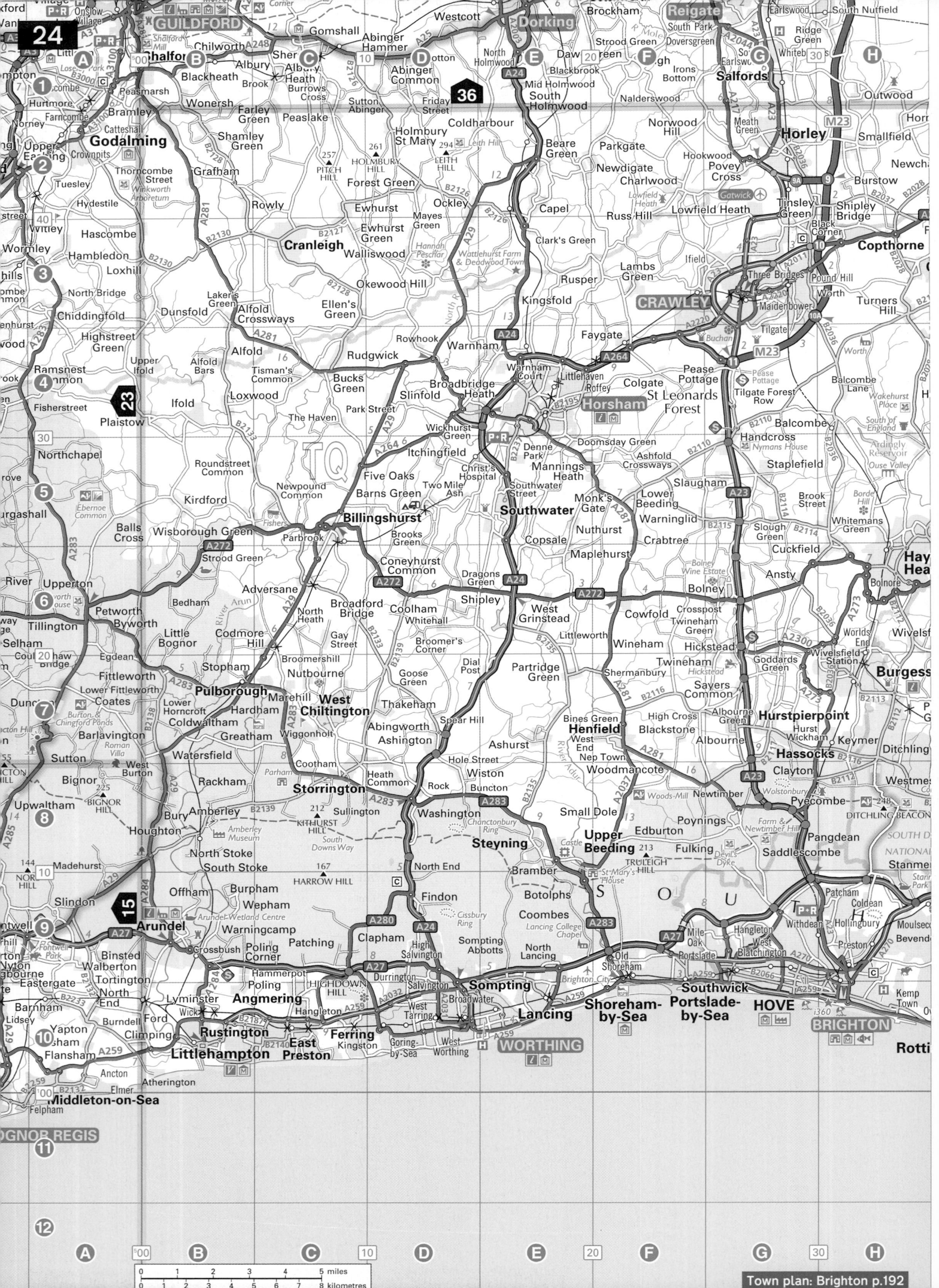

GUILDFORD

Onslow Village
P+R

Westcott
Brockham

Reigate
South Park
Doversgreen

Earlswood
South Nutfield
Ridge Green
Whiteb 30

DORKING

Gomshall
Abinger Hammer
A25

North Holmwood
Daw 20 een
Blackbrook
Mid Holmwood South Holmwood

Strood Green
gh

Salfords

Chalford
Chilworth
A248
Albury
Sher
Albury Heath
Dotton
A24

36

Nalderswood

M23

Horley
Smallfield

Blackheath
Wonersh
Brook
Burrows Cross
Abinger Common
Friday Street

Norwood Hill
Parkgate
Newdigate

Hookwood
Povey Cross

Horn

Godalming
Farley Green
Peaslake
Sutton Abinger
Holmbury St Mary
Coldharbour
294

Capel
Russ Hill
Charlwood
Lowfield Heath
Gatwick
Tinsley Green

Burstow

Thorncombe Street
Grafham
Shamley Green
Holmbury Hill
261
257
PITCH HILL
Forest Green
LEITH HILL
Leith Hill
Beare Green

Lowfield Heath

Black Corner
Shipley Bridge

Copthorne

Hascombe
Rowly
Ewhurst
Ockley
B2126
Clark's Green
Rusper
Lambs Green
Ifield
Three Bridges
Worth
Maidenbower
10A
Turners Hill

Cranleigh
Ewhurst Green
Mayes Green
Kingsfold
CRAWLEY
Pound Hill

Wormley
Chiddingfold
Walliswood
Okewood Hill
Hannah Peschar
Wattlehurst Farm & Deadwood Town
Buchan
M23

Dunsfold
Alfold Crossways
Ellen's Green
Rowhook
Warnham
Faygate
Pease Pottage
St Leonards Forest
Balcombe Lane
Wakehurst Place

North Bridge
Laker's Green
Alfold
Rudgwick
Warnham Court
Littlehaven
Roffey
Colgate
Tilgate Forest Row
Balcombe

23

Highstreet Green
Alfold Bars
Tisman's Common
Bucks Green
Broadbridge Heath
Slinfold
Horsham
Handcross
Nymans House

Plaistow
Ifold
Loxwood
Park Street
Wickhurst Green
Itchingfield
Christ's Hospital
Denne Park
Doomsday Green
Ashfold Crossways
Staplefield

Northchapel
Roundstreet Common
Five Oaks
Barns Green
Two Mile Ash
Southwater Street
Mannings Heath
Monk's Gate
Lower Beeding
Slaugham
Brook Street
Borde Hill

Kirdford
Newpound Common
Billingshurst
Brooks Green
Southwater
Copsale
Nuthurst
Warninglid
Slough Green
Cuckfield
Whitemans Green

Balls Cross
Wisborough Green
Parbrook
Coneyhurst Common
Dragons Green
Maplehurst
Crabtree
Bolney Wine Estate
Ansty
Hay Hea

Upperton
A272
Strood Green
Adversane
Broadford Bridge
Coolham Whitehall
Shipley
West Grinstead
Cowfold
Bolney
Crosspost
Twineham Green

Petworth
Byworth
North Heath
Gay Street
Broomer's Corner
Littleworth
Wineham
Hickstead
Worlds End
Wivels

Tillington
Selham
Egdean
Little Bognor
Codmore Hill
Goose Green
Dial Post
Partridge Green
Twineham
Shermanbury
Goddards Green
Wivelsfield Station
Burgess

Coates
Stopham
Broomershill
Nutbourne
West Grinstead
Sayers Common
Albourne Green

Fittleworth
Lower Fittleworth
Pulborough
Marehill
West Chiltington
Thakeham
Ashurst
High Cross
Blackstone
Albourne
Hurstpierpoint
Hurst
Keymer
Ditchling

Barlavington
Coldwaltham
Hardham
Greatham
Wiggonholt
Abingworth Ashington
Spear Hill
Henfield
West End
Nep Town
Woodmancote
Hassocks

Sutton
West Burton
Watersfield
Cootham
Rackham
Heath Common
Rock
Wiston
Buncton
Small Dole
Newtimber
Clayton

Bignor
Upwaltham
BIGNOR HILL
Amberley
Storrington
Washington
Chanctonbury Ring
Woods-Mill
Poynings
Edburton
Pyecombe
Westme

Houghton
Amberley Museum
KITHURST HILL
South Downs Way
Steyning
Castle
Upper Beeding
Fulking
Devil's Dyke
Saddlescombe
DITCHLING BEACON
SOUTH D

Madehurst
NOR HILL
North Stoke
South Stoke
HARROW HILL
North End
Bramber
Botolphs
TRULEIGH HILL
St Mary's House
Truleigh
Pangdean
SOUTH D
NATIONAL
Stanme

Slindon
Offham
Burpham
Wepham
Findon
Cissbury Ring
Coombes
SOU
Patcham
Coldean
Moulsecoomb

Arundel
Warningcamp
Patching
Clapham
High Salvington
Sompting Abbotts
North Lancing
Lancing College Chapel
Old Shoreham
Mile Oak Portslade
Hangleton West Blatchington
Hollingbury
Bevend

Crossbush
Poling Corner
A280
A24
Sompting
Brighton City
Portslade-by-Sea
HOVE

Binsted
Walberton
Tortington
North End
Hammerpot
Poling
HIGHDOWN HILL
Durrington
Salvington
West Tarring
Broadwater
Southwick
Preston

Lyminster
Angmering
Hangleton
West Worthing
Sompting
Lancing
Shoreham-by-Sea
Portslade-by-Sea
BRIGHTON

Rustington
Ford
Climping
Ferring
Kingston
Goring-by-Sea
West Worthing
WORTHING

Yapton
East Preston
Littlehampton
Goring-by-Sea
Rotti

Flansham
Atherington
Anton
Elmer

Middleton-on-Sea
Felpham

BOGNOR REGIS

Town plan: Brighton p.192

0 1 2 3 4 5 miles
0 1 2 3 4 5 6 7 8 kilometres

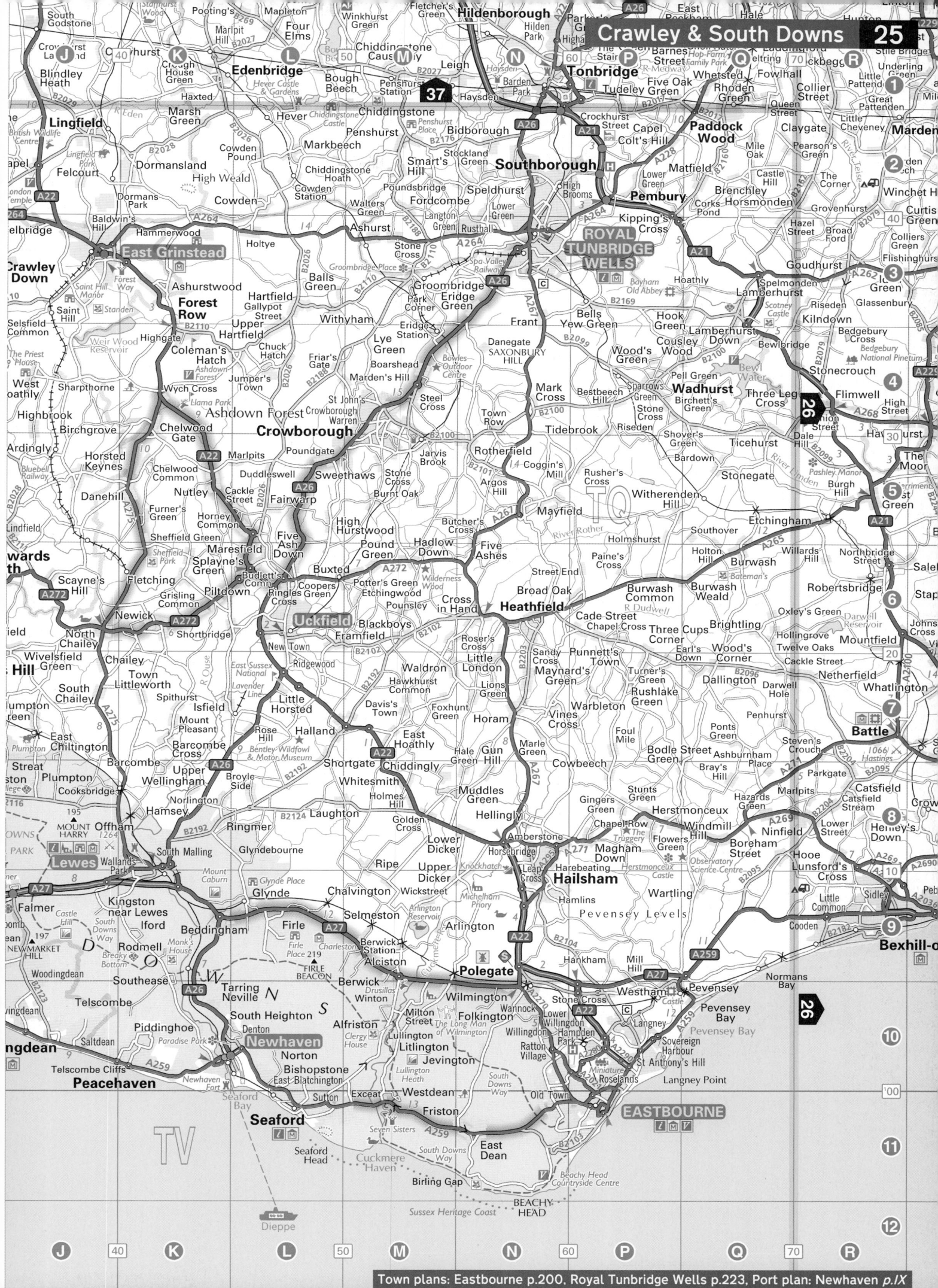

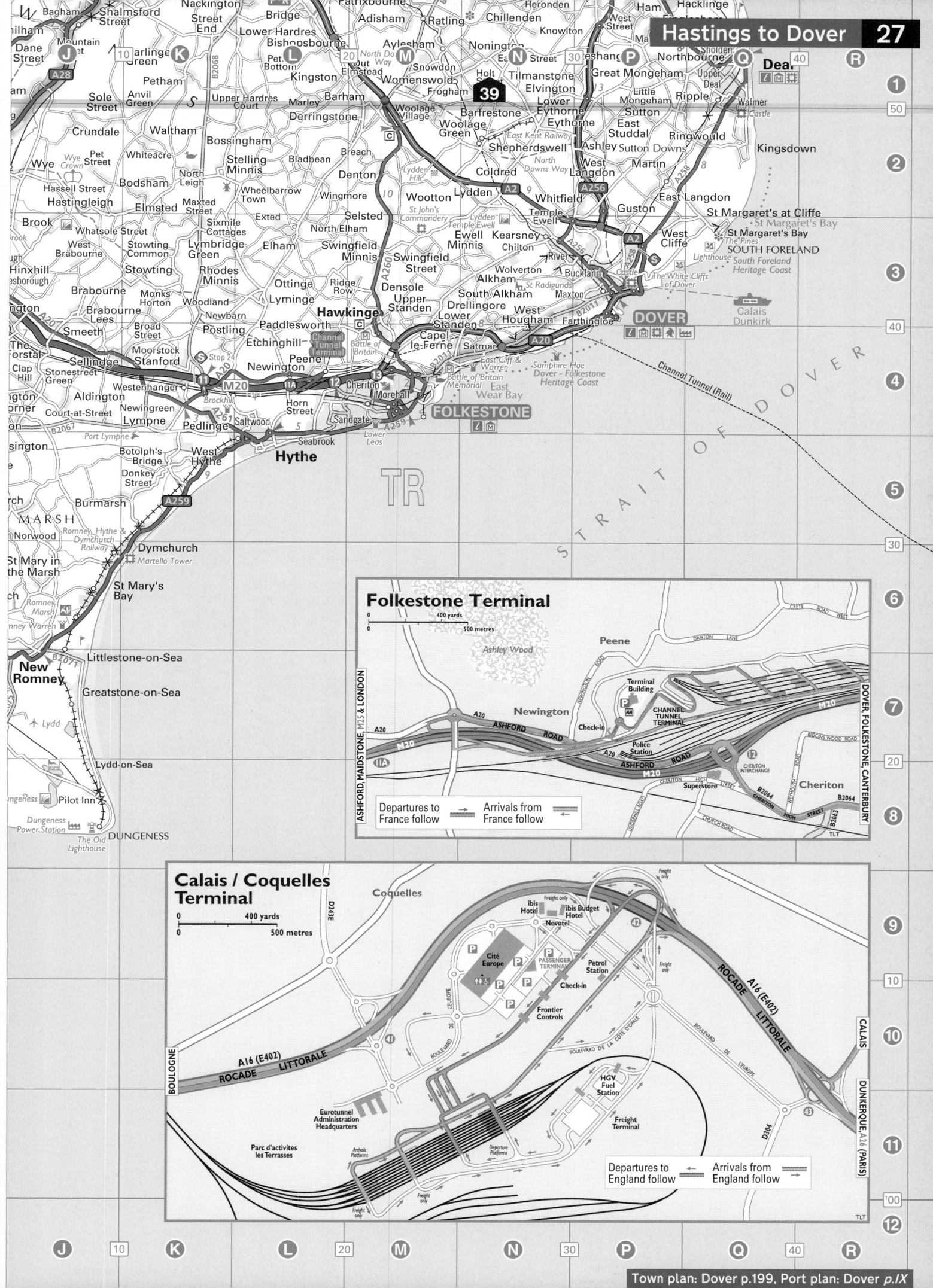

Folkestone Terminal

Departures to France follow →
Arrivals from France follow ←

Calais / Coquelles Terminal

Departures to England follow ←
Arrivals from England follow

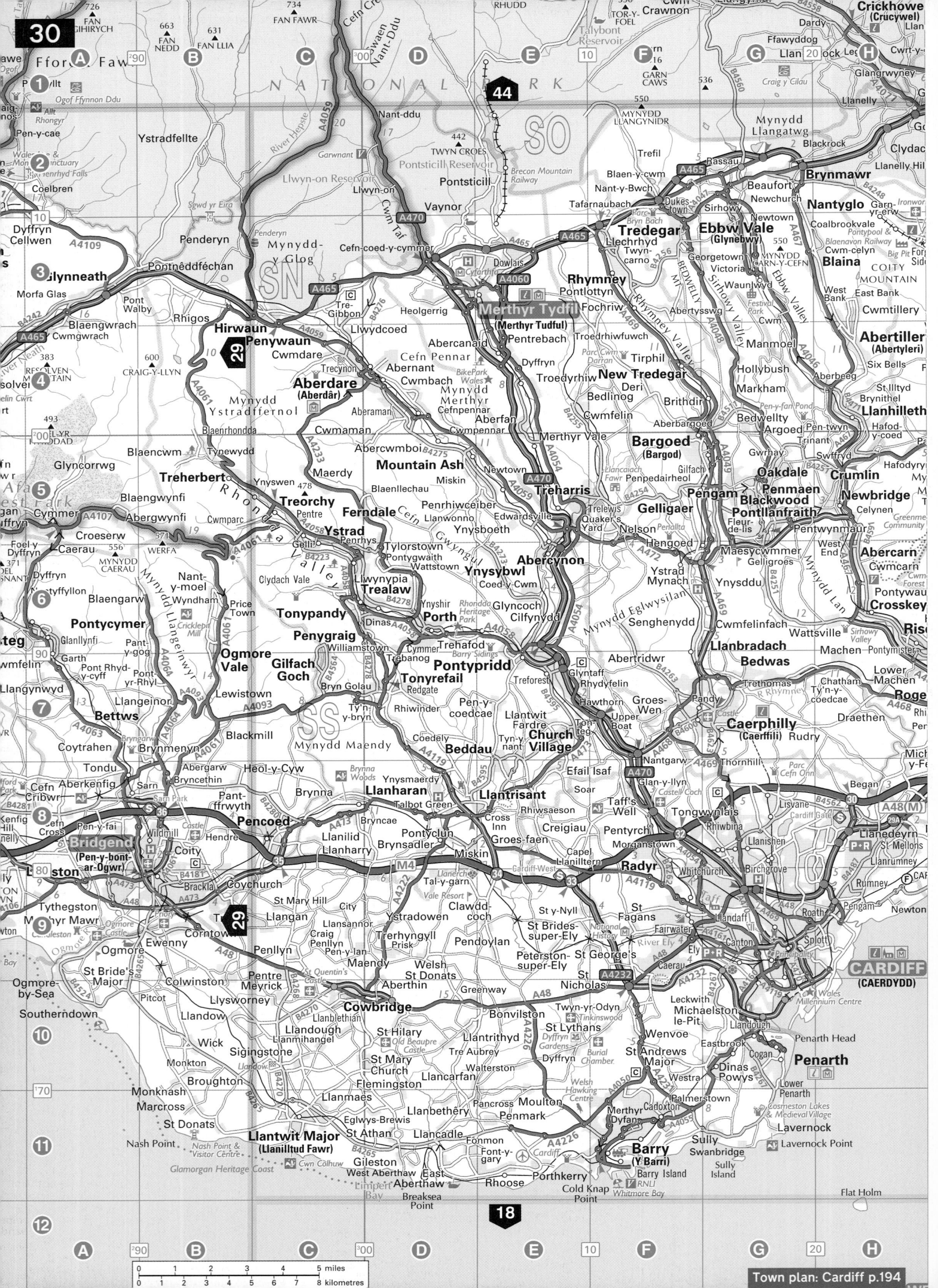

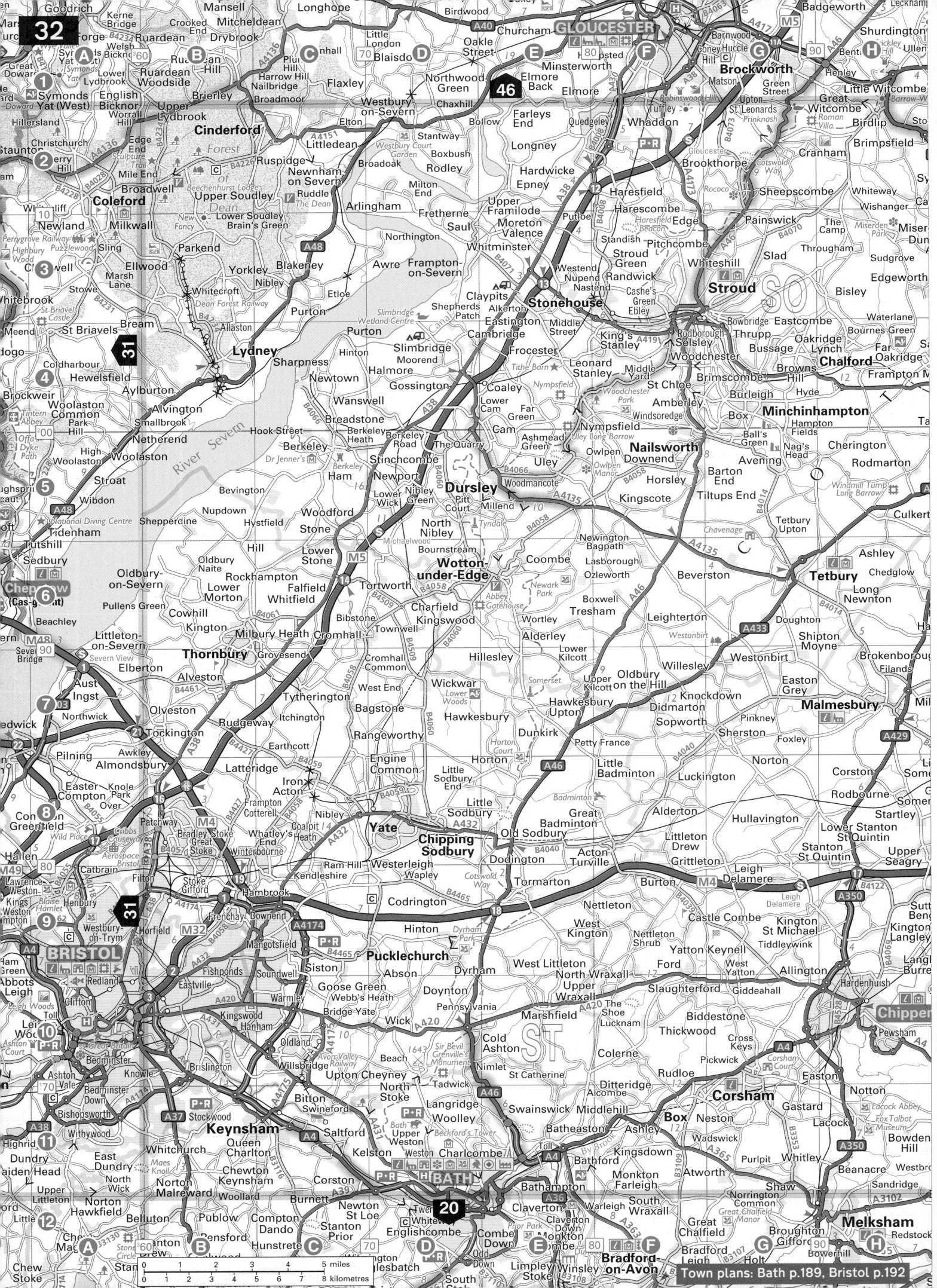

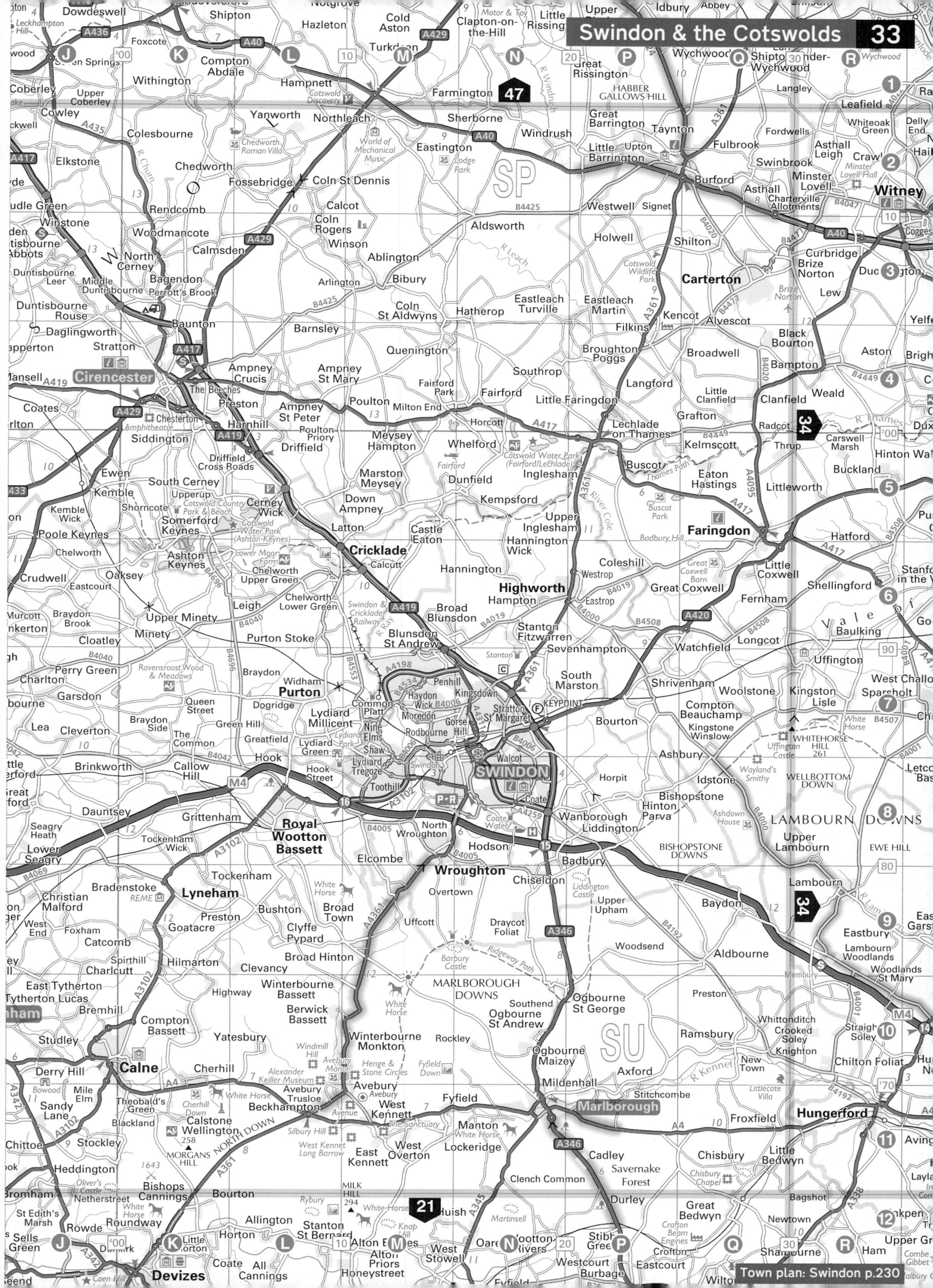

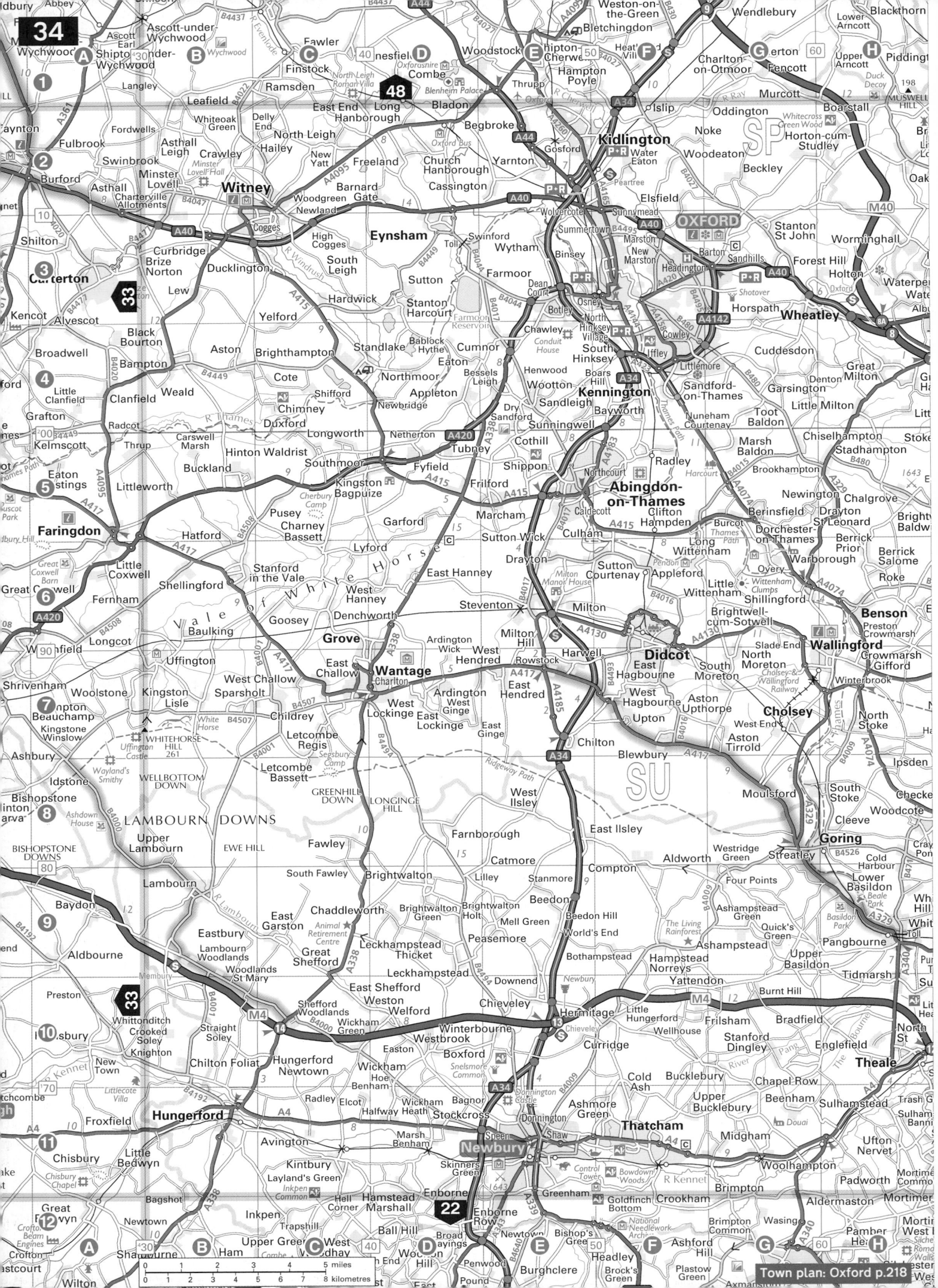

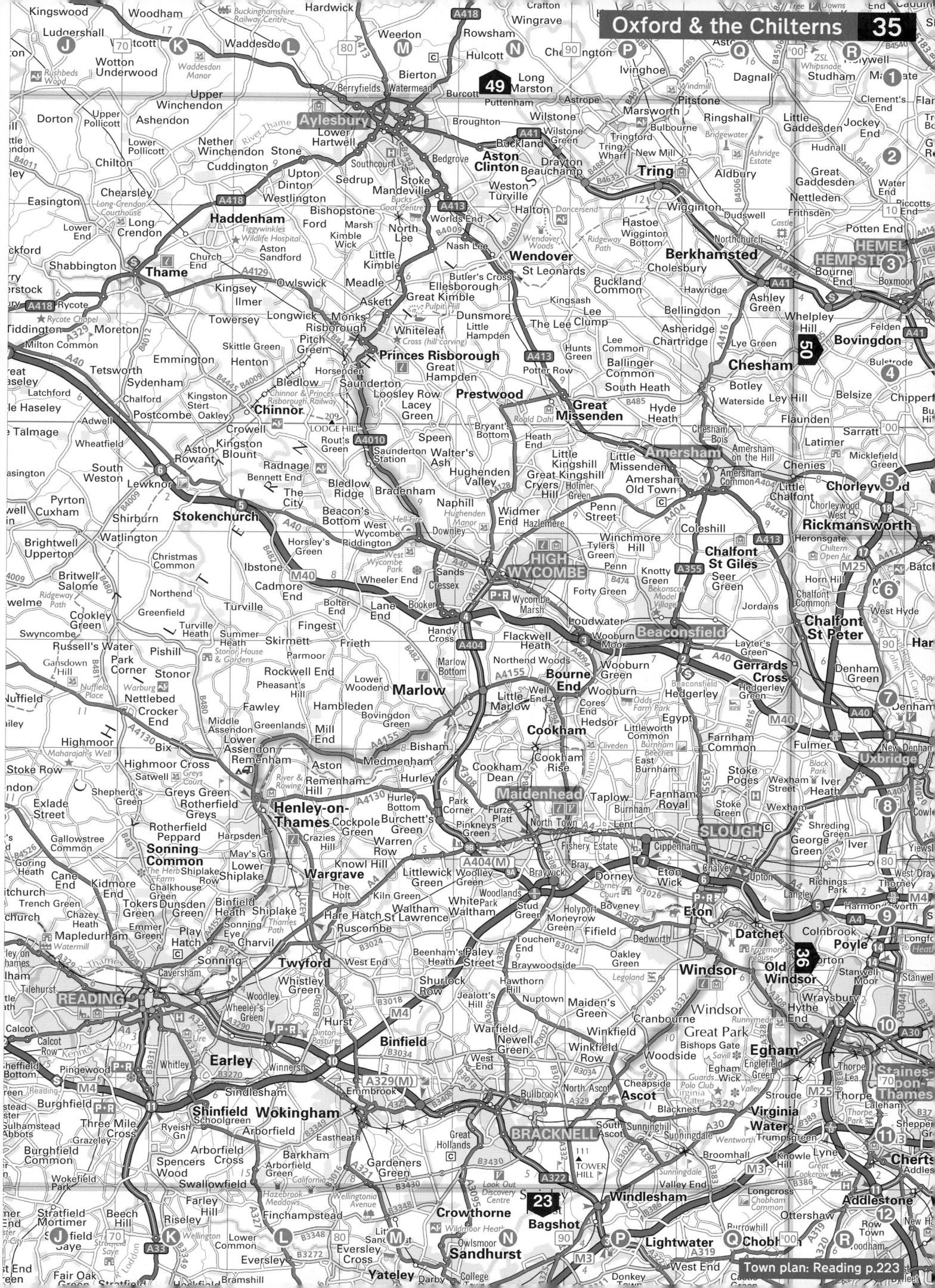

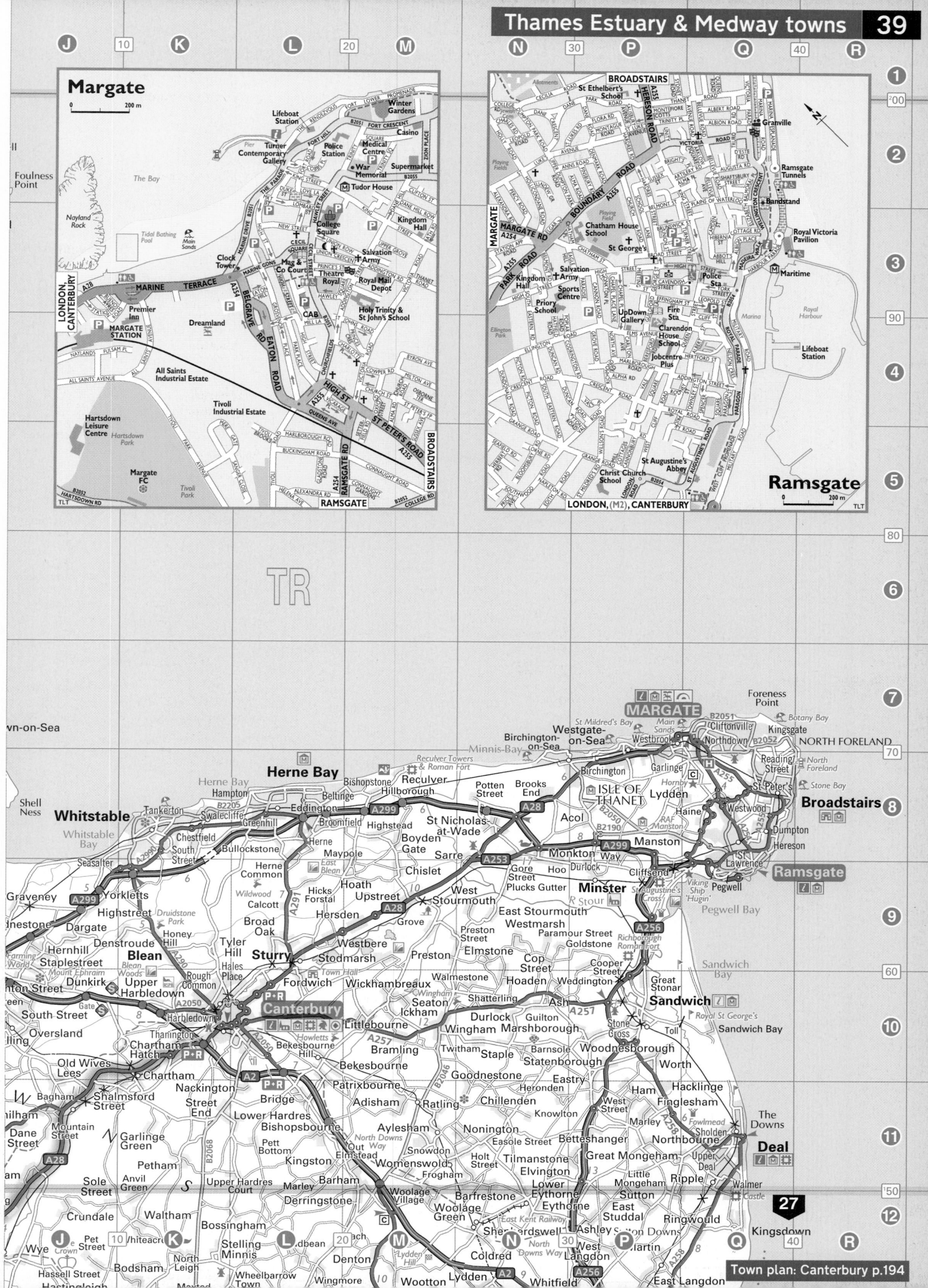

Margate

0   200 m

The Bay

Nayland Rock

Foulness Point

Tidal Bathing Pool

Main Sands

Lifeboat Station

Turner Contemporary Gallery

Pier

Winter Gardens

Fort Crescent

Casino

Police Station

Medical Centre

Supermarket

War Memorial

Tudor House

Kingdom Hall

Clock Tower

Mag & Co Court

MARINE TERRACE

Premier Inn

MARGATE STATION

Dreamland

College Square

Salvation Army

Theatre Royal

Royal Mail Depot

CAB

Holy Trinity & St John's School

All Saints Industrial Estate

Tivoli Industrial Estate

HIGH ST

QUEENS AVE

ST PETER'S RD

Hartsdown Leisure Centre

Hartsdown Park

Margate FC

Tivoli Park

LONDON, CANTERBURY

BROADSTAIRS

RAMSGATE

Ramsgate

0   200 m

MARGATE

MARGATE RD

BOUNDARY ROAD

HERESON ROAD

BROADSTAIRS

St Ethelbert's School

Chatham House School

St George's

Granville

Ramsgate Tunnels

Bandstand

Royal Victoria Pavilion

Maritime

Kingdom Hall

Salvation Army Sports Centre

Priory School

UpDown Gallery

Clarendon House School

Police Sta

Fire Sta

Jobcentre Plus

Royal Harbour

Marina

Lifeboat Station

St Augustine's Abbey

Christ Church School

LONDON, (M2), CANTERBURY

TR

Foulness Point

Shell Ness

Whitstable

Whitstable Bay

Seasalter

Graveney

Yorkletts

Highstreet

Dargate

Hernhill

Staplestreet

Dunkirk

Blean

Denstroude

Honey Hill

Upper Harbledown

Harbledown

South Street

Overland

Thanington

Chartham Hatch

Chartham

Shalmsford Street

Nackington

Bridge

Mountain Street

Garlinge Green

Petham

Sole Street

Anvil Green

Waltham

Crundale

Bodsham

Wye

Pet Street

Hassell Street

Hartingleigh

Herne Bay

Hampton

Tankerton

Chestfield

South Street

Bullockstone

Greenhill

Swalecliffe

Eddington

Broomfield

Herne

Maypole

Herne Common

Hicks Forstal

Calcott

Broad Oak

Tyler Hill

Hersden

Hoath

Upstreet

Hales Place

Sturry

Fordwich

Westbere

Rough Common

Canterbury

Bekesbourne Hill

Bekesbourne

Patrixbourne

Adisham

Lower Hardres

Bishopsbourne

Aylesham

Kingston

Barham

Derringstone

Upper Hardres Court

Marley

Womenswold

Elmsted

Frogham

Stelling Minnis

Denton

Wootton

Lydden

Whitfield

Bishopstone

Reculver

Hillborough

Reculver Towers & Roman Fort

Minnis Bay

Birchington-on-Sea

Westgate-on-Sea

Potten Street

Brooks End

St Nicholas-at-Wade

Boyden Gate

Sarre

Chislet

West Stourmouth

East Stourmouth

Westmarsh

Preston Street

Goldstone

Paramour Street

Cop Street

Hoaden

Weddington

Cooper Street

Great Stonar

Sandwich

Sandwich Bay

Royal St George's

Stonar

Toll

Ham

West Street

Hacklinge

Finglesham

Deal

The Downs

Sholden

Northbourne

Worth

Woodnesborough

Marshborough

Staple

Statenborough

Goodnestone

Eastry

Knowlton

Chillenden

Nonington

Easole Street

Tilmanstone

Betteshanger

Great Mongeham

Little Mongeham

Upper Deal

Ripple

Walmer

Castle

Kingsdown

Ringwould

Sutton

East Studdal

Sheperdswell

Ashley

Sutton Downs

West Langdon

East Langdon

Martin

Holt Street

Twitham

Guilton

Wingham

Ash

Durlock

Wingham Marshborough

Shatterling

Walmesham

Ickham

Seaton

Wickhambreaux

Littlebourne

Bramling

Westbere

Preston

Elmstone

East Stourmouth

Grove

Stodmarsh

Westbere

ISLE OF THANET

MARGATE

Foreness Point

Botany Bay

Cliftonville

Kingsgate

Northdown

NORTH FORELAND

Reading Street

North Foreland

Stone Bay

Broadstairs

Westwood

Dumpton

Hereson

Ramsgate

St Lawrence

Pegwell

Pegwell Bay

Viking Ship 'Hugin'

St Augustine's Cross

Richborough Roman Fort

Minster

Cliffsend

Manston

RAF Manston

Monkton

Gore Street

Plucks Gutter

Hoo

Durlock

Monkton Way

Birchington

Garlinge

Hornby

Lydden

Haine

Acol

R Stour

Town plan: Canterbury p.194

27

Town plan: Canterbury p.194

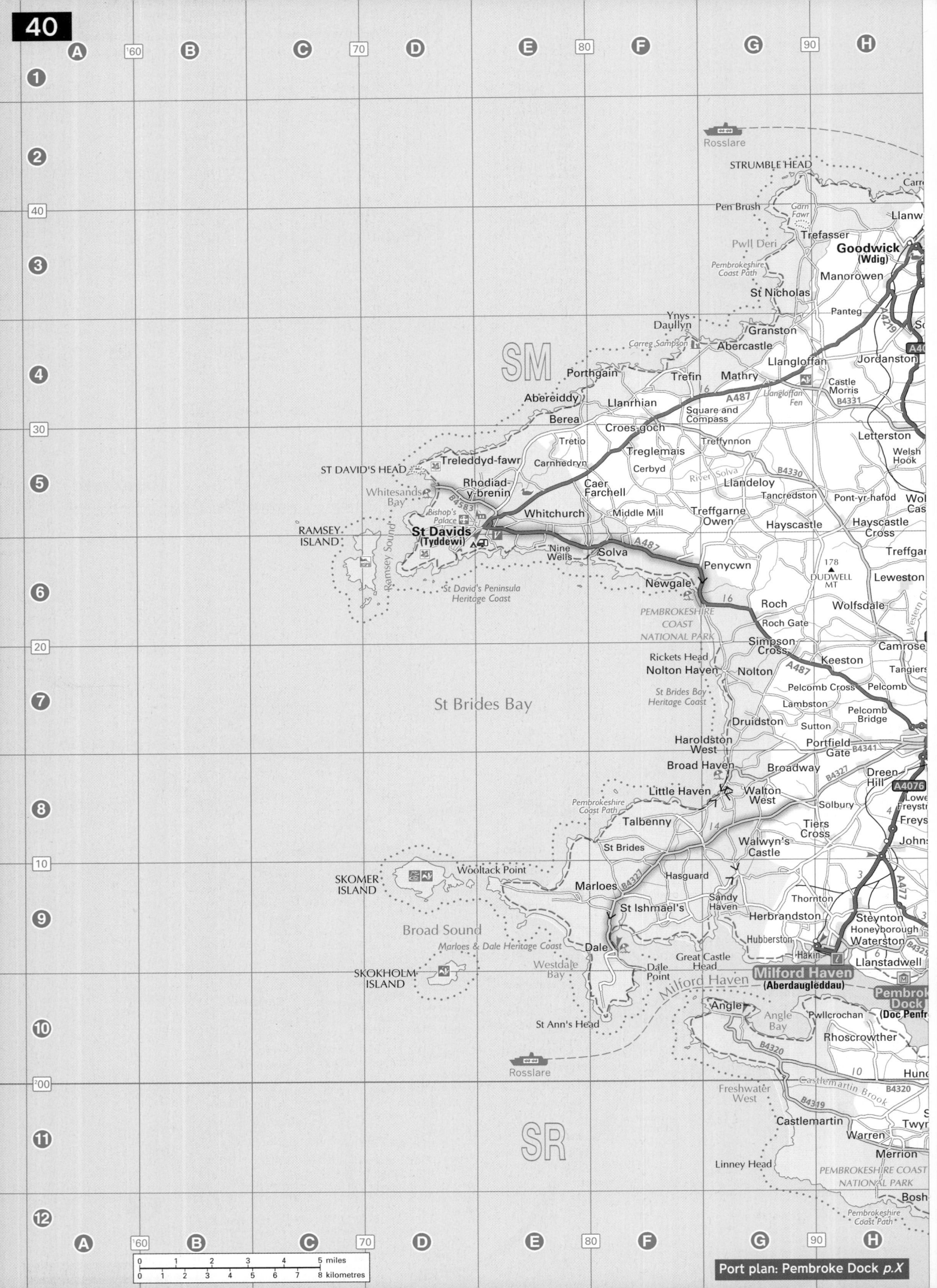

A '60 B C 70 D E 80 F G 90 H

1

2

Rosslare

STRUMBLE HEAD

40

Pen Brush   Garn Fawr   Llanw

Trefasser

Pwll Deri   **Goodwick (Wdig)**

Pembrokeshire Coast Path   Manorowen

St Nicholas   Panteg

Ynys Daullyn   Granston

Carreg Sampson   Abercastle

Jordanston   S

SM   Llangloffan

Porthgain   Trefin   Mathry   Castle Morris

Square and Compass   B4331

Abereiddy   Llanrhian   A487   Llangloffan Fen

Letterston

Berea   Croes-goch   Welsh Hook

30   Tretio   Treffynnon   Treglemais   B4330   Wol

Cerbyd   River Solva   Llandeloy   Cas

ST DAVID'S HEAD   Treleddyd-fawr   Carnhedryn   Tancredston   Pont-yr-hafod

Whitesands Bay   Rhodiad-y-brenin   Caer Farchell   Treffgarne Owen   Hayscastle   Hayscastle Cross

Bishop's Palace   Whitchurch   Middle Mill   Treffgar

RAMSEY ISLAND   **St Davids (Tyddewi)**   A487

Nine Wells   Solva   178   Leweston

St David's Peninsula Heritage Coast   Penycwn   **DUDWELL MT**   Wolfsdale

Newgale   16   Roch

PEMBROKESHIRE COAST NATIONAL PARK   Roch Gate   Camrose

20   Simpson Cross   Keeston   Tangiers

Rickets Head   Nolton Haven   Nolton   A487   Pelcomb

Pelcomb Cross   Pelcomb Bridge

St Brides Bay Heritage Coast   Lambston   Sutton

St Brides Bay   Druidston   B4341

Haroldston West   Portfield Gate   B4327   Dreen Hill   A4076

Broad Haven   Broadway   Lowe Freystr

SKOMER ISLAND   Wooltack Point   Little Haven   Walton West   Solbury   Freys

Pembrokeshire Coast Path   Talbenny   14   Tiers Cross   John

10   St Brides   Walwyn's Castle

Marloes   B4327   Hasguard   Thornton

Broad Sound   St Ishmael's   Sandy Haven   Herbrandston   Steynton   Honeyborough

Marloes & Dale Heritage Coast   Dale   Hubberston   Waterston

Westdale Bay   Dale Point   Great Castle Head   Hakin   **Milford Haven (Aberdaugleddau)**   Llanstadwell   Pembro Dock

SKOKHOLM ISLAND   Milford Haven   (Doc Penfr

St Ann's Head   Angle   Pwllcrochan

Angle Bay   Rhoscrowther

'00   B4320

Rosslare   Freshwater West   Castlemartin Brook   B4320

B4319

SR   Castlemartin   Twy

11   Warren

Linney Head   Merrion

PEMBROKESHIRE COAST NATIONAL PARK

12   Pembrokeshire Coast Path   Bosh

A '60 B C 70 D E 80 F G 90 H

0 1 2 3 4 5 miles
0 1 2 3 4 5 6 7 8 kilometres

Port plan: Pembroke Dock p.X

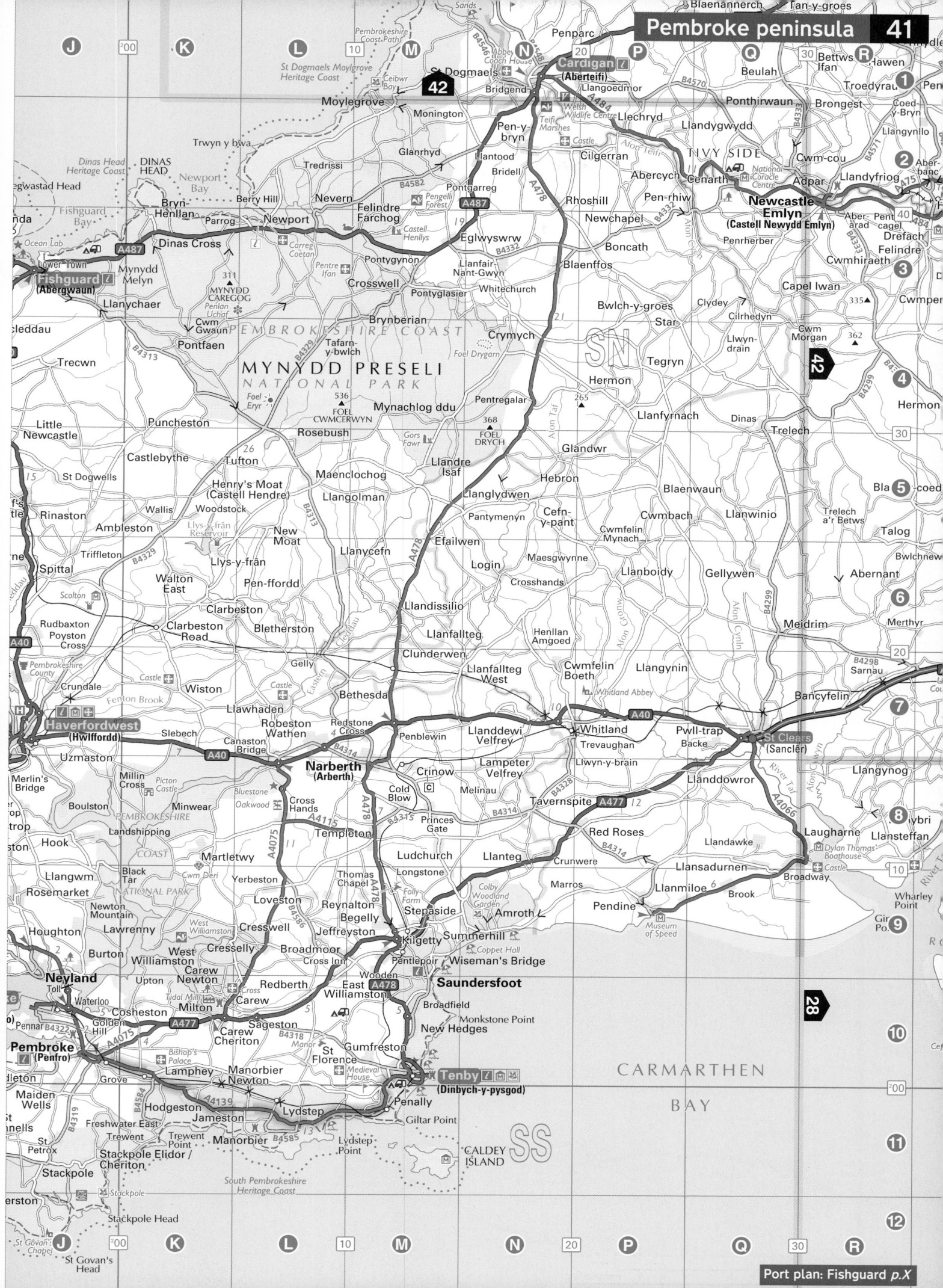

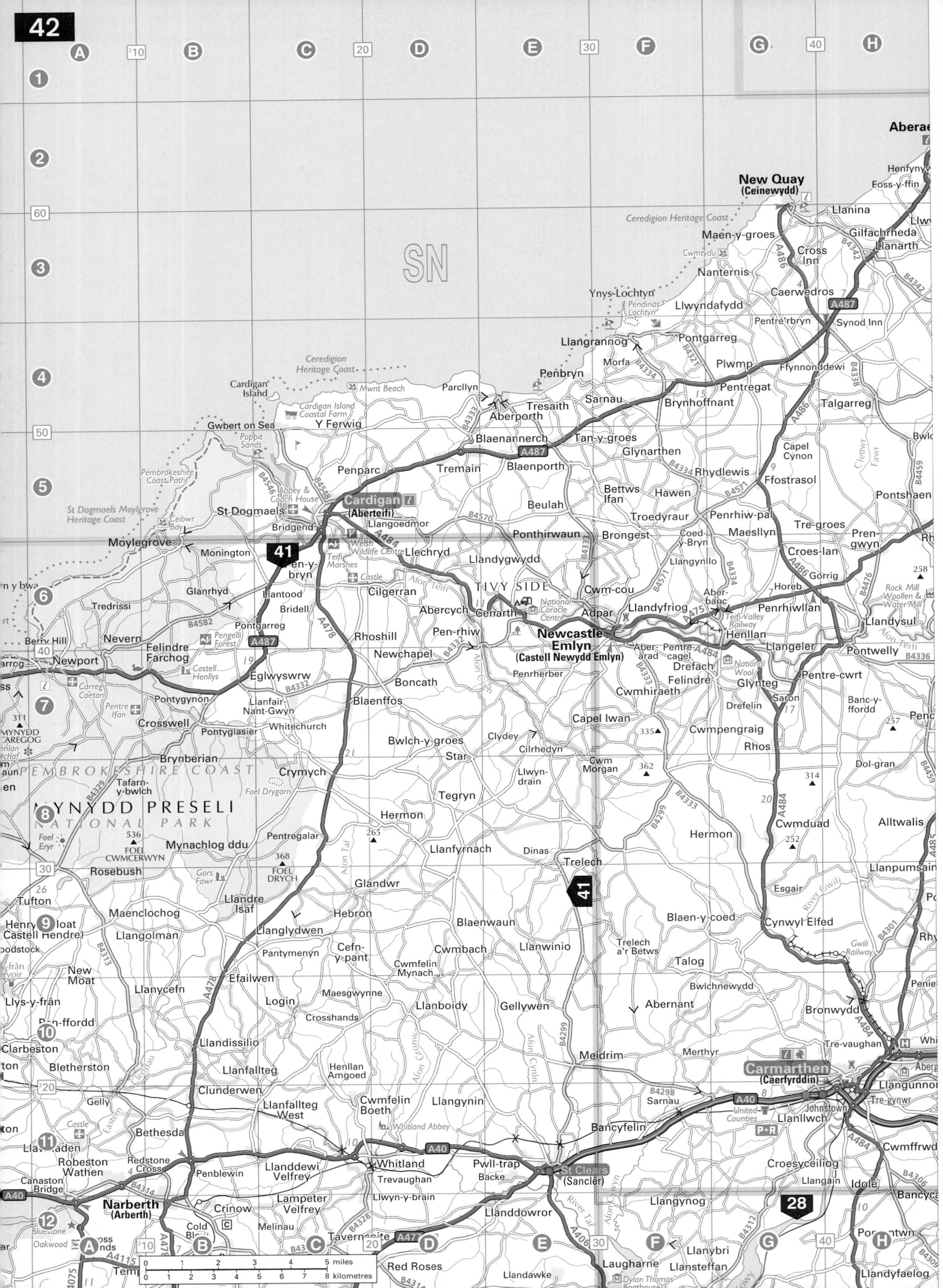

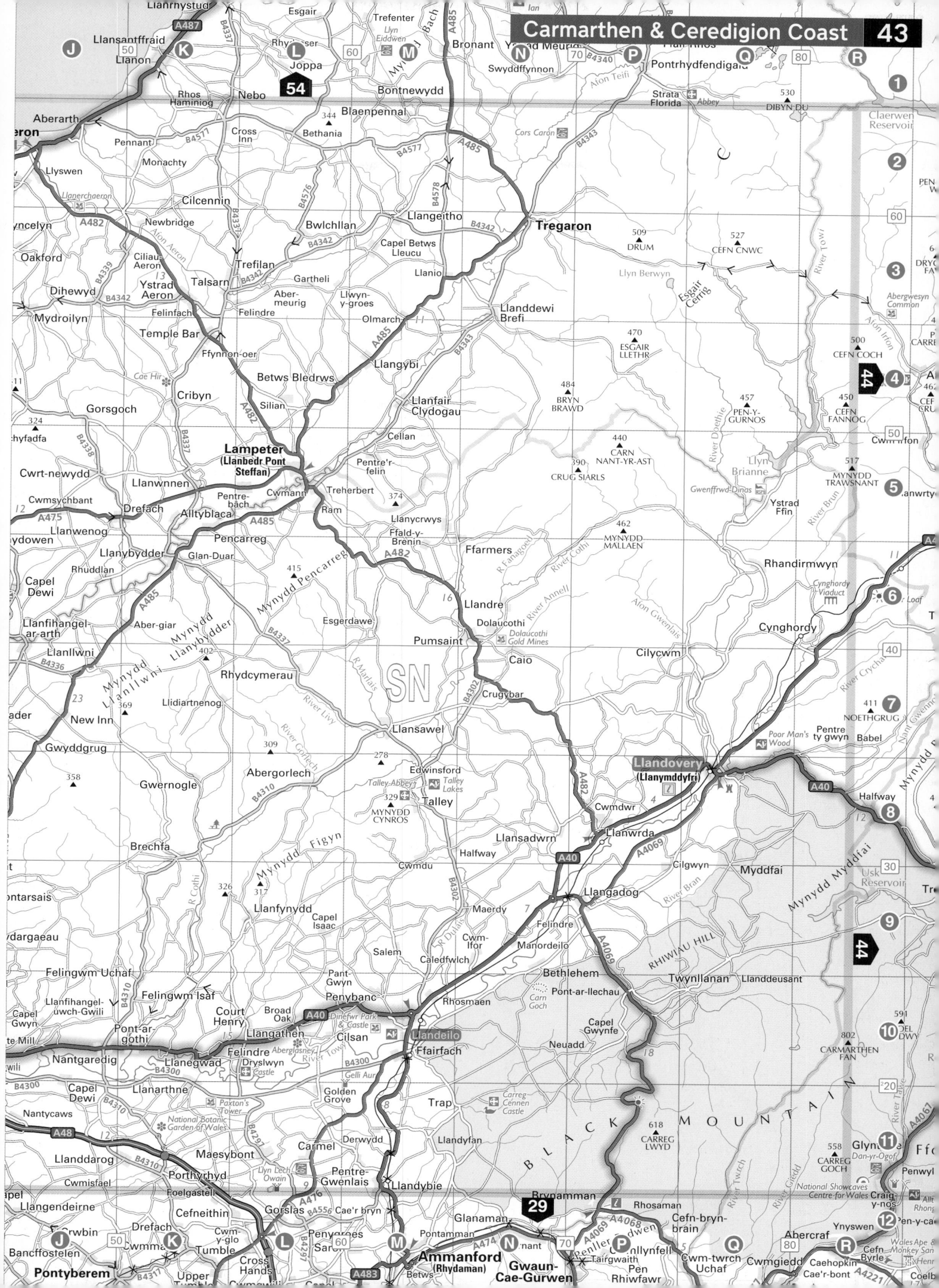

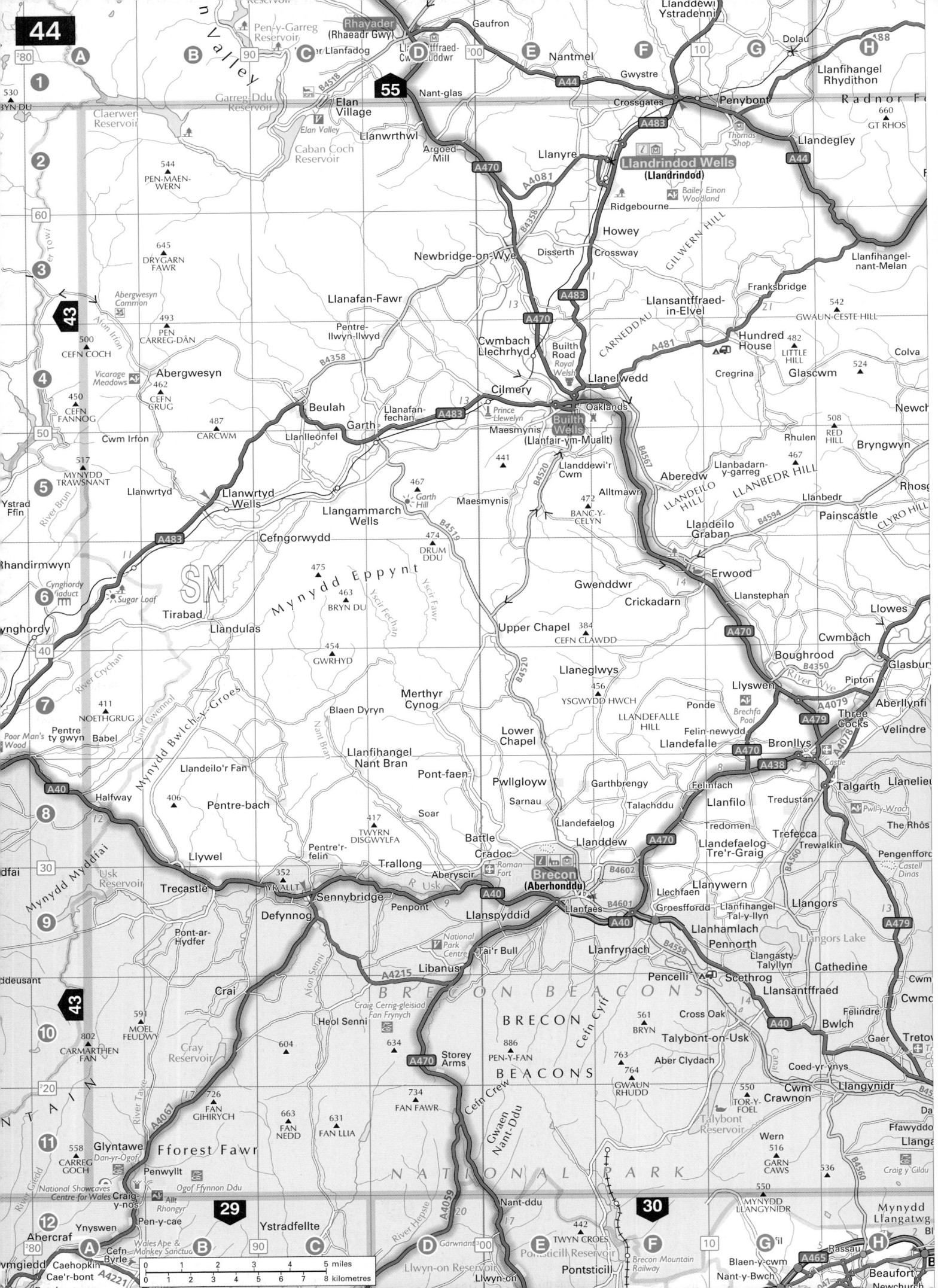

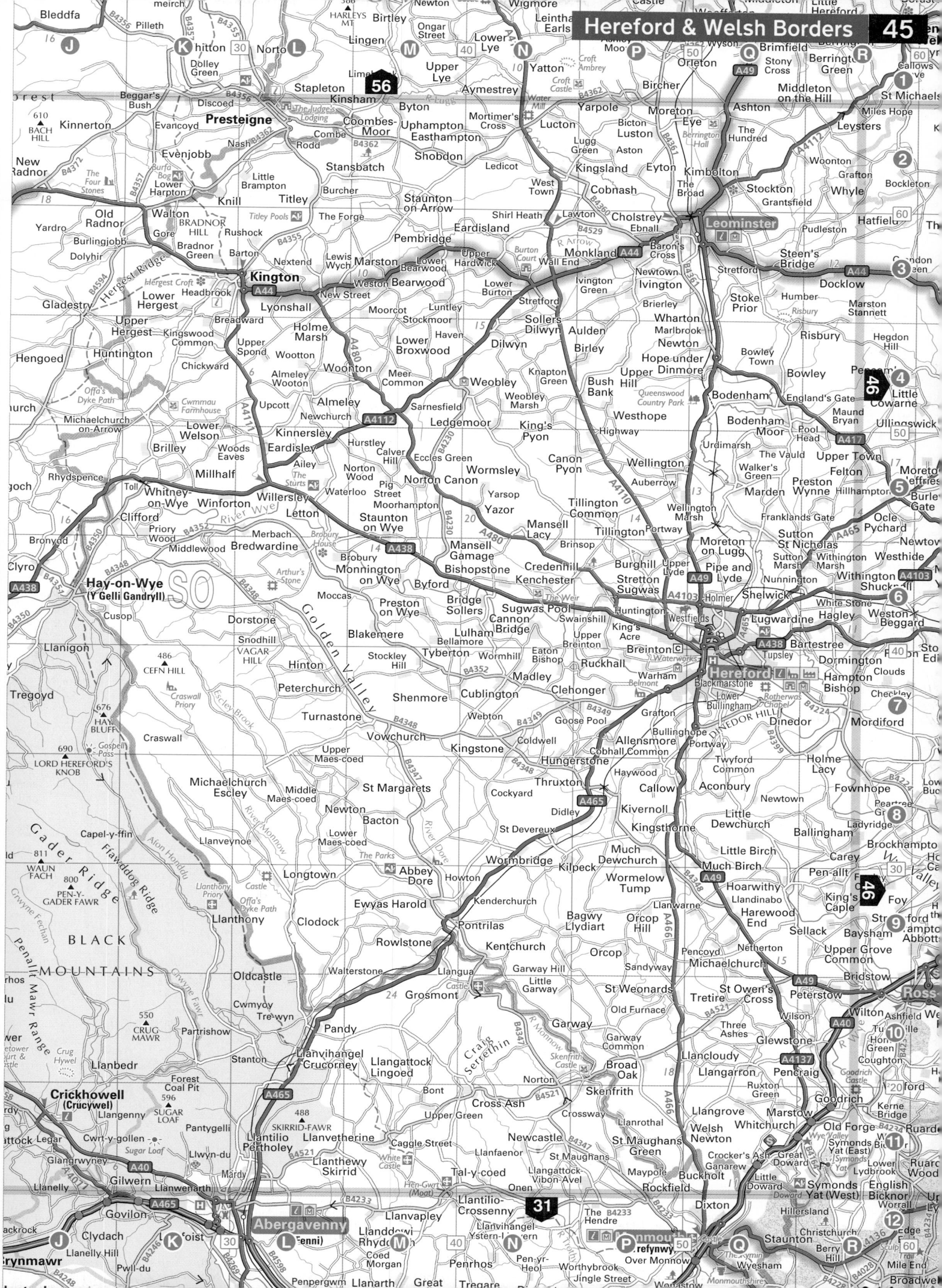

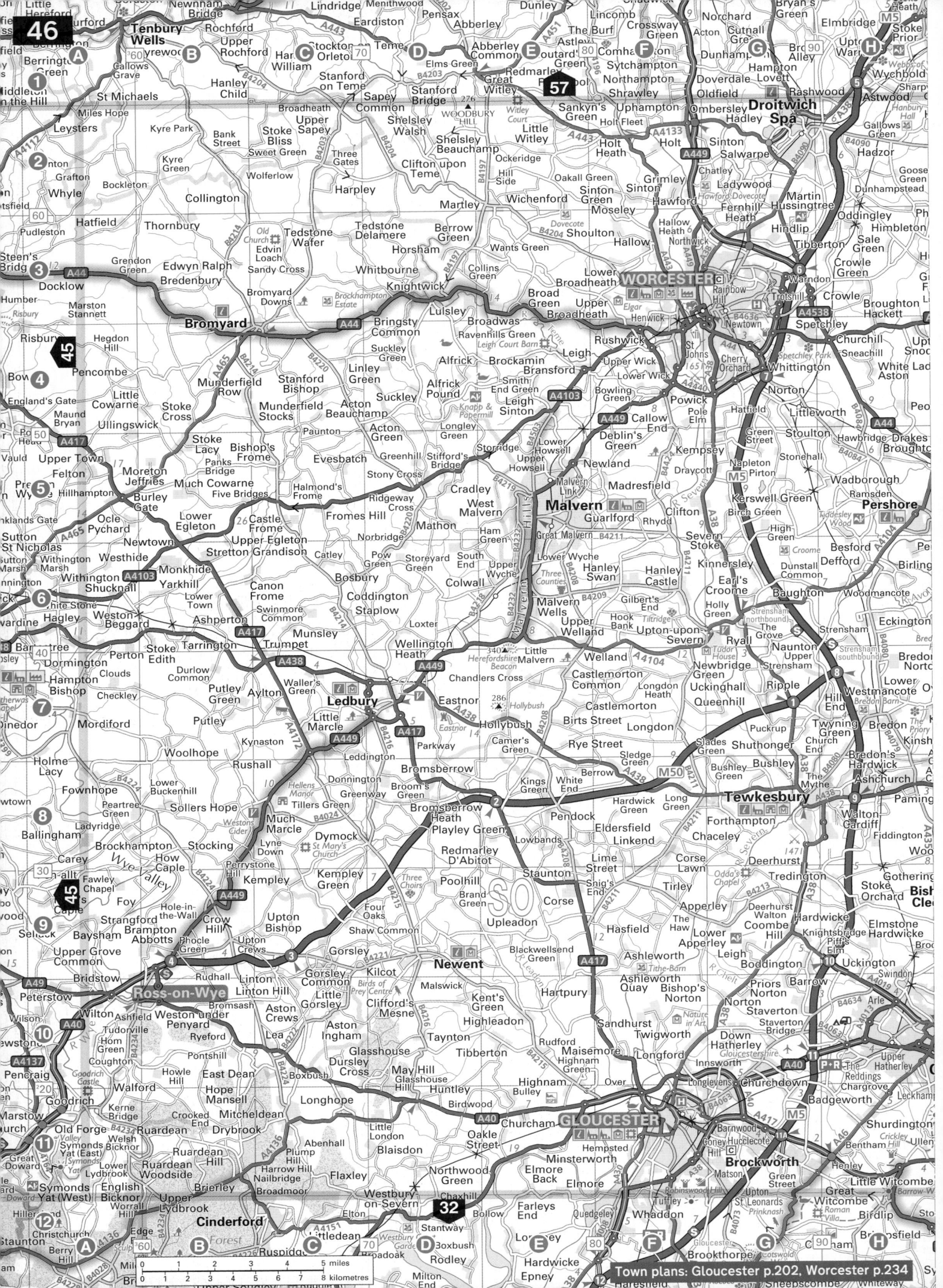

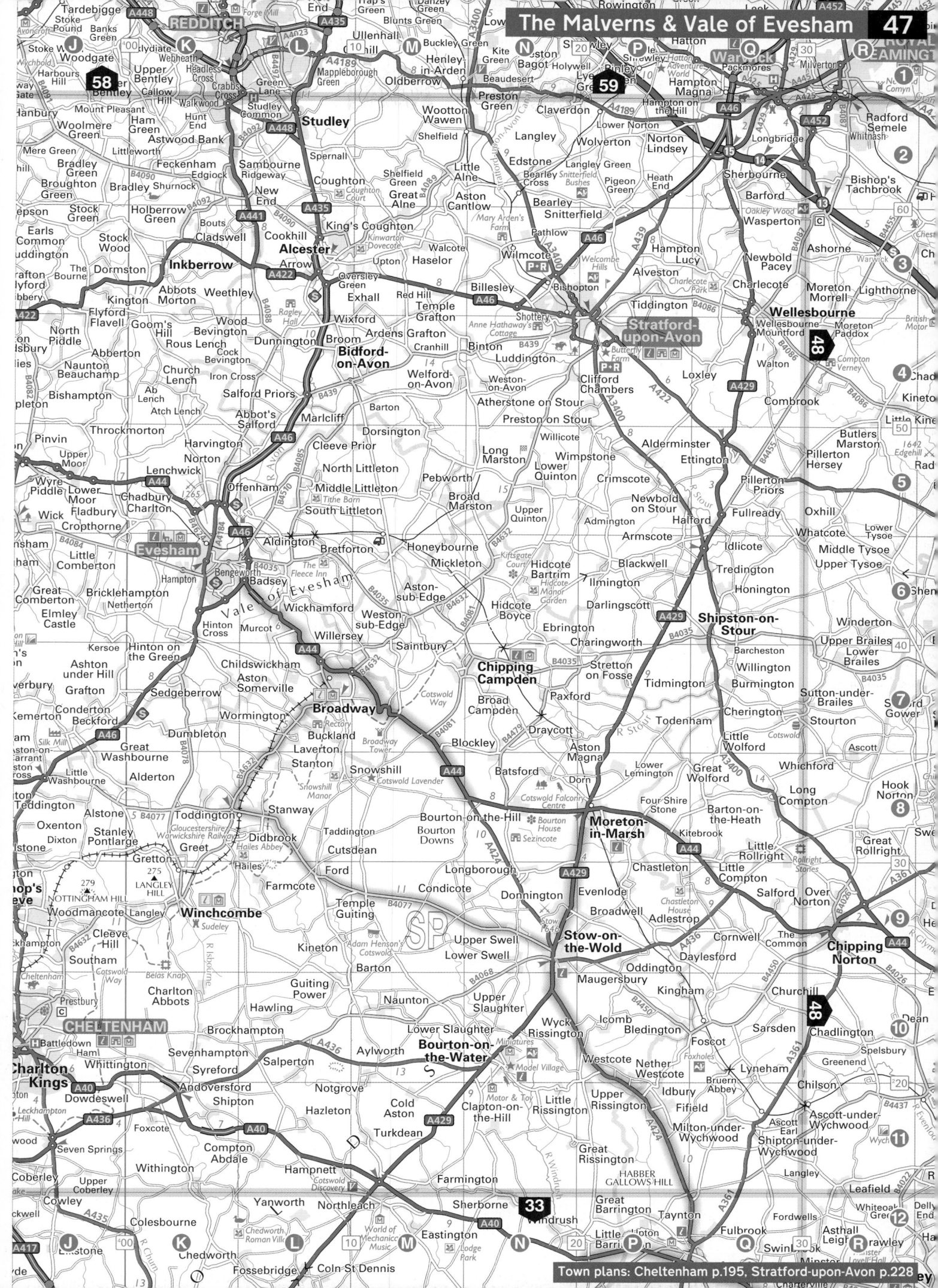

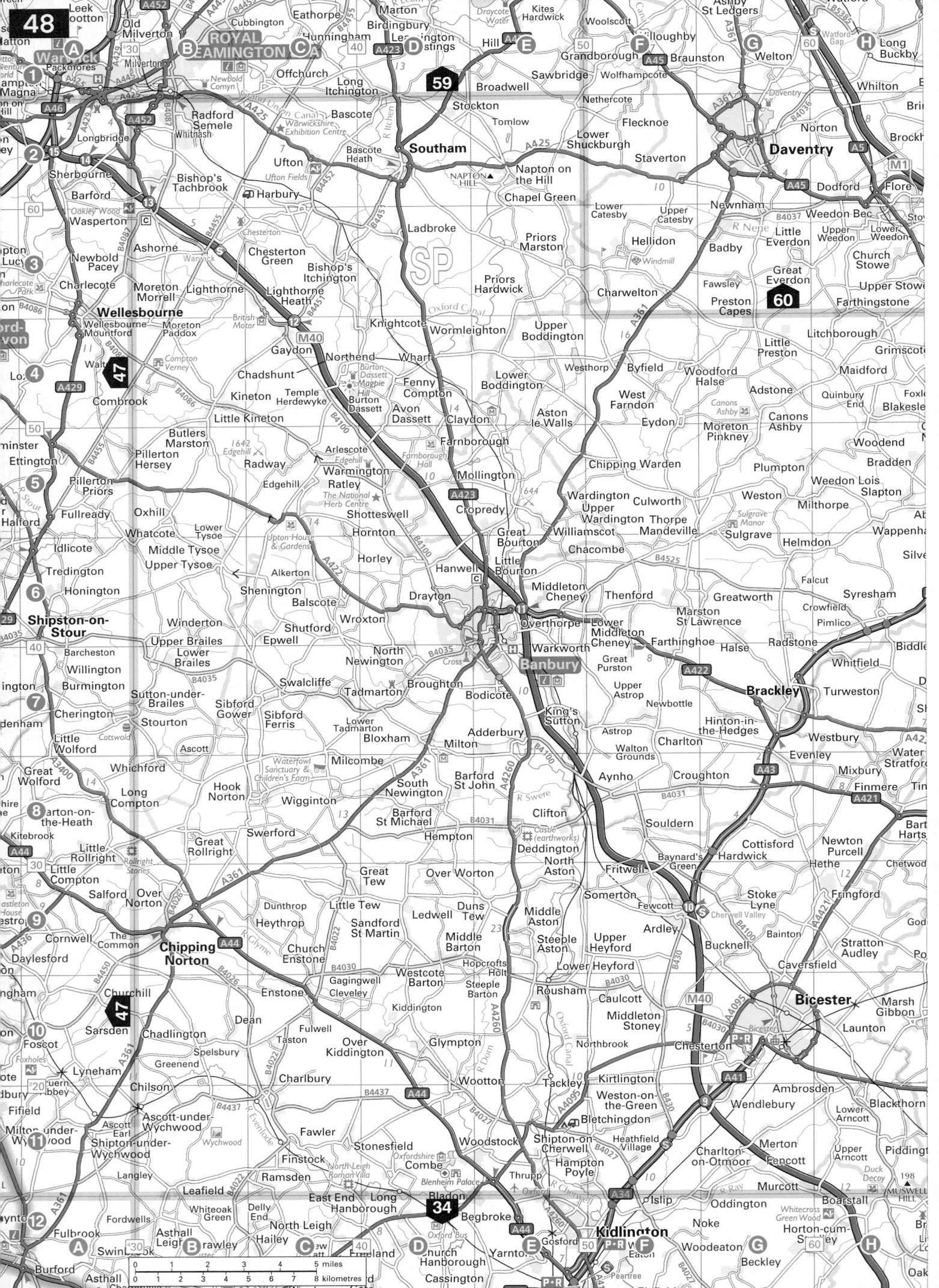

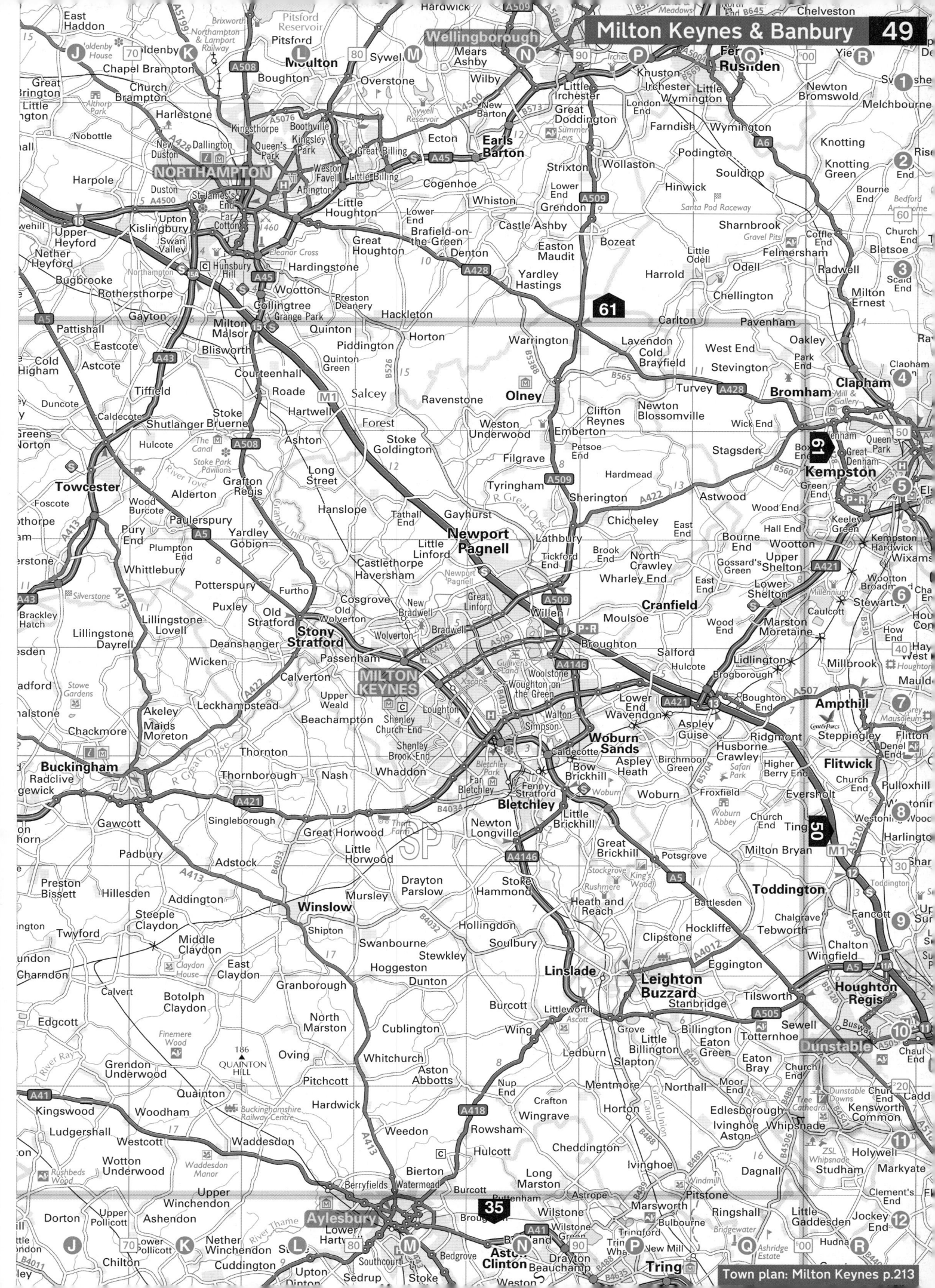

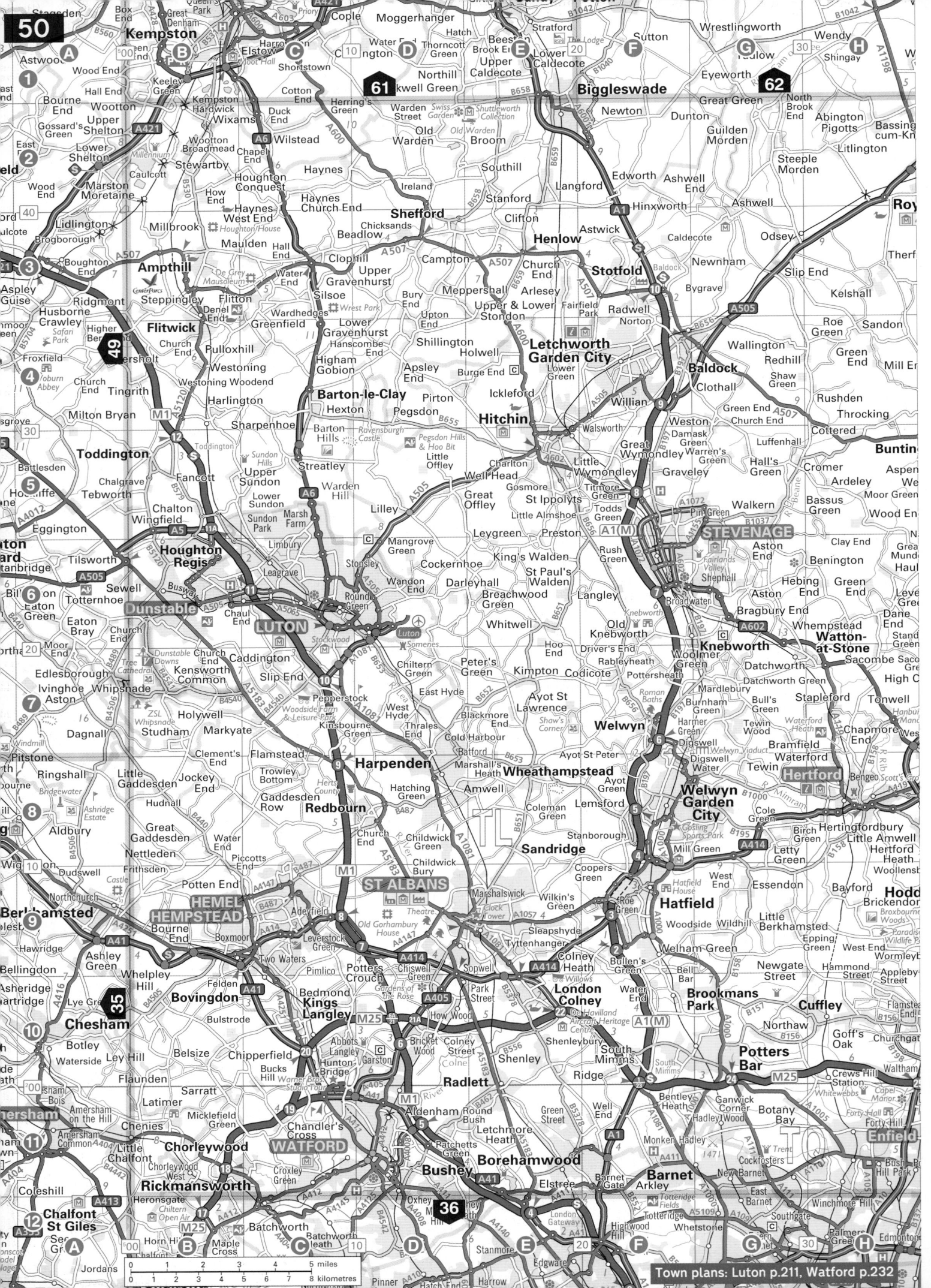

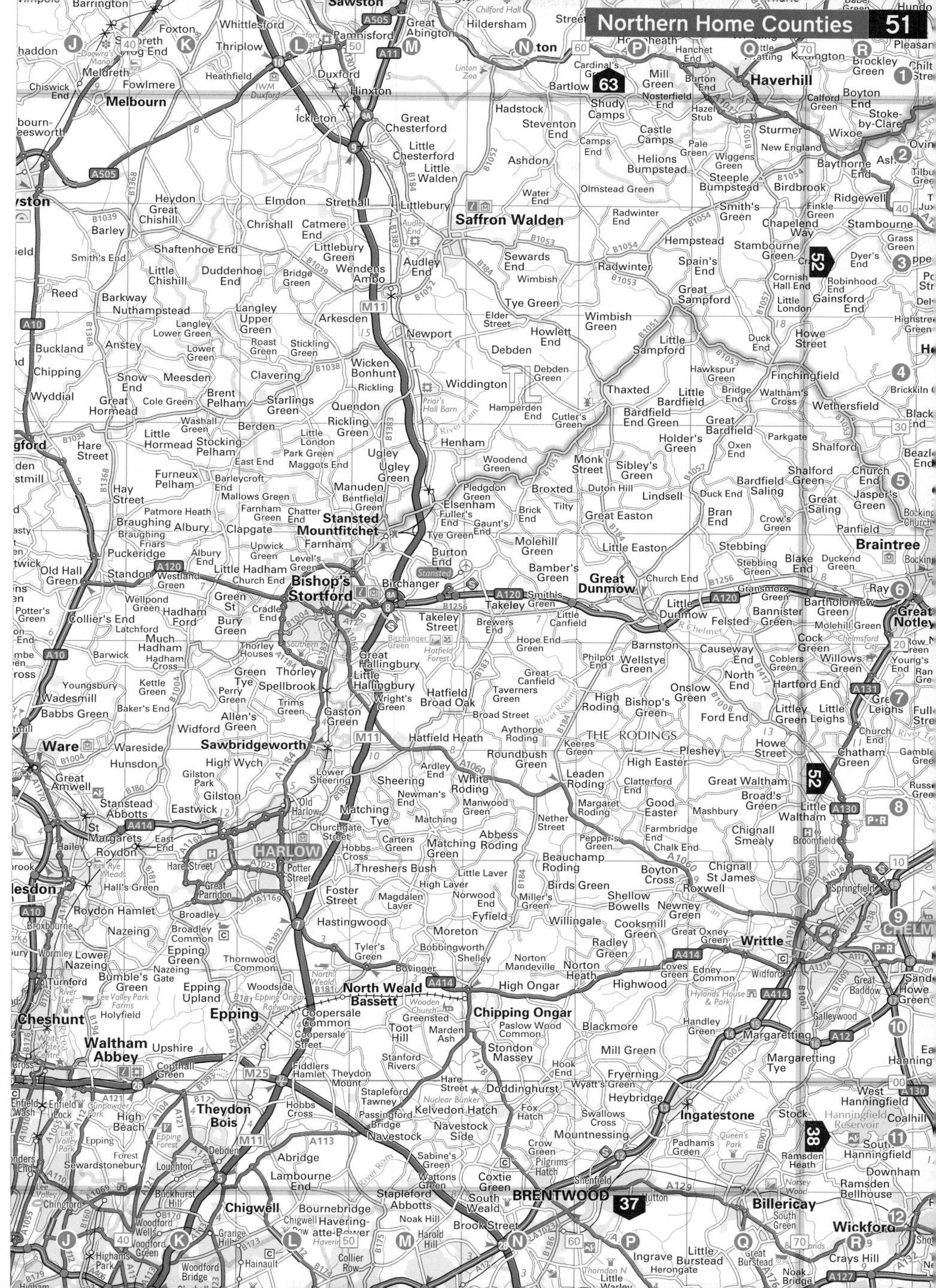

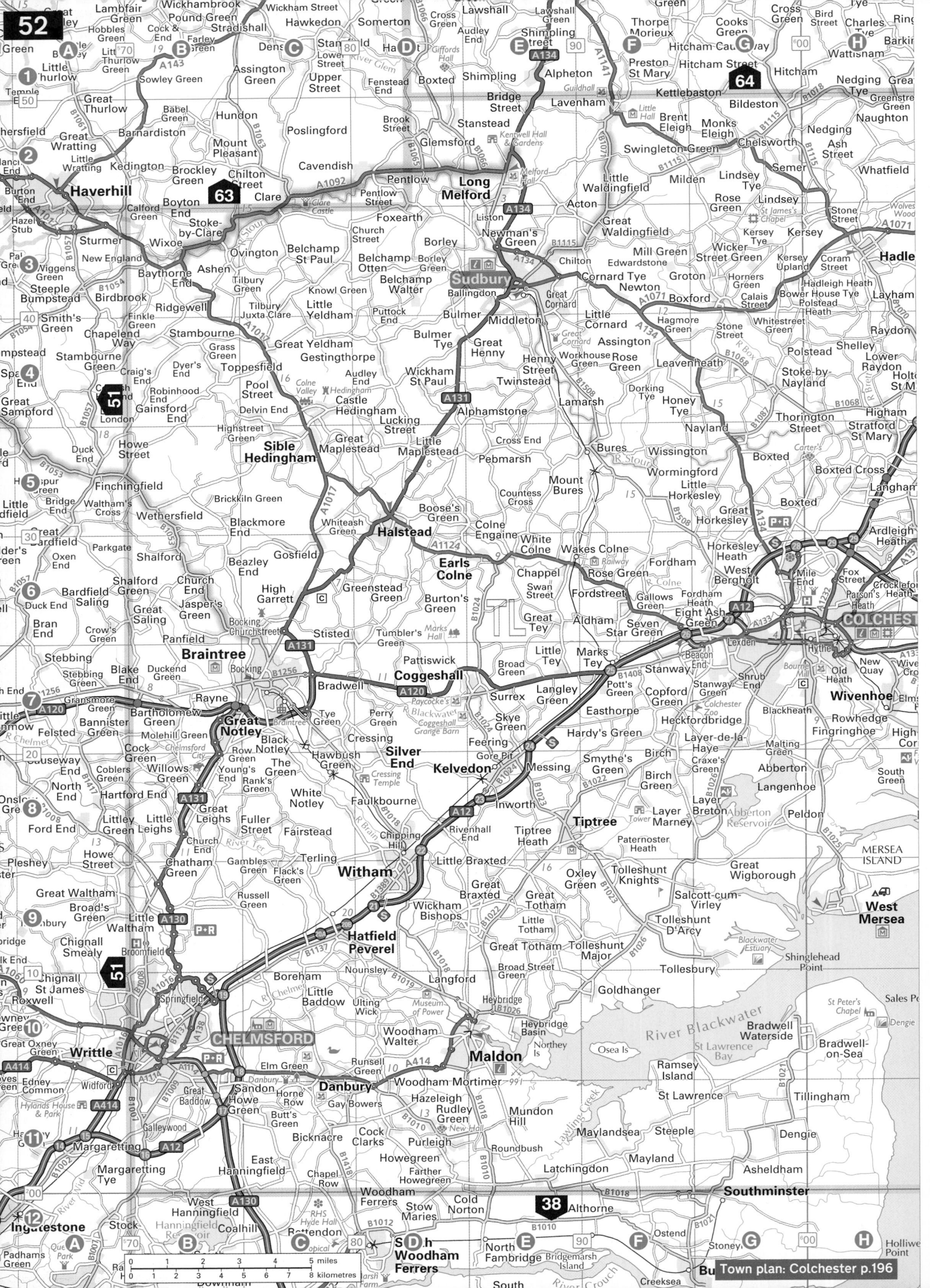

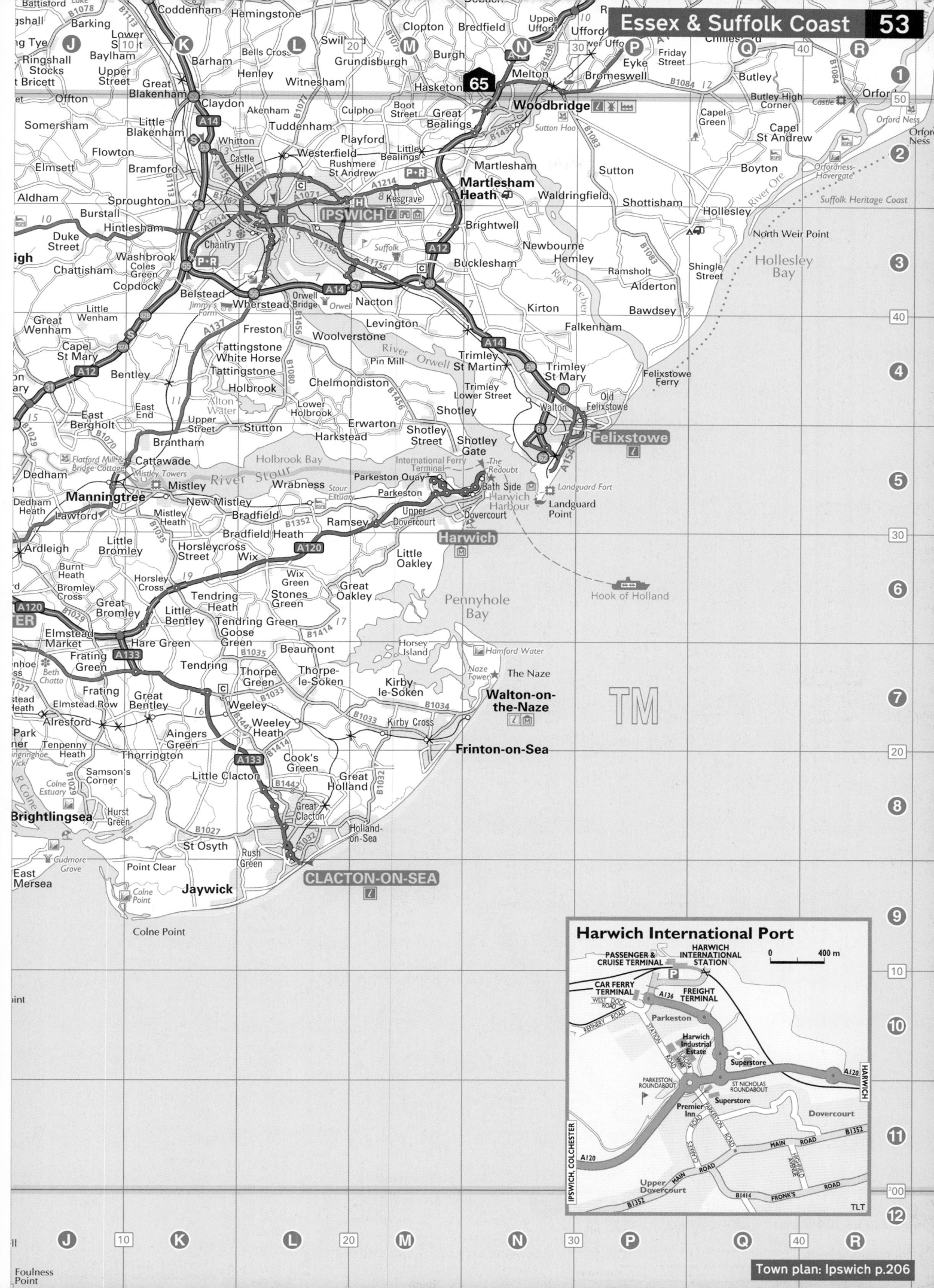

Harwich International Port

PASSENGER & CRUISE TERMINAL
HARWICH INTERNATIONAL STATION
CAR FERRY TERMINAL
FREIGHT TERMINAL
WEST DOCK ROAD
REFINERY ROAD
Parkeston
STATION ROAD
Harwich Industrial Estate
WEST DOCK ROAD
Superstore
PARKESTON ROUNDABOUT
ST NICHOLAS ROUNDABOUT
Superstore
Premier Inn
IPSWICH, COLCHESTER
A120
PARKESTON ROAD
Upper Dovercourt
MAIN ROAD
COKES LANE
MAIN ROAD
Dovercourt
SCHOOL AVENUE
FRONK'S ROAD
B1352
B1414
HARWICH
A120
TLT
0   400 m

Town plan: Ipswich p.206

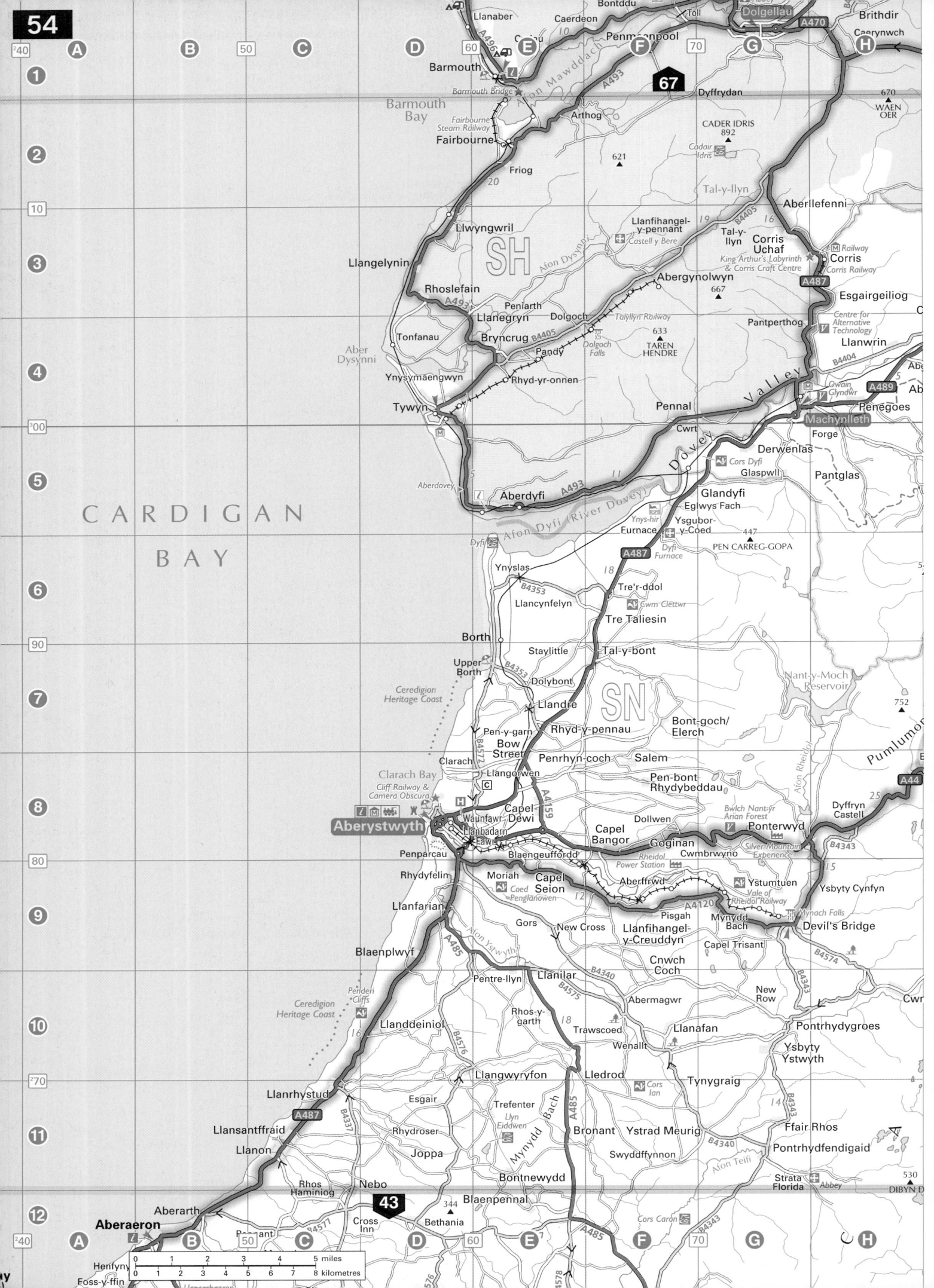

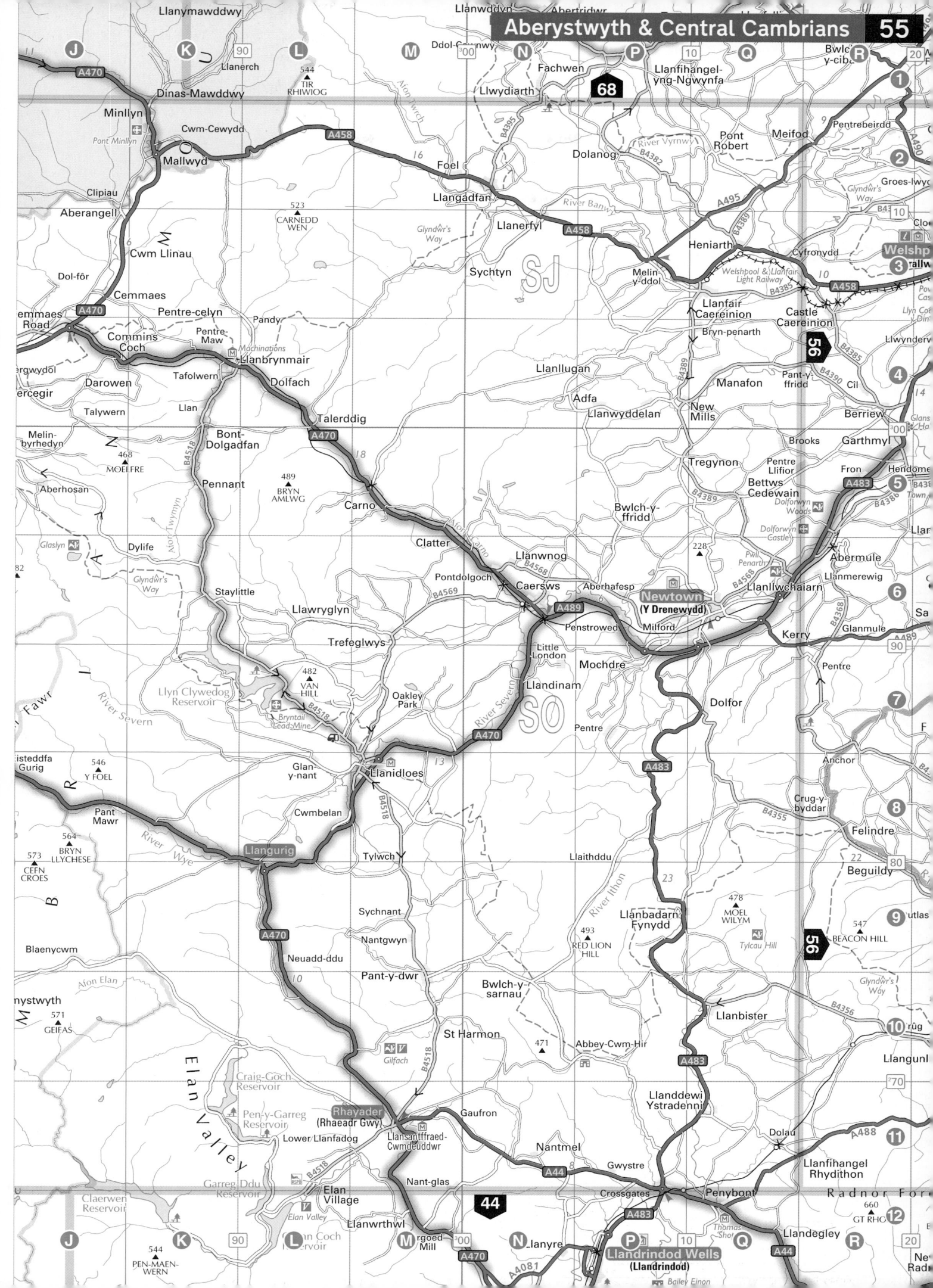

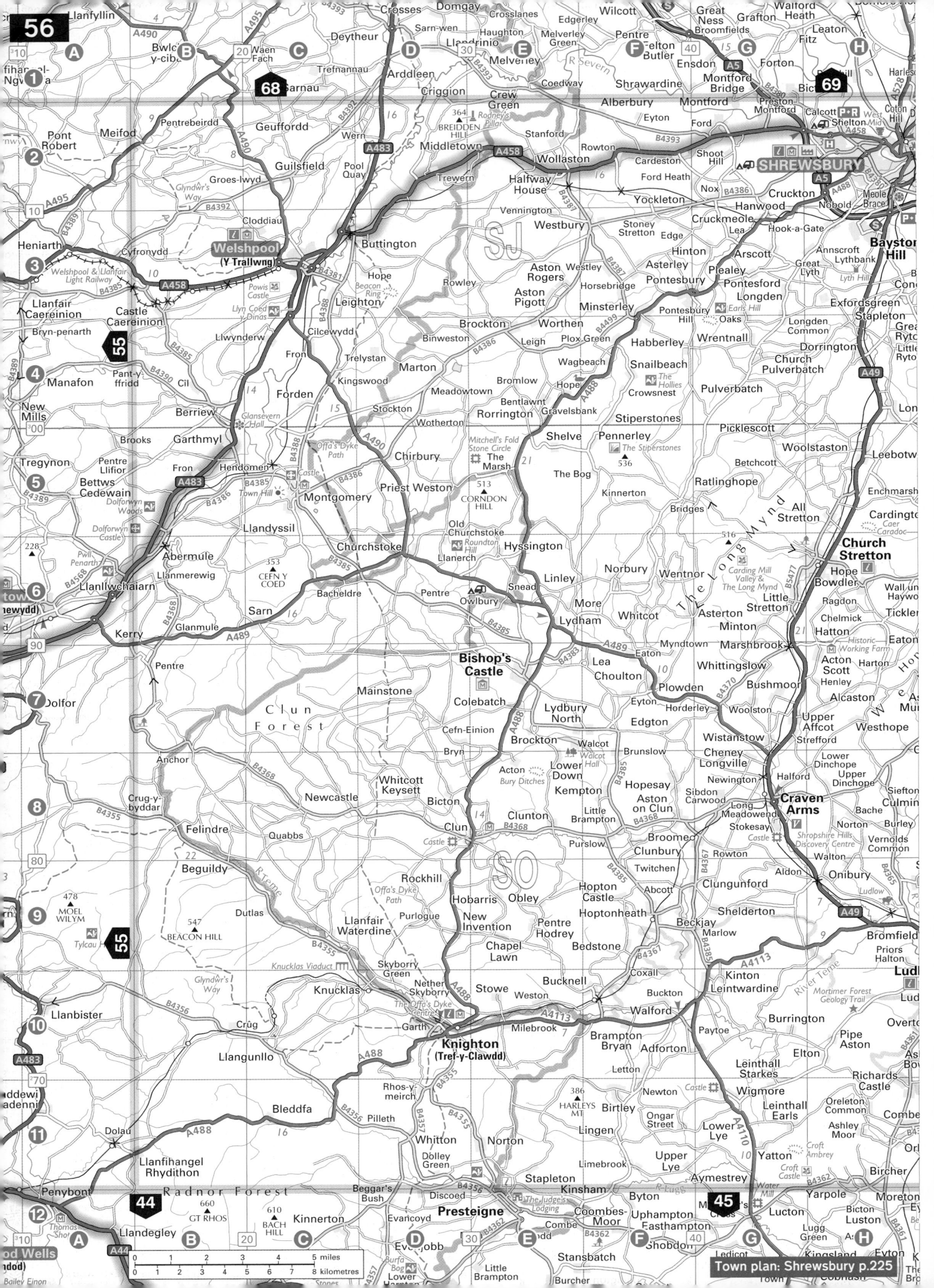

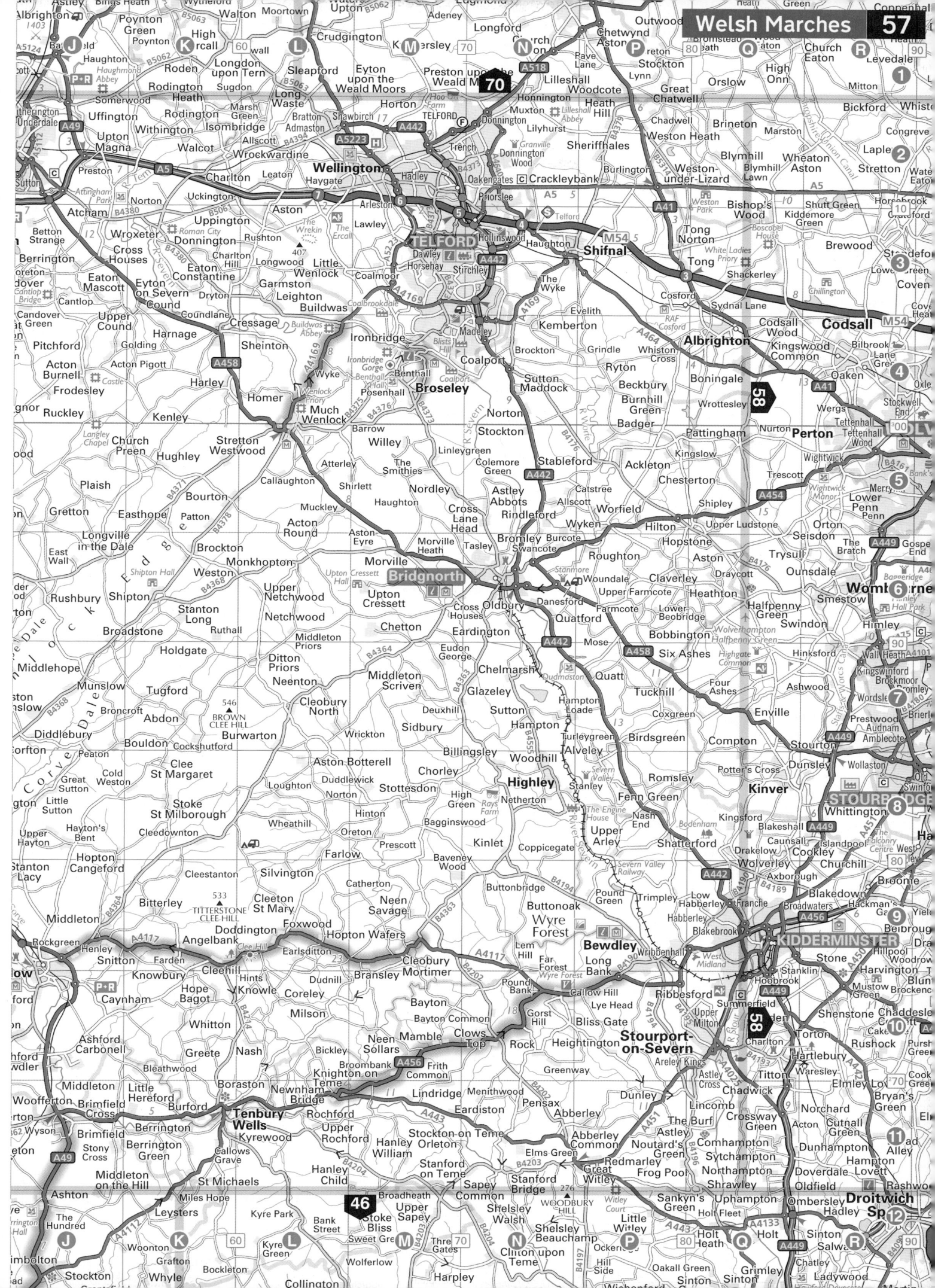

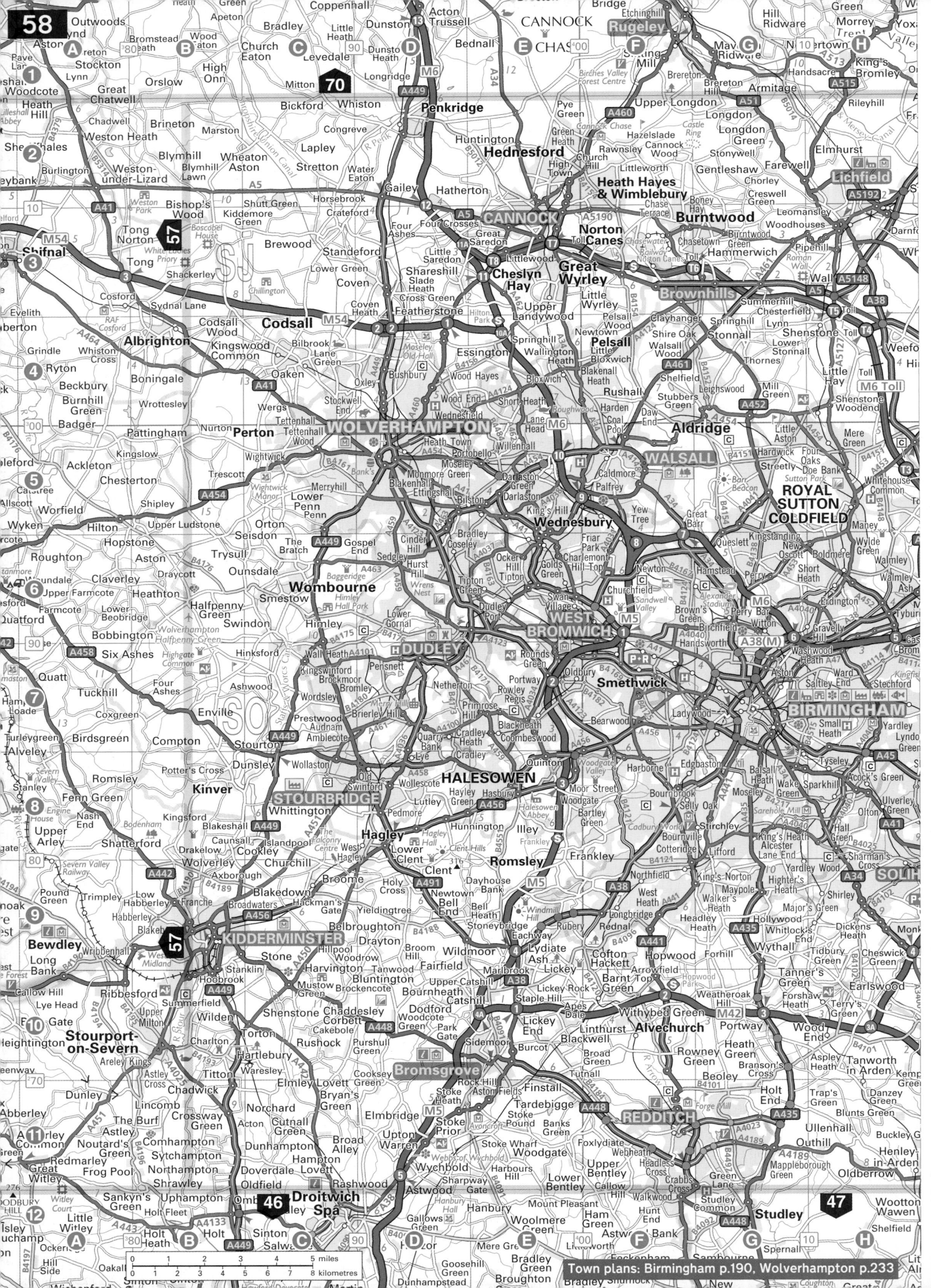

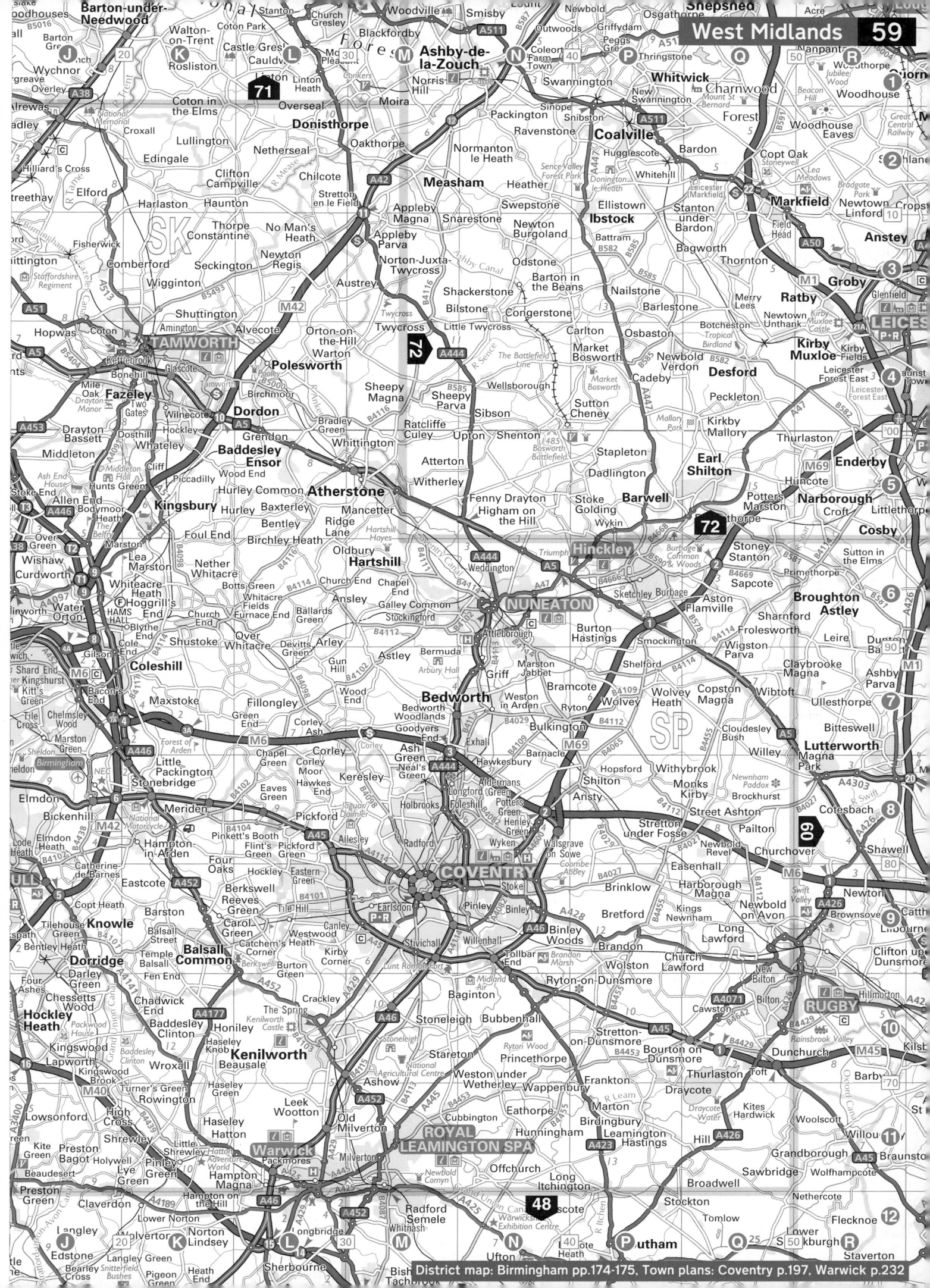

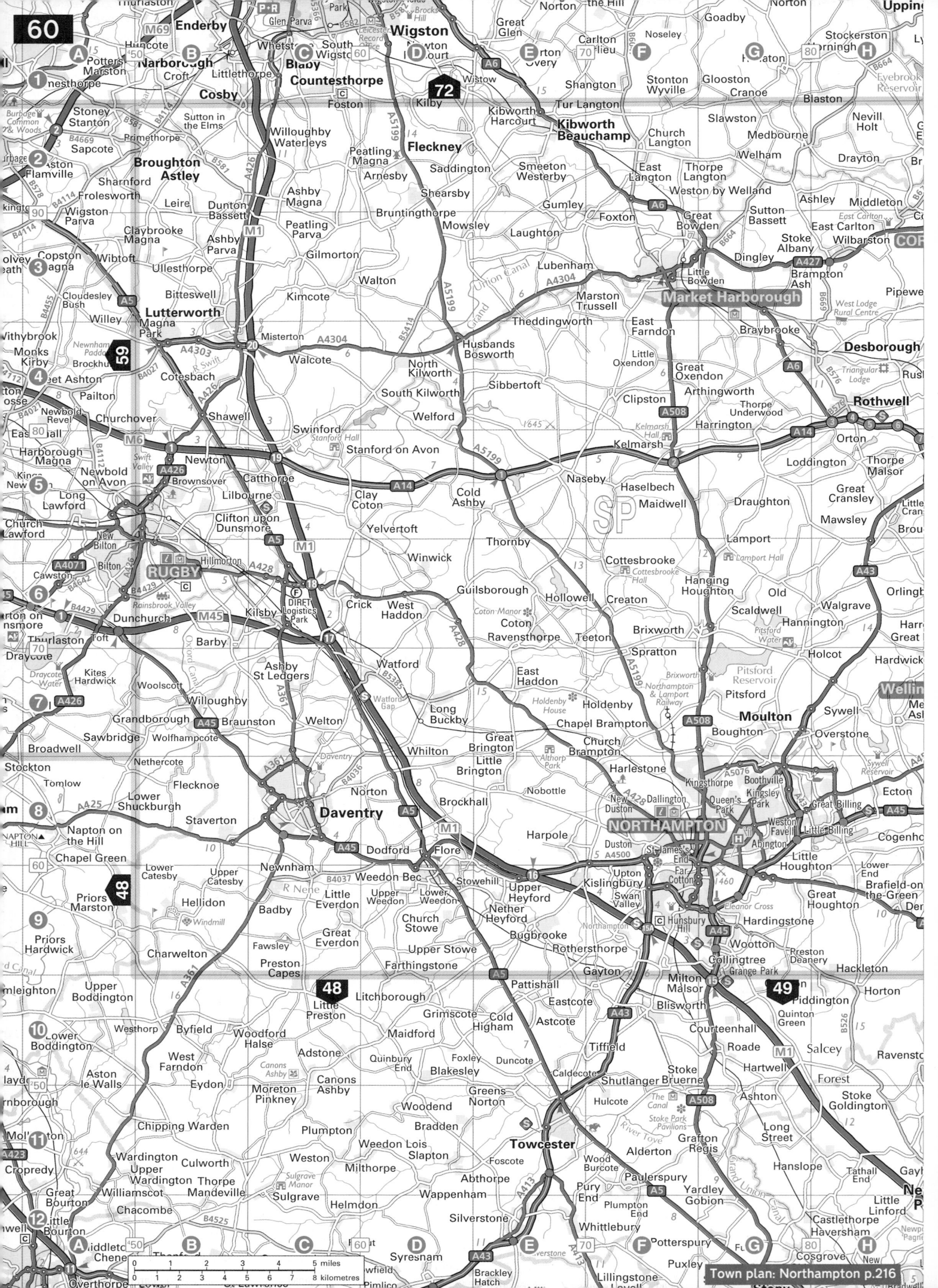

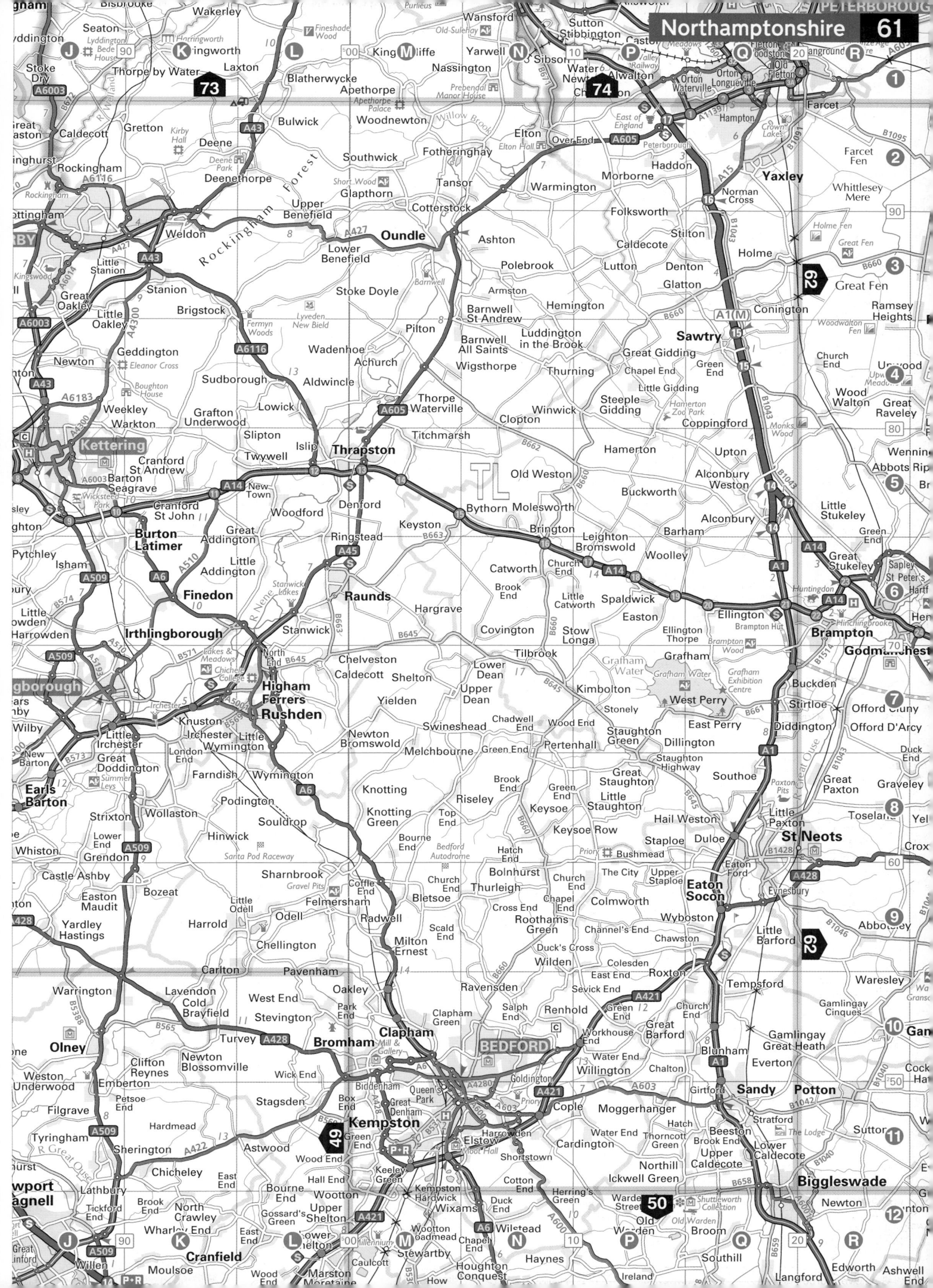

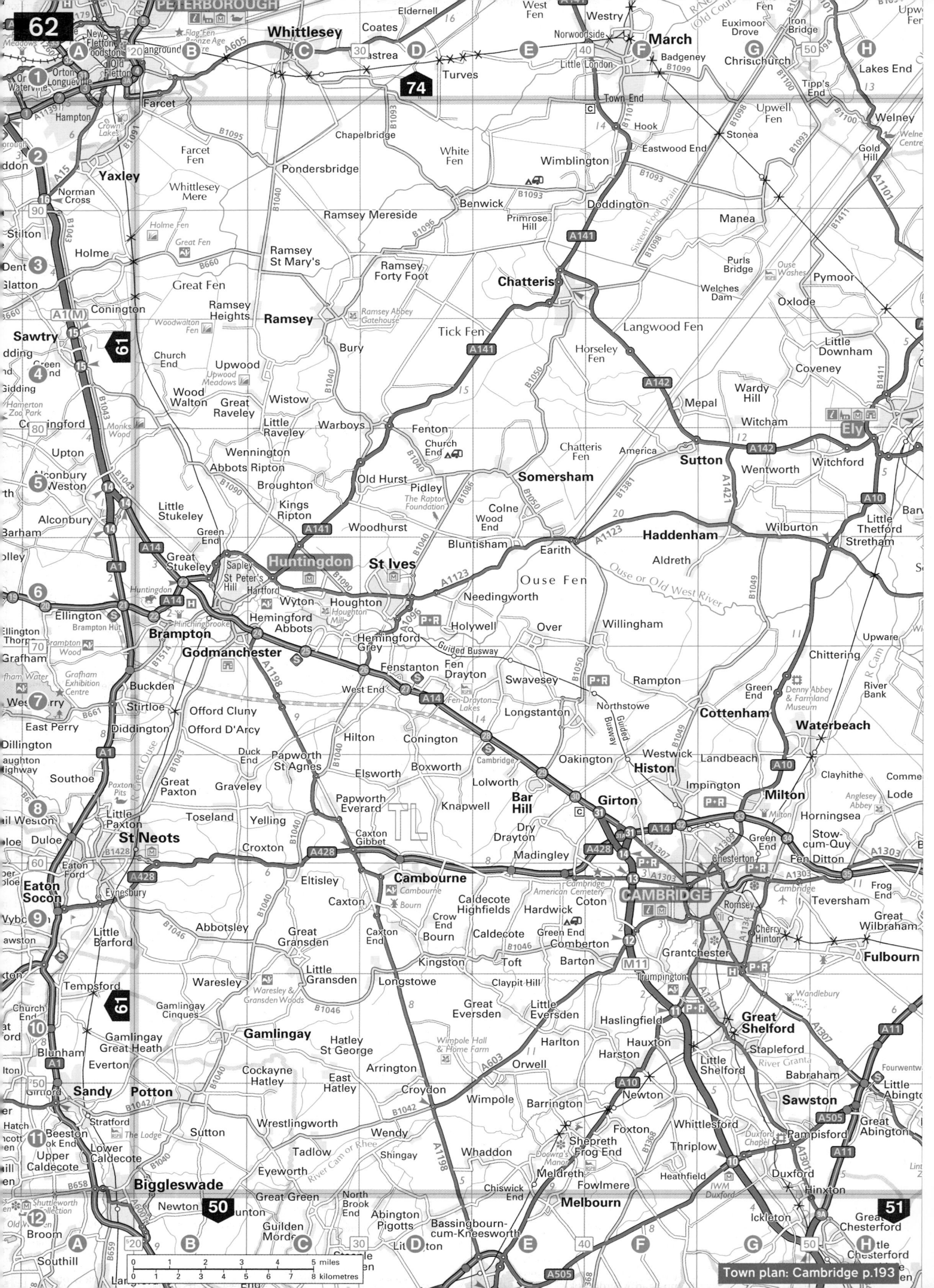

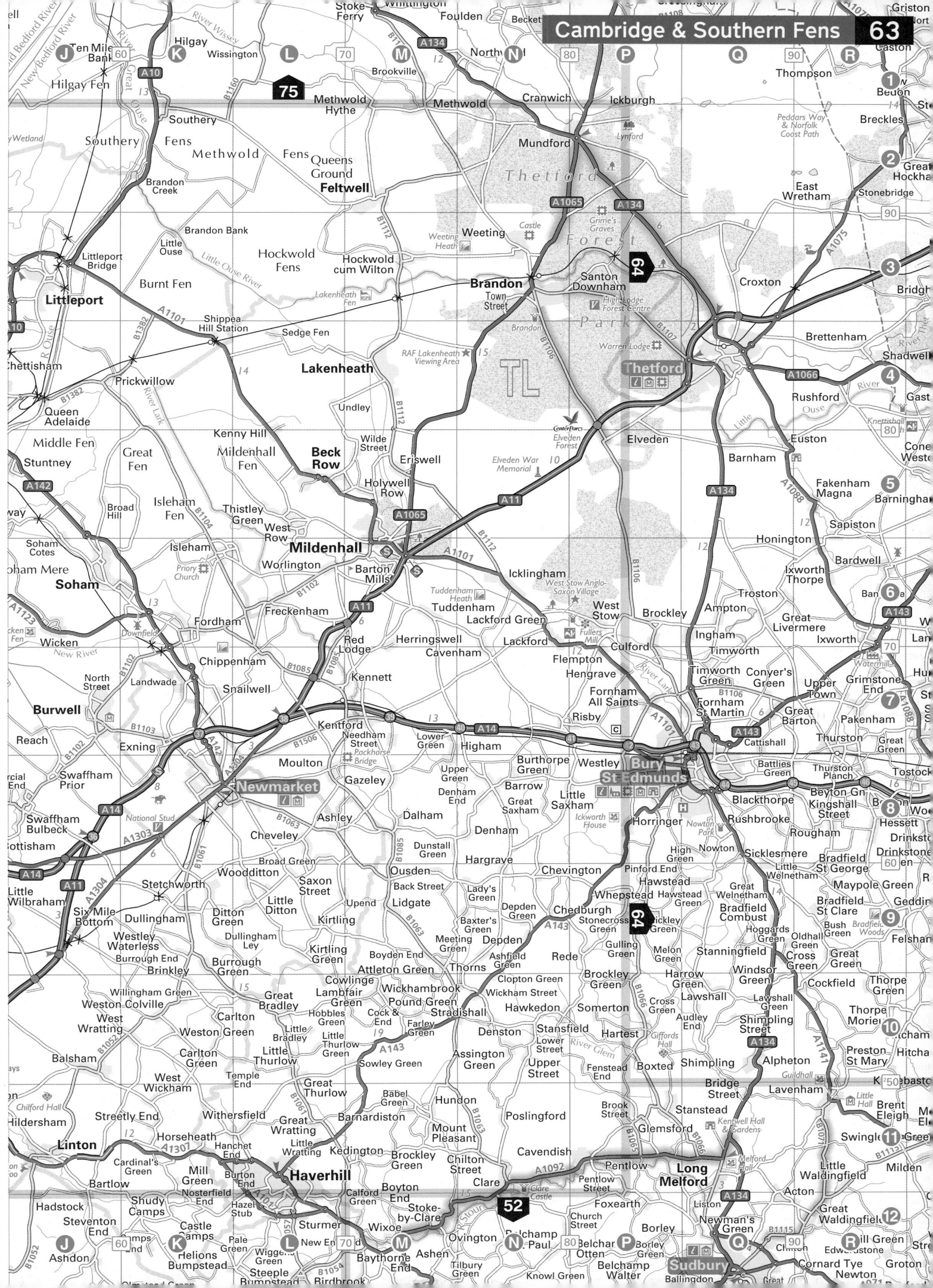

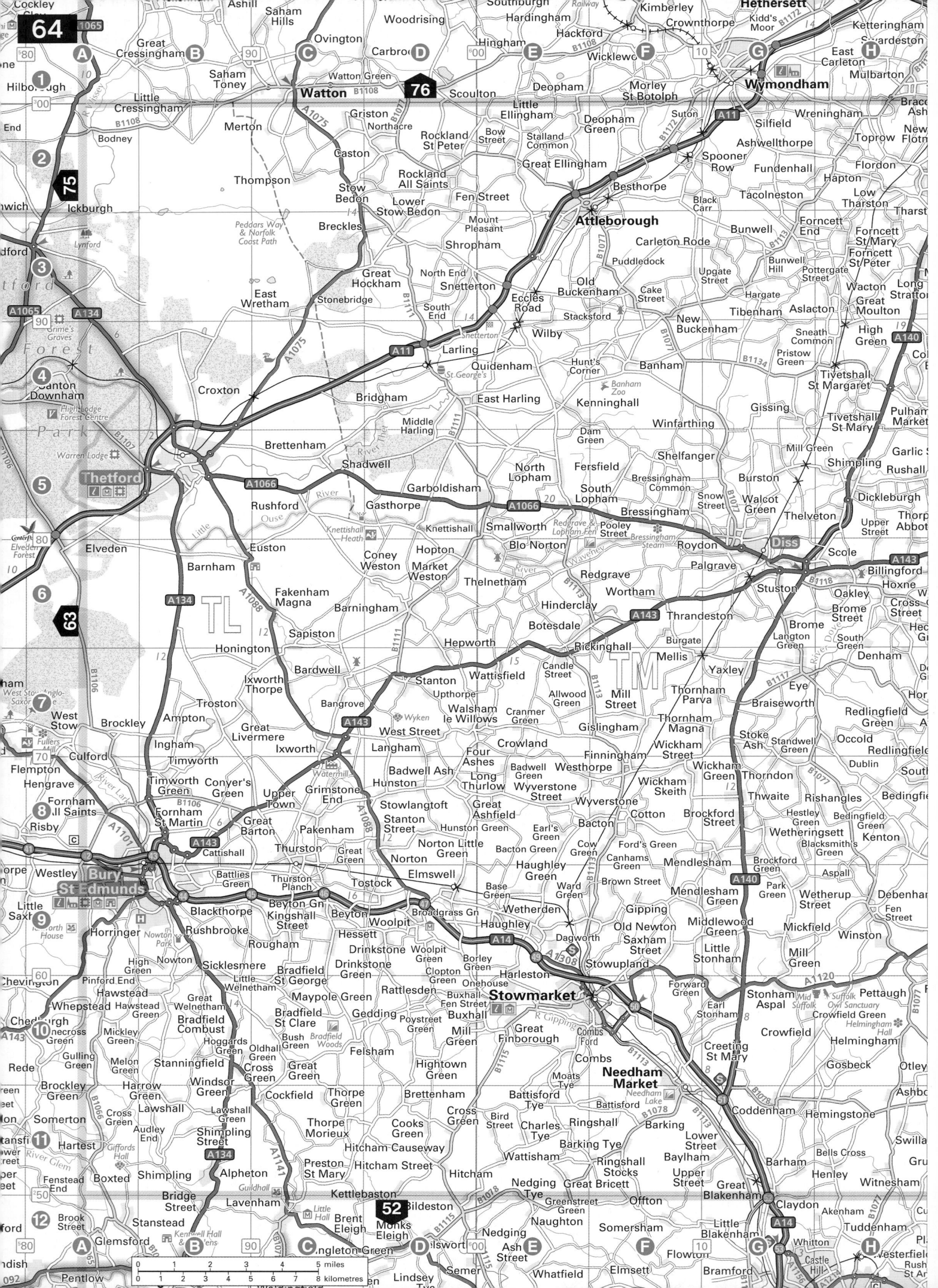

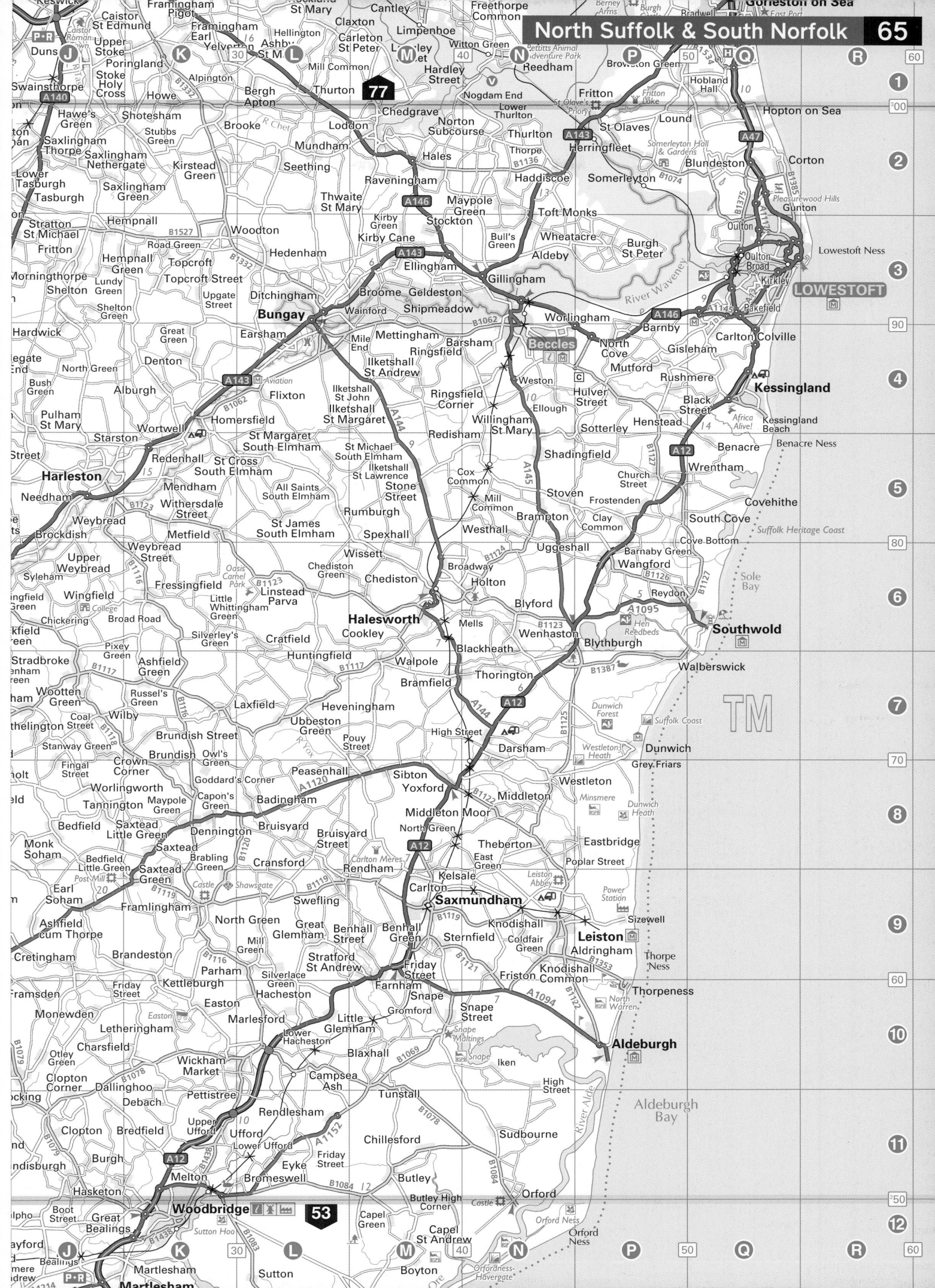

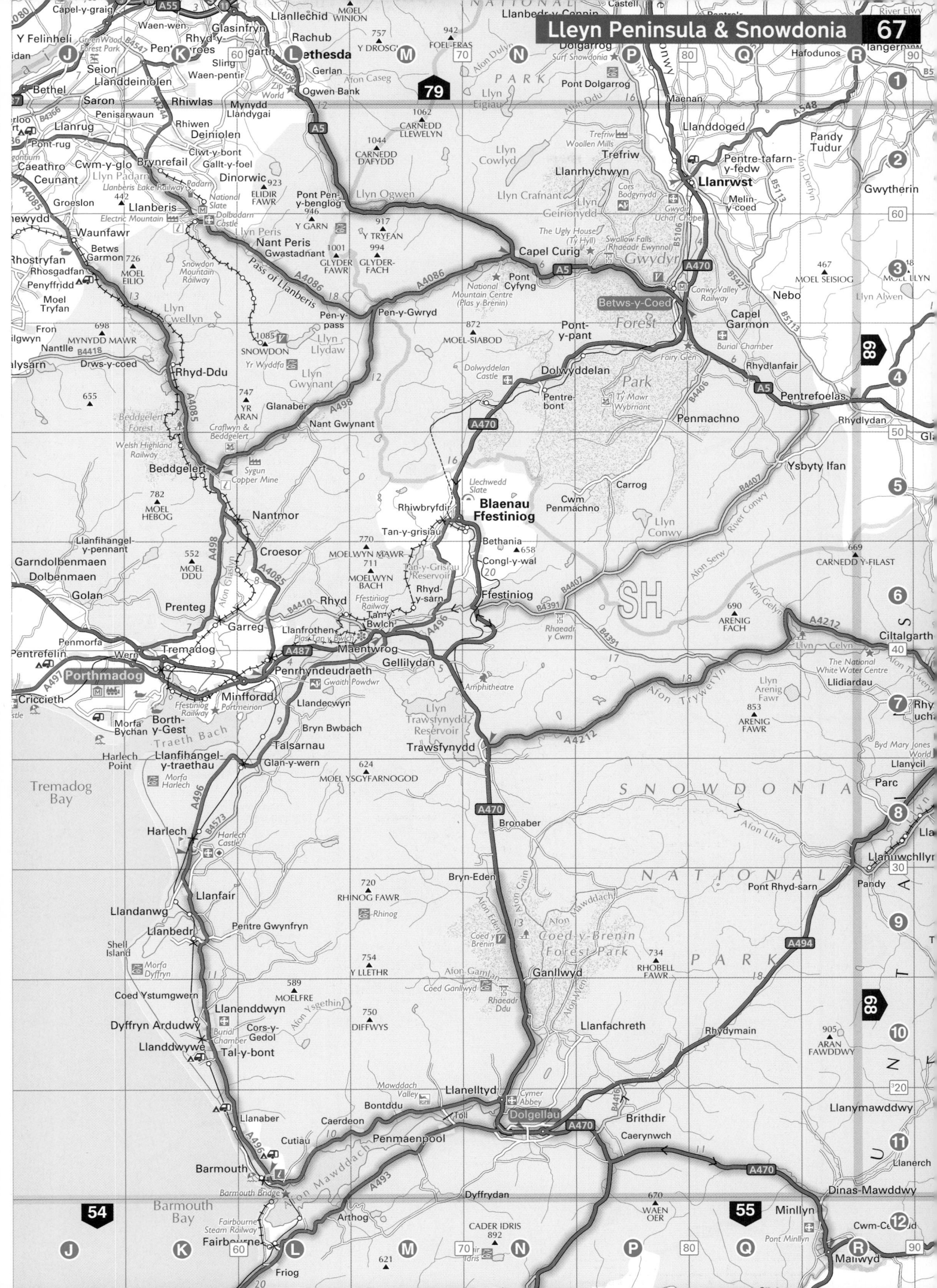

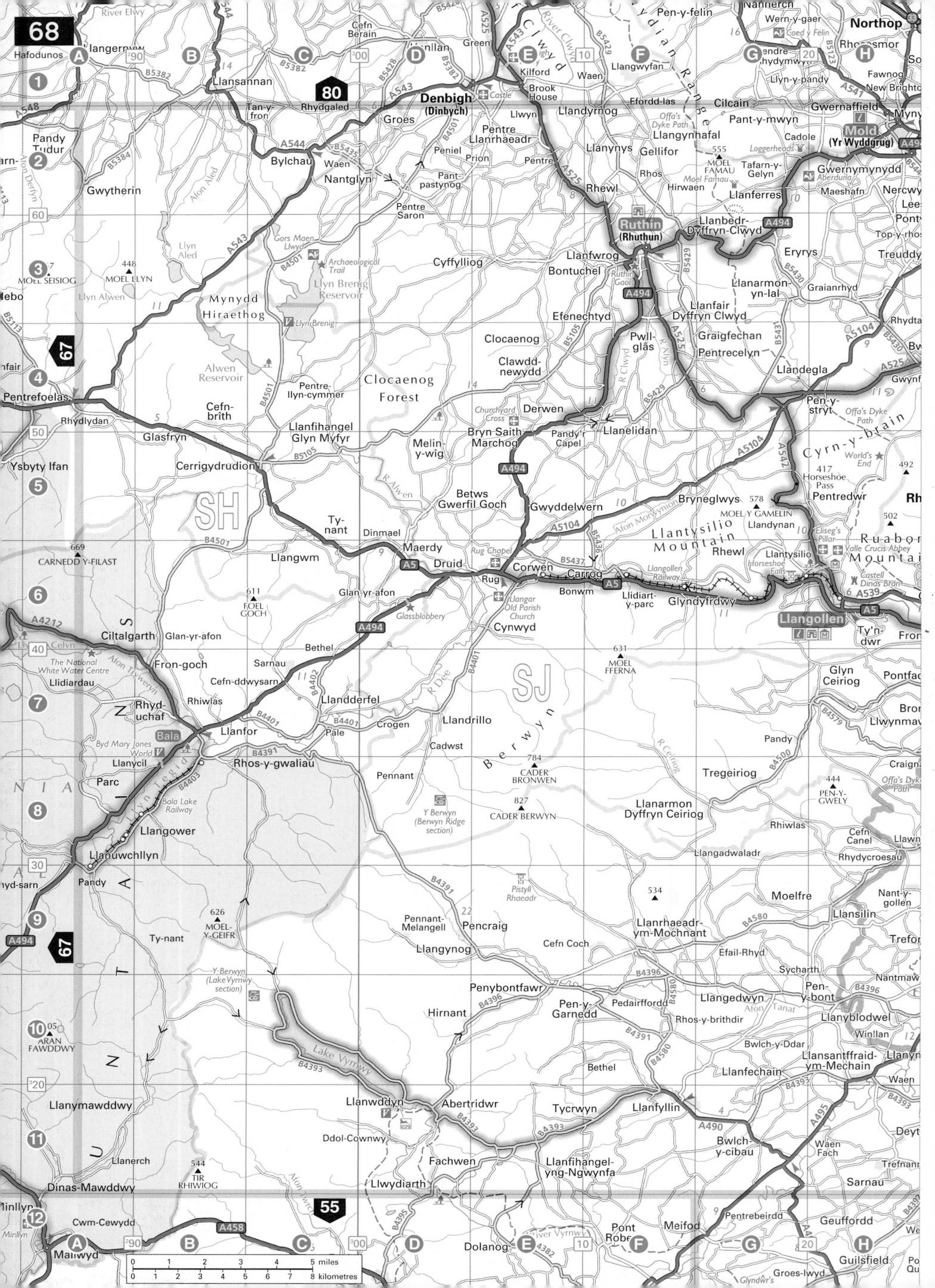

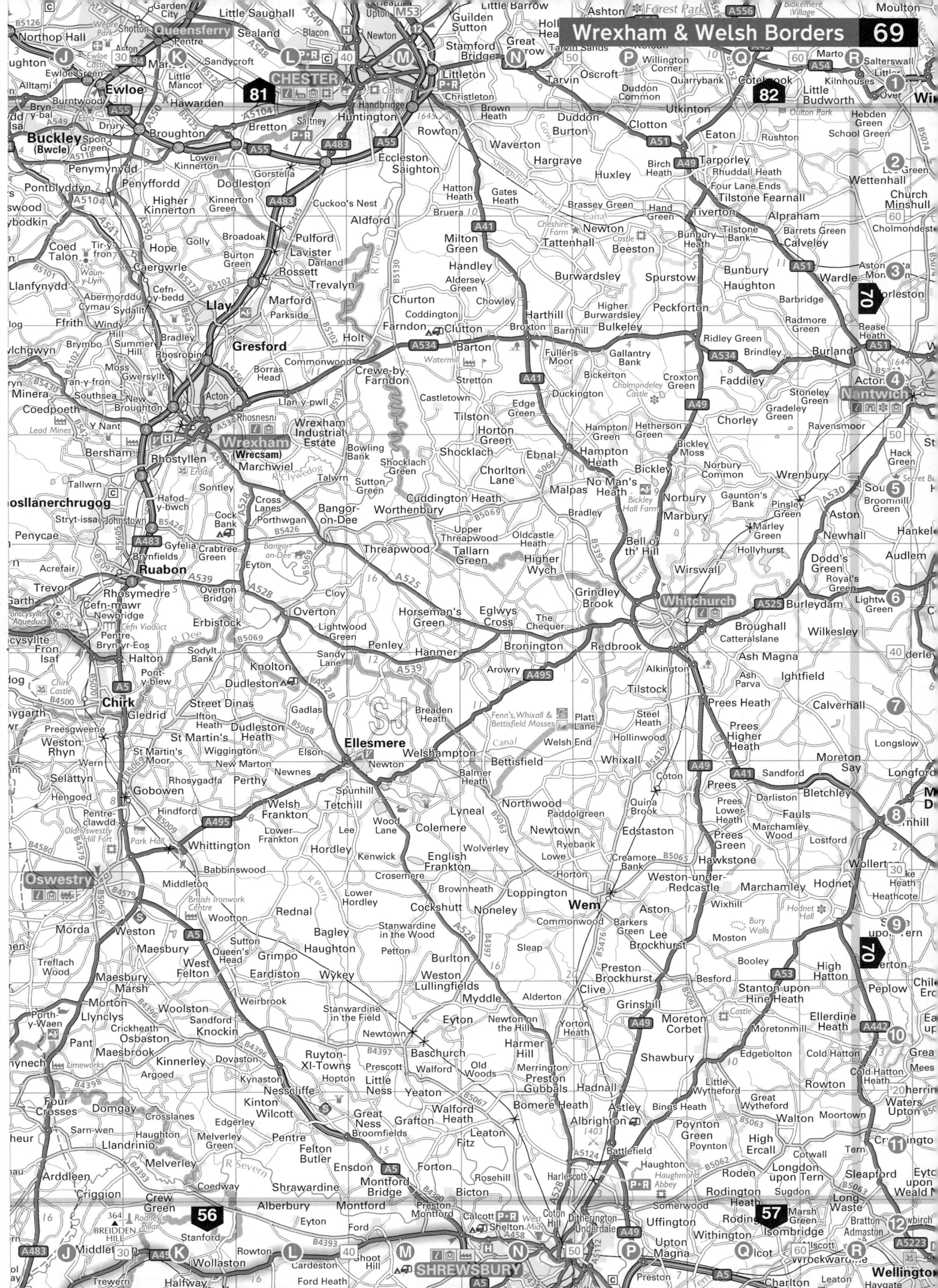

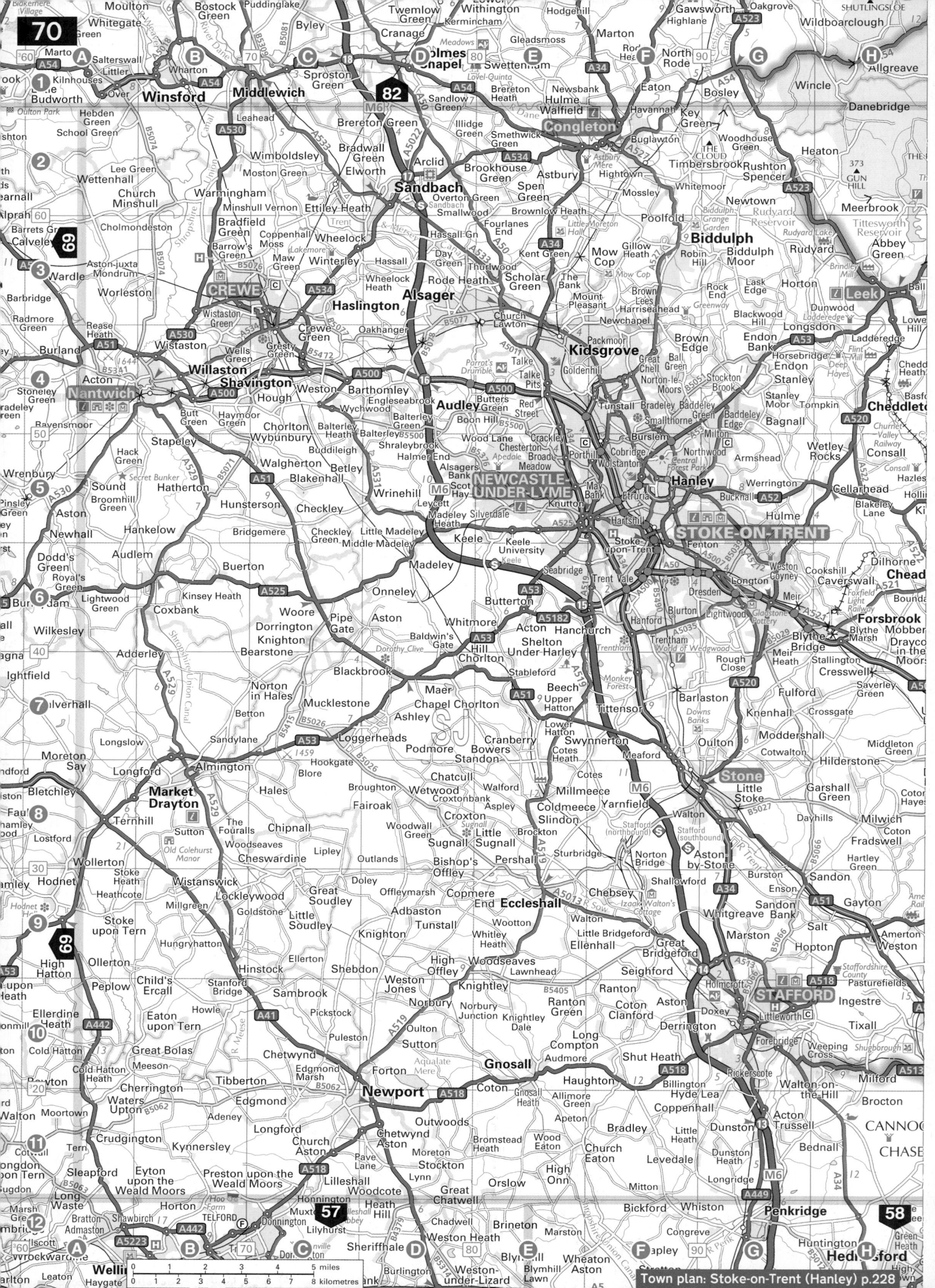

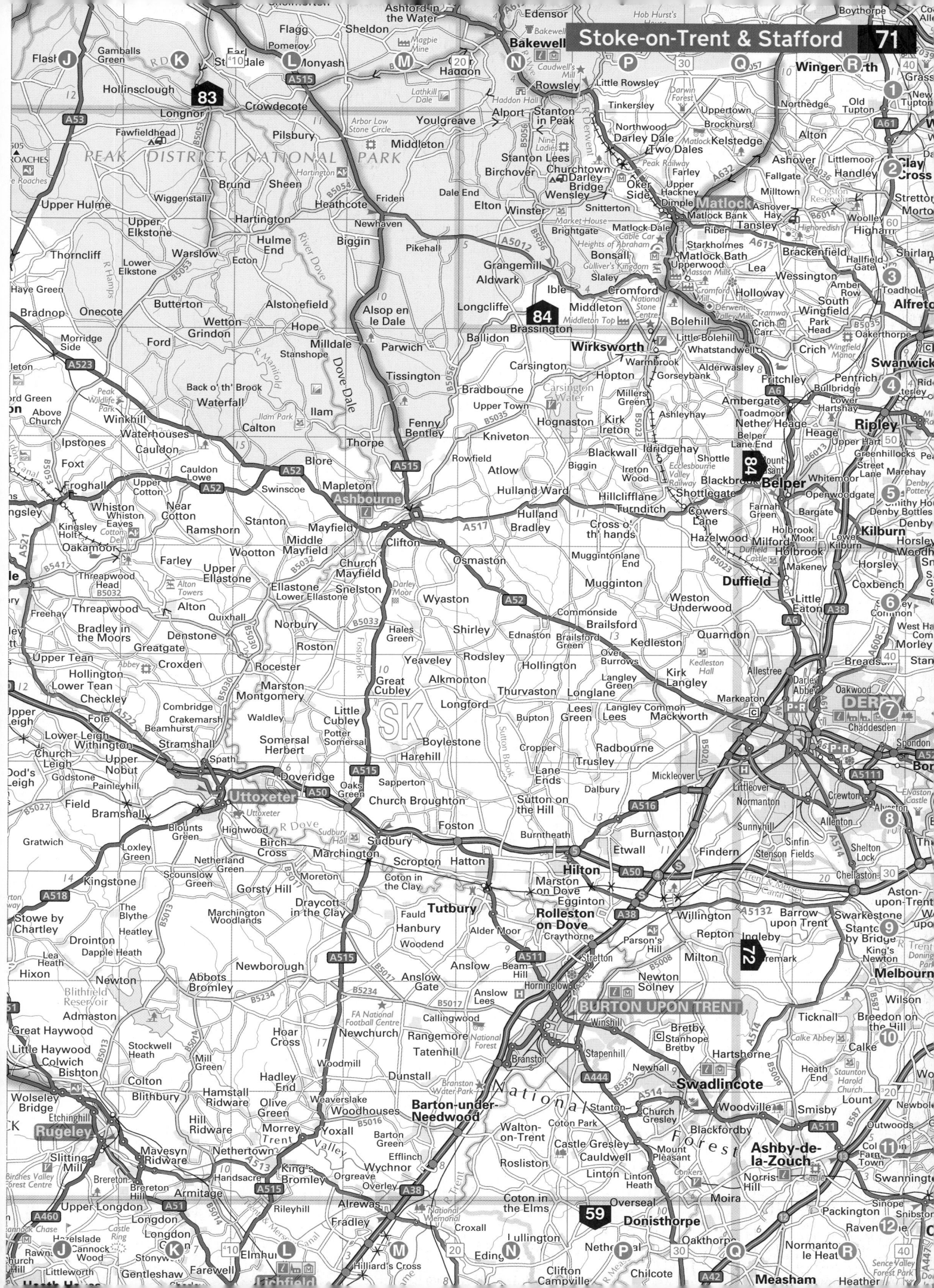

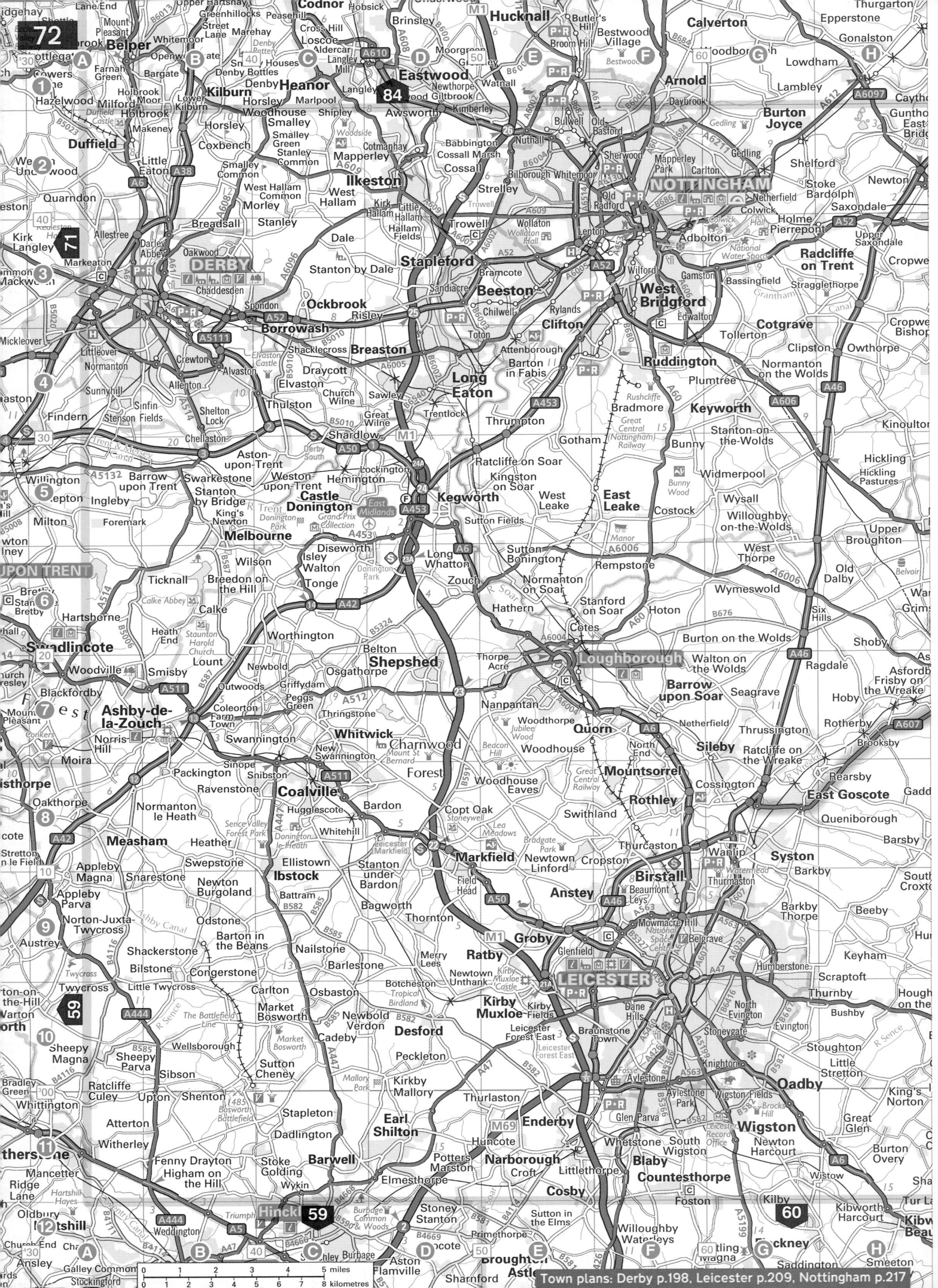

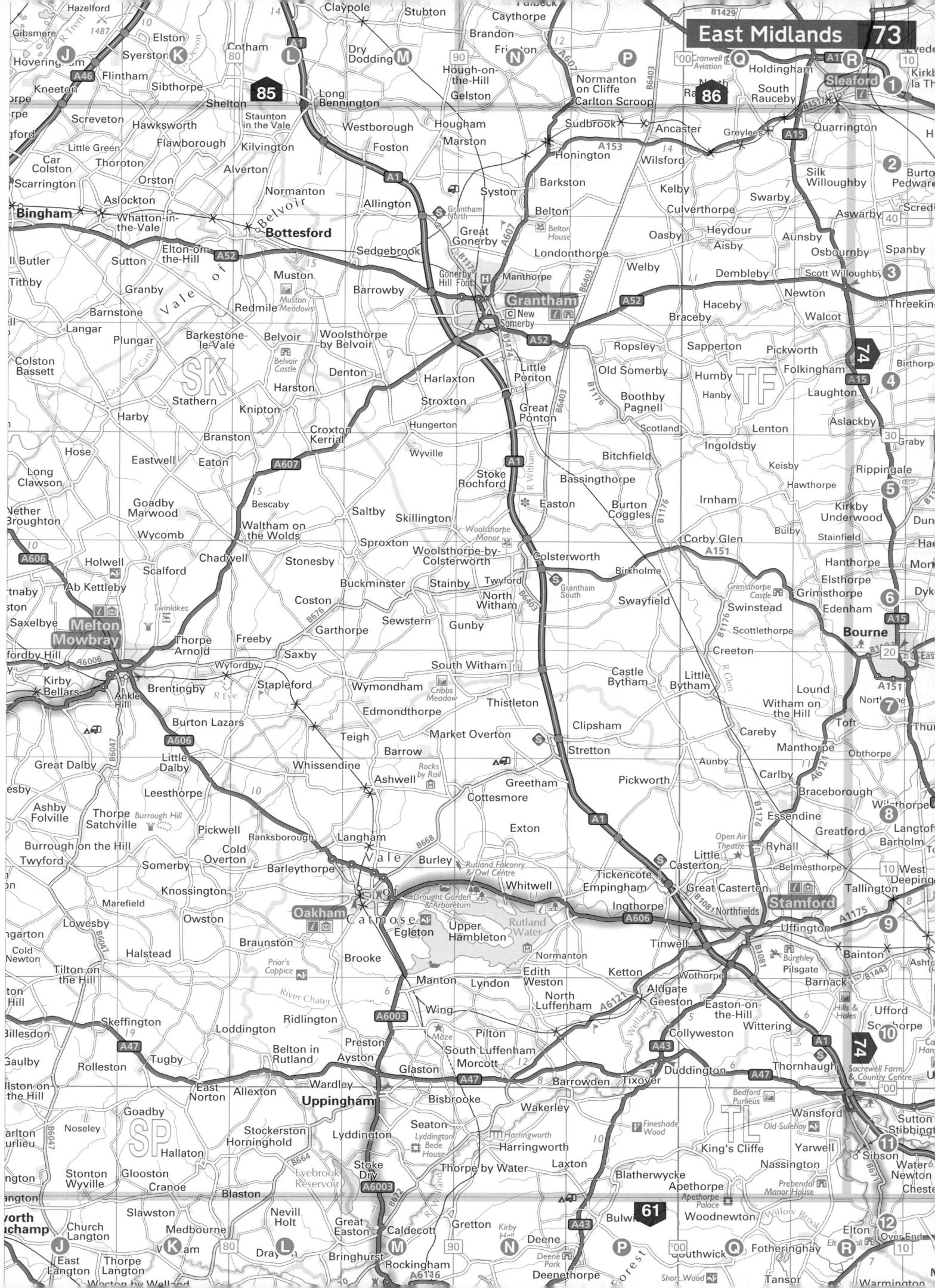

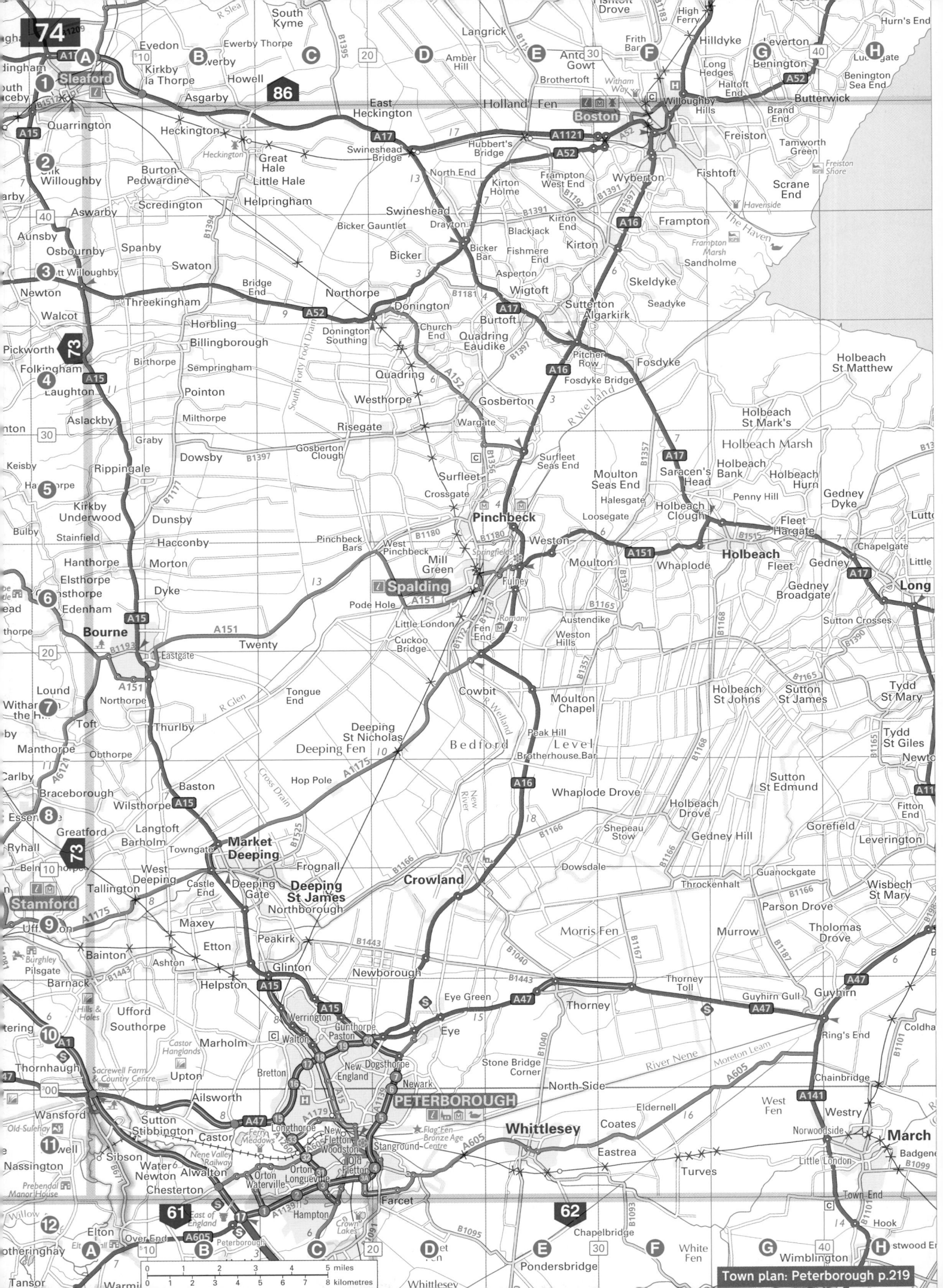

THE WASH

TF

87

Brancaster Bay
Scolt Head Island
Brancaster Staithe
Titchfield Marsh
Burnham Deepdale
Holme Dunes
Holme next the Sea
Brancaster
Burr Ov Sta

Old Hunstanton
Thornham
Titchwell
Branodunum Roman Fort
Burnham Norton
Burnha

Burnham Market
Ringstead
B1355

Hunstanton
Summerfield
North Creake
Stanhoe
Docking
South Creake

Heacham
Norfolk Lavender
Peddars Way & Norfolk Coast Path
B1454
B1155
B1153
Bircham Newton
Barmer
Syderstone
Wicker Village
76

Sedgeford
Fring
Great Bircham
Bircham Tofts
Tattersett
West Rudham
Broomsthorp
Snettisham
Southgate
Shernborne
Anmer
New Houghton
Houghton Hall
Harpley
Helhoughton
E Ruc

Snettisham Park
Ingoldisthorpe

Dersingham
Doddshill
Sandringham
West Newton
Flitcham
A148
West Raynha So Rayn

Dersingham Bog
Wolferton
Hillington
Little Massingham
Weasenham St Peter
6

Babingley River
A149
B1439
B1440
Congham
Roydon
Grimston
Great Massingham
Weasenham All Saints

The Wash
Castle Rising
North Wootton
A148
Roydon Common
Pott Row
Gayton
B1153
20
Rougham

London
Castle
South Wootton
A149
A1078
Bawsey
B1145
Gayton Thorpe
A1065

Sutton
Sutton Bridge
Little London
West Lynn
Gaywood
King's Lynn
Bawsey
Brow-of-the-Hill
Ashwicken
West Acre
Castle Acre
7
West Lexham

Wingland
Clenchwarton
South Lynn
Fairstead
Fair Green
East Winch
Gayton Thorpe
Priory
Newton

Walpole Cross Keys
A17
Tilney All Saints
A47
A148
H
A47
East Walton
Castle
Little Dunham

Tydd Gote
Hay Green
A10
North Runcton
Middleton
West Bilney
South Acre
8
Great Palgrave

Terrington St Clement
Tilney High End
Saddlebow
West Winch
Blackborough End
West Winch
Pentney
Spor

Four Gotes
Walpole St Andrew
St John's Highway
Tilney St Lawrence
Wiggenhall St Germans
Setchey
Narborough
River Nar
A47
Ecotech Discovery Centre
S

Walpole St Peter
Ingleborough
Terrington St John
Wiggenhall St Peter
Watlington
Wormegay
Marham
A1122
Swaffham
76

West Walton
St John's Fen End
Wiggenhall St Mary the Virgin
Lordsbridge
Tottenhill
Shouldham
11

Wisbech
Walton Highway
Walpole Highway
Wiggenhall St Mary Magdalen
Runcton Holme
South Runcton
Shouldham Thorpe
Fincham
Barton Bendish
Beachamwell
9
North Pickenham

Walsoken
New Walsoken
A47
Marshland St James
Chequers Corner
Thorpland
West Head
Stowbridge
Wimbotsham
Stow Bardolph
Stradsett
Crimplesham
Eastmoor
Cockley Cley
Iceni Village
A1065

Emneth
Emneth Hungate
Gaultree
Downham Market
Barroway Drove
Bexwell
Wereham
Boughton
Oxborough
Gooderstone
Hilborough
10
Great ssingh

Elm
Holly End
A1101
Stow Bardolph Fen
Denver
West Dereham
Oxburgh Hall
Little ssingham

Friday Bridge
Outwell
A1122
Fordham
Wretton
Whittington
Foulden
Beckett End
B1108
64
11

Laddus Fen
Upwell
Three Holes
Nordelph
Hilgay
Stoke Ferry
Northwold
A134
Bodney

Euximoor Fen
Iron Bridge
Upwell Fen
A1101
B1094
Wissington
B1112
Brookville
Ickburgh
12

Christchurch
Tipp's End
TL
Ten Mile Bank
Hilgay Fen
A10
Methwold Hythe
Methwold
Cranwich
Lynford

Stonea
Upwell Fen
Welney
Welney Wetland Centre
Southery Fens
63
Queens Ground
Feltwell
Mundford
Thetford

Brandon Creek

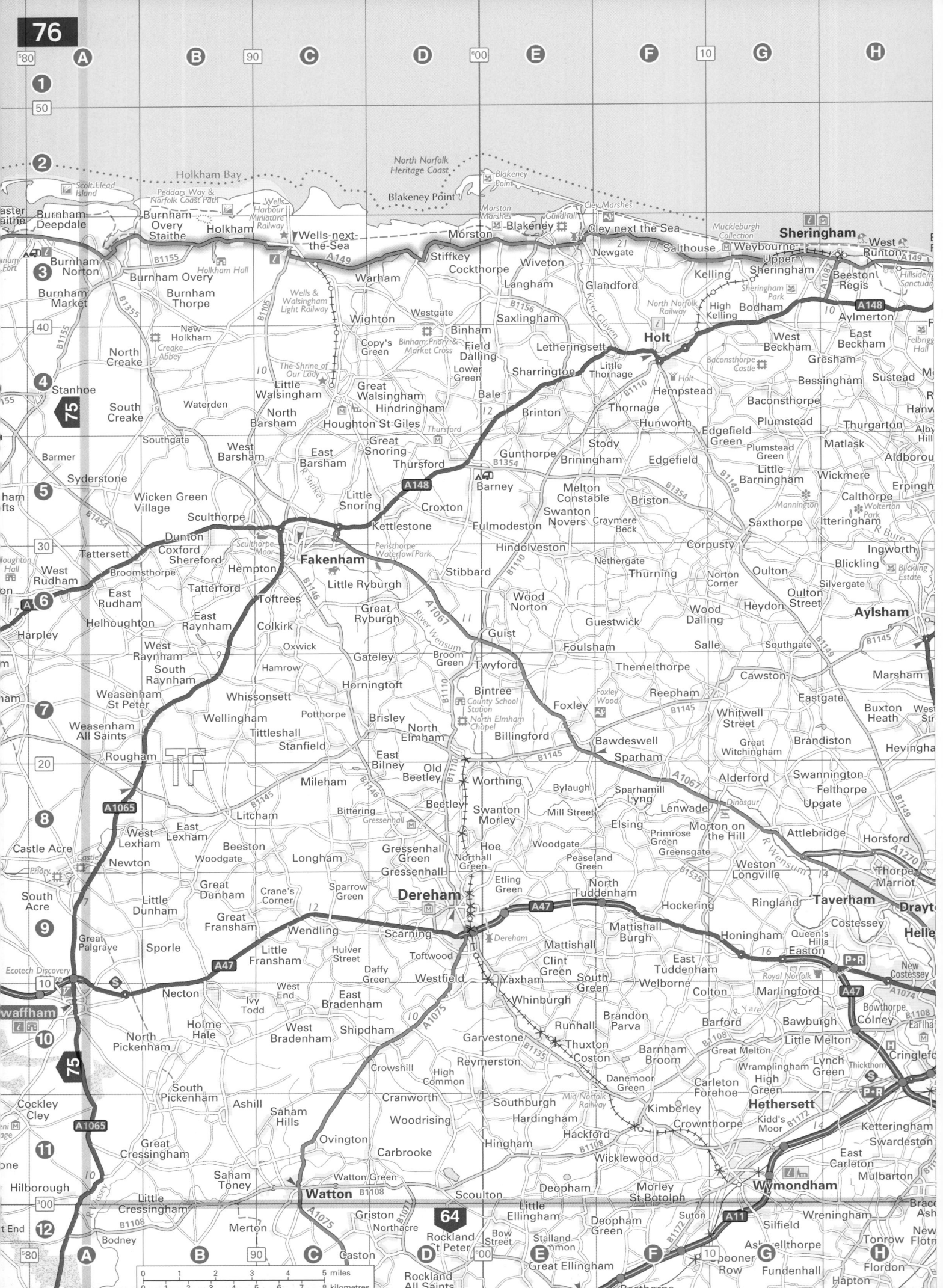

Holyhead Harbour

Marina
Maritime
BEACH ROAD
Porth-
y-Felin
Salt Island
PRINCE OF WALES ROAD
VICTORIA
WALTER STREET
A5154
ROAD
SOUTH STACK ROAD
Stryd
P+R Long Stay
Hertz Car Rental
FERRY TERMINAL
TERMINAL BUILDING
Short stay
HOLYHEAD
HOLYHEAD STATION
A5
A5
LLANFAWR ROAD
Môrawelon
LONDON ROAD
PLAS ROAD
Kingsland
KINGSLAND ROAD
A5
B4545
PORTHDAFARCH
CYTTIR ROAD
A5153
A5
BANGOR
TLT

0   500 m

North Anglesey Heritage Coast
The Skerries
Wylfa Head
Cemaes Bay
Porth Wen
Bull Bay
Amlwch
Point Lyna
Cemlyn Bay
Llanbadrig
Bull Bay
Hen Borth
Cemaes
Llaneilian
CARMEL HEAD
Tregele
A5025
Burwen
Pengorffwysfa
Pentrefelin
Llanfairynghornwy
Llanfechell
Rhosbeirio
Bodewryd
Penysarn
Nebo
Swtan Folk
17
Dulas
Holyhead Bay
Llanrhyddlad
Llanfflewyn
Rhosgoch
Gadfa
Church Bay
Carreglefn
Rhosybol
City Dulas
Dublin
Llanfaethlu
Llanbabo
Llyn Alaw
Capel Parc
Brynrefail
Rhôs Lli
Dublin
Llanddeusant
Din Llugwy
Porth Tywynmawr
Llynnon Mill
Gwredog
Llandyfrydog
Afon Alaw
Llanfwrog
Stryd-y-Facsen
Elim
Llantrisant
Maenaddwyn
North Stack
Breakwater
Llanerchymedd
Hebron
Gogarth Bay
Holyhead Mountain
Llaingoch
Hut Circles
Holyhead
(Caergybi)
Pen-llyn
Llanfigael
Bachau
Capel Coch
Brynteg
South Stack
3
Penrhos
Llanfachraeth
Llyn Llywenan
Cors Eddreiniog
Holyhead Mountain Heritage Coast
Ellins Tower
Penrhos Feilw
Kingsland
Llanynghenedl
A5
ANGLESEY
Llanbe
Presaddfed
B5112
Llechcynfarwy
Penrhyn Mawr
Trefignath
A5025
Valley
Bodedern
B5109
Trefor
Llangwyllog
Rhosmeirch
Trearddur Bay
A55
Caergeiliog
Llynfaes
B5110
Llanddy
B4545
4
Bodffordd
B5111
HOLY ISLAND
Four Mile Bridge
Llanfihangel yn Nhowyn
5
Bryngwran
Gwalchmai
A5
Cefni Reservoir
Oriel Ynys Môn
Llangefni
Llanfair-yn-Neubwll
Llechylched
6
A5114
Valley
A55
Rhoscolyn
Capel Gwyn
Heneglwys
Anglesey
Rhostrehwfa
Ceint
Rhoscolyn Head
Plas Cymyran
Ty Newydd
Dothan
Cerrigceinwen
18
Llangristiolus
Penm
Cymyran Bay
Pencarnisiog
Din Dryfol
Pentre Berw
SH
Rhosneigr
A4080
Llanfaelog
Bryn Du
Capel Mawr
Henblas
Bethel
Gaerwen
7
Llandaniel Fâb
Barclodiad y Gawres
Ty Croes
Trefdraeth
B4422
Bodwyr Burial Chamber
A4080
Capel Mawr
Porth Trecastell
Newborough
Malltraeth
Aberffraw
Llangadwaladr
A4080
Llangaffo
Brynsiencyn
Anglesey Circuit
Hermon
Bodorgan
B4421
21
Caer Lêb
Bryn Gwyn
Llan
Aberffraw Bay
Dwyran
Castell
Anglesey Sea Zoo
Aberffraw Bay Heritage Coast
Newborough
Pen-lôn
Foel Farm Park
Malltraeth Bay
Newborough Warren
Wate
Po
Llanddwyn Island
Caernarfon
Llanddwyn Bay
Caernarfon Castle
Welsh Highland
Abermenai
Bri

0 1 2 3 4 5 miles
0 1 2 3 4 5 6 7 8 kilometres

Llandudno

0   200 m

Great Orme Tramway
Great Orme
Victoria Station
Tabor Hill
Old Road
Flas Road
Ty-Coch Road
Hill Terrace
Church Walks
North Parade
Llandudno Pier
The Grand Hotel
North Shore Beach
Llandudno Bay

The Old Bank Gallery
Travelodge
Gloddaeth Street
South Parade
War Memorial
Abbey Road
Rectory Lane
Clement Ave
Caroline Road
New Street
Arvon Avenue
Mostyn Street
George Street
Ty Gwyn Road
Sea Road
Lloyd Street
The Promenade
Town Hall
St John's
A546
Victoria
Holy Trinity
Our Lady Star of the Sea
Clifton Road
Maelgwyn Road
St Andrew's Ave
St David's Road
James Street
Madoc Street
Brookes Street
Deganwy Avenue
Trinity Square
Augusta Street
Chapel Street
Bodafon Street
The Parade
Medical Centre
Adelphi
Mostyn Broadway
Conwy Road
Swimming Pool
Venue Cymru
St Paul's
Mostyn Ave
B5115

Conwy Archive Service
St Seiriol's Road
Jubilee Street
Central Place
Ffrwd Road
Trinity Avenue
Eryl Pl.
Llandudno Station
Ysgol Tudno
Police Station
Mostyn Gallery
Vaughan Street
Garage Street
Oxford Road
Argyll Road
Magistrates' Court
Parc Llandudno Retail Park
Cylch Tudur
Fire & Ambulance Station
Mostyn Champneys Retail Park
Charlotte Road
Clarence Crescent
Maes Clyd
Caer Clyd
Clarence Drive

Denness Pl.
Dinas Road
Ysgol Ffordd Dyffryn
King's Road
King's Ave
Dulyn Road
Mowbray Road
King's Avenue
Builder Street
Council Street West
Builder Street West
Norman Road
Howard Road
Wern
Wylan
Ffordd Penrhyn
Ffordd Gwynedd
Ffordd Dewi
Ffordd Tudno
Cwm Place
Cwm Road
Maesdu Road
Gwydir Road
Ffordd Dwyfor
Superstore
Ysgol Morfa Rhianedd
Ysgol John Bright
Llandudno FC
Coach
Ysgol Craig Y Don
Conway Road
A55, BETWS-Y-COED

SH

Dulas Bay
Seawatch Centre
Moelfre
Llanallgo
Marian-glas
Benllech
Red Wharf Bay
Cors Goch
Pentraeth
Llanddona
Hafoty Medieval House
Beaumaris Gaol
Beaumaris Castle
Beaumaris
Llansadwrn
Llandegfan
Llangoed
Llanfaes
Courthouse
Puffin Island
Penmon Priory
Toll
Black Point
Penmon
Caim
Glan-yr-afon

GREAT ORME'S HEAD
Great Orme Heritage Coast
Great Orme Tramway
Toll
Little Ormes Head
Penrhyn Bay
Rhôs-on-Sea
Colwyn B (Bae Colwyn)
Llandudno
Llanrhos
Penrhyn-side
Deganwy
Llandrillo yn-Rhos
Pydew
Esgyryn
Mochdre
Old Colwyn
A55
Llandudno Junction
Llanelian-yn-Rhos
Llysfaen
Rhy-
Bryn-y-Maen
Dolwen
Betws-yn-Rhos

Conwy Bay
Dwygyfylchi
Penmaenan
Conwy
Conwy Castle
Tywyn
Llansanffraid Glan Conwy
Capelulo
Penmaenmawr
Henryd
Llanfairfechan
Nant-y-pandy
Gorddinog
Abergwyngregyn
SNOWDONIA
TAL-Y-FAN 610
Rowen
Ty'n-y-Groes
Caerhun
Graig
Tal-y-Cafn
Bodnant
Eglwysbach
Trofarth
River Elwy

Menai Bridge (Porthaethwy)
Menai Strait
Bangor
Penrhyn Castle
Spinnies
Abergowen
Llandygai
Tal-y-bont
Coedydd Aber
Aber Falls
Llanllechid
MOEL WNION 580
Afon Anafon
NATIONAL
Llanbedr-y-Cennin
Castell
Tal-y-Bont
Dolgarrog
Surf Snowdonia
Pentre'r Felin
Vale of Conwy

Britannia Bridge
Plas Newydd
Menai Bridge
Waen-wen
Rhyd-y-groes
Glasinfryn
Pentir
Tregarth
Rachub
Gerlan
Y DROSGL 757
FOEL-FRAS 942
Afon Caseg
Ogwen Bank
Bethesda
PARK
Pont Dolgarrog
Llyn Eigiau
Hafodunos
Llangernyw

Y Felinheli
GreenWood Forest Park
Sling
Waen-pentir
Rhiwlas
Mynydd Llandygai
Rhiwen
Deiniolen
Y DROSGL
Llyn
Llanddeiniolen
Saron
Penisarwaun
Rhiwlas
Ogwen Bank
CARNEDD LLEWELYN 1062
CARNEDD DAFYDD 1044
Llyn Cowlyd
Trefriw Woollen Mills
Tre-
Llanddoged
Llanrwst
Pandy Tudur

Bethel
Llanrug
Cwm-y-glo
Brynrefail
Gallt-y-foel
Dinorwic
ELIDIR 923
Llyn Padarn
Llanberis Lake Railway
National
Pont Pen-
Llyn Ogwen
Llyn Crafnant
Llanrhychwyn
Pen-tafarn-y-fedw
Gwytherin

Isle of Man

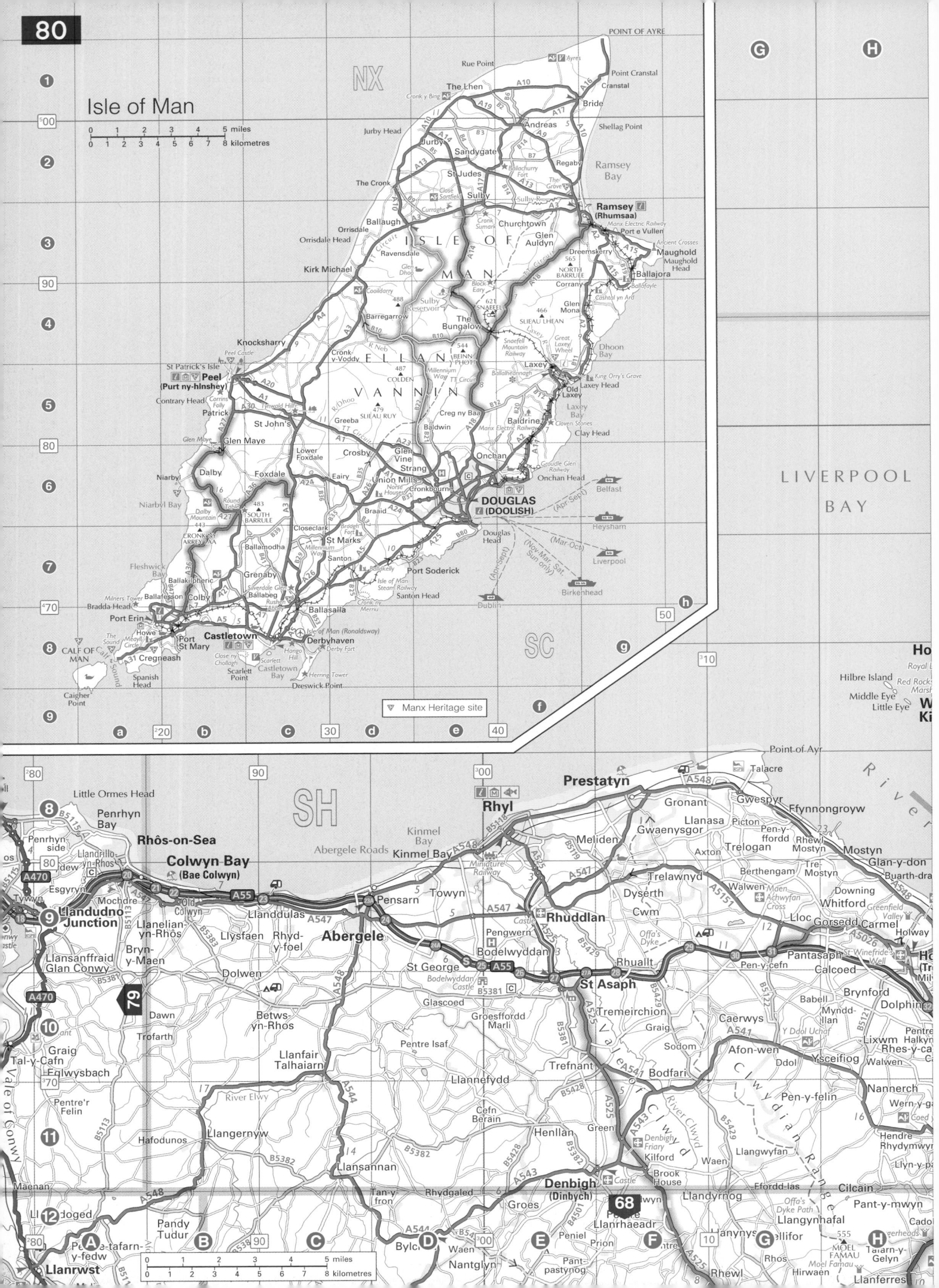

NX

POINT OF AYRE

Rue Point
The Lhen
Cronk y Bing
Jurby Head
Jurby
Sandygate
The Cronk
St Judes
Ballaugh
Orrisdale
Orrisdale Head
Kirk Michael
Ravensdale
Knocksharry
Peel Castle
St Patrick's Isle
Peel
(Purt ny-hInshey)
Contrary Head
Patrick
Corrins Folly
Glen Maye
Niarbyl
Dalby
Niarbyl Bay
Dalby Mountain
SOUTH BARRULE
CRONK NY ARREY LAA
Fleshwick Bay
Ballakilpheric
Bradda Head
Milners Tower
Ballafesson
Colby
Port Erin
Howe
The Meayll Circle
Port St Mary
CALF OF MAN
Cregneash
Caigher Point
Spanish Head

Point Cranstal
Cranstal
Bride
A10
Andreas
Shellag Point
Ramsey Bay
Ramsey (Rhumsaa)
Port e Vullen
Maughold
Maughold Head
Ballajora
Ballafayle
Dreemskerry
Ancient Crosses
Cashtal yn Ard
NORTH BARRULE
Corrany
Glen Mona
Dhoon Bay
Snaefell Mountain Railway
King Orry's Grave
Great Laxey Wheel
Laxey
Old Laxey
Laxey Head
Laxey Bay
Cloven Stones
Baldrine
Clay Head
Groudle Glen Railway
Onchan
Onchan Head

ISLE OF MAN
ELLAN VANNIN
SNAEFELL
The Bungalow
SLIEAU LHEAN
Laxey
BEINN PHOTT
Cronk-y-Voddy
COLDEN
SLIEAU RUY
Crosby
Glen Vine
Strang
Union Mills
Cronkbourne
Braaid
St Marks
Closeclark
Santon
Ballamodha
Grenaby
Ballabeg
Ballasalla
Silverdale Glen
Ballakelly
Castletown
Derbyhaven
Derby Fort
Hango Hill
Scarlett Point
Castletown Bay
Dreswick Point

Douglas (Doolish)
Douglas Head
Port Soderick
Isle of Man Steam Railway
Santon Head
Cronk ny Merriu

Belfast
Heysham
Liverpool
Birkenhead
Dublin

LIVERPOOL BAY

SC

Manx Heritage site

Manx Heritage site

SH

Point of Ayr
Talacre
Prestatyn
Gronant
Gwespyr
Ffynnongroyw
Llanasa
Picton
Gwaenysgor
Meliden
Pen-y-ffordd
Mostyn
Trelogan
Glan-y-don
Buarth-dra
Little Ormes Head
Penrhyn Bay
Rhos-on-Sea
Colwyn Bay (Bae Colwyn)
Penrhynside
Llandrillo-yn-Rhos
Esgyryn
Mochdre
Old Colwyn
Rhyl
Kinmel Bay
Abergele Roads
Kinmel Bay
Towyn
Pensarn
Rhuddlan
Downing
Whitford
Greenfield Valley
Gorsedd
Carmel
Holway
Berthengam
Tre-Mostyn
Walwen
Moel Achwyfan Cross
Lloc
Llandudno Junction
Llanelian-yn-Rhôs
Llysfaen
Rhyd-y-foel
Abergele
Bodelwyddan
St George
Bodelwyddan Castle
Glascoed
Pengwern
Offa's Dyke
Rhuallt
St Asaph
Pen-y-cefn
Pantasaph
Calcoed
St Winefride's Well
Babell
Brynford
Dolphin
Llansanffraid Glan Conwy
Bryn-y-Maen
Dolwen
Betws-yn-Rhos
Dawn
Trofarth
Groesffordd Marli
Glascoed
Tremeirchion
Caerwys
Y Dôl Uchaf
Mynydd-Ilan
Afon-wen
Ysceifiog
Walwen
Graig Tal-y-Cafn
Eglwysbach
Pentre'r Felin
Llanfair Talhaiarn
Pentre Isaf
Llannefydd
Trefnant
Bodfari
Graig
Sodom
Rhes-y-cae
Ddol
Pen-y-felin
Nannerch
Wern-y-g
Maenan
River Elwy
Cefn Berain
Llandyrnog
Llangwyfan
Llyn-p
Llangernyw
Hafodunos
Llansannan
Henllan
Denbigh Friary
Kilford
Waen
Llangynhafal
Llyn-p
Llandoged
Pandy Tudur
Rhydgaled
Tan-y-fron
Denbigh (Dinbych)
Brook House
Waen
Peniel
Prion
Eforddd-las
Cilcain
Moel Famau
Tafarn-y-Gelyn
Llanrwst
Pen-y-tafarn-y-fedw
Bylch
Nantglyn
Pant-pastynog
Llanrhaeadr
Groes
Offa's Dyke Path
Llanynys
Efenechtyd
Rhos
Moel Famau
Llanferres
Gellifor

Liverpool
Hilbre Island
Middle Eye
Little Eye
Red Rocks
Royal L

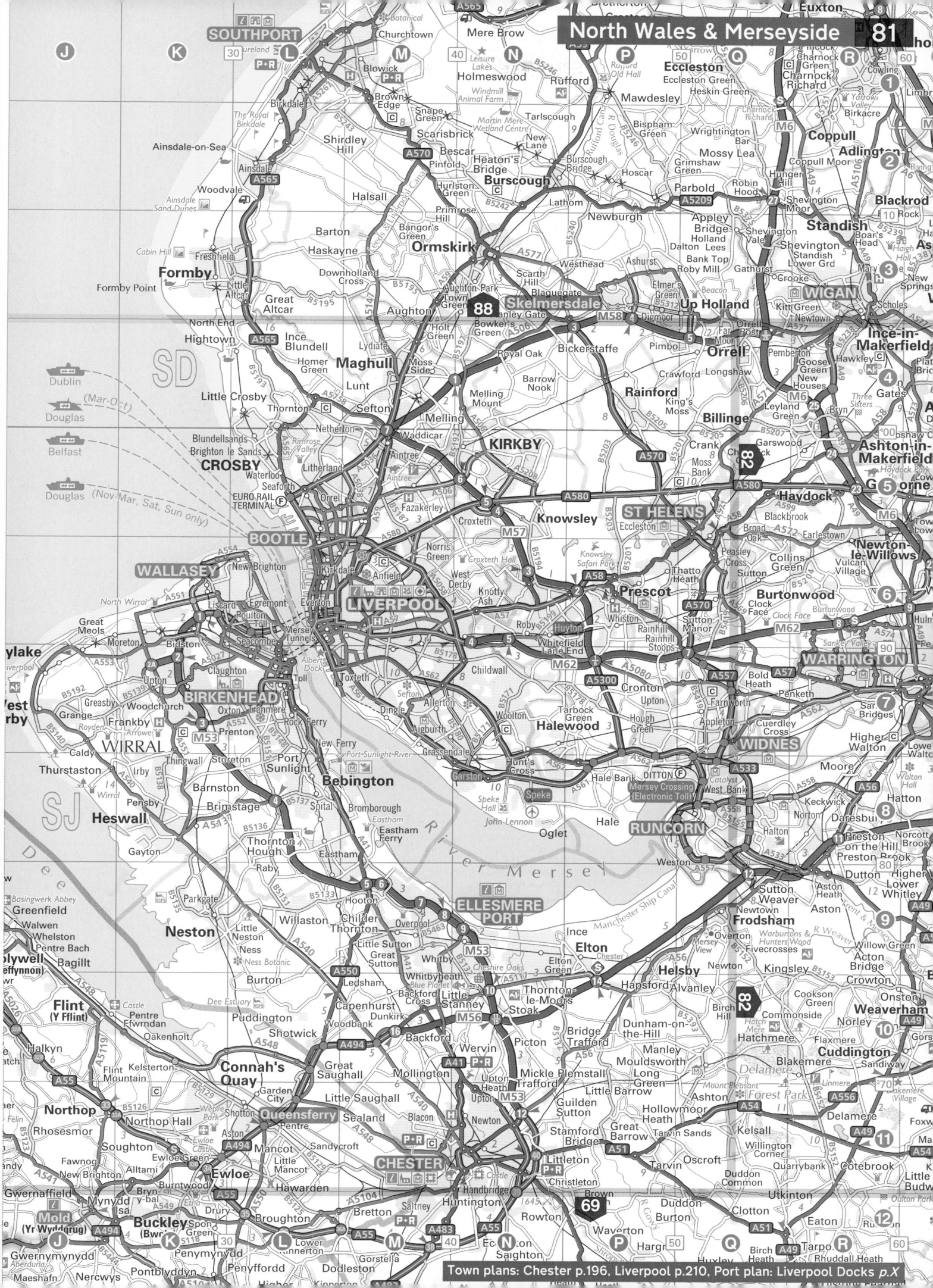

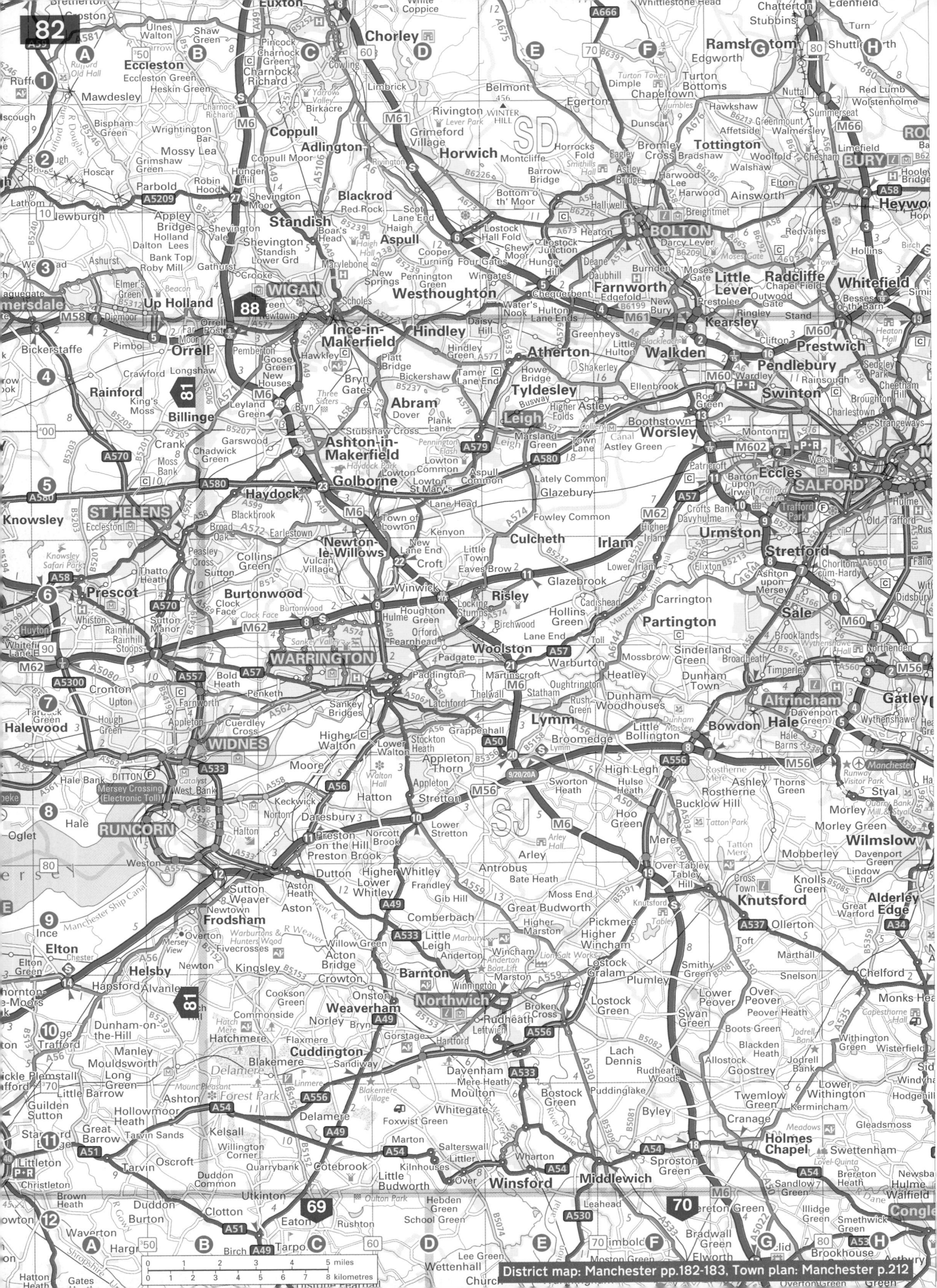

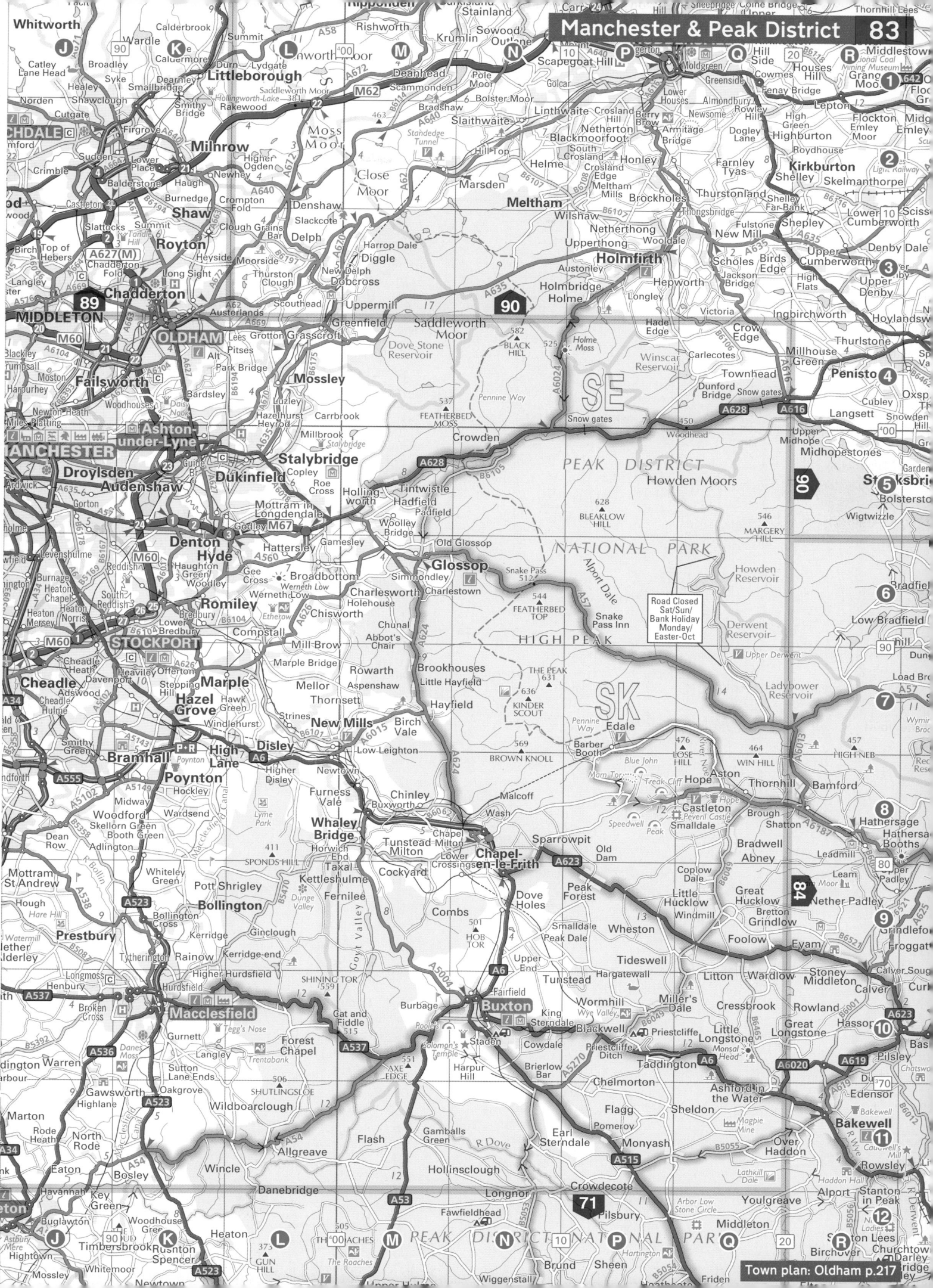

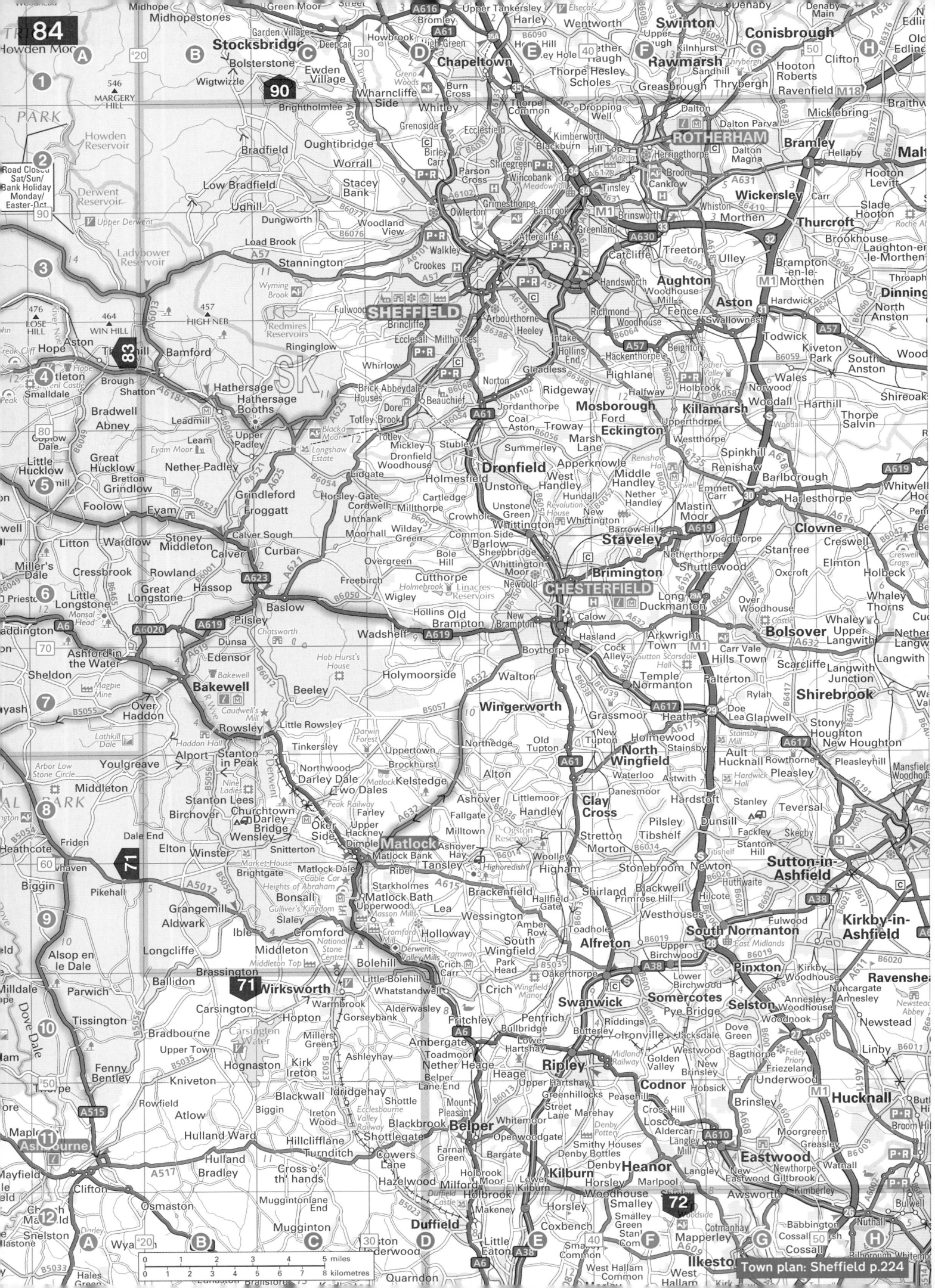

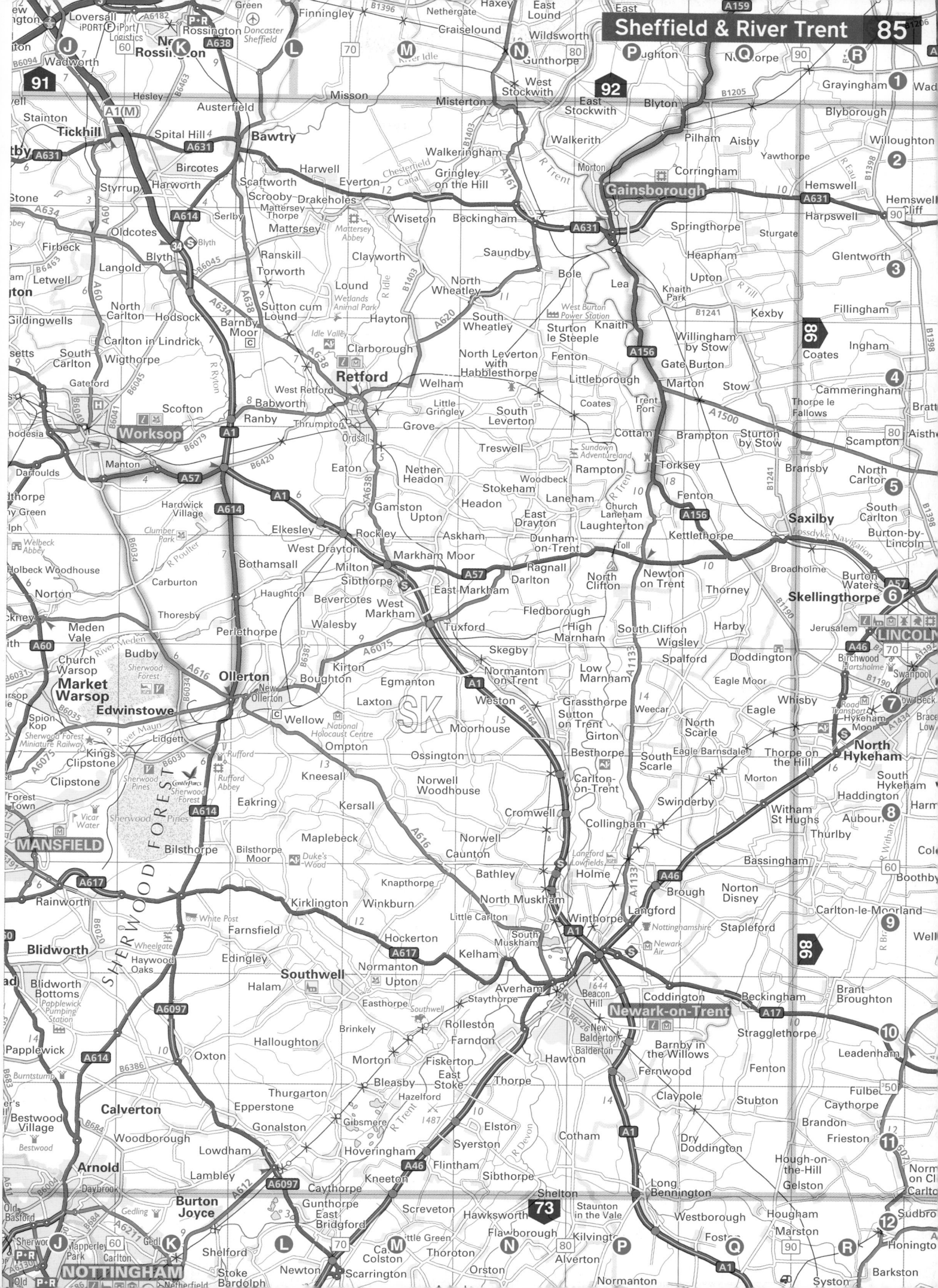

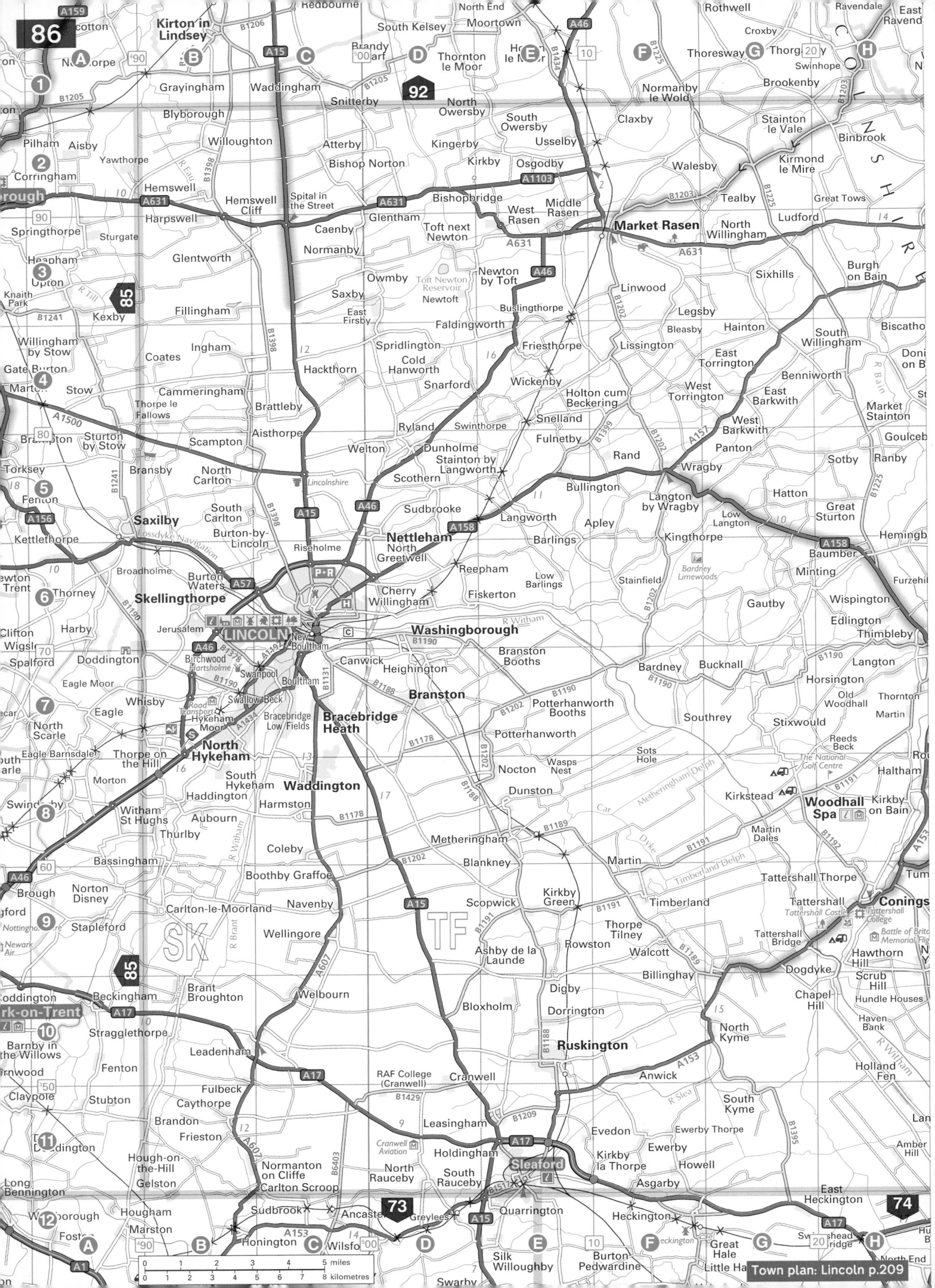

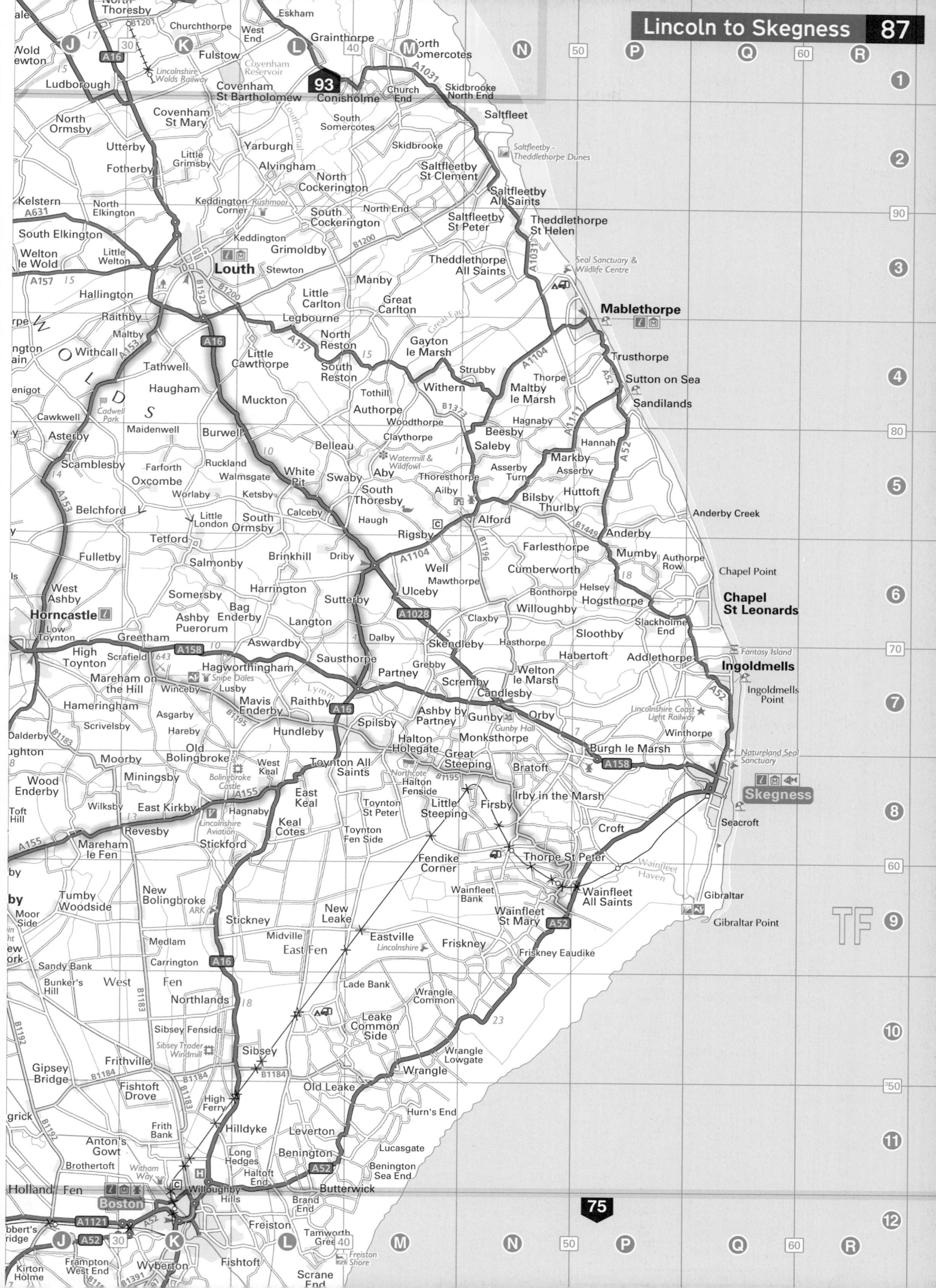

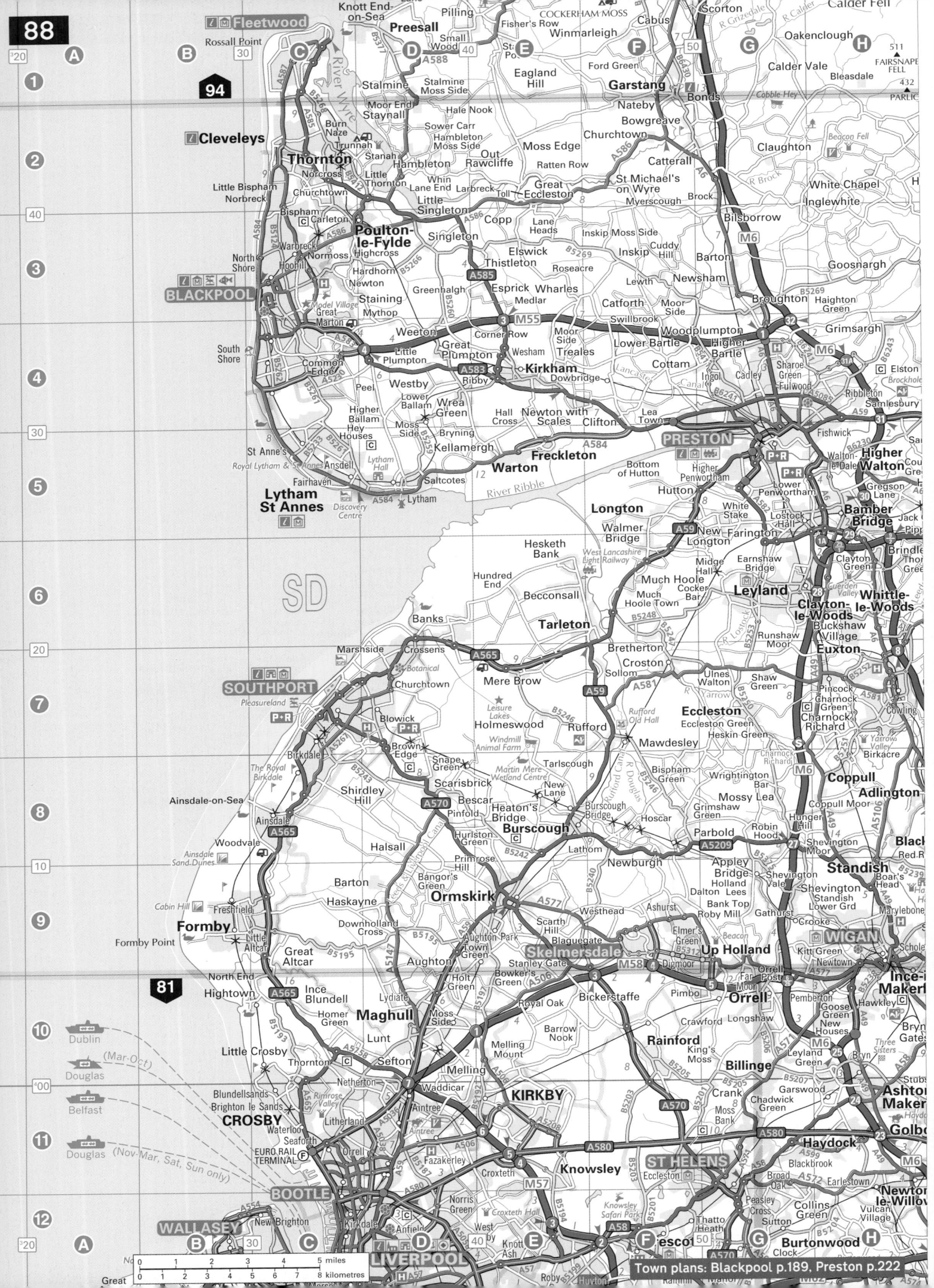

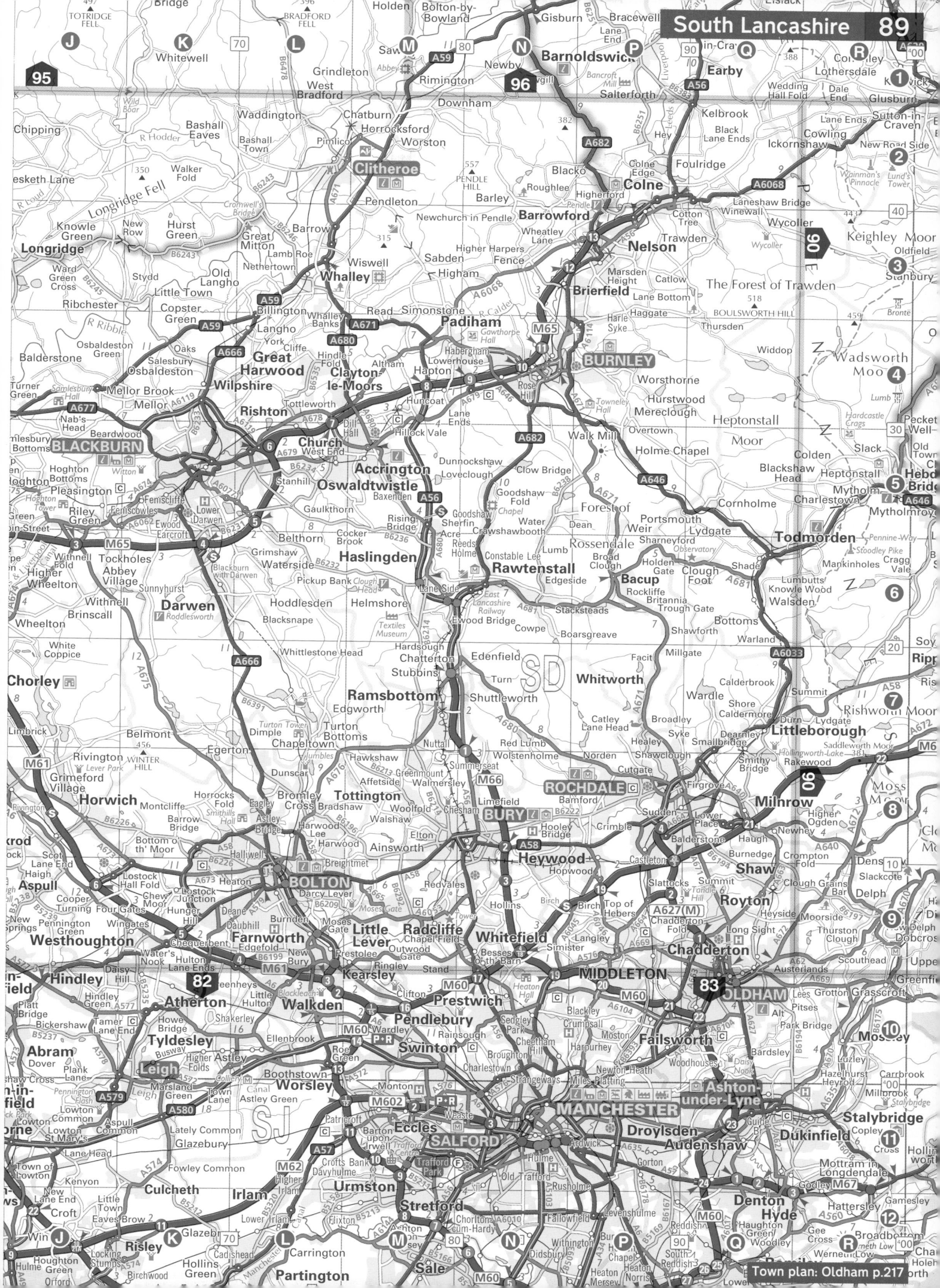

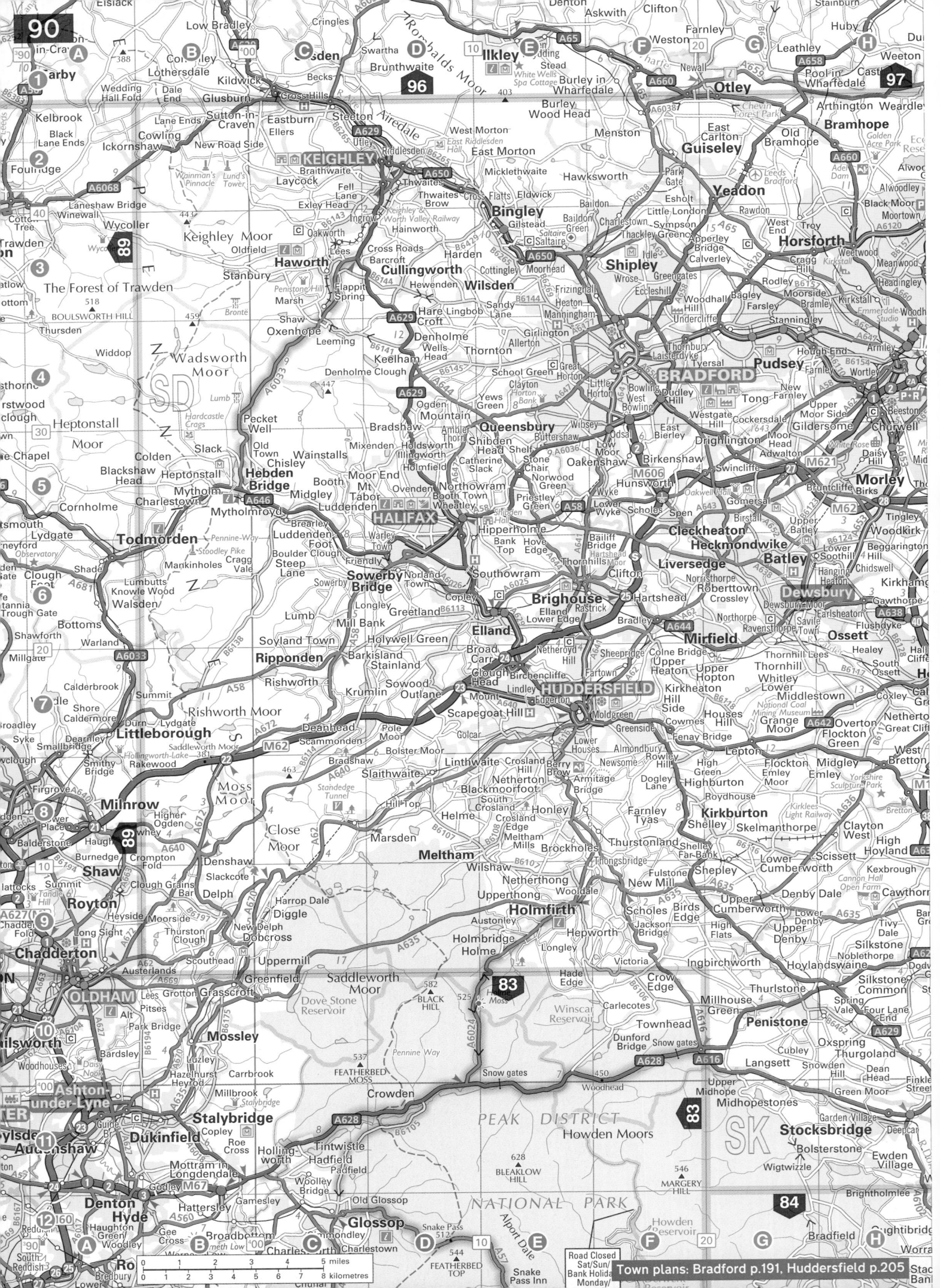

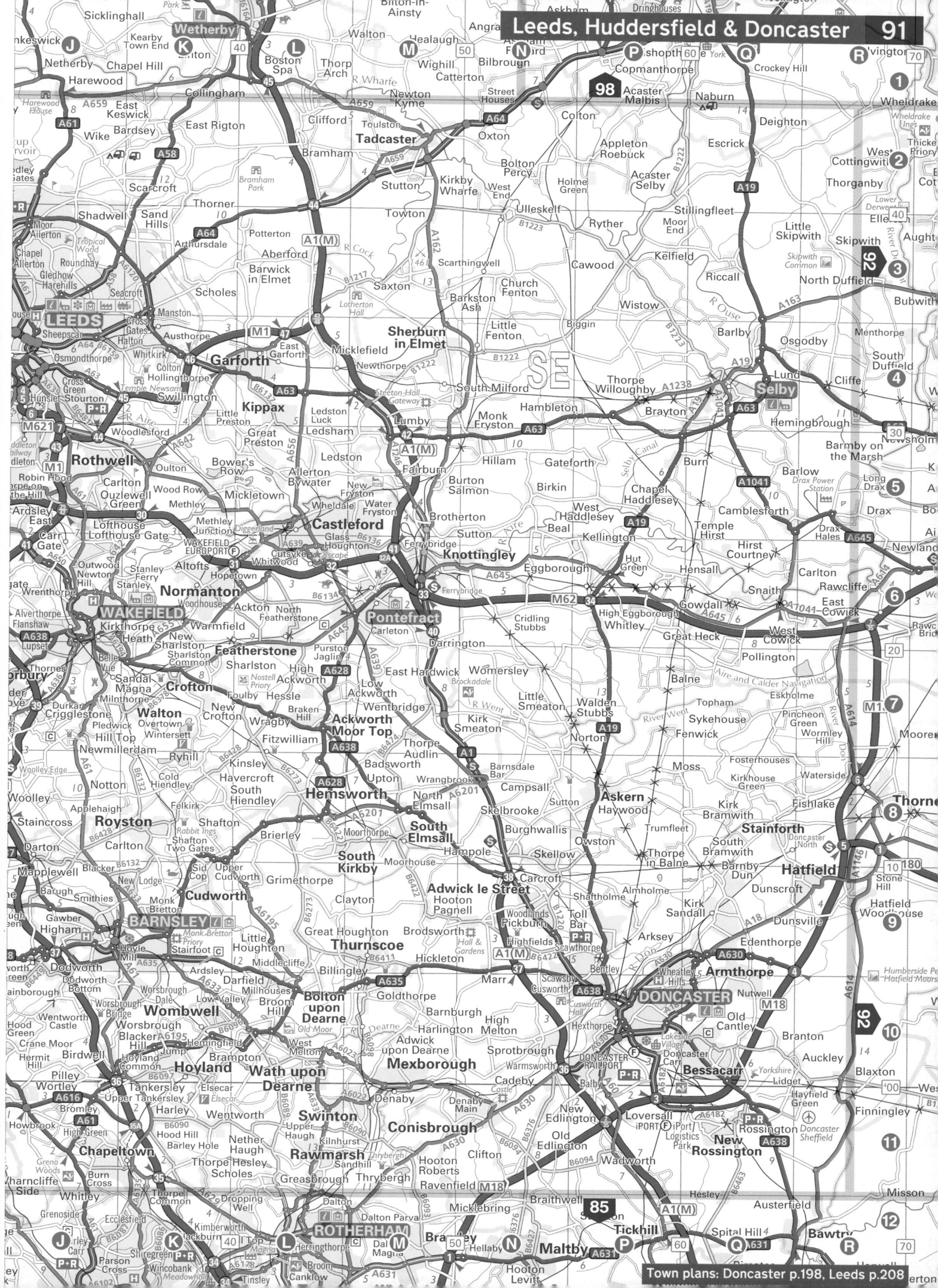

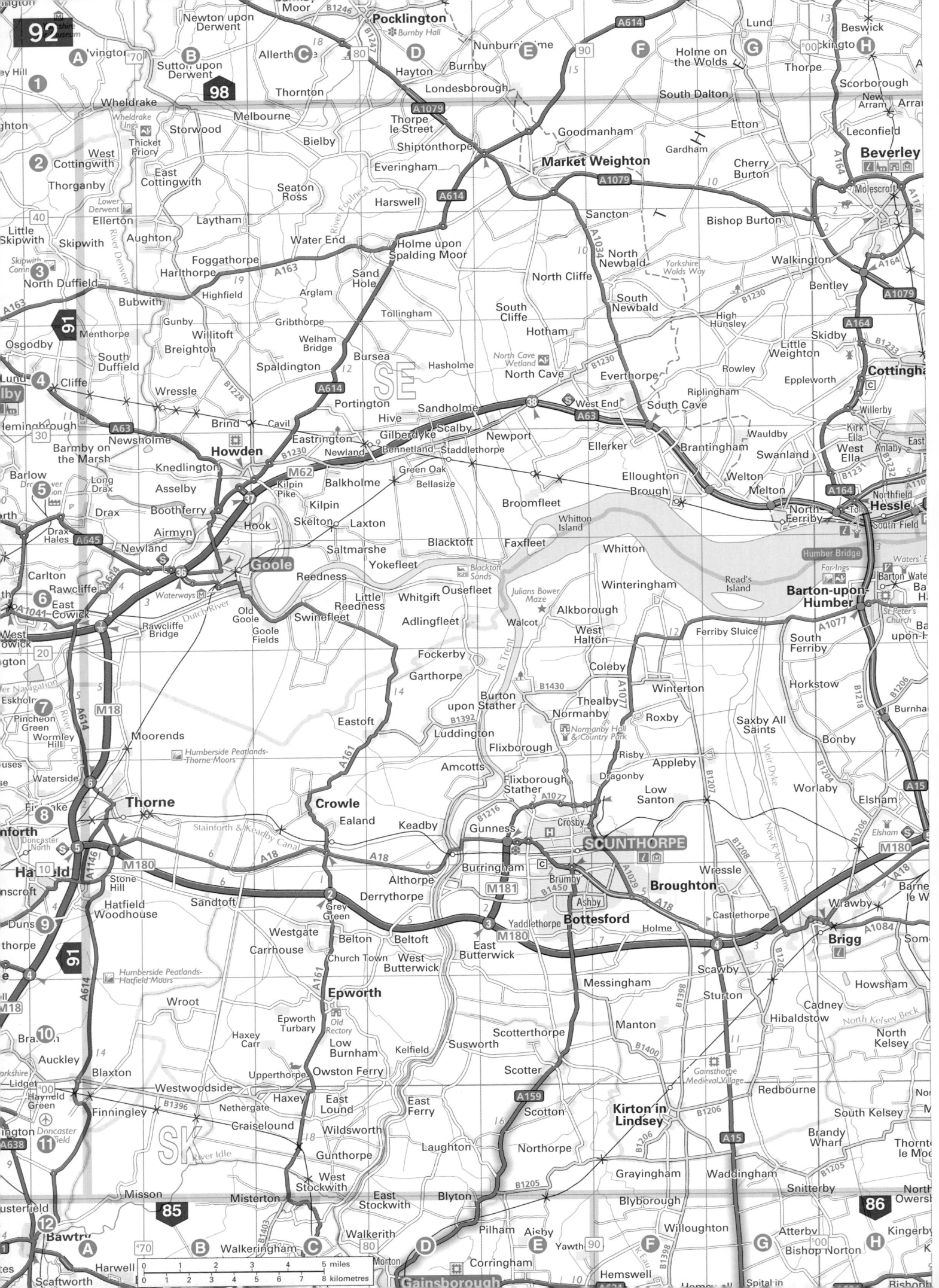

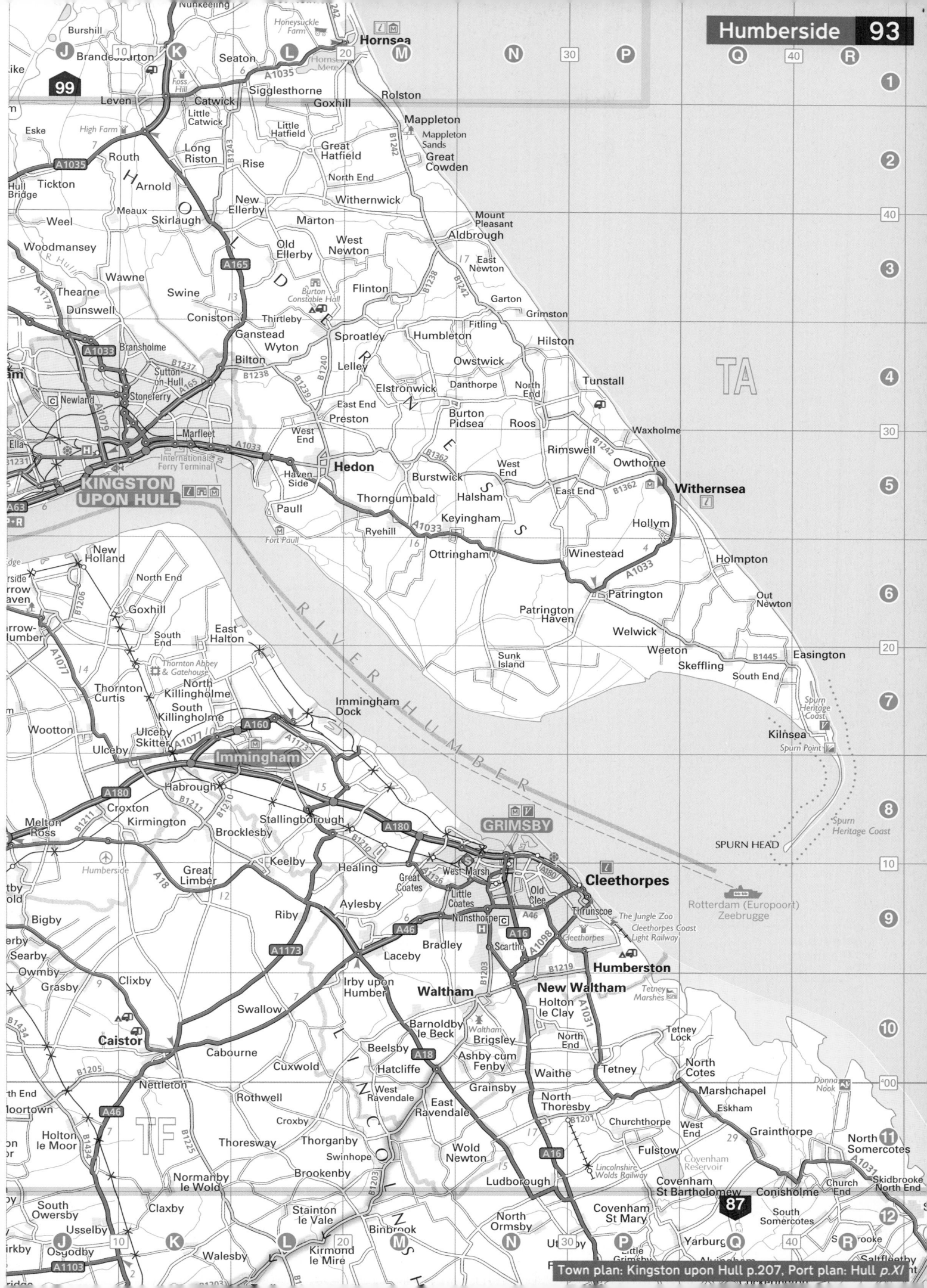

J K L M N 30 P Q 40 R

99

1
2
40
3
TA
4
30
5
6
20
7
8
10
9
00
11
12

Burshill
Nunkeeling
Honeysuckle Farm
Brandesburton
Seaton
Hornsea
Hornsea Mere
A1035
Leven
Sigglesthorne
Catwick
Goxhill
Rolston
Little Catwick
High Farm
Little Hatfield
Mappleton
Mappleton Sands
Eske
Routh
Long Riston
Rise
Great Hatfield
Great Cowden
Hull Bridge
Tickton
Meaux
Arnold
Skirlaugh
New Ellerby
North End
Withernwick
Weel
Woodmansey
Wawne
HOLDERNESS
Marton
West Newton
Mount Pleasant
Aldbrough
Thearne
Swine
Old Ellerby
Dunswell
Coniston
Thirtleby
Flinton
East Newton
Bransholme
Ganstead
Wyton
Sproatley
Humbleton
Garton
Grimston
Burton Constable Hall
Fitling
Sutton-on-Hull
Bilton
Lelley
Owstwick
Hilston
Newland
Stoneferry
Elstronwick
Danthorpe
North End
Tunstall
East End
Preston
Burton Pidsea
Roos
Marfleet
West End
Hedon
Halsham
Rimswell
Waxholme
KINGSTON UPON HULL
Haven Side
Burstwick
West End
Owthorne
Withernsea
Paull
Thorngumbald
Halsham
East End
Hollym
International Ferry Terminal
Ryehill
Keyingham
Winestead
Fort Paull
Ottringham
Patrington
Holmpton
New Holland
North End
Patrington Haven
Out Newton
Goxhill
South End
East Halton
Welwick
Weeton
Easington
Thornton Abbey & Gatehouse
Sunk Island
Skeffling
South End
Thornton Curtis
North Killingholme
Immingham Dock
Spurn Heritage Coast
Wootton
South Killingholme
Kilnsea
Ulceby Skitter
A160
A1173
Spurn Point
Ulceby
Immingham
Habrough
Melton Ross
Croxton
Kirmington
Stallingborough
A180
GRIMSBY
SPURN HEAD
Spurn Heritage Coast
Brocklesby
Keelby
Healing
West Marsh
Cleethorpes
Rotterdam (Europoort) Zeebrugge
Great Limber
Great Coates
Little Coates
Old Clee
Riby
Aylesby
Nunsthorpe
The Jungle Zoo
Cleethorpes Coast Light Railway
Bigby
Irby upon Humber
Bradley
Scartho
Humberston
Searby
Laceby
New Waltham
Owmby
Grasby
Clixby
Waltham
Holton le Clay
Tetney Marshes
Caistor
Swallow
Barnoldby le Beck
Brigsley
North End
Tetney
Tetney Lock
North Cotes
Cabourne
Beelsby
Ashby cum Fenby
Waithe
Cuxwold
Hatcliffe
Grainsby
North Thoresby
Marshchapel
Eskham
Nettleton
Rothwell
West Ravendale
East Ravendale
Donna Nook
Holton le Moor
Thoresway
Thorganby
Wold Newton
Churchthorpe
West End
Grainthorpe
North Somercotes
Normanby le Wold
Swinhope
Brookenby
Ludborough
Lincolnshire Wolds Railway
Covenham Reservoir
Fulstow
Skidbrooke North End
South Owersby
Claxby
Stainton le Vale
Kirmond le Mire
Binbrook
North Ormsby
Covenham St Bartholomew
Conisholme
Church End
Usselby
Osgodby
Walesby
North Somercotes
South Somercotes
Covenham St Mary
Yarburgh
Saltfleetby
Ludborough

87

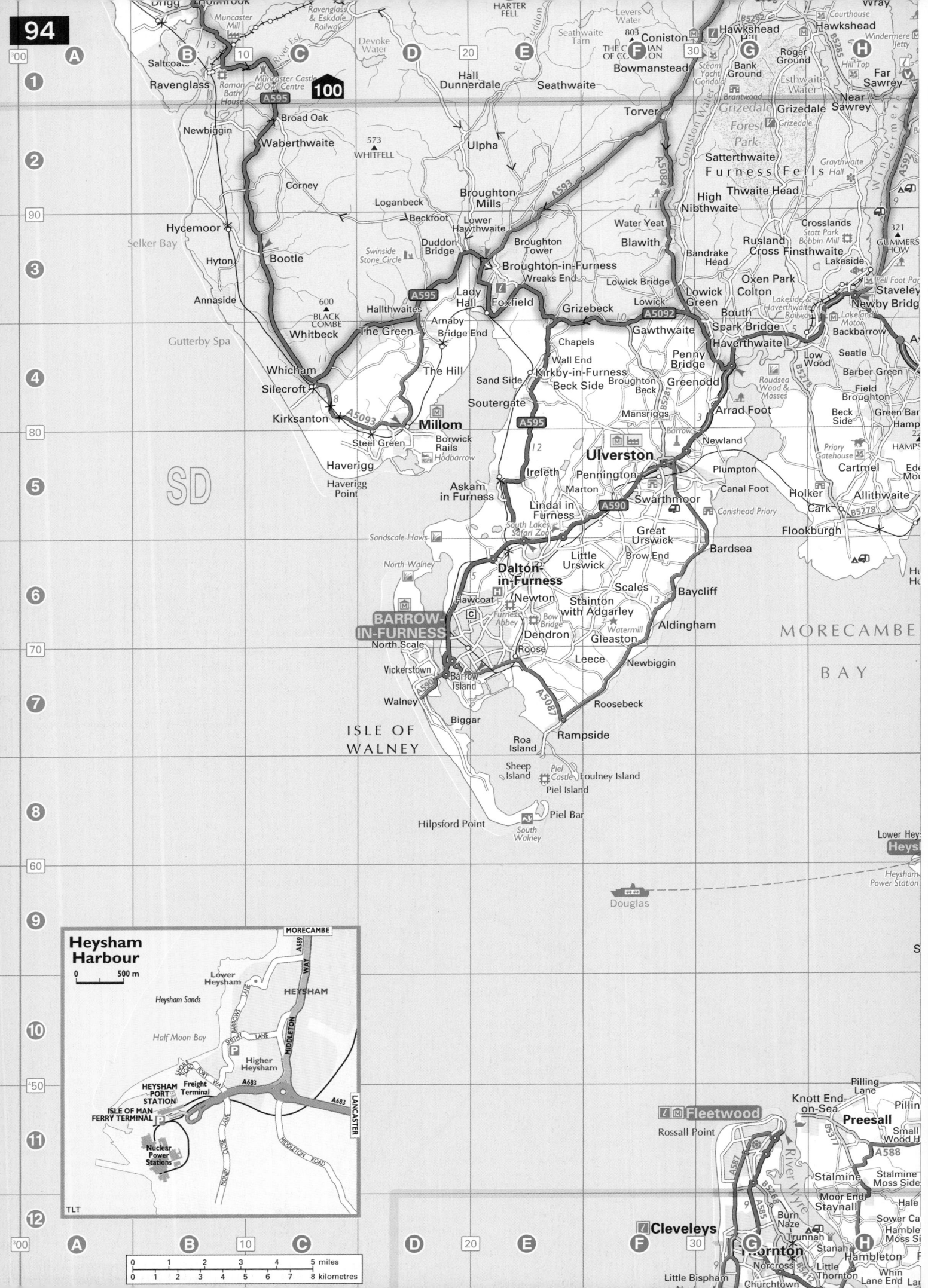

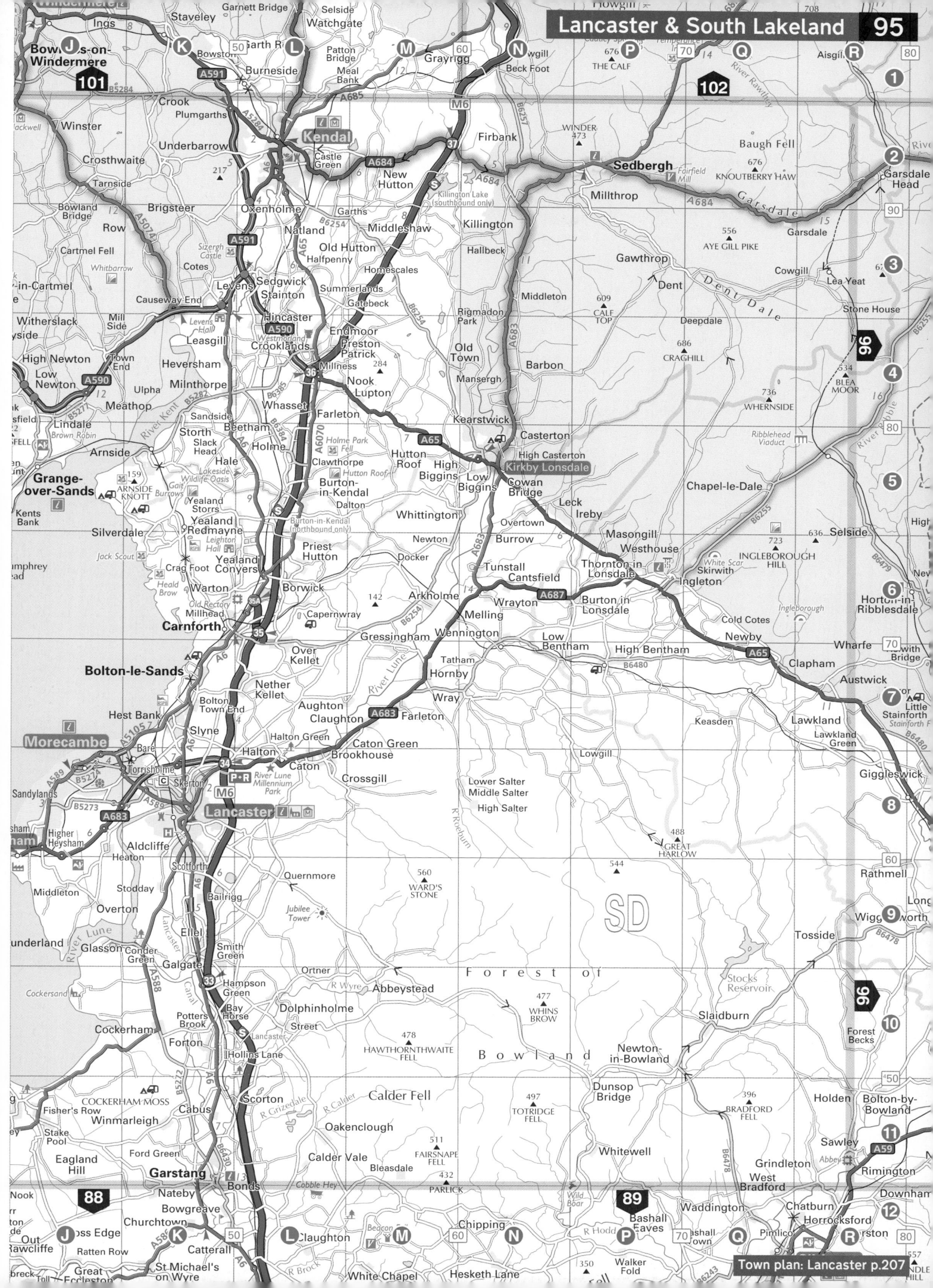

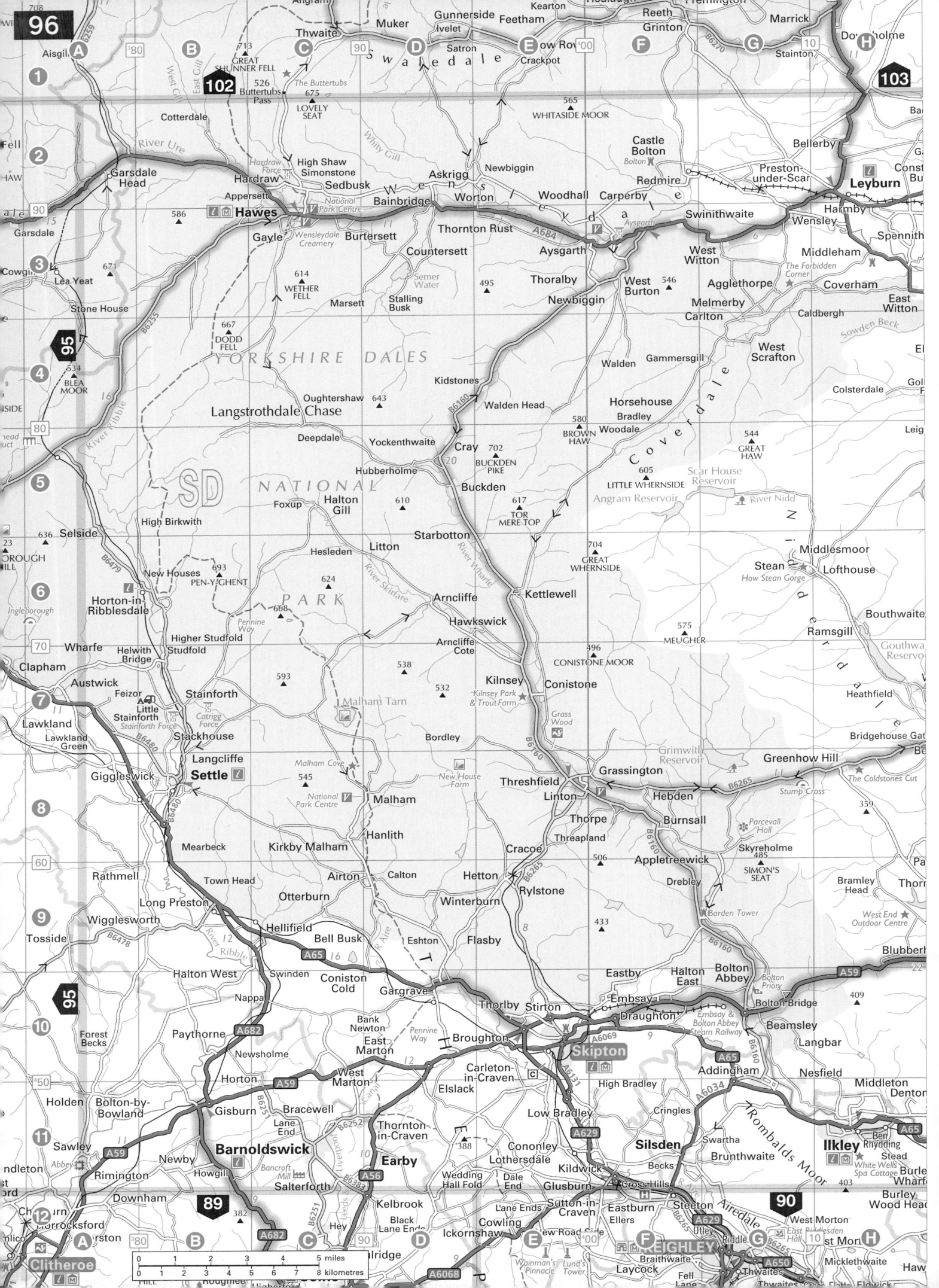

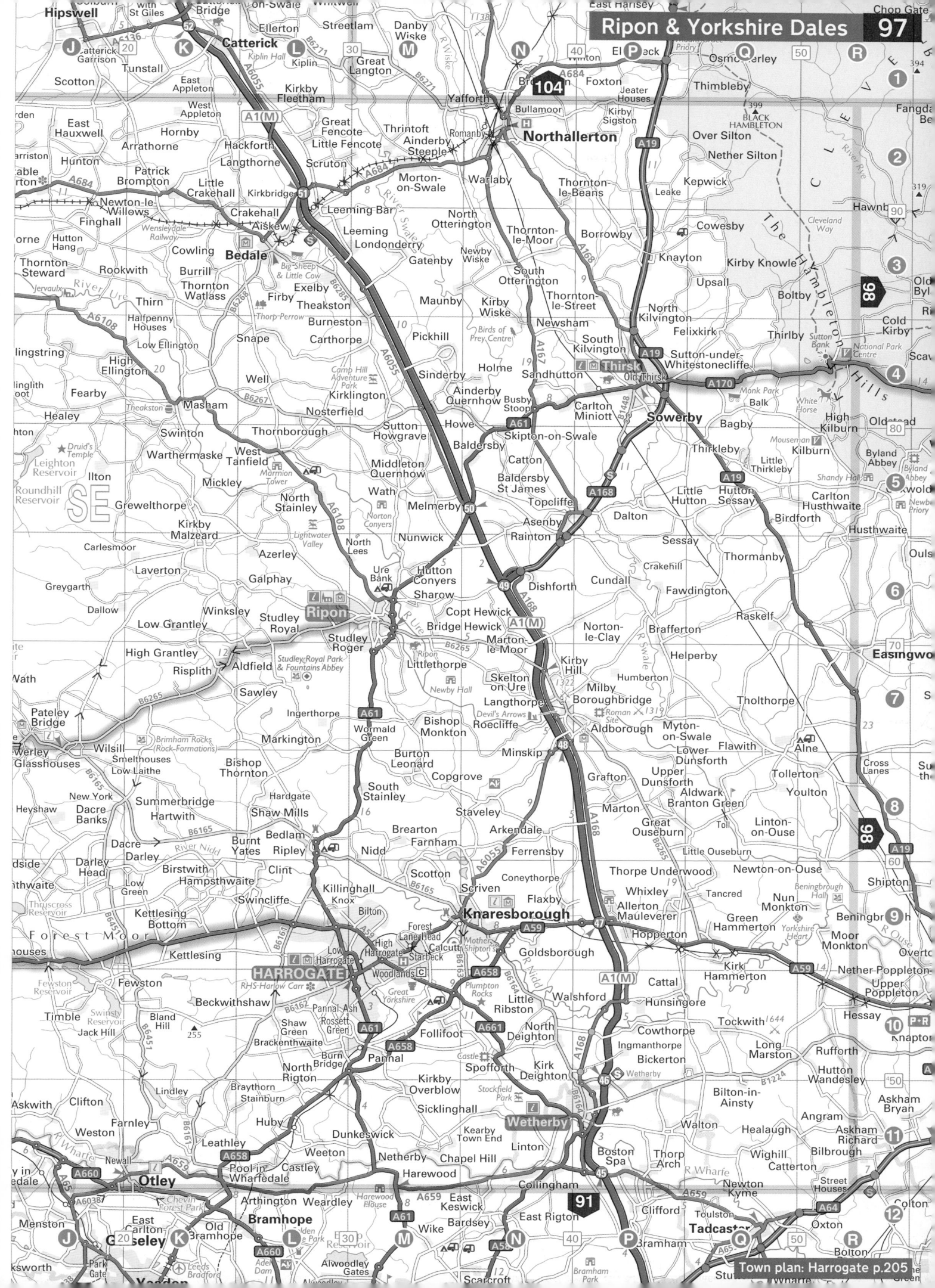

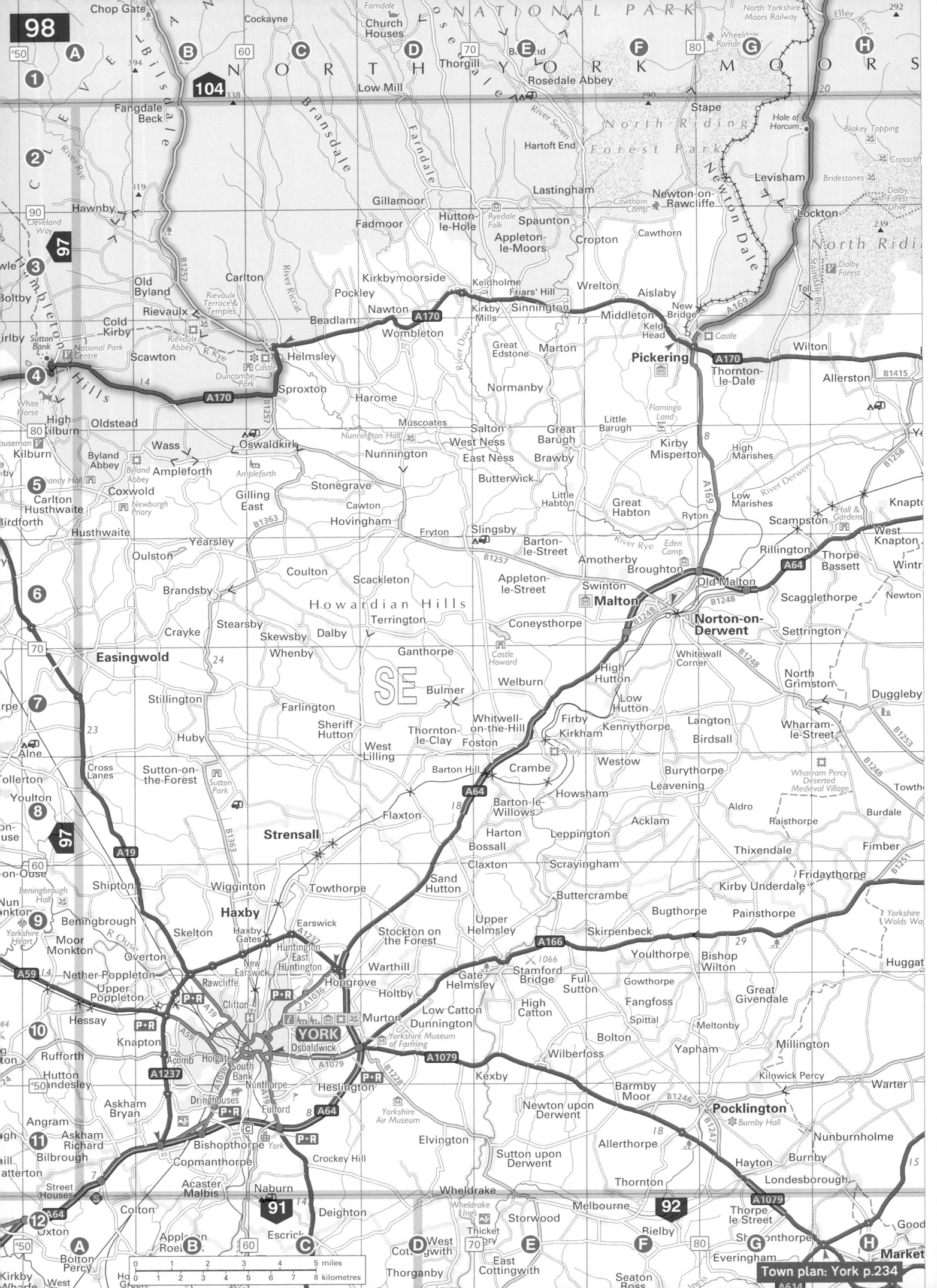

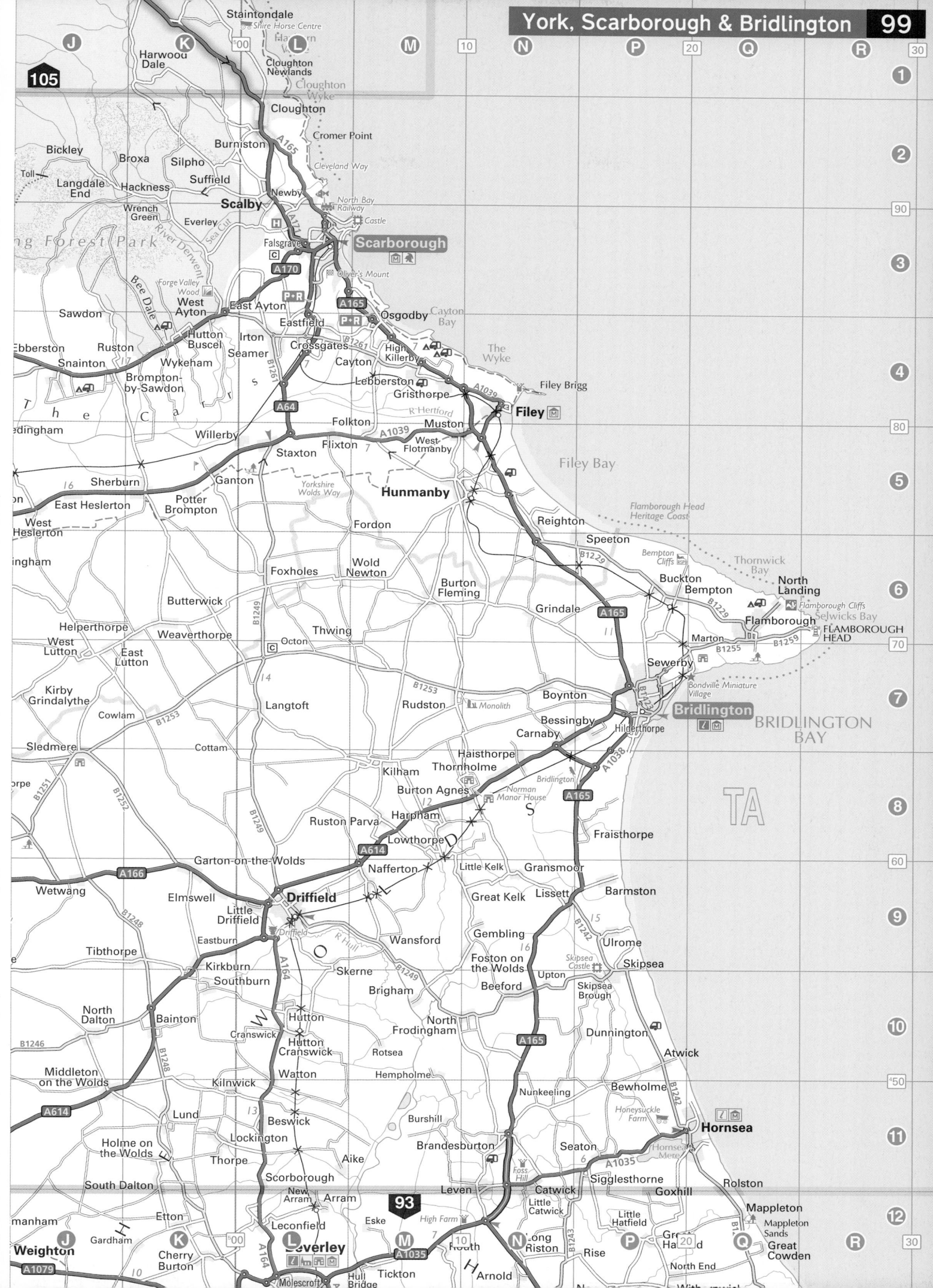

105

J K L M N P Q R
1 2 90 3 4 80 5 6 70 7 8 60 9 10 50 11 12 30

Staintondale
Shire Horse Centre
Harwood Dale
Cloughton Newlands
Cloughton Wyke
Cloughton
Bickley Broxa Silpho Suffield Cromer Point
Toll Langdale End Hackness
Wrench Green Everley Scalby Newby
Long Forest Park Bee Dale
Sawdon West Ayton East Ayton Falsgrave
Ruston Hutton Buscel Irton Eastfield
Ebberston Snainton Wykeham Seamer Crossgates
Brompton-by-Sawdon Cayton
The Ca Willerby Lebberston Gristhorpe
Bedingham Folkton Muston
Sherburn Flixton Staxton West Flotmanby
East Heslerton Potter Brompton Ganton
West Heslerton Fordon Hunmanby
Foxholes Wold Newton
Butterwick Burton Fleming
Helperthorpe Weaverthorpe Thwing
West Lutton East Lutton Octon
Kirby Grindalythe Langtoft Rudston
Cowlam Thorpe
Sledmere Cottam Kilham
Tibthorpe North Dalton Bainton Cranswick
Middleton on the Wolds Kilnwick Watton
Holme on the Wolds Lund Beswick
Weighton Gardham Cherry Burton Leconfield

Scarborough
Castle
North Bay Railway
Oliver's Mount
Osgodby Cayton Bay
High Killerby The Wyke
Filey Brigg
Filey
R Hertford
Filey Bay
Reighton
Speeton
Flamborough Head Heritage Coast
Bempton Cliffs Thornwick Bay
Buckton North Landing
Bempton Flamborough Cliffs Selwicks Bay
Grindale Flamborough
Marton FLAMBOROUGH HEAD
Sewerby
Bondville Miniature Village
Boynton Bridlington
Bessingby BRIDLINGTON BAY
Carnaby Hilderthorpe
Haisthorpe Norman Manor House
Thornholme Bridlington
Burton Agnes Fraisthorpe
Harpham
Ruston Parva Lowthorpe TA
Nafferton Little Kelk Gransmoor
Garton-on-the-Wolds Great Kelk Lissett Barmston
Wetwang Elmswell Driffield
Little Driffield Gembling Ulrome
Eastburn Wansford Foston on the Wolds Skipsea
Kirkburn Skerne Beeford Skipsea Brough
Southburn Brigham Upton
Hutton North Frodingham Dunnington
Hutton Cranswick Rotsea Atwick
Hempholme
Nunkeeling Bewholme
Thorpe Lockington Aike Burshill Honeysuckle Farm
Scorborough Brandesburton Seaton Hornsea
New Arram Leven Catwick Sigglesthorne Hornsea Mere
Arram Eske Little Catwick Goxhill Rolston
Beverley Tickton Rise Mappleton
Molescroft Hull Bridge Arnold Long Riston Mappleton Sands
Great Cowden

93

A165 A64 A1039 A170 A171 A614 A166 A164 A1035 A614 A1079
B1261 B1249 B1253 B1251 B1252 B1248 B1246 B1243 B1242 B1229 B1255 B1259 B1253 B1038

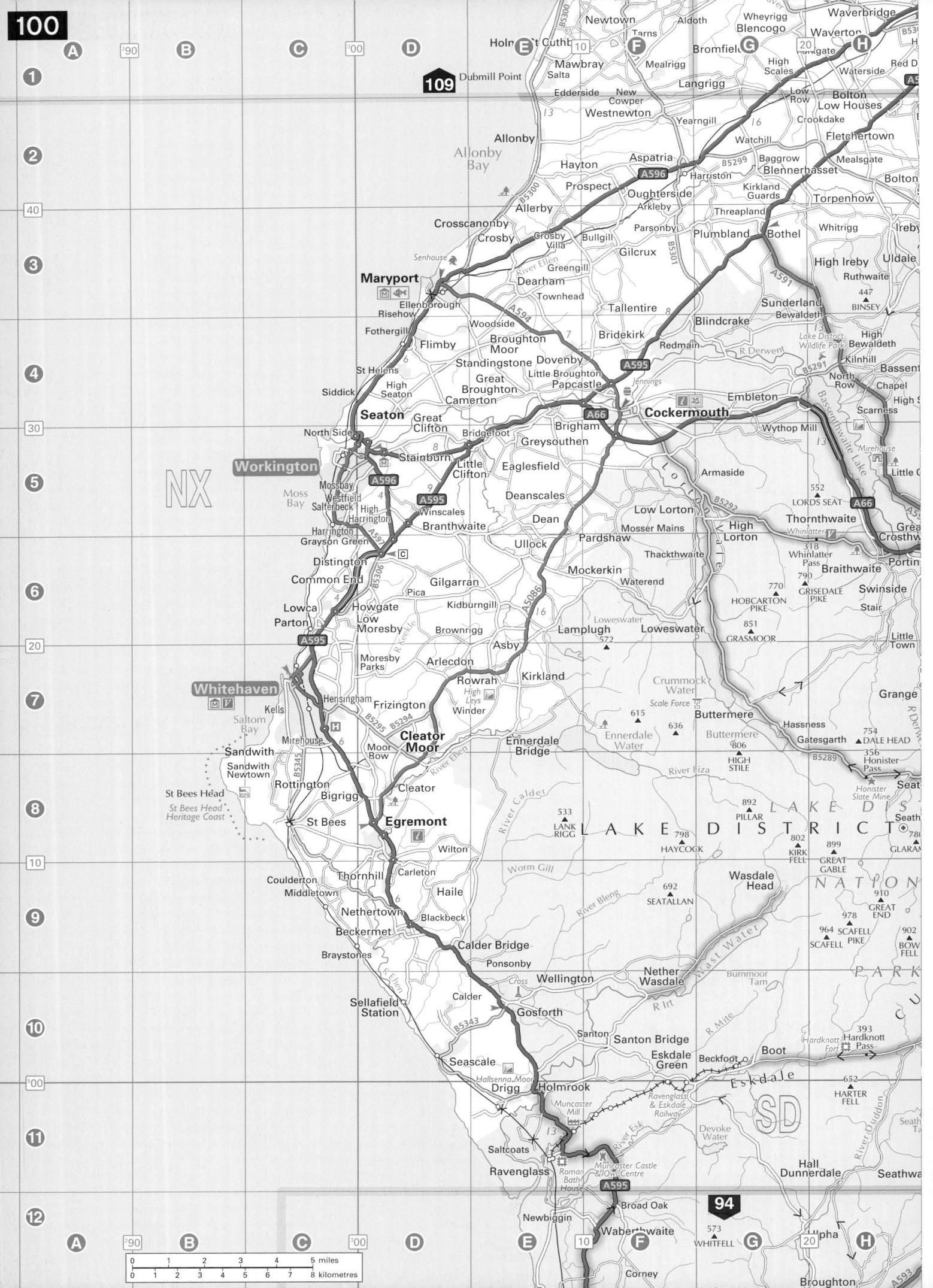

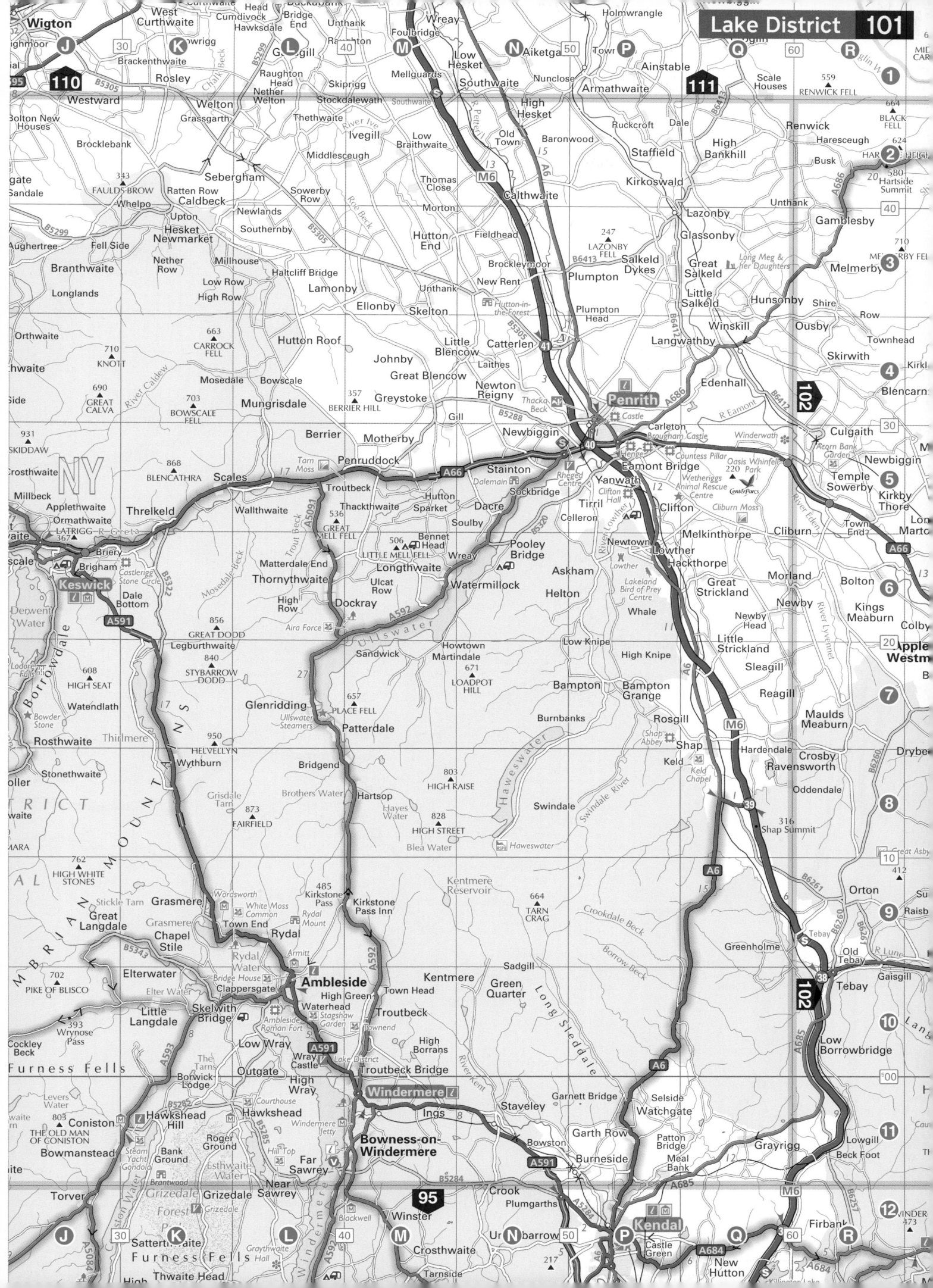

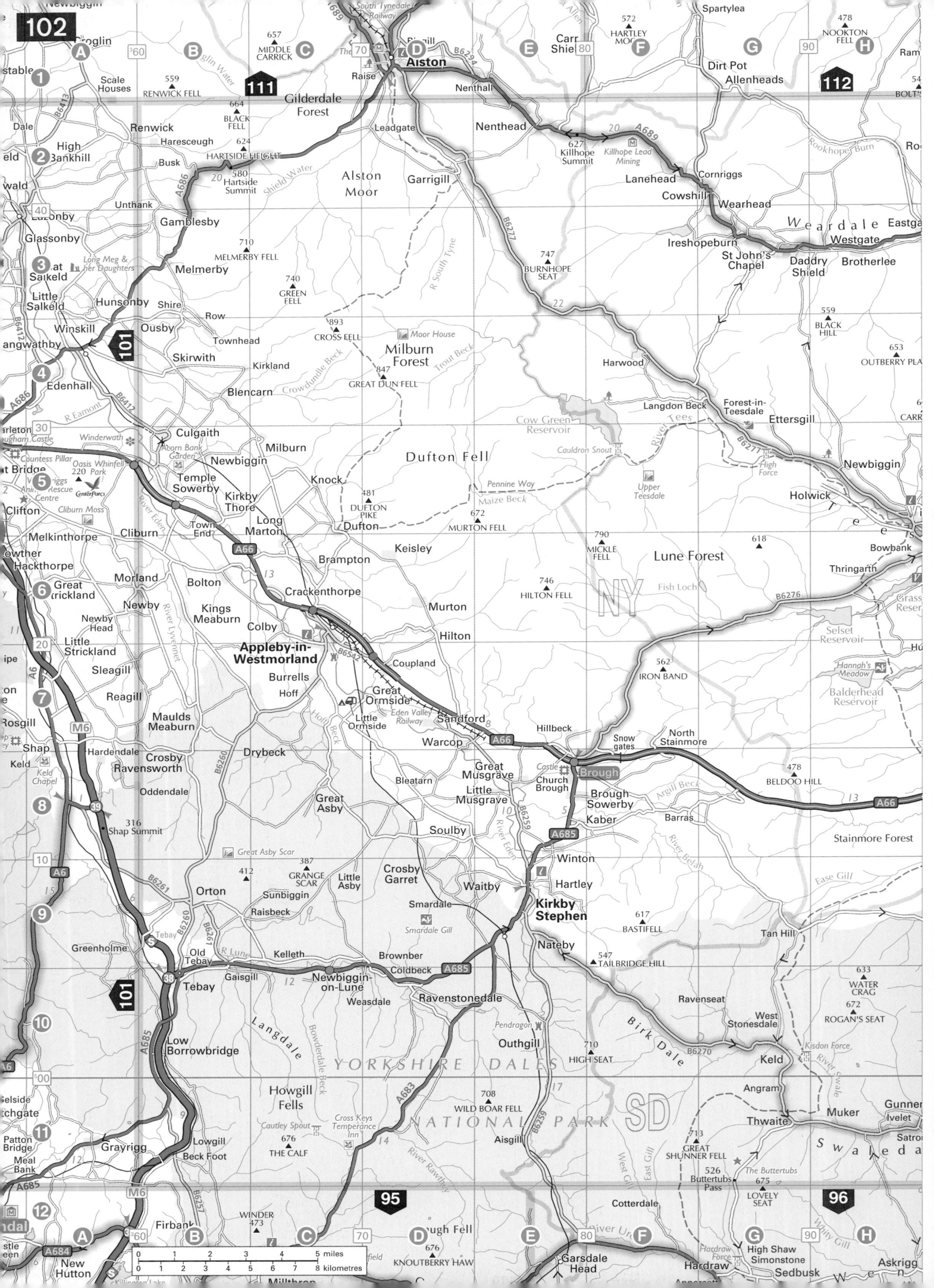

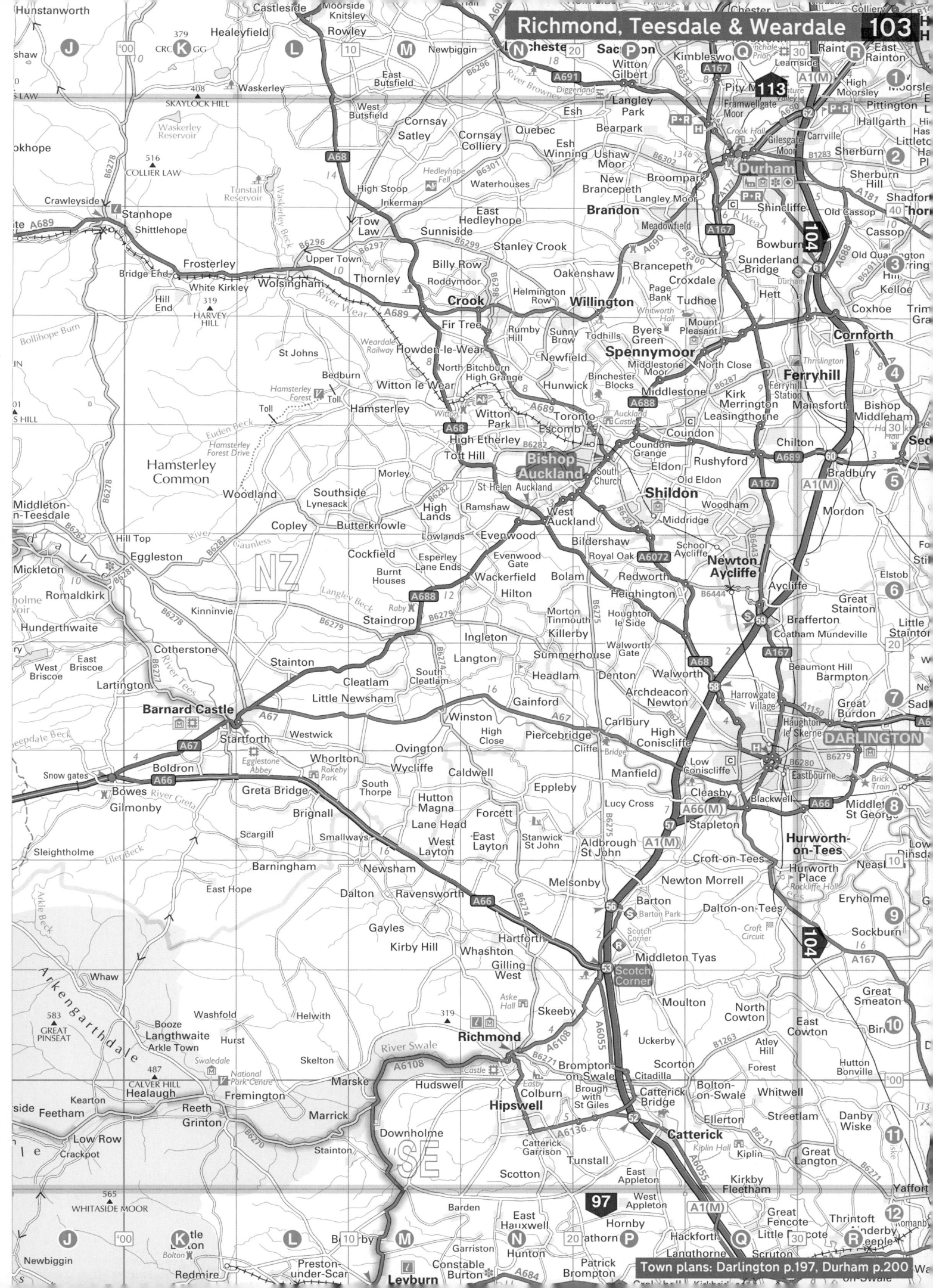

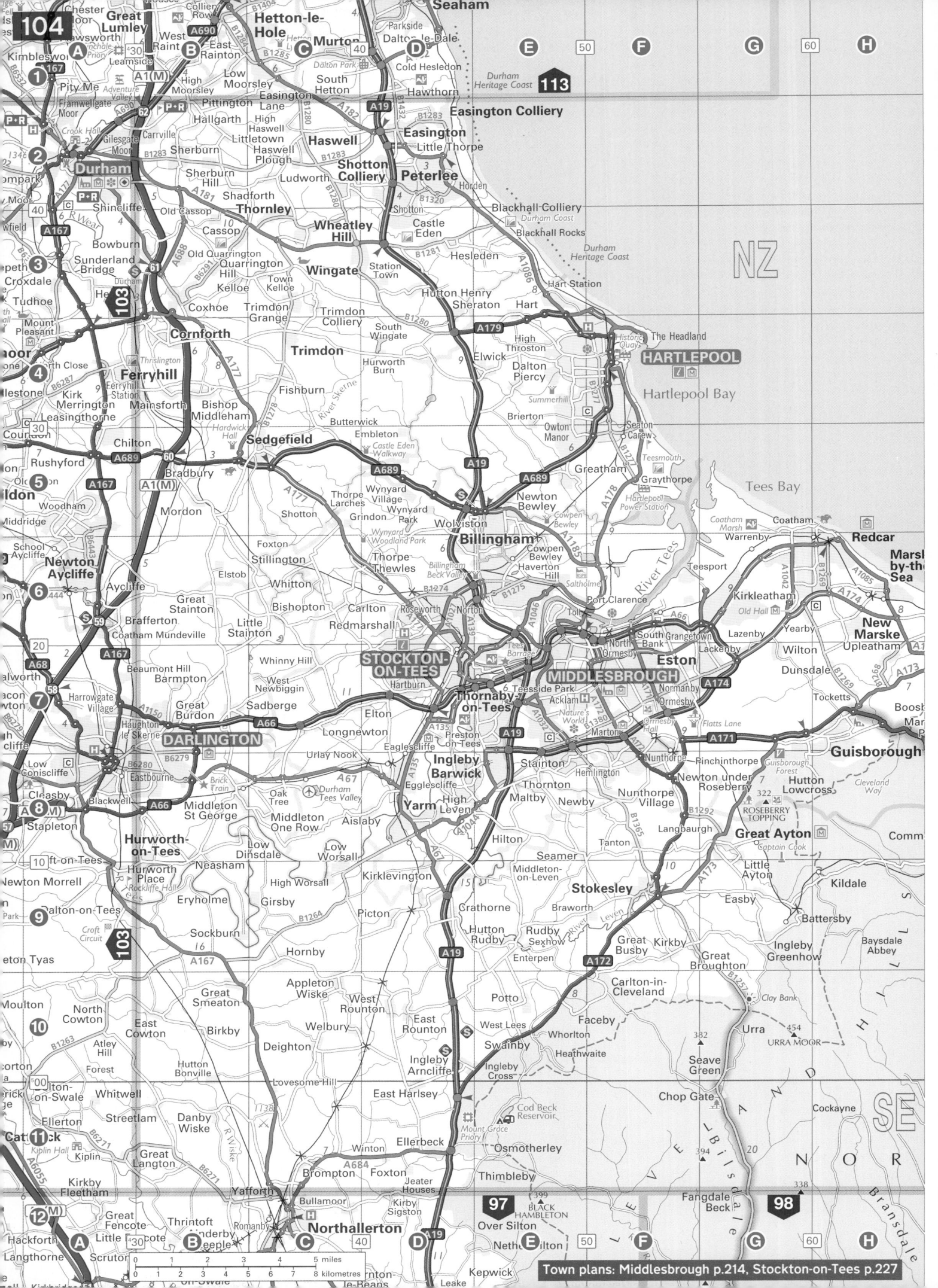

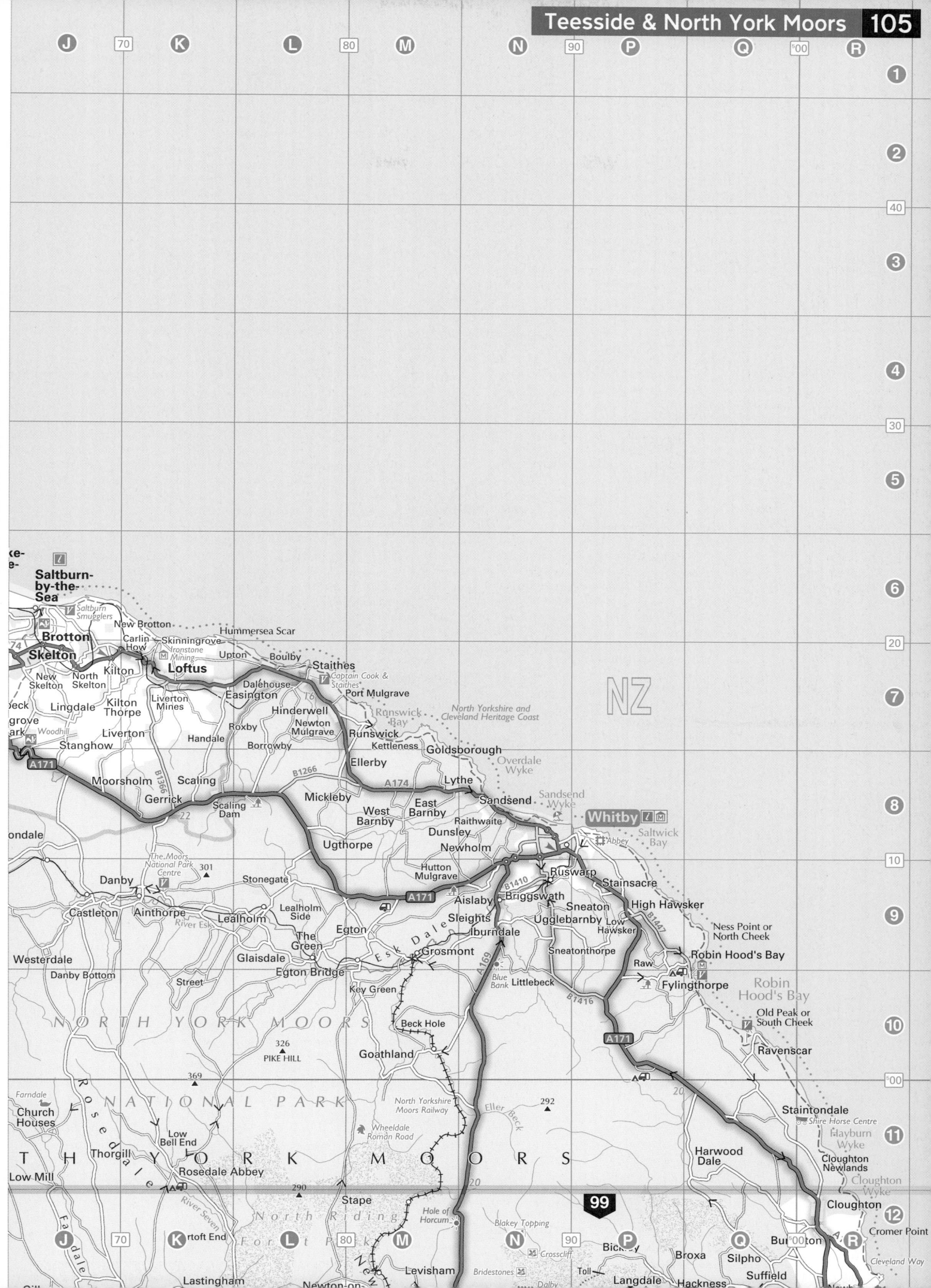

J 70 K L 80 M N 90 P Q '00 R

1
2
40
3
4
30
5
6
20
7

NZ

Saltburn-by-the-Sea
Saltburn Smugglers
New Brotton
Hummersea Scar
Brotton
Skelton
Carlin How
Skinningrove
Ironstone Mining
Upton
Boulby
Staithes
Loftus
Captain Cook & Staithes
New Skelton
North Skelton
Kilton
Dalehouse
Easington
Port Mulgrave
Lingdale
Kilton Thorpe
Liverton Mines
Hinderwell
Runswick
North Yorkshire and Cleveland Heritage Coast
Runswick Bay
Liverton
Roxby
Newton Mulgrave
New Brotton
Woodhill
Handale
Borrowby
Kettleness
Goldsborough
Stanghow
Moorsholm
Scaling
Ellerby
Lythe
Overdale Wyke
A171
Gerrick
Scaling Dam
Mickleby
A174
Sandsend
Sandsend Wyke
West Barnby
East Barnby
Raithwaite
Whitby
Saltwick Bay
Ugthorpe
Dunsley
Newholm
Abbey
The Moors National Park Centre
301
Hutton Mulgrave
Ruswarp
Danby
Stonegate
Aislaby
Briggswath
Sneaton
Stainsacre
High Hawsker
Castleton
Ainthorpe
Lealholm
Lealholm Side
Sleights
Ugglebarnby
Low Hawsker
Ness Point or North Cheek
Westerdale
The Green
Egton
Iburndale
Sneatonthorpe
Robin Hood's Bay
Glaisdale
Grosmont
Raw
Danby Bottom
Egton Bridge
Blue Bank
Littlebeck
Fylingthorpe
Robin Hood's Bay
Street
Key Green
Old Peak or South Cheek
NORTH YORK MOORS
Beck Hole
A171
Ravenscar
326
PIKE HILL
Goathland
Farndale
369
NATIONAL PARK
North Yorkshire Moors Railway
292
Staintondale
Church Houses
Rosedale
Wheeldale Roman Road
Eller Beck
Shire Horse Centre
Hayburn Wyke
Low Bell End
Harwood Dale
Cloughton Newlands
Thorgill
THE YORK MOORS
Cloughton Wyke
Low Mill
Rosedale Abbey
290
Cloughton
River Seven
Stape
North Riding
Hole of Horcum
99
Cromer Point
Lastingham
Newton-on-
Levisham
Blakey Topping
Crosscliff
Bickley
Broxa
Silpho
Cleveland Way
Forest Park
Bridestones
Toll
Langdale
Hackness
Suffield

J 70 K rtoft End L 80 M N 90 P Q Bur '00 R

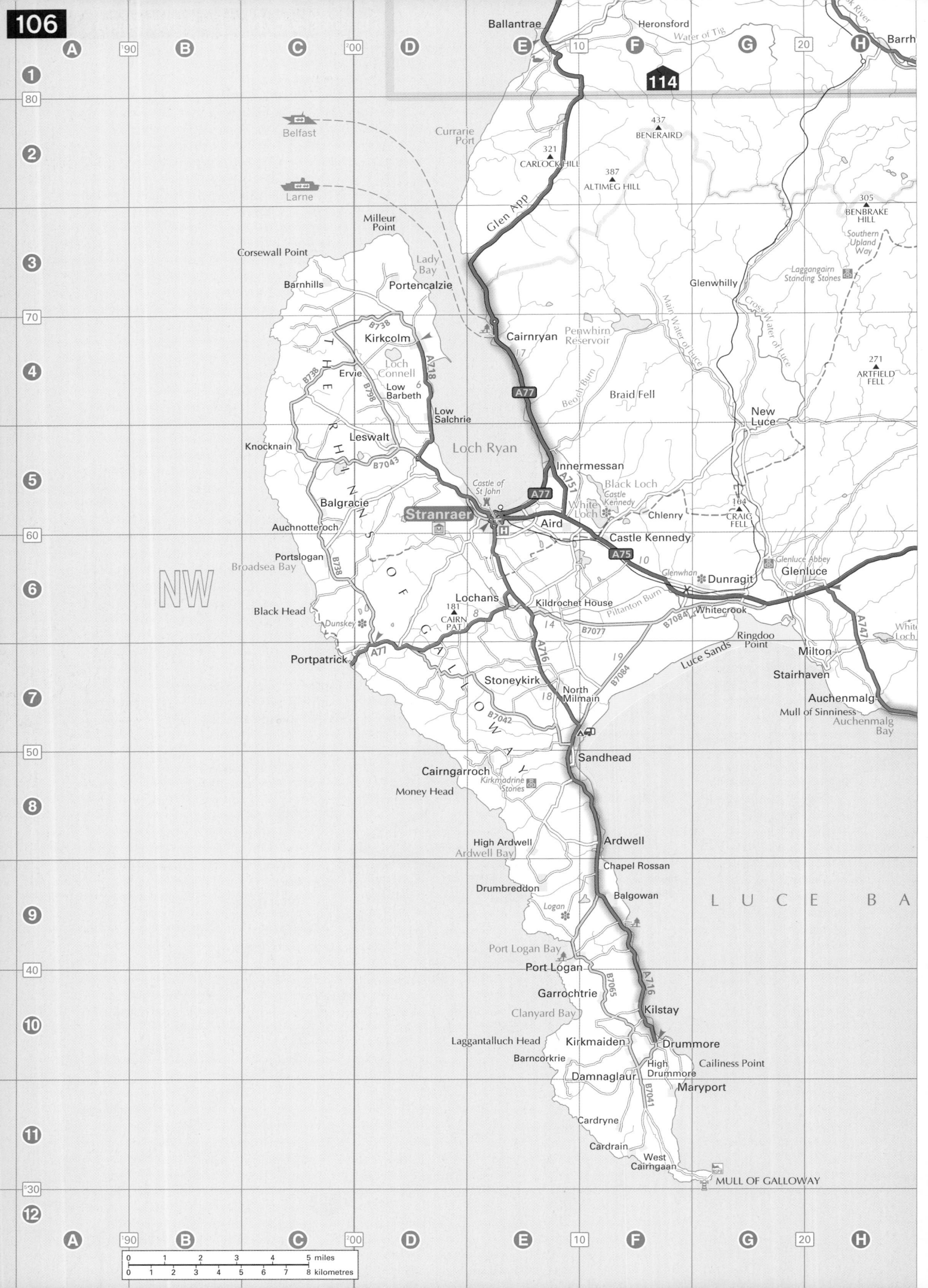

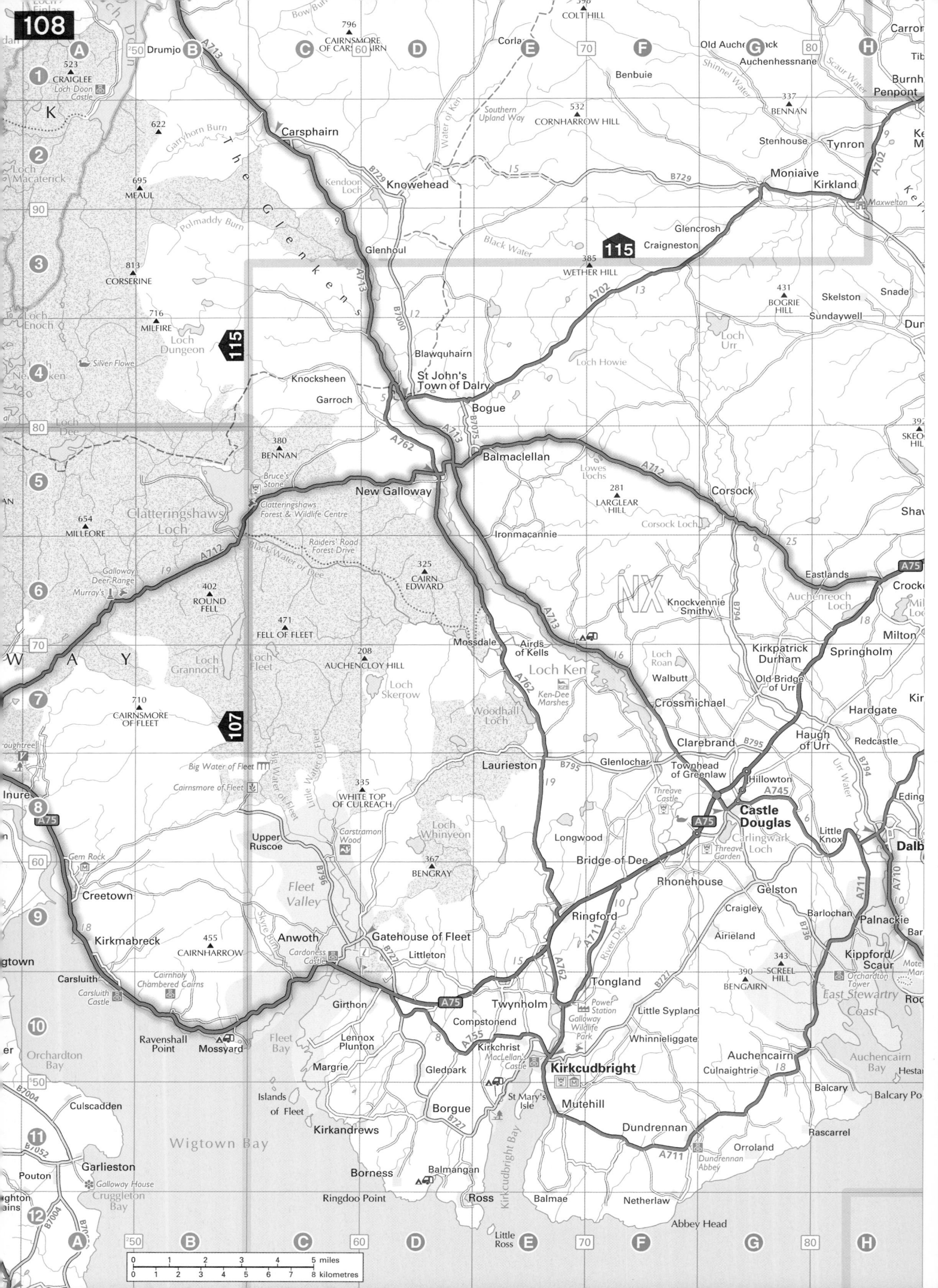

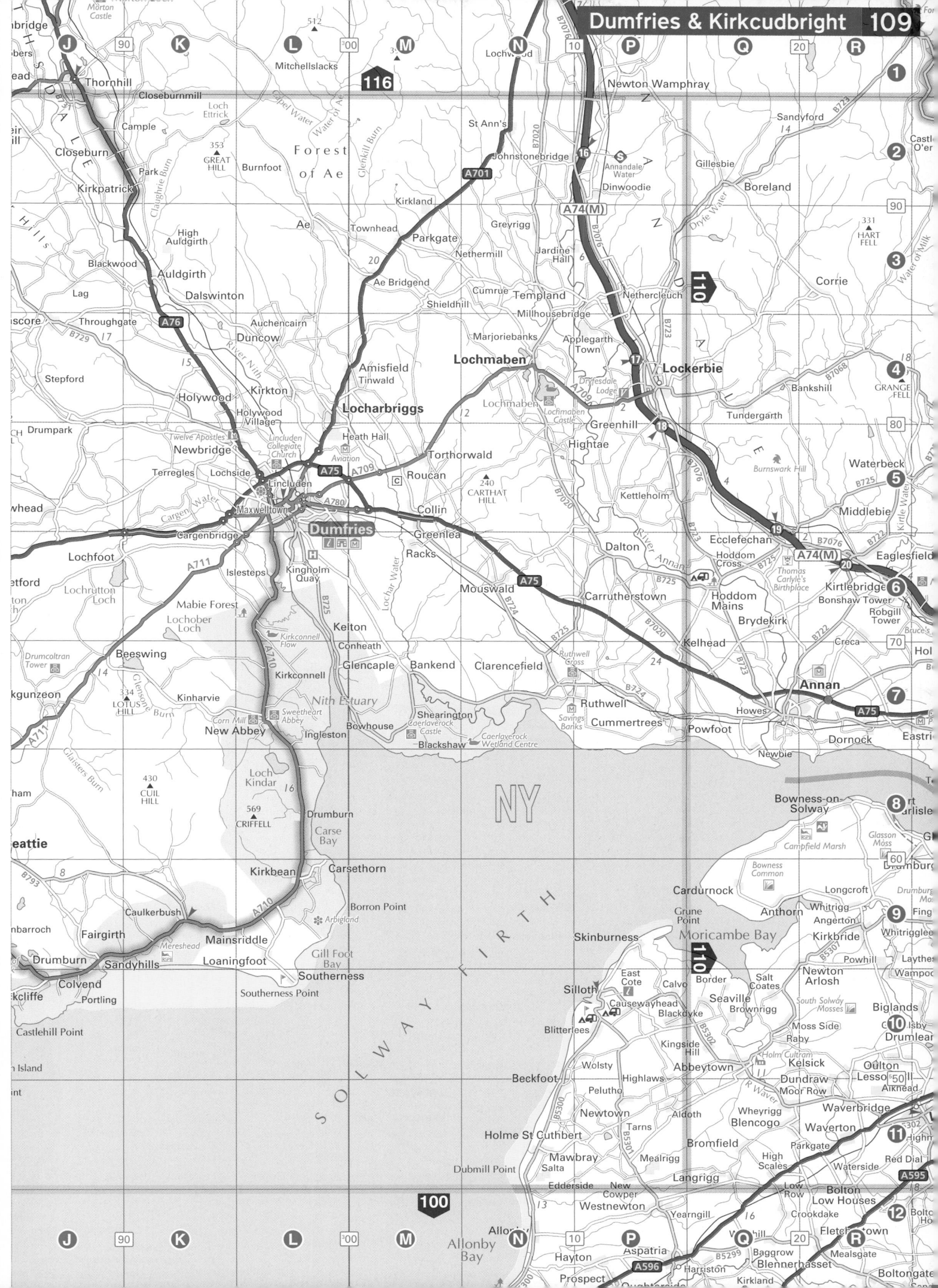

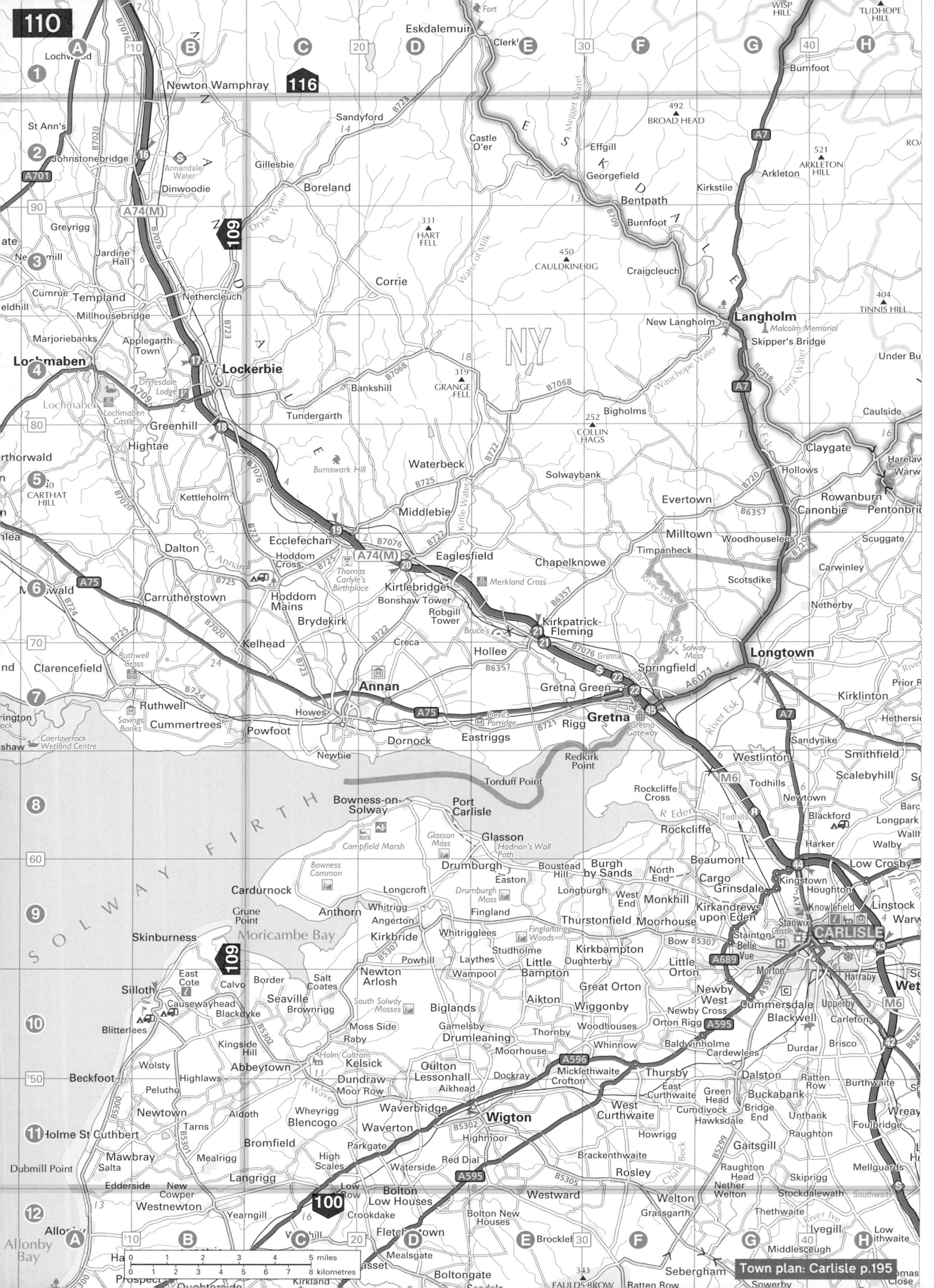

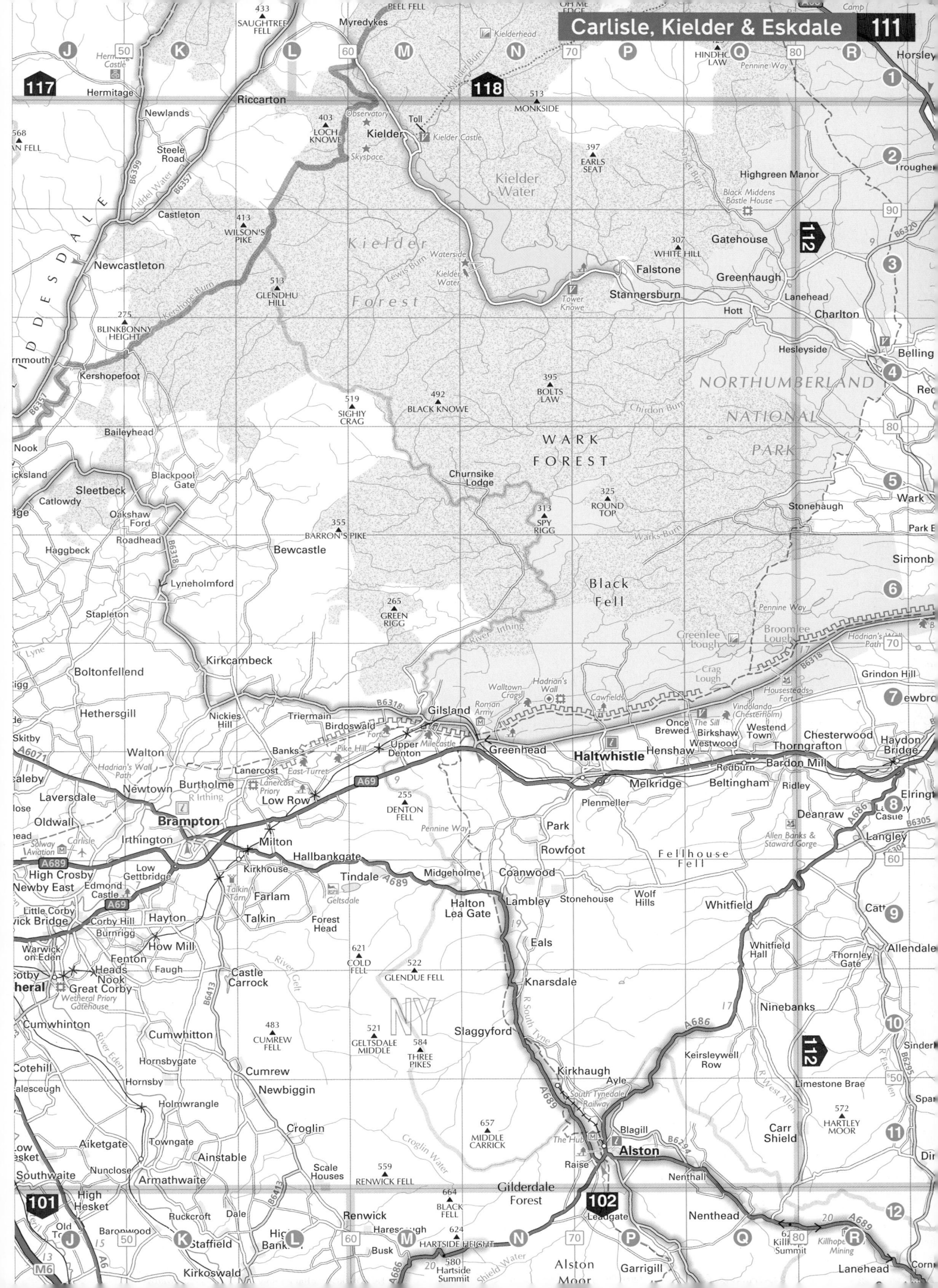

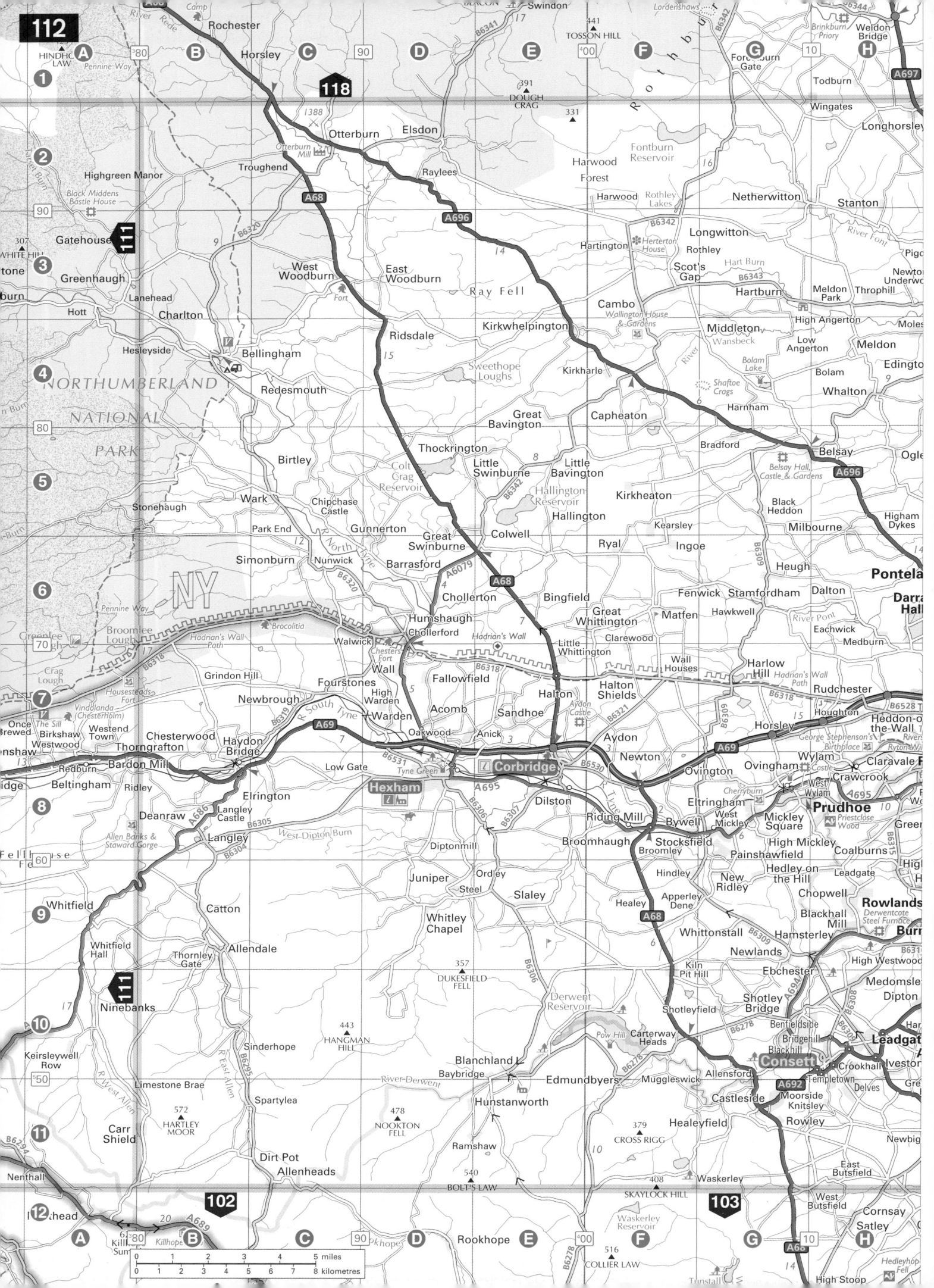

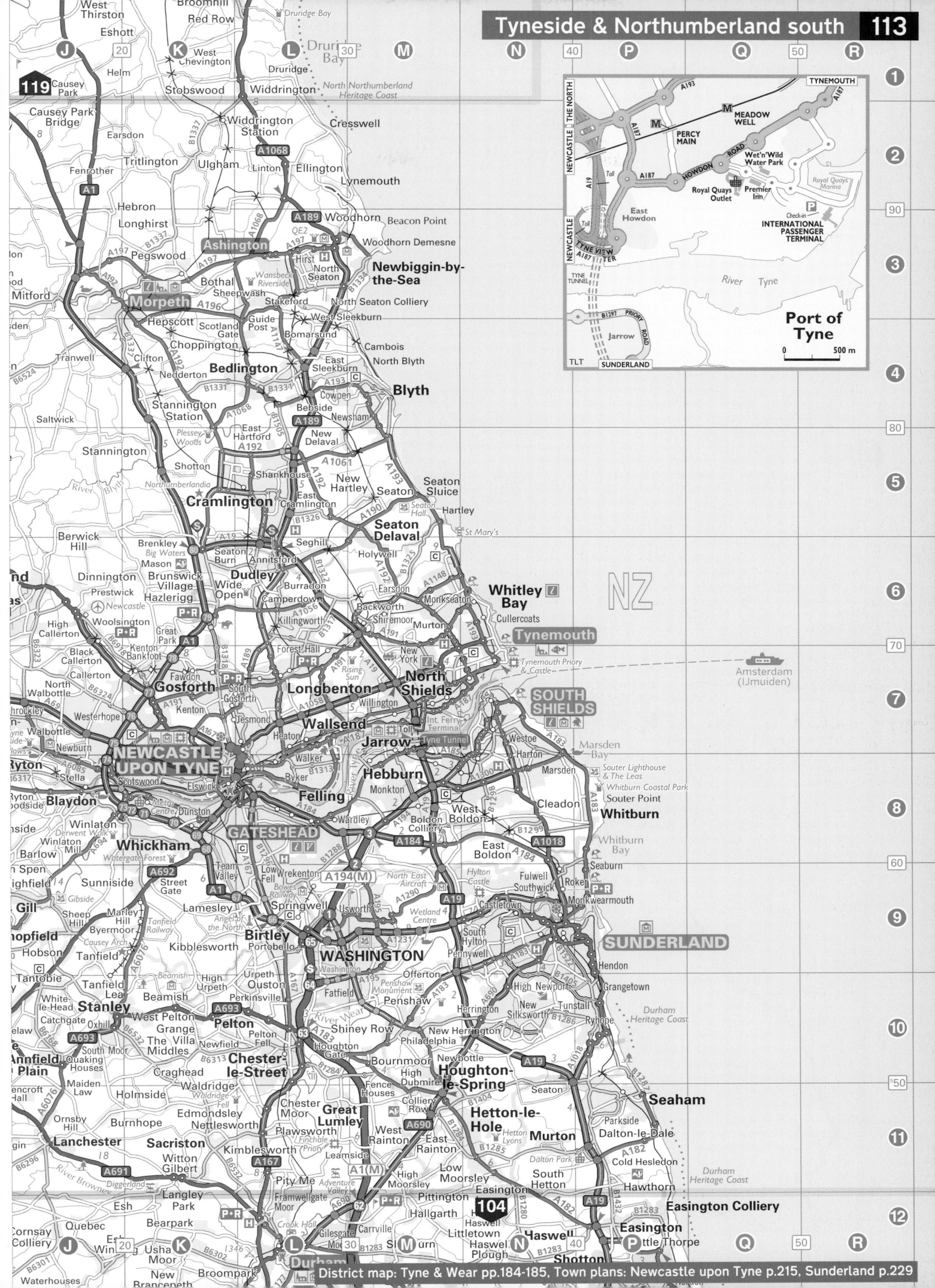

Port of Tyne

TYNEMOUTH

NEWCASTLE
THE NORTH

MEADOW WELL

PERCY MAIN

Wet'n'Wild Water Park

Royal Quays Outlet

Premier Inn

Royal Quays Marina

INTERNATIONAL PASSENGER TERMINAL

Check-in

East Howdon

HOWDON ROAD

East Howdon

TYNE VIEW

TYNE TUNNEL

Jarrow

PRIORY ROAD

SUNDERLAND

TLT

River Tyne

0   500 m

NZ

West Thirston
Eshott
Broomhill
Red Row
Druridge Bay
Druridge Bay

Causey Park
Helm
West Chevington
Druridge
North Northumberland Heritage Coast

Causey Park Bridge
Stobswood
Widdrington
Cresswell

Earsdon
Fenrother
Tritlington
Widdrington Station
Ulgham
Linton
Ellington
Lynemouth

Hebron
Longhirst
Woodhorn
Beacon Point
Woodhorn Demesne

Pegswood
Ashington
Hirst
North Seaton
Newbiggin-by-the-Sea

Mitford
Morpeth
Bothal
Sheepwash
Wansbeck Riverside
North Seaton Colliery

Hepscott
Scotland Gate
Guide Post
Stakeford
West Sleekburn

Tranwell
Choppington
Bomarsund
Cambois

Clifton
Nedderton
East Sleekburn
North Blyth

Bedlington
Cowpen
Blyth

Stannington Station
Bebside
Newsham

Saltwick
East Hartford
Plessey Woods
New Delaval

Stannington
Shotton
Northumberlandia
Shankhouse
New Hartley
Seaton Sluice

Cramlington
East Cramlington
Seaton
Hartley

Seaton Delaval
St Mary's

Brenkley
Big Waters
Seaton Burn
Annitsford
Seghill
Holywell

Berwick Hill
Mason
Dudley
Burradon
Earsdon
Whitley Bay

Dinnington
Brunswick Village
Wide Open
Camperdown
Backworth
Monkseaton
Cullercoats

Prestwick
Hazlerigg
Killingworth
Shiremoor
Murton
Tynemouth

Newcastle
Woolsington
Great Park
Forest Hall
New York
North Shields

High Callerton
Kenton Bankfoot
Rising Sun
Willington

Black Callerton
Fawdon
South Gosforth
Longbenton

North Walbottle
Gosforth
Jesmond
Wallsend
Int. Ferry Terminal
SOUTH SHIELDS

Westerhope
Kenton
Heaton
Jarrow
Tyne Tunnel
Westoe
Harton

Throckley
Walbottle
Newburn
Walker
Byker
Hebburn
Marsden
Marsden Bay

NEWCASTLE UPON TYNE
Elswick
Monkton
Souter Lighthouse & The Leas

Ryton
Stella
Scotswood
Dunston
Felling
Wardley
West Boldon
Cleadon
Souter Point

Blaydon
Metro Centre
GATESHEAD
Boldon Colliery
Whitburn Coastal Park

Winlaton
Winlaton Mill
Team Valley
Low Fell
Wrekenton
Boldon Colliery
Whitburn

Whickham
Watergate Forest
East Boldon
Whitburn Bay

Barlow
Sunniside
Street Gate
Lamesley
Angel of the North
Usworth
Hylton Castle
Fulwell
Roker

Gibside
Marley Hill
Byermoor
Tanfield Railway
Springwell
North East Aircraft
Wetland Centre
Castletown
Southwick
Monkwearmouth

Sheep Hill
Kibblesworth
Birtley
Portobello
WASHINGTON
South Hylton
SUNDERLAND

Hobson
Tantobie
Tanfield
Causey Arch
Beamish
High Urpeth
Urpeth
Ouston
Fatfield
Pennywell
Hendon

Tanfield Lea
Grange Villa
Offerton
High Newport
Grangetown

White-le-Head
Catchgate
West Pelton
Perkinsville
Penshaw Monument
Penshaw
Herrington
New Silksworth
Tunstall
Ryhope

Stanley
Oxhill
The Middles
Newfield
Pelton Fell
Shiney Row
Houghton Gate
Bournmoor
New Herrington
Philadelphia
Durham Heritage Coast

Pelton
Craghead
Waldridge
Chester Moor
Fence Houses
High Dubmire

Annfield Plain
South Moor
Quaking Houses
Plawsworth
Newbottle
Houghton-le-Spring

Maiden Law
Holmside
Edmondsley
Nettlesworth
Chester-le-Street
Great Lumley
Colliery Row
Seaham

Lanchester
Burnhope
Sacriston
Kimblesworth
Chester Moor
West Rainton
Hetton-le-Hole
Parkside
Dalton-le-Dale

Ornsby Hill
Witton Gilbert
Leamside
East Rainton
Hetton Lyons
Murton

Cornsay Colliery
Langley Park
Pity Me
High Moorsley
Seaton
Cold Hesleden

Quebec
Bearpark
Framwellgate Moor
Low Moorsley
South Hetton
Hawthorn

Esh
Adventure Valley
Pittington
Easington
Durham Heritage Coast

Durham
Crook Hall
Gilesgate Moor
Carrville
Hallgarth
Easington Colliery

Waterhouses
New Brancepeth
Gilesgate
Littletown
Haswell
Haswell Plough
Easington
Little Thorpe

Shotton

Amsterdam (IJmuiden)

District map: Tyne & Wear pp.184–185, Town plans: Newcastle upon Tyne p.215, Sunderland p.229

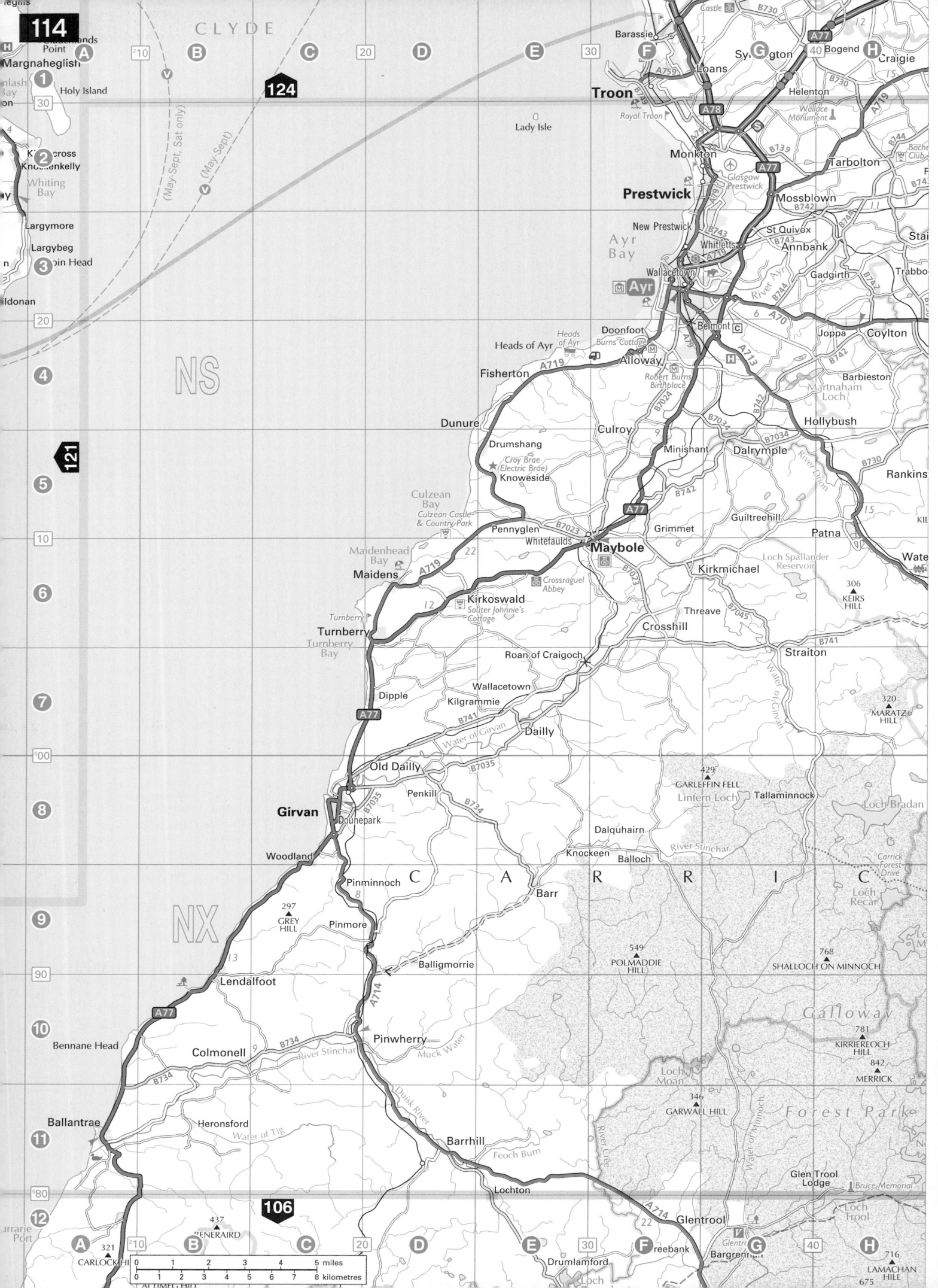

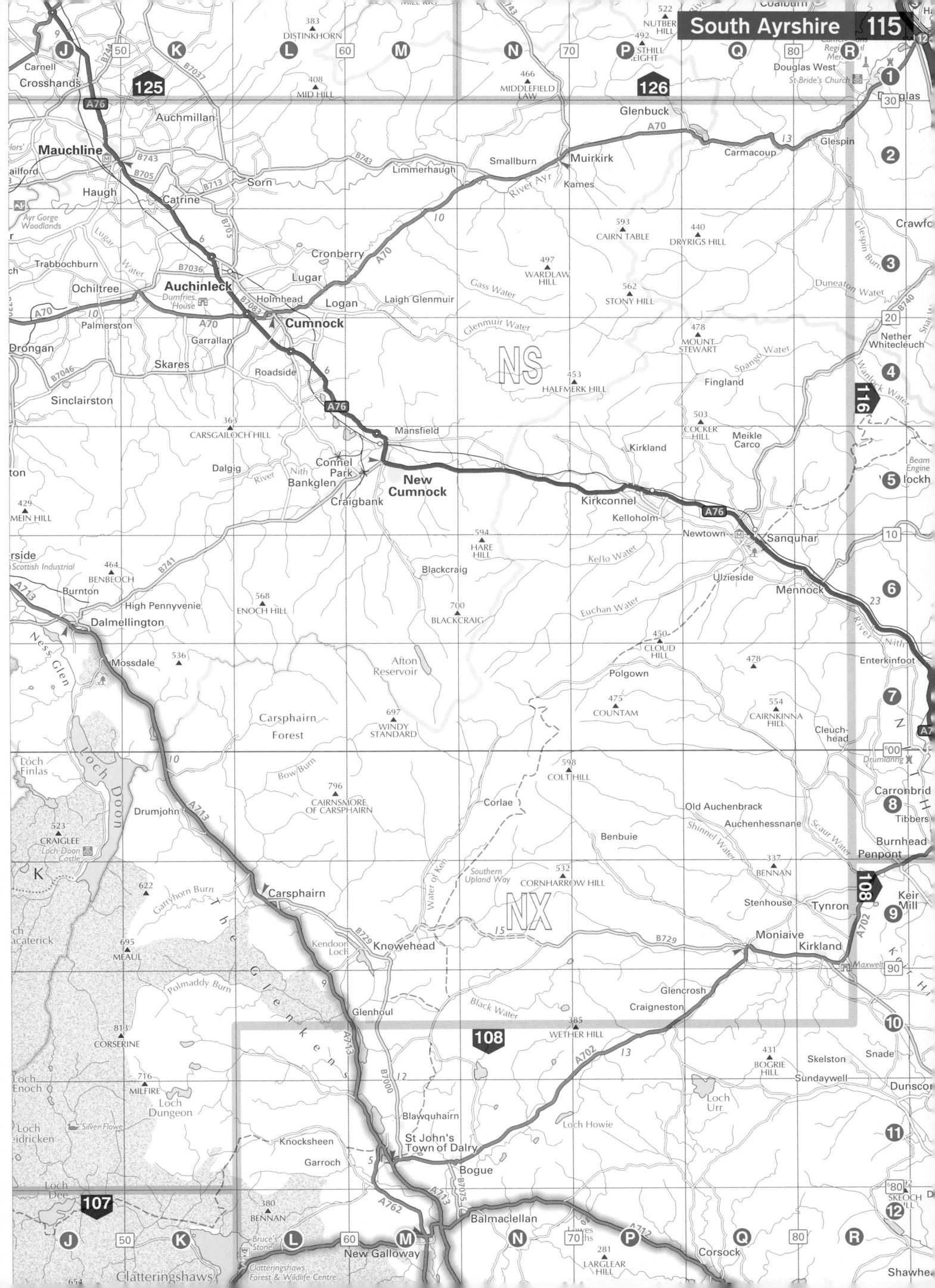

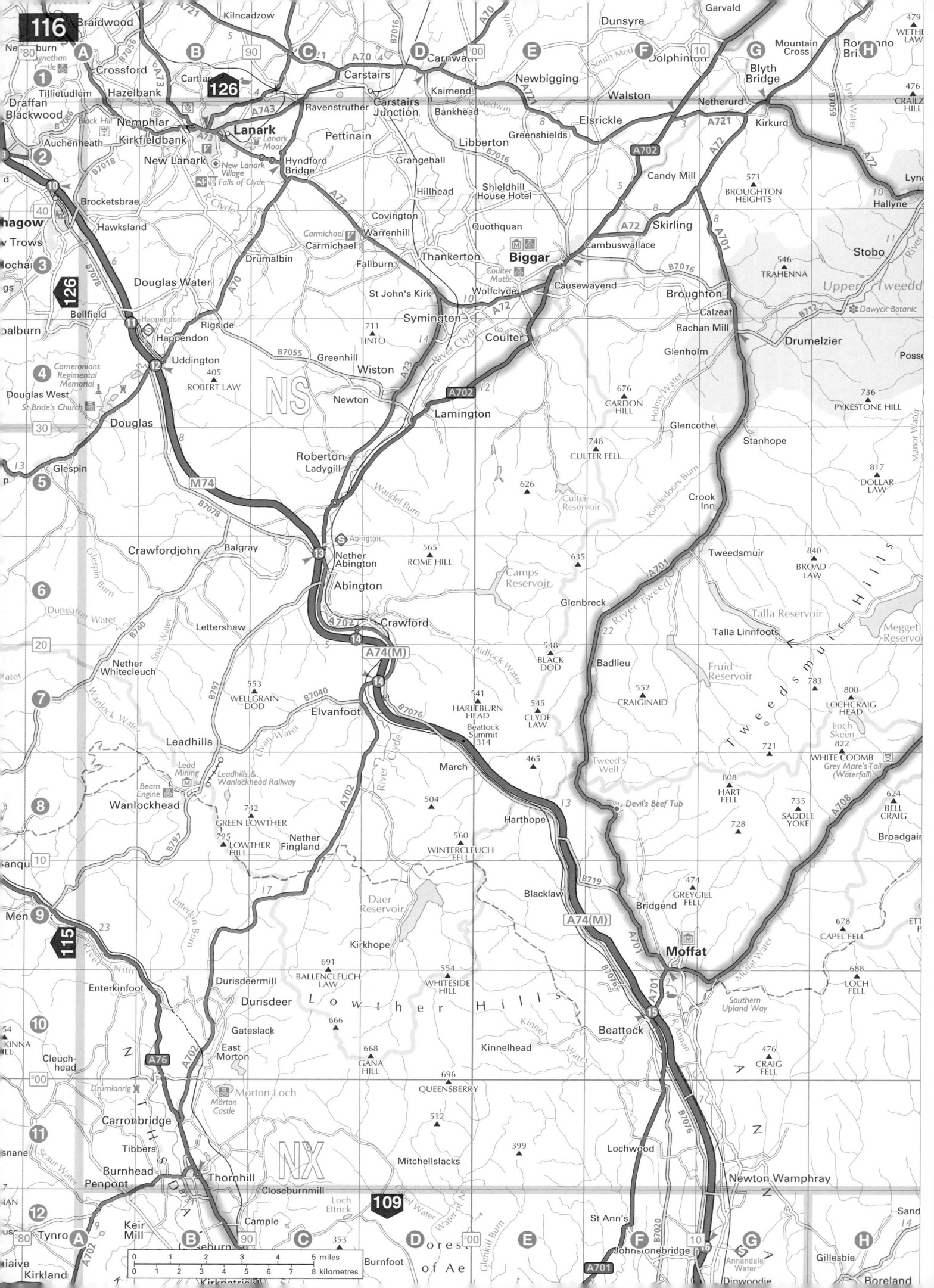

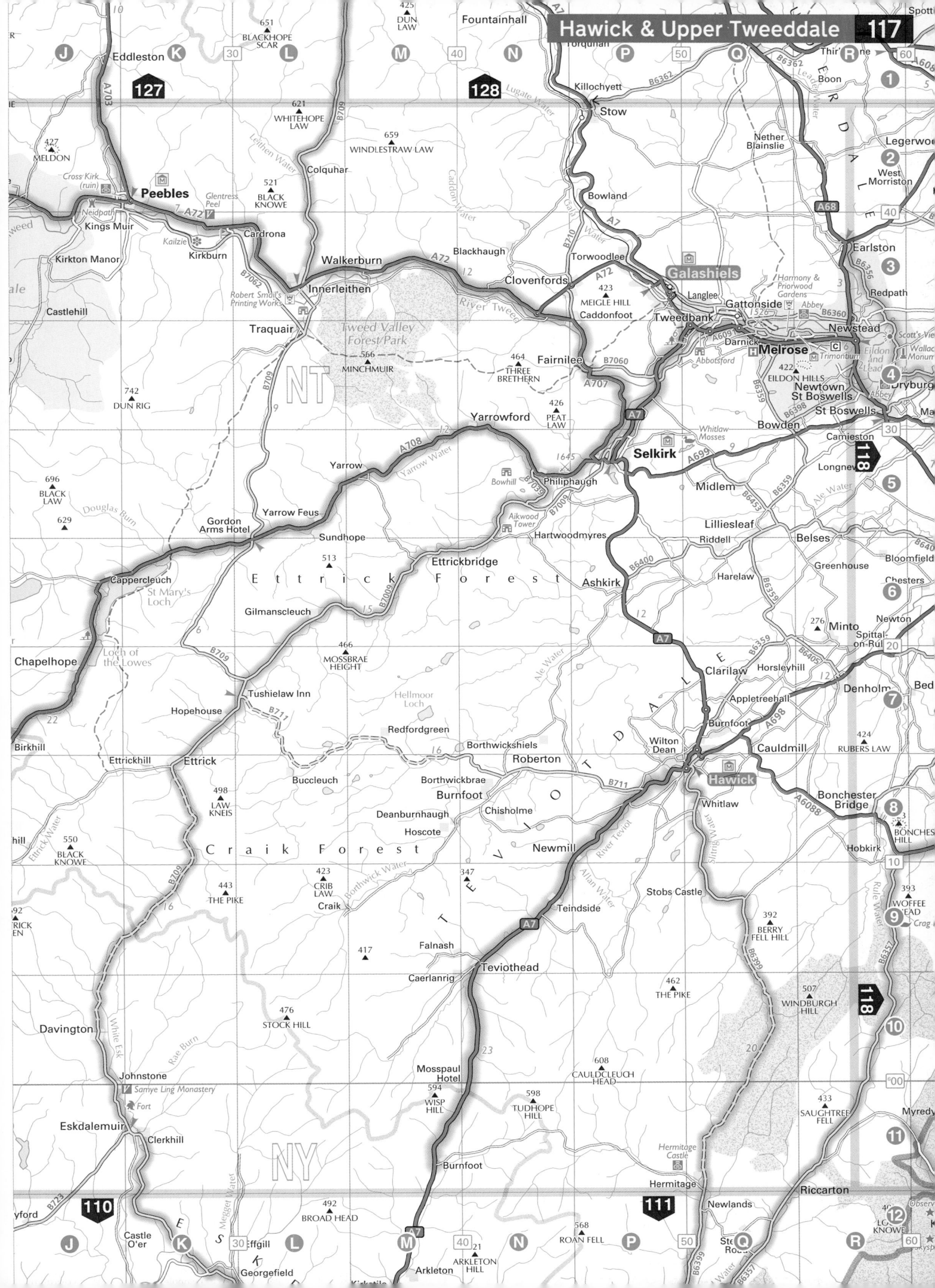

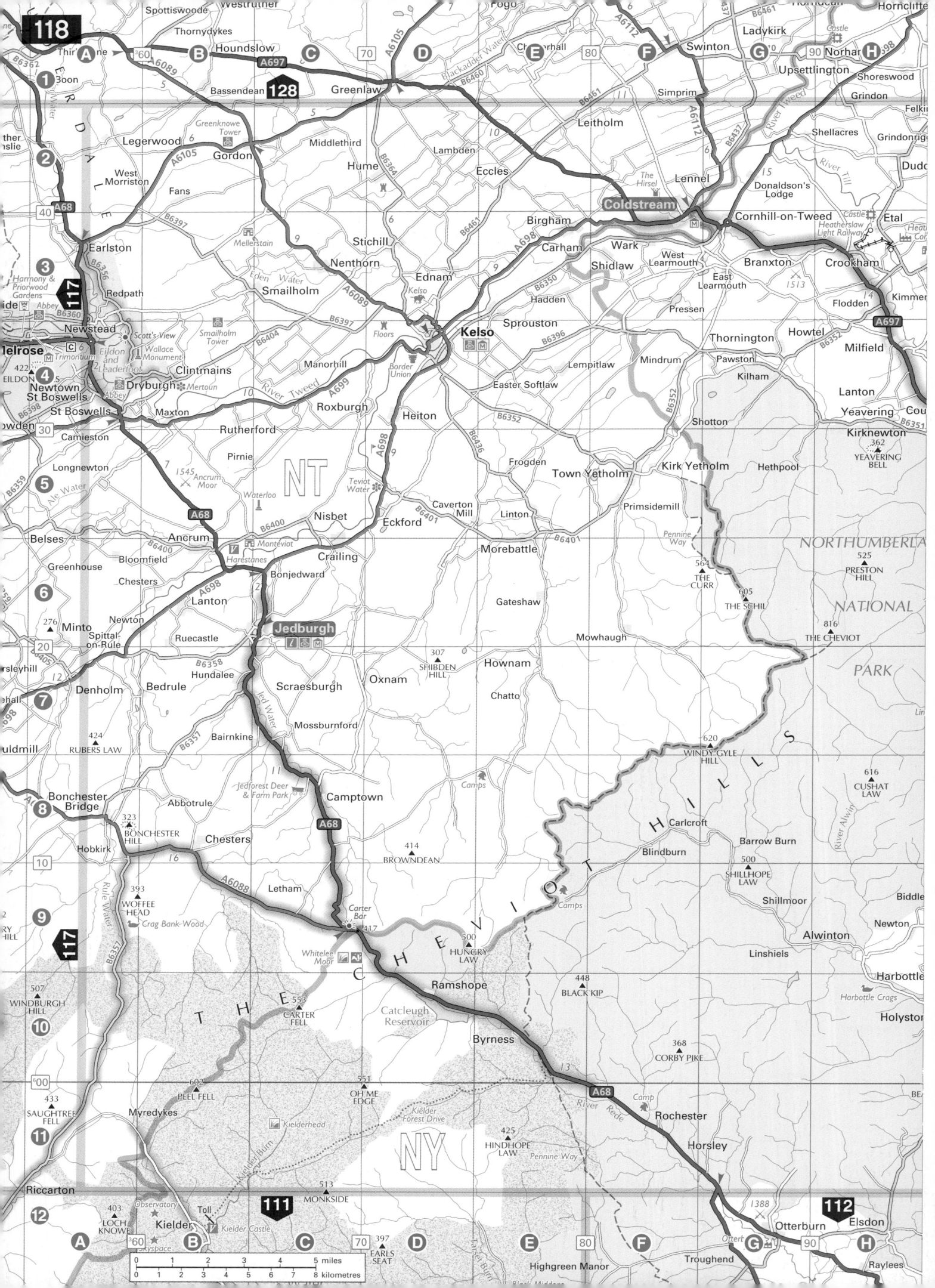

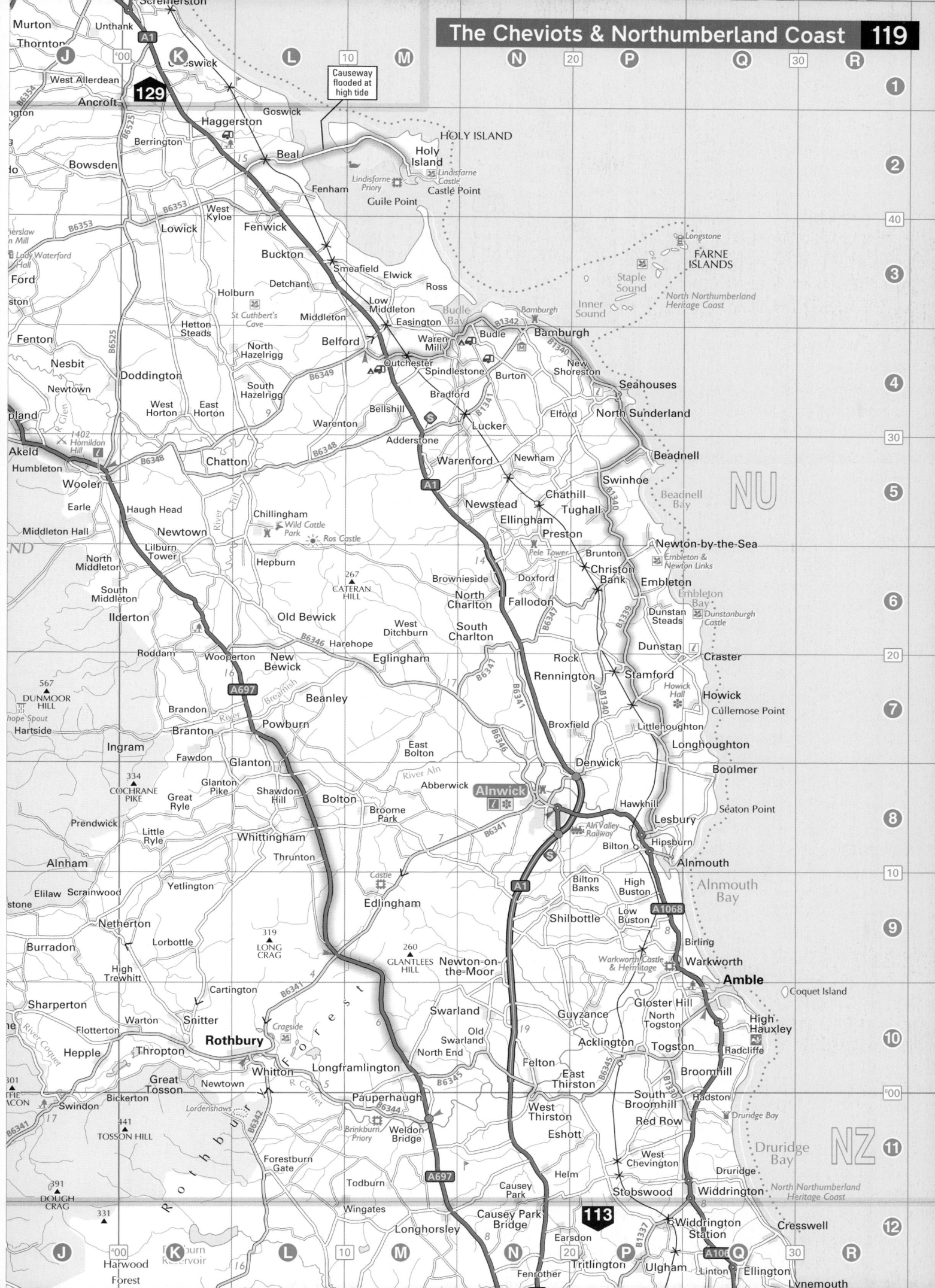

J K L M N P Q R

Murton
Thornton
West Allerdean
Ancroft
Berrington
Bowsden
Lowick
Fenton
Nesbit
Doddington
Newtown
Wooler
Humbleton
Akeld
Earle
Haugh Head
Newtown
Middleton Hall
Lilburn Tower
North Middleton
South Middleton
Ilderton
Roddam
Prendwick
Netherton
Alnham
Burradon
High Trewhitt
Sharperton
Hepple
Thropton
Rothbury
Great Tosson
Whitton
Bickerton
Swindon

Scremerston
Unthank
Keswick
Haggerston
Goswick
Beal
Fenham
West Kyloe
Fenwick
Buckton
Detchant
Holburn
Hetton Steads
Middleton
North Hazelrigg
Belford
South Hazelrigg
Warenton
Bellshill
Adderstone
Chatton
Chillingham
Wild Cattle Park
Ros Castle
Hepburn
CATERAN HILL
Old Bewick
West Ditchburn
Harehope
Eglingham
New Bewick
Wooperton
Beanley
Powburn
Branton
Ingram
Fawdon
Glanton
Glanton Pike
Shawdon Hill
Bolton
Whittingham
Thrunton
Yetlington
Little Ryle
Great Ryle
Brandon
COCHRANE PIKE
Lorbottle
LONG CRAG
Cartington
Snitter
Warton
Flotterton
Longframlington
Newtown
Pauperhaugh
Weldon Bridge
Forestburn Gate
Todburn
Wingates
Longhorsley

HOLY ISLAND
Holy Island
Lindisfarne Priory
Guile Point
Castle Point
Lindisfarne Castle
Elwick
Ross
Low Middleton
Easington
Bamburgh
Waren Mill
Budle
Outchester
Spindlestone
Burton
Bradford
Lucker
Warenford
Newham
Newstead
Ellingham
Chathill
Tughall
Preston
Pele Tower
Brownieside
Doxford
North Charlton
Fallodon
South Charlton
Rock
Rennington
Broxfield
Littlehoughton
Longhoughton
Denwick
Abberwick
Alnwick
Hawkhill
Lesbury
Aln Valley Railway
Bilton
Hipsburn
Alnmouth
Bilton Banks
High Buston
Low Buston
Shilbottle
Newton-on-the-Moor
Swarland
Old Swarland
North End
Guyzance
Acklington
Felton
East Thirston
West Thirston
Eshott
Helm
Causey Park
Causey Park Bridge
Earsdon
Tritlington
Fenrother

FARNE ISLANDS
Longstone
Staple Sound
Inner Sound
North Northumberland Heritage Coast
New Shoreston
Seahouses
North Sunderland
Elford
Beadnell
Swinhoe
Beadnell Bay
NU
Newton-by-the-Sea
Embleton & Newton Links
Christon Bank
Embleton
Embleton Bay
Dunstan Steads
Dunstanburgh Castle
Dunstan
Craster
Stamford
Howick Hall
Howick
Cullernose Point
Boulmer
Seaton Point
Birling
Warkworth Castle & Hermitage
Warkworth
Amble
Coquet Island
Gloster Hill
North Togston
Togston
High Hauxley
Radcliffe
Broomhill
South Broomhill
Red Row
Hadston
West Chevington
Druridge
Druridge Bay
Stobswood
Widdrington
Widdrington Station
Cresswell
North Northumberland Heritage Coast
NZ
Ulgham
Linton
Ellington
Lynemouth

A1
129
113
A697
A1068
A1

J K L M N P Q R

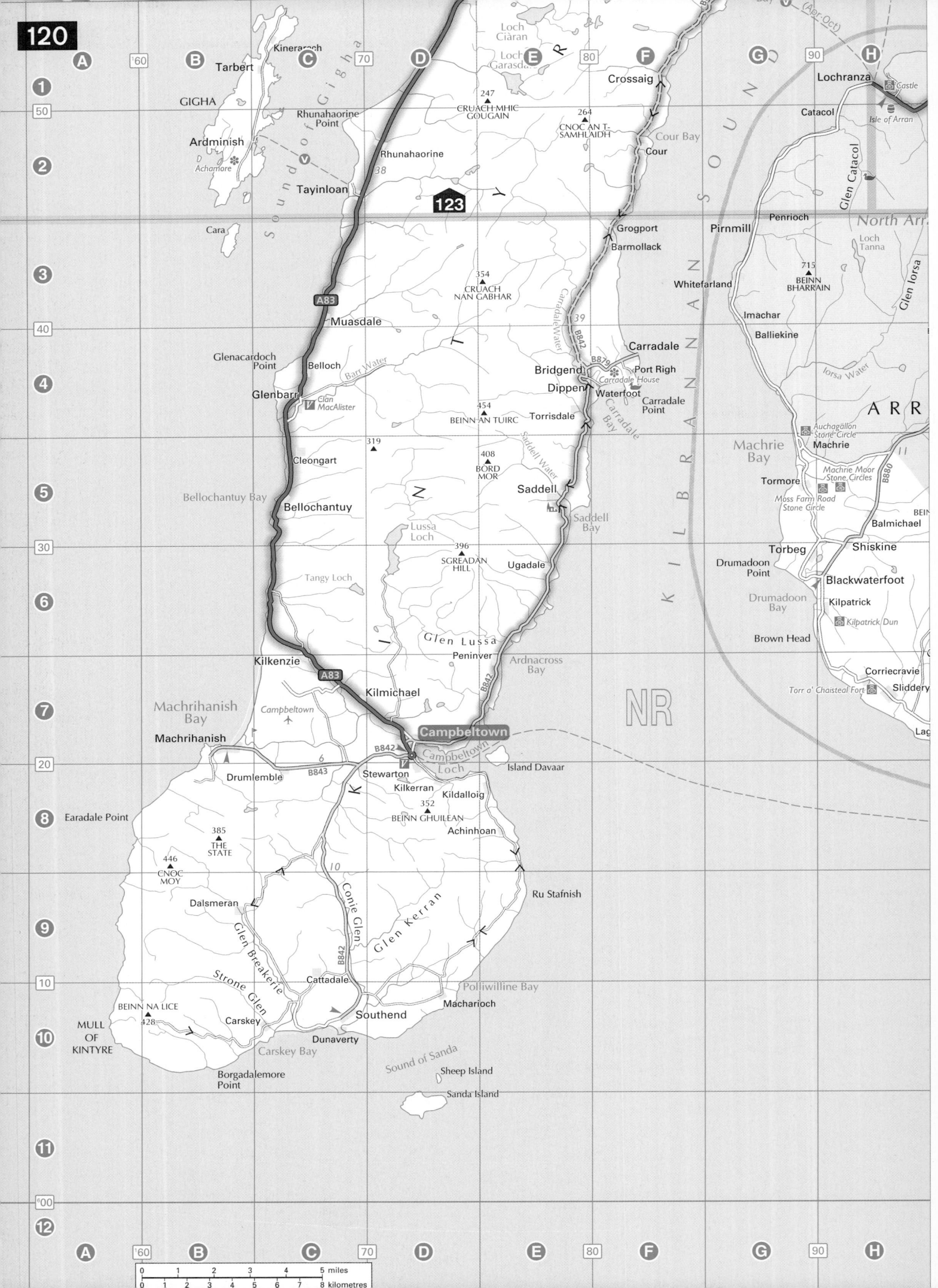

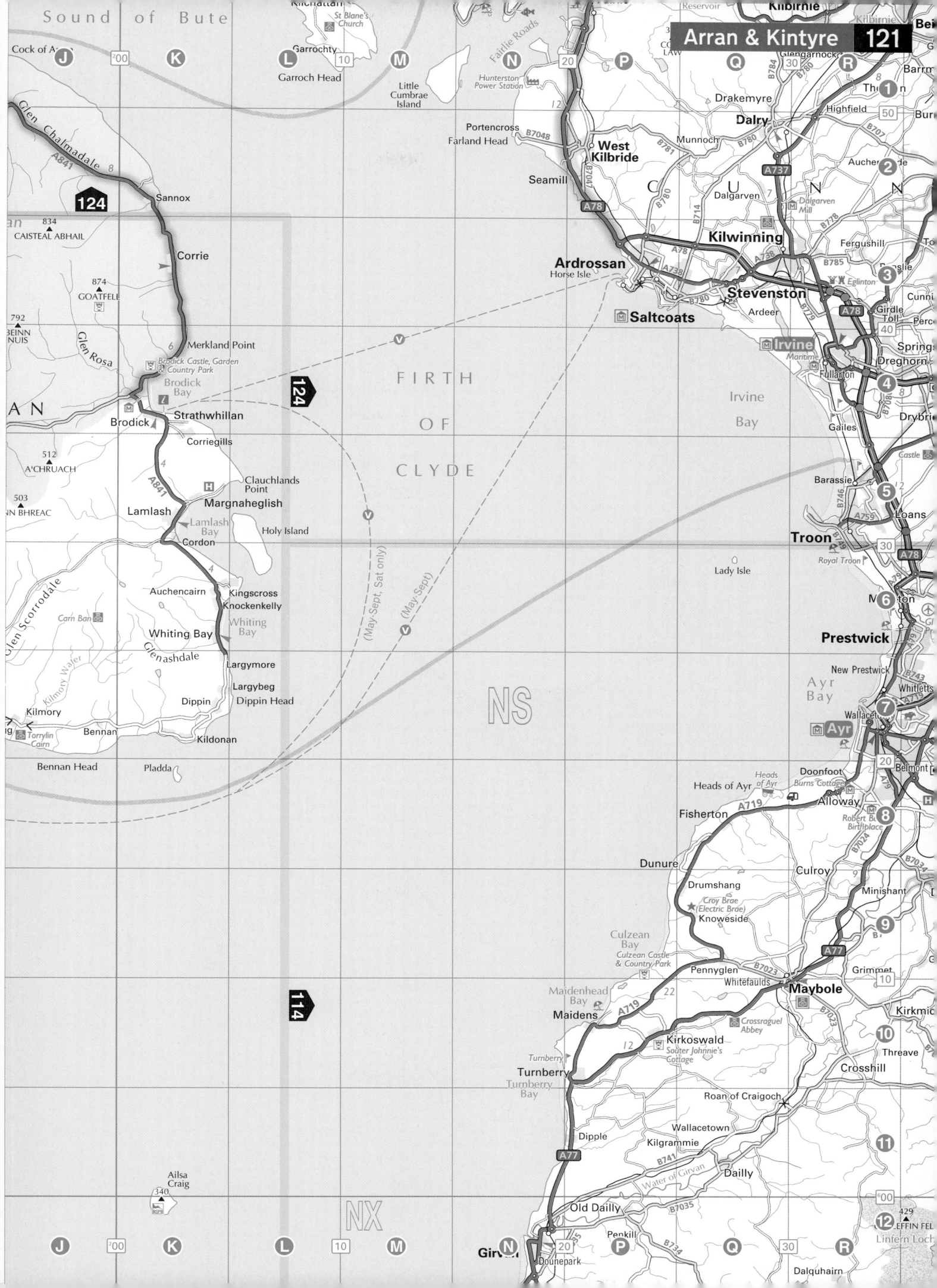

Sound of Bute

Kilbirnie

Kilchattan
St Blane's Church

Garrochty
Garroch Head

Little Cumbrae Island

Fairlie Roads

Hunterston Power Station

Reservoir
Glengarnock

Kilbirnie

Drakemyre
Highfield

Dalry

Barrm

Aucher

Portencross
Farland Head

West Kilbride

Munnoch

Dalgarven
Dalgarven Mill

Seamill

CUNN

Kilwinning

Fergushill

Roslie

Ardrossan
Horse Isle

Stevenston
Ardeer

Eglinton

Cunni
Perc

Saltcoats

Girdle Toll

Irvine
Maritime

Spring
Dreghorn

Cock of A

Glen Chalmadale
A841

124

Sannox

Corrie

834
CAISTEAL ABHAIL

874
GOATFELL

Merkland Point
Brodick Castle, Garden & Country Park

FIRTH OF CLYDE

Irvine Bay

Fullarton

Gailes

792
BEINN NUIS

Glen Rosa

6

Brodick Bay

124

AN

Brodick

Strathwhillan

Corriegills

Barassie

Castle

Drybri

512
A'CHRUACH

A841

Clauchlands Point

Margnaheglish

Troon

Royal Troon

Loans

503
NN BHREAC

Lamlash

Lamlash Bay

Holy Island

A759

Cordon

Glen Scorrodale

4

Auchencairn

Kingscross
Knockenkelly

Lady Isle

Prestwick

Carn Ban

Whiting Bay

Whiting Bay

New Prestwick

Ayr Bay

Glenashdale

Largymore

Kilmory Water

Largybeg
Dippin Head

(May-Sept, Sat only)

(May-Sept)

NS

Whitletts

Wallace

Kilmory

Dippin

Ayr

Torrylin Cairn

Bennan

Kildonan

Bennan Head

Pladda

Belmont

Doonfoot
Burns Cottage

Heads of Ayr
Heads of Ayr

Alloway
Robert B
Birthplace

A719

Fisherton

Dunure

Culroy

Drumshang
Croy Brae
(Electric Brae)
Knoweside

Minishant

114

Culzean Bay
Culzean Castle & Country Park

Pennyglen

Whitefaulds

Grimmet

Maidenhead Bay

A719

Maidens

12

Crossraguel Abbey

Maybole

Kirkmic

Kirkswald
Souter Johnnie's Cottage

Threave

Crosshill

Turnberry

Ailsa Craig

340

Turnberry
Turnberry Bay

Roan of Craigoch

Dipple

Wallacetown
Kilgrammie

Dailly

A77

B741
Water of Girvan

NX

Old Dailly

Penkill

Dounepark

Girvan

Dalquhairn

EFFIN FEL
Linfern Loch

429

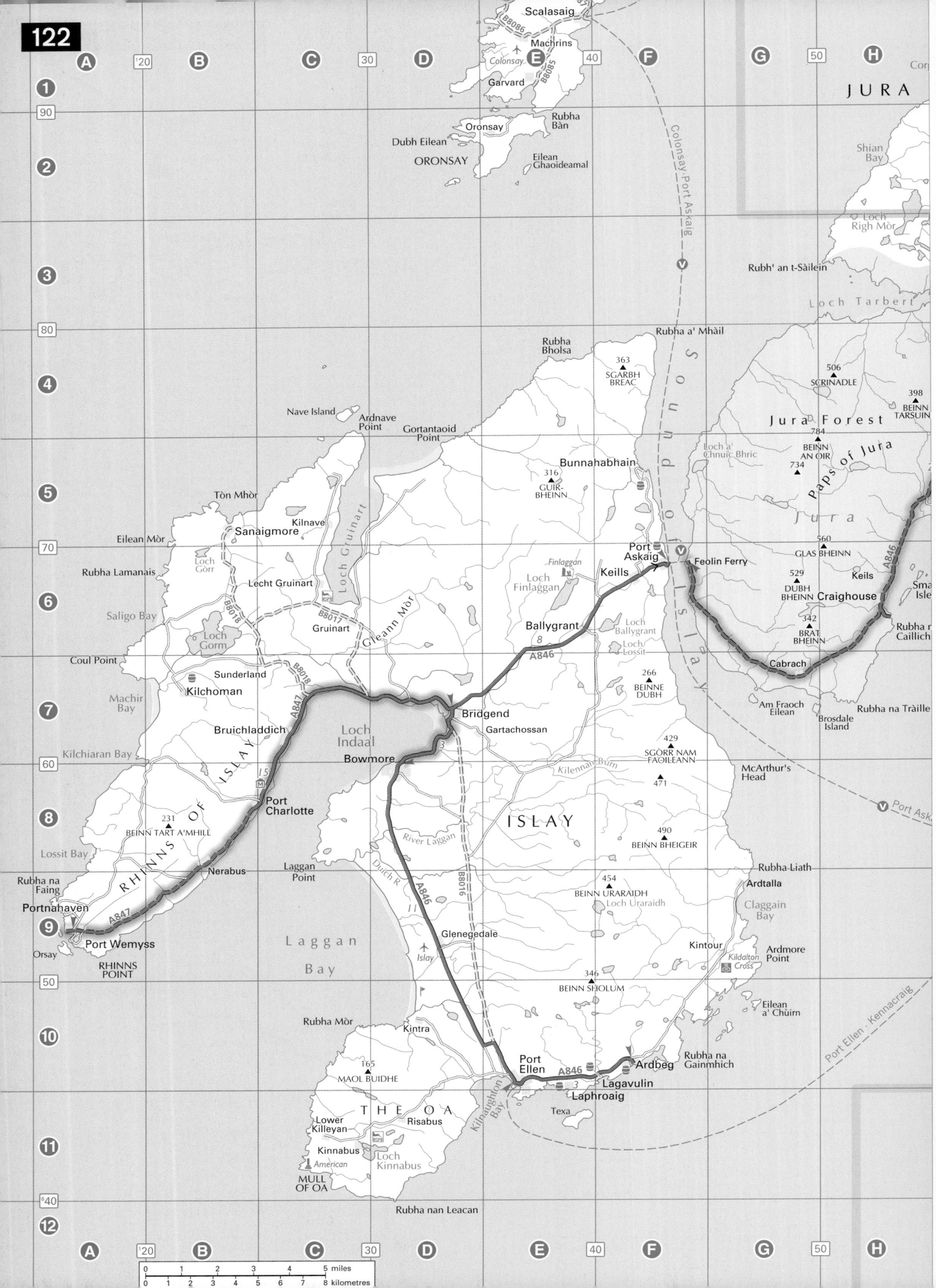

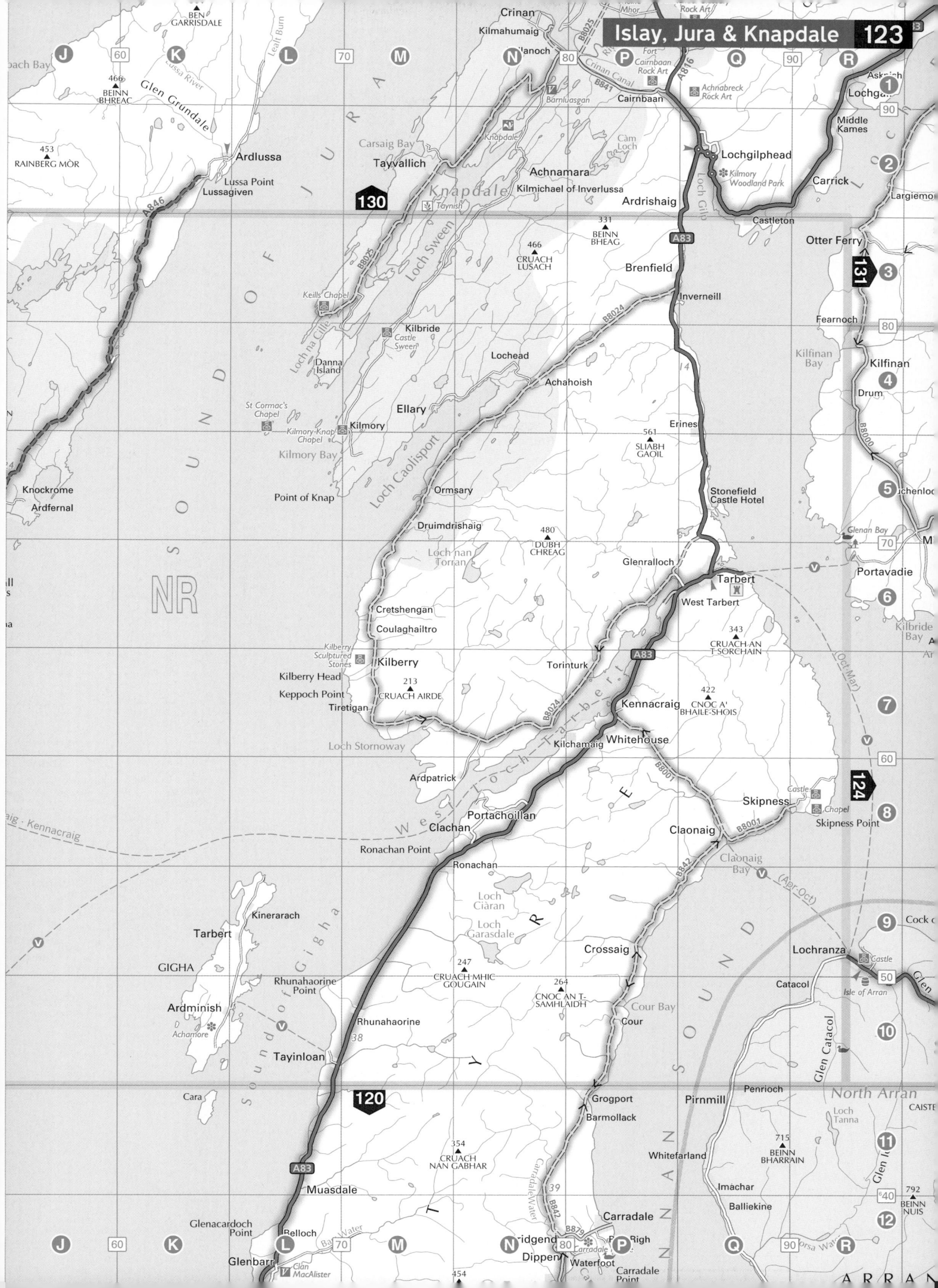

BEN GARRISDALE

Crinan

Kilmahumaig

Bellanoch

Fort Cairnbaan Rock Art

Cairnbaan

Achnabreck Rock Art

Askaig

Lochga...

Middle Kames

Loch

Carrick

Largiemo...

Lochgilphead

Kilmory Woodland Park

60

466 BEINN BHREAC

J

K

L

M

N

P

Q

R

1

2

70

Lussa River

Lealt Burn

Glen Grundale

453 RAINBERG MÒR

Ardlussa

Lussa Point Lussagiven

Carsaig Bay

Tayvallich

Knapdale

130

Achnamara

Kilmichael of Inverlussa

Ardrishaig

Castleton

Otter Ferry

3

131

331 BEINN BHEAG

Brenfield

A83

Inverneill

Fearnoch

80

S O U N D   O F   J U R A

B8025

Knapdale

Càm Loch

Taynish

466 CRUACH LUSACH

A846

Keills Chapel

Kilbride

Castle Sween

Lochead

Achahoish

Erines

Kilfinan Bay

Kilfinan

Drum

4

Loch na Cille

Danna Island

Ellary

Loch Sween

561 SLIABH GAOIL

B8000

Loch Caolisport

St Cormac's Chapel

Kilmory-Knap Chapel

Kilmory

Kilmory Bay

Ormsary

Stonefield Castle Hotel

5

chenlo...

NR

Point of Knap

Druimdrishaig

480 DUBH CHREAG

Glenralloch

Tarbert

West Tarbert

Glenan Bay

70

M

Portavadie

6

Loch nan Torran

Cretshengan

Coulaghailtro

Kilberry Sculptured Stones

Kilberry

213 CRUACH AIRDE

Torinturk

A83

343 CRUACH AN T-SORCHAIN

Kilbride Bay

Ar...

7

Kilberry Head

Keppoch Point

Tiretigan

Kennacraig

422 CNOC A' BHAILE-SHOIS

60

Loch Stornoway

Kilchamaig

Whitehouse

Castle

8

Ardpatrick

B8024

B8001

Skipness

Chapel

Skipness Point

124

g · Kennacraig

Portachoillan

Clachan

Claonaig

Claonaig Bay

(Apr-Oct)

Ronachan Point

Ronachan

B842

9

Cock o...

Kinerarach

Loch Ciaran

Loch Garasdale

Crossaig

Lochranza

Castle

Glen...

Tarbert

GIGHA

247 CRUACH MHIC GOUGAIN

264 CNOC AN T-SAMHLAIDH

Cour Bay

Catacol

50

10

Rhunahaorine Point

Cour

Isle of Arran

Ardminish

Achamore

Rhunahaorine

38

Glen Catacol

Loch Tanna

715 BEINN BHARRAIN

North Arran

792 BEINN NUIS

11

Tayinloan

Cara

120

Grogport

Barmollack

Pirnmill

Whitefarland

Imáchar

Balliekine

A83

354 CRUACH NAN GABHAR

B842

Carradale Water

39

Carradale

40

12

Muasdale

Glenacardoch Point

Belloch

Clan MacAlister

Glenbarr

454

B879

Bridgend

Dippen

Waterfoot

Carradale Point

Carradale R...

A R R A N

J

K

L

M

N

P

Q

R

60

70

80

90

SOUND of GIGHA

West Loch Tarbert

Kilgbride Bay

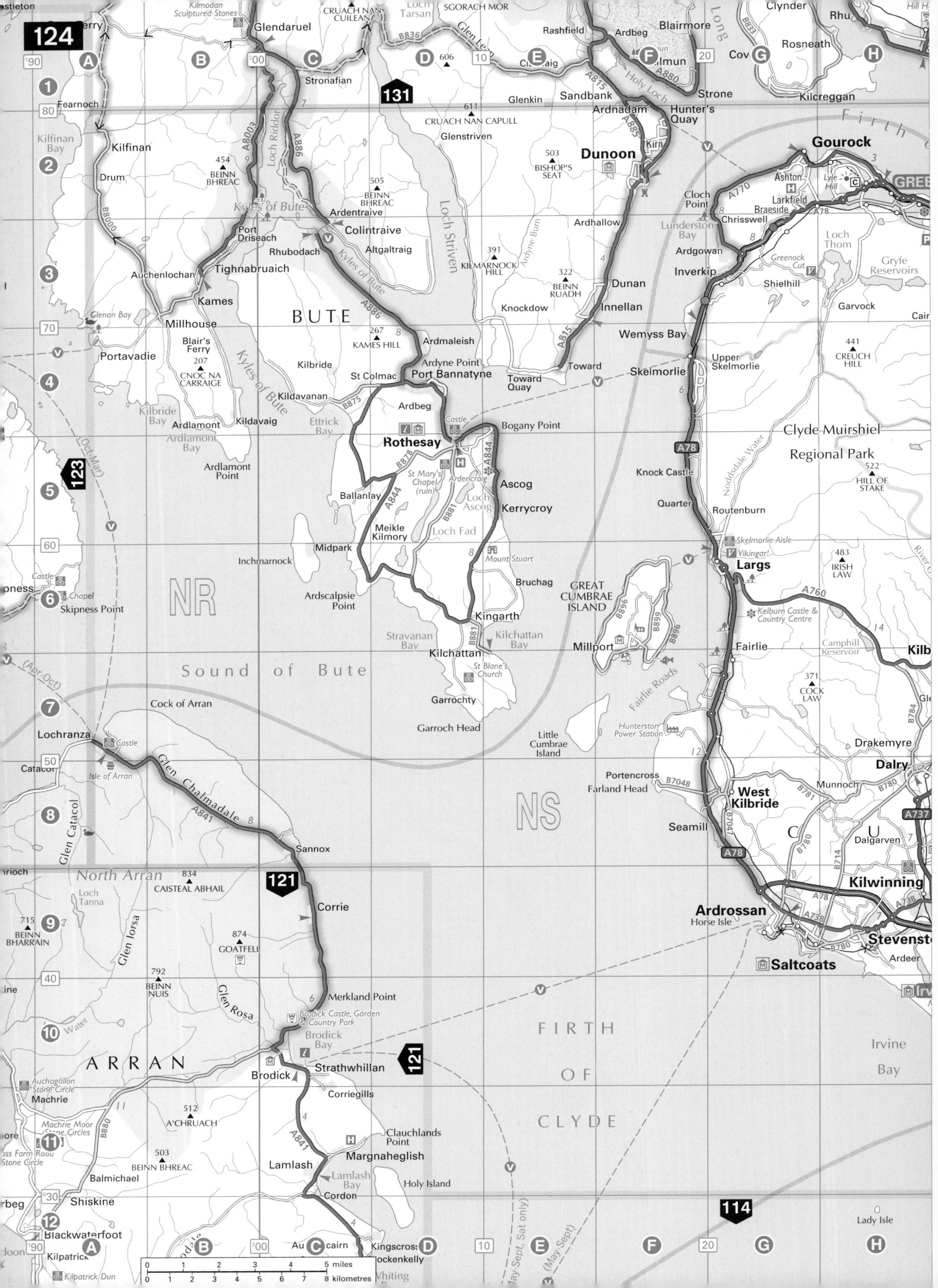

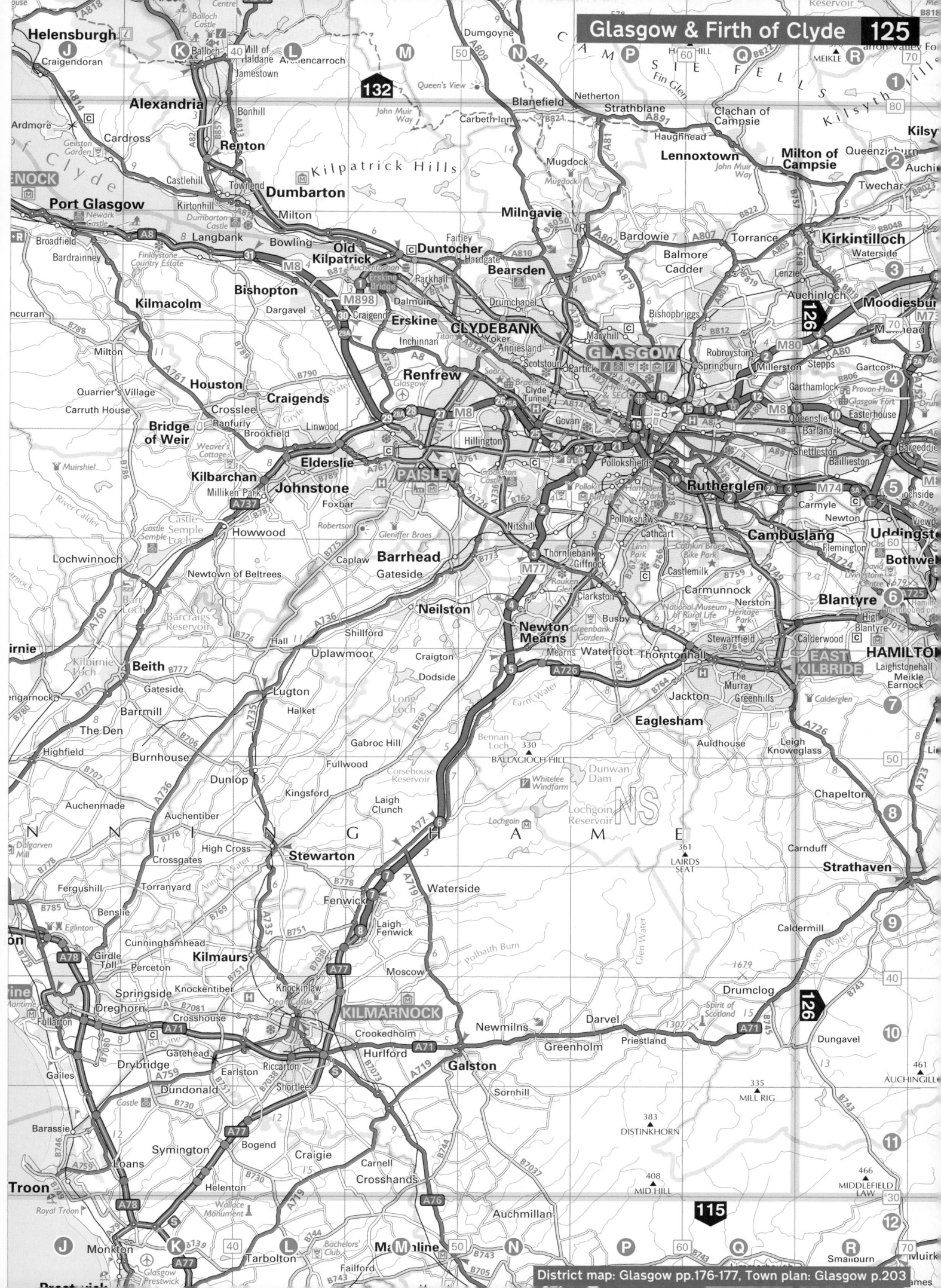

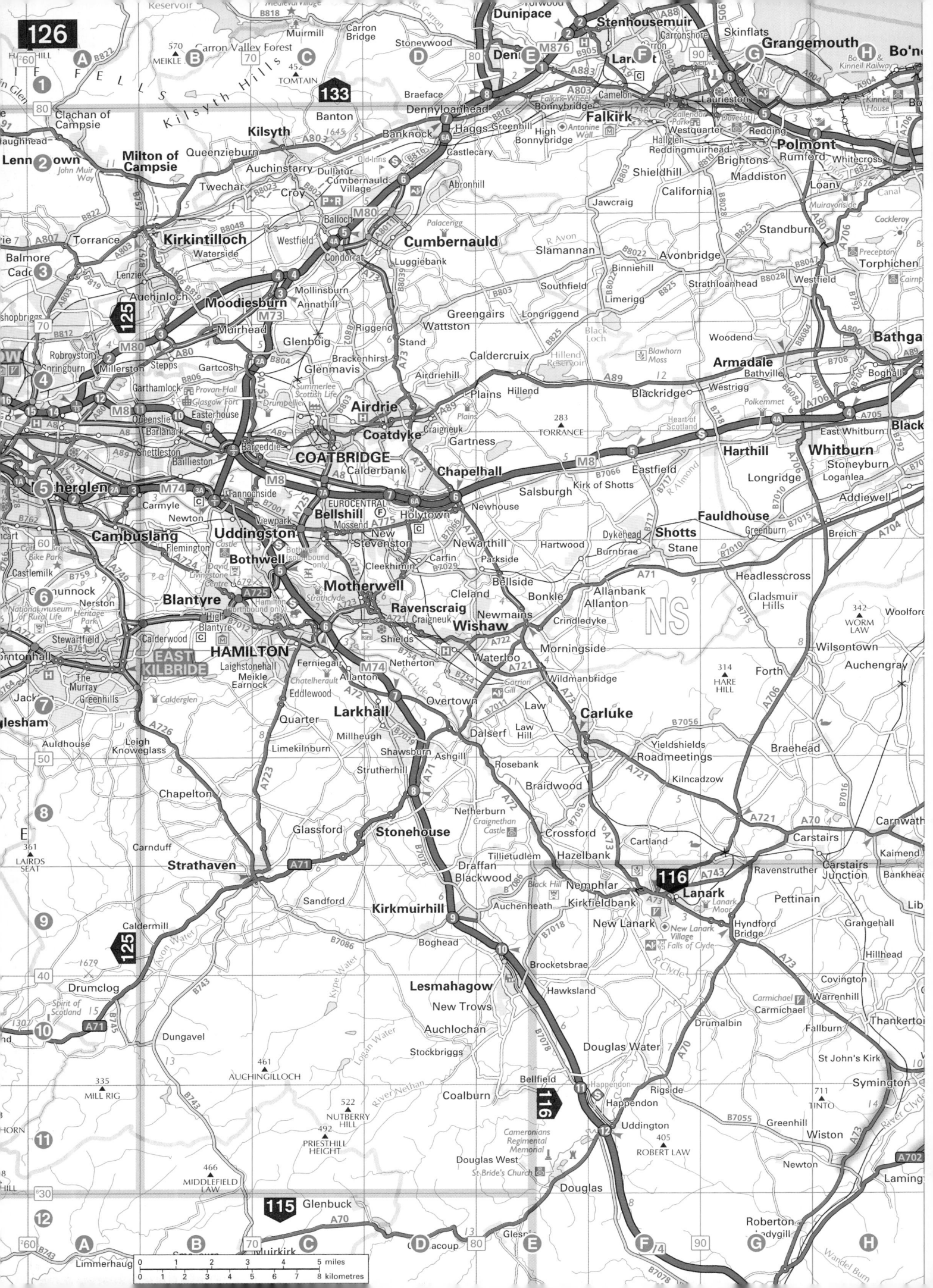

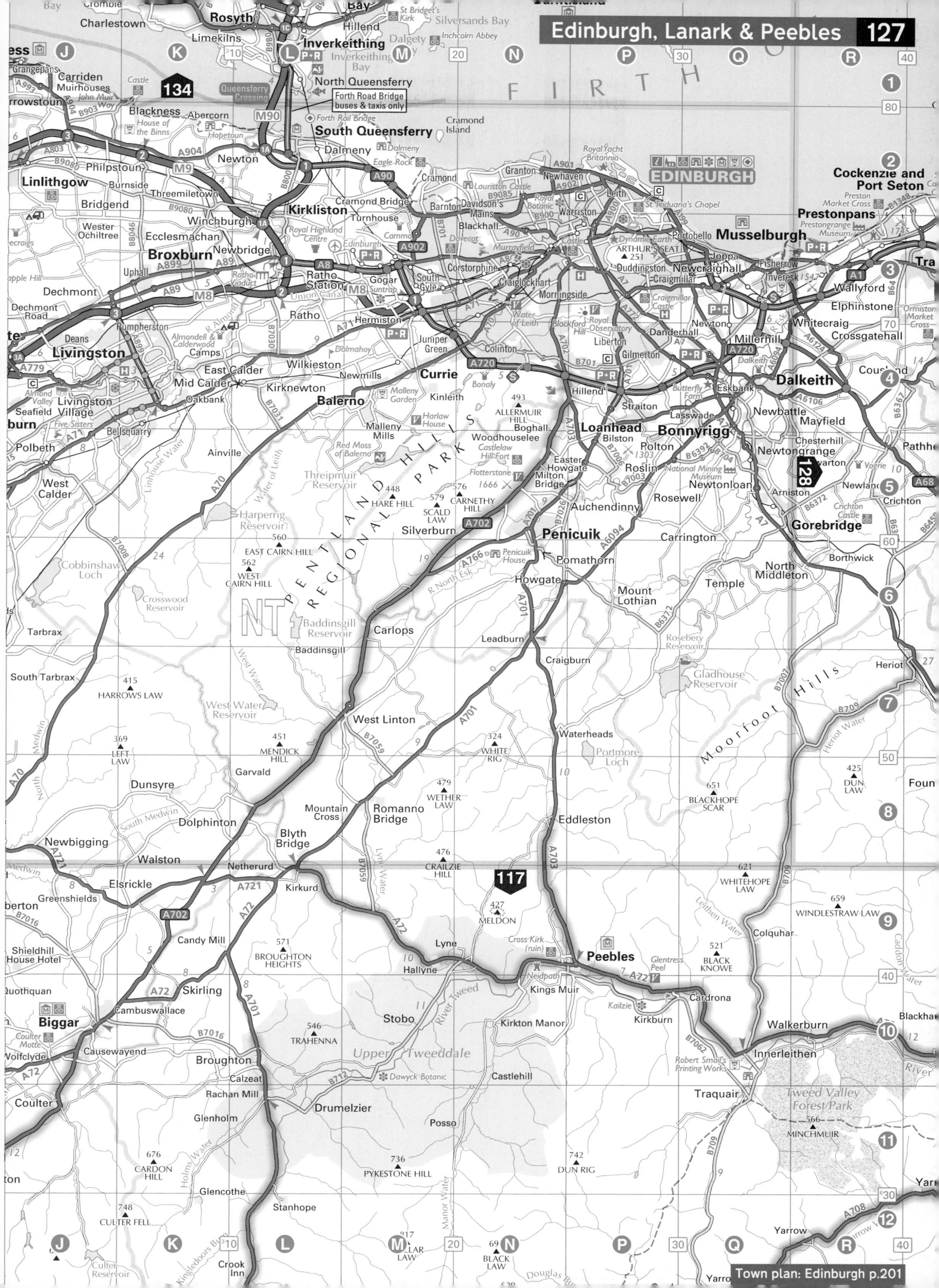

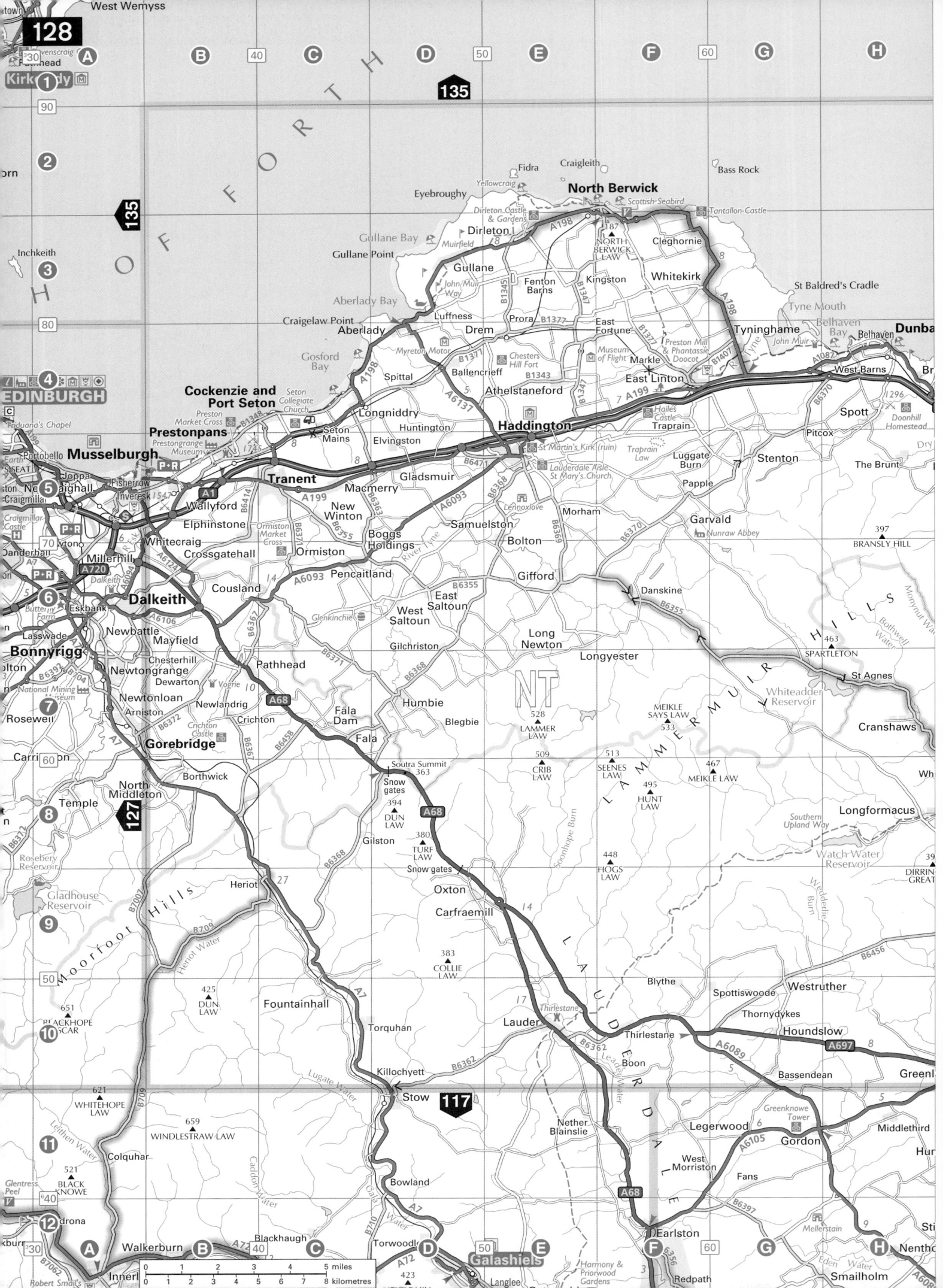

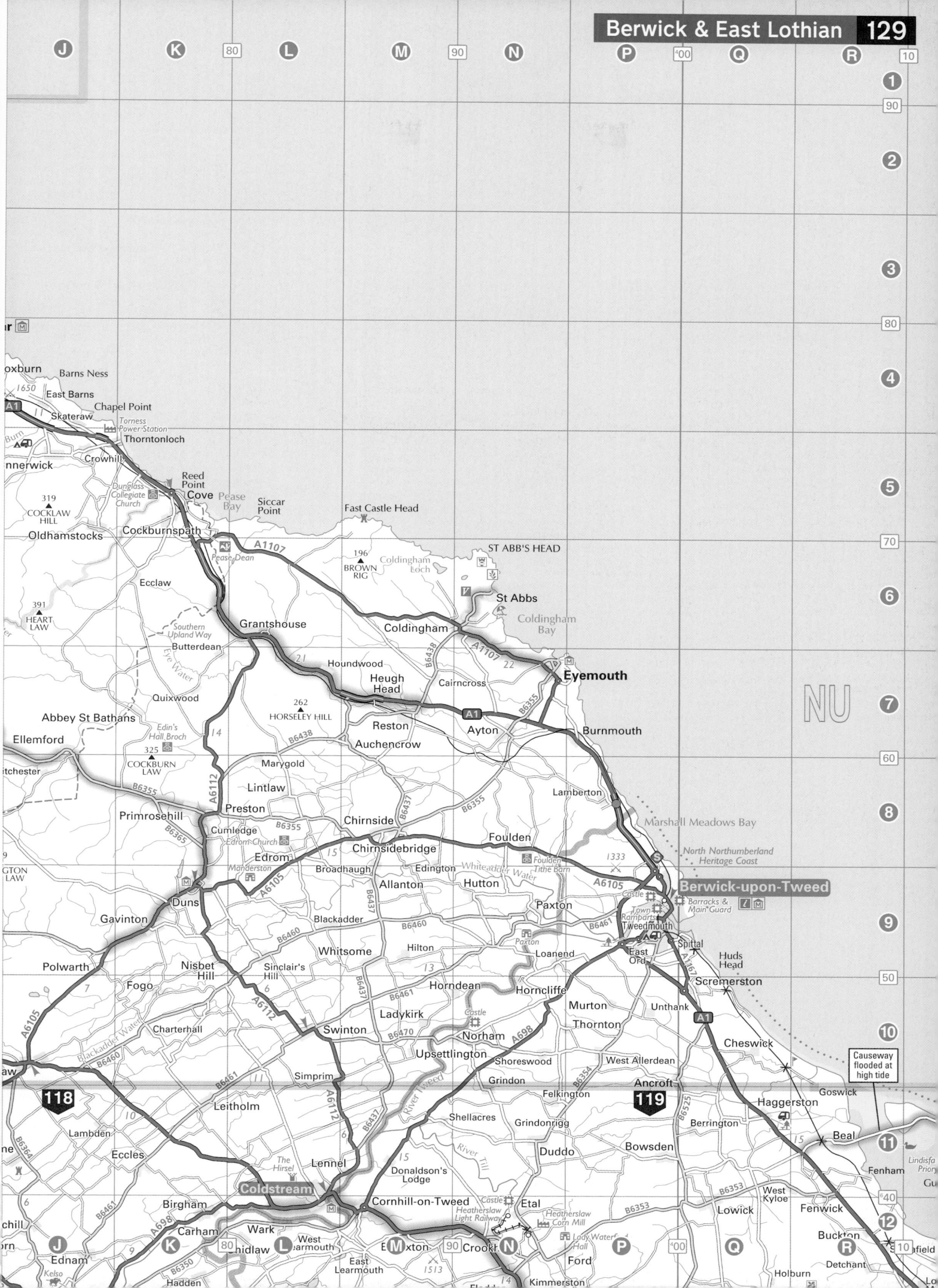

J K 80 L M 90 N P '00 Q R 10

1
90
2
3
80
4
70
5
6
70
6
60
7
NU 7
60
8
8
50
9
9
50
10
10
118
119
11
11
40
12
12
10

oxburn
Barns Ness
East Barns
Chapel Point
1650
A1
Skateraw
Torness
Power Station
Thorntonloch
nnerwick
Crowhill
319
COCKLAW
HILL
Oldhamstocks
Reed
Point
Cove
Pease
Bay
Siccar
Point
Fast Castle Head
Dunglass
Collegiate
Church
Cockburnspath
A1107
Pease Dean
196
BROWN
RIG
Coldingham
Loch
ST ABB'S HEAD
Ecclaw
391
HEART
LAW
Grantshouse
St Abbs
Southern
Upland Way
Butterdean
Coldingham
Coldingham
Bay
Lye Water
Quixwood
Houndwood
Heugh
Head
A1107
22
Eyemouth
Abbey St Bathans
Edin's
Hall Broch
262
HORSELEY HILL
Cairncross
21
Ellemford
14
Reston
A1
Burnmouth
itchester
325
COCKBURN
LAW
B6438
Auchencrow
Ayton
B6355
GTON
LAW
Marygold
Lamberton
Lintlaw
B6112
Primrosehill
Preston
Chirnside
Foulden
Marshall Meadows Bay
B6365
Cumledge
Edrom Church
B6355
B6437
B6355
Foulden
Tithe Barn
1333
North Northumberland
Heritage Coast
Edrom
Chirnsidebridge
15
Broadhaugh
Edington
Whiteadder Water
S
Duns
Manderston
A6105
Allanton
Hutton
A6105
Berwick-upon-Tweed
Gavinton
Castle
Town
Ramparts
Barracks &
Main Guard
Blackadder
Paxton
B6461
Tweedmouth
Polwarth
Nisbet
Hill
B6460
Whitsome
Hilton
Paxton
Spittal
Huds
Head
Fogo
Sinclair's
Hill
13
Loanend
East
Ord
Scremerston
A1167
Charterhall
B6437
Horndean
Horncliffe
Murton
Unthank
A1
A6112
Ladykirk
Castle
Norham
Thornton
Cheswick
Swinton
B6470
A698
Blackadder Water
B6460
Upsettlington
Shoreswood
West Allerdean
Causeway
flooded at
high tide
B6461
Simprim
Grindon
Ancroft
Goswick
118
Leitholm
10
Felkington
119
Berrington
Haggerston
Lambden
Eccles
The
Hirsel
Lennel
15
Shellacres
Grindonrigg
Duddo
Bowsden
Beal
Lindisfa
Priory
B6364
6
Birgham
Donaldson's
Lodge
River Till
Gu
Coldstream
Cornhill-on-Tweed
Castle
Etal
Heatherslaw
Light Railway
Heatherslaw
Corn Mill
B6353
West
Kyloe
Lowick
Fenwick
chill
Ednam
Carham
Wark
nidlaw
West
earmouth
E Mxton
90
Crookh
Lady Water
Hall
Ford
Buckton
Detchant
Kelso
B6350
Hadden
East
Learmouth
Kimmerston
1513
Holburn
Lo
afield

J K 80 L M 90 N P '00 Q R 10

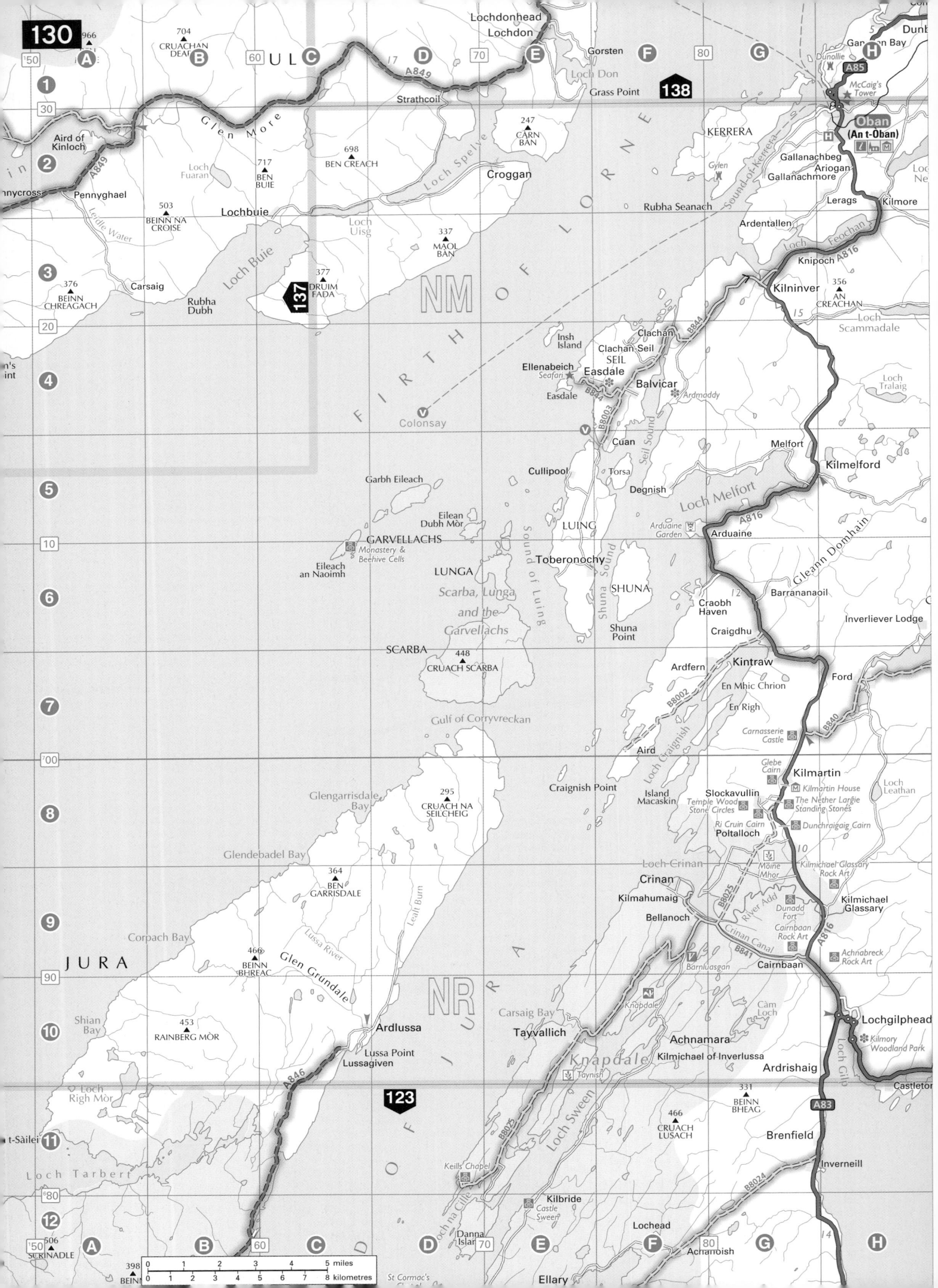

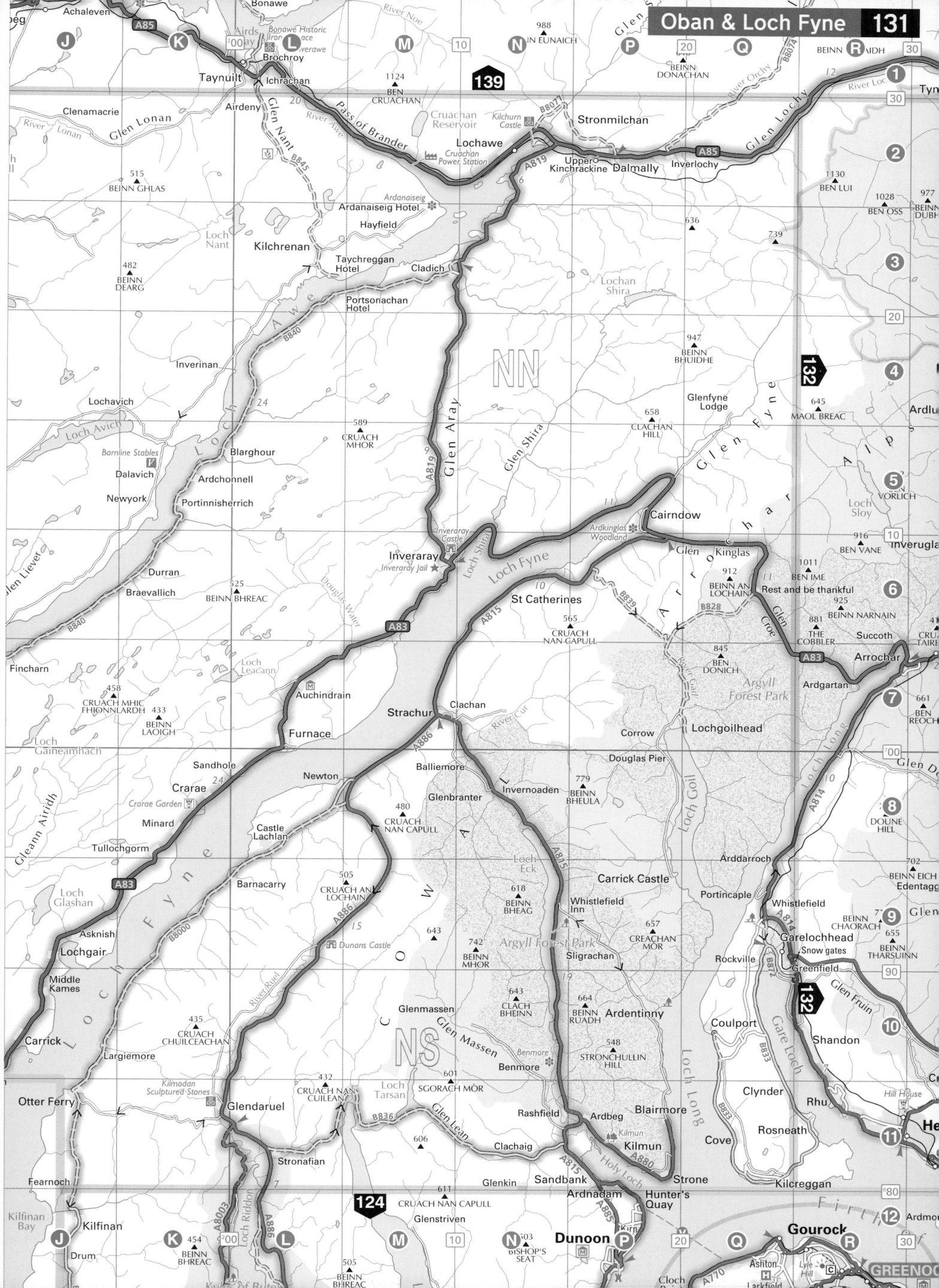

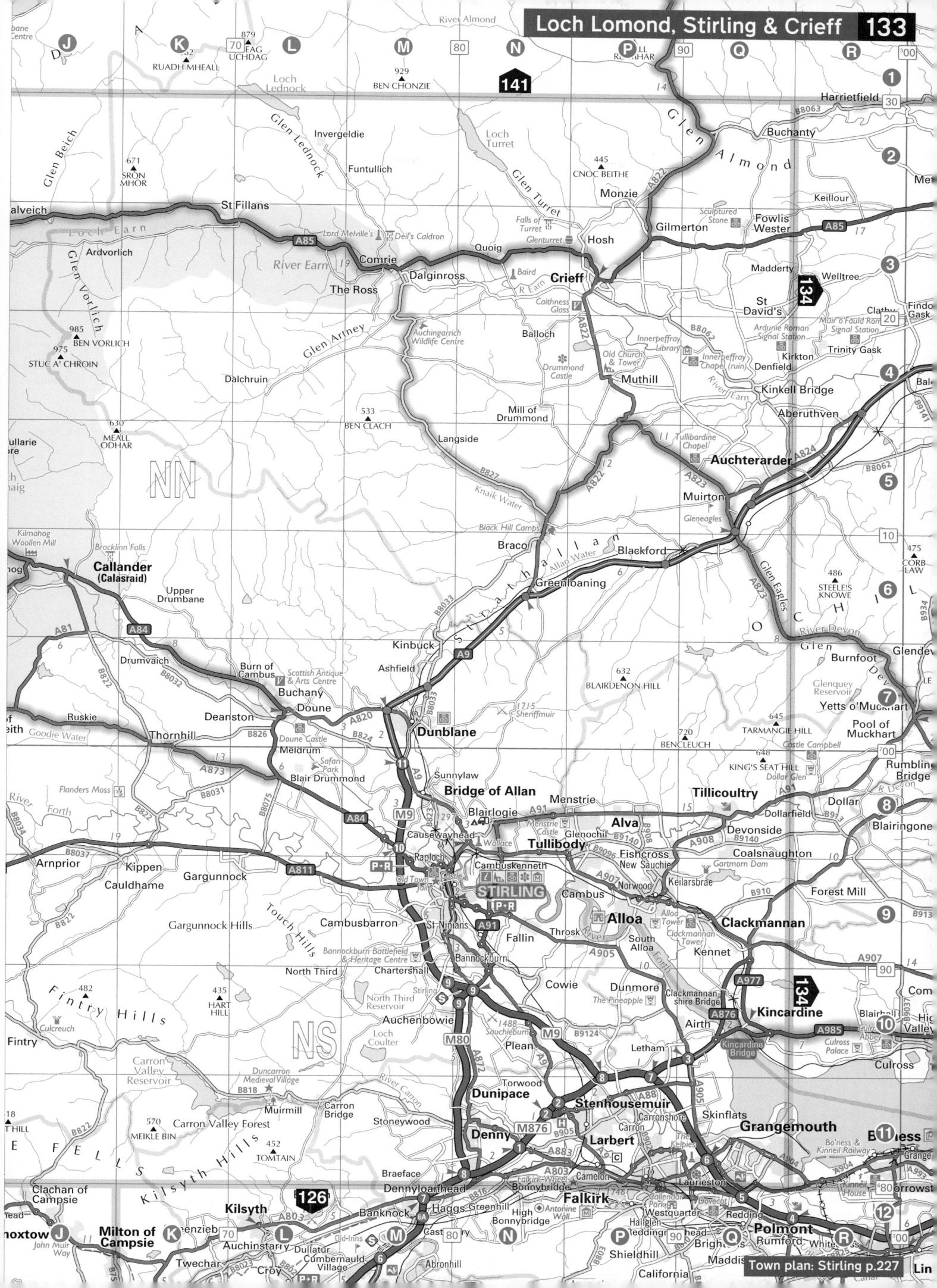

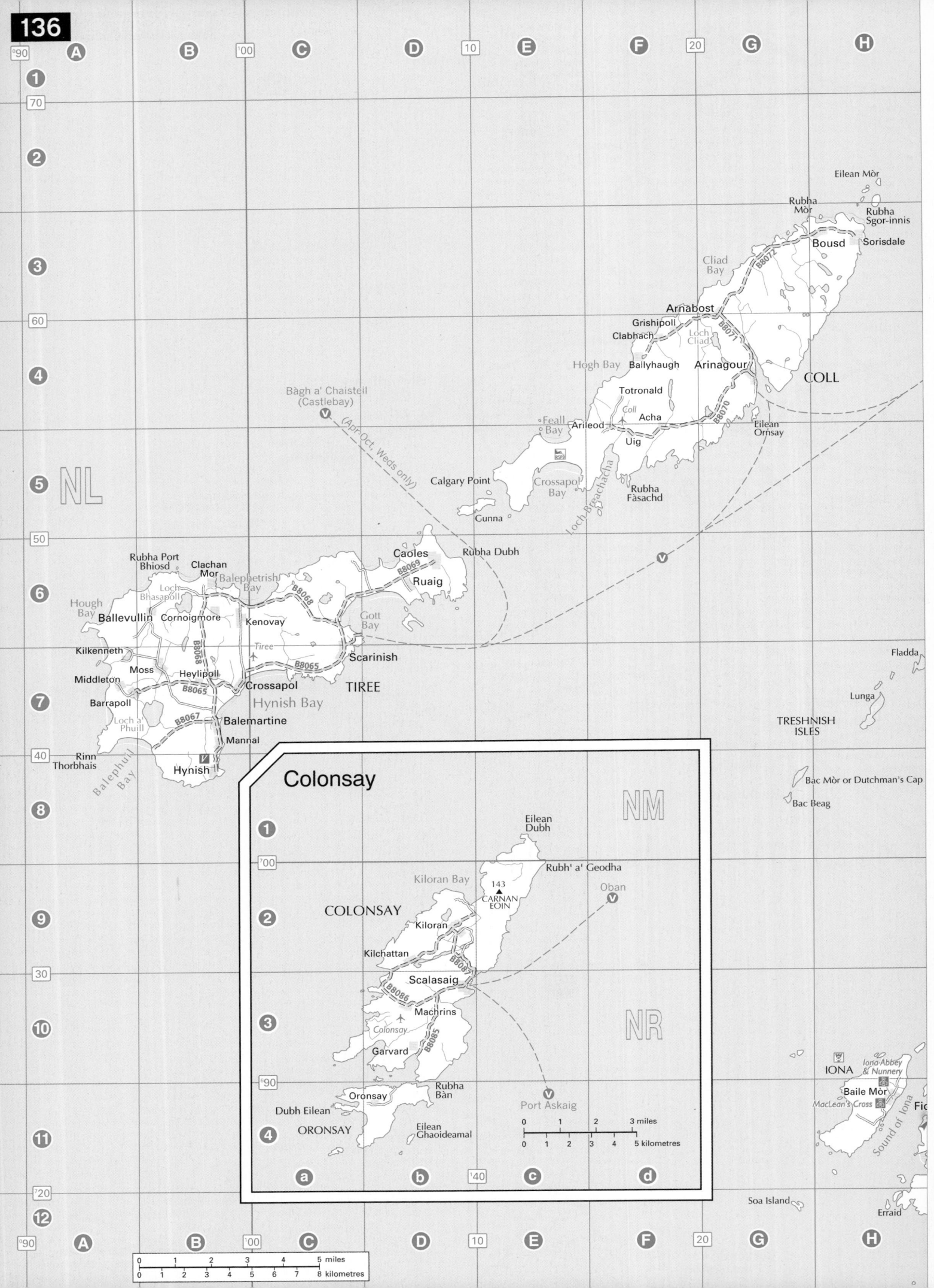

NL

COLL

Eilean Mòr
Rubha Mòr
Rubha Sgor-innis
Bousd
Sorisdale
B8072
Cliad Bay
Arnabost
Grishipoll
Clabhach
Loch Cliad
B8071
Hogh Bay
Ballyhaugh
Arinagour
B8070
Bàgh a' Chaisteil
(Castlebay)
Totronald
Coll
Acha
Feall Bay
Arileod
Uig
Eilean Ornsay
(Apr-Oct Weds only)
Calgary Point
Crossapol Bay
Loch Breachacha
Rubha Fàsachd
Gunna

Caoles
Rubha Dubh
B8069
Ruaig
Rubha Port Bhiosd
Clachan Mor
Balephetrish Bay
Loch Bhasapoll
B8068
Hough Bay
Ballevullin
Cornoigmore
Kenovay
Gott Bay
Tiree
B8068
Kilkenneth
Moss
Heylipoll
Scarinish
B8065
TIREE
Middleton
B8065
Crossapol
Barrapoll
Hynish Bay
Loch a' Phuill
B8067
Balemartine
Mannal
Rinn Thorbhais
Hynish
Balephuil Bay

Fladda

Lunga
TRESHNISH ISLES

Bac Mòr or Dutchman's Cap
Bac Beag

IONA
Iona Abbey & Nunrery
Baile Mòr
MacLean's Cross
Sound of Iona
Fi

Soa Island
Erraid

Colonsay

NM

Eilean Dubh
Kiloran Bay
143
CARNAN EOIN
Rubh' a' Geodha
Oban
COLONSAY
Kiloran
Kilchattan
B8087
Scalasaig
B8086
Machrins
NR
Colonsay
B8085
Garvard
'90
Oronsay
Rubha Bàn
Port Askaig
Dubh Eilean
Eilean Ghaoideamal
ORONSAY

0   1   2   3 miles
0   1   2   3   4   5 kilometres

0   1   2   3   4   5 miles
0   1   2   3   4   5   6   7   8 kilometres

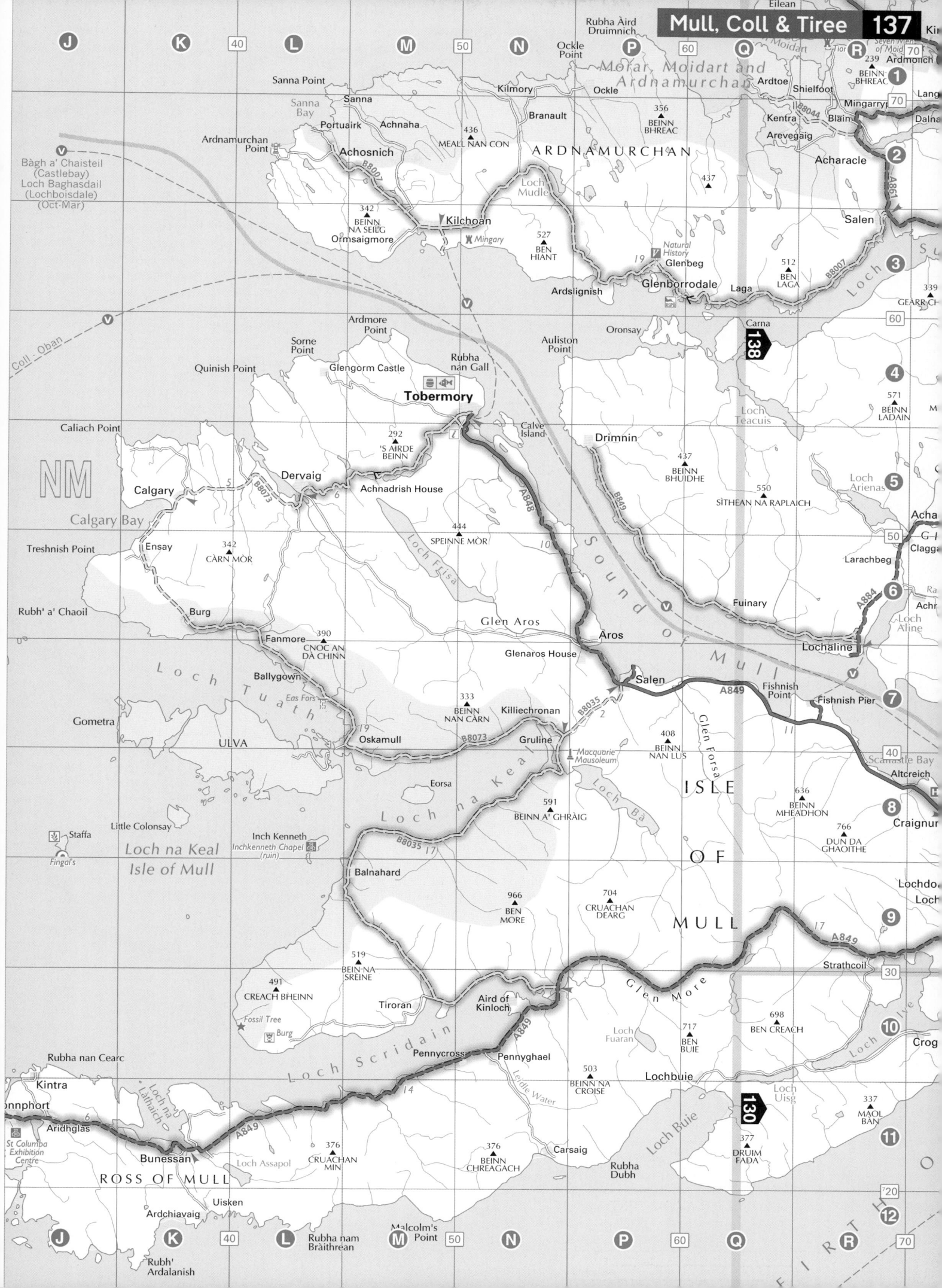

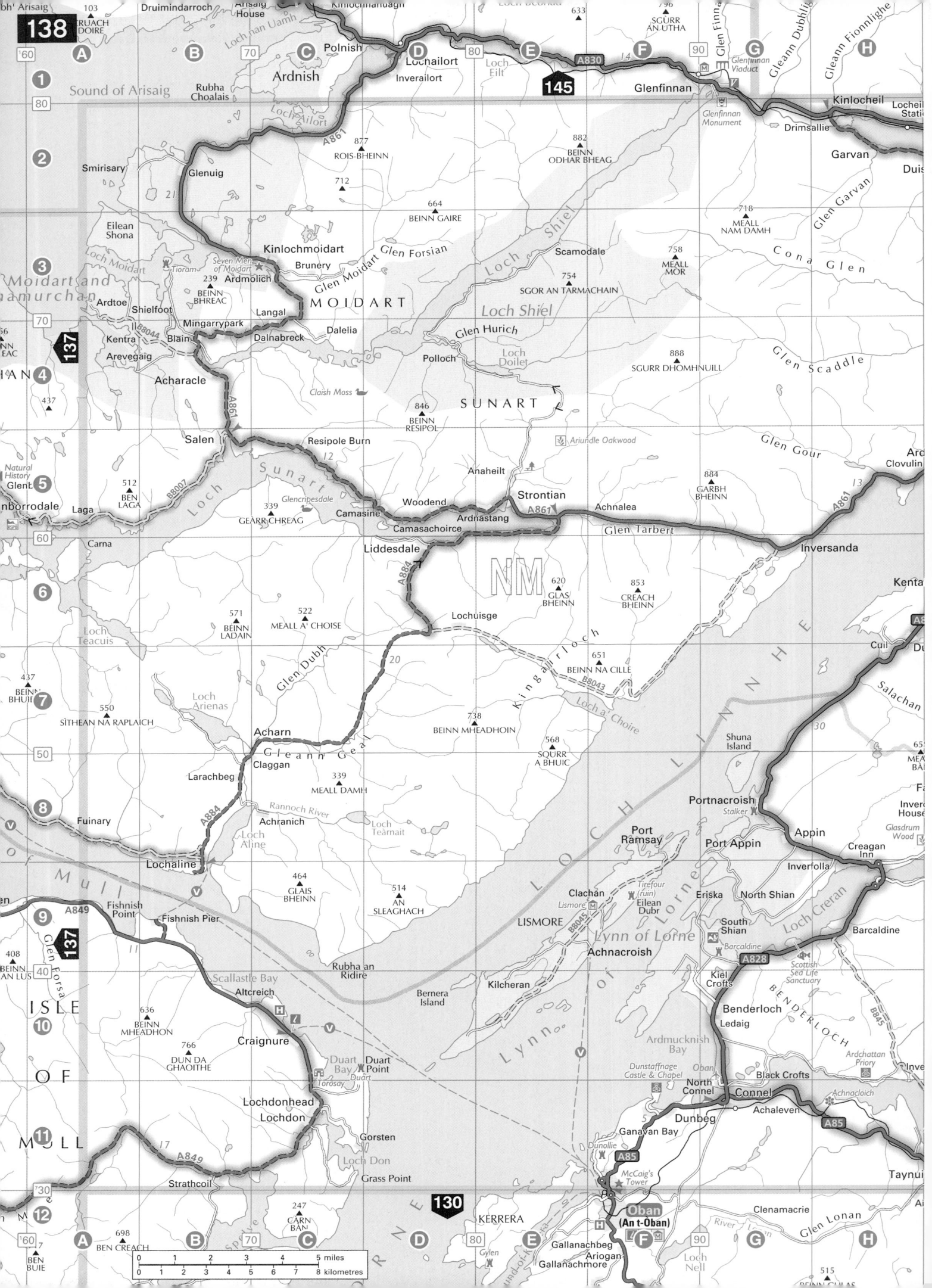

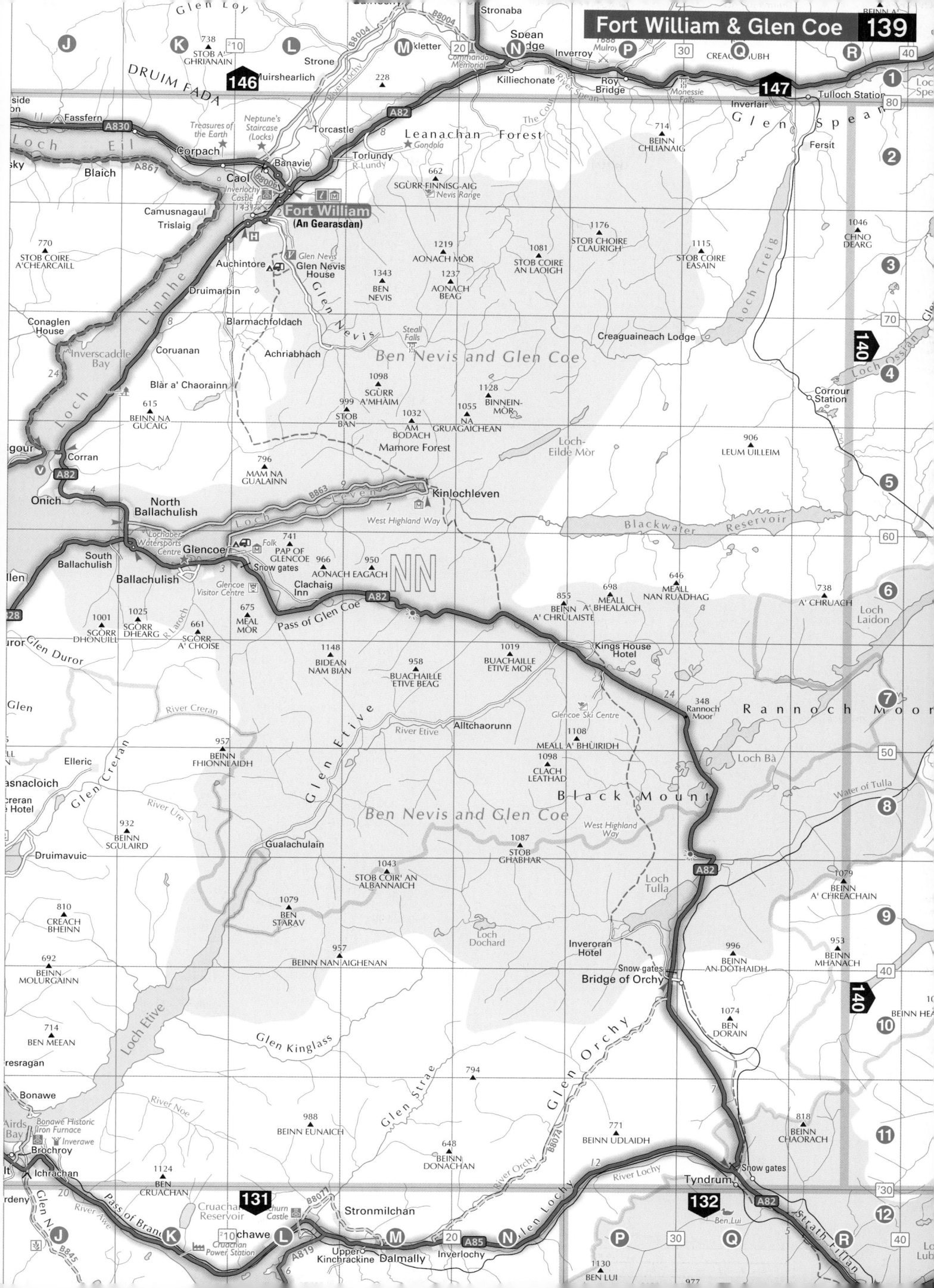

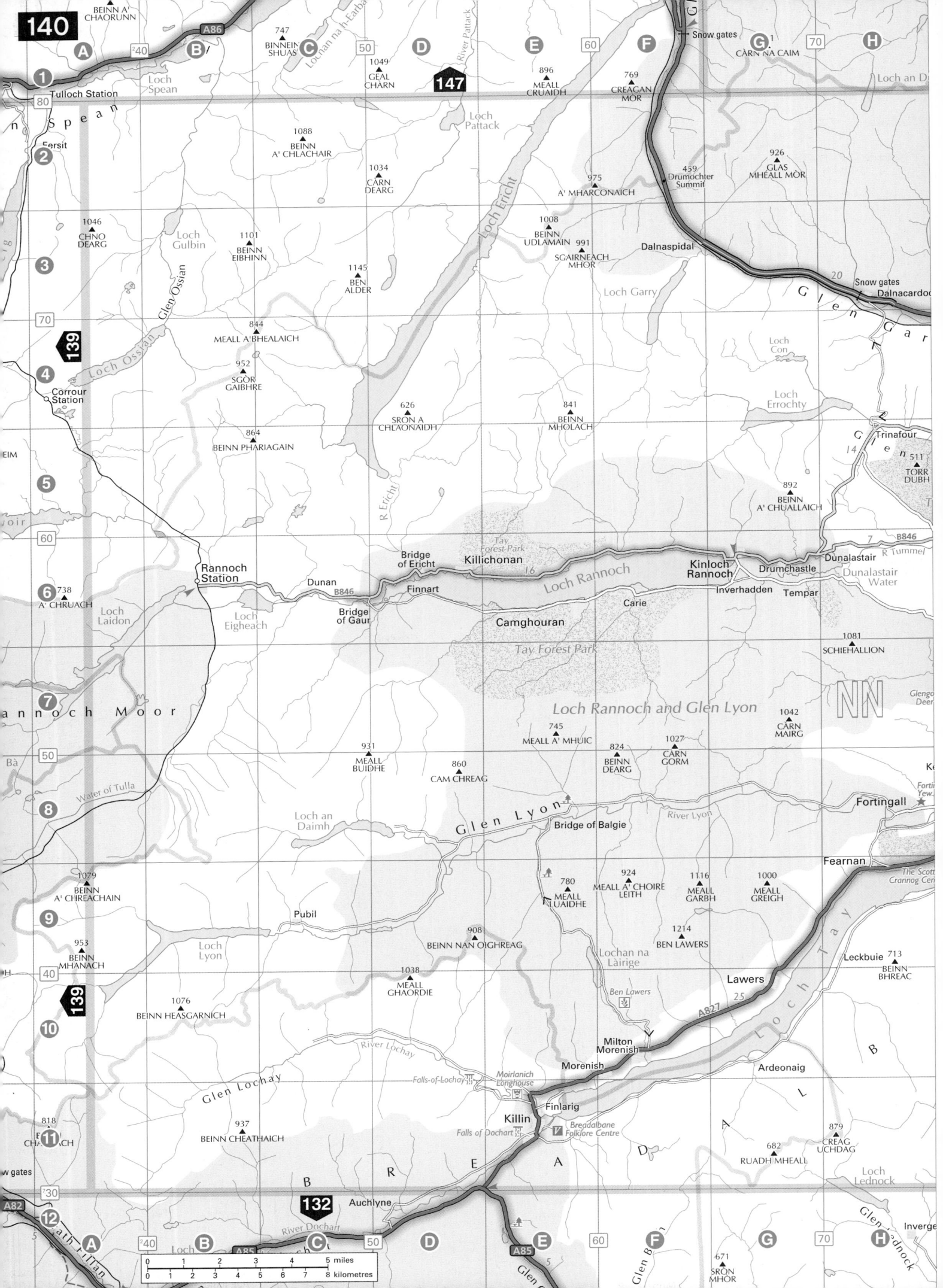

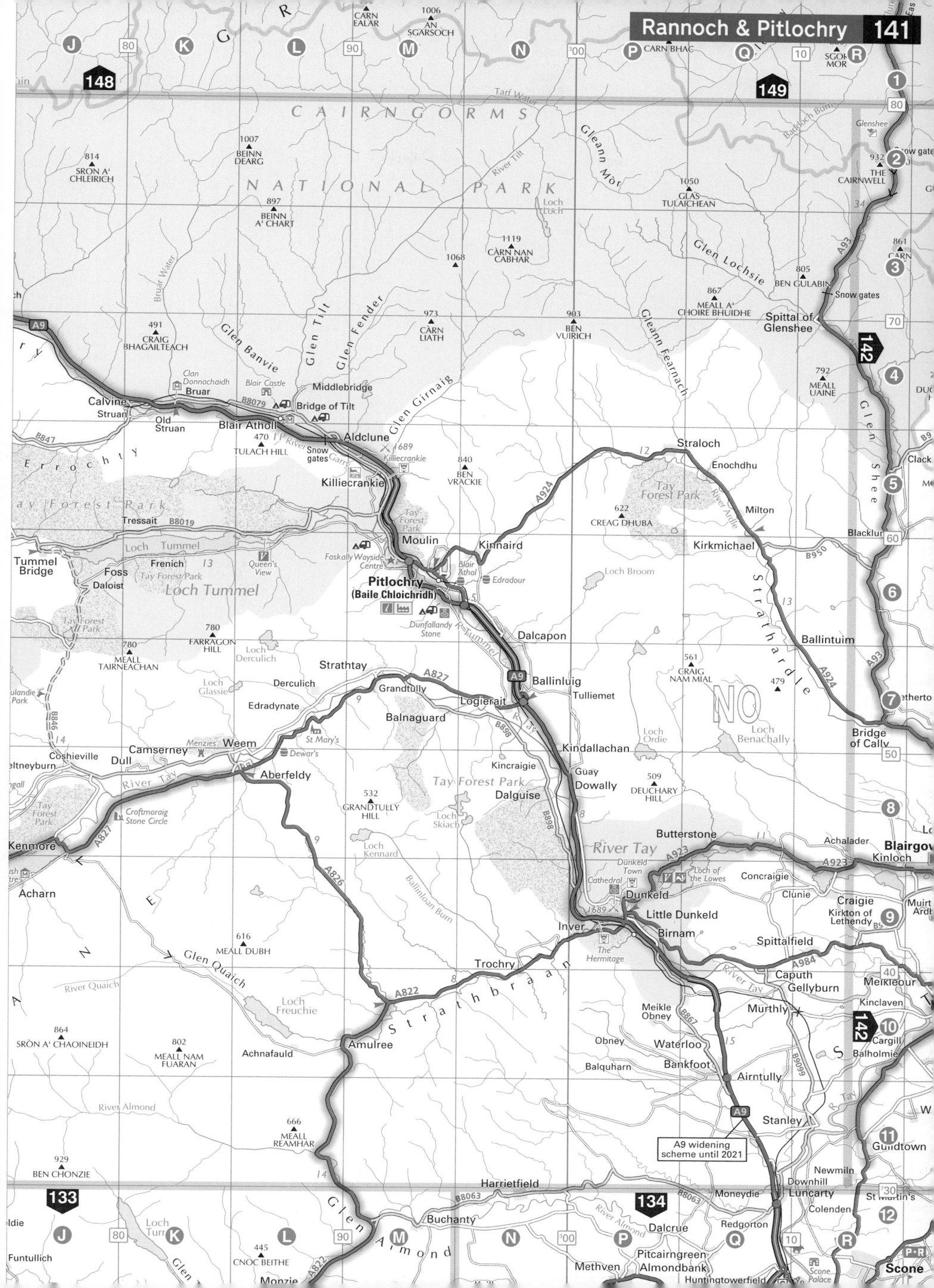

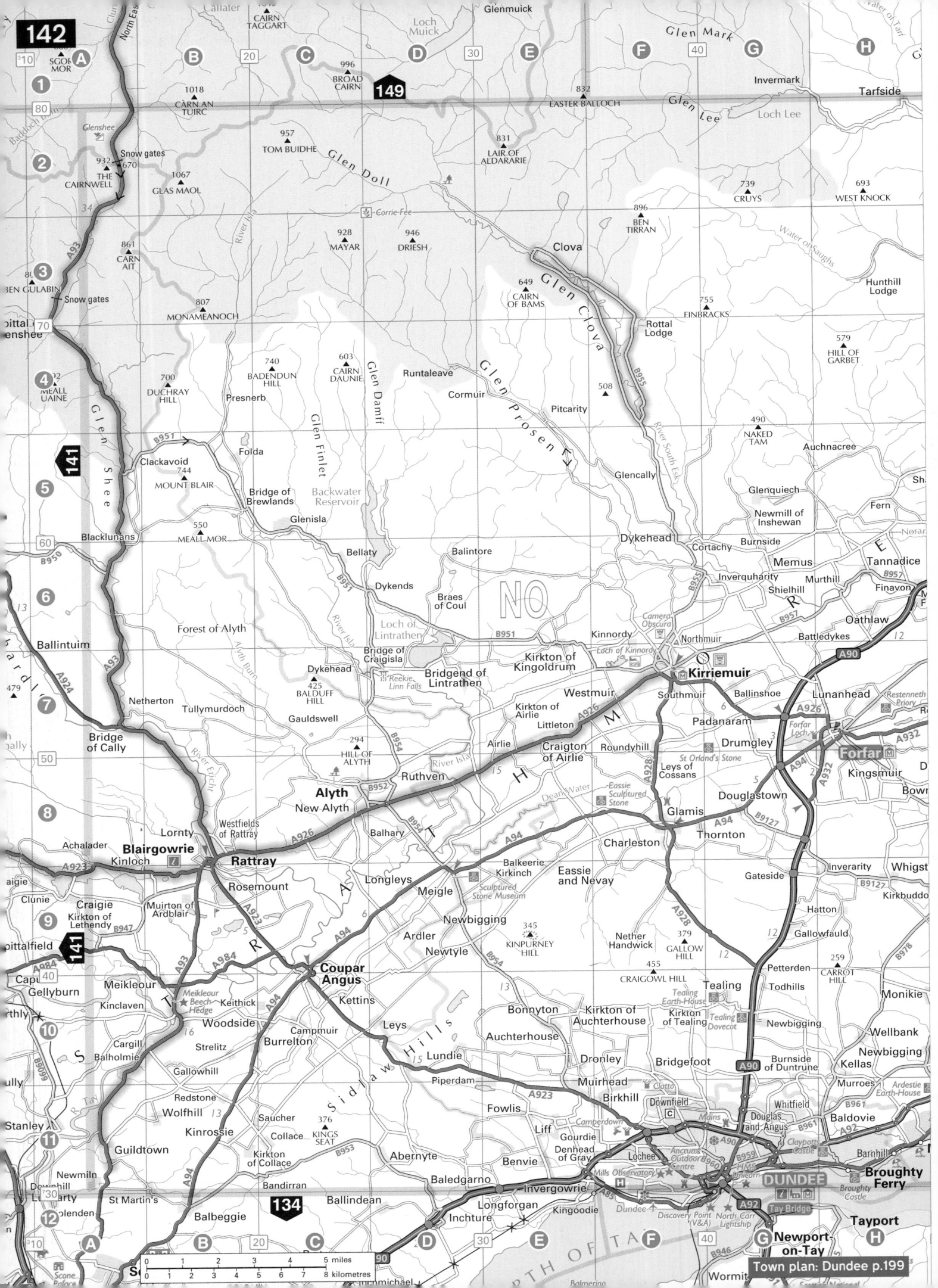

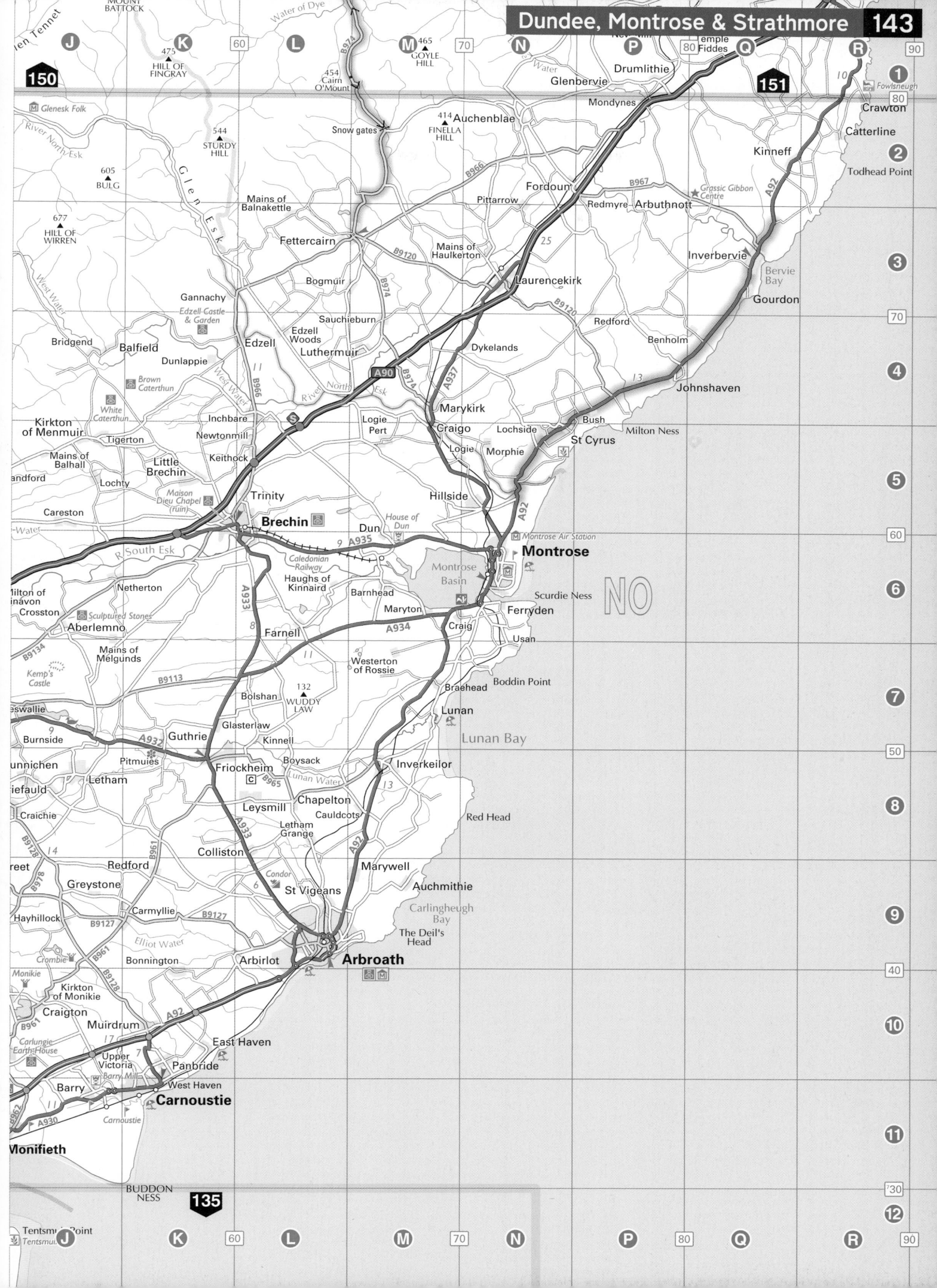

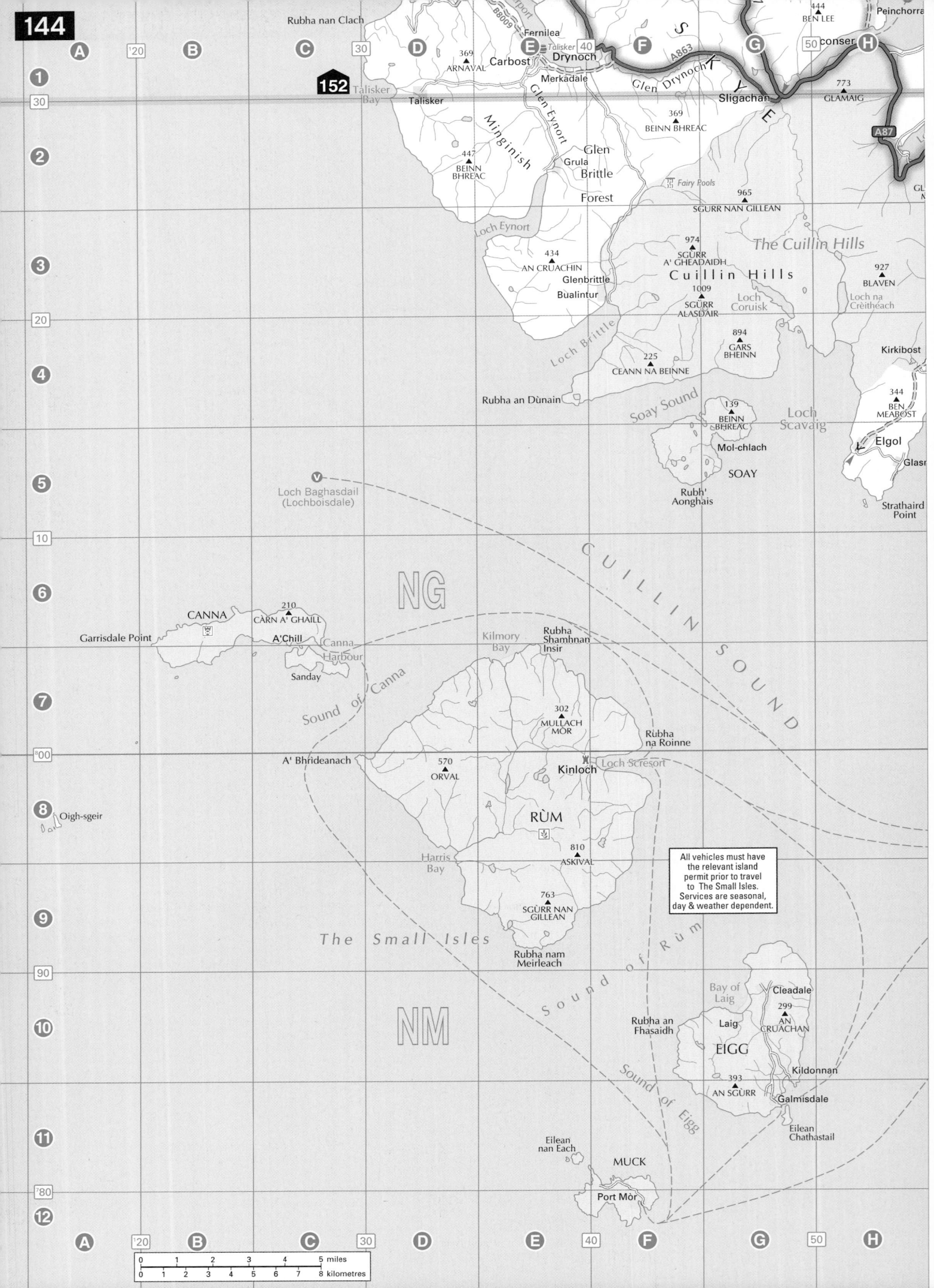

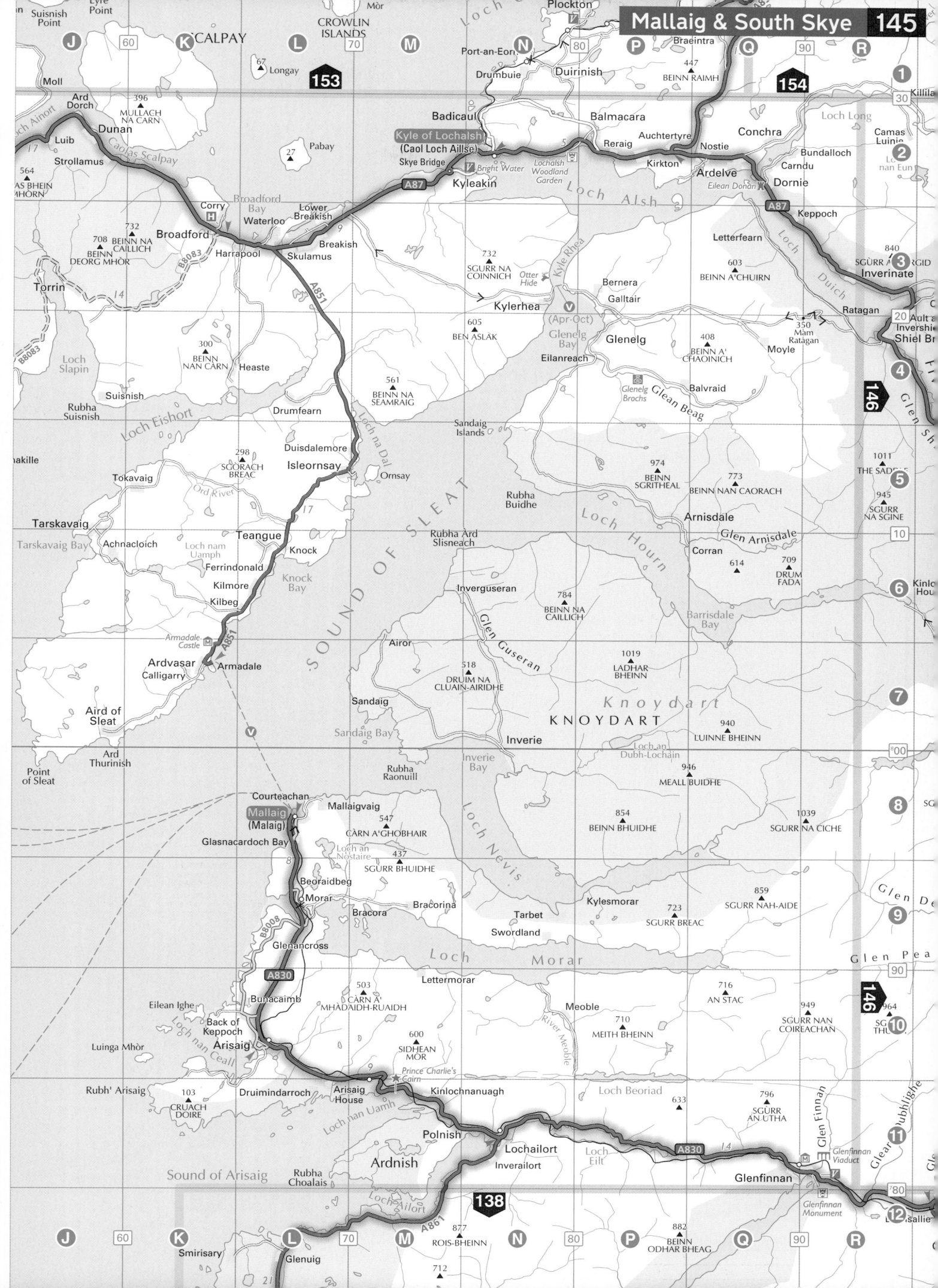

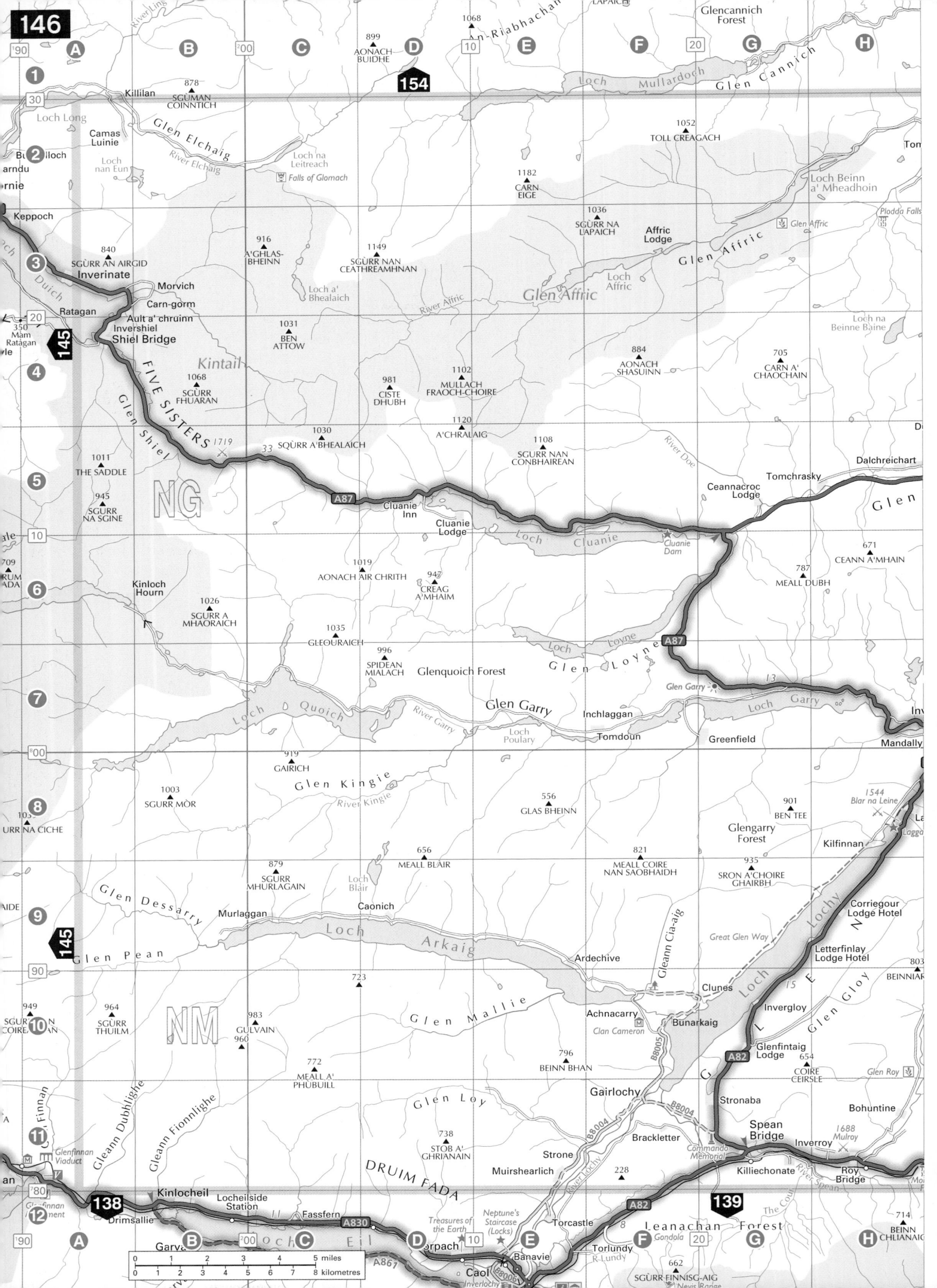

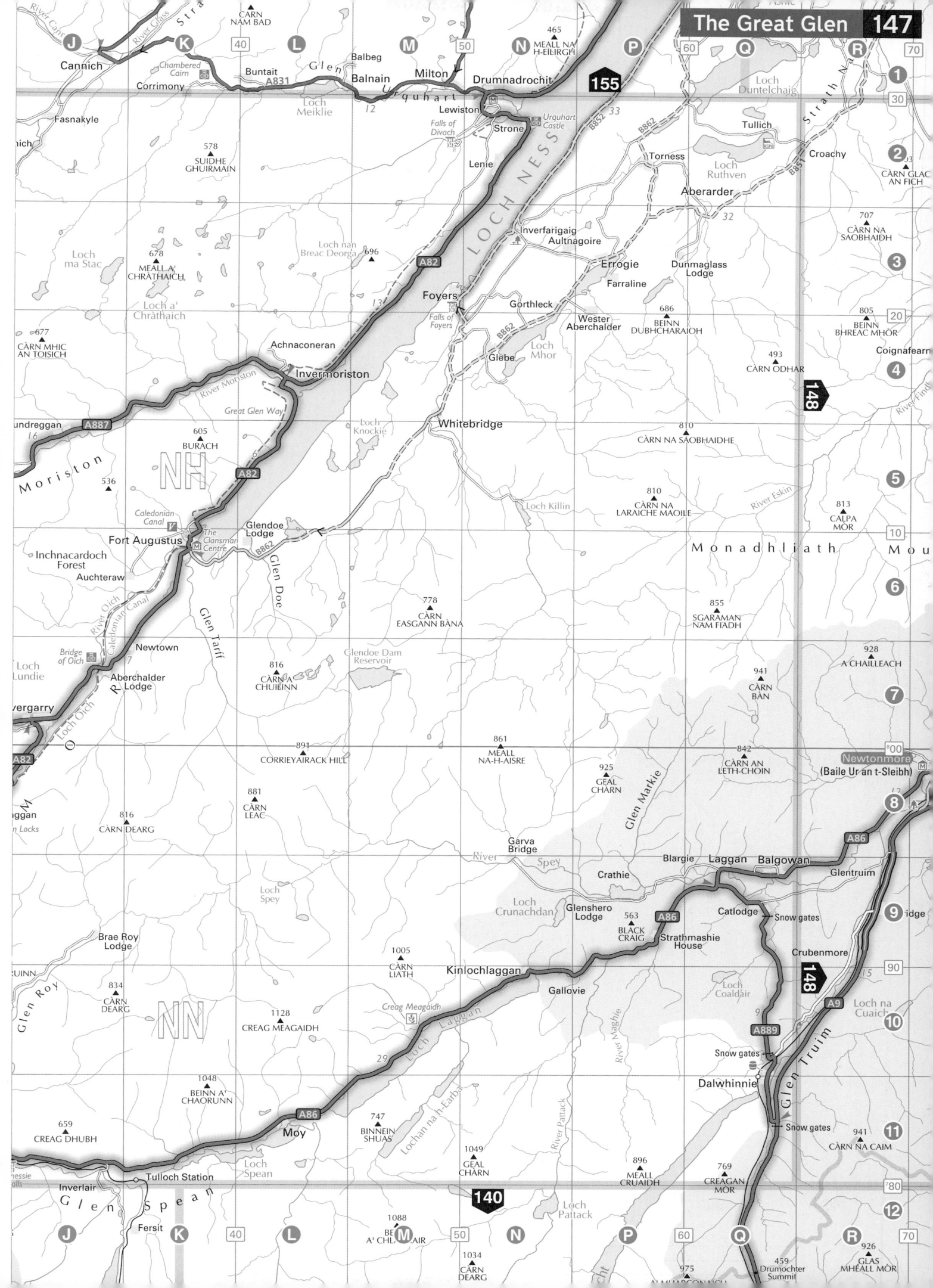

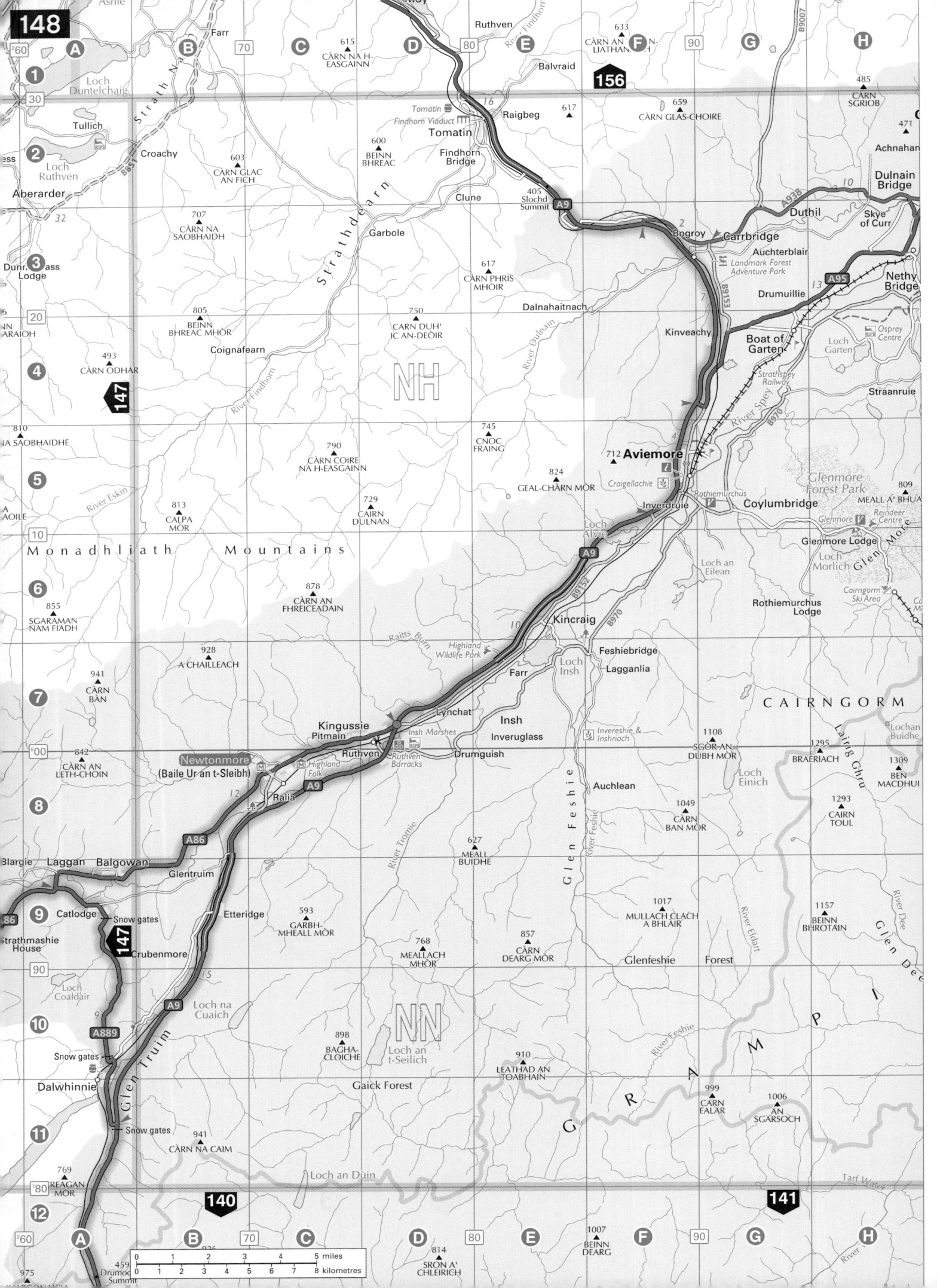

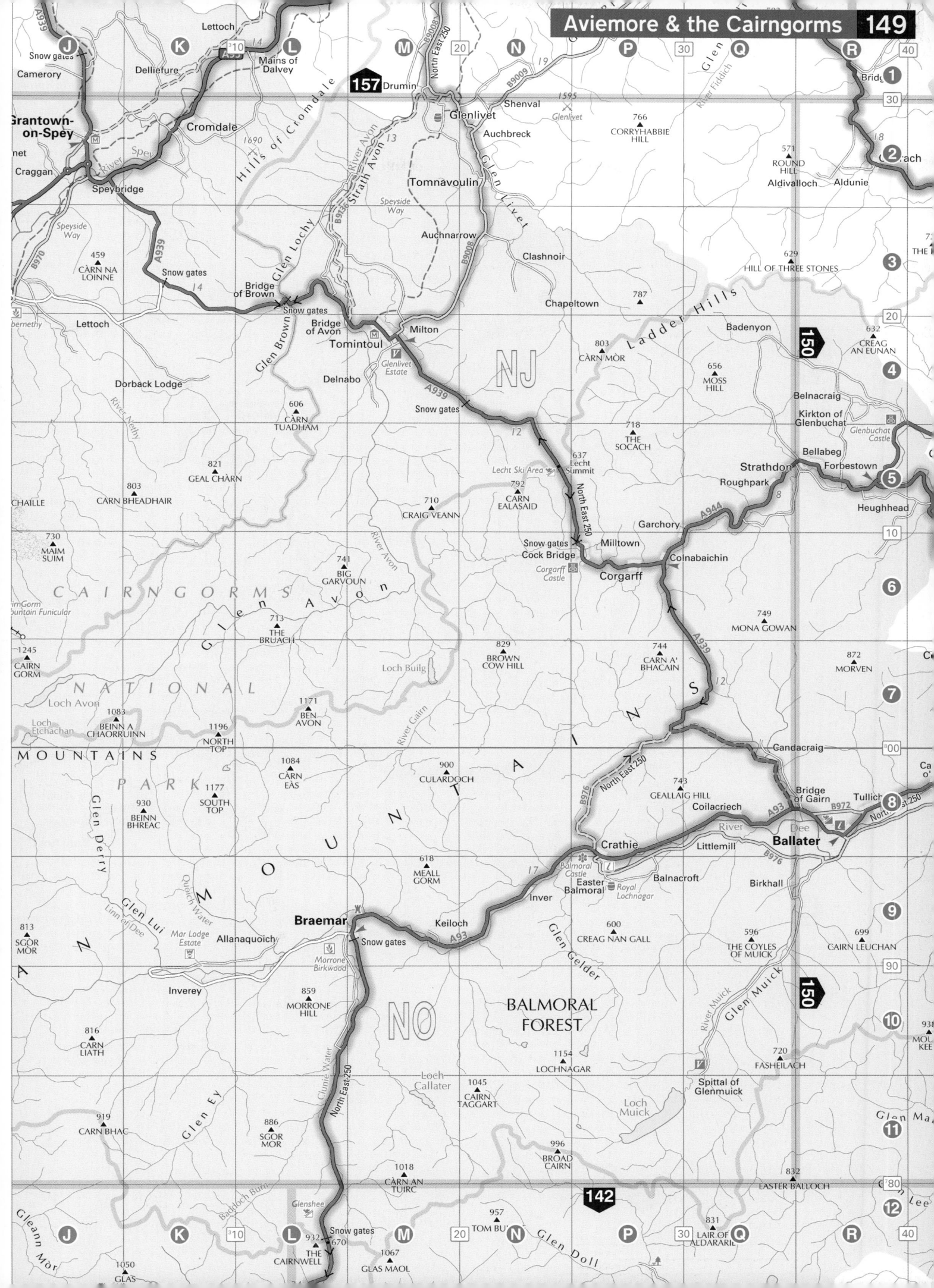

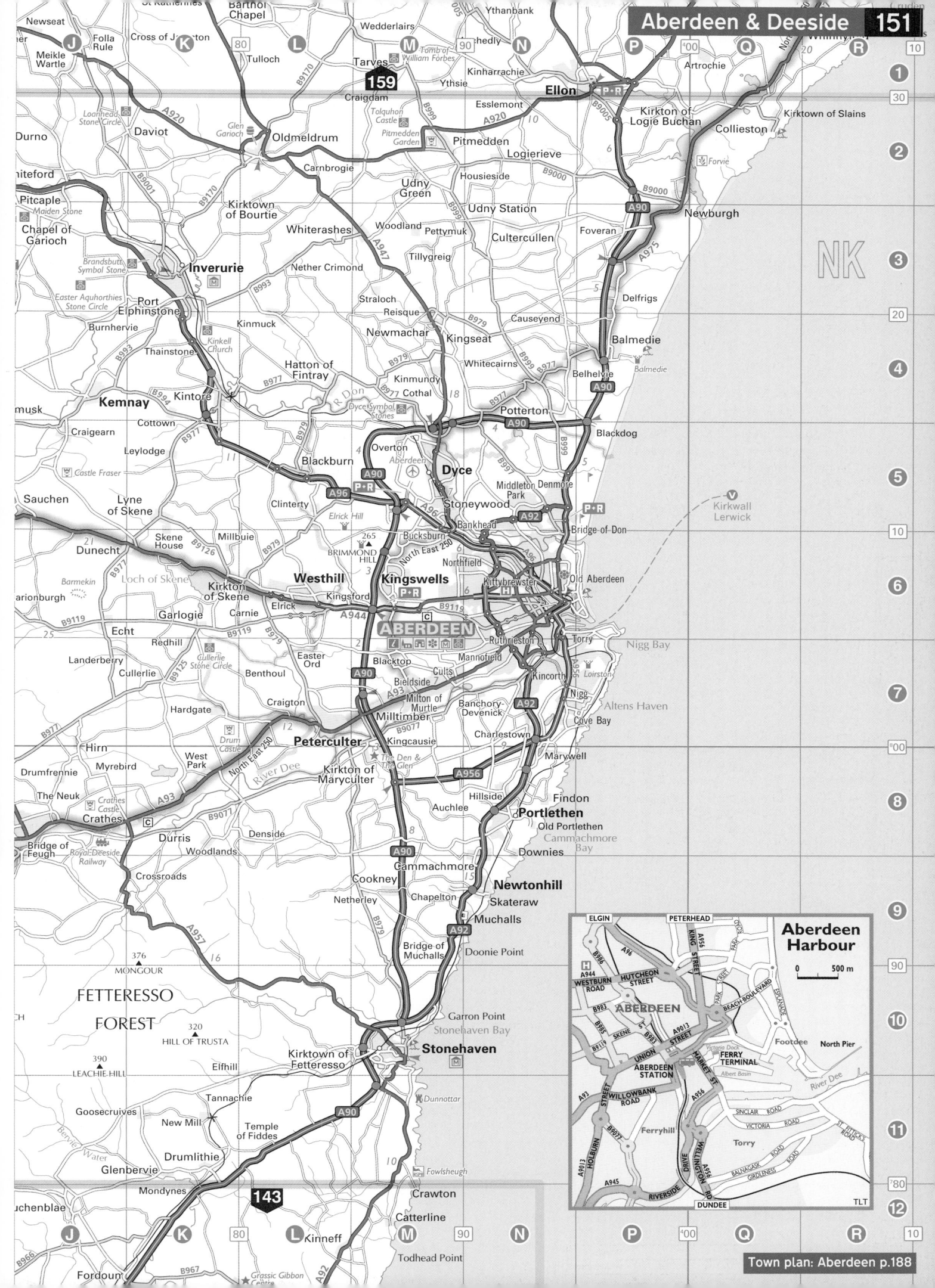

NK

Aberdeen Harbour

0   500 m

ELGIN   PETERHEAD
KING STREET
A956
A96
B986
HUTCHEON STREET
WESTBURN ROAD
A944
B983
B983
SKENE STREET
UNION STREET
ABERDEEN
A9013
MARKET ST
BEACH BOULEVARD
ESPLANADE
Victoria Dock
FERRY TERMINAL
Albert Basin
Footdee
North Pier
ABERDEEN STATION
WILLOWBANK ROAD
A93
HOLBURN STREET
A9013
SINCLAIR ROAD
VICTORIA ROAD
River Dee
Ferryhill
Torry
WELLINGTON ROAD
A956
BALNAGASK ROAD
GIRDLENESS ROAD
ST FITTICK'S ROAD
RIVERSIDE DRIVE
A945
A956
DUNDEE
TLT

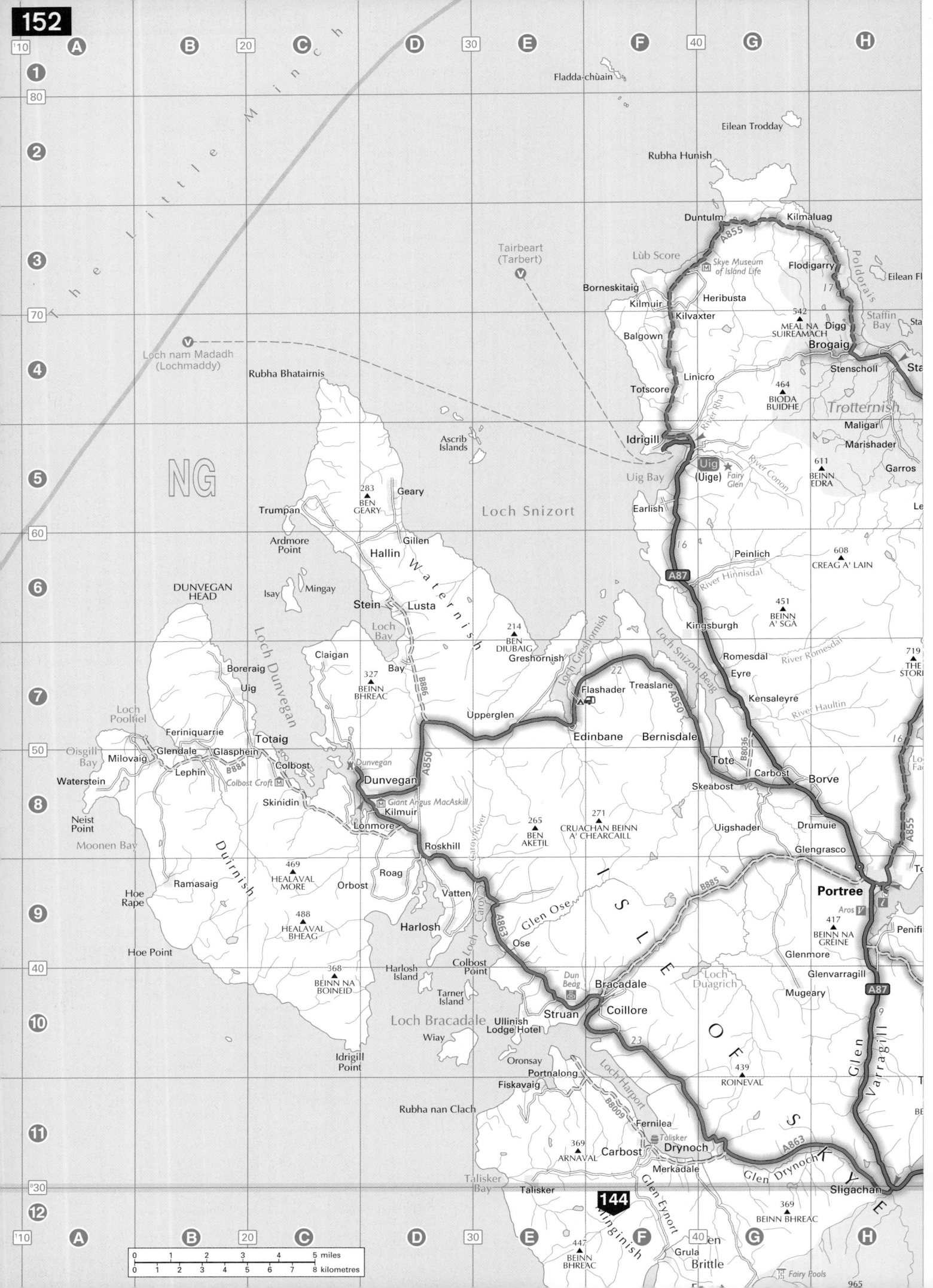

J K 60 L M 70 N P 80 Q R 90

CNOC BREAC

Garden 13

1

North Erradale

B8021

Poolewe

80

Londubh

Big Sand

160

Smithstown

Strath

A832

Heritage

2

Lonemore

Auchtercairn

Longa Island

Gairloch

Gairloch & Loch Ewe

Loch Gairloch

Charlestown

421 MEALL AN DOIREIN

Eilean Horrisdale

Port Henderson

B8056

Badachro

Opinan

Loch Bad an Sgalaig

3

70

Tal

South Erradale

Loch Ghaineamhach

4

Redpoint

154

875

Loch a' Ghodhainn

BAOSBHEINN

855

Red Point

619

BEINN BHREAC

Loch a' Bhealaich

BEINN AN EÒ

5

NG

Loch Torridon

985

914

Rubha na Fearn

BEINN ALLIGIN

BEINN DEARG

60

Fearnmore

Lower Diabaig

Ob Chuaig

Fearnbeg

Loch Diabaig

6

Arrina

Kenmore

Alligin Shuas

Inveralligin

Cuaig

Torridon House

Ardheslaig

Upper Loch Torridon

Tor

Callakille

Loch Shieldaig

Shieldaig

Annat

RONA

492

AN GARBH-MHEALL

493 CROIC-BHEINN

A896

Westerross

7

Lonbain

SOUND OF RAASAY

Eilean Tigh

Loch Damph

902

B 50 DAMPH

Glenshieldaig Forest

Eilean Fladday

Loch Leathan

Manish Point

Loch Arnish

Torran

Loch Lundie

8

North Coast 500

895

BEINN BHAN

Loch Coultrie

730 SGURR A GHARAIDH

Arnish

INNER SOUND

Brochel

River Applecross

Rassal Ashwood

9

312

RAASAY

Applecross Bay

Applecross

626 Pass of the Cattle

Kishorn

A896

Kirkton

orvaig

412 BEN TIANAVAIG

444 DUN CAAN

Milltown

Bealach na Bà

774 SGURR A'CHAORACHAIN

Camusteel

Camusterrach

40

10

Camastianavaig

Tianavaig Bay

Oskaig

Rubha na' Leac

Aird Dhubh

Culduie

Kishorn Island

Ardarroch

Lochcarron

Achintraid

Slumbay

154

Ollach

310 BEINN NA LEAC

Toscaig

River Toscaig

394 BAD A CHREAMHA

Strome

Clachan

Inverarish

Kishorn

Ardaneaskan

Stromeferry

A890

Ardnarff

The Braes

N LEE

Peinchorran

Suisnish Point

Eyre Point

Eilean Meadhonach

Eilean Mòr

Caolas Mòr

Loch Carron

Plockton

Braeintra

11

444

SCALPAY

CROWLIN ISLANDS

Port-an-Eorna

447 BEINN RAIMH

Achmore

30

Sconser

67 Longay

Duirinish

773 GLAMAIG

Moll

Ard Dorch

396 MULLACH NA CARN

145

Badicaul

Drumbuie

Balmacara

12

J A87 K 60 L 17 Dunan 60 L

M Pabay 70

N Kyle of Lochalsh

P 80 5 Rera Q Auchtertyre R 90

Strollamus

Caolas Scalpay

Bright Water

Lochalsh Woodland Garden

Kirkton

Conchra

Nostie

Carndu

564 GLAS BHEIN

2

Skye Bridge

A87

Kyleakin

Ardelve

Eilean Donan

Dornie

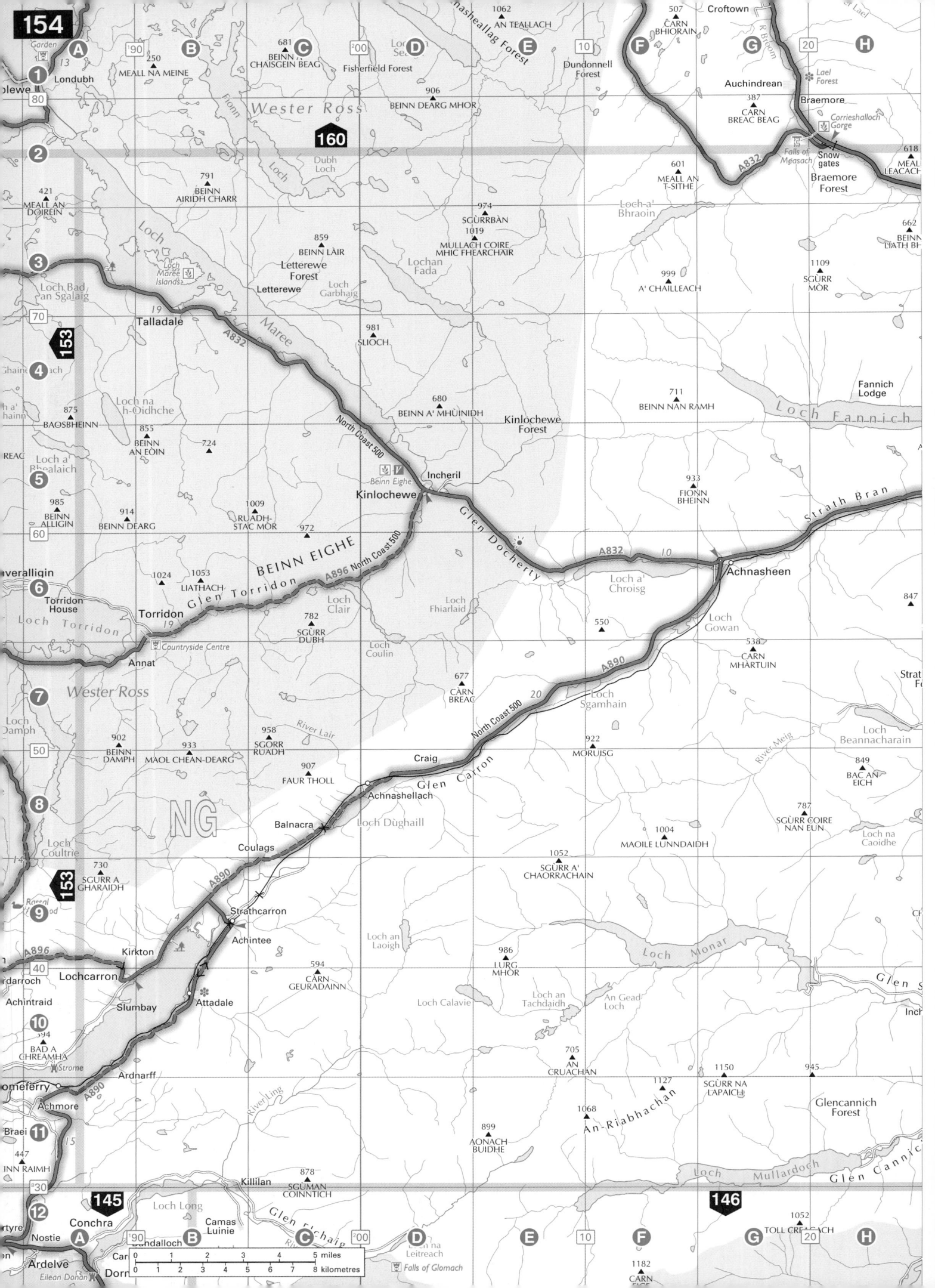

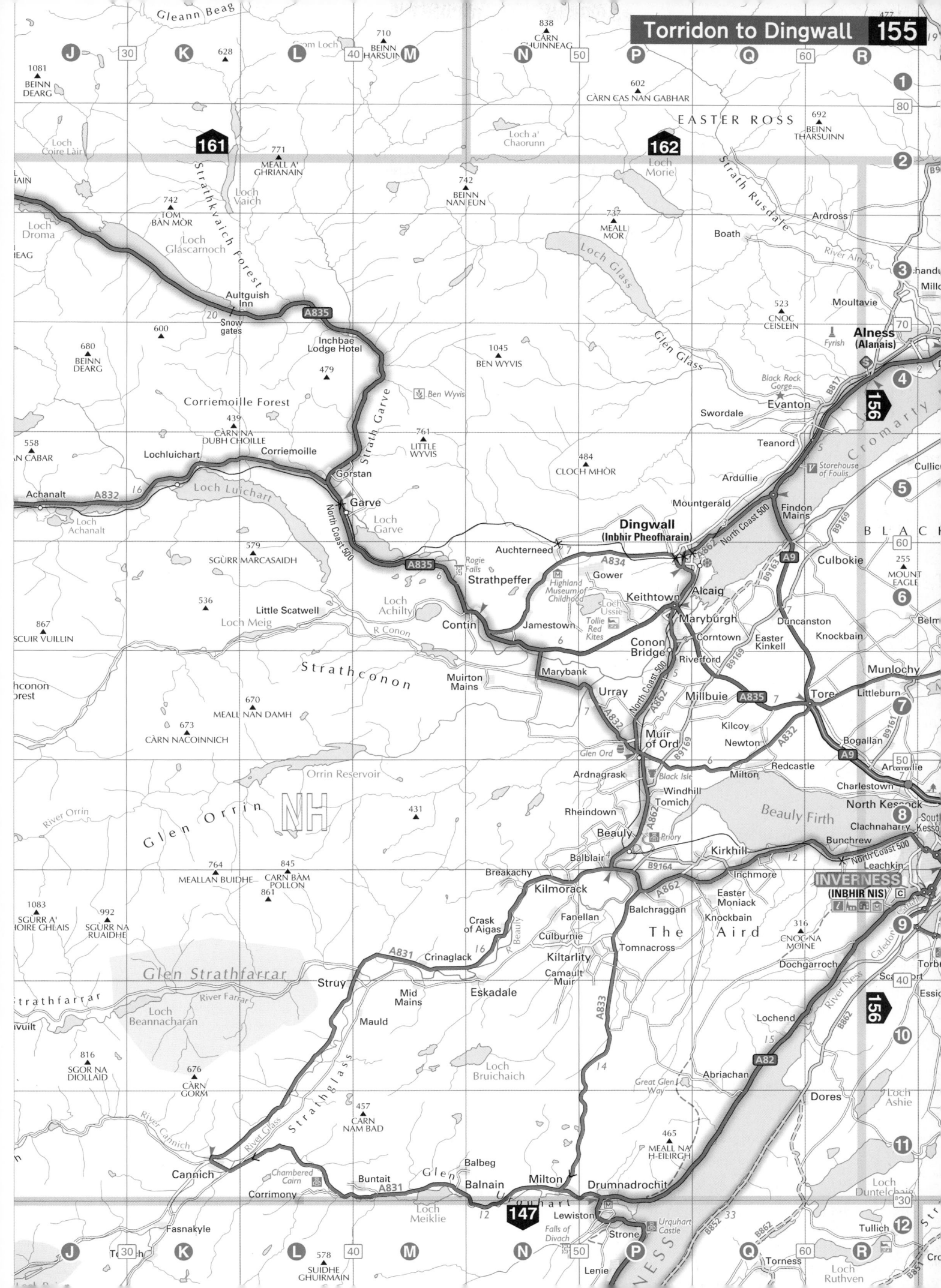

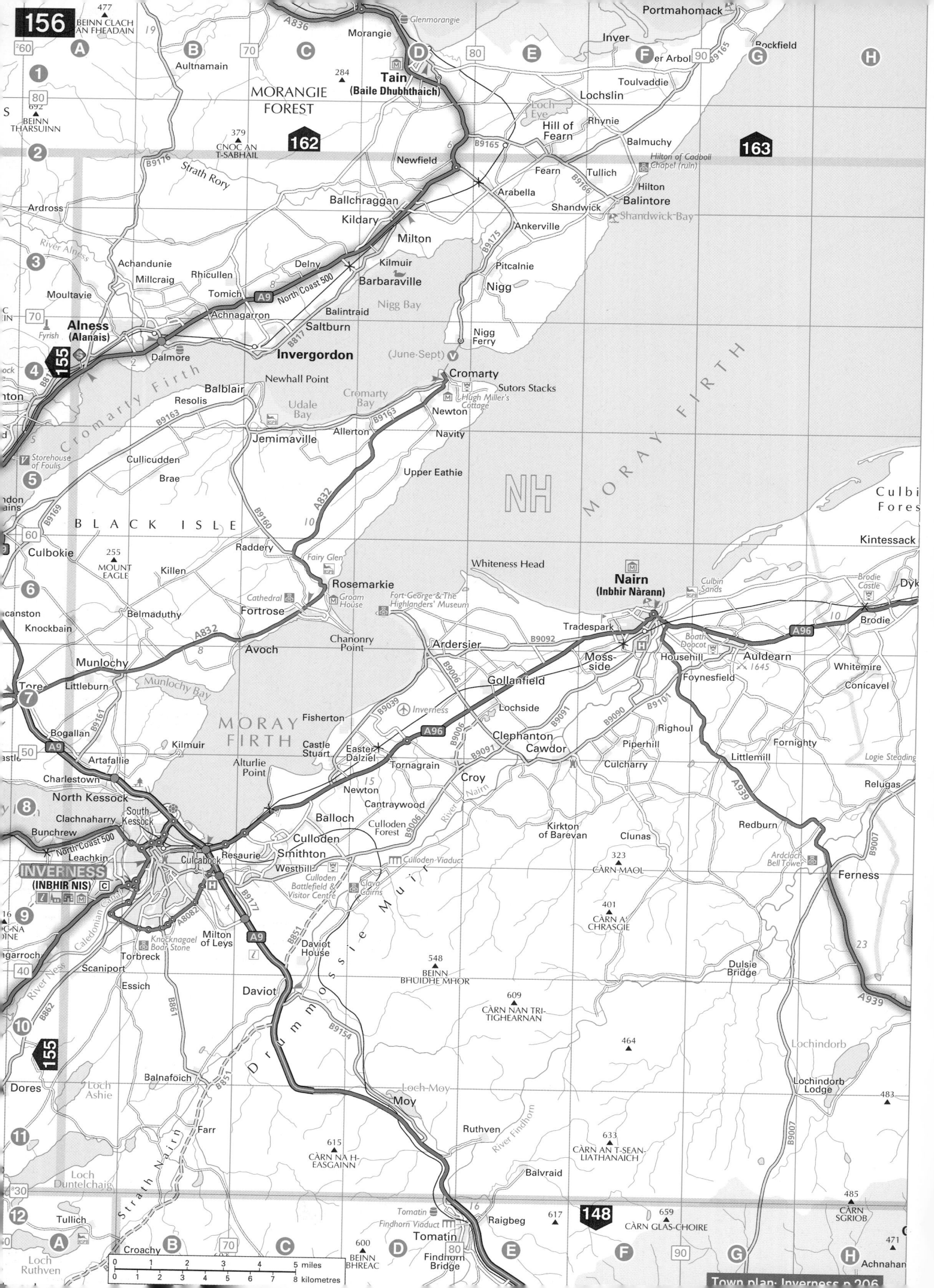

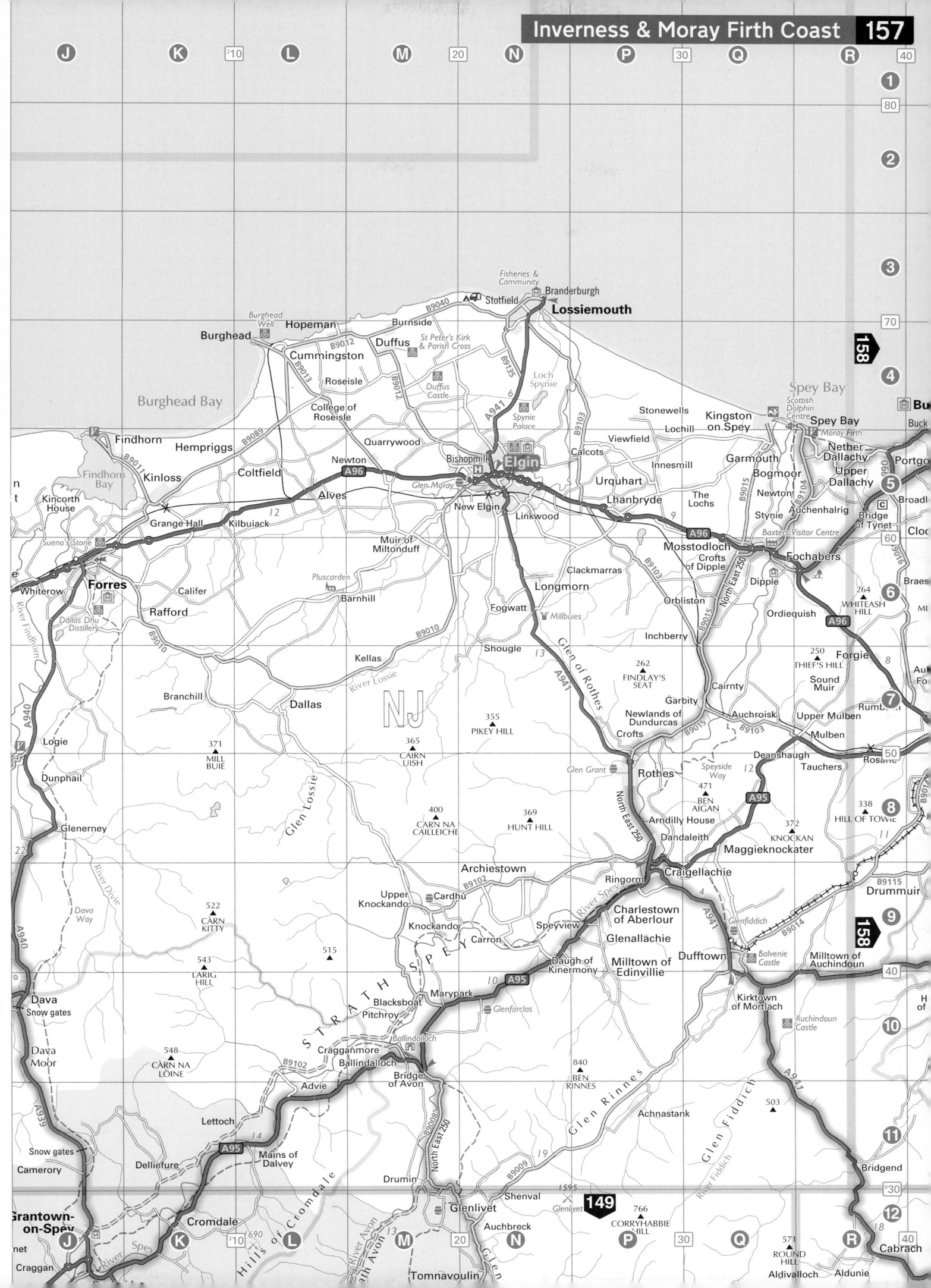

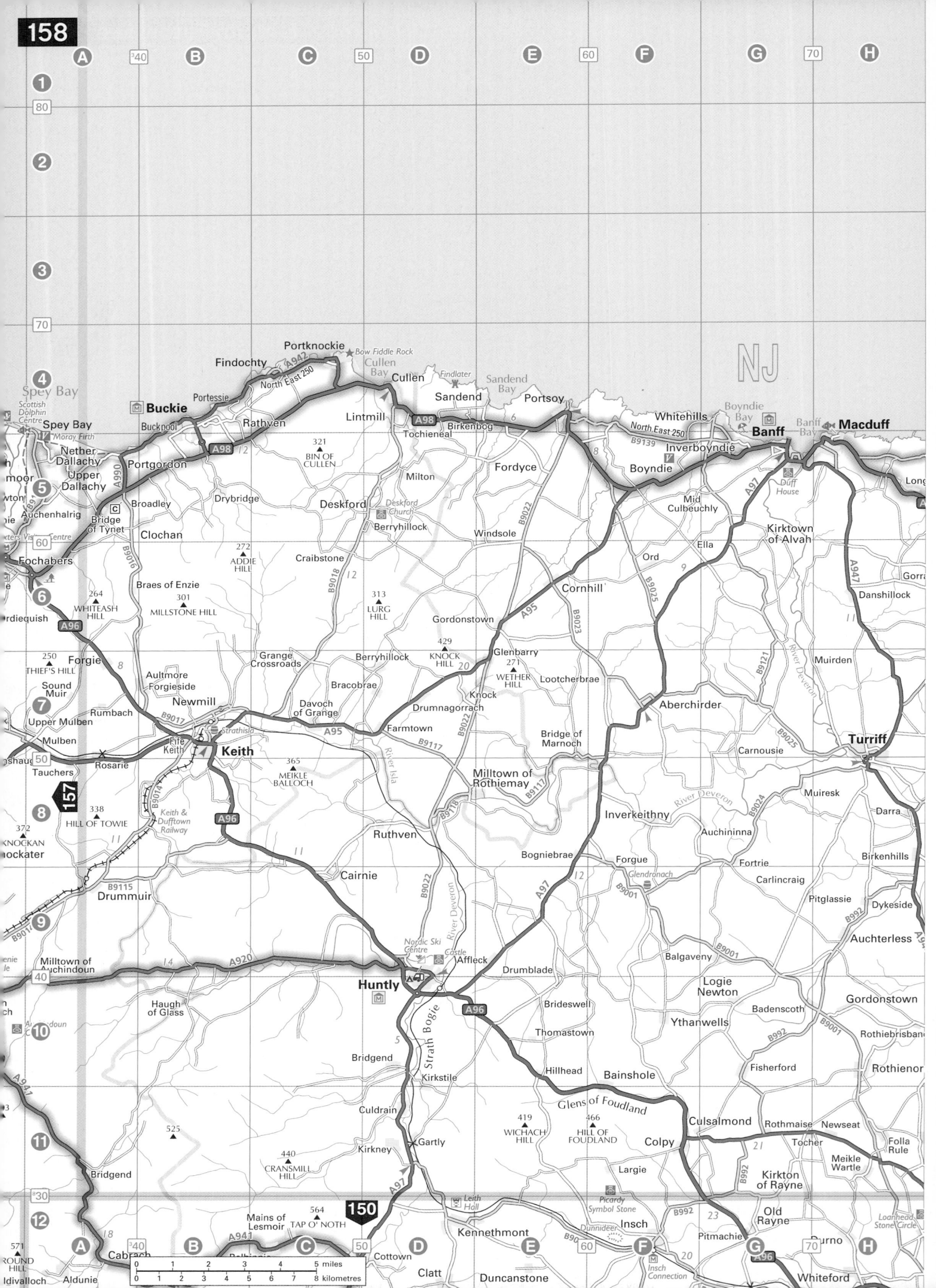

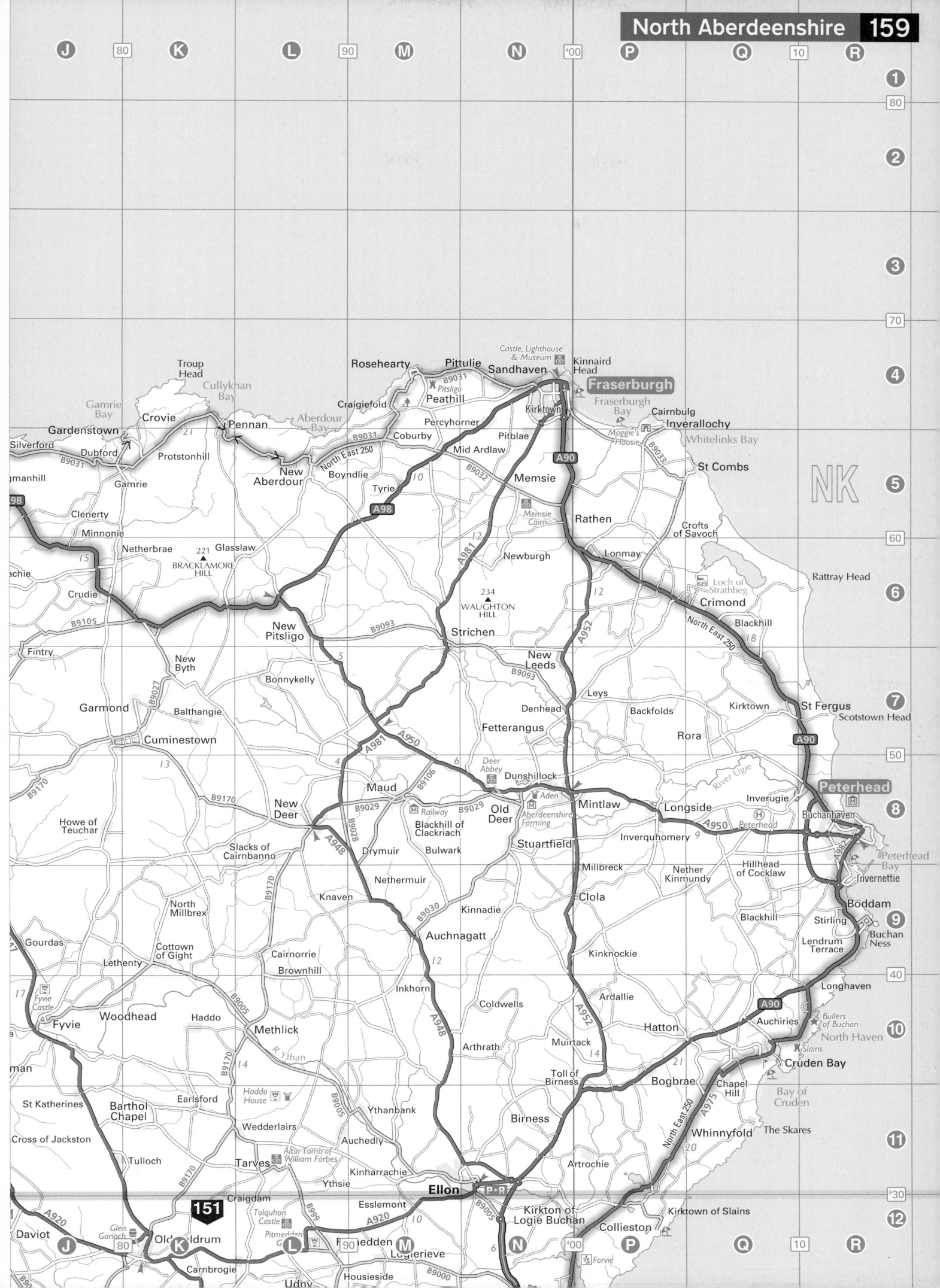

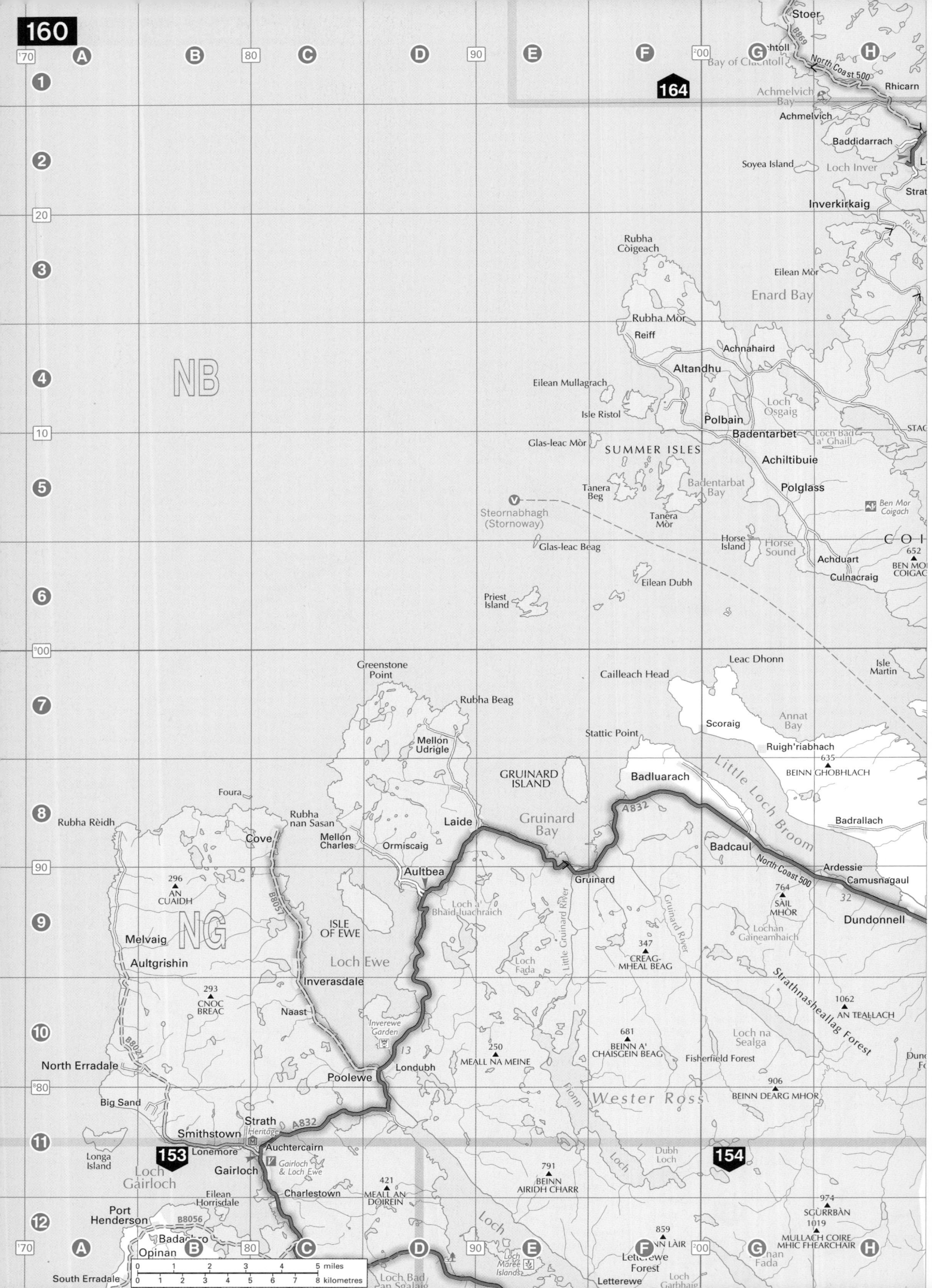

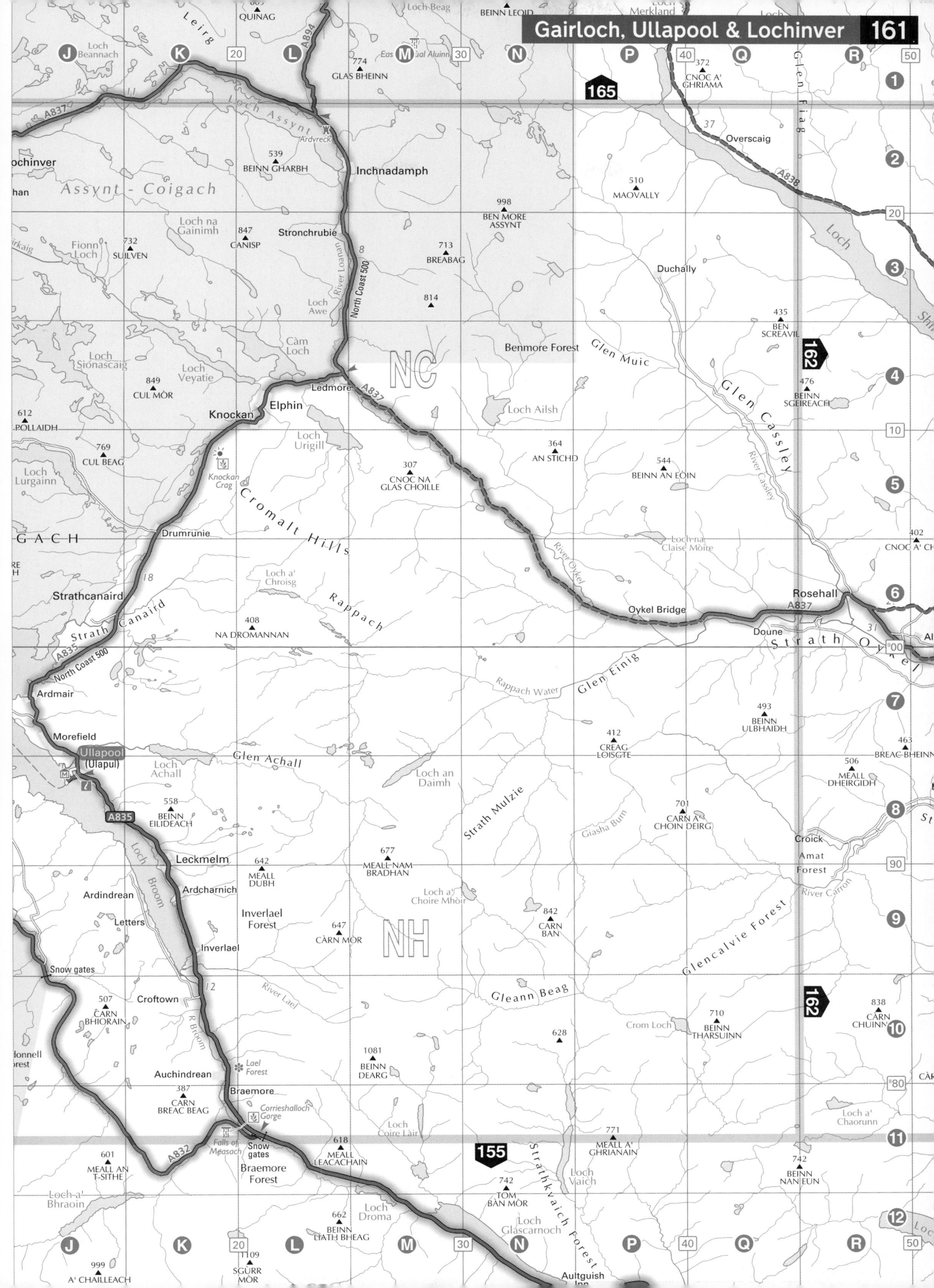

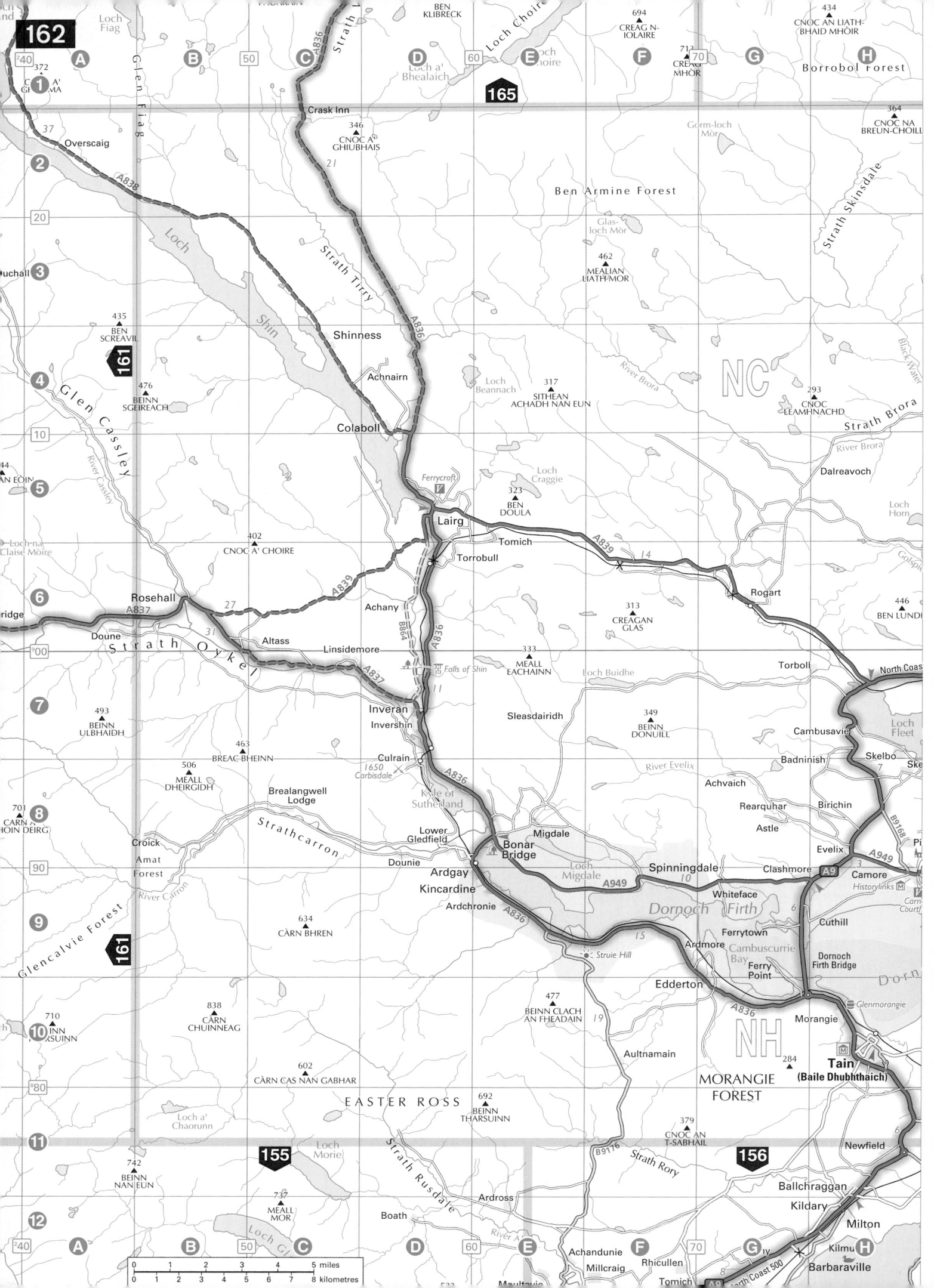

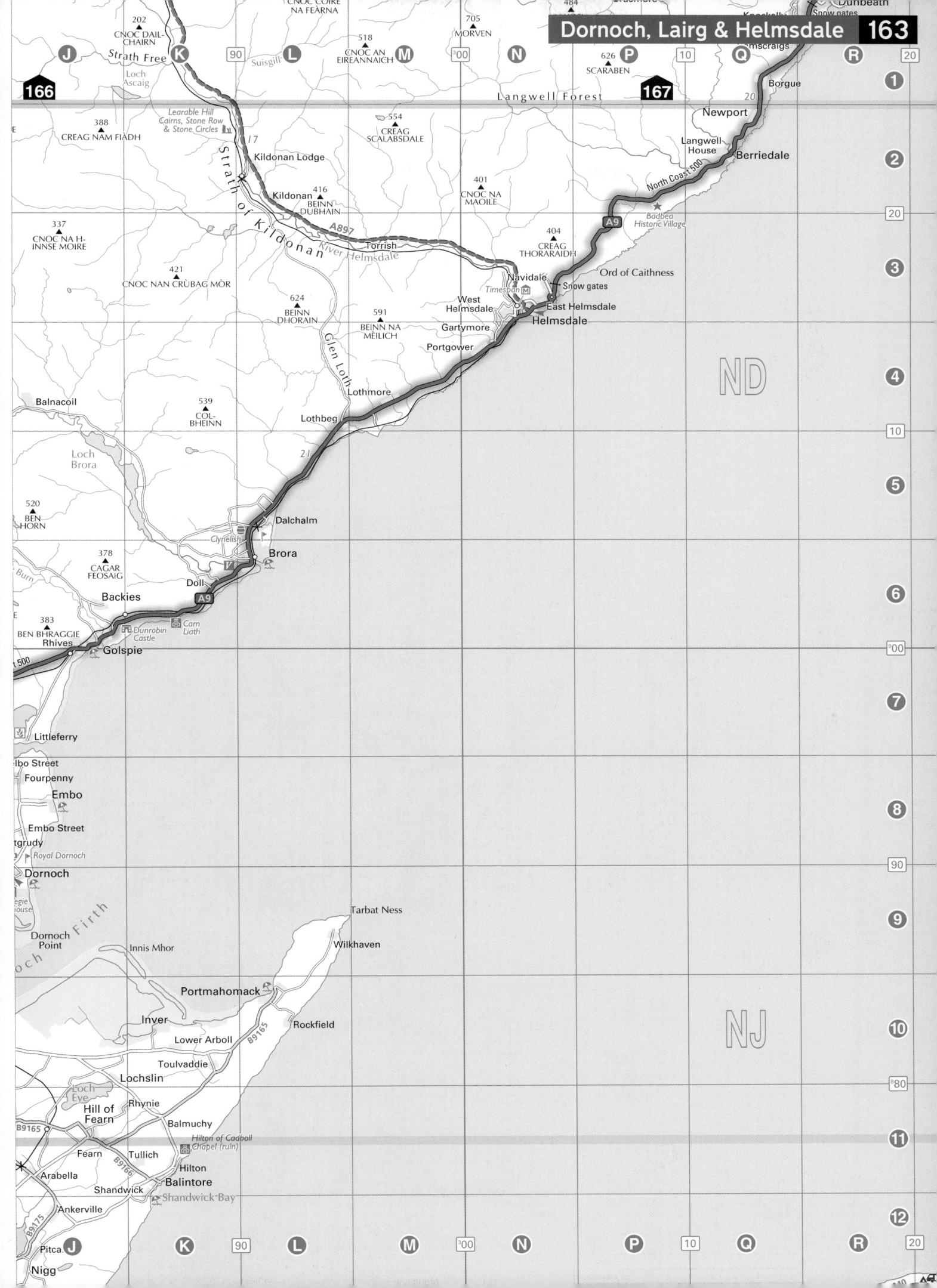

166

167

ND

NJ

Dunbeath

Snow gates

mscraigs

Borgue

Newport

Langwell Forest

Langwell House

Berriedale

North Coast 500

Badbea Historic Village

A9

Ord of Caithness

Snow gates

484

705 MORVEN

518 CNOC AN EIREANNAICH

626 SCARABEN

Keoaallh

202 CNOC DAIL-CHAIRN

Strath Free

Loch Ascaig

90 Suisgill

CNOC COIRE NA FEARNA

'00

'300

10

20

J K L M N P Q R 20

Learable Hill Cairns, Stone Row & Stone Circles

388 CREAG NAM FIADH

17

Kildonan Lodge

Strath of Kildonan

416 BEINN DUBHAIN

Kildonan

A897

River Helmsdale

Torrish

554 CREAG SCALABSDALE

401 CNOC NA MAOILE

404 CREAG THORARAIDH

337 CNOC NA H-INNSE MOIRE

421 CNOC NAN CRÙBAG MÒR

624 BEINN DHORAIN

591 BEINN NA MÈILICH

Glen Loth

Navidale

Timespan M

West Helmsdale

East Helmsdale

Helmsdale

Gartymore

Portgower

Lothmore

539 COL-BHEINN

Lothbeg

21

Balnacoil

Loch Brora

520 BEN HORN

Dalchalm

Clynelish

Brora

378 CAGAR FEOSAIG

Doll

A9

Backies

Burn

383 BEN BHRAGGIE

Rhives

Dunrobin Castle

Carn Liath

Golspie

'500

'00

Littleferry

lbo Street

Fourpenny

Embo

Embo Street

tgrudy

Royal Dornoch

egie ouse

Dornoch

Dornoch Point

Innis Mhor

Tarbat Ness

Wilkhaven

Portmahomack

Inver

B9165

Rockfield

Lower Arboll

Toulvaddie

Lochslin

Loch Eye

Rhynie

Hill of Fearn

Balmuchy

Hilton of Cadboll Chapel (ruin)

B9165

Fearn

B9166

Tullich

Hilton

Arabella

Balintore

Shandwick

Shandwick Bay

Ankerville

B9175

Pitca

Nigg

J K 90 L M '300 N P 10 Q R 20

1 2 20 3 4 10 5 6 '00 7 8 90 9 10 '80 11 12

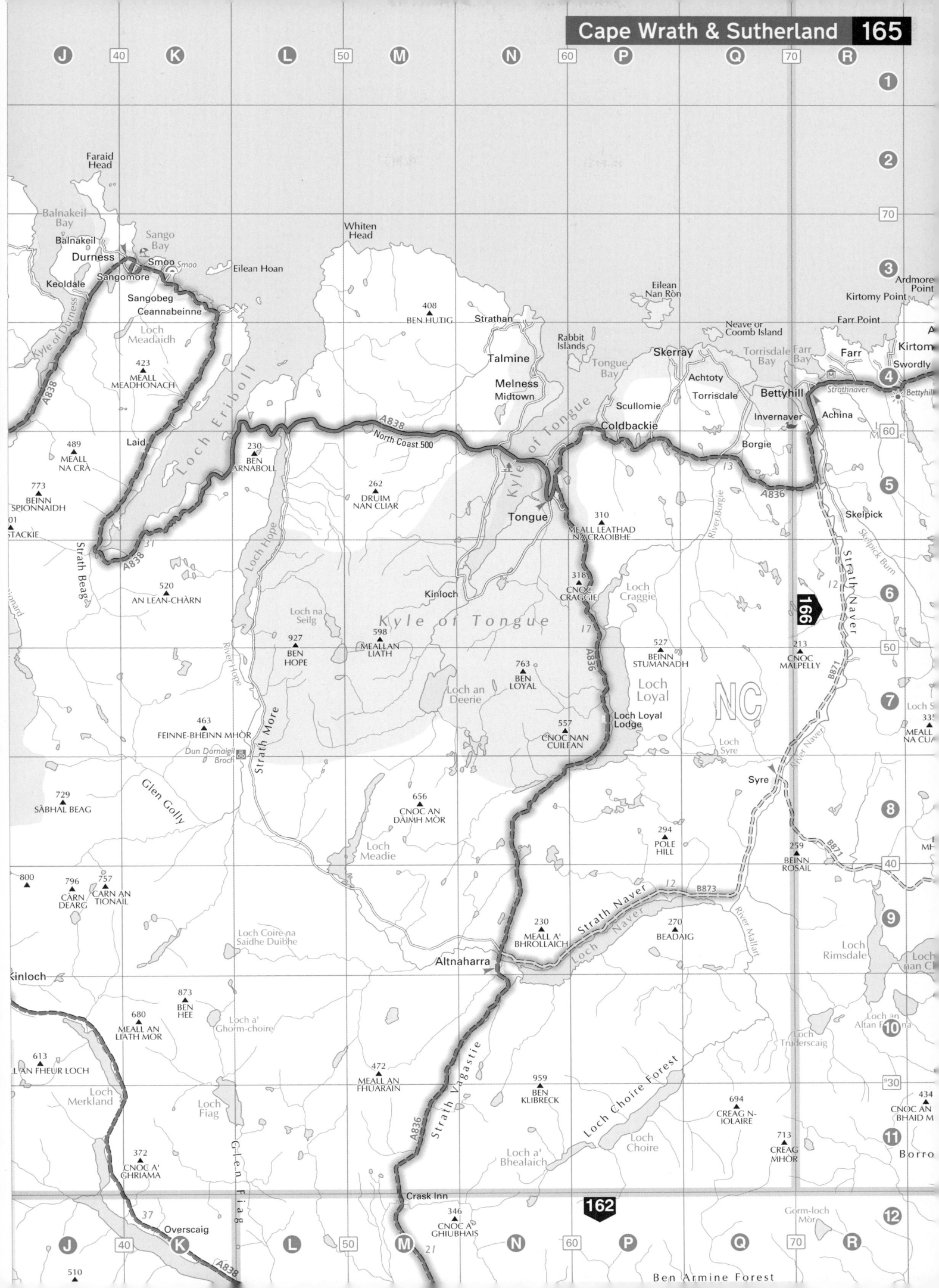

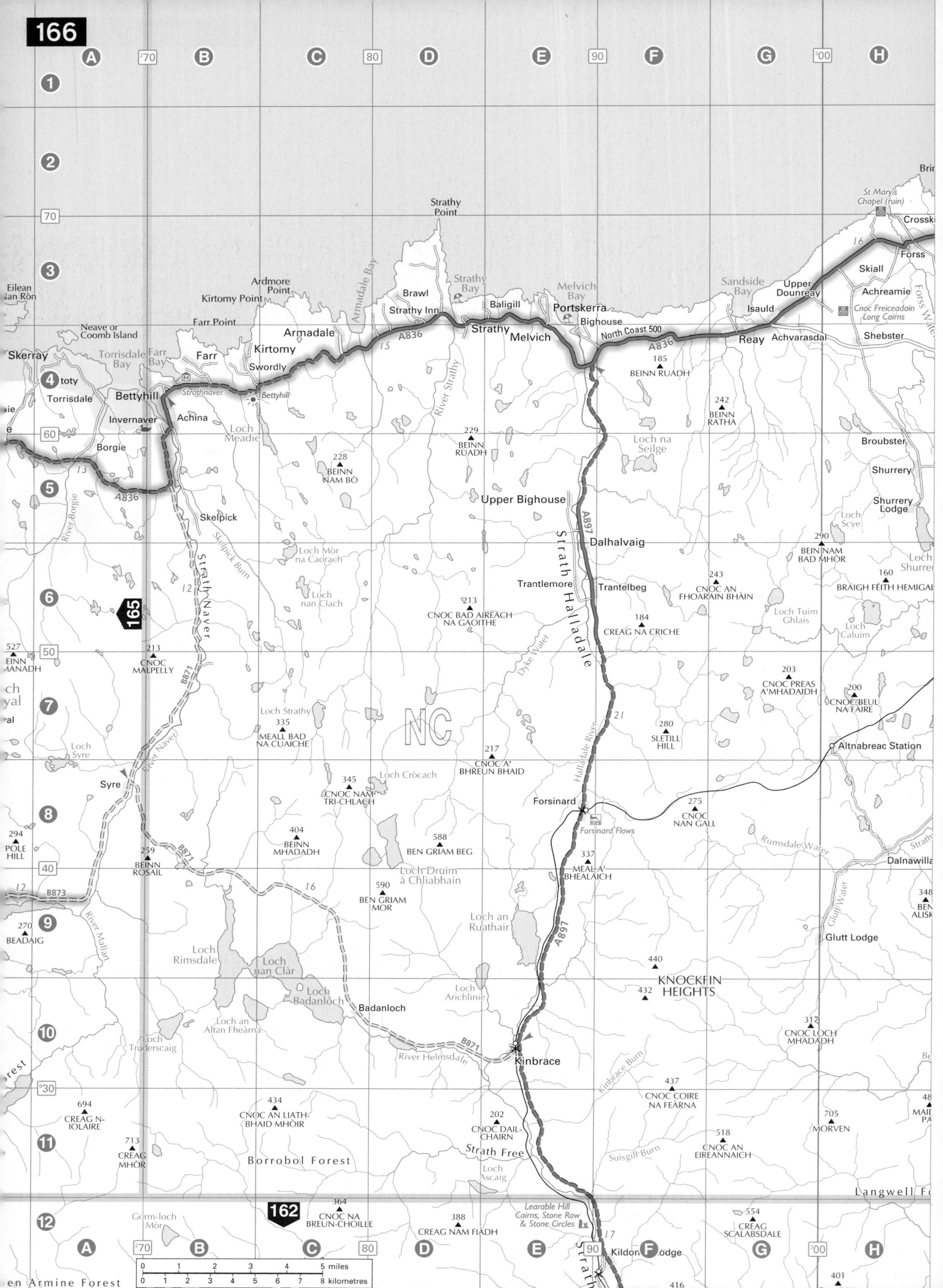

A 70 B 80 C D E 90 F G ³00 H

1

2

70

3

St Mary's
Chapel (ruin)
Crosski
Strathy
Point
16
Forss
Ardmore
Point
Brawl
Strathy Inn
Baligill
Melvich
Bay
Sandside
Bay
Skiall
Forss Water
Kirtomy Point
Strathy Bay
Portskerra
Achreamie
Upper
Dounreay
Kirtomy Point
Farr Point
Armadale Bay
Bighouse
Cnoc Freiceadain
Long Cairns
Isauld
Neave or
Coomb Island
Armadale
Strathy
Melvich
North Coast 500
Reay
Achvarasdal
Shebster
Eilean
nan Ròn
Kirtomy
A836
A836
Farr Bay
Skerray
Torrisdale Bay
Farr
15
185
Broubster
4 toty
Swordly
River Strathy
BEINN RUADH
242
Shurrery
Torrisdale
M
Bettyhill
Strathnaver
BEINN
RATHA
Shurrery
Lodge
Invernaver
Achina
Bettyhill
60
229
Loch na
Seilge
Loch
Scye
Borgie
Loch
Meadie
BEINN
RUADH
Loch
Shurrer
13
A836
228
BEINN
NAM BÒ
290
BEIN NAM
BAD MHÒR
160
BRAIGH FÉITH HEMIGAL
5
Skelpick
Upper Bighouse
Skelpick Burn
Loch Mòr
na Caoraich
Strath Halladale
Dalhalvaig
243
CNOC AN
FHOARAIN BHÀIN
165
Strath Naver
12
Loch
nan Clach
213
CNOC BAD AIREACH
NA GAOITHE
Trantlemore
Trantelbeg
184
CREAG NA CRICHE
Loch Tuim
Ghlais
Loch
Caluim
527
50
213
CNOC
MALPELLY
A897
203
CNOC PREAS
A'MHADAIDH
200
CNOC BEUL
NA FAIRE
EINN
MANADH
B871
Dyke Water
ch
yal
al
7
Loch Strathy
335
MEALL BAD
NA CUAICHE
NC
217
CNOC A'
BHREUN BHAID
Halladale River
21
280
SLETILL
HILL
Altnabreac Station
Loch
Syre
Loch Cròcach
345
CNOC NAM
TRI-CHLACH
Syre
River Naver
8
294
POLE
HILL
404
BEINN
MHADADH
588
BEN GRIAM BEG
Forsinard
275
CNOC
NAN GALL
Rumsdale Water
Strath
Forsinard Flows
Dalnawilla
40
259
BEINN
ROSAIL
B871
Loch Druim
à Chliabhain
337
MEAL-A'-
BHEALAICH
348
BEN
ALISK
12
B873
16
590
BEN GRIAM
MOR
Loch an
Ruathair
440
Glutt Water
9
270
BEADAIG
River Mallart
Loch
Rimsdale
432
KNOCKFIN
HEIGHTS
Glutt Lodge
Loch nan Clàr
Loch
Arichlinie
Loch
Badanlòch
30
10
Loch
Truderscaig
Loch an
Altan Fheàrna
Badanloch
B871
River Helmsdale
Kinbrace
317
CNOC LOCH
MHADADH
Be
694
CREAG N-
IOLAIRE
434
CNOC AN LIATH-
BHAID MHÒIR
437
CNOC COIRE
NA FEÀRNA
11
713
CREAG
MHÒR
202
CNOC DAIL-
CHAIRN
Suisgill Burn
518
CNOC AN
EIREANNAICH
705
MORVEN
48
MAI
PA
162
Borrobol Forest
Strath Free
Loch
Ascaig
Langwell Fo
12
Gorm-loch
Mòr
364
CNOC NA
BREUN-CHOILLE
388
CREAG NAM FIADH
Learable Hill
Cairns, Stone Row
& Stone Circles
554
CREAG
SCALABSDALE
401
en Armine Forest
90
Kildon
Lodge
17
Strath
416

A 70 B 80 C D E 90 F G ³00 H

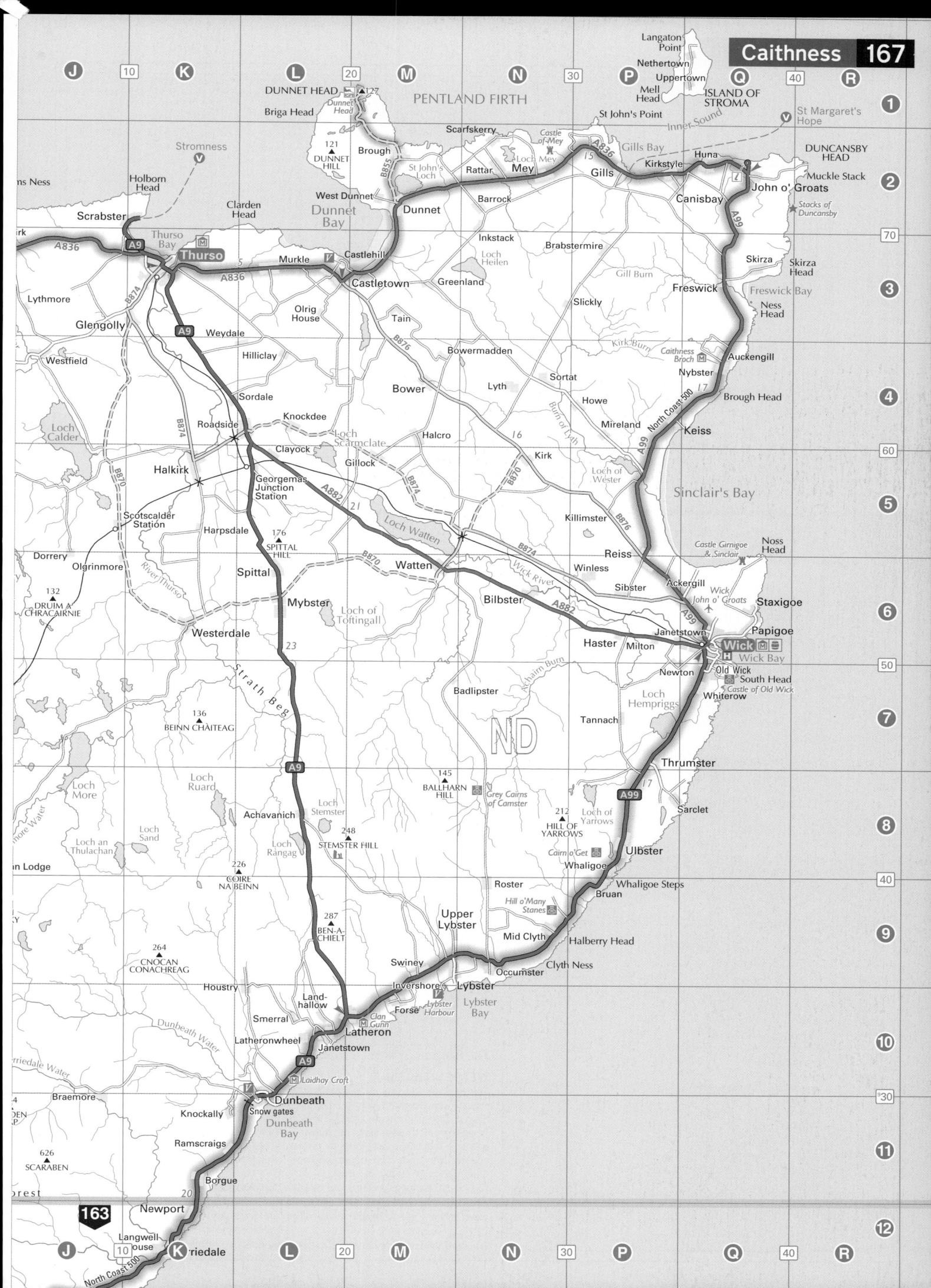

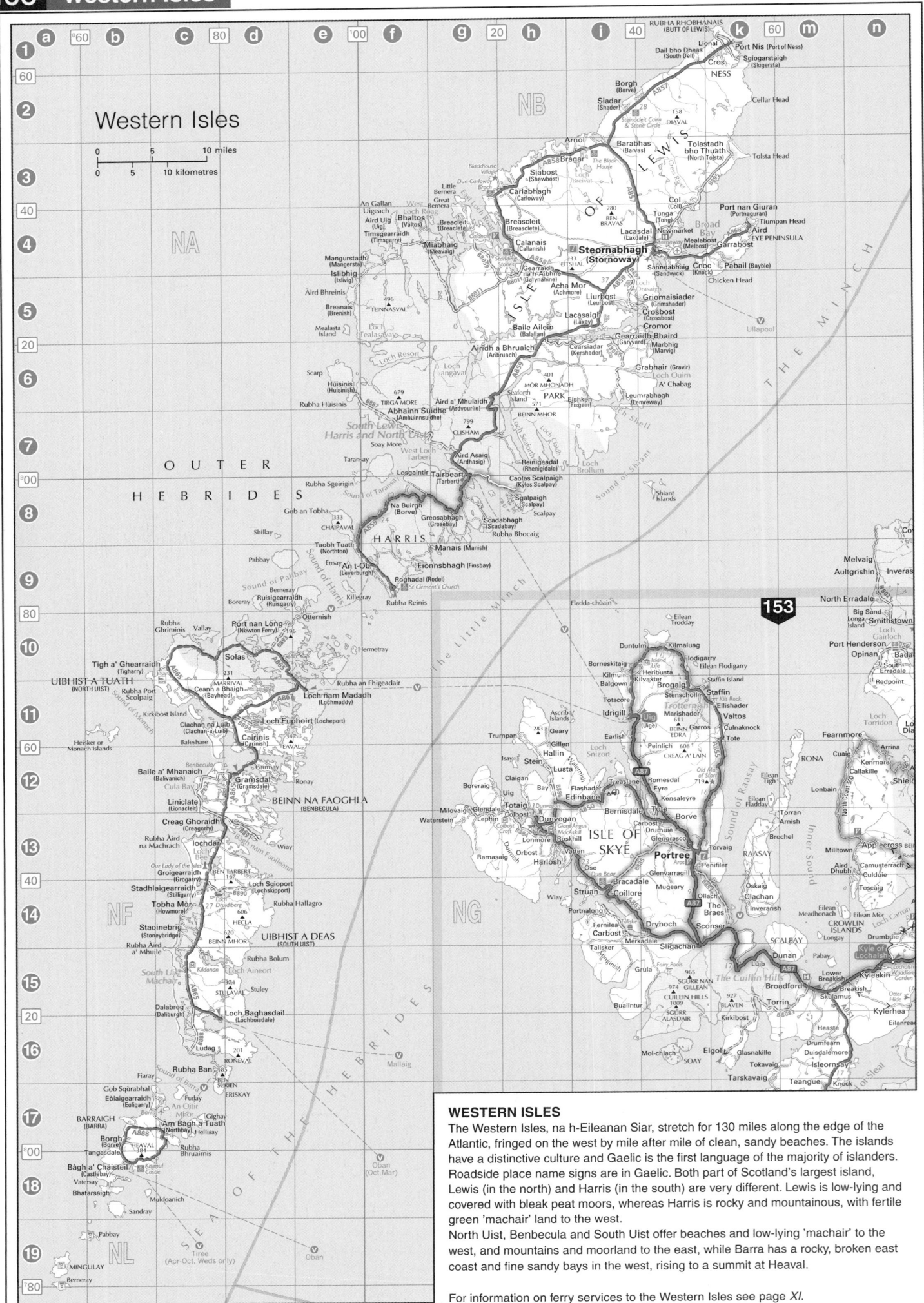

Western Isles

0   5   10 miles
0   5   10 kilometres

WESTERN ISLES

The Western Isles, na h-Eileanan Siar, stretch for 130 miles along the edge of the Atlantic, fringed on the west by mile after mile of clean, sandy beaches. The islands have a distinctive culture and Gaelic is the first language of the majority of islanders. Roadside place name signs are in Gaelic. Both part of Scotland's largest island, Lewis (in the north) and Harris (in the south) are very different. Lewis is low-lying and covered with bleak peat moors, whereas Harris is rocky and mountainous, with fertile green 'machair' land to the west.

North Uist, Benbecula and South Uist offer beaches and low-lying 'machair' to the west, and mountains and moorland to the east, while Barra has a rocky, broken east coast and fine sandy bays in the west, rising to a summit at Heaval.

For information on ferry services to the Western Isles see page XI.

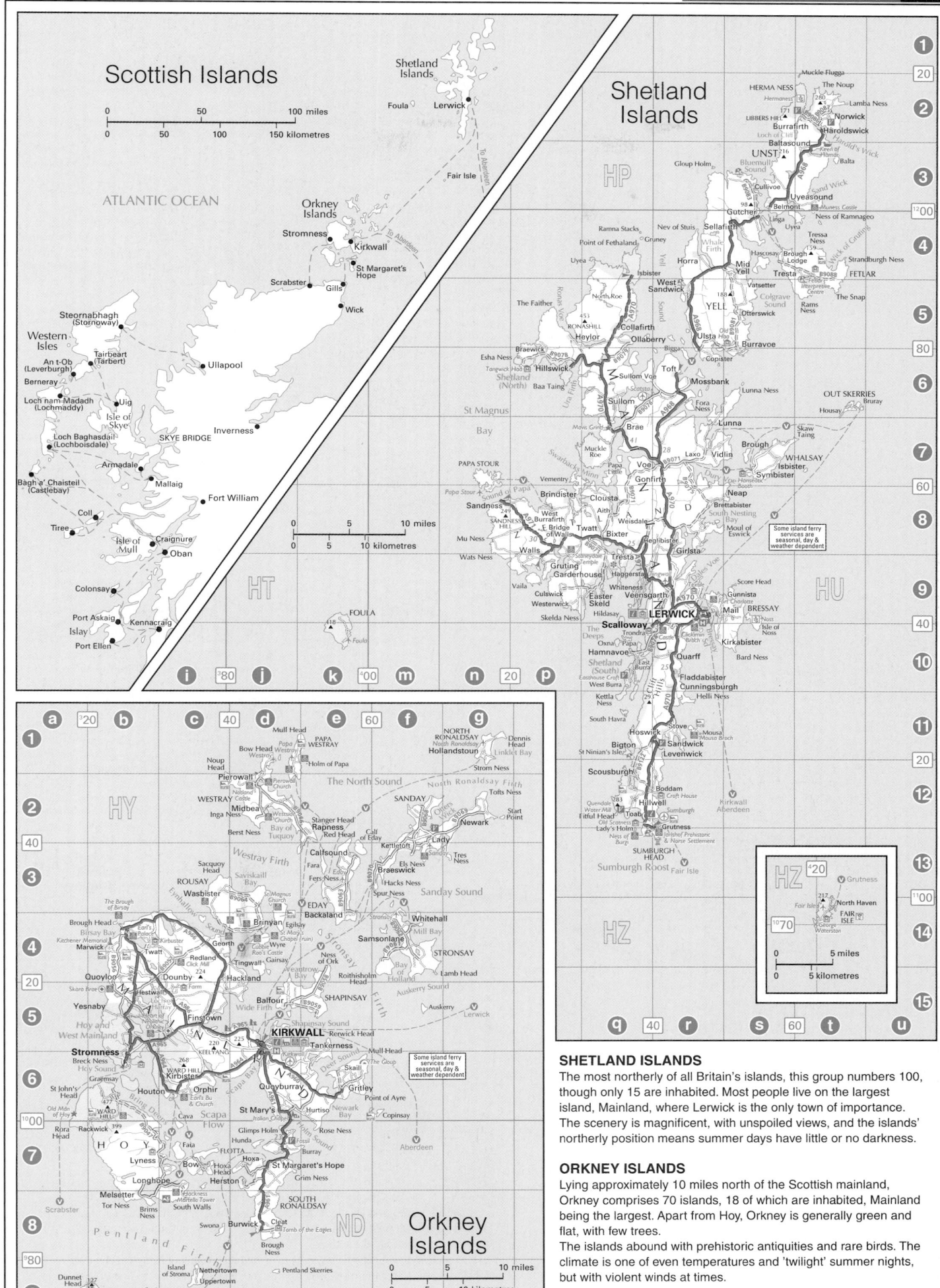

Scottish Islands

ATLANTIC OCEAN

Shetland Islands

Orkney Islands

Western Isles

Stornabhagh (Stornoway)
An t-Ob (Leverburgh)
Tairbeart (Tarbert)
Berneray
Loch nam Madadh (Lochmaddy)
Uig
Isle of Skye
Loch Baghasdail (Lochboisdale)
Bàgh a' Chaisteil (Castlebay)
Armadale
Mallaig
Coll
Tiree
Isle of Mull
Craignure
Oban
Colonsay
Port Askaig
Islay
Port Ellen
Kennacraig
Ullapool
Inverness
SKYE BRIDGE
Fort William

Foula
Lerwick
Fair Isle
Stromness
Kirkwall
St Margaret's Hope
Scrabster
Gills
Wick

To Aberdeen

Shetland Islands

SHETLAND ISLANDS

The most northerly of all Britain's islands, this group numbers 100, though only 15 are inhabited. Most people live on the largest island, Mainland, where Lerwick is the only town of importance. The scenery is magnificent, with unspoiled views, and the islands' northerly position means summer days have little or no darkness.

ORKNEY ISLANDS

Lying approximately 10 miles north of the Scottish mainland, Orkney comprises 70 islands, 18 of which are inhabited, Mainland being the largest. Apart from Hoy, Orkney is generally green and flat, with few trees.
The islands abound with prehistoric antiquities and rare birds. The climate is one of even temperatures and 'twilight' summer nights, but with violent winds at times.

For information on ferry services to the Shetland and Orkney Islands see page XI.

Orkney Islands

Some island ferry services are seasonal, day & weather dependent

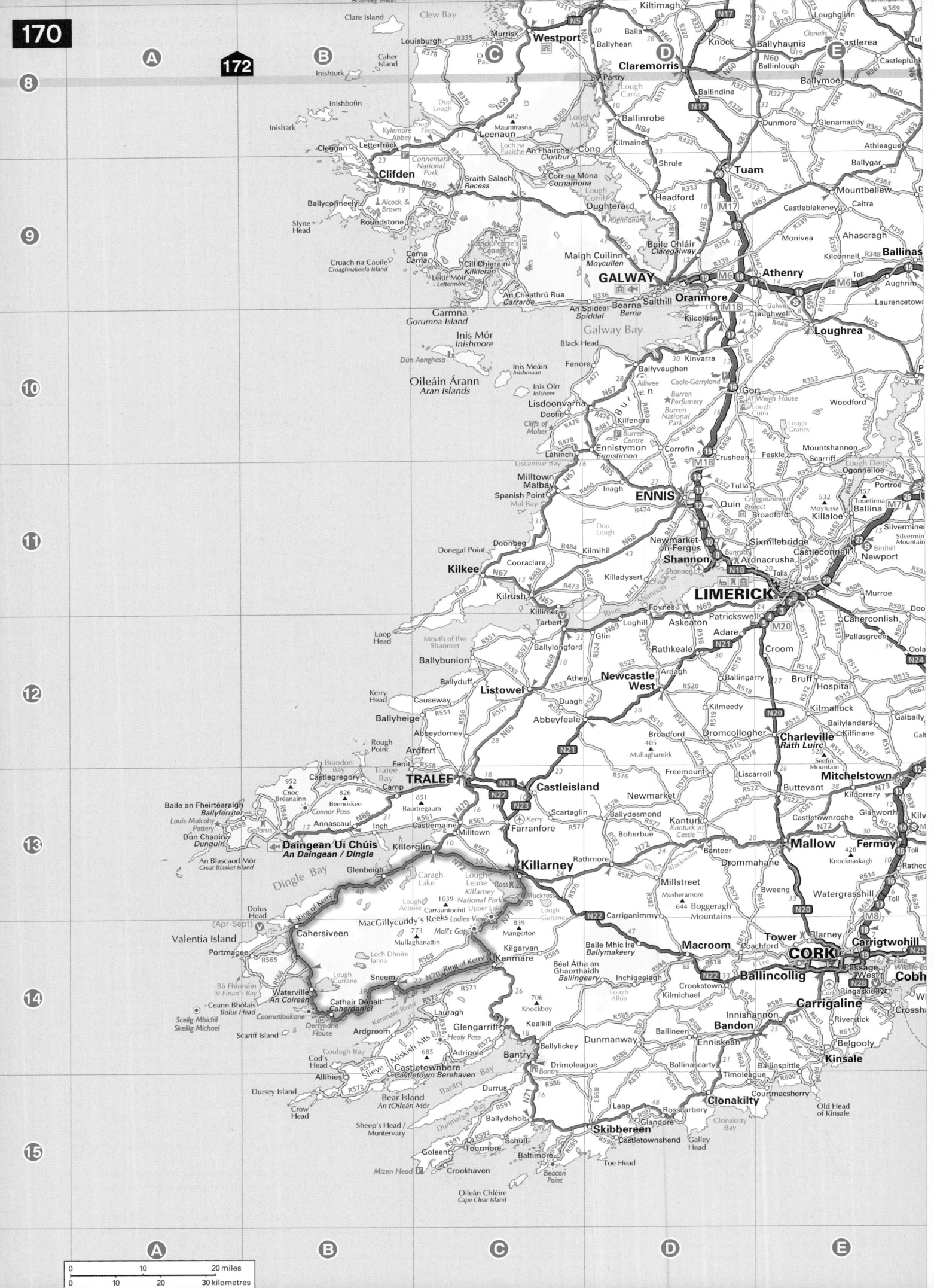

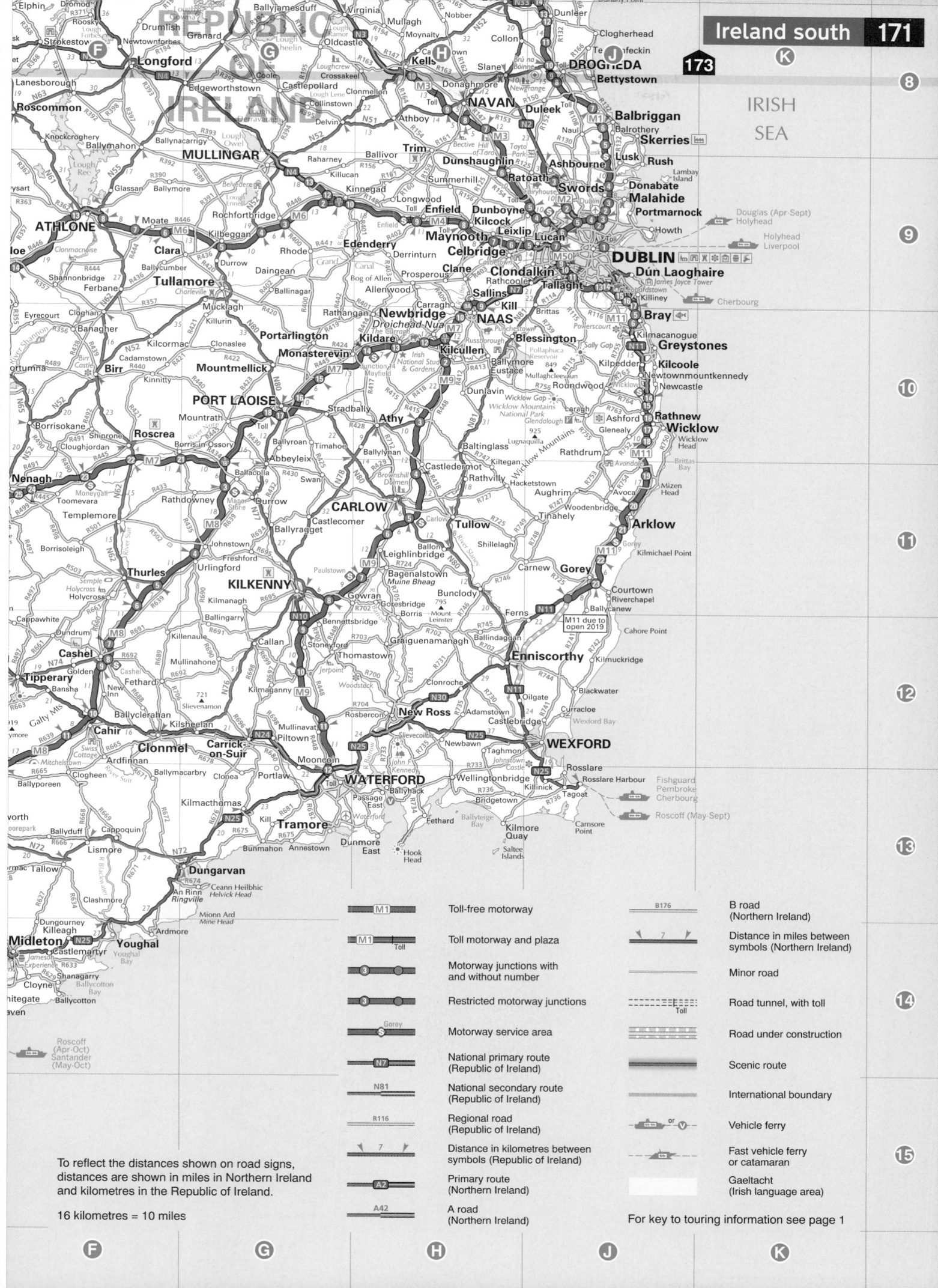

Ireland index

Abbeydorney.....C12
Abbeyfeale.....D12
Abbeyleix.....G11
Adamstown.....H12
Adare.....D12
Adrigole.....C14
Aghalee.....J5
Ahascragh.....E9
Aghoghill.....J4
Allenwood.....H9
Allihies.....B15
An Bun Beag.....E4
An Charraig.....E5
An Cheathrú Rua.....C9
An Clochán Liath.....E4
An Coireán.....B14
An Daingean.....B13
An Fál Carrach.....F3
An Fhairche.....C9
Annahilt.....J6
Annalong.....J7
Annascaul.....B13
Annestown.....G13
An Rinn.....G13
An Spidéal.....D9
Antrim.....J5
Ardagh.....D12
Ardara.....E5
Ardee.....H8
Ardfert.....C12
Ardfinnan.....F12
Ardglass.....K6
Ardgroom.....B14
Ardmore.....F14
Ardnacrusha.....E11
Arklow.....J11
Armagh.....H6
Armoy.....J3
Arvagh.....G7
Ashbourne.....J9
Ashford.....J10
Askeaton.....D12
Athea.....D12
Athenry.....E9
Athleague.....E8
Athlone.....F9
Athy.....H10
Augher.....G6
Aughnacloy.....H6
Aughrim.....E9
Aughrim.....J11
Avoca.....J11

Bagenalstown.....H11
Baile an Fheirtéaraigh.....B13
Baile Chláir.....D9
Baile Mhic Íre.....D14
Baile na Finne.....F4
Bailieborough.....H7
Balbriggan.....J8
Balla.....D8
Ballacolla.....G11
Ballaghaderreen.....E7
Ballina.....D7
Ballina.....E11
Ballinafad.....E7
Ballinagar.....G9
Ballinagh.....G7
Ballinamallard.....G6
Ballinamore.....F7
Ballinascarty.....D14
Ballinasloe.....E9
Ballincollig.....E14
Ballindaggan.....H12
Ballindine.....D8
Ballineen.....D14
Ballingarry.....D12
Ballingarry.....G12
Ballingeary.....D14
Ballinlough.....E8
Ballinrobe.....D8
Ballinspittle.....E14
Ballintra.....F5
Ballivor.....H9
Ballon.....H11
Ballybay.....H7
Ballybofey.....F5
Ballybunion.....C12
Ballycanew.....J11
Ballycarry.....K5

Ballycastle.....J3
Ballycastle.....C6
Ballyclare.....J5
Ballyclerahan.....F12
Ballyconneely.....B9
Ballyconnell.....G7
Ballycotton.....F14
Ballycumber.....F9
Ballydehob.....C15
Ballydesmond.....D13
Ballyduff.....C12
Ballyduff.....F13
Ballyfarnon.....E7
Ballyferriter.....B13
Ballygally.....J4
Ballygar.....E9
Ballygawley.....H6
Ballygawley.....E6
Ballygowan.....K5
Ballyhack.....H13
Ballyhaise.....G7
Ballyhalbert.....K5
Ballyhaunis.....E8
Ballyhean.....D8
Ballyheige.....C12
Ballyjamesduff.....G8
Ballylanders.....E14
Ballylynan.....H10
Ballylongford.....C12
Ballymacarbry.....F13
Ballymahon.....F8
Ballymakeery.....D14
Ballymena.....J4
Ballymoney.....H4
Ballymore.....F9
Ballymore Eustace.....H10
Ballymote.....E7
Ballynacarrigy.....G8
Ballynahinch.....J6
Ballynure.....J5
Ballyporeen.....F13
Ballyragget.....G11
Ballyroan.....G10
Ballysadare.....E6
Ballyshannon.....F5
Ballyvaughan.....D10
Ballywalter.....K5
Balrothery.....J8
Baltimore.....C15
Baltinglass.....H10
Banagher.....F10
Banbridge.....J6
Bandon.....E14
Bangor.....K5
Bangor Erris.....C7
Bansha.....F12
Banteer.....D13
Bantry.....C14
Barna.....D9
Béal an Mhuirthead.....B6
Béal Átha an Ghaorthaidh.....D14
Bearna.....D9
Belcoo.....F6
Belfast.....J5
Belgooly.....E14
Bellaghy.....H4
Belleek.....F6
Belmullet.....B6
Belturbet.....G7
Benburb.....H6
Bennettsbridge.....G12
Beragh.....G5
Bessbrook.....J6
Bettystown.....J8
Birr.....F10
Blacklion.....F6
Blackwater.....J12
Blarney.....E14
Blessington.....H10
Boherbue.....D13
Borris.....H11
Borris-in-Ossory.....F10
Borrisokane.....E10
Borrisoleigh.....F11
Boyle.....E7
Bray.....J10
Bridgetown.....H13

Brittas.....J9
Broadford.....E11
Broadford.....D12
Broughshane.....J4
Bruff.....E12
Bunbeg.....E4
Bunclody.....H11
Buncrana.....G3
Bundoran.....E6
Bunmahon.....G13
Bunnyconnellan.....D7
Bushmills.....H3
Buttevant.....E13
Bweeng.....E13

Cadamstown.....F10
Caherconlish.....E12
Caherdaniel.....B14
Cahersiveen.....B14
Cahir.....F12
Caledon.....H6
Callan.....G12
Caltra.....E9
Camp.....B13
Carndonagh.....G3
Cappawhite.....F12
Cappoquin.....F13
Carlanstown.....H8
Carlingford.....J7
Carlow.....H11
Carna.....C9
Carnew.....J11
Carnlough.....J4
Carragh.....H9
Carraig Airt.....F3
Carraroe.....C9
Carrick.....E5
Carrickfergus.....K5
Carrickmacross.....H7
Carrickmore.....G5
Carrick-on-Shannon.....F7
Carrick-on-Suir.....G12
Carrigaline.....E14
Carrigallen.....F7
Carriganimmy.....D13
Carrigart.....F3
Carrigtwohill.....E14
Carryduff.....J5
Cashel.....F12
Castlebar.....D8
Castlebellingham.....J7
Castleblakeney.....E9
Castleblayney.....H7
Castlebridge.....J12
Castlecomer.....G11
Castleconnell.....E11
Castlederg.....G5
Castledermot.....H11
Castlegregory.....B13
Castleisland.....C13
Castlemaine.....C13
Castlemartyr.....F14
Castleplunket.....E8
Castlepollard.....G8
Castlerea.....E8
Castlerock.....H3
Castletownbere.....B15
Castletownroche.....E13
Castletownshend.....D15
Castlewellan.....J6
Cathair Dónall.....B14
Causeway.....C12
Cavan.....G7
Celbridge.....H9
Charlestown.....D7
Charleville.....E12
Cill Charthaigh.....E5
Cill Chiaráin.....C9
Clady.....G4
Clane.....H9
Clara.....F9
Claregalway.....D9
Claremorris.....D8
Clashmore.....F13
Claudy.....G4
Cleggan.....B9
Clifden.....B9
Cliffoney.....E6
Cloghan.....F10
Clogheen.....F13
Clogher.....G6

Clogherhead.....J8
Clogh Mills.....J4
Clonakilty.....D15
Clonaslee.....G10
Clonbur.....C9
Clondalkin.....J9
Clonea.....G13
Clones.....G7
Clonmany.....G3
Clonmel.....F12
Clonmellon.....H8
Clonroche.....H12
Clough.....K6
Cloughjordan.....F10
Cloyne.....F14
Coachford.....D14
Coagh.....H5
Coalisland.....H5
Cobh.....E14
Coleraine.....H3
Collinstown.....G8
Collooney.....E7
Comber.....K5
Cong.....D9
Convoy.....F4
Cookstown.....H5
Coole.....G8
Cooraclare.....C11
Cootehill.....G7
Cork.....E14
Cornamona.....C9
Corr na Móna.....C9
Corrofin.....D10
Courtown.....J11
Courtmacsherry.....E15
Craughwell.....E10
Craigavon.....J6
Creeslough.....F4
Croithlí.....E4
Crolly.....E4
Crookhaven.....C15
Crookstown.....D14
Croom.....E12
Crossakeel.....H8
Crosshaven.....E14
Crossmaglen.....H7
Crossmolina.....D7
Crumlin.....J5
Crusheen.....D10
Culdaff.....G3
Cullybackey.....J4
Culmore.....G4
Curracloe.....J12
Curry.....E7
Cushendall.....J4
Cushendun.....J3

Daingean.....G9
Daingean Uí Chúis.....B13
Delvin.....G8
Derrinturn.....H9
Derry.....G4
Derrygonnelly.....F6
Derrylin.....G6
Dervock.....H3
Dingle.....B13
Doagh.....J5
Donabate.....J9
Donaghadee.....K5
Donaghmore.....H5
Donaghmore.....H8
Donegal.....F5
Donemana.....G4
Doolin.....C10
Doon.....E12
Doonbeg.....C11
Downings.....F3
Downpatrick.....K6
Dowra.....F6
Draperstown.....H5
Drimoleague.....D14
Drogheda.....J8
Droichead Nua.....H10
Dromahair.....E6
Dromara.....J6
Dromcollogher.....D12
Dromiskin.....J7
Drommahane.....E13
Dromod.....F8
Dromore.....J6

Dromore.....G5
Dromore West.....D6
Drumaness.....K6
Drumfries.....G3
Drumkeeran.....F7
Drumlish.....F8
Drumquin.....G5
Drumshanbo.....F7
Drumsna.....F7
Duagh.....C12
Dublin.....J9
Duleek.....J8
Dunboyne.....J9
Dún Chaoin.....A13
Dundalk.....J7
Dundonald.....K5
Dundrum.....F12
Dunfanaghy.....F3
Dungannon.....H5
Dungarvan.....G13
Dungiven.....H4
Dunglow.....E4
Dungourney.....F14
Dunkineely.....E5
Dunlavin.....H10
Dunleer.....J8
Dunloy.....J4
Dunmanway.....D14
Dunmore.....E8
Dunmore East.....H13
Dunquin.....A13
Dunshaughlin.....H9
Durrow.....G11
Durrow.....G9
Durrus.....C15
Dysart.....E9

Easky.....D6
Edenderry.....H9
Edgeworthstown.....G8
Eglinton.....G4
Elphin.....F8
Emyvale.....H6
Enfield.....H9
Ennis.....D11
Enniscorthy.....H12
Enniscrone.....D6
Enniskean.....D14
Enniskillen.....F6
Ennistymon.....D10
Eyrecourt.....F10

Fahan.....G4
Falcarragh.....F3
Fanore.....D10
Farranfore.....C13
Feakle.....E11
Fenagh.....F7
Fenit.....B13
Ferbane.....F9
Fermoy.....E13
Ferns.....J12
Fethard.....F12
Fethard.....H13
Fintona.....G6
Fintown.....F4
Fivemiletown.....G6
Foxford.....D7
Foynes.....D12
Freemount.....D13
Frenchpark.....E8
Freshford.....G11

Galbally.....E12
Galway.....D9
Garrison.....F6
Garvagh.....H4
Gilford.....J6
Glandore.....D15
Glaslough.....H6
Glassan.....F9
Gleann Cholm Cille.....E5
Glenamaddy.....E8
Glenarm.....J5
Glenavy.....J5
Glenbeigh.....B13
Glencolumbkille.....E5
Glenealy.....J10
Glengarriff.....C14
Glenties.....E5

Glin.....D12
Golden.....F12
Goleen.....C15
Goresbridge.....H11
Gorey.....J11
Gort.....D10
Gorteen.....E7
Gortin.....G5
Gowran.....G11
Graiguenamanagh.....H12
Granard.....G8
Grange.....E6
Greencastle.....H3
Greencastle.....H3
Greenore.....J7
Greyabbey.....K5
Greystones.....J10
Gulladuff.....H4

Hacketstown.....H11
Headford.....D9
Hillsborough.....J6
Hilltown.....J6
Holycross.....F11
Holywood.....K5
Hospital.....E12
Howth.....J9

Inagh.....D11
Inch.....B13
Inchigeelagh.....D14
Inishcrone.....D6
Innishannon.....E14
Irvinestown.....F6

Johnstown.....G11

Kanturk.....D13
Keadue.....F7
Keady.....H6
Kealkill.....C14
Keel.....B7
Kells.....J4
Kells.....H8
Kenmare.....C14
Kesh.....F5
Kilbeggan.....G9
Kilcar.....E5
Kilcock.....H9
Kilcolgan.....D10
Kilconnell.....E9
Kilcoole.....J10
Kilcormac.....F10
Kilcullen.....H10
Kildare.....H10
Kildorrery.....E13
Kilfenora.....D10
Kilfinane.....E12
Kilgarvan.....C14
Kilkee.....C11
Kilkeel.....J7
Kilkenny.....G11
Kilkieran.....C9
Kill.....H9
Kill.....G13
Killadysert.....D11
Killala.....D6
Killaloe.....E11
Killarney.....C13
Killashandra.....G7
Killeagh.....F14
Killenaule.....F12
Killimer.....C11
Killiney.....J9
Killinick.....J13
Killorglin.....C13
Killough.....K6
Killucan.....G9
Killurin.....G10
Killybegs.....E5
Killyleagh.....K6
Kilmacanogue.....J10
Kilmacrenan.....F4
Kilmacthomas.....G13
Kilmaganny.....G12
Kilmaine.....D8
Kilmallock.....E12
Kilmanagh.....G12
Kilmeedy.....D12
Kilmichael.....D14
Kilmihil.....C11
Kilmore Quay.....H13

Kilmuckridge.....J12
Kilpedder.....J10
Kilrea.....H4
Kilrush.....C11
Kilsheelan.....G12
Kiltegan.....H11
Kiltimagh.....D8
Kilworth.....E13
Kingscourt.....H7
Kinlough.....E6
Kinnegad.....G9
Kinnitty.....F10
Kinsale.....E14
Kinvarra.....D10
Kircubbin.....K5
Knock.....D8
Knockcroghery.....F8

Lahinch.....C10
Lanesborough.....F8
Laragh.....J10
Larne.....K4
Lauragh.....C14
Laurencetown.....F10
Leap.....D15
Leenaun.....C8
Leighlinbridge.....H11
Leitrim.....B9
Leitrim.....F7
Leixlip.....H9
Letterfrack.....B8

Letterkenny.....F4
Lifford.....G4
Limavady.....H4
Limerick.....E11
Lisbellaw.....G6
Lisburn.....J5
Liscarroll.....D13
Lisdoonvarna.....D10
Lismore.....F13
Lisnaskea.....G6
Listowel.....C12
Loghill.....D12
Londonderry.....G4
Longford.....F8
Longwood.....H9
Loughbrickland.....J6
Loughglinn.....E8
Loughrea.....E10
Louisburgh.....B8
Lucan.....J9
Lurgan.....J6
Lusk.....J9

Macroom.....D14
Maghera.....H4
Magherafelt.....H5
Maguiresbridge.....G6
Maigh Cuilinn.....D9
Malahide.....J9
Málainn Mhór.....E5
Malin.....G3

0   10   20 miles
0   10   20   30 kilometres

170

Malin More	E5	Muine Bheag	H11	Newtownbutler	G7	Portavogie	K6	Rathmore	D13	Salthill	D9	Stranorlar	F5	Tubbercurry	E7
Mallow	E13	Mullagh	H8	Newtown-		Portballintrae	H3	Rathmullan	G4	Scarriff	E11	Strokestown	F8	Tulla	D11
Manorhamilton	F6	Mullaghmore	E6	cunningham	G4	Portglenone	H4	Rathnew	J10	Scartaglin	C13	Summerhill	H9	Tullamore	G9
Markethill	H6	Mullinahone	G12	Newtownforbes	F8	Port Laoise	G10	Rathvilly	H11	Schull	C15	Swan	G11	Tullow	H11
Martinstown	J4	Mullinavat	G12	Newtownhamilton	H6	Portlaw	G13	Ratoath	J9	Seskinore	G5	Swanlinbar	F6	Tulsk	E8
Maynooth	H9	Mullingar	G9	Newtownmount-		Portmagee	B14	Recess	C9	Shanagarry	F14	Swinford	D7	Turlough	D7
Mayobridge	J6	Mulranny	C7	kennedy	J10	Portmarnock	J9	Rhode	G9	Shannon	D11	Swords	J9	
Midleton	F14	Murrisk	C8	Newtownstewart	G5	Portnablagh	F3	Ringaskiddy	E14	Shannonbridge	F9		Urlingford	G11
Milford	F4	Murroe	E11	Nobber	H8	Portnoo	E4	Ringville	G13	Shercock	H7	Taghmon	H12	Virginia	G8
Millstreet	D13	Naas	J9			Portroe	E11	Riverchapel	J11	Shillelagh	H11	Tagoat	J13	
Milltown	C13	Na Dúnaibh	F3	Ogonnelloe	E11	Portrush	H3	Riverstick	E14	Shinrone	F10	Tallaght	J9	Warrenpoint	J7
Milltown Malbay	C11	Naul	J8	Oilgate	H12	Portstewart	H3	Rochfortbridge	G9	Shrule	F13	Tallow	F13	Waterford	G13
Mitchelstown	E13	Navan	H8	Oldcastle	G8	Portumna	E10	Rockcorry	H7	Silvermines	E11	Tandragee	J6	Watergrasshill	E13
Moate	F9	Nenagh	E11	Omagh	G5	Poyntzpass	J6	Roosky	F8	Sion Mills	G5	Tarbert	C12	Waterville	B14
Mohill	F7	Newbawn	H12	Oola	E12	Prosperous	H9	Rosbercon	H12	Sixmilebridge	D11	Templemore	F11	Wellingtonbridge	H13
Monaghan	H6	Newbliss	G7	Oranmore	D9			Roscommon	F8	Skerries	J8	Termonfeckin	J8	Westport	C8
Monasterevin	G10	Newbridge	H10	Oughterard	D9	Quin	D11	Roscrea	F10	Skibbereen	D15	Thomastown	G12	Wexford	J12
Moneymore	H5	Newcastle	J10					Rosscarbery	D15	Slane	H8	Thurles	F11	Whitegate	E14
Monivea	E9	Newcastle West	D12	Pallasgreen	E12	Raharney	G9	Rosses Point	E6	Sligo	E6	Timahoe	G10	Whitehead	K5
Mooncoin	G13	New Inn	F12	Partry	D8	Ramelton	F4	Rosslare	J13	Smithborough	G6	Timoleague	D15	Wicklow	J10
Mountbellew	E9	Newmarket	D13	Passage East	H13	Randalstown	J5	Rosslare Harbour	J13	Sneem	B14	Tinahely	J11	Woodenbridge	J11
Mountcharles	F5	Newmarket-on-		Passage West	E14	Raphoe	G4	Rosslea	G6	Spanish Point	C11	Tipperary	F12	Woodford	E10
Mountmellick	G10	Fergus	D11	Patrickswell	E12	Rasharkin	H4	Rossnowlagh	E5	Spiddal	D9	Tobercurry	E7	
Mountrath	G10	Newport	C7	Pettigo	F5	Rathangan	H10	Rostrevor	J7	Sraith Salach	C9	Tobermore	H4	Youghal	F14
Mountshannon	E10	Newport	E11	Piltown	G13	Rathcoole	J9	Roundstone	B9	Stewartstown	H5	Toomevara	F11	
Moville	G3	New Ross	H12	Plumbridge	G5	Rathcormac	E13	Roundwood	J10	Stoneyford	G12	Toomore	C15	
Moy	H6	Newry	J6	Pomeroy	H5	Rathdowney	G11	Rush	J9	Strabane	G4	Tower	E14	
Moycullen	D9	Newtownabbey	J5	Portadown	H6	Rathdrum	J10			Stradbally	G10	Tralee	C13	
Moynalty	H8	Newtownards	K5	Portaferry	K6	Rathfriland	J6	Saintfield	K6	Stradone	G7	Tramore	G13	
Mucklagh	G9			Portarlington	G10	Rathkeale	D12	St Johnston	G4	Strandhill	E6	Trim	H8	
Muff	G4					Ráth Luirc	E12	Sallins	H9	Strangford	K6	Tuam	D9	

171

Central London Congestion Charge and Ultra Low Emission Zone

Rail interchange

0   1   2 miles
0   1   2   3 kilometres

For Central London see pages 238-247

Town plan : Central London p.238-247

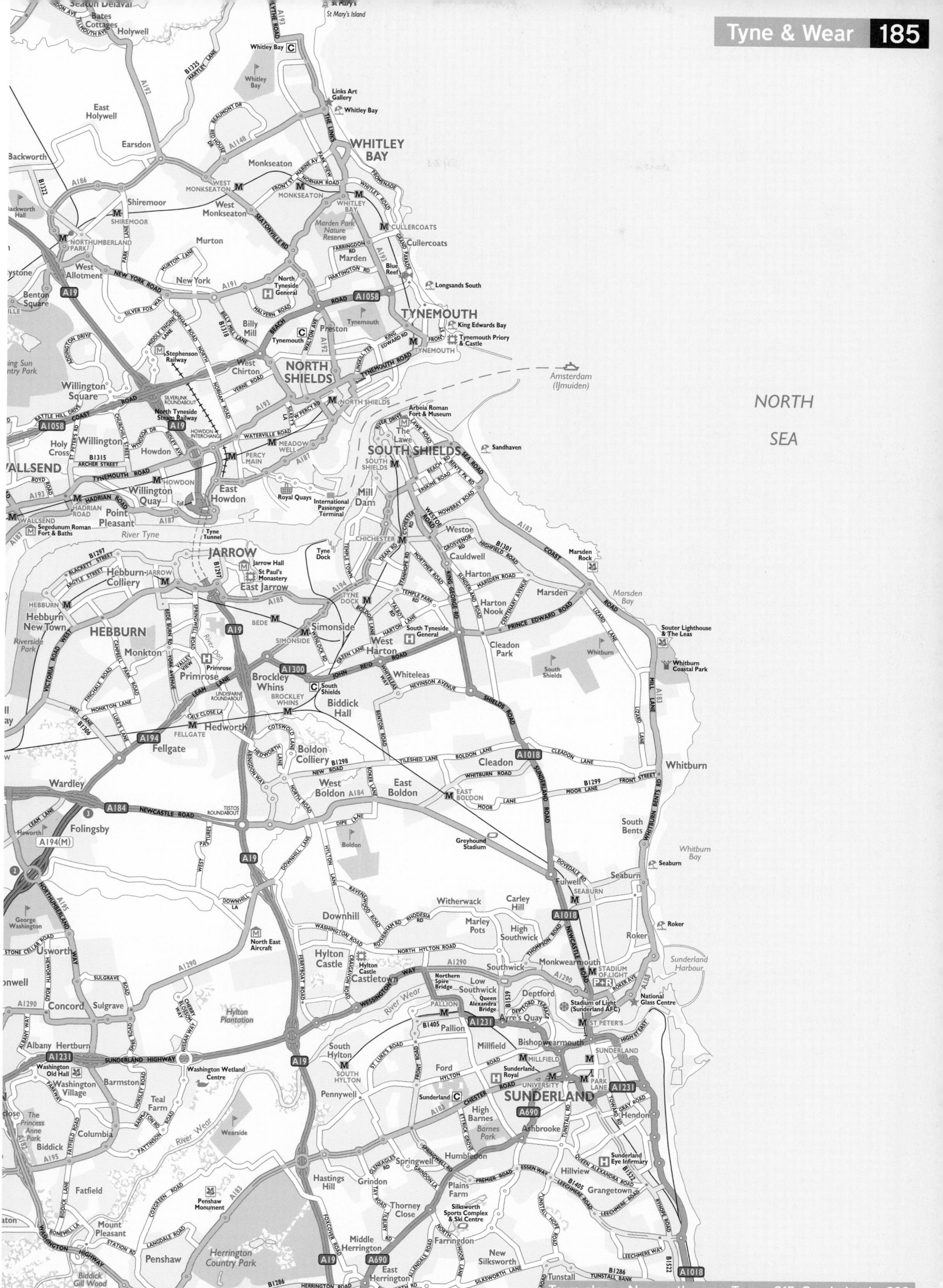

NORTH SEA

Amsterdam (IJmuiden)

WHITLEY BAY
Whitley Bay
Links Art Gallery
Monkseaton
West Monkseaton
Shiremoor
Murton
Seaton Delaval
Bates Cottages
Holywell
St Mary's Island
St Mary's
East Holywell
Earsdon
Backworth
Blackworth Hall
Benton Square
West Allotment
New York
New York Road
Northumberland Park
Cullercoats
Marden
Blue Reef
Longsands South
TYNEMOUTH
King Edwards Bay
Tynemouth Priory & Castle
Preston
North Tyneside General
Billy Mill
West Chirton
Stephenson Railway
NORTH SHIELDS
Willington Square
Willington
Holy Cross
Howdon
WALLSEND
Segedunum Roman Fort & Baths
Point Pleasant
Willington Quay
East Howdon
Royal Quays
International Passenger Terminal
Mill Dam
SOUTH SHIELDS
Arbeia Roman Fort & Museum
The Lawe
Sandhaven
Westoe
Cauldwell
Chichester
Harton
Harton Nook
Marsden
Marsden Rock
Marsden Bay
Souter Lighthouse & The Leas
Whitburn Coastal Park
Tyne Tunnel
JARROW
Jarrow Hall
St Paul's Monastery
East Jarrow
Hebburn Colliery
Tyne Dock
Simonside
West Harton
South Tyneside General
Whiteleas
South Shields
Cleadon Park
Whitburn
South Shields
HEBBURN
Hebburn New Town
Riverside Park
Monkton
Primrose
Brockley Whins
Biddick Hall
Hedworth
Fellgate
Boldon Colliery
West Boldon
East Boldon
Cleadon
Whitburn
Wardley
Folingsby
Heworth
George Washington
Usworth
North East Aircraft
Downhill
Hylton Castle
Castletown
Testos Roundabout
Greyhound Stadium
South Bents
Seaburn
Fulwell
Witherwack
Marley Pots
High Southwick
Carley Hill
Roker
Sunderland Harbour
Monkwearmouth
Stadium of Light
Stadium of Light (Sunderland AFC)
National Glass Centre
Southwick
Low Southwick
Northern Spire Bridge
Queen Alexandra Bridge
Deptford
St Peter's
Pallion
Ayre's Quay
Bishopwearmouth
Millfield
Concord
Sulgrave
Albany
Hertburn
Washington Old Hall
Washington Village
Washington Wetland Centre
Teal Farm
Barmston
South Hylton
South Hylton
Pennywell
Ford
Sunderland
Sunderland Royal
University
SUNDERLAND
Park Lane
Ashbrooke
Hendon
Sunderland Eye Infirmary
Hillview
Grangetown
High Barnes
Barnes Park
Humbledon
Biddick
Columbia
Wearside
Penshaw Monument
Herrington Country Park
Mount Pleasant
Penshaw
Biddick Gill Wood
Shiney
Fatfield
Springwell
Hastings Hill
Grindon
Thorney Close
Plains Farm
Middle Herrington
East Herrington
New Silksworth
Silksworth Sports Complex & Ski Centre
Silksworth
Tunstall
Farringdon

Street map symbols

Town, port and airport plans

Motorway and junction	One-way, gated/ closed road	Railway station	Car park, with electric charging point
Primary road single/ dual carriageway and numbered junction	Restricted access road	Light rapid transit system station	Park and Ride (at least 6 days per week)
A road single/ dual carriageway and numbered junction	Pedestrian area	Level crossing	Bus/coach station
B road single/ dual carriageway	Footpath	Tramway	Hospital
Local road single/ dual carriageway	Road under construction	Airport, heliport	24-hour Accident & Emergency hospital
Other road single/ dual carriageway, minor road	Road tunnel	Railair terminal	Beach (award winning)
Building of interest	Lighthouse	Theatre or performing arts centre	City wall
Ruined building	Castle	Cinema	Escarpment
Tourist Information Centre	Castle mound	Abbey, chapel, church	Cliff lift
Visitor or heritage centre	Monument, statue	Synagogue	River/canal, lake
World Heritage Site (UNESCO)	Post Office	Mosque	Lock, weir
Museum	Public library	Golf course	Viewpoint
English Heritage site	Shopping centre	Racecourse	Park/sports ground
Historic Scotland site	Shopmobility	Nature reserve	Cemetery
Cadw (Welsh heritage) site	Football stadium	Aquarium	Woodland
National Trust site	Rugby stadium	Agricultural showground	Built-up area
National Trust Scotland site	County cricket ground	Toilet, with facilities for the less able	Beach

Central London street map (see pages 238–247)

London Underground station	London Overground station
Docklands Light Railway (DLR) station	Central London Congestion Charge and Ultra Low Emission boundary

Royal Parks

Green Park	Park open 5am–midnight. Constitution Hill and The Mall closed to traffic Sundays and public holidays 8am–dusk.
Grosvenor Square Garden	Park open 7:30am–dusk.
Hyde Park	Park open 5am–midnight. Park roads closed to traffic midnight–5am.
Kensington Gardens	Park open 6am–dusk.
Regent's Park	Park open 5am–dusk. Park roads closed to traffic midnight–7am, except for residents.
St James's Park	Park open 5am–midnight. The Mall closed to traffic Sundays and public holidays 8am–dusk.
Victoria Tower Gardens	Park open dawn–dusk.

Traffic regulations in the City of London include security checkpoints and restrict the number of entry and exit points.

Note: Oxford Street is closed to through-traffic (except buses & taxis) 7am–7pm Monday–Saturday.

Central London Congestion Charge Zone (CCZ)

The charge for driving or parking a vehicle on public roads in this Central London area, during operating hours, is £11.50 per vehicle per day in advance or on the day of travel. Alternatively you can pay £10.50 by registering with CC Auto Pay, an automated payment system. Drivers can also pay the next charging day after travelling in the zone but this will cost £14. Payment permits entry, travel within and exit from the CCZ by the vehicle as often as required on that day.

The CCZ operates between 7am and 6pm, Mon–Fri only. There is no charge at weekends, on public holidays or between 25th Dec and 1st Jan inclusive.

For up to date information on the CCZ, exemptions, discounts or ways to pay, visit *www.tfl.gov.uk/modes/driving/congestion-charge*

Ultra Low Emission Zone (ULEZ)

All vehicles in Central London need to meet minimum exhaust emission standards or pay a daily Emission Surcharge. It applies to the same area covered by the Congestion Charge and operates 24 hours a day, every day of the year. The surcharge is £12.50 for motorcycles, cars and vans and is in addition to the Congestion Charge.

For further information visit *www.tfl.gov.uk/ULEZ*

In addition the Low Emission Zone (LEZ) operates across Greater London, 24 hours every day of the year and is aimed at the most heavy-polluting vehicles. It does not apply to cars or motorcycles. For details visit *www.tfl.gov.uk/LEZ*

Town Plans

Central London

Ferry Ports

Channel Tunnel

Airports

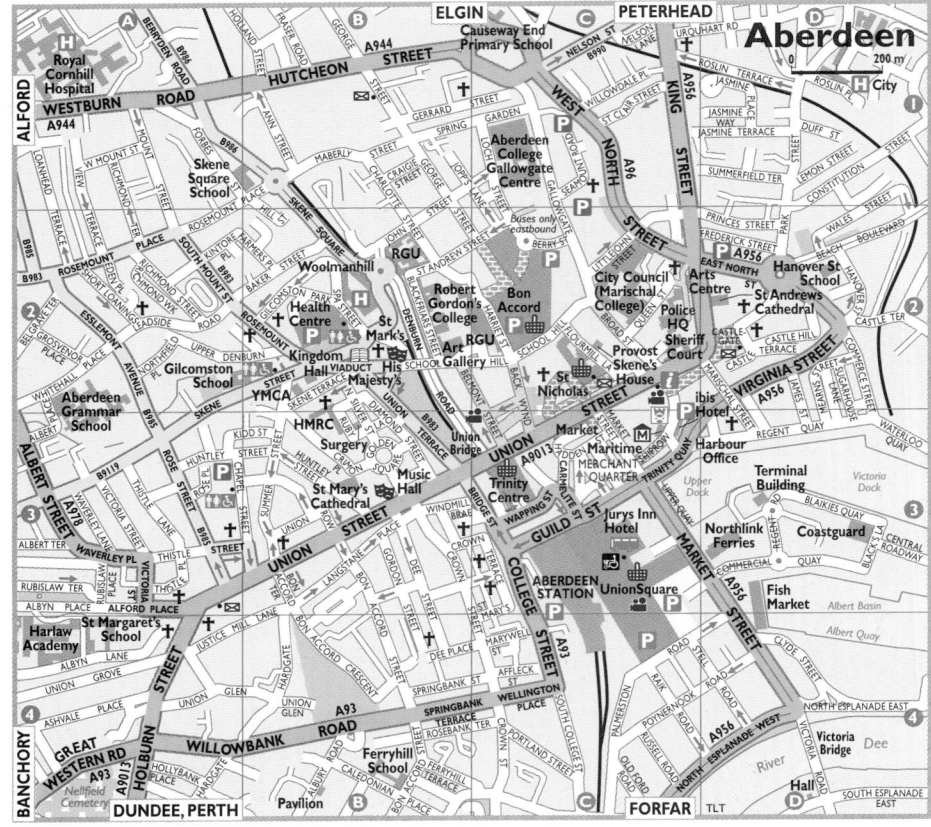

Aberdeen

Aberdeen is found on atlas page **151 N6**

Affleck Street	C4	Maberly Street	B1
Albert Street	A3	Marischal Street	D2
Albury Road	B4	Market Street	C3
Alford Place	A3	Nelson Street	C1
Ann Street	B1	Palmerston Road	C4
Beach Boulevard	D2	Park Street	D1
Belgrave Terrace	A2	Portland Street	C4
Berryden Road	A1	Poynernook Road	C4
Blackfriars Street	B2	Regent Quay	D3
Blaikies Quay	D3	Richmond Street	A2
Bon Accord Crescent	B4	Rose Place	A3
Bon Accord Street	B3	Rose Street	A3
Bridge Street	C3	Rosemount Place	A2
Caledonian Place	B4	Rosemount Viaduct	A2
Carmelite Street	C3	St Andrew Street	B2
Chapel Street	A3	St Clair Street	C1
Charlotte Street	B1	School Hill	C2
College Street	C3	Skene Square	B2
Constitution Street	D1	Skene Street	A3
Crimon Place	B3	Skene Terrace	B2
Crown Street	B3	South College Street	C4
Dee Street	B3	South Esplanade East	D4
Denburn Road	B2	South Mount Street	A2
Diamond Street	B3	Spa Street	B2
East North Street	D2	Springbank Street	B4
Esslemont Avenue	A2	Springbank Terrace	B4
Gallowgate	C1	Summer Street	B3
George Street	B1	Summerfield Terrace	D1
Gilcomston Park	B2	Thistle Lane	A3
Golden Square	B3	Thistle Place	A3
Gordon Street	B3	Thistle Street	A3
Great Western Road	A4	Trinity Quay	C3
Guild Street	C3	Union Bridge	B3
Hadden Street	C3	Union Grove	A4
Hanover Street	D2	Union Street	B3
Hardgate	B4	Union Terrace	B2
Harriet Street	C2	Upper Denburn	A2
Holburn Street	A4	Victoria Road	D4
Huntley Street	A3	Victoria Street	A3
Hutcheon Street	B1	View Terrace	A1
Jasmine Terrace	D1	Virginia Street	D2
John Street	B2	Wapping Street	C3
Justice Mill Lane	A4	Waverley Place	A3
King Street	C1	Wellington Place	C4
Langstane Place	B3	West North Street	C1
Leadside Road	A2	Westburn Road	A1
Loanhead Terrace	A1	Whitehall Place	A2
Loch Street	C1	Willowbank Road	A4

Basingstoke

Basingstoke is found on atlas page **22 H4**

Alencon Link	C1	London Street	C3
Allnutt Avenue	D2	Lower Brook Street	B4
Basing View	C1	Lytton Road	D3
Beaconsfield Road	C4	Market Place	B3
Bounty Rise	A4	May Place	C3
Bounty Road	A4	Montague Place	C4
Bramblys Close	A3	Mortimer Lane	A2
Bramblys Drive	A3	New Road	B3
Budd's Close	A3	New Road	C2
Castle Road	C4	New Street	B3
Chapel Hill	B1	Penrith Road	A3
Chequers Road	C2	Rayleigh Road	A2
Chester Road	A4	Red Lion Lane	C3
Churchill Way	B2	Rochford Road	A2
Churchill Way East	D1	St Mary's Court	C2
Churchill Way West	A2	Sarum Hill	A3
Church Square	B2	Seal Road	C2
Church Street	B2	Solby's Road	A2
Church Street	B3	Southend Road	A2
Cliddesden Road	C4	Southern Road	B4
Clifton Terrace	C1	Stukeley Road	A3
Cordale Road	A4	Sylvia Close	B4
Council Road	B4	Timberlake Road	B2
Crossborough Gardens	D3	Victoria Street	B3
Crossborough Hill	D3	Victory Roundabout	A2
Cross Street	B3	Vyne Road	B1
Devonshire Place	A4	Winchcombe Road	A4
Eastfield Avenue	D2	Winchester Road	A4
Eastrop Lane	D2	Winchester Street	B3
Eastrop Roundabout	C1	Winterthur Way	A1
Eastrop Way	D2	Worting Road	A3
Essex Road	A2	Wote Street	C3
Fairfields Road	B4		
Festival Way	C2		
Flaxfield Court	A2		
Flaxfield Road	A3		
Flaxfield Road	B3		
Frances Road	A4		
Frescade Crescent	A4		
Goat Lane	C2		
Hackwood Road	C4		
Hamelyn Road	A4		
Hardy Lane	A4		
Hawkfield Lane	A4		
Haymarket Yard	C3		
Joices Yard	B3		
Jubilee Road	B4		
London Road	D3		

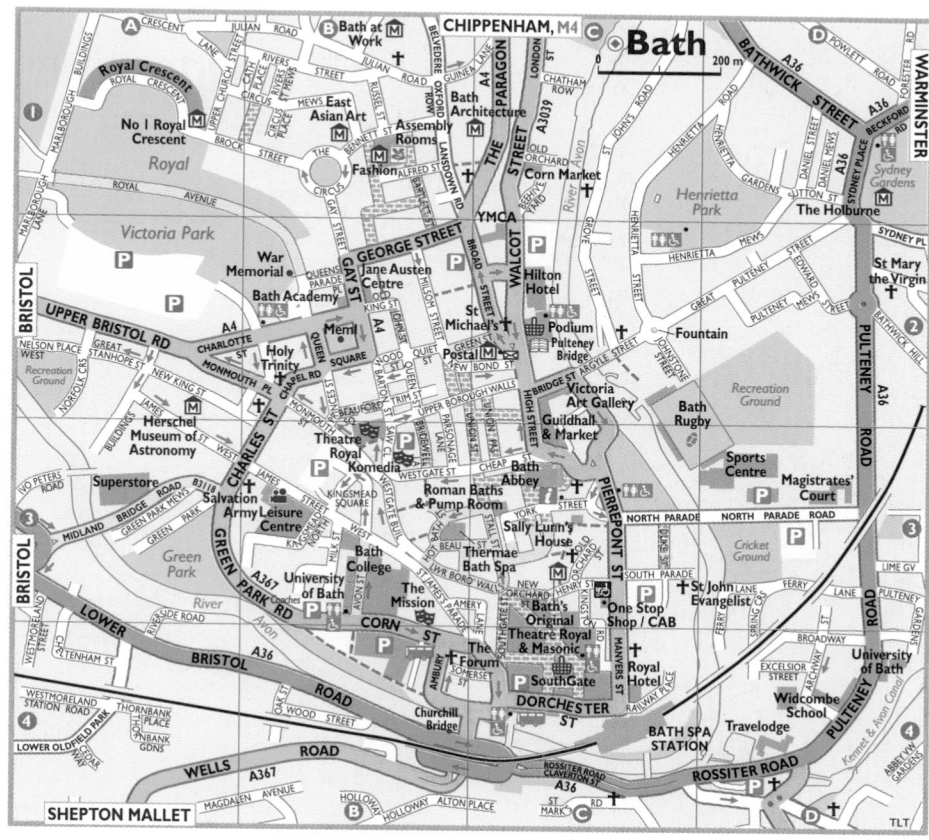

Bath

Bath is found on atlas page **20 D2**

Archway Street D4	Lower Borough Walls............B3
Argyle Street......................C2	Lower Bristol Road................A3
Avon Street B3	Lower Oldfield Park...............A4
Bartlett Street B1	Manvers Street.....................C3
Barton Street B2	Midland Bridge Road..............A3
Bathwick Street...................D1	Milk Street B3
Beauford Square B2	Milsom Street B2
Beau Street B3	Monmouth Place...................A2
Beckford Road D1	Monmouth Street B2
Bennett Street B1	New Bond Street...................B2
Bridge Street C2	New King Street.....................A2
Broad Street C2	New Orchard Street C3
Broadway D4	Norfolk Buildings A3
Brock Street A1	North Parade.......................C3
Chapel Road B2	North Parade Road D3
Charles Street A3	Old King Street B2
Charlotte Street A2	Oxford Row B1
Cheap Street C3	Pierrepont Street C3
Cheltenham Street................A4	Princes Street B2
Circus Mews B1	Pulteney Road D2
Claverton Street...................C4	Queen Square B2
Corn Street B4	Queen Street........................B2
Daniel Street D1	Railway Place C4
Dorchester Street C4	Rivers Street B1
Edward Street D2	Rossiter Road.......................C4
Ferry Lane D3	Royal Avenue A1
Gay Street B1	Royal Crescent......................A1
George Street B2	St James's Parade B3
Great Pulteney Street C2	St John's Road C1
Great Stanhope Street A2	Saw Close B3
Green Park Road A3	Southgate Street C4
Green Street B2	South Parade C3
Grove Street C2	Stall Street C3
Guinea Lane B1	Sutton Street D1
Henrietta Gardens................D1	Sydney Place D1
Henrietta Mews...................C2	The Circus B1
Henrietta Road....................C1	The Paragon C1
Henrietta Street...................C2	Thornbank Place A4
Henry Street C3	Union Street B2
High Street C2	Upper Borough Walls..............B2
Hot Bath Street B3	Upper Bristol Road.................A2
James Street West B3	Upper Church Street...............A1
John Street B2	Walcot Street.......................C2
Julian Road B1	Wells Road A4
Kingsmead North B3	Westgate Buildings B3
Kingston Road.....................C3	Westgate Street.....................B3
Lansdown Road...................B1	Westmoreland Station Road......A4
London Street C1	York Street...........................C3

Blackpool

Blackpool is found on atlas page **88 C3**

Abingdon Street....................B1	Havelock Street.....................C4
Adelaide Street......................B3	High Street C1
Albert Road B3	Hornby Road B3
Albert Road C3	Hornby Road D3
Alfred Street C2	Hull Road B3
Ashton Road D4	Kay Street C4
Bank Hey Street B2	Kent Road C4
Banks Street B1	King Street C2
Belmont Avenue C4	Leamington Road D2
Bennett Avenue D3	Leicester Road D2
Bethesda Road C4	Leopold Grove.......................C2
Birley Street B2	Lincoln Road D2
Blenheim Avenue D4	Livingstone Road C3
Bonny Street B4	Lord Street B1
Buchanan Street C1	Louise Street C4
Butler Street C1	Milbourne Street....................C1
Caunce Street D1	Montreal Avenue D3
Cedar Square C2	New Bonny Street B3
Central Drive........................C4	New Larkhill Street C1
Chapel Street B4	Palatine Road C4
Charles Street C1	Palatine Road D3
Charnley Road C3	Park Road D2
Cheapside B2	Park Road D4
Church Street B2	Peter Street D2
Church Street C2	Pier Street............................B4
Church Street D2	Princess Parade B1
Clifton Street B2	Promenade B1
Clinton Avenue D4	Queen Street B1
Cookson Street C2	Raikes Parade D2
Coop Street B4	Reads Avenue C3
Coronation Street..................B2	Reads Avenue D3
Corporation Street..................B2	Regent Road C2
Dale Street B4	Ribble Road C4
Deansgate...........................B2	Ripon Road D3
Dickson Road B1	Seasiders Way.......................B4
Edward Street C2	Selbourne Road D1
Elizabeth Street D1	South King Street C2
Fairhurst Street D1	Springfield Road B1
Fisher Street C1	Stanley Road C3
Fleet Street C3	Talbot Road B2
Foxhall Road B4	Talbot Road C1
Freckleton Street D4	Topping Street C2
General Street B1	Vance Road B3
George Street C1	Victoria Street B2
Gorton Street D1	Victory Road D1
Granville Road D2	West Street B2
Grosvenor Street...................C1	Woolman Road D4
Harrison Street D4	York Street............................B4

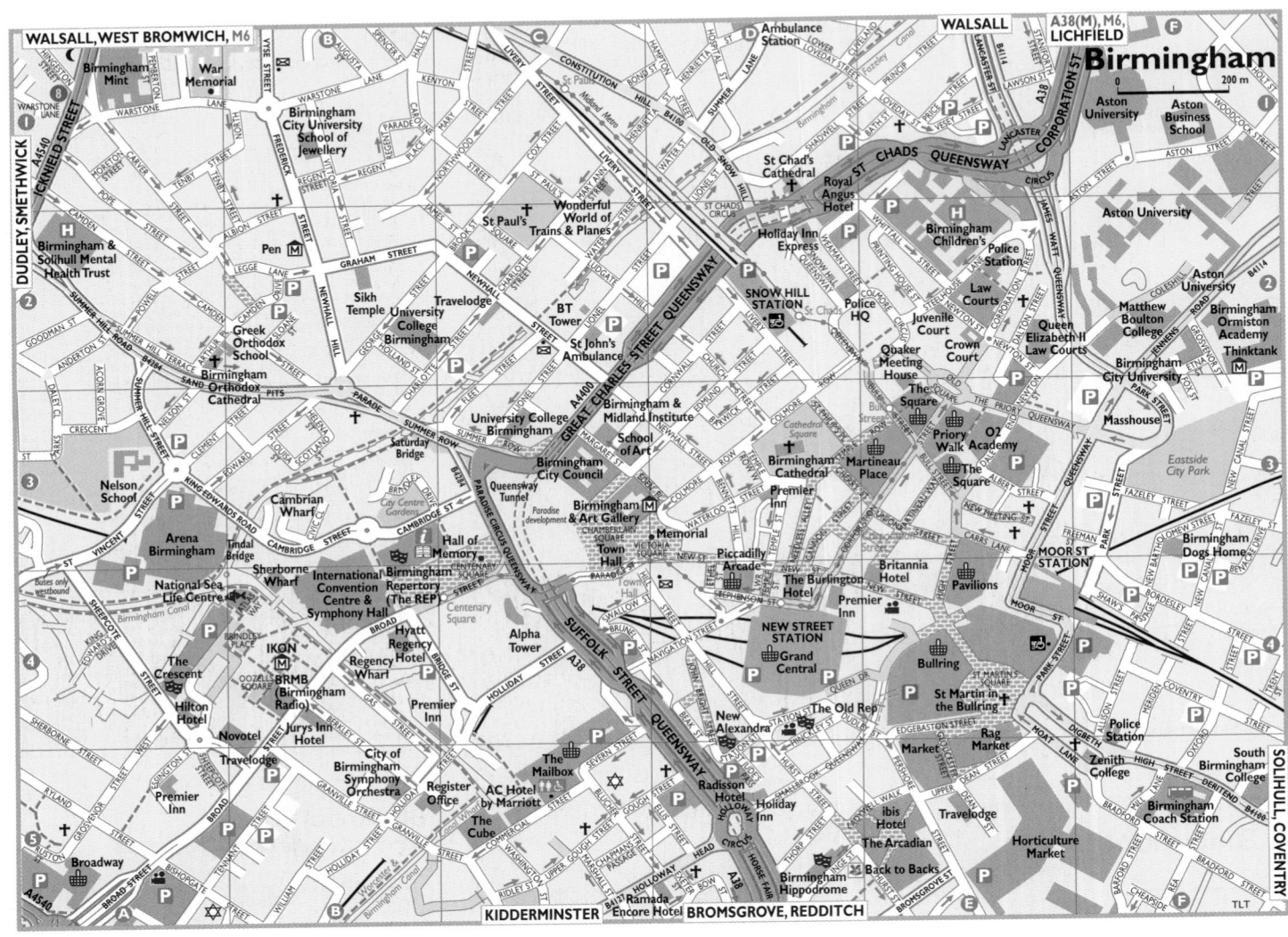

Birmingham

Birmingham is found on atlas page **58 G7**

Acorn Grove	A2	Caroline Street	B1
Albert Street	E3	Carrs Lane	E3
Albert Street	F3	Carver Street	A1
Albion Street	B2	Chamberlain Square	C3
Allison Street	F4	Chapmans Passage	C5
Anderton Street	A2	Charlotte Street	B3
Arthur Place	A2	Cheapside	F5
Aston Street	F1	Cherry Street	D3
Atlas Way	B4	Church Street	D2
Banbury Street	F3	Civic Close	B3
Barford Street	F5	Clement Street	A3
Bartholomew Street	F3	Cleveland Street	D1
Barwick Street	D3	Coleshill Street	F2
Bath Street	E1	Colmore Circus Queensway	E2
Beak Street	D4	Colmore Row	D3
Benacre Drive	F4	Commercial Street	C5
Bennetts Hill	D3	Constitution Hill	C1
Berkley Street	B4	Cornwall Street	D3
Bishopgate Street	A5	Corporation Street	E1
Blucher Street	C5	Corporation Street	E3
Bond Street	C1	Coventry Street	F4
Bordesley Street	F4	Cox Street	C1
Bow Street	D5	Dale End	E3
Bradford Street	F5	Daley Close	A3
Bridge Street	B4	Dalton Street	E2
Brindley Drive	B3	Dean Street	E5
Brindley Place	B4	Digbeth	E4
Broad Street	A5	Dudley Street	D4
Bromsgrove Birmingham	E5	Eden Place	C3
Brook Street	C2	Edgbaston Street	E4
Brunel Street	C4	Edmund Street	D3
Bull Street	E3	Edward Street	B3
Cambridge Street	B3	Ellis Street	D5
Camden Drive	B2	Essington Street	A5
Camden Street	A2	Ethel Street	D4
Cannon Street	D3	Etna Street	F2

Exeter Street	D5	King Edward's Drive	A4
Fazeley Street	F3	King Edwards Road	A3
Fleet Street	C3	Ladywell Walk	D5
Fox Street	F3	Lancaster Circus	E1
Frederick Street	B1	Lancaster Street	E1
Freeman Street	E3	Lawson Street	E1
Gas Street	B4	Legge Lane	B2
George Street	B2	Lighthouse Avenue	A3
Gloucester Street	E5	Lionel Street	C3
Goodman Street	A2	Livery Street	C1
Gough Street	C5	Louisa Street	B3
Graham Street	B2	Loveday Street	E1
Granville Street	B5	Lower Loveday Street	D1
Great Charles Street		Lower Temple Street	D4
Queensway	C3	Ludgate Hill	C2
Grosvenor Street	F2	Margaret Street	C3
Grosvenor Street West	A5	Marshall Street	C5
Hall Street	B1	Martineau Way	E3
Hampton Street	D1	Mary Ann Street	C1
Helena Street	B3	Mary Street	C1
Henrietta Street	C1	Meriden Street	F4
High Street	E4	Mill Lane	E4
High Street Deritend	F5	Moat Lane	E4
Hill Street	C4	Moor Street	E4
Hinckley Street	D4	Moor Street Queensway	E4
Hingeston Street	A1	Moreton Street	A1
Holland Street	B2	Navigation Street	C4
Holliday Street	B5	Needless Alley	D3
Holloway Circus	D5	Nelson Street	A3
Holloway Head	C5	New Bartholomew Street	F4
Holt Street	F1	New Canal Street	F4
Horse Fair	D5	Newhall Hill	B2
Hospital Street	D1	Newhall Street	C2
Hurst Street	D5	New Meeting Street	E3
Icknield Street	A1	Newton Street	E3
Inge Street	D5	Newton Street	E2
James Street	B2	Northwood Street	C1
James Watt Queensway	E2	Old Snow Hill	D1
Jennens Road	F2	Old Square	E3
John Bright Street	D4	Oozells Square	B4
Kenyon Street	B1	Oxford Street	F5

Parade	B3	Steelhouse Lane	E2
Paradise Circus Queensway	C3	Stephenson Street	D4
Paradise Street	C4	Suffolk Street Queensway	C4
Park Street	E4	Summer Hill Road	A2
Pemberton Street	A1	Summer Hill Street	A2
Pershore Street	E5	Summer Hill Terrace	A2
Pope Street	A1	Summer Lane	D1
Powell Street	A2	Summer Row	B3
Price Street	E1	Swallow Street	C4
Princip Street	E1	Temple Row	D3
Printing House Street	E2	Temple Row West	D3
Queens Drive	D4	Temple Street	D3
Queensway Tunnel	C3	Tenby Street	A1
Rea Street	F5	Tenby Street North	A1
Regent Parade	B1	Tennant Street	A5
Regent Place	B1	The Priory Queensway	E3
Regent Street	B1	Thorp Street	D5
Ridley Street	C5	Tindal Bridge	B3
Ruston Street	A5	Trent Street	F4
Ryland Street	A5	Union Street	E3
St Chads Queensway	E1	Upper Dean Street	E5
St Jude's Pass	D5	Upper Gough Street	C5
St Marks Crescent	A3	Vesey Street	E1
St Martin's Square	E4	Victoria Square	C3
St Paul's Square	C1	Vittoria Street	B1
St Philip's Place	D3	Vyse Street	B1
St Vincent Street	A3	Warstone Lane	A1
Sand Pitts	A2	Washington Street	C5
Saturday Bridge	B3	Waterloo Street	D3
Scotland Street	B3	Water Street	C2
Severn Street	C5	Weaman Street	D2
Shadwell Street	D1	Whittall Street	E2
Shaw's Passage	F4	William Street	B5
Sheepcote Street	A4	Woodcock Street	F1
Sherborne Street	A4		
Sloane Street	B2		
Smallbrook Queensway	D5		
Snow Hill Queensway	D1		
Spencer Street	B1		
Staniforth Street	E1		
Station Street	D5		

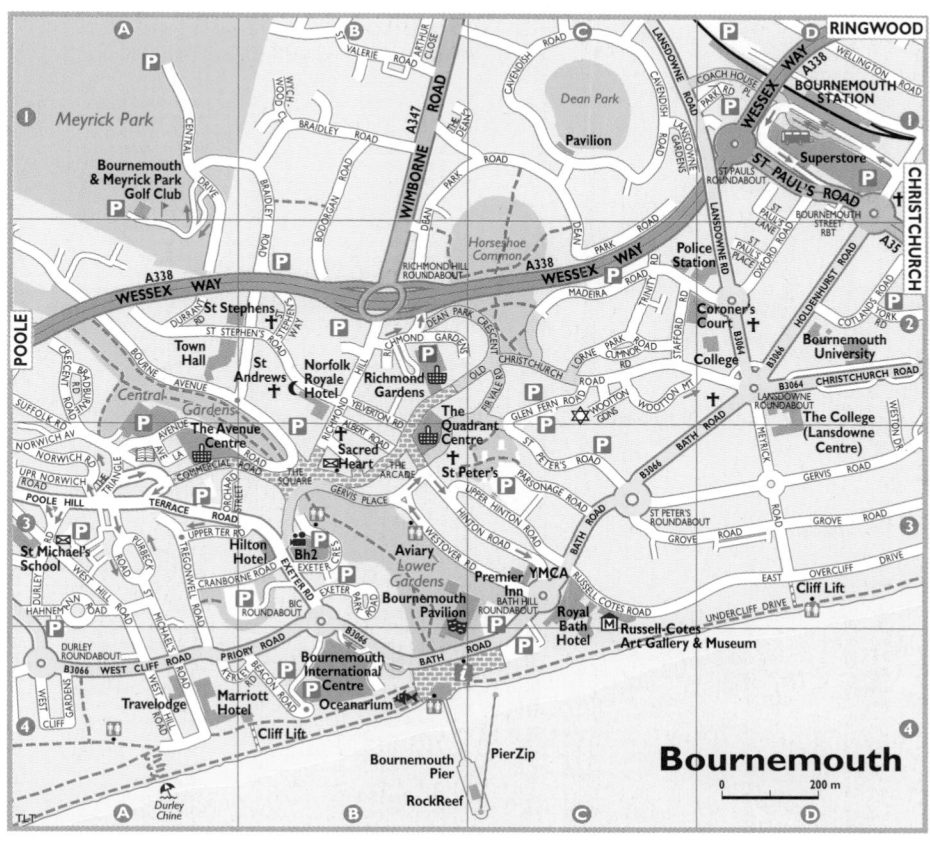

Bournemouth

Bournemouth is found on atlas page **13 J6**

Albert Road	B3	Old Christchurch Road	C2
Avenue Lane	A3	Orchard Street	A3
Avenue Road	A3	Oxford Road	D2
Bath Hill Roundabout	C3	Park Road	D1
Bath Road	B4	Parsonage Road	C3
Beacon Road	B4	Poole Hill	A3
BIC Roundabout	B3	Priory Road	A4
Bodorgan Road	B2	Purbeck Road	A3
Bourne Avenue	A2	Richmond Gardens	B2
Bournemouth Street		Richmond Hill	B3
Roundabout	D1	Richmond Hill Roundabout	B2
Bradburne Road	A2	Russell Cotes Road	C3
Braidley Road	B1	St Michael's Road	A3
Cavendish Road	C1	St Paul's Lane	D1
Central Drive	A1	St Paul's Place	D2
Christchurch Road	D2	St Paul's Road	D1
Coach House Place	D1	St Pauls Roundabout	D1
Commercial Road	A3	St Peter's Road	C3
Cotlands Road	D2	St Peter's Roundabout	C3
Cranborne Road	A3	St Stephen's Road	A2
Crescent Road	A2	St Stephen's Way	B2
Cumnor Road	C2	St Valerie Road	B1
Dean Park Crescent	B2	Stafford Road	C2
Dean Park Road	B2	Suffolk Road	A2
Durley Road	A3	Terrace Road	A3
Durley Roundabout	A4	The Arcade	B3
Durrant Road	A2	The Deans	B1
East Overcliff Drive	D3	The Square	B3
Exeter Crescent	B3	The Triangle	A3
Exeter Park Road	B3	Tregonwell Road	A3
Exeter Road	B3	Trinity Road	C2
Fir Vale Road	C2	Undercliff Drive	D3
Gervis Place	B3	Upper Hinton Road	C3
Gervis Road	D3	Upper Norwich Road	A3
Glen Fern Road	C2	Upper Terrace Road	A3
Grove Road	C3	Wellington Road	D1
Hahnemann Road	A3	Wessex Way	A2
Hinton Road	B3	West Cliff Gardens	A4
Holdenhurst Road	D2	West Cliff Road	A4
Kerley Road	A4	West Hill Road	A3
Lansdowne Gardens	C1	Weston Drive	D2
Lansdowne Road	C1	Westover Road	B3
Lansdowne Roundabout	D2	Wimborne Road	B1
Lorne Park Road	C2	Wootton Gardens	C2
Madeira Road	C2	Wootton Mount	C2
Meyrick Road	D3	Wychwood Close	B1
Norwich Avenue	A3	Yelverton Road	B2
Norwich Road	A3	York Road	D2

Bradford

Bradford is found on atlas page **90 F4**

Aldermanbury	B3	Lower Kirkgate	C2
Bank Street	B2	Lumb Lane	A1
Barkerend Road	D2	Manchester Road	B4
Barry Street	B2	Manningham Lane	A1
Bolling Road	C4	Manor Row	B1
Bolton Road	C2	Market Street	B3
Bridge Street	C3	Midland Road	B1
Broadway	C3	Morley Street	A4
Burnett Street	D2	Neal Street	B4
Canal Road	C1	Nelson Street	B4
Carlton Street	A3	North Brook Street	C1
Centenary Square	B3	Northgate	B2
Chandos Street	C4	North Parade	B1
Chapel Street	D3	North Street	C2
Cheapside	B2	North Wing	D1
Chester Street	A4	Otley Road	D1
Church Bank	C2	Paradise Street	A2
Claremont	A4	Peckover Street	D2
Croft Street	C4	Piccadilly	B2
Darfield Street	A1	Pine Street	C2
Darley Street	B2	Princes Way	B3
Drewton Road	A2	Randall Well Street	A3
Dryden Street	D4	Rawson Road	A2
Duke Street	B2	Rawson Square	B2
East Parade	D3	Rebecca Street	A2
Edmund Street	A4	St Blaise Way	C1
Edward Street	C4	St Thomas's Road	A2
Eldon Place	A1	Sawrey Place	A4
Filey Street	D3	Senior Way	B4
George Street	C3	Shipley Airedale Road	C1
Godwin Street	B2	Stott Hill	C2
Grattan Road	A2	Sunbridge Road	A2
Great Horton Road	A4	Tetley Street	A3
Grove Terrace	A4	Thornton Road	A3
Hallfield Road	A1	Trafalgar Street	B1
Hall Ings	B4	Tyrrel Street	B3
Hammerton Street	D3	Upper Park Gate	D2
Hamm Strasse	B1	Upper Piccadilly	B2
Holdsworth Street	C1	Valley Road	C1
Houghton Place	A1	Vicar Lane	C3
Howard Street	A4	Wakefield Road	D4
Hustlergate	B3	Wapping Road	D1
Infirmary Street	A1	Water Lane	A2
John Street	B2	Wellington Street	C2
Lansdowne Place	A4	Westgate	A2
Leeds Road	D3	Wharf Street	C1
Little Horton	A4	Wigan Street	A2
Little Horton Lane	B4	Wilton Street	A4

Brighton

Brighton is found on atlas page **24 H10**

Ardingly Street	D3	Madeira Place	D4
Ashton Rise	D1	Manchester Street	C4
Bartholomew Square	B3	Margaret Street	D4
Black Lion Street	B3	Marine Parade	D4
Blaker Street	D3	Market Street	B3
Bond Street	B2	Marlborough Place	C2
Boyces Street	A3	Meeting House Lane	B3
Brighton Place	B3	Middle Street	B3
Broad Street	D4	Morley Street	D1
Buckingham Road	A1	New Road	B2
Camelford Street	D4	New Steine	D4
Cannon Place	A3	Nile Street	B3
Carlton Hill	D2	North Gardens	B1
Centurion Road	A1	North Place	C2
Chapel Street	D3	North Road	B1
Charles Street	C4	North Street	B2
Cheltenham Place	C1	Old Steine	C3
Church Street	A1	Portland Street	B2
Church Street	B2	Powis Grove	A1
Circus Street	C2	Prince Albert Street	B3
Clifton Hill	A1	Prince's Street	C3
Clifton Terrace	A1	Queen's Gardens	B1
Devonshire Place	D3	Queen Square	A2
Dukes Lane	B3	Queen's Road	B2
Duke Street	B2	Regency Road	A2
East Street	C3	Regent Hill	A2
Edward Street	D3	Regent Street	C2
Elmore Street	D1	Robert Street	C1
Foundry Street	B1	St James's Street	D3
Frederick Street	B1	St Nicholas Road	A1
Gardner Street	B2	Ship Street	B3
George Street	D3	Spring Gardens	B1
Gloucester Place	C1	Steine Street	C4
Gloucester Road	B1	Sussex Street	D2
Gloucester Street	C1	Sydney Street	C1
Grand Junction Road	B4	Tichborne Street	B2
Grand Parade	C2	Tidy Street	C1
High Street	D3	Upper Gardner Street	B1
Ivory Place	D1	Upper Gloucester Road	A1
John Street	D2	Upper North Street	A2
Jubilee Street	C2	Vine Street	C1
Kensington Gardens	C1	Wentworth Street	D4
Kensington Street	C1	Western Road	A2
Kew Street	B1	West Street	A3
King's Road	A3	White Street	D3
Kingswood Street	C2	William Street	D2
Leopold Road	A1	Windsor Street	B2
Little East Street	B4		

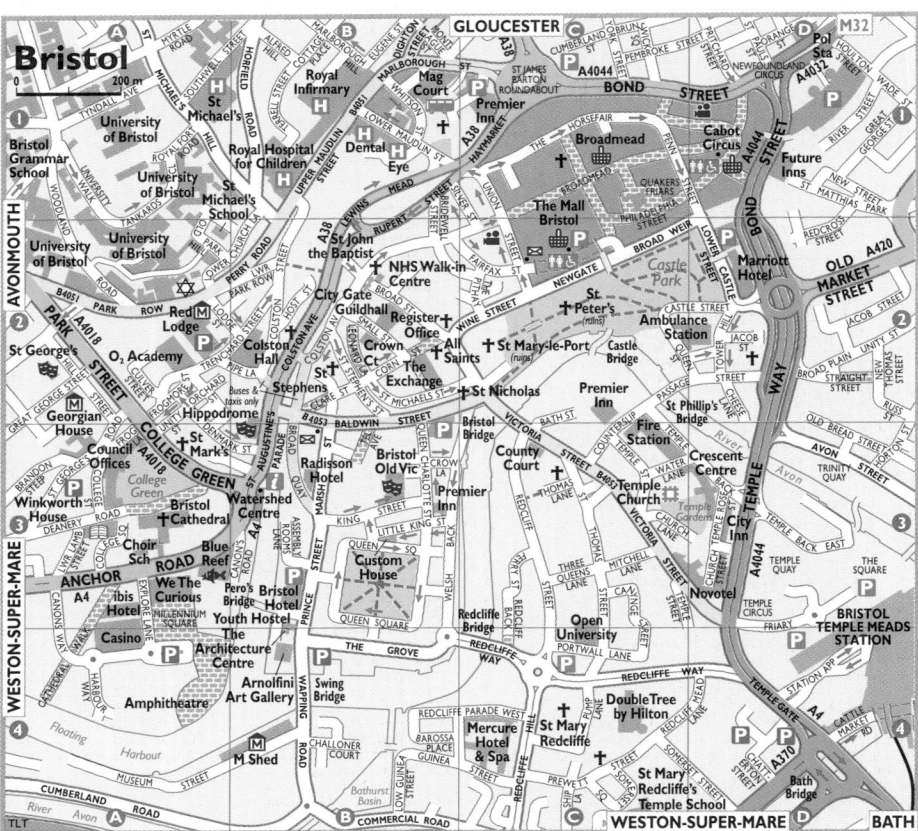

Bristol

Bristol is found on atlas page **31 Q10**

Anchor Road	A3	Passage Street	C2
Avon Street	D3	Pembroke Street	C1
Baldwin Street	B2	Penn Street	C1
Bath Bridge	D4	Pero's Bridge	B3
Bond Street	C1	Perry Road	A2
Bond Street	D2	Philadelphia Street	C2
Broadmead	C1	Portland Street	C4
Broad Plain	D2	Prewett Street	C4
Broad Quay	B3	Prince Street	B3
Broad Street	B2	Queen Charlotte Street	B3
Broad Weir	C2	Queen Square	B3
Canons Way	A3	Redcliffe Hill	C4
Canynge Street	C3	Redcliffe Parade West	B4
Castle Street	C2	Redcliffe Way	C4
College Green	A3	Redcliff Mead Lane	C4
Colston Avenue	B2	Redcliff Street	C3
Colston Street	B2	Royal Fort Road	A1
Commercial Road	B4	Rupert Street	B2
Corn Street	B2	St Augustine's Parade	B3
Counterslip	C3	St George's Road	A3
Cumberland Road	A4	St Matthias Park	D1
Deanery Road	A3	St Michael's Hill	A1
Denmark Street	A3	St Stephen's Street	B2
Explore Lane	A3	St Thomas Street	C3
Fairfax Street	C2	Small Street	B2
Ferry Street	C3	Somerset Street	C4
Friary	D3	Southwell Street	A1
Frogmore Street	A2	Tankards Close	A1
Great George Street	A3	Telephone Avenue	B3
Great George Street	D1	Temple Back	C3
Guinea Street	B4	Temple Back East	D3
Haymarket	C1	Temple Gate	D4
Hill Street	A2	Temple Street	C3
Horfield Road	B1	Temple Way	D3
Jacob Street	D2	The Grove	B4
King Street	B3	The Horsefair	C1
Lewins Mead	B2	The Pithay	C2
Lodge Street	A2	Tower Hill	D2
Lower Castle Street	D2	Trenchard Street	A2
Lower Church Lane	A2	Tyndall Avenue	A1
Lower Maudlin Street	B1	Union Street	C1
Marlborough Hill	B1	Upper Maudlin Street	B1
Marlborough Street	B1	Victoria Street	C2
Marsh Street	B3	Wapping Road	B4
Museum Street	A4	Welsh Back	B3
Newgate	C2	Whitson Street	B1
Old Market Street	D2	Wine Street	C2
Park Street	A2	Woodland Road	A1

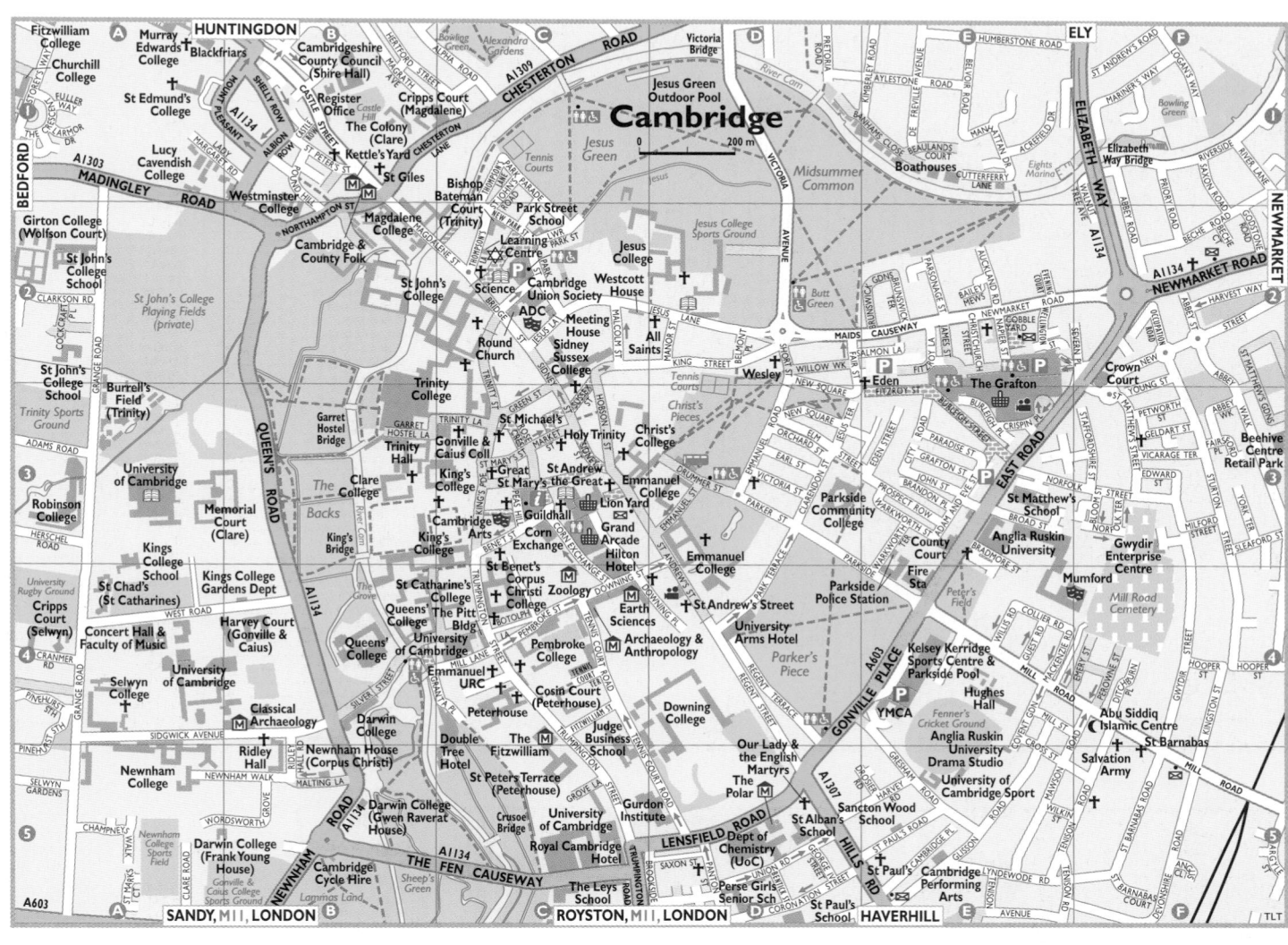

Cambridge

Cambridge is found on atlas page **62 G9**

Abbey Road	F1
Abbey Street	F2
Abbey Walk	F3
Acrefield Drive	E1
Adam and Eve Street	E3
Albion Row	B1
Alpha Road	C1
Auckland Road	E2
Aylestone Road	E1
Bailey Mews	E2
Banhams Close	D1
Beaulands Court	E1
Beche Road	F2
Belmont Place	D2
Belvoir Road	E1
Bene't Street	C3
Bloom Street	F3
Bradmore Street	E3
Brandon Place	E3
Bridge Street	C2
Broad Street	E3
Brookside	D5
Brunswick Gardens	E2
Brunswick Terrace	E2
Burleigh Place	E3
Burleigh Street	E3
Cambridge Place	E5
Castle Row	B1
Castle Street	B1
Champneys Walk	A5
Chesterton Lane	B1
Chesterton Road	C1
Christchurch Street	E2
City Road	E3
Clarendon Street	D3
Cobble Yard	E2

Collier Road	E4
Corn Exchange Street	C3
Coronation Street	D5
Covent Garden	E4
Crispin Place	E3
Cross Street	E4
Crusoe Bridge	B5
Cutler Ferry Close	E1
Cutterferry Lane	E1
De Freville Avenue	E1
Devonshire Road	F5
Ditchburn Place	F4
Downing Place	C4
Downing Street	C4
Drosier Road	D5
Drummer Street	D3
Earl Street	D3
East Road	E3
Eden Street	E3
Eden Street Back	E3
Edward Street	F3
Elizabeth Way	F1
Elm Street	D3
Emery Street	F4
Emmanuel Road	D3
Emmanuel Street	D3
Evening Court	E2
Fairsford Place	F3
Fair Street	D2
Fitzroy Lane	E2
Fitzroy Street	E3
Fitzwilliam Street	C4
Garret Hostel Bridge	B3
Garret Hostel Lane	B3
Geldart Street	F3
George IV Street	D5

Glisson Road	E5
Godstone Road	F2
Gonville Place	D4
Grange Road	A3
Grange Road	A4
Granta Place	B4
Green Street	C3
Gresham Road	E5
Gwydir Street	F4
Harvest Way	F2
Harvey Road	E5
Hertford Street	B1
Hills Road	D5
Hobson Street	C3
Humberstone Road	E1
James Street	E2
Jesus Lane	C2
Jesus Terrace	D3
John Street	E3
Kimberley Road	E1
King's Bridge	B3
King's Parade	C3
Kingston Street	F4
King Street	D2
Lady Margaret Road	A1
Lensfield Road	D5
Logan's Way	F1
Lwr Park Street	C2
Lyndewode Road	E5
Mackenzie Road	E4
Madingley Road	A1
Magdalene Street	B2
Magrath Avenue	B1
Maids Causeway	D2
Malcolm Street	C2
Malting Lane	B5
Manhattan Drive	E1
Manor Street	D2
Mariner's Way	F1
Market Street	C3
Mawson Road	E5

Milford Street	F3
Mill Lane	C4
Mill Road	E4
Mill Street	E4
Mortimer Road	E4
Mount Pleasant	B1
Napier Street	E2
Newmarket Road	E2
Newnham Road	B5
Newnham Walk	A5
New Park Street	C2
New Square	D3
New Street	F2
Norfolk Street	E3
Norfolk Terrace	F3
Northampton Street	B2
Occupation Road	F2
Orchard Street	D3
Panton Street	D5
Paradise Street	E3
Parker Street	D3
Parkside	D3
Park Street	C2
Park Terrace	D4
Parsonage Street	E2
Peas Hill	C3
Pembroke Street	C4
Perowne Street	F4
Petworth Street	F3
Pound Hill	B1
Priory Road	F1
Prospect Row	E3
Queen's Road	B3
Regent Street	D4
Regent Terrace	D4
River Lane	F1
Riverside	F1
St Andrew's Road	F1
St Andrew's Street	D3
St Barnabas Road	F5

St Mary's Street	C3
St Matthew's Gardens	F2
St Matthew's Street	F3
St Paul's Road	E5
St Peter's Street	B1
Salmon Lane	E2
Saxon Road	F1
Saxon Street	D5
Severn Place	F2
Shelly Row	B1
Short Street	D2
Sidgwick Avenue	A4
Sidney Street	C2
Silver Street	B4
Staffordshire Street	F3
Sturton Street	F3
Sussex Street	C3
Tenison Avenue	E5
Tenison Road	E5
Tennis Court Road	C4
Tennis Court Terrace	C4
The Fen Causeway	B5
Thompson's Lane	C2
Trinity Lane	C3
Trinity Street	C2
Trumpington Road	C5
Trumpington Street	C4
Union Road	D5
Vicarage Terrace	F3
Victoria Avenue	D1
Victoria Bridge	D1
Victoria Road	D3
Warkworth Street	E3
Warkworth Terrace	E4
Wellington Street	E3
West Road	A4
Wilkin Street	E5
Willis Road	E4
Willow Walk	D2
Wordsworth Grove	A5
Young Street	F3

University Colleges

Christ's College	C3
Clare College	A3
Clare College	B1
Clare College	B3
Corpus Christi College	C4
Darwin College	B4
Downing College	D4
Emmanuel College	C3
Emmanuel College	D3
Fitzwilliam College	A1
Girton College (Wolfson Court)	A2
Gonville & Caius College	C3
Gonville & Caius College	B4
Jesus College	C2
King's College	B3
Lucy Cavendish College	A1
Magdalene College	B2
Murray Edwards College	A1
Newnham College	A5
Pembroke College	C4
Peterhouse	C4
Queens' College	B4
Robinson College	A3
St Catharine's College	C4
St Edmund's College	A1
St John's College	B2
Selwyn College	A4
Sidney Sussex College	C2
Trinity College	B3
Westminster College	B1

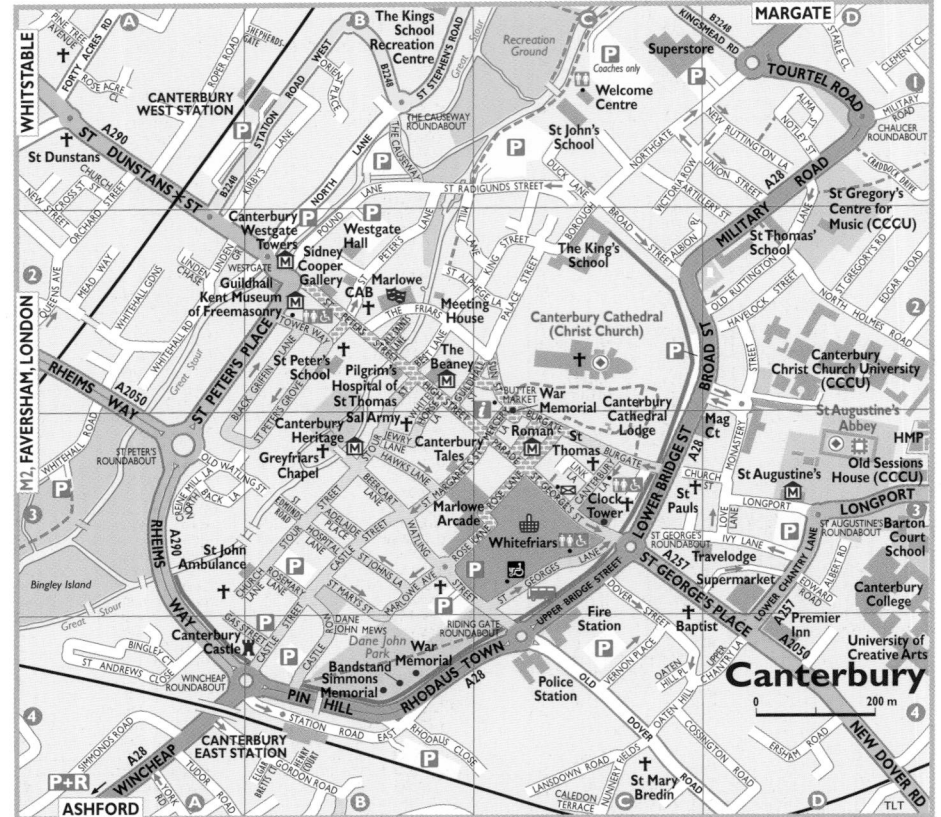

Canterbury

Canterbury is found on atlas page **39 K10**

Adelaide Place	B3	Nunnery Fields	C4
Albion Place	C2	Oaten Hill	C4
Alma Street	D1	Old Dover Road	C4
Artillery Street	C1	Old Ruttington Lane	D2
Beercart Lane	B3	Orchard Street	A2
Best Lane	B2	Palace Street	C2
Black Griffin Lane	A3	Parade	C3
Borough	C2	Pin Hill	B4
Broad Street	D2	Pound Lane	B2
Burgate	C3	Queens Avenue	A2
Butter Market	C2	Rheims Way	A3
Canterbury Lane	C3	Rhodaus Town	B4
Castle Row	B4	Rose Lane	B3
Castle Street	B3	Rosemary Lane	B3
Cossington Road	C4	St Alphege Lane	B2
Dover Street	C3	St Dunstans Street	A1
Duck Lane	C1	St Edmunds Road	B3
Edgar Road	D2	St George's Lane	C3
Edward Road	D3	St George's Place	C3
Ersham Road	D4	St George's Street	C3
Gas Street	A4	St Gregory's Road	D2
Gordon Road	B4	St Johns Lane	B3
Guildhall Street	B2	St Margaret's Street	B3
Havelock Street	C1	St Marys Street	B3
Hawks Lane	B3	St Peter's Grove	B3
High Street	B2	St Peter's Lane	B2
Hospital Lane	B3	St Peter's Place	A3
Ivy Lane	C3	St Peters Street	B2
Jewry Lane	B3	St Radigunds Street	B1
King Street	C2	Station Road East	B4
Kirby's Lane	B1	Station Road West	A1
Lansdown Road	C4	Stour Street	B3
Linden Grove	A2	Sturry Road	D1
Longport	D3	Sun Street	C2
Love Lane	D3	The Causeway	B1
Lower Bridge Street	C3	The Friars	B2
Lower Chantry Lane	D4	Tourtel Road	D1
Marlowe Avenue	B3	Tower Way	B2
Mead Way	A2	Tudor Road	A4
Mercery Lane	C3	Union Street	D1
Military Road	D2	Upper Bridge Street	C4
Mill Lane	B1	Vernon Place	C4
Monastery Street	D3	Victoria Row	C1
New Dover Road	D4	Watling Street	B3
New Ruttington Lane	D1	Whitehall Gardens	A2
North Lane	B1	Whitehall Road	A2
Northgate	C1	Wincheap	A4
Notley Street	D1	York Road	A4

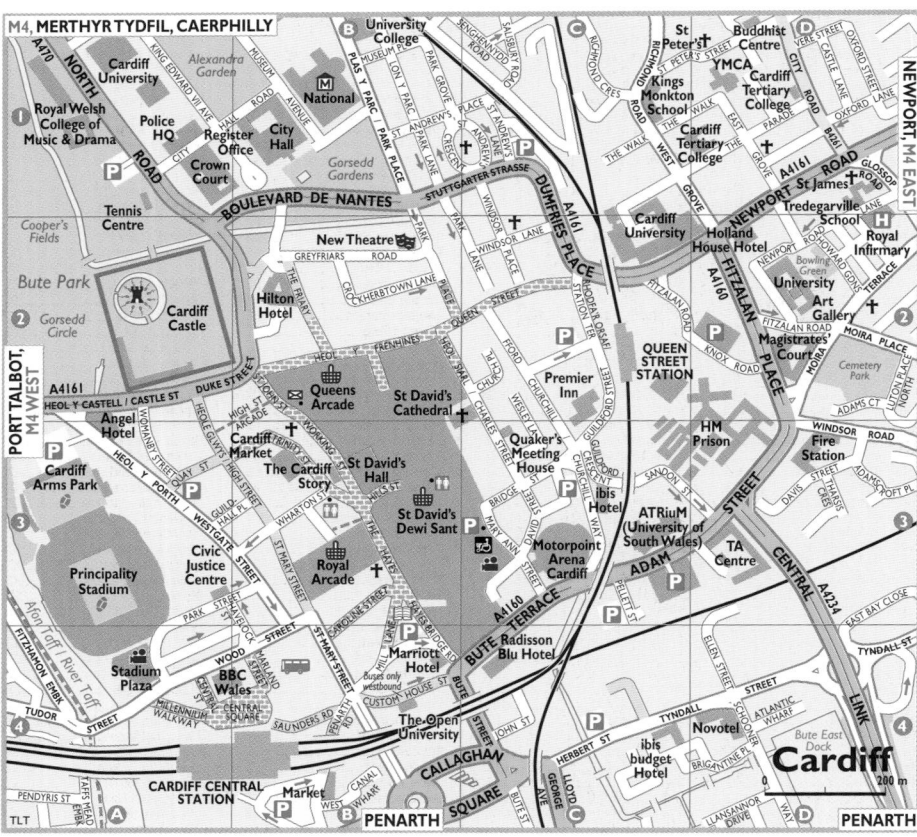

Cardiff

Cardiff is found on atlas page **30 G9**

Adam Street	C3	Museum Avenue	B1
Adams Court	D2	Museum Place	B1
Adamscroft Place	D3	Newport Road	D1
Atlantic Wharf	D4	Newport Road Lane	D2
Boulevard de Nantes	B1	North Luton Place	D2
Bridge Street	C3	North Road	A1
Brigantine Place	D4	Oxford Lane	D1
Bute Street	C4	Oxford Street	D1
Bute Terrace	C3	Park Grove	B1
Callaghan Square	B4	Park Lane	B1
Caroline Street	B3	Park Place	B1
Castle Lane	D1	Park Street	A3
Castle Street	A2	Pellett Street	C3
Central Link	D3	Pendyris Street	A4
Charles Street	B2	Quay Street	A3
Churchill Way	C2	Queen Street	B2
City Hall Road	A1	Richmond Crescent	C1
City Road	D1	Richmond Road	C1
Crockherbtown Lane	B2	St Andrew's Crescent	B1
Custom House Street	B4	St Andrew's Lane	C1
David Street	C3	St Andrew's Place	B1
Davis Street	D3	St John Street	B2
Duke Street	A2	St Mary Street	B3
Dumfries Place	C2	St Peter's Street	C1
East Bay Close	D3	Salisbury Road	C1
East Grove	D1	Sandon Street	C3
Fford Churchill	C2	Saunders Road	B4
Fitzalan Place	D2	Schooner Way	D4
Fitzalan Road	D2	Stuttgarter Strasse	B1
Fitzhamon Embankment	A4	The Friary	B2
Glossop Road	D1	The Hayes	B3
Greyfriars Road	B2	The Parade	D1
Guildford Street	C3	The Walk	C1
Guildhall Place	A3	Trinity Street	B3
Havelock Street	B3	Tudor Street	A4
Hayes Bridge Road	B3	Tyndall Street	D4
Heol Siarl	B2	Vere Street	D1
Herbert Street	C4	Wesley Lane	C2
High Street	B3	West Canal Wharf	B4
High Street Arcade	B2	West Grove	C1
Hills Street	B3	Westgate Street	A3
King Edward VII Avenue	A1	Wharton Street	B3
Knox Road	D2	Windsor Lane	C2
Lloyd George Avenue	C4	Windsor Place	C1
Mary Ann Street	C3	Windsor Road	D3
Mill Lane	B4	Womanby Street	A3
Moira Place	D2	Wood Street	A4
Moira Terrace	D2	Working Street	B3

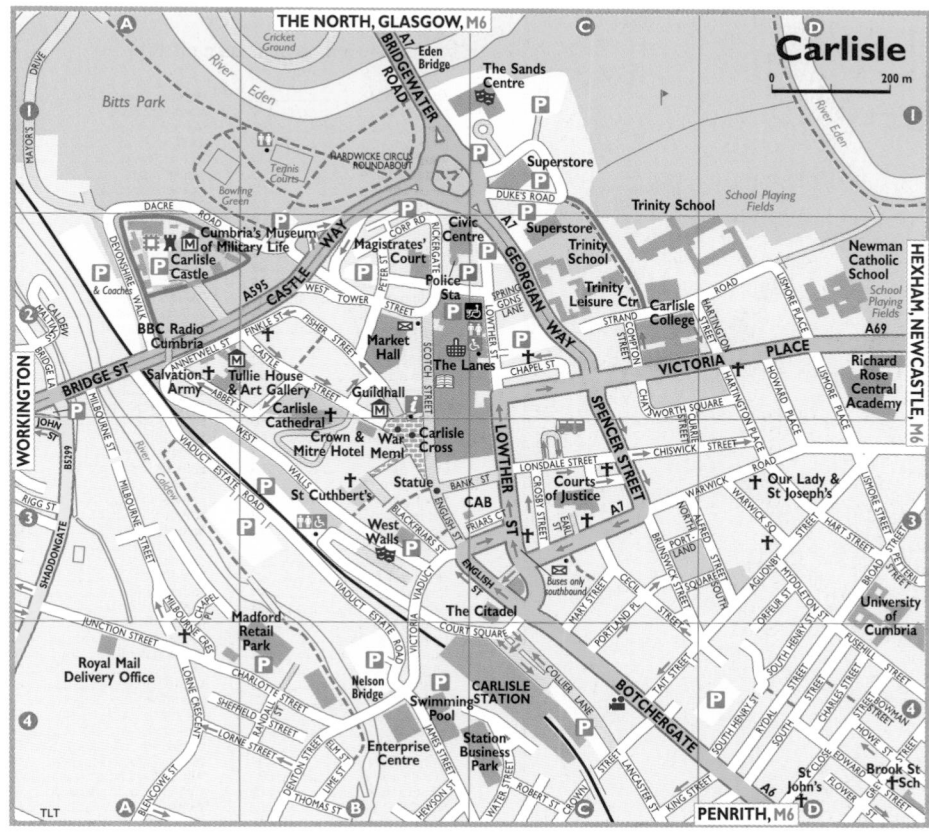

Carlisle

Carlisle is found on atlas page **110 G9**

Abbey Street	A2	Howard Place	D2
Aglionby Street	D3	Howe Street	D4
Annetwell Street	A2	James Street	B4
Bank Street	B3	John Street	A3
Blackfriars Street	B3	Junction Street	A4
Blencowe Street	A4	King Street	C4
Botchergate	C4	Lancaster Street	C4
Bridge Lane	A2	Lime Street	B4
Bridge Street	A2	Lismore Place	D2
Bridgewater Road	B1	Lismore Street	D3
Broad Street	D3	Lonsdale Street	C3
Brunswick Street	C3	Lorne Crescent	A4
Caldew Maltings	A2	Lorne Street	A4
Castle Street	B2	Lowther Street	C3
Castle Way	B2	Mary Street	C3
Cecil Street	C3	Mayor's Drive	A1
Chapel Place	A3	Milbourne Crescent	A3
Chapel Street	C2	Milbourne Street	A3
Charles Street	D4	Myddleton Street	D3
Charlotte Street	B4	North Alfred Street	D3
Chatsworth Square	C2	Orfeur Street	D3
Chiswick Street	C2	Peter Street	B2
Close Street	D4	Petteril Street	D3
Collier Lane	C4	Portland Place	C4
Compton Street	C2	Portland Square	C3
Corp Road	B2	Randall Street	B4
Court Square	B4	Rickergate	B2
Crosby Street	C3	Rigg Street	A3
Crown Street	C4	Robert Street	C4
Currie Street	C3	Rydal Street	D4
Dacre Road	A1	Scotch Street	B2
Denton Street	B4	Shaddongate	A3
Devonshire Walk	A2	Sheffield Street	A4
Duke's Road	C1	South Alfred Street	D3
Edward Street	D4	South Henry Street	D4
Elm Street	B4	Spencer Street	C2
English Street	B3	Spring Gardens Lane	C2
Finkle Street	B2	Strand Road	C2
Fisher Street	B2	Tait Street	C4
Flower Street	D4	Thomas Street	B4
Friars Court	C3	Viaduct Estate Road	A3
Fusehill Street	D4	Victoria Place	C2
Georgian Way	C2	Victoria Viaduct	B4
Grey Street	D4	Warwick Road	D3
Hartington Place	D2	Warwick Square	D3
Hartington Street	D2	Water Street	C4
Hart Street	D3	West Tower Street	B2
Hewson Street	B4	West Walls	B3

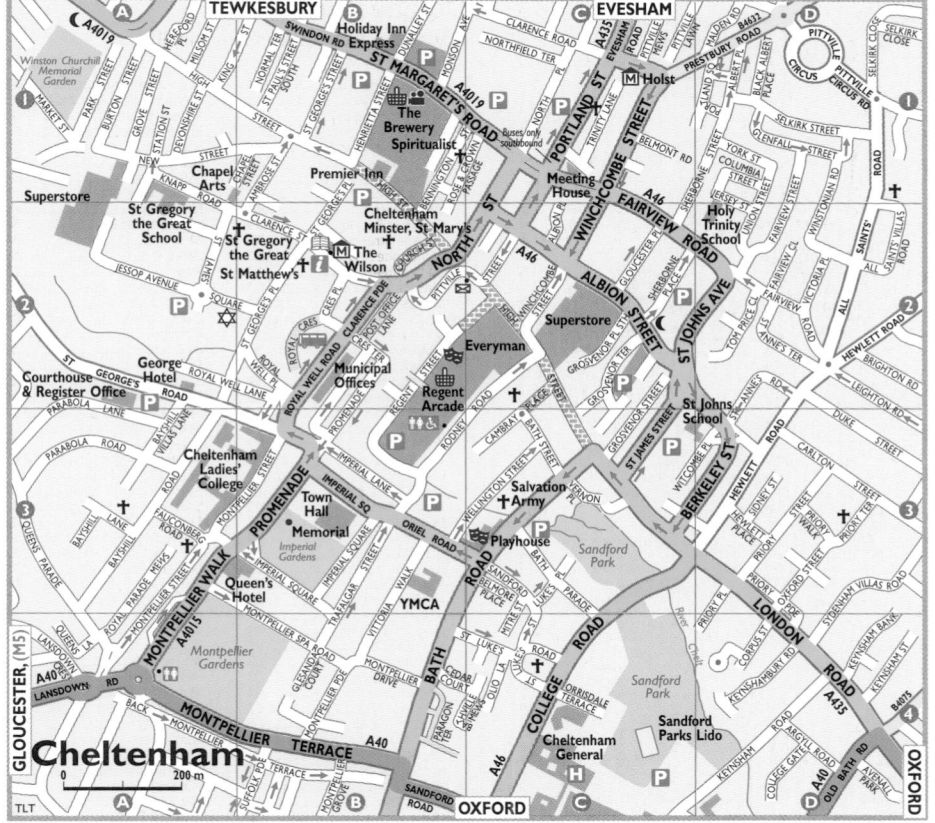

Cheltenham

Cheltenham is found on atlas page **46 H10**

Albion Street	C2	Montpellier Parade	B4
All Saints' Road	D2	Montpellier Spa Road	B4
Ambrose Street	B1	Montpellier Street	A4
Argyll Road	D4	Montpellier Terrace	A4
Back Montpellier Terrace	A4	Montpellier Walk	A4
Bath Road	B4	New Street	A1
Bath Street	C3	North Street	B2
Bayshill Road	A3	Old Bath Road	D4
Bayshill Villas Lane	A3	Oriel Road	B3
Bennington Street	B1	Parabola Lane	A3
Berkeley Street	C3	Parabola Road	A3
Burton Street	A1	Park Street	A1
Carlton Street	D3	Pittville Circus	D1
Church Street	B2	Pittville Circus Road	D1
Clarence Parade	B2	Pittville Street	B2
Clarence Road	C1	Portland Street	C1
Clarence Street	B2	Prestbury Road	C1
College Road	C4	Priory Street	D3
Crescent Terrace	B2	Promenade	B3
Devonshire Street	A1	Queens Parade	A3
Duke Street	D3	Regent Street	B2
Dunalley Street	B1	Rodney Road	B3
Evesham Road	C1	Royal Well Lane	A2
Fairview Road	C2	Royal Well Road	B2
Fairview Street	D2	St Anne's Road	D2
Fauconberg Road	A3	St Anne's Terrace	D2
Glenfall Street	D1	St George's Place	B2
Grosvenor Street	C3	St George's Road	A2
Grove Street	A1	St George's Street	B1
Henrietta Street	B1	St James' Square	A2
Hewlett Road	D3	St James Street	C3
High Street	A1	St Johns Avenue	C2
High Street	C2	St Margaret's Road	B1
Imperial Lane	B3	St Paul's Street South	B1
Imperial Square	B3	Sandford Street	C3
Jersey Street	D1	Selkirk Street	D1
Jessop Avenue	A2	Sherborne Street	C2
Keynsham Road	D4	Station Street	A1
King Street	A1	Suffolk Parade	B4
Knapp Road	A1	Swindon Road	B1
Lansdown Road	A4	Sydenham Villas Road	D3
Leighton Road	D2	Trafalgar Street	B4
London Road	D3	Union Street	D2
Malden Road	D1	Wellington Street	C3
Market Street	A1	Winchcombe Street	C2
Milsom Street	A1	Winstonian Road	D2
Monson Avenue	B1	Witcombe Place	C3
Montpellier Grove	B4	York Street	D1

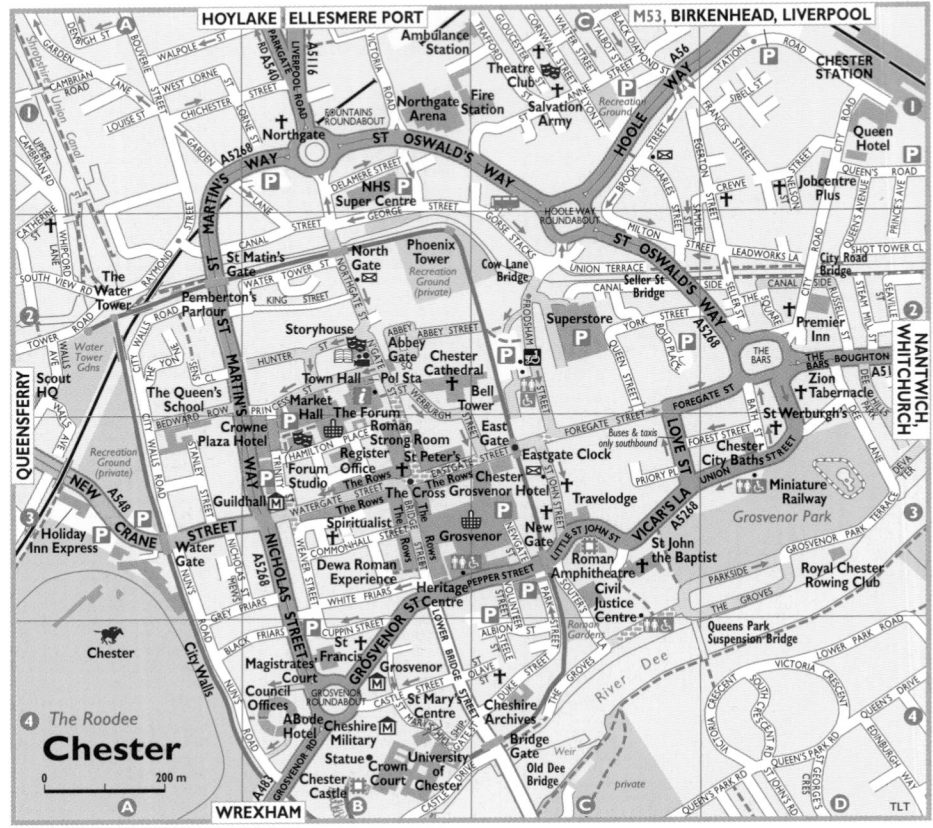

Chester

Chester is found on atlas page **81 N11**

Albion Street	C4	Nicholas Street	B3
Bath Street	D2	Northgate Street	B2
Black Diamond Street	C1	Nun's Road	A3
Boughton	D2	Parkgate Road	B1
Bouverie Street	A1	Park Street	C3
Bridge Street	B3	Pepper Street	C3
Brook Street	C1	Princess Street	B2
Canal Side	C2	Priory Place	C3
Castle Street	B4	Queen's Park Road	C4
Charles Street	C1	Queen's Road	D1
Chichester Street	A1	Queen Street	C2
City Road	D2	Raymond Street	A2
City Walls Road	A2	Russell Street	D2
Commonhall Street	B3	St Anne Street	C1
Cornwall Street	C1	St John's Road	D4
Crewe Street	D1	St John Street	C3
Cuppin Street	B4	St Martin's Way	A2
Dee Hills Park	D2	St Mary's Hill	B4
Dee Lane	D2	St Olave Street	C4
Delamere Street	B1	St Oswald's Way	B1
Duke Street	C4	St Werburgh Street	B2
Eastgate Street	B3	Samuel Street	C2
Egerton Street	C1	Seller Street	D2
Foregate Street	C2	Shipgate Street	B4
Forest Street	C3	Souter's Lane	C3
Francis Street	D1	South View Road	A2
Frodsham Street	C2	Stanley Street	A3
Garden Lane	A1	Station Road	D1
George Street	B2	Steam Mill Street	D2
Gloucester Street	C1	Steele Street	C4
Gorse Stacks	C2	Talbot Street	C1
Grosvenor Park Terrace	D3	Tower Road	A2
Grosvenor Road	B4	Trafford Street	C1
Grosvenor Street	B4	Trinity Street	B3
Hamilton Place	B3	Union Street	D3
Hoole Way	C1	Union Terrace	C2
Hunter Street	B2	Upper Cambrian Road	A1
King Street	B2	Vicar's Lane	C3
Leadworks Lane	D2	Victoria Crescent	D4
Little St John Street	C3	Victoria Road	B1
Liverpool Road	B1	Volunteer Street	C3
Lorne Street	A1	Walpole Street	A1
Love Street	C3	Walter Street	C1
Lower Bridge Street	B4	Watergate Street	B3
Lower Park Road	D4	Water Tower Street	B2
Milton Street	C2	Weaver Street	B3
New Crane Street	A3	White Friars	B3
Newgate Street	C3	York Street	C2

Colchester

Colchester is found on atlas page **52 G6**

Abbey Gates	C3	Middleborough	B1
Alexandra Road	A3	Middleborough Roundabout	A1
Alexandra Terrace	A4	Military Road	D4
Balkerne Hill	A3	Mill Street	D4
Beaconsfield Avenue	A4	Napier Road	C4
Burlington Road	A3	Nicholsons Green	D3
Butt Road	A4	North Bridge	B1
Castle Road	D1	Northgate Street	B1
Cedar Street	B3	North Hill	B1
Chapel Street North	B3	North Station Road	B1
Chapel Street South	B3	Nunn's Road	B1
Church Street	B3	Osborne Street	C3
Church Walk	B3	Papillon Road	A3
Circular Road East	C4	Pope's Lane	A2
Circular Road North	B4	Portland Road	C4
Creffield Road	A4	Priory Street	D3
Cromwell Road	C4	Queen Street	C3
Crouch Street	A3	Rawstorn Road	A2
Crouch Street	B3	Roman Road	D1
Crowhurst Road	A2	St Alban's Road	A2
Culver Street East	C2	St Augustine Mews	D2
Culver Street West	B2	St Botolph's Circus	C3
East Hill	D2	St Botolph's Street	C3
East Stockwell Street	C2	St Helen's Lane	C2
Essex Street	B3	St John's Avenue	B3
Fairfax Road	C4	St John's Street	B3
Flagstaff Road	C4	St Julian Grove	D3
Garland Road	A4	St Mary's Fields	A2
George Street	C2	St Peter's Street	B1
Golden Noble Hill	D4	Salisbury Avenue	A4
Gray Road	A3	Sheepen Place	A1
Headgate	B3	Sheepen Road	A1
Head Street	B2	Short Wyre Street	C3
Henry Laver Court	A2	Sir Isaac's Walk	B3
High Street	B2	South Street	B4
Hospital Road	A4	Southway	B3
Hospital Lane	A3	Stanwell Street	C3
Land Lane	D2	Trinity Street	B2
Lewis Gardens	D2	Walsingham Road	B3
Lexden Road	A3	Wellesley Road	A4
Lincoln Way	D1	Wellington Street	B3
Long Wyre Street	C2	West Stockwell Street	B1
Lucas Road	C4	West Street	B4
Magdalen Street	D3	Westway	A1
Maidenburgh Street	C1	Whitewell Road	C3
Maldon Road	A4	Wickham Road	A4
Manor Road	A3	William's Walk	C2
Mersea Road	C4	Winnock Road	D4

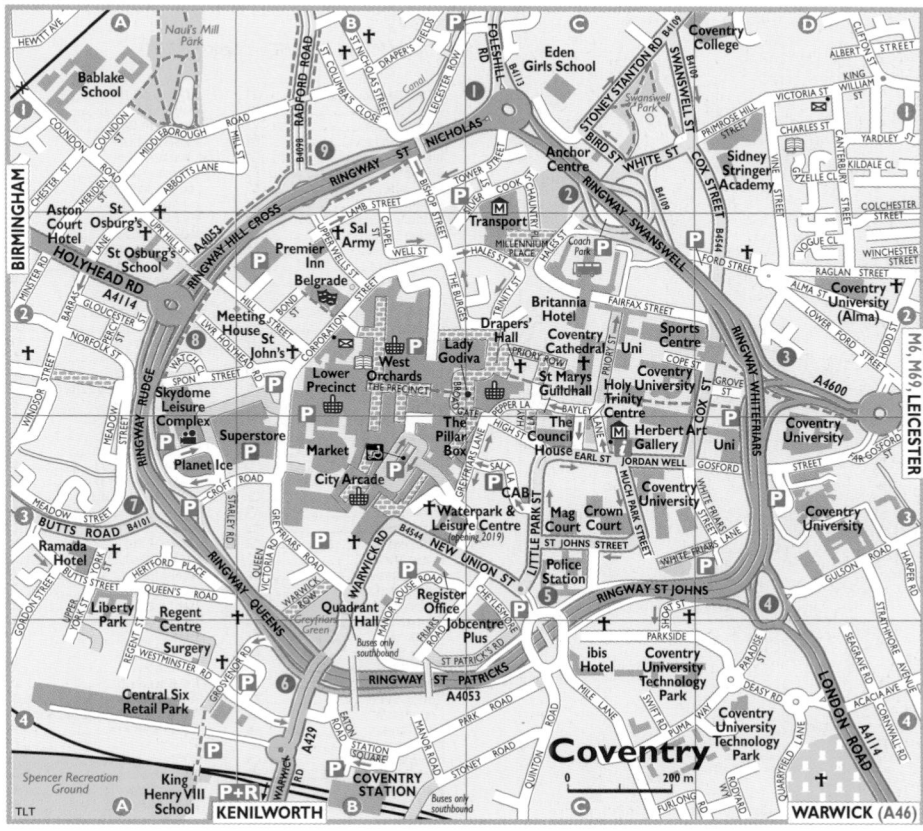

Coventry

Coventry is found on atlas page **59 M9**

Abbotts Lane	A1	Much Park Street	C3
Acacia Avenue	D4	New Union Street	B3
Alma Street	D2	Norfolk Street	A2
Barras Lane	A2	Park Road	B4
Bayley Lane	C2	Parkside	C4
Bird Street	C1	Primrose Hill Street	D1
Bishop Street	B1	Priory Row	C2
Broadgate	B2	Priory Street	C2
Butts Road	A3	Puma Way	C4
Butts Street	A3	Quarryfield Lane	D4
Canterbury Street	D1	Queen's Road	A3
Chester Street	A2	Queen Victoria Road	B3
Cheylesmore	C3	Quinton Road	C4
Cornwall Road	D4	Radford Road	B1
Corporation Street	B2	Raglan Street	D2
Coundon Road	A1	Regent Street	A4
Cox Street	D1	Ringway Hill Cross	A2
Cox Street	D2	Ringway Queens	A3
Croft Road	A3	Ringway Rudge	A3
Earl Street	C3	Ringway St Johns	C3
Eaton Road	B4	Ringway St Nicholas	B1
Fairfax Street	C2	Ringway St Patricks	B4
Foleshill Road	C1	Ringway Swanswell	C1
Gloucester Street	A2	Ringway Whitefriars	D2
Gosford Street	D3	St Johns Street	C3
Greyfriars Lane	B3	St Nicholas Street	B1
Greyfriars Road	B3	Salt Lane	C3
Grosvenor Road	A4	Seagrave Road	D4
Gulson Road	D3	Spon Street	A2
Hales Street	C2	Starley Road	A3
Hertford Place	A3	Stoney Road	B4
High Street	C3	Stoney Stanton Road	C1
Hill Street	B2	Strathmore Avenue	D3
Holyhead Road	A2	Swanswell Street	C1
Jordan Well	C3	The Burges	B2
Lamb Street	B2	Tower Street	B1
Leicester Row	B1	Trinity Street	C2
Little Park Street	C3	Upper Hill Street	B2
London Road	D4	Upper Wells Street	A4
Lower Ford Street	D2	Victoria Street	D1
Lower Holyhead Road	A2	Vine Street	D1
Manor House Road	B4	Warwick Road	B3
Manor Road	B4	Warwick Road	B4
Meadow Street	A3	Westminster Road	A4
Meriden Street	A1	White Friars Street	D3
Middleborough Road	A1	White Street	C1
Mile Lane	C4	Windsor Street	A3
Mill Street	A1	Yardley Street	D1

Darlington

Darlington is found on atlas page **103 Q8**

Abbey Road	A3	Maude Street	A2
Albert Street	D4	Melland Street	D3
Appleby Close	D4	Neasham Road	D4
Barningham Street	B1	Northgate	C2
Bartlett Street	B1	North Lodge Terrace	B2
Beaumont Street	B3	Northumberland Street	B4
Bedford Street	C4	Oakdene Avenue	A4
Beechwood Avenue	A4	Outram Street	A2
Blackwellgate	B3	Parkgate	D3
Bondgate	B2	Park Lane	D4
Borough Road	D3	Park Place	C4
Brunswick Street	C3	Pendower Street	B1
Brunton Street	D4	Pensbury Street	D4
Chestnut Street	C1	Polam Lane	B4
Cleveland Terrace	A4	Portland Place	A3
Clifton Road	C4	Powlett Street	B3
Commercial Street	B2	Priestgate	C3
Coniscliffe Road	A4	Raby Terrace	B3
Corporation Road	B1	Russell Street	C2
Crown Street	C2	St Augustine's Way	B2
Dodds Street	B1	St Cuthbert's Way	C2
Duke Street	A3	St Cuthbert's Way	C4
Easson Road	B1	St James Place	D4
East Mount Road	D1	Salisbury Terrace	A1
East Raby Street	B3	Salt Yard	B3
East Street	C3	Scarth Street	A4
Elms Road	A2	Skinnergate	B3
Elwin Lane	B4	Southend Avenue	A4
Feethams	C4	Stanhope Road North	A2
Fife Road	A3	Stanhope Road South	A3
Four Riggs	B2	Stonebridge	C3
Freeman's Place	C2	Sun Street	B2
Gladstone Street	B2	Swan Street	C4
Grange Road	B4	Swinburne Road	A3
Greenbank Road	A1	Trinity Road	A2
Greenbank Road	B2	Tubwell Row	B3
Hargreave Terrace	C4	Uplands Road	A3
Haughton Road	D2	Valley Street North	C2
High Northgate	C1	Vane Terrace	A2
High Row	B3	Victoria Embankment	C4
Hollyhurst Road	A1	Victoria Road	B4
Houndgate	B3	Victoria Road	C4
John Street	C1	West Crescent	A2
John Williams Boulevard	D3	West Powlett Street	A3
Kendrew Street	B2	West Row	B3
Kingston Street	B1	West Street	B4
Langholm Crescent	A4	Woodland Road	A2
Larchfield Street	A3	Yarm Road	D3

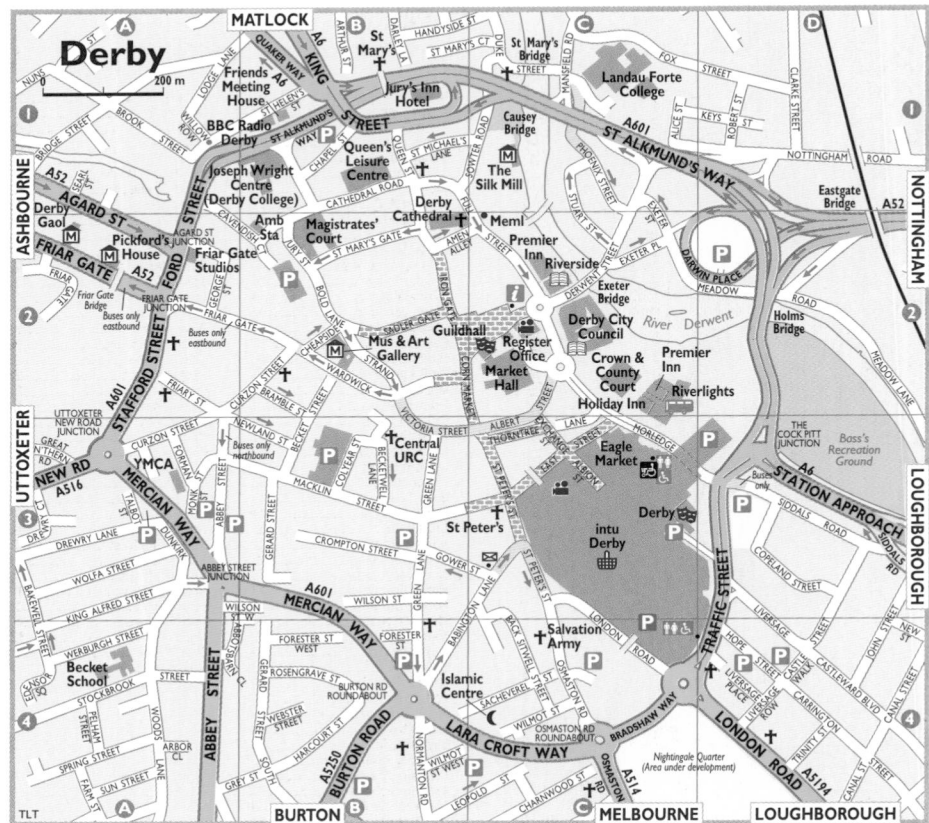

Derby

Derby is found on atlas page **72 B3**

Abbey Street	A4	King Alfred Street	A3
Agard Street	A1	King Street	B1
Albert Street	C3	Lara Croft Way	B4
Babington Lane	B4	Leopold Street	B4
Back Sitwell Street	C4	Liversage Row	D4
Becket Street	B3	Liversage Street	D3
Bold Lane	B2	Lodge Lane	A1
Bradshaw Way	C4	London Road	C3
Bramble Street	B2	Macklin Street	B3
Bridge Street	A1	Mansfield Road	C1
Brook Street	A1	Meadow Lane	D2
Burton Road	B4	Meadow Road	D2
Canal Street	D4	Mercian Way	B3
Carrington Street	D4	Morledge	C3
Cathedral Road	B1	Newland Street	A3
Cavendish Court	A2	New Road	A3
Chapel Street	B1	New Street	D4
Clarke Street	D1	Nottingham Road	D1
Copeland Street	D3	Osmaston Road	C4
Corn Market	B2	Phoenix Street	C1
Crompton Street	B3	Queen Street	B1
Curzon Street	A2	Robert Street	D1
Curzon Street	A3	Rosengrave Street	B4
Darwin Place	C2	Sacheverel Street	C4
Derwent Street	C2	Sadler Gate	B2
Drewry Lane	A3	St Alkmund's Way	C1
Duke Street	C1	St Helen's Street	B1
Dunkirk	A3	St Mary's Gate	B2
East Street	C3	St Peter's Street	C3
Exchange Street	C3	Siddals Road	D3
Exeter Place	C2	Sowter Road	C1
Exeter Street	C2	Spring Street	A4
Ford Street	A2	Stafford Street	A3
Forester Street West	B4	Station Approach	D3
Forman Street	A3	Stockbrook Street	A4
Fox Street	C1	Strand	B2
Friary Street	A2	Stuart Street	C1
Full Street	B1	Sun Street	A4
Gerard Street	B3	The Cock Pitt	D3
Gower Street	B3	Thorntree Lane	C3
Green Lane	B3	Traffic Street	D4
Grey Street	A4	Trinity Street	D4
Handyside Street	B1	Victoria Street	B2
Harcourt Street	B4	Wardwick	B2
Iron Gate	B2	Werburgh Street	A4
John Street	D4	Wilmot Street	C4
Jury Street	B2	Wolfa Street	A3
Keys Street	D1	Woods Lane	A4

Doncaster

Doncaster is found on atlas page **91 P10**

Alderson Drive	D3	Nelson Street	B4
Apley Road	B3	Nether Hall Road	B1
Balby Road Bridge	A4	North Bridge Road	A1
Beechfield Road	B3	North Street	C4
Broxholme Lane	C1	Osborne Road	D1
Carr House Road	C4	Palmer Street	C4
Carr Lane	B4	Park Road	B2
Chamber Road	B3	Park Terrace	B2
Chequer Avenue	C4	Prince's Street	B2
Chequer Road	C3	Priory Place	A2
Childers Street	C4	Prospect Place	B4
Christ Church Road	B1	Queen's Road	C1
Church View	A1	Rainton Road	C4
Church Way	B1	Ravensworth Road	C3
Clark Avenue	C4	Rectory Gardens	C1
Cleveland Street	A4	Regent Square	C2
College Road	B3	Roman Road	D3
Cooper Street	C4	Royal Avenue	C1
Coopers Terrace	B2	St Georges Gate	B2
Copley Road	B1	St James Street	B4
Cunningham Road	B3	St Mary's Road	C1
Danum Road	D3	St Sepulchre Gate	A2
Dockin Hill Road	B1	St Sepulchre Gate West	A3
Duke Street	A2	St Vincent Avenue	C1
East Laith Gate	B2	St Vincent Road	C1
Elmfield Road	C3	Scot Lane	B2
Firbeck Road	D3	Silver Street	B2
Frances Street	B2	Somerset Road	B3
Glyn Avenue	C1	South Parade	C2
Green Dyke Lane	A4	South Street	C4
Grey Friars' Road	A1	Spring Gardens	A2
Hall Cross Hill	C2	Stirling Street	A4
Hall Gate	B2	Stockil Road	C4
Hamilton Road	D4	Theobald Avenue	D4
Harrington Street	B1	Thorne Road	C1
High Street	A2	Town Fields	C2
Highfield Road	C1	Town Moor Avenue	D1
Jarratt Street	B4	Trafford Way	A2
King's Road	C1	Vaughan Avenue	C1
Lawn Avenue	C2	Waterdale	B3
Lawn Road	C2	Welbeck Road	D3
Lime Tree Avenue	D4	Welcome Way	A4
Manor Drive	D3	West Laith Gate	A2
Market Place	A2	West Street	A3
Market Road	B1	Whitburn Road	C3
Milbanke Street	B4	White Rose Way	B4
Milton Walk	B4	Windsor Road	D1
Montague Street	B1	Wood Street	B2

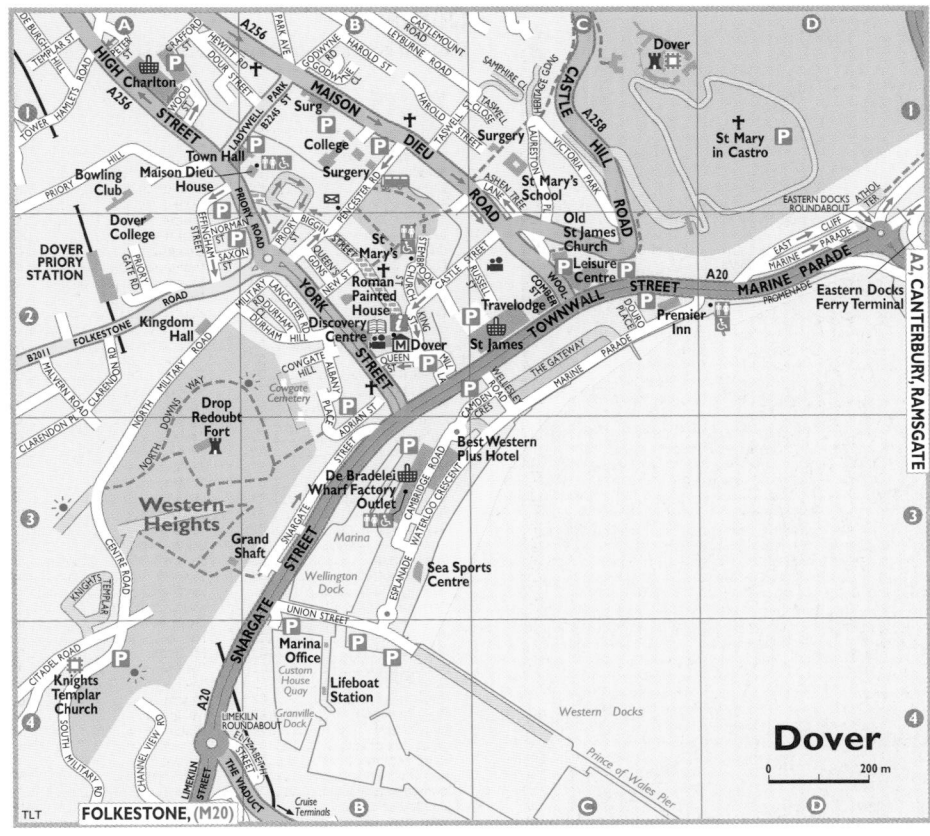

Dover

Dover

Dover is found on atlas page **27 P3**

Adrian Street	B3	Marine Parade	D2
Albany Place	B2	Military Road	B2
Ashen Tree Lane	C1	Mill Lane	B2
Athol Terrace	D1	New Street	B2
Biggin Street	B2	Norman Street	A2
Cambridge Road	B3	North Downs Way	A3
Camden Crescent	C2	North Military Road	A3
Castle Hill Road	C1	Park Avenue	B1
Castlemount Road	B1	Park Street	B1
Castle Street	B2	Pencester Road	B2
Centre Road	A3	Peter Street	A1
Channel View Road	A4	Priory Gate Road	A2
Church Street	B2	Priory Hill	A1
Citadel Road	A4	Priory Road	A1
Clarendon Place	A3	Priory Street	B2
Clarendon Road	A2	Promenade	D2
Cowgate Hill	B2	Queen's Gardens	B2
Crafford Street	A1	Queen Street	B2
De Burgh Hill	A1	Russell Street	B2
Douro Place	C2	Samphire Close	C1
Dour Street	A1	Saxon Street	A2
Durham Close	B2	Snargate Street	A4
Durham Hill	B2	South Military Road	A4
East Cliff	D2	Stembrook	B2
Eastern Docks		Taswell Close	C1
Roundabout	D2	Taswell Street	B1
Effingham Street	A2	Templar Street	A1
Elizabeth Street	A4	The Viaduct	A4
Esplanade	B3	Tower Hamlets Road	A1
Folkestone Road	A2	Townwall Street	C2
Godwyne Close	B1	Union Street	B3
Godwyne Road	B1	Victoria Park	C1
Harold Street	B1	Waterloo Crescent	B3
Harold Street	B1	Wellesley Road	C2
Heritage Gardens	C1	Wood Street	A1
Hewitt Road	A1	Woolcomber Street	C2
High Street	A1	York Street	B2
King Street	B2		
Knights Templar	A3		
Ladywell	A1		
Lancaster Road	B2		
Laureston Place	C1		
Leyburne Road	B1		
Limekiln Roundabout	A4		
Limekiln Street	A4		
Maison Dieu Road	B1		
Malvern Road	A2		
Marine Parade	C2		

Dundee

Dundee

Dundee is found on atlas page **142 G11**

Albert Square	B2	Laurel Bank	B1
Bank Street	B2	Lochee Road	A1
Barrack Road	A1	McDonald Street	D2
Barrack Road	B2	Meadowside	B2
Bell Street	B2	Miln Street	A2
Blackscroft	D1	Murraygate	C2
Blinshall Street	A1	Nethergate	A4
Blinshall Street	A2	North Lindsay Street	B2
Bonnybank Road	C1	North Marketgait	B1
Brown Street	A2	North Victoria Road	C1
Candle Lane	C2	Old Hawkhill	A3
Castle Street	C2	Panmure Street	B2
Chapel Street	C2	Perth Road	A4
City Square	C2	Princes Street	D1
Commercial Street	C2	Prospect Place	B1
Constable Street	D1	Queen Street	C1
Constitution Crescent	A1	Reform Street	B2
Constitution Road	A1	Riverside Drive	B4
Constitution Road	B2	Riverside Esplanade	C3
Court House Square	A2	Roseangle	A4
Cowgate	C1	St Andrews Street	C1
Cowgate	D1	Scrimgeour Place	A1
Crichton Street	C3	Seabraes Lane	A4
Dock Street	C3	Seagate	C2
Douglas Street	A2	Session Street	A2
Dudhope Street	B1	South Castle Street	C3
East Dock Street	D2	South Commercial Street	D3
East Marketgait	C1	South Crichton Street	C3
East Whale Lane	D1	South Marketgait	B3
Euclid Crescent	B2	South Tay Street	B3
Euclid Street	B2	South Union Street	C3
Exchange Street	C3	South Victoria Dock Road	D3
Forebank Road	C1	South Ward Road	B2
Foundry Lane	D1	Sugarhouse Wynd	C1
Gellatly Street	C2	Tay Road Bridge	D3
Greenmarket	B4	Tay Square	B3
Guthrie Street	A2	Thomson Avenue	C3
Hawkhill	A3	Trades Lane	C2
High Street	C3	Union Street	B3
Hilltown	B1	Union Terrace	B1
Hilltown Terrace	B1	Ward Road	B2
Hunter Street	A3	Weavers Yard	D1
Infirmary Brae	A1	West Marketgait	A2
Johnston Street	B2	West Port	A3
King Street	C1	West Victoria Dock Road	D2
Kirk Lane	A1	Whitehall Crescent	C3
Laburn Street	A1	Whitehall Street	C3
Ladywell Avenue	C1	Yeaman Shore	B3

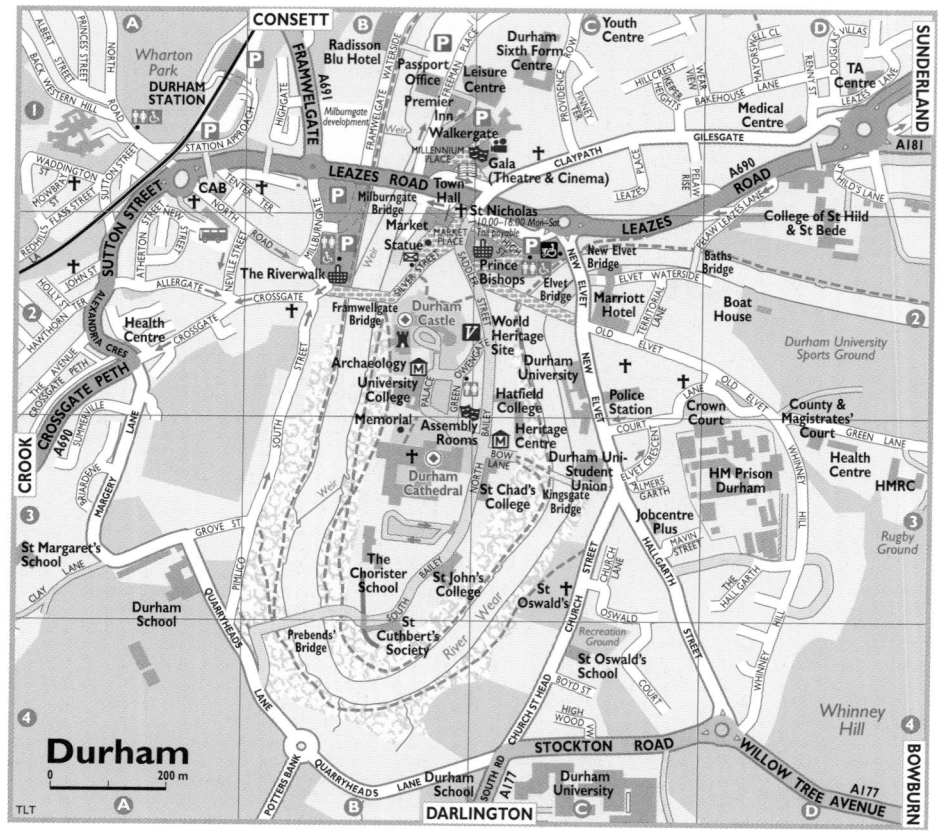

Durham

Durham is found on atlas page **103 Q2**

Albert Street	A1	Millburngate	B2
Alexandria Crescent	A2	Millennium Place	B1
Allergate	A2	Mowbray Street	A1
Atherton Street	A2	Neville Street	A2
Back Western Hill	A1	New Elvet	C2
Bakehouse Lane	C1	New Elvet Bridge	C2
Baths Bridge	C2	New Street	A2
Bow Lane	C3	North Bailey	C3
Boyd Street	C4	North Road	A1
Briardene	A3	Old Elvet	C2
Church Lane	C3	Oswald Court	C3
Church Street	C4	Owengate	B2
Church Street Head	C4	Palace Green	B2
Clay Lane	A3	Palmers Garth	C3
Claypath	C1	Pelaw Leazes Lane	D2
Court Lane	C3	Pelaw Rise	C1
Crossgate	A2	Pimlico	A3
Crossgate Peth	A3	Potters Bank	B4
Douglas Villas	D1	Prebends' Bridge	B4
Elvet Bridge	C2	Princes' Street	A1
Elvet Crescent	C3	Providence Row	C1
Elvet Waterside	C2	Quarryheads Lane	A3
Finney Terrace	C1	Redhills Lane	A2
Flass Street	A2	Renny Street	D1
Framwelgate	B1	Saddler Street	B2
Framwelgate Bridge	B2	St Hild's Lane	D1
Framwelgate Waterside	B1	Silver Street	B2
Freeman Place	B1	South Bailey	B3
Gilesgate	C1	South Road	C4
Green Lane	D3	South Street	B3
Grove Street	A3	Station Approach	A1
Hallgarth Street	C3	Stockton Road	C4
Hawthorn Terrace	A2	Summerville	A3
Highgate	B1	Sutton Street	A2
High Road View	C4	Tenter Terrace	A1
High Street	C2	Territorial Lane	C2
Hillcrest	C1	The Avenue	A2
Holly Street	A2	The Hall Garth	D3
John Street	A2	Waddington Street	A1
Keiper Heights	C1	Wear View	C1
Kingsgate Bridge	C3	Whinney Hill	D3
Leazes Place	C1	Willow Tree Avenue	D4
Leazes Road	B1		
Margery Lane	A3		
Market Square	B2		
Mavin Street	C3		
Mayorswell Close	D1		
Milburngate Bridge	B1		

Eastbourne

Eastbourne is found on atlas page **25 P11**

Arlington Road	A2	Langney Road	D1
Ashford Road	B2	Langney Road	C2
Ashford Road	C1	Lascelles Terrace	B4
Ashford Square	B1	Latimer Road	D1
Avenue Lane	A1	Leaf Road	B1
Belmore Road	C1	Lismore Road	B2
Blackwater Road	A4	Longstone Road	C1
Bolton Road	B3	Lushington Road	B3
Bourne Street	C1	Marine Parade	D2
Burlington Place	B3	Marine Road	D1
Burlington Road	C3	Mark Lane	B2
Camden Road	A3	Meads Road	A3
Carew Road	B1	Melbourne Road	C1
Carlisle Road	A4	Old Orchard Road	A2
Carlisle Road	B4	Old Wish Road	A4
Cavendish Avenue	C1	Pevensey Road	C2
Cavendish Place	C1	Promenade	C3
Ceylon Place	C2	Queen's Gardens	D2
Chiswick Place	B3	Saffrons Road	A2
College Road	B3	St Anne's Road	A1
Colonnade Gardens	D2	St Aubyn's Road	D1
Commercial Road	B1	St Leonard's Road	B1
Compton Street	B4	Seaside	D1
Compton Street	C3	Seaside Road	C2
Cornfield Lane	B3	Southfields Road	A2
Cornfield Road	B2	South Street	A3
Cornfield Terrace	B3	South Street	B3
Devonshire Place	B3	Spencer Road	B3
Dursley Road	C1	Station Parade	A2
Elms Road	C3	Station Street	B2
Enys Road	A1	Susan's Road	C2
Eversfield Road	A1	Sutton Road	B2
Furness Road	A3	Sydney Road	C1
Gildredge Road	B2	Terminus Road	A2
Grand Parade	C3	Terminus Road	C3
Grange Road	A3	The Avenue	A1
Grassington Road	A3	Tideswell Road	C2
Grove Road	A3	Trinity Place	C3
Hardwick Road	B3	Trinity Trees	B3
Hartfield Lane	A1	Upper Avenue	B1
Hartfield Road	A1	Upperton Gardens	A1
Hartington Place	C3	Upperton Road	A1
Howard Square	C4	West Street	A3
Hyde Gardens	B2	West Terrace	A2
Hyde Road	A2	Willowfield Road	D1
Ivy Terrace	A2	Wilmington Square	B4
Jevington Gardens	A4	Wish Road	B3
Junction Road	B2	York Road	A3

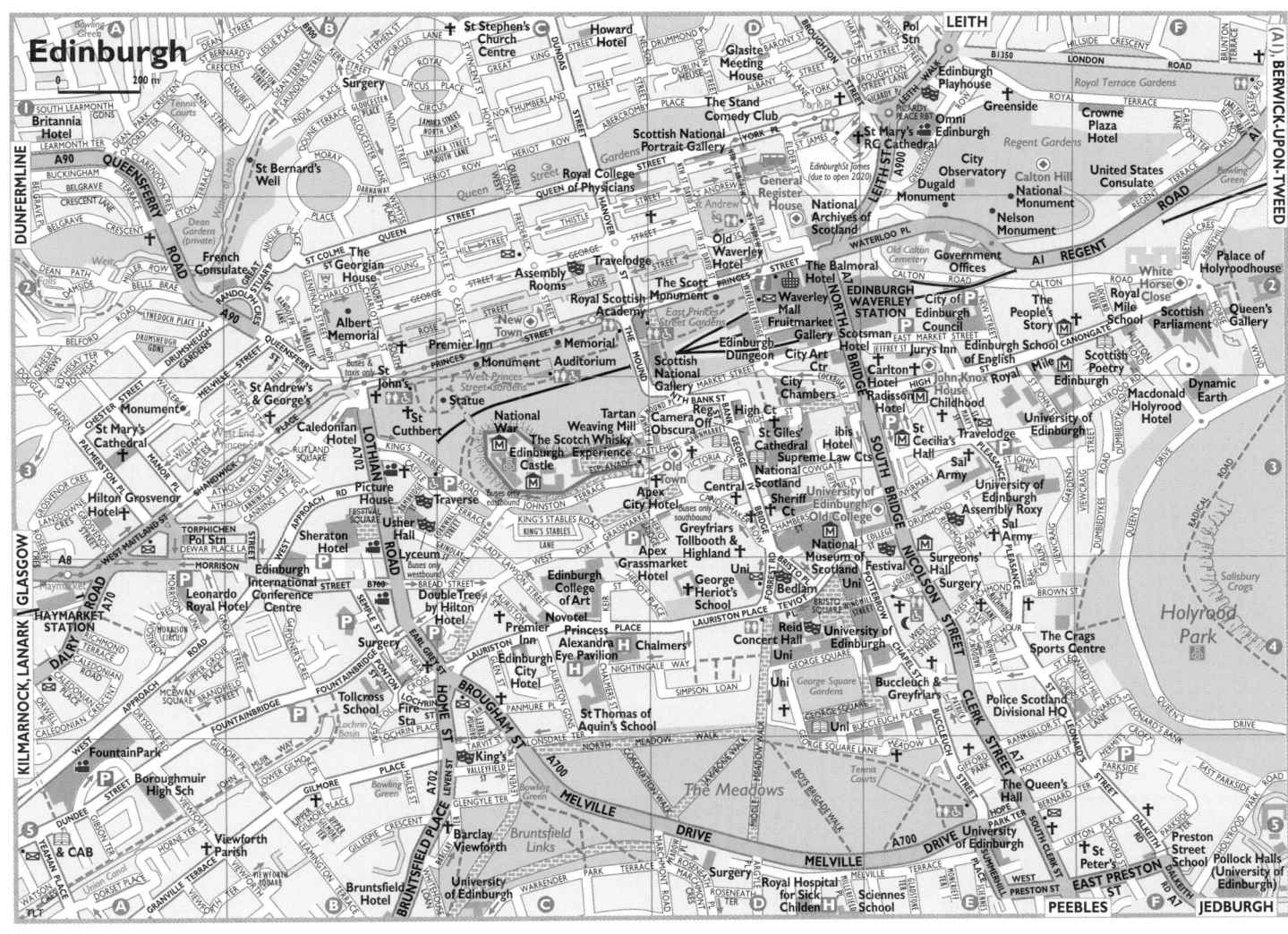

Edinburgh

Edinburgh is found on atlas page **127 P3**

Abbeyhill	F2
Abercromby Place	C1
Adam Street	E3
Albany Street	D1
Ann Street	A1
Argyle Place	D5
Atholl Crescent Lane	A3
Bank Street	D3
Barclay Terrace	C5
Belford Road	A2
Belgrave Crescent	A2
Bernard Terrace	E5
Boys Brigade Walk	D5
Brandfield Street	A4
Bread Street	B4
Bristo Place	D4
Brougham Street	C4
Broughton Street	D1
Broughton Street Lane	E1
Brunton Terrace	F1
Bruntsfield Place	B5
Buccleuch Place	D4
Buccleuch Street	E4
Caledonian Place	A4
Caledonian Road	A4
Caledonian Street	A4
Calton Road	E2
Candlemaker Row	D3
Canning Street	B3
Canongate	E2
Carlton Terrace	F1
Castle Hill	C3
Castle Street	C2
Castle Terrace	B3
Chalmers Street	C4
Chambers Street	D3

Chapel Street	E4
Charlotte Square	B2
Chester Street Gardens	A3
Circus Lane	B1
Circus Place	B1
Clarendon Crescent	A1
Clerk Street	E4
Cockburn Street	D2
Coronation Walk	C5
Cowan's Close	E4
Cowgate	D3
Dalkeith Road	F5
Dalry Road	A4
Danube Street	B1
Davie Street	E4
Dean Park Crescent	A1
Dean Street	A1
Dewar Place Lane	A3
Douglas Gardens	A3
Doune Terrace	B1
Drummond Street	E3
Dublin Street	D1
Dumbiedykes Road	F3
Dunbar Street	B4
Dundas Street	C1
Dundee Street	A5
Earl Grey Street	B4
Easter Road	F1
East Market Street	E2
East Parkside	F5
East Preston Street	F5
Elder Street	D1
Forrest Road	D4
Forth Street	D1
Fountainbridge	A4
Frederick Street	C2

Gardener's Crescent	B4
George IV Bridge	D3
George Square	D4
George Square Lane	D5
George Street	B2
George Street	C2
Gifford Park	E5
Gillespie Crescent	B5
Gilmore Park	A5
Gilmore Place	B5
Gilmour Street	E4
Glenfinlas Street	B2
Gloucester Lane	B1
Granville Terrace	A5
Great King Street	C1
Great Stuart Street	B2
Greenmarket	C3
Greenside Row	E1
Grindlay Street	B3
Grosvenor Street	A3
Grove Street	A4
Haddon's Court	E4
Hanover Street	C2
Haymarket Terrace	A4
Heriot Row	C1
Hermits Croft	F5
High Street	D3
High Street	E3
Hillside Crescent	E1
Hill Street	C2
Holyrood Park Road	F5
Holyrood Road	E3
Home Street	C4
Hope Street	B2
Horse Wynd	F2
Howden Street	E4
Howe Street	C1
India Place	B1
India Street	B1
Jamaica Street South Lane	B1
Jawbone Walk	D5

Jeffrey Street	E2
Johnston Terrace	C3
Keir Street	C4
Kerr Street	B1
King's Stables Road	B3
Lady Lawson Street	C3
Lansdowne Crescent	A3
Lauriston Gardens	C4
Lauriston Place	C4
Lauriston Street	C4
Lawnmarket	D3
Leamington Terrace	B5
Leith Street	E1
Leith Walk	E1
Lennox Street	A1
Leven Place	C5
Lochrin Place	B4
Lochrin Street	B4
London Road	E1
Lothian Road	B3
Lower Gilmore Place	B5
Lutton Place	E5
Lynedoch Place Lane	A2
Manor Place	A3
Marchmont Crescent	D5
Marchmont Road	D5
Market Street	D2
Meadow Lane	E5
Melville Drive	C5
Melville Street	B2
Melville Terrace	D5
Middle Meadow Walk	D5
Millerfield Place	D5
Miller Row	A2
Moncrieff Terrace	E5
Montague Street	E5
Moray Place	B1
Morrison Link	A4
Morrison Street	A4
Mound Place	D3
Nelson Street	C1

New Street	E2
Nicolson Square	E4
Nicolson Street	E4
Nightingale Way	C4
North Bridge	D2
North Castle Street	C2
North Meadow Walk	C5
North St Andrew Street	D1
North St David Street	D1
Northumberland Street	C1
Oxford Street	F5
Palmerston Place	A3
Panmure Place	C4
Pleasance	E3
Ponton Street	B4
Potterrow	E4
Princes Street	C2
Queens Drive	F3
Queensferry Road	A1
Queensferry Street	B2
Queen Street	B2
Radical Road	F3
Ramsay Lane	C3
Randolph Crescent	B2
Randolph Lane	B2
Rankeillor Street	E5
Regent Road	E2
Richmond Place	E3
Rose Street	B2
Roseneath Place	D5
Rothesay Place	A3
Royal Circus	B1
Royal Terrace	E1
St Andrew Square	D1
St Bernard's Crescent	A1
St Colme Street	B2
St James Place	D1
St Leonard's Bank	F4
St Leonard's Hill	F4
St Leonard's Lane	E4
St Leonard's Street	E4

St Patrick Street	E4
St Stephen Street	B1
St Vincent Street	C1
Saunders Street	B1
Sciennes	E5
Semple Street	B4
Shandwick Place	A3
Simpson Loan	D4
South Bridge	E3
South Charlotte Street	B2
South Clerk Street	E5
South Learmonth Gardens	A1
South St Andrew Street	D2
South St David Street	D2
Spittal Street	C4
Stafford Street	B3
Tarvit Street	C5
The Mound	C2
Thistle Street	C2
Torphichen Street	A3
Union Street	E1
Upper Gilmore Place	B5
Victoria Street	D3
Viewcraig Gardens	E4
Viewcraig Street	F3
Viewforth	A5
Walker Street	A3
Warrender Park Terrace	C5
Waterloo Place	D2
Waverley Bridge	D2
West Approach Road	A5
West Maitland Street	A3
West Nicolson Street	E4
West Port	C4
West Richmond Street	E4
West Toll Cross	B4
William Street	A3
Yeaman Place	A5
York Lane	D1
York Place	D1
Young Street	B2

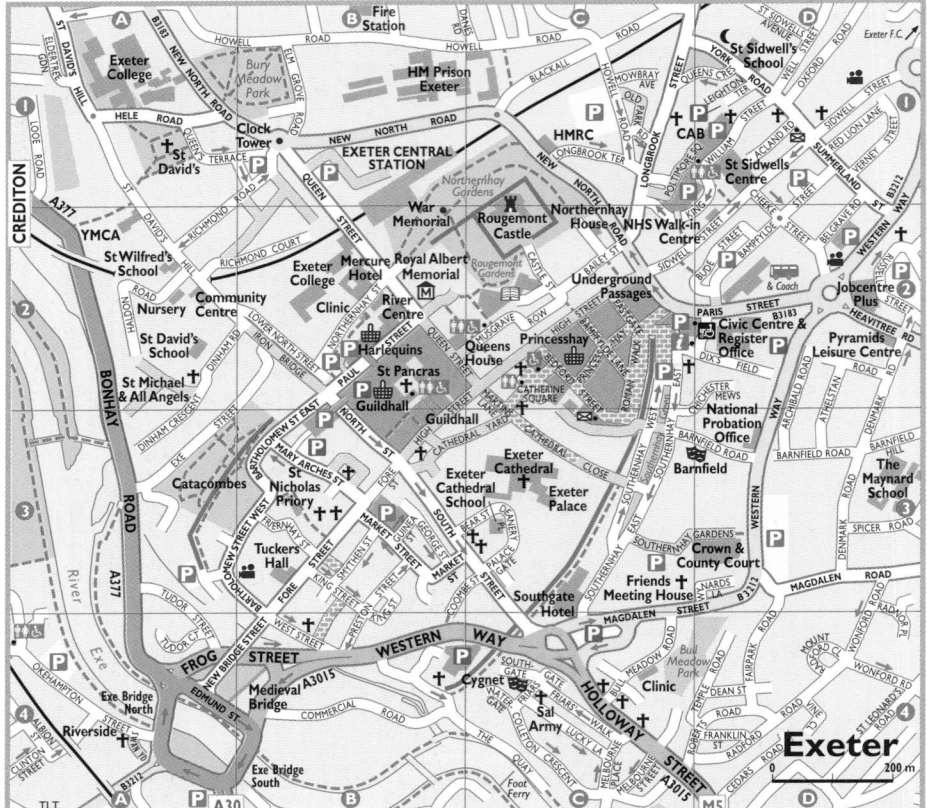

Exeter

Exeter is found on atlas page **9 M6**

Acland Road	D1	King Street	B3
Archibald Road	D3	King William Street	D1
Athelstan Road	D3	Longbrook Street	C1
Bailey Street	C2	Lower North Street	B2
Bampfylde Lane	C2	Magdalen Road	D3
Bampfylde Street	D2	Magdalen Street	C4
Barnfield Road	D3	Market Street	B3
Bartholomew Street East	B3	Martins Lane	C2
Bartholomew Street West	B3	Mary Arches Street	B3
Bear Street	C3	Musgrave Row	C2
Bedford Street	C2	New Bridge Street	A4
Belgrave Road	D2	New North Road	A1
Blackall Road	C1	Northernhay Street	B2
Bonhay Road	A2	North Street	B3
Bude Street	D2	Old Park Road	C1
Bull Meadow Road	C4	Oxford Road	D1
Castle Street	C2	Palace Gate	C3
Cathedral Close	C3	Paris Street	D2
Cathedral Yard	B3	Paul Street	B2
Cedars Road	D4	Preston Street	B4
Cheeke Street	D1	Princesshay	C2
Chichester Mews	C3	Queens Crescent	C1
Commercial Road	B4	Queen's Terrace	A1
Coombe Street	B3	Queen Street	B1
Deanery Place	C3	Radford Road	D4
Dean Street	D4	Richmond Court	B2
Denmark Road	D3	Richmond Road	A2
Dinham Crescent	A3	Roberts Road	C4
Dinham Road	A2	Roman Walk	C2
Dix's Field	D2	St David's Hill	A1
Eastgate	C2	Sidwell Street	C2
Edmund Street	A4	Sidwell Street	D1
Elm Grove Road	B1	Smythen Street	B3
Exe Street	A3	Southernhay East	C3
Fairpark Road	D4	Southernhay Gardens	C3
Fore Street	B3	Southernhay West	C3
Franklin Street	D4	South Street	B3
Friernhay Street	B3	Spicer Road	D3
Frog Street	A4	Summerland Street	D1
George Street	B3	Temple Road	D4
Guinea Street	B3	Tudor Court	A4
Haldon Road	A2	Tudor Street	A3
Heavitree Road	D2	Verney Street	D1
Hele Road	A1	Well Street	D1
High Street	C2	Western Way	B4
Holloway Street	C4	West Street	B4
Howell Road	B1	Wonford Road	D4
Iron Bridge	B2	York Road	D1

Gloucester

Gloucester is found on atlas page **46 F11**

Albert Street	D4	Millbrook Street	D4
Albion Street	B4	Montpellier	B4
All Saints' Road	D4	Napier Street	D4
Alvin Street	C2	Nettleton Road	C3
Archdeacon Street	B2	New Inn Lane	C3
Arthur Street	C4	Norfolk Street	B4
Barbican Road	B3	Northgate Street	C3
Barrack Square	B3	Old Tram Road	B4
Barton Street	D4	Over Causeway	A1
Bedford Street	C3	Oxford Road	D1
Belgrave Road	C4	Oxford Street	D2
Berkeley Street	B3	Park Road	C4
Black Dog Way	C2	Park Street	C2
Blenheim Road	D4	Parliament Street	B3
Brunswick Road	B4	Pembroke Street	C4
Brunswick Square	B4	Pitt Street	B2
Bruton Way	D3	Priory Road	B1
Bull Lane	B3	Quay Street	B2
Castle Meads Way	A2	Royal Oak Road	A2
Clarence Street	C3	Russell Street	C3
Clare Street	B2	St Aldate Street	C2
College Court	B2	St Catherine Street	C1
Commercial Road	B3	St John's Lane	B3
Cromwell Street	C4	St Mark Street	C1
Cross Keys Lane	B3	St Mary's Square	B2
Deans Walk	C1	St Mary's Street	B2
Eastgate Street	C3	St Michael's Square	C4
Gouda Way	B1	St Oswald's Road	B1
Great Western Road	D2	Sebert Street	C1
Greyfriars	C3	Severn Road	A3
Hampden Way	C3	Sherborne Street	D2
Hare Lane	C2	Sinope Street	D4
Heathville Road	D2	Southgate Street	B4
Henry Road	D1	Spa Road	B4
Henry Street	D2	Station Road	C3
High Orchard Street	A4	Swan Road	C1
Honyatt Road	D1	Sweetbriar Street	C1
Kings Barton Street	C4	The Cross	B3
Kingsholm Road	C1	The Oxebode	C3
King's Square	C2	The Quay	A2
Ladybellegate Street	B3	Union Street	C1
Llanthony Road	A4	Upper Quay Street	B2
London Road	D2	Vauxhall Road	D4
Longsmith Street	B3	Wellington Street	C4
Market Parade	C3	Westgate Street	A2
Merchants' Road	A4	Widden Street	D4
Mercia Road	B1	Worcester Parade	C2
Metz Way	D3	Worcester Street	C2

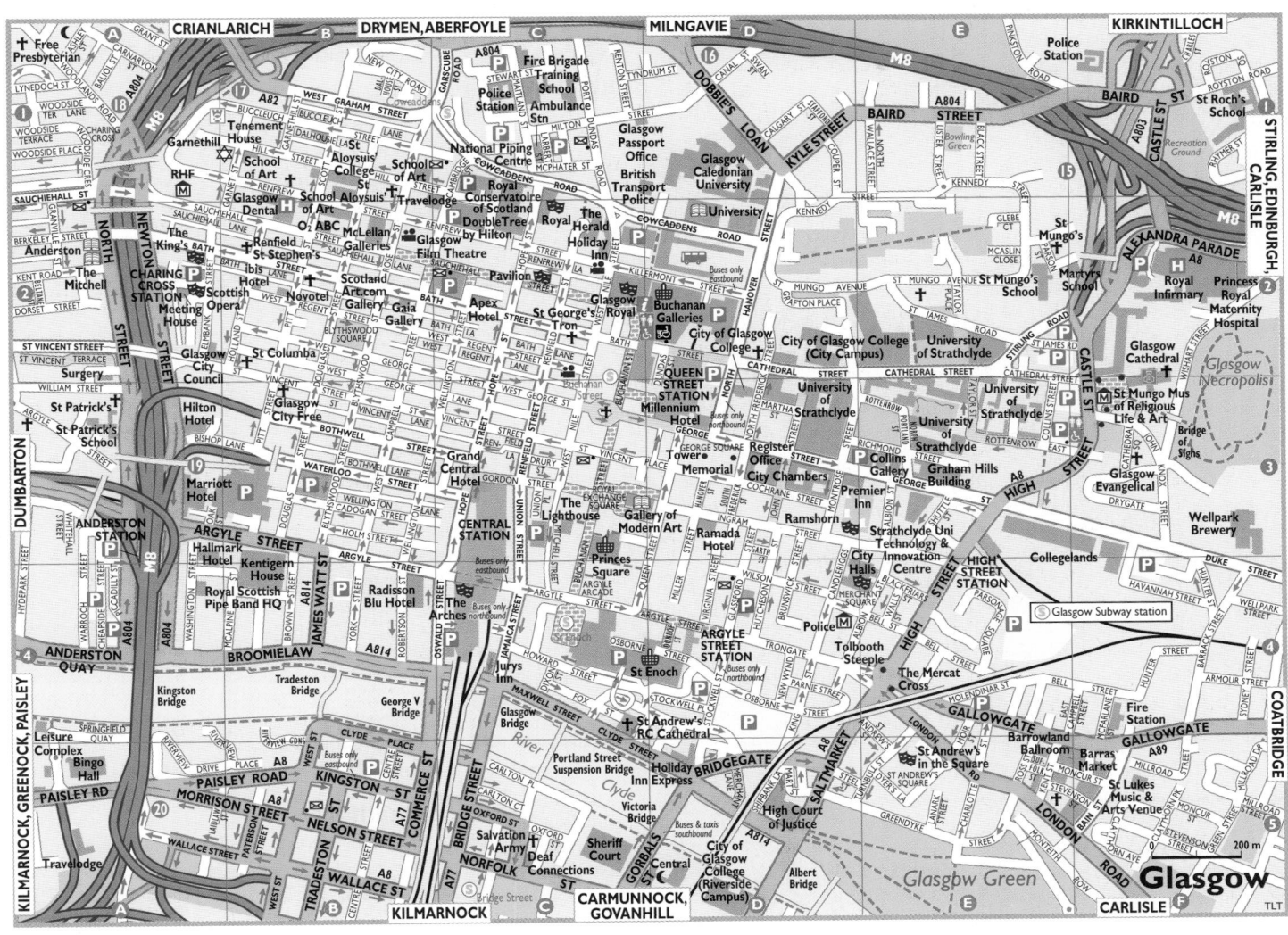

Glasgow

Glasgow is found on atlas page **125 P4**

Albert Bridge	D5	Candleriggs	D4	Gallowgate	E4
Albion Street	D4	Carlton Place	C5	Garnethill Street	B1
Albion Street	E3	Carnarvon Street	A1	Garnet Street	B2
Alexandra Parade	F2	Castle Street	F1	Garscube Road	C1
Anderston Quay	A4	Castle Street	F2	Garth Street	D3
Argyle Arcade	C4	Cathedral Square	F3	George Square	D3
Argyle Street	A3	Cathedral Street	D2	George Street	E3
Armour Street	F4	Centre Street	B5	George V Bridge	B4
Ashley Street	A1	Chalmer Street	F5	Glasgow Bridge	C5
Bain Street	F5	Charing Cross	A1	Glassford Street	D4
Baird Street	E1	Charles Street	F1	Glebe Court	E2
Baliol Street	A1	Charlotte Street	E5	Gorbals Street	C5
Barrack Street	F4	Cheapside Street	A4	Gordon Street	C3
Bath Lane	B2	Claythorn Avenue	F5	Grafton Place	D2
Bath Street	A2	Claythorn Park	F5	Granville Street	A2
Bell Street	E4	Clyde Place	B4	Greendyke Street	E5
Berkeley Street	A2	Clyde Street	C4	Green Street	F5
Blackfriars Street	E4	Cochrane Street	D3	Hanover Street	D3
Black Street	E1	Collins Street	E3	High Street	E4
Blythswood Square	B2	Commerce Street	B5	Hill Street	B1
Blythswood Street	B3	Couper Street	D1	Holland Street	B2
Bothwell Lane	B3	Cowcaddens Road	C1	Holm Street	B3
Bothwell Street	B3	Dalhousie Lane	B1	Hope Street	C3
Bridgegate	D5	Dixon Street	C4	Howard Street	C4
Bridge of Sighs	F3	Dobbie's Loan	C1	Hunter Street	F4
Bridge Street	C5	Dorset Street	A2	Hutcheson Street	D4
Broomielaw	B4	Douglas Street	B3	Hydepark Street	A4
Brown Street	B4	Drury Street	C3	Ingram Street	D3
Brunswick Street	D4	Drygate	F3	Jamaica Street	C4
Buccleuch Lane	B1	Duke Street	F4	James Watt Street	B4
Buccleuch Street	B1	Dundas Street	D3	John Knox Street	F3
Buchanan Street	C4	Dunlop Street	C4	John Street	D3
Cadogan Street	B3	Dyer's Lane	E5	Kennedy Street	D2
Calgary Street	D1	East Campbell Street	E4	Kennedy Street	E1
Cambridge Street	C1	Elmbank Street	A2	Kent Road	A2
Canal Street	D1	Fox Street	C4	Kent Street	E5
				Killermont Street	C2
				Kingston Bridge	A5
				Kingston Street	B5
				King Street	D4
				Kyle Street	D1

Lanark Street	E5	Paterson Street	B5	Steel Street	D5
Larbert Street	C1	Pinkston Road	E1	Stevenson Street	F5
Lister Street	E1	Pitt Street	B2	Stewart Street	C1
London Road	E4	Port Dundas Road	C1	Stirling Road	E2
Maitland Street	C1	Portland Street		Stockwell Place	D4
Martha Street	D3	Suspension Bridge	C5	Stockwell Street	D4
Mart Street	D5	Queen Street	C4	Suffolk Street	E5
Maxwell Street	C4	Renfield Lane	C3	Sydney Street	F4
McAlpine Street	B4	Renfield Street	C3	Taylor Place	E2
McAslin Close	E2	Renfrew Lane	C2	Taylor Street	E2
McFarlane Street	F4	Renfrew Street	B1	Tradeston Bridge	B4
McPhater Street	C1	Renton Street	C1	Tradeston Street	B5
Merchant Lane	D5	Rhymer Street	F1	Trongate	D4
Miller Street	D4	Richmond Street	E3	Turnbull Street	D5
Millroad Drive	F5	Riverview Drive	A4	Tyndrum Street	C1
Millroad Street	F5	Robertson Street	B4	Union Street	C3
Milton Street	C1	Rose Street	B2	Virginia Street	D4
Mitchell Street	C4	Ross Street	E5	Wallace Street	A5
Moir Street	E5	Rottenrow	E3	Walls Street	E4
Molendinar Street	E4	Rottenrow East	E3	Warroch Street	A4
Moncur Street	E5	Royal Exchange Square	C3	Washington Street	A4
Monteith Row	E5	Royston Road	F1	Waterloo Street	B3
Montrose Street	D3	Royston Square	F1	Wellington Lane	B3
Morrison Street	A5	St Andrew's Square	E5	Wellington Street	B3
Nelson Street	B5	St Andrew's Street	E4	Wellpark Street	F4
New City Road	B1	St James Road	E2	West Campbell Street	B3
Newton Street	A2	St Mungo Avenue	D2	West George Lane	B2
New Wynd	D4	St Vincent Lane	B3	West George Street	B2
Norfolk Street	C5	St Vincent Place	C3	West Graham Street	B1
North Frederick Street	D3	St Vincent Street	A2	West Nile Street	C3
North Hanover Street	D3	St Vincent Terrace	A2	West Regent Lane	C2
North Portland Street	E3	Saltmarket	D5	West Regent Street	B2
North Street	A2	Sauchiehall Lane	A2	West Street	B5
North Wallace Street	E1	Sauchiehall Lane	A1	William Street	A3
Osborne Street	C4	Sauchiehall Street	B2	Wilson Street	D4
Oswald Street	C4	Scott Street	B1	Wishart Street	F3
Oxford Street	C5	Shipbank Lane	D5	Woodlands Road	A1
Paisley Road	A5	Shuttle Street	E3	Woodside Crescent	A1
Parnie Street	D4	South Frederick Street	D3	Woodside Terrace	A1
Parsonage Square	E4	Springfield Quay	A4	Woodside Terrace Lane	A1
Parson Street	E2	Stafford Street	D1	York Street	B4

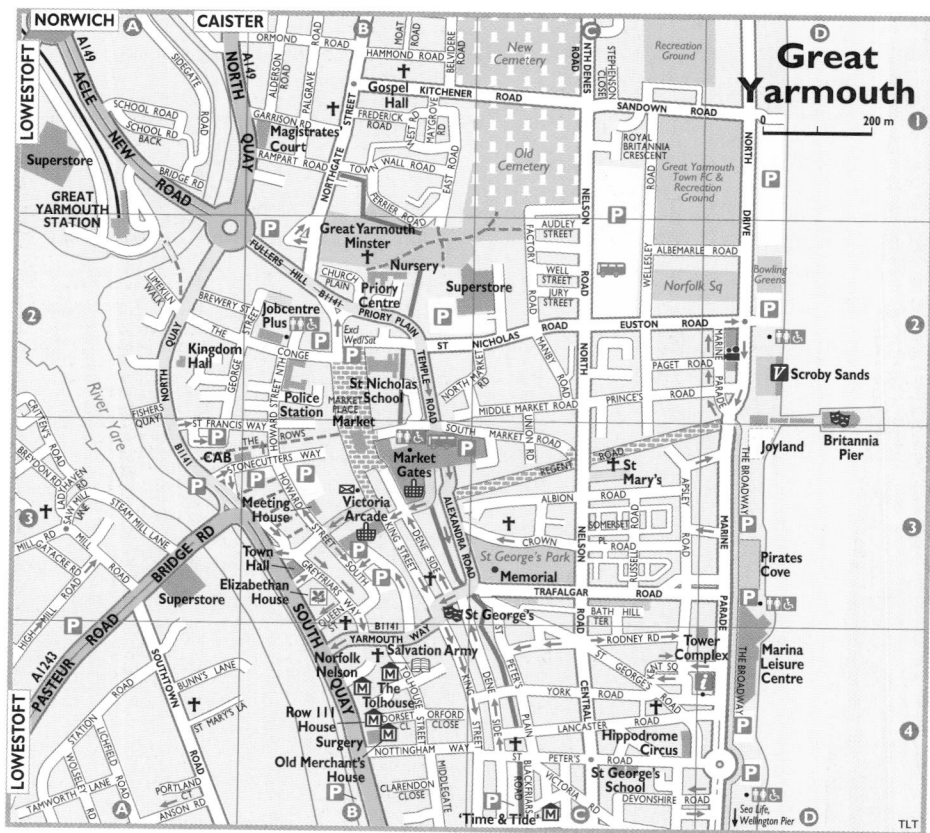

Great Yarmouth

Great Yarmouth is found on atlas page **77 Q10**

Acle New Road	A1	North Drive	D1
Albemarle Road	C2	North Market Road	C2
Albion Road	C3	North Quay	A2
Alderson Road	B1	Northgate Street	B1
Alexandra Road	B3	Nottingham Way	B4
Apsley Road	C3	Ormond Road	B1
Belvidere Road	B1	Paget Road	C2
Blackfriars Road	C4	Palgrave Road	B1
Brewery Street	A2	Pasteur Road	A4
Breydon Road	A3	Prince's Road	C2
Bridge Road	A1	Priory Plain	B2
Bridge Road	A3	Queen Street	B4
Bunn's Lane	A4	Rampart Road	B1
Church Plain	B2	Regent Road	C3
Critten's Road	A3	Rodney Road	C4
Crown Road	C3	Russell Road	C3
Dene Side	B3	St Francis Way	A3
Devonshire Road	C4	St George's Road	C4
East Road	B1	St Nicholas Road	B2
Euston Road	C2	St Peter's Plain	C4
Factory Road	C2	St Peter's Road	C4
Ferrier Road	B1	Sandown Road	C1
Fishers Quay	A2	Saw Mill Lane	A3
Frederick Road	B1	School Road	A1
Fullers Hill	B2	School Road Back	A1
Garrison Road	B1	Sidegate Road	A1
Gatacre Road	A3	South Market Road	C3
George Street	A2	South Quay	B3
Greyfriars Way	B3	Southtown Road	A4
Hammond Road	B1	Station Road	A4
High Mill Road	A3	Steam Mill Lane	A3
Howard Street North	B2	Stephenson Close	C1
Howard Street South	B3	Stonecutters Way	B3
King Street	B3	Tamworth Lane	A4
Kitchener Road	B1	Temple Road	B2
Ladyhaven Road	A3	The Broadway	D3
Lancaster Road	C4	The Conge	A2
Lichfield Road	A4	The Rows	B3
Limekiln Walk	A2	Tolhouse Street	B4
Manby Road	C2	Town Wall Road	B1
Marine Parade	D3	Trafalgar Road	C3
Maygrove Road	B1	Union Road	C3
Middle Market Road	C2	Victoria Road	C4
Middlegate	B4	Wellesley Road	C2
Moat Road	B1	West Road	B1
Nelson Road Central	C3	Wolseley Road	A4
Nelson Road North	C1	Yarmouth Way	B4
North Denes Road	C1	York Road	C4

Guildford

Guildford is found on atlas page **23 Q5**

Abbot Road	C4	Millmead	B3
Angel Gate	B3	Millmead Terrace	B4
Artillery Road	B1	Mount Pleasant	A4
Artillery Terrace	C1	Nightingale Road	D1
Bedford Road	A2	North Street	B3
Bridge Street	A3	Onslow Road	C1
Bright Hill	C3	Onslow Street	B2
Brodie Road	D3	Oxford Road	C3
Bury Fields	B4	Pannells Court	C2
Bury Street	B4	Park Street	B3
Castle Hill	C4	Pewley Bank	D3
Castle Street	C3	Pewley Fort Inner Court	D4
Chapel Street	B3	Pewley Hill	C3
Chertsey Street	C2	Pewley Way	D3
Cheselden Road	D2	Phoenix Court	B3
Church Road	B1	Porridge Pot Alley	B4
College Road	B2	Portsmouth Road	A4
Commercial Road	B2	Poyle Road	D4
Dene Road	D2	Quarry Street	B3
Denmark Road	D2	Sandfield Terrace	C2
Drummond Road	B1	Semaphore Road	D3
Eagle Road	C1	South Hill	C3
Epsom Road	D2	Springfield Road	C1
Falcon Road	C1	Station Approach	D1
Farnham Road	A3	Station View	A2
Fort Road	C4	Stoke Fields	C1
Foxenden Road	D1	Stoke Grove	C1
Friary Bridge	A3	Stoke Road	C1
Friary Street	B3	Swan Lane	B3
George Street	B1	Sydenham Road	C3
Guildford Park Road	A2	Testard Road	A3
Harvey Road	D3	The Bars	C2
Haydon Place	C2	The Mount	A4
High Pewley	D4	The Shambles	B3
High Street	C3	Tunsgate	C3
Jeffries Passage	C2	Upperton Road	A3
Jenner Road	D2	Victoria Road	D1
Laundry Road	B2	Walnut Tree Close	A1
Leapale Lane	B2	Ward Street	C2
Leapale Road	B2	Warwicks Bench	C4
Leas Road	B1	Wherwell Road	A3
London Road	D2	William Road	B1
Mareschal Road	A4	Wodeland Avenue	A3
Market Street	C3	Woodbridge Road	B1
Martyr Road	C2	York Road	B1
Mary Road	A1		
Millbrook	B3		
Mill Lane	B3		

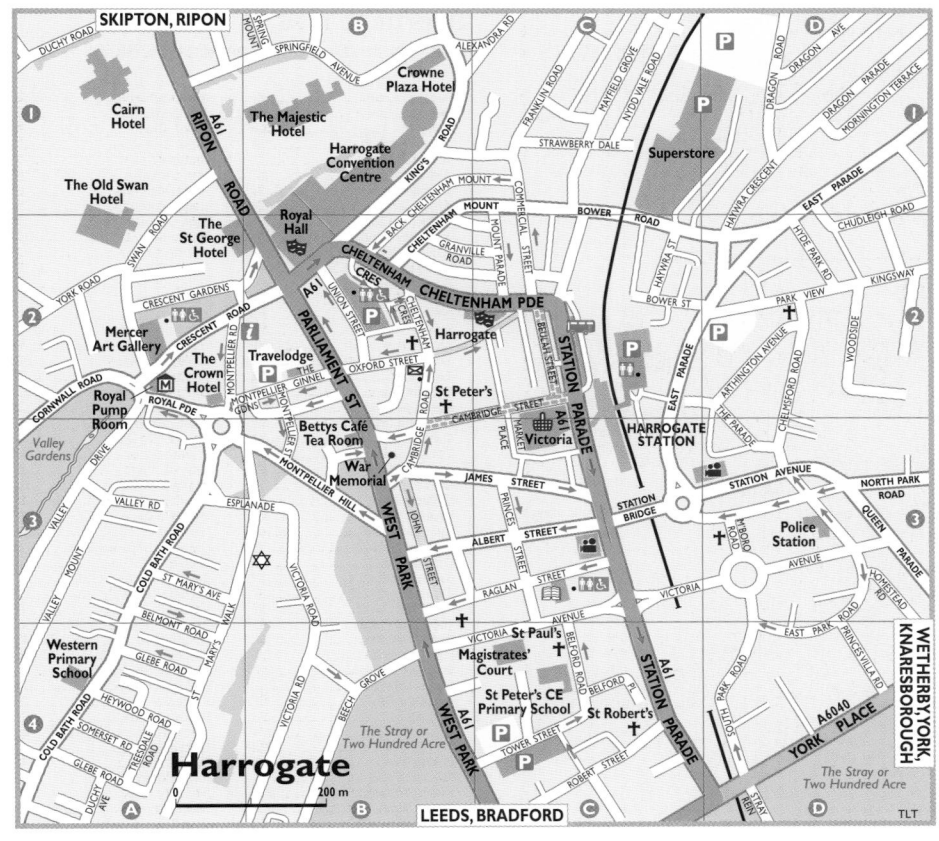

Harrogate

Harrogate is found on atlas page **97 M9**

Albert Street	C3	Montpellier Road	A2
Alexandra Road	B1	Montpellier Street	B2
Arthington Avenue	D2	Mornington Terrace	D1
Back Cheltenham Mount	B2	Mount Parade	C2
Beech Grove	B4	North Park Road	D3
Belford Place	C4	Nydd Vale Road	C1
Belford Road	C4	Oxford Street	B2
Belmont Road	A3	Park View	D2
Beulah Street	C2	Parliament Street	B2
Bower Road	C1	Princes Street	C3
Bower Street	C2	Princes Villa Road	D4
Cambridge Road	B3	Queen Parade	D3
Cambridge Street	C2	Raglan Street	C3
Chelmsford Road	D3	Ripon Road	A1
Cheltenham Crescent	B2	Robert Street	C4
Cheltenham Mount	B2	Royal Parade	A2
Cheltenham Parade	B2	St Mary's Avenue	A3
Chudleigh Road	D2	St Mary's Walk	A4
Cold Bath Road	A3	Somerset Road	A4
Commercial Street	C1	South Park Road	D4
Cornwall Road	A2	Springfield Avenue	B1
Crescent Gardens	A2	Spring Mount	B1
Crescent Road	A2	Station Avenue	D3
Dragon Avenue	D1	Station Bridge	C3
Dragon Parade	D1	Station Parade	C2
Dragon Road	D1	Strawberry Dale	C1
Duchy Avenue	A4	Stray Rein	D4
Duchy Road	A1	Swan Road	A2
East Parade	C2	The Ginnel	B2
East Park Road	D4	The Parade	D2
Esplanade	A3	Tower Street	C4
Franklin Road	C1	Treesdale Road	A4
Glebe Road	A4	Union Street	B2
Granville Road	B2	Valley Drive	A3
Haywra Street	C2	Valley Mount	A3
Heywood Road	A4	Valley Road	A3
Homestead Road	D3	Victoria Avenue	B4
Hyde Park Road	D2	Victoria Road	B3
Hywra Crescent	D2	West Park	B3
James Street	B3	West Park Street	B4
John Street	B3	Woodside	D2
King's Road	B1	York Place	D4
Kingsway	D2	York Road	A2
Market Place	C3		
Marlborough Road	D3		
Mayfield Grove	C1		
Montpellier Gardens	B2		
Montpellier Hill	B3		

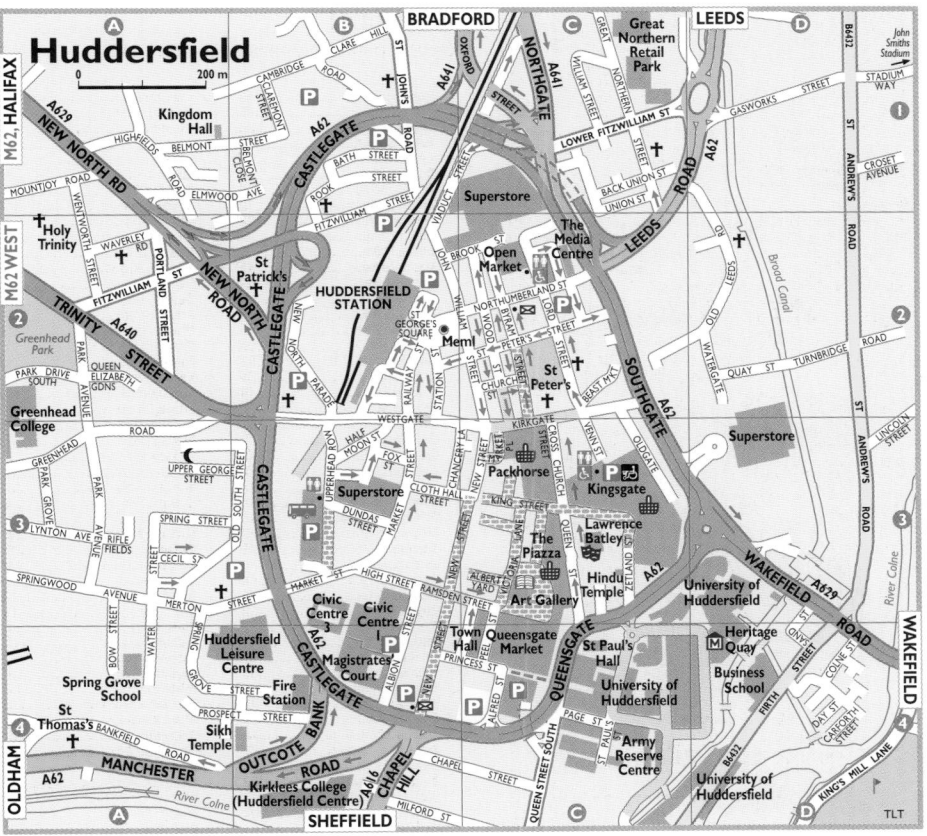

Huddersfield

Huddersfield is found on atlas page **90 E7**

Albion Street	B4	New North Road	A2
Alfred Street	C4	New Street	B4
Back Union Street	C1	Northgate	C1
Bankfield Road	A4	Northumberland Street	C2
Bath Street	B1	Old Leeds Road	D2
Belmont Street	A1	Old South Street	B3
Brook Street	C2	Outcote Bank	B4
Byram Street	C2	Oxford Street	C1
Cambridge Road	B1	Page Street	C4
Carforth Street	D4	Park Avenue	A2
Castlegate	B1	Park Drive South	A2
Chancery Lane	B3	Peel Street	C4
Chapel Hill	B4	Portland Street	A2
Chapel Street	B4	Princess Street	B4
Church Street	C2	Prospect Street	A4
Clare Hill	B1	Quay Street	D2
Claremont Street	B1	Queen Street	C3
Cloth Hall Street	B3	Queen Street South	C4
Cross Church Street	C3	Queensgate	C4
Dundas Street	B3	Railway Street	B2
Elizabeth Queen Gardens	B2	Ramsden Street	B3
Elmwood Avenue	A1	Rook Street	B1
Firth Street	D4	St Andrew's Road	D2
Fitzwilliam Street	A2	St George's Square	B2
Fitzwilliam Street	B2	St John's Road	B1
Gasworks Street	D1	St Peter's Street	C2
Great Northern Street	C1	Southgate	C2
Greenhead Road	A3	Spring Grove Street	A4
Half Moon Street	B3	Spring Street	A3
High Street	B3	Springwood Avenue	A3
Highfields Road	A1	Stadium Way	D1
John William Street	B2	Station Street	B2
King Street	C3	Trinity Street	A2
King's Mill Lane	D4	Turnbridge Road	D2
Kirkgate	C3	Union Street	C1
Leeds Road	C2	Upper George Street	A3
Lincoln Street	D3	Upperhead Row	B3
Lord Street	C2	Viaduct Street	B2
Lower Fitzwilliam Street	C1	Victoria Lane	C3
Lynton Avenue	A3	Wakefield Road	D3
Manchester Road	A4	Water Street	A3
Market Place	C3	Watergate	D2
Market Street	B3	Waverley Road	A2
Merton Street	A3	Wentworth Street	A2
Milford Street	B4	Westgate	B3
Mountjoy Road	A1	William Street	C1
New North Parade	B2	Wood Street	C2
New North Road	A1	Zetland Street	C3

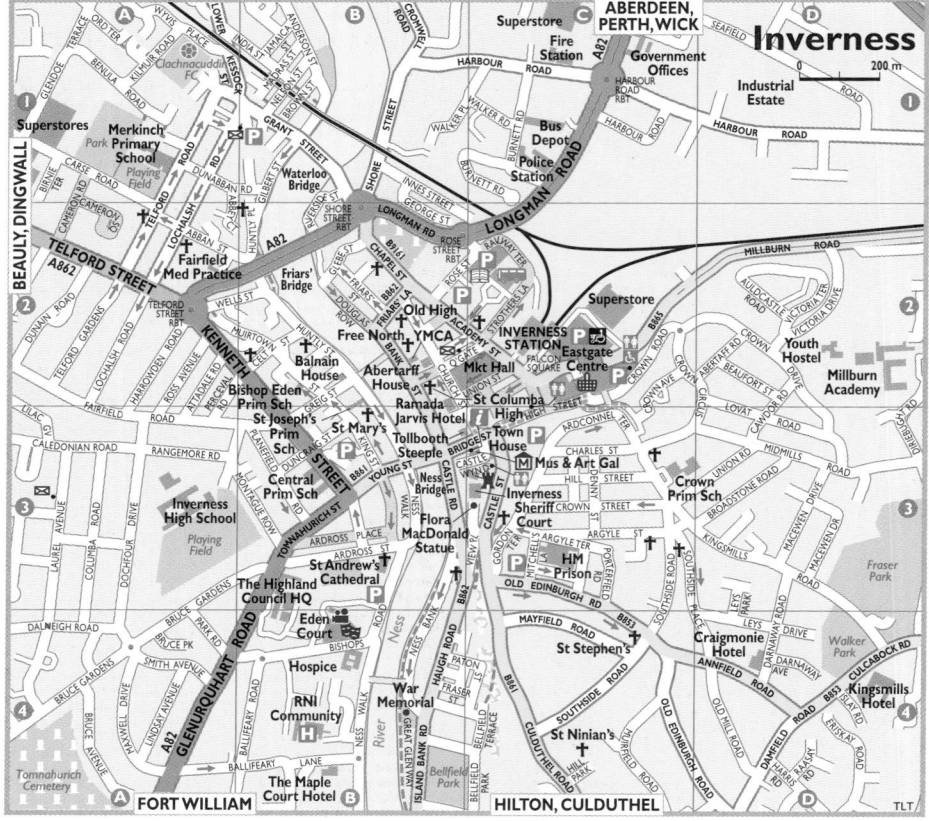

Inverness

Inverness is found on atlas page **156 B8**

Abertaff Road	D2	Glenurquhart Road	A4
Academy Street	B2	Gordon Terrace	C3
Anderson Street	B1	Grant Street	B1
Annfield Road	D4	Great Glen Way	B4
Ardconnel Terrace	C3	Harbour Road	C1
Ardross Street	B3	Harris Road	D4
Argyle Street	C3	Harrowden Road	A2
Argyle Terrace	C3	Haugh Road	B4
Ballifeary Lane	A4	High Street	C3
Ballifeary Road	B4	Hill Park	C4
Bank Street	B2	Hill Street	C3
Bellfield Terrace	C4	Huntly Street	B2
Benula Road	A1	Innes Street	B1
Birnie Terrace	A1	Kenneth Street	A2
Bishops Road	B4	King Street	B3
Bridge Street	B3	Kingsmills Road	D3
Broadstone Road	D3	Laurel Avenue	A3
Bruce Gardens	A4	Lindsay Avenue	A4
Bruce Park	A4	Lochalsh Road	A2
Burnett Road	C1	Longman Road	C2
Caledonian Road	A3	Lovat Road	D3
Cameron Road	A2	Lower Kessock Street	A1
Cameron Square	A2	Maxwell Drive	A4
Carse Road	A1	Mayfield Road	C4
Castle Road	B3	Midmills Road	D3
Castle Street	C3	Millburn Road	D2
Chapel Street	B2	Mitchell's Lane	C3
Charles Street	C3	Muirfield Road	C4
Columba Road	A3	Ness Bank	B4
Crown Circus	C2	Old Edinburgh Road	C3
Crown Drive	D2	Park Road	A4
Crown Road	C2	Planefield Road	B3
Crown Street	C3	Porterfield Road	C3
Culcabock Road	D4	Raasay Road	D4
Culduthel Road	C4	Rangemore Road	A3
Dalneigh Road	A4	Ross Avenue	A2
Damfield Road	D4	Seafield Road	D1
Darnaway Road	D4	Shore Street	B1
Denny Street	C3	Smith Avenue	A4
Dochfour Drive	A3	Southside Place	C3
Dunabban Road	A1	Southside Road	C4
Dunain Road	A2	Telford Gardens	A2
Duncraig Street	B3	Telford Road	A2
Eriskay Road	D4	Telford Street	A2
Fairfield Road	A3	Tomnahurich Street	B3
Falcon Square	C2	Union Road	D3
Friars' Lane	B2	Walker Road	C1
Glendoe Terrace	A1	Young Street	B3

Ipswich

Ipswich is found on atlas page **53 L3**

Alderman Road	A3	Key Street	C3
Anglesea Road	B1	King Street	B2
Argyle Street	D2	London Road	A2
Austin Street	C4	Lower Brook Street	C3
Barrack Lane	A1	Lower Orwell Street	C3
Belstead Road	B4	Museum Street	B2
Berners Street	B1	Neale Street	C1
Black Horse Lane	B2	Neptune Quay	D3
Blanche Street	D2	New Cardinal Street	B3
Bolton Lane	C1	Newson Street	A1
Bond Street	D3	Northgate Street	C2
Bramford Road	A1	Norwich Road	A1
Bridge Street	C4	Old Foundry Road	C2
Burlington Road	A2	Orchard Street	D2
Burrell Road	B4	Orford Street	A1
Cardigan Street	A1	Orwell Place	C3
Carr Street	C2	Orwell Quay	D4
Cecil Road	B1	Portman Road	A3
Cemetery Road	D1	Princes Street	A3
Chancery Road	A4	Quadling Street	B3
Charles Street	B1	Queen Street	B3
Christchurch Street	D1	Ranelagh Road	A4
Civic Drive	B2	Russell Road	A3
Clarkson Street	A1	St George's Street	B1
Cobbold Street	C2	St Helen's Street	D2
College Street	C3	St Margaret's Street	C2
Commercial Road	A4	St Matthews Street	B2
Constantine Road	A3	St Nicholas Street	B3
Crown Street	B2	St Peter's Street	B3
Cumberland Street	A1	Silent Street	B3
Dalton Road	A2	Sir Alf Ramsey Way	A3
Dock Street	C4	Soane Street	C2
Duke Street	D4	South Street	A1
Eagle Street	C3	Star Lane	C3
Elm Street	B2	Stoke Quay	C4
Falcon Street	B3	Suffolk Road	D1
Fonnereau Road	B1	Tacket Street	C3
Foundation Street	C3	Tavern Street	B3
Franciscan Way	B3	Tower Ramparts	B2
Geneva Road	A1	Tuddenham Avenue	D1
Grafton Way	B3	Turret Lane	C3
Great Gipping Street	A2	Upper Orwell Street	C3
Great Whip Street	C4	Vernon Street	C4
Grey Friars Road	B3	West End Road	A3
Grimwade Street	D3	Westgate Street	B2
Handford Road	A2	Willoughby Road	B4
Hervey Street	D1	Wolsey Street	B3
High Street	B1	Woodbridge Road	D2

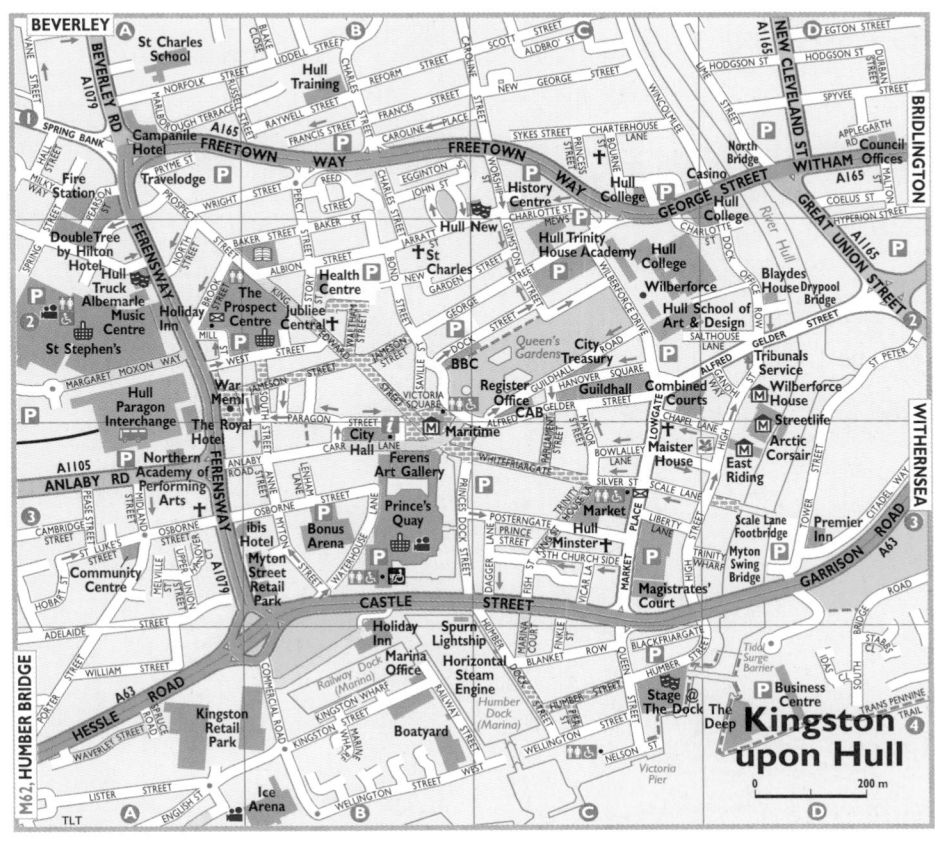

Kingston upon Hull

Kingston upon Hull is found on atlas page **93 J5**

Adelaide Street	A4	Market Place	C3
Albion Street	B2	Mill Street	A2
Alfred Gelder Street	C2	Myton Street	B3
Anlaby Road	A3	New Cleveland Street	D1
Baker Street	B2	New Garden Street	B2
Beverley Road	A1	New George Street	C1
Blackfriargate	C4	Norfolk Street	A1
Blanket Row	C4	Osborne Street	B3
Bond Street	B2	Osborne Street	A3
Brook Street	A2	Paragon Street	B2
Caroline Street	B1	Percy Street	B1
Carr Lane	B3	Porter Street	A3
Castle Street	B3	Portland Place	A2
Chapel Lane	C2	Portland Street	A2
Charles Street	B1	Postergate	C3
Charterhouse Lane	C1	Princes Dock Street	B3
Citadel Way	D3	Prospect Street	A1
Commercial Road	B4	Queen Street	C4
Dagger Lane	C3	Railway Street	B4
Dock Office Row	D2	Raywell Street	B1
Dock Street	B2	Reform Street	B1
Durban Street	D1	Russell Street	A1
Egginton Street	B1	St Luke's Street	A3
Ferensway	A2	St Peter Street	D2
Freetown Way	A1	Saville Street	B2
Gandhi Way	D2	Scale Lane	C3
Garrison Road	D3	Scott Street	C1
George Street	B2	Silver Street	C3
George Street	D1	South Bridge Road	D4
Great Union Street	D1	South Church Side	C3
Grimston Street	C2	South Street	B2
Guildhall Road	C2	Spring Bank	A1
Hanover Square	C2	Spyvee Street	D1
Hessle Road	A4	Sykes Street	C1
High Street	C3	Tower Street	D3
Hodgson Street	D1	Upper Union Street	A3
Humber Dock Street	C4	Victoria Square	B2
Humber Street	C4	Waterhouse Lane	B3
Hyperion Street	D1	Wellington Street	C4
Jameson Street	B2	Wellington Street West	B4
Jarratt Street	B2	West Street	A2
King Edward Street	B2	Whitefriargate	C3
Kingston Street	B4	Wilberforce Drive	C2
Liddell Street	B1	William Street	A4
Lime Street	C1	Wincolmlee	C1
Lister Street	A4	Witham	D1
Lowgate	C3	Worship Street	C1
Margaret Moxon Way	A2	Wright Street	A1

Lancaster

Lancaster is found on atlas page **95 K8**

Aberdeen Road	D4	Lincoln Road	A3
Aldcliffe Road	B4	Lindow Street	B4
Alfred Street	C2	Lodge Street	C2
Ambleside Road	D1	Long Marsh Lane	A2
Balmoral Road	D4	Lune Street	B1
Bath Street	D3	Market Street	B3
Blades Street	A3	Meeting House Lane	A3
Bond Street	D3	Middle Street	B3
Borrowdale Road	D2	Moor Gate	D3
Brewery Lane	B2	Moor Lane	C3
Bridge Lane	B2	Morecambe Road	B1
Brock Street	C3	Nelson Street	C3
Bulk Road	D2	North Road	C2
Bulk Street	C3	Owen Road	C1
Cable Street	B2	Park Road	D3
Castle Hill	B3	Parliament Street	C2
Castle Park	A3	Patterdale Road	D2
Caton Road	C2	Penny Street	B4
Cheapside	C3	Portland Street	B4
China Street	B3	Primrose Street	D4
Church Street	B2	Prospect Street	D4
Common Garden Street	B3	Quarry Road	C4
Dale Street	D4	Queen Street	B4
Dallas Road	B3	Regent Street	B4
Dalton Road	D2	Ridge Lane	D1
Dalton Square	C3	Ridge Street	D1
Damside Street	B2	Robert Street	C3
Derby Road	C1	Rosemary Lane	C2
De Vitre Street	C2	St George's Quay	A1
Dumbarton Road	D4	St Leonard's Gate	C2
East Road	D3	St Peter's Road	C4
Edward Street	C3	Sibsey Street	A3
Fairfield Road	A3	South Road	C4
Fenton Street	B3	Station Road	A3
Gage Street	C3	Stirling Road	D4
Garnet Street	D2	Sulyard Street	C3
George Street	C3	Sun Street	B3
Grasmere Road	D3	Thurnham Street	C4
Great John Street	C3	Troutbeck Road	D2
Gregson Road	D4	Ulleswater Road	D3
Greyhound Bridge Road	B1	West Road	A3
High Street	B4	Westbourne Road	A3
Kelsey Street	A3	Wheatfield Street	A3
Kentmere Road	D2	Williamson Road	D3
King Street	B3	Wingate-Saul Road	A3
Kingsway	C1	Wolseley Street	D2
Kirkes Road	D4	Woodville Street	D3
Langdale Road	D1	Wyresdale Road	D3

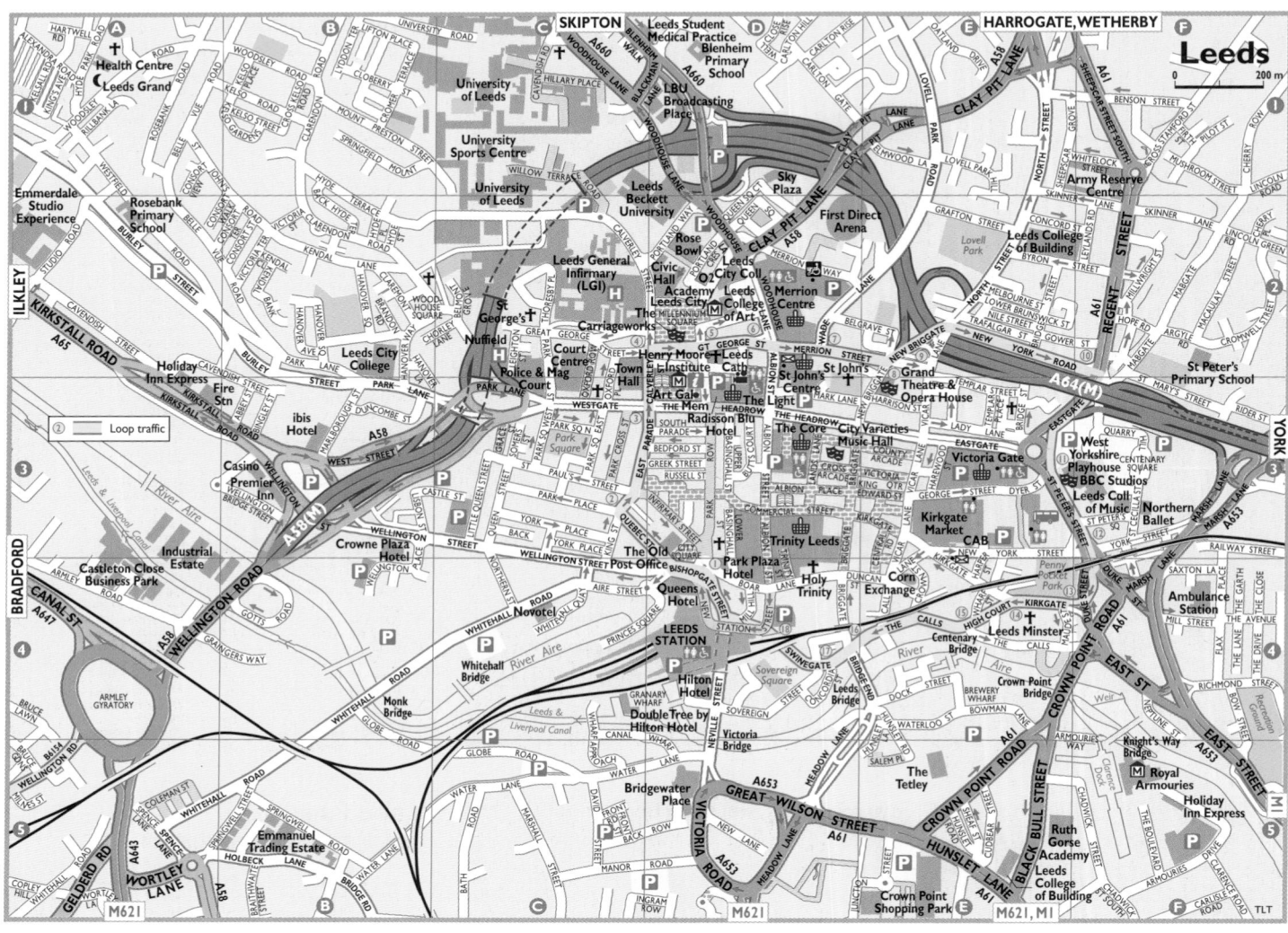

Leeds

Leeds is found on atlas page **90 H4**

Abbey Street....................B3
Aire Street.......................C4
Albion Place....................D3
Albion Street...................D2
Alexandra Road...............A1
Argyle Road.....................F2
Armley Gyratory..............A4
Armley Road....................A4
Armouries Drive..............F5
Armouries Way................E4
Back Hyde Terrace..........B2
Back Row........................C5
Bath Road........................C5
Bedford Street.................D3
Belgrave Street................D2
Belle Vue Road................A1
Belmont Grove.................C2
Benson Street...................F1
Bingley Street..................B3
Bishopgate Street.............D4
Black Bull Street..............E5
Blackman Lane.................C1
Blenheim Walk.................C1
Boar Lane.........................D4
Bowman Lane...................E4
Bow Street.......................F4
Brandon Road..................B2
Bridge End.......................D4
Bridge Road.....................B5
Bridge Street....................E2
Bridge Street....................E3
Briggate..........................D4
Burley Street....................A2
Butts Court.......................D3
Byron Street.....................E2
Call Lane..........................E4

Calverley Street...............C2
Canal Street......................A4
Canal Wharf.....................C4
Carlton Hill......................D1
Carlton Rise.....................D1
Castle Street.....................B3
Cavendish Road...............C1
Cavendish Street..............A2
Centenary Square.............F3
Central Road.....................E3
Chadwick Street...............F5
Cherry Row......................F1
Chorley Lane....................B2
City Square......................D3
Claremont........................B2
Clarence Road..................F5
Clarendon Road...............B1
Clay Pit Lane....................D2
Cloberry Street.................B1
Commercial Street............D3
Concordia Street..............D4
Concord Street.................E2
Consort Street..................B2
Consort View....................A1
County Arcade.................E3
Cromer Terrace................B1
Cromwell Street...............F2
Cross Arcade...................D3
Cross Kelso Road.............B1
Cross Stamford Street.......F1
Crown Point Road............E5
Crown Street....................E4
Cudbear Street.................E5
David Street.....................C5
Dock Street......................E4
Duke Street......................F4

Duke Street......................F4
Duncan Street...................D4
Duncombe Street..............B3
Dyer Street.......................E3
Eastgate...........................E3
East Parade......................C3
East Street........................F4
Elmwood Lane.................E1
Flax Place........................F4
Front Street......................C5
Gelderd Road...................A5
George Street....................E3
Globe Road......................B4
Gotts Road.......................B4
Gower Street....................E2
Grace Street.....................C3
Grafton Street...................E2
Graingers Way.................A4
Great George Street..........C2
Great Wilson Street..........D5
Greek Street.....................D3
Hanover Avenue...............B2
Hanover Lane...................B2
Hanover Square................B2
Harewood Street...............E3
Harper Street....................E4
Harrison Street.................E3
Hartwell Road..................A1
High Court.......................E4
Holbeck Lane...................B5
Hope Road.......................F2
Hunslet Road...................E4
Hunslet Road...................E5
Hyde Park Road...............A1
Hyde Street......................B2
Hyde Terrace....................B1
Infirmary Street...............D3
Junction Street.................D5
Kelso Road.......................B1
Kendal Lane.....................B2
King Edward Street..........E3

King's Avenue..................A1
King Street.......................C3
Kirkgate..........................E3
Kirkstall Road..................A2
Lady Lane........................E3
Lands Lane......................D3
Leighton Street.................C2
Leylands Road..................F2
Lifton Place.....................B1
Lincoln Green Road..........F2
Lisbon Street....................B3
Little Queen Street............C3
Lovell Park Hill................E1
Lovell Park Road..............E1
Lower Basinghall Street....D3
Lower Brunswick Street....E2
Lyddon Terrace................B1
Mabgate..........................F2
Macaulay Street...............F2
Manor Road.....................C5
Mark Lane.......................D3
Marlborough Street...........B3
Marshall Street.................C5
Marsh Lane......................F4
Maude Street...................E4
Meadow Lane...................D5
Melbourne Street..............E2
Merrion Street..................D2
Merrion Way....................D2
Millennium Square...........D2
Mill Street........................F4
Millwright Street..............F2
Mount Preston Street........B1
Mushroom Street..............F1
Neptune Street.................F4
Neville Street....................D4
New Briggate....................E3
New Lane.........................D5
New Station Street............D4
New York Road.................E2
New York Street...............E3

Northern Street.................C4
North Street......................E2
Oxford Place....................C3
Oxford Row.....................C3
Park Cross Street..............C3
Park Lane.........................B2
Park Place........................D3
Park Row.........................D3
Park Square East..............C3
Park Square North............C3
Park Square West.............C3
Park Street........................C3
Pilot Street.......................F1
Portland Crescent.............D2
Portland Way....................D2
Princes Square..................C4
Quarry Hill......................F3
Quebec Street..................C3
Queen Square...................D2
Queen Square Court..........D2
Queen Street....................C3
Railway Street..................F3
Regent Street....................E2
Richmond Street...............F4
Rider Street......................F3
Rillbank Lane...................A1
Rosebank Road.................A1
St Cecilla Street................F3
St John's Road..................A1
St Mary's Street................F3
St Paul's Street.................C3
St Peter's Square...............E3
St Peter's Street................E3
Salem Place......................E5
Saxton Lane.....................F4
Sheepscar Grove...............E1
Sheepscar Street South......F1
Skinner Lane....................E1
South Parade....................D3
Sovereign Street...............D4
Spence Lane.....................A5

Springfield Mount............B1
Springwell Road...............B5
Springwell Street..............B5
Studio Road.....................A2
Swinegate........................D4
Templar Street..................E3
The Avenue......................F4
The Boulevard..................F5
The Calls..........................E4
The Headrow....................D3
Thoresby Place.................C2
Trafalgar Street.................E2
Upper Basinghall Street....D3
Vicar Lane.......................E3
Victoria Road...................D5
Victoria Street..................B2
Victoria Terrace................B2
Wade Lane.......................D2
Water Lane.......................B5
Waterloo Street.................E4
Wellington Bridge Street...B3
Wellington Road...............A4
Wellington Road...............A5
Wellington Street..............B3
Westfield Road.................A1
Westgate..........................C3
West Street.......................B3
Wharf Approach...............C4
Wharf Street.....................E4
Whitehall Quay.................C4
Whitehall Road.................A5
Whitehall Road.................A5
Whitelock Street...............F1
Willow Terrace Road........C1
Woodhouse Lane..............C1
Woodhouse Square...........B2
Woodsley Road.................A1
Wortley Lane....................A5
Wortley Lane....................A5
York Place........................C3
York Street.......................F3

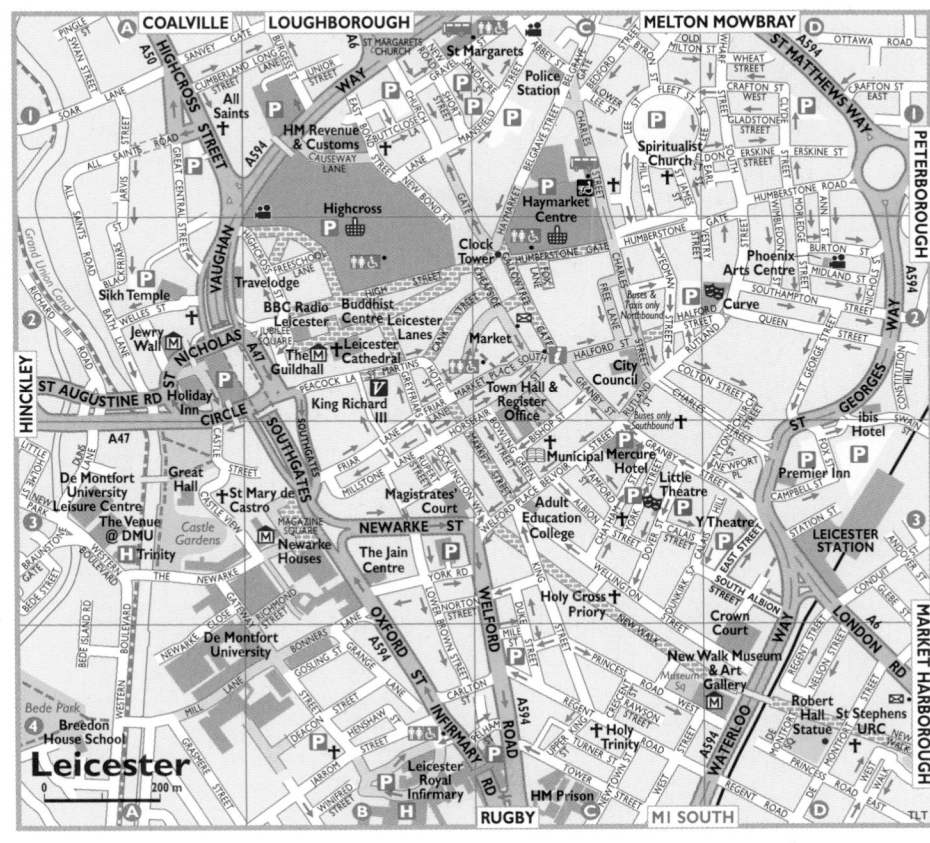

Leicester

Leicester is found on atlas page **72 F10**

Albion Street	C3	Infirmary Road	B4
All Saints Road	A1	Jarrom Street	B4
Bath Lane	A2	Jarvis Street	A1
Bedford Street	C1	King Street	C3
Belgrave Gate	C1	Lee Street	C1
Belvoir Street	C3	London Road	D3
Bishop Street	C3	Lower Brown Street	B3
Bonners Lane	B4	Magazine Square	B3
Bowling Green Street	C3	Mansfield Street	B1
Burgess Street	B1	Market Place South	B2
Burton Street	D2	Market Street	C3
Calais Hill	C3	Mill Lane	A4
Campbell Street	D3	Morledge Street	D1
Cank Street	B2	Newarke Street	B3
Castle Street	A3	New Walk	C3
Charles Street	C1	Oxford Street	B3
Chatham Street	C3	Peacock Lane	B2
Cheapside	C2	Pocklington Walk	B3
Church Gate	B1	Princess Road East	D4
Clyde Street	D1	Princess Road West	C4
Colton Street	C2	Queen Street	D2
Conduit Street	D3	Regent Road	C4
Crafton Street West	D1	Regent Street	D4
Deacon Street	B4	Richard III Road	A2
De Montfort Street	D4	Rutland Street	C2
Dover Street	C3	St Augustine Road	A2
Duke Street	C3	St George Street	D2
Duns Lane	A3	St Georges Way	D2
East Bond Street Lane	B1	St James Street	C1
Erskine Street	D1	St Matthews Way	D1
Fleet Street	C1	St Nicholas Circle	A2
Friar Lane	B3	Sanvey Gate	A1
Gallowtree Gate	C2	Soar Lane	A1
Gateway Street	A3	South Albion Street	D3
Granby Street	C2	Southampton Street	D2
Grasmere Street	A4	Southgates	B3
Gravel Street	B1	Station Street	D3
Great Central Street	A1	The Newarke	A3
Greyfriars	B2	Tower Street	C4
Halford Street	C2	Vaughan Way	A2
Haymarket	C2	Waterloo Way	D4
Highcross Street	A1	Welford Road	C3
Highcross Street	B2	Welles Street	A2
High Street	B2	Wellington Street	C3
Hill Street	C1	Western Boulevard	A4
Horsefair Street	B3	West Street	C4
Humberstone Gate	C2	Wharf Street South	D1
Humberstone Road	D1	Yeoman Street	C2

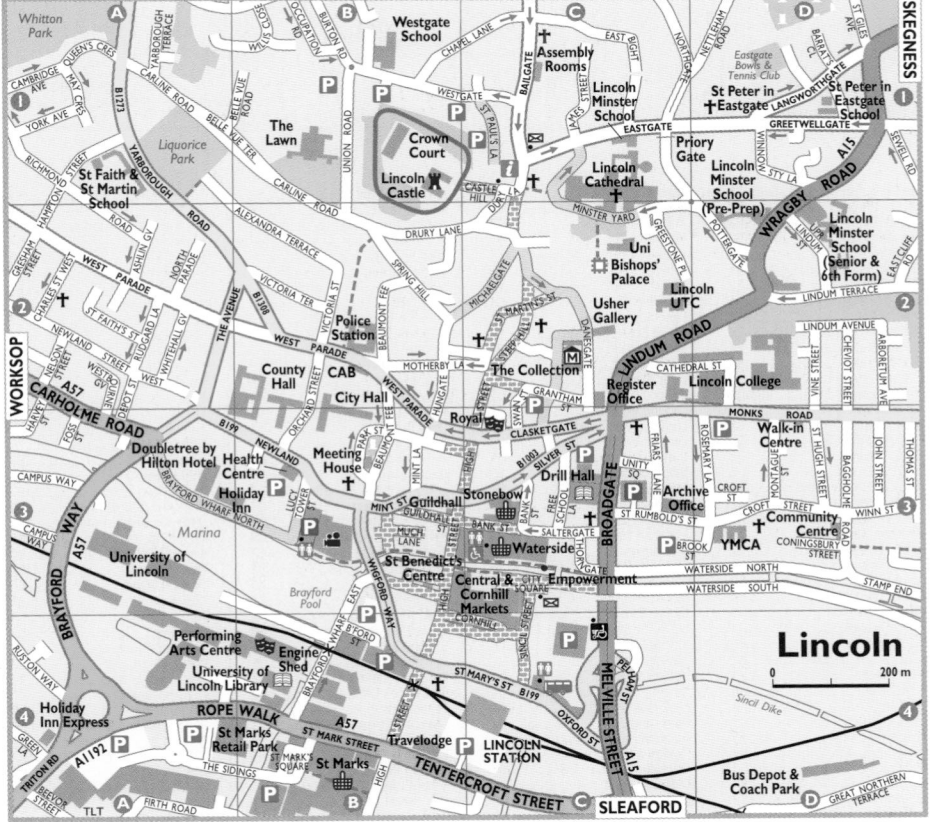

Lincoln

Lincoln is found on atlas page **86 C6**

Alexandra Terrace	B2	Montague Street	D3
Arboretum Avenue	D2	Motherby Lane	B2
Baggholme Road	D3	Nelson Street	A2
Bailgate	C1	Newland	B3
Bank Street	C3	Newland Street West	A2
Beaumont Fee	B3	Northgate	C1
Belle Vue Terrace	A1	Orchard Street	B3
Brayford Way	A4	Oxford Street	C4
Brayford Wharf East	B4	Park Street	B3
Brayford Wharf North	A3	Pelham Street	C4
Broadgate	C3	Pottergate	D2
Burton Road	B1	Queen's Crescent	A1
Carholme Road	A2	Richmond Road	A1
Carline Road	A1	Rope Walk	A4
Cathedral Street	C2	Rosemary Lane	D3
Chapel Lane	B1	Rudgard Lane	A2
Charles Street West	A2	St Hugh Street	D3
Cheviot Street	D2	St Mark Street	B4
City Square	C3	St Martin's Street	C2
Clasketgate	C3	St Mary's Street	B4
Cornhill	B4	St Rumbold's Street	C3
Croft Street	D3	Saltergate	C3
Danesgate	C2	Silver Street	C3
Depot Street	A3	Sincil Street	C4
Drury Lane	B2	Spring Hill	B2
East Bight	C1	Steep Hill	C2
Eastgate	C1	Swan Street	C3
Free School Lane	C3	Tentercroft Street	B4
Friars Lane	C3	The Avenue	A2
Grantham Street	C2	The Sidings	A4
Greetwellgate	D1	Thorngate	C3
Gresham Street	A2	Triton Road	A4
Guildhall Street	B3	Union Road	B1
Hampton Street	A1	Unity Square	C3
High Street	B3	Victoria Street	B2
Hungate	B3	Victoria Terrace	B2
John Street	D3	Vine Street	D2
Langworthgate	D1	Waterside North	C3
Lindum Road	C2	Waterside South	C3
Lindum Terrace	D2	Westgate	B1
Lucy Tower Street	B3	West Parade	A2
May Crescent	A1	Whitehall Grove	A2
Melville Street	C4	Wigford Way	B3
Michaelgate	C2	Winnow Sty Lane	D1
Minster Yard	C2	Winn Street	D3
Mint Lane	B3	Wragby Road	D2
Mint Street	B3	Yarborough Terrace	A1
Monks Road	D3	York Avenue	A1

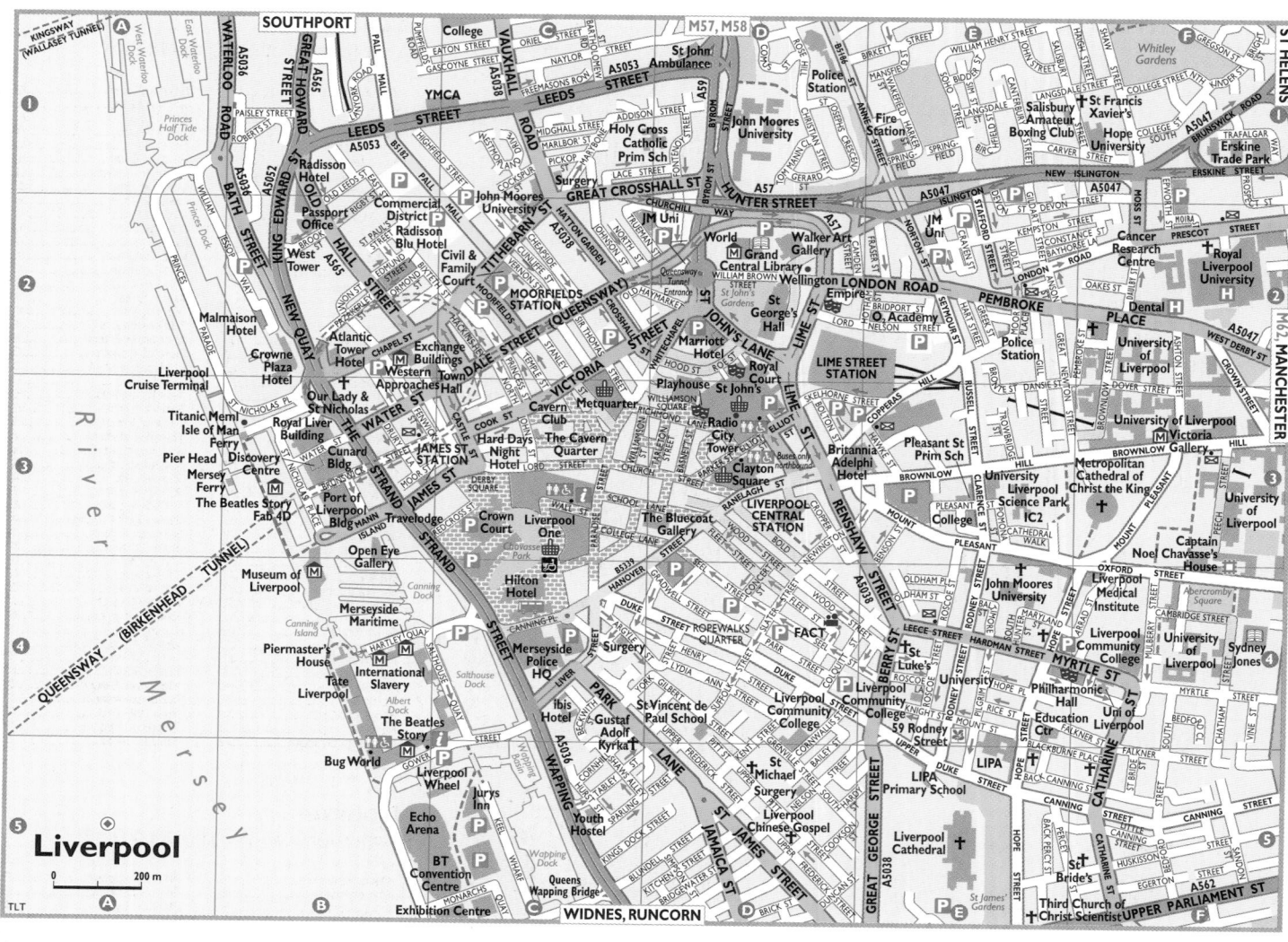

Liverpool

Liverpool is found on atlas page **81 L6**

Addison Street C1
Anson Street E2
Argyle Street C4
Arrad Street F4
Ashton Street F2
Audley Street E2
Back Canning Street E5
Baltimore Street E4
Bath Street B2
Beckwith Street C4
Bedford Street South F5
Benson Street E3
Berry Street E4
Bidder Street E1
Birkett Street D1
Bixteth Street B2
Blackburne Place E5
Blundell Street C5
Bold Street D3
Bosnett Street D3
Bridgewater Street D5
Bridport Street E2
Brook Street B2
Brownlow Hill E3
Brownlow Street F3
Brunswick Road F1
Brunswick Street B3
Byrom Street D1
Cambridge Street F4
Camden Street D2
Canning Place C4
Canning Street E5
Canterbury Street E1
Carver Street E1
Castle Street C3
Catharine Street F5

Cathedral Walk E3
Chapel Street B2
Chatham Street F4
Cheapside C2
Christian Street D1
Churchill Way D2
Church Street C3
Clarence Street E3
Cockspur Street C1
College Lane C3
College Street North F1
College Street South F1
Colquitt Street D4
Constance Street E2
Cook Street C3
Copperas Hill E3
Cornhill C5
Cornwallis Street D5
Craven Street E2
Cropper Street D3
Crosshall Street C2
Crown Street F2
Dale Street (Queensway) C2
Dansie Street E3
Daulby Street F2
Derby Square C3
Devon Street E2
Dover Street F3
Drury Lane B3
Duke Street D4
East Street B1
Eaton Street B1
Edmund Street B2
Egerton Street F5
Elliot Street D3
Epworth Street F1

Erskine Street F1
Falkner Street E4
Fazakerley Street B2
Fenwick Street B3
Fleet Street D3
Fontenoy Street D1
Fraser Street E2
Gascoyne Street B1
Gilbert Street D4
Gildart Street E2
Gill Street E2
Gower Street B5
Gradwell Street D4
Great Crosshall Street C1
Great George Street E5
Great Howard Street B1
Great Newton Street E2
Greek Street E2
Gregson Street F1
Grenville Street South D5
Hackins Hey C2
Hanover Street C4
Hardman Street E4
Harker Street E1
Hartley Quay B4
Hart Street E2
Hatton Garden C2
Hawke Street E3
Henry Street D4
Highfield Street B1
Hood Street D2
Hope Place E4
Hope Street E5
Hotham Street E2
Hunter Street D1
Huskisson Street F5
Islington E2
Jamaica Street D5
James Street B3
Johnson Street C2
Keel Wharf C5

Kempston Street E2
Kent Street D5
Kinder Street F1
King Edward Street B2
Kingsway (Wallasey Tunnel) A1
Kitchen Street D5
Knight Street E4
Lace Street C1
Langsdale Street E1
Leece Street E4
Leeds Street B1
Lime Street D2
Liver Street C4
London Road D2
London Road E2
Lord Nelson Street D2
Lord Street C3
Lydia Ann Street D4
Mann Island B3
Mansfield Street E1
Marybone C1
Maryland Street E4
Midghall Street C1
Moorfields C2
Moor Street B3
Moss Street F1
Mount Pleasant E3
Mount Street E4
Mulberry Street F4
Myrtle Street E4
Naylor Street C1
Nelson Street D5
Newington D4
New Islington E1
New Quay B2
North John Street C3
Norton Street E2
Old Hall Street B2
Oldham Street E4
Old Haymarket C2
Old Leeds Street B1

Ormond Street B2
Oxford Street F4
Paisley Street B1
Pall Mall B1
Paradise Street C3
Parker Street D3
Park Lane C4
Parr Street D4
Peech Street F3
Pembroke Place E2
Pembroke Street F2
Percey Street E5
Pilgrim Street E4
Pleasant Street E3
Pomona Street E3
Prescot Street F2
Princes Parade A2
Prospect Street F1
Queensway
(Birkenhead Tunnel) A4
Ranelagh Street D3
Redcross Street C3
Renshaw Street D3
Richmond Lane C3
Rigby Street B2
Rodney Street E4
Roscoe Street E4
Rose Hill D1
Russell Street E3
St Anne Street D1
St James Street D5
St John's Lane D2
St Josephs Crescent D1
St Nicholas Place B3
St Paul's Street B2
Salisbury Street E1
Salthouse Quay C4
Sandon Street F5
School Lane C3
Seel Street D4
Seymour Street E2

Shaw Street F1
Sir Thomas Street C2
Skelhorne Street D3
Slater Street D4
Soho Street E1
Sparling Street C5
Springfield E1
Stafford Street E2
Stanley Street C2
Strand Street B3
Suffolk Street D4
Tabley Street C5
Tarleton Street D3
Temple Street C2
The Strand B3
Tithe Barn Street C2
Trafalgar Way F1
Trowbridge Street E3
Trueman Street C2
Upper Duke Street E5
Upper Frederick Street D4
Upper Parliament Street F5
Upper Pitt Street D5
Vauxhall Road C1
Vernon Street C2
Victoria Street C3
Wakefield Street E1
Wall Street C3
Wapping C5
Waterloo Road A1
Water Street B3
West Derby Street F2
Westmorland Drive C1
Whitechapel D2
William Brown Street D2
William Henry Street E1
William Jessop Way A2
Williamson Square D3
Williamson Street C3
Wood Street D3
York Street C4

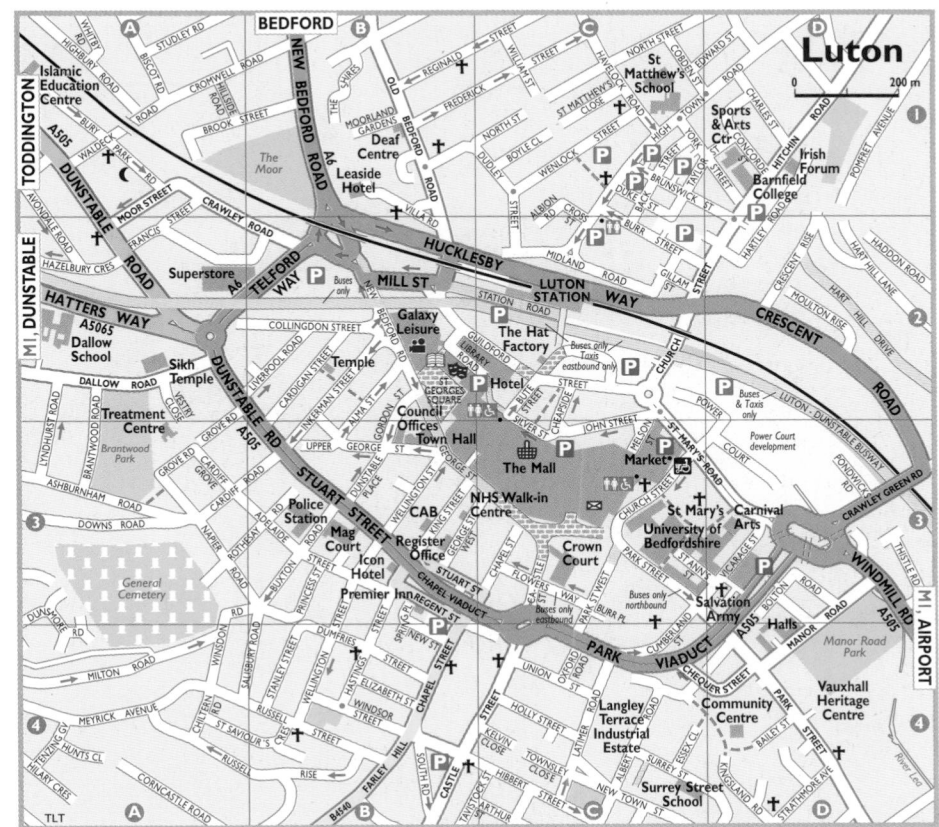

Luton

Luton is found on atlas page **50 C6**

Adelaide Street	B3	Hibbert Street	C4
Albert Road	C4	Highbury Road	A1
Alma Street	B2	High Town Road	C1
Arthur Street	C4	Hitchin Road	D1
Ashburnham Road	A3	Holly Street	C4
Biscot Road	A1	Hucklesby Way	B2
Brantwood Road	A3	Inkerman Street	B3
Brunswick Street	C1	John Street	C3
Burr Street	C2	King Street	B3
Bury Park Road	A1	Latimer Road	C4
Bute Street	C2	Liverpool Road	B2
Buxton Road	B3	Manor Road	D4
Cardiff Road	A3	Meyrick Avenue	A4
Cardigan Street	B2	Midland Road	C2
Castle Street	B4	Mill Street	B2
Chapel Street	B4	Milton Road	A4
Chapel Viaduct	B3	Moor Street	A1
Charles Street	D1	Napier Road	A3
Chequer Street	C4	New Bedford Road	B1
Church Street	C2	New Town Street	C4
Church Street	C3	Old Bedford Road	B1
Cobden Street	C1	Park Street	C3
Collingdon Street	B2	Park Street West	C3
Concorde Street	D1	Park Viaduct	C4
Crawley Green Road	D3	Princess Street	B3
Crawley Road	A1	Regent Street	B3
Crescent Road	D2	Reginald Street	B1
Cromwell Road	A1	Rothesay Road	A3
Cumberland Street	C4	Russell Rise	A4
Dallow Road	A2	Russell Street	B4
Dudley Street	C1	St Mary's Road	C3
Dumfries Street	B4	St Saviour's Crescent	A4
Dunstable Road	A1	Salisbury Road	A4
Farley Hill	B4	Stanley Street	B4
Flowers Way	C3	Station Road	C2
Frederick Street	B1	Strathmore Avenue	D4
George Street	B3	Stuart Street	B3
George Street West	B3	Surrey Street	C4
Gordon Street	B3	Tavistock Street	B4
Grove Road	A3	Telford Way	B2
Guildford Street	B2	Upper George Street	B3
Hart Hill Drive	D2	Vicarage Street	D3
Hart Hill Lane	D2	Waldeck Road	A1
Hartley Road	D2	Wellington Street	B4
Hastings Street	B4	Wenlock Street	C1
Hatters Way	A2	Windmill Road	D3
Havelock Road	C1	Windsor Street	B4
Hazelbury Crescent	A2	Winsdon Road	A4

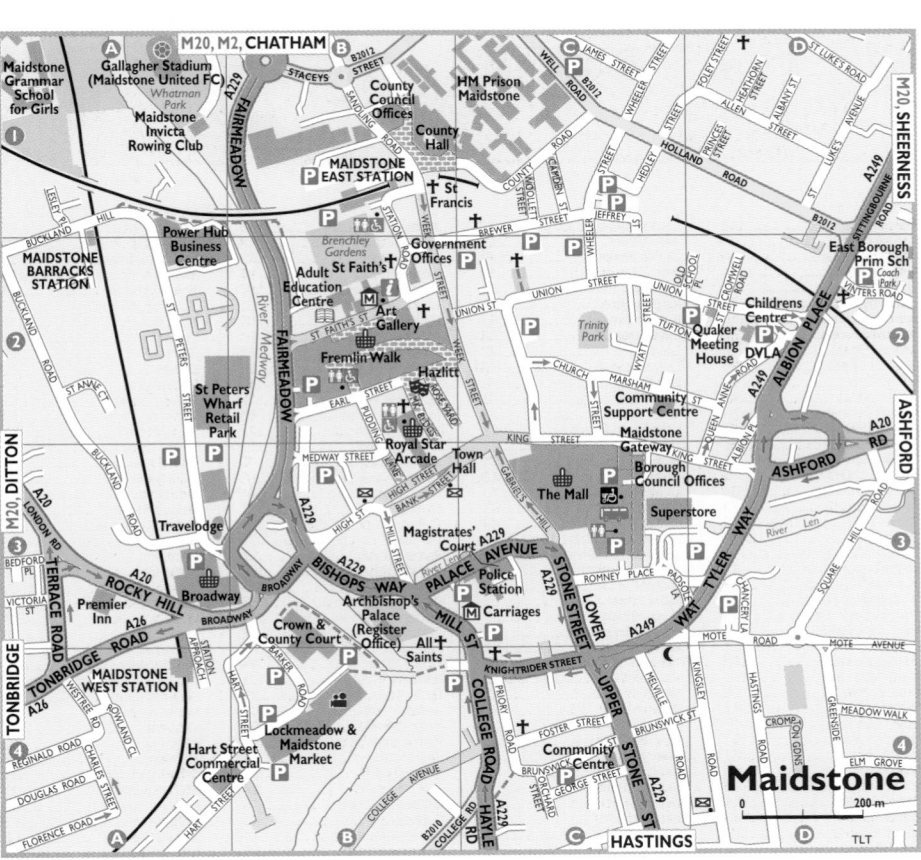

Maidstone

Maidstone is found on atlas page **38 C10**

Albany Street	D1	Market Buildings	B2
Albion Place	D2	Marsham Street	C2
Allen Street	D1	Meadow Walk	D4
Ashford Road	D3	Medway Street	B3
Bank Street	B3	Melville Road	C4
Barker Road	B4	Mill Street	B3
Bedford Place	A3	Mote Avenue	D3
Bishops Way	B3	Mote Road	D3
Brewer Street	C2	Old School Place	D2
Broadway	A3	Orchard Street	C4
Broadway	B3	Padsole Lane	C3
Brunswick Street	C4	Palace Avenue	B3
Buckland Hill	A2	Princes Street	D1
Buckland Road	A2	Priory Road	C4
Camden Street	C1	Pudding Lane	B2
Chancery Lane	D3	Queen Anne Road	D2
Charles Street	A4	Reginald Road	A4
Church Street	C2	Rocky Hill	A3
College Avenue	B4	Romney Place	C3
College Road	C4	Rose Yard	B2
County Road	C1	Rowland Close	A4
Crompton Gardens	D4	St Anne Court	A2
Cromwell Road	D2	St Faith's Street	B2
Douglas Road	A4	St Luke's Avenue	D1
Earl Street	B2	St Luke's Road	D1
Elm Grove	D4	St Peters Street	A2
Fairmeadow	B1	Sandling Road	B1
Florence Road	A4	Sittingbourne Road	D1
Foley Street	D1	Square Hill Road	D3
Foster Street	C4	Staceys Street	B1
Gabriel's Hill	C3	Station Approach	A4
George Street	C4	Station Road	B1
Greenside	D4	Terrace Road	A3
Hart Street	A4	Tonbridge Road	A4
Hastings Road	D4	Tufton Street	C2
Hayle Road	C4	Union Street	C2
Heathorn Street	D1	Upper Stone Street	C4
Hedley Street	C1	Victoria Street	A3
High Street	B3	Vinters Road	D2
Holland Road	D1	Wat Tyler Way	C3
James Street	C1	Week Street	B1
Jeffrey Street	C1	Well Road	C1
King Street	C2	Westree Road	A4
Kingsley Road	D4	Wheeler Street	C1
Knightrider Street	C4	Woollett Street	C1
Lesley Place	A1	Wyatt Street	C2
London Road	A3		
Lower Stone Street	C3		

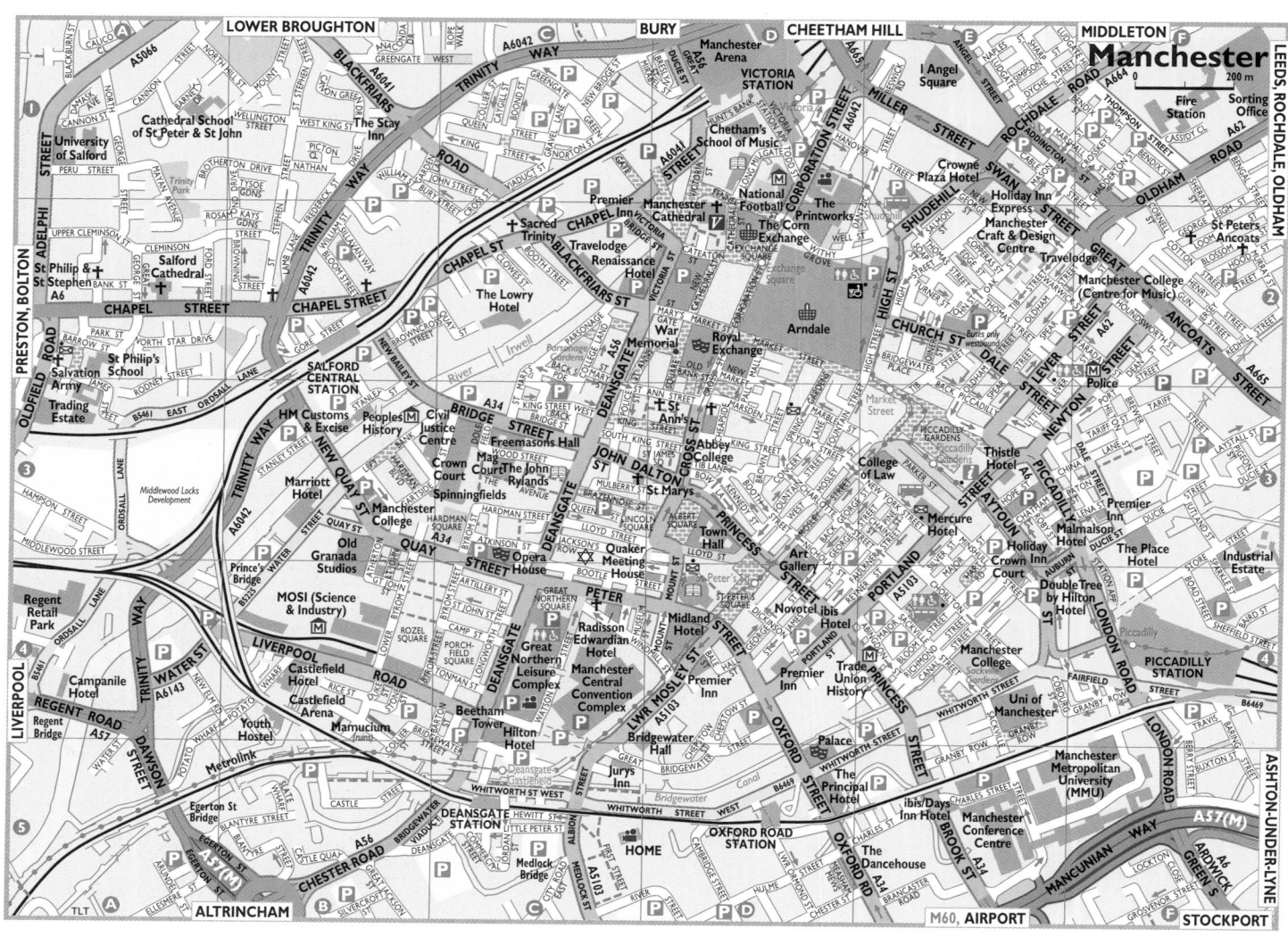

Manchester

Manchester is found on atlas page **82 H5**

Abingdon Street	E4	Browning Street	B2
Addington Street	E1	Brown Street	D3
Adelphi Street	A2	Bury Street	B1
Albion Street	C5	Byrom Street	B4
Angel Street	E1	Cable Street	E1
Ardwick Green South	F5	Cambridge Street	D5
Artillery Street	C4	Camp Street	C4
Atherton Street	B4	Canal Street	E4
Atkinson Street	C3	Cannon Street	A1
Auburn Street	E4	Canon Green Drive	B1
Aytoun Street	E3	Castle Street	B5
Back Piccadilly	E3	Cathedral Street	D2
Bank Street	A2	Chadderton Street	F1
Baring Street	F4	Chapel Street	A2
Barton Street	C4	Charles Street	E5
Berry Street	F4	Charlotte Street	D3
Blackfriars Road	B1	Chatham Street	E3
Blackfriars Street	C2	Cheapside	D3
Blantyre Street	B5	Chester Road	B5
Bloom Street	B2	China Lane	E3
Bloom Street	E4	Chorlton Street	E4
Blossom Street	F2	Church Street	E2
Boad Street	F4	City Road East	C5
Boond Street	C1	Cleminson Street	A2
Booth Street	D3	College Land	C2
Bootle Street	C4	Collier Street	C1
Brancaster Road	E5	Commercial Street	C5
Brazennose Street	C3	Copperas Street	E2
Brewer Street	F3	Cornell Street	F2
Bridge Street	C3	Corporation Street	D2
Bridgewater Place	E2	Cotton Street	F2
Bridgewater Street	B4	Crosskeys Street	F1
Bridgewater Viaduct	B5	Cross Street	C2
Brook Street	E5	Cross Street	D3
Brotherton Drive	A1	Dale Street	E2
Browncross Street	B2	Dantzic Street	D2

Dawson Street	A5	John Street	D1
Deansgate	C4	John Street	E2
Dickinson Street	D4	Joiner Street	E2
Duke Street	B4	Jutland Street	F3
Dulcie Street	F3	Kennedy Street	D3
East Ordsall Lane	A3	King Street	C1
Egerton Street	A5	King Street	C3
Exchange Square	D2	King Street West	C3
Fairfield Street	F4	Lamb Lane	B2
Faulkner Street	D4	Laystall Street	F3
Fennel Street	D1	Left Bank	B3
Ford Street	A2	Lena Street	F3
Fountain Street	D3	Lever Street	E2
Frederick Street	B2	Little Lever Street	E3
Garden Lane	B1	Little Peter Street	C5
Gartside Street	B3	Liverpool Road	B4
George Leigh Street	F2	Lloyd Street	C3
George Street	D4	London Road	F4
Gore Street	B2	Long Millgate	D1
Granby Row	E5	Longworth Street	C4
Gravel Lane	C1	Lower Byrom Street	B4
Great Ancoats Street	F2	Lower Mosley Street	C4
Great Bridgewater Street	C5	Lower Ormond Street	D5
Great Ducie Street	D1	Ludgate Street	E1
Great George Street	A2	Major Street	E4
Great Jackson Street	B5	Mancunian Way	E5
Great John Street	B4	Marble Street	D3
Greengate	C1	Market Street	D2
Greengate West	B1	Marsden Street	D3
Gun Street	F2	Marshall Street	E1
Hanover Street	D1	Mason Street	E1
Hardman Street	C3	Mayan Avenue	A1
Hewitt Street	C5	Medlock Street	C5
High Street	E2	Middlewood Street	A3
Hood Street	F2	Miller Street	E1
Hope Street	E3	Minshull Street	E3
Houndsworth Street	D5	Mirabel Street	C1
Hulme Street	D5	Mosley Street	D3
James Street	A3	Mount Street	B1
Jersey Street	F2	Mount Street	D4
John Dalton Street	C3	Museum Street	C4

John Street	D1	Nathan Drive	B1
John Street	E2	New Bailey Street	B2
Joiner Street	E2	New Bridge Street	C1
Jutland Street	F3	New Cathedral Street	D2
Kennedy Street	D3	New Elm Road	A4
King Street	C1	New George Street	E2
King Street	C3	New Quay Street	B3
King Street West	C3	Newton Street	E3
Lamb Lane	B2	New York Street	E3
Laystall Street	F3	Nicholas Street	D3
Left Bank	B3	North George Street	A1
Lena Street	F3	North Hill Street	A1
Lever Street	E2	North Star Drive	A2
Little Lever Street	E3	Norton Street	C1
Little Peter Street	C5	Oldfield Road	A3
Liverpool Road	B4	Oldham Road	F1
Lloyd Street	C3	Oldham Street	E2
London Road	F4	Ordsall Lane	A4
Long Millgate	D1	Oxford Road	D5
Longworth Street	C4	Oxford Street	D4
Lower Byrom Street	B4	Pall Mall	D3
Lower Mosley Street	C4	Parker Street	E3
Lower Ormond Street	D5	Peru Street	A1
Ludgate Street	E1	Peter Street	C4
Major Street	E4	Piccadilly	E3
Mancunian Way	E5	Piccadilly Gardens	E3
Marble Street	D3	Portland Street	D4
Market Street	D2	Port Street	F3
Marsden Street	D3	Potato Wharf	A5
Marshall Street	E1	Princess Street	D3
Mason Street	E1	Quay Street	B3
Mayan Avenue	A1	Queen Street	C1
Medlock Street	C5	Queen Street	C3
Middlewood Street	A3	Redhill Street	F2
Miller Street	E1	Regent Road	A4
Minshull Street	E3	Reyner Street	D4
Mirabel Street	C1	Rice Street	B4
Mosley Street	D3	Richmond Street	E4
Mount Street	B1	Rochdale Road	E1
Mount Street	D4	Rodney Street	A3
Museum Street	C4	Rosamond Drive	A2

Sackville Street	E4
St Anns Square	C2
St Ann Street	C3
St James Square	C3
St James Street	D4
St Mary's Parsonage	C3
St Stephen Street	B2
Store Street	F3
Sharp Street	E1
Shudehill	E2
Silk Street	A1
Simpson Street	E1
South King Street	C3
Spear Street	E3
Spring Gardens	D3
Station Approach	F3
Swan Street	E1
Tariff Street	F3
Thomas Street	E2
Thompson Street	F1
Tib Lane	D3
Tib Street	E2
Todd Street	D1
Tonman Street	C4
Travis Street	F4
Trinity Way	A4
Turner Street	E2
Victoria Bridge Street	C2
Victoria Station Approach	D1
Victoria	D2
Warwick Street	E2
Watson Street	C4
Well Street	D2
West King Street	B1
West Mosley Street	D3
Whitworth Street	D5
Whitworth Street West	C5
Windmill Street	C4
Withy Grove	D2
Wood Street	C3
York Street	D3

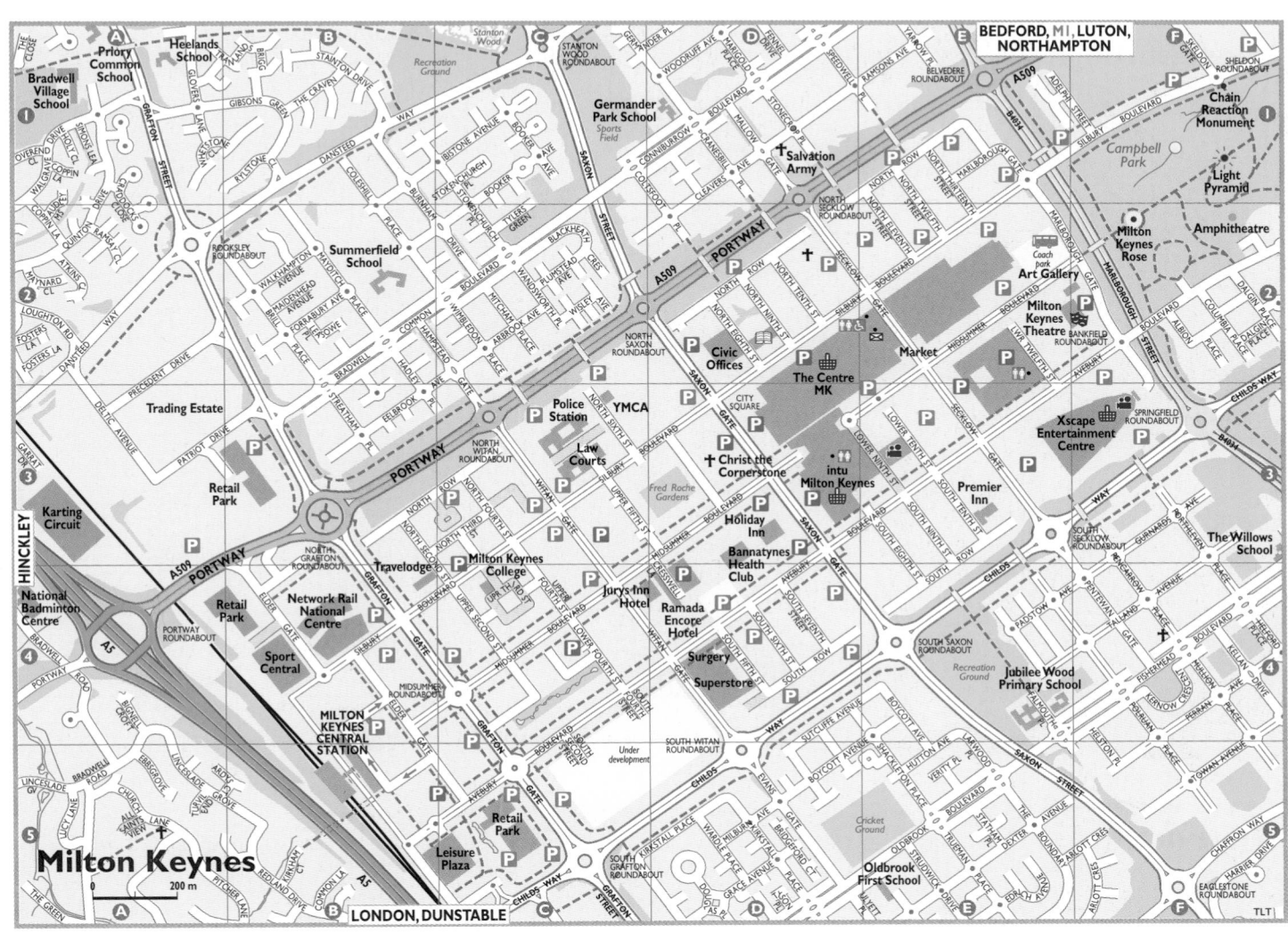

Milton Keynes

Milton Keynes is found on atlas page **49 N7**

Adelphi Street................E1	Cranesbill Place D1	Kellan Drive................F4	North Secklow	Simons Lea A1	Tyson Place................D5
Albion Place................F2	Cresswell Lane................D3	Kernow Crescent................F4	Roundabout D1	Skeldon Gate................F1	Ulyett Place................D5
All Saints View................A5	Dalgin Place................F2	Kirkham Court................B5	North Second Street................B3	South Eighth Street................E3	Upper Fifth Street................C3
Arbrook Avenue................C2	Dansteed Way................A2	Kirkstall Place................C5	North Sixth Street................C3	South Fifth Street D4	Upper Fourth Street................C4
Ardys Court................A5	Dansteed Way................B1	Larwood Place................E5	North Tenth Street................D2	South Fourth Street................C4	Upper Second Street................C4
Arlott Crescent................F5	Deltic Avenue................A3	Leasowe Place................B2	North Third Street................C3	South Grafton Roundabout................C5	Upper Third Street................C4
Atkins Close................A2	Dexter Avenue................E5	Linceslade Grove................A5	North Thirteenth Street................E1	South Ninth Street................E3	Verity Place................E5
Audley Mews................A2	Douglas Place................D5	Loughton Road................A2	North Twelfth Street................E1	South Row................D4	Walgrave Drive................A1
Avebury Boulevard................C5	Eaglestone Roundabout................F5	Lower Fourth Street................C4	Oldbrook Boulevard................E5	South Saxon Roundabout................E4	Walkhampton Avenue................B2
Bankfield Roundabout................E2	Ebbsgrove................A5	Lower Ninth Street................E3	Overend Close................A1	South Secklow Roundabout................E3	Wandsworth Place................C2
Belvedere Roundabout................E1	Edrich Avenue................E5	Lower Tenth Street................E3	Padstow Avenue................E4	South Second Street................C5	Wardle Place................D5
Bignell Croft................A4	Eelbrook Avenue................B3	Lower Twelfth Street................E2	Patriot Drive................A3	South Seventh Street................D4	Whetstone Close................A1
Blackheath Crescent................C2	Elder Gate................B4	Lucy Lane................A5	Pencarrow Place................F3	South Sixth Street................D4	Wimbledon Place................C2
Booker Avenue................C1	Evans Gate................D5	Maidenhead Avenue................B2	Pentewan Gate................F4	South Tenth Street................E3	Wisely Avenue................C2
Boycott Avenue................D5	Falmouth Place................E4	Mallow Gate................D1	Perran Avenue................F4	South Witan Roundabout................D5	Witan Gate................C3
Boycott Avenue................E4	Fennel Drive................D1	Marigold Place................D1	Pitcher Lane................A5	Speedwell Place................D1	Woodruff Avenue................D1
Bradwell Common	Fishermead Boulevard................F4	Marlborough Gate................E1	Plumstead Avenue................C2	Springfield Roundabout................F3	Yarrow Place................E1
Boulevard................B2	Forrabury Avenue................B2	Marlborough Gate................E2	Polruan Place................F4	Stainton Drive B1	
Bradwell Road................A4	Fosters Lane................A2	Marlborough Street................F2	Porthleven Place................F3	Stanton Wood	
Bradwell Road................A5	Garrat Drive................A3	Mayditch Place................B2	Portway................A4	Roundabout................C1	
Bridgeford Court................D5	Germander Place................C1	Maynard Close................A2	Portway Roundabout................A4	Statham Place................E5	
Brill Place................B2	Gibsons Green................B1	Midsummer Boulevard................C4	Precedent Drive................A3	Stokenchurch Place................C1	
Burnham Drive................B1	Glovers Lane................A1	Midsummer Boulevard................E2	Quinton Drive................A2	Stonecrop Place................D1	
Chaffron Way................F5	Grace Avenue................D5	Midsummer Roundabout................B4	Ramsay Close................A2	Streatham Place................B3	
Childs Way................C5	Grafton Gate................B4	Milburn Avenue................D5	Ramsons Avenue................E1	Strudwick Drive................E5	
Childs Way................F3	Grafton Street................A1	Mitcham Place................C2	Redland Drive................B5	Sutcliffe Avenue................D4	
Church Lane................A5	Grafton Street................C5	Mullion Place................F4	Rooksley Roundabout................A2	Talland Avenue................F4	
City Square................D3	Gurnards Avenue................F3	North Eighth Street................D2	Rylstone Close................B1	The Boundary................E5	
Cleavers Avenue................D1	Hadley Place................B2	North Eleventh Street................E1	Saxon Gate................D2	The Close................A1	
Coleshill Place................B1	Hampstead Gate................B2	North Fourth Street................C3	Saxon Street................C1	The Craven................B1	
Coltsfoot Place................C1	Harrier Drive................F5	North Grafton	Secklow Gate................D2	The Green................A5	
Columbia Place................F2	Helford Place................F4	Roundabout................B3	Shackleton Place................E5	Towan Avenue................F5	
Common Lane................B5	Helston Place................F4	North Ninth Street................D2	Sheldon Roundabout................F1	Tranlands Brigg................B1	
Conniburrow Boulevard................C1	Holy Close................A1	North Row................B3	Silbury Boulevard................B4	Trueman Place................E5	
Coppin Lane................A2	Hutton Avenue................E5	North Row................D2	Silbury Roundabout................B4	Turvil End................A5	
Craddocks Close................A1	Ibistone Avenue................C1	North Saxon Roundabout................C2		Tylers Green................C2	

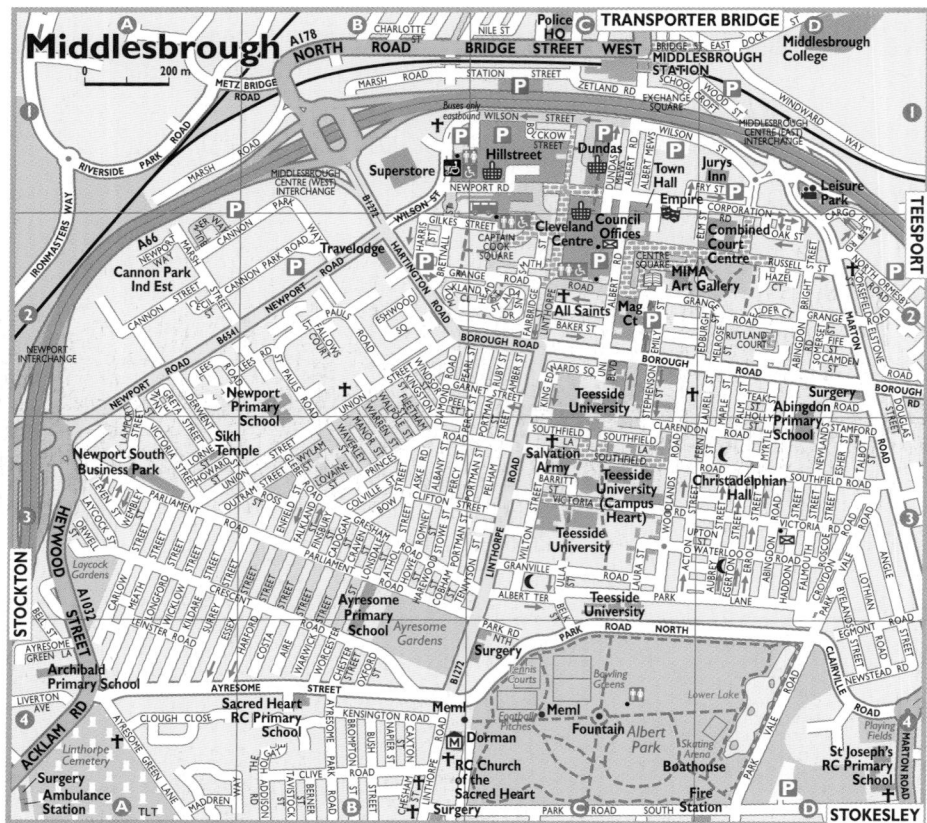

Middlesbrough

Middlesbrough is found on atlas page **104 E7**

Acklam Road	A4	Heywood Street	A3
Acton Street	C3	Ironmasters Way	A2
Aire Street	B4	Kensington Road	B4
Albert Road	C2	Kildare Street	A4
Amber Street	C2	Laurel Street	D3
Athol Street	B3	Lees Road	A2
Aubrey Street	D3	Linthorpe Road	B4
Ayresome Park Road	B4	Longford Street	A4
Ayresome Street	A4	Lorne Street	A3
Borough Road	C2	Lothian Road	D3
Bretnall Street	B2	Marsh Street	A2
Bridge Street East	C1	Marton Road	D2
Bridge Street West	C1	Melrose Street	D2
Bush Street	B4	Metz Bridge Road	A1
Cadogen Street	B3	Myrtle Street	D3
Camden Street	D2	Newlands Road	D3
Cannon Park Road	A2	Newport Road	A2
Cannon Park Way	A2	Palm Street	D3
Cannon Street	A2	Park Lane	C3
Carlow Street	A3	Park Road North	C2
Centre Square	C2	Park Vale Road	D4
Clairville Road	D4	Parliament Road	A3
Clarendon Road	C3	Pearl Street	C2
Clifton Street	B3	Pelham Street	C3
Corporation Road	D1	Portman Street	B3
Costa Street	B4	Princes Road	B3
Craven Street	B3	Riverside Park Road	A1
Crescent Road	A3	Ruby Street	C2
Croydon Road	D3	Russell Street	D2
Derwent Street	A2	St Pauls Road	B2
Diamond Road	B3	Southfield Road	C3
Egmont Road	D4	Station Street	C1
Emily Street	C2	Stowe Street	B3
Errol Street	D3	Tavistock Street	B4
Essex Street	A4	Tennyson Street	B3
Fairbridge Street	C2	Union Street	A3
Falmouth Street	D3	Victoria Road	C3
Finsbury Street	B3	Victoria Street	A3
Fleetham Street	B2	Warren Street	B2
Garnet Street	B2	Waterloo Road	D3
Glebe Road	B3	Waverley Street	B3
Grange Road	B2	Wembley Street	A3
Grange Road	D2	Wilson Street	B2
Granville Road	C3	Wilton Street	C3
Gresham Road	B3	Windsor Street	B2
Harewood Street	B3	Woodlands Road	C3
Harford Street	B4	Worcester Street	B4
Hartington Road	B2	Zetland Road	C1

Newport

Newport is found on atlas page **31 K7**

Albert Terrace	B3	Jones Street	B3
Allt-Yr-Yn Avenue	A2	Keynsham Avenue	C4
Bailey Street	B3	King Street	C4
Bedford Road	D2	Kingsway	C2
Blewitt Street	B3	Kingsway	C4
Bond Street	C1	Llanthewy Road	A3
Bridge Street	B2	Locke Street	B1
Bryngwyn Road	A3	Lower Dock Street	C4
Brynhyfryd Avenue	A4	Lucas Street	B1
Brynhyfryd Road	A4	Market Street	B2
Caerau Crescent	A4	Mellon Street	C4
Caerau Road	A3	Mill Street	B2
Cambrian Road	B2	North Street	B3
Caroline Street	D3	Oakfield Road	A3
Cedar Road	D2	Park Square	C4
Charles Street	C3	Queen's Hill	B1
Chepstow Road	D1	Queen's Hill Crescent	A1
Clarence Place	C1	Queen Street	C4
Clifton Place	B4	Queensway	B2
Clifton Road	B4	Risca Road	A4
Clyffard Crescent	A3	Rodney Road	C2
Clytha Park Road	A2	Rudry Street	D1
Clytha Square	C4	Ruperra Lane	C4
Colts Foot Close	A1	Ruperra Street	D4
Commercial Street	C3	St Edward Street	B3
Corelli Street	D1	St Julian Street	B4
Corn Street	C2	St Mark's Crescent	A2
Corporation Road	D2	St Mary Street	B3
Devon Place	B2	St Vincent Road	C2
Dewsland Park Road	B4	St Woolos Road	B3
Dumfries Place	D4	School Lane	C3
East Street	B3	Serpentine Road	A2
East Usk Road	C1	Skinner Street	C2
Factory Road	B1	Sorrel Drive	A1
Fields Road	A2	Spencer Road	A3
Friars Field	B4	Stow Hill	B3
Friars Road	B4	Stow Hill	B4
Friar Street	C3	Stow Park Avenue	A4
George Street	D4	Talbot Lane	C3
Godfrey Road	A2	Tregare Street	D1
Gold Tops	A2	Tunnel Terrace	A3
Grafton Road	C2	Upper Dock Street	C2
Granville Lane	D4	Upper Dock Street	C3
Granville Street	D4	Usk Way	D3
High Street	B2	Victoria Crescent	B3
Hill Street	C3	West Street	B3
John Frost Square	C3	Wyndham Stret	C1
John Street	D4	York Place	A4

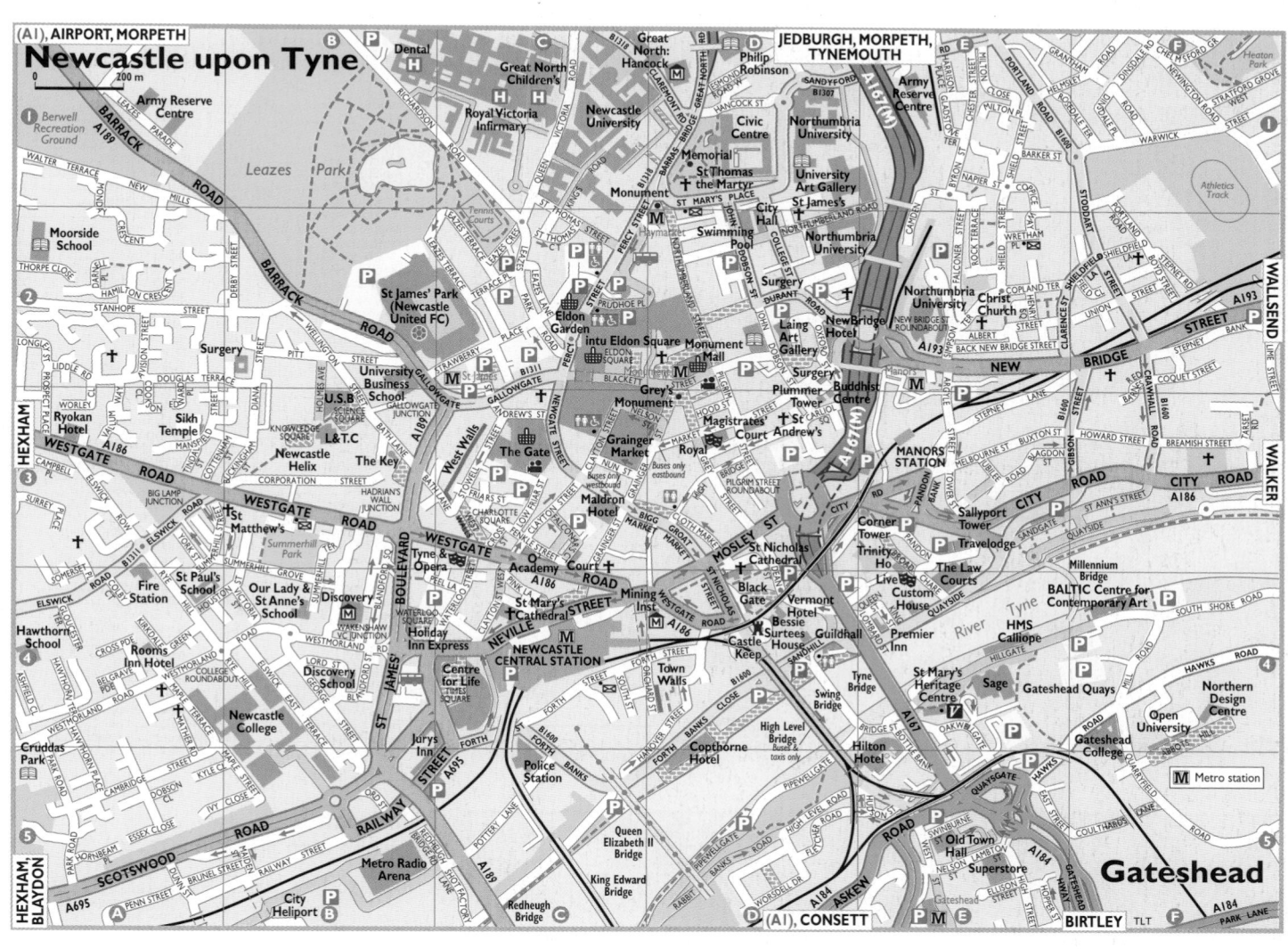

Newcastle upon Tyne

Newcastle upon Tyne is found on atlas page **113 K8**

Abbots Hill F4	Clayton Street West............C4	King Edward Bridge C5	Oxford Street D2	Scotswood Road A5
Albert Street E2	Cloth Market D3	King Street..........................E4	Pandon................................E3	Shieldfield Lane F2
Argyle Street E2	Colby Court.........................A4	Kirkdale Green A4	Pandon Bank E3	Shield Street E2
Askew Road D5	College Roundabout............A4	Kyle Close A5	Park Lane F5	Shot Factory Lane................C5
Avision Street A2	College Street......................D2	Lambton Street....................E5	Park Road A5	Simpson Terrace..................E2
Back New Bridge Street........E2	Cookson Close......................A3	Leazes Crescent C2	Peel Lane B4	Somerset Place....................A4
Barker Street E1	Copland Terrace E2	Leazes Lane C2	Penn Street A5	South Shore Road................F4
Barrack Road.......................A1	Coppice Way........................E1	Leazes Park Road.................C2	Percy Street C2	South Street C4
Barras Bridge D1	Coquet Street F2	Leazes Terrace C2	Pilgrim Street D2	Stanhope Street...................A2
Bath Lane B3	Corporation Street...............B3	Liddle Road A2	Pink Lane C4	Stepney Bank F2
Belgrave Parade A4	Cottenham Street A3	Lime Street F2	Pipewellgate.......................D5	Stepney Lane E3
Big Lamp Junction...............A3	Coulthards Lane...................F5	Lombard Street....................E4	Pitt Street B2	Stepney Road.......................F2
Blackett Street C2	Crawhall Road......................F2	Longley Street A5	Portland Road E1	Stoddart Street F1
Blagdon Street E3	Cross Parade.......................A4	Lord Street...........................B4	Portland Road F1	Stowell Street C3
Blandford Square B4	Cross Street C3	Low Friar Street...................C3	Pottery Lane C5	Stratford Grove West F1
Blandford Street B4	Darnell Place A2	Maiden Street B5	Prospect Place A2	Strawberry Place..................C2
Bottle Bank E4	Dean Street D3	Mansfield Street A3	Prudhoe Place C2	Summerhill Grove B3
Boyd Street F2	Derby Street B2	Maple Street B5	Quarryfield Road F5	Summerhill Street A3
Breamish Street F3	Diana Street B3	Maple Terrace......................A5	Quayside E5	Summerhill Terrace B4
Bridge Street E4	Dinsdale Place F1	Market Street D3	Quayside F3	Swinburne Street..................E5
Broad Chare E3	Dinsdale Road......................F1	Mather Road A4	Quayside E4	Tarset Road F3
Brunel Street A5	Dobson Close.......................A5	Melbourne Street E3	Queen Street E4	Terrace Place C2
Buckingham Street B3	Douglas Terrace A2	Mill Road F4	Queen Victoria Road C1	Tindal Street A3
Buxton Street E3	Duke Street E4	Milton Close E1	Rabbit Banks Road D5	Tower Street E3
Byron Street E1	Dunn Street A5	Milton Place E1	Railway Street......................B5	Tyne Bridge E4
Cambridge Street A5	Durant Road D2	Monday Crescent A1	Red Barnes F2	Union Street F2
Camden Street E2	East Street E5	Mosley Street D3	Redheugh Bridge Road.........B5	Vallum Way..........................A3
Campbell Place A3	Edward Place A3	Napier Street E1	Richardson Road..................B1	Victoria Street......................B4
Carliol Square D3	Eldon Square C2	Nelson Street C3	Rock Terrace E2	Walter Terrace.....................A1
Charlotte Square..................C3	Ellison Street E5	Nelson Street E5	Rosedale Terrace E1	Warwick Street F1
Chelmsford Grove F1	Elswick East Terrace............B4	Neville Street C4	Rye Hill A4	Waterloo Square B4
Chester Street E1	Elswick Road A3	New Bridge Street.................E2	St Andrew's Street C3	Waterloo Street C4
City Road E3	Elswick Row A4	Newgate Street.....................C3	St Ann's Street F3	Wellington Street B2
Claremont Road D1	Essex Close A5	Newington Road E1	St James' Boulevard B4	Westgate Road A3
Clarence Street E2	Falconar's Court...................C3	New Mills A1	St Mary's Place D1	Westmorland Road A4
Clayton Street C3	Falconer Street E2	Northumberland Road D2	St Nicholas Street D4	West Street E5
		Northumberland Street..........D2	St Thomas' Court C2	West Walls C3
	Fenkle Street C3	Nun Street C3	St Thomas' Street C1	Worley Close........................A3
	Field Close F2	Oakwellgate E4	Sandgate E3	Worsdell Drive D5
	Fletcher Road D5	Orchard Street C4	Sandhill D4	Wretham Place E2
	Forth Banks C4	Ord Street B5	Sandyford Road D1	York Street A3
	Forth Banks Close D5			
	Forth Street C4			
	Friars Street C3			
	Gallowgate B2			
	Gallowgate Junction............B3			
	Gateshead Highway E5			
	George Street B4			
	Gibson Street F3			
	Gladstone Terrace E1			
	Gloucester Terrace A4			
	Grainger Street C3			
	Grantham Road....................E1			
	Great North Road.................D1			
	Grey Street D3			
	Groat Market C3			
	Hamilton Crescent...............A2			
	Hanover Street C5			
	Harrison Place E1			
	Hawks Road E5			
	Hawthorn Place A4			
	Hawthorn Terrace A4			
	Helmsley Road E1			
	Henry Square E2			
	High Bridge D3			
	High Level Road D5			
	High Street E5			
	Hillgate E4			
	Hood Street D3			
	Hopper Street E5			
	Hornbeam Place A5			
	Houston Street A4			
	Howard Street F3			
	Hudson Street E5			
	Ivy Close A5			
	Jesmond Road West.............D1			
	John Dobson Street..............D2			
	Jubilee Road E3			

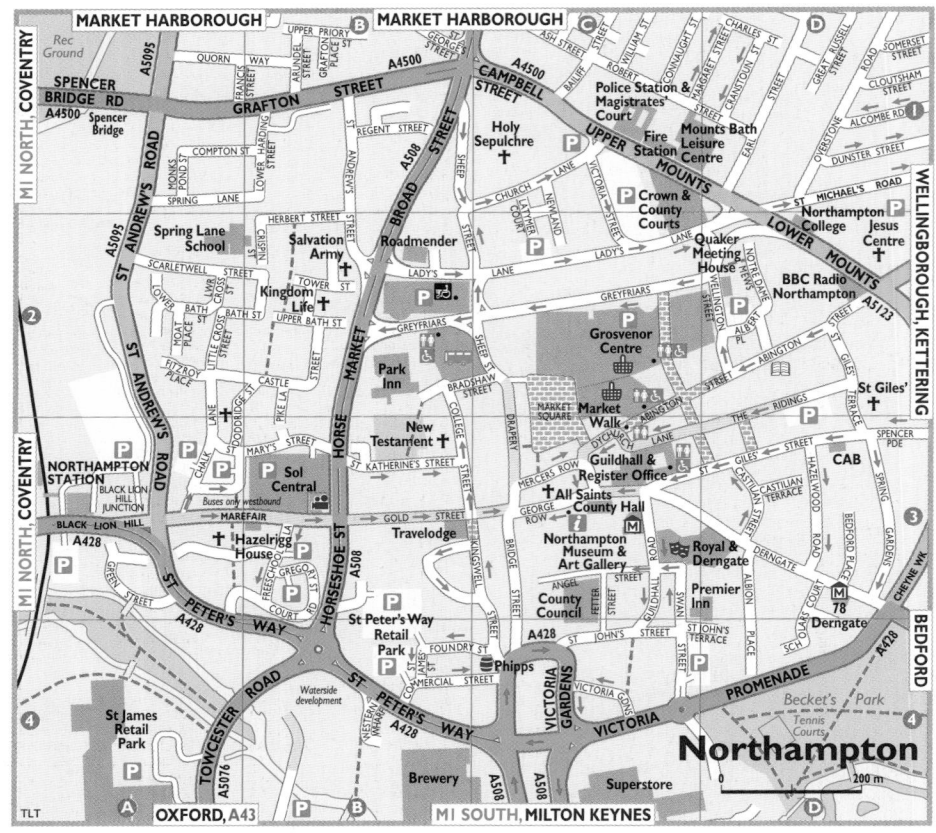

Northampton

Northampton is found on atlas page **60 G8**

Abington Street	C2	Little Cross Street	A2
Albert Place	D2	Lower Bath Street	A2
Albion Place	D3	Lower Cross Street	A2
Angel Street	C3	Lower Harding Street	B1
Arundel Street	B1	Lower Mounts	D2
Ash Street	C3	Marefair	A3
Bailiff Street	C1	Margaret Street	C1
Black Lion Hill	A3	Market Square	C2
Bradshaw Street	B2	Mercers Row	C3
Bridge Street	C3	Moat Place	A2
Broad Street	B1	Monkspond Street	A1
Campbell Street	C1	Newland	C1
Castilian Street	D3	Notredame Mews	D2
Castle Street	B2	Overstone Road	D1
Chalk Lane	A3	Pike Lane	B3
Cheyne Walk	D3	Quorn Way	A1
Church Lane	C1	Regent Street	B1
College Street	B2	Robert Street	C1
Commercial Street	B4	St Andrew's Road	A2
Connaught Street	C1	St Andrew's Street	B1
Court Road	B3	St Giles' Street	D3
Cranstoun Street	D1	St Giles' Terrace	D2
Crispin Street	B2	St John's Street	C4
Derngate	D3	St Katherine's Street	B3
Doddridge Street	A3	St Mary's Street	A3
Drapery	C3	St Michael's Road	D1
Dunster Street	D1	St Peter's Way	B4
Dychurch Lane	C3	Scarletwell Street	A2
Earl Street	D1	Scholars Court	D4
Fetter Street	C3	Sheep Street	B1
Fitzroy Place	A2	Sheep Street	C2
Foundry Street	B4	Spencer Bridge Road	A1
Francis Street	A1	Spencer Parade	D3
Freeschool Lane	B3	Spring Gardens	D3
George Row	C3	Spring Lane	A1
Gold Street	B3	Swan Street	C3
Grafton Street	A1	Tanner Street	A4
Great Russell Street	D1	The Ridings	D2
Green Street	A3	Towcester Road	A4
Gregory Street	B3	Tower Street	B2
Greyfriars	B2	Upper Bath Street	B2
Guildhall Road	C3	Upper Mounts	C1
Hazelwood Road	D3	Upper Priory Street	B1
Herbert Street	B2	Victoria Gardens	C4
Horse Market	B3	Victoria Promenade	C4
Horseshoe Street	B3	Victoria Street	C1
Kingswell Street	C3	Wellington Street	D2
Lady's Lane	B2	Western Wharf	B4

Norwich

Norwich is found on atlas page **77 J10**

All Saints Green	B4	Pottergate	A2
Bank Plain	C2	Prince of Wales Road	C2
Barn Road	A1	Princes Street	C2
Bedding Lane	C1	Quay Side	C1
Bedford Street	B2	Queens Road	B4
Ber Street	C4	Queen Street	C2
Bethel Street	A3	Rampant Horse Street	B3
Bishopgate	D1	Recorder Road	D2
Brigg Street	B3	Red Lion Street	B3
Calvert Street	B1	Riverside Road	D3
Castle Meadow	C3	Riverside Walk	D1
Cathedral Street	D2	Rose Lane	C3
Cattle Market Street	C3	Rouen Road	C3
Chantry Road	B3	Rupert Street	A4
Chapelfield East	A3	St Andrews Street	B2
Chapelfield North	A3	St Benedicts Street	A2
Chapelfield Road	A3	St Faiths Lane	D2
Cleveland Road	A3	St Georges Street	B1
Colegate	B1	St Giles Street	A2
Convent Road	A3	St Julians Alley	C4
Coslany Street	B2	St Marys Plain	B1
Cow Hill	A2	St Peters Street	B3
Davey Place	B3	St Stephens Road	B4
Dove Street	B2	St Stephens Square	A4
Duke Street	B2	St Stephens Street	B4
Elm Hill	C2	St Swithins Road	A2
Exchange Street	B2	St Verdast Street	D2
Farmers Avenue	C3	Surrey Street	B4
Ferry Lane	D2	Ten Bell Lane	A2
Fishergate	C1	Theatre Street	B3
Friars Quay	B1	Thorn Lane	C4
Gaol Hill	B3	Tombland	C2
Gentlemans Walk	B3	Unicorn Yard	A1
Goldenball Street	C3	Union Street	A4
Grapes Hill	A2	Unthank Road	A3
Haymarket	B3	Upper Goat Lane	B2
Heigham Street	A1	Upper King Street	C2
King Street	C2	Upper St Giles Street	A2
London Street	B2	Vauxhall Street	A3
Lower Goat Lane	B2	Walpole Street	A3
Magdalen Street	C1	Wensum Street	C1
Market Avenue	C3	Wessex Street	A4
Mountergate	D3	Westlegate	B3
Music House Lane	D4	Westwick Street	A1
Muspole Street	B1	Wherry Road	D4
New Mills Yard	A1	Whitefriars	C1
Oak Street	A1	White Lion Street	B3
Palace Street	C1	Willow Lane	A2

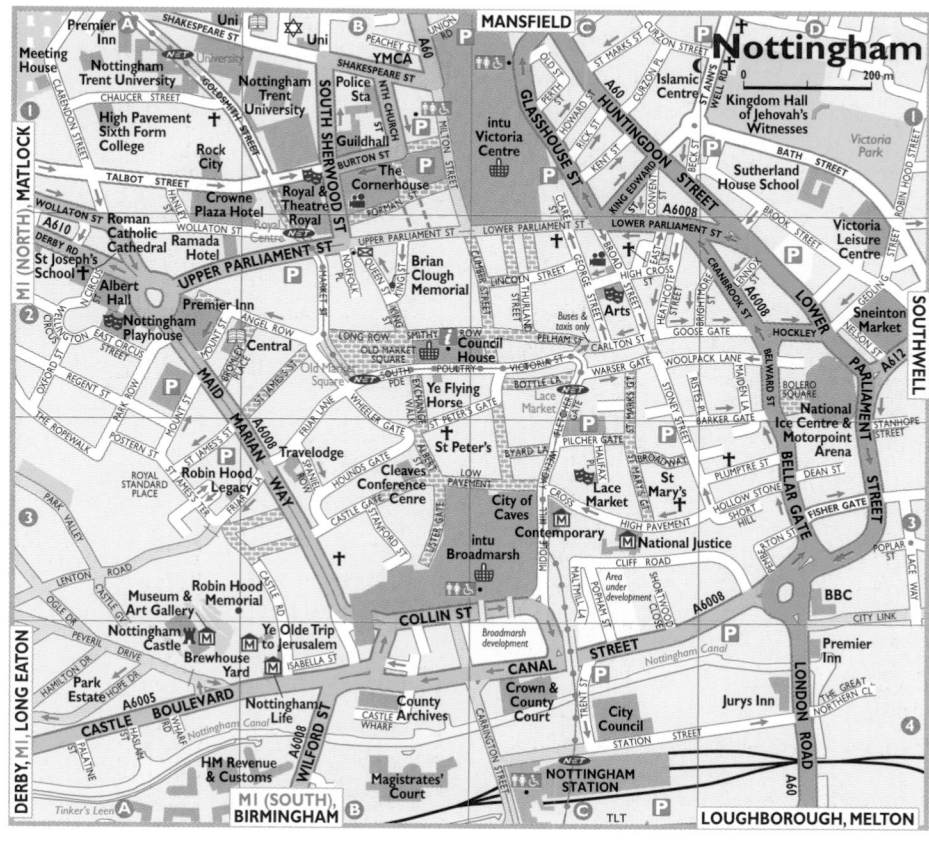

Nottingham

Nottingham is found on atlas page **72 F3**

Albert Street	B3	King Street	B2
Angel Row	B2	Lenton Road	A3
Barker Gate	D2	Lincoln Street	C2
Bath Street	D1	Lister Gate	B3
Bellar Gate	D3	London Road	D4
Belward Street	D2	Long Row	B2
Broad Street	C2	Lower Parliament Street	C2
Broadway	C3	Low Pavement	B3
Bromley Place	A2	Maid Marian Way	A2
Brook Street	D1	Market Street	B2
Burton Street	B1	Middle Hill	C3
Canal Street	C4	Milton Street	B1
Carlton Street	C2	Mount Street	A3
Carrington Street	C4	Norfolk Place	B2
Castle Boulevard	A4	North Circus Street	A2
Castle Gate	B3	Park Row	A3
Castle Road	B3	Pelham Street	C2
Chaucer Street	A1	Peveril Drive	A4
City Link	D3	Pilcher Gate	C3
Clarendon Street	A1	Popham Street	C3
Cliff Road	C3	Poultry	B2
Collin Street	B4	Queen Street	B2
Cranbrook Street	D2	Regent Street	A2
Cumber Street	C2	St Ann's Well Road	D1
Curzon Place	C1	St James's Street	A3
Derby Road	A2	St Marks Gate	C3
Exchange Walk	B2	St Marks Street	C1
Fisher Gate	D3	St Mary's Gate	C3
Fletcher Gate	C3	St Peter's Gate	B3
Forman Street	B1	Shakespeare Street	A1
Friar Lane	A3	Smithy Row	B2
Gedling Street	D2	South Parade	B2
George Street	C2	South Sherwood Street	B1
Glasshouse Street	C1	Spaniel Row	B3
Goldsmith Street	A1	Station Street	C4
Goose Gate	C2	Stoney Street	C2
Halifax Place	C3	Talbot Street	A1
Heathcote Street	C2	Thurland Street	C2
High Cross Street	C2	Trent Street	C4
High Pavement	C3	Upper Parliament Street	A2
Hockley	D2	Victoria Street	C2
Hollow Stone	D3	Warser Gate	C2
Hope Drive	A4	Weekday Cross	C3
Hounds Gate	B3	Wellington Circus	A2
Howard Street	C1	Wheeler Gate	B2
Huntingdon Street	C1	Wilford Street	B4
Kent Street	C1	Wollaton Street	A1
King Edward Street	C1	Woolpack Lane	C2

Oldham

Oldham is found on atlas page **83 K4**

Ascroft Street	B3	Napier Street East	A4
Bar Gap Road	B1	New Radcliffe Street	A2
Barlow Street	D4	Oldham Way	A3
Barn Street	B3	Park Road	B4
Beever Street	D2	Park Street	A4
Bell Street	D2	Peter Street	B3
Belmont Street	B1	Prince Street	D3
Booth Street	A3	Queen Street	C3
Bow Street	C3	Radcliffe Street	B1
Brook Street	D2	Ramsden Street	A1
Brunswick Street	B3	Regent Street	D2
Cardinal Street	C2	Rhodes Bank	C3
Chadderton Way	A1	Rhodes Street	C2
Chaucer Street	B3	Rifle Street	B1
Clegg Street	C3	Rochdale Road	A1
Coldhurst Road	B1	Rock Street	B2
Crossbank Street	B4	Roscoe Street	C3
Curzon Street	B2	Ruskin Street	A1
Dunbar Street	A1	St Hilda's Drive	A1
Eden Street	B2	St Marys Street	B1
Egerton Street	C2	St Mary's Way	B2
Emmott Way	C4	Shaw Road	D1
Firth Street	C3	Shaw Street	C1
Fountain Street	B2	Shore Street	D1
Franklin Street	B1	Siddall Street	C1
Gower Street	D2	Silver Street	B3
Grange Street	A2	Southgate Street	C3
Greaves Street	C3	South Hill Street	D4
Greengate Street	D4	Spencer Street	D2
Hardy Street	D4	Sunfield Road	B1
Harmony Street	C4	Thames Street	D1
Henshaw Street	B2	Trafalgar Street	A1
Higginshaw Road	C1	Trinity Street	B1
Highfield Street	A2	Tulbury Street	A1
High Street	B3	Union Street	B3
Hobson Street	B3	Union Street West	A4
Horsedge Street	C1	Union Street West	B3
John Street	A3	University Way	B4
King Street	B3	Wallshaw Street	D2
Lemnos Street	D2	Wall Street	B4
Malby Street	C1	Ward Street	A1
Malton Street	A4	Waterloo Street	C3
Manchester Street	A3	Wellington Street	B4
Market Place	B3	West End Street	A2
Marlborough Street	C4	West Street	B3
Middleton Road	A3	Willow Street	D2
Mortimer Street	D1	Woodstock Street	C4
Mumps	D2	Yorkshire Street	C3

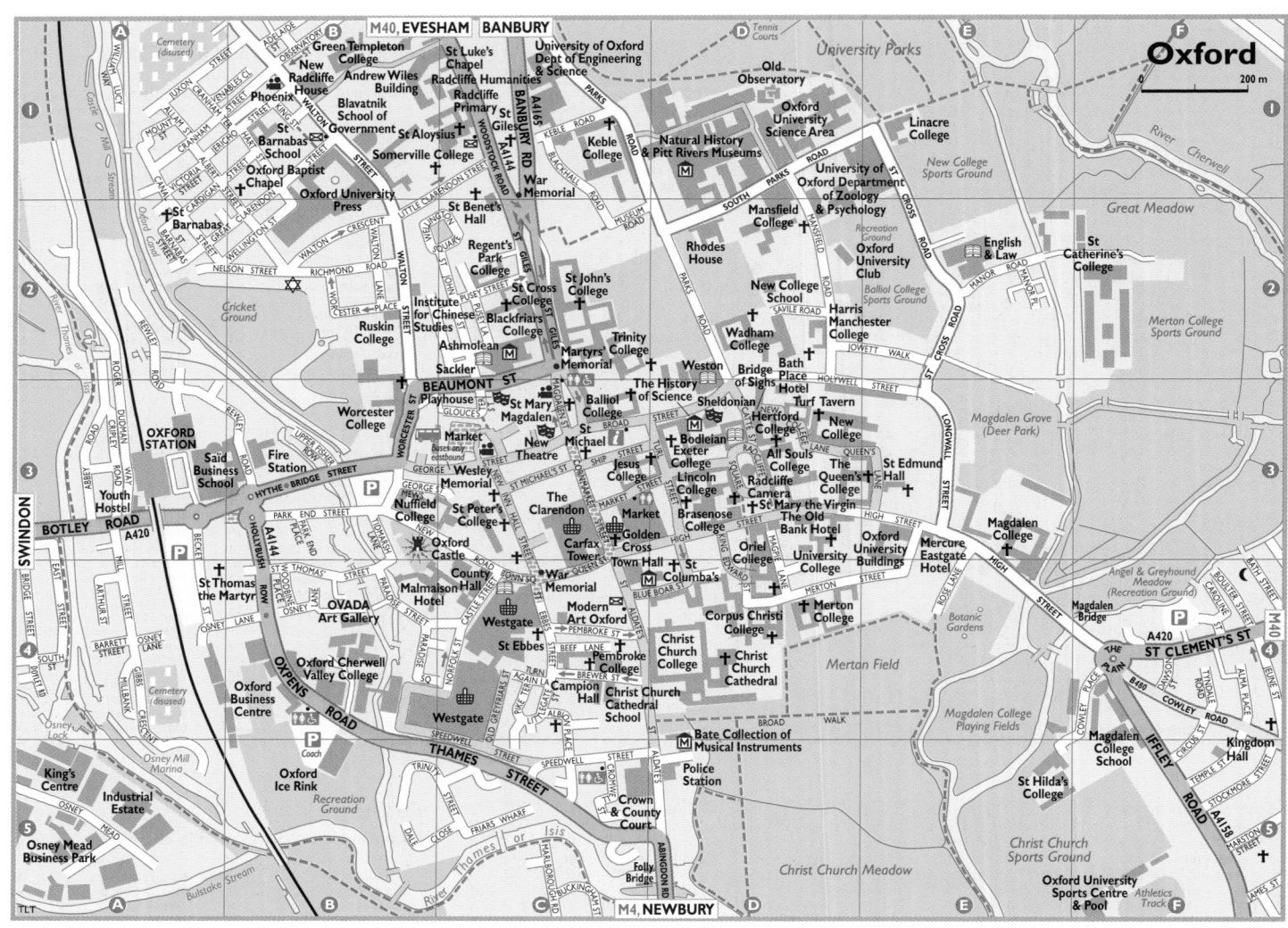

Oxford

Oxford is found on atlas page **34 F3**

Abbey Road	A3	Cromwell Street	C5	Marston Street	F5	St Barnabas Street	A2
Abingdon Road	D5	Dale Close	B5	Merton Street	D4	St Clement's Street	F4
Adelaide Street	B1	Dawson Street	F4	Millbank	A4	St Cross Road	E1
Albert Street	A1	East Street	A4	Mill Street	A4	St Cross Road	E2
Albion Place	C4	Folly Bridge	C5	Mount Street	A1	St Ebbes Street	C4
Allam Street	A1	Friars Wharf	C5	Museum Road	C2	St Giles	C2
Alma Place	F4	George Street	B3	Nelson Street	A2	St John Street	C2
Arthur Street	A4	George Street Mews	B3	New College Lane	D3	St Michael's Street	C3
Banbury Road	C1	Gibbs Crescent	A4	New Inn Hall Street	C3	St Thomas' Street	B4
Barrett Street	A4	Gloucester Street	C3	New Road	B3	Savile Road	D2
Bath Street	F4	Great Clarendon Street	A2	Norfolk Street	C4	Ship Street	C3
Beaumont Street	C3	Hart Street	B1	Observatory Street	B1	South Parks Road	D2
Becket Street	A3	High Street	D3	Old Greyfriars Street	C4	South Street	A4
Beef Lane	C4	High Street	E4	Osney Lane	A4	Speedwell Street	C5
Blackhall Road	C1	Hollybush Row	B3	Osney Lane	B4	Stockmore Street	F5
Blue Boar Street	C4	Holywell Street	D2	Osney Mead	A5	Temple Street	F5
Bonn Square	C4	Hythe Bridge Street	B3	Oxpens Road	B4	Thames Street	C5
Botley Road	A3	Iffley Road	F4	Paradise Square	B4	The Plain	F4
Boulter Street	F4	James Street	F5	Paradise Street	B4	Tidmarsh Lane	B3
Brewer Street	C4	Jericho Street	A1	Park End Street	B3	Trinity Street	B5
Bridge Street	A4	Jowett Walk	D2	Parks Road	C1	Turl Street	D3
Broad Street	C3	Juxon Street	A1	Parks Road	D2	Turn Again Lane	C4
Broad Walk	D4	Keble Road	C1	Pembroke Street	C4	Tyndale Road	F4
Buckingham Street	C5	King Edward Street	D3	Pike Terrace	C4	Upper Fisher Row	B3
Canal Street	A1	King Street	B1	Pusey Lane	C2	Venables Close	A1
Cardigan Street	A2	Little Clarendon Street	B2	Pusey Street	C2	Victoria Street	A1
Caroline Street	F4	Littlegate Street	C4	Queen's Lane	D3	Walton Crescent	B2
Castle Street	C4	Longwall Street	E3	Queen Street	C4	Walton Lane	B2
Catte Street	D3	Magdalen Bridge	E4	Radcliffe Square	D3	Walton Street	B1
Circus Street	F5	Magdalen Street	C3	Rewley Road	A2	Wellington Square	B2
Cornmarket Street	C3	Magpie Lane	D3	Rewley Road	B3	Wellington Street	B2
Cowley Place	F4	Manor Place	E2	Richmond Road	B2	William Lucy Way	A1
Cowley Road	F4	Manor Road	E2	Roger Dudman Way	A3	Woodbine Place	B4
Cranham Street	A1	Mansfield Road	D2	Rose Lane	E4	Woodstock Road	C1
Cranham Terrace	A1	Market Street	C3	St Aldate's	C4	Worcester Place	B2
Cripley Road	A3	Marlborough Road	C5	St Aldate's	D5	Worcester Street	B3

University Colleges

All Souls College	D3
Balliol College	C3
Brasenose College	D3
Christ Church College	D4
Corpus Christi College	D4
Exeter College	D3
Harris Manchester College	D2
Hertford College	D3
Jesus College	C3
Keble College	C1
Linacre College	E1
Lincoln College	D3
Magdalen College	E3
Mansfield College	D2
Merton College	D4
New College	D3
Nuffield College	B3
Oriel College	D3
Pembroke College	C4
Ruskin College	B2
St Catherine's College	F2
St Cross College	C2
St Hilda's College	E5
St John's College	C2
St Peter's College	C3
Somerville College	B1
The Queen's College	D3
Trinity College	C2
University College	D3
Wadham College	D2
Worcester College	B3

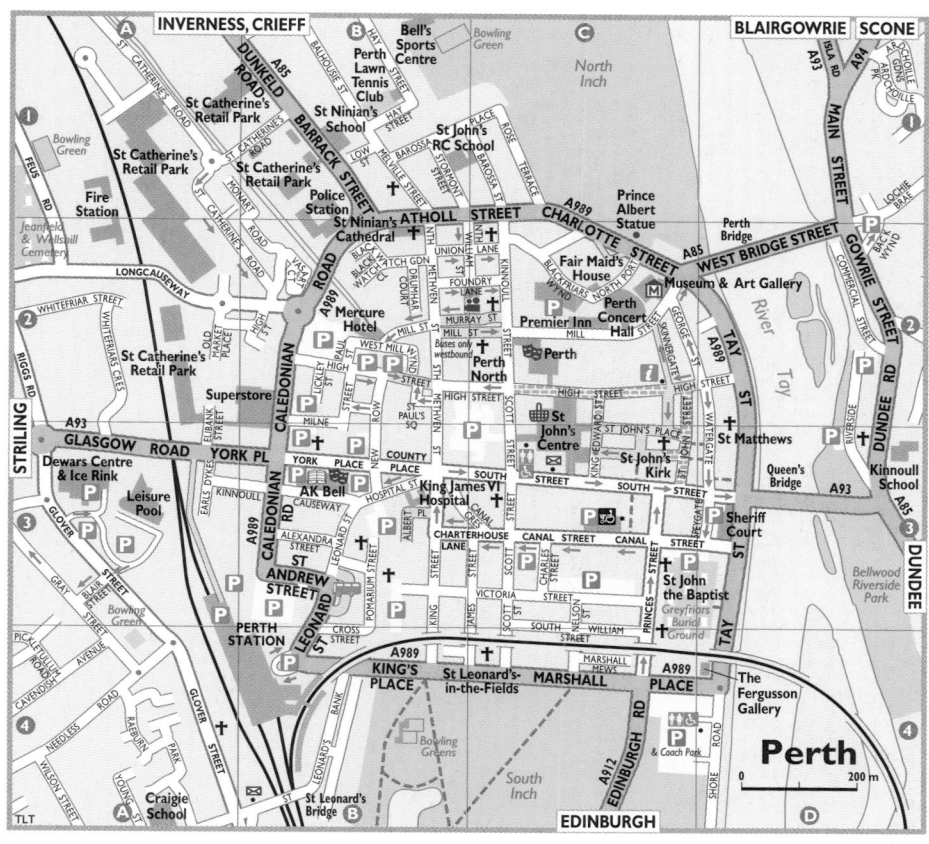

Perth

Perth is found on atlas page **134 E3**

Albert Place	B3	Melville Street	B1
Alexandra Street	B3	Mill Street	B2
Atholl Street	B1	Mill Street	C2
Back Wynd	D2	Milne Street	B2
Balhousie Street	B1	Monart Road	A1
Barossa Place	B1	Murray Street	B2
Barrack Street	B1	Needless Road	A4
Blackfriars Wynd	C2	New Row	B3
Black Watch Garden	B2	North Methven Street	B2
Caledonian Road	B2	North Port	C2
Caledonian Road	B3	North William Street	B2
Canal Street	C3	Old Market Place	A2
Cavendish Avenue	A4	Paul Street	B2
Charles Street	C3	Perth Bridge	D2
Charlotte Street	C2	Pickletullum Road	A4
Charterhouse Lane	B3	Pomarium Street	B3
Commercial Street	D2	Princes Street	C3
County Place	B3	Queen's Bridge	D3
Cross Street	B4	Raeburn Park	A4
Dundee Road	D3	Riggs Road	A2
Dunkeld Road	B1	Riverside	D3
Earls Dykes	A3	Rose Terrace	C1
Edinburgh Road	C4	St Andrew Street	B3
Elibank Street	A3	St Catherine's Road	A1
Feus Road	A1	St John's Place	C3
Foundry Lane	B2	St John Street	C3
George Street	C2	St Leonard's Bank	B4
Glasgow Road	A3	St Paul's Square	B2
Glover Street	A3	Scott Street	C3
Glover Street	A4	Shore Road	D4
Gowrie Street	D2	Skinnergate	C2
Gray Street	A3	South Methven Street	B2
Hay Street	B1	South Street	C3
High Street	B2	South William Street	C4
High Street	C2	Speygate	D3
Hospital Street	B3	Stormont Street	B1
Isla Road	D1	Tay Street	D2
James Street	C3	Tay Street	D4
King Edward Street	C3	Union Lane	B2
King's Place	B4	Victoria Street	C3
King Street	B3	Watergate	D2
Kinnoull Causeway	A3	West Bridge Street	D2
Kinnoull Street	C2	West Mill Wynd	B2
Leonard Street	B3	Whitefriars Crescent	A2
Lochie Brae	D1	Whitefriar Street	A2
Longcauseway	A2	Wilson Street	A4
Main Street	D1	York Place	A3
Marshall Place	C4	York Place	B3

Peterborough

Peterborough is found on atlas page **74 C11**

Albert Place	B3	New Road	C1
Bishop's Road	C3	Northminster	C1
Boongate	D1	North Street	B1
Bourges Boulevard	A1	Oundle Road	B4
Bridge Street	B3	Park Road	B1
Bright Street	A1	Pipe Lane	D2
Broadway	B2	Priestgate	A2
Brook Street	C1	Rivergate	B3
Cathedral Square	B2	River Lane	A2
Cattle Market Street	B1	Russell Street	A1
Chapel Street	C1	St John's Street	C2
Church Street	B2	St Peters Road	B3
Church Walk	C1	South Street	D2
City Road	C2	Star Road	D2
Cowgate	B2	Station Road	A2
Craig Street	B1	Thorpe Lea Road	A3
Crawthorne Road	C1	Thorpe Road	A2
Cromwell Road	A1	Trinity Street	B3
Cross Street	B2	Viersen Platz	B3
Cubitt Way	B4	Vineyard Road	C3
Deacon Street	A1	Wake Road	D2
Dickens Street	D1	Wareley Road	A4
Eastfield Road	D1	Wellington Street	D1
Eastgate	D2	Wentworth Street	B3
East Station Road	C4	Westgate	A1
Embankment Road	C3		
Exchange Street	B2		
Fengate Close	D2		
Field Walk	D1		
Fitzwilliam Street	B1		
Frank Perkins Parkway	D4		
Geneva Street	B1		
Gladstone Street	A1		
Granby Street	C2		
Hawksbill Way	B4		
Hereward Close	D2		
Hereward Road	D2		
King Street	B2		
Laxton Square	C2		
Lea Gardens	A3		
Lincoln Road	B1		
London Road	B4		
Long Causeway	B2		
Manor House Street	B1		
Mayor's Walk	A1		
Midgate	B2		
Morris Street	D1		
Nene Street	D2		

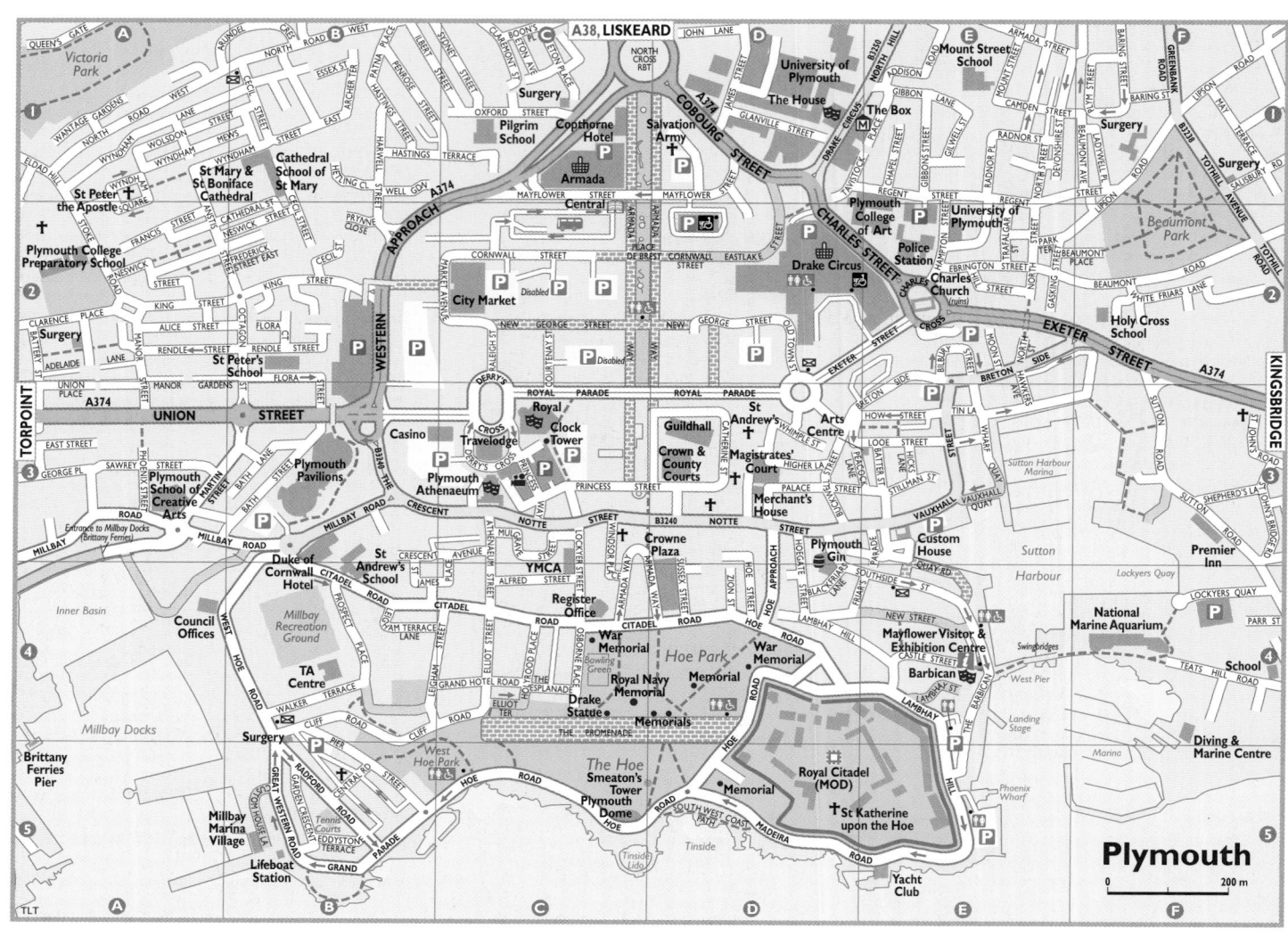

Plymouth

Plymouth is found on atlas page **6 D8**

Addison Road................E1
Adelaide Lane................A2
Alfred Street................C4
Alice Street................A2
Anstis Street................A2
Archer Terrace................B1
Armada Street................E1
Armada Way................C2
Armada Way................C4
Arundel Crescent................A1
Athenaeum Street................C3
Baring Street................F1
Bath Lane................B3
Bath Street................B3
Batter Street................E3
Battery Street................A2
Beaumont Avenue................F1
Beaumont Place................E2
Beaumont Road................F2
Bilbury Street................E2
Blackfriars Lane................D4
Boon's Place................C1
Breton Side................D3
Buckwell Street................D3
Camden Street................E1
Castle Street................E4
Cathedral Street................A2
Catherine Street................D3
Cecil Street................B1
Central Road................B5
Chapel Street................E1
Charles Cross................E2
Charles Street................D2
Citadel Road................B4
Citadel Road................C4
Claremont Street................C1

Clarence Place................A2
Cliff Road................B4
Cobourg Street................D1
Cornwall Street................C2
Courtenay Street................C3
Crescent Avenue................B3
Custom House Lane................B5
Derry's Cross................C3
Devonshire Street................E1
Drake Circus................D1
Eastlake Street................D2
East Street................A3
Ebrington Street................E2
Eddystone Terrace................B5
Eldad Hill................A1
Elliot Street................C4
Elliot Terrace................C4
Essex Street................B1
Eton Avenue................C1
Eton Place................C1
Exeter Street................D2
Exeter Street................E2
Flora Court................B2
Flora Street................B2
Francis Street................A2
Frederick Street East................B2
Friar's Parade................D4
Garden Crescent................B5
Gasking Street................E2
George Place................A3
Gibbon Lane................E1
Gibbons Street................E1
Gilwell Street................E1
Glanville Street................D1
Grand Hotel Road................C4
Grand Parade................B5

Great Western Road................B5
Greenbank Road................F1
Hampton Street................E2
Harwell Street................B1
Hastings Street................B1
Hastings Terrace................B1
Hawkers Avenue................E2
Hetling Close................B1
Hicks Lane................E3
Higher Lane................D3
Hill Street................E2
Hoe Approach................D4
Hoegate Street................D3
Hoe Road................C5
Hoe Street................D3
Holyrood Place................C4
How Street................E3
Ilbert Street................B1
James Street................D1
John Lane................D1
King Street................A2
Ladywell Place................F1
Lambhay Hill................D4
Lambhay Street................E4
Leigham Street................B4
Leigham Terrace Lane................B4
Lipson Road................F1
Lockyers Quay................F4
Lockyer Street................C3
Looe Street................E3
Madeira Road................D5
Manor Gardens................A3
Manor Street................A2
Market Avenue................C2
Martin Street................A3
Mayflower Street................C1

Mayflower Street................D1
May Terrace................F1
Millbay Road................A3
Moon Street................E2
Mount Street................E1
Mulgrave Street................C3
Neswick Street................A2
New George Street................C2
New Street................E4
North Cross Roundabout................C1
North Hill................E1
North Road West................A1
North Street................E2
Notte Street................C3
Octagon Street................B2
Old Town Street................D2
Osborne Place................C4
Oxford Street................C1
Palace Street................D3
Park Terrace................E2
Parr Street................F4
Patna Place................B1
Peacock Lane................D3
Penrose Street................B1
Phoenix Street................A3
Pier Street................B5
Place de Brest................C2
Plym Street................F1
Princess Street................C3
Princess Way................C3
Prospect Place................B4
Prynne Close................B2
Quay Road................E4
Queen's Gate................A1
Radford Road................B5
Radnor Place................E1

Radnor Street................E1
Raleigh Street................C2
Regent Street................E1
Rendle Street................A2
Royal Parade................C3
St James Place................B4
St John's Bridge Road................F3
St John's Road................F3
Salisbury Road................F1
Sawrey Street................A3
Shepherd's Lane................F3
Southside Street................D4
South West Coast Path................D5
Stillman Street................E3
Stoke Road................A2
Sussex Street................D3
Sutton Road................F3
Sydney Street................B1
Tavistock Place................D1
Teats Hill Road................F4
The Barbican................E4
The Crescent................B3
The Esplanade................C4
The Promenade................C4
Tin Lane................E3
Tothill Avenue................F1
Tothill Road................F2
Trafalgar Street................E2
Union Place................A3
Union Street................A3
Vauxhall Quay................E3
Vauxhall Street................E3
Walker Terrace................B4
Wantage Gardens................A1
Well Garden................B1
Western Approach................B2

West Hoe Road................A4
Wharf Quay................E3
Whimple Street................D3
White Friars Lane................F2
Windsor Place................C3
Wolsdon Street................A1
Wyndham Lane................A1
Wyndham Mews................A1
Wyndham Square................A1
Wyndham Street East................A1
Zion Street................D4

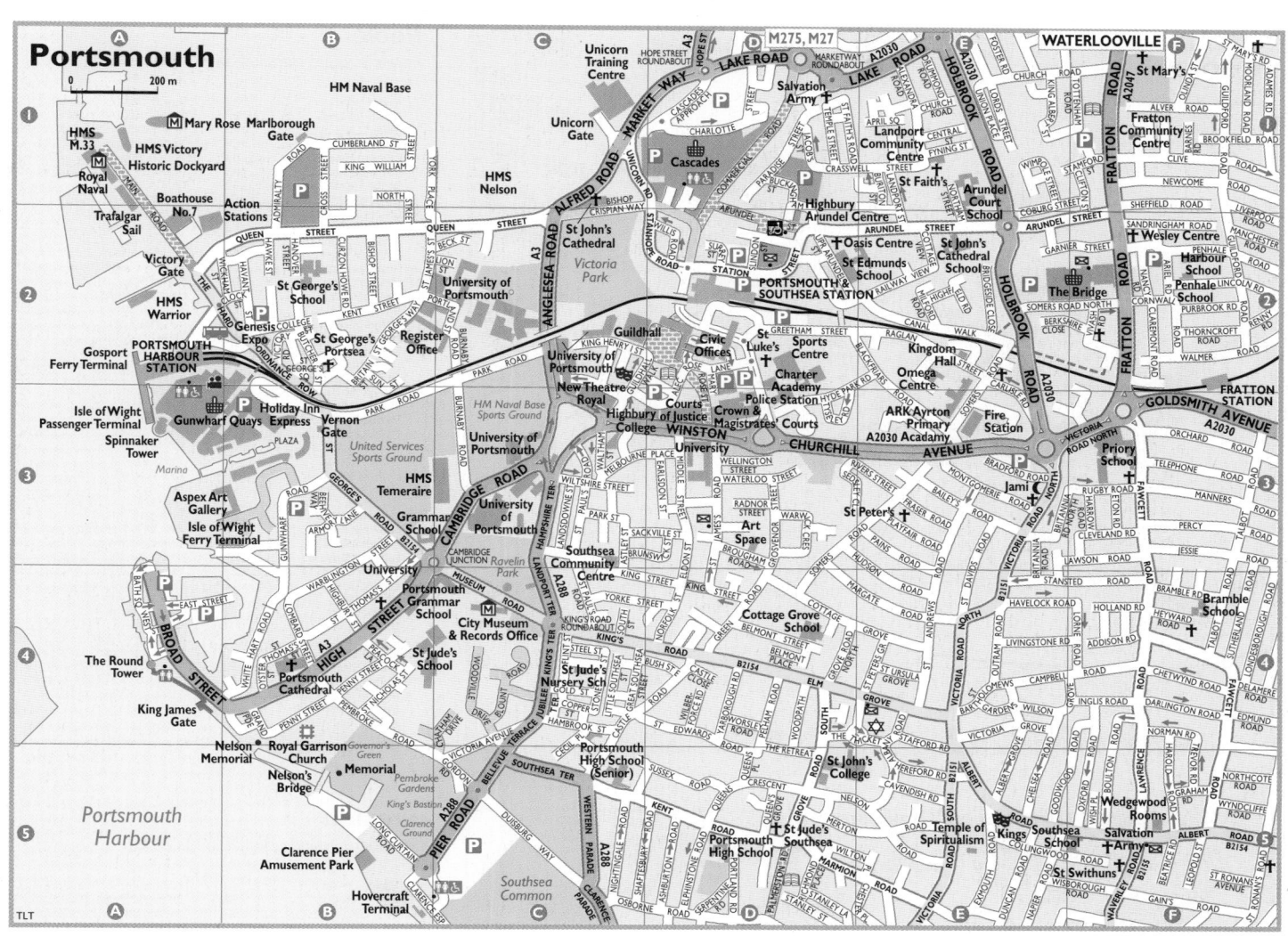

Portsmouth

Portsmouth is found on atlas page **14 H7**

Admiralty Road	B2	Cavendish Road	E5
Albany Road	E5	Central Street	E1
Albert Grove	E5	Charlotte Street	D1
Albert Road	E5	Chelsea Road	E5
Alec Rose Lane	D3	Chester Place	E5
Alexandra Road	E1	Chetwynd Road	F4
Alfred Road	C1	Churchill Avenue	D3
Alver Road	F1	Church Road	E1
Anglesea Road	C2	Claremont Road	F2
Ariel Road	F2	Clarence Parade	C5
Armory Lane	B3	Cleveland Road	F3
Arundel Street	D2	Clive Road	F1
Arundel Street	E2	Clock Street	B2
Ashburton Road	D5	College Street	B2
Bailey's Road	E3	Collingwood Road	E5
Bath Square	A4	Commercial Road	D1
Bellevue Terrace	C5	Cornwall Road	F2
Belmont Place	D4	Cottage Grove	D4
Bishop Crispian Way	C2	Cottage View	E2
Bishop Street	B2	Crasswell Street	D1
Blackfriars Road	E2	Cross Street	B2
Blount Road	C4	Cumberland Street	B1
Boulton Road	F5	Curzon Howe Road	B2
Bramble Road	F4	Darlington Road	F4
Bridgeside Close	E2	Drummond Road	E1
Britain Street	B2	Duisburg Way	C5
Broad Street	A4	Duncan Road	E5
Brookfield Road	F1	Earlsdon Street	D3
Brunswick Street	C3	East Street	A4
Buckingham Street	D1	Eldon Street	D4
Cambridge Road	C3	Elm Grove	D4
Campbell Road	E4	Elphinstone Road	D5
Canal Walk	E2	Exmouth Road	E5
Carlisle Road	E2	Fawcett Road	F3
Cascades Approach	D1	Fawcett Road	F4
Castle Road	C4	Flint Street	C4

Foster Road	E1	Lake Road	D1
Fratton Road	F2	Landport Street	E1
Gain's Road	F5	Landport Terrace	C3
Garnier Street	E2	Lansdowne Road	C3
Goldsmith Avenue	F3	Lawrence Road	F5
Gold Street	C4	Lawson Road	F3
Goodwood Road	E5	Leopold Street	F5
Gordon Road	C5	Lincoln Road	F2
Great Southsea Street	C4	Little Southsea Street	C4
Green Road	D4	Livingstone Road	E4
Greetham Street	D2	Lombard Street	B4
Grosvenor Street	D3	Londesborough Road	F4
Grove Road North	D4	Lords Road	E1
Grove Road South	D5	Lorne Road	F4
Guildford Road	F1	Main Road	A1
Guildhall Walk	C2	Manners Road	F3
Gunwharf Road	B3	Margate Road	D4
Hambrook Street	C4	Market Way	C1
Hampshire Terrace	C3	Marmion Road	D5
Harold Road	F5	Mary Rose Street	D2
Havant Street	B2	Melbourne Place	C3
Havelock Road	E4	Merton Road	D5
Hawke Street	B2	Middle Street	D3
Hereford Road	E5	Milford Road	E2
Highbury Street	B4	Montgomerie Road	E3
High Street	B4	Moorland Road	F1
Holbrook Road	E1	Museum Road	C4
Holland Road	F4	Napier Road	E5
Hudson Road	E3	Nelson Road	D5
Hyde Park Road	D3	Newcome Road	F1
Inglis Road	F4	Nightingale Road	C5
Jessie Road	F3	Norfolk Street	D3
Jubilee Terrace	C4	Norman Road	E5
Kent Road	D5	Olinda Street	F1
Kent Street	B2	Orchard Road	E4
King Albert Street	E1	Ordnance Row	B2
King Henry I Street	C2	Osborne Road	C5
King's Road	C4	Outram Road	E4
King's Terrace	C4	Oxford Road	F5
King William Street	B1	Oyster Street	B4
		Pains Road	E3

Palmerston Road	D5	Stamford Street	E1
Paradise Street	D1	Stanhope Road	D2
Park Road	B3	Stansted Road	E4
Pelham Road	D4	Station Street	D2
Pembroke Road	B4	Steel Street	C4
Penhale Road	F2	Stone Street	C4
Penny Street	B4	Sussex Road	D5
Percy Road	F3	Sutherland Road	F4
Pier Road	C5	Talbot Road	F4
Playfair Road	E3	Telephone Road	F3
Portland Street	D1	Temple Street	D1
Portsmouth Road	D5	The Hard	A2
Purbrook Road	F2	The Retreat	D5
Queen Crescent	D5	The Thicket	D4
Queen Street	B2	Thorncroft Road	F2
Raglan Street	E2	Tottenham Road	F1
Railway View	E2	Trevor Road	F4
Richmond Place	D5	Unicorn Road	C1
Rivers Street	D3	Upper Arundel Street	D2
Rugby Road	F3	Victoria Avenue	C5
Sackville Street	C3	Victoria Grove	E5
St Andrews Road	E4	Victoria Road North	E4
St Bartholomews Gardens	E4	Victoria Road North	F3
St Davids Road	E4	Victoria Road South	E5
St Edwards Road	D4	Vivash Road	F2
St Faith's Road	D1	Walmer Road	F2
St George's Square	B3	Warblington Street	B4
St George's Square	B2	Warwick Crescent	D3
St George's Way	B2	Waterloo Street	D3
St James's Road	D3	Waverley Road	F5
St James's Street	B2	Western Parade	C5
St Nicholas Street	B4	West Street	A4
St Paul's Road	C3	White Hart Road	B4
St Peters Grove	E4	Wilson Grove	E4
St Thomas's Street	B4	Wiltshire Street	C3
Sandringham Road	F2	Winston Churchill Avenue	D3
Shaftesbury Road	C5	Wisborough Road	E5
Somers Road	D4	Woodpath	D4
Somers Road	E3	Woodville Drive	C4
Somers Road North	E2	Yarborough Road	D4
Southsea Terrace	C5	Yorke Street	C4
Stafford Road	E4		

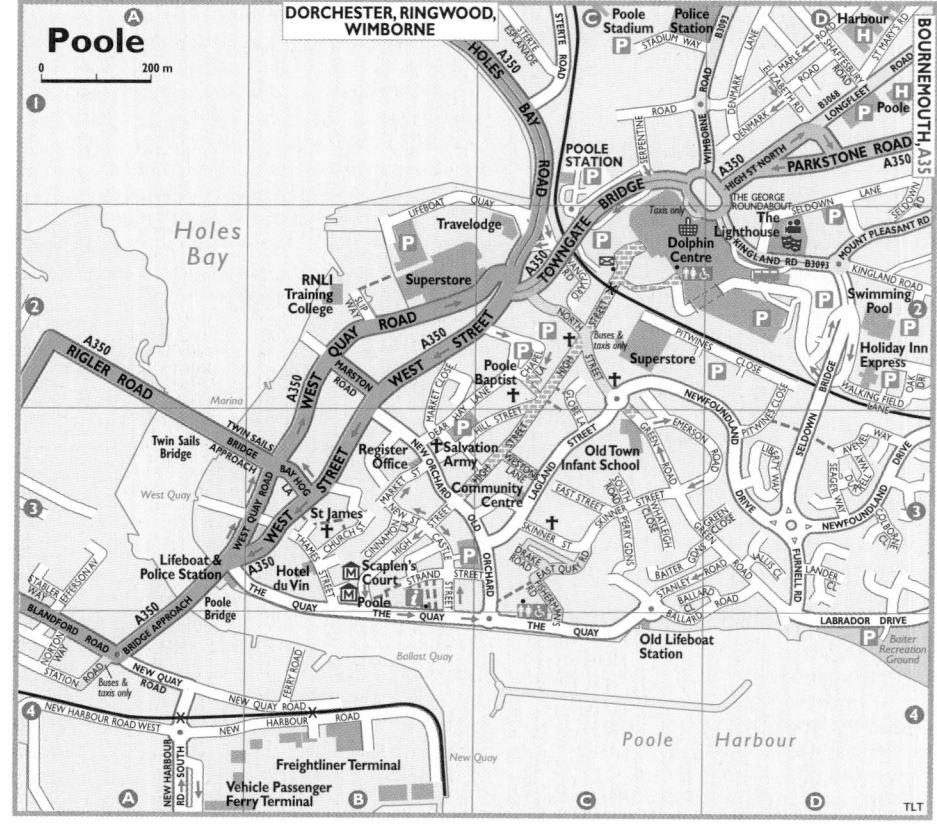

Poole

Poole is found on atlas page **12 H6**

Avenel Way	D3
Baiter Gardens	C3
Ballard Close	C3
Ballard Road	C4
Bay Hog Lane	B3
Blandford Road	A3
Bridge Approach	A4
Castle Street	B3
Chapel Lane	C2
Church Street	B3
Cinnamon Lane	B3
Colborne Close	D3
Dear Hay Lane	B3
Denmark Lane	D1
Denmark Road	D1
Drake Road	C3
Durrell Way	D3
East Quay Road	C3
East Street	C3
Elizabeth Road	D1
Emerson Road	C3
Ferry Road	B4
Fisherman's Road	C3
Furnell Road	D3
Globe Lane	C2
Green Close	D3
Green Road	C3
High Street	B3
High Street North	D1
Hill Street	C3
Holes Bay Road	C1
Jefferson Avenue	A3
Kingland Road	D2
Labrador Drive	D4
Lagland Street	C3
Lander Close	D3
Liberty Way	D3
Lifeboat Quay	B2
Longfleet Road	D1
Maple Road	D1
Market Close	B2
Market Street	B3
Marston Road	B2
Mount Pleasant Road	D2
Newfoundland Drive	C2
New Harbour Road	A4
New Harbour Road South	A4
New Harbour Road West	A4
New Orchard	B3
New Quay Road	A4
New Street	B3
North Street	C2
Norton Way	A4
Oak Drive	D2
Old Orchard	B3
Parkstone Road	D1
Perry Gardens	C3
Pitwines Close	C2
Poole Bridge	A3
Rigler Road	A2
St Mary's Road	D1
Seager Way	D3
Seldown Bridge	D3
Seldown Lane	D2
Seldown Road	D2
Serpentine Road	C1
Shaftesbury Road	D1
Skinner Street	C3
Slip Way	B2
South Road	C3
Stabler Way	A3
Stadium Way	C1
Stanley Road	C3
Sterte Esplanade	C1
Sterte Road	C1
Strand Street	B3
Thames Street	B3
The Quay	B3
Towngate Bridge	C2
Twin Sails Bridge Approach	A3
Twin Sails Bridge	A3
Vallis Close	D3
Vanguard Road	C2
Walking Field Lane	D2
Westons Lane	C3
West Quay Road	B2
West Street	B3
Whatleigh Close	C3
Wimborne Road	D1

Preston

Preston is found on atlas page **88 G5**

Adelphi Street	A1
Arthur Street	A3
Avenham Lane	C4
Avenham Road	C3
Avenham Street	C3
Berwick Road	C4
Birley Street	C2
Boltons Court	C3
Bow Lane	A3
Butler Street	B3
Cannon Street	C3
Carlisle Street	C2
Chaddock Street	C4
Chapel Street	B3
Charlotte Street	D4
Cheapside	C3
Christ Church Street	A3
Church Street	C3
Clarendon Street	D4
Corporation Street	B2
Corporation Street	B3
Craggs Row	B1
Cross Street	C3
Crown Street	B1
Deepdale Road	D1
Derby Street	D2
Earl Street	C2
East Cliff	B4
East Street	D1
Edmund Street	D2
Edward Street	A2
Elizabeth Street	B1
Fishergate	B3
Fishergate Hill	A4
Fleet Street	B3
Fox Street	B2
Friargate	B2
Friargate	C2
Fylde Road	A1
Glover's Court	C3
Glover Street	C3
Great Avenham Street	C4
Great Shaw Street	B2
Grimshaw Street	D2
Guildhall Street	C3
Harrington Street	B1
Heatley Street	B2
Herschell Street	D4
Holstein Street	D1
Hopwood Street	D2
Jutland Street	D1
Lancaster Road	C2
Lancaster Road North	C1
Latham Street	C4
Lawson Street	B1
Leighton Street	A2
Lund Street	C1
Lune Street	B3
Main Sprit Weind	C3
Manchester Road	D3
Market Street	C2
Market Street West	B2
Marsh Lane	A2
Maudland Road	A1
Meadow Street	C1
Moor Lane	B1
Mount Street	B3
North Road	C1
Oak Street	D3
Ormskirk Road	C2
Oxford Street	C3
Pedder Street	A1
Percy Street	D2
Pitt Street	A3
Pole Street	D2
Pump Street	D1
Queen Street	D3
Ribblesdale Place	B4
Ring Way	B2
Rose Street	D3
St Austin's Road	D3
St Paul's Road	D1
St Paul's Square	D1
St Peter's Street	B1
Sedgwick Street	C1
Selborne Street	D4
Shepherd Street	D3
Snow Hill	B2
Syke Street	D3
Tithebarn Street	C2
Walker Street	B1
Walton's Parade	A3
Ward's End	C2
Warwick Street	B1
West Cliff	A4
Winkley Square	B3

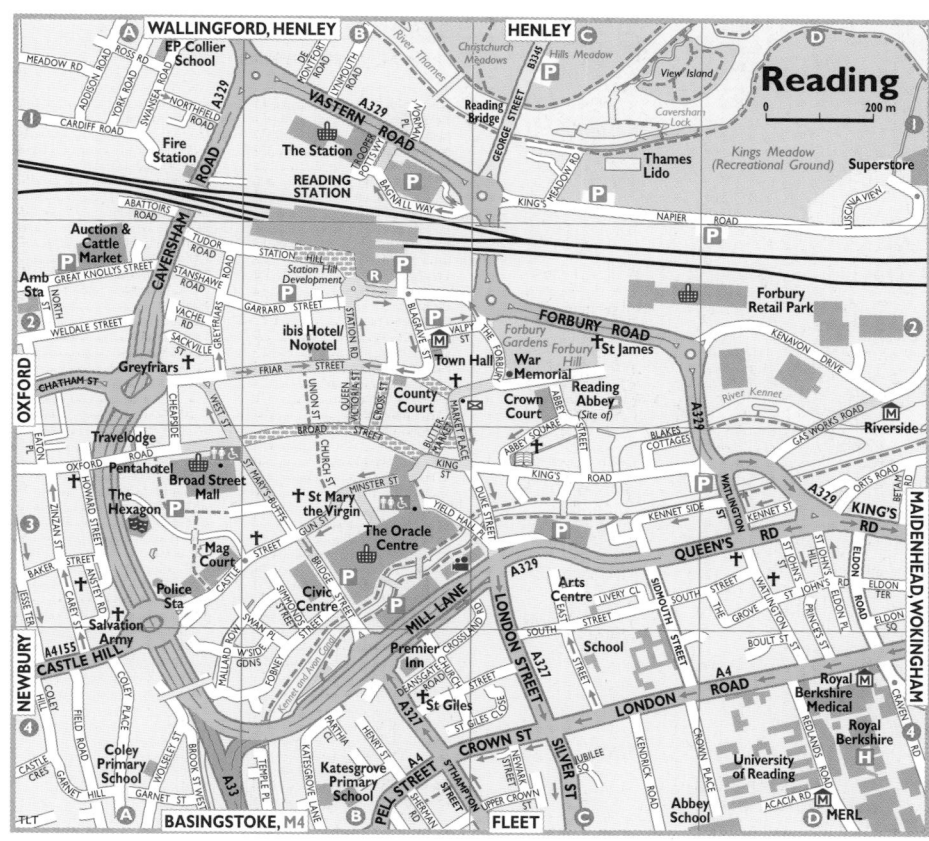

Reading

Reading is found on atlas page **35 K10**

Abbey Square	C3	King's Meadow Road	C1
Abbey Street	C2	King's Road	D3
Addison Road	A1	King Street	B3
Anstey Road	A3	Livery Close	C3
Baker Street	A3	London Road	C4
Blagrave Street	B2	London Street	C3
Blakes Cottages	C3	Mallard Row	A4
Boult Street	D4	Market Place	B2
Bridge Street	B3	Mill Lane	B4
Broad Street	B3	Minster Street	B3
Brook Street West	A4	Napier Road	C1
Buttermarket	B3	Newark Street	C4
Cardiff Road	A1	Northfield Road	A1
Carey Street	A3	Oxford Road	A3
Castle Hill	A4	Parthia Close	B4
Castle Street	A3	Pell Street	B4
Caversham Road	A2	Prince's Street	D3
Chatham Street	A2	Queen's Road	C3
Cheapside	A2	Queen Victoria Street	B2
Church Street	B3	Redlands Road	D4
Church Street	B4	Ross Road	A1
Coley Place	A4	Sackville Street	A2
Craven Road	D4	St Giles Close	B4
Crossland Road	B4	St John's Road	D3
Cross Street	B2	St Mary's Butts	B3
Crown Street	C4	Sidmouth Street	C3
Deansgate Road	B4	Silver Street	C4
Duke Street	C3	Simmonds Street	B3
East Street	C3	Southampton Street	B4
Eldon Road	D3	South Street	C3
Field Road	A4	Station Hill	B2
Fobney Street	B4	Station Road	B2
Forbury Road	C2	Swan Place	B3
Friar Street	B2	Swansea Road	A1
Garnet Street	A4	The Forbury	C2
Garrard Street	B2	Tudor Road	A2
Gas Works Road	D3	Union Street	B2
George Street	C1	Upper Crown Street	C4
Great Knollys Street	A2	Vachel Road	A2
Greyfriars Road	A2	Valpy Street	B2
Gun Street	B3	Vastern Road	B1
Henry Street	B4	Watlington Street	D3
Howard Street	A3	Weldale Street	A2
Katesgrove Lane	B4	West Street	A2
Kenavon Drive	D2	Wolseley Street	A4
Kendrick Road	C4	Yield Hall Place	B3
Kennet Side	C3	York Road	A1
Kennet Street	D3	Zinzan Street	A3

Royal Tunbridge Wells

Royal Tunbridge Wells is found on atlas page **25 N3**

Albert Street	C1	Lansdowne Road	C2
Arundel Road	C4	Lime Hill Road	B1
Bayhall Road	D2	Linden Park Road	A4
Belgrave Road	C1	Little Mount Sion	B4
Berkeley Road	B4	London Road	A2
Boyne Park	A1	Lonsdale Gardens	B2
Buckingham Road	C4	Madeira Park	B4
Calverley Park	C2	Major York's Road	A4
Calverley Park Gardens	D2	Meadow Road	B1
Calverley Road	C2	Molyneux Park Road	A1
Calverley Street	C2	Monson Road	C2
Cambridge Gardens	D4	Monson Way	B2
Cambridge Street	D3	Mount Edgcumbe Road	A3
Camden Hill	D3	Mount Ephraim	A2
Camden Park	D3	Mount Ephraim Road	B1
Camden Road	C1	Mountfield Gardens	C3
Carlton Road	D2	Mountfield Road	C3
Castle Road	A2	Mount Pleasant Avenue	B2
Castle Street	B3	Mount Pleasant Road	B2
Chapel Place	B4	Mount Sion	B4
Christchurch Avenue	B3	Nevill Street	B4
Church Road	A2	Newton Road	B1
Civic Way	B2	Norfolk Road	C4
Claremont Gardens	C4	North Street	D2
Claremont Road	C4	Oakfield Court Road	D3
Clarence Road	B2	Park Street	D3
Crescent Road	C2	Pembury Road	D2
Culverden Street	B1	Poona Road	C4
Dale Street	C1	Prince's Street	D3
Dudley Road	B1	Prospect Road	D3
Eden Road	B4	Rock Villa Road	B1
Eridge Road	A4	Royal Chase	A1
Farmcombe Lane	C4	St James' Road	D1
Farmcombe Road	C4	Sandrock Road	D1
Ferndale	D1	Somerville Gardens	A1
Frant Road	A4	South Green	B3
Frog Lane	B4	Station Approach	B3
Garden Road	C1	Stone Street	D1
Garden Street	C1	Sussex Mews	A4
George Street	C1	Sutherland Road	C3
Goods Station Road	B1	Tunnel Road	C1
Grecian Road	C4	Upper Grosvenor Road	B1
Grosvenor Road	B1	Vale Avenue	B3
Grove Hill Gardens	C3	Vale Road	B3
Grove Hill Road	C3	Victoria Road	C1
Guildford Road	C3	Warwick Park	B4
Hanover Road	B1	Wood Street	C1
High Street	B4	York Road	B2

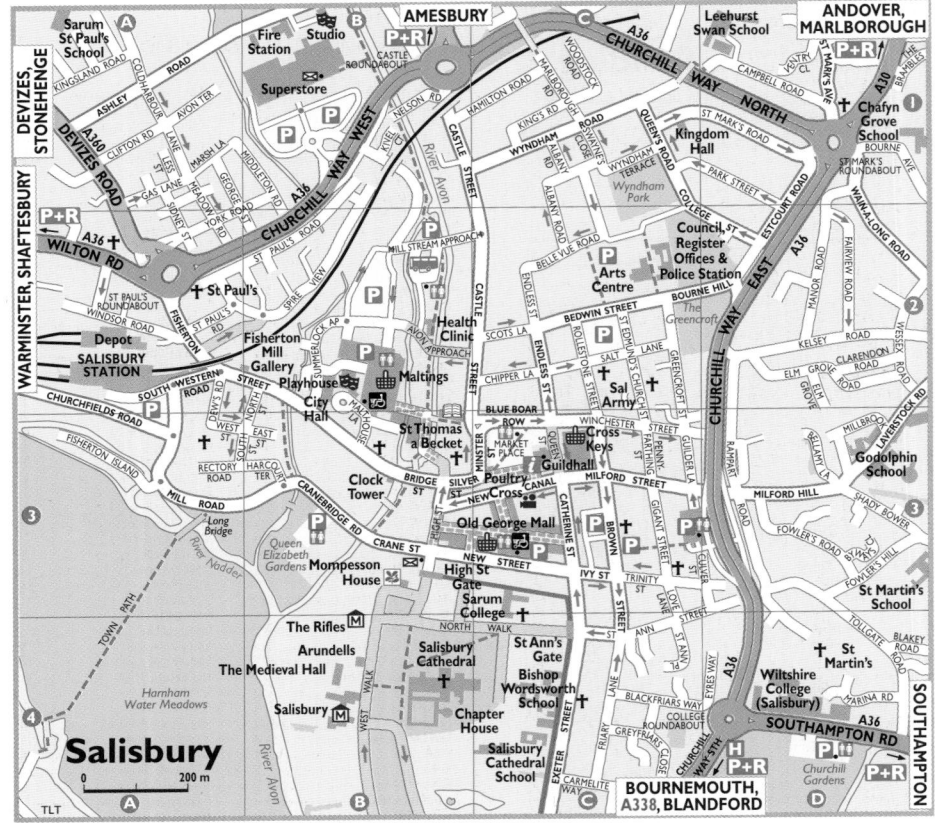

Salisbury

Salisbury is found on atlas page **21 M9**

Albany Road	C1	Kingsland Road	A1
Ashley Road	A1	King's Road	C1
Avon Approach	B2	Laverstock Road	D3
Bedwin Street	C2	Malthouse Lane	B3
Belle Vue Road	C2	Manor Road	D2
Blackfriars Way	C4	Marlborough Road	C1
Blue Boar Row	C3	Meadow Road	A1
Bourne Avenue	D1	Middleton Road	A1
Bourne Hill	C2	Milford Hill	D3
Bridge Street	B3	Milford Street	C3
Brown Street	C3	Mill Road	A3
Campbell Road	D1	Minster Street	C3
Castle Street	B1	Nelson Road	B1
Catherine Street	C3	New Canal	B3
Chipper Lane	C2	New Street	B3
Churchfields Road	A2	North Street	B3
Churchill Way East	D3	Park Street	D1
Churchill Way North	C1	Pennyfarthing Street	C3
Churchill Way South	C4	Queen's Road	C1
Churchill Way West	B2	Queen Street	C3
Clarendon Road	D2	Rampart Road	D3
Clifton Road	A1	Rectory Road	A3
Coldharbour Lane	A2	Rollestone Street	C2
College Street	C1	St Ann Street	C4
Cranebridge Road	B3	St Edmund's Church Street	C2
Crane Street	B3	St Mark's Avenue	D1
Devizes Road	A1	St Mark's Road	D1
Dew's Road	A3	St Paul's Road	B2
East Street	B3	Salt Lane	C2
Elm Grove	D2	Scots Lane	C2
Elm Grove Road	D2	Sidney Street	A1
Endless Street	C2	Silver Street	B3
Estcourt Road	D2	Southampton Road	D4
Exeter Street	C4	South Street	A3
Eyres Way	D4	South Western Road	A2
Fairview Road	D2	Spire View	B2
Fisherton Street	A2	Summerlock Approach	B2
Fowler's Road	D3	Tollgate Road	D4
Friary Lane	C4	Trinity Street	C3
Gas Lane	A1	Wain-A-Long Road	D1
George Street	A1	Wessex Road	D2
Gigant Street	C3	West Street	A3
Greencroft Street	C2	Wilton Road	A2
Guilder Lane	C3	Winchester Street	C3
Hamilton Road	C1	Windsor Road	A2
High Street	B3	Woodstock Road	C1
Ivy Street	C3	Wyndham Road	C1
Kelsey Road	D2	York Road	A2

Sheffield

Sheffield is found on atlas page **84 E3**

Angel Street	C2	Howard Street	C4
Arundel Gate	C3	Hoyle Street	A1
Arundel Street	C4	King Street	C2
Backfields	B3	Lambert Street	B1
Bailey Street	A2	Leopold Street	B3
Balm Green	B3	Mappin Street	A3
Bank Street	C2	Meetinghouse Lane	C2
Barkers Pool	B3	Mulberry Street	C2
Broad Lane	A2	Newcastle Street	A2
Broad Street	D2	New Street	C2
Brown Street	C4	Norfolk Street	C3
Cambridge Street	B3	North Church Street	B2
Campo Lane	B2	Orchard Street	B3
Carver Street	B3	Paradise Street	B2
Castlegate	C1	Pinstone Street	B3
Castle Street	C2	Pond Hill	C3
Charles Street	B4	Pond Street	C3
Charter Row	B4	Portobello Street	A3
Church Street	B2	Queen Street	B2
Commercial Street	C2	Rockingham Street	A2
Corporation Street	B1	St James Street	B2
Cross Burgess Street	B3	Scargill Croft	C2
Cutlers Gate	D1	Scotland Street	A1
Derek Dooley Way	D1	Sheaf Street	D4
Devonshire Street	A3	Shoreham Street	C4
Division Street	A3	Shrewsbury Road	D4
Dixon Lane	C2	Silver Street	B2
Duke Street	D2	Smithfield	A1
Exchange Street	D2	Snig Hill	C2
Eyre Street	B4	Solly Street	A2
Fig Tree Lane	C2	South Street Park	D3
Fitzwilliam Street	A4	Suffolk Road	C4
Flat Street	C3	Surrey Street	C3
Furnace Hill	B1	Talbot Street	D4
Furnival Gate	B4	Tenter Street	B2
Furnival Road	D1	Townhead Street	B2
Furnival Street	C4	Trafalgar Street	A4
Garden Street	A2	Trippet Lane	B3
George Street	C2	Union Street	B4
Gibraltar Street	B1	Vicar Lane	B2
Harmer Lane	C3	Victoria Station Road	D1
Harts Head	C2	Waingate	C2
Hawley Street	B2	Wellington Street	A4
Haymarket	C2	West Bar	B2
High Street	C2	West Bar Green	B2
Holland Street	A3	West Street	A3
Hollis Croft	A2	White Croft	A2
Holly Street	B3	York Street	C2

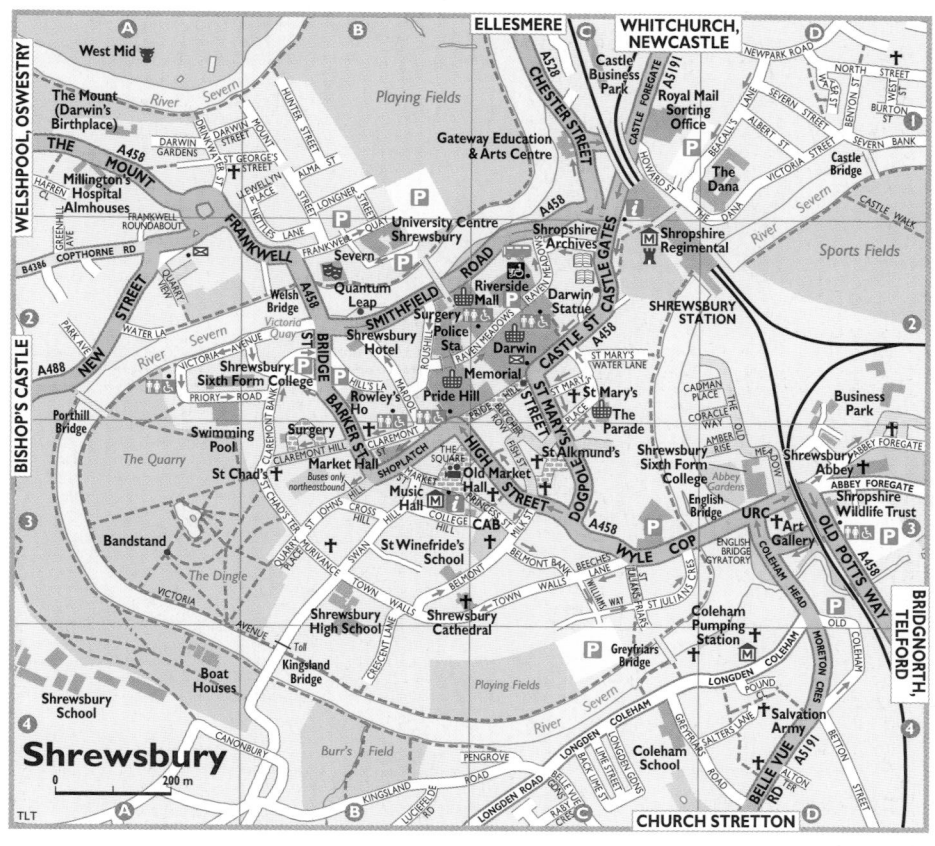

Shrewsbury

Shrewsbury

Shrewsbury is found on atlas page **56 H2**

Abbey Foregate...................D3	Mardol.................................B2
Albert Street......................D1	Market Street.....................B3
Alma Street........................B1	Milk Street..........................C3
Amber Rise.........................D3	Moreton Crescent.............D4
Barker Street......................B2	Mount Street.......................B1
Beacall's Lane....................D1	Murivance...........................B3
Beeches Lane.....................C3	Nettles Lane........................B1
Belle Vue Gardens.............C4	Newpark Road.....................D1
Belle Vue Road...................D4	New Street...........................A2
Belmont..............................B3	North Street.........................D1
Belmont Bank.....................C3	Old Coleham.......................D3
Benyon Street.....................D1	Old Potts Way......................D3
Betton Street......................D4	Park Avenue........................A2
Bridge Street.......................B2	Pengrove.............................C4
Burton Street......................D1	Pound Close........................D4
Butcher Row.......................C2	Pride Hill.............................C2
Canonbury...........................A4	Princess Street....................B3
Castle Foregate...................C1	Priory Road.........................A2
Castle Gates........................C2	Quarry Place.......................B3
Castle Street.......................C2	Quarry View........................A2
Chester Street.....................C1	Raven Meadows..................B2
Claremont Bank..................B3	Roushill...............................B2
Claremont Hill....................B3	St Chad's Terrace................B3
Claremont Street.................B3	St George's Street................A1
Coleham Head.....................D3	St Johns Hill........................B3
College Hill.........................B3	St Julians Crescent.............C3
Copthorne Road..................A2	St Julians Friars..................C3
Coracle Way........................D2	St Mary's Place...................C2
Crescent Lane.....................B4	St Mary's Street...................C2
Cross Hill............................B3	St Mary's Water Lane..........C2
Darwin Gardens..................A1	Salters Lane........................D4
Darwin Street......................A1	Severn Bank........................D1
Dogpole..............................C3	Severn Street.......................D1
Drinkwater Street................A1	Shoplatch...........................B3
Fish Street...........................C3	Smithfield Road..................B2
Frankwell............................A2	Swan Hill.............................B3
Frankwell Quay....................B2	The Dana.............................D1
Greenhill Avenue................A2	The Mount...........................A1
Greyfriars Road...................C4	The Old Meadow.................D3
High Street..........................C3	The Square..........................B3
Hill's Lane...........................B2	Town Walls..........................B3
Howard Street.....................C1	Victoria Avenue...................A2
Hunter Street......................B1	Victoria Street.....................D1
Kingsland Road....................B4	Water Lane..........................A2
Lime Street..........................C4	Water Street........................D1
Longden Coleham...............C4	West Street..........................D1
Longden Road.....................C4	Williams Way......................C3
Longner Street.....................B1	Wyle Cop............................C3

Southend-on-Sea

Southend-on-Sea is found on atlas page **38 E4**

Albert Road.........................C3	Lancaster Gardens..............C2
Alexandra Road...................A3	Leamington Road................D2
Alexandra Street.................A3	London Road.......................A2
Ambleside Drive..................D2	Lucy Road............................C4
Ashburnham Road...............A2	Luker Road...........................A2
Baltic Avenue......................B3	Marine Parade.....................C4
Baxter Avenue.....................A1	Milton Street.......................B1
Beach Road.........................D4	Napier Avenue.....................A2
Boscombe Road...................C1	Nelson Street.......................A3
Bournemouth Park Road......D1	Oban Road...........................D1
Cambridge Road..................A3	Old Southend Road.............D3
Capel Terrace......................A3	Outing Close.......................D3
Chancellor Road..................B3	Pitmans Close.....................B2
Cheltenham Road................D2	Pleasant Road.....................C3
Chichester Road..................B1	Portland Avenue..................B3
Christchurch Road...............D1	Princes Street......................A2
Church Road........................B3	Prittlewell Square...............A3
Clarence Road.....................A3	Quebec Avenue...................B2
Clarence Street...................B3	Queen's Road.......................A2
Clifftown Parade.................A4	Queensway..........................A1
Clifftown Road....................B3	Queensway..........................C3
Coleman Street...................B1	Royal Terrace......................B4
Cromer Road.......................C2	Runwell Terrace..................A3
Devereux Road....................A4	St Ann's Road......................B1
Eastern Esplanade..............D4	St Leonard's Road...............C3
Elmer Approach..................A2	Scratton Road.....................A3
Elmer Avenue......................A2	Short Street........................B1
Essex Street.........................B1	Southchurch Avenue...........D2
Ferndown Close...................D1	Southchurch Road...............B2
Fowler Close........................D2	Stanier Close.......................D2
Gordon Place.......................A2	Stanley Road.......................C3
Gordon Road.......................A2	Sutton Road.........................C1
Grange Gardens..................C2	Swanage Road.....................C1
Grover Street.......................B3	Toledo Road........................C2
Guildford Road....................B1	Tylers Avenue......................B3
Hamlet Road........................A3	Tyrrel Drive..........................C2
Hartington Place.................C4	Victoria Avenue...................A1
Hartington Road..................C3	Warrior Square East.............B2
Hastings Road.....................C2	Warrior Square North...........B2
Hawtree Close.....................D4	Warrior Square....................B2
Herbert Grove......................C3	Wesley Road........................C3
Heygate Avenue..................B3	Western Esplanade..............A4
High Street..........................B2	Weston Road........................B2
Hillcrest Road......................C2	Whitegate Road...................B2
Honiton Road.......................D2	Wimborne Road...................C1
Horace Road........................C3	Windermere Road................D2
Kilworth Avenue..................C2	Woodgrange Drive...............D3
Kursaal Way.........................D4	York Road............................B3

Southend-on-Sea

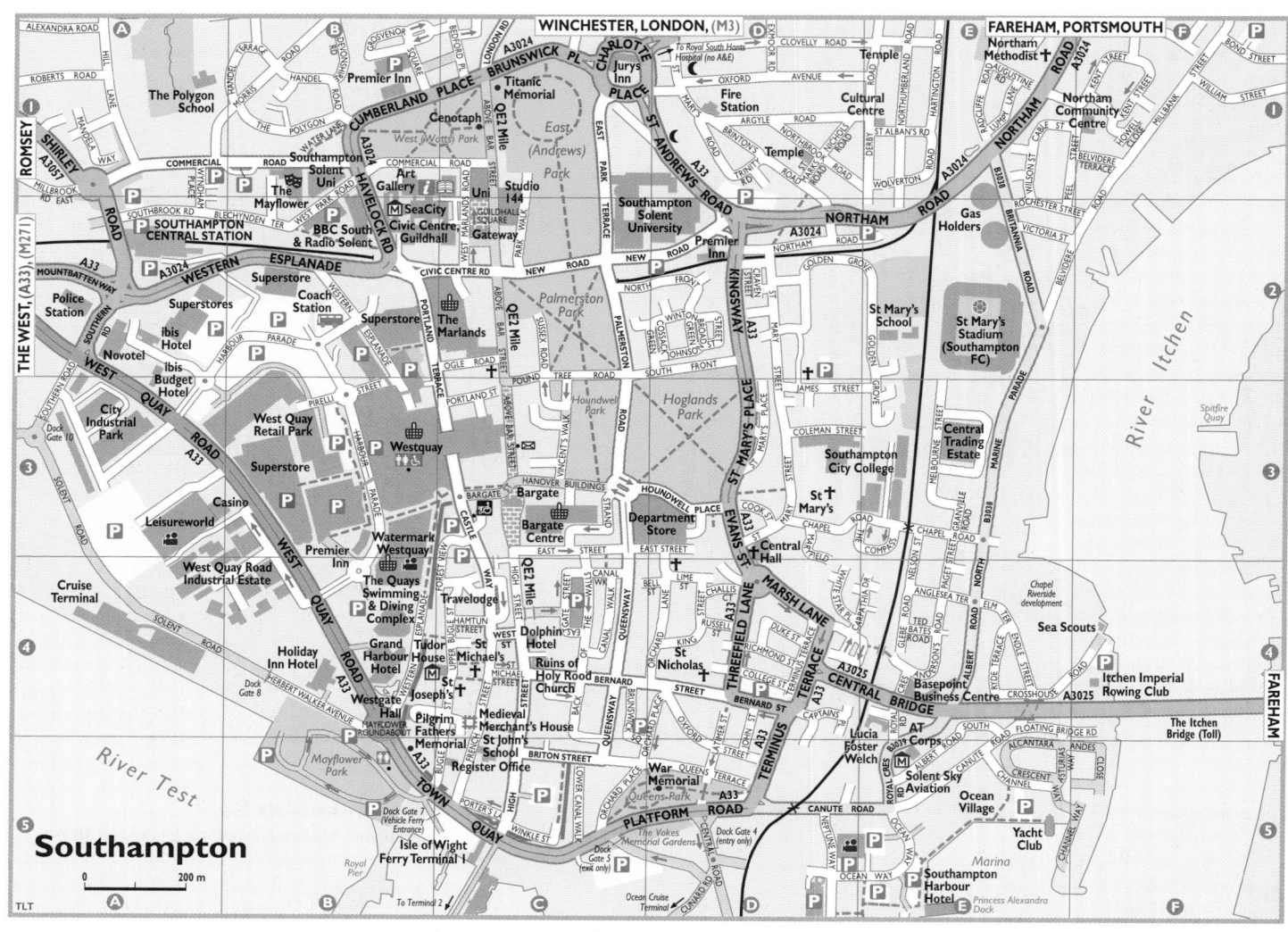

Southampton

Southampton is found on atlas page **14 D4**

Above Bar Street...................C1	Channel Way E5	Hartington Road E1	Northumberland Road E1	South Front...........................C2
Albert Road North...............E4	Chapel Road.......................D3	Havelock Road B1	Ocean Way D5	Strand..................................C3
Albert Road South...............E5	Charlotte Place...................C1	Herbert Walker Avenue B4	Ogle Road C2	Sussex Road........................C2
Alcantara Crescent..............E5	Civic Centre Road B2	High Street C4	Orchard Place C5	Ted Bates Road....................E4
Alexandra Road...................A1	Clovelly Road D1	Hill Lane A1	Oxford Avenue D1	Terminus Terrace..................D5
Anderson's Road E4	Coleman Street....................D3	Houndwell Place D3	Oxford Street D4	The Compass D3
Andes Close F5	College Street.....................D4	Howell Close F1	Paget Street........................E4	The Polygon B1
Anglesea Terrace.................E4	Commercial Road A1	Itchen Bridge F4	Palmerston Road C2	Threefield Lane D4
Argyle Road D1	Cook Street........................D3	James Street D3	Park Walk C2	Town Quay B5
Asturias Way......................E5	Cossack Green D2	Johnson Street....................D2	Peel Street D4	Trinity Road D1
Augustine Road...................E1	Craven Street......................D2	John Street D5	Pirelli Street........................B3	Upper Bugle Street C4
Back Of The Walls C4	Crosshouse Road E4	Kent Street.........................F1	Platform Road......................C5	Victoria Street......................E2
Bargate Street C3	Cumberland Place.................B1	King Street D4	Porter's Lane.......................C5	Vincent's Walk C3
Bedford Place C1	Cunard Road D5	Kingsway...........................D2	Portland Street.....................C3	Water Lane B1
Bell Street D4	Derby Road E1	Latimer Street.....................D5	Portland Terrace...................B2	Western Esplanade A2
Belvidere Road E2	Devonshire Road..................B1	Lime Street D4	Pound Tree Road..................C3	Western Esplanade B4
Belvidere Terrace.................F1	Duke Street........................D4	London Road.......................C1	Queens Terrace D5	West Marlands Road..............C2
Bernard Street C4	Eastgate Street C4	Lower Canal Walk C5	Queensway.........................C4	West Park Road B2
Blechynden Terrace..............B2	East Park Terrace C1	Lumpy Lane........................A1	Radcliffe Road E1	West Quay Road A2
Bond Street F1	East Street C3	Mandela Way A1	Richmond Street D4	West Street C4
Brinton's Road D1	Elm Terrace E4	Marine Parade.....................E3	Roberts Road A1	White Star Place...................D4
Britannia Road E1	Endle Street E4	Marsh Lane D4	Rochester Street...................E2	William Street.......................F1
Briton Street.......................C5	Evans Street.......................D3	Maryfield D3	Royal Crescent Road.............E5	Wilson Street........................E1
Broad Green D2	Exmoor Road......................D1	Mayflower Roundabout..........B4	Russell Street D4	Winkle Street........................C5
Brunswick Place..................C1	Floating Bridge Road E4	Melbourne Street E3	Ryde Terrace E4	Winton Street.......................D2
Brunswick Square C4	Forest View C4	Millbank Street F1	St Alban's Road E1	Wolverton Road....................E1
Bugle Street C5	French Street C5	Millbrook Road East..............A1	St Andrews Road..................D1	Wyndham Place A1
Cable Street E1	Glebe Road E4	Morris Road B1	St Mary's Place....................D3	
Canal Walk.........................C4	Golden Grove D2	Mountbatten Way A2	St Mary's Road D1	
Canute Road D5	Granville Road E3	Nelson Street......................E4	St Mary Street D2	
Captains Place D4	Grosvenor Square B1	Neptune Way D5	St Michael Street..................C4	
Carpathia Drive D4	Hamtun Street.....................C4	New Road C2	Shirley Road.........................A1	
Castle Way C3	Handel Road B1	Nichols Road D1	Solent Road A3	
Central Bridge D4	Handel Terrace....................B1	Northam Road D2	Southbrook Road..................A2	
Central Road D5	Hanover Buildings................C3	Northbrook Road..................D1	Southern Road......................A2	
Challis Court D4	Harbour Parade...................B2	North Front C2		

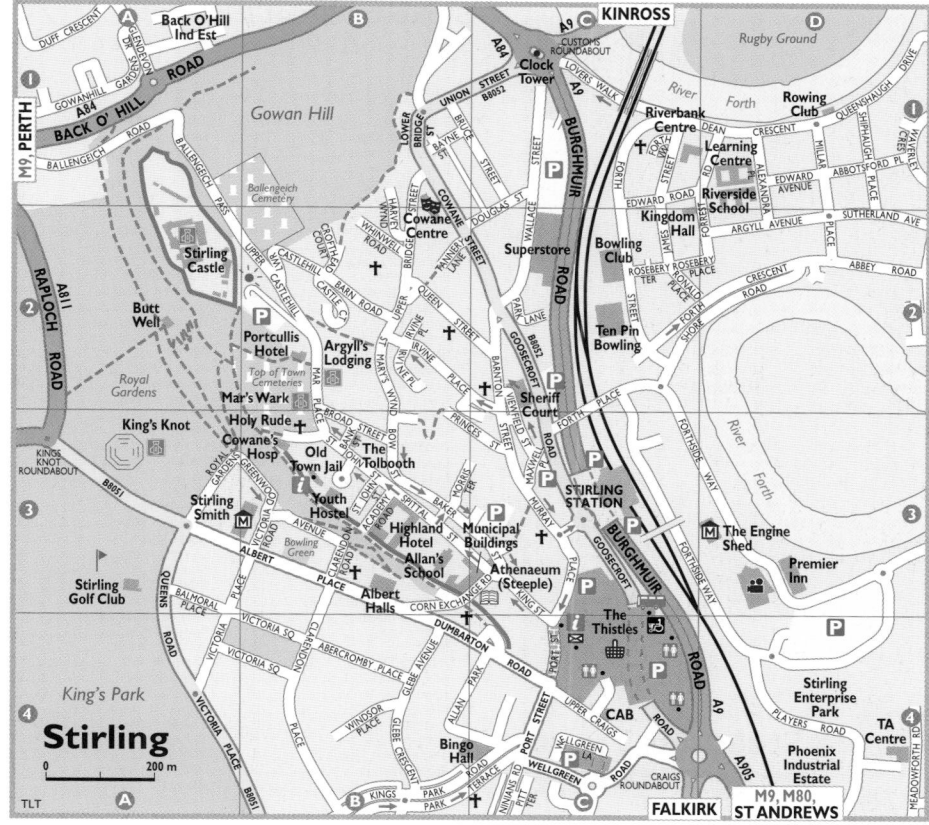

Stirling

Stirling is found on atlas page **133 M9**

Abbey Road	D2	James Street	C2
Abbotsford Place	D1	Kings Knot Roundabout	A3
Abercromby Place	B4	Kings Park Road	B4
Academy Road	B3	King Street	C3
Albert Place	A3	Lovers Walk	C1
Alexandra Place	D1	Lower Bridge Street	B1
Allan Park	B4	Lower Castlehill	B2
Argyll Avenue	D2	Mar Place	B2
Back O' Hill Road	A1	Maxwell Place	C3
Baker Street	B3	Meadowforth Road	D4
Ballengeich Road	A1	Millar Place	D1
Ballengeich Pass	A1	Morris Terrace	B3
Balmoral Place	A3	Murray Place	C3
Bank Street	B3	Ninians Road	C4
Barn Road	B2	Park Lane	C2
Barnton Street	C2	Park Terrace	B4
Bayne Street	B1	Players Road	D4
Bow Street	B3	Port Street	C4
Broad Street	B3	Princes Street	B3
Bruce Street	B1	Queenshaugh Drive	D1
Burghmuir Road	C1	Queens Road	A3
Castle Court	B2	Queen Street	B2
Clarendon Place	B4	Raploch Road	A2
Clarendon Road	B3	Ronald Place	C2
Corn Exchange Road	C1	Rosebery Place	C2
Cowane Street	B1	Rosebery Terrace	C2
Craigs Roundabout	C4	Royal Gardens	A3
Crofthead Court	B2	St John Street	B3
Customs Roundabout	C1	St Mary's Wynd	B2
Dean Crescent	D1	Shiphaugh Place	D1
Douglas Street	C2	Shore Road	C2
Dumbarton Road	B4	Spittal Street	B3
Edward Avenue	D1	Sutherland Avenue	D2
Edward Road	C1	Tannery Lane	B2
Forrest Road	D2	Union Street	B1
Forth Crescent	C2	Upper Bridge Street	B2
Forthside Way	C3	Upper Castlehill	A2
Forth Street	C1	Upper Craigs	C4
Forth Place	C3	Victoria Place	A4
Forth View	C1	Victoria Road	B3
Glebe Avenue	B4	Victoria Square	A4
Glebe Crescent	B4	Viewfield Street	C2
Glendevon Drive	A1	Wallace Street	C2
Goosecroft Road	C2	Waverley Crescent	D1
Gowanhill Gardens	A1	Wellgreen Lane	C4
Greenwood Avenue	A3	Wellgreen Road	C4
Harvey Wynd	B1	Whinwell Road	B2
Irvine Place	B2	Windsor Place	B4

Stockton-on-Tees

Stockton-on-Tees is found on atlas page **104 D7**

1825 Way	B4	Massey Road	D3
Allison Street	B1	Melbourne Street	A2
Alma Street	B1	Middle Street	B2
Bath Lane	C1	Mill Street West	A2
Bedford Street	A1	Nelson Terrace	B2
Bishop Street	B2	North Shore Road	D2
Bishopton Lane	A1	Northport Road	D1
Bishopton Road	A1	Northshore Link	C2
Bowesfield Lane	A4	Norton Road	B1
Bridge Road	B3	Palmerston Street	A2
Bridge Road	C4	Park Road	A4
Bright Street	B2	Park Terrace	C3
Britannia Road	A1	Parkfield Road	B4
Brunswick Street	B3	Parliament Street	B4
Bute Street	A2	Portrack Lane	D1
Church Road	D1	Prince Regent Street	B3
Clarence Row	C1	Princess Avenue	C1
Corportion Street	A2	Princeton Drive	D4
Council of Europe		Quayside Road	C3
Boulevard	C2	Raddcliffe Crescent	D3
Cromwell Avenue	B1	Ramsgate	B3
Dixon Street	A2	Riverside	C3
Dovecot Street	A3	Russell Street	B2
Dugdale Street	D1	St Paul's Street	A1
Durham Road	A1	Silver Street	B2
Durham Street	A2	Skinner Street	B3
Edwards Street	A4	Station Street	D4
Farrer Street	B1	Sydney Street	B2
Finkle Street	B3	The Square	D2
Frederick Street	B1	Thistle Green	C2
Fudan Way	D3	Thomas Street	B1
Gooseport Road	D1	Thompson Street	B1
Hartington Road	A3	Tower Street	B4
Harvard Avenue	D3	Union Street East	C1
High Street	B2	University Boulevard	C3
Hill Street East	D1	Vane Street	B2
Hume Street	B1	Vicarage Street	A1
Hutchinson Street	A2	Wellington Street	A2
John Street	B2	West Row	B3
King Street	B2	Westbourne Street	A4
Knightport Road	D1	Westpoint Road	C3
Knowles Street	C2	Wharf Street	B4
Laing Street	B1	William Street	B3
Leeds Street	B2	Woodland Street	A4
Lobdon Street	B2	Worthing Street	A3
Lodge Street	B3	Yale Crescent	C4
Mandale Road	D4	Yarm Lane	A4
Maritime Road	C1	Yarm Road	A4

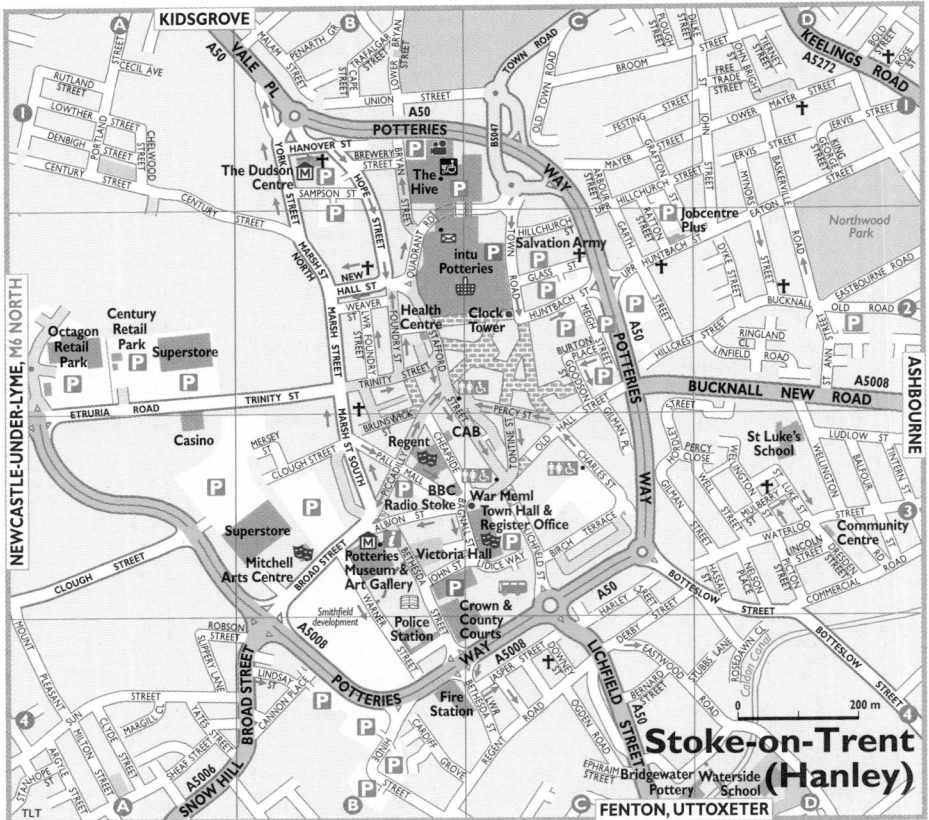

Stoke-on-Trent (Hanley)

Stoke-on-Trent (Hanley) is found on atlas page **70 F5**

Albion Street	B3	Linfield Road	D2
Bagnall Street	B3	Lower Mayer Street	D1
Balfour Street	D3	Lowther Street	A1
Baskerville Road	D1	Ludlow Street	D3
Bathesda Street	B4	Malam Street	B1
Bernard Street	C4	Marsh Street	B2
Bethesda Street	B3	Marsh Street North	B2
Birch Terrace	C3	Marsh Street South	B3
Botteslow Street	C3	Mayer Street	C1
Broad Street	B4	Mersey Street	B3
Broom Street	C1	Milton Street	A4
Brunswick Street	B3	Mount Pleasant	A4
Bryan Street	B1	Mynors Street	D1
Bucknall New Road	C2	New Hall Street	B2
Bucknall Old Road	D2	Ogden Road	C4
Cardiff Grove	B4	Old Hall Street	C3
Century Street	A1	Old Town Road	C1
Charles Street	C3	Pall Mall	B3
Cheapside	B3	Percy Street	C2
Chelwood Street	A1	Piccadilly	B3
Clough Street	A3	Portland Street	A1
Clyde Street	A4	Potteries Way	B1
Commercial Road	D3	Potteries Way	B4
Denbigh Street	A1	Quadrant Road	B2
Derby Street	B2	Regent Road	C4
Dyke Street	D2	Rutland Street	A1
Eastwood Road	C4	St John Street	D1
Eaton Street	B2	St Luke Street	D3
Etruria Road	A2	Sampson Street	B1
Foundry Street	B2	Sheaf Street	A4
Garth Street	C2	Slippery Lane	A4
Gilman Street	C3	Snow Hill	A4
Goodson Street	C2	Stafford Street	B2
Grafton Street	C1	Sun Street	A4
Hanover Street	B1	Tontine Street	C3
Harley Street	C4	Town Road	C2
Hillchurch	C2	Trafalgar Street	B1
Hillcrest Street	C2	Trinity Street	B2
Hinde Street	B4	Union Street	B1
Hope Street	B1	Upper Hillchurch Street	C2
Hordley Street	C3	Upper Huntbach Street	C2
Huntbach Street	C2	Warner Street	B3
Jasper Street	C4	Waterloo Street	D3
Jervis Street	D1	Well Street	D3
John Street	B3	Wellington Road	D3
Keelings Road	D1	Wellington Street	D3
Lichfield Street	C3	Yates Street	A4
Lidice Way	C3	York Street	B1

Stratford-upon-Avon

Stratford-upon-Avon is found on atlas page **47 P3**

Albany Road	A3	New Broad Street	B4
Alcester Road	A2	New Street	B4
Arden Street	B2	Old Red Lion Court	C2
Avenue Road	C1	Old Town	C2
Bancroft Place	C2	Orchard Way	A4
Birmingham Road	B1	Payton Street	C2
Brewery Street	B1	Percy Street	C1
Bridge Foot	D2	Rother Street	B3
Bridge Street	C2	Rowley Crescent	D1
Bridgeway	B2	Ryland Road	B4
Broad Street	B4	St Andrew's Crescent	A3
Brookvale Road	A4	St Gregory's Road	C1
Brunel Way	A2	St Martin's Close	A3
Bull Street	B4	Sanctus Drive	B4
Cedar Close	D1	Sanctus Road	A4
Chapel Lane	C3	Sanctus Street	B4
Chapel Street	C3	Sandfield Road	A4
Cherry Orchard	A4	Scholars Lane	B3
Cherry Street	B4	Seven Meadows Road	A4
Chestnut Walk	B3	Shakespeare Street	B1
Church Street	B3	Sheep Street	C3
Clopton Bridge	D3	Shipston Road	D4
Clopton Road	B1	Shottery Road	A3
College Lane	B4	Shrieves Walk	C3
College Mews	B4	Southern Lane	C3
College Street	B4	Swan's Nest	D3
Ely Gardens	B3	The Willows	A3
Ely Street	B3	Tiddington Road	D3
Evesham Place	B3	Town Square	B2
Evesham Road	A4	Tramway Bridge	D3
Garrick Way	A4	Tyler Street	C2
Great William Street	C1	Union Street	C2
Greenhill Street	B2	Warwick Court	C1
Grove Road	B3	Warwick Crescent	D1
Guild Street	C2	Warwick Road	C2
Henley Street	B2	Waterside	C3
High Street	C3	Welcombe Road	D1
Holtom Street	B4	Wellesbourne Grove	B2
John Street	C2	Western Road	B1
Kendall Avenue	B1	West Street	B4
Lock Close	C2	Willows Drive North	A2
Maidenhead Road	C1	Windsor Street	B2
Mansell Street	B2	Wood Street	B2
Mayfield Avenue	C1		
Meer Street	B2		
Mill Lane	C4		
Mulberry Street	C1		
Narrow Lane	B4		

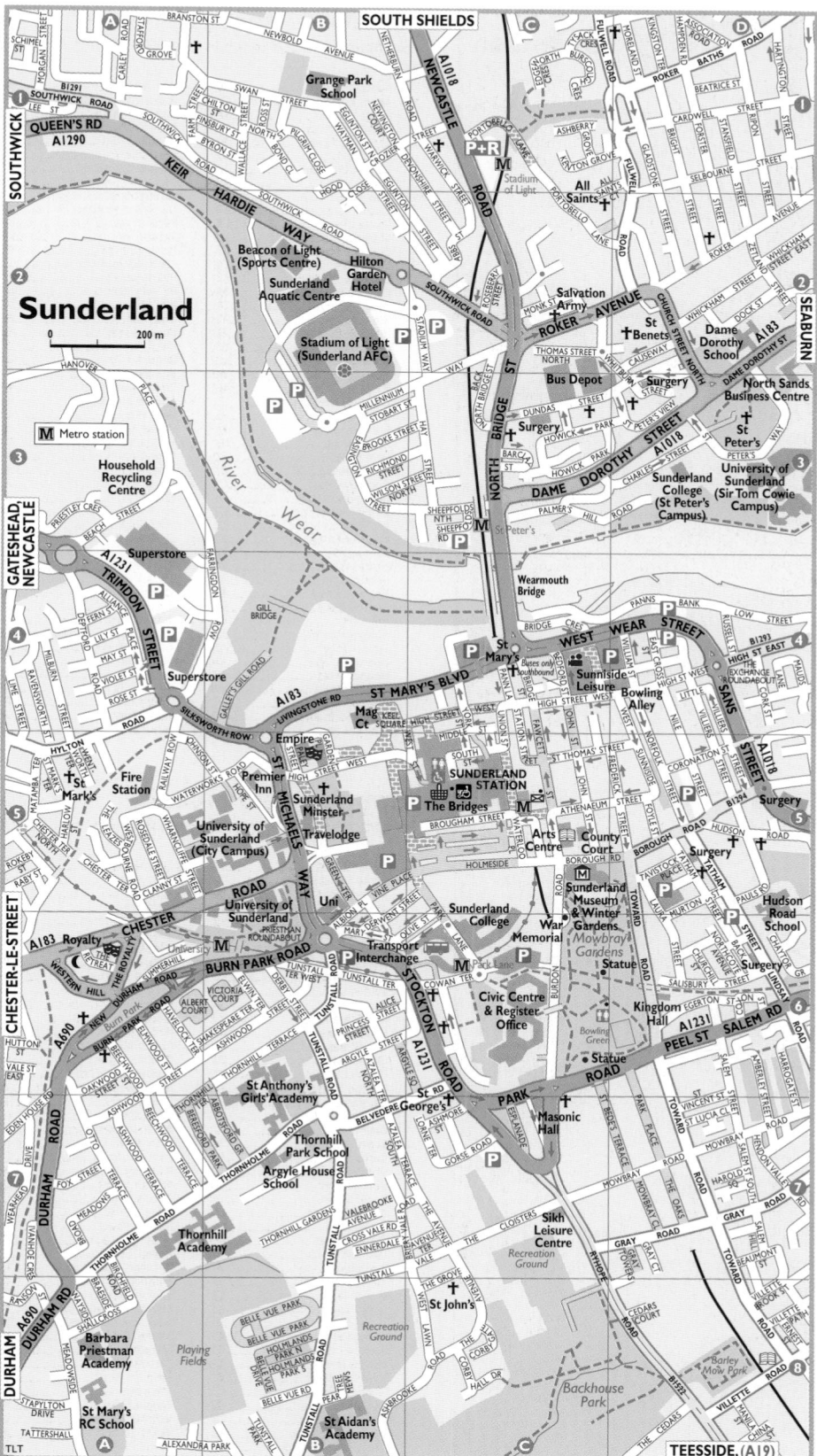

Sunderland

Sunderland is found on atlas page **113 N9**

Abbotsford Green	B7
Abbs Street	C2
Albion Place	B6
Alice Street	B6
Alliance Place	A4
Amberley Street	D6
Argyle Square	B6
Argyle Street	B6
Ashbrooke Road	B8
Ashmore Street	C7
Ashwood Street	A7
Ashwood Terrace	A7
Association Road	D1
Athenaeum Street	C5
Azalea Terrace North	B6
Azalea Terrace South	B7
Back North Bridge Street	C3
Beach Street	A3
Bedford Street	C4
Beechwood Street	A6
Beechwood Terrace	A7
Belvedere Road	B7
Beresford Park	A7
Birchfield Road	A7
Borough Road	D5
Bridge Crescent	C4
Bridge Street	C4
Briery Vale Road	C7
Bright Street	D1
Brooke Street	B3
Brougham Street	C5
Burdon Road	C5
Burn Park Road	B6
Cardwell Street	D1
Carley Road	A1
Charles Street	D3
Chester Road	A6
Churchill Street	D6
Church Street North	D2
Clanny Street	A5
Cork Street	D4
Coronation Street	D5
Cowan Terrace	C6
Cross Vale Road	B7
Crozier Street	B1
Dame Dorothy Street	C3
Deptford Road	A4
Derby Street	B6
Derwent Street	B6
Devonshire Street	B1
Dock Street	D2
Dundas Street	C3
Durham Road	A7
Easington Street	B3
East Cross Street	D4
Eden House Road	A7
Egerton Street	D6
Eglinton Street	B1
Eglinton Street North	B1
Elmwood Street	A6
Ennerdale	B7
Farm Street	A1
Farringdon Row	B4
Fawcett Street	C4
Forster Street	D1
Fox Street	A7
Foyle Street	D5
Frederick Street	D5
Fulwell Road	C1
Galley's Gill Road	B4
Gladstone Street	D1
Gorse Road	C7
Gray Road	D7
Green Terrace	B5
Hampden Road	D1
Hanover Place	A2
Harlow Street	A5
Harrogate Street	D6
Hartington Street	D1
Havelock Terrace	A6
Hay Street	C3
Hendon Valley Road	D7
High Street East	D4
High Street West	B5
Holmeside	C5
Hope Street	B5
Howick Park	C3
Hudson Road	D5
Hylton Road	A5
Johnson Street	A5
John Street	C4
Keir Hardie Way	A1
Laura Street	D5
Lindsay Road	D6
Little Villiers Street	D4
Livingstone Road	B4
Low Street	D4
Mary Street	B6
Mauds Lane	D4
Meadowside	A8
Middle Street	C5

Milburn Street	A4
Millennium Way	B3
Monk Street	C2
Moreland Street	D1
Morgan Street	A1
Mowbray Road	D7
Netherburn Road	B1
Newbold Avenue	B1
Newcastle Road	C1
New Durham Road	A6
Nile Street	D4
Norfolk Street	D5
North Bridge Street	C3
Northcote Avenue	D6
North Street	B1
Oakwood Street	A6
Olive Street	B6
Otto Terrace	A7
Palmer's Hill Road	C3
Panns Bank	D4
Park Lane	C5
Park Place	D6
Park Road	C6
Pauls Road	D5
Peel Street	D6
Portobello Lane	C1
Queen's Road	A1
Railway Row	A5
Ravensworth Street	A4
Richmond Street	B3
Ripon Street	D1
Roker Avenue	C2
Roker Baths Road	D1
Rosedale Street	A5
Ross Street	B1
Russell Street	D4
Ryhope Road	C7
St Bede's Terrace	D7
St Mary's Boulevard	B4
St Michaels Way	B5
St Peter's View	D3
St Thomas' Street	C5
St Vincent Street	D7
Salem Road	D6
Salem Street	D6
Salem Street South	D7
Salisbury Street	D6
Sans Street	D4
Selbourne Street	D1
Shakespeare Terrace	A6
Shallcross	A8
Sheepfolds Road	C3
Silksworth Row	A4
South Street	C5
Southwick Road	A1
Southwick Road	C2
Stadium Way	C2
Stansfield Street	D1
Station Street	C4
Stobart Street	B3
Stockton Road	C6
Swan Street	B1
Tatham Street	D5
Tatham Street Back	D5
The Avenue	C7
The Cloisters	C7
The Royalty	A6
Thomas Street North	C2
Thornhill Terrace	B6
Thornholme Road	A7
Toward Road	D5
Trimdon Street	A4
Tunstall Road	B7
Tunstall Terrace	B6
Tunstall Terrace West	B6
Tunstall Vale	B8
Union Street	C4
Valebrooke Avenue	B7
Villette Road	D8
Villiers Street	D4
Vine Place	B5
Wallace Street	B1
Warwick Street	C1
Waterloo Place	C5
Waterworks Road	A5
Wayman Street	B1
Wearhead Drive	A7
Westbourne Road	A5
Western Hill	A6
West Lawn	C8
West Street	C5
West Sunniside	D4
West Wear Street	C4
Wharncliffe Street	A5
Whickham Street	D2
Whickham Street East	D2
Whitburn Street	D3
William Street	D4
Wilson Street North	B3
York Street	C4
Zetland Street	D2

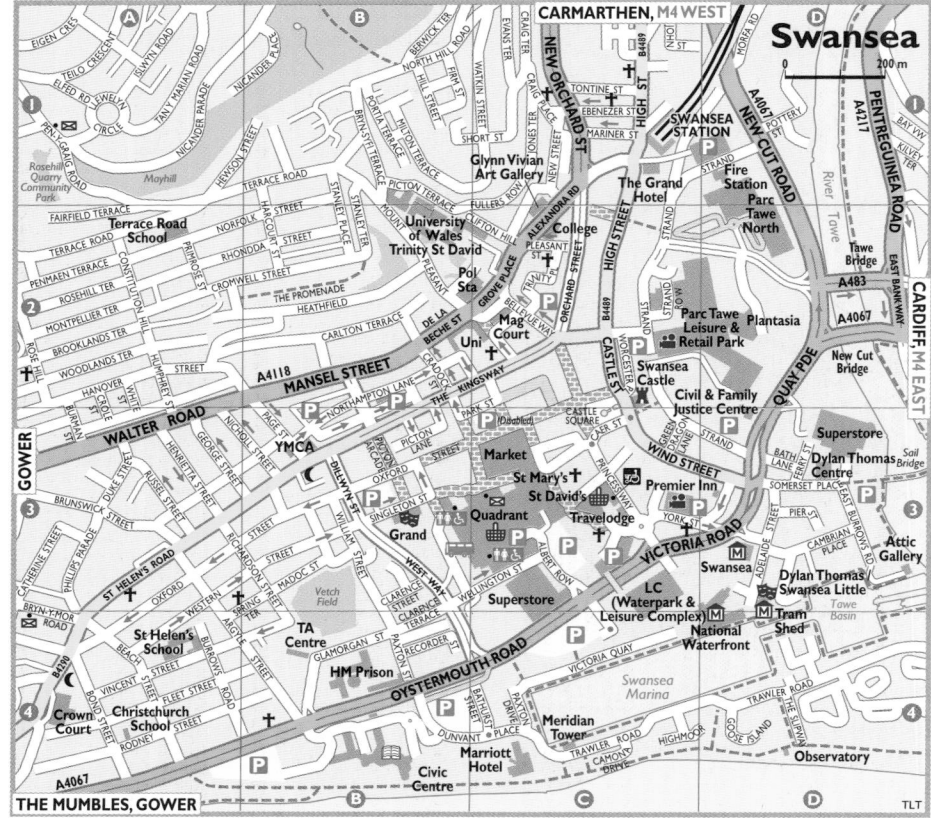

Swansea

Swansea is found on atlas page **29 J6**

Adelaide Street	D3	New Orchard Street	C1
Alexandra Road	C2	New Street	C1
Argyle Street	A4	Nicander Parade	A1
Bath Lane	D3	Nicholl Street	A3
Beach Street	A4	Norfolk Street	A2
Bond Street	A4	North Hill Road	B1
Brunswick Street	A3	Northampton Lane	B2
Burrows Road	A4	Orchard Street	C2
Caer Street	C3	Oxford Street	A3
Carlton Terrace	B2	Oystermouth Road	B4
Castle Street	C2	Page Street	B3
Catherine Street	A3	Park Street	B3
Clarence Street	B3	Paxton Street	B4
Clifton Hill	C2	Pentreguinea Road	D1
Constituion Hill	A2	Pen-Y-Graig Road	A1
Cradock Street	B2	Picton Lane	B3
Craig Place	C1	Pier Street	D3
Cromwell Street	A2	Primrose Street	A2
De La Beche Street	B2	Princess Way	C3
Dillwyn Street	B3	Quay Parade	D2
Duke Street	A3	Recorder Street	B4
Dunvant Place	B4	Rhondda Street	A2
East Bank Way	D2	Richardson Street	A3
East Burrows Road	D3	Rodney Street	A4
Ebenezer Street	C1	Rose Hill	A2
Elfed Road	A1	Russel Street	A3
Ferry Street	D3	St Helen's Road	A3
Firm Street	B1	Short Street	B1
Fleet Street	A4	Singleton Street	B3
George Street	A3	Somerset Place	D3
Glamorgan Street	B4	Strand	C1
Green Dragon Lane	C3	Tan Y Marian Road	A1
Grove Place	C2	Teilo Crescent	A1
Hanover Street	A2	Terrace Road	A2
Harcourt Street	B2	The Kingsway	B2
Heathfield	B2	Tontine Street	C1
Henrietta Street	A3	Trawler Road	C4
Hewson Street	A1	Victoria Quay	C4
High Street	C2	Victoria Road	C4
Hill Street	B1	Vincent Street	A4
Humphrey Street	A2	Walter Road	A3
Islwyn Road	A1	Watkin Street	C1
Llewelyn Circle	A1	Wellington Street	C3
Madoc Street	B3	West Way	B3
Mansel Street	B2	Western Street	A4
Mariner Street	C1	William Street	B3
Mount Pleasant	B2	Wind Street	C3
New Cut Road	D1	York Street	C3

Swindon

Swindon is found on atlas page **33 M8**

Albion Street	A4	Islington Street	C3
Alfred Street	C2	John Street	B3
Ashford Road	B4	King Street	B3
Aylesbury Street	B2	London Street	A3
Bathurst Road	C2	Manchester Road	C2
Beckhampton Street	C3	Market Street	B3
Bridge Street	B2	Maxwell Street	A3
Bristol Street	A3	Medgbury Road	C2
Broad Street	C2	Milford Street	B2
Cambria Bridge Road	A4	Milton Road	B3
Canal Walk	B3	Morley Street	B3
Carr Street	B3	Morse Street	B4
Chester Street	A3	Newcastle Street	D3
Church Place	A3	Newcombe Drive	A1
Cirencester Way	D1	Newhall Street	B4
Clarence Street	C3	Northampton Street	D3
College Street	B3	North Star Avenue	B1
Commercial Road	B3	Ocotal Way	D1
Corporation Street	C2	Park Lane	A3
County Road	D2	Plymouth Street	D3
Crombey Street	B4	Polaris Way	B1
Curtis Street	A4	Ponting Street	C2
Deacon Street	B4	Portsmouth Street	D3
Dixon Street	B4	Princes Street	C3
Dover Street	C4	Prospect Hill	C4
Dowling Street	B4	Queen Street	B3
Drove Road	D4	Radnor Street	A4
Dryden Street	A4	Regent Place	C3
Eastcott Hill	C4	Regent Street	B3
East Street	B2	Rosebery Street	C2
Edgeware Road	B3	Salisbury Street	C2
Elmina Road	C1	Sanford Street	B3
Emlyn Square	A3	Sheppard Street	B2
Euclid Street	C3	Southampton Street	D3
Faringdon Road	A3	Stafford Street	B4
Farnsby Street	B3	Stanier Street	B4
Fire Fly Avenue	A2	Station Road	B2
Fleet Street	B2	Swindon Road	C4
Fleming Way	C3	Tennyson Street	A3
Gladstone Street	C2	Theobald Street	A3
Gooch Street	C2	Victoria Road	C4
Graham Street	C2	Villett Street	B3
Great Western Way	A1	Westcott Place	A4
Groundwell Road	C3	Western Street	C4
Havelock Street	B3	Whitehead Street	B4
Hawksworth Way	A1	Whitney Street	B4
Haydon Street	C2	William Street	A4
Holbrook Way	B2	York Road	D3

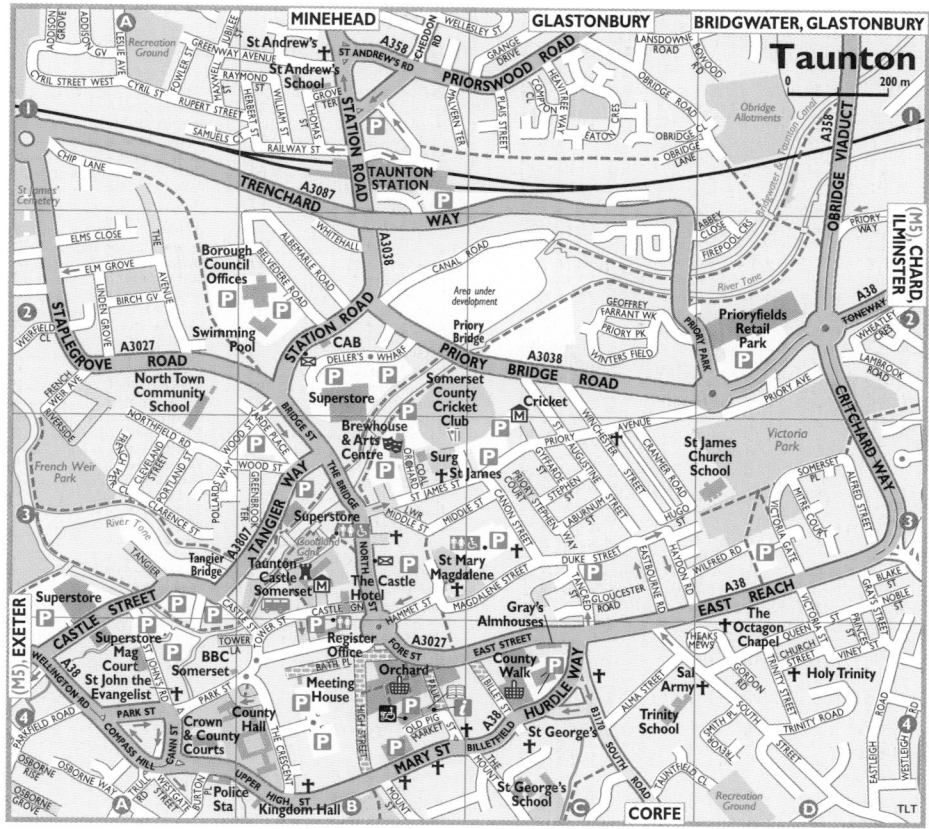

Taunton

Taunton is found on atlas page **18 H10**

Abbey Close	D2	Maxwell Street	A1
Albemarle Road	B2	Middle Street	B3
Alfred Street	D3	Northfield Road	A3
Alma Street	C4	North Street	A3
Belvedere Road	B2	Obridge Road	C1
Billetfield	C4	Obridge Viaduct	D2
Billet Street	C4	Old Pig Market	B4
Bridge Street	B2	Parkfield Road	A4
Canal Road	B2	Park Street	A4
Cann Street	A4	Paul Street	B4
Canon Street	C3	Plais Street	C1
Castle Street	A4	Portland Street	A3
Cheddon Road	B1	Priorswood Road	B1
Chip Lane	A1	Priory Avenue	C3
Church Street	D4	Priory Bridge Road	B2
Clarence Street	A3	Queen Street	D4
Cleveland Street	A3	Railway Street	B1
Compass Hill	A4	Raymond Street	A1
Cranmer Road	C3	Rupert Street	A1
Critchard Way	D2	St Andrew's Road	B1
Cyril Street	A1	St Augustine Street	C3
Deller's Wharf	B2	St James Street	B3
Duke Street	C3	St John's Road	A4
Eastbourne Road	C3	Samuels Court	A1
Eastleigh Road	D4	South Road	C4
East Reach	D3	South Street	D4
East Street	C4	Staplegrove Road	A2
Fore Street	B4	Station Road	B2
Fowler Street	A1	Stephen Street	C3
French Weir Avenue	A2	Stephen Way	C3
Gloucester Road	C3	Tancred Street	C3
Grange Drive	C1	The Avenue	A2
Grays Street	D3	The Bridge	B3
Greenway Avenue	A1	The Crescent	B4
Gyffarde Street	C3	Thomas Street	B1
Hammet Street	B4	Toneway	D2
Haydon Road	C3	Tower Street	B4
Herbert Street	B1	Trenchard Way	B1
High Street	B4	Trinity Street	D4
Hugo Street	C3	Upper High Street	B4
Hurdle Way	C4	Victoria Gate	D3
Laburnum Street	C3	Victoria Street	D3
Lansdowne Road	C1	Viney Street	D4
Leslie Avenue	A1	Wellington Road	A4
Linden Grove	A2	Wilfred Road	C3
Lower Middle Street	B3	William Street	B1
Magdalene Street	B3	Winchester Street	C2
Mary Street	B4	Wood Street	B3

Torquay

Torquay is found on atlas page **7 N6**

Abbey Road	B1	Middle Warbury Road	D1
Alexandra Road	C1	Mill Lane	A1
Alpine Road	C2	Montpellier Road	D3
Ash Hill Road	C1	Morgan Avenue	B1
Avenue Road	A1	Palm Road	B1
Bampfylde Road	A2	Parkhill Road	D4
Beacon Hill	D4	Pembroke Road	C1
Belgrave Road	A1	Pennsylvania Road	D1
Braddons Hill Road East	D3	Pimlico	C2
Braddons Hill Road West	C2	Potters Hill	C1
Braddons Street	D2	Princes Road	C1
Bridge Road	A1	Queen Street	C2
Camden Road	D1	Rathmore Road	A2
Cary Parade	C3	Rock Road	C2
Cary Road	C3	Rosehill Road	D1
Castle Lane	C1	St Efride's Road	A1
Castle Road	C1	St Luke's Road	B2
Cavern Road	D1	St Marychurch Road	C1
Chestnut Avenue	A2	Scarborough Road	B2
Church Lane	A1	Seaway Lane	A4
Church Street	A1	Shedden Hill Road	B3
Cleveland Road	A1	Solbro Road	A3
Croft Hill	B2	South Hill Road	D3
Croft Road	B2	South Street	A1
East Street	A1	Stentiford Hill Road	C2
Ellacombe Road	C1	Strand	D3
Falkland Road	A2	Sutherland Road	D1
Fleet Street	C3	Temperance Street	C2
Grafton Road	D2	The King's Drive	A3
Hennapyn Road	A4	The Terrace	D3
Higher Union Lane	B1	Torbay Road	A4
Hillesdon Road	D2	Tor Church Road	A1
Hoxton Road	D1	Tor Hill Road	B1
Hunsdon Road	D3	Torwood Street	D3
Laburnum Street	A1	Trematon Ave	B1
Lime Avenue	A2	Trinity Hill	D3
Lower Ellacombe		Union Street	B1
Church Road	D1	Upper Braddons Hill	D2
Lower Union Lane	C2	Vanehill Road	D4
Lower Warbury Road	D2	Vansittart Road	A1
Lucius Street	A1	Vaughan Parade	C3
Lymington Road	B1	Victoria Parade	D4
Magdalene Road	B1	Victoria Road	C1
Market Street	C2	Vine Road	A1
Marion View	D3	Walnut Road	A2
Meadfoot Lane	D4	Warberry Road West	C1
Melville Lane	C2	Warren Road	B2
Melville Street	C2	Wellington Road	C1

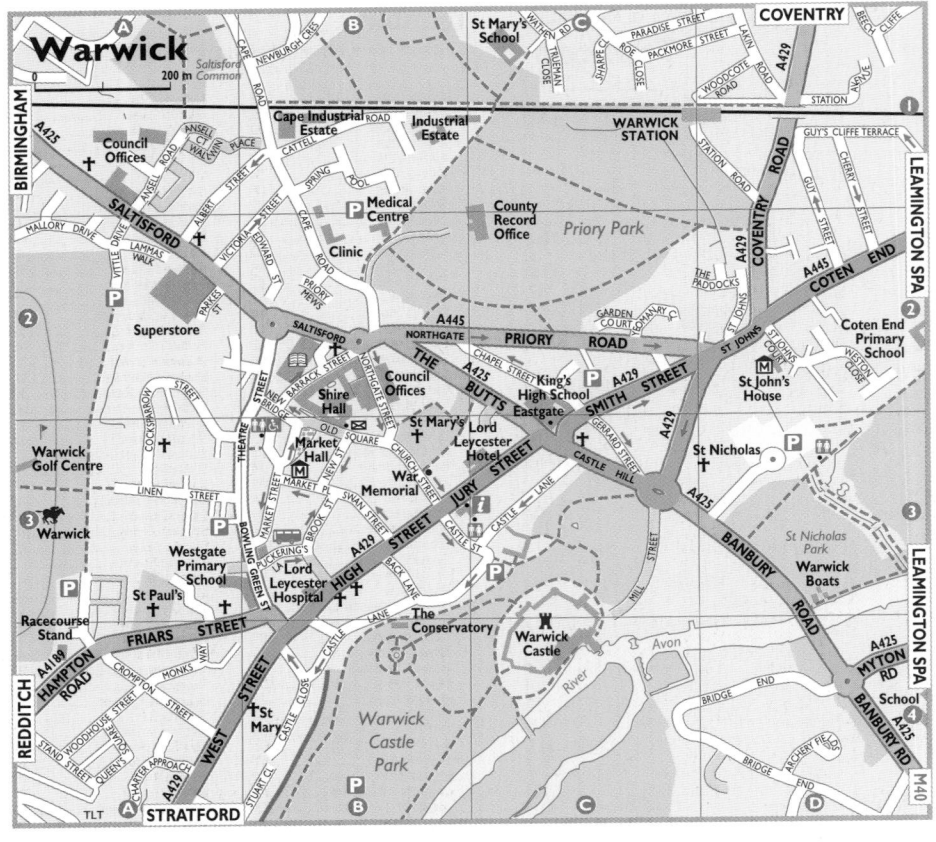

Warwick

Warwick is found on atlas page **59 L11**

Albert Street A2	Old Square B3
Ansell Court A1	Packmore Street C1
Ansell Road A1	Paradise Street C1
Archery Fields D4	Parkes Street A2
Back Lane B3	Priory Mews B2
Banbury Road D3	Priory Road C2
Barrack Street B2	Puckering's Lane B3
Beech Cliffe D1	Queen's Square A4
Bowling Green Street B3	Roe Close...........................C1
Bridge End D4	St Johns D2
Brook Street B3	St Johns Court D2
Cape Road B1	Saltisford A1
Castle Close B4	Sharpe Close.......................C1
Castle Hill C3	Smith Street C2
Castle Lane B4	Spring Pool B1
Castle Street B3	Stand Street A4
Cattell Road B1	Station Avenue D1
Chapel Street C2	Station Road D1
Charter Approach A4	Stuart Close B4
Cherry Street D1	Swan Street B3
Church Street B3	Theatre Street B3
Cocksparrow Street A3	The Butts B2
Coten End D2	The Paddocks.......................D2
Coventry Road D2	Trueman Close C1
Crompton Street A4	Victoria Street A2
Edward Street B2	Vittle Drive A2
Friars Street A4	Wallwin Place A1
Garden Court C2	Wathen Road C1
Gerrard Street C3	Weston Close D2
Guy's Cliffe Terrace D1	West Street A4
Guy Street D1	Woodcote Road D1
Hampton Road.....................A4	Woodhouse Street A4
High Street B3	Yeomanry Close C2
Jury Street B3	
Lakin Road D1	
Lammas Walk A2	
Linen Street A3	
Mallory Drive A2	
Market Place B3	
Market Street B3	
Mill Street C3	
Monks Way A4	
Myton Road D4	
New Bridge B2	
Newburgh Crescent B1	
New Street B3	
Northgate...........................B2	
Northgate Street B2	

Watford

Watford is found on atlas page **50 D11**

Addiscombe Road B3	Marlborough Road B3
Albert Road North B2	Merton Road B4
Albert Road South B2	Mildred Avenue A3
Alexandra Road....................A1	Monica Close D1
Anglian Close......................D1	Nascot Street B1
Beechen Grove.....................C3	New Road D4
Brocklesbury Close D2	New Street C3
Burton Avenue A4	Orphanage Road C1
Cassiobury Drive..................A2	Park Avenue A3
Cassio Road A3	Peace Prospect A2
Chester Road A4	Percy Road B3
Chester Street.....................A4	Pretoria Road.......................A4
Clarendon Road C1	Prince Street C2
Cross Street C2	Queen's Road C2
Denmark Street A1	Queen Street C3
Derby Road C3	Radlett Road D2
Duke Street C2	Raphael Drive D1
Durban Road East A4	Reeds Crescent C1
Durban Road West A4	Rickmansworth Road A3
Earl Street C3	Rosslyn Road B3
Ebury Road D2	St Albans Road B1
Essex Road A1	St John's Road B1
Estcourt Road C2	St Mary's Road B4
Exchange Road B3	St Pauls Way D1
Farraline Road B4	Shady Lane B1
Feranley Street B4	Shaftesbury Road D2
Francis Road B3	Smith Street C4
Franklin Road B3	Sotheron Road C2
Gartlet Road C2	Southsea Avenue A4
Gaumont Approach B2	Stanley Road C3
George Street C4	Station Road B1
Gladstone Road D3	Stephenson Way D3
Granville Road C4	Sutton Road C2
Grosvenor Road C3	The Avenue A1
Halsey Road B2	The Broadway C3
Harwoods Road....................A4	The Crescent C4
Hempstead Road A1	The Parade B2
High Street C3	Upton Road B3
Hyde Road A2	Vicarage Road B4
Keele Close C1	Water Lane D4
King Street C4	Wellington Road B1
Lady's Close C4	Wellstones B3
Link Road D1	Westland Road B1
Loates Lane C3	West Street..........................B1
Lord Street C3	Whippendell Road A4
Lower High Street D4	Wiggenhall Road....................B4
Malden Road A1	Woodford Road C1
Market Street B4	

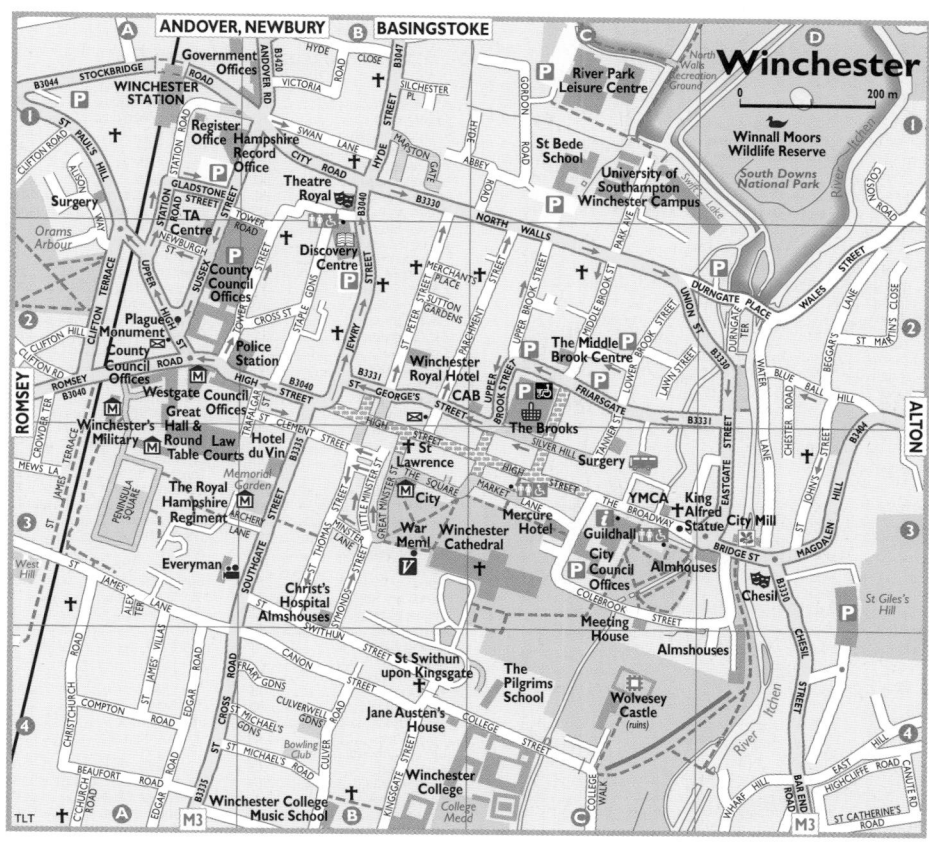

Winchester

Winchester is found on atlas page **22 E9**

Alex Terrace	A3	Market Lane	C3
Alison Way	A1	Marston Gate	B1
Andover Road	B1	Merchants Place	B2
Archery Lane	A3	Mews Lane	A3
Bar End Road	D4	Middle Brook Street	C2
Beaufort Road	A4	Minster Lane	B3
Beggar's Lane	D2	Newburgh Street	A2
Blue Ball Hill	D2	North Walls	C1
Bridge Street	D3	Parchment Street	B2
Canon Street	B4	Park Avenue	C2
Canute Road	D4	Romsey Road	A2
Chesil Street	D3	St Clement Street	B2
Chester Road	D2	St Cross Road	A4
Christchurch Road	A4	St George's Street	B2
City Road	B1	St James' Lane	A3
Clifton Hill	A2	St James Terrace	A3
Clifton Road	A1	St James' Villas	A4
Clifton Terrace	A2	St John's Street	D3
Colebrook Street	C3	St Martin's Close	D2
College Street	B4	St Michael's Gardens	B4
College Walk	C4	St Michael's Road	B4
Colson Road	D1	St Paul's Hill	A1
Compton Road	A4	St Peter Street	B2
Cross Street	B2	St Swithun Street	B3
Crowder Terrace	A3	St Thomas Street	B3
Culver Road	B4	Silchester Place	B1
Culverwell Gardens	B4	Silver Hill	C3
Durngate Place	D2	Southgate Street	B3
Durngate Terrace	D2	Staple Gardens	B2
Eastgate Street	D3	Station Road	A1
East Hill	D4	Stockbridge Road	A1
Edgar Road	A4	Sussex Street	A2
Friarsgate	C2	Sutton Gardens	B2
Friary Gardens	B4	Swan Lane	B1
Gladstone Street	A1	Symonds Street	B3
Gordon Road	C1	Tanner Street	C3
Great Minster Street	B3	The Broadway	C3
Highcliffe Road	D4	The Square	B3
High Street	B2	Tower Road	A1
Hyde Abbey Road	B1	Tower Street	A2
Hyde Close	B1	Trafalgar Street	B3
Hyde Street	B1	Union Street	C2
Jewry Street	B2	Upper Brook Street	C2
Kingsgate Street	B4	Upper High Street	A2
Lawn Street	C2	Victoria Road	B1
Little Minster Street	B3	Wales Street	D2
Lower Brook Street	C2	Water Lane	D3
Magdalen Hill	D3	Wharf Hill	D4

Wolverhampton

Wolverhampton is found on atlas page **58 D5**

Bath Avenue	A1	Peel Street	B3
Bath Road	A2	Penn Road	B4
Bell Street	B3	Piper's Row	D2
Berry Street	C2	Pitt Street	B3
Bilston Road	D3	Powlett Street	D4
Bilston Street	C3	Princess Street	C2
Birch Street	B2	Queen Square	B2
Broad Street	C2	Queen Street	C2
Castle Street	C3	Raby Street	D4
Chapel Ash	A3	Raglan Street	A3
Church Lane	B4	Red Lion Street	B2
Church Street	B4	Retreat Street	A4
Clarence Road	B2	Ring Road St Andrews	A2
Clarence Street	B2	Ring Road St Davids	D2
Cleveland Road	D4	Ring Road St Georges	C4
Cleveland Street	B3	Ring Road St Johns	B4
Corn Hill	D2	Ring Road St Marks	B3
Culwell Street	D1	Ring Road St Patricks	C1
Dale Street	A4	Ring Road St Peters	B2
Darlington Street	B3	Russell Street	A4
Dudley Road	C4	St George's Parade	C3
Dudley Street	C2	St John's Square	C4
Fold Street	B3	St Mark's Road	A3
Fryer Street	C2	St Mark's Street	A3
Garrick Street	C3	Salop Street	B3
Graiseley Street	A4	School Street	B3
Great Brickkiln Street	A4	Skinner Street	B3
Great Western Street	C1	Snow Hill	C3
Grimstone Street	D1	Stafford Street	C1
Horseley Fields	D2	Stephenson Street	A3
Hospital Street	D4	Stewart Street	B4
Lansdown Road	A1	Summer Row	B3
Lever Street	C4	Tempest Street	C3
Lichfield Street	C2	Temple Street	B3
Little's Lane	C1	Thomas Street	B4
Long Street	C2	Tower Street	C3
Lord Street	A3	Vicarage Road	D4
Mander Street	A4	Victoria Street	B3
Market Street	C3	Walsall Street	D3
Merridale Street	A4	Warwick Street	D3
Middle Cross	D3	Waterloo Road	B1
Mitre Fold	B2	Wednesfield Road	D1
Molineux Street	B1	Westbury Street	C2
New Hampton Road East	A1	Whitemore Hill	B1
North Street	B2	Whitmore Street	C2
Park Avenue	A1	Worcester Street	B4
Park Road East	B1	Wulfruna Street	C2
Park Road West	A2	Zoar Street	A4

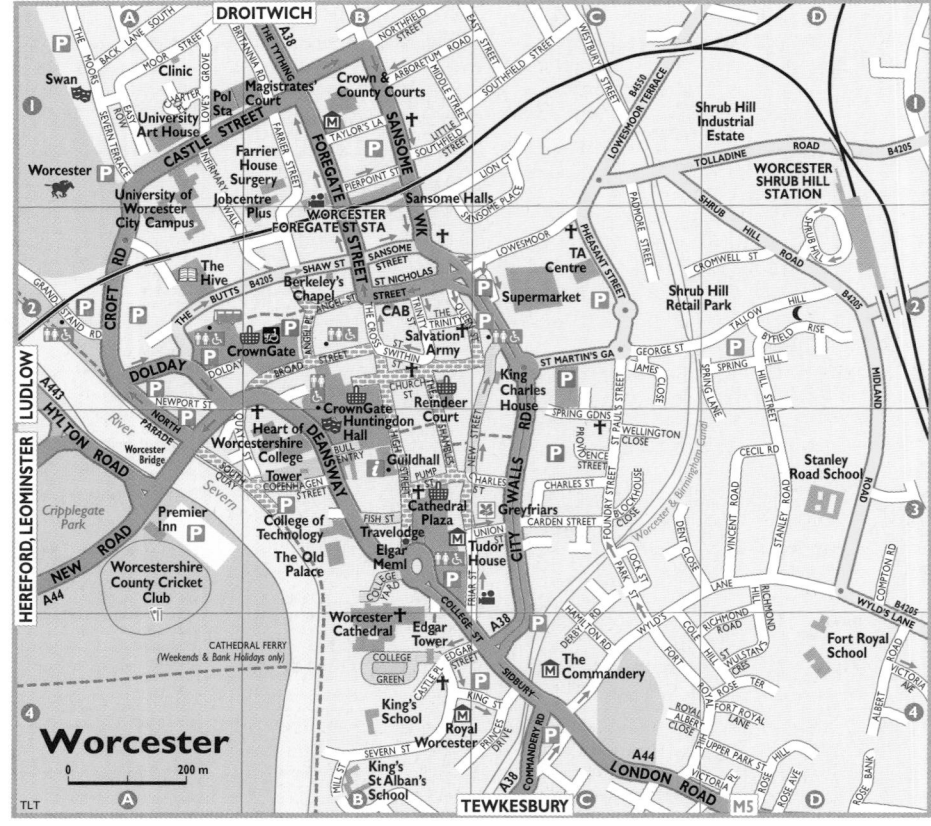

Worcester

Worcester is found on atlas page **46 G4**

Albert Road	D4	Middle Street	B1
Angel Street	B2	Midland Road	D2
Arboretum Road	B1	Mill Street	B4
Back Lane South	A1	Moor Street	A1
Blockhouse Close	C3	Newport Street	A2
Britannia Road	A1	New Road	A3
Broad Street	B2	New Street	C3
Byfield Rise	D2	Northfield Street	B1
Carden Street	C3	North Parade	A3
Castle Street	A1	Padmore Street	C1
Cathedral Ferry	A4	Park Street	C3
Cecil Road	D3	Pheasant Street	C2
Charles Street	C3	Pierpoint Street	B1
Charter Place	A1	Providence Street	C3
Church Street	B2	Pump Street	B3
City Walls Road	C3	Quay Street	A3
Cole Hill	C4	Queen Street	B2
College Street	B3	Richmond Road	D4
Commandery Road	C4	Rose Hill	D4
Compton Road	D3	Rose Terrace	D4
Copenhagen Street	B3	St Martin's Gate	C2
Croft Road	A2	St Nicholas Street	B2
Cromwell Street	D2	St Paul's Street	C3
Deansway	B3	St Swithin Street	B2
Dent Close	C3	Sansome Walk	B1
Derby Road	C4	Severn Street	B4
Dolday	A2	Severn Terrace	A1
East Street	B1	Shaw Street	B2
Edgar Street	B4	Shrub Hill Road	D2
Farrier Street	B1	Sidbury	C4
Fish Street	B3	Southfield Street	C1
Foregate Street	B1	Spring Hill	D2
Fort Royal Hill	C4	Stanley Road	D3
Foundry Street	C3	Tallow Hill	D2
Friar Street	C3	Taylor's Lane	B1
George Street	C2	The Butts	A2
Grandstand Road	A2	The Cross	B2
Hamilton Road	C3	The Moors	A1
High Street	B3	The Shambles	B2
Hill Street	D2	The Tything	B1
Hylton Road	A3	Tolladine Road	C1
King Street	B4	Trinity Street	B2
Little Southfield Street	B1	Union Street	C3
Lock Street	C3	Upper Park Street	D4
London Road	C4	Vincent Road	D3
Love's Grove	A1	Wellington Close	C3
Lowesmoor	C2	Westbury Street	C1
Lowesmoor Terrace	C1	Wyld's Lane	C4

York

York is found on atlas page **98 C10**

Aldwark	C2	Lower Ousegate	C3
Barbican Road	D4	Lower Priory Street	B3
Bishopgate Street	B4	Low Petergate	C2
Bishophill Senior	B3	Margaret Street	D3
Black Horse Lane	D2	Market Street	C2
Blake Street	B2	Micklegate	A3
Blossom Street	A4	Minster Yard	B1
Bootham	B1	Monkgate	C1
Bridge Street	B3	Museum Street	B2
Buckingham Street	B3	Navigation Road	D3
Cemetery Road	D4	New Street	B2
Church Street	C2	North Street	B2
Clifford Street	C3	Nunnery Lane	A3
College Street	C1	Ogleforth	C1
Colliergate	C2	Palmer Lane	D2
Coney Street	B2	Palmer Street	D2
Coppergate	C3	Paragon Street	D4
Cromwell Road	B4	Parliament Street	C2
Davygate	B2	Pavement	C2
Deangate	C1	Peasholme Green	D2
Dove Street	B4	Percy's Lane	D3
Duncombe Place	B2	Piccadilly	C3
Dundas Street	D2	Price's Lane	B4
Fairfax Street	B3	Priory Street	C3
Fawcett Street	D4	Queen Street	A3
Feasegate	C2	Rougier Street	B2
Fetter Lane	B3	St Andrewgate	C2
Finkle Street	C2	St Denys' Road	D3
Fishergate	D4	St Leonard's Place	B1
Foss Bank	D1	St Martins Lane	B3
Fossgate	C2	St Maurice's Road	C1
Foss Islands Road	D2	St Saviourgate	C2
George Street	D3	St Saviours Place	C2
Gillygate	B1	Scarcroft Road	A4
Goodramgate	C2	Shambles	C2
Hampden Street	B4	Skeldergate	B3
High Ousegate	C3	Spen Lane	C2
High Petergate	B1	Spurriergate	B2
Holgate Road	A4	Station Road	A3
Hope Street	D4	Stonegate	B2
Hungate	D2	Swinegate	C2
Jewbury	D1	The Stonebow	C2
Kent Street	D4	Toft Green	A3
King Street	C3	Tower Street	C3
Kyme Street	B4	Trinity Lane	B3
Lendal	B2	Victor Street	B4
Long Close Lane	D4	Walmgate	D3
Lord Mayor's Walk	C1	Wellington Road	B2

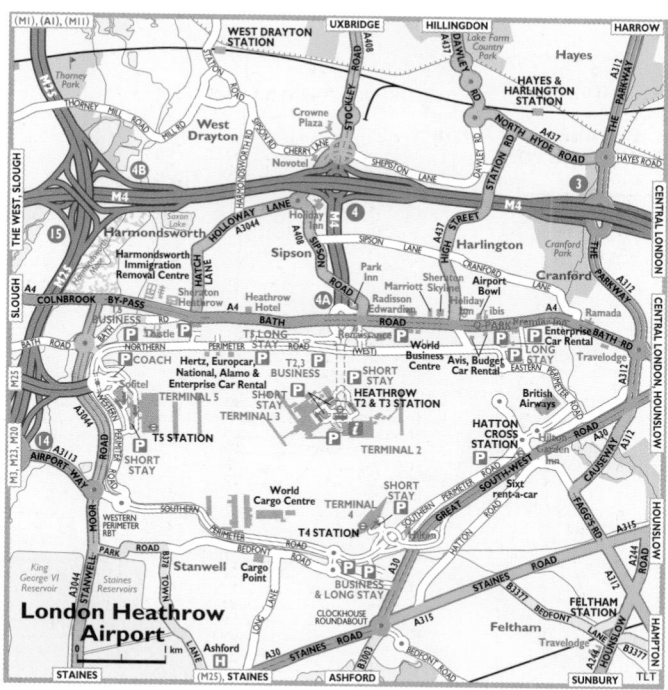

London Heathrow Airport – 17 miles west of central London, M25 junction 14 and M4 junction 4A

Satnav Location: TW6 1EW (Terminal 2), TW6 1QG (T3), TW6 3XA (T4), TW6 2GA (T5)
Information: visit www.heathrow.com
Parking: short-stay, long-stay and business parking is available.
Public Transport: coach, bus, rail and London Underground.
There are several 4-star and 3-star hotels within easy reach of the airport.
Car hire facilities are available.

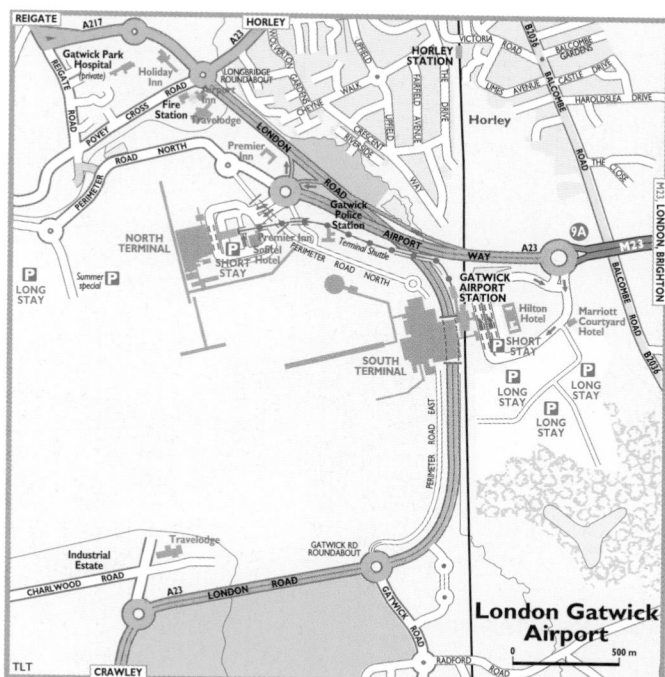

London Gatwick Airport – 29 miles south of central London, M23 junction 9A

Satnav Location: RH6 0NP (South terminal), RH6 0PJ (North terminal)
Information: visit www.gatwickairport.com
Parking: short and long-stay parking is available at both the North and South terminals.
Public Transport: coach, bus and rail.
There are several 4-star and 3-star hotels within easy reach of the airport.
Car hire facilities are available.

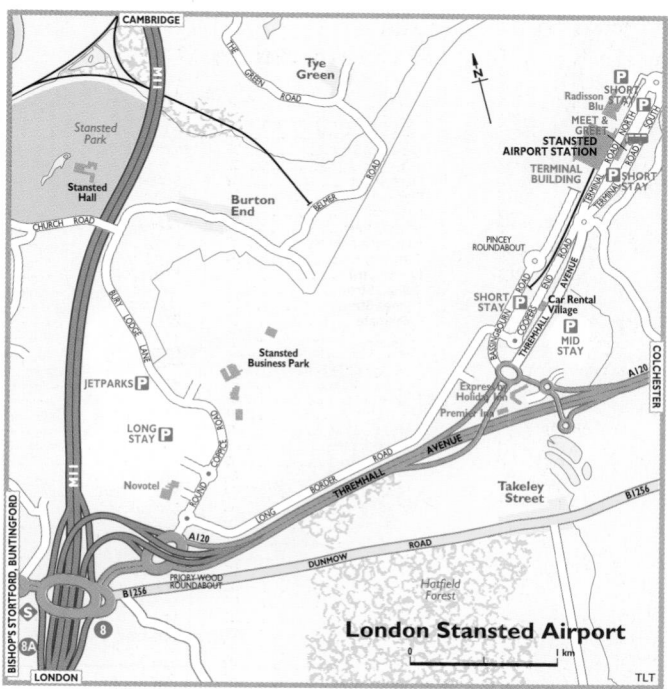

London Stansted Airport – 36 miles north-east of central London, M11 junction 8/8A

Satnav Location: CM24 1RW
Information: visit www.stanstedairport.com
Parking: short, mid and long-stay open-air parking is available.
Public Transport: coach, bus and direct rail link to London on the Stansted Express.
There are several hotels within easy reach of the airport.
Car hire facilities are available.

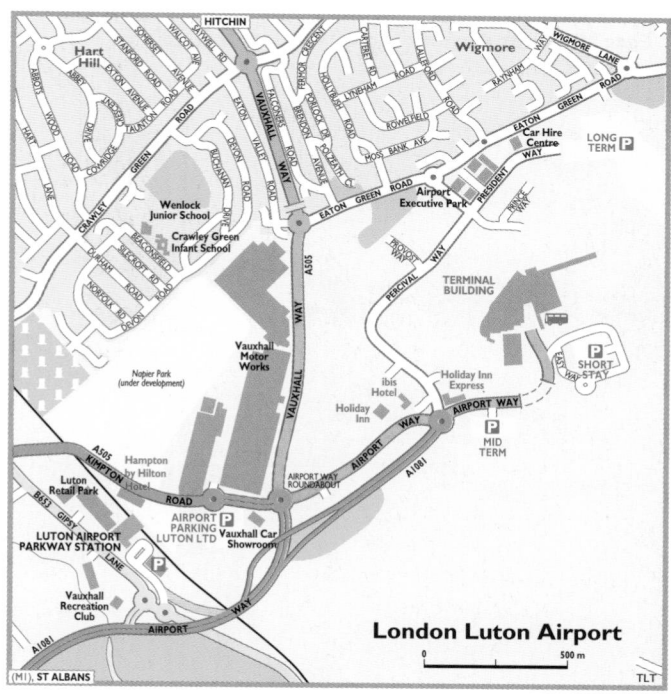

London Luton Airport – 34 miles north of central London

Satnav Location: LU2 9QT
Information: visit www.london-luton.co.uk
Parking: short-term, mid-term and long-stay parking is available.
Public Transport: coach, bus and rail.
There are several hotels within easy reach of the airport.
Car hire facilities are available.

London City Airport – 8 miles east of central London

Satnav Location: E16 2PX
Information: visit *www.londoncityairport.com*
Parking: short and long-stay open-air parking is available.
Public Transport: easy access to the rail network, Docklands Light Railway and the London Underground.
There are 5-star, 4-star and 3-star hotels within easy reach of the airport.
Car hire facilities are available.

Birmingham Airport – 10 miles east of Birmingham, M42 junction 6

Satnav Location: B26 3QJ
Information: visit *www.birminghamairport.co.uk*
Parking: short and long-stay parking is available.
Public Transport: Air-Rail Link service operates every 2 minutes to and from Birmingham International Railway Station & Interchange.
There are several 4-star and 3-star hotels within easy reach of the airport.
Car hire facilities are available.

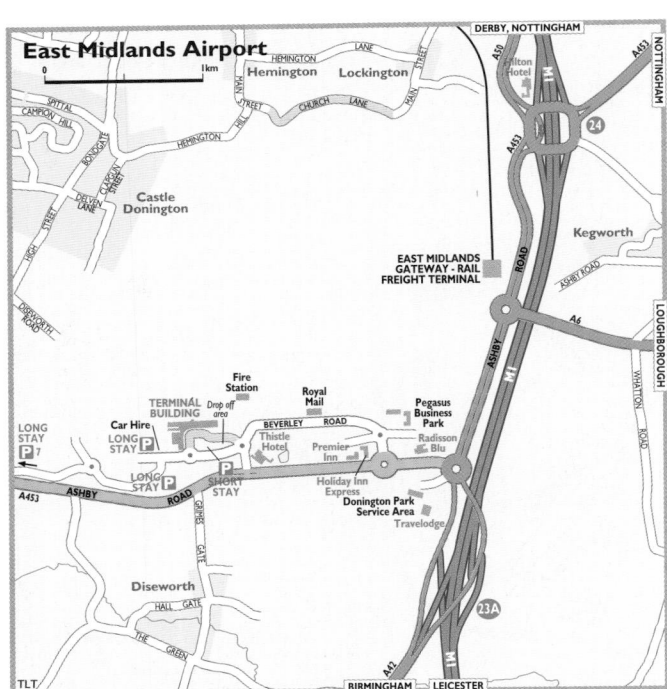

East Midlands Airport – 14 miles south-west of Nottingham, M1 junction 23A/24

Satnav Location: DE74 2SA
Information: visit *www.eastmidlandsairport.com*
Parking: short and long-stay parking is available.
Public Transport: bus and coach services to major towns and cities in the East Midlands.
There are several 3-star hotels within easy reach of the airport.
Car hire facilities are available.

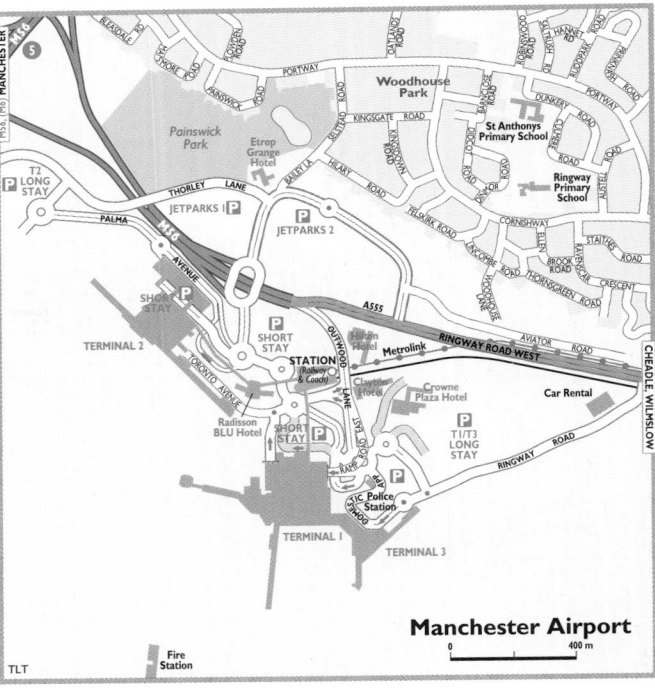

Manchester Airport – 10 miles south of Manchester, M56 junction 5

Satnav Location: M90 1QX
Information visit *www.manchesterairport.co.uk*
Parking: short and long-stay parking is available.
Public Transport: coach, bus and rail.
There are several 4-star and 3-star hotels within easy reach of the airport.
Car hire facilities are available.

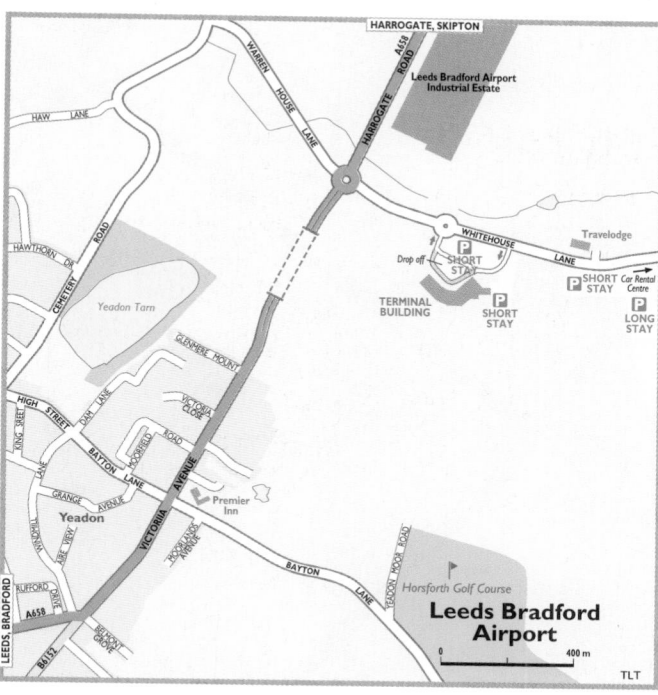

Leeds Bradford Airport – 8 miles north-east of Bradford and 8 miles north-west of Leeds

Satnav Location: LS19 7TU
Information: visit *www.leedsbradfordairport.co.uk*
Parking: short, mid-term and long-stay parking is available.
Public Transport: bus service operates every 30 minutes from Bradford, Leeds and Otley.
There are several 4-star and 3-star hotels within easy reach of the airport.
Car hire facilities are available.

Aberdeen Airport – 7 miles north-west of Aberdeen

Satnav Location: AB21 7DU
Information: visit *www.aberdeenairport.com*
Parking: short and long-stay parking is available.
Public Transport: regular bus service to central Aberdeen.
There are several 4-star and 3-star hotels within easy reach of the airport.
Car hire facilities are available.

Edinburgh Airport – 9 miles west of Edinburgh

Satnav Location: EH12 9DN
Information: visit *www.edinburghairport.com*
Parking: short and long-stay parking is available.
Public Transport: regular bus services to central Edinburgh, Glasgow and Fife
and a tram service to Edinburgh.
There are several 4-star and 3-star hotels within easy reach of the airport.
Car hire and valet parking facilities are available.

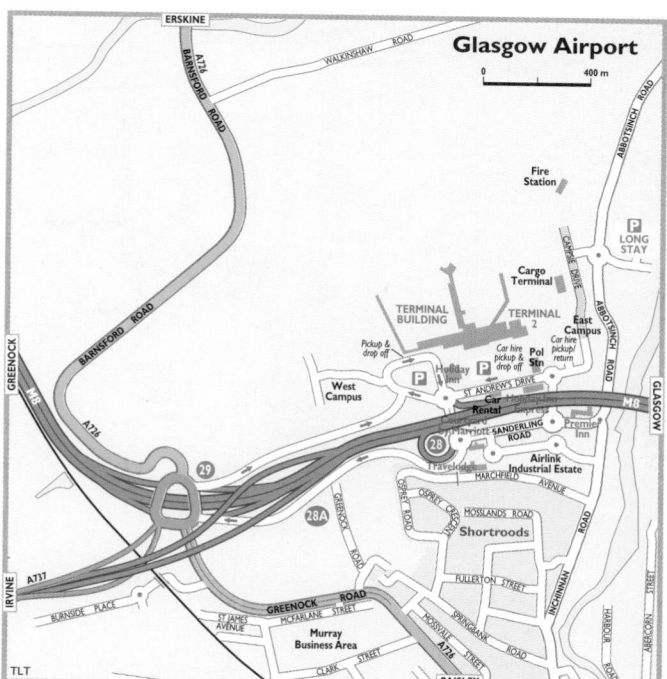

Glasgow Airport – 10 miles west of Glasgow, M8 junction 28/29

Satnav Location: PA3 2SW
Information: visit *www.glasgowairport.com*
Parking: short and long-stay parking is available.
Public Transport: regular coach services operate direct to central Glasgow.
There are several 3-star hotels within easy reach of the airport.
Car hire facilities are available.

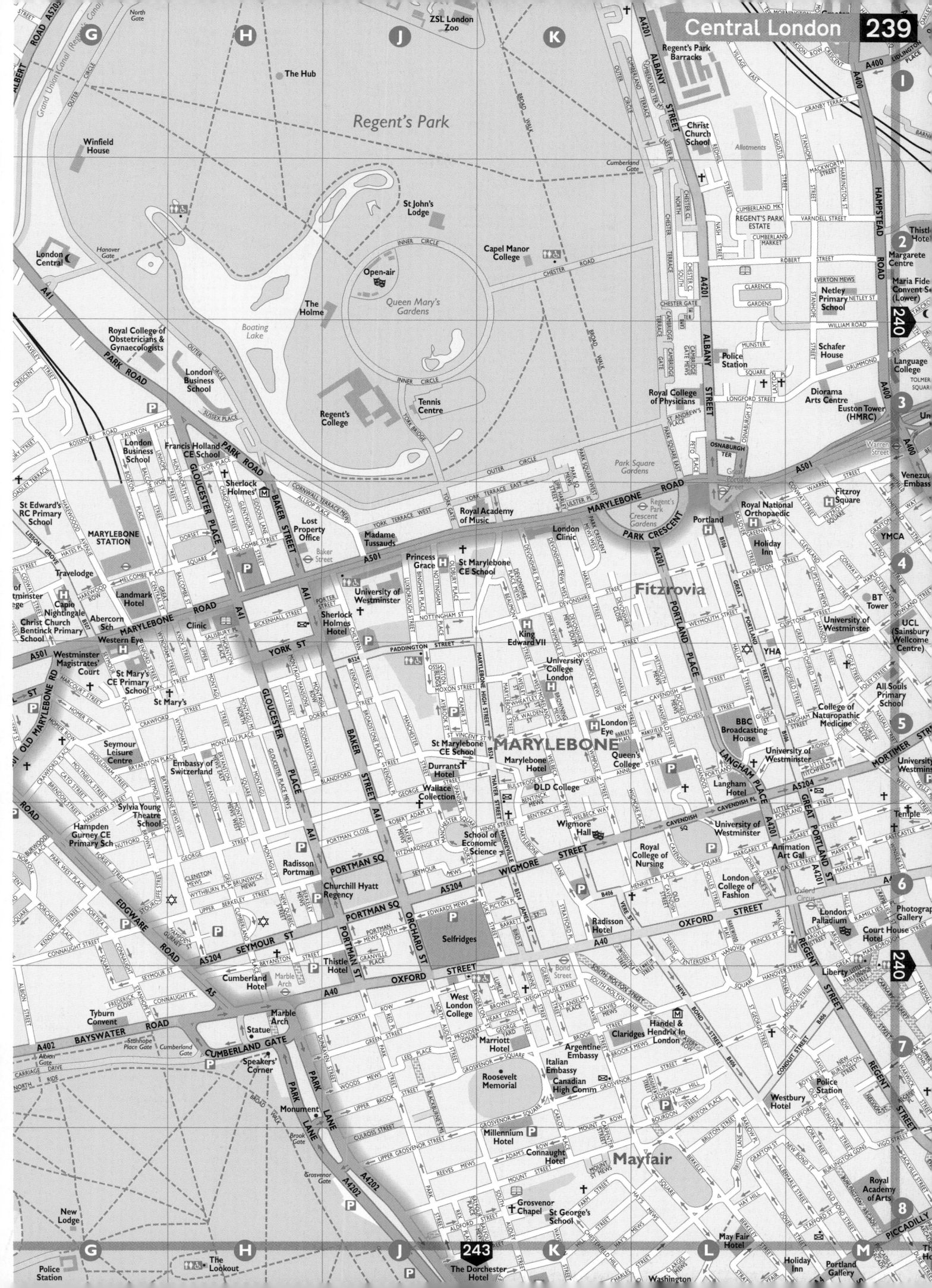

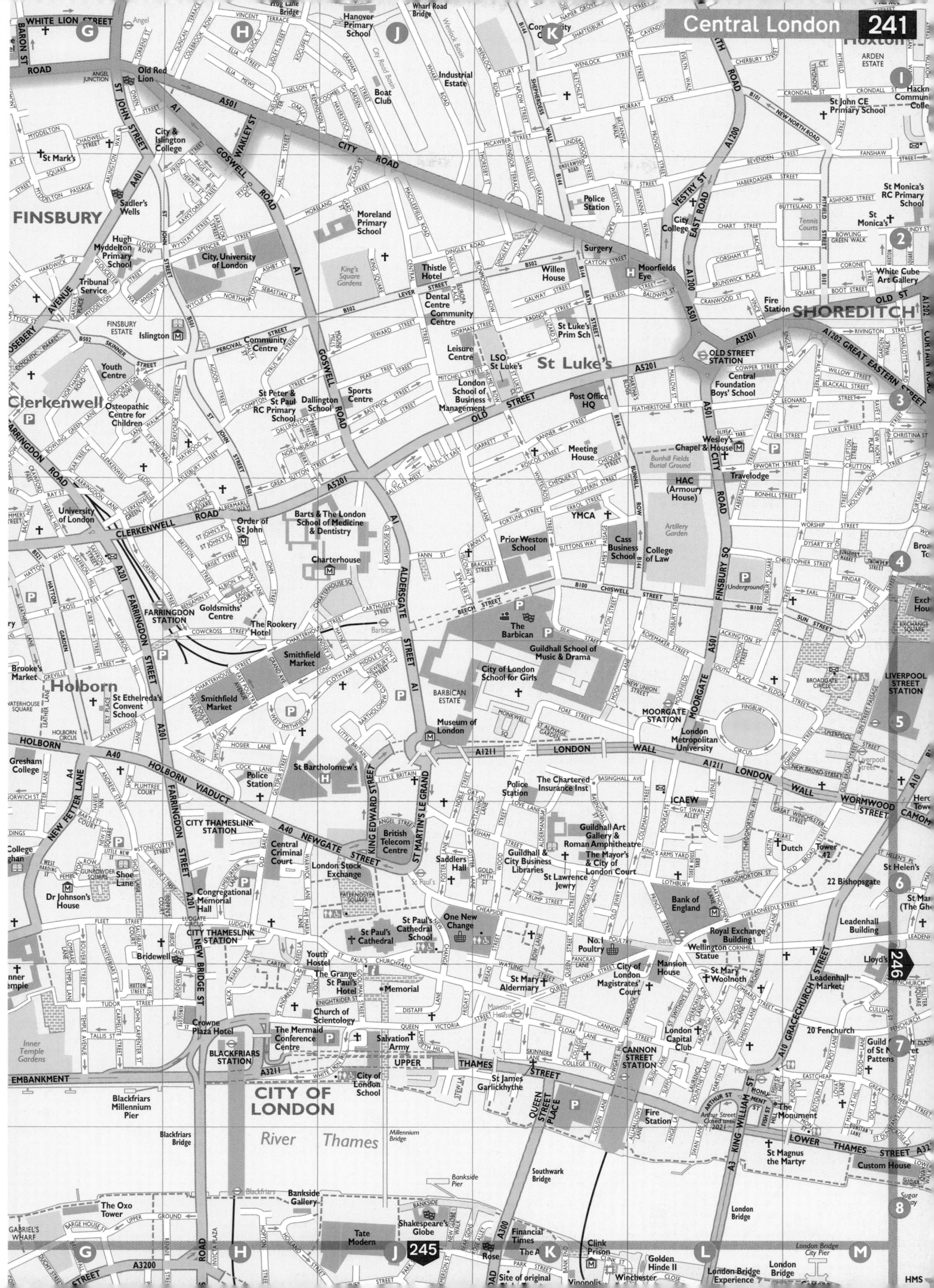

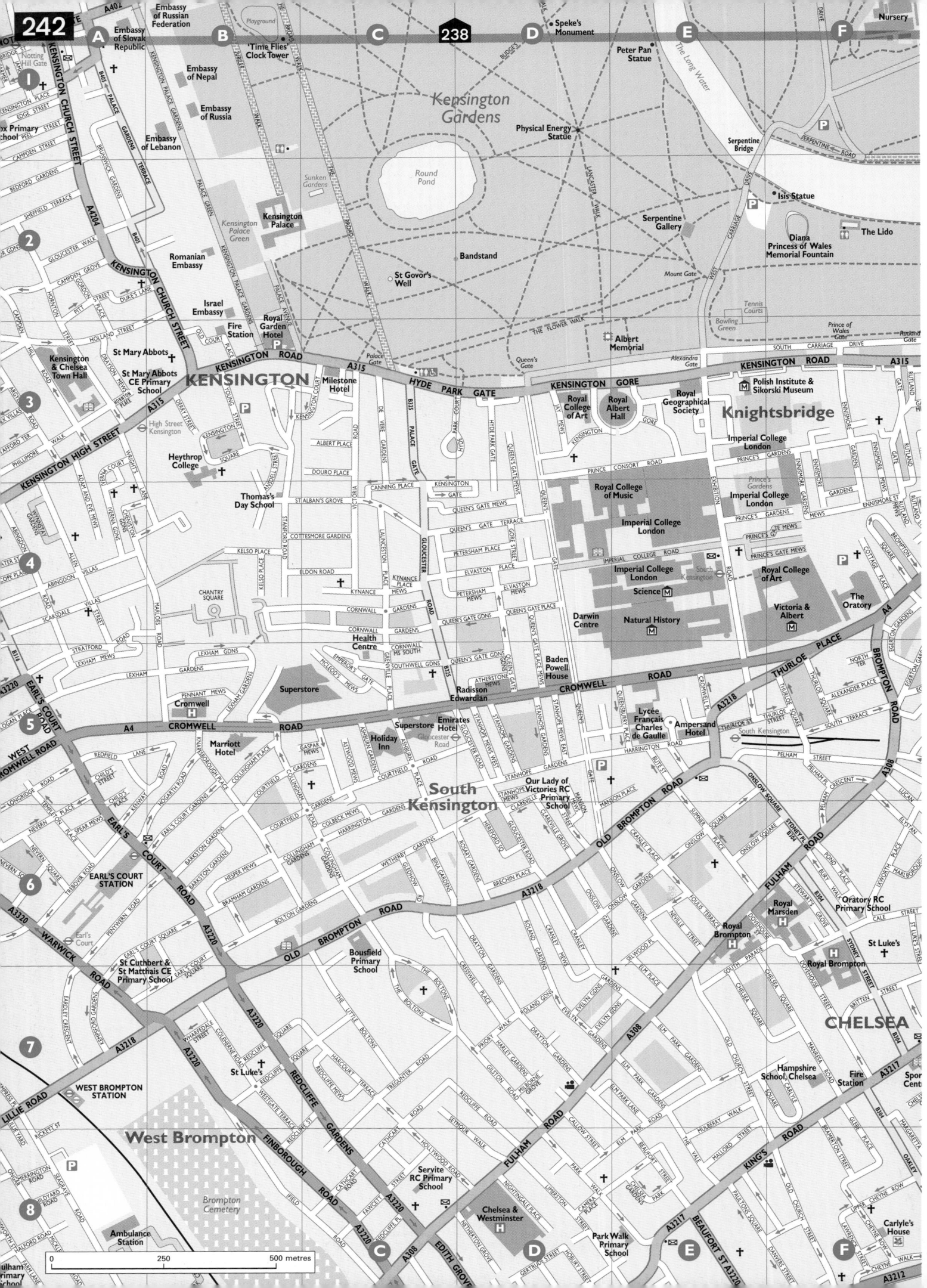

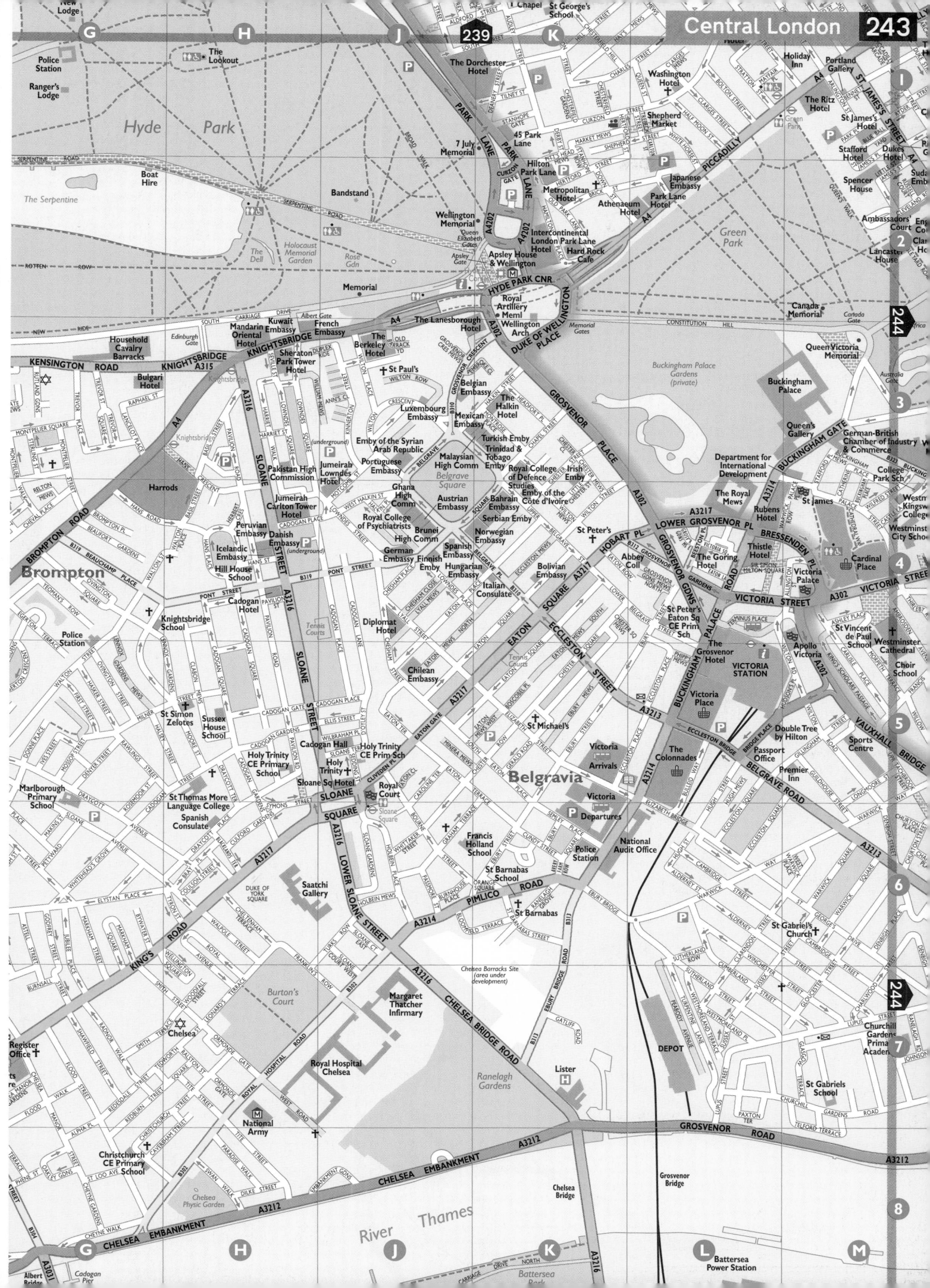

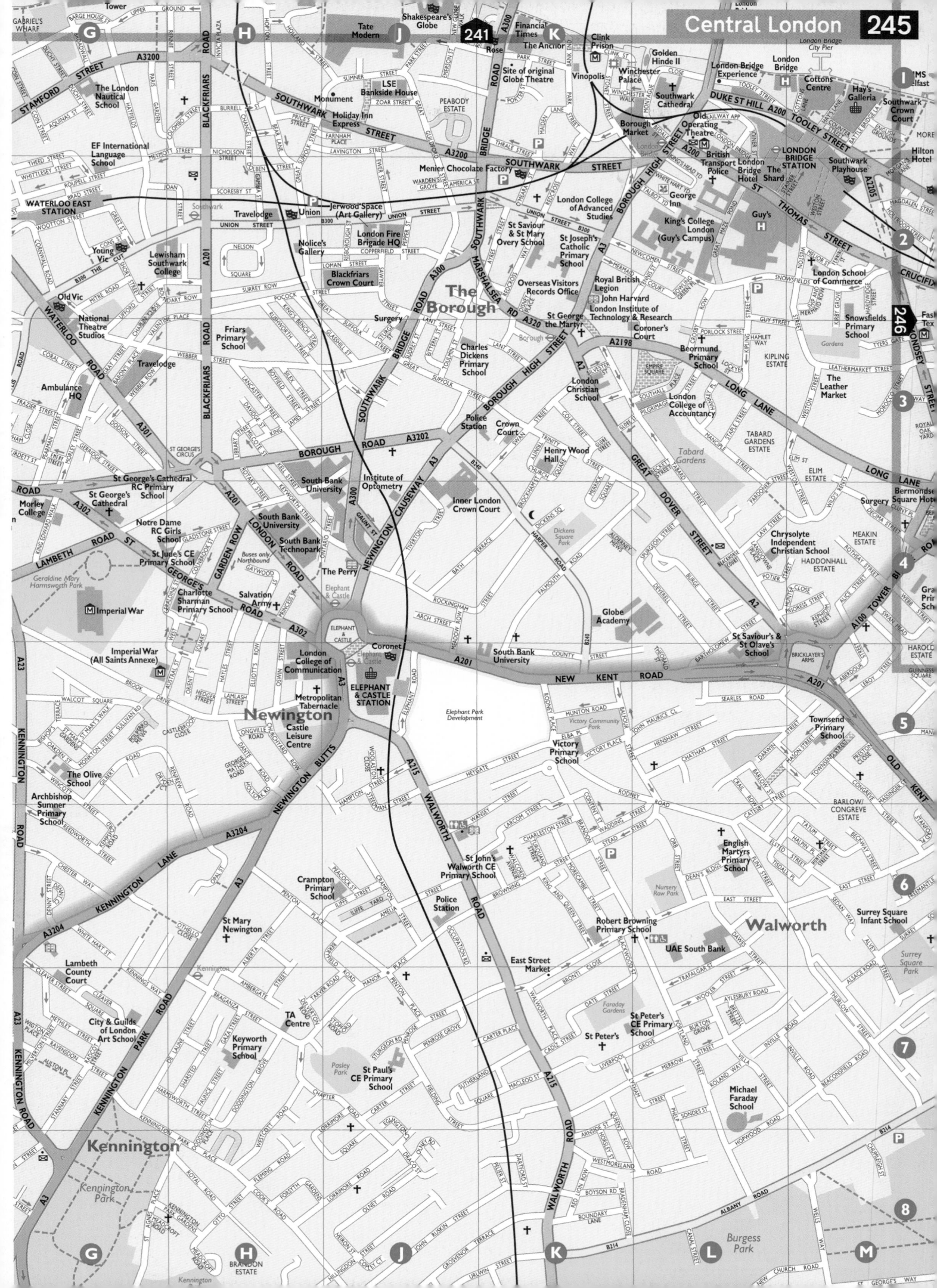

This index lists street and station names, and top places of tourist interest shown in red. Names are listed in alphabetical order and written in full, but may be abbreviated on the map. Each entry is followed by its Postcode District and then the page number and grid reference to the square in which the name is found. Names are asterisked (*) in the index where there is insufficient space to show them on the map.

A

Abbey Gardens NW8....238 C1
Abbey Orchard Street SW1P....244 B4
Abbey Road NW8....238 D1
Abbey Street SE1....246 B7
Abchurch Lane EC4N....241 L7
Abercorn Close NW8....238 C1
Abercorn Place NW8....238 C1
Aberdeen Place NW8....238 E3
Abingdon Road W8....242 A4
Abingdon Street SW1P....244 C3
Abingdon Villas W8....242 A4
Ackroyd Drive E3....247 L1
Acorn Walk SE16....247 K5
Acton Street WC1X....240 E2
Adam and Eve Mews W8....242 A3
Adam's Row W1K....239 K8
Adam Street WC2N....240 D8
Addington Street SE1....244 E3
Addle Hill EC4V....241 H7
Adelina Grove E1....246 F1
Adeline Place WC1B....240 B5
Adler Street E1....246 D2
Admiral Place SE16....247 K5
Admiral Walk W9....238 A4
Adpar Street W2....238 E4
Agar Street WC2N....240 D8
Agdon Street EC1V....241 H3
Agnes Street E14....247 L2
Ainsty Street SE16....247 G6
Air Street W1B....240 A8
Alaska Street SE1....244 F2
Albany Road SE5....245 L8
Albany Street NW1....239 L1
Albemarle Street W1S....239 L8
Albemarle Way EC1V....241 H4
Alberta Street SE17....245 H6
Albert Bridge SW3....243 G8
Albert Embankment SE1....244 D7
Albert Gardens E1....247 H3
Albert Gate SW1X....243 H2
Albert Place W8....242 C3
Albion Gate W2....239 G7
Albion Place EC1M....241 H4
Albion Place SE16....247 H4
Albion Street W2....239 G7
Aldenham Street NW1....240 A1
Aldermanbury EC2V....241 K6
Alderney Mews SE1....245 L4
Alderney Street SW1V....243 L6
Aldford Street W1K....239 J8
Aldgate EC3M....246 B3
Aldgate EC3M....246 B3
Aldgate East E1....246 C2
Aldgate High Street EC3N....246 B3
Aldgate Square EC3N....246 B3
Aldsworth Close W9....238 B4
Aldwych WC2E....240 E7
Alexander Place SW7....242 F5
Alexander Street W2....238 A6
Alexandra Gate SW7....242 E3
Alfred Mews WC1E....240 B4
Alfred Place WC1E....240 B4
Alfred Road W2....238 A5
Alice Street SE1....245 M4
Alie Street E1....246 C3
Allen Street W8....242 A4
Allhallows Lane EC4R....241 L8
Allington Street SW1E....243 M4
Allitsen Road NW8....238 F1
Allsop Place NW1....239 H4
Alma Square NW8....238 D1
Alpha Place SW3....243 G8
Alsace Road SE17....245 M6
Alscot Road * SE1....246 C8
Alvey Street SE17....245 M6
Ambergate Street SE17....245 H7
Amberley Road W9....238 A4
Ambrosden Avenue SW1P....244 A4
Amelia Street SE17....245 J6
America Square EC3N....246 B3
America Street SE1....245 J2
Ampton Street WC1X....240 E2
Amwell Street EC1R....240 F2
Anchorage Point E14....247 M6
Andover Place NW6....238 B1
Angel N1....241 G1
Angela Hooper Place * SW1E....244 A4
Angel Junction N1....241 G1
Angel Lane EC4R....241 L8
Angel Street EC1A....241 J6
Ann Moss Way SE16....246 F8
Ann's Close SW1X....243 J3
Ansdell Street W8....242 B4
Antill Terrace E1....247 H2
Antizan Street E1....246 B2
Apple Tree Yard SW1Y....240 A8
Appold Street EC2A....241 M4
Apsley Gate SW1X....243 J2
Apsley House & Wellington Museum W1J....243 K2
Aquinas Street SE1....245 G1
Arbour Square E1....247 H2
Archangel Street SE16....247 J7
Archer Street W1B....240 B7
Arch Street SE1....245 J4
Arden Estate N1....241 M1
Argyle Square WC1H....240 D2
Argyle Street WC1H....240 D2
Argyll Road W8....242 A3
Argyll Street W1F....239 M6
Arlington Street SW1A....243 M1
Arlington Way EC1R....241 G2
Arne Street WC2H....240 D6
Arneway Street SW1P....244 B5
Arnhem Place E14....247 M8
Arnold Estate SE1....246 C7
Arnside Street SE17....245 K8
Artesian Road W11....238 A6
Arthur Street EC4V....241 L7
Artichoke Hill E1....246 E4
Artillery Lane E1....246 A1
Artillery Row SW1P....244 B4
Arundel Street WC2R....240 F7

Ashbridge Street NW8....238 F4
Ashburn Gardens SW7....242 C5
Ashburn Place SW7....242 C5
Ashby Street EC1V....241 H2
Asher Way E1W....246 D4
Ashfield Street E1....246 E2
Ashford Street N1....241 M2
Ashley Place SW1P....243 M4
Ashmill Street NW1....238 F4
Ashmole Street SW8....244 F8
Ashworth Road W9....238 B2
Assam Street E1....246 C2
Assembly Passage E1....247 G1
Astell Street SW3....243 G6
Aston Street E14....247 K1
Astwood Mews SW7....242 C5
Atherstone Mews SW7....242 D5
Atterbury Street SW1P....244 C6
Attneave Street WC1X....240 F3
Augustus Street NW1....239 L1
Aulton Place SE11....245 G7
Austin Friars EC2N....241 L6
Australia Gate SW1A....243 M3
Austral Street SE11....245 H5
Aveline Street SE11....244 F7
Ave Maria Lane EC1A....241 H6
Avenue Dock Hill SE16....247 J6
Avery Farm Row SW1W....243 K6
Avery Row W1K....239 L7
Aybrook Street W1U....239 J5
Aylesbury Road SE17....245 L7
Aylesbury Street EC1R....241 H4
Aylesford Street SW1V....244 B7
Aylward Street E1....247 G2
Ayres Street SE1....245 K2

B

Babmaes Street SW1Y....240 B8
Bache's Street N1....241 L2
Back Church Lane E1....246 D3
Back Hill EC1R....241 G4
Bacon Grove SE1....246 B8
Bainbridge Street WC1A....240 C6
Bakers Mews W1U....239 J6
Baker's Row EC1R....241 G4
Baker Street NW1....239 H4
Baker Street W1U....239 J5
Balcombe Street NW1....239 G3
Balderton Street W1K....239 J7
Baldwin's Gardens EC1N....240 F5
Baldwin Street EC1V....241 L2
Bale Road E1....247 J1
Balfe Street N1....240 D1
Balfour Mews W1K....239 K8
Balfour Place W1K....239 J8
Balfour Street SE17....245 K5
Baltic Street East EC1Y....241 J3
Baltic Street West EC1Y....241 J4
Balvaird Place SW1V....244 C7
Bank EC2R....241 L6
Bank End SE1....245 K1
Bankside SE1....241 J8
Banner Street EC1Y....241 K3
Banqueting House SW1A....244 C2
Banyard Road SE16....246 E8
Barbican EC1A....241 J4
Barbican Estate EC2Y....241 J5
Barge House Street SE1....245 G1
Bark Place W2....238 B7
Barkston Gardens SW5....242 B6
Barley Corn Way E14....247 L4
Barlow/Congreve Estate SE17....245 M5
Barlow Place W1J....239 L7
Barlow Street SE17....245 L5
Barnardo Street E1....247 H3
Barnby Street NW1....240 A1
Barnes Street E14....247 J2
Barnham Street SE1....246 A6
Baron's Place SE1....245 G3
Baron Street N1....241 G1
Barrett Street W1U....239 K6
Barrow Hill Estate NW8....238 F1
Barrow Hill Road NW8....238 F1
Barter Street WC1A....240 D5
Bartholomew Close EC1A....241 J5
Bartholomew Lane EC2R....241 L6
Bartholomew Street SE1....245 L5
Bartlett Court EC4A....241 G6
Barton Street SW1P....244 C4
Basil Street SW3....243 H4
Basin Approach E14....247 K3
Basinghall Avenue EC2V....241 K5
Basinghall Street EC2V....241 K5
Bastwick Street EC1V....241 J3
Bateman's Buildings W1D....240 B6
Bateman Street W1D....240 B6
Bath Street EC1V....241 K2
Bath Terrace SE1....245 J4
Bathurst Mews W2....238 E7
Bathurst Street W2....238 E7
Battle Bridge Lane SE1....245 M1
Batty Street E1....246 D2
Bayley Street WC1B....240 B5
Baylis Road SE1....244 F3
Bayswater W2....238 B7
Bayswater Road W2....238 E7
Baythorne Street E3....247 L1
Beaconsfield Road SE17....245 M7
Beak Street W1F....240 A7
Bear Gardens SE1....241 J8
Bear Lane SE1....245 H1
Beauchamp Place SW3....243 G4
Beaufort Gardens SW3....243 G4
Beaufort Street SW3....242 E8
Beaumont Place W1T....240 A3
Beaumont Street W1G....239 K4
Beccles Street E14....247 M3
Beckett Street E1....245 L3
Beckway Street SE17....245 M6
Bedale Street SE1....245 L1
Bedford Avenue WC1B....240 C5
Bedfordbury WC2N....240 C7
Bedford Gardens W8....242 A2
Bedford Place WC1N....240 D4

Bedford Row WC1R....240 E4
Bedford Square WC1B....240 B5
Bedford Street WC2E....240 D7
Bedford Way WC1H....240 C3
Bedlow Close NW8....238 F3
Beech Street EC2Y....241 J4
Beeston Place SW1W....243 L4
Belgrave Mews North * SW1X....243 J3
Belgrave Mews South * SW1X....243 K4
Belgrave Place SW1X....243 J4
Belgrave Road SW1V....243 L5
Belgrave Road SW1V....244 A6
Belgrave Square SW1X....243 J3
Belgrave Street E1....247 J2
Belgrove Street WC1H....240 D2
Bell Lane E1....246 B1
Bell Street NW1....238 F4
Bell Yard WC2A....240 F6
Belvedere Road SE1....244 E2
Benjamin Street EC1M....241 H4
Ben Jonson Road E1....247 J1
Bennett Street SW1A....243 M1
Ben Smith Way SE16....246 D7
Benson Quay E1W....246 F4
Bentinck Mews W1U....239 K6
Bentinck Street W1U....239 K6
Bere Street E1W....247 H3
Bergen Square SE16....247 K8
Berkeley Mews W1H....239 H6
Berkeley Square W1J....239 L8
Berkeley Street W1J....239 L8
Bermondsey SE16....246 A7
Bermondsey Spa SE16....246 C8
Bermondsey Square SE1....246 A8
Bermondsey Street SE1....246 A6
Bermondsey Wall East SE16....246 D6
Bermondsey Wall Estate SE16....246 D7
Bermondsey Wall West SE16....246 C6
Bernard Street WC1N....240 D4
Berners Mews W1T....240 A5
Berners Place W1F....240 A6
Berners Street W1T....240 A5
Bernhardt Crescent NW8....238 F3
Berryfield Road SE17....245 J6
Berry Street EC1V....241 H3
Berwick Street W1F....240 A6
Bessborough Gardens SW1V....244 C6
Bessborough Street SW1V....244 B6
Betterton Street WC2H....240 D6
Bevenden Street N1....241 L2
Bevin Close SE16....247 J5
Bevington Street SE16....246 D7
Bevin Way WC1X....240 F1
Bevis Marks EC3A....246 A2
Bewley Street E1....246 F3
Bickenhall Street W1U....239 H4
Bidborough Street WC1H....240 C2
Biddulph Road W9....238 B2
Big Ben (Elizabeth Tower) SW1A....244 D3
Bigland Street E1....246 E3
Billiter Square EC3M....246 A3
Billiter Street EC3M....246 A3
Bina Gardens SW5....242 C6
Bingham Place W1U....239 J4
Binney Street W1K....239 K7
Birchfield Street E14....247 M3
Birchin Lane EC3V....241 L7
Birdcage Walk SW1H....244 A3
Birde Lane EC4Y....241 H6
Bird Street W1C....239 K6
Birkenhead Street N1....240 D1
Bishop's Bridge Road W2....238 C6
Bishopsgate EC2M....246 A2
Bishops Square E1....246 B1
Bishop's Terrace SE11....245 G5
Bittern Street SE1....245 J3
Blackall Street EC2A....241 M3
Blackburne's Mews W1K....239 J7
Blackfriars EC4V....241 H7
Blackfriars Bridge SE1....241 H8
Blacklands Terrace SW3....243 H6
Black Friars Lane EC4V....241 H7
Blackfriars Road SE1....245 H3
Blackhorse Court SE1....245 L4
Black Lion Gate W2....238 B8
Black Prince Road SE11....244 E6
Blackwood Street SE17....245 K6
Blandford Street W1U....239 H5
Blenheim Street W1S....239 L7
Bletchley Street N1....241 K1
Blomfield Mews W2....238 C5
Blomfield Road W9....238 C4
Blomfield Street EC2M....241 M5
Blomfield Villas W2....238 C5
Bloomfield Terrace SW1W....243 J6
Bloomsbury Square WC1A....240 D5
Bloomsbury Street WC1B....240 C5
Bloomsbury Way WC1A....240 C5
Blount Street E14....247 K2
Blue Ball Yard SW1A....243 M1
Bohn Road E1....247 J1
Bolsover Street W1W....239 L4
Bolton Gardens SW5....242 B6
Bolton Street W1J....243 L1
Bond Street W1C....239 K6
Bondway SW8....244 D8
Bonhill Street EC2A....241 L4
Bonnington Square SW8....244 E8
Boot Street N1....241 M2
Borough SE1....245 K3
Borough High Street SE1....245 K3
Borough Road SE1....245 H3
Boscobel Place SW1W....243 K5
Boscobel Street NW8....238 E4
Boss Street SE1....246 B6
Boston Place NW1....239 G3
Botolph Lane EC3R....241 M7
Boundary Lane SE17....245 K8
Boundary Row SE1....245 G2
Bourdon Street W1K....239 L7
Bourlet Close W1W....239 M5
Bourne Estate EC1N....241 G4
Bourne Street SW1W....243 J6
Bourne Terrace W2....238 B5
Bouverie Place W2....238 F6
Bouverie Street EC4Y....241 G6
Bowland Yard * SW1X....243 J3
Bow Lane EC4M....241 K6

Bowling Green Lane EC1R....241 G3
Bowling Green Place SE1....245 L2
Bowling Green Street SE11....244 F8
Bowling Green Walk N1....241 M2
Boswell Street WC1N....240 D4
Bow Street WC2E....240 D7
Boyd Street E1....246 D3
Boyfield Street SE1....245 H3
Boyle Street W1S....239 M7
Boyson Road SE17....245 K8
Brackley Street EC1Y....241 J4
Bradenham Close SE17....245 K8
Brad Street SE1....245 G2
Braganza Street SE17....245 H7
Braham Street E1....246 C3
Bramerton Street SW3....242 F7
Bramham Gardens SW5....242 B6
Branch Road E14....247 J3
Brandon Estate SE17....245 H8
Brandon Street SE17....245 K6
Brangton Road SE11....244 F7
Bray Crescent SE16....247 H6
Bray Place SW3....243 H6
Bread Street EC4M....241 K7
Bream's Buildings EC4A....240 F6
Brechin Place SW7....242 D6
Breezer's Hill E1W....246 D4
Brendon Street W1H....239 G5
Bressenden Place SW1W....243 L4
Brettell Street SE17....245 L7
Brewers Green SW1H....244 A3
Brewer Street W1F....240 A7
Brewhouse Lane E1W....246 F6
Brewhouse Walk SE16....247 J5
Brick Court WC2R....240 F7
Brick Lane E1....246 C1
Brick Street W1J....243 K2
Bridewell Place EC4V....241 H7
Bridgeman Street NW8....238 F1
Bridge Place SW1V....243 L5
Bridgeport Place E1W....246 D4
Bridge Street SW1A....244 D3
Bridgewater Street EC2Y....241 J4
Bridgeway Street NW1....240 A1
Bridle Lane W1F....240 A7
Bridstow Place W2....238 A6
Brightlingsea Place E14....247 L4
Brill Place NW1....240 C1
Briset Street EC1M....241 H4
Bristol Gardens W9....238 B4
Britannia Street WC1X....240 E2
Britannia Walk N1....241 L2
Britannia Way N1....241 K1
Britten Street SW3....242 F7
Britton Street EC1M....241 H4
Broadbent Street W1K....239 L7
Broadgate Circle EC2M....241 M5
Broadley Street NW8....238 F4
Broadley Terrace NW1....239 G4
Broadstone Place W1U....239 J5
Broad Walk NW1....239 K1
Broad Walk W2....239 H7
Broadwall SE1....245 G1
Broadway SW1H....244 B4
Broadwick Street W1F....240 A7
Brockham Street SE1....245 K4
Brodlove Lane E1W....247 H3
Bromley Street E1....247 J2
Brompton Place SW3....243 G4
Brompton Road SW3....243 G4
Brompton Road SW7....242 F5
Brompton Square SW3....243 G4
Bronti Close SE17....245 K7
Brook Drive SE11....245 G5
Brooke Street EC1N....240 F5
Brook Gate W1K....239 H8
Brook Mews North W2....238 D7
Brook's Mews W1K....239 L7
Brook Street W1K....239 K7
Brook Street W2....238 E7
Brown Heart Gardens W1K....239 K7
Browning Mews W1G....239 K5
Browning Street SE17....245 K6
Brownlow Mews WC1N....240 E3
Brownlow Street WC1V....240 E5
Brown Street W1H....239 G6
Brunel Road SE16....247 G6
Brune Street E1....246 B1
Brunswick Close SE1....246 A6
Brunswick Gardens W8....242 A1
Brunswick Place N1....241 L2
Brunswick Quay SE16....247 J8
Brunswick Square WC1N....240 D3
Brunton Place E14....247 K3
Brushfield Street E1....246 B1
Bruton Lane W1J....239 L8
Bruton Place W1J....239 L8
Bruton Street W1J....239 L8
Bryan Road SE16....247 K6
Bryanston Mews West W1H....239 G5
Bryanston Mews East W1H....239 H5
Bryanston Place W1H....239 G5
Bryanston Square W1H....239 H5
Bryanston Street W1C....239 H7
Buck Hill Walk W2....238 E8
Buckingham Gate SW1E....243 L3
Buckingham Mews SW1E....243 M3
Buckingham Palace SW1A....243 L3
Buckingham Palace Road SW1W....243 L5
Buckingham Place SW1E....243 M4
Buckland Street N1....241 L1
Buckle Street E1....246 C2
Bucknall Street WC2H....240 C6
Buckters Rents SE16....247 J5
Budge's Walk W2....238 C8
Bulleid Way SW1V....243 L5
Bulstrode Street W1U....239 K5
Bunhill Row EC1Y....241 L3
Burdett Estate E14....247 L2
Burdett Road E14....247 L2
Burdett Street SE1....244 F4
Burgess Street E14....247 M1
Burge Street SE1....245 L4
Burlington Arcade W1J....239 M8
Burlington Gardens W1S....239 M8
Burnhouse Place SW1W....243 J6
Burnsall Street SW3....243 G7

Burnside Close SE16....247 J5
Burrell Street SE1....245 H1
Burslem Street E1....246 D3
Burton Grove SE17....245 L7
Burton Street WC1H....240 C3
Burwood Place W2....239 G6
Bury Close SE16....247 H5
Bury Court EC3A....246 A2
Bury Place WC1A....240 D5
Bury Street EC3A....246 A2
Bury Street SW1Y....244 A1
Bury Walk SW3....242 F6
Bushell Street E1W....246 D5
Bush Lane EC4V....241 L7
Butcher Row E14....247 J3
Bute Street SW7....242 E5
Butler Place SW1H....244 B4
Butler's Wharf SE1....246 C6
Buttesland Street N1....241 L2
Byefield Close SE16....247 K6
Bylands Close SE16....247 J5
Byng Place WC1E....240 B4
Byng Street E14....247 M6
Byward Street EC3R....246 A4
Bywater Place SE16....247 K5
Bywater Street SW3....243 G6

C

Cabbell Street NW1....238 F5
Cable Street E1....246 F3
Cadiz Street SE17....245 K7
Cadogan Gardens SW3....243 H5
Cadogan Gate SW1X....243 H5
Cadogan Lane SW1X....243 J4
Cadogan Place SW1X....243 J4
Cadogan Square SW1X....243 H5
Cadogan Street SW3....243 G5
Caledonian Road N1....240 D1
Caledonia Street N1....240 D1
Cale Street SW3....242 F6
Callow Street SW3....242 D7
Calshot Street N1....240 E1
Calthorpe Street WC1X....240 E3
Cambridge Circus WC2H....240 C7
Cambridge Gardens NW6....238 A1
Cambridge Gate NW1....239 L3
Cambridge Road NW6....238 A1
Cambridge Road NW6....238 A2
Cambridge Square W2....238 F6
Cambridge Street SW1V....243 L6
Cambridge Terrace NW1....239 L3
Cambridge Terrace Mews NW1....239 L3
Camdenhurst Street E14....247 K2
Camera Place SW10....242 D8
Camomile Street EC3A....246 A2
Campden Grove W8....242 A2
Campden Hill Road W8....242 A2
Campden Street W8....242 A1
Camperdown Street E1....246 C3
Canada Estate SE16....247 G7
Canada Gate SW1A....243 M3
Canada Water SE16....247 H7
Canada Wharf SE16....247 L5
Canal Street SE5....245 L8
Canary Riverside E14....247 L4
Candle Street E1....247 K1
Canning Place W8....242 C4
Cannon Drive E14....247 M4
Cannon Street EC4N....241 K7
Cannon Street EC4R....241 K7
Cannon Street Road E1....246 E3
Canon Beck Road SE16....247 G6
Canon Row SW1A....244 D3
Canton Street E14....247 M3
Capeners Close * SW1X....243 J3
Capland Street NW8....238 E3
Capper Street WC1E....240 A4
Capstan Way SE16....247 K5
Carbis Road E14....247 L2
Cardigan Street SE11....244 F6
Cardington Street NW1....240 A2
Carey Street WC2A....240 F6
Carlisle Avenue EC3N....246 B3
Carlisle Lane SE1....244 E4
Carlisle Place SW1P....243 M4
Carlisle Street W1D....240 B6
Carlos Place W1K....239 K7
Carlton Gardens SW1Y....244 B2
Carlton Hill NW6....238 B1
Carlton House Terrace SW1Y....244 B1
Carlton Vale NW6....238 A1
Carlton Vale NW6....238 B1
Carlyle Square SW3....242 F7
Carmelite Street EC4Y....241 G7
Carnaby Street W1F....239 M7
Caroline Place W2....238 B7
Caroline Street E1....247 H3
Caroline Terrace SW1W....243 J5
Carpenter Street W1K....239 K7
Carrington Street W1J....243 L1
Carr Street E14....247 K1
Carteret Street SW1H....244 B3
Carter Lane EC4V....241 H7
Carter Place SE17....245 K7
Carter Street SE17....245 J7
Carthusian Street EC1M....241 J4
Carting Lane WC2R....240 D8
Cartwright Gardens WC1H....240 C2
Cartwright Street E1....246 C4
Casey Close NW8....238 F3
Casson Street E1....246 C1
Castellain Road W9....238 B3
Castle Lane SW1E....243 M4
Castlebrook Close SE11....245 H5
Catesby Street SE17....245 L6
Cathay Street SE16....246 F7
Cathcart Road SW10....242 C8
Cathedral Walk SW1E....243 M4
Catherine Place SW1E....243 M4
Catherine Street WC2E....240 D7
Cato Street W1H....239 G5
Causton Street SW1P....244 B6

Cavell Street E1 .... 246 F1
Cavendish Avenue NW8 .... 238 E1
Cavendish Place W1G 239 L6
Cavendish Square W1G 239 L6
Cavendish Street N1 .... 241 L1
Caversham Street SW3 .... 243 G8
Caxton Street SW1H 244 B4
Cayton Street EC1V 241 K2
Centaur Street SE1 .... 244 F4
Central Street EC1V 241 J2
Chadwell Street EC1R 241 G1
Chadwick Street SW1P 244 B4
Chagford Street NW1 .... 239 H4
Chalton Street NW1 .... 240 B1
Chambers Street SE16 .... 246 D7
Chamber Street E1 .... 246 C3
Chambers Wharf SE16 .... 246 D6
Chancel Street SE1 .... 245 H1
Chancery Lane WC2A 240 F5
Chancery Lane WC1V 240 F5
Chandos Place WC2N 240 C8
Chandos Street W1G 239 L5
Chantry Square W8 .... 242 B4
Chapel Market N1 .... 240 F1
Chapel Street NW1 .... 238 F5
Chapel Street SW1X 243 K3
Chaplin Close SE1 .... 245 G3
Chapman Street E1 .... 246 E3
Chapter Road SE17 .... 245 H7
Chapter Street SW1P 244 B6
Chargrove Close SE16 .... 247 H6
Charing Cross ⇌ ⊖ WC2N 244 D1
Charing Cross Road WC2H 244 B6
Charing Cross Road WC2N 240 C7
Charlbert Street NW8 .... 238 F1
Charles II Street SW1Y 240 B8
Charles Square N1 .... 241 M2
Charles Street W1J 243 K1
Charleston Street SE17 .... 245 K6
Charlotte Road EC2A 241 M3
Charlotte Street W1T 240 A4
Charlwood Place SW1V 244 A6
Charlwood Street SW1V 243 M7
Charlwood Street SW1V 244 A6
Charrington Street NW1 .... 240 B1
Charterhouse Square EC1M 241 H4
Charterhouse Street EC1M 241 G5
Chart Street N1 .... 241 L2
Chaseley Street E14 .... 247 J2
Chatham Street SE17 .... 245 L5
Cheapside EC2V 241 K6
Chelsea Bridge SW1W 243 K8
Chelsea Bridge Road SW1W 243 J7
Chelsea Embankment SW3 .... 243 G8
Chelsea Manor Gardens SW3 .... 242 F7
Chelsea Manor Street SW3 .... 242 F7
Chelsea Park Gardens SW3 .... 242 D7
Chelsea Physic Garden SW3 .... 243 H8
Chelsea Square SW3 .... 242 E7
Cheltenham Terrace SW3 .... 243 H6
Chenies Mews WC1E 240 B4
Chenies Street WC1E 240 B4
Cheniston Gardens W8 .... 242 A4
Chepstow Place W2 .... 238 A7
Chepstow Road W2 .... 238 A6
Chequer Street EC1Y 241 K3
Cherbury Street N1 .... 241 L1
Cherry Garden Street SE16 .... 246 E7
Chesham Close SW1X 243 J4
Chesham Place SW1X 243 J4
Chesham Street SW1X 243 J4
Chester Close SW1X 243 K3
Chester Close North NW1 .... 239 L2
Chester Close South NW1 .... 239 L2
Chesterfield Gardens W1J 243 K1
Chesterfield Hill W1J 239 K8
Chesterfield Street W1J 243 K1
Chester Gate NW1 .... 239 L2
Chester Mews SW1X 243 K3
Chester Place NW1 .... 239 L1
Chester Road NW1 .... 239 K2
Chester Row SW1W 243 J5
Chester Square SW1W 243 K5
Chester Square Mews SW1W 243 K4
Chester Street SW1X 243 K4
Chester Terrace NW1 .... 239 L2
Chester Way SE11 .... 245 G6
Cheval Place SW7 .... 243 G4
Cheval Street E14 .... 247 M7
Cheyne Gardens SW3 .... 243 G8
Cheyne Row SW3 .... 242 F8
Cheyne Walk SW3 .... 242 F8
Chicheley Street SE1 .... 244 E2
Chichester Road NW6 .... 238 A1
Chichester Road W2 .... 238 C5
Chichester Street SW1V 244 A7
Chicksand Street E1 .... 246 C1
Chigwell Hill E1W 246 E4
Child's Place SW5 .... 242 A5
Child's Street SW5 .... 242 A5
Chiltern Street W1U 239 J4
Chilworth Mews W2 .... 238 D6
Chilworth Street W2 .... 238 C6
China Hall Mews SE16 .... 247 G8
Chinatown W1D 240 B7
Chippenham Mews W9 .... 238 A4
Chiswell Street EC1Y 241 K4
Chitty Street W1T 240 A4
Christchurch Street SW3 .... 243 G8
Christian Street E1 .... 246 D3
Christina Street EC2A 241 M3
Christopher Close SE16 .... 247 H6
Christopher Street EC2A 241 L4
Chudleigh Street E1 .... 247 H2
Chumleigh Street SE5 .... 245 M8
Churchill Gardens Road SW1V 243 L7
Churchill War Rooms SW1A 244 C3
Church Street NW8 .... 238 F4
Church Way NW1 .... 240 B2
Churchyard Row SE1 .... 245 H5
Churton Place SW1V 244 A6
Churton Street SW1V 244 A6
Circus Road NW8 .... 238 E1
Cirencester Square W2 .... 238 A5
City Garden Row N1 .... 241 J1
City Road N1 .... 241 J1
City Road EC1Y 241 L3
City Thameslink ⇌ EC4M 241 H6
Clabon Mews SW1X 243 H5
Clack Street SE16 .... 247 G7
Clanricarde Gardens W2 .... 238 A8
Clarkson Row N1 .... 239 M1
Claremont Square N1 .... 240 F1
Clarence Gardens NW1 .... 239 L2
Clarence Mews SE16 .... 247 G6
Clarendon Gardens W9 .... 238 D4

Clarendon Gate W2 .... 238 F7
Clarendon Place W2 .... 238 F7
Clarendon Street SW1V 243 L6
Clareville Grove SW7 .... 242 D6
Clareville Street SW7 .... 242 D6
Clarges Mews W1J 243 L1
Clarges Street W1J 243 L1
Clark Street E1 .... 246 F2
Carkson Row E1 .... 239 M1
Claverton Street SW1V 244 A7
Clave Street E1W 246 F5
Clay Street W1U 239 H5
Clayton Street SE11 .... 244 F8
Cleaver Square SE11 .... 245 G7
Cleaver Street SE11 .... 245 G7
Clegg Street E1W 246 F5
Clemence Street E14 .... 247 L2
Clements Lane EC4N 241 L7
Clement's Road SE16 .... 246 E8
Clenston Mews W1H 239 H6
Clere Street EC2A 241 L3
Clerkenwell Close EC1R 241 G3
Clerkenwell Green EC1R 241 G4
Clerkenwell Road EC1M 241 G4
Cleveland Gardens W2 .... 238 C6
Cleveland Mews W1T 239 M4
Cleveland Place SW1Y 244 A1
Cleveland Row SW1A 244 A2
Cleveland Square W2 .... 238 C6
Cleveland Street W1T 239 M4
Cleveland Terrace W2 .... 238 D6
Clifford Street W1S 239 M7
Clifton Gardens W9 .... 238 C4
Clifton Place SE16 .... 247 G6
Clifton Place W2 .... 238 E7
Clifton Road W9 .... 238 D3
Clifton Street EC2A 241 M3
Clifton Villas W9 .... 238 C4
Clink Street SE1 .... 245 K1
Clipper Close SE16 .... 247 H6
Clipstone Mews W1W 239 M4
Clipstone Street W1W 239 L4
Cliveden Place SW1W 243 J5
Cloak Lane EC4R 241 K7
Cloth Fair EC1A 241 J5
Cloth Street EC1A 241 J5
Cluny Place SE1 .... 246 A8
Cobb Street E1 .... 246 B2
Cobourg Street NW1 .... 240 A2
Coburg Close SW1P 244 A5
Cochrane Mews NW8 .... 238 E1
Cochrane Street NW8 .... 238 E1
Cock Lane EC1A 241 H5
Cockspur Street SW1Y 244 C1
Codling Close * E1W 246 D5
Coin Street SE1 .... 245 G1
Coke Street E1 .... 246 D2
Colbeck Mews SW7 .... 242 C6
Colebrook Row N1 .... 241 H1
Coleherne Road SW10 .... 242 B7
Coleman Street EC2R 241 L6
Cole Street SE1 .... 245 K3
Coley Street WC1X 240 F3
College Hill EC4R 241 K7
College Street EC4R 241 K7
Collett Road SE16 .... 246 D8
Collier Street N1 .... 240 E1
Collingham Gardens SW5 .... 242 B6
Collingham Place SW5 .... 242 B5
Collingham Road SW5 .... 242 B5
Colnbrook Street SE1 .... 245 H4
Colombo Street SE1 .... 245 H1
Colonnade WC1N 240 D4
Coltman Street E14 .... 247 K2
Commercial Road E1 .... 246 D2
Commercial Road E14 .... 247 K3
Commercial Street E1 .... 246 B1
Compton Street EC1V 241 H3
Concert Hall Approach SE1 .... 244 E2
Conder Street E14 .... 247 K2
Conduit Mews W2 .... 238 E6
Conduit Place W2 .... 238 E6
Conduit Street W1S 239 L7
Congreve Street SE17 .... 245 M5
Connaught Close W2 .... 238 F7
Connaught Place W2 .... 239 G7
Connaught Square W2 .... 239 G6
Connaught Street W2 .... 239 G6
Cons Street SE1 .... 245 G2
Constitution Hill SW1A 243 L3
Content Street SE17 .... 245 K5
Conway Street W1T 239 M4
Cookham Crescent SE16 .... 247 H6
Cook's Road SE17 .... 245 H8
Coombs Street N1 .... 241 J1
Cooper's Lane Estate NW1 .... 240 B1
Cooper's Row EC3N 246 B3
Copenhagen Place E14 .... 247 L2
Cope Place W8 .... 242 A4
Copley Court SE17 .... 245 J8
Copley Street E1 .... 247 H1
Copperfield Road E3 .... 247 K1
Copperfield Street SE1 .... 245 J2
Copthall Avenue EC2R 241 L6
Coptic Street WC1A 240 C5
Coral Street SE1 .... 245 G3
Coram Street WC1H 240 C3
Cork Square E1W 246 E5
Cork Street W1S 239 M8
Corlett Street NW1 .... 238 F5
Cornhill EC3V 241 L6
Cornwall Gardens SW7 .... 242 C4
Cornwall Mews South SW7 .... 242 C5
Cornwall Road SE1 .... 244 F1
Cornwall Road SE1 .... 245 G2
Cornwall Street E1 .... 246 E3
Cornwall Terrace Mews NW1 .... 239 H4
Cornwood Drive E1 .... 247 G2
Coronet Street N1 .... 241 M2
Corporation Row EC1R 241 G3
Corsham Street N1 .... 241 L2
Cosser Street SE1 .... 244 F4
Cosway Street NW1 .... 239 G4
Cottage Place SW3 .... 242 F4
Cottesmore Gardens W8 .... 242 B4
Cottons Lane SE1 .... 245 M1
Coulson Street SW3 .... 243 H6
Counter Street SE1 .... 245 M1
County Street SE1 .... 245 K5
Courtenay Square SE11 .... 244 F7
Courtenay Street SE11 .... 244 F6
Courtfield Gardens SW5 .... 242 B5
Courtfield Mews * SW5 .... 242 C5
Courtfield Road SW7 .... 242 C5
Court Street E1 .... 246 E1
Cousin Lane SE1 .... 241 K8

Covent Garden ⊖ WC2E 240 D7
Covent Garden WC2E 240 D7
Coventry Street W1D 240 B8
Cowcross Street EC1M 241 H4
Cowper Street EC2A 241 L3
Crail Row SE17 .... 245 L5
Cramer Street W1U 239 J5
Crampton Street SE17 .... 245 J6
Cranbourn Street WC2H 240 C7
Cranleigh Street NW1 .... 240 A1
Cranley Gardens SW7 .... 242 D6
Cranley Mews SW7 .... 242 D6
Cranley Place SW7 .... 242 E6
Cranston Estate N1 .... 241 L1
Cranwood Street EC1V 241 L2
Craven Hill W2 .... 238 D7
Craven Hill Gardens W2 .... 238 C7
Craven Road W2 .... 238 D7
Craven Street WC2N 244 D1
Craven Terrace W2 .... 238 D7
Crawford Passage EC1R 241 G3
Crawford Place W1H 239 G5
Crawford Street W1H 239 G5
Creechurch Lane EC3A 246 A3
Creed Lane EC4V 241 H7
Cresswell Place SW10 .... 242 D6
Cressy Place E1 .... 247 G1
Crestfield Street WC1H 240 D2
Crimscott Street SE1 .... 246 A8
Crispin Street E1 .... 246 B1
Cromer Street WC1H 240 D2
Crompton Street W2 .... 238 D4
Cromwell Mews * SW7 .... 242 E5
Cromwell Place SW7 .... 242 E5
Cromwell Road SW5 .... 242 B5
Cromwell Road SW7 .... 242 E5
Crondall Court N1 .... 241 M1
Crondall Street N1 .... 241 L1
Cropley Street N1 .... 241 K1
Crosby Row SE1 .... 245 L3
Cross Lane EC3R 246 A4
Crosswall EC3N 246 B3
Crowder Street E1 .... 246 E3
Crucifix Lane SE1 .... 246 A6
Cruikshank Street WC1X 240 F1
Crutched Friars EC3N 246 A3
Cuba Street E14 .... 247 M6
Cubitt Street WC1X 240 E2
Culford Gardens SW3 .... 243 H6
Culling Road SE16 .... 246 F7
Cullum Street EC3M 241 M7
Culross Street W1K 239 J8
Culworth Street NW8 .... 238 F1
Cumberland Gardens WC1X 240 F2
Cumberland Gate W2 .... 239 H7
Cumberland Market NW1 .... 239 L2
Cumberland Street SW1V 243 L6
Cumberland Terrace NW1 .... 239 K1
Cumberland Terrace Mews NW1 .... 239 L1
Cumberland Wharf SE16 .... 247 G6
Cumming Street N1 .... 240 E1
Cundy Street SW1W 243 K6
Cunningham Place NW8 .... 238 E3
Cureton Street SW1P 244 C6
Curlew Street SE1 .... 246 B6
Cursitor Street EC4A 240 F6
Curtain Road EC2A 241 M3
Curtain Road EC2A 241 M4
Curzon Gate W2 .... 243 K2
Curzon Street W1J 243 K1
Cuthbert Street W2 .... 238 E4
Cutler Street EC3A 246 A2
Cynthia Street N1 .... 240 F1
Cypress Place W1T 240 A4
Cyrus Street EC1V 241 H3

D

Dacre Street SW1H 244 B3
Dakin Place E1 .... 247 J1
Dallington Street EC1V 241 H3
Damien Street E1 .... 246 F2
Dane Street WC1R 240 E5
Dansey Place W1D 240 B7
Dante Road SE11 .... 245 H5
Danvers Street SW3 .... 242 F8
D'Arblay Street W1F 240 A6
Dartford Street SE17 .... 245 K8
Dartmouth Street SW1H 244 B3
Darwin Street SE17 .... 245 L5
Date Street SE17 .... 245 K7
Davenant Street E1 .... 246 D1
Daventry Street NW1 .... 238 F4
Davidge Street SE1 .... 245 H3
Davies Mews W1K 239 K7
Davies Street W1K 239 K7
Dawes Street SE17 .... 245 L6
Dawson Place W2 .... 238 A7
Deal Porters Way SE16 .... 247 G8
Deal Street E1 .... 246 D1
Dean Bradley Street SW1P 244 C5
Dean Close SE16 .... 247 H6
Deancross Street E1 .... 246 F3
Deanery Street W1K 243 K1
Dean Farrar Street SW1H 244 B3
Dean Ryle Street SW1P 244 C5
Dean's Buildings SE17 .... 245 L6
Dean Stanley Street SW1P 244 C4
Dean Street W1D 240 B6
Dean's Yard SW1P 244 C4
Decima Street SE1 .... 245 M4
Deck Close SE16 .... 247 J6
Defoe Close SE16 .... 247 K7
Delamere Street W2 .... 238 C5
Delamere Terrace W2 .... 238 B4
De Laune Street SE17 .... 245 H7
Delaware Road W9 .... 238 B3
Dellow Street E1 .... 246 F3
Delverton Road SE17 .... 245 H7
Denbigh Place SW1V 243 M6
Denbigh Street SW1V 243 M6
Denbigh Street SW1V 244 A6
Denman Street W1D 240 B7
Denmark Street WC2H 240 C6
Denny Close SE11 .... 245 G6
Denny Street SE11 .... 245 G6
Denyer Street SW3 .... 243 G5
Derby Gate SW1A 244 D3
Derby Street W1J 243 K1
Dering Street W1S 239 L6
Derry Street W8 .... 242 B3
De Vere Gardens W8 .... 242 C3
Deverell Street SE1 .... 245 L4
Devonport Street E1 .... 247 G3

Devonshire Close W1G 239 K4
Devonshire Mews South W1G 239 K4
Devonshire Mews West W1G 239 K4
Devonshire Place W1G 239 K4
Devonshire Place Mews W1G 239 K4
Devonshire Row EC2M 246 A2
Devonshire Square EC2M 246 A2
Devonshire Street W1G 239 K4
Devonshire Terrace W2 .... 238 D7
De Walden Street W1G 239 K5
Dickens Estate SE16 .... 246 D7
Dickens Square SE1 .... 245 K4
Dilke Street SW3 .... 243 H8
Dingley Place EC1V 241 K2
Dingley Road EC1V 241 J2
Disney Place SE1 .... 245 K2
Distaff Lane EC4V 241 J7
Distin Street SE11 .... 244 F6
Dockhead SE1 .... 246 C7
Dockley Road SE16 .... 246 D8
Dock Street E1 .... 246 D4
Doddington Grove SE17 .... 245 H7
Doddington Place SE17 .... 245 H8
Dodson Street SE1 .... 245 G3
Dod Street E14 .... 247 M2
Dolben Street SE1 .... 245 H2
Dolland Street SE11 .... 244 E7
Dolphin Square SW1V 244 A7
Dolphin Square SW1V 244 B7
Dombey Street WC1N 240 E4
Dominion Drive SE16 .... 247 H7
Dominion Street EC2A 241 L5
Donegal Street N1 .... 240 F1
Dongola Road E1 .... 247 J1
Donne Place SW3 .... 243 G5
Doon Street SE1 .... 245 G1
Dora Street E14 .... 247 L2
Doric Way NW1 .... 240 B2
Dorset Rise EC4Y 241 G7
Dorset Square NW1 .... 239 H4
Dorset Street W1U 239 H5
Doughty Mews WC1N 240 E3
Doughty Street WC1N 240 E3
Douglas Street SW1P 244 B6
Douro Place W8 .... 242 C4
Douthwaite Square * E1W 246 D5
Dovehouse Street SW3 .... 242 F6
Dover Street W1J 243 L1
Dover Street W1S 239 L8
Dowgate Hill EC4R 241 K7
Downfield Close W9 .... 238 B4
Downing Street SW1A 244 C2
Down Street W1J 243 K2
Downtown Road SE16 .... 247 K6
D'Oyley Street SW1X 243 J5
Draco Street SE17 .... 245 J8
Drake Close SE16 .... 247 H6
Draycott Avenue SW3 .... 243 G5
Draycott Place SW3 .... 243 H5
Draycott Terrace SW3 .... 243 H5
Drayson Mews W8 .... 242 A3
Drayton Gardens SW10 .... 242 D6
Druid Street SE1 .... 246 A6
Druid Street SE1 .... 246 B6
Drummond Crescent NW1 .... 240 B2
Drummond Gate * SW1V 244 B6
Drummond Road SE16 .... 246 E8
Drummond Street NW1 .... 240 A3
Drury Lane WC2B 240 D6
Dryden Court SE11 .... 245 G5
Dryden Street WC2B 240 D6
Duchess Mews W1G 239 L5
Duchess Street W1B 239 L5
Duchy Street SE1 .... 245 G1
Duckett Street E1 .... 247 J1
Duck Lane W1F 240 B6
Dufferin Street EC1Y 241 K4
Duke of Wellington Place SW1W 243 K3
Duke of York Square SW3 .... 243 H6
Duke of York Street SW1Y 244 A1
Duke Shore Wharf E14 .... 247 K4
Duke's Lane W8 .... 242 A2
Duke's Place EC3A 246 B2
Duke's Road WC1H 240 C2
Duke Street W1K 239 J6
Duke Street W1U 239 J6
Duke Street Hill SE1 .... 245 L1
Duke Street St James's SW1Y 244 A1
Dunbar Wharf E14 .... 247 L4
Duncannon Street WC2N 240 C8
Duncan Terrace N1 .... 241 H1
Dundee Street E1W 246 E5
Dundee Wharf E14 .... 247 L4
Dunelm Street E1 .... 247 H2
Dunlop Place SE16 .... 246 C8
Dunraven Street W1K 239 H7
Dunster Court EC3R 246 A4
Duplex Ride SW1X 243 H3
Durand's Wharf SE16 .... 247 H7
Durham Row E1 .... 247 J1
Durham Street SE11 .... 244 E7
Durham Terrace W2 .... 238 A6
Dyott Street WC1A 240 C6
Dysart Street EC2A 241 M4

E

Eagle Court EC1M 241 H4
Eagle Street EC1M 240 E5
Eamont Street NW8 .... 239 G1
Eardley Crescent SW5 .... 242 A7
Earlham Street WC2H 240 C7
Earl's Court ⊖ SW5 .... 242 A6
Earl's Court Gardens SW5 .... 242 B6
Earl's Court Road SW5 .... 242 A6
Earl's Court Square SW5 .... 242 A6
Earlstoke Street EC1V 241 H2
Earl Street EC2A 241 M4
Earnshaw Street WC2H 240 C6
East Arbour Street E1 .... 247 H2
Eastbourne Mews W2 .... 238 D6
Eastbourne Terrace W2 .... 238 D6
Eastcastle Street W1W 240 A6
Eastcheap EC3M 241 M7
Eastfield Street E14 .... 247 K1
East India Dock Road E14 .... 247 M3
East Lane SE16 .... 246 D6
Easton Street WC1X 240 F3
East Poultry Avenue EC1A 241 H5
East Road N1 .... 241 L2
East Smithfield E1W 246 C4
East Street SE17 .... 245 L6
East Tenter Street E1 .... 246 C3
Eaton Close SW1W 243 J5

Eaton Gate SW1W 243 J5
Eaton Lane SW1W 243 L4
Eaton Mews North SW1W 243 J5
Eaton Mews South SW1W 243 K5
Eaton Mews West SW1W 243 K5
Eaton Place SW1X 243 J4
Eaton Row SW1W 243 K4
Eaton Square SW1W 243 K5
Eaton Terrace SW1W 243 J5
Ebbisham Drive SW8 .... 244 E8
Ebury Bridge SW1W 243 K6
Ebury Bridge Road SW1W 243 K6
Ebury Mews SW1W 243 K5
Ebury Square SW1W 243 K6
Ebury Street SW1W 243 K5
Eccleston Bridge SW1W 243 L5
Eccleston Mews SW1X 243 K4
Eccleston Place SW1W 243 L5
Eccleston Square SW1V 243 L6
Eccleston Street SW1X 243 K4
Edbrooke Road W9 .... 238 A3
Edge Street W8 .... 242 A1
Edgware Road W2 .... 238 F5
Edgware Road ⊖ NW1 .... 238 F5
Edinburgh Gate SW1X 243 H3
Edith Grove SW10 .... 242 C8
Edwards Mews W1H 239 J6
Egerton Crescent SW3 .... 242 F5
Egerton Gardens SW3 .... 242 F5
Egerton Terrace SW3 .... 243 G4
Eglinton Court SE17 .... 245 J7
Elba Place SE17 .... 245 K5
Eldon Road W8 .... 242 B4
Eldon Street EC2M 241 L5
Eleanor Close SE16 .... 247 H6
Elephant & Castle SE1 .... 245 J4
Elephant & Castle ⇌ ⊖ SE1 .... 245 J5
Elephant Lane SE16 .... 246 F6
Elephant Road SE17 .... 245 J5
Elf Row E1W 247 G3
Elgar Street SE16 .... 247 K7
Elgin Avenue W9 .... 238 B2
Elgin Mews North W9 .... 238 C2
Elgin Mews South W9 .... 238 C2
Elia Mews N1 .... 241 H1
Elia Street N1 .... 241 H1
Elim Estate SE1 .... 245 M3
Elim Street SE1 .... 245 M3
Elizabeth Bridge SW1V 243 L6
Elizabeth Street SW1W 243 K5
Ellen Street E1 .... 246 D3
Elliott's Row SE11 .... 245 H5
Ellis Street SW1X 243 J5
Elmfield Way W9 .... 238 A4
Elm Park Gardens SW10 .... 242 E7
Elm Park Lane SW3 .... 242 E7
Elm Park Road SW3 .... 242 E8
Elm Place SW7 .... 242 E7
Elms Mews W2 .... 238 D7
Elm Street WC1X 240 F4
Elm Tree Road NW8 .... 238 E2
Elnathan Mews W9 .... 238 B4
Elsa Street E1 .... 247 J1
Elsted Street SE17 .... 245 L6
Elvaston Mews SW7 .... 242 D4
Elvaston Place SW7 .... 242 D4
Elverton Street SW1P 244 B5
Ely Place EC1N 241 G5
Elystan Place SW3 .... 243 G6
Elystan Street SW3 .... 242 F6
Embankment ⊖ WC2N 244 D1
Embankment Gardens SW3 .... 243 H8
Embankment Place WC2N 244 D1
Emba Street SE16 .... 246 D7
Emerald Street WC1N 240 E4
Emerson Street SE1 .... 245 J1
Emery Hill Street SW1P 244 A5
Emery Street SE1 .... 245 G3
Emperor's Gate SW7 .... 242 C5
Empire Square SE1 .... 245 L3
Empress Place SW6 .... 242 A7
Endell Street WC2H 240 C6
Endsleigh Gardens WC1H 240 B3
Endsleigh Place WC1H 240 B3
Endsleigh Street WC1H 240 B3
Enford Street W1H 239 G5
English Grounds SE1 .... 245 M1
Enid Street SE16 .... 246 C8
Ennismore Gardens SW7 .... 242 F3
Ennismore Gardens Mews SW7 .... 242 F3
Ennismore Mews SW7 .... 242 F3
Ennismore Street SW7 .... 242 F4
Ensign Street E1 .... 246 D4
Epworth Street EC2A 241 L3
Erasmus Street SW1P 244 C6
Errol Street EC1Y 241 K4
Essendine Road W9 .... 238 A3
Essex Street WC2R 240 F7
Essex Villas W8 .... 242 A3
Europa Place EC1V 241 J2
Euston ⇌ ⊖ NW1 .... 240 B2
Euston Road NW1 .... 240 B3
Euston Square ⊖ NW1 .... 240 A3
Euston Square NW1 .... 240 A3
Euston Street NW1 .... 240 A2
Evelyn Gardens SW7 .... 242 D7
Evelyn Walk N1 .... 241 L1
Eversholt Street NW1 .... 240 A1
Everton Mews NW1 .... 239 M2
Ewer Street SE1 .... 245 J2
Ewhurst Close E1 .... 247 G1
Exchange Square EC2A 241 M4
Exeter Street WC2E 240 D7
Exhibition Road SW7 .... 242 E3
Exmouth Market EC1R 241 G3
Exon Street SE17 .... 245 M6
Exton Street SE1 .... 244 F2
Eyre Street Hill EC1R 240 F4

F

Fairclough Street E1 .... 246 D3
Fair Street SE1 .... 246 B6
Falmouth Road SE1 .... 245 K4
Fane Street EC1M 241 J4
Fanshaw Street N1 .... 241 M1
Farmer Street W8 .... 242 A1
Farm Lane SW6 .... 242 A8
Farm Street W1K 239 K8
Farnham Place SE1 .... 245 J1
Farrance Street E14 .... 247 M3
Farringdon ⇌ ⊖ EC1M 241 G4
Farringdon Lane EC1R 241 G4
Farringdon Road EC1R 240 F3

Farringdon Street EC1M 241 H5
Farrins Rents SE16 .... 247 J5
Farrow Place SE16 .... 247 K7
Farthing Fields * E1W 246 F5
Fashion Street E1 .... 246 B1
Faunce Street SE17 .... 245 H7
Fawcett Street SW10 .... 242 C8
Featherstone Street EC1Y 241 L3
Fenchurch Avenue EC3M 246 A3
Fenchurch Buildings EC3M 246 A3
Fenchurch Place EC3M 246 A3
Fenchurch Street EC3M 246 A3
Fenchurch Street ⇌ EC3M 246 A3
Fendall Street SE1 .... 246 B8
Fenning Street SE1 .... 245 M2
Fentiman Road SW8 .... 244 D8
Fernsbury Street WC1X 240 F2
Fetter Lane EC4A 241 G6
Fieldgate Street E1 .... 246 D2
Fielding Street SE17 .... 245 J7
Field Street WC1X 240 E1
Finborough Road SW10 .... 241 B8
Finch Lane EC3V 241 L6
Finland Street SE16 .... 247 K8
Finsbury Circus EC2M 241 L5
Finsbury Estate EC1R 241 G3
Finsbury Market EC2A 241 M4
Finsbury Square EC2A 241 L4
Finsbury Street EC2Y 241 L4
First Street SW3 .... 243 G5
Fishermans Drive SE16 .... 247 J6
Fisher Street WC1R 240 D5
Fisherton Street NW8 .... 238 E3
Fish Street Hill EC3R 241 L7
Fitzalan Street SE11 .... 244 F5
Fitzhardinge Street W1H 239 J6
Fitzroy Square W1T 239 M4
Fitzroy Street W1T 239 M4
Flamborough Street E14 .... 247 J3
Flank Street E1 .... 246 C4
Flaxman Terrace WC1H 240 C3
Fleet Street EC4A 241 G6
Fleming Road SE17 .... 245 H8
Fletcher Street E1 .... 246 D3
Flint Street SE17 .... 245 L6
Flitcroft Street WC2H 240 C6
Flockton Street SE16 .... 246 D7
Flood Street SW3 .... 243 G7
Flood Walk SW3 .... 243 G7
Floral Street WC2E 240 D7
Foley Street W1W 239 M5
Forbes Street E1 .... 246 D3
Fordham Street E1 .... 246 D2
Ford Square E1 .... 246 F2
Fore Street EC2Y 241 K5
Formosa Street W9 .... 238 C4
Forset Street W1H 239 G6
Forsyth Gardens SE17 .... 245 H8
Fort Street E1 .... 246 B1
Fortune Street EC1Y 241 K4
Forum Magnum Square SE1 .... 244 E3
Foster Lane EC2V 241 J6
Foulis Terrace SW7 .... 242 E6
Foundry Close SE16 .... 247 J5
Fournier Street E1 .... 246 B1
Fowey Close E1W 246 E5
Frampton Street NW8 .... 238 E4
Francis Street SW1P 244 A5
Frankland Road * SE16 .... 246 F8
Franklin's Row SW3 .... 243 H6
Frazier Street SE1 .... 245 G3
Frean Street SE16 .... 246 C8
Frederick Close W2 .... 239 G7
Frederick Street WC1X 240 E2
Frederic Mews * SW1X 243 J3
Freemantle Street SE17 .... 245 M6
Friday Street EC4V 241 J7
Friend Street EC1V 241 H2
Frith Street W1D 240 B6
Fulbourne Street E1 .... 246 E1
Fulford Street SE16 .... 246 F7
Fulham Road SW10 .... 242 D8
Fulham Road SW3 .... 242 F6
Furnival Street EC4A 240 F5
Fynes Street SW1P 244 B5

G

Gabriel's Wharf SE1 .... 245 G1
Gainsford Street SE1 .... 246 B6
Galleon Close SE16 .... 247 G6
Galsworthy Avenue E14 .... 247 K2
Galway Street EC1V 241 K2
Gambia Street SE1 .... 245 H2
Garden Road NW8 .... 238 D1
Garden Row SE1 .... 245 H4
Garden Street E1 .... 247 H1
Garden Terrace * SW1V 244 B6
Garden Walk EC2A 241 M3
Gard Street EC1V 241 J2
Garford Street E14 .... 247 M4
Garnault Place EC1R 241 G3
Garnet Street E1W 246 F4
Garrett Street EC1Y 241 K3
Garrick Street WC2E 240 C7
Garterway SE16 .... 247 H7
Garway Road W2 .... 238 B6
Gaspar Mews SW7 .... 242 C5
Gataker Street * SE16 .... 246 E8
Gate Mews SW7 .... 242 F3
Gateforth Street NW8 .... 238 F3
Gate Mews NW1 .... 239 L3
Gatesborough Street * EC2A 241 M3
Gate Street WC2A 240 E5
Gatliff Road SW1W 243 K7
Gaunt Street SE1 .... 245 J4
Gayfere Street SW1P 244 C4
Gaywood Street SE1 .... 245 H4
Gaza Street SE17 .... 245 H7
Gedling Place SE1 .... 246 C7
Gee Street EC1V 241 J3
George Mathew Road SE11 .... 245 H5
George Row SE16 .... 246 C7
George Street W1H 239 H6
George Yard W1K 239 K7
Geraldine Street SE11 .... 245 H4
Gerald Road SW1W 243 K5
Gerrard Street W1D 240 B7
Gerridge Street SE1 .... 245 G3
Gertrude Street SW10 .... 242 D8
Gibson Road SE11 .... 244 F4
Gilbert Place WC1A 240 C5
Gilbert Road SE11 .... 245 G5
Gilbert Street W1K 239 K7

Gildea Street W1W 239 L5
Gillingham Street SW1V 243 M5
Gill Street E14 .... 247 L7
Gilston Road SW10 .... 242 D7
Giltspur Street EC1A 241 H5
Gladstone Street SE1 .... 245 H4
Glamis Place E1W 247 G4
Glamis Road E1W 247 G4
Glasgow Terrace SW1V 243 M7
Glasshill Street SE1 .... 245 J3
Glasshouse Street W1B 240 A8
Glasshouse Walk SE11 .... 244 D7
Glasshouse Yard EC1 .... 241 J4
Glebe Place SW3 .... 242 F7
Gledhow Road SW5 .... 242 C6
Glentworth Street NW1 .... 239 H4
Globe Pond Road SE16 .... 247 J5
Globe Street SE1 .... 245 K3
Gloucester Court * EC3R 246 A4
Gloucester Gardens W2 .... 238 C6
Gloucester Mews W2 .... 238 D6
Gloucester Mews West W2 .... 238 C6
Gloucester Place NW1 .... 239 H3
Gloucester Place W1U 239 H5
Gloucester Place Mews W1U 239 H5
Gloucester Road SW7 .... 242 C4
Gloucester Road SW7 .... 242 D6
Gloucester Road ⊖ SW7 .... 242 C5
Gloucester Square W2 .... 238 F6
Gloucester Street SW1V 243 M7
Gloucester Terrace W2 .... 238 B5
Gloucester Terrace W2 .... 238 D6
Gloucester Walk W8 .... 242 A2
Gloucester Way EC1R 241 G2
Glyn Street SE11 .... 244 E7
Godfrey Street SW3 .... 243 G6
Goding Street SE11 .... 244 D7
Godliman Street EC4V 241 J7
Godwin Close N1 .... 241 K1
Golden Hinde II SE1 .... 245 L1
Golden Jubilee Bridge WC2N 244 D1
Golden Lane EC1Y 241 J4
Golden Square W1F 240 A7
Golding Street E1 .... 246 E3
Goldney Road W9 .... 238 A4
Goldsmith Street EC2V 241 K6
Goodge Place W1T 240 A5
Goodge Street W1T 240 A5
Goodge Street ⊖ W1T 240 B5
Goodwin Close SE16 .... 246 C8
Gordon Place W8 .... 242 A2
Gordon Square WC1H 240 B3
Gordon Street WC1H 240 B3
Gore Street SW7 .... 242 D4
Goring Street * EC3A 246 A2
Gosfield Street W1W 239 L5
Goslett Yard WC2H 240 B6
Goswell Road EC1V 241 H1
Gough Street WC1X 240 F3
Goulston Street E1 .... 246 B2
Gower Mews WC1E 240 B5
Gower Place NW1 .... 240 A3
Gower Street WC1E 240 B3
Gower's Walk E1 .... 246 D2
Gracechurch Street EC3V 241 M7
Grafton Place NW1 .... 240 B2
Grafton Street W1S 239 L8
Grafton Way W1T 240 A4
Graham Street N1 .... 241 J1
Graham Terrace SW1W 243 J6
Granby Terrace NW1 .... 239 M1
Grand Avenue EC1A 241 H5
Grange Road SE1 .... 246 B8
Grange Walk SE1 .... 246 A8
Grange Yard SE1 .... 246 B8
Grantully Road W9 .... 238 B2
Granville Place W1H 239 J6
Granville Road NW6 .... 238 A1
Granville Square WC1X 240 F2
Grape Street WC2H 240 C6
Gravel Lane E1 .... 246 B2
Gray's Inn Road WC1X 240 D2
Gray's Inn Square WC1R 240 F5
Gray Street SE1 .... 245 G3
Great Castle Street W1G 239 L6
Great Central Street NW1 .... 239 G4
Great Chapel Street W1D 240 B6
Great College Street SW1P 244 C4
Great Cumberland Place W1H 239 H6
Great Dover Street SE1 .... 245 K3
Great Eastern Street EC2A 241 M3
Great George Street SW1P 244 C3
Great Guildford Street SE1 .... 245 J1
Great James Street WC1N 240 E4
Great Marlborough Street W1F 239 M7
Great Maze Pond SE1 .... 245 L2
Great New Portland Street WC2H 240 C7
Greatorex Street E1 .... 246 D1
Great Ormond Street WC1N 240 D4
Great Percy Street WC1X 240 F2
Great Peter Street SW1P 244 B4
Great Portland Street W1W 239 L4
Great Portland Street ⊖ W1W 239 L4
Great Pulteney Street W1F 240 A7
Great Queen Street WC2B 240 D6
Great Russell Street WC1B 240 C5
Great Scotland Yard SW1A 244 C1
Great Smith Street SW1P 244 C4
Great Suffolk Street SE1 .... 245 H2
Great Sutton Street EC1V 241 H4
Great Swan Alley EC2R 241 L6
Great Titchfield Street W1W 239 M4
Great Tower Street EC3M 241 M7
Great Tower Street EC3R 246 A4
Great Winchester Street EC2N 241 L6
Great Windmill Street W1D 240 B7
Greek Street W1D 240 B6
Greenacre Square SE16 .... 247 J6
Green Bank E1W 246 E5
Greenberry Street NW8 .... 238 F1
Greencoat Place SW1P 244 A5
Green Coat Row SW1P 244 A4
Greenfield Road E1 .... 246 D2
Greenham Close SE1 .... 244 F3
Green Street W1K 239 J7
Greenwell Street W1W 239 L4
Greet Street SE1 .... 245 G2
Grenade Street E14 .... 247 L4
Grendon Street NW8 .... 238 F3
Grenville Place SW7 .... 242 C5
Grenville Street WC1N 240 D4
Gresham Street EC2V 241 J6
Gresse Street W1T 240 B5
Greville Street EC1N 241 G5
Greycoat Place SW1P 244 B4

Greycoat Street SW1P 244 B4
Grigg's Place SE1 .... 246 A8
Grosvenor Bridge SW8 .... 243 L8
Grosvenor Crescent SW1X 243 J3
Grosvenor Crescent Mews SW1X 243 J3
Grosvenor Gardens SW1W 243 L4
Grosvenor Gardens
 Mews East SW1W 243 L4
Grosvenor Gardens
 Mews North SW1W 243 L4
Grosvenor Gardens
 Mews South * SW1W 243 L4
Grosvenor Gate W2 .... 239 H8
Grosvenor Hill W1K 239 L7
Grosvenor Place SW1X 243 K3
Grosvenor Road SW1V 243 L8
Grosvenor Square W1K 239 J7
Grosvenor Street W1K 239 K7
Grosvenor Terrace SE5 .... 245 J8
Grove End Road NW8 .... 238 D2
Guildhouse Street SW1V 243 M5
Guilford Street WC1N 240 D4
Guinness Square SE1 .... 245 M5
Gulliver Street SE16 .... 247 K8
Gun Street E1 .... 246 B1
Gunthorpe Street E1 .... 246 C2
Gutter Lane EC2V 241 J6
Guy Street SE1 .... 245 L3

H

Haberdasher Street N1 .... 241 L2
Haddonhall Estate SE1 .... 245 M4
Hainton Close E1 .... 246 F3
Halcrow Street * E1 .... 246 F2
Half Moon Street W1J 243 L1
Halford Road SW6 .... 242 A8
Halkin Place SW1X 243 J4
Halkin Street SW1X 243 K3
Hallam Street W1W 239 L5
Halley Street E14 .... 247 K1
Hallfield Estate W2 .... 238 C6
Hall Place W2 .... 238 E4
Hall Road NW8 .... 238 D2
Hall Street EC1V 241 H2
Halpin Place SE17 .... 245 M6
Halsey Street SW3 .... 243 G5
Hamilton Close NW8 .... 238 D2
Hamilton Close SE16 .... 247 K7
Hamilton Gardens NW8 .... 238 D2
Hamilton Place W1J 243 K2
Hamilton Terrace NW8 .... 238 C1
Hamlet Way SE1 .... 245 L3
Hammett Street EC3N 246 B4
Hampden Close NW1 .... 240 B1
Hampden Gurney Street W2 .... 239 H6
Hampstead Road NW1 .... 239 M2
Hampton Street SE17 .... 245 J6
Hanbury Street E1 .... 246 C1
Hand Court WC1V 240 E5
Handel Street WC1N 240 D3
Hankey Place SE1 .... 245 L3
Hannibal Road E1 .... 247 G1
Hanover Square W1S 239 L6
Hanover Street W1S 239 L7
Hans Crescent SW3 .... 243 H3
Hanson Street W1W 239 M4
Hans Place SW1X 243 H4
Hans Road SW3 .... 243 G4
Hans Street SW1X 243 H4
Hanway Place W1T 240 B6
Hanway Street W1T 240 B6
Harbet Road W2 .... 238 F5
Harcourt Street W1H 239 G5
Harcourt Terrace SW10 .... 242 C7
Hardinge Street E1W 247 G3
Hardwick Street EC1R 241 G2
Hardwidge Street SE1 .... 245 M2
Hardy Close SE16 .... 247 H6
Harewood Place W1G 239 L6
Harewood Row NW1 .... 239 G4
Harewoood Avenue NW1 .... 239 G4
Harford Street E1 .... 247 J1
Harleyford Road SE11 .... 244 E8
Harley Gardens SW10 .... 242 D7
Harley Place W1G 239 K5
Harley Street W1G 239 K4
Harmsworth Street SE17 .... 245 G7
Harold Estate SE1 .... 246 A8
Harper Road SE1 .... 245 K4
Harpour Street WC1N 240 E4
Harriet Street SW1X 243 H3
Harriet Walk SW1X 243 H3
Harrington Gardens SW7 .... 242 C6
Harrington Road SW7 .... 242 E5
Harrington Square NW1 .... 239 M1
Harrington Street NW1 .... 239 M2
Harrison Street WC1H 240 D2
Harrods SW1X 243 G4
Harrowby Street W1H 239 G6
Harrow Place E1 .... 246 B2
Harrow Road W2 .... 238 A4
Hart Street EC3R 246 A3
Hasker Street SW3 .... 243 G5
Hastings Street WC1H 240 C2
Hatfields SE1 .... 245 G1
Hatherley Grove W2 .... 238 B6
Hatteraick Road SE16 .... 247 G6
Hatton Garden EC1N 241 G4
Hatton Street W2 .... 238 E4
Hatton Wall EC1N 241 G4
Havering Street E1 .... 247 H3
Haverstock Street N1 .... 241 J1
Hawke Place * SE16 .... 247 H6
Haydon Street EC3N 246 B3
Hayes Place NW1 .... 239 G4
Hay Hill W1J 239 L8
Hayles Street SE11 .... 245 H5
Haymarket SW1Y 240 B8
Hay's Lane SE1 .... 245 M1
Hay's Mews W1J 239 L8
Haywood Place EC1R 241 H3
Headfort Place SW1X 243 K3
Head Street E1 .... 247 H2
Hearnshaw Street E14 .... 247 K2
Hearn Street EC2A 241 M4
Heathcote Street WC1N 240 E3
Heddon Street W1B 239 M7
Heddon Street W1S 240 A7
Hedger Street SE11 .... 245 H5
Heiron Street SE17 .... 245 J8
Hellings Street E1W 246 D5

Helmet Row EC1V 241 K3
Helsinki Square SE16 .... 247 L8
Henderson Drive NW8 .... 238 E3
Heneage Lane EC3A 246 A3
Heneage Street E1 .... 246 C1
Henrietta Place W1G 239 L6
Henrietta Street WC2E 240 D7
Henriques Street E1 .... 246 D2
Henshaw Street SE17 .... 245 L5
Herbal Hill EC1R 241 G4
Herbert Crescent SW1X 243 H4
Herbrand Street WC1H 240 C3
Hercules Road SE1 .... 244 F4
Hereford Road W2 .... 238 A6
Hereford Square SW7 .... 242 D6
Hermitage Street W2 .... 238 E5
Hermitage Wall E1W 246 D5
Hermit Street EC1V 241 H2
Heron Place SE16 .... 247 K5
Heron Quay E14 .... 247 M5
Herrick Street SW1P 244 C6
Hertford Street W1J 243 K2
Hertsmere Road E14 .... 247 M4
Hesper Mews SW5 .... 242 B6
Hessel Street E1 .... 246 E3
Hewett Street EC2A 241 M3
Heygate Street SE17 .... 245 J5
Hide Place SW1P 244 B6
High Holborn WC1V 240 E5
High Street Kensington ⊖ W8 .... 242 A3
Hildyard Road SW6 .... 242 A8
Hilliards Court E1W 246 F5
Hillingdon Street SE17 .... 245 J8
Hill Road NW8 .... 238 D1
Hills Place W1F 239 M6
Hill Street W1J 239 K8
Hinde Street W1U 239 K6
Hind Grove E14 .... 247 M3
Hindgrove Area E14 .... 247 M3
Hithe Grove SE16 .... 247 G8
HMS Belfast SE1 .... 246 A5
Hobart Place SW1W 243 K4
Hobury Street SW10 .... 242 D8
Hogarth Road SW5 .... 242 B6
Holbein Mews SW1W 243 J6
Holbein Place SW1W 243 J6
Holborn EC1N 241 G5
Holborn ⊖ WC2B 240 E5
Holborn Circus EC1N 241 G5
Holborn Viaduct EC1A 241 G5
Holford Street WC1X 240 F2
Holland Street SE1 .... 245 H1
Holland Street W8 .... 242 A3
Hollen Street W1F 240 A6
Holles Street W1C 239 L6
Hollywood Road SW10 .... 242 C8
Holyoak Road SE11 .... 245 H5
Holyrood Street SE1 .... 245 M2
Holyrood Street SE1 .... 246 A6
Holywell Row EC2A 241 M4
Homefield Street * N1 .... 241 M1
Homer Row W1H 239 G5
Homer Street W1H 239 G5
Hooper Street E1 .... 246 D3
Hopetown Street E1 .... 246 C1
Hopkins Street W1F 240 A7
Hopton Street SE1 .... 245 H1
Hopwood Road SE17 .... 245 L8
Hornton Place W8 .... 242 A3
Hornton Street W8 .... 242 A2
Horse & Dolphin Yard W1D 240 B7
Horseferry Road E14 .... 247 J3
Horseferry Road SW1P 244 B4
Horse Guards Avenue SW1A 244 C2
Horse Guards Parade SW1A 244 C2
Horse Guards Road SW1A 244 C2
Horselydown Lane SE1 .... 246 B6
Horsley Street SE17 .... 245 K8
Hosier Lane EC1A 241 H5
Hothfield Place SE16 .... 247 G8
Hotspur Street SE11 .... 244 F6
Houghton Street WC2A 240 E6
Houndsditch EC3A 246 A2
Houses of Parliament SW1A 244 D3
Howick Place SW1P 244 A4
Howland Street W1T 240 A4
Howland Way SE16 .... 247 K7
Hoxton Square N1 .... 241 M2
Hoxton Street N1 .... 241 M1
Hudson's Place SW1V 243 M5
Hugh Mews SW1V 243 L6
Hugh Street SW1V 243 L6
Hugh Street SW1V 243 L6
Hull Close SE16 .... 247 J6
Hull Street EC1V 241 J2
Hungerford Bridge SE1 .... 244 E1
Hunter Close SE1 .... 245 M4
Hunter Street WC1N 240 D3
Huntley Street WC1E 240 A4
Huntsman Street SE17 .... 245 M6
Huntsworth Mews NW1 .... 239 H3
Hurley Crescent SE16 .... 247 H6
Hutching's Street E14 .... 247 M7
Hutton Street EC4Y 241 G7
Hyde Park W2 .... 243 G1
Hyde Park Corner W1J 243 K2
Hyde Park Corner ⊖ W1J 243 K2
Hyde Park Court SW7 .... 242 D3
Hyde Park Crescent W2 .... 238 F6
Hyde Park Gardens W2 .... 238 F7
Hyde Park Gardens Mews W2 .... 238 F7
Hyde Park Gate SW7 .... 242 C3
Hyde Park Gate SW7 .... 242 D3
Hyde Park Square W2 .... 238 F7
Hyde Park Street W2 .... 238 F7

I

Idol Lane EC3R 241 M7
Ifield Road SW10 .... 242 B8
Iliffe Street SE17 .... 245 J6
Iliffe Yard SE17 .... 245 J6
Imperial College Road SW7 .... 242 D4
Imperial War Museum SE1 .... 245 G4
India Street EC3N 246 B3
Ingestre Place W1F 240 A7
Ingleburt Street EC1R 240 F2
Ingram Close SE11 .... 244 E5
Inner Circle NW1 .... 239 J2
Inverness Terrace W2 .... 238 B6
Inverness Terrace Gate W2 .... 238 C8
Invicta Plaza SE1 .... 245 H1
Inville Road SE17 .... 245 L7

Ironmonger Lane EC2V 241 K6
Ironmonger Row EC1V 241 K2
Irving Street WC2N 240 C8
Isambard Place SE16 .... 247 G6
Island Row E14 .... 247 K3
Iverna Court W8 .... 242 A4
Iverna Gardens W8 .... 242 A4
Ives Street SW3 .... 243 G5
Ivor Place NW1 .... 239 G4
Ixworth Place SW3 .... 242 F6

J

Jacob Street SE1 .... 246 C6
Jamaica Gate SE16 .... 246 F8
Jamaica Road SE1 .... 246 C7
Jamaica Road SE16 .... 246 E7
Jamaica Street E1 .... 247 G2
Jamaica Wharf SE1 .... 246 C6
James Street W1U 239 K6
James Street WC2E 240 D7
Jameson Street W8 .... 242 A1
Jamuna Close E14 .... 247 K1
Janeway Street SE16 .... 246 D7
Jardine Road E1W 247 J4
Java Wharf SE1 .... 246 C6
Jay Mews SW7 .... 242 D3
Jermyn Street SW1Y 240 A8
Jerome Crescent NW8 .... 238 F3
Jewery Street EC3N 246 B3
Joan Street SE1 .... 245 G2
Jockey's Fields WC1R 240 E4
Johanna Street SE1 .... 244 F3
John Adam Street WC2N 240 D8
John Carpenter Street EC4Y 241 G7
John Fisher Street E1 .... 246 C4
John Islip Street SW1P 244 C5
John Prince's Street W1G 239 L6
John Roll Way SE16 .... 246 D7
John Ruskin Street SE5 .... 245 J8
John's Mews WC1N 240 E4
Johnson's Place SW1V 244 A7
Johnson Street E1 .... 247 G3
John Street WC1N 240 E4
Joiner Street SE1 .... 245 L1
Jonathan Street SE11 .... 244 E6
Jubilee Place SW3 .... 243 G6
Jubilee Street E1 .... 247 G2
Jubilee Walk SE1 .... 242 B1
Judd Street WC1H 240 C2
Junction Mews W2 .... 238 F5
Juxon Street SE11 .... 244 E5

K

Katherine Close SE16 .... 247 H5
Kean Street WC2B 240 E6
Keel Close SE16 .... 247 J6
Keeley Street WC2B 240 E6
Keeton's Road SE16 .... 246 E7
Kell Street SE1 .... 245 H3
Kelso Place W8 .... 242 B4
Kemble Street WC2B 240 E6
Kempsford Gardens SW5 .... 242 A7
Kempsford Road SE11 .... 245 G6
Kendall Place W1U 239 J5
Kendal Street W2 .... 239 G6
Kennet Street E1W 246 D5
Kenning Street SE16 .... 247 G6
Kennings Way SE11 .... 245 G7
Kennington ⊖ SE11 .... 245 H7
Kennington Lane SE11 .... 244 E7
Kennington Oval SE11 .... 244 E8
Kennington Park Gardens SE11 .... 245 G8
Kennington Park Place SE11 .... 245 G8
Kennington Park Road SE11 .... 245 G7
Kennington Road SE1 .... 244 F4
Kennington Road SE11 .... 245 G5
Kennnington Oval SE11 .... 244 F8
Kenrick Place W1U 239 J5
Kensington Church Street W8 .... 242 A1
Kensington Court W8 .... 242 B3
Kensington Gardens W2 .... 242 C1
Kensington Gardens Square W2 .... 238 B6
Kensington Gate W8 .... 242 C4
Kensington Gore SW7 .... 242 D3
Kensington High Street W8 .... 242 A4
Kensington Palace W8 .... 242 B2
Kensington Palace Gardens W8 .... 242 B1
Kensington Palace Gardens W8 .... 242 B2
Kensington Place W8 .... 242 A1
Kensington Road SW7 .... 242 D3
Kensington Road W8 .... 242 B3
Kensington Square W8 .... 242 B3
Kenton Street WC1H 240 C3
Kenway Road SW5 .... 242 A6
Keystone Close N1 .... 240 D1
Keyworth Street SE1 .... 245 H4
Kia Oval (Surrey County
 Cricket Ground) SE11 .... 244 F8
Kilburn Park Road NW6 .... 238 A2
Kildare Terrace W2 .... 238 A6
Killick Street N1 .... 240 E1
Kinburn Street SE16 .... 247 H6
Kinder Street E1 .... 246 E2
King & Queen Wharf SE16 .... 247 H5
King and Queen Street SE17 .... 245 K6
King Charles Street SW1A 244 C2
King David Lane E1 .... 247 G3
Kingdom Street W2 .... 238 C5
King Edward Street EC1A 241 J6
King Edward Walk SE1 .... 245 G4
King James Street SE1 .... 245 H3
Kingly Street W1F 239 M7
King's Arms Street EC2R 241 L6
King's Bench Street SE1 .... 245 H2
Kingscote Street EC4V 241 H7
King's Cross ⇌ N1C 240 D1
King's Cross Road WC1X 240 E2
King's Cross Square N1C 240 D1
King's Cross St Pancras ⊖ N1C 240 D1
Kingsgate Walk * SW1E 244 A4
King's Head Yard SE1 .... 245 L1
King's Mews WC1N 240 F4
Kingsmill Terrace NW8 .... 238 E1
King Square EC1V 241 J2
King's Road SW3 .... 242 D8
King's Scholars Passage SW1P 244 M5
King's Stairs Close SE16 .... 246 E6
King Street WC2E 240 D7
King Street SW1Y 244 A1
King Street EC2V 241 K6

Kingsway WC2B............240 E6
King William Street EC4N............241 L7
Kinnerton Place North * SW1X............243 J3
Kinnerton Place South * SW1X............243 J3
Kinnerton Street SW1X............243 J3
Kinnerton Yard * SW1X............243 J3
Kipling Estate SE1............245 L3
Kipling Street SE1............245 L3
Kirby Estate SE16............246 D7
Kirby Grove SE1............245 M3
Kirby Street EC1N............241 G4
Knaresborough Place SW5............242 B5
Knightrider Street EC4V............241 H7
Knightsbridge SW1X............243 H3
Knightsbridge SW3............243 H3
Knox Street W1H............239 H4
Kynance Mews SW7............242 C4
Kynance Place SW7............242 C4

L

Lackington Street EC2A............241 L4
Lafone Street SE1............246 B6
Lagado Mews SE16............247 H5
Lambeth Bridge SW1P............244 D5
Lambeth High Street SE1............244 E5
Lambeth Hill EC4V............241 J7
Lambeth North ⊖ SE1............244 F3
Lambeth Palace Road SE1............244 E4
Lambeth Road SE1............244 F4
Lambeth Walk SE11............244 F4
Lamb's Conduit Street WC1N............240 E4
Lamb's Passage EC1Y............241 K4
Lamb Street E1............246 B1
Lamb Way SE1............246 A7
Lamlash Street SE11............245 H5
Lanark Place W9............238 D3
Lanark Road W9............238 B1
Lancaster Gate W2............238 D7
Lancaster Gate ⊖ W2............238 D8
Lancaster Gate ⊖ W2............238 E7
Lancaster Mews W2............238 D7
Lancaster Place WC2E............240 E7
Lancaster Street SE1............245 H3
Lancaster Terrace W2............238 E7
Lancaster Walk W2............238 D8
Lancelot Place SW7............243 G3
Lancing Street NW1............240 B2
Lanesborough Place * SW1X............243 J3
Langdale Street E1............246 E3
Langford Place NW8............238 D1
Langham Place W1B............239 L5
Langham Street W1W............239 L5
Langham Street W1W............239 M5
Langley Lane SW8............244 D8
Langley Street WC2H............240 C7
Langton Close WC1X............240 E3
Lanhill Road W9............238 A3
Lansdowne Place SE1............245 L4
Lant Street SE1............245 J3
Larcom Street SE17............245 K6
Lauderdale Road W9............238 B3
Laud Street SE11............244 E7
Launcelot Street SE1............244 F3
Launceston Place W8............242 C4
Laurence Pountney Lane EC4V............241 L7
Lavender Road SE16............247 K5
Lavender Wharf SE16............247 K4
Lavington Street SE1............245 J1
Lawn Lane SW8............244 D8
Lawrence Street SW3............242 F8
Lawrence Wharf SE16............247 L6
Law Street SE1............245 L4
Laxton Place NW1............239 L3
Laystall Street EC1R............240 F4
Leadenhall Place EC3A............246 A3
Leadenhall Street EC3V............241 M6
Leake Street SE1............244 E2
Leather Lane EC1N............241 G4
Leathermarket Street SE1............245 M3
Leeke Street WC1X............240 E2
Lees Place W1K............239 J7
Leicester Square ⊖ WC2H............240 C7
Leicester Square WC2H............240 C7
Leicester Street WC2H............240 B7
Leigh Street WC1H............240 C3
Leinster Gardens W2............238 C6
Leinster Mews W2............238 C7
Leinster Place W2............238 C7
Leinster Square W2............238 A7
Leinster Terrace W2............238 C7
Leman Street E1............246 C3
Lennox Gardens SW1X............243 G4
Lennox Gardens Mews SW1X............243 G5
Leonard Street EC2A............241 L3
Leopold Estate E3............247 M1
Leopold Street E3............247 L1
Leroy Street SE1............245 M5
Lever Street EC1V............241 J2
Lewisham Street SW1H............244 B3
Lexham Gardens W8............242 A5
Lexham Mews W8............242 A5
Lexington Street W1F............240 A7
Leyden Street E1............246 B2
Leydon Close SE16............247 H5
Library Street SE1............245 H3
Lidlington Place NW1............240 A1
Lilestone Street NW8............238 F3
Lilley Close E1W............246 D5
Lillie Road SW6............242 A7
Lillie Yard SW6............242 A7
Limeburner Lane EC4M............241 H6
Lime Close E1W............246 D5
Limehouse Causeway E14............247 L4
Limehouse Link E14............247 L3
Limehouse ⇌ E14............247 J3
Limerston Street SW10............242 D8
Lime Street EC3M............246 A4
Lincoln's Inn Fields WC2A............240 E6
Linden Gardens W2............238 A8
Lindley Street E1............246 F1
Lindsay Square SW1V............244 B7
Lindsey Street EC1A............241 H4
Linhope Street NW1............239 G3
Linsey Street SE16............246 D8
Lisle Street WC2H............240 B7
Lisson Green Estate NW8............238 F3
Lisson Grove NW1............239 G4
Lisson Grove NW8............238 F3
Lisson Street NW1............238 F4
Litchfield Street WC2H............240 C7
Little Argyll Street W1F............239 M6
Little Britain EC1A............241 J5
Little Chester Street SW1X............243 K4

Little George Street SW1P............244 C3
Little Marlborough Street W1F............240 A7
Little New Street EC4A............241 G6
Little Portland Street W1G............239 L6
Little Russell Street WC1A............240 C5
Little St James's Street SW1A............243 M2
Little Sanctuary SW1A............244 C3
Little Somerset Street E1............246 B3
Little Titchfield Street W1W............239 M5
Liverpool Grove SE17............245 K7
Liverpool Street EC2M............241 M5
Liverpool Street ⇌ EC2M............241 M5
Lizard Street EC1V............241 K3
Llewellyn Street SE16............246 D7
Lloyd Baker Street WC1X............240 F2
Lloyd's Avenue EC3N............246 B3
Lloyd Square WC1X............240 F2
Lloyds Row EC1R............241 G2
Lloyd Street WC1X............240 F2
Locksley Estate E14............247 L2
Locksley Street E14............247 L1
Lockyer Street SE1............245 L3
Lodge Road NW8............238 F3
Loftie Street SE16............246 D7
Logan Place W8............242 A5
Lolesworth Close E1............246 B1
Lollard Street SE11............244 F5
Lollard Street SE11............244 F6
Loman Street SE1............245 J2
Lomas Street E1............246 D1
Lombard Lane EC4Y............241 G6
Lombard Street EC3V............241 L7
London Bridge EC4R............241 L8
London Bridge ⊖ ⇌ SE1............245 L1
London Bridge Street SE1............245 L1
London Dungeon SE1............244 E2
London Eye SE1............244 E2
London Mews W2............238 E6
London Road SE1............245 H4
London Street EC3R............246 A3
London Street W2............238 E6
London Transport
  Museum WC2E............240 D7
London Wall EC2M............241 K5
London Zoo ZSL NW1............239 J1
Long Acre WC2E............240 D7
Longford Street NW1............239 L3
Long Lane EC1A............241 J5
Long Lane SE1............245 L3
Longmoore Street SW1V............243 M5
Longridge Road SW5............242 A5
Longville Road SE11............245 H5
Long Walk SE1............246 A8
Long Yard WC1N............240 E4
Lord North Street SW1P............244 C4
Lorenzo Street WC1X............240 E1
Lorrimore Road SE17............245 J8
Lorrimore Square SE17............245 H8
Lothbury EC2R............241 L6
Loughborough Street SE11............244 F7
Lovat Lane EC3R............241 M7
Love Lane EC2V............241 K6
Lovell Place SE16............247 K7
Lowell Street E14............247 K2
Lower Belgrave Street SW1W............243 K4
Lower Grosvenor Place SW1W............243 L4
Lower James Street W1F............240 A7
Lower John Street W1F............240 A7
Lower Marsh SE1............244 F3
Lower Road SE16............247 G7
Lower Sloane Street SW1W............243 J6
Lower Thames Street EC3R............246 A4
Lower Thames Street EC3R............241 M8
Lowndes Close * SW1X............243 J4
Lowndes Place SW1X............243 J4
Lowndes Square SW1X............243 H3
Lowndes Street SW1X............243 J4
Lucan Place SW3............242 F5
Lucey Road SE16............246 C8
Ludgate Circus EC4M............241 H6
Ludgate Hill EC4M............241 H6
Luke Street EC2A............241 M3
Lukin Street E1............247 G3
Lumley Street W1K............239 K7
Lupus Street SW1V............243 L7
Lupus Street SW1V............244 B7
Luton Street NW8............238 E4
Luxborough Street W1U............239 J4
Lyall Mews SW1X............243 J4
Lyall Street SW1X............243 J4
Lyons Place NW8............238 E3
Lytham Street SE17............245 K7

M

Macclesfield Road EC1V............241 J2
Macclesfield Street * W1D............240 B7
Mace Close E1W............246 E5
Macklin Street WC2B............240 D6
Mackworth Street NW1............239 M2
Macleod Street SE17............245 K7
Madame Tussauds NW1............239 J4
Maddox Street W1S............239 M7
Magdalen Street SE1............245 M2
Magee Street SE11............244 F8
Maguire Street SE1............246 C6
Maida Avenue W9............238 D4
Maida Vale W9............238 C2
Maida Vale ⊖ W9............238 C2
Maiden Lane SE1............245 K1
Maiden Lane WC2E............240 D7
Major Road SE16............246 D7
Makins Street SW3............243 G6
Malet Street WC1E............240 B4
Mallord Street SW3............242 E8
Mallory Street NW8............238 F3
Mallow Street EC1Y............241 L3
Malta Street EC1V............241 H3
Maltby Street SE1............246 B7
Manchester Square W1U............239 J6
Manchester Street W1U............239 J5
Manciple Street SE1............245 L3
Mandeville Place W1U............239 K6
Manette Street W1D............240 B6
Manilla Street E14............247 M6
Manningford Close EC1V............241 H2
Manor Place SE17............245 J7
Manresa Road SW3............242 F7
Mansell Street E1............246 C3
Mansfield Mews W1G............239 L5
Mansfield Street W1G............239 L5
Mansion House ⊖ EC4V............241 K7
Manson Mews SW7............242 D5

Manson Place SW7............242 D6
Mapleleaf Square SE16............247 J6
Maples Place E1............246 F1
Maple Street W1T............239 M4
Marble Arch ⊖ W1C............239 H7
Marchmont Street WC1N............240 C3
Margaret Street W1W............239 L6
Margaretta Terrace SW3............242 F7
Margery Street WC1X............240 F3
Marigold Street SE16............246 E7
Marine Street SE16............246 C7
Market Mews W1J............243 K1
Market Place W1W............239 M6
Markham Square SW3............243 G6
Markham Street SW3............243 G6
Mark Lane EC3R............246 A4
Marlborough Gate W2............238 E7
Marlborough Place NW8............238 C1
Marlborough Road SW1A............244 A2
Marlborough Street SW3............242 F6
Marloes Road W8............242 B4
Marlow Way SE16............247 H6
Maroon Street E14............247 K2
Marshall Street W1F............240 A7
Marshalsea Road SE1............245 K2
Marsham Street SW1P............244 C5
Marsh Wall E14............247 M5
Martha's Buildings EC1V............241 K3
Martha Street E1............246 F3
Martin Lane EC4V............241 L7
Maryland Road W9............238 A4
Marylands Road W9............238 A4
Marylebone ⊖ ⇌ NW1............239 G4
Marylebone Flyover W2............238 E5
Marylebone High Street W1U............239 K5
Marylebone Lane W1U............239 K6
Marylebone Road NW1............239 G4
Marylebone Street W1G............239 K5
Marylee Way SE11............244 F6
Masjid Lane E14............247 M2
Mason Street SE17............245 M5
Massinger Street SE17............245 M6
Masters Street E1............247 J1
Matlock Street E14............247 J2
Matthew Parker Street SW1H............244 C3
Maunsel Street SW1P............244 B5
Mayfair Place W1J............243 L1
Mayflower Street SE16............246 F7
Mayford Estate NW1............240 A1
Maynards Quay E1W............246 F4
May's Court WC2N............240 C8
McAuley Close SE1............244 F4
McLeod's Mews SW7............242 C5
Meadcroft Road SE11............245 G8
Meadcroft Road SE11............245 H8
Meadow Road SW8............244 D8
Meadow Row SE1............245 J5
Mead Row SE1............244 F4
Meakin Estate SE1............245 M4
Mecklenburgh Square WC1N............240 E3
Medway Street SW1P............244 B5
Meeting House Alley E1W............246 E5
Melcombe Place NW1............239 G4
Melcombe Street W1U............239 H4
Melina Place NW8............238 D2
Melior Street SE1............245 M2
Melton Street NW1............240 A2
Memorial Gates SW1W............243 K3
Mepham Street SE1............244 F2
Mercer Street WC2H............240 C7
Merchant Square W2............238 E5
Merlin Street EC1R............240 F2
Mermaid Court SE1............245 K2
Merrick Square SE1............245 K4
Merrington Road SW6............242 A8
Merrow Street SE17............245 L7
Methley Street SE11............245 G7
Meymott Street SE1............245 G2
Micawber Street N1............241 K1
Micklethwaite Road SW6............242 A8
Middlesex Street E1............246 A1
Middlesex Street E1............246 B2
Middle Street EC1A............241 J5
Middle Temple WC2R............240 F7
Middle Temple Lane EC4Y............240 F7
Middleton Drive SE16............247 H6
Midland Road NW1............240 C1
Midship Close SE16............247 H6
Milborne Grove SW10............242 D7
Milcote Street SE1............245 H3
Miles Street SW8............244 D8
Milford Lane WC2R............240 F7
Milk Street EC2V............241 K6
Milk Yard E1W............247 G4
Millbank SW1P............244 D4
Millennium Bridge SE1............241 J8
Millennium Harbour E14............247 M6
Milligan Street E14............247 L4
Millman Mews WC1N............240 E4
Millman Street WC1N............240 E4
Mill Place E14............247 K3
Millstream Road SE1............246 B7
Mill Street SE1............246 C6
Mill Street W1S............239 L7
Milner Street SW3............243 G5
Milton Street EC2Y............241 K4
Milverton Street SE11............245 G7
Mincing Lane EC3M............246 A4
Minera Mews SW1W............243 J5
Minories EC3N............246 B3
Mitchell Street EC1V............241 J3
Mitre Road SE1............245 G2
Mitre Street EC3A............246 A3
Molyneux Street W1H............239 G5
Monck Street SW1P............244 C4
Monkton Street SE11............245 G5
Monkwell Square EC2Y............241 K5
Monmouth Place W2............238 A6
Monmouth Road W2............238 A6
Monmouth Street WC2H............240 C6
Montague Close SE1............245 L1
Montague Place WC1E............240 C5
Montague Street WC1B............240 C5
Montagu Mansions W1U............239 H5
Montagu Mews North W1H............239 H5
Montagu Mews West W1H............239 H6
Montagu Place W1H............239 H5
Montagu Row W1U............239 H5
Montagu Square W1H............239 H5
Montagu Street W1H............239 H6
Montford Place SE11............244 F7
Monthorpe Road E1............246 C1
Montpelier Square SW7............243 G3
Montpelier Street SW7............243 G3
Montpelier Walk SW7............242 G3
Montrose Place SW1X............243 K3

Monument ⊖ EC4R............241 L7
Monument Street EC3R............241 L7
Monument Street EC3R............241 M7
Monza Street E1W............247 G4
Moodkee Street SE16............247 G7
Moore Street SW3............243 H5
Moorfields EC2Y............241 L5
Moorgate EC2R............241 L6
Moorgate ⊖ ⇌ EC2Y............241 L5
Moor Lane EC2Y............241 K5
Moor Street W1D............240 C7
Mora Street EC1V............241 K2
Morecambe Street SE17............245 K6
Moreland Street EC1V............241 H2
More London SE1............246 A5
Moreton Place SW1V............244 A6
Moreton Street SW1V............244 A6
Moreton Terrace SW1V............244 A6
Morgan's Lane SE1............245 M2
Morgan's Lane SE1............246 A5
Morley Street SE1............245 G3
Mornington Crescent NW1............239 M1
Mornington Place NW1............239 L1
Mornington Terrace NW1............239 L1
Morocco Street SE1............246 A7
Morpeth Terrace SW1P............243 M5
Morris Street E1............246 F3
Morshead Road W9............238 A2
Mortimer Market WC1E............240 A4
Mortimer Street W1T............240 A5
Mortimer Street W1W............239 M5
Morton Place SE1............244 F4
Morwell Street WC1B............240 B5
Moscow Place W2............238 B7
Moscow Road W2............238 B7
Mossop Street SW3............243 G5
Motcomb Street SW1X............243 J4
Mount Gate W2............242 C2
Mount Mills EC1V............241 J3
Mount Pleasant WC1X............240 F4
Mount Row W1K............239 K8
Mount Street W1K............239 K8
Mount Street Mews W1K............239 K8
Mount Terrace E1............246 E1
Moxon Street W1U............239 J5
Mulberry Street E1............246 D2
Mulberry Walk SW3............242 E8
Mulready Street NW8............238 F4
Mundy Street N1............241 M2
Munster Square NW1............239 L3
Munton Road SE17............245 K5
Murphy Street SE1............244 F3
Murray Grove N1............241 K1
Musbury Street E1............247 G2
Muscovy Street EC3N............246 A4
Museum of London EC2Y............241 J5
Museum Street WC1A............240 C5
Myddelton Passage EC1R............241 G2
Myddelton Square EC1R............241 G1
Myddelton Street EC1R............241 G3
Myrdle Street E1............246 D2

N

Naoroji Street WC1X............240 F2
Napier Grove N1............241 K1
Narrow Street E14............247 K4
Nash Street NW1............239 L2
Nassau Street W1W............239 M5
Nathaniel Close * E1............246 C2
National Portrait
  Gallery WC2H............240 C8
Natural History Museum SW7............242 E4
Neal Street WC2H............240 C6
Neathouse Place * SW1V............243 M5
Neckinger SE1............246 C8
Needleman Street SE16............247 H7
Nelson Close NW6............238 A1
Nelson Place N1............241 H1
Nelson's Column WC2N............240 C8
Nelson Square SE1............245 H2
Nelson Street E1............246 E2
Nelson Terrace N1............241 H1
Neptune Street SE16............247 G7
Nesham Street E1W............246 D4
Netherton Grove SW10............242 D8
Netley Street NW1............239 M2
Nevern Place SW5............242 A6
Nevern Square SW5............242 A6
Neville Street SW7............242 E6
Newark Street E1............246 E2
New Atlas Wharf E14............247 M8
New Bond Street W1S............239 L7
New Bond Street W1S............239 L8
New Bridge Street EC4V............241 H6
New Broad Street EC2M............241 M5
New Burlington Street W1S............239 M7
Newburn Street SE11............244 F7
Newbury Street EC1A............241 J5
Newcastle Place W2............238 E5
New Cavendish Street W1G............239 L5
New Change EC4M............241 J6
New Church Road SE5............245 L8
Newcomen Street SE1............245 K2
New Compton Street WC2H............240 C6
Newcourt Street NW8............238 E1
Newell Street E14............247 L3
New Fetter Lane EC4A............241 G6
Newgate Street EC1A............241 H6
New Globe Walk SE1............241 J8
New Goulston Street E1............246 B2
Newham's Row SE1............246 A7
Newington Butts SE1............245 H5
Newington Causeway SE1............245 J4
New Kent Road SE1............245 K5
Newlands Quay E1W............246 F4
Newman Street W1T............240 A5
New North Place EC2A............241 M3
New North Road N1............241 L1
New North Street WC1N............240 D4
New Oxford Street WC1A............240 C6
Newport Street SE11............244 E5
New Quebec Street W1H............239 H6
New Ride SW7............242 E3
New Road E1............246 E2
New Row WC2N............240 C7
New Spring Gardens Walk SE1............244 D7
New Square WC2A............240 F6
New Street EC2M............246 A2
New Street Square EC4A............241 G6
Newton Road W2............238 A6
Newton Street WC2B............240 D6
New Union Street EC2Y............241 K5
Nicholas Lane EC3V............241 L7

Nicholson Street SE1............245 H1
Nightingale Place SW10............242 D8
Nile Street N1............241 K2
Nine Elms Lane SW8............244 C8
Noble Street EC2V............241 J6
Noel Road N1............241 J1
Noel Street W1F............240 A6
Norbiton Road E14............247 L2
Norfolk Crescent W2............239 G6
Norfolk Place W2............238 E6
Norfolk Square W2............238 E6
Norman Street EC1V............241 J3
Norris Street SW1Y............240 B8
Northampton Road EC1R............241 G3
Northampton Square EC1V............241 H2
North Audley Street W1K............239 J7
North Bank NW8............238 F2
Northburgh Street EC1V............241 H3
North Carriage Drive W2............238 F7
Northdown Street N1............240 D1
Northey Street E14............247 K4
North Gower Street NW1............240 A2
Northington Street WC1N............240 E4
North Mews WC1N............240 E4
North Ride W2............239 G7
North Row W1K............239 J7
North Terrace SW3............242 F5
Northumberland Alley EC3N............246 B3
Northumberland
  Avenue WC2N............244 C1
Northumberland Place W2............238 A6
Northumberland Street WC2N............244 C1
North Wharf Road W2............238 E5
Northwick Terrace NW8............238 D3
Norway Gate SE16............247 K7
Norway Place E14............247 L3
Norwich Street EC4A............240 F5
Nottingham Place W1U............239 J4
Nottingham Street W1U............239 J4
Notting Hill Gate W11............238 A8
Notting Hill Gate ⊖ W11............242 A1
Nugent Terrace NW8............238 D1
Nutford Place W1H............239 G6

O

Oakden Street SE11............245 G5
Oakington Road W9............238 A3
Oak Lane E14............247 L3
Oakley Close EC1V............241 H1
Oakley Gardens SW3............243 G8
Oakley Square NW1............240 A1
Oakley Street SW3............242 F8
Oak Tree Road NW8............238 F2
Oat Lane EC2V............241 J5
Occupation Road SE17............245 J6
Ocean Square E1............247 J1
Ocean Street E1............247 J1
Odessa Street SE16............247 L7
Ogle Street W1W............239 M5
Old Bailey EC4M............241 H6
Old Barrack Yard SW1X............243 J3
Old Bond Street W1S............239 M8
Old Broad Street EC2N............241 M6
Old Brompton Road SW5............242 B6
Old Brompton Road SW7............242 D6
Old Burlington Street W1S............239 M7
Oldbury Place W1U............239 J4
Old Castle Street E1............246 B2
Old Cavendish Street W1G............239 L6
Old Church Road E1............247 H2
Old Church Street SW3............242 E7
Old Compton Street W1D............240 B7
Old Court Place W8............242 B3
Old Gloucester Street WC1N............240 D4
Old Jamaica Road SE16............246 C7
Old Jewry EC2R............241 K6
Old Kent Road SE1............245 M5
Old Marylebone Road NW1............239 G5
Old Montague Street E1............246 C1
Old North Street WC1X............240 E4
Old Paradise Street SE11............244 E5
Old Park Lane W1J............243 K2
Old Pye Street SW1P............244 B4
Old Queen Street SW1H............244 B3
Old Square WC2A............240 F6
Old Street EC1V............241 J3
Old Street ⊖ EC1Y............241 L3
Old Street Junction EC1Y............241 L3
Oliver's Yard EC1Y............241 L3
Olney Road SE17............245 J8
O'Meara Street SE1............245 K2
Omega Place N1............240 D1
Onega Gate SE16............247 K8
Ongar Road SW6............242 A8
Onslow Gardens SW7............242 D6
Onslow Square SW7............242 E5
Onslow Square SW7............242 E6
Ontario Street SE1............245 H4
Ontario Way E14............247 M4
Opal Street SE11............245 H6
Orange Place SE16............247 G8
Orange Square SW1W............243 K6
Orange Street E1W............246 D5
Orange Street WC2H............240 B8
Orb Street SE17............245 L6
Orchardson Street NW8............238 E4
Orchard Street W1H............239 J6
Orde Hall Street WC1N............240 E4
Orient Street SE11............245 H5
Orme Court W2............238 B8
Orme Lane W2............238 B8
Orme Square Gate W2............238 B8
Ormond Close WC1N............240 D4
Ormonde Gate SW3............243 H7
Ormond Yard SW1Y............244 A8
Orsett Mews W2............238 C6
Orsett Street SE11............244 E6
Orsett Terrace W2............238 C5
Orton Street E1W............246 D5
Osbert Street SW1V............244 B6
Osborn Street E1............246 C2
Oslo Square SE16............247 K7
Osnaburgh Street NW1............239 L3
Osnaburgh Terrace NW1............239 L3
Ossington Buildings W1U............239 J5
Ossington Street W2............238 A7
Ossulston Street NW1............240 B1
Oswin Street SE11............245 H5
Othello Close SE1............245 H6
Otto Street SE17............245 H8
Outer Circle NW1............239 H3
Outer Circle NW1............239 K1
Oval ⊖ SE11............244 F8

Oval Way SE11....244 E7
Ovington Square SW3....243 G4
Ovington Street SW3....243 G5
Owen Street EC1V....241 G1
Oxendon Street SW1Y....240 B8
Oxford Circus ⊖ W1B....239 M6
Oxford Road NW6....238 A1
Oxford Square W2....238 F6
Oxford Street W1C....239 L6
Oxford Street WC1A....240 A6

P

Pace Place E1....246 E3
Pacific Wharf SE16....247 H5
Paddington ⇌⊖ W2....238 D6
Paddington Green W2....238 E5
Paddington Street W1U....239 J5
Pageant Crescent SE16....247 K5
Page Street SW1P....244 B5
Paget Street EC1V....241 H2
Pakenham Street WC1X....240 E3
Palace Avenue W8....242 B2
Palace Court W2....238 A7
Palace Gardens Terrace W8....242 A1
Palace Gate W8....242 C3
Palace Green W8....242 B2
Palace of Westminster SW1A....244 D3
Palace Place SW1E....243 M4
Palace Street SW1E....243 M4
Pall Mall SW1Y....244 A1
Pall Mall East SW1Y....244 B1
Palmer Street SW1H....244 B3
Pancras Lane EC4N....241 K6
Pancras Road N1C....240 C1
Panton Street SW1Y....240 B8
Paradise Street SE16....246 E7
Paradise Walk SW3....243 H8
Pardoner Street SE1....245 L4
Pardon Street EC1V....241 H3
Parfett Street E1....246 D2
Paris Garden SE1....245 G1
Park Crescent W1B....239 K4
Park Crescent Mews West W1G....239 K4
Parker's Row SE1....246 C7
Parker Street WC2B....240 D6
Park Lane W1K....239 H7
Park Lane W2....243 J1
Park Place SW1A....243 M1
Park Place Villas W2....238 D4
Park Road NW1....239 H3
Park Square East NW1....239 L3
Park Square Mews NW1....239 K3
Park Square West NW1....239 K3
Park Street SE1....245 K1
Park Street W1K....239 J7
Park Village East NW1....239 L1
Park Walk SW10....242 D8
Park West Place W2....239 G6
Parliament Street SW1A....244 C2
Parry Street SW8....244 D8
Passmore Street SW1W....243 J6
Paternoster Square....241 J6
Pater Street W8....242 A4
Pattina Walk SE16....247 K5
Paul Street EC2A....241 M3
Paultons Square SW3....242 E8
Paveley Street NW1....239 G3
Pavilion Road SW1X....243 H3
Pavilion Street SW1X....243 H4
Paxton Terrace SW1V....243 L7
Peabody Avenue SW1V....243 L7
Peabody Estate SE1....245 J1
Peacock Street SE17....245 J6
Pearl Street E1W....246 F5
Pearman Street SE1....245 G3
Pear Tree Court EC1R....241 G3
Peartree Lane E1W....247 G4
Pear Tree Street EC1V....241 J3
Peel Street W8....242 A1
Peerless Street EC1V....241 K2
Pelham Crescent SW7....242 F6
Pelham Place SW7....242 F5
Pelham Street SW7....242 F5
Pelier Street SE17....245 K8
Pemberton Row EC4A....241 G6
Pembridge Gardens W2....238 A8
Pembridge Place W2....238 A7
Pembridge Square W2....238 A7
Pembridge Villas W11....238 A7
Pembroke Close SW1X....243 J3
Penang Street E1W....246 F5
Penfold Place NW8....238 F5
Penfold Street NW8....238 E4
Pennant Mews W8....242 B5
Pennington Street E1W....246 D4
Pennyfields E14....247 M4
Penrose Grove SE17....245 J7
Penrose Street SE17....245 J7
Penton Place SE17....245 H6
Penton Rise WC1X....240 E2
Penton Street N1....240 F1
Pentonville Road N1....240 E1
Penywern Road SW5....242 A6
Pepper Street SE1....245 J2
Pepys Street EC3N....246 A4
Percival Street EC1V....241 H3
Percy Circus WC1X....240 F2
Percy Street W1T....240 B5
Perkin's Rents SW1P....244 B4
Perryn Road SE16....246 E7
Petersham Mews SW7....242 D4
Petersham Place SW7....242 C4
Peter Street W1F....240 B7
Peto Place NW1....239 L3
Petticoat Lane E1....246 B2
Petty France SW1H....244 A3
Petty Wales EC3R....246 A4
Petyward SW3....243 G6
Phelp Street SE17....245 L7
Phene Street SW3....243 G8
Phillimore Walk W8....242 A3
Phipp's Mews SW1W....243 L5
Phipp Street EC2A....241 M3
Phoenix Place WC1X....240 F3
Phoenix Road NW1....240 B1
Phoenix Street WC2H....240 C6
Piccadilly W1J....243 L2
Piccadilly Arcade SW1Y....243 M1
Piccadilly Circus W1B....240 A8
Piccadilly Circus ⊖ W1J....240 B8
Pickard Street EC1V....241 J2

Picton Place W1U....239 K6
Pier Head E1W....246 E6
Pigott Street E14....247 M3
Pilgrimage Street SE1....245 L3
Pimlico ⊖ SW1V....244 B6
Pimlico Road SW1W....243 J6
Pinchin Street E1....246 D3
Pindar Street EC2A....241 M4
Pindock Mews W9....238 B3
Pine Street EC1R....240 F3
Pitfield Street N1....241 M1
Pitsea Street E1....247 H3
Pitt's Head Mews W1J....243 K2
Pitt Street W8....242 A2
Pixley Street E14....247 L2
Platina Street * EC2A....241 L3
Plover Way SE16....247 K8
Plumbers Row E1....246 D2
Plumtree Court EC4A....241 G6
Plympton Street NW8....238 F4
Pocock Street SE1....245 H2
Poland Street W1F....240 A6
Pollen Street W1S....239 L7
Pollitt Street SE1....238 E3
Polperro Mews SE11....245 G5
Polygon Road NW1....240 B1
Pond Place SW3....242 F6
Ponler Street E1....246 E3
Ponsonby Place SW1P....244 C6
Ponsonby Terrace SW1P....244 C6
Ponton Road SW1V....244 B8
Pont Street SW1X....243 H4
Poolmans Street SE16....247 H6
Pope Street SE1....246 B7
Poplar Place W2....238 B7
Poppin's Court EC4A....241 H6
Porchester Gardens W2....238 B7
Porchester Gate W2....238 C8
Porchester Place W2....239 G6
Porchester Road W2....238 B5
Porchester Square W2....238 B6
Porchester Terrace W2....238 C7
Porchester Terrace North W2....238 C6
Porlock Street SE1....245 L3
Porter Street NW1....239 H4
Porteus Road W2....238 D5
Portland Place W1B....239 L4
Portland Place W1B....239 L5
Portland Square E1W....246 E5
Portland Street SE17....245 L7
Portman Close W1H....239 J6
Portman Mews South W1H....239 J6
Portman Square W1H....239 J6
Portman Street W1H....239 J6
Portpool Lane EC1N....240 F4
Portsea Place W2....239 G6
Portsmouth Street WC2A....240 E6
Portsoken Street E1....246 B3
Portugal Street WC2A....240 E6
Potier Street SE1....245 L4
Potters Fields SE1....246 B6
Pottery Street SE16....246 E7
Poultry EC2V....241 K6
Powis Place WC1N....240 D4
Praed Mews W2....238 E6
Praed Street W2....238 E6
Pratt Walk SE1....244 E5
Premier Place E14....247 M4
Prescot Street E1....246 C3
Preston Close SE1....245 M5
Price's Street SE1....245 H1
Prideaux Place WC1X....240 F2
Primrose Street EC2A....246 A1
Prince Albert Road NW8....238 F1
Prince Consort Road SW7....242 D3
Princelet Street E1....246 C1
Prince of Wales Gate SW7....242 F3
Princes Arcade SW1Y....240 A8
Prince's Gardens SW7....242 E3
Prince's Gate Mews SW7....242 E4
Princes Riverside Road SE16....247 H5
Princess Road NW6....238 A1
Princess Street SE1....245 H4
Princes Street W1B....239 L6
Prince's Street EC2R....241 L6
Princeton Street WC1R....240 E5
Prioress Street SE1....245 L4
Priory Green Estate N1....240 E1
Priory Walk SW10....242 D7
Proctor Street WC1V....240 E5
Prospect Place E1W....247 G5
Prospect Street SE16....246 E7
Provident Court W1K....239 J7
Provost Street N1....241 L1
Prusom Street E1W....246 F5
Pudding Lane EC3R....241 M7
Pumphouse Mews E1....246 D3
Purbrook Street SE1....246 A7
Purcell Street N1....241 M1
Purchese Street NW1....240 B1

Q

Quebec Way SE16....247 J7
Queen Anne's Gate SW1H....244 B3
Queen Anne Street W1G....239 K5
Queen Elizabeth Street SE1....246 B6
Queen Mother Gate W2....243 J2
Queensborough Terrace W2....238 C7
Queensbury Place SW7....242 E5
Queen's Gardens W2....238 C7
Queen's Gate SW7....242 D3
Queen's Gate SW7....242 D4
Queen's Gate Gardens SW7....242 D5
Queen's Gate Mews SW7....242 D4
Queen's Gate Place SW7....242 D4
Queen's Gate Place Mews SW7....242 D4
Queen's Gate Terrace SW7....242 C4
Queen's Mews W2....238 B7
Queen Square WC1N....240 D4
Queen's Row SE17....245 K7
Queen Street EC4N....241 K7
Queen Street W1J....243 L1
Queen Street Place EC4R....241 K7
Queen's Walk SE1....246 A5
Queen's Walk SW1A....243 M2
Queensway W2....238 B6
Queensway ⊖ W2....238 B8
Queen Victoria Street EC4V....241 J7
Quick Street N1....241 H1

R

Raby Street E14....247 K2
Radcliffe Road SE1....246 B8
Radcot Street SE11....245 G7
Radnor Mews W2....238 E6
Radnor Place W2....238 F6
Radnor Street EC1V....241 K3
Radnor Walk SW3....243 G7
Railway Approach SE1....245 L1
Railway Avenue SE16....247 G6
Railway Street N1....240 D1
Raine Street E1W....246 F5
Ralston Street SW3....243 H7
Ramillies Place W1F....239 M6
Ramillies Street W1F....239 M6
Rampart Street E1....246 E2
Rampayne Street SW1V....244 B6
Randall Road SE11....244 D6
Randall Row SE11....244 E6
Randolph Avenue W9....238 B3
Randolph Crescent W9....238 C3
Randolph Gardens NW6....238 B1
Randolph Mews W9....238 D4
Randolph Road W9....238 C4
Ranelagh Grove SW1W....243 K6
Ranelagh Road SW1V....244 A7
Rangoon Street * EC3N....246 B3
Ranston Street NW8....238 F4
Raphael Street SW7....243 G3
Ratcliffe Cross Street E1W....247 J3
Ratcliffe Lane E14....247 J3
Rathbone Place W1T....240 B5
Rathbone Street W1T....240 A5
Raven Row E1....246 F1
Ravensdon Street SE11....245 G7
Ravey Street EC2A....241 M3
Rawlings Street SW3....243 G5
Rawstorne Street EC1V....241 H2
Ray Street EC1R....241 G4
Reardon Place E1W....246 F5
Reardon Street E1W....246 E5
Rectory Square E1....247 H1
Redan Place W2....238 B6
Redburn Street SW3....243 G7
Redcastle Close E1W....247 G4
Redcliffe Gardens SW10....242 B7
Redcliffe Mews SW10....242 C7
Redcliffe Place SW10....242 C8
Redcliffe Road SW10....242 D7
Redcliffe Square SW10....242 B7
Redcliffe Street SW10....242 B8
Redcross Way SE1....245 K2
Redesdale Street SW3....243 G7
Redfield Lane SW5....242 A5
Redhill Street NW1....239 L1
Red Lion Row SE5....245 K8
Red Lion Square WC1R....240 E5
Red Lion Street WC2B....240 E5
Redman's Road E1....247 G1
Red Place W1K....239 J7
Redriff Road SE16....247 J8
Reedworth Street SE11....245 G6
Reeves Mews W1K....239 J8
Regal Close E1....246 D1
Regan Way N1....241 M1
Regency Street SW1P....244 B5
Regent Place W1B....240 A7
Regent's Park ⊖ W1B....239 L4
Regent's Park NW1....239 J1
Regent's Park Estate NW1....239 L2
Regent Square WC1H....240 D2
Regent Street SW1Y....240 B8
Regent Street W1S....239 M7
Relton Mews SW7....243 G4
Remington Street N1....241 H1
Remnant Street WC2A....240 E6
Renforth Street SE16....247 G7
Renfrew Road SE11....245 H5
Rennie Street SE1....245 H1
Rephidim Street SE1....245 M4
Repton Street E14....247 K2
Reveley Square SE16....247 K7
Rex Place W1K....239 J8
Rhodeswell Road E14....247 L2
Rich Street E14....247 M3
Rickett Street SW6....242 A8
Ridgemount Street WC1E....240 B4
Ridgemount Gardens WC1E....240 B4
Riding House Street W1W....239 M5
Riley Road SE1....246 B7
Risborough Street SE1....245 J2
Risdon Street SE16....247 G6
Rissinghill Street N1....240 F1
River Street EC1R....240 F2
Rivington Street EC2A....241 M3
Robert Adam Street W1U....239 J6
Roberts Close SE16....247 J7
Robert Street NW1....239 L2
Rochester Row SW1P....244 A5
Rochester Street SW1P....244 B5
Rockingham Street SE1....245 J4
Rocliffe Street N1....241 H1
Roding Mews E1W....246 D5
Rodmarton Street W1U....239 H5
Rodney Place SE17....245 K5
Rodney Road SE17....245 K5
Rodney Street N1....240 E1
Roger Street WC1N....240 E4
Roland Gardens SW7....242 D6
Roland Way SE17....245 L7
Romford Street E1....246 E2
Romilly Street W1D....240 B7
Romney Street SW1P....244 C5
Rood Lane EC3M....241 M7
Ropemaker Road SE16....247 K7
Ropemaker Street EC2Y....241 L4
Roper Lane SE1....246 B7
Rope Street SE16....247 K8
Rope Walk Gardens E1....246 E2
Rosary Gardens SW7....242 D6
Roscoe Street EC1Y....241 K3
Rose Alley SE1....241 K8
Rosebery Avenue EC1R....240 F3
Rosemoor Street SW3....243 G6
Rose Street WC2E....240 C7
Rossmore Road NW1....239 G3
Rotary Street SE1....245 H3
Rotherhithe ⊖ SE16....247 G6
Rotherhithe Street SE16....247 G5
Rotherhithe Street SE16....247 J6
Rotherhithe Tunnel SE16....247 H5
Rothsay Street SE1....245 M4
Rotten Row W2....242 F2

Rouel Road SE16....246 C8
Roupell Street SE1....245 G2
Royal Albert Hall SW7....242 E3
Royal Avenue SW3....243 H6
Royal Hospital Road SW3....243 H7
Royal Mint Street E1....246 C4
Royal Oak ⊖ W2....238 B5
Royal Oak Yard SE1....246 A7
Royal Opera House WC2E....240 D7
Royal Road SE17....245 H8
Royal Street SE1....244 E3
Rudolph Road NW6....238 A1
Rugby Street WC1N....240 E4
Rum Close E1W....246 F4
Rupack Street SE16....247 G6
Rupert Street W1D....240 B7
Rushworth Street SE1....245 H2
Russell Court SW1A....244 A2
Russell Square WC1B....240 C4
Russell Square ⊖ WC1B....240 D4
Russell Street WC2B....240 D7
Russia Dock Road SE16....247 K6
Rutherford Street SW1P....244 B5
Rutland Gardens SW7....243 G3
Rutland Gate SW7....242 F4
Rutland Mews SW7....242 F4
Rutland Street SW7....242 F4
Ryder Street SW1Y....244 A1

S

Sackville Street W1S....240 A8
Saffron Hill EC1N....241 G4
Saffron Street EC1N....241 G4
Sail Street SE11....244 F5
St Agnes Place SE11....245 G8
St Alban's Grove W8....242 B4
St Alban's Street W1Y....240 B8
St Alphage Garden EC2Y....241 K5
St Andrews Hill EC4V....241 H7
St Andrew's Place NW1....239 L3
St Andrew Street EC4A....241 G5
St Anne's Court W1F....240 B6
St Ann's Street SW1....244 C4
St Anselm's Place W1K....239 K7
St Barnabas Street SW1W....243 K6
St Botolph Street EC3N....246 B2
St Bride Street EC4A....241 G6
St Chad's Street WC1H....240 D2
St Clare Street EC3....246 B3
St Clements Lane WC2A....240 E6
St Cross Street EC1N....241 G4
St Dunstan's Hill EC3R....241 M8
St Dunstan's Lane EC3R....241 M7
St Elmos Road SE16....247 J7
St Ermin's Hill SW1....244 B3
St George's Circus SE1....245 H3
St George's Drive SW1V....243 M6
St George's Lane * EC3R....241 M7
St George's Road SE1....245 G4
St George's Square SW1V....244 B7
St George Street W1S....239 L7
St Giles High Street WC2H....240 C6
St Helen's Place EC3A....241 M6
St James Market * SW1Y....240 B8
St James's Park ⊖ SW1H....244 B3
St James's Park SW1A....244 B3
St James's Place SW1A....243 M2
St James's Road SE16....246 D8
St James's Square SW1Y....244 A1
St James's Street SW1A....243 M1
St James Walk EC1R....241 G3
St John's Lane EC1M....241 H4
St John's Place EC1M....241 H4
St John's Square EC1V....241 H4
St John Street EC1V....241 H2
St John's Wood High Street NW8....238 E1
St John's Wood Road NW8....238 E3
St Katharine's Way E1W....246 C5
St Leonard's Terrace SW3....243 H7
St Loo Avenue SW3....243 G8
St Luke's Close EC1V....241 K3
St Luke's Street SW3....242 F6
St Manningtree E1....246 C2
St Mark Street E1....246 C3
St Martin's Lane WC2N....240 C7
St Martin's le Grand EC1A....241 J6
St Martin's Place WC2N....240 C8
St Mary at Hill EC3R....241 M8
St Mary Axe EC3A....246 A3
St Marychurch Street SE16....246 F7
St Mary's Gardens SE11....245 G5
St Mary's Terrace W2....238 D4
St Mary's Walk SE11....245 G5
St Matthew Street SW1P....244 B4
St Michael's Street W2....238 E6
St Olav's Square SE16....246 F7
St Oswald's Place SE11....244 E7
St Oswulf Street * SW1P....244 C6
St Pancras International ⇌ N1C....240 C1
St Paul's ⊖ EC1A....241 J6
St Paul's Avenue SE16....247 J5
St Paul's Cathedral EC4M....241 J6
St Paul's Churchyard EC4M....241 J6
St Paul's Way E3....247 L1
St Petersburgh Mews W2....238 B7
St Petersburgh Place W2....238 B7
St Saviours Wharf SE1....246 C6
St Stephen's Gardens W2....238 A5
St Swithin's Lane EC4N....241 L7
St Thomas Street SE1....245 L2
St Vincent Street W1U....239 J5
Salamanca Street SE1....244 D6
Salem Road W2....238 B7
Sale Place W2....238 F5
Salisbury Court EC4Y....241 G6
Salisbury Place W1H....239 H4
Salisbury Street NW8....238 F4
Salmon Lane E14....247 J2
Salter Road SE16....247 J5
Salter Street E14....247 M4
Samford Street NW8....238 F4
Sampson Street E1W....246 D5
Sancroft Street SE11....244 F6
Sandland Street WC1R....240 E5
Sandpiper Close SE16....247 K6
Sandwich Street WC1H....240 C2
Sandy's Row E1....246 B1
Sans Walk EC1R....241 G3
Sardinia Street WC2A....240 E6
Savage Gardens EC3N....246 B3
Savile Row W1S....239 M7
Savoy Hill WC2R....240 E8

Savoy Place WC2R....240 D8
Savoy Street WC2E....240 E7
Sawyer Street SE1....245 J2
Scala Street W1T....240 A5
Scandrett Street E1W....246 E5
Scarborough Street E1....246 C3
Scarsdale Villas W8....242 A4
Schooner Close * SE16....247 H6
Science Museum SW7....242 E4
Scoresby Street SE1....245 H2
Scotch House Junction SW1X....243 H3
Scotland Place SW1A....244 C1
Scott Ellis Gardens NW8....238 E2
Scott Lidgett Crescent SE16....246 D7
Scrutton Street EC2A....241 M3
Seaford Street WC1H....240 D2
Seagrave Road SW6....242 A8
Sea Life London Aquarium SE1....244 E3
Searles Road SE1....245 L5
Sebastian Street EC1V....241 H2
Secker Street SE1....244 F2
Sedan Way SE17....245 M6
Sedding Street SW1X....243 J5
Seddon Street WC1X....240 E3
Seething Lane EC3N....246 A4
Sekforde Street EC1R....241 H3
Selfridges W1A....239 J6
Selsey Street E14....247 M1
Selwood Place SW7....242 E6
Semley Place SW1W....243 K6
Senior Street W2....238 B4
Senrab Street E1....247 H2
Serle Street WC2A....240 F6
Serpentine Bridge W2....242 E1
Serpentine Road W2....242 F2
Seth Street SE16....247 G6
Settles Street E1....246 D2
Seven Dials WC2H....240 C6
Seville Street SW1X....243 H3
Seward Street EC1V....241 J3
Seymour Mews W1H....239 J6
Seymour Place W1H....239 G5
Seymour Street W1H....239 H6
Seymour Street W2....239 G7
Seymour Walk SW10....242 C7
Shad Thames SE1....246 B6
Shad Thames SE1....246 C6
Shadwell ⊖ E1....246 F3
Shadwell Gardens E1....246 F3
Shaftesbury Avenue W1D....240 B7
Shaftesbury Avenue WC2H....240 C6
Shaftesbury Street N1....241 K1
Shakespeare's Globe SE1....241 J8
Shand Street SE1....246 A6
Sharsted Street SE17....245 H7
Shaw Crescent E14....247 K2
Shawfield Street SW3....243 G7
Sheffield Terrace W8....242 A2
Sheldon Square W2....238 D5
Shelmerdine Close E3....247 M1
Shelton Street WC2H....240 D6
Shepherdess Walk N1....241 K1
Shepherd Street W1J....243 K1
Sheraton Street W1F....240 B6
Sherborne Lane EC4N....241 L7
Sherwood Street W1D....240 A7
Ship and Mermaid Row SE1....245 M2
Shipwright Road SE16....247 K7
Shirland Road W9....238 A3
Shoe Lane EC4A....241 G5
Shorter Street EC3N....246 B4
Shorts Gardens WC2H....240 C6
Short Street SE1....245 G2
Shoulder of Mutton Alley E14....247 K4
Shouldham Street W1H....239 G5
Shroton Street NW1....238 F4
Siddons Lane W1H....239 H4
Sidmouth Street WC1N....240 D3
Sidney Square E1....246 F2
Sidney Street E1....246 F1
Silex Street SE1....245 H3
Silk Street EC2Y....241 K4
Silver Walk SE16....247 K5
Silvester Street SE1....245 K3
Singer Street EC2A....241 L3
Sir John Soane's Museum WC2A....240 E5
Sir Simon Milton Square SW1V....243 L4
Skinner Place * SW3....243 J6
Skinners Lane EC4V....241 K7
Skinner Street EC1R....241 G3
Slippers Place SE16....246 F8
Sloane Avenue SW3....243 G6
Sloane Court East SW3....243 J6
Sloane Court West SW3....243 J6
Sloane Gardens SW1W....243 J6
Sloane Square SW1W....243 J5
Sloane Square ⊖ SW1W....243 J6
Sloane Street SW1X....243 H3
Sloane Terrace SW1X....243 J5
Smeaton Street E1W....246 E5
Smithfield Street EC1A....241 H5
Smith Square SW1P....244 C4
Smith Street SW3....243 G7
Smith Terrace SW3....243 G7
Smithy Street E1....247 G1
Snowden Street EC2A....241 M4
Snow Hill EC1A....241 H5
Snowsfields SE1....245 L2
Soho Square W1D....240 B6
Soho Street W1D....240 B6
Somerford Way SE16....247 K7
Somers Crescent W2....238 F6
Somerset House WC2R....240 E7
Somerston Estate NW1....240 A1
Sondes Street SE17....245 L7
South & West Africa Gate SW1A....244 A3
Southall Place SE1....245 L3
Southampton Buildings WC2A....240 F5
Southampton Place WC1A....240 D5
Southampton Row WC1B....240 D4
Southampton Street WC2E....240 D7
South Audley Street W1K....239 J8
South Carriage Drive SW1X....243 H3
South Carriage Drive SW7....242 F3
South Eaton Place SW1W....243 J5
South Kensington ⊖ SW7....242 E5
South Lambeth Road SW8....244 D8
South Molton Lane W1K....239 K7
South Molton Street W1K....239 K7
South Parade SW3....242 E7
South Place EC2M....241 L5
South Sea Street SE16....247 L8
South Square WC1R....240 F5

South Street W1K ... 243 J1
South Tenter Street E1 ... 246 C3
South Terrace SW7 ... 242 F5
Southwark ⊖ SE1 ... 245 H2
Southwark Bridge SE1 ... 241 K8
Southwark Bridge Road SE1 ... 245 J3
Southwark Park Road SE16 ... 246 E8
Southwell Gardens SW7 ... 242 C5
South Wharf Road W2 ... 238 E6
Southwick Mews W2 ... 238 F6
Southwick Place W2 ... 238 F6
Southwick Street W2 ... 238 F6
Sovereign Close E1W ... 246 F4
Sovereign Crescent SE16 ... 247 J4
Spanish Place W1U ... 239 J5
Spa Road SE16 ... 246 C8
Spear Mews SW5 ... 242 A6
Spelman Street E1 ... 246 C1
Spence Close SE16 ... 247 K7
Spencer Street EC1V ... 241 H2
Spenser Street SW1E ... 244 A4
Spert Street E14 ... 247 J4
Spital Square E1 ... 246 A1
Spring Gardens SW1A ... 244 C1
Spring Street W2 ... 238 E6
Spurgeon Street SE1 ... 245 L4
Spur Road SE1 ... 244 F3
Stables Way SE11 ... 244 F7
Stable Yard Road SW1A ... 244 A2
Stacey Street WC2H ... 240 C6
Stafford Place SW1E ... 243 M3
Stafford Road NW6 ... 238 A2
Stafford Street W1S ... 239 M8
Stafford Terrace W8 ... 242 A3
Stainer Street SE1 ... 245 L2
Staining Lane EC2V ... 241 K6
Stainsby Road E14 ... 247 M2
Stalham Street SE16 ... 246 F8
Stamford Street SE1 ... 245 G1
Stanford Place SE1 ... 245 M6
Stanford Road W8 ... 242 B4
Stanford Street * SW1V ... 244 B6
Stanhope Close * SE16 ... 247 H6
Stanhope Gardens SW7 ... 242 D5
Stanhope Gate W1K ... 243 K1
Stanhope Mews SW7 ... 242 D5
Stanhope Mews East SW7 ... 242 D5
Stanhope Mews West SW7 ... 242 D5
Stanhope Place W2 ... 239 G7
Stanhope Place Gate W2 ... 239 G7
Stanhope Row W1J ... 243 K1
Stanhope Street NW1 ... 239 M1
Stanhope Terrace W2 ... 238 E7
Stannary Street SE11 ... 245 G7
Staples Close SE16 ... 247 J5
Staple Street SE1 ... 245 L3
Starcross Street NW1 ... 240 A2
Star Street W2 ... 238 F6
Station Approach SE1 ... 244 F3
Stave Yard Road SE16 ... 247 J5
Stead Street SE17 ... 245 K6
Steedman Street SE17 ... 245 J5
Steel's Lane E1 ... 247 G3
Steeres Way SE14 ... 247 K7
Stephenson Way NW1 ... 240 A3
Stephen Street W1T ... 240 B5
Stepney Green E1 ... 247 H1
Stepney High Street E1 ... 247 J1
Stepney Way E1 ... 246 E1
Sterling Street SW7 ... 243 G3
Stevedore Street E1W ... 246 E5
Stevens Street SE1 ... 246 A7
Steward Street * E1 ... 246 B1
Stewart's Grove SW3 ... 242 F6
Stew Lane EC4V ... 241 J7
Stillington Street SW1P ... 244 A5
Stockholm Way E1W ... 246 D5
Stocks Place E14 ... 247 M3
Stone Buildings WC2A ... 240 F5
Stonecutter Street EC4A ... 241 G6
Stoney Lane E1 ... 246 B2
Stoney Street SE1 ... 245 K1
Stopford Road SE17 ... 245 J7
Store Street WC1E ... 240 B5
Storey's Gate SW1H ... 244 C3
Storks Road SE16 ... 246 D8
Stoughton Close SE11 ... 244 E6
Stourcliffe Street W1H ... 239 G6
Strafford Street E14 ... 247 M6
Strand WC2R ... 240 D8
Stratford Place W1C ... 239 K6
Stratford Road W8 ... 242 A5
Strathearn Place W2 ... 238 F7
Stratton Street W1J ... 243 L1
Strutton Ground SW1P ... 244 B4
Strype Street E1 ... 246 B2
Stuart Road NW6 ... 238 A2
Stukeley Street WC2B ... 240 D6
Sturgeon Road SE17 ... 245 J7
Sturge Street SE1 ... 245 J3
Sturt Street N1 ... 241 K1
Stutfield Street E1 ... 246 D3
Sudley Street N1 ... 241 H1
Sudrey Street SE1 ... 245 J3
Suffolk Lane EC4V ... 241 L7
Suffolk Street SW1Y ... 240 B8
Sugar Lane SE16 ... 246 D7
Sugar Quay Walk EC3R ... 246 A4
Sullivan Road SE11 ... 245 G5
Summercourt Road E1 ... 247 G2
Summers Street EC1R ... 240 F4
Sumner Place SW7 ... 242 E6
Sumner Street SE1 ... 245 J1
Sunderland Terrace W2 ... 238 A6
Sun Passage SE16 ... 246 D8
Sun Street EC2M ... 241 M4
Sun Street Passage EC2M ... 241 M5
Surrendale Place W9 ... 238 A4
Surrey Quays Road SE16 ... 247 H7
Surrey Row SE1 ... 245 H2
Surrey Square SE17 ... 245 M6
Surrey Street WC2E ... 240 E7
Surrey Water Road SE16 ... 247 H6
Sussex Gardens W2 ... 238 E6
Sussex Mews East W2 ... 238 E7
Sussex Place NW1 ... 239 H3
Sussex Place W2 ... 238 E6
Sussex Square W2 ... 238 E7
Sussex Street SW1V ... 243 L7
Sutherland Avenue W9 ... 238 A4
Sutherland Row SW1V ... 243 L6
Sutherland Square SE17 ... 245 J7
Sutherland Street SW1V ... 243 L7
Sutton Row W1D ... 240 B6
Sutton Street E1 ... 247 G3

Suttons Way EC1Y ... 241 K4
Swain Street NW8 ... 238 F3
Swallow Place W1B ... 239 L6
Swallow Street W1B ... 240 A8
Swan Lane EC4R ... 241 L8
Swan Mead SE1 ... 245 M4
Swan Road SE16 ... 247 G6
Swan Street SE1 ... 245 K3
Swan Walk SW3 ... 243 H8
Swedenborg Gardens E1 ... 246 E4
Sweeney Crescent SE1 ... 246 C7
Swinton Street WC1X ... 240 E2
Sydney Place SW7 ... 242 F6
Sydney Street SW3 ... 242 F6
Symons Street SW3 ... 243 H6

T

Tabard Gardens Estate SE1 ... 245 L3
Tabard Street SE1 ... 245 L3
Tabernacle Street EC2A ... 241 L3
Tachbrook Street SW1V ... 244 A6
Talbot Road W2 ... 238 A6
Talbot Square W2 ... 238 E6
Talbot Yard SE1 ... 245 L2
Tallis Street EC4Y ... 241 G7
Tamworth Street SW6 ... 242 A8
Tanner Street SE1 ... 246 A7
Taplow Street N1 ... 241 K1
Tarling Street E1 ... 246 F3
Tarver Road SE17 ... 245 H7
Tatum Street SE17 ... 245 M6
Taunton Place NW1 ... 239 G3
Tavistock Place WC1H ... 240 C3
Tavistock Square WC1H ... 240 C3
Tavistock Street WC2E ... 240 D7
Taviton Street WC1H ... 240 B3
Teak Close SE16 ... 247 K6
Tedworth Square SW3 ... 243 G7
Telford Terrace SW1V ... 243 M7
Temeraire Street SE16 ... 247 G6
Temple ⊖ WC2R ... 240 F7
Temple Avenue EC4Y ... 241 G7
Temple Lane EC4Y ... 241 G7
Temple Place WC2R ... 240 F7
Templeton Place SW5 ... 242 A5
Tench Street E1W ... 246 E5
Tenniel Close W2 ... 238 C7
Tennis Street SE1 ... 245 L2
Tenterden Street W1S ... 239 L6
Tenterground E1 ... 246 B1
Teredo Street SE16 ... 247 J8
Terminus Place SW1V ... 243 L4
Thame Road SE16 ... 247 H6
Thanet Street WC1H ... 240 C2
Thavies Inn EC4A ... 241 G6
Thayer Street W1U ... 239 K5
The Arches WC2N ... 240 D8
The Boltons SW10 ... 242 C7
The Broad Walk W2 ... 238 B8
The Broad Walk W8 ... 242 C2
The Cut SE1 ... 245 G2
Theed Street SE1 ... 245 G2
The Flower Walk W2 ... 242 D3
The Grange SE1 ... 246 B8
The Highway E1W ... 246 E4
The Little Boltons SW10 ... 242 C7
The Mall SW1A ... 244 B2
The Mitre E14 ... 247 L3
The Monument EC3R ... 241 L7
The National Gallery WC2N ... 240 C8
Theobald's Road WC1X ... 240 E4
Theobald Street SE1 ... 245 L5
The Oval (Surrey County Cricket Ground) SE11 ... 244 F8
The Shard SE1 ... 245 L2
The Vale SW3 ... 242 E8
Thirleby Road SW1P ... 244 A4
Thomas More Street E1W ... 246 D4
Thomas Road E14 ... 247 M2
Thoresby Street N1 ... 241 K1
Thorney Street SW1P ... 244 C5
Thornton Place W1H ... 239 H4
Thrale Street SE1 ... 245 K1
Thrawl Street E1 ... 246 C1
Threadneedle Street EC2R ... 241 L6
Three Colt Street E14 ... 247 L3
Three Oak Lane SE1 ... 246 B6
Throgmorton Avenue EC2N ... 241 L6
Throgmorton Street EC2N ... 241 L6
Thurland Road SE16 ... 246 D8
Thurloe Place SW7 ... 242 F5
Thurloe Square SW7 ... 242 F5
Thurloe Street SW7 ... 242 E5
Thurlow Street SE17 ... 245 M7
Tichbourne Row W2 ... 238 F6
Tiller Road E14 ... 247 M8
Tillman Street E1 ... 246 E3
Tilney Street W1J ... 243 K1
Timber Pond Road SE16 ... 247 J6
Tinsley Road E1 ... 247 G1
Tinworth Street SE11 ... 244 D6
Tisdall Place SE17 ... 245 L6
Tite Street SW3 ... 243 H8
Tiverton Street SE1 ... 245 J4
Token House Yard EC2R ... 241 L6
Tolmer's Square NW1 ... 240 A3
Tomlin's Terrace E14 ... 247 K2
Tonbridge Street WC1H ... 240 D2
Tooley Street SE1 ... 245 L1
Tooley Street SE1 ... 246 B6
Tor Gardens W8 ... 242 A2
Torquay Street W2 ... 238 A5
Torrens Street EC1V ... 241 G1
Torrington Place EC2R ... 241 L6
Torrington Place WC1E ... 240 B4
Torrington Square WC1E ... 240 B4
Tothill Street SW1H ... 244 B3
Tottenham Court Road W1T ... 240 A4
Tottenham Court Road ⊖ W1D ... 240 B6
Tottenham Street W1T ... 240 A5
Toulmin Street SE1 ... 245 J3
Tower Bridge EC3N ... 246 B5
Tower Bridge Approach EC3N ... 246 B5
Tower Bridge Road SE1 ... 246 A7
Tower Bridge Wharf E1W ... 246 C5
Tower Gateway ⊖ EC3N ... 246 B4
Tower Hill EC3N ... 246 B4
Tower Hill * EC3N ... 246 B4
Tower of London EC3N ... 246 B4

Tower Place EC3R ... 246 A4
Tower Street WC2H ... 240 C7
Townsend Street SE17 ... 245 M5
Toynbee Street E1 ... 246 B1
Trafalgar Gardens E1 ... 247 H1
Trafalgar Square WC2N ... 240 C8
Transept Street NW1 ... 238 F5
Trebeck Street W1J ... 243 L1
Trebovir Road SW5 ... 242 A6
Tregunter Road SW10 ... 242 C7
Trenton Road SE16 ... 246 E8
Tresham Crescent NW8 ... 238 F3
Trevor Place SW7 ... 243 G3
Trevor Square SW7 ... 243 G3
Trevor Street SW7 ... 243 G3
Trinidad Street E14 ... 247 M4
Trinity Church Square SE1 ... 245 K3
Trinity Square EC3N ... 246 B4
Trinity Street SE1 ... 245 K3
Trump Street EC2V ... 241 K6
Tufton Street SW1P ... 244 C4
Tunnel Road SE16 ... 247 G6
Turks Row SW3 ... 243 J6
Turner's Road E3 ... 247 L2
Turner Street E1 ... 246 E2
Turnmill Street EC1N ... 241 G4
Turpentine Lane SW1V ... 243 L7
Turquand Street SE17 ... 245 K6
Tyers Gate SE1 ... 245 M3
Tyers Street SE11 ... 244 E7
Tyers Terrace SE11 ... 244 E7
Tyron Street SW3 ... 243 H6
Tysoe Street EC1R ... 241 G3

U

Udall Street SW1P ... 244 A5
Ufford Street SE1 ... 245 G2
Ulster Place NW1 ... 239 K4
Umberston Street E1 ... 246 E2
Undershaft EC3A ... 246 A2
Underwood Road N1 ... 241 K2
Underwood Street N1 ... 241 K1
Union Street SE1 ... 245 H2
University Street WC1E ... 240 A4
Upbrook Mews W2 ... 238 D6
Upper Belgrave Street SW1X ... 243 K4
Upper Berkeley Street W1H ... 239 H6
Upper Brook Street W1K ... 239 J7
Upper Cheyne Row SW3 ... 242 F8
Upper Grosvenor Street W1K ... 239 J8
Upper Ground SE1 ... 244 F1
Upper Harley Street NW1 ... 239 K3
Upper James Street W1F ... 240 A7
Upper John Street W1F ... 240 A7
Upper Marsh SE1 ... 244 E3
Upper Montagu Street W1H ... 239 H5
Upper St Martin's WC2H ... 240 C7
Upper Tachbrook Street SW1V ... 244 A5
Upper Thames Street EC4V ... 241 J7
Upper Wimpole Street W1G ... 239 K4
Upper Woburn Place WC1H ... 240 B2
Urlwin Street SE5 ... 245 J8
Uxbridge Street W8 ... 242 A1

V

Valentine Place SE1 ... 245 G3
Vandon Passage SW1H ... 244 A3
Vandon Street SW1H ... 244 A4
Varden Street E1 ... 246 E2
Varndell Street NW1 ... 239 M2
Vauban Street SE16 ... 246 C8
Vaughan Street SE16 ... 247 L7
Vaughan Way E1W ... 246 D5
Vauxhall ⇌ ⊖ SW8 ... 244 D7
Vauxhall Bridge SW1V ... 244 C7
Vauxhall Bridgefoot SE1 ... 244 D7
Vauxhall Bridge Road SW1V ... 243 M5
Vauxhall Cross SE1 ... 244 D7
Vauxhall Grove SW8 ... 244 D8
Vauxhall Street SE11 ... 244 E6
Vauxhall Walk SE11 ... 244 E6
Venables Street W2 ... 238 E4
Vere Street W1G ... 239 K6
Vernon Place WC1A ... 240 D5
Vernon Rise WC1X ... 240 E2
Verulam Street WC1X ... 240 F4
Vestry Street N1 ... 241 L2
Victoria ⇌ ⊖ SW1V ... 243 L5
Victoria & Albert Museum SW7 ... 242 F4
Victoria Embankment SW1A ... 244 D2
Victoria Embankment WC2R ... 240 F7
Victoria Gate W2 ... 238 F7
Victoria Road W8 ... 242 C4
Victoria Square SW1W ... 243 L4
Victoria Street SW1E ... 243 L4
Victory Place SE17 ... 245 K5
Victory Way SE16 ... 247 K7
Vigo Street W1S ... 239 M8
Villa Street SE17 ... 245 L7
Villiers Street WC2N ... 240 D8
Vincent Close SE16 ... 247 K7
Vincent Square SW1P ... 244 B5
Vincent Street SW1P ... 244 B5
Vincent Terrace N1 ... 241 H1
Vince Street EC1V ... 241 L2
Vine Court E1 ... 246 D1
Vinegar Street E1W ... 246 E5
Vine Hill EC1R ... 240 F4
Vine Lane SE1 ... 246 A6
Vine Street EC3N ... 246 B3
Violet Hill NW8 ... 238 C1
Virgil Street SE1 ... 244 F4
Virginia Street E1W ... 246 D4
Viscount Street EC2Y ... 241 J4

W

Wadding Street SE17 ... 245 K6
Wakefield Street WC1H ... 240 D3
Wakeling Street E14 ... 247 J3
Wakley Street EC1V ... 241 H2
Walbrook EC4N ... 241 L7
Walcorde Avenue SE17 ... 245 K6
Walcot Square SE11 ... 245 G5
Walden Street E1 ... 246 E2
Waley Street E1 ... 247 J1

Wallwood Street E14 ... 247 M1
Walnut Tree Walk SE11 ... 244 F5
Walpole Street SW3 ... 243 H6
Walter Terrace E1 ... 247 H2
Walton Place SW3 ... 243 H4
Walton Street SW3 ... 243 G4
Walworth Place SE17 ... 245 K7
Walworth Road SE17 ... 245 J5
Wandsworth Road SW8 ... 244 C8
Wansey Street SE17 ... 245 J6
Wapping ⊖ E1W ... 246 F5
Wapping High Street E1W ... 246 E6
Wapping Lane E1W ... 246 F4
Wapping Wall E1W ... 247 G5
Warden's Grove SE1 ... 245 J2
Wardour Street W1F ... 240 B6
Warner Street EC1R ... 240 F4
Warren Street ⊖ W1T ... 239 M4
Warren Street W1T ... 239 M3
Warrington Crescent W9 ... 238 C3
Warrington Gardens W9 ... 238 C4
Warwick Avenue ⊖ W9 ... 238 C4
Warwick Avenue W9 ... 238 C4
Warwick Crescent W2 ... 238 C5
Warwick House Street SW1Y ... 244 B1
Warwick Lane EC4M ... 241 H6
Warwick Place W9 ... 238 C4
Warwick Road SW5 ... 242 A6
Warwick Row SW1E ... 243 L4
Warwick Square SW1V ... 243 M6
Warwick Street W1B ... 240 A7
Warwick Way SW1V ... 243 L6
Waterhouse Square EC1N ... 241 G5
Waterloo ⇌ ⊖ SE1 ... 244 F2
Waterloo Bridge SE1 ... 244 E1
Waterloo Bridge WC2R ... 240 E8
Waterloo East SE1 ... 245 G2
Waterloo Place SW1Y ... 244 B1
Waterloo Road SE1 ... 244 F1
Waterloo Road SE1 ... 245 G2
Waterman Way E1W ... 246 E5
Waterside Close SE16 ... 246 D7
Watling Street EC4N ... 241 K7
Watney Street E1 ... 246 F2
Watts Street E1W ... 246 E5
Waveney Close E1W ... 246 D5
Waverton Street W1J ... 239 K8
Weavers Lane SE1 ... 246 A6
Webber Row SE1 ... 245 G3
Webber Street SE1 ... 245 H3
Webb Street SE1 ... 246 A8
Webster Road SE16 ... 246 D8
Weigh House Street W1K ... 239 K7
Welbeck Street W1G ... 239 K5
Welbeck Way W1G ... 239 K6
Welland Mews E1W ... 246 E5
Wellclose Square E1 ... 246 D4
Wellesley Street E1 ... 247 H2
Wellesley Terrace N1 ... 241 K2
Wellington Arch W1J ... 243 K2
Wellington Square SW3 ... 243 H6
Wellington Place NW8 ... 238 E2
Wellington Road NW8 ... 238 E1
Wellington Street WC2E ... 240 D7
Wells Mews W1T ... 240 A5
Wells Street W1T ... 240 A5
Wells Way SE5 ... 245 M8
Wenlock Road N1 ... 241 K1
Wenlock Street N1 ... 241 K1
Wentworth Street E1 ... 246 B2
Werrington Street NW1 ... 240 A1
Wesley Street W1G ... 239 K5
West Arbour Street E1 ... 247 G2
Westbourne Crescent W2 ... 238 D7
Westbourne Gardens W2 ... 238 B6
Westbourne Gate W2 ... 238 E7
Westbourne Grove W2 ... 238 A6
Westbourne Grove Terrace W2 ... 238 B6
Westbourne Park Road W2 ... 238 A5
Westbourne Park Villas W2 ... 238 A5
Westbourne Street W2 ... 238 E7
Westbourne Terrace W2 ... 238 D6
Westbourne Terrace Mews W2 ... 238 C6
Westbourne Terrace Road W2 ... 238 C5
West Brompton ⇌ ⊖ SW5 ... 242 A7
West Carriage Drive W2 ... 242 E2
Westcott Road SE17 ... 245 H8
West Cromwell Road SW5 ... 242 A5
Western Place SE16 ... 247 G6
Westferry ⊖ E14 ... 247 M4
Westferry Circus E14 ... 247 M5
Westferry Road E14 ... 247 M5
West Gardens E1W ... 246 F4
Westgate Terrace SW6 ... 242 B7
West Halkin Street SW1X ... 243 J4
West Harding Street EC4A ... 241 G6
West India Avenue E14 ... 247 M5
West India Dock Road E14 ... 247 M3
Westland Place N1 ... 241 K2
West Lane SE16 ... 246 E7
Westminster ⊖ SW1A ... 244 D3
Westminster Abbey SW1P ... 244 C3
Westminster Bridge SE1 ... 244 D3
Westminster Bridge Road SE1 ... 244 F3
Westmoreland Place SW1V ... 243 L7
Westmoreland Road SE17 ... 245 K8
Westmoreland Street W1G ... 239 K5
Westmoreland Terrace SW1V ... 243 L7
Weston Rise WC1X ... 240 E1
Weston Street SE1 ... 245 M2
Weston Street SE1 ... 245 M3
Westport Street E1 ... 247 H2
West Poultry Avenue EC1A ... 241 H5
West Road SW3 ... 243 H7
West Smithfield EC1A ... 241 H5
West Square SE11 ... 245 H4
West Street WC2H ... 240 C7
West Tenter Street E1 ... 246 C3
West Warwick Place SW1V ... 243 M6
Westway W2 ... 238 B5
Wetherby Gardens SW5 ... 242 C6
Weyhill Road E1 ... 246 D2
Weymouth Mews W1G ... 239 L5
Weymouth Street W1G ... 239 K5
Wharfdale Road N1 ... 240 D1
Wharfedale Street SW10 ... 242 B7
Wharf Road N1 ... 241 J1
Wharton Street WC1X ... 240 F2
Wheatley Street W1G ... 239 K5
Whetstone Park WC2A ... 240 E5
Whidborne Street WC1H ... 240 D2
Whiskin Street EC1R ... 241 G2
Whitcomb Street WC2H ... 240 B8
Whitechapel ⇌ ⊖ E1 ... 246 E1
Whitechapel Estate E1 ... 246 E1
Whitechapel High Street E1 ... 246 C2

Whitechapel Road E1 ... 246 D1
Whitecross Street EC1Y ... 241 K3
Whitefriars Street EC4Y ... 241 G6
Whitehall SW1A ... 244 C2
Whitehall Court SW1A ... 244 D2
Whitehall Place SW1A ... 244 D1
White Hart Street SE11 ... 245 G6
White Hart Yard SE1 ... 245 L2
Whitehaven Street NW8 ... 238 F4
White Horse Lane E1 ... 247 H1
Whitehorse Road E1 ... 247 J3
White Horse Street W1J ... 243 L1
White Kennett Street E1 ... 246 B2
White Lion Hill EC4V ... 241 H7
White Lion Street N1 ... 240 F1
White's Grounds SE1 ... 246 A7
White's Row E1 ... 246 B1
White Tower Way E1 ... 247 J1
Whitfield Place W1T ... 240 A4
Whitfield Street W1T ... 240 A4
Whitgift Street SE11 ... 244 E5
Whittaker Street SW1W ... 243 J6
Whittlesey Street SE1 ... 245 G2
Wicker Street E1 ... 246 E3
Wickham Close E1 ... 247 G1
Wickham Street SE11 ... 244 E7
Wicklow Street WC1X ... 240 E2
Widegate Street E1 ... 246 A1
Widley Road W9 ... 238 A3
Wigmore Place W1G ... 239 K5
Wigmore Street W1U ... 239 K6
Wigton Place SE11 ... 245 G7
Wilbraham Place SW1X ... 243 J5
Wilcox Place * SW1E ... 244 A4
Wild Court WC2B ... 240 E6
Wild's Rents SE1 ... 245 M4
Wild Street WC2B ... 240 D6
Wilfred Street SW1E ... 243 M4
Wilkes Street E1 ... 246 B1
William IV Street WC2N ... 240 C8
William Mews SW1X ... 243 H3
William Road NW1 ... 239 M3
Willow Place SW1P ... 244 A5
Willow Street EC2A ... 241 M3
Wilmington Square WC1X ... 240 F3
Wilmington Street WC1X ... 240 F2
Wilson Grove SE16 ... 246 E7
Wilson Street EC2A ... 241 L4
Wilton Crescent SW1X ... 243 J3
Wilton Mews SW1X ... 243 K4
Wilton Place SW1X ... 243 J3
Wilton Road SW1V ... 243 M5
Wilton Row SW1X ... 243 J3
Wilton Street SW1X ... 243 K4
Wimpole Mews W1G ... 239 K5
Wimpole Street W1G ... 239 K5
Winchester Street SW1V ... 243 L6
Winchester Walk SE1 ... 245 K1
Wincott Street SE11 ... 245 G5
Windmill Road SE11 ... 244 F7
Windmill Street W1T ... 240 B5
Windrose Close SE16 ... 247 H6
Windsor Terrace N1 ... 241 K1
Wine Close E1W ... 246 F5
Winnett Street W1D ... 240 B7
Winsland Mews W2 ... 238 E6
Winsland Street W2 ... 238 E6
Winsley Street W1W ... 240 A6
Winthrop Street E1 ... 246 E1
Woburn Place WC1H ... 240 C3
Woburn Square WC1H ... 240 C4
Wodeham Gardens E1 ... 246 E1
Wolfe Crescent SE16 ... 247 H7
Wolseley Street SE1 ... 246 C6
Woodbridge Street EC1R ... 241 G3
Woodchester Square W9 ... 238 A4
Woodfall Street SW3 ... 243 H7
Woodland Crescent SE16 ... 247 H7
Woodseer Street E1 ... 246 C1
Woods Mews W1K ... 239 J7
Woods Place SE1 ... 246 A8
Woodstock Street W1C ... 239 K6
Wood Street EC2V ... 241 K6
Woolaston Close SE1 ... 245 J5
Wooler Street SE17 ... 245 L7
Wootton Street SE1 ... 245 G2
Worgan Street SE11 ... 244 E6
Worgan Street SE16 ... 247 H7
Wormwood Street EC2M ... 241 M5
Worship Street EC2A ... 241 M4
Wren Street WC1X ... 240 E3
Wright's Lane W8 ... 242 A3
Wyatt Close SE16 ... 247 L7
Wyclif Street EC1V ... 241 H2
Wymering Road W9 ... 238 A2
Wynard Terrace SE11 ... 244 F7
Wyndham Place W1H ... 239 H5
Wyndham Street W1H ... 239 G4
Wynnstay Gardens W8 ... 242 A4
Wynyatt Street EC1V ... 241 H2
Wythburn Place W1H ... 239 H6

Y

Yalding Road * SE16 ... 246 C8
Yardley Street WC1X ... 240 F2
Yeoman's Row SW3 ... 243 G4
York Boulevard WC2N ... 240 D8
York Bridge NW1 ... 239 J3
York Gate NW1 ... 239 J4
York Road SE1 ... 244 E2
Yorkshire Road E14 ... 247 K3
York Square E14 ... 247 J2
York Street W1H ... 239 G5
York Street W1U ... 239 H5
York Terrace East NW1 ... 239 J4
York Terrace West NW1 ... 239 J4
York Way N1 ... 240 D1
Young Street W8 ... 242 B3

Z

Zoar Street SE1 ... 245 J1
ZSL London Zoo NW1 ... 239 J1

This index lists places appearing in the main map section of the atlas in alphabetical order. The reference following each name gives the atlas page number and grid reference of the square in which the place appears. The map shows counties, unitary authorities and administrative areas, together with a list of the abbreviated name forms used in the index. The top 100 places of tourist interest are indexed in red, World Heritage sites in green, motorway service areas in blue, airports in blue italic and National Parks in green italic.

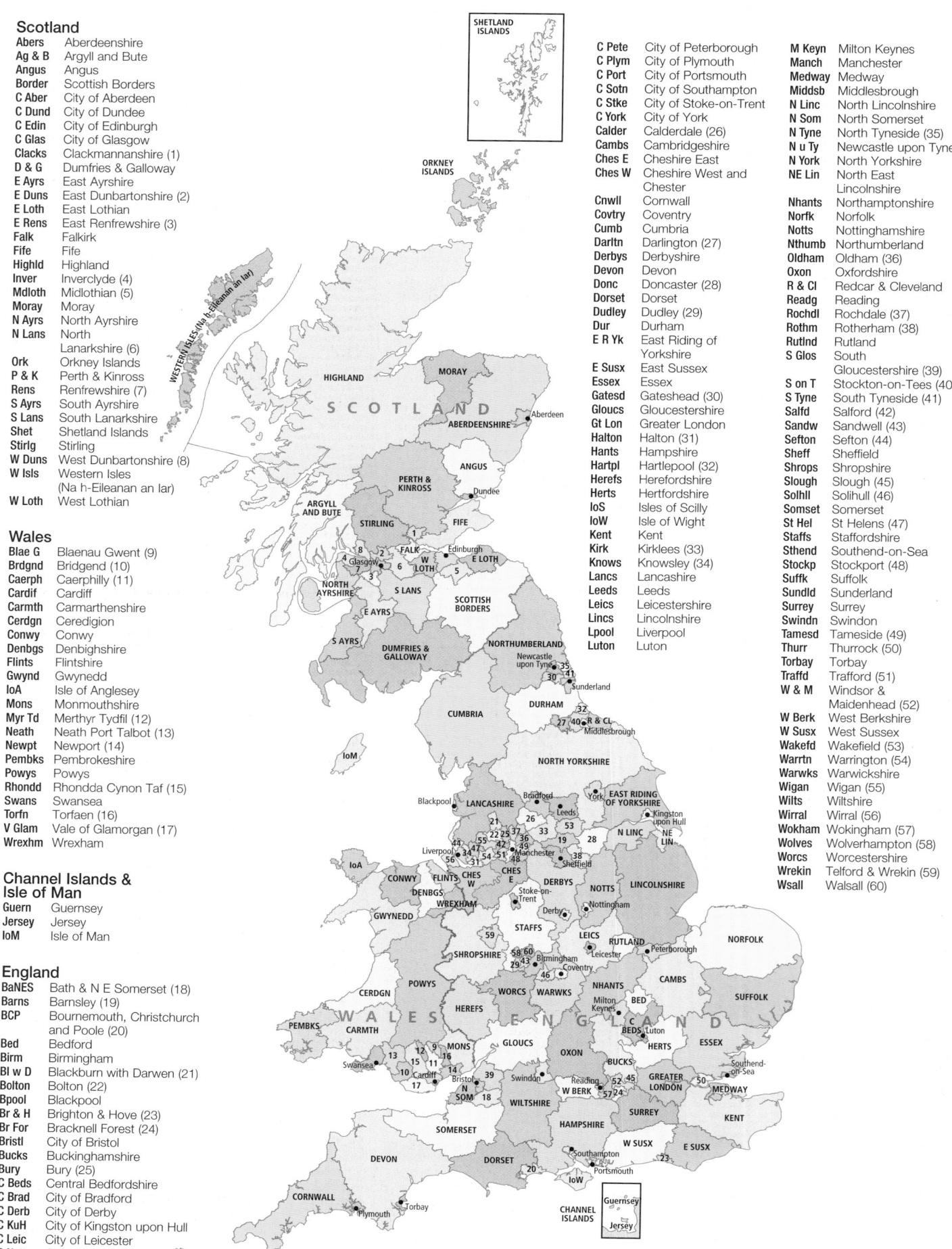

Scotland

Abers	Aberdeenshire
Ag & B	Argyll and Bute
Angus	Angus
Border	Scottish Borders
C Aber	City of Aberdeen
C Dund	City of Dundee
C Edin	City of Edinburgh
C Glas	City of Glasgow
Clacks	Clackmannanshire (1)
D & G	Dumfries & Galloway
E Ayrs	East Ayrshire
E Duns	East Dunbartonshire (2)
E Loth	East Lothian
E Rens	East Renfrewshire (3)
Falk	Falkirk
Fife	Fife
Highld	Highland
Inver	Inverclyde (4)
Mdloth	Midlothian (5)
Moray	Moray
N Ayrs	North Ayrshire
N Lans	North Lanarkshire (6)
Ork	Orkney Islands
P & K	Perth & Kinross
Rens	Renfrewshire (7)
S Ayrs	South Ayrshire
S Lans	South Lanarkshire
Shet	Shetland Islands
Stirlg	Stirling
W Duns	West Dunbartonshire (8)
W Isls	Western Isles (Na h-Eileanan an Iar)
W Loth	West Lothian

Wales

Blae G	Blaenau Gwent (9)
Brdgnd	Bridgend (10)
Caerph	Caerphilly (11)
Cardif	Cardiff
Carmth	Carmarthenshire
Cerdgn	Ceredigion
Conwy	Conwy
Denbgs	Denbighshire
Flints	Flintshire
Gwynd	Gwynedd
IoA	Isle of Anglesey
Mons	Monmouthshire
Myr Td	Merthyr Tydfil (12)
Neath	Neath Port Talbot (13)
Newpt	Newport (14)
Pembks	Pembrokeshire
Powys	Powys
Rhondd	Rhondda Cynon Taf (15)
Swans	Swansea
Torfn	Torfaen (16)
V Glam	Vale of Glamorgan (17)
Wrexhm	Wrexham

Channel Islands & Isle of Man

Guern	Guernsey
Jersey	Jersey
IoM	Isle of Man

England

BaNES	Bath & N E Somerset (18)
Barns	Barnsley (19)
BCP	Bournemouth, Christchurch and Poole (20)
Bed	Bedford
Birm	Birmingham
Bl w D	Blackburn with Darwen (21)
Bolton	Bolton (22)
Bpool	Blackpool
Br & H	Brighton & Hove (23)
Br For	Bracknell Forest (24)
Bristl	City of Bristol
Bucks	Buckinghamshire
Bury	Bury (25)
C Beds	Central Bedfordshire
C Brad	City of Bradford
C Derb	City of Derby
C KuH	City of Kingston upon Hull
C Leic	City of Leicester
C Nott	City of Nottingham

C Pete	City of Peterborough
C Plym	City of Plymouth
C Port	City of Portsmouth
C Sotn	City of Southampton
C Stke	City of Stoke-on-Trent
C York	City of York
Calder	Calderdale (26)
Cambs	Cambridgeshire
Ches E	Cheshire East
Ches W	Cheshire West and Chester
Cnwll	Cornwall
Covtry	Coventry
Cumb	Cumbria
Darltn	Darlington (27)
Derbys	Derbyshire
Devon	Devon
Donc	Doncaster (28)
Dorset	Dorset
Dudley	Dudley (29)
Dur	Durham
E R Yk	East Riding of Yorkshire
E Susx	East Sussex
Essex	Essex
Gatesd	Gateshead (30)
Gloucs	Gloucestershire
Gt Lon	Greater London
Halton	Halton (31)
Hants	Hampshire
Hartpl	Hartlepool (32)
Herefs	Herefordshire
Herts	Hertfordshire
IoS	Isles of Scilly
IoW	Isle of Wight
Kent	Kent
Kirk	Kirklees (33)
Knows	Knowsley (34)
Lancs	Lancashire
Leeds	Leeds
Leics	Leicestershire
Lincs	Lincolnshire
Lpool	Liverpool
Luton	Luton

M Keyn	Milton Keynes
Manch	Manchester
Medway	Medway
Middsb	Middlesbrough
N Linc	North Lincolnshire
N Som	North Somerset
N Tyne	North Tyneside (35)
N u Ty	Newcastle upon Tyne
N York	North Yorkshire
NE Lin	North East Lincolnshire
Nhants	Northamptonshire
Norfk	Norfolk
Notts	Nottinghamshire
Nthumb	Northumberland
Oldham	Oldham (36)
Oxon	Oxfordshire
R & Cl	Redcar & Cleveland
Readg	Reading
Rochdl	Rochdale (37)
Rothm	Rotherham (38)
Rutlnd	Rutland
S Glos	South Gloucestershire (39)
S on T	Stockton-on-Tees (40)
S Tyne	South Tyneside (41)
Salfd	Salford (42)
Sandw	Sandwell (43)
Sefton	Sefton (44)
Sheff	Sheffield
Shrops	Shropshire
Slough	Slough (45)
Solhll	Solihull (46)
Somset	Somerset
St Hel	St Helens (47)
Staffs	Staffordshire
Sthend	Southend-on-Sea
Stockp	Stockport (48)
Suffk	Suffolk
Sundld	Sunderland
Surrey	Surrey
Swindn	Swindon
Tamesd	Tameside (49)
Thurr	Thurrock (50)
Torbay	Torbay
Traffd	Trafford (51)
W & M	Windsor & Maidenhead (52)
W Berk	West Berkshire
W Susx	West Sussex
Wakefd	Wakefield (53)
Warrtn	Warrington (54)
Warwks	Warwickshire
Wigan	Wigan (55)
Wilts	Wiltshire
Wirral	Wirral (56)
Wokham	Wokingham (57)
Wolves	Wolverhampton (58)
Worcs	Worcestershire
Wrekin	Telford & Wrekin (59)
Wsall	Walsall (60)

Abbas Combe – Ansley 255

A

Abbas Combe Somset 20 D10
Abberley Worcs 57 P11
Abberley Common Worcs 57 N11
Abberton Essex 52 H8
Abberton Worcs 47 J4
Abberwick Nthumb 119 M8
Abbess Roding Essex 51 N8
Abbey Devon 10 C2
Abbey-Cwm-Hir Powys 55 P10
Abbeydale Sheff 84 D4
Abbey Dore Herefs 45 M8
Abbey Green Staffs 70 H3
Abbey Hill Somset 19 J11
Abbey St Bathans Border 129 K7
Abbeystead Lancs 95 M10
Abbeytown Cumb 110 C10
Abbey Village Lancs 89 J6
Abbey Wood Gt Lon 37 L5
Abbotrule Border 118 B8
Abbots Bickington Devon 16 F9
Abbots Bromley Staffs 71 K10
Abbotsbury Dorset 11 M7
Abbot's Chair Derbys 83 M6
Abbots Deuglie P & K 134 E5
Abbotsham Devon 16 G6
Abbotskerswell Devon 7 M5
Abbots Langley Herts 50 C10
Abbotsleigh Devon 7 L9
Abbots Leigh N Som 31 P10
Abbotsley Cambs 62 B9
Abbots Morton Worcs 47 K3
Abbots Ripton Cambs 62 B5
Abbot's Salford Warwks 47 L4
Abbotstone Hants 22 G8
Abbotswood Hants 22 C10
Abbots Worthy Hants 22 E8
Abbotts Ann Hants 22 B6
Abbott Street Dorset 12 G4
Abcott Shrops 56 F9
Abdon Shrops 57 K7
Abenhall Gloucs 46 C11
Aberaeron Cerdgn 43 J2
Aberaman Rhondd 30 D4
Aberangell Gwynd 55 J2
Aber-arad Carmth 42 F6
Aberarder Highld 147 Q2
Aberargie P & K 134 F4
Aberarth Cerdgn 43 J2
Aberavon Neath 29 K7
Aber-banc Cerdgn 42 G6
Aberbargoed Caerph 30 G4
Aberbeeg Blae G 30 H4
Abercanaid Myr Td 30 E4
Abercarn Caerph 30 H6
Abercastle Pembks 40 G4
Abercegir Powys 55 J4
Aberchalder Lodge Highld 147 J7
Aberchirder Abers 158 F7
Aber Clydach Powys 44 G10
Abercorn W Loth 127 K2
Abercraf Powys 29 M2
Abercregan Neath 29 M5
Abercwmboi Rhondd 30 D5
Abercych Pembks 41 P2
Abercynon Rhondd 30 E6
Aberdalgie P & K 134 D3
Aberdare Rhondd 30 D4
Aberdaron Gwynd 66 B9
Aberdeen C Aber 151 N6
Aberdeen Airport C Aber 151 M5
Aberdesach Gwynd 66 G4
Aberdour Fife 134 F10
Aberdulais Neath 29 L5
Aberdyfi Gwynd 54 E5
Aberedw Powys 44 F5
Abereiddy Pembks 40 E4
Abererch Gwynd 66 F7
Aberfan Myr Td 30 E4
Aberfeldy P & K 141 L8
Aberffraw IoA 78 F11
Aberffrwd Cerdgn 54 F9
Aberford Leeds 91 L3
Aberfoyle Stirlg 132 G7
Abergarw Brdgnd 29 P8
Abergarwed Neath 29 M4
Abergavenny Mons 31 J2
Abergele Conwy 80 C9
Aber-giar Carmth 43 K6
Abergorlech Carmth 43 L8
Abergwesyn Powys 44 B4
Abergwili Carmth 42 H10
Abergwydol Powys 54 H4
Abergwynfi Neath 29 N5
Abergwyngregyn Gwynd 79 M10
Abergynolwyn Gwynd 54 F3
Aberhafesp Powys 55 P6
Aberhosan Powys 55 J5
Aberkenfig Brdgnd 29 N8
Aberlady E Loth 128 D4
Aberlemno Angus 143 J6
Aberllefenni Gwynd 54 H3
Aberllynfi Powys 44 H7
Aberlour, Charlestown of Moray 157 P9
Abermagwr Cerdgn 54 F10
Aber-meurig Cerdgn 43 L3
Abermorddu Flints 69 K3
Abermule Powys 56 B6
Abernant Carmth 42 F10
Abernant Rhondd 30 D4
Abernethy P & K 134 F4
Abernyte P & K 142 D11
Aberporth Cerdgn 42 E4
Abersoch Gwynd 66 E9
Abersychan Torfn 31 J4
Aberthin V Glam 30 D10
Abertillery Blae G 30 H4
Abertridwr Caerph 30 F7
Abertridwr Powys 68 D11
Abertysswg Caerph 30 F3
Aberuthven P & K 134 B4
Aberyscir Powys 44 D9
Aberystwyth Cerdgn 54 D8
Abingdon-on-Thames Oxon 34 E5
Abinger Common Surrey 36 D11
Abinger Hammer Surrey 36 C11
Abington Nhants 60 G8
Abington S Lans 116 C6
Abington Pigotts Cambs 50 H2
Abington Services S Lans 116 C6
Abingworth W Susx 24 D7
Ab Kettleby Leics 73 J6
Ab Lench Worcs 47 K4
Ablington Gloucs 33 M3
Ablington Wilts 21 N5
Abney Derbys 83 Q8
Above Church Staffs 71 J4
Aboyne Abers 150 E8
Abhainn Suidhe W Isls 168 f7
Abram Wigan 82 D4
Abriachan Highld 155 Q10
Abridge Essex 51 L11
Abronhill N Lans 126 D2
Abson S Glos 32 D10
Abthorpe Nhants 48 H5
Aby Lincs 87 M5
Acaster Malbis C York 98 B11
Acaster Selby N York 91 P2
Accrington Lancs 89 M5
Acha Ag & B 136 F5
Achahoish Ag & B 123 N4
Achalader P & K 141 R8
Achaleven Ag & B 138 G11
Acha Mor W Isls 168 i5
Achanalt Highld 155 J5
Achandunie Highld 156 A3
Achany Highld 162 D6
Acharacle Highld 138 B4
Acharn Highld 138 C7
Acharn P & K 141 J9
Achavanich Highld 167 L8
Achduart Highld 160 G6
Achfary Highld 164 G9
A'Chill Highld 144 C6
Achiltibuie Highld 160 G5
Achina Highld 166 B4
Achinhoan Ag & B 120 E8
Achintee Highld 154 B9
Achintraid Highld 153 Q10
Achmelvich Highld 160 H2
Achmore Highld 153 R11
Achmore W Isls 168 i5
Achnacarnin Highld 164 B10
Achnacarry Highld 146 F10
Achnacloich Highld 145 J6
Achnaconeran Highld 147 L4
Achnacroish Ag & B 138 F9
Achnadrish House Ag & B 137 M5
Achnafauld P & K 141 L10
Achnagarron Highld 156 B3
Achnaha Highld 137 M2
Achnahaird Highld 160 G4
Achnahannet Highld 148 H2
Achnairn Highld 162 D4
Achnalea Highld 138 F5
Achnamara Ag & B 130 F10
Achnasheen Highld 154 G6
Achnashellach Highld 154 D8
Achnastank Moray 157 P11
Achosnich Highld 137 L2
Achranich Highld 138 C8
Achreamie Highld 166 H3
Achriabhach Highld 139 L4
Achriesgill Highld 164 G6
Achtoty Highld 165 Q4
Achurch Nhants 61 M4
Achvaich Highld 162 G8
Achvarasdal Highld 166 G4
Ackergill Highld 167 Q6
Acklam Middsb 104 E7
Acklam N York 98 F8
Ackleton Shrops 57 P5
Acklington Nthumb 119 P10
Ackton Wakefd 91 L6
Ackworth Moor Top Wakefd 91 L7
Acle Norfk 77 N9
Acock's Green Birm 58 H8
Acol Kent 39 P8
Acomb C York 98 B10
Acomb Nthumb 112 D7
Acombe Somset 10 D2
Aconbury Herefs 45 Q8
Acre Lancs 89 M6
Acrefair Wrexhm 69 J6
Acton Ches E 70 A4
Acton Dorset 12 G9
Acton Gt Lon 36 F4
Acton Shrops 56 E8
Acton Staffs 70 E6
Acton Suffk 52 E2
Acton Worcs 58 B11
Acton Wrexhm 69 K4
Acton Beauchamp Herefs 46 C4
Acton Bridge Ches W 82 C9
Acton Burnell Shrops 57 J4
Acton Green Herefs 46 C4
Acton Pigott Shrops 57 J4
Acton Round Shrops 57 L5
Acton Scott Shrops 56 H7
Acton Trussell Staffs 70 G11
Acton Turville S Glos 32 F8
Adbaston Staffs 70 D9
Adber Dorset 19 Q10
Adbolton Notts 72 F3
Adderbury Oxon 48 E7
Adderley Shrops 70 B7
Adderstone Nthumb 119 M4
Addiewell W Loth 126 H5
Addingham C Brad 96 G11
Addington Bucks 49 K9
Addington Gt Lon 37 J8
Addington Kent 37 Q9
Addiscombe Gt Lon 36 H7
Addlestone Surrey 36 C8
Addlestonemoor Surrey 36 C7
Addlethorpe Lincs 87 P7
Adeney Wrekin 70 B11
Adeyfield Herts 50 C9
Adfa Powys 55 P4
Adforton Herefs 56 G10
Adisham Kent 39 M11
Adlestrop Gloucs 47 P9
Adlingfleet E R Yk 92 D6
Adlington Ches E 83 K8
Adlington Lancs 89 J8
Admaston Staffs 71 J10
Admaston Wrekin 57 L2
Admington Warwks 47 P5
Adpar Cerdgn 42 F6
Adsborough Somset 19 J9
Adscombe Somset 18 G7
Adstock Bucks 49 K9
Adstone Nhants 48 G4
Adswood Stockp 83 J7
Adversane W Susx 24 C6
Advie Highld 157 L11
Adwalton Leeds 90 G5
Adwell Oxon 35 J5
Adwick le Street Donc 91 N9
Adwick upon Dearne Donc 91 M10
Ae D & G 109 L3
Ae Bridgend D & G 109 M3
Afan Forest Park Neath 29 N5
Affetside Bury 89 M8
Affleck Abers 158 E9
Affpuddle Dorset 12 D6
Affric Lodge Highld 146 F3
Afon-wen Flints 80 G10
Afon Wen Gwynd 66 G7
Afton Devon 7 L6
Afton IoW 13 P7
Agglethorpe N York 96 G3
Aigburth Lpool 81 M7
Aike E R Yk 99 L11
Aiketgate Cumb 111 J11
Aikhead Cumb 110 D11
Aikton Cumb 110 E10
Ailby Lincs 87 M5
Ailey Herefs 45 L5
Ailsworth C Pete 74 B11
Ainderby Quernhow N York 97 M4
Ainderby Steeple N York 97 M2
Aingers Green Essex 53 K7
Ainsdale Sefton 88 C8
Ainsdale-on-Sea Sefton 88 B8
Ainstable Cumb 111 K11
Ainsworth Bury 89 M8
Ainthorpe N York 105 K9
Aintree Sefton 81 M5
Ainville W Loth 127 L5
Aird Ag & B 130 F7
Aird D & G 106 E5
Aird W Isls 168 k4
Àird a' Mhulaidh W Isls 168 g6
Aird Asaig W Isls 168 g7
Aird Dhubh Highld 153 N9
Airdeny Ag & B 131 K2
Aird of Kinloch Ag & B 137 N10
Aird of Sleat Highld 145 J7
Airdrie N Lans 126 D4
Airdriehill N Lans 126 D4
Airds of Kells D & G 108 E6
Àird Uig W Isls 168 f4
Airidh a bhruaich W Isls 168 h6
Airieland D & G 108 G9
Airlie Angus 142 E7
Airmyn E R Yk 92 B6
Airntully P & K 141 Q10
Airor Highld 145 M6
Airth Falk 133 Q10
Airton N York 96 D9
Aisby Lincs 73 Q3
Aisby Lincs 85 Q2
Aisgill Cumb 102 E11
Aish Devon 6 H6
Aish Devon 7 L7
Aisholt Somset 18 G7
Aiskew N York 97 L3
Aislaby N York 98 F3
Aislaby N York 105 N9
Aislaby S on T 104 D8
Aisthorpe Lincs 86 B4
Aith Shet 169 q8
Akeld Nthumb 119 J5
Akeley Bucks 49 K7
Akenham Suffk 53 L2
Albaston Cnwll 5 Q7
Alberbury Shrops 56 F2
Albourne W Susx 24 G7
Albourne Green W Susx 24 G7
Albrighton Shrops 57 Q4
Albrighton Shrops 69 N11
Alburgh Norfk 65 K4
Albury Herts 51 K6
Albury Oxon 35 J3
Albury Surrey 36 B11
Albury End Herts 51 K6
Albury Heath Surrey 36 C11
Alby Hill Norfk 76 H5
Alcaig Highld 155 Q6
Alcaston Shrops 56 H7
Alcester Warwks 47 L3
Alcester Lane End Birm 58 G8
Alciston E Susx 25 M9
Alcombe Somset 18 C5
Alcombe Wilts 32 F11
Alconbury Cambs 61 Q5
Alconbury Weston Cambs 61 Q5
Aldborough N York 97 P7
Aldborough Norfk 76 H5
Aldbourne Wilts 33 Q9
Aldbrough E R Yk 93 M3
Aldbrough St John N York 103 P8
Aldbury Herts 35 Q2
Aldcliffe Lancs 95 K8
Aldclune P & K 141 L5
Aldeburgh Suffk 65 P10
Aldeby Norfk 65 N3
Aldenham Herts 50 D11
Alderbury Wilts 21 N9
Aldercar Derbys 84 F11
Alderford Norfk 76 G8
Alderholt Dorset 13 K2
Alderley Gloucs 32 E6
Alderley Edge Ches E 82 H9
Aldermans Green Covtry 59 N8
Aldermaston W Berk 34 G11
Alderminster Warwks 47 P5
Alder Moor Staffs 71 N9
Aldersey Green Ches W 69 N3
Aldershot Hants 23 N4
Alderton Gloucs 47 K8
Alderton Nhants 49 K5
Alderton Shrops 69 N10
Alderton Suffk 53 P3
Alderton Wilts 32 F8
Alderwasley Derbys 71 Q4
Aldfield N York 97 L7
Aldford Ches W 69 M3
Aldgate Rutlnd 73 P10
Aldham Essex 52 F6
Aldham Suffk 52 J2
Aldingbourne W Susx 15 P5
Aldingham Cumb 94 F6
Aldington Kent 27 J4
Aldington Worcs 47 L6
Aldington Corner Kent 27 J4
Aldivalloch Moray 150 B2
Aldochlay Ag & B 132 D9
Aldon Shrops 56 G9
Aldoth Cumb 109 P11
Aldreth Cambs 62 F6
Aldridge Wsall 58 G4
Aldringham Suffk 65 N9
Aldro N York 98 G8
Aldsworth Gloucs 33 N3
Aldsworth W Susx 15 L5
Aldunie Moray 150 B2
Aldwark Derbys 84 B9
Aldwark N York 97 Q8
Aldwick W Susx 15 P7
Aldwincle Nhants 61 M4
Aldworth W Berk 34 G9
Alexandria W Duns 125 K2
Aley Somset 18 G7
Alfardisworthy Devon 16 D9
Alfington Devon 10 C5
Alfold Surrey 24 B4
Alfold Bars W Susx 24 B4
Alfold Crossways Surrey 24 B3
Alford Abers 150 F4
Alford Lincs 87 N5
Alford Somset 20 B8
Alfreton Derbys 84 F9
Alfrick Worcs 46 D4
Alfrick Pound Worcs 46 D4
Alfriston E Susx 25 M10
Algarkirk Lincs 74 E3
Alhampton Somset 20 B8
Alkborough N Linc 92 E6
Alkerton Gloucs 32 E3
Alkerton Oxon 48 C6
Alkham Kent 27 N3
Alkington Shrops 69 P7
Alkmonton Derbys 71 M7
Allaleigh Devon 7 L8
Allanaquoich Abers 149 L9
Allanbank N Lans 126 E6
Allanton Border 129 M9
Allanton N Lans 126 E6
Allanton S Lans 126 C7
Allaston Gloucs 32 B4
Allbrook Hants 22 E10
All Cannings Wilts 21 L2
Allendale Nthumb 112 B9
Allen End Warwks 59 J5
Allenheads Nthumb 112 C11
Allensford Dur 112 G10
Allen's Green Herts 51 L7
Allensmore Herefs 45 P7
Allenton C Derb 72 B4
Aller Devon 17 P6
Aller Somset 19 M9
Allerby Cumb 100 E3
Allercombe Devon 9 P6
Aller Cross Devon 17 N6
Allerford Somset 18 B5
Allerston N York 98 H4
Allerthorpe E R Yk 98 F11
Allerton C Brad 90 E4
Allerton Highld 156 D4
Allerton Lpool 81 M7
Allerton Bywater Leeds 91 L5
Allerton Mauleverer N York 97 P9
Allesley Covtry 59 M8
Allestree C Derb 72 A3
Allet Common Cnwll 3 K4
Allexton Leics 73 L10
Allgreave Ches E 83 L11
Allhallows Medway 38 D6
Allhallows-on-Sea Medway 38 D6
Alligin Shuas Highld 153 Q6
Allimore Green Staffs 70 F11
Allington Dorset 11 K6
Allington Kent 38 C10
Allington Lincs 73 M2
Allington Wilts 21 L2
Allington Wilts 21 P7
Allington Wilts 32 G9
Allithwaite Cumb 94 H5
Alloa Clacks 133 P9
Allonby Cumb 100 E2
Allostock Ches W 82 F10
Alloway S Ayrs 114 F4
Allowenshay Somset 10 H2
All Saints South Elmham Suffk 65 L5
Allscott Shrops 57 N5
Allscott Wrekin 57 L2
All Stretton Shrops 56 H5
Alltami Flints 81 K11
Alltchaorunn Highld 139 M7
Alltmawr Powys 44 F5
Alltwalis Carmth 42 H8
Alltwen Neath 29 K4
Alltyblaca Cerdgn 43 K5
Allweston Dorset 11 P2
Allwood Green Suffk 64 E7
Almeley Herefs 45 L4
Almeley Wooton Herefs 45 L4
Almer Dorset 12 F5
Almholme Donc 91 P9
Almington Staffs 70 C8
Almodington W Susx 15 M7
Almondbank P & K 134 D2
Almondbury Kirk 90 F8
Almondsbury S Glos 32 B8
Alne N York 97 Q7
Alness Highld 156 B4
Alnham Nthumb 119 J8
Alnmouth Nthumb 119 P8
Alnwick Nthumb 119 N8
Alperton Gt Lon 36 E4
Alphamstone Essex 52 E4
Alpheton Suffk 64 B11
Alphington Devon 9 M6
Alpington Norfk 77 K11
Alport Derbys 84 B8
Alpraham Ches E 69 Q3
Alresford Essex 53 J7
Alrewas Staffs 59 J2
Alsager Ches E 70 D3
Alsagers Bank Staffs 70 D5
Alsop en le Dale Derbys 71 M4
Alston Cumb 111 P11
Alston Devon 10 G4
Alstone Gloucs 47 J8
Alstone Somset 19 K5
Alstonefield Staffs 71 L3
Alston Sutton Somset 19 M4
Alswear Devon 17 N7
Alt Oldham 83 K4
Altandhu Highld 160 F4
Altarnun Cnwll 5 L5
Altass Highld 162 C6
Altcreich Ag & B 138 B10
Altgaltraig Ag & B 124 C3
Altham Lancs 89 M4
Althorne Essex 38 F2
Althorpe N Linc 92 D9
Altnabreac Station Highld 166 H7
Altnaharra Highld 165 N9
Altofts Wakefd 91 K6
Alton Derbys 84 E8
Alton Hants 23 K7
Alton Staffs 71 K6
Alton Wilts 21 N5
Alton Barnes Wilts 21 M2
Alton Pancras Dorset 11 Q4
Alton Priors Wilts 21 M2
Alton Towers Staffs 71 K6
Altrincham Traffd 82 G7
Altskeith Hotel Stirlg 132 F7
Alva Clacks 133 P8
Alvanley Ches W 81 P10
Alvaston C Derb 72 B4
Alvechurch Worcs 58 F10
Alvecote Warwks 59 K4
Alvediston Wilts 21 J10
Alveley Shrops 57 P8
Alverdiscott Devon 17 J6
Alverstoke Hants 14 H7
Alverstone IoW 14 G9
Alverthorpe Wakefd 91 J6
Alverton Notts 73 K2
Alves Moray 157 L5
Alvescot Oxon 33 Q4
Alveston S Glos 32 B7
Alveston Warwks 47 P3
Alvingham Lincs 87 L2
Alvington Gloucs 32 B4
Alwalton C Pete 74 B11
Alwinton Nthumb 118 H9
Alwoodley Leeds 90 H2
Alwoodley Gates Leeds 91 J2
Alyth P & K 142 C8
Am Bàgh a Tuath W Isls 168 c17
Ambergate Derbys 84 D10
Amber Hill Lincs 86 H11
Amberley Gloucs 32 G4
Amberley W Susx 24 B8
Amber Row Derbys 84 E9
Amberstone E Susx 25 N8
Amble Nthumb 119 Q10
Amblecote Dudley 58 C7
Ambler Thorn C Brad 90 D5
Ambleside Cumb 101 L10
Ambleston Pembks 41 K5
Ambrosden Oxon 48 H11
Amcotts N Linc 92 E8
America Cambs 62 F5
Amersham Bucks 35 Q5
Amersham Common Bucks 35 Q5
Amersham Old Town Bucks 35 Q5
Amersham on the Hill Bucks 35 Q5
Amerton Staffs 70 H9
Amesbury Wilts 21 N6
Amhuinnsuidhe W Isls 168 f7
Amington Staffs 59 K4
Amisfield D & G 109 M4
Amlwch IoA 78 G6
Ammanford Carmth 28 H2
Amotherby N York 98 E6
Ampfield Hants 22 D10
Ampleforth N York 98 B5
Ampney Crucis Gloucs 33 L4
Ampney St Mary Gloucs 33 L4
Ampney St Peter Gloucs 33 L4
Amport Hants 22 B6
Ampthill C Beds 50 B3
Ampton Suffk 64 B7
Amroth Pembks 41 N9
Amulree P & K 141 L10
Amwell Herts 50 E8
Anaheilt Highld 138 E5
Ancaster Lincs 73 P2
Ancells Farm Hants 23 M3
Anchor Shrops 56 B7
Ancroft Nthumb 129 P11
Ancrum Border 118 B6
Ancton W Susx 15 Q6
Anderby Lincs 87 P5
Anderby Creek Lincs 87 Q5
Andersea Somset 19 K8
Andersfield Somset 18 H8
Anderson Dorset 12 E5
Anderton Ches W 82 D9
Anderton Cnwll 6 C8
Andover Hants 22 C5
Andoversford Gloucs 47 K11
Andreas IoM 80 f2
Anelog Gwynd 66 B9
Anerley Gt Lon 36 H7
Anfield Lpool 81 M6
Angarrack Cnwll 2 F6
Angarrick Cnwll 3 K6
Angelbank Shrops 57 K9
Angersleigh Somset 18 G11
Angerton Cumb 110 D9
Angle Pembks 40 G10
Anglesey IoA 78 G8
Anglesey Abbey Cambs 62 H8
Angmering W Susx 24 C10
Angram N York 97 R11
Angram N York 102 G11
Angrouse Cnwll 2 H10
Anick Nthumb 112 D7
Ankerville Highld 156 E3
Ankle Hill Leics 73 K7
Anlaby E R Yk 92 H5
Anmer Norfk 75 P5
Anmore Hants 15 J4
Annan D & G 110 C7
Annandale Water Services D & G 109 P2
Annaside Cumb 94 B3
Annat Highld 154 A7
Annathill N Lans 126 C3
Anna Valley Hants 22 C6
Annbank S Ayrs 114 H3
Anne Hathaway's Cottage Warwks 47 N4
Annesley Notts 84 H10
Annesley Woodhouse Notts 84 G10
Annfield Plain Dur 113 J10
Anniesland C Glas 125 N4
Annitsford N Tyne 113 L6
Annscroft Shrops 56 H3
Ansdell Lancs 88 C5
Ansford Somset 20 B8
Ansley Warwks 59 M6

Anslow Staffs — 71 N9
Anslow Gate Staffs — 71 M10
Anslow Lees Staffs — 71 N10
Ansteadbrook Surrey — 23 P8
Anstey Hants — 23 K6
Anstey Herts — 51 K4
Anstey Leics — 72 F9
Anstruther Fife — 135 P7
Ansty W Susx — 24 G6
Ansty Warwks — 59 P8
Ansty Wilts — 21 J9
Ansty Cross Dorset — 12 C4
Anthill Common Hants — 14 H4
Anthonys Surrey — 36 B8
Anthorn Cumb — 110 C9
Antingham Norfk — 77 K5
An t-Ob W Isls — 168 f9
Antonine Wall — 126 E2
Anton's Gowt Lincs — 87 K11
Antony Cnwll — 5 Q11
Antrobus Ches W — 82 D9
Anvil Corner Devon — 16 F11
Anvil Green Kent — 27 K2
Anwick Lincs — 86 F10
Anwoth D & G — 108 C9
Aperfield Gt Lon — 37 K9
Apes Dale Worcs — 58 E10
Apethorpe Nhants — 73 Q11
Apeton Staffs — 70 F11
Apley Lincs — 86 F5
Apperknowle Derbys — 84 E5
Apperley Gloucs — 46 G9
Apperley Bridge C Brad — 90 F3
Apperley Dene Nthumb — 112 G9
Appersett N York — 96 C2
Appin Ag & B — 138 G8
Appleby N Linc — 92 G8
Appleby-in-Westmorland Cumb — 102 C6
Appleby Magna Leics — 59 M3
Appleby Parva Leics — 59 M3
Appleby Street Herts — 50 H10
Applecross Highld — 153 N9
Appledore Devon — 9 Q2
Appledore Devon — 16 H5
Appledore Kent — 26 G6
Appledore Heath Kent — 26 G5
Appleford Oxon — 34 F6
Applegarth Town D & G — 109 P4
Applehaigh Wakefd — 91 K8
Appleshaw Hants — 22 B5
Applethwaite Cumb — 101 J5
Appleton Halton — 81 Q7
Appleton Oxon — 34 D4
Appleton Warrtn — 82 D8
Appleton-le-Moors N York — 98 E3
Appleton-le-Street N York — 98 E6
Appleton Roebuck N York — 91 P2
Appleton Thorn Warrtn — 82 D8
Appleton Wiske N York — 104 C10
Appletreehall Border — 117 Q7
Appletreewick N York — 96 H8
Appley Somset — 18 E10
Appley Bridge Lancs — 88 G9
Apse Heath IoW — 14 G10
Apsley End C Beds — 50 D4
Apuldram W Susx — 15 M6
Arabella Highld — 156 E2
Arbirlot Angus — 143 L9
Arborfield Wokham — 35 L11
Arborfield Cross Wokham — 35 L11
Arborfield Green Wokham — 35 L11
Arbourthorne Sheff — 84 E3
Arbroath Angus — 143 L9
Arbuthnott Abers — 143 P2
Arcadia Kent — 26 E4
Archdeacon Newton Darltn — 103 Q7
Archencarroch W Duns — 132 E11
Archiestown Moray — 157 N9
Archirondel Jersey — 11 c1
Arclid Ches E — 70 D2
Ardallie Abers — 159 P10
Ardanaiseig Hotel Ag & B — 131 M3
Ardaneaskan Highld — 153 Q10
Ardarroch Highld — 153 Q10
Ardbeg Ag & B — 122 F10
Ardbeg Ag & B — 124 D4
Ardbeg Ag & B — 131 P11
Ardcharnich Highld — 161 K9
Ardchiavaig Ag & B — 137 K12
Ardchonnell Ag & B — 131 K5
Ardchronie Highld — 162 E9
Ardchullarie More Stirlg — 132 H5
Arddarroch Ag & B — 131 Q9
Arddleen Powys — 69 J11
Ard Dorch Highld — 145 J2
Ardechive Highld — 146 E9
Ardeer N Ayrs — 124 H9
Ardeley Herts — 50 H5
Ardelve Highld — 145 Q2
Arden Ag & B — 132 D11
Ardens Grafton Warwks — 47 M4
Ardentallen Ag & B — 130 G3
Ardentinny Ag & B — 131 P10
Ardentraive Ag & B — 124 C3
Ardeonaig Stirlg — 140 G10
Ardersier Highld — 156 D7
Ardessie Highld — 160 H9
Ardfern Ag & B — 130 G7
Ardfernal Ag & B — 123 J5
Ardgartan Ag & B — 132 B7
Ardgay Highld — 162 D8
Ardgour Highld — 139 J5
Ardgowan Inver — 124 G3
Ardhallow Ag & B — 124 F3
Ardhasig W Isls — 168 g7
Ardindrean Highld — 161 K9
Ardingly W Susx — 24 H5
Ardington Oxon — 34 D7
Ardington Wick Oxon — 34 D7
Ardlamont Ag & B — 124 B4
Ardleigh Essex — 53 J6
Ardleigh Heath Essex — 52 H5
Ardler P & K — 142 D9
Ardley Oxon — 48 F9
Ardley End Essex — 51 M8
Ardlui Ag & B — 132 C4
Ardlussa Ag & B — 130 C10
Ardmair Highld — 161 J7
Ardmaleish Ag & B — 124 D4
Ardminish Ag & B — 123 K10
Ardmolich Highld — 138 C3
Ardmore Ag & B — 125 J2

Ardmore Highld — 162 G9
Ardnadam Ag & B — 131 P11
Ardnagrask Highld — 155 P8
Ardnamurchan Highld — 137 P2
Ardnarff Highld — 154 A10
Ardnastang Highld — 138 E5
Ardpatrick Ag & B — 123 N8
Ardrishaig Ag & B — 130 H10
Ardross Highld — 155 R3
Ardrossan N Ayrs — 124 G9
Ardsley Barns — 91 K9
Ardsley East Leeds — 91 J5
Ardslignish Highld — 137 P3
Ardtalla Ag & B — 122 G9
Ardtoe Highld — 138 A3
Arduaine Ag & B — 130 F5
Ardullie Highld — 155 Q5
Ardvasar Highld — 145 K7
Ardvorlich P & K — 133 J3
Ardvourlie W Isls — 168 g6
Ardwell D & G — 106 F8
Ardwick Manch — 83 J5
Areley Kings Worcs — 57 P10
Arevegaig Highld — 138 B4
Arford Hants — 23 M7
Argoed Caerph — 30 G5
Argoed Shrops — 69 K10
Argoed Mill Powys — 44 D2
Argos Hill E Susx — 25 N5
Argyll Forest Park Ag & B — 131 Q7
Aribruach W Isls — 168 h6
Aridhglas Ag & B — 137 J11
Arileod Ag & B — 136 F5
Arinagour Ag & B — 136 G4
Ariogan Ag & B — 130 H2
Arisaig Highld — 145 L10
Arisaig House Highld — 145 L11
Arkendale N York — 97 N8
Arkesden Essex — 51 L4
Arkholme Lancs — 95 M6
Arkleby Cumb — 100 F3
Arkleton D & G — 110 G2
Arkle Town N York — 103 K10
Arkley Gt Lon — 50 F11
Arksey Donc — 91 P9
Arkwright Town Derbys — 84 F6
Arle Gloucs — 46 H10
Arlecdon Cumb — 100 D7
Arlescote Warwks — 48 C5
Arlesey C Beds — 50 E3
Arleston Wrekin — 57 M2
Arley Ches E — 82 E8
Arley Warwks — 59 L6
Arlingham Gloucs — 32 D2
Arlington Devon — 17 L3
Arlington E Susx — 25 M9
Arlington Gloucs — 33 M3
Arlington Beccott Devon — 17 L3
Armadale Highld — 145 K7
Armadale Highld — 166 C4
Armadale W Loth — 126 G4
Armaside Cumb — 100 G5
Armathwaite Cumb — 111 K11
Arminghall Norfk — 77 K11
Armitage Staffs — 71 K11
Armitage Bridge Kirk — 90 E8
Armley Leeds — 90 H4
Armscote Warwks — 47 P6
Armshead Staffs — 70 G5
Armston Nhants — 61 N3
Armthorpe Donc — 91 Q10
Arnabost Ag & B — 136 G3
Arnaby Cumb — 94 D4
Arncliffe N York — 96 F6
Arncliffe Cote N York — 96 D6
Arncroach Fife — 135 N6
Arndilly House Moray — 157 P8
Arne Dorset — 12 G7
Arnesby Leics — 60 D2
Arngask P & K — 134 E5
Arnisdale Highld — 145 P5
Arnish Highld — 153 K8
Arniston Mdloth — 127 Q5
Arnol W Isls — 168 i3
Arnold E R Yk — 93 K2
Arnold Notts — 85 J11
Arnprior Stirlg — 133 J9
Arnside Cumb — 95 K5
Aros Ag & B — 137 P6
Arowry Wrexhm — 69 N7
Arrad Foot Cumb — 94 G4
Arram E R Yk — 92 H2
Arran N Ayrs — 120 H4
Arrathorne N York — 97 K2
Arreton IoW — 14
Arrina Highld — 153 N6
Arrington Cambs — 62 D10
Arrochar Ag & B — 132 B7
Arrow Warwks — 47 L3
Arrowfield Top Worcs — 58 F10
Arscott Shrops — 56 G3
Artafallie Highld — 156 A8
Arthington Leeds — 90 H2
Arthingworth Nhants — 60 G4
Arthog Gwynd — 54 E2
Arthrath Abers — 159 N10
Arthursdale Leeds — 91 K3
Artrochie Abers — 159 P11
Arundel W Susx — 24 B9
Asby Cumb — 100 E6
Ascog Ag & B — 124 E5
Ascot W & M — 35 P11
Ascott Warwks — 48 B8
Ascott Earl Oxon — 48 B11
Ascott-under-Wychwood Oxon — 48 B11
Asenby N York — 97 N5
Asfordby Leics — 73 J7
Asfordby Hill Leics — 73 J7
Asgarby Lincs — 86 F11
Asgarby Lincs — 87 K7
Ash Devon — 7 L9
Ash Devon — 17 J10
Ash Dorset — 12 E2
Ash Kent — 27 P8
Ash Kent — 39 N10
Ash Somset — 19 J10
Ash Somset — 19 N10
Ash Surrey — 23 P4
Ashampstead W Berk — 34 G9
Ashampstead Green W Berk — 34 G9
Ashbocking Suffk — 64 H10
Ashbourne Derbys — 71 M5
Ashbrittle Somset — 18 E10

Ashburnham Place E Susx — 25 Q8
Ashburton Devon — 7 K4
Ashbury Devon — 8 D5
Ashbury Oxon — 33 Q7
Ashby by Partney Lincs — 87 M7
Ashby cum Fenby NE Lin — 93 N10
Ashby de la Laude Lincs — 86 E9
Ashby-de-la-Zouch Leics — 72 B7
Ashby Folville Leics — 73 J8
Ashby Magna Leics — 60 C2
Ashby Parva Leics — 60 B3
Ashby Puerorum Lincs — 87 K6
Ashby St Ledgers Nhants — 60 C7
Ashby St Mary Norfk — 77 L11
Ashchurch Gloucs — 46 H8
Ashcombe Devon — 9 M9
Ashcombe N Som — 19 L2
Ashcott Somset — 19 M7
Ashdon Essex — 51 N4
Ashdown Forest E Susx — 25 L4
Ashe Hants — 22 H4
Asheldham Essex — 52 G11
Ashen Essex — 52 B3
Ashendon Bucks — 35 K2
Asheridge Bucks — 35 P4
Ashfield Hants — 22 C11
Ashfield Herefs — 46 A10
Ashfield Stirlg — 133 M7
Ashfield cum Thorpe Suffk — 65 J9
Ashfield Green Suffk — 63 N9
Ashfield Green Suffk — 65 K7
Ashfold Crossways W Susx — 24 F5
Ashford Devon — 6 H9
Ashford Devon — 17 J4
Ashford Kent — 26 H3
Ashford Surrey — 36 C6
Ashford Bowdler Shrops — 57 J10
Ashford Carbonell Shrops — 57 J10
Ashford Hill Hants — 22 G2
Ashford in the Water Derbys — 83 Q11
Ashgill S Lans — 126 D7
Ash Green Surrey — 23 P5
Ash Green Warwks — 59 M8
Ashill Devon — 10 B2
Ashill Norfk — 76 B11
Ashill Somset — 19 K11
Ashingdon Essex — 38 E3
Ashington BCP — 12 H5
Ashington Nthumb — 113 L3
Ashington Somset — 19 Q10
Ashington W Susx — 24 D7
Ashkirk Border — 117 P6
Ashlett Hants — 14 E6
Ashleworth Gloucs — 46 F9
Ashleworth Quay Gloucs — 46 F9
Ashley Cambs — 63 L8
Ashley Ches E — 82 G8
Ashley Devon — 17 M9
Ashley Dorset — 13 K4
Ashley Gloucs — 33 H6
Ashley Hants — 13 N5
Ashley Hants — 22 C8
Ashley Kent — 27 P2
Ashley Nhants — 60 G2
Ashley Staffs — 70 D7
Ashley Wilts — 32 F11
Ashley Green Bucks — 35 Q3
Ashleyhay Derbys — 71 P4
Ashley Heath Dorset — 13 K4
Ashley Moor Herefs — 56 H11
Ash Magna Shrops — 69 Q7
Ashmansworth Hants — 22 D3
Ashmansworthy Devon — 16 E8
Ashmead Green Gloucs — 32 E5
Ashmill Devon — 5 P2
Ash Mill Devon — 17 P7
Ashmore Dorset — 20 H11
Ashmore Green W Berk — 34 F11
Ashorne Warwks — 48 B3
Ashover Derbys — 84 D8
Ashover Hay Derbys — 84 D8
Ashow Warwks — 59 M10
Ash Parva Shrops — 69 Q7
Ashperton Herefs — 46 B6
Ashprington Devon — 7 L7
Ash Priors Somset — 18 G9
Ashreigney Devon — 17 L9
Ash Street Suffk — 52 H2
Ash Thomas Devon — 9 P2
Ashton C Pete — 74 B9
Ashton Ches W — 81 Q11
Ashton Cnwll — 2 G8
Ashton Devon — 9 L8
Ashton Herefs — 45 Q2
Ashton Inver — 124 G2
Ashton Nhants — 49 L5
Ashton Nhants — 61 N3
Ashton Somset — 19 M5
Ashton Common Wilts — 20 G3
Ashton Hill Wilts — 20 H3
Ashton-in-Makerfield Wigan — 82 C5
Ashton Keynes Wilts — 33 K6
Ashton under Hill Worcs — 47 J7
Ashton-under-Lyne Tamesd — 83 K5
Ashton upon Mersey Traffd — 82 G6
Ashton Vale Bristl — 31 Q10
Ashurst Hants — 13 P2
Ashurst Kent — 25 M3
Ashurst Lancs — 88 F9
Ashurst W Susx — 24 E7
Ashurstwood W Susx — 25 K3
Ash Vale Surrey — 23 N4
Ashwater Devon — 5 P3
Ashwell Herts — 50 G3
Ashwell Rutlnd — 73 M8
Ashwell End Herts — 50 G3
Ashwellthorpe Norfk — 64 H2
Ashwick Somset — 20 B5
Ashwicken Norfk — 75 P7
Ashwood Staffs — 58 C7
Askam in Furness Cumb — 94 E5
Askern Donc — 91 P7
Askerswell Dorset — 11 L6
Askett Bucks — 35 M3
Askham Cumb — 101 P6
Askham Notts — 85 M6
Askham Bryan C York — 98 B11
Askham Richard C York — 98 A11
Asknish Ag & B — 131 J9

Askrigg N York — 96 D2
Askwith N York — 97 J11
Aslackby Lincs — 74 A4
Aslacton Norfk — 64 H3
Aslockton Notts — 73 J3
Asney Somset — 19 N7
Aspall Suffk — 64 H9
Aspatria Cumb — 100 F2
Aspenden Herts — 51 J5
Aspenshaw Derbys — 83 M7
Asperton Lincs — 74 D2
Aspley Staffs — 70 B3
Aspley Guise C Beds — 49 P7
Aspley Heath C Beds — 49 P8
Aspley Heath Warwks — 58 G10
Aspull Wigan — 89 J9
Aspull Common Wigan — 82 D5
Asselby E R Yk — 92 B5
Asserby Lincs — 87 N5
Asserby Turn Lincs — 87 N5
Assington Suffk — 52 F4
Assington Green Suffk — 63 N10
Astbury Ches E — 70 E2
Astcote Nhants — 49 J4
Asterby Lincs — 87 J5
Asterley Shrops — 56 F3
Asterton Shrops — 56 F6
Asthall Oxon — 33 Q2
Asthall Leigh Oxon — 34 B2
Astle Highld — 162 G8
Astley Shrops — 69 P11
Astley Warwks — 59 M7
Astley Wigan — 82 F4
Astley Worcs — 57 P11
Astley Abbots Shrops — 57 N5
Astley Bridge Bolton — 89 L8
Astley Cross Worcs — 57 Q10
Astley Green Wigan — 82 F5
Aston Birm — 58 G7
Aston Ches E — 69 R5
Aston Ches W — 82 C9
Aston Derbys — 83 Q8
Aston Flints — 81 L11
Aston Herefs — 45 P2
Aston Herts — 50 G6
Aston Oxon — 34 B4
Aston Rothm — 84 G3
Aston Shrops — 57 Q6
Aston Shrops — 69 P9
Aston Staffs — 70 D6
Aston Staffs — 70 F10
Aston Wokham — 35 L8
Aston Wrekin — 57 L3
Aston Abbotts Bucks — 49 M10
Aston Botterell Shrops — 57 L8
Aston-by-Stone Staffs — 70 G8
Aston Cantlow Warwks — 47 M2
Aston Clinton Bucks — 35 N2
Aston Crews Herefs — 46 C10
Aston Cross Gloucs — 46 H8
Aston End Herts — 50 G6
Aston-Eyre Shrops — 57 M6
Aston Fields Worcs — 58 E11
Aston Flamville Leics — 59 Q6
Aston Heath Ches W — 82 C9
Aston juxta Mondrum Ches E — 70 A3
Aston le Walls Nhants — 48 E4
Aston Magna Gloucs — 47 N7
Aston Munslow Shrops — 57 J7
Aston-on-Carrant Gloucs — 46 H8
Aston on Clun Shrops — 56 F8
Aston Pigott Shrops — 56 E3
Aston Rogers Shrops — 56 E3
Aston Rowant Oxon — 35 K5
Aston Sandford Bucks — 35 K3
Aston Somerville Worcs — 47 K7
Aston-sub-Edge Gloucs — 47 M6
Aston Tirrold Oxon — 34 G7
Aston-upon-Trent Derbys — 72 C5
Aston Upthorpe Oxon — 34 G7
Astrop Nhants — 48 E7
Astrope Herts — 35 N2
Astwick C Beds — 50 F3
Astwith Derbys — 84 F8
Astwood M Keyn — 49 Q5
Astwood Worcs — 58 D11
Astwood Bank Worcs — 47 K2
Aswarby Lincs — 73 R3
Aswardby Lincs — 87 L6
Atcham Shrops — 57 J3
Atch Lench Worcs — 47 K4
Athelhampton Dorset — 12 C6
Athelington Suffk — 65 J7
Athelney Somset — 19 K9
Athelstaneford E Loth — 128 E4
Atherfield Green IoW — 14 E11
Atherington Devon — 17 K7
Atherington W Susx — 24 B10
Atherstone Somset — 19 L11
Atherstone Warwks — 59 M5
Atherstone on Stour Warwks — 47 P4
Atherton Wigan — 82 E4
Atley Hill N York — 103 Q10
Atlow Derbys — 71 N5
Attadale Highld — 154 B10
Attenborough Notts — 72 E4
Atterby Lincs — 86 C2
Attercliffe Sheff — 84 E3
Atterley Shrops — 57 L5
Atterton Leics — 72 B11
Attingham Park Shrops — 57 J2
Attleborough Norfk — 64 E2
Attleborough Warwks — 59 N6
Attlebridge Norfk — 76 H8
Attleton Green Suffk — 63 M10
Atwick E R Yk — 99 P8
Atworth Wilts — 32 G11
Auberrow Herefs — 45 P5
Aubourn Lincs — 86 B8
Auchbreck Moray — 149 N2
Auchedly Abers — 159 L11
Auchenblae Abers — 143 N2
Auchenbowie Stirlg — 133 M10
Auchencairn D & G — 108 G10
Auchencairn D & G — 109 L4
Auchencairn N Ayrs — 121 K6
Auchencrow Border — 129 M7
Auchendinny Mdloth — 127 N4
Auchengray S Lans — 126 H5
Auchenhalrig Moray — 157 Q5
Auchenheath S Lans — 126 E9
Auchenhessnane D & G — 115 R8

Auchenlochan Ag & B — 124 B3
Auchenmade N Ayrs — 125 K8
Auchenmalg D & G — 106 H7
Auchentiber N Ayrs — 125 K8
Auchindrain Ag & B — 131 L7
Auchindrean Highld — 161 K10
Auchininna Abers — 158 G8
Auchinleck E Ayrs — 115 L3
Auchinloch N Lans — 126 B3
Auchinstarry N Lans — 126 C2
Auchintore Highld — 139 K3
Auchiries Abers — 159 Q10
Auchlean Highld — 148 H8
Auchlee Abers — 151 M8
Auchleven Abers — 150 G3
Auchlochan S Lans — 126 E10
Auchlossan Abers — 150 F7
Auchlyne Stirlg — 132 G2
Auchmillan E Ayrs — 115 K2
Auchmithie Angus — 143 M9
Auchmuirbridge Fife — 134 G7
Auchnacree Angus — 142 H5
Auchnagatt Abers — 159 M9
Auchnarrow Moray — 149 N3
Auchnotteroch D & G — 106 C5
Auchroisk Moray — 157 Q7
Auchterarder P & K — 133 Q5
Auchteraw Highld — 147 K6
Auchterblair Highld — 148 G3
Auchtercairn Highld — 153 Q2
Auchterderran Fife — 134 G8
Auchterhouse Angus — 142 E10
Auchterless Abers — 158 H9
Auchtermuchty Fife — 134 G5
Auchterneed Highld — 155 N6
Auchtertool Fife — 134 G9
Auchtertyre Highld — 145 P2
Auchtubh Stirlg — 132 H3
Auckengill Highld — 167 Q4
Auckley Donc — 91 Q10
Audenshaw Tamesd — 83 K5
Audlem Ches E — 70 B4
Audley Staffs — 70 D4
Audley End Essex — 51 M3
Audley End Essex — 52 D4
Audley End Suffk — 64 B11
Audley End House & Gardens Essex — 51 M3
Audmore Staffs — 70 E10
Audnam Dudley — 58 C7
Aughertree Cumb — 101 J3
Aughton E R Yk — 92 B3
Aughton Lancs — 88 D9
Aughton Lancs — 95 M7
Aughton Rothm — 84 G3
Aughton Wilts — 21 P3
Aughton Park Lancs — 88 E9
Auldearn Highld — 156 G6
Aulden Herefs — 45 P3
Auldgirth D & G — 109 K3
Auldhouse S Lans — 125 Q6
Ault a' chruinn Highld — 146 A3
Aultbea Highld — 160 B9
Aultgrishin Highld — 160 A9
Aultguish Inn Highld — 155 L3
Ault Hucknall Derbys — 84 G7
Aultmore Moray — 158 B7
Aultnagoire Highld — 147 N3
Aultnamain Highld — 162 F10
Aunby Lincs — 73 Q8
Aunk Devon — 9 P4
Aunsby Lincs — 73 Q3
Aust S Glos — 31 Q7
Austendike Lincs — 74 E6
Austerfield Donc — 85 L2
Austerlands Oldham — 90 B9
Austhorpe Leeds — 91 K4
Austonley Kirk — 90 E9
Austrey Warwks — 59 L3
Austwick N York — 95 R7
Authorpe Lincs — 87 L4
Authorpe Row Lincs — 87 P6
Avebury Wilts — 33 M11
Avebury Trusloe Wilts — 33 L11
Aveley Thurr — 37 N4
Avening Gloucs — 32 G5
Averham Notts — 85 N10
Aveton Gifford Devon — 6 H9
Aviemore Highld — 148 F5
Avington W Berk — 34 C11
Avoch Highld — 156 C6
Avon Hants — 13 K5
Avonbridge Falk — 126 G3
Avon Dassett Warwks — 48 D4
Avonmouth Bristl — 31 P9
Avonwick Devon — 7 J7
Awbridge Hants — 22 B10
Awkley S Glos — 31 Q7
Awliscombe Devon — 10 C4
Awre Gloucs — 32 D3
Awsworth Notts — 72 D2
Axborough Worcs — 58 C9
Axbridge Somset — 19 M4
Axford Hants — 22 H6
Axford Wilts — 33 P10
Axmansford Hants — 22 G2
Axminster Devon — 10 F5
Axmouth Devon — 10 F6
Axton Flints — 80 G8
Aycliffe Dur — 103 Q6
Aydon Nthumb — 112 F7
Aylburton Gloucs — 32 B4
Ayle Nthumb — 111 P11
Aylesbeare Devon — 9 P6
Aylesbury Bucks — 35 M2
Aylesby NE Lin — 93 M9
Aylesford Kent — 38 B10
Aylesham Kent — 39 M11
Aylestone C Leic — 72 F10
Aylestone Park C Leic — 72 F10
Aylmerton Norfk — 76 H4
Aylsham Norfk — 76 H6
Aylton Herefs — 46 C7
Aylworth Gloucs — 47 M10
Aymestrey Herefs — 56 G11
Aynho Nhants — 48 F8
Ayot Green Herts — 50 F8
Ayot St Lawrence Herts — 50 E7
Ayot St Peter Herts — 50 F7
Ayr S Ayrs — 114 F3
Aysgarth N York — 96 H3
Ayshford Devon — 18 D11
Ayside Cumb — 94 H4
Ayston Rutlnd — 73 M10

Aythorpe Roding – Beadlow 257

Aythorpe Roding Essex 51 N7
Ayton Border 129 N7
Azerley N York 97 L6

B

Babbacombe Torbay 7 N5
Babbington Notts 72 D2
Babbinswood Shrops 69 K9
Babbs Green Herts 51 J7
Babcary Somset 19 Q9
Babel Carmth 44 A7
Babel Green Suffk 63 M11
Babell Flints 80 H10
Babeny Devon 8 G9
Bablock Hythe Oxon 34 D4
Babraham Cambs 62 H10
Babworth Notts 85 L4
Bachau IoA 78 G8
Bache Shrops 56 H8
Bacheldre Powys 56 C6
Bachelor's Bump E Susx 26 D9
Backaland Ork 169 e3
Backbarrow Cumb 94 H4
Backe Carmth 41 Q7
Backfolds Abers 159 P7
Backford Ches W 81 M10
Backford Cross Ches W 81 M10
Backies Highld 163 J6
Back of Keppoch Highld 145 L10
Back o' th' Brook Staffs 71 K4
Back Street Suffk 63 M9
Backwell N Som 31 N11
Backworth N Tyne 113 M6
Bacon's End Solhll 59 J7
Baconsthorpe Norfk 76 G4
Bacton Herefs 45 M8
Bacton Norfk 77 L5
Bacton Suffk 64 F8
Bacton Green Suffk 64 E8
Bacup Lancs 89 P6
Badachro Highld 153 P3
Badanloch Highld 166 C10
Badbury Swindn 33 N8
Badby Nhants 60 C9
Badcall Highld 164 F5
Badcaul Highld 160 G8
Baddeley Edge C Stke 70 G4
Baddeley Green C Stke 70 G4
Baddesley Clinton Warwks 59 K10
Baddesley Ensor Warwks 59 L5
Baddidarrach Highld 160 H2
Baddinsgill Border 127 L7
Badenscoth Abers 158 G10
Badentarbet Highld 160 G5
Badenyon Abers 149 Q4
Badersfield Norfk 77 K7
Badgall Cnwll 5 L4
Badgeney Cambs 74 H11
Badger Shrops 57 P5
Badger's Cross Cnwll 2 D7
Badgers Mount Kent 37 L8
Badgeworth Gloucs 46 H11
Badgworth Somset 19 L4
Badharlick Cnwll 5 M4
Badicaul Highld 145 N2
Badingham Suffk 65 L8
Badlesmere Kent 38 H11
Badlieu Border 116 F7
Badlipster Highld 167 M7
Badluarach Highld 160 F8
Badninish Highld 162 H8
Badrallach Highld 160 H8
Badsey Worcs 47 L6
Badshot Lea Surrey 23 N5
Badsworth Wakefd 91 M8
Badwell Ash Suffk 64 D8
Badwell Green Suffk 64 E8
Bagber Dorset 12 C2
Bagby N York 97 Q4
Bag Enderby Lincs 87 L6
Bagendon Gloucs 33 K3
Bagginswood Shrops 57 M8
Baggrow Cumb 100 G2
Bàgh a' Chaisteil W Isls 168 b18
Bagham Kent 39 J11
Bagillt Flints 81 J9
Baginton Warwks 59 M10
Baglan Neath 29 K6
Bagley Leeds 90 G3
Bagley Shrops 69 M9
Bagley Somset 19 N5
Bagmore Hants 23 J6
Bagnall Staffs 70 G4
Bagnor W Berk 34 E11
Bagshot Surrey 23 P2
Bagshot Wilts 34 B11
Bagstone S Glos 32 C7
Bagthorpe Notts 84 G10
Bagworth Leics 72 C9
Bagwy Llydiart Herefs 45 N9
Baildon C Brad 90 F3
Baildon Green C Brad 90 E3
Baile Ailein W Isls 168 h5
Baile a' Mhanaich W Isls 168 c12
Baile Mòr Ag & B 136 H11
Bailey Green Hants 23 J9
Baileyhead Cumb 111 K5
Bailiff Bridge Calder 90 E5
Baillieston C Glas 126 B5
Bailrigg Lancs 95 K9
Bainbridge N York 96 D2
Bainshole Abers 158 F10
Bainton C Pete 74 A9
Bainton E R Yk 99 K10
Bainton Oxon 48 G9
Baintown Fife 135 K7
Bairnkine Border 118 C7
Baker's End Herts 51 J7
Baker Street Thurr 37 P4
Bakewell Derbys 84 B7
Bala Gwynd 68 B7
Balallan W Isls 168 h5
Balbeg Highld 155 M11
Balbeggie P & K 134 F2
Balblair Highld 155 P8
Balblair Highld 156 C4
Balby Donc 91 P10
Balcary D & G 108 H11
Balchraggan Highld 155 P9
Balchreick Highld 164 E4
Balcombe W Susx 24 H4
Balcombe Lane W Susx 24 H4
Balcomie Links Fife 135 Q6
Baldersby N York 97 N5
Baldersby St James N York 97 N5
Balderstone Lancs 89 J4
Balderstone Rochdl 89 Q8
Balderton Notts 85 P10
Baldhu Cnwll 3 K5
Baldinnie Fife 135 L5
Baldinnies P & K 134 C4
Baldock Herts 50 F4
Baldock Services Herts 50 F3
Baldovie C Dund 142 H11
Baldrine IoM 80 f5
Baldslow E Susx 26 D9
Baldwin IoM 80 e5
Baldwinholme Cumb 110 F10
Baldwin's Gate Staffs 70 D7
Baldwin's Hill W Susx 25 J3
Bale Norfk 76 E4
Baledgarno P & K 142 D11
Balemartine Ag & B 136 B7
Balerno C Edin 127 M4
Balfarg Fife 134 H7
Balfield Angus 143 J4
Balfour Ork 169 d5
Balfron Stirlg 132 G10
Balgaveny Abers 158 G9
Balgonar Fife 134 C9
Balgowan D & G 106 F9
Balgowan Highld 147 Q9
Balgown Highld 152 F4
Balgracie D & G 106 C5
Balgray S Lans 116 B6
Balham Gt Lon 36 G6
Balhary P & K 142 D8
Balholmie P & K 142 A10
Baligill Highld 166 E3
Balintore Angus 142 D6
Balintore Highld 156 F2
Balintraid Highld 156 C3
Balivanich W Isls 168 c12
Balk N York 97 Q4
Balkeerie Angus 142 E9
Balkholme E R Yk 92 C5
Ballabeg IoM 80 c7
Ballachulish Highld 139 K6
Ballafesson IoM 80 b7
Ballajora IoM 80 g3
Ballakilpheric IoM 80 b7
Ballamodha IoM 80 c7
Ballanlay Ag & B 124 C5
Ballantrae S Ayrs 114 A11
Ballards Gore Essex 38 F3
Ballards Green Warwks 59 L6
Ballasalla IoM 80 c7
Ballater Abers 150 B8
Ballaugh IoM 80 d3
Ballchraggan Highld 156 D2
Ballencrieff E Loth 128 D4
Ballevullin Ag & B 136 B6
Ball Green C Stke 70 F4
Ball Haye Green Staffs 70 H3
Ball Hill Hants 22 D2
Ballidon Derbys 71 N4
Balliekine N Ayrs 120 G4
Balliemore Ag & B 131 N8
Balligmorrie S Ayrs 114 D9
Ballimore Stirlg 132 G4
Ballindalloch Moray 157 M10
Ballindean P & K 134 H2
Ballingdon Suffk 52 E3
Ballinger Common Bucks 35 P4
Ballingham Herefs 46 A8
Ballingry Fife 134 F8
Ballinluig P & K 141 N7
Ballinshoe Angus 142 G7
Ballintuim P & K 141 R6
Balloch Highld 156 C8
Balloch N Lans 126 C3
Balloch P & K 133 N4
Balloch S Ayrs 114 F8
Balloch W Duns 132 D11
Balls Cross W Susx 23 Q9
Balls Green E Susx 25 L3
Ball's Green Gloucs 32 G5
Ballygown Ag & B 137 L7
Ballygrant Ag & B 122 E6
Ballyhaugh Ag & B 136 F4
Balmacara Highld 145 P2
Balmaclellan D & G 108 E5
Balmae D & G 108 E12
Balmaha Stirlg 132 E9
Balmalcolm Fife 135 J6
Balmangan D & G 108 D11
Balmedie Abers 151 P4
Balmer Heath Shrops 69 M8
Balmerino Fife 135 K3
Balmerlawn Hants 13 P4
Balmichael N Ayrs 120 H5
Balmore E Duns 125 P3
Balmuchy Highld 163 K11
Balmule Fife 134 G10
Balmullo Fife 135 L3
Balnacoil Highld 163 J4
Balnacra Highld 154 C8
Balnacroft Abers 149 P9
Balnafoich Highld 156 B10
Balnaguard P & K 141 M7
Balnahard Ag & B 137 M9
Balnain Highld 155 M11
Balnakeil Highld 165 J3
Balne N York 91 P7
Balquharn P & K 141 P10
Balquhidder Stirlg 132 G3
Balsall Common Solhll 59 K9
Balsall Heath Birm 58 G8
Balsall Street Solhll 59 K9
Balscote Oxon 48 C6
Balsham Cambs 63 J10
Baltasound Shet 169 t3
Balterley Staffs 70 D4
Balterley Green Staffs 70 D4
Balterley Heath Staffs 70 C4
Baltersan D & G 107 M5
Balthangie Abers 159 K7
Baltonsborough Somset 19 P8
Balvicar Ag & B 130 F4
Balvraid Highld 145 P4
Balvraid Highld 156 E11
Balwest Cnwll 2 F7
Bamber Bridge Lancs 88 H5
Bamber's Green Essex 51 N6
Bamburgh Nthumb 119 N4
Bamburgh Castle Nthumb 119 N3
Bamford Derbys 84 B4
Bamford Rochdl 89 P8
Bampton Cumb 101 P7
Bampton Devon 18 C10
Bampton Oxon 34 B4
Bampton Grange Cumb 101 P7
Banavie Highld 139 L2
Banbury Oxon 48 E6
Bancffosfelen Carmth 28 E2
Banchory Abers 150 H8
Banchory-Devenick Abers 151 N7
Bancycapel Carmth 28 D2
Bancyfelin Carmth 42 F11
Banc-y-ffordd Carmth 42 H7
Bandirran P & K 142 C11
Bandrake Head Cumb 94 G3
Banff Abers 158 G5
Bangor Gwynd 79 K10
Bangor-on-Dee Wrexhm 69 L5
Bangors Cnwll 5 L2
Bangor's Green Lancs 88 D9
Bangrove Suffk 64 C7
Banham Norfk 64 F4
Bank Hants 13 N3
Bankend D & G 109 M7
Bankfoot P & K 141 Q10
Bankglen E Ayrs 115 L5
Bank Ground Cumb 101 K11
Bankhead C Aber 151 N6
Bankhead S Lans 116 D2
Bank Newton N York 96 D10
Banknock Falk 126 D2
Banks Cumb 111 L8
Banks Lancs 88 D6
Banks Green Worcs 58 E11
Bankshill D & G 110 C4
Bank Street Worcs 46 B2
Bank Top Calder 90 E6
Bank Top Lancs 88 G9
Banningham Norfk 77 J6
Bannister Green Essex 51 Q6
Bannockburn Stirlg 133 N9
Banstead Surrey 36 G9
Bantham Devon 6 H10
Banton N Lans 126 C2
Banwell N Som 19 L3
Bapchild Kent 38 F9
Bapton Wilts 21 J7
Barabhas W Isls 168 i3
Barassie S Ayrs 125 J11
Barbaraville Highld 156 C3
Barber Booth Derbys 83 P8
Barber Green Cumb 94 H4
Barbieston S Ayrs 114 H4
Barbon Cumb 95 N4
Barbridge Ches E 69 R3
Barbrook Devon 17 N2
Barby Nhants 60 B6
Barcaldine Ag & B 138 H9
Barcheston Warwks 47 Q7
Barclose Cumb 110 H8
Barcombe E Susx 25 K8
Barcombe Cross E Susx 25 K7
Barcroft C Brad 90 C3
Barden N York 96 H2
Barden Park Kent 37 N11
Bardfield End Green Essex 51 P4
Bardfield Saling Essex 51 Q5
Bardney Lincs 86 F7
Bardon Leics 72 C8
Bardon Mill Nthumb 111 Q8
Bardowie E Duns 125 P3
Bardown E Susx 25 Q5
Bardrainney Inver 125 J3
Bardsea Cumb 94 G6
Bardsey Leeds 91 K2
Bardsey Island Gwynd 66 A10
Bardsley Oldham 83 K4
Bardwell Suffk 64 C7
Bare Lancs 95 K8
Bareppa Cnwll 3 K8
Barfad D & G 107 K4
Barford Norfk 76 G10
Barford Warwks 47 Q2
Barford St John Oxon 48 D8
Barford St Martin Wilts 21 L8
Barford St Michael Oxon 48 D8
Barfrestone Kent 39 N11
Bargate Derbys 84 E11
Bargeddie N Lans 126 B5
Bargoed Caerph 30 G5
Bargrennan D & G 107 L2
Barham Cambs 61 P5
Barham Kent 39 M11
Barham Suffk 64 G11
Bar Hill Cambs 62 E8
Barholm Lincs 74 A8
Barkby Leics 72 G9
Barkby Thorpe Leics 72 G9
Barkers Green Shrops 69 P9
Barkestone-le-Vale Leics 73 K4
Barkham Wokham 35 L11
Barking Gt Lon 37 K4
Barking Suffk 64 F11
Barkingside Gt Lon 37 K3
Barking Tye Suffk 64 F11
Barkisland Calder 90 D7
Barkla Shop Cnwll 3 J3
Barkston Lincs 73 N2
Barkston Ash N York 91 M3
Barkway Herts 51 J3
Barlanark C Glas 126 B5
Barlaston Staffs 70 F7
Barlavington W Susx 23 Q11
Barlborough Derbys 84 G5
Barlby N York 91 Q4
Barlestone Leics 72 C9
Barley Herts 51 K3
Barley Lancs 89 N2
Barleycroft End Herts 51 K5
Barley Hole Rothm 91 K11
Barleythorpe Rutlnd 73 L9
Barling Essex 38 F4
Barlings Lincs 86 E6
Barlochan D & G 108 H9
Barlow Derbys 84 D6
Barlow Gatesd 113 J8
Barlow N York 91 Q5
Barmby Moor E R Yk 98 F11
Barmby on the Marsh E R Yk 92 A5
Barmer Norfk 75 R4
Barming Heath Kent 38 B10
Barmollack Ag & B 120 F3
Barmouth Gwynd 67 L11
Barmpton Darltn 104 B7
Barmston E R Yk 99 P9
Barnaby Green Suffk 65 P5
Barnacarry Ag & B 131 L9
Barnack C Pete 74 A9
Barnacle Warwks 59 N8
Barnard Castle Dur 103 L7
Barnard Gate Oxon 34 D2
Barnardiston Suffk 63 M11
Barnbarroch D & G 108 H9
Barnburgh Donc 91 M10
Barnby Suffk 65 P4
Barnby Dun Donc 91 Q9
Barnby in the Willows Notts 85 Q10
Barnby Moor Notts 85 L4
Barncorkrie D & G 106 E10
Barnehurst Gt Lon 37 L5
Barnes Gt Lon 36 F5
Barnes Street Kent 37 P11
Barnet Gt Lon 50 F11
Barnetby le Wold N Linc 93 J9
Barnet Gate Gt Lon 50 F11
Barney Norfk 76 D5
Barnham Suffk 64 B6
Barnham W Susx 15 Q6
Barnham Broom Norfk 76 F10
Barnhead Angus 143 M6
Barnhill C Dund 142 H11
Barnhill Ches W 69 N4
Barnhill Moray 157 L6
Barnhills D & G 106 C3
Barningham Dur 103 L8
Barningham Suffk 64 D6
Barnoldby le Beck NE Lin 93 M10
Barnoldswick Lancs 96 C11
Barnsdale Bar Donc 91 N8
Barns Green W Susx 24 D5
Barnsley Barns 91 J9
Barnsley Gloucs 33 L4
Barnsole Kent 39 N10
Barnstaple Devon 17 K5
Barnston Essex 51 P7
Barnston Wirral 81 K8
Barnstone Notts 73 J3
Barnt Green Worcs 58 F10
Barnton C Edin 127 M3
Barnton Ches W 82 D10
Barnwell All Saints Nhants 61 M4
Barnwell St Andrew Nhants 61 N4
Barnwood Gloucs 46 G11
Baron's Cross Herefs 45 P3
Baronwood Cumb 101 P2
Barr S Ayrs 114 E9
Barra W Isls 168 b17
Barra Airport W Isls 168 c17
Barrachan D & G 107 L8
Barraigh W Isls 168 b17
Barrananaoil Ag & B 130 G6
Barrapoll Ag & B 136 A7
Barras Cumb 102 F8
Barrasford Nthumb 112 D6
Barregarrow IoM 80 d4
Barrets Green Ches E 69 Q3
Barrhead E Rens 125 M6
Barrhill S Ayrs 114 D11
Barrington Cambs 62 E11
Barrington Somset 19 L11
Barripper Cnwll 2 G6
Barrmill N Ayrs 125 K7
Barrock Highld 167 N2
Barrow Gloucs 46 G10
Barrow Lancs 89 L3
Barrow Rutlnd 73 M7
Barrow Shrops 57 M4
Barrow Somset 20 D8
Barrow Suffk 63 N8
Barroway Drove Norfk 75 L10
Barrow Bridge Bolton 89 K8
Barrow Burn Nthumb 118 G8
Barrowby Lincs 73 M3
Barrowden Rutlnd 73 N10
Barrowford Lancs 89 P3
Barrow Gurney N Som 31 P11
Barrow Haven N Linc 93 J6
Barrow Hill Derbys 84 F5
Barrow-in-Furness Cumb 94 E7
Barrow Island Cumb 94 D7
Barrow Nook Lancs 81 N4
Barrow's Green Ches E 70 B3
Barrow Street Wilts 20 F8
Barrow-upon-Humber N Linc 93 J6
Barrow upon Soar Leics 72 F7
Barrow upon Trent Derbys 72 B5
Barrow Vale BaNES 20 B2
Barry Angus 143 J11
Barry V Glam 30 F11
Barry Island V Glam 30 F11
Barsby Leics 72 H8
Barsham Suffk 65 M4
Barston Solhll 59 K9
Bartestree Herefs 45 R6
Barthol Chapel Abers 159 K11
Bartholomew Green Essex 52 B7
Barthomley Ches E 70 D4
Bartley Hants 13 P2
Bartley Green Birm 58 F8
Bartlow Cambs 63 J11
Barton Cambs 62 F9
Barton Ches W 69 M4
Barton Gloucs 47 L9
Barton Herefs 45 K3
Barton Lancs 88 D9
Barton Lancs 88 G3
Barton N York 103 P9
Barton Oxon 34 G3
Barton Torbay 7 N5
Barton Warwks 47 M4
Barton Bendish Norfk 75 P9
Barton End Gloucs 32 F5
Barton Green Staffs 71 M11
Barton Hartshorn Bucks 48 H8
Barton Hill N York 98 E8
Barton in Fabis Notts 72 E4
Barton in the Beans Leics 72 B9
Barton-le-Clay C Beds 50 C4
Barton-le-Street N York 98 E6
Barton-le-Willows N York 98 E8
Barton Mills Suffk 63 M6
Barton-on-Sea Hants 13 M6
Barton-on-the-Heath Warwks 47 Q8
Barton Park Services N York 103 P9
Barton St David Somset 19 P8
Barton Seagrave Nhants 61 J5
Barton Stacey Hants 22 D6
Barton Town Devon 17 M3
Barton Turf Norfk 77 M7
Barton-under-Needwood Staffs 71 M11
Barton-upon-Humber N Linc 92 H6
Barton upon Irwell Salfd 82 G5
Barton Waterside N Linc 92 H6
Barugh Barns 91 J9
Barugh Green Barns 91 J9
Barvas W Isls 168 i3
Barway Cambs 63 J5
Barwell Leics 72 C11
Barwick Devon 17 K10
Barwick Herts 51 J7
Barwick Somset 11 M2
Barwick in Elmet Leeds 91 L3
Baschurch Shrops 69 M10
Bascote Warwks 48 D2
Bascote Heath Warwks 48 C2
Base Green Suffk 64 E9
Basford Green Staffs 70 H4
Bashall Eaves Lancs 89 K2
Bashall Town Lancs 89 L2
Bashley Hants 13 M5
Basildon Essex 38 B4
Basingstoke Hants 22 H4
Baslow Derbys 84 C6
Bason Bridge Somset 19 K5
Bassaleg Newpt 31 J7
Bassendean Border 128 G10
Bassenthwaite Cumb 100 H4
Bassett C Sotn 22 D11
Bassingbourn-cum-Kneesworth Cambs 50 H2
Bassingfield Notts 72 G3
Bassingham Lincs 86 B9
Bassingthorpe Lincs 73 P5
Bassus Green Herts 50 H5
Basted Kent 37 P9
Baston Lincs 74 B8
Bastwick Norfk 77 N8
Batch Somset 19 K3
Batchworth Herts 36 C2
Batchworth Heath Herts 36 C2
Batcombe Dorset 11 N4
Batcombe Somset 20 C7
Bate Heath Ches E 82 E9
Batford Herts 50 D7
Bath BaNES 20 D2
Bath BaNES 20 E2
Bathampton BaNES 32 E11
Bathealton Somset 18 E10
Batheaston BaNES 32 E11
Bathford BaNES 32 E11
Bathgate W Loth 126 H4
Bathley Notts 85 N9
Bathpool Cnwll 5 M7
Bathpool Somset 19 J9
Bath Side Essex 53 N5
Bathville W Loth 126 G4
Bathway Somset 19 Q4
Batley Kirk 90 G6
Batsford Gloucs 47 N8
Batson Devon 7 J11
Battersby N York 104 G9
Battersea Gt Lon 36 G5
Battisborough Cross Devon 6 F9
Battisford Suffk 64 F11
Battisford Tye Suffk 64 E11
Battle E Susx 26 C8
Battle Powys 44 E8
Battleborough Somset 19 K4
Battledown Gloucs 47 J10
Battledykes Angus 142 H6
Battlefield Shrops 69 P11
Battlesbridge Essex 38 C3
Battlesden C Beds 49 Q9
Battleton Somset 18 B9
Battlies Green Suffk 64 C9
Battram Leics 72 C9
Battramsley Cross Hants 13 P5
Batt's Corner Hants 23 M6
Baughton Worcs 46 G6
Baughurst Hants 22 G2
Baulds Abers 150 G9
Baulking Oxon 34 B6
Baumber Lincs 86 H6
Baunton Gloucs 33 K4
Baveney Wood Shrops 57 M9
Baverstock Wilts 21 K8
Bawburgh Norfk 76 H10
Bawdeswell Norfk 76 E7
Bawdrip Somset 19 K7
Bawdsey Suffk 53 P3
Bawsey Norfk 75 N6
Bawtry Donc 85 K2
Baxenden Lancs 89 M5
Baxterley Warwks 59 L5
Baxter's Green Suffk 63 N9
Bay Highld 152 D7
Bayble W Isls 168 k4
Baybridge Hants 22 F10
Baybridge Nthumb 112 E10
Baycliff Cumb 94 F6
Baydon Wilts 33 Q9
Bayford Herts 50 H9
Bayford Somset 20 D9
Bayhead W Isls 168 c11
Bay Horse Lancs 95 K10
Bayley's Hill Kent 37 M10
Baylham Suffk 64 G11
Baynard's Green Oxon 48 F9
Baysdale Abbey N York 104 H9
Baysham Herefs 45 R9
Bayston Hill Shrops 56 H3
Baythorne End Essex 52 B3
Bayton Worcs 57 M10
Bayton Common Worcs 57 N10
Bayworth Oxon 34 E4
Beach S Glos 32 D10
Beachampton Bucks 49 L7
Beachamwell Norfk 75 Q9
Beachley Gloucs 31 Q6
Beachy Head E Susx 25 N11
Beacon Devon 10 D3
Beacon End Essex 52 G7
Beacon Hill Kent 26 D5
Beacon Hill Notts 85 P10
Beacon Hill Surrey 23 N7
Beacon's Bottom Bucks 35 L5
Beaconsfield Bucks 35 P6
Beaconsfield Services Bucks 35 Q7
Beadlam N York 98 D4
Beadlow C Beds 50 D3

Place	Region	Page	Grid
Beadnell	Nthumb	119	P5
Beaford	Devon	17	K8
Beal	N York	91	N5
Beal	Nthumb	119	L2
Bealbury	Cnwll	5	P8
Bealsmill	Cnwll	5	P6
Beam Hill	Staffs	71	N9
Beamhurst	Staffs	71	K7
Beaminster	Dorset	11	K4
Beamish	Dur	113	K10
Beamish Museum	Dur	113	K10
Beamsley	N York	96	G10
Bean	Kent	37	N6
Beanacre	Wilts	32	H11
Beanley	Nthumb	119	L7
Beardon	Devon	8	D8
Beardwood	Bl w D	89	K5
Beare	Devon	9	N4
Beare Green	Surrey	24	E2
Bearley	Warwks	47	N2
Bearley Cross	Warwks	47	N2
Bearpark	Dur	103	P2
Bearsden	E Duns	125	N3
Bearsted	Kent	38	D10
Bearstone	Shrops	70	C7
Bearwood	BCP	12	H5
Bearwood	Birm	58	F7
Bearwood	Herefs	45	M3
Beattock	D & G	116	F10
Beauchamp Roding	Essex	51	N9
Beauchief	Sheff	84	D4
Beaudesert	Warwks	59	J11
Beaufort	Blae G	30	G2
Beaulieu	Hants	14	C6
Beaulieu Road Station	Hants	13	P3
Beauly	Highld	155	P8
Beaumaris	IoA	79	L9
Beaumaris Castle	IoA	79	L9
Beaumont	Cumb	110	F9
Beaumont	Essex	53	L7
Beaumont	Jersey	11	b2
Beaumont Hill	Darltn	103	Q7
Beaumont Leys	C Leic	72	F9
Beausale	Warwks	59	K10
Beauworth	Hants	22	G9
Beaworthy	Devon	8	C5
Beazley End	Essex	52	B6
Bebington	Wirral	81	L8
Bebside	Nthumb	113	L4
Beccles	Suffk	65	N4
Becconsall	Lancs	88	F6
Beckbury	Shrops	57	P4
Beckenham	Gt Lon	37	J7
Beckermet	Cumb	100	D9
Beckett End	Norfk	75	Q11
Beckfoot	Cumb	94	D3
Beckfoot	Cumb	100	G10
Beck Foot	Cumb	102	B11
Beckfoot	Cumb	109	N11
Beckford	Worcs	47	J7
Beckhampton	Wilts	33	L11
Beck Hole	N York	105	M10
Beckingham	Lincs	85	Q10
Beckingham	Notts	85	N3
Beckington	Somset	20	F4
Beckjay	Shrops	56	F9
Beckley	E Susx	26	E7
Beckley	Hants	13	M5
Beckley	Oxon	34	G2
Beck Row	Suffk	63	L5
Becks	C Brad	96	F11
Beck Side	Cumb	94	E4
Beck Side	Cumb	94	H4
Beckton	Gt Lon	37	K4
Beckwithshaw	N York	97	L10
Becontree	Gt Lon	37	L3
Becquet Vincent	Jersey	11	b1
Bedale	N York	97	L3
Bedburn	Dur	103	L4
Bedchester	Dorset	20	G11
Beddau	Rhondd	30	E7
Beddgelert	Gwynd	67	K5
Beddingham	E Susx	25	K9
Beddington	Gt Lon	36	H7
Beddington Corner	Gt Lon	36	H7
Bedfield	Suffk	65	J8
Bedfield Little Green	Suffk	65	J8
Bedford	Bed	61	M11
Bedgebury Cross	Kent	26	B5
Bedgrove	Bucks	35	M2
Bedham	W Susx	24	B6
Bedhampton	Hants	15	K5
Bedingfield	Suffk	64	H8
Bedingfield Green	Suffk	64	H8
Bedlam	N York	97	L10
Bedlington	Nthumb	113	L4
Bedlinog	Myr Td	30	E4
Bedminster	Bristl	31	Q10
Bedminster Down	Bristl	31	Q10
Bedmond	Herts	50	C10
Bednall	Staffs	70	H11
Bedrule	Border	118	B7
Bedstone	Shrops	56	F9
Bedwas	Caerph	30	G4
Bedwellty	Caerph	30	G4
Bedworth	Warwks	59	N7
Bedworth Woodlands	Warwks	59	M7
Beeby	Leics	72	H9
Beech	Hants	23	J7
Beech	Staffs	70	F7
Beech Hill	W Berk	23	J2
Beechingstoke	Wilts	21	L3
Beedon	W Berk	34	E9
Beedon Hill	W Berk	34	E9
Beeford	E R Yk	99	N10
Beeley	Derbys	84	C7
Beelsby	NE Lin	93	M10
Beenham	W Berk	34	G11
Beenham's Heath	W & M	35	M9
Beeny	Cnwll	5	J3
Beer	Devon	10	E7
Beer	Somset	19	M8
Beercrocombe	Somset	19	K10
Beer Hackett	Dorset	11	N2
Beesands	Devon	7	L10
Beesby	Lincs	87	N4
Beeson	Devon	7	L10
Beeston	C Beds	61	Q10
Beeston	Ches W	69	P3
Beeston	Leeds	90	H4
Beeston	Norfk	76	C8
Beeston	Notts	72	E3
Beeston Regis	Norfk	76	H3
Beeswing	D & G	109	J7
Beetham	Cumb	95	K5
Beetham	Somset	10	H2
Beetley	Norfk	76	D8
Began	Cardif	30	H8
Begbroke	Oxon	34	E2
Begdale	Cambs	75	J9
Begelly	Pembks	41	M9
Beggarington Hill	Leeds	90	H6
Beggar's Bush	Powys	45	K2
Beguildy	Powys	56	B9
Beighton	Norfk	77	M10
Beighton	Sheff	84	F4
Beinn Na Faoghla	W Isls	168	d12
Beith	N Ayrs	125	K7
Bekesbourne	Kent	39	L10
Bekesbourne Hill	Kent	39	L10
Belaugh	Norfk	77	K8
Belbroughton	Worcs	58	D9
Belchalwell	Dorset	12	C3
Belchalwell Street	Dorset	12	C3
Belchamp Otten	Essex	52	D3
Belchamp St Paul	Essex	52	C3
Belchamp Walter	Essex	52	D3
Belchford	Lincs	87	J5
Belford	Nthumb	119	M4
Belgrave	C Leic	72	F9
Belhaven	E Loth	128	H4
Belhelvie	Abers	151	N4
Belhinnie	Abers	150	D2
Bellabeg	Abers	150	B5
Bellamore	Herefs	45	M6
Bellanoch	Ag & B	130	F9
Bellasize	E R Yk	92	D5
Bellaty	Angus	142	C6
Bell Bar	Herts	50	G9
Bell Busk	N York	96	D9
Belleau	Lincs	87	M5
Bell End	Worcs	58	D9
Bellerby	N York	96	H2
Bellever	Devon	8	G9
Belle Vue	Cumb	110	G9
Belle Vue	Wakefd	91	J7
Bellfield	S Lans	126	E11
Bell Heath	Worcs	58	D9
Bell Hill	Hants	23	K10
Bellingdon	Bucks	35	P3
Bellingham	Nthumb	112	B4
Belloch	Ag & B	120	C4
Bellochantuy	Ag & B	120	C5
Bell o' th' Hill	Ches W	69	P5
Bellows Cross	Dorset	13	J2
Bells Cross	Suffk	64	H11
Bellshill	N Lans	126	C5
Bellshill	Nthumb	119	M4
Bellside	N Lans	126	E6
Bellsquarry	W Loth	127	K4
Bells Yew Green	E Susx	25	P3
Belluton	BaNES	20	B2
Belmaduthy	Highld	156	A6
Belmesthorpe	Rutlnd	73	Q8
Belmont	Bl w D	89	K7
Belmont	Gt Lon	36	G8
Belmont	S Ayrs	114	F4
Belmont	Shet	169	s3
Belnacraig	Abers	150	B4
Belowda	Cnwll	4	F9
Belper	Derbys	84	D11
Belper Lane End	Derbys	84	D11
Belph	Derbys	84	H5
Belsay	Nthumb	112	G5
Belses	Border	117	R5
Belsford	Devon	7	K7
Belsize	Herts	50	B10
Belstead	Suffk	53	K3
Belstone	Devon	8	F6
Belthorn	Bl w D	89	L6
Beltinge	Kent	39	L8
Beltingham	Nthumb	111	Q8
Beltoft	N Linc	92	D9
Belton	Leics	72	C6
Belton	Lincs	73	N3
Belton	N Linc	92	C9
Belton	Norfk	77	P11
Belton House	Lincs	73	N3
Belton in Rutland	Rutlnd	73	L10
Beltring	Kent	37	Q11
Belvedere	Gt Lon	37	L5
Belvoir	Leics	73	L4
Bembridge	IoW	14	H9
Bemerton	Wilts	21	M8
Bempton	E R Yk	99	P6
Benacre	Suffk	65	Q5
Benbecula	W Isls	168	d12
Benbecula Airport	W Isls	168	c12
Benbuie	D & G	115	P8
Benderloch	Ag & B	138	G10
Benenden	Kent	26	D5
Benfieldside	Dur	112	G10
Bengates	Norfk	77	L6
Bengeworth	Worcs	47	K6
Benhall Green	Suffk	65	M9
Benhall Street	Suffk	65	M9
Benholm	Abers	143	Q4
Beningbrough	N York	98	A9
Benington	Herts	50	G6
Benington	Lincs	87	L11
Benington Sea End	Lincs	87	M11
Benllech	IoA	79	J8
Benmore	Ag & B	131	N10
Bennacott	Cnwll	5	M3
Bennan	N Ayrs	121	J7
Bennet Head	Cumb	101	M6
Bennetland	E R Yk	92	D5
Bennett End	Bucks	35	L5
Ben Nevis	Highld	139	M3
Benniworth	Lincs	86	H4
Benover	Kent	26	B3
Ben Rhydding	C Brad	96	H11
Benslie	N Ayrs	125	J9
Benson	Oxon	34	H6
Bentfield Green	Essex	51	M5
Benthall	Shrops	57	M4
Benthoul	C Aber	151	L7
Bentlawnt	Shrops	56	E4
Bentley	Donc	91	P9
Bentley	E R Yk	92	H3
Bentley	Hants	23	L6
Bentley	Suffk	53	K4
Bentley	Warwks	59	L5
Bentley Heath	Herts	50	G11
Bentley Heath	Solhll	59	J9
Benton	Devon	17	M4
Bentpath	D & G	110	F2
Bentwichen	Devon	17	N5
Bentworth	Hants	23	J6
Benvie	Angus	142	E11
Benville	Dorset	11	L4
Benwick	Cambs	62	D2
Beoley	Worcs	58	G11
Beoraidbeg	Highld	145	L9
Bepton	W Susx	23	N11
Berden	Essex	51	L5
Berea	Pembks	40	E4
Bere Alston	Devon	6	C5
Bere Ferrers	Devon	6	C5
Berepper	Cnwll	2	H9
Bere Regis	Dorset	12	D6
Bergh Apton	Norfk	77	L11
Berhill	Somset	19	M7
Berinsfield	Oxon	34	G5
Berkeley	Gloucs	32	C5
Berkeley Heath	Gloucs	32	C5
Berkeley Road	Gloucs	32	D4
Berkhamsted	Herts	35	Q3
Berkley	Somset	20	F5
Berkswell	Solhll	59	K9
Bermondsey	Gt Lon	36	H5
Bermuda	Warwks	59	N7
Bernera	Highld	145	P3
Bernisdale	Highld	152	G7
Berrick Prior	Oxon	34	H6
Berrick Salome	Oxon	34	H6
Berriedale	Highld	163	Q2
Berrier	Cumb	101	L5
Berriew	Powys	56	B4
Berrington	Nthumb	119	K2
Berrington	Shrops	57	J3
Berrington	Worcs	57	K11
Berrington Green	Worcs	57	K11
Berrow	Somset	19	J4
Berrow	Worcs	46	E8
Berrow Green	Worcs	46	D3
Berry Brow	Kirk	90	D7
Berry Cross	Devon	16	H9
Berry Down Cross	Devon	17	K3
Berryfields	Bucks	49	L11
Berry Hill	Gloucs	31	Q3
Berry Hill	Pembks	41	L2
Berryhillock	Moray	158	C5
Berryhillock	Moray	158	D7
Berrynarbor	Devon	17	K2
Berry Pomeroy	Devon	7	L6
Berry's Green	Gt Lon	37	K9
Bersham	Wrexhm	69	K5
Bersted	W Susx	15	P6
Berthengam	Flints	80	G9
Berwick	E Susx	25	M9
Berwick Bassett	Wilts	33	L10
Berwick Hill	Nthumb	113	J5
Berwick St James	Wilts	21	L7
Berwick St John	Wilts	20	H10
Berwick St Leonard	Wilts	20	H8
Berwick Station	E Susx	25	M9
Berwick-upon-Tweed	Nthumb	129	P9
Bescaby	Leics	73	L5
Bescar	Lancs	88	D8
Besford	Shrops	69	Q9
Besford	Worcs	46	H6
Bessacarr	Donc	91	Q10
Bessels Leigh	Oxon	34	E4
Besses o' th' Barn	Bury	89	N9
Bessingby	E R Yk	99	P7
Bessingham	Norfk	76	H4
Bestbeech Hill	E Susx	25	P4
Besthorpe	Norfk	64	F2
Besthorpe	Notts	85	P8
Bestwood Village	Notts	85	J11
Beswick	E R Yk	99	L11
Betchcott	Shrops	56	G5
Betchworth	Surrey	36	F10
Bethania	Cerdgn	43	L2
Bethania	Gwynd	67	N6
Bethel	Gwynd	68	C7
Bethel	Gwynd	79	J11
Bethel	IoA	78	F10
Bethel	Pembks	41	L7
Bethersden	Kent	26	F3
Bethesda	Gwynd	79	L11
Bethesda	Pembks	41	L7
Bethlehem	Carmth	43	N9
Bethnal Green	Gt Lon	36	H4
Betley	Staffs	70	D5
Betsham	Kent	37	P6
Betteshanger	Kent	39	P11
Bettiscombe	Dorset	10	H4
Bettisfield	Wrexhm	69	N7
Betton	Shrops	70	B7
Betton Strange	Shrops	57	J3
Bettws	Brdgnd	29	P7
Bettws	Newpt	31	J6
Bettws Cedewain	Powys	55	Q5
Bettws Ifan	Cerdgn	42	F5
Bettws-Newydd	Mons	31	L3
Bettyhill	Highld	166	B4
Betws	Carmth	28	H2
Betws Bledrws	Cerdgn	43	L4
Betws Garmon	Gwynd	67	J3
Betws Gwerfil Goch	Denbgs	68	D5
Betws-y-Coed	Conwy	67	P3
Betws-yn-Rhos	Conwy	80	C10
Beulah	Cerdgn	42	E5
Beulah	Powys	44	C4
Bevendean	Br & H	24	H9
Bevercotes	Notts	85	L6
Beverley	E R Yk	92	H3
Beverston	Gloucs	32	G6
Bevington	Gloucs	32	C5
Bewaldeth	Cumb	100	H4
Bewcastle	Cumb	111	L6
Bewdley	Worcs	57	P9
Bewerley	N York	97	J7
Bewholme	E R Yk	99	N11
Bewlbridge	Kent	25	Q4
Bexhill-on-Sea	E Susx	26	B10
Bexley	Gt Lon	37	L6
Bexleyheath	Gt Lon	37	L5
Bexleyhill	W Susx	23	P9
Bexon	Kent	38	E10
Bexwell	Norfk	75	M10
Beyton	Suffk	64	C9
Beyton Green	Suffk	64	C9
Bhaltos	W Isls	168	f4
Bhatarsaigh	W Isls	168	b18
Bibstone	S Glos	32	C6
Bibury	Gloucs	33	M3
Bicester	Oxon	48	G10
Bickenhill	Solhll	59	J8
Bicker	Lincs	74	D3
Bicker Bar	Lincs	74	D3
Bicker Gauntlet	Lincs	74	D3
Bickershaw	Wigan	82	D4
Bickerstaffe	Lancs	81	N4
Bickerton	Ches E	69	P4
Bickerton	Devon	7	L11
Bickerton	N York	97	Q10
Bickerton	Nthumb	119	J10
Bickford	Staffs	58	C2
Bickington	Devon	7	L4
Bickington	Devon	17	J5
Bickleigh	Devon	6	E6
Bickleigh	Devon	9	M3
Bickleton	Devon	17	J5
Bickley	Ches W	69	P5
Bickley	Gt Lon	37	K7
Bickley	N York	99	J2
Bickley	Worcs	57	L10
Bickley Moss	Ches W	69	P5
Bicknacre	Essex	52	C11
Bicknoller	Somset	18	F7
Bicknor	Kent	38	E10
Bickton	Hants	13	K2
Bicton	Herefs	45	P2
Bicton	Shrops	56	D8
Bicton	Shrops	69	M11
Bidborough	Kent	25	N2
Bidden	Hants	23	K5
Biddenden	Kent	26	E4
Biddenden Green	Kent	26	E3
Biddenham	Bed	61	M10
Biddestone	Wilts	32	G10
Biddisham	Somset	19	L4
Biddlesden	Bucks	48	H7
Biddlestone	Nthumb	119	J9
Biddulph	Staffs	70	F3
Biddulph Moor	Staffs	70	G3
Bideford	Devon	16	H6
Bidford-on-Avon	Warwks	47	M4
Bidston	Wirral	81	K6
Bielby	E R Yk	92	C3
Bieldside	C Aber	151	M7
Bierley	IoW	14	F11
Bierton	Bucks	49	M11
Big Balcraig	D & G	107	L9
Bigbury	Devon	6	H9
Bigbury-on-Sea	Devon	6	H10
Bigby	Lincs	93	J9
Biggar	Cumb	94	D7
Biggar	S Lans	116	E3
Biggin	Derbys	71	M3
Biggin	Derbys	71	P5
Biggin	N York	91	N4
Biggin Hill	Gt Lon	37	K9
Biggleswade	C Beds	50	E2
Bigholms	D & G	110	F4
Bighouse	Highld	166	E4
Bighton	Hants	22	H8
Biglands	Cumb	110	E10
Bignor	W Susx	15	P5
Bigrigg	Cumb	100	D8
Big Sand	Highld	160	B11
Bigton	Shet	169	q11
Bilborough	C Nott	72	E2
Bilbrook	Somset	18	D6
Bilbrook	Staffs	58	C4
Bilbrough	N York	98	A11
Bilbster	Highld	167	N6
Bildershaw	Dur	103	P7
Bildeston	Suffk	52	G2
Billacott	Cnwll	5	M3
Billericay	Essex	37	Q2
Billesdon	Leics	73	J10
Billesley	Warwks	47	M3
Billingborough	Lincs	74	B4
Billinge	St Hel	82	B4
Billingford	Norfk	64	H7
Billingford	Norfk	76	E7
Billingham	S on T	104	E6
Billinghay	Lincs	86	G10
Billingley	Barns	91	L10
Billingshurst	W Susx	24	C5
Billingsley	Shrops	57	N8
Billington	C Beds	49	P10
Billington	Lancs	89	L3
Billington	Staffs	70	F10
Billockby	Norfk	77	N9
Billy Row	Dur	103	N3
Bilsborrow	Lancs	88	G3
Bilsby	Lincs	87	N5
Bilsham	W Susx	15	Q6
Bilsington	Kent	26	H5
Bilsthorpe	Notts	85	K8
Bilsthorpe Moor	Notts	85	K9
Bilston	Mdloth	127	P5
Bilston	Wolves	58	E5
Bilstone	Leics	72	B9
Bilting	Kent	27	J2
Bilton	E R Yk	93	L4
Bilton	N York	97	M9
Bilton	Nthumb	119	P8
Bilton	Warwks	59	Q10
Bilton Banks	Nthumb	119	P8
Bilton-in-Ainsty	N York	97	Q10
Binbrook	Lincs	86	H2
Binchester Blocks	Dur	103	P4
Bincombe	Dorset	11	P8
Binegar	Somset	20	B5
Bines Green	W Susx	24	E7
Binfield	Br For	35	M10
Binfield Heath	Oxon	35	K9
Bingfield	Nthumb	112	E6
Bingham	Notts	73	J3
Bingham's Melcombe	Dorset	12	C4
Bingley	C Brad	90	E3
Bings Heath	Shrops	69	P11
Binham	Norfk	76	D4
Binley	Covtry	59	N9
Binley	Hants	22	D4
Binley Woods	Warwks	59	N9
Binnegar	Dorset	12	E7
Binniehill	Falk	126	F2
Binscombe	Surrey	23	Q5
Binsey	Oxon	34	E3
Binstead	IoW	14	G8
Binsted	Hants	23	L6
Binsted	W Susx	15	N5
Binton	Warwks	47	M4
Bintree	Norfk	76	E7
Binweston	Shrops	56	E4
Birch	Essex	52	F8
Birch	Rochdl	89	P9
Bircham Newton	Norfk	75	Q4
Bircham Tofts	Norfk	75	Q4
Birchanger	Essex	51	M6
Birchanger Green Services	Essex	51	M6
Birch Cross	Staffs	71	L8
Birchencliffe	Kirk	90	E7
Bircher	Herefs	56	H11
Birchett's Green	E Susx	25	Q4
Birchfield	Birm	58	G6
Birch Green	Essex	52	F8
Birch Green	Herts	50	G8
Birch Green	Worcs	46	G5
Birchgrove	Cardif	30	G9
Birchgrove	Swans	29	K5
Birch Heath	Ches W	69	P2
Birch Hill	Ches W	81	Q10
Birchington	Kent	39	P8
Birchington-on-Sea	Kent	39	N8
Birchley Heath	Warwks	59	L6
Birchmoor	Warwks	59	L4
Birchmoor Green	C Beds	49	Q8
Birchover	Derbys	84	B8
Birch Services	Rochdl	89	N9
Birch Vale	Derbys	83	M7
Birchwood	Lincs	86	B7
Birch Wood	Somset	10	E2
Birchwood	Warrtn	82	E6
Bircotes	Notts	85	K2
Birdbrook	Essex	52	B3
Birdforth	N York	97	Q5
Birdham	W Susx	15	M6
Birdingbury	Warwks	59	P11
Birdlip	Gloucs	32	H2
Birdoswald	Cumb	111	M7
Birdsall	N York	98	G7
Birds Edge	Kirk	90	G9
Birds Green	Essex	51	N9
Birdsgreen	Shrops	57	P7
Birdsmoorgate	Dorset	10	H4
Bird Street	Suffk	64	E11
Birdwell	Barns	91	J10
Birdwood	Gloucs	46	D11
Birgham	Border	118	E3
Birichin	Highld	162	H8
Birkacre	Lancs	88	H4
Birkby	N York	104	B10
Birkdale	Sefton	88	C8
Birkenbog	Abers	158	D4
Birkenhead	Wirral	81	L7
Birkenhead (Queensway) Tunnel	Lpool	81	L7
Birkenhills	Abers	158	H8
Birkenshaw	Kirk	90	G5
Birkhall	Abers	149	Q9
Birkhill	Angus	142	F11
Birkhill	D & G	117	J7
Birkholme	Lincs	73	P6
Birkin	N York	91	N5
Birks	Leeds	90	H5
Birkshaw	Nthumb	111	Q7
Birley	Herefs	45	P4
Birley Carr	Sheff	84	D2
Birling	Kent	37	Q8
Birling	Nthumb	119	P9
Birling Gap	E Susx	25	N11
Birlingham	Worcs	46	H6
Birmingham	Birm	58	G7
Birmingham Airport	Solhll	59	J8
Birnam	P & K	141	P9
Birness	Abers	159	N11
Birse	Abers	150	F8
Birsemore	Abers	150	E8
Birstall	Kirk	90	G5
Birstall	Leics	72	F9
Birstwith	N York	97	K9
Birthorpe	Lincs	74	B4
Birtley	Gatesd	113	L9
Birtley	Herefs	56	F11
Birtley	Nthumb	112	C5
Birts Street	Worcs	46	E7
Bisbrooke	Rutlnd	73	M11
Biscathorpe	Lincs	86	H4
Biscovey	Cnwll	3	R3
Bisham	W & M	35	M7
Bishampton	Worcs	47	J4
Bish Mill	Devon	17	N6
Bishop Auckland	Dur	103	P5
Bishopbridge	Lincs	86	D2
Bishopbriggs	E Duns	125	Q3
Bishop Burton	E R Yk	92	G3
Bishop Middleham	Dur	104	B4
Bishopmill	Moray	157	N5
Bishop Monkton	N York	97	M7
Bishop Norton	Lincs	86	C2
Bishopsbourne	Kent	39	L11
Bishops Cannings	Wilts	21	K2
Bishop's Castle	Shrops	56	E7
Bishop's Caundle	Dorset	11	P2
Bishop's Cleeve	Gloucs	47	J9
Bishop's Frome	Herefs	46	C5
Bishops Gate	Surrey	35	Q10
Bishop's Green	Essex	51	P7
Bishop's Green	Hants	22	G2
Bishop's Hull	Somset	18	H10
Bishop's Itchington	Warwks	48	C3
Bishops Lydeard	Somset	18	G9
Bishop's Norton	Gloucs	46	F10
Bishop's Nympton	Devon	17	P7
Bishop's Offley	Staffs	70	D9
Bishop's Stortford	Herts	51	L6
Bishop's Sutton	Hants	22	H8
Bishop's Tachbrook	Warwks	48	B2
Bishop's Tawton	Devon	17	K6
Bishopsteignton	Devon	7	N4
Bishopstoke	Hants	22	E11
Bishopston	Swans	28	G7
Bishopstone	Bucks	35	M2
Bishopstone	E Susx	25	L10
Bishopstone	Herefs	45	N6
Bishopstone	Kent	39	L8
Bishopstone	Swindn	33	P8
Bishopstone	Wilts	21	L9
Bishopstrow	Wilts	20	G6
Bishop Sutton	BaNES	19	Q3
Bishop's Waltham	Hants	22	G11
Bishop's Wood	Staffs	58	B3
Bishopswood	Somset	10	F2
Bishopsworth	Bristl	31	Q11
Bishop Thornton	N York	97	L8
Bishopthorpe	C York	98	B11
Bishopton	Darltn	104	C6
Bishopton	Rens	125	L3
Bishopton	Warwks	47	N3

Bishop Wilton E R Yk....98 F9
Bishton Newpt....31 L7
Bishton Staffs....71 J10
Bisley Gloucs....32 H3
Bisley Surrey....23 Q3
Bisley Camp Surrey....23 P3
Bispham Bpool....88 C2
Bispham Green Lancs....88 F8
Bissoe Cnwll....3 K5
Bisterne Hants....13 K4
Bitchet Green Kent....37 M10
Bitchfield Lincs....73 P5
Bittadon Devon....17 J3
Bittaford Devon....6 H7
Bittering Norfk....76 C8
Bitterley Shrops....57 K9
Bitterne C Sotn....14 E4
Bitteswell Leics....60 B3
Bitton S Glos....32 C11
Bix Oxon....35 K8
Bixter Shet....169 q8
Blaby Leics....72 F11
Blackadder Border....129 L9
Blackawton Devon....7 L8
Blackbeck Cumb....100 D9
Blackborough Devon....10 B3
Blackborough End Norfk....75 N7
Black Bourton Oxon....33 Q4
Blackboys E Susx....25 M6
Blackbrook Derbys....84 D11
Blackbrook St Hel....82 B5
Blackbrook Staffs....70 D2
Blackbrook Surrey....36 E11
Blackburn Abers....151 L5
Blackburn Bl w D....89 K7
Blackburn Rothm....84 E2
Blackburn W Loth....126 H4
Blackburn with Darwen
  Services Bl w D....89 K6
Black Callerton N u Ty....113 J7
Black Carr Norfk....64 F2
Black Corner W Susx....24 G3
Blackcraig E Ayrs....115 M6
Black Crofts Ag & B....138 G11
Black Cross Cnwll....4 E9
Blackden Heath Ches E....82 G10
Blackdog Abers....151 P5
Black Dog Devon....9 K3
Blackdown Devon....8 D9
Blackdown Dorset....10 H4
Blackdyke Cumb....109 P10
Blacker Barns....91 J9
Blacker Hill Barns....91 K10
Blackfen Gt Lon....37 L6
Blackfield Hants....14 D6
Blackford Cumb....110 G8
Blackford P & K....133 P6
Blackford Somset....19 M5
Blackford Somset....20 C9
Blackfordby Leics....72 A7
Blackgang IoW....14 E11
Blackhall C Edin....127 N3
Blackhall Colliery Dur....104 E3
Blackhall Mill Gatesd....112 H8
Blackhall Rocks Dur....104 E3
Blackhaugh Border....117 N3
Blackheath Essex....52 H7
Blackheath Gt Lon....37 J5
Blackheath Sandw....58 E7
Blackheath Suffk....65 N7
Blackheath Surrey....36 B11
Black Heddon Nthumb....112 G5
Blackhill Abers....159 Q6
Blackhill Abers....159 Q9
Blackhill Dur....112 G10
Blackhill of Clackriach
  Abers....159 M8
Blackhorse Devon....9 N6
Blackjack Lincs....74 E3
Blackland Wilts....33 K11
Black Lane Ends Lancs....89 Q2
Blackley Manch....83 J4
Blacklunans P & K....142 A5
Blackmarstone Herefs....45 Q7
Blackmill Brdgnd....29 P7
Blackmoor Hants....23 L8
Black Moor Leeds....90 H3
Blackmoor N Som....19 N2
Blackmoorfoot Kirk....90 D8
Blackmoor Gate Devon....17 L3
Blackmore Essex....51 P10
Blackmore End Essex....52 B5
Blackmore End Herts....50 E7
Black Mountains....45 K9
Blackness Falk....127 K2
Blacknest Hants....23 L6
Blacknest W & M....35 Q11
Black Notley Essex....52 C7
Blacko Lancs....89 P2
Black Pill Swans....28 H6
Blackpool Bpool....88 C3
Blackpool Devon....7 L4
Blackpool Devon....7 M9
Blackpool Gate Cumb....111 K5
Blackpool Zoo Bpool....88 C3
Blackridge W Loth....126 F4
Blackrock Cnwll....2 H7
Blackrock Mons....30 H2
Blackrod Bolton....89 J8
Blacksboat Moray....157 M10
Blackshaw D & G....109 M7
Blackshaw Head Calder....90 B6
Blacksmith's Green Suffk....64 G8
Blacksnape Bl w D....89 L6
Blackstone W Susx....24 F7
Black Street Suffk....65 Q4
Black Tar Pembks....41 J9
Blackthorn Oxon....48 H11
Blackthorpe Suffk....64 C9
Blacktoft E R Yk....92 D5
Blacktop C Aber....151 M7
Black Torrington Devon....8 C3
Blackwall Derbys....71 P5
Blackwall Tunnel Gt Lon....37 J4
Blackwater Cnwll....3 J4
Blackwater Hants....23 M3
Blackwater IoW....14 F9
Blackwater Somset....19 J11
Blackwaterfoot N Ayrs....120 H6
Blackwell Cumb....110 H10
Blackwell Darltn....103 Q8
Blackwell Derbys....83 P10
Blackwell Derbys....84 F9
Blackwell Warwks....47 P6

Blackwell Worcs....58 E10
Blackwellsend Green Gloucs....46 E9
Blackwood Caerph....30 G5
Blackwood D & G....109 K3
Blackwood S Lans....126 D9
Blackwood Hill Staffs....70 G3
Blacon Ches W....81 M11
Bladbean Kent....27 L2
Bladnoch D & G....107 M7
Bladon Oxon....34 E2
Bladon Somset....19 M10
Blaenannerch Cerdgn....42 D5
Blaenau Ffestiniog Gwynd....67 N5
Blaenavon Torfn....31 J3
Blaenavon Industrial
  Landscape Torfn....30 H3
Blaencwm Rhondd....29 P5
Blaen Dyryn Powys....44 C7
Blaenffos Pembks....41 N3
Blaengarw Brdgnd....29 P6
Blaengeuffordd Cerdgn....54 E8
Blaengwrach Neath....29 N3
Blaengwynfi Neath....29 N5
Blaenllechau Rhondd....30 D5
Blaenpennal Cerdgn....43 M2
Blaenplwyf Cerdgn....54 D9
Blaenporth Cerdgn....42 E5
Blaenrhondda Rhondd....29 P5
Blaenwaun Carmth....41 P5
Blaen-y-coed Carmth....42 F9
Blaen-y-cwm Blae G....30 F2
Blaenycwm Cerdgn....55 J9
Blagdon N Som....19 P3
Blagdon Somset....18 H11
Blagdon Torbay....7 M6
Blagdon Hill Somset....18 H11
Blagill Cumb....111 P11
Blaguegate Lancs....88 F9
Blaich Highld....139 J2
Blain Highld....138 B4
Blaina Blae G....30 H3
Blair Atholl P & K....141 L4
Blair Drummond Stirlg....133 L8
Blairgowrie P & K....142 B8
Blairhall Fife....134 B10
Blairingone P & K....134 B8
Blairlogie Stirlg....133 N8
Blairmore Ag & B....131 P11
Blairmore Highld....164 E5
Blair's Ferry Ag & B....124 B4
Blaisdon Gloucs....46 D11
Blakebrook Worcs....57 Q9
Blakedown Worcs....58 C9
Blake End Essex....52 B7
Blakeley Lane Staffs....70 H5
Blakemere Ches W....82 C10
Blakemere Herefs....45 M6
Blakemore Devon....7 K4
Blakenall Heath Wsall....58 F4
Blakeney Gloucs....32 C3
Blakeney Norfk....76 E3
Blakenhall Ches E....70 C5
Blakenhall Wolves....58 D5
Blakeshall Worcs....58 B8
Blakesley Nhants....48 H4
Blanchland Nthumb....112 D10
Blandford Camp Dorset....12 F3
Blandford Forum Dorset....12 E3
Blandford St Mary Dorset....12 E3
Bland Hill N York....97 K10
Blanefield Stirlg....125 N2
Blankney Lincs....86 E8
Blantyre S Lans....126 B6
Blàr a' Chaorainn Highld....139 L4
Blarghour Ag & B....131 K5
Blargie Highld....147 Q9
Blarmachfoldach Highld....139 K4
Blashford Hants....13 L3
Blaston Leics....73 L11
Blatherwycke Nhants....73 P11
Blawith Cumb....94 F3
Blawquhairn D & G....108 D4
Blaxhall Suffk....65 M10
Blaxton Donc....91 R10
Blaydon Gatesd....113 J8
Bleadney Somset....19 N5
Bleadon N Som....19 K3
Bleak Street Somset....20 E8
Blean Kent....39 K9
Bleasby Lincs....86 F4
Bleasby Notts....85 M11
Bleasdale Lancs....95 M11
Bleatarn Cumb....102 D8
Bleathwood Herefs....57 K10
Blebocraigs Fife....135 L4
Bleddfa Powys....56 C11
Bledington Gloucs....47 P10
Bledlow Bucks....35 L4
Bledlow Ridge Bucks....35 L5
Bleet Wilts....20 G3
Blegbie E Loth....128 C5
Blencarn Cumb....102 B4
Blencogo Cumb....110 C11
Blendworth Hants....15 K4
Blenheim Palace Oxon....48 D11
Blennerhasset Cumb....100 G2
Bletchingdon Oxon....48 F11
Bletchingley Surrey....36 H10
Bletchley M Keyn....49 N8
Bletchley Shrops....69 R8
Bletchley Park Museum
  M Keyn....49 N8
Bletherston Pembks....41 L6
Bletsoe Bed....61 M9
Blewbury Oxon....34 F7
Blickling Norfk....76 H6
Blidworth Notts....85 J9
Blidworth Bottoms Notts....85 J10
Blindburn Nthumb....118 F8
Blindcrake Cumb....100 F4
Blindley Heath Surrey....37 J11
Blisland Cnwll....5 J7
Blissford Hants....13 L2
Bliss Gate Worcs....57 N10
Blisworth Nhants....49 K4
Blithbury Staffs....71 K11
Blitterlees Cumb....109 P10
Blockley Gloucs....47 N7
Blofield Norfk....77 L10
Blofield Heath Norfk....77 L9
Blo Norton Norfk....64 E6
Bloomfield Border....118 A6
Blore Staffs....70 C8
Blore Staffs....71 L5
Blounce Hants....23 J6

Blounts Green Staffs....71 K8
Blowick Sefton....88 D7
Bloxham Oxon....48 D7
Bloxholm Lincs....86 E10
Bloxwich Wsall....58 E4
Bloxworth Dorset....12 E6
Blubberhouses N York....97 J9
Blue Anchor Cnwll....4 E10
Blue Anchor Somset....18 D6
Blue Bell Hill Kent....38 C9
Blue John Cavern Derbys....83 P8
Blundellsands Sefton....81 L5
Blundeston Suffk....65 Q2
Blunham C Beds....61 Q10
Blunsdon St Andrew Swindn....33 M7
Bluntington Worcs....58 D10
Bluntisham Cambs....62 E6
Blunts Cnwll....5 N9
Blunts Green Warwks....58 H11
Blurton C Stke....70 F6
Blyborough Lincs....86 B2
Blyford Suffk....65 N6
Blymhill Staffs....57 Q2
Blymhill Lawn Staffs....57 Q2
Blyth Notts....85 K3
Blyth Nthumb....113 M4
Blyth Bridge Border....127 L8
Blythburgh Suffk....65 N6
Blythe Border....128 F10
Blythe Bridge Staffs....70 H6
Blythe End Warwks....59 H6
Blythe Marsh Staffs....70 H6
Blyth Services Notts....85 K3
Blyton Lincs....85 Q2
Boarhills Fife....135 P5
Boarhunt Hants....14 H5
Boarley Kent....38 C10
Boarsgreave Lancs....89 N6
Boarshead E Susx....25 M4
Boar's Head Wigan....88 H9
Boars Hill Oxon....34 E4
Boarstall Bucks....34 H2
Boasley Cross Devon....8 D6
Boath Highld....155 Q3
Boat of Garten Highld....148 G5
Bobbing Kent....38 E8
Bobbington Staffs....57 Q6
Bobbingworth Essex....51 M9
Bocaddon Cnwll....5 K10
Bocking Essex....52 C7
Bocking Churchstreet Essex....52 C7
Bockleton Worcs....46 A2
Boconnoc Cnwll....5 K9
Boddam Abers....159 R9
Boddam Shet....169 q12
Boddington Gloucs....46 G9
Bodedern IoA....78 E8
Bodelwyddan Denbgs....80 E9
Bodenham Herefs....45 Q4
Bodenham Wilts....21 N9
Bodenham Moor Herefs....45 Q4
Bodewryd IoA....78 G6
Bodfari Denbgs....80 F10
Bodffordd IoA....78 G9
Bodham Norfk....76 G3
Bodiam E Susx....26 C6
Bodicote Oxon....48 E7
Bodieve Cnwll....4 F7
Bodinnick Cnwll....5 J11
Bodle Street Green E Susx....25 Q8
Bodmin Cnwll....4 H8
Bodmin Moor Cnwll....5 K6
Bodney Norfk....64 A2
Bodorgan IoA....78 F11
Bodsham Kent....27 K2
Boduan Gwynd....66 E7
Bodwen Cnwll....4 G9
Bodymoor Heath Warwks....59 J5
Bogallan Highld....156 A7
Bogbrae Abers....159 P10
Bogend S Ayrs....125 L11
Boggs Holdings E Loth....128 C5
Boghall Mdloth....127 N4
Boghall W Loth....126 H4
Boghead S Lans....126 D9
Bogmoor Moray....157 R5
Bogmuir Abers....143 L3
Bogniebrae Abers....158 E8
Bognor Regis W Susx....15 P7
Bogroy Highld....148 G3
Bogue D & G....108 D4
Bohetherick Cnwll....5 Q8
Bohortha Cnwll....3 M7
Bohuntine Highld....146 H11
Bojewyan Cnwll....2 B7
Bokiddick Cnwll....4 H9
Bolam Dur....103 N6
Bolam Nthumb....112 H4
Bolberry Devon....6 H11
Bold Heath St Hel....82 B7
Boldmere Birm....58 H6
Boldon Colliery S Tyne....113 M8
Boldre Hants....13 P5
Boldron Dur....103 K8
Bole Notts....85 N3
Bolehill Derbys....84 C9
Bole Hill Derbys....84 D6
Bolenowe Cnwll....3 K3
Bolham Devon....18 C11
Bolham Water Devon....10 D2
Bolingey Cnwll....3 K3
Bollington Ches E....83 K9
Bollington Cross Ches E....83 K9
Bollow Gloucs....32 D2
Bolney W Susx....24 G6
Bolnhurst Bed....61 N9
Bolnore W Susx....24 H6
Bolshan Angus....143 L7
Bolsover Derbys....84 G6
Bolster Moor Kirk....90 D7
Bolsterstone Sheff....90 H11
Boltby N York....97 Q3
Boltenstone Abers....150 C5
Bolter End Bucks....35 L6
Bolton Bolton....89 L9
Bolton Cumb....102 B6
Bolton E Loth....128 E6
Bolton E R Yk....98 F10
Bolton Nthumb....119 M8
Bolton Abbey N York....96 G10
Bolton Bridge N York....96 G10
Bolton-by-Bowland Lancs....96 A11
Bolton Town End Lancs....95 K7
Boltonfellend Cumb....111 J7
Boltongate Cumb....100 H2
Bolton-le-Sands Lancs....95 K7

Bolton Low Houses Cumb....100 H2
Bolton New Houses Cumb....100 H2
Bolton-on-Swale N York....103 Q11
Bolton Percy N York....91 N2
Bolton Town End Lancs....95 K7
Bolton upon Dearne Barns....91 M10
Bolventor Cnwll....5 K6
Bomarsund Nthumb....113 L4
Bomere Heath Shrops....69 N11
Bonar Bridge Highld....162 E8
Bonawe Ag & B....139 J11
Bonby N Linc....92 H7
Boncath Pembks....41 P3
Bonchester Bridge Border....118 A8
Bonchurch IoW....14 G11
Bondleigh Devon....8 G4
Bonds Lancs....88 F2
Bonehill Devon....8 H9
Bonehill Staffs....59 J4
Bo'ness Falk....134 C11
Boney Hay Staffs....58 F2
Bonhill W Duns....125 K2
Boningale Shrops....57 Q4
Bonjedward Border....118 C6
Bonkle N Lans....126 E6
Bonnington Angus....143 K10
Bonnington Kent....27 J4
Bonnybank Fife....135 K7
Bonnybridge Falk....126 E2
Bonnykelly Abers....159 L7
Bonnyrigg Mdloth....127 Q4
Bonnyton Angus....142 E10
Bonsall Derbys....84 C9
Bonshaw Tower D & G....110 D6
Bont Mons....45 M11
Bontddu Gwynd....67 M11
Bont-Dolgadfan Powys....55 K4
Bont-goch Cerdgn....54 F7
Bonthorpe Lincs....87 N6
Bontnewydd Cerdgn....54 E11
Bontnewydd Gwynd....66 H3
Bontuchel Denbgs....68 E3
Bonvilston V Glam....30 E10
Bonwm Denbgs....68 F6
Bon-y-maen Swans....29 J5
Boode Devon....17 J4
Booker Bucks....35 M6
Booley Shrops....69 Q9
Boon Border....128 F10
Boon Hill Staffs....70 E4
Boorley Green Hants....14 F4
Boosbeck R & Cl....105 J7
Boose's Green Essex....52 D5
Boot Cumb....100 G10
Booth Calder....90 C5
Boothby Graffoe Lincs....86 C9
Boothby Pagnell Lincs....73 P4
Boothferry E R Yk....92 B5
Booth Green Ches E....83 K8
Boothstown Salfd....82 F4
Booth Town Calder....90 D5
Boothville Nhants....60 G8
Bootle Cumb....94 C3
Bootle Sefton....81 L5
Boots Green Ches W....82 G10
Boot Street Suffk....53 M2
Booze N York....103 K10
Boraston Shrops....57 L11
Bordeaux Guern....10 c1
Borden Kent....38 E9
Borden W Susx....23 M10
Border Cumb....110 C10
Bordley N York....96 D7
Boreham Essex....52 C10
Boreham Wilts....20 G6
Boreham Street E Susx....25 Q8
Borehamwood Herts....50 E11
Boreland D & G....110 C2
Boreland Highld....152 B7
Boreraig Highld....152 B7
Boreton Shrops....57 J3
Borgh W Isls....168 b17
Borgh W Isls....168 j2
Borgie Highld....165 Q5
Borgue D & G....108 D11
Borgue Highld....167 K11
Borley Essex....52 D3
Borley Green Essex....52 D3
Borley Green Suffk....64 D9
Borneskitaig Highld....152 F3
Borness D & G....108 D11
Boroughbridge N York....97 N7
Borough Green Kent....37 P9
Borras Head Wrexhm....69 L4
Borrowash Derbys....72 C4
Borrowby N York....97 P3
Borrowby N York....105 L7
Borrowdale Cumb....101 J7
Borrowstoun Falk....134 B11
Borstal Medway....38 B8
Borth Cerdgn....54 E6
Borthwick Mdloth....128 B8
Borthwickbrae Border....117 N8
Borthwickshiels Border....117 N7
Borth-y-Gest Gwynd....67 K7
Borve Highld....152 G8
Borve W Isls....168 b17
Borve W Isls....168 f8
Borve W Isls....168 j2
Borwick Lancs....95 L6
Borwick Lodge Cumb....101 L11
Borwick Rails Cumb....94 D5
Bosavern Cnwll....2 B7
Bosbury Herefs....46 C6
Boscarne Cnwll....4 G8
Boscastle Cnwll....4 H3
Boscombe BCP....13 K6
Boscombe Wilts....21 P7
Boscoppa Cnwll....3 Q3
Bosham W Susx....15 M6
Bosham Hoe W Susx....15 M6
Bosherston Pembks....41 J12
Boskednan Cnwll....2 C7
Boskenna Cnwll....2 C9
Bosley Ches E....83 K11
Bosoughan Cnwll....4 E9
Bossall N York....98 E8
Bossiney Cnwll....4 H4
Bossingham Kent....27 L2
Bossington Somset....18 A4
Bostock Green Ches W....82 E11
Boston Lincs....74 F2
Boston Spa Leeds....97 P11
Boswarthan Cnwll....2 C7
Boswinger Cnwll....3 P5
Botallack Cnwll....2 B7

Botany Bay Gt Lon....50 G11
Botcheston Leics....72 D10
Botesdale Suffk....64 E6
Bothal Nthumb....113 K3
Bothampstead W Berk....34 F9
Bothamsall Notts....85 L6
Bothel Cumb....100 G3
Bothenhampton Dorset....11 K6
Bothwell S Lans....126 C6
Bothwell Services S Lans....126 C6
Botley Bucks....35 Q2
Botley Hants....14 F4
Botley Oxon....34 E3
Botolph Claydon Bucks....49 K10
Botolphs W Susx....24 E9
Botolph's Bridge Kent....27 K5
Bottesford Leics....73 L3
Bottesford N Linc....92 E9
Bottisham Cambs....62 H8
Bottomcraig Fife....135 K3
Bottom of Hutton Lancs....88 F5
Bottom o' th' Moor Bolton....89 K8
Bottoms Calder....89 Q6
Bottoms Cnwll....2 B9
Botts Green Warwks....59 K6
Botusfleming Cnwll....5 Q9
Botwnnog Gwynd....66 D8
Bough Beech Kent....37 L11
Boughrood Powys....44 G7
Boughspring Gloucs....31 Q5
Boughton Nhants....60 G7
Boughton Norfk....75 P10
Boughton Notts....85 L7
Boughton Aluph Kent....26 H2
Boughton End C Beds....49 Q7
Boughton Green Kent....38 C11
Boughton Malherbe Kent....26 E2
Boughton Monchelsea Kent....38 C11
Boughton Street Kent....39 J10
Boulby R & Cl....105 L7
Boulder Clough Calder....90 C6
Bouldnor IoW....14 C9
Bouldon Shrops....57 J7
Boulmer Nthumb....119 Q8
Boulston Pembks....41 J8
Boultham Lincs....86 C7
Boundary Staffs....70 H6
Bourn Cambs....62 D9
Bournbrook Birm....58 F8
Bourne Lincs....74 A6
Bournebridge Essex....37 M2
Bourne End Bed....61 M8
Bourne End Bucks....35 N7
Bourne End C Beds....49 Q6
Bourne End Herts....50 B9
Bournemouth BCP....13 J6
Bournemouth Airport BCP....13 K5
Bournes Green Gloucs....32 H4
Bournes Green Sthend....38 F4
Bournheath Worcs....58 E10
Bournmoor Dur....113 M10
Bournstream Gloucs....32 D6
Bournville Birm....58 F8
Bourton Dorset....20 E8
Bourton N Som....19 L2
Bourton Oxon....33 P7
Bourton Shrops....57 K5
Bourton Wilts....21 K2
Bourton on Dunsmore
  Warwks....59 P10
Bourton-on-the-Hill Gloucs....47 N8
Bourton-on-the-Water
  Gloucs....47 N10
Bousd Ag & B....136 H3
Boustead Hill Cumb....110 E9
Bouth Cumb....94 G3
Bouthwaite N York....96 H6
Bouts Worcs....47 K3
Boveney Bucks....35 P9
Boveridge Dorset....13 J2
Bovey Tracey Devon....9 K9
Bovingdon Herts....50 B9
Bovingdon Green Bucks....35 M7
Bovinger Essex....51 M9
Bovington Dorset....12 D7
Bovington Camp Dorset....12 D7
Bow Cumb....110 F9
Bow Devon....7 L7
Bow Devon....8 H4
Bow Gt Lon....37 J4
Bow Ork....169 c7
Bowbank Dur....102 H6
Bow Brickhill M Keyn....49 P8
Bowbridge Gloucs....32 G3
Bowburn Dur....104 B3
Bowcombe IoW....14 E9
Bowd Devon....10 C6
Bowden Border....117 R4
Bowden Devon....7 L9
Bowden Hill Wilts....32 H11
Bowdon Traffd....82 G7
Bower Highld....167 M4
Bowerchalke Wilts....21 K10
Bowerhill Wilts....20 H2
Bower Hinton Somset....19 N11
Bower House Tye Suffk....52 G3
Bowermadden Highld....167 M4
Bowers Staffs....70 E7
Bowers Gifford Essex....38 C4
Bowershall Fife....134 D9
Bowes Dur....103 J8
Bowgreave Lancs....88 F2
Bowhouse D & G....109 M7
Bowithick Cnwll....5 K5
Bowker's Green Lancs....81 N4
Bowland Border....117 P2
Bowland Bridge Cumb....95 J3
Bowley Herefs....45 Q4
Bowley Town Herefs....45 Q4
Bowlhead Green Surrey....23 P7
Bowling C Brad....90 F4
Bowling W Duns....125 L3
Bowling Bank Wrexhm....69 L5
Bowling Green Worcs....46 F4
Bowmanstead Cumb....101 K11
Bowmore Ag & B....122 D8
Bowness-on-Solway Cumb....110 D8
Bowness-on-Windermere
  Cumb....101 M11
Bow of Fife Fife....135 J5
Bowriefauld Angus....143 J8
Bowscale Cumb....101 L4
Bowsden Nthumb....119 J2
Bowston Cumb....101 N11

260 Bow Street – Brockton

Bow Street Cerdgn 54 E7
Bow Street Norfk 64 E2
Bowthorpe Norfk 76 H10
Box Gloucs 32 G4
Box Wilts 32 F11
Boxbush Gloucs 32 D2
Boxbush Gloucs 46 C10
Box End Bed 61 M11
Boxford Suffk 52 G3
Boxford W Berk 34 D10
Boxgrove W Susx 15 P5
Box Hill Surrey 36 E10
Boxley Kent 38 C10
Boxmoor Herts 50 B9
Box's Shop Cnwll 16 C11
Boxted Essex 52 G5
Boxted Essex 52 H5
Boxted Suffk 64 A11
Boxted Cross Essex 52 H5
Boxwell Gloucs 32 F6
Boxworth Cambs 62 D8
Boyden End Suffk 63 M9
Boyden Gate Kent 39 M8
Boylestone Derbys 71 M7
Boyndie Abers 158 F5
Boyndlie Abers 159 M5
Boynton E R Yk 99 N7
Boysack Angus 143 L8
Boys Hill Dorset 11 P2
Boythorpe Derbys 84 E7
Boyton Cnwll 5 N3
Boyton Suffk 53 Q2
Boyton Wilts 21 J7
Boyton Cross Essex 51 P9
Boyton End Suffk 52 B3
Bozeat Nhants 61 K9
Braaid IoM 80 d6
Brabling Green Suffk 65 K9
Brabourne Kent 27 K3
Brabourne Lees Kent 27 J3
Brabstermire Highld 167 P3
Bracadale Highld 152 F10
Braceborough Lincs 74 A8
Bracebridge Heath Lincs 86 C7
Bracebridge Low Fields Lincs 86 C7
Braceby Lincs 73 Q3
Bracewell Lancs 96 C11
Brackenfield Derbys 84 E9
Brackenhirst N Lans 126 C4
Brackenthwaite Cumb 110 E11
Brackenthwaite N York 97 L10
Brackla Brdgnd 29 P9
Bracklesham W Susx 15 M7
Brackletter Highld 146 F11
Brackley Nhants 48 G7
Brackley Hatch Nhants 48 H6
Bracknell Br For 35 N11
Braco P & K 133 N6
Bracobrae Moray 158 D7
Bracon Ash Norfk 64 H2
Bracora Highld 145 M9
Bracorina Highld 145 M9
Bradaford Devon 5 P3
Bradbourne Derbys 71 N4
Bradbury Dur 104 B5
Bradden Nhants 48 H5
Braddock Cnwll 5 K9
Bradeley C Stke 70 F4
Bradenham Bucks 35 M5
Bradenstoke Wilts 33 K9
Bradfield Devon 9 Q3
Bradfield Essex 53 K5
Bradfield Norfk 77 K5
Bradfield Sheff 84 C2
Bradfield W Berk 34 H10
Bradfield Combust Suffk 64 B10
Bradfield Green Ches E 70 B3
Bradfield Heath Essex 53 K5
Bradfield St Clare Suffk 64 C10
Bradfield St George Suffk 64 C10
Bradford C Brad 90 F4
Bradford Cnwll 5 J6
Bradford Devon 16 G10
Bradford Nthumb 112 G5
Bradford Nthumb 119 N4
Bradford Abbas Dorset 11 M2
Bradford Leigh Wilts 20 F2
Bradford-on-Avon Wilts 20 F2
Bradford-on-Tone Somset 18 G10
Bradford Peverell Dorset 11 P6
Bradiford Devon 17 K5
Brading IoW 14 H9
Bradley Ches W 69 P5
Bradley Derbys 71 N5
Bradley Hants 22 H6
Bradley Kirk 90 F6
Bradley N York 96 F4
Bradley NE Lin 93 M9
Bradley Staffs 70 F11
Bradley Wolves 58 E5
Bradley Worcs 47 J2
Bradley Wrexhm 69 K4
Bradley Green Somset 19 J7
Bradley Green Warwks 59 L4
Bradley Green Worcs 47 J2
Bradley in the Moors Staffs 71 K6
Bradley Stoke S Glos 32 B8
Bradmore Notts 72 F4
Bradney Somset 19 K7
Bradninch Devon 9 N4
Bradninch Devon 17 L5
Bradnop Staffs 71 J3
Bradnor Green Herefs 45 K3
Bradpole Dorset 11 K6
Bradshaw Bolton 89 L8
Bradshaw Calder 90 D5
Bradshaw Kirk 90 D8
Bradstone Devon 5 P5
Bradwall Green Ches E 70 D2
Bradwell Derbys 83 Q8
Bradwell Devon 17 J3
Bradwell Essex 52 D7
Bradwell M Keyn 49 M6
Bradwell Norfk 77 Q11
Bradwell-on-Sea Essex 52 H10
Bradwell Waterside Essex 52 G10
Bradworthy Devon 16 E9
Brae Highld 156 B5
Brae Shet 169 q7
Braeface Falk 133 M11
Braehead Angus 143 M7
Braehead D & G 107 M7
Braehead S Lans 126 H7
Braeintra Highld 153 R11
Braemar Abers 149 M9
Braemore Highld 161 K11
Braemore Highld 167 J11
Brae Roy Lodge Highld 147 J9
Braeside Inver 124 G3
Braes of Coul Angus 142 D6
Braes of Enzie Moray 158 A6
Braeswick Ork 169 f3
Braevallich Ag & B 131 K6
Braewick Shet 169 p6
Brafferton Darltn 103 Q6
Brafferton N York 97 P6
Brafield-on-the-Green Nhants 60 H9
Bragar W Isls 168 h3
Bragbury End Herts 50 G6
Braidwood S Lans 126 E8
Brailsford Derbys 71 P6
Brailsford Green Derbys 71 P6
Brain's Green Gloucs 32 C3
Braintree Essex 52 C7
Braiseworth Suffk 64 G7
Braishfield Hants 22 C9
Braithwaite C Brad 90 C2
Braithwaite Cumb 100 H6
Braithwell Donc 84 H2
Braken Hill Wakefd 91 L7
Bramber W Susx 24 E8
Brambridge Hants 22 E10
Bramcote Notts 72 E3
Bramcote Warwks 59 P7
Bramdean Hants 22 H9
Bramerton Norfk 77 K11
Bramfield Herts 50 G7
Bramfield Suffk 65 M7
Bramford Suffk 53 K2
Bramhall Stockp 83 J8
Bramham Leeds 91 L2
Bramhope Leeds 90 H2
Bramley Hants 23 J3
Bramley Leeds 90 G3
Bramley Rothm 84 G2
Bramley Surrey 24 B2
Bramley Corner Hants 22 H3
Bramley Green Hants 23 J3
Bramley Head N York 96 H9
Bramling Kent 39 M10
Brampford Speke Devon 9 M5
Brampton Cambs 62 B6
Brampton Cumb 102 C6
Brampton Cumb 111 K8
Brampton Lincs 85 P5
Brampton Norfk 77 J7
Brampton Rothm 91 L10
Brampton Suffk 65 N5
Brampton Abbotts Herefs 46 B9
Brampton Ash Nhants 60 G3
Brampton Bryan Herefs 56 F10
Brampton-en-le-Morthen Rothm 84 G3
Bramshall Staffs 71 K8
Bramshaw Hants 21 Q11
Bramshill Hants 23 K2
Bramshott Hants 23 M8
Bramwell Somset 19 M9
Branault Highld 137 N2
Brancaster Norfk 75 Q2
Brancaster Staithe Norfk 75 Q2
Brancepeth Dur 103 P3
Branchill Moray 157 K7
Brand End Lincs 87 L11
Branderburgh Moray 157 N3
Brandesburton E R Yk 99 N11
Brandeston Suffk 65 J9
Brand Green Gloucs 46 D9
Brandis Corner Devon 16 G11
Brandiston Norfk 76 G7
Brandon Dur 103 P2
Brandon Lincs 86 B11
Brandon Nthumb 119 K7
Brandon Suffk 63 N3
Brandon Warwks 59 P9
Brandon Bank Norfk 63 K3
Brandon Creek Norfk 63 K2
Brandon Parva Norfk 76 F10
Brandsby N York 98 B6
Brandy Wharf Lincs 92 H11
Brane Cnwll 2 C8
Bran End Essex 51 Q5
Branksome BCP 12 H6
Branksome Park BCP 13 J6
Bransbury Hants 22 D6
Bransby Lincs 85 Q5
Branscombe Devon 10 D7
Bransford Worcs 46 E4
Bransgore Hants 13 L5
Bransholme C KuH 93 K4
Bransley Shrops 57 M9
Branson's Cross Worcs 58 G10
Branston Leics 73 L5
Branston Lincs 86 D7
Branston Staffs 71 N10
Branston Booths Lincs 86 E7
Branstone IoW 14 G10
Brant Broughton Lincs 86 B10
Brantham Suffk 53 K5
Branthwaite Cumb 100 E6
Branthwaite Cumb 101 J3
Brantingham E R Yk 92 F5
Branton Donc 91 Q10
Branton Nthumb 119 K7
Branton Green N York 97 P8
Branxton Nthumb 118 G3
Brassey Green Ches W 69 P2
Brassington Derbys 71 N4
Brasted Kent 37 L9
Brasted Chart Kent 37 L10
Brathens Abers 150 H8
Bratoft Lincs 87 N8
Brattleby Lincs 86 B4
Bratton Somset 18 B5
Bratton Wilts 20 H4
Bratton Wrekin 57 L2
Bratton Clovelly Devon 8 C6
Bratton Fleming Devon 17 L4
Bratton Seymour Somset 20 C9
Braughing Herts 51 J5
Braughing Friars Herts 51 K6
Braunston Nhants 60 B7
Braunston Rutlnd 73 L9
Braunstone Town Leics 72 F10
Braunton Devon 16 H4
Brawby N York 98 E5
Brawl Highld 166 D3
Braworth N York 104 F9
Bray W & M 35 P9
Braybrooke Nhants 60 G4
Braydon Wilts 33 L7
Braydon Brook Wilts 33 J6
Braydon Side Wilts 33 K7
Brayford Devon 17 M5
Bray's Hill E Susx 25 Q8
Bray Shop Cnwll 5 N7
Braystones Cumb 100 D9
Braythorn N York 97 K11
Brayton N York 91 Q4
Braywick W & M 35 N9
Braywoodside W & M 35 N9
Brazacott Cnwll 5 M3
Breach Kent 27 L2
Breach Kent 38 D8
Breachwood Green Herts 50 E6
Breacleit W Isls 168 g4
Breaclete W Isls 168 g4
Breaden Heath Shrops 69 M7
Breadsall Derbys 72 B3
Breadstone Gloucs 32 D4
Breadward Herefs 45 K4
Breage Cnwll 2 G8
Breakachy Highld 155 N9
Breakish Highld 145 L3
Brealangwell Lodge Highld 162 C8
Bream Gloucs 32 B3
Breamore Hants 21 N11
Brean Somset 19 J3
Breanais W Isls 168 e5
Brearley Calder 90 C5
Brearton N York 97 M8
Breascleit W Isls 168 h4
Breasclete W Isls 168 h4
Breaston Derbys 72 D4
Brechfa Carmth 43 K8
Brechin Angus 143 L5
Breckles Norfk 64 D3
Brecon Powys 44 E9
Brecon Beacons National Park 44 E10
Bredbury Stockp 83 K6
Brede E Susx 26 D8
Bredenbury Herefs 46 B3
Bredfield Suffk 65 K11
Bredgar Kent 38 E9
Bredhurst Kent 38 C9
Bredon Worcs 46 H7
Bredon's Hardwick Worcs 46 H7
Bredon's Norton Worcs 46 H7
Bredwardine Herefs 45 L6
Breedon on the Hill Leics 72 C6
Breich W Loth 126 H5
Breightmet Bolton 89 L9
Breighton E R Yk 92 B4
Breinton Herefs 45 P7
Bremhill Wilts 33 J10
Bremridge Devon 17 M6
Brenchley Kent 25 Q2
Brendon Devon 16 F10
Brendon Devon 17 P2
Brendon Hill Somset 18 D8
Brenfield Ag & B 123 P3
Brenish W Isls 168 e5
Brenkley N u Ty 113 K5
Brent Cross Gt Lon 36 F3
Brent Eleigh Suffk 52 F2
Brentford Gt Lon 36 E5
Brentingby Leics 73 K7
Brent Knoll Somset 19 K4
Brent Mill Devon 6 H7
Brent Pelham Herts 51 K4
Brentwood Essex 37 N2
Brenzett Kent 26 H6
Brenzett Green Kent 26 H6
Brereton Staffs 71 K11
Brereton Green Ches E 70 D2
Brereton Heath Ches E 82 H11
Brereton Hill Staffs 71 K11
Bressay Shet 169 s9
Bressingham Norfk 64 F5
Bressingham Common Norfk 64 F5
Bretby Derbys 71 P10
Bretford Warwks 59 P9
Bretforton Worcs 47 L6
Bretherton Lancs 88 F6
Brettabister Shet 169 r8
Brettenham Norfk 64 C5
Brettenham Suffk 64 D11
Bretton C Pete 74 C10
Bretton Derbys 84 B5
Bretton Flints 69 L2
Brewers End Essex 51 N6
Brewer Street Surrey 36 H10
Brewood Staffs 58 C3
Briantspuddle Dorset 12 D6
Brick End Essex 51 N5
Brickendon Herts 50 H9
Bricket Wood Herts 50 D10
Brick Houses Sheff 84 D4
Brickkiln Green Essex 52 B5
Bricklehampton Worcs 47 J6
Bride IoM 80 f1
Bridekirk Cumb 100 F4
Bridell Pembks 41 N2
Bridestowe Devon 8 D7
Brideswell Abers 158 E10
Bridford Devon 9 K7
Bridge Kent 39 L11
Bridge End Cumb 94 D4
Bridge End Cumb 110 G11
Bridge End Devon 6 H9
Bridge End Dur 103 K3
Bridge End Essex 51 Q4
Bridge End Lincs 74 B3
Bridgefoot Angus 142 F10
Bridgefoot Cumb 100 E5
Bridge Green Essex 51 L3
Bridgehampton Somset 19 Q10
Bridge Hewick N York 97 M6
Bridgehill Dur 112 G10
Bridgehouse Gate N York 97 J7
Bridgemary Hants 14 G6
Bridgemere Ches E 70 C5
Bridgend Abers 158 D10
Bridgend Ag & B 120 E4
Bridgend Ag & B 122 D7
Bridgend Angus 143 J4
Bridgend Brdgnd 29 P9
Bridgend Cerdgn 42 C5
Bridgend Cumb 101 M8
Bridgend D & G 116 F9
Bridgend Devon 6 F9
Bridgend Fife 135 K5
Bridgend Moray 158 A11
Bridgend P & K 134 E3
Bridgend W Loth 127 J2
Bridgend of Lintrathen Angus 142 D7
Bridge of Alford Abers 150 F4
Bridge of Allan Stirlg 133 M8
Bridge of Avon Moray 149 M4
Bridge of Avon Moray 157 M10
Bridge of Balgie P & K 140 E8
Bridge of Brewlands Angus 142 B5
Bridge of Brown Highld 149 L3
Bridge of Cally P & K 142 A7
Bridge of Canny Abers 150 H8
Bridge of Craigisla Angus 142 D7
Bridge of Dee D & G 108 F9
Bridge of Don C Aber 151 N6
Bridge of Dye Abers 150 H10
Bridge of Earn P & K 134 E4
Bridge of Ericht P & K 140 D6
Bridge of Feugh Abers 151 J8
Bridge of Gairn Abers 150 B8
Bridge of Gaur P & K 140 D6
Bridge of Marnoch Abers 158 E7
Bridge of Muchalls Abers 151 M9
Bridge of Orchy Ag & B 139 P10
Bridge of Tilt P & K 141 L4
Bridge of Tynet Moray 158 A5
Bridge of Walls Shet 169 p8
Bridge of Weir Rens 125 K4
Bridge Reeve Devon 17 M9
Bridgerule Devon 16 D11
Bridges Shrops 56 F5
Bridge Sollers Herefs 45 N6
Bridge Street Suffk 52 E2
Bridgetown Cnwll 5 N4
Bridgetown Somset 18 B8
Bridge Trafford Ches W 81 P10
Bridge Yate S Glos 32 C10
Bridgham Norfk 64 D4
Bridgnorth Shrops 57 N6
Bridgwater Somset 19 J7
Bridgwater Services Somset 19 K8
Bridlington E R Yk 99 P7
Bridport Dorset 11 K6
Bridstow Herefs 46 A10
Brierfield Lancs 89 N3
Brierley Barns 91 L8
Brierley Gloucs 46 B11
Brierley Herefs 45 P3
Brierley Hill Dudley 58 D7
Brierlow Bar Derbys 83 N11
Brierton Hartpl 104 E4
Briery Cumb 101 J6
Brigg N Linc 92 H9
Briggate Norfk 77 L6
Briggswath N York 105 N9
Brigham Cumb 100 E4
Brigham Cumb 101 J6
Brigham E R Yk 99 M10
Brighouse Calder 90 E6
Brighstone IoW 14 D10
Brightgate Derbys 84 C9
Brighthampton Oxon 34 C4
Brightholmlee Sheff 90 H11
Brightley Devon 8 F5
Brightling E Susx 25 Q6
Brightlingsea Essex 53 J8
Brighton Br & H 24 H10
Brighton Cnwll 3 N3
Brighton City Airport W Susx 24 E9
Brighton le Sands Sefton 81 L5
Brightons Falk 126 G2
Brightwalton W Berk 34 D9
Brightwalton Green W Berk 34 D9
Brightwalton Holt W Berk 34 D9
Brightwell Suffk 53 N3
Brightwell Baldwin Oxon 35 J5
Brightwell-cum-Sotwell Oxon 34 G6
Brightwell Upperton Oxon 35 J6
Brignall Dur 103 L8
Brig o'Turk Stirlg 132 G6
Brigsley NE Lin 93 N10
Brigsteer Cumb 95 K3
Brigstock Nhants 61 K3
Brill Bucks 35 J2
Brill Cnwll 3 J8
Brilley Herefs 45 K5
Brimfield Herefs 57 J11
Brimfield Cross Herefs 57 J11
Brimington Derbys 84 F6
Brimley Devon 9 K9
Brimpsfield Gloucs 32 H2
Brimpton W Berk 22 G2
Brimpton Common W Berk 22 G2
Brimscombe Gloucs 32 G4
Brimstage Wirral 81 L8
Brincliffe Sheff 84 D4
Brind E R Yk 92 B4
Brindham Somset 19 P7
Brindister Shet 169 p8
Brindle Lancs 88 H6
Brindley Ches E 69 Q4
Brineton Staffs 57 Q2
Bringhurst Leics 60 H2
Bringsty Common Herefs 46 D3
Brington Cambs 61 N5
Briningham Norfk 76 E5
Brinkely Notts 85 M10
Brinkhill Lincs 87 L6
Brinkley Cambs 63 K10
Brinklow Warwks 59 P9
Brinkworth Wilts 33 K8
Brinscall Lancs 89 J6
Brinscombe Somset 19 M4
Brinsea N Som 19 M2
Brinsley Notts 84 G11
Brinsop Herefs 45 N6
Brinsworth Rothm 84 F3
Brinton Norfk 76 E4
Brinyan Ork 169 d4
Brisco Cumb 110 H10
Brisley Norfk 76 C7
Brislington Bristl 32 B10
Brissenden Green Kent 26 F4
Bristol Bristl 31 Q10
Bristol Airport N Som 31 P11
Bristol Zoo Gardens Bristl 31 Q10
Briston Norfk 76 F5
Brisworthy Devon 6 F5
Britannia Lancs 89 P6
Britford Wilts 21 N9
Brithdir Caerph 30 F4
Brithdir Gwynd 67 P11
British Legion Village Kent 38 B10
Briton Ferry Neath 29 K6
Britwell Salome Oxon 35 J6
Brixham Torbay 7 N7
Brixton Devon 6 F8
Brixton Gt Lon 36 H5
Brixton Deverill Wilts 20 G7
Brixworth Nhants 60 F6
Brize Norton Oxon 33 Q3
Brize Norton Airport Oxon 33 Q3
Broad Alley Worcs 58 C11
Broad Blunsdon Swindn 33 M6
Broadbottom Tamesd 83 L6
Broadbridge W Susx 15 M5
Broadbridge Heath W Susx 24 D4
Broad Campden Gloucs 47 N7
Broad Carr Calder 90 D7
Broad Chalke Wilts 21 K9
Broad Clough Lancs 89 P6
Broadclyst Devon 9 N5
Broadfield Inver 125 J3
Broadfield Pembks 41 M10
Broadford Highld 145 K3
Broad Ford Kent 26 B4
Broadford Bridge W Susx 24 C6
Broadgairhill Border 117 J8
Broadgrass Green Suffk 64 D9
Broad Green Cambs 63 L8
Broad Green Essex 52 E7
Broad Green Worcs 46 E3
Broad Green Worcs 58 E10
Broadhaugh Border 129 M9
Broad Haven Pembks 40 G8
Broadheath Traffd 82 G7
Broadheath Worcs 57 M11
Broadhembury Devon 10 C4
Broadhempston Devon 7 L5
Broad Hill Cambs 63 J5
Broad Hinton Wilts 33 M9
Broadholme Lincs 85 Q6
Broadland Row E Susx 26 D8
Broadlay Carmth 28 C3
Broad Layings Hants 22 D2
Broadley Essex 51 K9
Broadley Lancs 89 P7
Broadley Moray 158 A5
Broadley Common Essex 51 K9
Broad Marston Worcs 47 M5
Broadmayne Dorset 12 B7
Broad Meadow Staffs 70 E5
Broadmere Hants 22 H5
Broadmoor Gloucs 46 B11
Broadmoor Pembks 41 L9
Broadnymett Devon 8 H4
Broad Oak Carmth 43 L10
Broad Oak Cumb 94 C2
Broadoak Dorset 11 J5
Broad Oak E Susx 25 P6
Broad Oak E Susx 26 D8
Broadoak Gloucs 32 C2
Broad Oak Hants 23 L4
Broad Oak Herefs 45 P10
Broad Oak Kent 39 L9
Broad Oak St Hel 82 B5
Broadoak Wrexhm 69 L3
Broad Road Suffk 65 K6
Broadsands Torbay 7 M7
Broad's Green Essex 51 Q8
Broadstairs Kent 39 Q8
Broadstone BCP 12 H5
Broadstone Mons 31 P4
Broadstone Shrops 57 J7
Broad Street E Susx 26 E8
Broad Street Essex 51 N7
Broad Street Kent 27 K3
Broad Street Kent 38 D10
Broad Street Medway 38 C7
Broad Street Wilts 21 M3
Broad Street Green Essex 52 E10
Broad Town Wilts 33 L9
Broadwas Worcs 46 E3
Broadwater Herts 50 F6
Broadwater W Susx 24 D10
Broadwaters Worcs 58 B9
Broadway Carmth 28 C3
Broadway Carmth 41 Q8
Broadway Pembks 40 G8
Broadway Somset 19 K11
Broadway Suffk 65 M6
Broadway Worcs 47 L7
Broadwell Gloucs 31 Q2
Broadwell Gloucs 47 P9
Broadwell Oxon 33 Q4
Broadwell Warwks 59 Q11
Broadwey Dorset 11 P8
Broadwindsor Dorset 11 J4
Broadwood Kelly Devon 8 F3
Broadwoodwidger Devon 5 Q4
Brobury Herefs 45 L6
Brochel Highld 153 K8
Brochroy Ag & B 139 J11
Brock Lancs 88 G2
Brockamin Worcs 46 E4
Brockbridge Hants 22 H11
Brockdish Norfk 65 J6
Brockencote Worcs 58 C10
Brockenhurst Hants 13 P4
Brocketsbrae S Lans 126 E10
Brockford Green Suffk 64 G8
Brockford Street Suffk 64 G8
Brockhall Nhants 60 D8
Brockham Surrey 36 E11
Brockhampton Gloucs 46 H9
Brockhampton Gloucs 47 K10
Brockhampton Hants 15 K5
Brockhampton Herefs 46 A8
Brockhampton Green Dorset 11 Q3
Brockholes Kirk 90 F8
Brockhurst Derbys 84 D8
Brockhurst Warwks 59 Q8
Brocklebank Cumb 101 K2
Brocklesby Lincs 93 K8
Brockley N Som 31 N11
Brockley Suffk 64 A7
Brockley Green Suffk 63 M11
Brockley Green Suffk 64 A11
Brockleymoor Cumb 101 N3
Brockmoor Dudley 58 D7
Brockscombe Devon 8 C5
Brock's Green Hants 22 F2
Brockton Shrops 56 E4
Brockton Shrops 56 E7

Brockton Shrops 57 K6
Brockton Shrops 57 N4
Brockton Staffs 70 L8
Brockweir Gloucs 31 P4
Brockwood Park Hants 22 H9
Brockworth Gloucs 46 G11
Brocton Cnwll 4 G8
Brocton Staffs 70 H11
Brodick N Ayrs 121 K4
Brodie Moray 156 H6
Brodsworth Donc 91 N9
Brogaig Highld 152 H4
Brogborough C Beds 49 Q7
Brokenborough Wilts 32 H7
Broken Cross Ches E 83 J10
Broken Cross Ches W 82 E10
Brokerswood Wilts 20 F4
Bromborough Wirral 81 M8
Brome Suffk 64 G6
Brome Street Suffk 64 H6
Bromeswell Suffk 65 L11
Bromfield Cumb 110 C11
Bromfield Shrops 56 H9
Bromham Bed 61 M10
Bromham Wilts 33 J11
Bromley Barns 91 J11
Bromley Dudley 58 D7
Bromley Gt Lon 37 K7
Bromley Shrops 57 N5
Bromley Common Gt Lon 37 K7
Bromley Cross Bolton 89 L8
Bromley Cross Essex 53 J6
Bromley Green Kent 26 G4
Bromlow Shrops 56 E4
Brompton Medway 38 C8
Brompton N York 104 C11
Brompton-by-Sawdon
  N York 99 J4
Brompton-on-Swale N York 103 P11
Brompton Ralph Somset 18 E8
Brompton Regis Somset 18 C8
Bromsash Herefs 46 C10
Bromsberrow Gloucs 46 D8
Bromsberrow Heath Gloucs 46 D8
Bromsgrove Worcs 58 E10
Bromstead Heath Staffs 70 D11
Bromyard Herefs 46 C4
Bromyard Downs Herefs 46 C3
Bronaber Gwynd 67 N8
Bronant Cerdgn 54 E11
Broncroft Shrops 57 J7
Brongest Cerdgn 42 F5
Bronington Wrexhm 69 N7
Bronllys Powys 44 G8
Bronwydd Carmth 42 H10
Bronydd Powys 45 J5
Bronygarth Shrops 69 J7
Brook Carmth 41 Q9
Brook Hants 13 N2
Brook Hants 22 B9
Brook IoW 14 C10
Brook Kent 27 J3
Brook Surrey 23 P7
Brook Surrey 36 C11
Brooke Norfk 65 K2
Brooke Rutlnd 73 L9
Brookenby Lincs 93 M11
Brook End Bed 61 N8
Brook End C Beds 61 Q11
Brook End Cambs 61 N6
Brook End M Keyn 49 P6
Brookfield Rens 125 L5
Brookhampton Oxon 34 H5
Brookhampton Somset 20 B9
Brook Hill Hants 13 N2
Brook House Denbgs 80 F11
Brookhouse Lancs 95 L8
Brookhouse Rothm 84 H3
Brookhouse Green Ches E 70 E2
Brookhouses Derbys 83 M7
Brookland Kent 26 G6
Brooklands Traffd 82 G6
Brookmans Park Herts 50 F10
Brooks Powys 55 Q5
Brooksby Leics 72 H7
Brooks End Kent 39 N8
Brooks Green W Susx 24 D6
Brook Street Essex 37 N2
Brook Street Kent 26 F6
Brook Street Suffk 52 D2
Brook Street W Susx 24 H5
Brookthorpe Gloucs 32 F2
Brookville Norfk 75 P11
Brookwood Surrey 23 Q3
Broom C Beds 50 E2
Broom Rothm 84 F2
Broom Warwks 47 L4
Broombank Worcs 57 M10
Broome Norfk 65 M3
Broome Shrops 56 G9
Broome Worcs 58 D9
Broomedge Warrtn 82 F7
Broome Park Nthumb 119 M8
Broomer's Corner W Susx 24 D6
Broomershill W Susx 24 C7
Broomfield Essex 52 B9
Broomfield Kent 38 D11
Broomfield Kent 39 L8
Broomfield Somset 18 H8
Broomfields Shrops 69 M11
Broomfleet E R Yk 92 E5
Broom Green Norfk 76 D7
Broomhall W & M 35 Q10
Broomhaugh Nthumb 112 F8
Broom Hill Barns 91 L10
Broom Hill Dorset 12 H4
Broom Hill Notts 84 H11
Broomhill Nthumb 119 P10
Broom Hill Worcs 58 D9
Broomhill Green Ches E 70 A5
Broomley Nthumb 112 H8
Broompark Dur 103 P2
Broom's Green Gloucs 46 D8
Broomsthorpe Norfk 76 A6
Broom Street Kent 38 H9
Brora Highld 163 L6
Broseley Shrops 57 M4
Brotherhouse Bar Lincs 74 E8
Brotherlee Dur 102 H3
Brothertoft Lincs 87 J11
Brotherton N York 91 M5
Brotton R & Cl 105 J7
Broubster Highld 166 H4
Brough Cumb 102 E8
Brough Derbys 83 Q8

Brough E R Yk 92 F5
Brough Highld 167 M2
Brough Notts 85 P9
Brough Shet 169 s7
Broughall Shrops 69 Q6
Brough Lodge Shet 169 s4
Brough Sowerby Cumb 102 E8
Broughton Border 116 G3
Broughton Bucks 35 M2
Broughton Cambs 62 C5
Broughton Flints 69 K2
Broughton Hants 22 B8
Broughton Lancs 88 G4
Broughton M Keyn 49 N7
Broughton N Linc 92 G9
Broughton N York 96 D10
Broughton N York 98 F6
Broughton Nhants 60 H5
Broughton Oxon 48 D7
Broughton Salfd 82 H4
Broughton Staffs 70 D8
Broughton V Glam 29 P10
Broughton Astley Leics 60 B2
Broughton Beck Cumb 94 F4
Broughton Gifford Wilts 20 G2
Broughton Green Worcs 47 J2
Broughton Hackett Worcs 46 H4
Broughton-in-Furness
  Cumb 94 E3
Broughton Mains D & G 107 N8
Broughton Mills Cumb 94 E2
Broughton Moor Cumb 100 E4
Broughton Poggs Oxon 33 P4
Broughton Tower Cumb 94 E3
Broughty Ferry C Dund 142 H11
Brow with St Giles N York 103 P11
Brow End Cumb 94 F6
Brownber Cumb 102 D9
Brown Candover Hants 22 G7
Brown Edge Lancs 88 D8
Brown Edge Staffs 70 G4
Brown Heath Ches W 69 N2
Brownhill Shrops 69 N9
Brownhill Abers 159 L9
Brownhills Fife 135 N4
Brownhills Wsall 58 F3
Brownieside Nthumb 119 N6
Browninghill Green Hants 22 G3
Brown Lees Staffs 70 F3
Brownlow Heath Ches E 70 E2
Brownrigg Cumb 100 D6
Brownrigg Cumb 110 C10
Brownsea Island Dorset 12 H7
Brown's Green Birm 58 G6
Brownsham Devon 16 D6
Browns Hill Gloucs 32 G4
Brownsover Warwks 60 B5
Brownston Devon 6 H8
Brown Street Suffk 64 F9
Brow-of-the-Hill Norfk 75 N7
Browston Green Norfk 77 P11
Broxa N York 99 J2
Broxbourne Herts 51 J9
Broxburn E Loth 128 H4
Broxburn W Loth 127 K3
Broxfield Nthumb 119 P7
Broxted Essex 51 N5
Broxton Ches W 69 N4
Broyle Side E Susx 25 L8
Bruan Highld 167 P9
Bruar P & K 141 K4
Bruchag Ag & B 124 E6
Bruera Ches W 69 M2
Bruern Abbey Oxon 47 Q10
Bruichladdich Ag & B 122 C7
Bruisyard Suffk 65 L8
Bruisyard Street Suffk 65 L8
Brumby N Linc 92 E9
Brund Staffs 71 L2
Brundall Norfk 77 L10
Brundish Suffk 65 K8
Brundish Street Suffk 65 K7
Brunery Highld 138 C3
Brunnion Cnwll 2 E6
Brunslow Shrops 56 F8
Brunswick Village N u Ty 113 K6
Bruntcliffe Leeds 90 H5
Brunthwaite C Brad 96 G11
Bruntingthorpe Leics 60 D3
Brunton Fife 135 J3
Brunton Nthumb 119 P6
Brunton Wilts 21 P3
Brushford Devon 17 M10
Brushford Somset 18 B9
Bruton Somset 20 C7
Bryan's Green Worcs 58 C11
Bryanston Dorset 12 E3
Bryant's Bottom Bucks 35 N5
Brydekirk D & G 110 C6
Bryher IoS 2 b2
Brymbo Wrexhm 69 J4
Brympton Somset 19 P11
Bryn Carmth 28 F4
Bryn Ches W 82 D10
Bryn Neath 29 M6
Bryn Shrops 56 D7
Bryn Wigan 82 C4
Brynamman Carmth 29 K2
Brynberian Pembks 41 M3
Brynbryddan Neath 29 L6
Bryn Bwbach Gwynd 67 L7
Bryncae Rhondd 30 C8
Bryncethin Brdgnd 29 P8
Bryncir Gwynd 66 H6
Bryn-coch Neath 29 K5
Bryncroes Gwynd 66 C8
Bryncrug Gwynd 54 E4
Bryn Du IoA 78 E10
Bryneglwys Denbgs 68 F5
Brynfields Wrexhm 69 K6
Brynford Flints 80 H10
Bryn Gates Wigan 82 C4
Bryn Golau Rhondd 30 D7
Bryngwran IoA 78 F9
Bryngwyn Mons 31 L3
Bryngwyn Powys 44 H5
Bryn-Henllan Pembks 41 K3
Brynhoffnant Cerdgn 42 F4
Bryning Lancs 88 E5
Brynithel Blae G 30 H4
Brynmawr Blae G 30 G2
Brynmawr Gwynd 66 C8
Brynmenyn Brdgnd 29 P8
Brynmill Swans 28 H6

Brynna Rhondd 30 C8
Bryn-penarth Powys 55 Q4
Brynrefail Gwynd 67 K2
Brynrefail IoA 78 H7
Brynsadler Rhondd 30 D8
Bryn Saith Marchog Denbgs 68 E4
Brynsiencyn IoA 78 H11
Brynteg IoA 78 H8
Bryn-y-bal Flints 69 J2
Bryn-y-Maen Conwy 79 Q9
Bryn-yr-Eos Wrexhm 69 J6
Bualintur Highld 144 F3
Buarth-draw Flints 80 H9
Bubbenhall Warwks 59 N10
Bubwith E R Yk 92 B3
Buccleuch Border 117 L8
Buchanan Smithy Stirlg 132 F10
Buchanhaven Abers 159 R8
Buchanty P & K 133 Q2
Buchlyvie Stirlg 133 L7
Buckabank Cumb 110 G11
Buckden Cambs 61 Q7
Buckden N York 96 H5
Buckenham Norfk 77 M10
Buckerell Devon 10 C4
Buckfast Devon 7 J5
Buckfastleigh Devon 7 J5
Buckhaven Fife 135 K8
Buckholt Mons 45 Q11
Buckhorn Devon 5 P2
Buckhorn Weston Dorset 20 E10
Buckhurst Hill Essex 37 K2
Buckie Moray 158 B4
Buckingham Bucks 49 J8
Buckland Bucks 35 N2
Buckland Devon 6 H10
Buckland Gloucs 47 L7
Buckland Hants 13 P5
Buckland Herts 51 J4
Buckland Kent 27 P3
Buckland Oxon 34 B5
Buckland Surrey 36 F10
Buckland Brewer Devon 16 G7
Buckland Common Bucks 35 P3
Buckland Dinham Somset 20 E4
Buckland Filleigh Devon 16 H10
Buckland in the Moor
  Devon 7 J4
Buckland Monachorum
  Devon 6 D5
Buckland Newton Dorset 11 P3
Buckland Ripers Dorset 11 P8
Buckland St Mary Somset 10 F2
Buckland-Tout-Saints
  Devon 7 K9
Bucklebury W Berk 34 G10
Bucklers Hard Hants 14 D6
Bucklesham Suffk 53 M3
Buckley Flints 69 J2
Buckley Green Warwks 59 J11
Bucklow Hill Ches E 82 F8
Buckminster Leics 73 M6
Bucknall C Stke 70 G5
Bucknall Lincs 86 G7
Bucknell Oxon 48 G9
Bucknell Shrops 56 F10
Buckpool Moray 158 B4
Bucksburn C Aber 151 M6
Buck's Cross Devon 16 F7
Bucks Green W Susx 24 C4
Buckshaw Village Lancs 88 H6
Bucks Hill Herts 50 C10
Buck's Horn Oak Hants 23 M6
Buck's Mills Devon 16 F7
Buckton E R Yk 99 P6
Buckton Herefs 56 F10
Buckton Nthumb 119 L3
Buckworth Cambs 61 P5
Budby Notts 85 K7
Buddileigh Staffs 70 D5
Bude Cnwll 16 C10
Budge's Shop Cnwll 5 N10
Budlake Devon 9 N4
Budle Nthumb 119 N3
Budleigh Salterton Devon 9 Q8
Budlett's Common E Susx 25 L6
Budock Water Cnwll 3 K7
Buerton Ches E 70 B6
Bugbrooke Nhants 60 E9
Bugford Devon 7 L8
Buglawton Ches E 70 F2
Bugle Cnwll 4 G10
Bugley Dorset 20 E10
Bugthorpe E R Yk 98 F9
Buildwas Shrops 57 L4
Builth Road Powys 44 E4
Builth Wells Powys 44 E4
Bulbourne Herts 35 P2
Bulbridge Wilts 21 L8
Bulby Lincs 73 R5
Bulford Wilts 21 N6
Bulford Camp Wilts 21 N6
Bulkeley Ches E 69 P4
Bulkington Warwks 59 N7
Bulkington Wilts 20 H3
Bulkworthy Devon 16 F9
Bullamoor N York 97 N2
Bull Bay IoA 78 G6
Bullbridge Derbys 84 E10
Bullbrook Br For 35 N11
Bullen's Green Herts 50 F9
Bulley Gloucs 46 E11
Bullgill Cumb 100 D3
Bullinghope Herefs 45 Q7
Bullington Hants 22 E6
Bullington Lincs 86 E5
Bullockstone Kent 39 L8
Bull's Green Herts 50 G7
Bull's Green Norfk 65 N3
Bulmer Essex 52 D3
Bulmer N York 98 D7
Bulmer Tye Essex 52 D4
Bulphan Thurr 37 P3
Bulstone Devon 10 D7
Bulstrode Herts 50 B10
Bulverhythe E Susx 26 C10
Bulwark Abers 159 M8
Bulwell C Nott 72 E2
Bulwick Nhants 61 L2
Bumble's Green Essex 51 K9
Bunacaimb Highld 145 L10
Bunarkaig Highld 146 F10
Bunbury Ches E 69 Q3
Bunbury Heath Ches E 69 Q3

Bunchrew Highld 155 R8
Buncton W Susx 24 D8
Bundalloch Highld 145 Q2
Bunessan Ag & B 137 K11
Bunker's Hill Lincs 87 J10
Bunnahabhain Ag & B 122 F5
Bunny Notts 72 F5
Buntait Highld 155 M11
Buntingford Herts 51 J5
Bunwell Norfk 64 G3
Bunwell Hill Norfk 64 G3
Bupton Derbys 71 N7
Burbage Derbys 83 M10
Burbage Leics 59 P6
Burbage Wilts 21 P2
Burcher Herefs 45 L2
Burchett's Green W & M 35 M8
Burcombe Wilts 21 L8
Burcot Oxon 34 G5
Burcot Worcs 58 E10
Burcote Shrops 57 N5
Burcott Bucks 49 M11
Burcott Bucks 49 N10
Burdale N York 98 H8
Bures Essex 52 F5
Burford Oxon 33 Q2
Burford Shrops 57 K11
Burg Ag & B 137 K6
Burgate Suffk 64 F6
Burgates Hants 23 L9
Burge End Herts 50 D4
Burgess Hill W Susx 24 H7
Burgh Suffk 65 J11
Burgh by Sands Cumb 110 F9
Burgh Castle Norfk 77 P10
Burghclere Hants 22 E2
Burghead Moray 157 L4
Burghfield W Berk 35 J11
Burghfield Common W Berk 35 J11
Burgh Heath Surrey 36 F9
Burgh Hill E Susx 26 B6
Burghill Herefs 45 P6
Burgh Island Devon 6 G10
Burgh le Marsh Lincs 87 P7
Burgh next Aylsham Norfk 77 J6
Burgh on Bain Lincs 86 H3
Burgh St Margaret Norfk 77 N9
Burgh St Peter Norfk 65 P3
Burghwallis Donc 91 N8
Burham Kent 38 B9
Buriton Hants 23 K11
Burland Ches E 69 R4
Burlawn Cnwll 4 F7
Burleigh Gloucs 32 G4
Burlescombe Devon 18 E11
Burleston Dorset 12 C6
Burlestone Devon 7 L9
Burley Hants 13 M4
Burley Rutlnd 73 M8
Burley Shrops 56 H8
Burleydam Ches E 69 R6
Burley Gate Herefs 46 A5
Burley in Wharfedale C Brad 97 J11
Burley Lawn Hants 13 M4
Burley Street Hants 13 M4
Burley Wood Head C Brad 90 F2
Burlingham Green Norfk 77 M9
Burlingjobb Powys 45 K3
Burlington Shrops 57 P2
Burlton Shrops 69 N9
Burmarsh Kent 27 K5
Burmington Warwks 47 Q7
Burn N York 91 P5
Burnage Manch 83 J6
Burnaston Derbys 71 P8
Burnbanks Cumb 101 P7
Burnbrae N Lans 126 F6
Burn Bridge N York 97 L10
Burnby E R Yk 98 F11
Burn Cross Sheff 91 J11
Burndell W Susx 15 Q6
Burnden Bolton 89 L9
Burnedge Rochdl 89 Q8
Burneside Cumb 101 P11
Burneston N York 97 M4
Burnett BaNES 32 C11
Burnfoot Border 117 N8
Burnfoot Border 117 Q7
Burnfoot D & G 109 L2
Burnfoot D & G 117 F3
Burnfoot D & G 117 M11
Burnfoot P & K 134 B7
Burnham Bucks 35 P8
Burnham N Linc 93 J7
Burnham Deepdale Norfk 75 R2
Burnham Green Herts 50 G7
Burnham Market Norfk 76 A3
Burnham Norton Norfk 76 A3
Burnham-on-Crouch Essex 38 F2
Burnham-on-Sea Somset 19 K5
Burnham Overy Norfk 76 A3
Burnham Overy Staithe
  Norfk 76 A3
Burnham Thorpe Norfk 76 B3
Burnhead D & G 116 B11
Burnhervie Abers 151 J4
Burnhill Green Staffs 57 P4
Burnhope Dur 113 J11
Burnhouse N Ayrs 125 K6
Burniston N York 99 L2
Burnley Lancs 89 N4
Burnmouth Border 129 P7
Burn Naze Lancs 88 C2
Burn of Cambus Stirlg 133 L7
Burnopfield Dur 113 J9
Burnrigg Cumb 111 J9
Burnsall N York 96 H7
Burnside Angus 142 G6
Burnside Angus 143 J7
Burnside Fife 134 F6
Burnside Moray 157 M4
Burnside W Loth 127 L4
Burnside of Duntrune
  Angus 142 G11
Burntcommon Surrey 36 B10
Burntheath Derbys 71 N8
Burnt Heath Essex 53 J6
Burnt Hill W Berk 34 G10
Burnthouse Cnwll 3 K6
Burnt Houses Dur 103 N6
Burntisland Fife 134 G10
Burnt Oak E Susx 25 L4
Burnton E Ayrs 115 J6
Burntwood Flints 69 J2

Burntwood Staffs 58 G3
Burntwood Green Staffs 58 G3
Burnt Yates N York 97 L8
Burnworthy Somset 18 G11
Burpham Surrey 36 B10
Burpham W Susx 24 B9
Burradon N Tyne 113 L6
Burradon Nthumb 119 J9
Burrafirth Shet 169 t2
Burras Cnwll 2 H7
Burraton Cnwll 5 Q8
Burravoe Shet 169 s5
Burrells Cumb 102 C9
Burrelton P & K 142 C10
Burridge Devon 10 G3
Burridge Devon 17 K4
Burridge Hants 14 F4
Burrill N York 97 K3
Burringham N Linc 92 D9
Burrington Devon 17 L8
Burrington Herefs 56 G10
Burrington N Som 19 N3
Burrough End Cambs 63 K9
Burrough Green Cambs 63 K9
Burrough on the Hill Leics 73 K8
Burrow Lancs 95 N6
Burrow Somset 18 B6
Burrow Bridge Somset 19 L8
Burrowhill Surrey 23 Q2
Burrows Cross Surrey 36 C11
Burry Swans 28 E6
Burry Green Swans 28 E6
Burry Port Carmth 28 D4
Burscough Lancs 88 E8
Burscough Bridge Lancs 88 E8
Bursea E R Yk 92 D4
Burshill E R Yk 99 M11
Bursledon Hants 14 F5
Burslem C Stke 70 F5
Burstall Suffk 53 J3
Burstock Dorset 11 J4
Burston Norfk 64 G5
Burston Staffs 70 G8
Burstow Surrey 24 H2
Burstwick E R Yk 93 M5
Burtersett N York 96 C3
Burtholme Cumb 111 K8
Burthorpe Green Suffk 63 N8
Burthwaite Cumb 110 H11
Burthy Cnwll 4 E10
Burtle Hill Somset 19 L6
Burtoft Lincs 74 E3
Burton BCP 13 L6
Burton Ches W 69 P2
Burton Ches W 81 L10
Burton Dorset 11 P6
Burton Nthumb 119 N4
Burton Pembks 41 J9
Burton Somset 11 L2
Burton Somset 18 G6
Burton Wilts 20 F8
Burton Wilts 32 F9
Burton Agnes E R Yk 99 N8
Burton Bradstock Dorset 11 K7
Burton-by-Lincoln Lincs 86 C6
Burton Coggles Lincs 73 P5
Burton Dassett Warwks 48 C4
Burton End Essex 51 M6
Burton End Suffk 63 L11
Burton Fleming E R Yk 99 M6
Burton Green Warwks 59 L9
Burton Green Wrexhm 69 K3
Burton Hastings Warwks 59 P7
Burton-in-Kendal Cumb 95 L7
Burton-in-Kendal Services
  Cumb 95 L5
Burton in Lonsdale N York 95 P6
Burton Joyce Notts 72 G2
Burton Latimer Nhants 61 K6
Burton Lazars Leics 73 K7
Burton Leonard N York 97 M8
Burton on the Wolds Leics 72 F6
Burton Overy Leics 72 H11
Burton Pedwardine Lincs 74 B2
Burton Pidsea E R Yk 93 M4
Burton Salmon N York 91 M5
Burton's Green Essex 52 D6
Burton upon Stather N Linc 92 E7
Burton upon Trent Staffs 71 N10
Burton Waters Lincs 86 B6
Burtonwood Warrtn 82 C6
Burtonwood Services
  Warrtn 82 C6
Burwardsley Ches W 69 P3
Burwarton Shrops 57 L7
Burwash E Susx 25 Q6
Burwash Common E Susx 25 P6
Burwash Weald E Susx 25 Q6
Burwell Cambs 63 J7
Burwell Lincs 87 L5
Burwen IoA 78 G6
Burwick Ork 169 d8
Bury Bury 89 N8
Bury Cambs 62 C4
Bury Somset 18 B9
Bury W Susx 24 B8
Bury End C Beds 50 D3
Bury Green Herts 51 L6
Bury St Edmunds Suffk 64 B9
Burythorpe N York 98 F8
Busby E Rens 125 P6
Busby Stoop N York 97 N4
Buscot Oxon 33 P5
Bush Abers 143 N4
Bush Cnwll 16 C10
Bush Bank Herefs 45 P4
Bushbury Wolves 58 D4
Bushby Leics 72 H10
Bushey Herts 50 D11
Bushey Heath Herts 36 D2
Bush Green Norfk 65 J4
Bush Green Suffk 64 C9
Bush Hill Park Gt Lon 50 H11
Bushley Worcs 46 G8
Bushley Green Worcs 46 G8
Bushmead Bed 61 P8
Bushmoor Shrops 56 G7
Bushton Wilts 33 L9
Busk Cumb 102 B2
Buslingthorpe Lincs 86 E3
Bussage Gloucs 32 G4
Bussex Somset 19 L7
Butcher's Cross E Susx 25 N5
Butcombe N Som 19 P2
Bute Ag & B 124 C4

Butleigh Somset 19 P8
Butleigh Wootton Somset 19 P7
Butler's Cross Bucks 35 M3
Butler's Hill Notts 84 H11
Butlers Marston Warwks 48 B4
Butley Suffk 65 M11
Butley High Corner Suffk 53 Q2
Buttercrambe N York 98 E9
Butterdean Dur 129 K7
Butterknowle Dur 103 M5
Butterleigh Devon 9 N3
Butterley Derbys 84 F10
Buttermere Cumb 100 G8
Buttermere Wilts 22 B2
Butters Green Staffs 70 K4
Buttershaw C Brad 90 E5
Butterstone P & K 141 Q8
Butterton Staffs 70 E6
Butterton Staffs 71 K3
Butterwick Dur 104 C4
Butterwick Lincs 87 L11
Butterwick N York 98 E5
Butterwick N York 99 K6
Butt Green Ches E 70 B4
Buttington Powys 56 C3
Buttonbridge Shrops 57 N9
Buttonoak Shrops 57 P9
Buttsash Hants 14 D5
Buttsbear Cross Cnwll 16 D11
Butt's Green Essex 52 C11
Buxhall Suffk 64 E10
Buxhall Fen Street Suffk 64 E10
Buxted E Susx 25 L6
Buxton Derbys 83 N10
Buxton Norfk 77 J7
Buxton Heath Norfk 76 H7
Buxworth Derbys 83 M8
Bwlch Powys 44 H10
Bwlchgwyn Wrexhm 69 J4
Bwlchllan Cerdgn 43 L3
Bwlchnewydd Carmth 42 G10
Bwlchtocyn Gwynd 66 E9
Bwlch-y-cibau Powys 68 G11
Bwlch-y-Ddar Powys 68 G10
Bwlchyfadfa Cerdgn 42 H5
Bwlch-y-ffridd Powys 55 P5
Bwlch-y-groes Pembks 41 P3
Bwlchymyrdd Swans 28 G5
Bwlch-y-sarnau Powys 55 N10
Byermoor Gatesd 113 J9
Byers Green Dur 103 P4
Byfield Nhants 48 F4
Byfleet Surrey 36 C8
Byford Herefs 45 M6
Bygrave Herts 50 G3
Byker N u Ty 113 L8
Byland Abbey N York 98 A5
Bylaugh Norfk 76 E8
Bylchau Conwy 68 C2
Byley Ches W 82 F11
Bynea Carmth 28 F5
Byrness Nthumb 118 E10
Bystock Devon 9 P8
Bythorn Cambs 61 N5
Byton Herefs 45 M2
Bywell Nthumb 112 F8
Byworth W Susx 23 Q10

C

Cabbacott Devon 16 G7
Cabourne Lincs 93 K10
Cabrach Ag & B 122 G7
Cabrach Moray 150 B2
Cabus Lancs 95 K11
Cackle Street E Susx 25 L5
Cackle Street E Susx 25 Q7
Cackle Street E Susx 26 D8
Cadbury Devon 9 M3
Cadbury Barton Devon 17 M8
Cadbury World Birm 58 F8
Cadder E Duns 125 Q3
Caddington C Beds 50 C7
Caddonfoot Border 117 P3
Cadeby Donc 91 N10
Cadeby Leics 72 C10
Cadeleigh Devon 9 M3
Cade Street E Susx 25 P6
Cadgwith Cnwll 3 J11
Cadham Fife 134 H7
Cadishead Salfd 82 F6
Cadle Swans 28 H5
Cadley Lancs 88 G4
Cadley Wilts 21 P4
Cadley Wilts 33 P11
Cadmore End Bucks 35 L6
Cadnam Hants 13 P2
Cadney N Linc 92 H10
Cadole Flints 68 H2
Cadoxton V Glam 30 F11
Cadoxton Juxta-Neath Neath 29 L5
Cadwst Denbgs 68 D7
Caeathro Gwynd 67 J2
Caehopkin Powys 29 M2
Caenby Lincs 86 C3
Caerau Brdgnd 29 N6
Caerau Cardif 30 F7
Cae'r-bont Powys 29 M2
Cae'r bryn Carmth 28 G2
Caerdeon Gwynd 67 M11
Caer Farchell Pembks 40 E9
Caergeiliog IoA 78 E9
Caergwrle Flints 69 K3
Caerhun Conwy 79 P10
Caerlanrig Border 117 M10
Caerleon Newpt 31 K6
Caernarfon Gwynd 66 H2
Caernarfon Castle Gwynd 66 H2
Caerphilly Caerph 30 G7
Caersws Powys 55 N6
Caerwedros Cerdgn 42 G3
Caerwent Mons 31 N6
Caerwys Flints 80 G10
Caerynwch Gwynd 67 P11
Caggle Street Mons 45 M11
Caim IoA 79 L8
Caio Carmth 43 N7
Cairinis W Isls 168 d11
Cairnbaan Ag & B 130 G3
Cairnbulg Abers 159 P4
Cairncross Border 129 M7
Cairncurran Inver 125 J3

Cairndow Ag & B 131 P5
Cairneyhill Fife 134 C10
Cairngarroch D & G 106 C8
Cairngorms National Park 149 K7
Cairnie Abers 158 C9
Cairnorrie Abers 159 L9
Cairnryan D & G 106 C6
Cairnty Moray 157 Q7
Caister-on-Sea Norfk 77 Q9
Caistor Lincs 93 K10
Caistor St Edmund Norfk 77 J11
Cakebole Worcs 58 C10
Cake Street Norfk 64 F3
Calais Street Suffk 52 G4
Calanais W Isls 168 h4
Calbourne IoW 14 D9
Calceby Lincs 87 L5
Calcoed Flints 80 H10
Calcot Gloucs 33 L2
Calcot W Berk 35 J10
Calcot Row W Berk 35 J10
Calcots Moray 157 N5
Calcott Shrops 56 G2
Calcutt N York 97 M9
Calcutt Wilts 33 M6
Caldbeck Cumb 101 K2
Caldbergh N York 96 G3
Caldecote Cambs 61 P3
Caldecote Cambs 62 D9
Caldecote Herts 50 F3
Caldecote Nhants 49 J4
Caldecote Highfields Cambs 62 E9
Caldecott Nhants 61 L7
Caldecott Oxon 34 E5
Caldecott Rutlnd 61 J2
Caldecotte M Keyn 49 N7
Calder Cumb 100 D10
Calderbank N Lans 126 D5
Calder Bridge Cumb 100 D9
Calderbrook Rochdl 89 Q7
Caldercruix N Lans 126 E4
Calder Grove Wakefd 91 J7
Caldermill S Lans 126 B9
Caldermore Rochdl 89 Q7
Calder Vale Lancs 95 L11
Calderwood S Lans 126 B6
Caldey Island Pembks 41 M11
Caldicot Mons 31 N7
Caldmore Wsall 58 F5
Caldwell N York 103 M8
Caldy Wirral 81 J7
Caledfwlch Carmth 43 N9
Calenick Cnwll 3 L5
Calf of Man IoM 80 a8
Calford Green Suffk 63 M11
Calfsound Ork 169 e3
Calgary Ag & B 137 K5
Califer Moray 157 K6
California Falk 126 G2
California Norfk 77 Q8
California Cross Devon 7 J8
Calke Derbys 72 B6
Calke Abbey Derbys 72 B6
Callakille Highld 153 M6
Callander Stirlg 133 J6
Callanish W Isls 168 h4
Callaughton Shrops 57 L5
Callerton N u Ty 113 J7
Callestick Cnwll 3 K3
Calligarry Highld 145 K7
Callington Cnwll 5 P8
Callingwood Staffs 71 M10
Callow Herefs 45 P8
Callow End Worcs 46 F4
Callow Hill Wilts 33 K8
Callow Hill Worcs 47 K2
Callow Hill Worcs 57 N10
Callows Grave Worcs 57 K11
Calmore Hants 13 P2
Calmsden Gloucs 33 K3
Calne Wilts 33 J10
Calow Derbys 84 F6
Calshot Hants 14 E6
Calstock Cnwll 6 C5
Calstone Wellington Wilts 33 K11
Calthorpe Norfk 76 H5
Calthorpe Street Norfk 77 N6
Calthwaite Cumb 101 N2
Calton N York 96 D9
Calton Staffs 71 L5
Calveley Ches E 69 Q3
Calver Derbys 84 B6
Calverhall Shrops 69 R7
Calver Hill Herefs 45 M5
Calverleigh Devon 9 M2
Calverley Leeds 90 G3
Calver Sough Derbys 84 B6
Calvert Bucks 49 J10
Calverton M Keyn 49 L7
Calverton Notts 85 K11
Calvine P & K 141 K4
Calvo Cumb 109 P10
Calzeat Border 116 G3
Cam Gloucs 32 E5
Camasachoirce Highld 138 D5
Camasine Highld 138 D5
Camas Luinie Highld 146 A2
Camastianavaig Highld 153 J10
Camault Muir Highld 155 P9
Camber E Susx 26 G8
Camberley Surrey 23 N2
Camberwell Gt Lon 36 H5
Camblesforth N York 91 Q5
Cambo Nthumb 112 F3
Cambois Nthumb 113 M4
Camborne Cnwll 2 G5
Camborne & Redruth
   Mining District Cnwll 2 G5
Cambourne Cambs 62 D9
Cambridge Cambs 62 G9
Cambridge Gloucs 32 D4
Cambridge Airport Cambs 62 G9
Cambrose Cnwll 2 H4
Cambus Clacks 133 P9
Cambusavie Highld 162 H7
Cambusbarron Stirlg 133 M9
Cambuskenneth Stirlg 133 N9
Cambuslang S Lans 125 Q5
Cambus o' May Abers 150 C8
Cambuswallace S Lans 116 E3
Camden Town Gt Lon 36 G4
Cameley BaNES 20 B3
Camelford Cnwll 5 J5
Camelon Falk 133 P11

Camerory Highld 157 J11
Camer's Green Worcs 46 E8
Camerton BaNES 20 C3
Camerton Cumb 100 D4
Camghouran P & K 140 E6
Camieston Border 117 R4
Cammachmore Abers 151 N6
Cammeringham Lincs 86 B4
Camore Highld 162 H9
Campbeltown Ag & B 120 D7
Campbeltown Airport
   Ag & B 120 C7
Camperdown N Tyne 113 L6
Cample D & G 109 J2
Campmuir P & K 142 C10
Camps W Loth 127 K4
Campsall Donc 91 N8
Campsea Ash Suffk 65 L11
Camps End Cambs 51 P2
Campton C Beds 50 D3
Camptown Border 118 C8
Camrose Pembks 40 H6
Camserney P & K 141 K8
Camusnagaul Highld 139 K3
Camusnagaul Highld 160 H9
Camusteel Highld 153 M6
Camusterrach Highld 153 N9
Canada Hants 21 Q11
Canal Foot Cumb 94 G5
Canaston Bridge Pembks 41 L7
Candacraig Abers 149 Q8
Candlesby Lincs 87 N7
Candle Street Suffk 64 E7
Candover Green Shrops 57 J3
Candy Mill Border 116 F2
Cane End Oxon 35 J9
Canewdon Essex 38 F3
Canford Bottom Dorset 12 H4
Canford Cliffs BCP 13 J7
Canford Heath BCP 12 H6
Canford Magna BCP 12 H5
Canhams Green Suffk 64 F8
Canisbay Highld 167 Q2
Canklow Rothm 84 F2
Canley Covtry 59 M9
Cann Dorset 20 G10
Canna Highld 144 B6
Cann Common Dorset 20 G10
Cannich Highld 155 K11
Cannington Somset 19 J7
Canning Town Gt Lon 37 K4
Cannock Staffs 58 E2
Cannock Chase Staffs 70 H11
Cannock Wood Staffs 58 F2
Cannon Bridge Herefs 45 N6
Canonbie D & G 110 G5
Canon Frome Herefs 46 B6
Canon Pyon Herefs 45 P5
Canons Ashby Nhants 48 G4
Canonstown Cnwll 2 E6
Canterbury Kent 39 K10
Canterbury Cathedral Kent 39 L10
Cantley Norfk 77 M11
Cantlop Shrops 57 J3
Canton Cardif 30 G9
Cantraywood Highld 156 D8
Cantsfield Lancs 95 N6
Canvey Island Essex 38 C5
Canwick Lincs 86 C7
Canworthy Water Cnwll 5 L3
Caol Highld 139 L2
Caolas Scalpaigh W Isls 168 h8
Caoles Ag & B 136 D6
Caonich Highld 146 D9
Capel Kent 25 P2
Capel Surrey 24 E2
Capel Bangor Cerdgn 54 F8
Capel Betws Lleucu Cerdgn 43 M3
Capel Coch IoA 78 H8
Capel Curig Conwy 67 N3
Capel Cynon Cerdgn 42 G5
Capel Dewi Carmth 43 J10
Capel Dewi Cerdgn 43 J6
Capel-Dewi Cerdgn 54 E8
Capel Garmon Conwy 67 Q3
Capel Green Suffk 53 Q2
Capel Gwyn Carmth 43 J10
Capel Gwyn IoA 78 E9
Capel Gwynfe Carmth 43 P10
Capel Hendre Carmth 28 G2
Capel Isaac Carmth 43 L9
Capel Iwan Carmth 41 Q3
Capel-le-Ferne Kent 27 M4
Capelles Guern 10 c1
Capel Llanilltern Cardif 30 E9
Capel Mawr IoA 78 G10
Capel Parc IoA 78 G7
Capel St Andrew Suffk 53 Q2
Capel St Mary Suffk 53 J4
Capel Seion Cerdgn 54 E9
Capel Trisant Cerdgn 54 G9
Capeluchaf Gwynd 66 G5
Capelulo Conwy 79 N9
Capel-y-ffin Powys 45 K8
Capel-y-graig Gwynd 79 J11
Capenhurst Ches W 81 M10
Capernwray Lancs 95 L6
Cape Wrath Highld 164 G1
Capheaton Nthumb 112 F4
Caplaw E Rens 125 L6
Capon's Green Suffk 65 K8
Cappercleuch Border 117 J7
Capstone Medway 38 C8
Capton Devon 7 L8
Capton Somset 18 E7
Caputh P & K 141 Q9
Caradon Mining District
   Cnwll 5 M7
Caradon Town Cnwll 5 M7
Carbeth Inn Stirlg 125 N2
Carbis Cnwll 4 G10
Carbis Bay Cnwll 2 E6
Carbost Highld 152 F11
Carbost Highld 152 G8
Carbrook Sheff 84 E3
Carbrooke Norfk 76 C11
Carburton Notts 85 K6
Carclaze Cnwll 3 Q3
Car Colston Notts 85 J2
Carcroft Donc 91 N9
Cardenden Fife 134 G8
Cardeston Shrops 56 F2
Cardewlees Cumb 110 G10
Cardhu Moray 157 M9
Cardiff Cardif 30 G9

Cardiff Airport V Glam 30 E11
Cardiff Gate Services Cardif 30 H8
Cardiff West Services Cardif 30 E9
Cardigan Cerdgn 42 C5
Cardinal's Green Cambs 63 K11
Cardington Bed 61 N11
Cardington Shrops 57 J4
Cardinham Cnwll 5 J8
Cardrain D & G 106 F11
Cardrona Border 117 L3
Cardross Ag & B 125 J2
Cardryne D & G 106 F11
Cardurnock Cumb 110 C9
Careby Lincs 73 Q7
Careston Angus 143 J5
Carew Pembks 41 K10
Carew Cheriton Pembks 41 K10
Carew Newton Pembks 41 K10
Carey Herefs 45 R8
Carfin N Lans 126 D6
Carfraemill Border 128 E9
Cargate Green Norfk 77 M9
Cargenbridge D & G 109 L6
Cargill P & K 142 B10
Cargo Cumb 110 G9
Cargreen Cnwll 6 C6
Cargurrel Cnwll 3 M6
Carham Nthumb 118 E3
Carhampton Somset 18 D6
Carharrack Cnwll 3 J5
Carie P & K 140 F6
Carinish W Isls 168 d11
Carisbrooke IoW 14 E9
Cark Cumb 94 H5
Carkeel Cnwll 5 C6
Càrlabhagh W Isls 168 h3
Carland Cross Cnwll 3 M3
Carlbury Darltn 103 P7
Carlby Lincs 73 Q8
Carlcroft Nthumb 118 F8
Carlecotes Barns 83 Q4
Carleen Cnwll 2 G6
Carlesmoor N York 97 K6
Carleton Cumb 100 D9
Carleton Cumb 101 P5
Carleton Cumb 110 H10
Carleton Lancs 88 C3
Carleton Wakefd 91 M6
Carleton Forehoe Norfk 76 F10
Carleton Rode Norfk 64 G4
Carleton St Peter Norfk 77 L11
Carlidnack Cnwll 3 K8
Carlincraig Abers 158 G9
Carlingcott BaNES 20 C3
Carlin How R & Cl 105 K7
Carlisle Cumb 110 H9
Carlisle Airport Cumb 111 J8
Carloggas Cnwll 4 D8
Carlops Border 127 M6
Carloway W Isls 168 h3
Carlton Barns 91 K8
Carlton Bed 61 L9
Carlton Cambs 63 K10
Carlton Leeds 91 J5
Carlton Leics 72 B10
Carlton N York 91 Q6
Carlton N York 96 G4
Carlton N York 98 C3
Carlton Notts 72 G2
Carlton S on T 104 C6
Carlton Suffk 65 M9
Carlton Colville Suffk 65 Q4
Carlton Curlieu Leics 72 H11
Carlton Green Cambs 63 K10
Carlton Husthwaite N York 97 Q5
Carlton-in-Cleveland N York 104 F10
Carlton in Lindrick Notts 85 J4
Carlton-le-Moorland Lincs 86 B9
Carlton Miniott N York 97 N4
Carlton-on-Trent Notts 85 N8
Carlton Scroop Lincs 86 B11
Carluke S Lans 126 E7
Carlyon Bay Cnwll 3 R3
Carmacoup S Lans 115 Q2
Carmarthen Carmth 42 H10
Carmel Carmth 43 L11
Carmel Flints 80 H9
Carmel Gwynd 66 H4
Carmichael S Lans 116 C3
Carmunnock C Glas 125 Q5
Carmyle C Glas 125 Q5
Carmyllie Angus 143 J9
Carnaby E R Yk 99 N7
Carnbee Fife 135 N6
Carnbo P & K 134 D7
Carn Brea Cnwll 2 H5
Carnbrogie Abers 151 M2
Carndu Highld 145 Q2
Carnduff S Lans 126 B8
Carne Cnwll 3 K9
Carne Cnwll 3 M6
Carne Cnwll 4 F10
Carnell E Ayrs 125 M11
Carnewas Cnwll 4 D8
Carnforth Lancs 95 K6
Carn-gorm Highld 146 B3
Carnhedryn Pembks 40 F5
Carnhell Green Cnwll 2 G6
Carnie Abers 151 L6
Carnkie Cnwll 2 H5
Carnkie Cnwll 3 J7
Carnkief Cnwll 3 K3
Carno Powys 55 M5
Carnock Fife 134 C10
Carnon Downs Cnwll 3 K5
Carnousie Abers 158 G7
Carnoustie Angus 143 K11
Carnwath S Lans 126 H8
Carnyorth Cnwll 2 B7
Carol Green Solhll 59 L9
Carpalla Cnwll 3 P3
Carperby N York 96 F3
Carr Rothm 84 H2
Carradale Ag & B 120 F4
Carrbridge Highld 148 G3
Carrbrook Tamesd 83 L4
Carrefour Jersey 11 b1
Carreglefn IoA 78 F7
Carr Gate Wakefd 91 J5
Carrhouse N Linc 92 C9
Carrick Ag & B 131 J10
Carrick Castle Ag & B 131 P9
Carriden Falk 134 C11

Carrington Lincs 87 K9
Carrington Mdloth 127 Q5
Carrington Traffd 82 F6
Carrog Conwy 67 P5
Carrog Denbgs 68 F6
Carron Falk 133 P11
Carron Moray 157 N9
Carronbridge D & G 116 B11
Carron Bridge Stirlg 133 L11
Carronshore Falk 133 P11
Carrow Hill Mons 31 M6
Carr Shield Nthumb 112 B11
Carruth House Inver 125 K4
Carrutherstown D & G 109 P6
Carr Vale Derbys 84 G7
Carrville Dur 104 B2
Carsaig Ag & B 137 N11
Carseriggan D & G 107 K4
Carsethorn D & G 109 L9
Carshalton Gt Lon 36 G8
Carsington Derbys 71 P4
Carskey Ag & B 120 C10
Carsluith D & G 107 N7
Carsphairn D & G 115 L9
Carstairs S Lans 126 G8
Carstairs Junction S Lans 126 H8
Carswell Marsh Oxon 34 B5
Carter's Clay Hants 22 B10
Carters Green Essex 51 M8
Carterton Oxon 33 Q3
Carterway Heads Nthumb 112 F10
Carthew Cnwll 3 G10
Carthorpe N York 97 M4
Cartington Nthumb 119 K10
Cartland S Lans 126 F8
Cartledge Derbys 84 D5
Cartmel Cumb 94 H5
Cartmel Fell Cumb 95 J3
Carway Carmth 28 E3
Carwinley Cumb 110 H6
Cashe's Green Gloucs 32 F3
Cashmoor Dorset 12 G2
Cassington Oxon 34 E2
Cassop Dur 104 B3
Castallack Cnwll 2 D8
Castel Guern 10 b2
Castell Conwy 79 P11
Castell-y-bwch Torfn 31 J6
Casterton Cumb 95 N5
Castle Cnwll 4 H10
Castle Acre Norfk 75 R7
Castle Ashby Nhants 61 J9
Castlebay W Isls 168 b18
Castle Bolton N York 96 F2
Castle Bromwich Solhll 58 H7
Castle Bytham Lincs 73 P7
Castlebythe Pembks 41 K5
Castle Caereinion Powys 56 B3
Castle Camps Cambs 51 P2
Castle Carrock Cumb 111 K9
Castlecary Falk 126 D2
Castle Cary Somset 20 B8
Castle Combe Wilts 32 F9
Castle Donington Leics 72 C5
Castle Douglas D & G 108 G8
Castle Eaton Swindn 33 M5
Castle Eden Dur 104 D3
Castle End C Pete 74 B9
Castleford Wakefd 91 L5
Castle Frome Herefs 46 C5
Castle Gate Cnwll 2 D7
Castle Green Cumb 95 L2
Castle Green Surrey 23 Q2
Castle Gresley Derbys 71 P11
Castle Hedingham Essex 52 C4
Castlehill Border 117 J3
Castlehill Highld 167 L3
Castle Hill Kent 25 Q2
Castle Hill Suffk 53 K2
Castlehill W Duns 125 K2
Castle Howard N York 98 E6
Castle Kennedy D & G 106 F6
Castle Lachlan Ag & B 131 L8
Castlemartin Pembks 40 H11
Castlemilk C Glas 125 P6
Castle Morris Pembks 40 H4
Castlemorton Worcs 46 E7
Castlemorton Common
   Worcs 46 E7
Castle O'er D & G 110 D2
Castle Rising Norfk 75 N6
Castleside Dur 112 G11
Castle Stuart Highld 156 C8
Castlethorpe M Keyn 49 M6
Castlethorpe N Linc 92 G9
Castleton Ag & B 130 H11
Castleton Border 111 K3
Castleton Derbys 83 Q8
Castleton N York 105 J9
Castleton Newpt 31 J8
Castleton Rochdl 89 P8
Castletown Ches W 69 M4
Castletown Dorset 11 P10
Castletown Highld 167 L3
Castletown IoM 80 c8
Castletown Sundld 113 N9
Castley N York 97 L11
Caston Norfk 64 D2
Castor C Pete 74 B11
Caswell Bay Swans 28 G7
Cat and Fiddle Derbys 83 M10
Catacol N Ayrs 123 R10
Catbrain S Glos 31 Q8
Catbrook Mons 31 P4
Catch Flints 81 J10
Catchall Cnwll 2 C8
Catchem's Corner Solhll 59 L9
Catchgate Dur 113 J10
Catcliffe Rothm 84 F3
Catcomb Wilts 33 K9
Catcott Somset 19 L7
Catcott Burtle Somset 19 M6
Caterham Surrey 36 H9
Catfield Norfk 77 M7
Catfield Common Norfk 77 N7
Catford Gt Lon 37 J6
Catforth Lancs 88 F4
Cathcart C Glas 125 P5
Cathedine Powys 44 G9
Catherine-de-Barnes Solhll 59 J8
Catherine Slack C Brad 90 D5
Catherington Hants 15 J4
Catherston Leweston
   Dorset 10 H6
Catherton Shrops 57 M9

Catisfield Hants	14	G5
Catley Herefs	46	C6
Catley Lane Head Rochdl	89	P7
Catlodge Highld	147	Q9
Catlow Lancs	89	P3
Catlowdy Cumb	111	J5
Catmere End Essex	51	L3
Catmore W Berk	34	E8
Caton Devon	7	K4
Caton Lancs	95	L8
Caton Green Lancs	95	M7
Cator Court Devon	8	G9
Catrine E Ayrs	115	K2
Cat's Ash Newpt	31	L6
Catsfield E Susx	26	B9
Catsfield Stream E Susx	26	B9
Catsgore Somset	19	P9
Catsham Somset	19	Q8
Catshill Worcs	58	E10
Catstree Shrops	57	N5
Cattadale Ag & B	120	C9
Cattal N York	97	P10
Cattawade Suffk	53	K5
Catterall Lancs	88	F2
Catteralslane Shrops	69	Q6
Catterick N York	103	P11
Catterick Bridge N York	103	P11
Catterick Garrison N York	103	N11
Catterlen Cumb	101	N4
Catterline Abers	143	R2
Catterton N York	97	R11
Catteshall Surrey	23	Q6
Catthorpe Leics	60	C5
Cattishall Suffk	64	B8
Cattistock Dorset	11	M4
Catton N York	97	N5
Catton Nthumb	112	B9
Catwick E R Yk	99	N11
Catworth Cambs	61	N6
Caudle Green Gloucs	32	H2
Caulcott C Beds	50	B2
Caulcott Oxon	48	F10
Cauldcots Angus	143	M8
Cauldhame Stirlg	133	J9
Cauldmill Border	117	Q7
Cauldon Staffs	71	K5
Cauldon Lowe Staffs	71	K5
Cauldwell Derbys	71	P11
Caulkerbush D & G	109	K9
Caulside D & G	110	H4
Caundle Marsh Dorset	11	P2
Caunsall Worcs	58	C8
Caunton Notts	85	M8
Causeway Hants	23	K10
Causeway End Cumb	95	K3
Causeway End D & G	107	M6
Causeway End Essex	51	Q7
Causewayend S Lans	116	E3
Causewayhead Cumb	109	P10
Causewayhead Stirlg	133	N8
Causeyend Abers	151	N4
Causey Park Nthumb	113	J2
Causey Park Bridge Nthumb	113	J2
Cavendish Suffk	63	P11
Cavenham Suffk	63	N6
Caversfield Oxon	48	G9
Caversham Readg	35	K10
Caverswall Staffs	70	H6
Caverton Mill Border	118	D5
Cavil E R Yk	92	C4
Cawdor Highld	156	E7
Cawkwell Lincs	87	J5
Cawood N York	91	P3
Cawsand Cnwll	6	C8
Cawston Norfk	76	G7
Cawston Warwks	59	Q10
Cawthorn N York	98	F3
Cawthorne Barns	90	H9
Cawton N York	98	C5
Caxton Cambs	62	D9
Caxton End Cambs	62	D9
Caxton Gibbet Cambs	62	C8
Caynham Shrops	57	K10
Caythorpe Lincs	86	B11
Caythorpe Notts	85	L11
Cayton N York	99	M4
Ceannabeinne Highld	165	K3
Ceann a Bhaigh W Isls	168	c11
Ceannacroc Lodge Highld	146	G5
Cearsiadar W Isls	168	i6
Ceciliford Mons	31	P4
Cefn Newpt	31	J7
Cefn Berain Conwy	80	D11
Cefn-brith Conwy	68	B4
Cefn-bryn-brain Carmth	29	K2
Cefn Byrle Powys	29	M2
Cefn Canel Powys	68	H8
Cefn Coch Powys	68	F9
Cefn-coed-y-cymmer Myr Td	30	D3
Cefn Cribwr Brdgnd	29	N8
Cefn Cross Brdgnd	29	N8
Cefn-ddwysarn Gwynd	68	C7
Cefn-Einion Shrops	56	D7
Cefneithin Carmth	28	G2
Cefngorwydd Powys	44	C5
Cefn-mawr Wrexhm	69	J6
Cefnpennar Rhondd	30	D3
Cefn-y-bedd Flints	69	K3
Cefn-y-pant Carmth	41	N5
Ceint IoA	78	H9
Cellan Cerdgn	43	M5
Cellardyke Fife	135	P7
Cellarhead Staffs	70	H5
Celleron Cumb	101	N5
Celynen Caerph	30	H5
Cemaes IoA	78	F6
Cemmaes Powys	55	J3
Cemmaes Road Powys	55	J4
Cenarth Cerdgn	41	Q2
Cerbyd Pembks	40	F5
Ceres Fife	135	L5
Cerne Abbas Dorset	11	P4
Cerney Wick Gloucs	33	L5
Cerrigceinwen IoA	78	G10
Cerrigydrudion Conwy	68	C5
Cess Norfk	77	N8
Ceunant Gwynd	67	J2
Chaceley Gloucs	46	G8
Chacewater Cnwll	3	K5
Chackmore Bucks	49	J7
Chacombe Nhants	48	E6
Chadbury Worcs	47	K5
Chadderton Oldham	89	Q9
Chadderton Fold Oldham	89	Q9
Chaddesden C Derb	72	B3
Chaddesley Corbett Worcs	58	C10
Chaddlehanger Devon	8	C9
Chaddleworth W Berk	34	D9
Chadlington Oxon	48	B10
Chadshunt Warwks	48	B4
Chadwell Leics	73	K6
Chadwell Shrops	57	P2
Chadwell End Bed	61	N7
Chadwell Heath Gt Lon	37	L3
Chadwell St Mary Thurr	37	P5
Chadwick Worcs	58	B11
Chadwick End Solhll	59	K10
Chadwick Green St Hel	82	B5
Chaffcombe Somset	10	H2
Chafford Hundred Thurr	37	P5
Chagford Devon	8	H7
Chailey E Susx	25	J7
Chainbridge Cambs	74	H10
Chainhurst Kent	26	B2
Chalbury Dorset	12	H3
Chalbury Common Dorset	12	H3
Chaldon Surrey	36	H9
Chaldon Herring Dorset	12	C8
Chale IoW	14	E11
Chale Green IoW	14	E11
Chalfont Common Bucks	36	B2
Chalfont St Giles Bucks	35	Q6
Chalfont St Peter Bucks	36	B2
Chalford Gloucs	32	G4
Chalford Oxon	35	K4
Chalford Wilts	20	G4
Chalgrave C Beds	50	B5
Chalgrove Oxon	34	H5
Chalk Kent	37	Q6
Chalk End Essex	51	P8
Chalkhouse Green Oxon	35	K9
Chalkway Somset	10	H3
Chalkwell Kent	38	E9
Challaborough Devon	6	H10
Challacombe Devon	17	M3
Challoch D & G	107	L4
Challock Kent	38	H11
Chalmington Dorset	11	M4
Chalton C Beds	50	B5
Chalton C Beds	61	P10
Chalton Hants	23	K11
Chalvey Slough	35	Q9
Chalvington E Susx	25	M9
Chambers Green Kent	26	F3
Chandler's Cross Herts	50	C11
Chandler's Cross Worcs	46	F2
Chandler's Ford Hants	22	D11
Channel's End Bed	61	P9
Channel Tunnel Terminal Kent	27	L4
Chantry Somset	20	D5
Chantry Suffk	53	K3
Chapel Cumb	100	H4
Chapel Fife	134	H9
Chapel Allerton Leeds	91	J3
Chapel Allerton Somset	19	M4
Chapel Amble Cnwll	4	F6
Chapel Brampton Nhants	60	F7
Chapelbridge Cambs	62	C2
Chapel Chorlton Staffs	70	E7
Chapel Cross E Susx	25	P6
Chapel End Bed	61	P9
Chapel End C Beds	50	C2
Chapel End Cambs	61	P4
Chapel End Warwks	59	M6
Chapelend Way Essex	52	B4
Chapel-en-le-Frith Derbys	83	N8
Chapel Field Bury	89	M9
Chapelgate Lincs	74	H6
Chapel Green Warwks	48	E2
Chapel Green Warwks	59	L7
Chapel Haddlesey N York	91	P5
Chapelhall N Lans	126	D5
Chapel Hill Abers	159	Q10
Chapel Hill Lincs	86	H10
Chapel Hill Mons	31	P5
Chapel Hill N York	97	M11
Chapelhope Border	117	J7
Chapelknowe D & G	110	F6
Chapel Lawn Shrops	56	E9
Chapel-le-Dale N York	95	Q5
Chapel Leigh Somset	18	F9
Chapel Milton Derbys	83	N8
Chapel of Garioch Abers	151	J3
Chapel Rossan D & G	106	F9
Chapel Row E Susx	25	P8
Chapel Row Essex	52	C11
Chapel Row W Berk	34	G11
Chapels Cumb	94	E4
Chapel St Leonards Lincs	87	Q6
Chapel Stile Cumb	101	K9
Chapelton Abers	151	M9
Chapelton Angus	143	L8
Chapelton Devon	17	K6
Chapelton S Lans	126	B8
Chapeltown Bl w D	89	L7
Chapel Town Cnwll	4	D10
Chapeltown Moray	149	N3
Chapeltown Sheff	91	K11
Chapmanslade Wilts	20	F5
Chapmans Well Devon	5	P3
Chapmore End Herts	50	H7
Chappel Essex	52	E6
Charaton Cnwll	5	N8
Chard Somset	10	G3
Chard Junction Somset	10	G4
Chardleigh Green Somset	10	G2
Chardstock Devon	10	G4
Charfield S Glos	32	D6
Chargrove Gloucs	46	H11
Charing Kent	26	G2
Charing Heath Kent	26	F2
Charing Hill Kent	38	G11
Charingworth Gloucs	47	N7
Charlbury Oxon	48	C11
Charlcombe BaNES	32	D11
Charlcutt Wilts	33	J9
Charlecote Warwks	47	Q3
Charlemont Sandw	58	F6
Charles Devon	17	M5
Charleshill Surrey	23	N6
Charleston Angus	142	F8
Charlestown C Aber	151	N7
Charlestown C Brad	90	F3
Charlestown Calder	90	B5
Charlestown Cnwll	3	Q3
Charlestown Cnwll	3	N3
Charlestown Derbys	83	M6
Charlestown Dorset	11	
Charlestown Fife	134	D11
Charlestown Highld	153	Q3
Charlestown Highld	156	A8
Charlestown Salfd	82	H4
Charlestown of Aberlour Moray	157	P9
Charles Tye Suffk	64	E11
Charlesworth Derbys	83	M6
Charlinch Somset	18	H7
Charlottetown Fife	134	H5
Charlton Gt Lon	37	K5
Charlton Hants	22	C5
Charlton Herts	50	E5
Charlton Nhants	48	F7
Charlton Nthumb	112	B4
Charlton Oxon	34	D7
Charlton Somset	19	J9
Charlton Somset	20	B6
Charlton Somset	20	C4
Charlton Surrey	36	C7
Charlton W Susx	15	N4
Charlton Wilts	20	H10
Charlton Wilts	33	J7
Charlton Worcs	47	K5
Charlton Worcs	58	B10
Charlton Wrekin	57	K2
Charlton Abbots Gloucs	47	K10
Charlton Adam Somset	19	P9
Charlton All Saints Wilts	21	N10
Charlton Down Dorset	11	P5
Charlton Hill Shrops	57	K3
Charlton Horethorne Somset	20	C10
Charlton Kings Gloucs	47	J10
Charlton Mackrell Somset	19	P9
Charlton Marshall Dorset	12	F4
Charlton Musgrove Somset	20	D9
Charlton-on-Otmoor Oxon	48	G11
Charlton on the Hill Dorset	12	E4
Charlton St Peter Wilts	21	M3
Charlwood Hants	23	J8
Charlwood Surrey	24	F2
Charminster Dorset	11	P6
Charmouth Dorset	10	H6
Charndon Bucks	49	J10
Charney Bassett Oxon	34	C6
Charnock Green Lancs	88	H7
Charnock Richard Lancs	88	H7
Charnock Richard Services Lancs	88	H7
Charsfield Suffk	65	K10
Chart Corner Kent	38	C11
Charter Alley Hants	22	G3
Charterhall Border	129	K10
Charterhouse Somset	19	N3
Chartershall Stirlg	133	M9
Charterville Allotments Oxon	34	B2
Chartham Kent	39	K11
Chartham Hatch Kent	39	K10
Chart Hill Kent	26	C2
Chartridge Bucks	35	P4
Chart Sutton Kent	26	D2
Chartway Street Kent	38	D11
Charvil Wokham	35	L9
Charwelton Nhants	60	B9
Chase Terrace Staffs	58	F3
Chasetown Staffs	58	F3
Chastleton Oxon	47	P9
Chasty Devon	16	E11
Chatburn Lancs	89	M2
Chatcull Staffs	70	D8
Chatham Caerph	30	H7
Chatham Medway	38	C8
Chatham Green Essex	52	B8
Chathill Nthumb	119	N5
Chatley Worcs	46	G2
Chatsworth House Derbys	84	C6
Chattenden Medway	38	C7
Chatter End Essex	51	L5
Chatteris Cambs	62	E3
Chatterton Lancs	89	M7
Chattisham Suffk	53	J3
Chatto Border	118	E7
Chatton Nthumb	119	L5
Chaul End C Beds	50	C6
Chawleigh Devon	17	N9
Chawley Oxon	34	E4
Chawston Bed	61	Q9
Chawton Hants	23	K7
Chaxhill Gloucs	32	D2
Chazey Heath Oxon	35	J9
Cheadle Staffs	71	J6
Cheadle Stockp	83	J7
Cheadle Heath Stockp	83	J7
Cheadle Hulme Stockp	83	J7
Cheam Gt Lon	36	F8
Cheapside W & M	35	P11
Chearsley Bucks	35	K2
Chebsey Staffs	70	F9
Checkendon Oxon	35	J8
Checkley Ches E	70	C5
Checkley Herefs	46	A7
Checkley Staffs	71	J7
Checkley Green Ches E	70	C5
Chedburgh Suffk	63	N9
Cheddar Somset	19	N4
Cheddington Bucks	49	P11
Cheddleton Staffs	70	H4
Cheddleton Heath Staffs	70	H4
Cheddon Fitzpaine Somset	18	H9
Chedglow Wilts	32	H6
Chedgrave Norfk	65	M2
Chedington Dorset	11	K3
Chediston Suffk	65	M6
Chediston Green Suffk	65	M6
Chedworth Gloucs	33	L2
Chedzoy Somset	19	K7
Cheeseman's Green Kent	26	H4
Cheetham Hill Manch	82	H4
Cheldon Devon	8	H2
Chelford Ches E	82	H10
Chellaston C Derb	72	B4
Chellington Bed	61	L9
Chelmarsh Shrops	57	N7
Chelmick Shrops	57	H6
Chelmondiston Suffk	53	M4
Chelmorton Derbys	83	P11
Chelmsford Essex	52	B10
Chelmsley Wood Solhll	59	J7
Chelsea Gt Lon	36	G5
Chelsfield Gt Lon	37	L8
Chelsham Surrey	37	J9
Chelston Somset	18	G10
Chelsworth Suffk	52	G2
Cheltenham Gloucs	46	H10
Chelveston Nhants	61	L7
Chelvey N Som	31	N11
Chelwood BaNES	20	B2
Chelwood Common E Susx	25	K5
Chelwood Gate E Susx	25	K4
Chelworth Wilts	33	J6
Chelworth Lower Green Wilts	33	L6
Chelworth Upper Green Wilts	33	L6
Cheney Longville Shrops	56	G8
Chenies Bucks	50	B11
Chepstow Mons	31	P6
Chequerbent Bolton	89	K9
Chequers Corner Norfk	75	J3
Cherhill Wilts	33	K10
Cherington Gloucs	32	H5
Cherington Warwks	47	Q7
Cheriton Devon	17	N2
Cheriton Hants	22	G9
Cheriton Kent	27	M4
Cheriton Pembks	41	J11
Cheriton Swans	28	E6
Cheriton Bishop Devon	9	J6
Cheriton Fitzpaine Devon	9	L3
Cherrington Wrekin	70	B11
Cherry Burton E R Yk	92	G2
Cherry Hinton Cambs	62	G9
Cherry Orchard Worcs	46	G4
Cherry Willingham Lincs	86	D6
Chertsey Surrey	36	B7
Cherwell Valley Services Oxon	48	F9
Cheselbourne Dorset	12	C5
Chesham Bucks	35	Q4
Chesham Bury	89	N8
Chesham Bois Bucks	35	Q5
Cheshunt Herts	51	J10
Chesil Beach Dorset	11	N9
Chesley Kent	38	E9
Cheslyn Hay Staffs	58	E3
Chessetts Wood Warwks	59	J10
Chessington Gt Lon	36	E8
Chessington World of Adventures Gt Lon	36	E8
Chester Ches W	81	N11
Chesterblade Somset	20	C6
Chesterfield Derbys	84	E6
Chesterfield Staffs	58	G3
Chesterhill Mdloth	128	B7
Chester-le-Street Dur	113	L10
Chester Moor Dur	113	L11
Chesters Border	118	B6
Chesters Border	118	B8
Chester Services Ches W	81	P11
Chesterton Cambs	62	G8
Chesterton Cambs	74	B11
Chesterton Gloucs	33	K4
Chesterton Oxon	48	G10
Chesterton Shrops	57	P5
Chesterton Staffs	70	E5
Chesterton Green Warwks	48	C3
Chesterwood Nthumb	112	B7
Chester Zoo Ches W	81	N10
Chestfield Kent	39	K8
Chestnut Street Kent	38	E9
Cheston Devon	6	H7
Cheswardine Shrops	70	C8
Cheswick Nthumb	129	Q10
Cheswick Green Solhll	58	H9
Chetnole Dorset	11	N3
Chettiscombe Devon	9	J2
Chettisham Cambs	62	H4
Chettle Dorset	12	G2
Chetton Shrops	57	M6
Chetwode Bucks	48	H9
Chetwynd Wrekin	70	C10
Chetwynd Aston Wrekin	70	D11
Cheveley Cambs	63	L8
Chevening Kent	37	L9
Cheverton IoW	14	E10
Chevington Suffk	63	N9
Cheviot Hills	118	E9
Chevithorne Devon	18	C11
Chew Magna BaNES	19	Q2
Chew Moor Bolton	89	K9
Chew Stoke BaNES	19	Q2
Chewton Keynsham BaNES	32	C11
Chewton Mendip Somset	19	Q4
Chicacott Devon	8	F5
Chicheley M Keyn	49	P5
Chichester W Susx	15	N6
Chickerell Dorset	11	N8
Chickering Suffk	65	J6
Chicklade Wilts	20	H8
Chicksands C Beds	50	D3
Chickward Herefs	45	K4
Chidden Hants	23	J11
Chiddingfold Surrey	23	Q7
Chiddingly E Susx	25	M8
Chiddingstone Kent	25	M2
Chiddingstone Causeway Kent	37	M11
Chiddingstone Hoath Kent	25	L2
Chideock Dorset	11	J6
Chidham W Susx	15	L6
Chidswell Kirk	90	H6
Chieveley W Berk	34	E10
Chieveley Services W Berk	34	E10
Chignall St James Essex	51	Q8
Chignall Smealy Essex	51	Q8
Chigwell Essex	37	K2
Chigwell Row Essex	37	L2
Chilbolton Hants	22	C6
Chilcomb Hants	22	F9
Chilcombe Dorset	11	L6
Chilcompton Somset	20	B4
Chilcote Leics	59	L2
Child Thornton Ches W	81	M9
Child Okeford Dorset	12	D2
Childrey Oxon	34	C7
Child's Ercall Shrops	70	B9
Childswickham Worcs	47	L7
Childwall Lpool	81	N7
Childwick Bury Herts	50	D8
Childwick Green Herts	50	D8
Chilfrome Dorset	11	M5
Chilgrove W Susx	15	M4
Chilham Kent	39	J11
Chilla Devon	8	B4
Chillaton Devon	8	B8
Chillenden Kent	39	N11
Chillerton IoW	14	E10
Chillesford Suffk	65	M11
Chillingham Nthumb	119	L5
Chillington Devon	7	K10
Chillington Somset	10	H2
Chilmark Wilts	21	J8
Chilmington Green Kent	26	G3
Chilson Oxon	48	B11
Chilsworthy Cnwll	5	Q7
Chilsworthy Devon	16	E10
Chiltern Green C Beds	50	D7
Chiltern Hills	35	L5
Chilthorne Domer Somset	19	P11
Chilton Bucks	35	J2
Chilton Devon	9	L4
Chilton Dur	103	Q5
Chilton Kent	27	N3
Chilton Oxon	34	E7
Chilton Suffk	52	E3
Chilton Candover Hants	22	G6
Chilton Cantelo Somset	19	Q10
Chilton Foliat Wilts	34	B10
Chilton Polden Somset	19	L6
Chilton Street Suffk	63	N11
Chilton Trinity Somset	19	J7
Chilwell Notts	72	E3
Chilworth Hants	22	D11
Chilworth Surrey	36	B11
Chimney Oxon	34	C4
Chineham Hants	23	J3
Chingford Gt Lon	37	J2
Chinley Derbys	83	M8
Chinnor Oxon	35	L4
Chipchase Castle Nthumb	112	C5
Chipnall Shrops	70	C8
Chippenham Cambs	63	L7
Chippenham Wilts	32	H10
Chipperfield Herts	50	B10
Chipping Herts	51	J4
Chipping Lancs	89	J2
Chipping Campden Gloucs	47	N7
Chipping Hill Essex	52	D8
Chipping Norton Oxon	48	B9
Chipping Ongar Essex	51	N10
Chipping Sodbury S Glos	32	D8
Chipping Warden Nhants	48	E5
Chipshop Devon	8	B9
Chipstable Somset	18	D9
Chipstead Kent	37	M9
Chipstead Surrey	36	G9
Chirbury Shrops	56	D5
Chirk Wrexhm	69	J7
Chirnside Border	129	M8
Chirnsidebridge Border	129	M8
Chirton Wilts	21	L3
Chisbury Wilts	33	Q11
Chiselborough Somset	11	K2
Chiseldon Swindn	33	N8
Chiselhampton Oxon	34	G5
Chisholme Border	117	N8
Chislehurst Gt Lon	37	K6
Chislet Kent	39	M9
Chisley Calder	90	C5
Chiswell Green Herts	50	D10
Chiswick Gt Lon	36	F5
Chiswick End Cambs	62	E11
Chisworth Derbys	83	L6
Chitcombe E Susx	26	D7
Chithurst W Susx	23	M10
Chittering Cambs	62	G7
Chitterne Wilts	21	J6
Chittlehamholt Devon	17	M7
Chittlehampton Devon	17	L6
Chittoe Wilts	33	J11
Chivelstone Devon	7	K11
Chivenor Devon	17	J5
Chlenry D & G	106	F5
Chobham Surrey	23	Q2
Cholderton Wilts	21	P6
Cholesbury Bucks	35	P3
Chollerford Nthumb	112	D6
Chollerton Nthumb	112	D6
Cholmondeston Ches E	70	A3
Cholsey Oxon	34	G7
Cholstrey Herefs	45	P3
Chop Gate N York	104	G11
Choppington Nthumb	113	L4
Chopwell Gatesd	112	H9
Chorley Ches E	69	Q4
Chorley Lancs	88	H7
Chorley Shrops	57	M8
Chorley Staffs	58	G2
Chorleywood Herts	50	B11
Chorleywood West Herts	50	B11
Chorlton Ches E	70	C4
Chorlton-cum-Hardy Manch	82	H6
Chorlton Lane Ches W	69	N5
Choulton Shrops	56	F7
Chowley Ches W	69	N3
Chrishall Essex	51	K3
Chrisswell Inver	124	G3
Christchurch BCP	13	L6
Christchurch Cambs	75	J11
Christchurch Gloucs	31	Q2
Christchurch Newpt	31	K7
Christian Malford Wilts	33	J9
Christleton Ches W	81	N11
Christmas Common Oxon	35	K6
Christmas Pie Surrey	23	P5
Christon N Som	19	L3
Christon Bank Nthumb	119	P6
Christow Devon	9	K7
Christ's Hospital W Susx	24	D5
Chuck Hatch E Susx	25	L4
Chudleigh Devon	9	L9
Chudleigh Knighton Devon	9	K9
Chulmleigh Devon	17	M9
Chunal Derbys	83	M6
Church Lancs	89	L5
Churcham Gloucs	46	E11
Church Aston Wrekin	70	C11
Church Brampton Nhants	60	F7
Church Brough Cumb	102	E8
Church Broughton Derbys	71	N8
Church Cove Cnwll	3	J11
Church Crookham Hants	23	M4
Churchdown Gloucs	46	G11
Church Eaton Staffs	70	E11
Church End Bed	61	N9
Church End Bed	61	N9
Church End Bucks	35	K3
Church End C Beds	49	Q10
Church End C Beds	49	Q8
Church End C Beds	50	B4
Church End C Beds	50	B7
Church End C Beds	50	E3

Church End C Beds 61 Q10
Church End Cambs 61 N6
Church End Cambs 62 B4
Church End Cambs 62 D5
Churchend Essex 38 H3
Church End Essex 51 P6
Church End Essex 52 B6
Church End Essex 52 B8
Church End Gloucs 46 G7
Church End Gt Lon 36 F2
Church End Herts 50 D8
Church End Herts 50 G4
Church End Herts 51 K6
Church End Lincs 74 D4
Church End Lincs 93 R11
Church End Warwks 59 K6
Church End Warwks 59 L6
Church Enstone Oxon 48 C9
Church Fenton N York 91 N3
Churchfield Sandw 58 F6
Churchgate Herts 50 H10
Churchgate Street Essex 51 L8
Church Green Devon 10 D5
Church Gresley Derbys 71 P11
Church Hanborough Oxon 34 D2
Church Hill Staffs 58 F2
Church Houses N York 105 J11
Churchill Devon 10 F4
Churchill Devon 17 K3
Churchill N Som 19 M3
Churchill Oxon 47 Q10
Churchill Worcs 46 H4
Churchill Worcs 58 C9
Churchinford Somset 10 E2
Church Knowle Dorset 12 F8
Church Laneham Notts 85 P5
Church Langton Leics 60 F2
Church Lawford Warwks 59 Q9
Church Lawton Ches E 70 E3
Church Leigh Staffs 71 J7
Church Lench Worcs 47 K4
Church Mayfield Staffs 71 M6
Church Minshull Ches E 70 B2
Church Norton W Susx 15 N7
Churchover Warwks 60 B4
Church Preen Shrops 57 J5
Church Pulverbatch Shrops 56 G4
Churchstanton Somset 10 D2
Churchstoke Powys 56 D6
Churchstow Devon 7 J9
Church Stowe Nhants 60 D9
Church Street Essex 52 C3
Church Street Kent 38 B7
Church Street Kent 65 P6
Church Stretton Shrops 56 H6
Churchthorpe Lincs 93 P11
Churchtown Bpool 88 C2
Churchtown Cnwll 4 H6
Churchtown Derbys 84 C8
Churchtown Devon 17 M3
Churchtown IoM 80 f3
Churchtown Lancs 88 F2
Church Town N Linc 92 C9
Churchtown Sefton 88 D7
Church Village Rhondd 30 E7
Church Warsop Notts 85 J7
Church Wilne Derbys 72 C4
Churnsike Lodge Nthumb 111 N5
Churston Ferrers Torbay 7 N7
Churt Surrey 23 N7
Churton Ches W 69 M3
Churwell Leeds 90 H5
Chwilog Gwynd 66 G7
Chyandour Cnwll 2 D7
Chyanvounder Cnwll 2 H9
Chyeowling Cnwll 3 K5
Chyvarloe Cnwll 2 H9
Cil Powys 56 B4
Cilcain Flints 80 H11
Cilcennin Cerdgn 43 K2
Cilcewydd Powys 56 C4
Cilfrew Neath 29 L4
Cilfynydd Rhondd 30 E6
Cilgerran Pembks 41 N2
Cilgwyn Carmth 43 P9
Cilgwyn Gwynd 66 H4
Ciliau-Aeron Cerdgn 43 K3
Cilmaengwyn Neath 29 K3
Cilmery Powys 44 E4
Cilrhedyn Pembks 41 Q4
Cilsan Carmth 43 L10
Ciltalgarth Gwynd 68 A6
Cilycwm Carmth 43 Q2
Cimla Neath 29 L5
Cinderford Gloucs 32 C2
Cinder Hill Wolves 58 D6
Cippenham Slough 35 Q8
Cirencester Gloucs 33 K4
Citadilla N York 103 P11
City Gt Lon 36 H4
City V Glam 30 C9
City Airport Gt Lon 37 K4
City Dulas IoA 78 H7
Clabhach Ag & B 136 F4
Clachaig Ag & B 131 N11
Clachaig Inn Highld 139 L6
Clachan Ag & B 123 N8
Clachan Ag & B 130 F4
Clachan Ag & B 131 M7
Clachan Ag & B 138 F9
Clachan Highld 153 J10
Clachan-a-Luib W Isls 168 d11
Clachan Mor Ag & B 136 B6
Clachan na Luib W Isls 168 d11
Clachan of Campsie E Duns 125 Q2
Clachan-Seil Ag & B 130 F4
Clachnaharry Highld 156 A8
Clachtoll Highld 164 B11
Clackavoid Ag & B 142 K4
Clacket Lane Services
  Surrey 37 K10
Clackmannan Clacks 133 Q9
Clackmannanshire Bridge
  Fife 133 Q10
Clackmarras Moray 157 N6
Clacton-on-Sea Essex 53 L8
Cladich Ag & B 131 M3
Cladswell Worcs 47 L3
Claggan Highld 138 C8
Claigan Highld 152 C7
Clandown BaNES 20 C3
Clanfield Hants 23 J11
Clanfield Oxon 33 Q4
Clannaborough Devon 8 H4
Clanville Hants 22 B5

Clanville Somset 20 B8
Claonaig Ag & B 123 Q8
Clapgate Dorset 12 H4
Clapgate Herts 51 K6
Clapham Bed 61 M10
Clapham Devon 9 L7
Clapham Gt Lon 36 G5
Clapham N York 95 Q7
Clapham W Susx 24 C9
Clapham Green Bed 61 M10
Clappersgate Cumb 101 L10
Clapton Somset 11 J3
Clapton Somset 20 B4
Clapton-in-Gordano N Som 31 N10
Clapton-on-the-Hill Gloucs 47 M10
Clapworthy Devon 17 M7
Clarach Cerdgn 54 E8
Clarbeston Pembks 41 L6
Clarbeston Road Pembks 41 K6
Clarborough Notts 85 M4
Clare Suffk 63 N11
Clarebrand D & G 108 G7
Clarencefield D & G 109 N7
Clarewood Nthumb 112 F7
Clarilaw Border 117 Q7
Clark's Green Surrey 24 E3
Clarkston E Rens 125 P6
Clashmore Highld 162 G9
Clashmore Highld 164 B10
Clashnessie Highld 164 C10
Clashnoir Moray 149 N3
Clathy P & K 134 B3
Clathymore P & K 134 C3
Clatt Abers 150 E2
Clatter Powys 55 M6
Clatterford End Essex 51 P8
Clatworthy Somset 18 E8
Claughton Lancs 88 G2
Claughton Lancs 95 M7
Claughton Wirral 81 L7
Clavelshay Somset 19 J8
Claverdon Warwks 59 J11
Claverham N Som 31 N11
Clavering Essex 51 L4
Claverley Shrops 57 P6
Claverton BaNES 20 E2
Claverton Down BaNES 20 E2
Clawdd-coch V Glam 30 E9
Clawdd-newydd Denbgs 68 E4
Clawthorpe Cumb 95 L5
Clawton Devon 5 P2
Claxby Lincs 86 F2
Claxby Lincs 87 N6
Claxton N York 98 D9
Claxton Norfk 77 L11
Claybrooke Magna Leics 59 Q7
Clay Common Suffk 65 P5
Clay Coton Nhants 60 C5
Clay Cross Derbys 84 E8
Claydon Oxon 48 E5
Claydon Suffk 53 K2
Clay End Herts 50 H6
Claygate D & G 110 G5
Claygate Kent 26 B3
Claygate Surrey 36 E8
Claygate Cross Kent 37 P9
Clayhall Gt Lon 37 K2
Clayhanger Devon 18 D10
Clayhanger Wsall 58 F4
Clayhidon Devon 18 G11
Clayhill E Susx 26 D7
Clayhithe Cambs 62 H8
Clayock Highld 167 L5
Claypit Hill Cambs 62 E10
Claypits Gloucs 32 E3
Claypole Lincs 85 P11
Claythorpe Lincs 87 M5
Clayton C Brad 90 E4
Clayton Donc 91 M9
Clayton W Susx 24 G8
Clayton Green Lancs 88 H6
Clayton-le-Moors Lancs 89 M4
Clayton-le-Woods Lancs 88 H6
Clayton West Kirk 90 H8
Clayworth Notts 85 M3
Cleadale Highld 144 G10
Cleadon S Tyne 113 N8
Clearbrook Devon 6 E5
Clearwell Gloucs 31 Q3
Cleasby N York 103 Q8
Cleat Ork 169 d8
Cleatlam Dur 103 M7
Cleator Cumb 100 D8
Cleator Moor Cumb 100 D7
Cleckheaton Kirk 90 F5
Cleedownton Shrops 57 K8
Cleehill Shrops 57 K9
Cleekhimin N Lans 126 D6
Clee St Margaret Shrops 57 K8
Cleestanton Shrops 57 K9
Cleethorpes NE Lin 93 P9
Cleeton St Mary Shrops 57 L9
Cleeve N Som 31 N11
Cleeve Oxon 34 H8
Cleeve Hill Gloucs 47 J9
Cleeve Prior Worcs 47 L5
Cleghornie E Loth 128 F3
Clehonger Herefs 45 N7
Cleish P & K 134 D8
Cleland N Lans 126 D6
Clement's End C Beds 50 B8
Clement Street Kent 37 M6
Clenamacrie Ag & B 131 J2
Clench Common Wilts 33 N11
Clenchwarton Norfk 75 L6
Clenerty Abers 159 J5
Clent Worcs 58 D9
Cleobury Mortimer Shrops 57 M9
Cleobury North Shrops 57 L7
Cleongart Ag & B 120 C5
Clephanton Highld 156 E7
Clerkhill D & G 117 K11
Cleuch-head D & G 115 R7
Clevancy Wilts 33 L9
Clevedon N Som 31 M10
Cleveley Oxon 48 C10
Cleveleys Lancs 88 C2
Cleverton Wilts 33 J7
Clewer Somset 19 M4
Cley next the Sea Norfk 76 E3
Cliburn Cumb 101 Q6
Cliddesden Hants 22 H5

Cliff Warwks 59 K5
Cliffe Lancs 89 L4
Cliffe Medway 38 B6
Cliffe N York 91 R4
Cliffe N York 103 P7
Cliff End E Susx 26 E9
Cliffe Woods Medway 38 B7
Clifford Herefs 45 J5
Clifford Leeds 91 L2
Clifford Chambers Warwks 47 N4
Clifford's Mesne Gloucs 46 D10
Cliffsend Kent 39 P9
Clifton Bristl 31 Q10
Clifton C Beds 50 E3
Clifton C Nott 72 E4
Clifton C York 98 B9
Clifton Calder 90 F6
Clifton Cumb 101 P5
Clifton Derbys 71 M10
Clifton Devon 17 L3
Clifton Donc 91 N11
Clifton Lancs 88 F4
Clifton Nthumb 113 K4
Clifton Oxon 48 E8
Clifton Salfd 82 G4
Clifton Worcs 46 F5
Clifton Campville Staffs 59 L2
Clifton Hampden Oxon 34 F5
Clifton Reynes M Keyn 49 P4
Clifton upon Dunsmore
  Warwks 60 B5
Clifton upon Teme Worcs 46 D2
Cliftonville Kent 39 Q7
Climping W Susx 15 Q6
Clink Somset 20 E5
Clint N York 97 L9
Clinterty C Aber 151 L5
Clint Green Norfk 76 E9
Clintmains Border 118 B4
Clipiau Gwynd 55 J2
Clippesby Norfk 77 N9
Clipsham Rutlnd 73 P7
Clipston Nhants 60 F4
Clipston Notts 72 G4
Clipstone C Beds 49 P9
Clipstone Notts 85 J8
Clitheroe Lancs 89 L2
Clive Shrops 69 P10
Clixby Lincs 93 J10
Cloatley Wilts 33 J6
Clocaenog Denbgs 68 E4
Clochan Moray 158 B5
Clock Face St Hel 82 B6
Cloddiau Powys 56 C3
Clodock Herefs 45 L9
Cloford Somset 20 D6
Clola Abers 159 P9
Clophill C Beds 50 C3
Clopton Nhants 61 N4
Clopton Suffk 65 J11
Clopton Corner Suffk 65 J11
Clopton Green Suffk 63 N10
Clopton Green Suffk 64 D10
Clos du Valle Guern 10 c1
Closeburn D & G 109 J2
Closeburnmill D & G 109 K2
Closeclark IoM 80 c6
Closworth Somset 11 M2
Clothall Herts 50 G4
Clotton Ches W 69 P2
Cloudesley Bush Warwks 59 Q7
Clouds Herefs 46 A7
Clough Oldham 89 Q9
Clough Foot Calder 89 Q6
Clough Head Calder 90 D7
Cloughton N York 99 L2
Cloughton Newlands N York 105 R11
Clousta Shet 169 q8
Clova Angus 142 E3
Clovelly Devon 16 E7
Clovenfords Border 117 P3
Clovulin Highld 139 J5
Clow Bridge Lancs 89 N5
Clowne Derbys 84 G5
Clows Top Worcs 57 N10
Cloy Wrexhm 69 L6
Cluanie Inn Highld 146 D5
Cluanie Lodge Highld 146 D5
Clubworthy Cnwll 5 M3
Clugston D & G 107 L6
Clun Shrops 56 F8
Clunas Highld 156 F8
Clunbury Shrops 56 F8
Clunderwen Carmth 41 M7
Clune Highld 148 D2
Clunes Highld 146 F10
Clungunford Shrops 56 F9
Clunie P & K 141 R9
Clunton Shrops 56 F8
Cluny Fife 134 G8
Clutton BaNES 20 B3
Clutton Ches W 69 N4
Clutton Hill BaNES 20 B3
Clwt-y-bont Gwynd 67 K2
Clydach Mons 30 H2
Clydach Swans 29 J4
Clydach Vale Rhondd 30 C6
Clydebank W Duns 125 M3
Clydey Pembks 41 Q3
Clyffe Pypard Wilts 33 L9
Clynder Ag & B 131 Q11
Clyne Neath 29 M4
Clynnog Fawr Gwynd 66 G5
Clyro Powys 45 J6
Clyst Honiton Devon 9 N6
Clyst Hydon Devon 9 P4
Clyst St George Devon 9 N7
Clyst St Lawrence Devon 9 P4
Clyst St Mary Devon 9 N6
Cnoc W Isls 168 j4
Cnwch Coch Cerdgn 54 F10
Coad's Green Cnwll 5 M6
Coal Aston Derbys 84 E5
Coalbrookvale Blae G 30 G3
Coalburn S Lans 126 E11
Coalburns Gatesd 112 H8
Coaley Gloucs 32 E4
Coalhill Essex 38 C2
Coalmoor Wrekin 57 M3
Coalpit Heath S Glos 32 C8
Coal Pool Wsall 58 F5
Coalport Wrekin 57 M4
Coalsnaughton Clacks 133 Q8

Coal Street Suffk 65 J7
Coaltown of Balgonie Fife 134 H8
Coaltown of Wemyss Fife 135 J8
Coalville Leics 72 C8
Coanwood Nthumb 111 N9
Coat Somset 19 N10
Coatbridge N Lans 126 C4
Coatdyke N Lans 126 C4
Coate Swindn 33 N8
Coate Wilts 21 N4
Coates Cambs 74 F11
Coates Gloucs 33 G4
Coates Lincs 86 B4
Coates Notts 85 P4
Coates W Susx 23 Q11
Coatham R & Cl 104 G5
Coatham Mundeville Darltn 103 Q6
Cobbaton Devon 17 L6
Coberley Gloucs 47 J11
Cobhall Common Herefs 45 P7
Cobham Kent 37 Q7
Cobham Surrey 36 D8
Cobham Services Surrey 36 D9
Cobley Dorset 21 K10
Cobnash Herefs 45 P2
Cobo Guern 10 b1
Cobridge C Stke 70 F5
Coburby Abers 159 M5
Cockayne N York 104 H11
Cockayne Hatley C Beds 62 C11
Cock Bank Wrexhm 69 L5
Cock Bevington Warwks 47 L4
Cock Bridge Abers 149 P6
Cockburnspath Border 129 K5
Cock Clarks Essex 52 D11
Cock & End Suffk 63 M10
Cockenzie and Port Seton
  E Loth 128 C4
Cocker Bar Lancs 88 G6
Cocker Brook Lancs 89 L5
Cockerham Lancs 95 K10
Cockermouth Cumb 100 F4
Cockernhoe Herts 50 D6
Cockersdale Leeds 90 G5
Cockett Swans 28 H6
Cockfield Dur 103 M6
Cockfield Suffk 64 C11
Cockfosters Gt Lon 50 G11
Cock Green Essex 51 Q7
Cocking W Susx 23 N11
Cocking Causeway W Susx 23 N11
Cockington Torbay 7 M6
Cocklake Somset 19 M5
Cockley Beck Cumb 100 H11
Cockley Cley Norfk 75 Q10
Cock Marling E Susx 26 E8
Cockpole Green Wokham 35 L8
Cocks Cnwll 3 K3
Cockshutford Shrops 57 K7
Cockshutt Shrops 69 M9
Cock Street Kent 38 C11
Cockthorpe Norfk 76 D3
Cockwells Cnwll 2 E7
Cockwood Devon 9 N8
Cockwood Somset 18 H6
Cockyard Derbys 83 M9
Cockyard Herefs 45 N8
Coddenham Suffk 64 G11
Coddington Ches W 69 N3
Coddington Herefs 46 D6
Coddington Notts 85 P10
Codford St Mary Wilts 21 J7
Codford St Peter Wilts 21 J7
Codicote Herts 50 F7
Codmore Hill W Susx 24 C6
Codnor Derbys 84 F11
Codrington S Glos 32 D9
Codsall Staffs 58 C4
Codsall Wood Staffs 58 B4
Coedely Rhondd 30 D7
Coed Hirwaun Neath 29 M8
Coedkernew Newpt 31 J8
Coed Morgan Mons 31 L2
Coedpoeth Wrexhm 69 J4
Coed Talon Flints 69 J3
Coedway Powys 69 K11
Coed-y-Bryn Cerdgn 42 G5
Coed-y-caerau Newpt 31 L6
Coed-y-Cwm Rhondd 30 E6
Coed-y-paen Mons 31 K5
Coed-yr-ynys Powys 44 H10
Coed Ystumgwern Gwynd 67 K10
Coelbren Powys 29 N2
Coffinswell Devon 7 M5
Coffle End Bed 61 M9
Cofton Devon 9 N8
Cofton Hackett Worcs 58 F9
Cogan V Glam 30 G10
Cogenhoe Nhants 60 H8
Cogges Oxon 34 C3
Coggeshall Essex 52 E7
Coggin's Mill E Susx 25 N5
Coignafearn Highld 148 C4
Coilacriech Abers 149 Q8
Coilantogle Stirlg 132 H6
Coillore Highld 152 F10
Coity Brdgnd 29 P8
Col W Isls 168 j4
Colaboll Highld 162 D4
Colan Cnwll 4 D9
Colaton Raleigh Devon 10 B7
Colbost Highld 152 C8
Colburn N York 103 N11
Colby Cumb 102 C6
Colby IoM 80 b7
Colby Norfk 77 J5
Colchester Essex 52 H6
Colchester Zoo Essex 52 G7
Cold Ash W Berk 34 F11
Cold Ashby Nhants 60 E5
Cold Ashton S Glos 32 E10
Cold Aston Gloucs 47 M11
Coldbackie Highld 165 P4
Cold Blow Pembks 41 M8
Cold Brayfield M Keyn 49 P4
Cold Cotes N York 95 Q6
Coldean Br & H 24 H9
Coldeast Devon 7 L3
Colden Calder 90 B5
Colden Common Hants 22 E10
Coldfair Green Suffk 65 N9
Coldham Cambs 74 H10

Cold Hanworth Lincs 86 D4
Coldharbour Cnwll 3 K4
Coldharbour Devon 9 Q2
Coldharbour Gloucs 31 Q4
Cold Harbour Herts 50 D7
Cold Harbour Oxon 34 H9
Coldharbour Surrey 24 D2
Cold Hatton Wrekin 70 A10
Cold Hatton Heath Wrekin 70 A10
Cold Hesledon Dur 113 P11
Cold Higham Nhants 49 J4
Coldingham Border 129 M6
Cold Kirby N York 98 A4
Coldmeece Staffs 70 F8
Cold Newton Leics 73 J9
Cold Northcott Cnwll 5 L4
Cold Norton Essex 52 E11
Cold Overton Leics 73 L8
Coldred Kent 27 N2
Coldridge Devon 17 M10
Coldstream Border 118 F3
Coldwaltham W Susx 24 B7
Coldwell Herefs 45 N7
Coldwells Abers 159 N10
Cold Weston Shrops 57 K8
Cole Somset 20 C8
Colebatch Shrops 56 E7
Colebrook C Plym 6 E7
Colebrook Devon 9 P3
Colebrooke Devon 9 J5
Coleby Lincs 86 C8
Coleby N Linc 92 E7
Cole End Warwks 59 K7
Coleford Devon 9 J4
Coleford Gloucs 31 Q2
Coleford Somset 20 C5
Coleford Water Somset 18 E8
Colegate End Norfk 64 H4
Cole Green Herts 50 G8
Cole Green Herts 51 J5
Cole Henley Hants 22 E4
Colehill Dorset 12 H4
Coleman Green Herts 50 E8
Coleman's Hatch E Susx 25 K4
Colemere Shrops 69 M8
Colemore Hants 23 K8
Colemore Green Shrops 57 N5
Colenden P & K 134 E2
Coleorton Leics 72 C7
Colerne Wilts 32 F10
Colesbourne Gloucs 33 K2
Cole's Cross Devon 7 K9
Coles Cross Dorset 10 H4
Colesden Bed 61 P9
Coles Green Suffk 53 K3
Coleshill Bucks 35 P5
Coleshill Oxon 33 P6
Coleshill Warwks 59 K7
Colestocks Devon 10 B4
Coley BaNES 19 Q3
Colgate W Susx 24 F4
Colinsburgh Fife 135 M7
Colinton C Edin 127 N4
Colintraive Ag & B 124 C3
Colkirk Norfk 76 C6
Coll Ag & B 136 G4
Coll W Isls 168 j4
Collace P & K 142 C11
Collafirth Shet 169 q5
Coll Airport Ag & B 136 F4
Collaton Devon 7 J11
Collaton St Mary Torbay 7 M6
College of Roseisle Moray 157 L4
College Town Br For 23 N2
Collessie Fife 134 H5
Colleton Mills Devon 17 M8
Collier Row Gt Lon 37 M2
Collier's End Herts 51 J6
Collier's Green E Susx 26 C4
Colliers Green Kent 26 C4
Collier Street Kent 26 B2
Colliery Row Sundld 113 M11
Collieston Abers 151 Q2
Collin D & G 109 M5
Collingbourne Ducis Wilts 21 P4
Collingbourne Kingston
  Wilts 21 P3
Collingham Leeds 97 N11
Collingham Notts 85 P9
Collington Herefs 46 B2
Collingtree Nhants 60 G9
Collins Green Warrtn 82 C6
Collins Green Worcs 46 D3
Colliston Angus 143 L8
Colliton Devon 10 B4
Collyweston Nhants 73 P10
Colmonell S Ayrs 114 B10
Colmworth Bed 61 P9
Colnabaichin Abers 149 P6
Colnbrook Slough 36 B5
Colne Cambs 62 E5
Colne Lancs 89 P3
Colne Bridge Kirk 90 F6
Colne Edge Lancs 89 P2
Colne Engaine Essex 52 D5
Colney Norfk 76 H10
Colney Heath Herts 50 F9
Colney Street Herts 50 E10
Coln Rogers Gloucs 33 L3
Coln St Aldwyns Gloucs 33 M3
Coln St Dennis Gloucs 33 L2
Colonsay Ag & B 136 b2
Colonsay Airport Ag & B 136 b3
Colpy Abers 158 F11
Colquhar Border 117 J2
Colquite Cnwll 4 H7
Colscott Devon 16 G9
Colsterdale N York 96 H4
Colsterworth Lincs 73 N6
Colston Bassett Notts 72 H4
Coltfield Moray 157 L5
Colt Hill Hants 23 L4
Coltishall Norfk 77 K8
Colton Cumb 94 G3
Colton Leeds 91 K4
Colton N York 91 N2
Colton Norfk 76 G10
Colton Staffs 71 J9
Colt's Hill Kent 25 P2
Columbjohn Devon 9 N5
Colva Powys 44 H4
Colvend Border 109 J10
Colwall Herefs 46 E6
Colwell Nthumb 112 E5

Colwich Staffs 71 J10
Colwick Notts 72 G2
Colwinston V Glam 29 P9
Colworth W Susx 15 P6
Colwyn Bay Conwy 80 B9
Colyford Devon 10 F6
Colyton Devon 10 E6
Combe Devon 7 J11
Combe Herefs 45 L2
Combe Oxon 48 D11
Combe W Berk 22 C2
Combe Almer Dorset 12 G5
Combe Down BaNES 20 E2
Combe Fishacre Devon 7 L5
Combe Florey Somset 18 G8
Combe Hay BaNES 20 D3
Combeinteignhead Devon 7 N4
Combe Martin Devon 17 K2
Combe Raleigh Devon 10 D4
Comberbach Ches W 82 D9
Comberford Staffs 59 J3
Comberton Cambs 62 E9
Comberton Herefs 56 H11
Combe St Nicholas Somset 10 G2
Combpyne Devon 10 F6
Combridge Staffs 71 K7
Combrook Warwks 48 B4
Combs Derbys 83 M9
Combs Suffk 64 E10
Combs Ford Suffk 64 E10
Combwich Somset 19 J6
Comers Abers 150 H6
Comhampton Worcs 58 B11
Commercial End Cambs 63 J8
Commins Coch Powys 55 J4
Commondale N York 105 J8
Common Edge Bpool 88 C4
Common End Cumb 100 D6
Common Moor Cnwll 5 L8
Common Platt Wilts 33 M7
Commonside Ches W 82 B10
Commonside Derbys 71 N6
Common Side Derbys 84 D5
Commonwood Wrexhm 69 L4
Compass Somset 19 J8
Compstall Stockp 83 L6
Compstonend D & G 108 E10
Compton Devon 7 M6
Compton Hants 22 B9
Compton Hants 22 E9
Compton Staffs 57 Q8
Compton Surrey 23 Q5
Compton W Berk 34 F8
Compton W Susx 15 L4
Compton Wilts 21 M4
Compton Abbas Dorset 20 G11
Compton Bassett Wilts 33 K10
Compton Beauchamp Oxon 33 Q7
Compton Bishop Somset 19 L3
Compton Chamberlayne Wilts 21 K9
Compton Dando BaNES 20 B2
Compton Dundon Somset 19 N8
Compton Durville Somset 19 M11
Compton Greenfield S Glos 31 Q8
Compton Martin BaNES 19 P3
Compton Pauncefoot Somset 20 B9
Compton Valence Dorset 11 M6
Comrie Fife 134 C10
Comrie P & K 133 M3
Conaglen House Highld 139 J4
Conchra Highld 145 Q2
Concraigie P & K 141 Q9
Conder Green Lancs 95 K9
Conderton Worcs 47 J7
Condicote Gloucs 47 N9
Condorrat N Lans 126 C3
Condover Shrops 56 H3
Coney Hill Gloucs 46 G11
Coneyhurst Common W Susx 24 D6
Coneysthorpe N York 98 E6
Coneythorpe N York 97 N9
Coney Weston Suffk 64 D6
Conford Hants 23 M8
Congdon's Shop Cnwll 5 M6
Congerstone Leics 72 B9
Congham Norfk 75 P6
Congleton Ches E 70 F2
Congl-y-wal Gwynd 67 N6
Congresbury N Som 19 M2
Congreve Staffs 58 D2
Conheath D & G 109 L7
Conicavel Moray 156 H7
Coningsby Lincs 86 H9
Conington Cambs 61 Q3
Conington Cambs 62 D7
Conisbrough Donc 91 N11
Conisholme Lincs 93 R11
Coniston Cumb 101 K11
Coniston E R Yk 93 L3
Coniston Cold N York 96 D10
Conistone N York 96 E7
Connah's Quay Flints 81 K11
Connel Ag & B 138 G11
Connel Park E Ayrs 115 M5
Connor Downs Cnwll 2 F6
Conon Bridge Highld 155 P6
Cononley N York 96 E11
Consall Staffs 70 H5
Consett Dur 112 H10
Constable Burton N York 97 J2
Constable Lee Lancs 89 N6
Constantine Cnwll 3 J8
Constantine Bay Cnwll 4 D7
Contin Highld 155 N6
Conwy Conwy 79 P9
Conwy Castle Conwy 79 P9
Conyer Kent 38 G9
Conyer's Green Suffk 64 B8
Cooden E Susx 26 B10
Cookbury Devon 16 G10
Cookbury Wick Devon 16 F10
Cookham W & M 35 N7
Cookham Dean W & M 35 N7
Cookham Rise W & M 35 N7
Cookhill Worcs 47 L3
Cookley Suffk 65 L6
Cookley Worcs 58 B8
Cookley Green Oxon 35 J6
Cookney Abers 151 M9

Cooksbridge E Susx 25 K8
Cooksey Green Worcs 58 D11
Cook's Green Essex 53 L8
Cooks Green Suffk 64 D11
Cookshill Staffs 70 H5
Cooksland Cnwll 4 H8
Cooksmill Green Essex 51 P9
Cookson Green Ches W 82 C10
Coolham W Susx 24 D6
Cooling Medway 38 C6
Cooling Street Medway 38 B7
Coombe Cnwll 2 G5
Coombe Cnwll 2 L5
Coombe Cnwll 3 N3
Coombe Cnwll 3 N4
Coombe Devon 9 K8
Coombe Devon 10 C6
Coombe Gloucs 32 E6
Coombe Hants 23 J10
Coombe Wilts 21 M4
Coombe Bissett Wilts 21 M9
Coombe Cellars Devon 7 N4
Coombe Cross Hants 23 J10
Coombe Hill Gloucs 46 G9
Coombe Keynes Dorset 12 D8
Coombe Pafford Torbay 7 N5
Coombes W Susx 24 E9
Coombes-Moor Herefs 45 M2
Coombe Street Somset 20 E8
Coombeswood Dudley 58 E7
Coopersale Common Essex 51 L10
Coopersale Street Essex 51 L10
Cooper's Corner Kent 37 L11
Coopers Green E Susx 25 L6
Coopers Green Herts 50 E9
Cooper Street Kent 39 P9
Cooper Turning Bolton 89 J9
Cootham W Susx 24 C8
Copdock Suffk 53 K3
Copford Green Essex 52 F7
Copgrove N York 97 M8
Copister Shet 169 r6
Cople Bed 61 P11
Copley Calder 90 D6
Copley Dur 103 L5
Copley Tamesd 83 L5
Coplow Dale Derbys 83 Q9
Copmanthorpe C York 98 B11
Copmere End Staffs 70 E3
Copp Lancs 88 E3
Coppathorne Cnwll 16 C11
Coppenhall Staffs 70 G11
Coppenhall Moss Ches E 70 C3
Copperhouse Cnwll 2 F6
Coppicegate Shrops 57 N8
Coppingford Cambs 61 Q5
Coppins Corner Kent 26 F2
Copplestone Devon 9 J4
Coppull Lancs 88 H8
Coppull Moor Lancs 88 H8
Copsale W Susx 24 E6
Copster Green Lancs 89 K4
Copston Magna Warwks 59 Q7
Cop Street Kent 39 N9
Copthall Green Essex 51 K10
Copt Heath Solhll 59 J9
Copt Hewick N York 97 M6
Copthorne Cnwll 5 M3
Copthorne W Susx 24 H3
Copt Oak Leics 72 C8
Copy's Green Norfk 76 C4
Copythorne Hants 13 P2
Coram Street Suffk 52 H3
Corbets Tey Gt Lon 37 N3
Corbière Jersey 11 a2
Corbridge Nthumb 112 E8
Corby Nhants 61 J3
Corby Glen Lincs 73 Q6
Corby Hill Cumb 111 J9
Cordon N Ayrs 121 K5
Cordwell Derbys 84 D5
Coreley Shrops 57 L10
Cores End Bucks 35 P7
Corfe Somset 18 H11
Corfe Castle Dorset 12 G8
Corfe Mullen Dorset 12 G5
Corfton Shrops 56 H7
Corgarff Abers 149 P6
Corhampton Hants 22 H10
Corks Pond Kent 25 Q2
Corlae D & G 115 N8
Corley Warwks 59 M7
Corley Ash Warwks 59 L8
Corley Moor Warwks 59 L8
Corley Services Warwks 59 M7
Cormuir Angus 142 E4
Cornard Tye Suffk 52 F3
Corndon Devon 8 G7
Corner Row Lancs 88 E4
Corney Cumb 94 C2
Cornforth Dur 104 B4
Cornhill Abers 158 E6
Cornhill-on-Tweed Nthumb 118 G3
Cornholme Calder 89 Q5
Cornish Hall End Essex 51 Q3
Cornoigmore Ag & B 136 B6
Cornriggs Dur 102 F2
Cornsay Dur 103 M2
Cornsay Colliery Dur 103 N2
Corntown Highld 155 Q6
Corntown V Glam 29 P9
Cornwall Airport Newquay Cnwll 4 D9
Cornwell Oxon 47 Q9
Cornwood Devon 6 G7
Cornworthy Devon 7 L7
Corpach Highld 139 K2
Corpusty Norfk 76 G6
Corrachree Abers 150 D7
Corran Highld 139 J5
Corran Highld 145 P6
Corrany IoM 80 g4
Corrie D & G 110 D3
Corrie N Ayrs 121 K3
Corriecravie N Ayrs 120 H7
Corriegills N Ayrs 121 K4
Corriegour Lodge Hotel Highld 146 H9
Corriemoille Highld 155 L5
Corrimony Highld 155 L10
Corringham Lincs 85 Q2
Corringham Thurr 38 B5
Corris Gwynd 54 H3
Corris Uchaf Gwynd 54 G3
Corrow Ag & B 131 P7

Corry Highld 145 K3
Corscombe Devon 8 F5
Corscombe Dorset 11 L3
Corse Gloucs 46 E9
Corse Lawn Gloucs 46 F8
Corsham Wilts 32 G10
Corsindae Abers 150 H6
Corsley Wilts 20 F5
Corsley Heath Wilts 20 F5
Corsock D & G 108 G5
Corston BaNES 32 C11
Corston Wilts 32 H8
Corstorphine C Edin 127 M3
Cors-y-Gedol Gwynd 67 L10
Cortachy Angus 142 F6
Corton Suffk 65 Q2
Corton Wilts 21 H6
Corton Denham Somset 20 B10
Coruanan Highld 139 K4
Corwen Denbgs 68 G6
Coryates Dorset 11 N7
Coryton Devon 8 C7
Coryton Thurr 38 B5
Cosby Leics 72 E11
Coscote Oxon 34 C4
Coseley Dudley 58 D6
Cosford Shrops 57 Q3
Cosgrove Nhants 49 L6
Cosham C Port 15 J5
Cosheston Pembks 41 K10
Coshieville P & K 141 J8
Cossall Notts 72 D2
Cossall Marsh Notts 72 D2
Cossington Leics 72 G8
Cossington Somset 19 L6
Costessey Norfk 76 H9
Costock Notts 72 F5
Coston Leics 73 L6
Coston Norfk 76 F10
Cote Oxon 34 C4
Cote Somset 19 K6
Cotebrook Ches W 82 C11
Cotehill Cumb 111 J10
Cotes Cumb 95 K4
Cotes Leics 72 F6
Cotes Staffs 70 E6
Cotesbach Leics 60 B4
Cotes Heath Staffs 70 E6
Cotford St Luke Somset 18 G9
Cotgrave Notts 72 G3
Cothal Abers 151 M4
Cotham Notts 85 N11
Cothelstone Somset 18 G8
Cotherstone Dur 103 K7
Cothill Oxon 34 E4
Cotleigh Devon 10 E4
Cotmanhay Derbys 72 D2
Coton Cambs 62 F9
Coton Nhants 60 E6
Coton Shrops 69 P8
Coton Staffs 59 J4
Coton Staffs 70 E10
Coton Staffs 70 H8
Coton Clanford Staffs 70 F10
Coton Hayes Staffs 70 H8
Coton Hill Shrops 56 H2
Coton in the Clay Staffs 71 M9
Coton in the Elms Derbys 71 N11
Coton Park Derbys 71 P11
Cotswolds 33 J3
Cotswold Wildlife Park & Gardens Oxon 33 P3
Cott Devon 7 K7
Cottam E R Yk 99 K7
Cottam Lancs 88 G4
Cottam Notts 85 P5
Cottenham Cambs 62 F7
Cotterdale N York 96 B2
Cottered Herts 50 H5
Cotteridge Birm 58 F8
Cotterstock Nhants 61 M2
Cottesbrooke Nhants 60 F6
Cottesmore Rutlnd 73 N8
Cottingham E R Yk 92 H4
Cottingham Nhants 60 H2
Cottingley C Brad 90 E3
Cottisford Oxon 48 G8
Cotton Suffk 64 F8
Cotton End Bed 61 N11
Cotton Tree Lancs 89 Q3
Cottown Abers 150 E2
Cottown Abers 151 K4
Cottown of Gight Abers 159 K9
Cotts Devon 6 C5
Cotwall Wrekin 69 R11
Cotwalton Staffs 70 G8
Couch's Mill Cnwll 5 J10
Coughton Herefs 46 A10
Coughton Warwks 47 L2
Coulaghailtro Ag & B 123 M6
Coulags Highld 154 C9
Coulderton Cumb 100 C9
Coull Abers 150 E7
Coulport Ag & B 131 Q10
Coulsdon Gt Lon 36 G9
Coulston Wilts 21 J4
Coulter S Lans 116 L4
Coultershaw Bridge W Susx 23 Q11
Coultings Somset 18 H7
Coulton N York 98 C6
Coultra Fife 135 K3
Cound Shrops 57 J3
Coundlane Shrops 57 K4
Coundon Dur 103 P5
Coundon Grange Dur 103 P5
Countersett N York 96 D3
Countess Wilts 21 N6
Countess Cross Essex 52 E5
Countess Wear Devon 9 M7
Countesthorpe Leics 72 F11
Countisbury Devon 17 N2
Coupar Angus P & K 142 C10
Coup Green Lancs 88 H5
Coupland Cumb 102 D7
Coupland Nthumb 118 H4
Cour Ag & B 123 J7
Court-at-Street Kent 27 J4
Courteachan Highld 145 L8
Courteenhall Nhants 49 L4
Court Henry Carmth 43 L10
Courtsend Essex 38 H3
Courtway Somset 18 H8
Cousland Mdloth 128 B6
Cousley Wood E Susx 25 Q4
Cove Ag & B 131 Q10
Cove Border 129 K5

Cove Devon 18 C11
Cove Hants 23 N3
Cove Highld 160 G8
Cove Bay C Aber 151 P7
Cove Bottom Suffk 65 P6
Covehithe Suffk 65 Q5
Coven Staffs 58 D3
Coveney Cambs 62 G4
Covenham St Bartholomew Lincs 87 K2
Covenham St Mary Lincs 87 K2
Coven Heath Staffs 58 D3
Coventry Covtry 59 M9
Coverack Cnwll 3 K10
Coverack Bridges Cnwll 2 H7
Coverham N York 96 H3
Covington Cambs 61 N6
Covington S Lans 116 D3
Cowan Bridge Lancs 95 N5
Cowbeech E Susx 25 P8
Cowbit Lincs 74 E7
Cowbridge V Glam 30 C10
Cowdale Derbys 83 N10
Cowden Kent 25 L2
Cowdenbeath Fife 134 F9
Cowden Pound Kent 25 L2
Cowden Station Kent 25 L2
Cowers Lane Derbys 71 Q5
Cowes IoW 14 E7
Cowesby N York 97 Q3
Cowesfield Green Wilts 21 Q5
Cowfold W Susx 24 F6
Cowgill Cumb 95 R3
Cow Green Suffk 64 F8
Cowhill S Glos 32 B6
Cowie Abers 151 M4
Cowie Stirlg 133 N10
Cowlam E R Yk 99 K7
Cowley Devon 9 M5
Cowley Gloucs 33 J2
Cowley Gt Lon 36 C4
Cowley Oxon 34 F4
Cowling Lancs 88 H7
Cowling N York 90 B2
Cowling N York 97 K3
Cowlinge Suffk 63 M10
Cowmes Kirk 90 F7
Cowpe Lancs 89 N6
Cowpen Nthumb 113 L4
Cowpen Bewley S on T 104 E6
Cowplain Hants 15 J4
Cowshill Dur 102 F2
Cowslip Green N Som 19 N2
Cowthorpe N York 97 P10
Coxall Herefs 56 F10
Coxbank Ches E 70 B6
Coxbench Derbys 72 B2
Coxbridge Somset 19 P7
Cox Common Suffk 65 N5
Coxford Cnwll 5 K2
Coxford Norfk 76 B6
Coxgreen Staffs 57 Q7
Coxheath Kent 38 B11
Coxhoe Dur 104 B3
Coxley Somset 19 P6
Coxley Wakefd 90 H7
Coxley Wick Somset 19 P6
Coxpark Cnwll 5 Q7
Coxtie Green Essex 51 N11
Coxwold N York 98 A5
Coychurch Brdgnd 29 P9
Coylton S Ayrs 114 H4
Coylumbridge Highld 148 G5
Coytrahen Brdgnd 29 N7
Crabbs Cross Worcs 58 F11
Crab Orchard Dorset 13 J3
Crabtree W Susx 24 F5
Crabtree Green Wrexhm 69 K6
Crackenthorpe Cumb 102 C6
Crackington Haven Cnwll 5 J2
Crackley Staffs 70 E4
Crackley Warwks 59 L10
Crackleybank Shrops 57 P2
Crackpot N York 103 J11
Cracoe N York 96 E8
Craddock Devon 10 B2
Cradle End Herts 51 L6
Cradley Dudley 58 D7
Cradley Herefs 46 D5
Cradley Heath Sandw 58 D7
Cradoc Powys 44 D7
Crafthole Cnwll 5 P11
Crafton Bucks 49 N11
Crag Foot Lancs 95 K6
Craggan Highld 149 J2
Cragganmore Moray 157 M10
Cragg Hill Leeds 90 G3
Cragg Vale Calder 90 C6
Craghead Dur 113 L10
Cragside House & Garden Nthumb 119 L10
Crai Powys 44 B10
Craibstone Moray 158 C6
Craichie Angus 143 J8
Craig Angus 143 M6
Craig Highld 154 D8
Craigbank E Ayrs 115 L5
Craigburn Border 127 N7
Craig-cefn-parc Swans 29 J4
Craigcleuch D & G 110 F3
Craigdam Abers 159 K11
Craigdhu Ag & B 130 G6
Craigearn Abers 151 J5
Craigellachie Moray 157 P9
Craigend P & K 134 E3
Craigend Rens 125 M3
Craigends Rens 125 L4
Craighat Ag & B 132 C11
Craighlaw D & G 107 K5
Craighouse Ag & B 122 H6
Craigie P & K 141 R9
Craigie S Ayrs 125 L11
Craigiefold Abers 159 M4
Craiglockhart C Edin 127 N3
Craig Llangiwg Neath 29 K4
Craigmillar C Edin 127 Q3
Craignant Shrops 69 J7
Craigneston D & G 115 Q10
Craigneuk N Lans 126 D4
Craigneuk N Lans 126 E4
Craignure Ag & B 138 C10
Craigo Angus 143 M5
Craig Penllyn V Glam 30 C9
Craigrothie Fife 135 K5
Craigruie Stirlg 132 F3

Craig's End Essex 52 B4
Craigton Angus 143 J10
Craigton C Aber 151 L7
Craigton E Rens 125 M7
Craigton of Airlie Angus 142 E7
Craigy-Duke Neath 29 K4
Craig-y-nos Powys 44 A11
Craik Border 117 L9
Crail Fife 135 Q6
Crailing Border 118 C6
Craiselound N Linc 92 C11
Crakehall N York 97 K3
Crakehill N York 97 P6
Crakemarsh Staffs 71 K7
Crambe N York 98 E8
Cramlington Nthumb 113 L5
Cramond C Edin 127 M2
Cramond Bridge C Edin 127 M2
Crampmoor Hants 22 C10
Cranage Ches E 82 G11
Cranberry Staffs 70 E7
Cranborne Dorset 13 J2
Cranbourne Br For 35 P10
Cranbrook Devon 9 N6
Cranbrook Kent 26 C4
Cranbrook Common Kent 26 C4
Crane Moor Barns 91 J10
Crane's Corner Norfk 76 C9
Cranfield C Beds 49 Q6
Cranford Devon 16 E7
Cranford Gt Lon 36 D5
Cranford St Andrew Nhants 61 K5
Cranford St John Nhants 61 K5
Cranham Gloucs 32 G2
Cranham Gt Lon 37 N3
Cranhill Warwks 47 M4
Crank St Hel 81 Q5
Cranleigh Surrey 24 C3
Cranmer Green Suffk 64 E7
Cranmore IoW 14 C8
Cranmore Somset 20 C6
Cranoe Leics 73 K11
Cransford Suffk 65 L9
Cranshaws Border 128 H7
Cranstal IoM 80 g1
Cranswick E R Yk 99 L10
Crantock Cnwll 4 B9
Cranwell Lincs 86 D11
Cranwich Norfk 63 N2
Cranworth Norfk 76 D11
Craobh Haven Ag & B 130 F6
Crapstone Devon 6 E5
Crarae Ag & B 131 K8
Crask Inn Highld 162 C2
Crask of Aigas Highld 155 N9
Craster Nthumb 119 Q7
Craswall Herefs 45 K7
Crateford Staffs 58 D3
Cratfield Suffk 65 L6
Crathes Abers 151 K8
Crathie Abers 149 P8
Crathie Highld 147 P9
Crathorne N York 104 D9
Craven Arms Shrops 56 G8
Crawcrook Gatesd 112 H8
Crawford Lancs 81 P4
Crawford S Lans 116 D6
Crawfordjohn S Lans 116 B6
Crawley Hants 22 D8
Crawley Oxon 34 B2
Crawley W Susx 24 G3
Crawley Down W Susx 24 H3
Crawleyside Dur 103 J2
Crawshawbooth Lancs 89 N5
Crawton Abers 143 R2
Craxe's Green Essex 52 F8
Cray N York 96 D5
Crayford Gt Lon 37 M5
Crayke N York 98 B6
Craymere Beck Norfk 76 F5
Crays Hill Essex 38 B3
Cray's Pond Oxon 34 H8
Craythorne Staffs 71 N9
Craze Lowman Devon 9 N2
Crazies Hill Wokham 35 L8
Creacombe Devon 17 Q8
Creagan Ag & B 138 H9
Creag Ghoraidh W Isls 168 c13
Creagorry W Isls 168 c13
Creaguaineach Lodge Highld 139 Q4
Creamore Bank Shrops 69 P8
Creaton Nhants 60 F6
Creca D & G 110 D6
Credenhill Herefs 45 P6
Crediton Devon 9 K4
Creebank D & G 107 K2
Creebridge D & G 107 M4
Creech Dorset 12 F8
Creech Heathfield Somset 19 J9
Creech St Michael Somset 19 J9
Creed Cnwll 3 N4
Creekmoor BCP 12 H6
Creekmouth Gt Lon 37 L4
Creeksea Essex 38 F2
Creeting St Mary Suffk 64 F10
Creeton Lincs 73 Q6
Creetown D & G 107 N6
Cregneash IoM 80 a8
Creg ny Baa IoM 80 e5
Cregrina Powys 44 G4
Creich Fife 135 J3
Creigiau Cardif 30 E8
Cremyll Cnwll 6 D8
Cressage Shrops 57 K4
Cressbrook Derbys 83 Q10
Cresselly Pembks 41 L9
Cressex Bucks 35 M6
Cressing Essex 52 C7
Cresswell Nthumb 113 L2
Cresswell Pembks 41 L9
Cresswell Staffs 70 H7
Creswell Derbys 84 H6
Creswell Green Staffs 58 G2
Cretingham Suffk 65 J9
Cretshengan Ag & B 123 M6
Crewe Ches E 70 C3
Crewe-by-Farndon Ches W 69 M4
Crewe Green Ches E 70 C3
Crew Green Powys 69 K11
Crewkerne Somset 11 J3
Crews Hill Station Gt Lon 50 H10
Crewton C Derb 72 B4
Crianlarich Stirlg 132 D2
Cribyn Cerdgn 43 K4

Criccieth Gwynd...66 H7
Crich Derbys...84 D10
Crich Carr Derbys...84 D10
Crichton Mdloth...128 B7
Crick Mons...31 N6
Crick Nhants...60 C6
Crickadarn Powys...44 F6
Cricket St Thomas Somset...10 H3
Crickheath Shrops...69 J10
Crickhowell Powys...45 J11
Cricklade Wilts...33 L6
Cricklewood Gt Lon...36 F3
Cridling Stubbs N York...91 N6
Crieff P & K...133 P3
Criggan Cnwll...4 G9
Criggion Powys...69 J11
Crigglestone Wakefd...91 J7
Crimble Rochdl...89 P8
Crimond Abers...159 Q6
Crimplesham Norfk...75 N10
Crimscote Warwks...47 P5
Crinaglack Highld...155 M9
Crinan Ag & B...130 F9
Crindledyke N Lans...126 E6
Cringleford Norfk...76 H10
Cringles C Brad...96 F11
Crinow Pembks...41 M8
Cripplesease Cnwll...2 E6
Cripplestyle Dorset...13 J2
Cripp's Corner E Susx...26 C7
Croachy Highld...148 B2
Croanford Cnwll...4 G7
Crockenhill Kent...37 M7
Crocker End Oxon...35 K7
Crockerhill W Susx...15 P5
Crockernwell Devon...9 J6
Crocker's Ash Herefs...45 Q11
Crockerton Wilts...20 G7
Crocketford D & G...108 H6
Crockey Hill C York...98 C11
Crockham Hill Kent...37 K10
Crockhurst Street Kent...37 P11
Crockleford Heath Essex...52 H6
Crock Street Somset...10 G2
Croeserw Neath...29 N5
Croes-goch Pembks...40 F4
Croes-lan Cerdgn...42 G6
Croesor Gwynd...67 L6
Croesyceiliog Carmth...42 H11
Croesyceiliog Torfn...31 K5
Croes-y-mwyalch Torfn...31 K6
Croes-y-pant Mons...31 K4
Croft Leics...72 E11
Croft Lincs...87 P8
Croft Warrtn...82 D6
Croftamie Stirlg...132 F10
Croft Mitchell Cnwll...2 H6
Crofton Cumb...110 F10
Crofton Wakefd...91 K7
Crofton Wilts...21 Q2
Croft-on-Tees N York...103 Q9
Croftown Highld...161 K10
Crofts Moray...157 P7
Crofts Bank Traffd...82 G5
Crofts of Dipple Moray...157 Q6
Crofts of Savoch Abers...159 P5
Crofty Swans...28 F6
Crogen Gwynd...68 D7
Croggan Ag & B...130 E2
Croglin Cumb...111 L11
Croick Highld...162 B8
Cromarty Highld...156 D4
Crombie Fife...134 D11
Cromdale Highld...149 K2
Cromer Herts...50 G5
Cromer Norfk...77 J3
Cromford Derbys...84 C9
Cromhall S Glos...32 C6
Cromhall Common S Glos...32 C6
Cromor W Isls...168 j5
Crompton Fold Oldham...89 Q9
Cromwell Notts...85 N8
Cronberry E Ayrs...115 M3
Crondall Hants...23 L5
Cronkbourne IoM...80 e6
Cronk-y-Voddy IoM...80 d4
Cronton Knows...81 P7
Crook Cumb...101 N11
Crook Dur...103 N3
Crookdake Cumb...100 G2
Crooke Wigan...88 H9
Crooked End Gloucs...46 B11
Crookedholm E Ayrs...125 M10
Crooked Soley Wilts...34 B10
Crookes Sheff...84 D3
Crookhall Dur...112 H10
Crookham Nthumb...118 H3
Crookham W Berk...22 F2
Crookham Village Hants...23 L4
Crook Inn Border...116 G5
Crooklands Cumb...95 L4
Crook of Devon P & K...134 C7
Cropper Derbys...71 N7
Cropredy Oxon...48 E5
Cropston Leics...72 F8
Cropthorne Worcs...47 J5
Cropton N York...98 F3
Cropwell Bishop Notts...72 H3
Cropwell Butler Notts...72 H3
Cros W Isls...168 k1
Crosbost W Isls...168 i5
Crosby Cumb...100 E3
Crosby IoM...80 d6
Crosby N Linc...92 E8
Crosby Sefton...81 L5
Crosby Garret Cumb...102 D9
Crosby Ravensworth Cumb...102 B8
Crosby Villa Cumb...100 E3
Croscombe Somset...19 Q6
Crosemere Shrops...69 M9
Crosland Edge Kirk...90 E8
Crosland Hill Kirk...90 E8
Cross Somset...19 M4
Crossaig Ag & B...123 P9
Crossapol Ag & B...136 B7
Cross Ash Mons...45 N11
Cross-at-Hand Kent...26 C2
Crossbost W Isls...168 i5
Crossbush W Susx...24 B9
Crosscanonby Cumb...100 E3
Cross Coombe Cnwll...3 J3
Crossdale Street Norfk...77 J4
Cross End Bed...61 N9
Cross End Essex...52 E4
Crossens Sefton...88 D6

Cross Flatts C Brad...90 E2
Crossford Fife...134 D10
Crossford S Lans...126 E8
Crossgate Cnwll...5 N4
Crossgate Lincs...74 D5
Crossgate Staffs...70 G7
Crossgatehall E Loth...128 B6
Crossgates E Ayrs...125 K9
Crossgates Fife...134 E10
Cross Gates Leeds...91 K4
Crossgates N York...99 L4
Crossgates Powys...44 F2
Crossgill Lancs...95 M8
Cross Green Devon...5 P4
Cross Green Leeds...91 J4
Cross Green Staffs...58 D3
Cross Green Suffk...64 A11
Cross Green Suffk...64 B10
Cross Green Suffk...64 D11
Cross Hands Carmth...28 G2
Crosshands Carmth...41 N6
Crosshands E Ayrs...125 M11
Cross Hands Pembks...41 L8
Cross Hill Derbys...84 F11
Crosshill Fife...134 F8
Crosshill S Ayrs...114 F6
Cross Hills N York...96 F11
Crosshouse E Ayrs...125 K10
Cross Houses Shrops...57 J4
Cross Houses Shrops...57 M6
Cross in Hand E Susx...25 N6
Cross Inn Cerdgn...42 G3
Cross Inn Cerdgn...43 K2
Cross Inn Pembks...41 M9
Cross Inn Rhondd...30 E8
Cross Keys Ag & B...132 C10
Crosskeys Caerph...30 H6
Cross Keys Wilts...32 G10
Crosskirk Highld...166 H3
Crosslands Cumb...94 G3
Cross Lane IoW...14 F9
Cross Lane Head Shrops...57 N5
Cross Lanes Cnwll...2 H9
Cross Lanes Cnwll...3 K5
Cross Lanes N York...98 A4
Crosslanes Shrops...69 K11
Cross Lanes Wrexhm...69 L5
Crosslee Rens...125 L4
Crossley Kirk...90 G6
Crossmichael D & G...108 F7
Cross Oak Powys...44 G10
Cross of Jackston Abers...158 H11
Cross o' th' hands Derbys...71 P5
Crosspost W Susx...24 G6
Crossroads Abers...150 F6
Crossroads Abers...151 K9
Cross Roads C Brad...90 D3
Cross Street Suffk...64 H6
Crosston Angus...143 J6
Cross Town Ches E...82 G9
Crossway Mons...45 N11
Crossway Powys...44 F3
Crossway Green Mons...31 P6
Crossway Green Worcs...58 B11
Crossways Dorset...12 C7
Crosswell Pembks...41 M3
Crosthwaite Cumb...95 J2
Croston Lancs...88 F7
Crostwick Norfk...77 K8
Crostwight Norfk...77 L6
Crouch Kent...37 P9
Crouch Kent...39 J10
Crouch End Gt Lon...36 H3
Croucheston Wilts...21 L9
Crough House Green Kent...37 K11
Croughton Nhants...48 F8
Crovie Abers...159 K4
Crow Hants...13 L4
Crowan Cnwll...2 G7
Crowborough E Susx...25 M4
Crowborough Warren E Susx...25 M4
Crowcombe Somset...18 F7
Crowdecote Derbys...83 P11
Crowden Derbys...83 N5
Crowden Devon...8 C5
Crowdhill Hants...22 H4
Crowdleham Kent...37 N9
Crow Edge Barns...83 Q4
Crowell Oxon...35 K5
Crow End Cambs...62 D9
Crowfield Nhants...48 H6
Crowfield Suffk...64 G10
Crowfield Green Suffk...64 G10
Crowgate Street Norfk...77 L7
Crow Green Essex...51 N11
Crowhill E Loth...129 J5
Crow Hill Herefs...46 B9
Crowhole Derbys...84 D5
Crowhurst E Susx...26 C9
Crowhurst Surrey...37 J11
Crowhurst Lane End Surrey...37 J11
Crowland Lincs...74 D9
Crowland Suffk...64 E7
Crowlas Cnwll...2 D8
Crowle N Linc...92 C8
Crowle Worcs...46 H3
Crowle Green Worcs...46 H3
Crowmarsh Gifford Oxon...34 H7
Crown Corner Suffk...65 K7
Crownhill C Plym...6 D7
Crownpits Surrey...23 Q6
Crownthorpe Norfk...76 F11
Crowntown Cnwll...2 G7
Crows-an-Wra Cnwll...2 B8
Crow's Green Essex...51 Q5
Crowshill Norfk...76 D10
Crow's Nest Cnwll...5 M8
Crowsnest Shrops...56 F4
Crowthorne Wokham...23 M2
Crowton Ches W...82 C10
Croxall Staffs...59 J2
Croxby Lincs...93 L11
Croxdale Dur...103 Q3
Croxden Staffs...71 K7
Croxley Green Herts...50 C11
Croxteth Lpool...81 N5
Croxton Cambs...62 B8
Croxton N Linc...93 J8
Croxton Norfk...64 B4
Croxton Norfk...76 D5
Croxton Staffs...70 D8
Croxtonbank Staffs...70 D8
Croxton Green Ches E...69 Q4

Croxton Kerrial Leics...73 L5
Croy Highld...156 D8
Croy N Lans...126 C2
Croyde Devon...16 G4
Croyde Bay Devon...16 G4
Croydon Cambs...62 D11
Croydon Gt Lon...36 H7
Crubenmore Highld...148 B9
Cruckmeole Shrops...56 G3
Cruckton Shrops...56 G2
Cruden Bay Abers...159 Q10
Crudgington Wrekin...70 A11
Crudie Abers...159 J6
Crudwell Wilts...33 J6
Cruft Devon...8 D5
Crûg Powys...56 B10
Crugmeer Cnwll...4 E6
Crugybar Carmth...43 N7
Crug-y-byddar Powys...56 B8
Crumlin Caerph...30 H5
Crumplehorn Cnwll...5 L11
Crumpsall Manch...82 H4
Crundale Kent...27 J2
Crundale Pembks...41 J7
Crunwere Pembks...41 N8
Cruwys Morchard Devon...9 L2
Crux Easton Hants...22 D3
Cruxton Dorset...11 N5
Crwbin Carmth...28 E2
Cryers Hill Bucks...35 N5
Crymmych Pembks...41 N4
Crynant Neath...29 L4
Crystal Palace Gt Lon...36 H6
Cuaig Highld...153 N6
Cuan Ag & B...130 F5
Cubbington Warwks...59 M11
Cubert Cnwll...4 B10
Cubley Barns...90 G10
Cublington Bucks...49 M10
Cublington Herefs...45 N7
Cuckfield W Susx...24 H5
Cucklington Somset...20 E9
Cuckney Notts...85 J6
Cuckoo Bridge Lincs...74 D6
Cuckoo's Corner Hants...23 K6
Cuckoo's Nest Ches W...69 L2
Cuddesdon Oxon...34 G4
Cuddington Bucks...35 K2
Cuddington Ches W...82 C10
Cuddington Heath Ches W...69 N5
Cuddy Hill Lancs...88 F3
Cudham Gt Lon...37 K9
Cudliptown Devon...8 D9
Cudnell BCP...13 J5
Cudworth Barns...91 K9
Cudworth Somset...10 H2
Cuerdley Cross Warrtn...82 B7
Cufaude Hants...23 J3
Cuffley Herts...50 H10
Cuil Highld...138 H6
Culbokie Highld...155 R6
Culbone Somset...17 Q2
Culburnie Highld...155 N9
Culcabock Highld...156 B9
Culcharry Highld...156 F7
Culcheth Warrtn...82 E6
Culdrain Abers...158 D11
Culduie Highld...153 N9
Culford Suffk...64 A7
Culgaith Cumb...102 B5
Culham Oxon...34 F5
Culkein Highld...164 B10
Culkein Drumbeg Highld...164 D10
Culkerton Gloucs...32 H5
Cullen Moray...158 D4
Cullercoats N Tyne...113 N6
Cullerlie Abers...151 K7
Cullicudden Highld...156 A5
Cullingworth C Brad...90 D3
Cuillin Hills Highld...144 G3
Cullipool Ag & B...130 E5
Cullivoe Shet...169 s3
Culloden Highld...156 C8
Cullompton Devon...9 P3
Cullompton Services Devon...9 P3
Culm Davy Devon...18 F11
Culmington Shrops...56 H8
Culmstock Devon...10 C2
Culnacraig Highld...160 H6
Culnaightrie D & G...108 G10
Culnaknock Highld...153 J5
Culpho Suffk...53 M2
Culrain Highld...162 D8
Culross Fife...134 B10
Culroy S Ayrs...114 F5
Culsalmond Abers...158 G11
Culscadden D & G...107 N8
Culshabbin D & G...107 K7
Culswick Shet...169 p9
Cultercullen Abers...151 N3
Cults C Aber...151 M7
Culverstone Green Kent...37 P8
Culverthorpe Lincs...73 Q2
Culworth Nhants...48 F5
Culzean Castle & Country Park S Ayrs...114 D5
Cumbernauld N Lans...126 D3
Cumbernauld Village N Lans...126 D2
Cumberworth Lincs...87 P6
Cumdivock Cumb...110 F11
Cuminestown Abers...159 K7
Cumledge Border...129 K8
Cummersdale Cumb...110 G10
Cummertrees D & G...109 P7
Cummingston Moray...157 L4
Cumnock E Ayrs...115 L3
Cumnor Oxon...34 E4
Cumrew Cumb...111 L10
Cumrue D & G...109 N3
Cumwhinton Cumb...111 J10
Cumwhitton Cumb...111 K10
Cundall N York...97 P6
Cunninghamhead N Ayrs...125 K9
Cunningsburgh Shet...169 r10
Cupar Fife...135 K5
Cupar Muir Fife...135 K5
Curbar Derbys...84 C6
Curbridge Hants...14 F4
Curbridge Oxon...34 B3
Curdridge Hants...14 F4
Curdworth Warwks...59 J6
Curland Somset...19 J11
Curridge W Berk...34 E10
Currie C Edin...127 M4
Curry Mallet Somset...19 K10

Curry Rivel Somset...19 L9
Curteis Corner Kent...26 E4
Curtisden Green Kent...26 B3
Curtisknowle Devon...7 J8
Cury Cnwll...2 H9
Cushnie Abers...150 E5
Cushuish Somset...18 G8
Cusop Herefs...45 J6
Cusworth Donc...91 N10
Cutcloy D & G...107 N11
Cutcombe Somset...18 B7
Cutgate Rochdl...89 P8
Cuthill Highld...162 H9
Cutiau Gwynd...67 L11
Cutler's Green Essex...51 N4
Cutmadoc Cnwll...4 H9
Cutmere Cnwll...5 N9
Cutnall Green Worcs...58 C11
Cutsdean Gloucs...47 L8
Cutsyke Wakefd...91 L6
Cutthorpe Derbys...84 D6
Cuttivett Cnwll...5 P9
Cuxham Oxon...35 J5
Cuxton Medway...38 B8
Cuxwold Lincs...93 L10
Cwm Blae G...30 G3
Cwm Denbgs...80 F9
Cwmafan Neath...29 L6
Cwmaman Rhondd...30 D5
Cwmann Carmth...43 L5
Cwmavon Torfn...31 J3
Cwmbach Carmth...28 E4
Cwmbach Carmth...28 E4
Cwmbâch Powys...44 H7
Cwmbach Rhondd...30 D4
Cwmbach Llechrhyd Powys...44 E4
Cwmbelan Powys...55 L8
Cwmbran Torfn...31 J6
Cwmbrwyno Cerdgn...54 G8
Cwm Capel Carmth...28 E4
Cwmcarn Caerph...30 H6
Cwmcarvan Mons...31 N3
Cwm-celyn Blae G...30 H3
Cwm-Cewydd Gwynd...55 K2
Cwm-cou Cerdgn...41 Q2
Cwm Crawnon Powys...44 G11
Cwmdare Rhondd...30 C4
Cwmdu Carmth...43 M8
Cwmdu Powys...44 H10
Cwmdu Swans...28 H6
Cwmduad Carmth...42 G8
Cwm Dulais Swans...28 H4
Cwmdwr Carmth...43 P8
Cwmfelin Brdgnd...29 N7
Cwmfelin Myr Td...30 E4
Cwmfelin Boeth Carmth...41 N7
Cwmfelinfach Caerph...30 G6
Cwmfelin Mynach Carmth...41 P6
Cwmffrwd Carmth...42 H11
Cwmgiedd Powys...29 L2
Cwmgorse Carmth...29 K2
Cwmgwili Carmth...28 G2
Cwmgwrach Neath...29 N4
Cwmhiraeth Carmth...42 F7
Cwm-Ifor Carmth...43 N9
Cwm Irfon Powys...44 B5
Cwmisfael Carmth...43 J11
Cwm Llinau Powys...55 J3
Cwmllynfell Neath...29 K2
Cwmmawr Carmth...28 F2
Cwm Morgan Carmth...41 Q4
Cwmparc Rhondd...29 P5
Cwmpengraig Carmth...42 G7
Cwm Penmachno Conwy...67 P5
Cwmpennar Rhondd...30 D4
Cwmrhos Powys...44 H10
Cwmrhydyceirw Swans...29 J5
Cwmsychbant Cerdgn...43 J5
Cwmtillery Blae G...30 H3
Cwm-twrch Isaf Powys...29 L2
Cwm-twrch Uchaf Powys...29 L2
Cwm-y-glo Carmth...28 G2
Cwm-y-glo Gwynd...67 K2
Cwmyoy Mons...45 K10
Cwmystwyth Cerdgn...54 H10
Cwrt Gwynd...54 F5
Cwrt-newydd Cerdgn...43 J5
Cwrt-y-gollen Powys...45 J11
Cyfarthfa Castle Museum Myr Td...30 D3
Cyffylliog Denbgs...68 E3
Cyfronydd Powys...55 Q3
Cylibebyll Neath...29 K4
Cymau Flints...69 J3
Cymmer Neath...29 N5
Cymmer Rhondd...30 D6
Cynghordy Carmth...43 R6
Cynheidre Carmth...28 E3
Cynonville Neath...29 M5
Cynwyd Denbgs...68 E6
Cynwyl Elfed Carmth...42 G9

D

Daccombe Devon...7 N5
Dacre Cumb...101 N5
Dacre N York...97 J8
Dacre Banks N York...97 J8
Daddry Shield Dur...102 G3
Dadford Bucks...49 J7
Dadlington Leics...72 C11
Dafen Carmth...28 F4
Daffy Green Norfk...76 D10
Dagenham Gt Lon...37 M4
Daglingworth Gloucs...33 J3
Dagnall Bucks...49 Q11
Dagworth Suffk...64 E9
Dail bho Dheas W Isls...168 j1
Dailly S Ayrs...114 E7
Dainton Devon...7 M5
Dairsie Fife...135 L4
Daisy Hill Bolton...82 E4
Daisy Hill Leeds...90 H5
Dalabrog W Isls...168 c15
Dalavich Ag & B...131 K5
Dalbeattie D & G...108 H8
Dalbury Derbys...71 P8
Dalby IoM...80 b6
Dalby Lincs...87 M7
Dalby N York...98 C6
Dalcapon P & K...141 N7
Dalchalm Highld...163 L5

Dalchreichart Highld...146 H5
Dalchruin P & K...133 L4
Dalcrue P & K...134 C2
Dalderby Lincs...87 J7
Dalditch Devon...9 P5
Dale Cumb...101 P2
Dale Derbys...72 C3
Dale Pembks...40 F9
Dale Bottom Cumb...101 J6
Dale End Derbys...84 B8
Dale End N York...96 E11
Dale Hill E Susx...26 B5
Dalehouse N York...105 L7
Dalelia Highld...138 C4
Dalgarven N Ayrs...124 H8
Dalgety Bay Fife...134 F11
Dalgig E Ayrs...115 L5
Dalginross P & K...133 M3
Dalguise P & K...141 N8
Dalhalvaig Highld...166 E6
Dalham Suffk...63 M8
Daliburgh W Isls...168 c15
Dalkeith Mdloth...127 Q4
Dallas Moray...157 L7
Dallinghoo Suffk...65 K10
Dallington E Susx...25 Q7
Dallington Nhants...60 F8
Dallow N York...97 J6
Dalmally Ag & B...131 P2
Dalmary Stirlg...132 G8
Dalmellington E Ayrs...115 J6
Dalmeny C Edin...127 L2
Dalmore Highld...156 B4
Dalmuir W Duns...125 M3
Dalnabreck Highld...138 C4
Dalnacardoch P & K...140 H3
Dalnahaitnach Highld...148 H4
Dalnaspidal P & K...140 F3
Dalnawillan Lodge Highld...166 H8
Daloist P & K...141 J6
Dalqueich P & K...134 C7
Dalquhairn S Ayrs...114 F8
Dalreavoch Highld...162 H6
Dalry N Ayrs...124 H8
Dalrymple E Ayrs...114 G5
Dalserf S Lans...126 D7
Dalsmeran Ag & B...120 B9
Dalston Cumb...110 G10
Dalston Gt Lon...36 H4
Dalswinton D & G...109 K3
Dalton Cumb...95 L5
Dalton D & G...109 P6
Dalton Lancs...88 F9
Dalton N York...97 P5
Dalton N York...103 M9
Dalton Nthumb...112 H6
Dalton Rothm...84 G2
Dalton-in-Furness Cumb...94 E6
Dalton-le-Dale Dur...113 P11
Dalton Magna Rothm...84 G2
Dalton-on-Tees N York...103 Q9
Dalton Parva Rothm...84 G2
Dalton Piercy Hartpl...104 E4
Dalveich Stirlg...133 J3
Dalwhinnie Highld...147 Q11
Dalwood Devon...10 E4
Damask Green Herts...50 G5
Damerham Hants...21 M11
Damgate Norfk...77 N10
Dam Green Norfk...64 E4
Damnaglaur D & G...106 F10
Danaway Kent...38 E9
Danbury Essex...52 C10
Danby N York...105 K9
Danby Bottom N York...105 J10
Danby Wiske N York...104 B11
Dandaleith Moray...157 N9
Danderhall Mdloth...127 Q4
Danebridge Ches E...83 L11
Dane End Herts...50 H6
Danegate E Susx...25 N4
Danehill E Susx...25 K5
Dane Hills C Leic...72 F10
Danemoor Green Norfk...76 F10
Danesford Shrops...57 N6
Danesmoor Derbys...84 F8
Dane Street Kent...39 J11
Daniel's Water Kent...26 G3
Danshillock Abers...158 H6
Danskine E Loth...128 F6
Danthorpe E R Yk...93 M4
Danzey Green Warwks...58 H11
Dapple Heath Staffs...71 J9
Darby Green Hants...23 M2
Darcy Lever Bolton...89 L9
Dardy Powys...45 J11
Darenth Kent...37 N6
Daresbury Halton...82 C8
Darfield Barns...91 L10
Darfoulds Notts...85 J5
Dargate Kent...39 J9
Dargavel Rens...125 L3
Darite Cnwll...5 M8
Darland Medway...38 C8
Darland Wrexhm...69 L3
Darlaston Wsall...58 E5
Darlaston Green Wsall...58 E5
Darley N York...97 K9
Darley Abbey C Derb...72 B3
Darley Bridge Derbys...84 C8
Darley Dale Derbys...84 C8
Darley Green Solhll...59 J10
Darleyhall Herts...50 D6
Darley Head N York...97 J9
Darlingscott Warwks...47 P6
Darlington Darltn...103 Q8
Darliston Shrops...69 Q8
Darlton Notts...85 N6
Darnford Staffs...59 H3
Darnick Border...117 Q4
Darowen Powys...55 J4
Darra Abers...158 H8
Darracott Devon...16 C8
Darracott Devon...16 H4
Darras Hall Nthumb...113 J6
Darrington Wakefd...91 M7
Darsham Suffk...65 N8
Darshill Somset...20 B6
Dartford Kent...37 N6
Dartford Crossing Kent...37 P8
Dartington Devon...7 K6
Dartmeet Devon...6 H4
Dartmoor National Park Devon...8 G9
Dartmouth Devon...7 M8

Darton – Dudley 267

Darton Barns 91 J8
Darvel E Ayrs 125 P10
Darwell Hole E Susx 25 Q7
Darwen Bl w D 89 K6
Datchet W & M 35 Q9
Datchworth Herts 50 G7
Datchworth Green Herts 50 G7
Daubhill Bolton 89 L9
Daugh of Kinermony Moray 157 N9
Dauntsey Wilts 33 J8
Dava Highld 157 J10
Davenham Ches W 82 E10
Davenport Stockp 83 K7
Davenport Green Ches E 82 H9
Davenport Green Traffd 82 H7
Daventry Nhants 60 C8
Davidson's Mains C Edin 127 N2
Davidstow Cnwll 5 K4
David Street Kent 37 P8
Davington D & G 117 J10
Davington Hill Kent 38 H9
Daviot Abers 151 J2
Daviot Highld 156 C10
Daviot House Highld 156 C9
Davis's Town E Susx 25 M7
Davoch of Grange Moray 158 C7
Davyhulme Traffd 82 G5
Daw End Wsall 58 F4
Dawesgreen Surrey 36 F11
Dawley Wrekin 57 M3
Dawlish Devon 9 N9
Dawlish Warren Devon 9 N9
Dawn Conwy 80 B10
Daws Green Somset 18 G10
Daws Heath Essex 38 D4
Daw's House Cnwll 5 N5
Dawsmere Lincs 74 H4
Daybrook Notts 85 J11
Day Green Ches E 70 D3
Dayhills Staffs 70 H8
Dayhouse Bank Worcs 58 E9
Daylesford Gloucs 47 P9
Ddol Flints 80 G10
Ddol-Cownwy Powys 68 D11
Deal Kent 39 Q11
Dean Cumb 100 E5
Dean Devon 7 J6
Dean Devon 17 L2
Dean Devon 17 N2
Dean Dorset 21 J11
Dean Hants 22 D8
Dean Hants 22 G11
Dean Lancs 89 P5
Dean Oxon 48 B10
Dean Somset 20 C6
Dean Bottom Kent 37 N7
Deanburnhaugh Border 117 M8
Deancombe Devon 7 J6
Dean Court Oxon 34 E3
Deane Bolton 89 K9
Deane Hants 22 F4
Dean End Dorset 21 J11
Dean Head Barns 90 H10
Deanhead Kirk 90 C7
Deanland Dorset 21 J11
Deanlane End W Susx 15 K4
Dean Prior Devon 7 J6
Deanraw Nthumb 112 B8
Dean Row Ches E 83 J8
Deans W Loth 127 J4
Deanscales Cumb 100 E5
Deanshanger Nhants 49 L7
Deanshaugh Moray 157 R7
Deanston Stirlg 133 L7
Dean Street Kent 38 B11
Dearham Cumb 100 E3
Dearnley Rochdl 89 Q7
Debach Suffk 65 J11
Debden Essex 51 K11
Debden Essex 51 N4
Debden Green Essex 51 N4
Debenham Suffk 64 H9
Deblin's Green Worcs 46 F5
Dechmont W Loth 127 J3
Dechmont Road W Loth 127 J4
Deddington Oxon 48 E8
Dedham Essex 53 J5
Dedham Heath Essex 53 J5
Dedworth W & M 35 P9
Deene Nhants 61 K2
Deenethorpe Nhants 61 L2
Deepcar Sheff 90 H11
Deepcut Surrey 23 P3
Deepdale Cumb 95 Q4
Deepdale N York 96 C5
Deeping Gate C Pete 74 B9
Deeping St James Lincs 74 C9
Deeping St Nicholas Lincs 74 D7
Deerhurst Gloucs 46 G8
Deerhurst Walton Gloucs 46 G9
Deerton Street Kent 38 G9
Defford Worcs 46 H6
Defynnog Powys 44 C9
Deganwy Conwy 79 P9
Degnish Ag & B 130 F5
Deighton C York 91 Q2
Deighton N York 104 C10
Deiniolen Gwynd 67 K2
Delabole Cnwll 4 H5
Delamere Ches W 82 C11
Delfrigs Abers 151 P3
Delley Devon 17 J7
Delliefure Highld 157 K11
Dell Quay W Susx 15 M6
Delly End Oxon 34 C2
Delnabo Moray 149 M4
Delny Highld 156 C3
Delph Oldham 90 B9
Delves Dur 112 H11
Delvin End Essex 52 C4
Dembleby Lincs 73 Q3
Demelza Cnwll 4 F9
Denaby Donc 91 M11
Denaby Main Donc 91 M11
Denbies Surrey 36 D10
Denbigh Denbgs 80 F11
Denbrae Fife 135 K4
Denbury Devon 7 L5
Denby Derbys 84 E11
Denby Bottles Derbys 84 E11
Denby Dale Kirk 90 G9
Denchworth Oxon 34 C6
Dendron Cumb 94 E6
Denel End C Beds 50 B3
Denfield P & K 134 B4
Denford Nhants 61 L5
Dengie Essex 52 G11
Denham Bucks 36 B3
Denham Suffk 63 N8
Denham Suffk 64 H7
Denham End Suffk 63 N8
Denham Green Bucks 36 B3
Denham Green Suffk 64 H7
Denhead Abers 159 N7
Denhead Fife 135 M5
Denhead of Gray C Dund 142 F11
Denholm Border 117 R7
Denholme C Brad 90 D4
Denholme Clough C Brad 90 D4
Denio Gwynd 66 F7
Denmead Hants 15 J4
Denmore C Aber 151 N5
Denne Park W Susx 24 E5
Dennington Suffk 65 K8
Denny Falk 133 N11
Dennyloanhead Falk 133 N11
Den of Lindores Fife 134 H4
Denshaw Oldham 90 B8
Denside Abers 151 L8
Densole Kent 27 M3
Denston Suffk 63 N10
Denstone Staffs 71 K6
Denstroude Kent 39 K9
Dent Cumb 95 Q3
Denton Cambs 61 Q3
Denton Darltn 103 P7
Denton E Susx 25 L10
Denton Kent 27 M2
Denton Kent 37 Q6
Denton Lincs 73 M4
Denton N York 96 H11
Denton Nhants 60 H9
Denton Norfk 65 K4
Denton Oxon 34 G4
Denton Tamesd 83 K5
Denver Norfk 75 M10
Denwick Nthumb 119 P8
Deopham Norfk 76 E11
Deopham Green Norfk 64 E2
Depden Suffk 63 N9
Depden Green Suffk 63 N9
Deptford Gt Lon 37 J5
Deptford Wilts 21 K7
Derby C Derb 72 B3
Derby Devon 17 K5
Derbyhaven IoM 80 c8
Derculich P & K 141 L7
Dereham Norfk 76 D9
Deri Caerph 30 F4
Derril Devon 16 E11
Derringstone Kent 27 M2
Derrington Staffs 70 F10
Derriton Devon 16 E11
Derry Hill Wilts 33 J10
Derrythorpe N Linc 92 D9
Dersingham Norfk 75 N4
Dervaig Ag & B 137 L5
Derwen Denbgs 68 E4
Derwenlas Powys 54 G5
Derwent Valley Mills Derbys 84 D9
Derwent Water Cumb 101 J6
Derwydd Carmth 43 M11
Desborough Nhants 60 H4
Desford Leics 72 D10
Deskford Moray 158 D5
Detchant Nthumb 119 L3
Detling Kent 38 C10
Deuxhill Shrops 57 M7
Devauden Mons 31 N5
Devil's Bridge Cerdgn 54 G9
Devitts Green Warwks 59 L6
Devizes Wilts 21 K2
Devonport C Plym 6 D8
Devonside Clacks 133 Q8
Devoran Cnwll 3 K6
Devoran & Perran Cnwll 3 K6
Dewarton Mdloth 128 B7
Dewlish Dorset 12 C5
Dewsbury Kirk 90 G6
Dewsbury Moor Kirk 90 G6
Deytheur Powys 68 H11
Dial N Som 31 P11
Dial Green W Susx 23 P9
Dial Post W Susx 24 E7
Dibberford Dorset 11 K4
Dibden Hants 14 D5
Dibden Purlieu Hants 14 D5
Dickens Heath Solhll 58 H9
Dickleburgh Norfk 64 H5
Didbrook Gloucs 47 L8
Didcot Oxon 34 F6
Diddington Cambs 61 Q7
Diddlebury Shrops 57 J7
Didley Herefs 45 P8
Didling W Susx 23 M11
Didmarton Gloucs 32 F7
Didsbury Manch 82 H6
Didworthy Devon 6 H6
Digby Lincs 86 E10
Digg Highld 152 H4
Diggle Oldham 90 C9
Digmoor Lancs 88 F9
Digswell Herts 50 F7
Digswell Water Herts 50 G8
Dihewyd Cerdgn 43 J3
Dilham Norfk 77 L6
Dilhorne Staffs 70 H6
Dill Hall Lancs 89 M5
Dillington Cambs 61 P7
Dilston Nthumb 112 E8
Dilton Wilts 20 G5
Dilton Marsh Wilts 20 F5
Dilwyn Herefs 45 N4
Dimple Bolton 89 L7
Dimple Derbys 84 C8
Dinas Carmth 41 Q4
Dinas Cnwll 4 E7
Dinas Gwynd 66 D7
Dinas Gwynd 66 H3
Dinas Rhondd 30 D6
Dinas Cross Pembks 41 K3
Dinas Dinlle Gwynd 66 G3
Dinas-Mawddwy Gwynd 67 R11
Dinas Powys V Glam 30 G10
Dinder Somset 19 Q6
Dinedor Herefs 45 Q7
Dingestow Mons 31 N2
Dingle Lpool 81 M7
Dingleden Kent 26 D5
Dingley Nhants 60 G3
Dingwall Highld 155 P6
Dinmael Conwy 68 D6
Dinnet Abers 150 D8
Dinnington N u Ty 113 K6
Dinnington Rothm 84 H3
Dinnington Somset 11 J2
Dinorwic Gwynd 67 K2
Dinton Bucks 35 L2
Dinton Wilts 21 K8
Dinwoodie D & G 109 P2
Dinworthy Devon 16 E8
Dipford Somset 18 H10
Dipley Hants 23 K3
Dippen Ag & B 120 F4
Dippenhall Surrey 23 M5
Dippermill Devon 8 B3
Dippertown Devon 8 B8
Dippin N Ayrs 121 K7
Dipple Moray 157 Q6
Dipple S Ayrs 114 D7
Diptford Devon 7 J7
Dipton Dur 113 J10
Diptonmill Nthumb 112 D8
Dirleton E Loth 128 E3
Dirt Pot Nthumb 112 C11
Discoed Powys 45 K2
Diseworth Leics 72 D6
Dishforth N York 97 N6
Disley Ches E 83 L8
Diss Norfk 64 G5
Disserth Powys 44 E3
Distington Cumb 100 D6
Ditchampton Wilts 21 L8
Ditcheat Somset 20 B7
Ditchingham Norfk 65 L3
Ditchling E Susx 24 H7
Ditherington Shrops 57 J2
Ditteridge Wilts 32 F11
Dittisham Devon 7 M7
Ditton Kent 38 B10
Ditton Green Cambs 63 L9
Ditton Priors Shrops 57 L7
Dixton Gloucs 47 J8
Dixton Mons 31 P2
Dizzard Cnwll 5 K2
Dobcross Oldham 90 B9
Dobwalls Cnwll 5 L8
Doccombe Devon 9 J7
Dochgarroch Highld 155 R9
Dockenfield Surrey 23 M6
Docker Lancs 95 M6
Docking Norfk 75 Q3
Docklow Herefs 45 R3
Dockray Cumb 101 L6
Dockray Cumb 110 E11
Dodbrooke Devon 7 J10
Doddinghurst Essex 51 N11
Doddington Cambs 62 F2
Doddington Kent 38 F10
Doddington Lincs 85 Q6
Doddington Nthumb 119 J4
Doddington Shrops 57 L9
Doddiscombsleigh Devon 9 L7
Dodd's Green Ches E 69 R6
Doddshill Norfk 75 N4
Doddy Cross Cnwll 5 N9
Dodford Nhants 60 D8
Dodford Worcs 58 D10
Dodington S Glos 32 E8
Dodington Somset 18 G6
Dodleston Ches W 69 L2
Dodscott Devon 17 J8
Dodside E Rens 125 N7
Dod's Leigh Staffs 71 J8
Dodworth Barns 91 J9
Dodworth Bottom Barns 91 J10
Dodworth Green Barns 91 J10
Doe Bank Birm 58 H5
Doe Lea Derbys 84 G7
Dogdyke Lincs 86 H9
Dogley Lane Kirk 90 F8
Dogmersfield Hants 23 L4
Dogridge Wilts 33 L7
Dogsthorpe C Pete 74 C10
Dog Village Devon 9 N5
Dolanog Powys 55 P2
Dolau Powys 55 Q11
Dolaucothi Carmth 43 N6
Dolbenmaen Gwynd 67 J6
Doley Staffs 70 C9
Dolfach Powys 55 L4
Dol-fôr Powys 55 J3
Dolfor Powys 55 Q7
Dolgarrog Conwy 79 P11
Dolgellau Gwynd 67 N11
Dolgoch Gwynd 54 F4
Dol-gran Carmth 42 H8
Doll Highld 163 K6
Dollar Clacks 134 B8
Dollarfield Clacks 134 B8
Dolley Green Powys 56 D11
Dollwen Cerdgn 54 F8
Dolphin Flints 80 H10
Dolphinholme Lancs 95 L10
Dolphinton S Lans 127 L8
Dolton Devon 17 K9
Dolwen Conwy 80 B10
Dolwyddelan Conwy 67 N4
Dolybont Cerdgn 54 E7
Dolyhir Powys 45 J3
Domgay Powys 69 J11
Donaldson's Lodge Nthumb 118 G2
Doncaster Donc 91 P10
Doncaster Carr Donc 91 P10
Doncaster North Services Donc 91 R8
Doncaster Sheffield Airport Donc 91 R11
Donhead St Andrew Wilts 20 H10
Donhead St Mary Wilts 20 H10
Donibristle Fife 134 F10
Doniford Somset 18 E6
Donington Lincs 74 D3
Donington on Bain Lincs 86 H4
Donington Park Services Leics 72 D5
Donington Southing Lincs 74 D4
Donisthorpe Leics 59 M2
Donkey Street Kent 27 K5
Donkey Town Surrey 23 P2
Donnington Gloucs 47 N9
Donnington Herefs 46 D8
Donnington Shrops 57 K3
Donnington W Berk 34 E11
Donnington W Susx 15 N6
Donnington Wrekin 57 N2
Donnington Wood Wrekin 57 N2
Donyatt Somset 10 G2
Doomsday Green W Susx 24 E5
Doonfoot S Ayrs 114 F4
Dora's Green Hants 23 M5
Dorback Lodge Highld 149 K4
Dorchester Dorset 11 P6
Dorchester-on-Thames Oxon 34 G6
Dordon Warwks 59 L4
Dore Sheff 84 D4
Dores Highld 155 Q11
Dorking Surrey 36 E11
Dorking Tye Suffk 52 F4
Dormansland Surrey 25 K2
Dormans Park Surrey 25 J2
Dormington Herefs 46 A6
Dormston Worcs 47 J3
Dorn Gloucs 47 P8
Dorney Bucks 35 P9
Dornie Highld 145 Q2
Dornoch Highld 162 H9
Dornock D & G 110 D7
Dorrery Highld 167 J6
Dorridge Solhll 59 J10
Dorrington Lincs 86 E10
Dorrington Shrops 56 H4
Dorrington Shrops 70 C6
Dorsington Warwks 47 M5
Dorstone Herefs 45 L6
Dorton Bucks 35 J2
Dosthill Staffs 59 K5
Dothan IoA 78 F10
Dottery Dorset 11 K5
Doublebois Cnwll 5 K9
Doughton Gloucs 32 G6
Douglas IoM 80 e6
Douglas S Lans 116 A4
Douglas and Angus C Dund 142 G11
Douglas Pier Ag & B 131 P8
Douglastown Angus 142 G8
Douglas Water S Lans 116 B3
Douglas West S Lans 126 E11
Doulting Somset 20 B6
Dounby Ork 169 b4
Doune Highld 161 Q6
Doune Stirlg 133 L7
Dounepark S Ayrs 114 C8
Dounie Highld 162 D8
Dousland Devon 6 E5
Dovaston Shrops 69 L10
Dove Dale Derbys 71 L4
Dove Green Notts 84 G10
Dove Holes Derbys 83 N9
Dovenby Cumb 100 E4
Dover Kent 27 P3
Dover Wigan 82 D4
Dover Castle Kent 27 P3
Dovercourt Essex 53 M5
Doverdale Worcs 58 C11
Doveridge Derbys 71 L8
Doversgreen Surrey 36 G11
Dowally P & K 141 P8
Dowbridge Lancs 88 E4
Dowdeswell Gloucs 47 K11
Dowlais Myr Td 30 E3
Dowland Devon 17 K9
Dowlish Ford Somset 10 H2
Dowlish Wake Somset 10 H2
Down Ampney Gloucs 33 L5
Downderry Cnwll 5 N11
Downe Gt Lon 37 K8
Downend Gloucs 32 F5
Downend IoW 14 F9
Downend S Glos 32 C9
Downend W Berk 34 E9
Downfield C Dund 142 F11
Downgate Cnwll 5 M7
Downgate Cnwll 5 P7
Downham Essex 38 B2
Downham Gt Lon 37 J6
Downham Lancs 89 M2
Downham Market Norfk 75 M10
Down Hatherley Gloucs 46 G10
Downhead Somset 19 Q9
Downhead Somset 20 C5
Downhill Cnwll 4 D8
Downhill P & K 134 D2
Downholland Cross Lancs 88 D9
Downholme N York 103 M11
Downicarey Devon 5 P3
Downies Abers 151 N9
Downing Flints 80 H9
Downley Bucks 35 M5
Down St Mary Devon 8 H4
Downside Somset 20 B4
Downside Somset 20 B6
Downside Surrey 36 D9
Down Thomas Devon 6 E8
Downton Hants 13 N6
Downton Wilts 21 N10
Dowsby Lincs 74 B5
Dowsdale Lincs 74 E8
Doxey Staffs 70 F10
Doxford Nthumb 119 N6
Doynton S Glos 32 D10
Draethen Caerph 30 H7
Draffan S Lans 126 D8
Dragonby N Linc 92 F8
Dragons Green W Susx 24 D6
Drakeholes Notts 85 M2
Drakelow Worcs 57 Q8
Drakemyre N Ayrs 124 H7
Drakes Broughton Worcs 46 H5
Drakewalls Cnwll 6 C4
Draughton N York 96 F10
Draughton Nhants 60 G5
Drax N York 92 A5
Drax Hales N York 91 R5
Draycote Warwks 59 P10
Draycot Foliat Swindn 33 N9
Draycott Derbys 72 C4
Draycott Gloucs 47 N7
Draycott Shrops 57 Q6
Draycott Somset 19 N4
Draycott Somset 19 Q10
Draycott Worcs 46 G5
Draycott in the Clay Staffs 71 M9
Draycott in the Moors Staffs 70 H6
Drayford Devon 9 J2
Drayton C Port 15 J5
Drayton Leics 60 H2
Drayton Lincs 74 D3
Drayton Norfk 76 H9
Drayton Oxon 34 E6
Drayton Oxon 48 D6
Drayton Somset 19 M10
Drayton Worcs 58 D9
Drayton Bassett Staffs 59 J4
Drayton Beauchamp Bucks 35 P2
Drayton Manor Park Staffs 59 J4
Drayton Parslow Bucks 49 M9
Drayton St Leonard Oxon 34 G5
Drebley N York 96 G9
Dreemskerry IoM 80 g3
Dreen Hill Pembks 40 H8
Drefach Carmth 28 F2
Drefach Carmth 42 G7
Drefach Cerdgn 43 J5
Drefelin Carmth 42 G7
Dreghorn N Ayrs 125 K10
Drellingore Kent 27 M3
Drem E Loth 128 E4
Dresden C Stke 70 G6
Drewsteignton Devon 8 H6
Driby Lincs 87 L6
Driffield E R Yk 99 L9
Driffield Gloucs 33 L5
Driffield Cross Roads Gloucs 33 L5
Drift Cnwll 2 C8
Drigg Cumb 100 E11
Drighlington Leeds 90 G5
Drimnin Highld 137 P5
Drimpton Dorset 11 J4
Drimsallie Highld 138 H2
Dringhouses C York 98 B11
Drinkstone Suffk 64 D9
Drinkstone Green Suffk 64 D9
Drive End Dorset 11 M3
Driver's End Herts 50 F6
Drointon Staffs 71 J9
Droitwich Spa Worcs 46 G2
Dron P & K 134 E4
Dronfield Derbys 84 E5
Dronfield Woodhouse Derbys 84 D5
Drongan E Ayrs 114 H4
Dronley Angus 142 E10
Droop Dorset 12 C3
Dropping Well Rothm 84 E2
Droxford Hants 22 H11
Droylsden Tamesd 83 K5
Druid Denbgs 68 D6
Druidston Pembks 40 G7
Druimarbin Highld 139 K3
Druimavuic Ag & B 139 J8
Druimdrishaig Ag & B 123 M5
Druimindarroch Highld 145 L11
Drum Ag & B 124 A2
Drum P & K 134 C7
Drumalbin S Lans 116 C3
Drumbeg Highld 164 D10
Drumblade Abers 158 E9
Drumbreddon D & G 106 E9
Drumbuie Highld 153 P11
Drumburgh Cumb 110 E9
Drumburn D & G 109 J10
Drumburn D & G 109 L8
Drumchapel C Glas 125 N3
Drumchastle P & K 140 G6
Drumclog S Lans 125 Q10
Drumeldrie Fife 135 L7
Drumelzier Border 116 G4
Drumfearn Highld 145 L4
Drumfrennie Abers 151 J8
Drumgley Angus 142 G7
Drumguish Highld 148 D7
Drumin Moray 157 M11
Drumjohn D & G 115 K8
Drumlamford S Ayrs 107 J2
Drumlasie Abers 150 G6
Drumleaning Cumb 110 E10
Drumlemble Ag & B 120 C8
Drumlithie Abers 151 K11
Drummoddie D & G 107 L8
Drummore D & G 106 F10
Drummuir Moray 158 A9
Drumnadrochit Highld 155 P11
Drumnagorrach Moray 158 D7
Drumpark D & G 109 J5
Drumrunie Highld 161 K5
Drumshang S Ayrs 114 E5
Drumuie Highld 152 H8
Drumuillie Highld 148 G3
Drumvaich Stirlg 133 K7
Drunzie P & K 134 E6
Druridge Nthumb 119 Q11
Drury Flints 69 J2
Drws-y-coed Gwynd 67 J4
Drybeck Cumb 102 C7
Drybridge Moray 158 B5
Drybridge N Ayrs 125 K10
Drybrook Gloucs 46 B11
Dryburgh Border 118 A4
Dry Doddington Lincs 85 Q11
Dry Drayton Cambs 62 E8
Drymen Stirlg 132 F10
Drymuir Abers 159 M8
Drynoch Highld 152 G11
Dry Sandford Oxon 34 E4
Dryslwyn Carmth 43 L10
Dry Street Essex 37 Q3
Dryton Shrops 57 K3
Dubford Abers 159 J5
Dublin Suffk 64 H8
Duchally Highld 161 P3
Duck End Bed 50 C2
Duck End Cambs 62 B8
Duck End Essex 51 Q4
Duck End Essex 51 Q5
Duckend Green Essex 52 B7
Duckington Ches W 69 N4
Ducklington Oxon 34 C3
Duck's Cross Bed 61 P9
Duddenhoe End Essex 51 L3
Duddingston C Edin 127 P3
Duddington Nhants 73 P10
Duddlestone Somset 18 H10
Duddleswell E Susx 25 L5
Duddlewick Shrops 57 M8
Duddo Nthumb 118 H2
Duddon Ches W 69 P2
Duddon Bridge Cumb 94 D3
Duddon Common Ches W 81 Q11
Dudleston Shrops 69 K7
Dudleston Heath Shrops 69 L7
Dudley Dudley 58 D6

268 Dudley – Eaton Socon

Dudley N Tyne 113 L6
Dudley Hill C Brad 90 F4
Dudley Port Sandw 58 E6
Dudnill Shrops 57 L10
Dudsbury Dorset 13 J5
Dudswell Herts 35 Q3
Duffield Derbys 72 A2
Duffryn Neath 29 M5
Dufftown Moray 157 Q9
Duffus Moray 157 M4
Dufton Cumb 102 C5
Duggleby N York 98 H7
Duirinish Highld 153 P11
Duisdalemore Highld 145 M5
Duisky Highld 139 J2
Dukestown Blae G 30 F2
Duke Street Suffk 53 J3
Dukinfield Tamesd 83 K5
Dulas IoA 78 H7
Dulcote Somset 19 Q6
Dulford Devon 9 Q3
Dull P & K 141 K8
Dullatur N Lans 126 C2
Dullingham Cambs 63 K9
Dullingham Ley Cambs 63 K9
Dulnain Bridge Highld 148 H3
Duloe Bed 61 Q8
Duloe Cnwll 5 L10
Dulsie Bridge Highld 156 G9
Dulverton Somset 18 B9
Dulwich Gt Lon 36 H6
Dumbarton W Duns 125 L2
Dumbleton Gloucs 47 K7
Dumfries D & G 109 L5
Dumgoyne Stirlg 132 G11
Dummer Hants 22 G5
Dumpton Kent 39 Q8
Dun Angus 143 M6
Dunalastair P & K 140 H6
Dunan Ag & B 124 F3
Dunan Highld 145 J2
Dunan P & K 140 C6
Dunaverty Ag & B 120 C10
Dunball Somset 19 K6
Dunbar E Loth 128 H4
Dunbeath Highld 167 L11
Dunbeg Ag & B 138 F11
Dunblane Stirlg 133 M7
Dunbog Fife 134 H4
Dunbridge Hants 22 B9
Duncanston Highld 155 Q6
Duncanstone Abers 150 F2
Dunchideock Devon 9 L7
Dunchurch Warwks 59 Q10
Duncote Nhants 49 J4
Duncow D & G 109 L4
Duncrievie P & K 134 E6
Duncton W Susx 23 Q11
Dundee C Dund 142 G11
Dundee Airport C Dund 135 K2
Dundon Somset 19 N8
Dundonald S Ayrs 125 K11
Dundonnell Highld 160 H9
Dundraw Cumb 110 D11
Dundreggan Highld 147 J5
Dundrennan D & G 108 F11
Dundry N Som 31 Q11
Dunecht Abers 151 K6
Dunfermline Fife 134 D10
Dunfield Gloucs 33 M5
Dunford Bridge Barns 83 Q4
Dungate Kent 38 F10
Dungavel S Lans 126 B10
Dunge Wilts 20 G4
Dungeness Kent 27 J8
Dungworth Sheff 84 C3
Dunham Massey Traffd 82 F7
Dunham-on-the-Hill Ches W 81 P10
Dunham-on-Trent Notts 85 P6
Dunhampstead Worcs 46 H2
Dunhampton Worcs 58 B11
Dunham Town Traffd 82 F7
Dunham Woodhouses Traffd 82 F7
Dunholme Lincs 86 D5
Dunino Fife 135 N5
Dunipace Falk 133 N11
Dunkeld P & K 141 P9
Dunkerton BaNES 20 D3
Dunkeswell Devon 10 C3
Dunkeswick N York 97 M11
Dunkirk Ches W 81 M10
Dunkirk Kent 39 J10
Dunkirk S Glos 32 E7
Dunkirk Wilts 21 J2
Dunk's Green Kent 37 P10
Dunlappie Angus 143 K4
Dunley Hants 22 E4
Dunley Worcs 57 P11
Dunlop E Ayrs 125 L8
Dunmaglass Highld 147 P3
Dunmere Cnwll 4 G8
Dunmore Falk 133 P10
Dunnet Highld 167 M2
Dunnichen Angus 143 J8
Dunning P & K 134 C5
Dunnington C York 98 D10
Dunnington E R Yk 99 P10
Dunnington Warwks 47 L4
Dunnockshaw Lancs 89 N5
Dunn Street Kent 38 C9
Dunoon Ag & B 124 F2
Dunphail Moray 157 J8
Dunragit D & G 106 G6
Duns Border 129 K9
Dunsa Derbys 84 B6
Dunsby Lincs 74 B5
Dunscar Bolton 89 L8
Dunscore D & G 109 J4
Dunscroft Donc 91 Q9
Dunsdale R & Cl 104 H7
Dunsden Green Oxon 35 K9
Dunsdon Devon 16 E10
Dunsfold Surrey 24 B3
Dunsford Devon 9 K7
Dunshalt Fife 134 G5
Dunshillock Abers 159 N8
Dunsill Notts 84 G8
Dunsley N York 105 N8
Dunsley Staffs 58 C8
Dunsmore Bucks 35 N3
Dunsop Bridge Lancs 95 P11
Dunstable C Beds 50 B6
Dunstall Staffs 71 M10
Dunstall Common Worcs 46 G6
Dunstall Green Suffk 63 M8
Dunstan Nthumb 119 P7
Dunstan Steads Nthumb 119 P6
Dunster Somset 18 C6
Duns Tew Oxon 48 E9
Dunston Gatesd 113 K8
Dunston Lincs 86 E8
Dunston Norfk 77 J11
Dunston Staffs 70 G11
Dunstone Devon 6 F8
Dunstone Devon 8 H9
Dunston Heath Staffs 70 G11
Dunsville Donc 91 Q9
Dunswell E R Yk 93 J3
Dunsyre S Lans 127 K8
Dunterton Devon 5 P6
Dunthrop Oxon 48 C9
Duntisbourne Abbots Gloucs 33 J3
Duntisbourne Leer Gloucs 33 J3
Duntisbourne Rouse Gloucs 33 J3
Duntish Dorset 11 P3
Duntocher W Duns 125 M3
Dunton Bucks 49 M10
Dunton C Beds 50 F2
Dunton Norfk 76 B5
Dunton Bassett Leics 60 B2
Dunton Green Kent 37 M9
Dunton Wayletts Essex 37 Q2
Duntulm Highld 152 G3
Dunure S Ayrs 114 E4
Dunvant Swans 28 G6
Dunvegan Highld 152 D8
Dunwich Suffk 65 P7
Dunwood Staffs 70 G3
Durdar Cumb 110 H10
Durgan Cnwll 3 K8
Durham Dur 103 Q2
Durham Cathedral Dur 103 Q2
Durham Services Dur 104 B3
Durham Tees Valley Airport S on T 104 C8
Durisdeer D & G 116 B10
Durisdeermill D & G 116 B10
Durkar Wakefd 91 J7
Durleigh Somset 19 J7
Durley Hants 22 F11
Durley Wilts 21 P2
Durley Street Hants 22 F11
Durlock Kent 39 N10
Durlock Kent 39 P9
Durlow Common Herefs 46 B7
Durn Rochdl 89 Q7
Durness Highld 165 K3
Durno Abers 151 J2
Duror Highld 138 H6
Durran Ag & B 131 K6
Durrington W Susx 24 D9
Durrington Wilts 21 N6
Durris Abers 151 K8
Dursley Gloucs 32 E5
Dursley Cross Gloucs 46 C10
Durston Somset 19 J9
Durweston Dorset 12 E3
Duston Nhants 60 F8
Duthil Highld 148 G3
Dutlas Powys 56 C9
Duton Hill Essex 51 P5
Dutson Cnwll 5 N4
Dutton Ches W 82 C9
Duxford Cambs 62 G11
Duxford Oxon 34 C5
Duxford IWM Cambs 62 G11
Dwygyfylchi Conwy 79 N9
Dwyran IoA 78 G11
Dyce C Aber 151 M5
Dyer's End Essex 52 B4
Dyfatty Carmth 28 E4
Dyffrydan Gwynd 54 F2
Dyffryn Brdgnd 29 N6
Dyffryn Myr Td 30 E4
Dyffryn V Glam 30 E10
Dyffryn Ardudwy Gwynd 67 K10
Dyffryn Castell Cerdgn 54 H8
Dyffryn Cellwen Neath 29 N2
Dyke Lincs 74 B6
Dyke Moray 156 H6
Dykehead Angus 142 C7
Dykehead Angus 142 F6
Dykehead N Lans 126 F6
Dykehead Stirlg 132 H8
Dykelands Abers 143 N4
Dykends Angus 142 D6
Dykeside Abers 158 H9
Dylife Powys 55 K6
Dymchurch Kent 27 K6
Dymock Gloucs 46 D8
Dyrham S Glos 32 D9
Dysart Fife 135 J9
Dyserth Denbgs 80 F9

E

Eachway Worcs 58 E9
Eachwick Nthumb 112 H6
Eagland Hill Lancs 95 J11
Eagle Lincs 85 Q7
Eagle Barnsdale Lincs 85 Q7
Eagle Moor Lincs 85 Q7
Eaglescliffe S on T 104 D7
Eaglesfield Cumb 100 E5
Eaglesfield D & G 110 D6
Eaglesham E Rens 125 P7
Eagley Bolton 89 L8
Eairy IoM 80 c6
Eakring Notts 85 L8
Ealand N Linc 92 C8
Ealing Gt Lon 36 E4
Eals Nthumb 111 N9
Eamont Bridge Cumb 101 P5
Earby Lancs 96 D11
Earcroft Bl w D 89 K6
Eardington Shrops 57 N6
Eardisland Herefs 45 N3
Eardisley Herefs 45 L5
Eardiston Shrops 69 L9
Eardiston Worcs 57 M11
Earith Cambs 62 E5
Earle Nthumb 119 J5
Earlestown St Hel 82 C5
Earley Wokham 35 K10
Earlham Norfk 76 H10
Earlish Highld 152 F5
Earls Barton Nhants 61 J8
Earls Colne Essex 52 E6
Earls Common Worcs 47 J3
Earl's Croome Worcs 46 G6
Earlsditton Shrops 57 L9
Earlsdon Covtry 59 M9
Earl's Down E Susx 25 P7
Earlsferry Fife 135 M7
Earlsfield Gt Lon 36 G6
Earlsford Abers 159 K11
Earl's Green Suffk 64 E8
Earlsheaton Kirk 90 H6
Earl Shilton Leics 72 D11
Earl Soham Suffk 65 J9
Earl Sterndale Derbys 83 N11
Earlston Border 117 R3
Earlston E Ayrs 125 L10
Earl Stonham Suffk 64 G10
Earlswood Surrey 36 G11
Earlswood Warwks 58 H10
Earlswood Common Mons 31 N6
Earnley W Susx 15 M7
Earnshaw Bridge Lancs 88 G6
Earsdon N Tyne 113 M6
Earsdon Nthumb 113 J2
Earsham Norfk 65 L4
Earswick C York 98 C9
Eartham W Susx 15 P5
Earthcott S Glos 32 C7
Easby N York 104 G9
Easdale Ag & B 130 E4
Easebourne W Susx 23 P10
Easenhall Warwks 59 Q9
Eashing Surrey 23 P6
Easington Bucks 35 J2
Easington Dur 104 D2
Easington E R Yk 93 Q7
Easington Nthumb 119 M4
Easington Oxon 35 J5
Easington R & Cl 105 K7
Easington Colliery Dur 104 D2
Easington Lane Sundld 113 N11
Easingwold N York 98 A7
Easole Street Kent 39 N11
Eassie and Nevay Angus 142 E9
East Aberthaw V Glam 30 D11
East Allington Devon 7 K9
East Anstey Devon 17 R6
East Anton Hants 22 C5
East Appleton N York 103 P11
East Ashey IoW 14 G9
East Ashling W Susx 15 M5
East Aston Hants 22 D5
East Ayton N York 99 K3
East Balsdon Cnwll 5 M2
East Bank Blae G 30 H3
East Barkwith Lincs 86 G4
East Barming Kent 38 B11
East Barnby N York 105 M8
East Barnet Gt Lon 50 G11
East Barns E Loth 129 J4
East Barsham Norfk 76 C5
East Beckham Norfk 76 H4
East Bedfont Gt Lon 36 C6
East Bergholt Suffk 53 J5
East Bierley Kirk 90 F5
East Bilney Norfk 76 D8
East Blatchington E Susx 25 L10
East Bloxworth Dorset 12 E6
East Boldon S Tyne 113 N8
East Boldre Hants 14 C6
East Bolton Nthumb 119 M7
Eastbourne Darltn 104 B8
Eastbourne E Susx 25 P11
East Bower Somset 19 K7
East Bradenham Norfk 76 C10
East Brent Somset 19 K4
Eastbridge Suffk 65 P8
East Bridgford Notts 72 H2
East Briscoe Dur 103 J7
Eastbrook V Glam 30 G10
East Buckland Devon 17 M5
East Budleigh Devon 9 Q8
Eastburn C Brad 90 C2
Eastburn E R Yk 99 K9
East Burnham Bucks 35 Q8
East Burton Dorset 12 D7
Eastbury W Berk 34 B9
East Butsfield Dur 112 H11
East Butterwick N Linc 92 D9
Eastby N York 96 F10
East Calder W Loth 127 K4
East Carleton Norfk 76 H11
East Carlton Leeds 90 G2
East Carlton Nhants 60 H3
East Chaldon Dorset 12 C8
East Challow Oxon 34 C7
East Charleton Devon 7 K10
East Chelborough Dorset 11 M3
East Chiltington E Susx 25 J7
East Chinnock Somset 11 K2
East Chisenbury Wilts 21 M4
East Cholderton Hants 21 Q5
Eastchurch Kent 38 G7
East Clandon Surrey 36 C10
East Claydon Bucks 49 K9
East Clevedon N Som 31 M10
East Coker Somset 11 L2
Eastcombe Gloucs 32 G4
Eastcombe Somset 18 G8
East Compton Somset 20 B6
East Cornworthy Devon 7 L7
East Cote Cumb 109 P9
Eastcote Gt Lon 36 D3
Eastcote Nhants 49 J4
Eastcote Solhll 59 J9
Eastcott Cnwll 16 D8
Eastcott Wilts 21 K3
East Cottingwith E R Yk 92 B2
Eastcourt Wilts 21 P2
Eastcourt Wilts 33 J6
East Cowes IoW 14 F7
East Cowick E R Yk 91 R6
East Cowton N York 104 B10
East Cramlington Nthumb 113 L5
East Cranmore Somset 20 C6
East Creech Dorset 12 F8
East Curthwaite Cumb 110 F11
East Dean E Susx 25 N11
East Dean Gloucs 46 C10
East Dean Hants 21 Q9
East Dean W Susx 15 P4
Eastdown Devon 7 L9
East Down Devon 17 L3
East Drayton Notts 85 N5
East Dulwich Gt Lon 36 H5
East Dundry N Som 31 Q11
East Ella C KuH 93 J5
East End Bed 61 P9
East End C Beds 49 Q6
East End E R Yk 93 L4
East End E R Yk 93 N5
Eastend Essex 38 F3
East End Essex 51 K8
East End Hants 14 C7
East End Hants 22 D2
East End Herts 51 L5
East End Kent 26 D4
East End Kent 38 G7
East End M Keyn 49 P6
East End Oxon 48 C11
East End Somset 20 C5
East End Suffk 53 K4
Easter Balmoral Abers 149 P9
Easter Compton S Glos 31 Q8
Easter Dalziel Highld 156 D7
Eastergate W Susx 15 P5
Easterhouse C Glas 126 B4
Easter Howgate Mdloth 127 N5
Easter Kinkell Highld 155 Q6
Easter Moniack Highld 155 Q9
Eastern Green Covtry 59 L9
Easter Ord Abers 151 L7
Easter Pitkierie Fife 135 P6
Easter Skeld Shet 169 q9
Easter Softlaw Border 118 E4
Easterton Wilts 21 K4
Eastertown Somset 19 K4
East Everleigh Wilts 21 P4
East Farleigh Kent 38 B11
East Farndon Nhants 60 F4
East Ferry Lincs 92 D11
Eastfield N Lans 126 F5
Eastfield N York 99 L4
East Firsby Lincs 86 D3
East Fortune E Loth 128 E4
East Garforth Leeds 91 L4
East Garston W Berk 34 C9
Eastgate Dur 103 J3
Eastgate Lincs 74 B7
Eastgate Norfk 76 G7
East Ginge Oxon 34 D7
East Goscote Leics 72 G8
East Grafton Wilts 21 Q2
East Green Suffk 65 N8
East Grimstead Wilts 21 P9
East Grinstead W Susx 25 J3
East Guldeford E Susx 26 F7
East Haddon Nhants 60 E7
East Hagbourne Oxon 34 F7
East Halton N Linc 93 K7
East Ham Gt Lon 37 K4
Eastham Wirral 81 M8
Eastham Ferry Wirral 81 M8
Easthampton Herefs 45 N2
East Hanney Oxon 34 D6
East Hanningfield Essex 52 C11
East Hardwick Wakefd 91 M7
East Harling Norfk 64 D4
East Harlsey N York 104 D11
East Harnham Wilts 21 M9
East Harptree BaNES 19 Q3
East Hartford Nthumb 113 L5
East Harting W Susx 23 L11
East Hatch Wilts 20 H9
East Hatley Cambs 62 C10
East Hauxwell N York 97 J2
East Haven Angus 143 K10
Eastheath Wokham 35 L11
East Heckington Lincs 74 C2
East Hedleyhope Dur 103 N2
East Helmsdale Highld 163 N3
East Hendred Oxon 34 E7
East Heslerton N York 99 J5
East Hewish N Som 19 M2
East Hoathly E Susx 25 M7
East Holme Dorset 12 E7
East Hope Dur 103 K9
Easthope Shrops 57 K5
Easthorpe Essex 52 F7
Easthorpe Notts 85 M10
East Horrington Somset 19 Q5
East Horsley Surrey 36 C10
East Horton Nthumb 119 K4
East Howe BCP 13 J5
East Huntington C York 98 C9
East Huntspill Somset 19 K5
East Hyde C Beds 50 D7
East Ilkerton Devon 17 N2
East Ilsley W Berk 34 E8
Eastington Devon 8 H3
Eastington Gloucs 32 E3
Eastington Gloucs 33 M2
East Keal Lincs 87 L8
East Kennett Wilts 33 M11
East Keswick Leeds 91 K2
East Kilbride S Lans 125 Q7
East Kimber Devon 8 C5
East Kirkby Lincs 87 K8
East Knighton Dorset 12 D7
East Knowstone Devon 17 Q7
East Knoyle Wilts 20 G8
East Lambrook Somset 19 M11
Eastlands D & G 108 H6
East Langdon Kent 27 P2
East Langton Leics 60 F2
East Lavant W Susx 15 N5
East Lavington W Susx 23 P11
East Layton N York 103 N9
Eastleach Martin Gloucs 33 P4
Eastleach Turville Gloucs 33 N3
East Leake Notts 72 F5
East Learmouth Nthumb 118 G3
East Leigh Devon 6 H8
East Leigh Devon 7 K7
East Leigh Devon 8 G3
Eastleigh Devon 16 H6
Eastleigh Hants 22 E11
East Lexham Norfk 76 B8
Eastling Kent 38 G10
East Linton E Loth 128 F4
East Liss Hants 23 L9
East Lockinge Oxon 34 D7
East Lound N Linc 92 C11
East Lulworth Dorset 12 E8
East Lutton N York 99 J7
East Lydeard Somset 18 G9
East Lydford Somset 19 Q8
East Malling Kent 38 B10
East Malling Heath Kent 37 Q9
East Marden W Susx 15 M4
East Markham Notts 85 M6
East Martin Hants 21 L11
East Marton N York 96 D10
East Meon Hants 23 J10
East Mere Devon 18 C11
East Mersea Essex 52 H9
East Midlands Airport Leics 72 D5
East Molesey Surrey 36 D7
Eastmoor Norfk 75 P10
East Morden Dorset 12 F6
East Morton C Brad 90 D2
East Morton D & G 116 B10
East Ness N York 98 D5
East Newton E R Yk 93 N3
Eastney C Port 15 J7
Eastnor Herefs 46 D7
East Norton Leics 73 K10
Eastoft N Linc 92 D7
East Ogwell Devon 7 L4
Easton Cambs 61 P6
Easton Cumb 110 E9
Easton Devon 8 H7
Easton Dorset 11 P10
Easton Hants 22 F8
Easton Lincs 73 N5
Easton Norfk 76 G9
Easton Somset 19 P5
Easton Suffk 65 K10
Easton W Berk 34 D10
Easton Wilts 32 G10
Easton Grey Wilts 32 G7
Easton-in-Gordano N Som 31 P9
Easton Maudit Nhants 61 J9
Easton-on-the-Hill Nhants 73 Q10
Easton Royal Wilts 21 P2
East Orchard Dorset 20 F11
East Ord Nthumb 129 P9
East Panson Devon 5 P3
East Parley BCP 13 J5
East Peckham Kent 37 Q11
East Pennard Somset 19 Q7
East Perry Cambs 61 Q7
East Portlemouth Devon 7 K11
East Prawle Devon 7 K11
East Preston W Susx 24 C10
East Pulham Dorset 11 Q3
East Putford Devon 16 F8
East Quantoxhead Somset 18 F6
East Rainham Medway 38 D8
East Rainton Sundld 113 M11
East Ravendale NE Lin 93 M11
East Raynham Norfk 76 B6
Eastrea Cambs 74 E11
Eastriggs D & G 110 D7
East Rigton Leeds 91 K2
Eastrington E R Yk 92 C5
East Rolstone N Som 19 L2
Eastrop Swindn 33 P6
East Rounton N York 104 D10
East Rudham Norfk 76 A6
East Runton Norfk 76 H3
East Ruston Norfk 77 L6
Eastry Kent 39 P11
East Saltoun E Loth 128 D6
Eastshaw W Susx 23 N10
East Sheen Gt Lon 36 F6
East Shefford W Berk 34 C10
East Sleekburn Nthumb 113 L4
East Somerton Norfk 77 P8
East Stockwith Lincs 85 N2
East Stoke Dorset 12 E7
East Stoke Notts 85 N11
East Stour Dorset 20 F10
East Stour Common Dorset 20 F10
East Stourmouth Kent 39 N9
East Stowford Devon 17 L6
East Stratton Hants 22 F6
East Studdal Kent 27 P2
East Sutton Kent 26 D2
East Taphouse Cnwll 5 K9
East-the-Water Devon 16 H6
East Thirston Nthumb 119 N10
East Tilbury Thurr 37 Q5
East Tilbury Village Thurr 37 Q5
East Tisted Hants 23 K8
East Torrington Lincs 86 F4
East Tuddenham Norfk 76 F9
East Tytherley Hants 21 Q9
East Tytherton Wilts 33 J10
East Village Devon 9 K3
Eastville Bristl 32 B10
Eastville Lincs 87 M9
East Wall Shrops 57 J6
East Walton Norfk 75 P7
East Water Somset 19 P4
East Week Devon 8 G6
Eastwell Leics 73 K5
East Wellow Hants 22 B10
East Wemyss Fife 135 J8
East Whitburn W Loth 126 H4
Eastwick Herts 51 K8
East Wickham Gt Lon 37 L5
East Williamston Pembks 41 L10
East Winch Norfk 75 N7
East Winterslow Wilts 21 P8
East Wittering W Susx 15 L7
East Witton N York 96 H3
Eastwood Notts 84 G11
Eastwood Sthend 38 D4
East Woodburn Nthumb 112 D3
Eastwood End Cambs 62 F2
East Woodhay Hants 22 D2
East Woodlands Somset 20 E6
East Worldham Hants 23 L7
East Wretham Norfk 64 C3
East Youlstone Devon 16 D8
Eathorpe Warwks 59 N11
Eaton Ches E 83 J11
Eaton Ches W 69 Q2
Eaton Leics 73 K5
Eaton Norfk 77 J10
Eaton Notts 85 M5
Eaton Oxon 34 D4
Eaton Shrops 56 F7
Eaton Shrops 57 J7
Eaton Bishop Herefs 45 N7
Eaton Bray C Beds 49 Q10
Eaton Constantine Shrops 57 K3
Eaton Ford Cambs 61 Q9
Eaton Green C Beds 49 Q10
Eaton Hastings Oxon 33 Q5
Eaton Mascott Shrops 57 J3
Eaton Socon Cambs 61 Q9

Eaton upon Tern Shrops 70 B10
Eaves Brow Warrtn 82 D6
Eaves Green Solhll 59 L8
Ebberston N York 98 H4
Ebbesborne Wake Wilts 21 J10
Ebbw Vale Blae G 30 G3
Ebchester Dur 112 H9
Ebdon N Som 19 L2
Ebford Devon 9 N7
Ebley Gloucs 32 F3
Ebnal Ches W 69 N5
Ebnall Herefs 45 P3
Ebrington Gloucs 47 N6
Ebsworthy Devon 8 D6
Ecchinswell Hants 22 E3
Ecclaw Border 129 K6
Ecclefechan D & G 110 C6
Eccles Border 118 E2
Eccles Kent 38 B9
Eccles Salfd 82 G5
Ecclesall Sheff 84 D4
Ecclesfield Sheff 84 E2
Eccles Green Herefs 45 M5
Eccleshall Staffs 70 E9
Eccleshill C Brad 90 F3
Ecclesmachan W Loth 127 K3
Eccles on Sea Norfk 77 N6
Eccles Road Norfk 64 E4
Eccleston Ches W 69 M2
Eccleston Lancs 88 G7
Eccleston St Hel 81 P5
Eccleston Green Lancs 88 G7
Echt Abers 151 J6
Eckford Border 118 D5
Eckington Derbys 84 F5
Eckington Worcs 46 H6
Ecton Nhants 60 H8
Ecton Staffs 71 K3
Edale Derbys 83 P7
Eday Ork 169 e2
Eday Airport Ork 169 e3
Edburton W Susx 24 F8
Edderside Cumb 109 P11
Edderton Highld 162 G10
Eddington Kent 39 L8
Eddleston Border 127 N8
Eddlewood S Lans 126 C7
Edenbridge Kent 37 K11
Edenfield Lancs 89 N7
Edenhall Cumb 101 Q4
Edenham Lincs 73 R6
Eden Mount Cumb 95 J5
Eden Park Gt Lon 37 J7
Eden Project Cnwll 3 Q3
Edensor Derbys 84 B7
Edentaggart Ag & B 132 C9
Edenthorpe Donc 91 Q9
Edern Gwynd 66 D7
Edgarley Somset 19 P7
Edgbaston Birm 58 G8
Edgcombe Cnwll 3 J7
Edgcott Bucks 49 J10
Edgcott Somset 17 Q4
Edge Gloucs 32 F3
Edge Shrops 56 F3
Edgebolton Shrops 69 Q10
Edge End Gloucs 31 Q2
Edgefield Norfk 76 F5
Edgefield Green Norfk 76 F5
Edgefold Bolton 89 L9
Edge Green Ches W 69 N4
Edgehill Warwks 48 C5
Edgerley Shrops 69 L11
Edgerton Kirk 90 E7
Edgeside Lancs 89 N6
Edgeworth Gloucs 32 H3
Edgeworthy Devon 9 K2
Edginswell Torbay 7 M5
Edgiock Worcs 47 K2
Edgmond Wrekin 70 C11
Edgmond Marsh Wrekin 70 C10
Edgton Shrops 56 F7
Edgware Gt Lon 36 E2
Edgworth Bl w D 89 L7
Edinbane Highld 152 E7
Edinburgh C Edin 127 P3
Edinburgh Airport C Edin 127 L3
Edinburgh Castle C Edin 127 P3
Edinburgh Old & New
  Town C Edin 127 P3
Edinburgh Royal Botanic
  Gardens C Edin 127 N2
Edinburgh Zoo RZSS C Edin 127 N3
Edingale Staffs 59 K2
Edingham D & G 108 H8
Edingley Notts 85 L9
Edingthorpe Norfk 77 L5
Edingthorpe Green Norfk 77 L5
Edington Border 129 M9
Edington Nthumb 113 J4
Edington Somset 19 L7
Edington Wilts 20 H4
Edington Burtle Somset 19 L6
Edingworth Somset 19 L4
Edistone Devon 16 D7
Edithmead Somset 19 K5
Edith Weston Rutlnd 73 N9
Edlesborough Bucks 49 Q11
Edlingham Nthumb 119 M9
Edlington Lincs 86 H6
Edmond Castle Cumb 111 J9
Edmondsham Dorset 13 J2
Edmondsley Dur 113 K11
Edmondthorpe Leics 73 M7
Edmonton Cnwll 4 F7
Edmonton Gt Lon 36 H2
Edmundbyers Dur 112 F10
Ednam Border 118 D3
Ednaston Derbys 71 N6
Edney Common Essex 51 Q10
Edradynate P & K 141 L7
Edrom Border 129 L8
Edstaston Shrops 69 P8
Edstone Warwks 47 N2
Edvin Loach Herefs 46 C3
Edwalton Notts 72 F3
Edwardstone Suffk 52 F3
Edwardsville Myr Td 30 E5
Edwinsford Carmth 43 M8
Edwinstowe Notts 85 K7
Edworth C Beds 50 F2
Edwyn Ralph Herefs 46 B3
Edzell Angus 143 L4
Edzell Woods Abers 143 L4
Efail-fach Neath 29 L5

Efail Isaf Rhondd 30 E8
Efailnewydd Gwynd 66 F7
Efail-Rhyd Powys 68 G9
Efailwen Carmth 41 M5
Efenechtyd Denbgs 68 F3
Effgill D & G 110 F2
Effingham Surrey 36 D10
Effingham Junction Surrey 36 D9
Efflinch Staffs 71 M11
Efford Devon 9 L4
Egbury Hants 22 D4
Egdean W Susx 23 Q10
Egerton Bolton 89 L8
Egerton Kent 26 F2
Egerton Forstal Kent 26 E2
Eggborough N York 91 P6
Eggbuckland C Plym 6 E7
Eggesford Devon 17 M9
Eggington C Beds 49 Q9
Egginton Derbys 71 P9
Egglescliffe S on T 104 D8
Eggleston Dur 103 J6
Egham Surrey 36 B6
Egham Wick Surrey 35 Q10
Egleton Rutlnd 73 M9
Eglingham Nthumb 119 M7
Egloshayle Cnwll 4 G7
Egloskerry Cnwll 5 M4
Eglwysbach Conwy 79 Q10
Eglwys Cross Wrexhm 69 N6
Eglwys Fach Cerdgn 54 F5
Eglwyswrw Pembks 41 M3
Egmanton Notts 85 M7
Egremont Cumb 100 D8
Egremont Wirral 81 L6
Egton N York 105 M9
Egton Bridge N York 105 M10
Egypt Bucks 35 Q7
Egypt Hants 22 E6
Eigg Highld 144 G10
Eight Ash Green Essex 52 F6
Eilanreach Highld 145 P4
Eilean Donan Castle Highld 145 Q2
Eisgein W Isls 168 i6
Eishken W Isls 168 i6
Eisteddfa Gurig Cerdgn 54 H8
Elan Valley Powys 55 K11
Elan Village Powys 44 C2
Elberton S Glos 32 B7
Elbridge W Susx 15 P6
Elburton C Plym 6 E8
Elcombe Swindn 33 M8
Elcot W Berk 34 C11
Eldernell Cambs 74 F11
Eldersfield Worcs 46 E8
Elderslie Rens 125 L5
Elder Street Essex 51 N4
Eldon Dur 103 P5
Eldwick C Brad 90 E2
Elerch Cerdgn 54 F7
Elfhill Abers 151 L10
Elford Nthumb 119 N4
Elford Staffs 59 J2
Elgin Moray 157 N5
Elgol Highld 144 H5
Elham Kent 27 L3
Elie Fife 135 M7
Elilaw Nthumb 119 J9
Elim IoA 78 F8
Eling Hants 14 C4
Elkesley Notts 85 L5
Elkstone Gloucs 33 J2
Ella Abers 158 F6
Ellacombe Torbay 7 N4
Elland Calder 90 E6
Elland Lower Edge Calder 90 E6
Ellary Ag & B 123 M4
Ellastone Staffs 71 L6
Ellel Lancs 95 K9
Ellemford Border 129 J7
Ellenabeich Ag & B 130 E4
Ellenborough Cumb 100 D3
Ellenbrook Salfd 82 F4
Ellenhall Staffs 70 E9
Ellen's Green Surrey 24 C3
Ellerbeck N York 104 D11
Ellerby N York 105 L8
Ellerdine Heath Wrekin 69 R10
Ellerhayes Devon 9 N4
Elleric Ag & B 139 J8
Ellerker E R Yk 92 F5
Ellers N York 90 C2
Ellerton E R Yk 92 B3
Ellerton N York 103 Q11
Ellerton Shrops 70 C9
Ellesborough Bucks 35 M3
Ellesmere Shrops 69 L8
Ellesmere Port Ches W 81 N9
Ellingham Hants 13 K3
Ellingham Norfk 65 M3
Ellingham Nthumb 119 N5
Ellingstring N York 97 J4
Ellington Cambs 61 Q6
Ellington Nthumb 113 L2
Ellington Thorpe Cambs 61 Q6
Elliots Green Somset 20 E5
Ellisfield Hants 23 H5
Ellishader Highld 153 J4
Ellistown Leics 72 C8
Ellon Abers 159 N11
Ellonby Cumb 101 M3
Ellough Suffk 65 N4
Elloughton E R Yk 92 F5
Ellwood Gloucs 31 Q3
Elm Cambs 75 J9
Elmbridge Worcs 58 D11
Elmdon Essex 51 L3
Elmdon Solhll 59 J8
Elmdon Heath Solhll 59 J8
Elmer W Susx 15 Q6
Elmers End Gt Lon 37 J7
Elmer's Green Lancs 88 G9
Elmesthorpe Leics 72 D11
Elm Green Essex 52 C10
Elmhurst Staffs 58 H2
Elmley Castle Worcs 47 J6
Elmley Lovett Worcs 58 C11
Elmore Gloucs 46 E11
Elmore Back Gloucs 46 E11
Elm Park Gt Lon 37 M3
Elmscott Devon 16 C7
Elmsett Suffk 53 J2
Elms Green Worcs 57 N11
Elmstead Heath Essex 53 J7

Elmstead Market Essex 53 J7
Elmstead Row Essex 53 J7
Elmsted Kent 27 K3
Elmstone Kent 39 N9
Elmstone Hardwicke Gloucs 46 H9
Elmswell E R Yk 99 H3
Elmswell Suffk 64 D9
Elmton Derbys 84 H6
Elphin Highld 161 L4
Elphinstone E Loth 128 B6
Elrick Abers 151 L6
Elrig D & G 107 K8
Elrington Nthumb 112 C8
Elsdon Nthumb 112 D2
Elsecar Barns 91 K11
Elsenham Essex 51 M5
Elsfield Oxon 34 F2
Elsham N Linc 92 H8
Elsing Norfk 76 F8
Elslack N York 96 D11
Elson Hants 14 H6
Elson Shrops 69 L7
Elsrickle S Lans 116 F2
Elstead Surrey 23 P6
Elsted W Susx 23 M11
Elsthorpe Lincs 73 R6
Elstob Dur 104 B6
Elston Lancs 88 H4
Elston Notts 85 N11
Elston Wilts 21 L6
Elstone Devon 17 M8
Elstow Bed 61 N11
Elstree Herts 50 E11
Elstronwick E R Yk 93 M4
Elswick Lancs 88 E3
Elswick N u Ty 113 K8
Elsworth Cambs 62 D8
Elterwater Cumb 101 K10
Eltham Gt Lon 37 K6
Eltisley Cambs 62 C9
Elton Bury 89 M8
Elton Cambs 61 N2
Elton Ches W 81 P9
Elton Derbys 84 B8
Elton Gloucs 32 D2
Elton Herefs 56 H10
Elton S on T 104 D7
Elton Green Ches W 81 P10
Elton-on-the-Hill Notts 73 K3
Eltringham Nthumb 112 G8
Elvanfoot S Lans 116 D7
Elvaston Derbys 72 C4
Elveden Suffk 63 P4
Elvetham Heath Hants 23 M4
Elvingston E Loth 128 D5
Elvington C York 98 E11
Elvington Kent 39 N11
Elwell Devon 17 M5
Elwick Hartpl 104 E4
Elwick Nthumb 119 M3
Elworth Ches E 70 C2
Elworthy Somset 18 E8
Ely Cambs 62 H4
Ely Cardif 30 F9
Emberton M Keyn 49 N5
Embleton Cumb 100 G4
Embleton Cumb 104 D5
Embleton Nthumb 119 P6
Embo Highld 163 J4
Emborough Somset 20 B4
Embo Street Highld 163 J8
Embsay N York 96 F10
Emery Down Hants 13 N3
Emley Kirk 90 G8
Emley Moor Kirk 90 G8
Emmbrook Wokam 35 M11
Emmer Green Readg 35 K9
Emmett Carr Derbys 84 G5
Emmington Oxon 35 K4
Emneth Norfk 75 J9
Emneth Hungate Norfk 75 N9
Empingham Rutlnd 73 N9
Empshott Hants 23 L8
Empshott Green Hants 23 L8
Emsworth Hants 15 K5
Enborne W Berk 34 D11
Enborne Row W Berk 22 D2
Enchmarsh Shrops 57 J5
Endmoor Cumb 95 L4
Endon Staffs 70 G4
Endon Bank Staffs 70 G4
Enfield Gt Lon 51 J11
Enfield Lock Gt Lon 51 J11
Enfield Wash Gt Lon 51 J11
Enford Wilts 21 M4
Engine Common S Glos 32 C8
England's Gate Herefs 45 Q4
Englefield W Berk 34 H10
Englefield Green Surrey 35 Q10
Engleseabrook Ches E 70 D4
English Bicknor Gloucs 46 A11
Englishcombe BaNES 20 D2
English Frankton Shrops 69 N9
Engollan Cnwll 4 F7
Enham Alamein Hants 22 C5
Enmore Somset 18 H7
Enmore Green Dorset 20 G10
Ennerdale Bridge Cumb 100 F7
Enniscaven Cnwll 4 F10
Enochdhu P & K 141 Q5
Ensay Ag & B 137 K6
Ensbury BCP 13 J5
Ensdon Shrops 69 M11
Ensis Devon 17 K6
Enson Staffs 70 G9
Enstone Oxon 48 C10
Enterkinfoot D & G 116 B10
Enterpen N York 104 E9
Enville Staffs 58 B7
Eòlaigearraidh W Isls 168 c17
Eoligarry W Isls 168 c17
Epney Gloucs 32 E2
Epperstone Notts 85 L11
Epping Essex 51 L10
Epping Green Essex 51 K9
Epping Green Herts 51 J9
Epping Upland Essex 51 K10
Eppleby N York 103 N8
Eppleworth E R Yk 92 H4
Epsom Surrey 36 F8
Epwell Oxon 48 C6
Epworth N Linc 92 C10
Epworth Turbary N Linc 92 C10
Erbistock Wrexhm 69 L6

Erdington Birm 58 H6
Eridge Green E Susx 25 N3
Eridge Station E Susx 25 M4
Erines Ag & B 123 Q4
Eriska Ag & B 138 G9
Eriskay W Isls 168 c17
Eriswell Suffk 63 M5
Erith Gt Lon 37 M5
Erlestoke Wilts 21 J4
Ermington Devon 6 G8
Erpingham Norfk 76 H5
Erriottwood Kent 38 F10
Errogie Highld 147 P3
Errol P & K 134 G3
Erskine Rens 125 M3
Erskine Bridge Rens 125 M3
Ervie D & G 106 D4
Erwarton Suffk 53 M5
Erwood Powys 44 F5
Eryholme N York 104 B9
Eryrys Denbgs 68 H3
Escalls Cnwll 2 B8
Escomb Dur 103 N4
Escott Somset 18 E7
Escrick N York 91 Q2
Esgair Carmth 42 G9
Esgair Cerdgn 54 D11
Esgairgeiliog Powys 54 H3
Esgerdawe Carmth 43 M6
Esgyryn Conwy 79 Q9
Esh Dur 103 N2
Esher Surrey 36 D8
Esholt C Brad 90 F2
Eshott Nthumb 119 P11
Eshton N York 96 D9
Esh Winning Dur 103 N2
Eskadale Highld 155 N9
Eskbank Mdloth 127 Q4
Eskdale Green Cumb 100 F10
Eskdalemuir D & G 117 K11
Eske E R Yk 93 J2
Eskham Lincs 93 Q11
Eskholme Donc 91 Q7
Esperley Lane Ends Dur 103 M6
Esprick Lancs 88 E3
Essendine Rutlnd 73 Q8
Essendon Herts 50 G9
Essich Highld 156 A10
Essington Staffs 58 E4
Esslemont Abers 151 N2
Eston R & Cl 104 F7
Etal Nthumb 118 H3
Etchilhampton Wilts 21 K2
Etchingham E Susx 26 B6
Etchinghill Kent 27 L4
Etchinghill Staffs 71 J11
Etchingwood E Susx 25 M6
Etling Green Norfk 76 E9
Etloe Gloucs 32 C3
Eton W & M 35 Q9
Eton Wick W & M 35 Q9
Etruria C Stke 70 F5
Etteridge Highld 148 B9
Ettersgill Dur 102 G5
Ettiley Heath Ches E 70 C2
Ettingshall Wolves 58 D5
Ettington Warwks 47 Q5
Etton C Pete 74 B9
Etton E R Yk 92 H2
Ettrick Border 117 K8
Ettrickbridge Border 117 M6
Ettrickhill Border 117 K8
Etwall Derbys 71 P8
Eudon George Shrops 57 M7
Euston Suffk 64 B6
Euximoor Drove Cambs 75 J11
Euxton Lancs 88 H7
Evancoyd Powys 45 K4
Evanton Highld 155 R4
Evedon Lincs 86 E11
Evelith Shrops 57 N3
Evelix Highld 162 H9
Evenjobb Powys 45 K2
Evenley Nhants 48 G8
Evenlode Gloucs 47 P9
Evenwood Dur 103 N6
Evenwood Gate Dur 103 N6
Evercreech Somset 20 B7
Everingham E R Yk 92 D2
Everleigh Wilts 21 N4
Everley N York 99 K3
Eversholt C Beds 49 Q8
Evershot Dorset 11 M4
Eversley Hants 23 L2
Eversley Cross Hants 23 L2
Everthorpe E R Yk 92 F4
Everton C Beds 62 B10
Everton Hants 13 N6
Everton Lpool 81 L6
Everton Notts 85 L2
Evertown D & G 110 G4
Evesbatch Herefs 46 C5
Evesham Worcs 47 K6
Evington C Leic 72 G10
Ewden Village Sheff 90 H11
Ewell Surrey 36 F8
Ewell Minnis Kent 27 N3
Ewelme Oxon 34 H6
Ewen Gloucs 33 K5
Ewenny V Glam 29 P9
Ewerby Lincs 86 F11
Ewerby Thorpe Lincs 86 F11
Ewhurst Surrey 24 C2
Ewhurst Green E Susx 26 C7
Ewhurst Green Surrey 24 C2
Ewloe Flints 81 L11
Ewloe Green Flints 81 K11
Ewood Bl w D 89 K5
Ewood Bridge Lancs 89 M6
Eworthy Devon 8 D7
Ewshot Hants 23 M5
Ewyas Harold Herefs 45 M9
Exbourne Devon 8 F4
Exbury Hants 14 D6
Exceat E Susx 25 M11
Exebridge Somset 18 B9
Exelby N York 97 L3
Exeter Devon 9 N6
Exeter Airport Devon 9 N6
Exeter Services Devon 9 N6
Exford Somset 17 Q4
Exfordsgreen Shrops 56 H3
Exhall Warwks 47 M3
Exhall Warwks 59 N7
Exlade Street Oxon 35 J8

Exley Head C Brad 90 C2
Exminster Devon 9 M7
Exmoor National Park 17 R4
Exmouth Devon 9 P8
Exning Suffk 63 K7
Exted Kent 27 L3
Exton Devon 9 N7
Exton Hants 22 H10
Exton Rutlnd 73 N8
Exton Somset 18 B8
Exwick Devon 9 M6
Eyam Derbys 84 B5
Eydon Nhants 48 F5
Eye C Pete 74 D10
Eye Herefs 45 P2
Eye Suffk 64 G7
Eye Green C Pete 74 D10
Eyemouth Border 129 N7
Eyeworth C Beds 62 C11
Eyhorne Street Kent 38 D11
Eyke Suffk 65 L11
Eynesbury Cambs 61 Q9
Eynsford Kent 37 M7
Eynsham Oxon 34 D3
Eype Dorset 11 J6
Eyre Highld 152 G7
Eythorne Kent 27 N2
Eyton Herefs 45 P2
Eyton Shrops 56 F7
Eyton Shrops 56 F7
Eyton Shrops 69 M10
Eyton Wrexhm 69 L6
Eyton on Severn Shrops 57 K3
Eyton upon the Weald
  Moors Wrekin 57 M2

F

Faccombe Hants 22 C3
Faceby N York 104 E10
Fachwen Powys 68 D11
Facit Lancs 89 P7
Fackley Notts 84 G8
Faddiley Ches E 69 Q4
Fadmoor N York 98 D3
Faerdre Swans 29 J4
Faifley W Duns 125 M3
Failand N Som 31 P10
Failford S Ayrs 115 J2
Failsworth Oldham 83 J4
Fairbourne Gwynd 54 E2
Fairburn N York 91 M5
Fairfield Derbys 83 N10
Fairfield Kent 26 G6
Fairfield Worcs 58 D9
Fairfield Park Herts 50 F4
Fairford Gloucs 33 N4
Fairford Park Gloucs 33 N4
Fairgirth D & G 109 J9
Fair Green Norfk 75 N7
Fairhaven Lancs 88 C5
Fair Isle Shet 169 t14
Fair Isle Airport Shet 169 t14
Fairlands Surrey 23 Q4
Fairlie N Ayrs 124 G7
Fairlight E Susx 26 E9
Fairlight Cove E Susx 26 E9
Fairmile Devon 10 B5
Fairmile Surrey 36 D8
Fairnilee Border 117 P4
Fair Oak Hants 22 E11
Fairoak Staffs 70 D8
Fair Oak Green Hants 23 J2
Fairseat Kent 37 P8
Fairstead Essex 52 C8
Fairstead Norfk 75 M6
Fairstead Norfk 77 K7
Fairwarp E Susx 25 L5
Fairwater Cardif 30 F9
Fairy Cross Devon 16 G7
Fakenham Norfk 76 C6
Fakenham Magna Suffk 64 C6
Fala Mdloth 128 C7
Fala Dam Mdloth 128 C7
Falcut Nhants 48 G6
Faldingworth Lincs 86 E4
Faldouët Jersey 11 c2
Falfield S Glos 32 C6
Falkenham Suffk 53 N4
Falkirk Falk 133 P11
Falkirk Wheel Falk 133 P11
Falkland Fife 134 H6
Fallburn S Lans 116 D3
Fallgate Derbys 84 E8
Fallin Stirlg 133 N9
Fallodon Nthumb 119 N6
Fallowfield Manch 83 J6
Fallowfield Nthumb 112 D7
Falmer E Susx 25 J9
Falmouth Cnwll 3 L7
Falnash Border 117 M9
Falsgrave N York 99 L3
Falstone Nthumb 111 P3
Fanagmore Highld 164 E7
Fancott C Beds 50 B5
Fanellan Highld 155 N9
Fangdale Beck N York 98 B2
Fangfoss E R Yk 98 F10
Fannich Lodge Highld 154 H4
Fans Border 118 B2
Far Bletchley M Keyn 49 N8
Farcet Cambs 62 B2
Far Cotton Nhants 60 G9
Farden Shrops 57 K9
Fareham Hants 14 G5
Farewell Staffs 58 G2
Far Forest Worcs 57 N9
Farforth Lincs 87 K5
Far Green Gloucs 32 E4
Faringdon Oxon 33 Q5
Farington Lancs 88 G5
Farlam Cumb 111 L9
Farleigh Surrey 37 J8
Farleigh Hungerford Somset 20 F3
Farleigh Wallop Hants 22 H5
Farlesthorpe Lincs 87 N6
Farleton Cumb 95 L4
Farleton Lancs 95 M7
Farley Derbys 84 C8
Farley Staffs 71 K6
Farley Wilts 21 P9

Farley Green Suffk 63 M10
Farley Green Surrey 36 C11
Farley Hill Wokam 23 K2
Farleys End Gloucs 32 E2
Farlington C Port 15 J5
Farlington N York 98 C7
Farlow Shrops 57 L8
Farmborough BaNES 20 C2
Farmbridge End Essex 51 P8
Farmcote Gloucs 47 L9
Farmcote Shrops 57 P6
Farmington Gloucs 47 M11
Farmoor Oxon 34 E3
Far Moor Wigan 82 B4
Farms Common Cnwll 2 H7
Farm Town Leics 72 B7
Farmtown Moray 158 D7
Farnah Green Derbys 84 D11
Farnborough Gt Lon 37 K8
Farnborough Hants 23 N4
Farnborough W Berk 34 D8
Farnborough Warwks 48 D5
Farnborough Park Hants 23 N3
Farncombe Surrey 23 Q6
Farndish Bed 61 K8
Farndon Ches W 69 M4
Farndon Notts 85 N10
Farne Islands Nthumb 119 P3
Farnell Angus 143 L6
Farnham Dorset 21 J11
Farnham Essex 51 L6
Farnham N York 97 M8
Farnham Suffk 65 M9
Farnham Surrey 23 M5
Farnham Common Bucks 35 Q7
Farnham Green Essex 51 L5
Farnham Royal Bucks 35 Q8
Farningham Kent 37 M7
Farnley Leeds 90 H4
Farnley N York 97 K11
Farnley Tyas Kirk 90 F8
Farnsfield Notts 85 K9
Farnworth Bolton 89 L9
Farnworth Halton 81 Q7
Far Oakridge Gloucs 32 H4
Farr Highld 148 J7
Farr Highld 156 B11
Farr Highld 166 B4
Farraline Highld 147 P3
Farringdon Devon 9 P6
Farrington Gurney BaNES 20 B3
Far Sawrey Cumb 101 L11
Farsley Leeds 90 G3
Farther Howegreen Essex 52 D11
Farthing Green Kent 26 D2
Farthinghoe Nhants 48 F7
Farthingloe Kent 27 N3
Farthingstone Nhants 48 H4
Farthing Street Gt Lon 37 K8
Fartown Kirk 90 F7
Farway Devon 10 D5
Fasnacloich Ag & B 139 J8
Fasnakyle Highld 147 J2
Fassfern Highld 139 J2
Fatfield Sundld 113 M10
Faugh Cumb 111 K10
Fauld Staffs 71 M9
Fauldhouse W Loth 126 G5
Faulkbourne Essex 52 C8
Faulkland Somset 20 D4
Fauls Shrops 69 Q8
Faversham Kent 38 H9
Fawdington N York 97 P6
Fawdon N u Ty 113 K7
Fawdon Nthumb 119 K7
Fawfieldhead Staffs 71 K2
Fawkham Green Kent 37 N7
Fawler Oxon 48 C11
Fawley Bucks 35 L7
Fawley Hants 14 E6
Fawley W Berk 34 C8
Fawley Chapel Herefs 46 A9
Fawnog Flints 81 J11
Fawsley Nhants 60 C9
Faxfleet E R Yk 92 E6
Faygate W Susx 24 F4
Fazakerley Lpool 81 M5
Fazeley Staffs 59 K4
Fearby N York 97 J4
Fearn Highld 156 E2
Fearnan P & K 140 H9
Fearnbeg Highld 153 N6
Fearnhead Warrtn 82 D6
Fearnmore Highld 153 N5
Fearnoch Ag & B 124 A2
Featherstone Staffs 58 D3
Featherstone Wakefd 91 L7
Feckenham Worcs 47 K2
Feering Essex 52 E7
Feetham N York 103 J11
Feizor N York 96 A7
Felbridge Surrey 25 J3
Felbrigg Norfk 77 J4
Felcourt Surrey 25 J2
Felden Herts 50 B10
Felindre Carmth 43 G7
Felindre Carmth 43 L10
Felindre Carmth 43 P9
Felindre Cerdgn 43 L3
Felindre Powys 44 H10
Felindre Powys 56 B8
Felindre Swans 28 H4
Felindre Farchog Pembks 41 M3
Felinfach Cerdgn 43 K3
Felinfach Powys 44 F8
Felinfoel Carmth 28 F4
Felingwm Isaf Carmth 43 K10
Felingwm Uchaf Carmth 43 K10
Felin-newydd Powys 44 G7
Felixkirk N York 97 Q4
Felixstowe Suffk 53 P5
Felixstowe Ferry Suffk 53 P4
Felkington Nthumb 118 H2
Felkirk Wakefd 91 K8
Felling Gatesd 113 L8
Fell Lane C Brad 90 C2
Fell Side Cumb 101 K3
Felmersham Bed 61 L9
Felmingham Norfk 77 K6
Felpham W Susx 15 P7
Felsham Suffk 64 C10
Felsted Essex 51 Q6
Feltham Gt Lon 36 D6
Felthamhill Surrey 36 C6
Felthorpe Norfk 76 H8

Felton Herefs 46 A5
Felton N Som 31 P11
Felton Nthumb 119 N10
Felton Butler Shrops 69 L11
Feltwell Norfk 63 M2
Fenay Bridge Kirk 90 F7
Fence Lancs 89 N3
Fence Rothm 84 F3
Fence Houses Sundld 113 M11
Fencott Oxon 48 G11
Fendike Corner Lincs 87 N8
Fen Ditton Cambs 62 G8
Fen Drayton Cambs 62 D7
Fen End Lincs 74 D6
Fen End Solhll 59 K10
Fenham Nthumb 119 L2
Feniscliffe Bl w D 89 K5
Feniscowles Bl w D 89 J5
Feniton Devon 10 C5
Fenn Green Shrops 57 P8
Fenn Street Medway 38 C6
Fenny Bentley Derbys 71 M5
Fenny Bridges Devon 10 C5
Fenny Compton Warwks 48 D4
Fenny Drayton Leics 72 B11
Fenny Stratford M Keyn 49 N8
Fenrother Nthumb 113 J2
Fenstanton Cambs 62 D7
Fenstead End Suffk 63 P10
Fen Street Norfk 64 D2
Fen Street Suffk 64 H9
Fenton C Stke 70 F6
Fenton Cambs 62 D5
Fenton Cumb 111 K9
Fenton Lincs 85 P5
Fenton Lincs 85 Q10
Fenton Notts 85 N4
Fenton Nthumb 119 J4
Fenton Barns E Loth 128 E3
Fenwick Donc 91 P7
Fenwick E Ayrs 125 M9
Fenwick Nthumb 112 G6
Fenwick Nthumb 119 L2
Feock Cnwll 3 L6
Feolin Ferry Ag & B 122 B10
Fergushill N Ayrs 125 J9
Feriniquarrie Highld 152 B7
Fermain Bay Guern 10 c2
Fern Angus 142 H5
Ferndale Rhondd 30 C5
Ferndown Dorset 13 J4
Ferness Highld 156 H8
Fernham Oxon 33 Q6
Fernhill Heath Worcs 46 G3
Fernhurst W Susx 23 N9
Fernie Fife 135 J4
Ferniegair S Lans 126 C7
Fernilea Highld 152 F11
Fernilee Derbys 83 M9
Fernwood Notts 85 P10
Ferrensby N York 97 N8
Ferriby Sluice N Linc 92 G6
Ferrindonald Highld 145 L6
Ferring W Susx 24 C10
Ferrybridge Wakefd 91 M6
Ferrybridge Services
  Wakefd 91 M6
Ferryden Angus 143 N6
Ferryhill Dur 103 Q4
Ferryhill Station Dur 103 Q4
Ferry Point Highld 162 G9
Ferryside Carmth 28 C2
Ferrytown Highld 162 G9
Fersfield Norfk 64 F5
Fersit Highld 139 R2
Feshiebridge Highld 148 F7
Fetcham Surrey 36 D9
Fetlar Shet 169 t4
Fetterangus Abers 159 N7
Fettercairn Abers 143 M3
Fewcott Oxon 48 F9
Fewston N York 97 J10
Ffairfach Carmth 43 M10
Ffair Rhos Cerdgn 54 G11
Ffald-y-Brenin Carmth 43 M6
Ffarmers Carmth 43 N6
Ffawyddog Powys 45 J11
Ffestiniog Gwynd 67 N6
Ffestiniog Railway Gwynd 67 M6
Ffordd-las Denbgs 68 F2
Fforest Carmth 28 G4
Fforest Gôch Neath 29 K4
Ffostrasol Cerdgn 42 G5
Ffrith Flints 69 J3
Ffynnondewi Cerdgn 42 G4
Ffynnongroyw Flints 80 G8
Ffynnon-oer Cerdgn 43 K4
Fickleshole Surrey 37 J8
Fiddington Gloucs 46 H8
Fiddington Somset 18 H6
Fiddleford Dorset 12 D2
Fiddlers Green Cnwll 4 C10
Fiddlers Hamlet Essex 51 L10
Field Staffs 71 J8
Field Broughton Cumb 94 H4
Field Dalling Norfk 76 E4
Fieldhead Cumb 101 N3
Field Head Leics 72 D9
Fifehead Magdalen Dorset 20 E10
Fifehead Neville Dorset 12 C2
Fifehead St Quintin Dorset 12 C2
Fife Keith Moray 158 B7
Fifield Oxon 47 P11
Fifield W & M 35 P9
Fifield Wilts 21 M4
Figheldean Wilts 21 N5
Filands Wilts 32 H7
Filby Norfk 77 P9
Filey N York 99 N4
Filgrave M Keyn 49 N5
Filkins Oxon 33 P4
Filleigh Devon 17 M6
Filleigh Devon 17 M6
Fillingham Lincs 86 B3
Fillongley Warwks 59 L7
Filmore Hill Hants 23 J9
Filton S Glos 32 B9
Fimber E R Yk 98 H8
Finavon Angus 142 H6
Fincham Norfk 75 N9
Finchampstead Wokam 23 L2
Fincharn Ag & B 131 J7
Finchdean Hants 15 K4
Finchingfield Essex 51 Q4
Finchley Gt Lon 36 G2

Findern Derbys 71 Q8
Findhorn Moray 157 J5
Findhorn Bridge Highld 148 E2
Findochty Moray 158 C4
Findo Gask P & K 134 C4
Findon Abers 151 N8
Findon W Susx 24 D9
Findon Mains Highld 155 R5
Findrack House Abers 150 G7
Finedon Nhants 61 K6
Fingal Street Suffk 65 J8
Fingask P & K 134 F4
Fingest Bucks 35 L6
Finghall N York 97 J3
Fingland D & G 115 Q4
Finglesham Kent 39 P11
Fingringhoe Essex 52 H7
Finkle Green Essex 52 B3
Finkle Street Barns 91 J11
Finlarig Stirlg 140 E11
Finmere Oxon 48 H8
Finnart P & K 140 D6
Finningham Suffk 64 F8
Finningley Donc 91 R11
Finsbay W Isls 168 f9
Finstall Worcs 58 E10
Finsthwaite Cumb 94 H3
Finstock Oxon 48 C11
Finstown Ork 169 c5
Fintry Abers 159 J7
Fintry Stirlg 133 J10
Finzean Abers 150 G9
Fionnphort Ag & B 137 J11
Fionnsbhagh W Isls 168 f9
Firbank Cumb 95 N2
Firbeck Rothm 85 J3
Firby N York 97 L3
Firby N York 98 E7
Firgrove Rochdl 89 Q8
Firle E Susx 25 L9
Firsby Lincs 87 N8
Firsdown Wilts 21 P8
Fir Tree Dur 103 M4
Fishbourne IoW 14 G8
Fishbourne W Susx 15 M6
Fishbourne Roman Palace
  W Susx 15 M6
Fishburn Dur 104 C4
Fishcross Clacks 133 P8
Fisher W Susx 15 N6
Fisherford Abers 158 G10
Fisherrow E Loth 127 Q3
Fisher's Pond Hants 22 E10
Fisher's Row Lancs 95 J11
Fisherstreet W Susx 23 P8
Fisherton Highld 156 C7
Fisherton S Ayrs 114 E4
Fisherton de la Mere Wilts 21 K7
Fisherwick Staffs 59 J3
Fishery Estate W & M 35 N8
Fishguard Pembks 41 J3
Fishlake Donc 91 R8
Fishleigh Devon 8 D3
Fishmere End Lincs 74 E3
Fishnish Pier Ag & B 138 B9
Fishpond Bottom Dorset 10 H5
Fishponds Bristl 32 B9
Fishtoft Lincs 74 E2
Fishtoft Drove Lincs 87 K11
Fishwick Lancs 88 H5
Fiskavaig Highld 152 E11
Fiskerton Lincs 86 D6
Fiskerton Notts 85 M10
Fitling E R Yk 93 N4
Fittleton Wilts 21 M5
Fittleworth W Susx 24 B7
Fitton End Cambs 74 H8
Fitz Shrops 69 M11
Fitzhead Somset 18 F9
Fitzroy Somset 18 G9
Fitzwilliam Wakefd 91 L7
Five Ash Down E Susx 25 L6
Five Ashes E Susx 25 N5
Five Bells Somset 18 E6
Five Bridges Herefs 46 B5
Fivecrosses Ches W 82 B9
Fivehead Somset 19 L10
Fivelanes Cnwll 5 L5
Five Lanes Mons 31 N6
Five Oak Green Kent 37 P11
Five Oaks Jersey 11 c2
Five Oaks W Susx 24 C5
Five Roads Carmth 28 E3
Five Wents Kent 38 D11
Flack's Green Essex 52 C9
Flackwell Heath Bucks 35 N7
Fladbury Worcs 47 J5
Fladdabister Shet 169 r10
Flagg Derbys 83 P11
Flamborough E R Yk 99 Q6
Flamborough Head E R Yk 99 R6
Flamingo Land Theme
  Park N York 98 F5
Flamstead Herts 50 C8
Flamstead End Herts 50 H10
Flansham W Susx 15 Q6
Flanshaw Wakefd 91 J6
Flappit Spring C Brad 90 D3
Flasby N York 96 D9
Flash Staffs 83 M11
Flashader Highld 152 E7
Flaunden Herts 50 B10
Flawborough Notts 73 K2
Flawith N York 97 Q7
Flax Bourton N Som 31 N11
Flaxby N York 97 N9
Flaxley Gloucs 46 C11
Flaxmere Ches W 82 C10
Flaxpool Somset 18 F7
Flaxton N York 98 D8
Fleckney Leics 60 D2
Flecknoe Warwks 60 B8
Fledborough Notts 85 N6
Fleet Dorset 11 N8
Fleet Hants 15 N4
Fleet Hants 23 M4
Fleet Lincs 74 G6
Fleetend Hants 14 F5
Fleet Hargate Lincs 74 G6
Fleet Services Hants 23 L3
Fleetwood Lancs 94 G11
Fleggburgh Norfk 77 N9
Flemingston V Glam 30 D11
Flemington S Lans 126 B6

Flempton Suffk 63 P7
Fletcherbridge Cnwll 5 J8
Fletcher's Green Kent 37 M11
Fletchertown Cumb 100 H2
Fletching E Susx 25 K6
Fleur-de-lis Caerph 30 G5
Flexbury Cnwll 16 C10
Flexford Surrey 23 P4
Flimby Cumb 100 D4
Flimwell E Susx 26 B5
Flint Flints 81 J10
Flintham Notts 85 M11
Flint Mountain Flints 81 J10
Flinton E R Yk 93 M3
Flint's Green Solhll 59 L8
Flishinghurst Kent 26 C4
Flitcham Norfk 75 P5
Flitton C Beds 50 C3
Flitwick C Beds 50 B4
Flixborough N Linc 92 E8
Flixborough Stather N Linc 92 E8
Flixton N York 99 L5
Flixton Suffk 65 L4
Flixton Traffd 82 F6
Flockton Kirk 90 G8
Flockton Green Kirk 90 H7
Flodden Nthumb 118 H3
Flodigarry Highld 152 H3
Flookburgh Cumb 94 H5
Flordon Norfk 64 H2
Flore Nhants 60 D8
Flotterton Nthumb 119 J10
Flowers Green E Susx 25 P8
Flowton Suffk 53 J2
Flushdyke Wakefd 90 H6
Flushing Cnwll 3 L7
Fluxton Devon 10 B6
Flyford Flavell Worcs 47 J3
Fobbing Thurr 38 B5
Fochabers Moray 157 Q6
Fochriw Caerph 30 F3
Fockerby N Linc 92 D7
Foddington Somset 19 Q9
Foel Powys 55 M2
Foelgastell Carmth 28 F2
Foel y Dyffryn Brdgnd 29 N6
Foggathorpe E R Yk 92 C3
Fogo Border 129 K10
Fogwatt Moray 157 N6
Foindle Highld 164 E7
Folda Angus 142 B5
Fole Staffs 71 J7
Foleshill Covtry 59 N8
Folke Dorset 11 P2
Folkestone Kent 27 M4
Folkingham Lincs 73 R4
Folkington E Susx 25 N10
Folksworth Cambs 61 P3
Folkton N York 99 M5
Folla Rule Abers 158 H11
Follifoot N York 97 M10
Folly Gate Devon 8 E5
Folly Hill Surrey 23 M5
Fonmon V Glam 30 D11
Fonthill Bishop Wilts 20 H8
Fonthill Gifford Wilts 20 H8
Fontmell Magna Dorset 20 G11
Fontmell Parva Dorset 12 D2
Fontwell W Susx 15 P5
Font-y-gary V Glam 30 E11
Foolow Derbys 83 Q9
Foots Cray Gt Lon 37 L6
Forbestown Abers 150 B5
Forcett N York 103 N8
Ford Ag & B 130 H7
Ford Bucks 35 L3
Ford Derbys 84 F4
Ford Devon 6 G8
Ford Devon 7 K10
Ford Devon 16 G7
Ford Gloucs 47 L9
Ford Nthumb 118 H3
Ford Shrops 56 G2
Ford Somset 18 E9
Ford Somset 19 Q4
Ford Staffs 71 K4
Ford W Susx 15 Q6
Ford Wilts 32 F9
Forda Devon 8 D6
Fordcombe Kent 25 M2
Fordell Fife 134 F10
Forden Powys 56 C4
Ford End Essex 51 Q7
Forder Green Devon 7 K5
Ford Green Lancs 95 K11
Fordham Cambs 63 K6
Fordham Essex 52 F6
Fordham Norfk 75 M11
Fordham Heath Essex 52 F6
Fordingbridge Hants 13 K2
Fordon E R Yk 99 L5
Fordoun Abers 143 N2
Ford's Green Suffk 64 F8
Fordstreet Essex 52 F6
Ford Street Somset 18 G11
Fordton Devon 9 K5
Fordwells Oxon 34 B2
Fordwich Kent 39 L10
Fordyce Abers 158 E4
Forebridge Staffs 70 G10
Foremark Derbys 72 A5
Forest Guern 10 b2
Forest N York 103 Q10
Forest Becks Lancs 96 A10
Forest Chapel Ches E 83 L10
Forest Coal Pit Mons 45 L10
Forest Gate Gt Lon 37 K3
Forest Green Surrey 24 D2
Forest Hall N Tyne 113 L7
Forest Head Cumb 111 L9
Forest Hill Oxon 34 G3
Forest-in-Teesdale Dur 102 H4
Forest Lane Head N York 97 M9
Forest Mill Clacks 134 B9
Forest of Bowland Lancs 95 N10
Forest of Dean Gloucs 32 B2
Forest Row E Susx 25 K4
Forest Side IoW 14 F9
Forestside W Susx 15 L4
Forest Town Notts 85 J9

Forgandenny P & K 134 D4
Forge Powys 54 H5
Forge Hammer Torfn 31 J5
Forge Side Torfn 30 H3
Forgie Moray 158 A7
Forgieside Moray 158 B7
Forhill Worcs 58 F8
Formby Sefton 88 C9
Forncett End Norfk 64 G3
Forncett St Mary Norfk 64 H3
Forncett St Peter Norfk 64 H3
Fornham All Saints Suffk 64 A8
Fornham St Martin Suffk 64 B8
Fornighty Highld 156 G7
Forres Moray 157 J6
Forsbrook Staffs 70 H6
Forse Highld 167 M10
Forshaw Heath Warwks 58 G10
Forsinard Highld 166 E8
Forss Highld 166 H3
Forston Dorset 11 P5
Fort Augustus Highld 147 K6
Forteviot P & K 134 D4
Forth S Lans 126 G7
Forthampton Gloucs 46 G8
Fort Hommet Guern 10 b1
Forth Rail Bridge C Edin 127 L2
Forth Road Bridge Fife 127 L2
Fortingall P & K 140 H8
Forton Hants 22 D6
Forton Lancs 95 K10
Forton Shrops 69 M11
Forton Somset 10 G3
Forton Staffs 70 D10
Fort Richmond Guern 10 b2
Fortrie Abers 158 G8
Fortrose Highld 156 C6
Fortuneswell Dorset 11 P10
Fort William Highld 139 L3
Forty Green Bucks 35 P6
Forty Hill Gt Lon 50 H11
Forward Green Suffk 64 G10
Fosbury Wilts 22 B3
Foscot Oxon 47 P10
Foscote Nhants 49 J5
Fosdyke Lincs 74 F4
Fosdyke Bridge Lincs 74 F4
Foss P & K 141 J6
Fossebridge Gloucs 33 J2
Foss-y-ffin Cerdgn 42 H2
Fosterhouses Donc 91 R8
Foster Street Essex 51 L9
Foston Derbys 71 M8
Foston Leics 60 D2
Foston Lincs 73 M2
Foston N York 98 D7
Foston on the Wolds E R Yk 99 N9
Fotherby Lincs 87 K2
Fothergill Cumb 100 D4
Fotheringhay Nhants 61 N2
Foula Shet 169 k10
Foula Airport Shet 169 k10
Foulbridge Cumb 110 H11
Foulby Wakefd 91 K7
Foulden Border 129 N8
Foulden Norfk 75 Q11
Foul End Warwks 59 K6
Foul Mile E Susx 25 P7
Foulness Island Essex 38 G3
Foulridge Lancs 89 P2
Foulsham Norfk 76 E7
Fountainhall Border 128 C10
Four Ashes Solhll 59 J9
Four Ashes Staffs 57 Q7
Four Ashes Staffs 58 D3
Four Ashes Suffk 64 E7
Four Cabots Guern 10 b2
Four Crosses Powys 69 J11
Four Crosses Staffs 58 E3
Four Elms Kent 37 L11
Four Foot Somset 19 Q8
Four Forks Somset 18 H7
Four Gates Bolton 89 J9
Four Gotes Cambs 75 J7
Four Lane End Barns 90 H10
Four Lane Ends Ches W 69 Q2
Four Lanes Cnwll 2 H6
Fourlanes End Ches E 70 E3
Four Marks Hants 23 J7
Four Mile Bridge IoA 78 D9
Four Oaks Birm 58 H5
Four Oaks E Susx 26 E7
Four Oaks Gloucs 46 C9
Four Oaks Solhll 59 K8
Fourpenny Highld 163 J8
Four Points W Berk 34 G9
Four Roads Carmth 28 D3
Four Shire Stone Warwks 47 P8
Fourstones Nthumb 112 C7
Four Throws Kent 26 C6
Four Wents Kent 37 P10
Fovant Wilts 21 K9
Foveran Abers 151 P3
Fowey Cnwll 5 J11
Fowley Common Warrtn 82 E5
Fowlhall Kent 37 Q11
Fowlis Angus 142 E11
Fowlis Wester P & K 133 Q3
Fowlmere Cambs 62 F11
Fownhope Herefs 46 A8
Foxbar Rens 125 M5
Foxcombe Devon 8 C7
Fox Corner Surrey 23 Q4
Foxcote Gloucs 47 K11
Foxcote Somset 20 D4
Foxdale IoM 80 c6
Foxearth Essex 52 D3
Foxendown Kent 37 P7
Foxfield Cumb 94 E3
Foxham Wilts 33 J9
Fox Hatch Essex 51 N11
Foxhills Hants 13 P2
Foxhole Cnwll 3 P3
Foxholes N York 99 L6
Foxhunt Green E Susx 25 M7
Foxley Nhants 48 H4
Foxley Norfk 76 F7
Foxley Wilts 32 G7
Foxlydiate Worcs 58 F11
Fox Street Essex 52 H6
Foxt Staffs 71 J5
Foxton Cambs 62 F11
Foxton Dur 104 C6
Foxton Leics 60 F3

Foxton N York 104 D11
Foxup N York 96 C5
Foxwist Green Ches W 82 D11
Foxwood Shrops 57 L9
Foy Herefs 46 A9
Foyers Highld 147 M3
Foynesfield Highld 156 F7
Fraddam Cnwll 2 F7
Fraddon Cnwll 4 E10
Fradley Staffs 59 J2
Fradswell Staffs 70 H8
Fraisthorpe E R Yk 99 P8
Framfield E Susx 25 L6
Framingham Earl Norfk 77 K11
Framingham Pigot Norfk 77 K11
Framlingham Suffk 65 K9
Frampton Dorset 11 N5
Frampton Lincs 74 F3
Frampton Cotterell S Glos 32 C8
Frampton Mansell Gloucs 32 H4
Frampton-on-Severn Gloucs 32 D3
Frampton West End Lincs 74 F2
Framsden Suffk 64 H10
Framwellgate Moor Dur 103 Q2
Franche Worcs 57 Q9
Frandley Ches W 82 D9
Frankaborough Devon 5 P3
Frankby Wirral 81 J7
Frankfort Norfk 77 L7
Franklands Gate Herefs 45 Q5
Frankley Worcs 58 E8
Frankley Services Worcs 58 E8
Franksbridge Powys 44 G3
Frankton Warwks 59 P10
Frant E Susx 25 N3
Fraserburgh Abers 159 N4
Frating Essex 53 J7
Frating Green Essex 53 J7
Fratton C Port 15 J7
Freathy Cnwll 5 P11
Freckenham Suffk 63 L6
Freckleton Lancs 88 E5
Freebirch Derbys 84 D6
Freeby Leics 73 L6
Freefolk Hants 22 E5
Freehay Staffs 71 J6
Freeland Oxon 34 D2
Freethorpe Norfk 77 N10
Freethorpe Common Norfk 77 N11
Freiston Lincs 74 G2
Fremington Devon 17 J5
Fremington N York 103 K11
Frenchay S Glos 32 B9
Frenchbeer Devon 8 G7
French Street Kent 37 L10
Frenich P & K 141 K6
Frensham Surrey 23 M6
Freshfield Sefton 88 B9
Freshford Wilts 20 E2
Freshwater IoW 13 P7
Freshwater Bay IoW 13 P7
Freshwater East Pembks 41 K11
Fressingfield Suffk 65 K6
Freston Suffk 53 L4
Freswick Highld 167 Q3
Fretherne Gloucs 32 D2
Frettenham Norfk 77 J8
Freuchie Fife 134 H6
Freystrop Pembks 41 J8
Friar Park Sandw 58 F6
Friar's Gate E Susx 25 L4
Friars' Hill N York 98 E3
Friar Waddon Dorset 11 N7
Friday Bridge Cambs 75 J10
Friday Street Suffk 65 J10
Friday Street Suffk 65 L11
Friday Street Suffk 65 M9
Friday Street Surrey 36 D11
Fridaythorpe E R Yk 98 H9
Friden Derbys 71 M2
Friendly Calder 90 D6
Friern Barnet Gt Lon 36 G2
Friesthorpe Lincs 86 E4
Frieston Lincs 86 B11
Frieth Bucks 35 L6
Friezeland Notts 84 G10
Frilford Oxon 34 D5
Frilsham W Berk 34 F10
Frimley Surrey 23 N3
Frimley Green Surrey 23 N3
Frindsbury Medway 38 B8
Fring Norfk 75 P4
Fringford Oxon 48 H9
Frinsted Kent 38 E10
Frinton-on-Sea Essex 53 M7
Friockheim Angus 143 K8
Friog Gwynd 54 E2
Frisby on the Wreake Leics 72 H7
Friskney Lincs 87 N9
Friskney Eaudike Lincs 87 N9
Friston E Susx 25 N11
Friston Suffk 65 N9
Fritchley Derbys 84 E10
Fritham Hants 13 M2
Frith Bank Lincs 87 K11
Frith Common Worcs 57 M11
Frithelstock Devon 16 H8
Frithelstock Stone Devon 16 H8
Frithend Hants 23 M7
Frithsden Herts 50 B9
Frithville Lincs 87 K10
Frittenden Kent 26 D3
Frittiscombe Devon 7 L10
Fritton Norfk 65 J3
Fritton Norfk 77 P11
Fritwell Oxon 48 F9
Frizinghall C Brad 90 E3
Frizington Cumb 100 D7
Frocester Gloucs 32 E4
Frodesley Shrops 57 J4
Frodsham Ches W 81 Q9
Frogden Border 118 E3
Frog End Cambs 62 E11
Frog End Cambs 62 H9
Froggatt Derbys 84 B5
Froghall Staffs 71 J5
Frogham Hants 13 L2
Frogham Kent 39 N11
Frogmore Devon 7 K10
Frognall Lincs 74 C8
Frog Pool Worcs 57 Q11
Frogwell Cnwll 5 N8
Frolesworth Leics 60 B2

Frome Somset 20 E5
Frome St Quintin Dorset 11 M4
Fromes Hill Herefs 46 C5
Fron Gwynd 66 F7
Fron Gwynd 67 J4
Fron Powys 56 B5
Fron Powys 56 C4
Froncysyllte Wrexhm 69 J6
Fron-goch Gwynd 68 B7
Fron Isaf Wrexhm 69 J6
Frostenden Suffk 65 P5
Frosterley Dur 103 K3
Froxfield C Beds 49 Q8
Froxfield Wilts 33 Q11
Froxfield Green Hants 23 K9
Fryern Hill Hants 22 D10
Fryerning Essex 51 P10
Fryton N York 98 D6
Fuinary Highld 137 Q6
Fulbeck Lincs 86 B10
Fulbourn Cambs 62 H9
Fulbrook Oxon 33 Q2
Fulflood Hants 22 E8
Fulford Somset 18 H9
Fulford Staffs 70 H7
Fulford York 98 C11
Fulham Gt Lon 36 G5
Fulking W Susx 24 F8
Fullaford Devon 17 M4
Fullarton N Ayrs 125 J10
Fuller's End Essex 51 M5
Fuller's Moor Ches W 69 N4
Fuller Street Essex 52 B8
Fuller Street Kent 37 N9
Fullerton Hants 22 C7
Fulletby Lincs 87 J6
Full Sutton E R Yk 98 E9
Fullready Warwks 47 Q5
Fullwood E Ayrs 125 L7
Fulmer Bucks 35 Q7
Fulmodeston Norfk 76 D5
Fulnetby Lincs 86 E5
Fulney Lincs 74 E6
Fulstone Kirk 90 F9
Fulstow Lincs 93 P11
Fulwell Oxon 48 C10
Fulwell Sundld 113 N9
Fulwood Lancs 88 G4
Fulwood Notts 84 G9
Fulwood Sheff 84 D3
Fulwood Somset 18 H10
Fundenhall Norfk 64 H2
Funtington W Susx 15 M5
Funtley Hants 14 G5
Funtullich P & K 133 M2
Furley Devon 10 F4
Furnace Ag & B 131 L7
Furnace Carmth 28 F4
Furnace Cerdgn 54 F5
Furnace End Warwks 59 K6
Furner's Green E Susx 25 K5
Furness Vale Derbys 83 M8
Furneux Pelham Herts 51 K5
Further Quarter Kent 26 E4
Furtho Nhants 49 L6
Furzehill Devon 17 N2
Furzehill Dorset 12 H4
Furzehills Lincs 87 J6
Furzeley Corner Hants 15 J4
Furze Platt W & M 35 N8
Furzley Hants 21 Q11
Fyfett Somset 10 E2
Fyfield Essex 51 N9
Fyfield Hants 21 Q5
Fyfield Oxon 34 D5
Fyfield Wilts 33 N2
Fyfield Wilts 33 M11
Fyfield Bavant Wilts 21 K9
Fylingthorpe N York 105 P10
Fyning W Susx 23 M10
Fyvie Abers 159 J10

G

Gabroc Hill E Ayrs 125 M7
Gaddesby Leics 72 H8
Gaddesden Row Herts 50 C8
Gadfa IoA 78 H7
Gadgirth S Ayrs 114 H3
Gadlas Shrops 69 L7
Gaer Powys 44 H10
Gaerllwyd Mons 31 M5
Gaerwen IoA 78 H10
Gagingwell Oxon 48 D9
Gailes N Ayrs 125 J10
Gailey Staffs 58 D2
Gainford Dur 103 N7
Gainsborough Lincs 85 P3
Gainsford End Essex 52 B4
Gairloch Highld 153 Q2
Gairlochy Highld 146 F11
Gairneybridge P & K 134 E8
Gaisgill Cumb 102 B9
Gaitsgill Cumb 110 G11
Galashiels Border 117 P3
Galgate Lancs 95 K9
Galhampton Somset 20 B9
Gallanach Ag & B 130 G2
Gallanachmore Ag & B 130 G2
Gallantry Bank Ches E 69 P4
Gallatown Fife 134 H9
Galley Common Warwks 59 M6
Galleywood Essex 52 B11
Gallovie Highld 147 P10
Galloway Forest Park 114 H10
Gallowfauld Angus 142 G9
Gallowhill P & K 142 B10
Gallows Green Essex 52 F6
Gallows Green Worcs 46 H2
Gallowstree Common Oxon 35 J8
Galltair Highld 145 P3
Gallt-y-foel Gwynd 67 K2
Gally Hill Hants 23 M4
Gallypot Street E Susx 25 L3
Galmisdale Highld 144 G11
Galmpton Devon 6 H10
Galmpton Torbay 7 M7
Galphay N York 97 L6
Galston E Ayrs 125 N10
Gamballs Green Staffs 83 M11
Gamblesby Cumb 102 B3
Gambles Green Essex 52 C9
Gamelsby Cumb 110 E10

Gamesley Derbys 83 M6
Gamlingay Cambs 62 B10
Gamlingay Cinques Cambs 62 B10
Gamlingay Great Heath 62 B10
Gammersgill N York 96 G4
Gamrie Abers 159 J5
Gamston Notts 72 F3
Gamston Notts 85 M5
Ganarew Herefs 45 Q11
Ganavan Bay Ag & B 138 F11
Gang Cnwll 5 N8
Ganllwyd Gwynd 67 N10
Gannachy Angus 143 K3
Ganstead E R Yk 93 K4
Ganthorpe N York 98 D6
Ganton N York 99 K5
Ganwick Corner Herts 50 G11
Gappah Devon 9 L9
Garbity Moray 157 Q7
Garboldisham Norfk 64 E5
Garbole Highld 148 D3
Garchory Abers 149 Q5
Garden City Flints 81 L11
Gardeners Green Wokham 35 M11
Gardenstown Abers 159 K5
Garden Village Sheff 90 H11
Garderhouse Shet 169 q9
Gardham E R Yk 92 G2
Gare Hill Somset 20 E6
Garelochhead Ag & B 131 Q9
Garford Oxon 34 D5
Garforth Leeds 91 L4
Gargrave N York 96 D10
Gargunnock Stirlg 133 L9
Garlic Street Norfk 65 J5
Garlieston D & G 107 N8
Garlinge Kent 39 P8
Garlinge Green Kent 39 K11
Garlogie Abers 151 K6
Garmond Abers 159 K7
Garmouth Moray 157 Q5
Garmston Shrops 57 L3
Garnant Carmth 29 J2
Garndolbenmaen Gwynd 66 H6
Garnett Bridge Cumb 101 P11
Garnfadryn Gwynd 66 D8
Garnkirk N Lans 126 B4
Garnswllt Swans 28 H3
Garn-yr-erw Torfn 30 H3
Garrabost W Isls 168 k4
Garrallan E Ayrs 115 K4
Garras Cnwll 3 J9
Garreg Gwynd 67 L6
Garrigill Cumb 102 D2
Garriston N York 97 J2
Garroch D & G 108 C4
Garrochtie D & G 106 F10
Garrochty Ag & B 124 D7
Garros Highld 152 H5
Garsdale Cumb 95 Q3
Garsdale Head Cumb 96 A2
Garsdon Wilts 33 J7
Garshall Green Staffs 70 H6
Garsington Oxon 34 G4
Garstang Lancs 95 K11
Garston Herts 50 D10
Garston Lpool 81 N8
Garswood St Hel 82 C5
Gartachossan Ag & B 122 D7
Gartcosh N Lans 126 B4
Garth Brdgnd 29 N6
Garth Mons 31 K4
Garth Powys 44 D5
Garth Powys 56 D10
Garth Wrexhm 69 J6
Garthamlock C Glas 126 B4
Garthbrengy Powys 44 E8
Gartheli Cerdgn 43 L3
Garthmyl Powys 56 B5
Garthorpe Leics 73 L6
Garthorpe N Linc 92 D7
Garth Row Cumb 101 P11
Garths Cumb 95 L3
Gartly Abers 158 D11
Gartmore Stirlg 132 G8
Gartness N Lans 126 D5
Gartness Stirlg 132 G10
Gartocharn W Duns 132 E10
Garton E R Yk 93 N3
Garton-on-the-Wolds E R Yk 99 K9
Gartymore Highld 163 N4
Garva Bridge Highld 147 N9
Garvald Border 127 L8
Garvald E Loth 128 F5
Garvan Highld 138 H2
Garvard Ag & B 136 b3
Garve Highld 155 L5
Garvellachs Ag & B 130 D5
Garvestone Norfk 76 E10
Garvock Inver 124 H3
Garway Herefs 45 P10
Garway Common Herefs 45 P10
Garway Hill Herefs 45 N9
Garynahine W Isls 168 h4
Garyvard W Isls 168 i6
Gasper Wilts 20 E8
Gastard Wilts 32 G11
Gasthorpe Norfk 64 D5
Gaston Green Essex 51 L7
Gatcombe IoW 14 E9
Gateback Cumb 95 L3
Gate Burton Lincs 85 P4
Gateford Notts 85 J4
Gateforth N York 91 P5
Gatehead E Ayrs 125 K10
Gate Helmsley N York 98 D9
Gatehouse Nthumb 111 J3
Gatehouse of Fleet D & G 108 C9
Gateley Norfk 76 D7
Gatenby N York 97 M3
Gatesgarth Cumb 100 G7
Gateshaw Border 118 E4
Gateshead Gatesd 113 L8
Gates Heath Ches W 69 N2
Gateside Angus 142 G9
Gateside E Rens 125 M6
Gateside Fife 134 F6
Gateside N Ayrs 125 K7
Gateslack D & G 116 B10
Gathurst Wigan 88 G9
Gatley Stockp 82 H7
Gatton Surrey 36 G10
Gattonside Border 117 Q3
Gatwick Airport W Susx 24 G2

Gaufron Powys 55 M11
Gaulby Leics 72 H10
Gauldry Fife 135 K3
Gauldswell P & K 142 C7
Gaulkthorn Lancs 89 M5
Gaultree Norfk 75 J9
Gaunt's Bank Ches E 69 Q5
Gaunt's Common Dorset 12 H3
Gaunt's End Essex 51 N5
Gautby Lincs 86 G6
Gavinton Border 129 K9
Gawber Barns 91 J9
Gawcott Bucks 49 J8
Gawsworth Ches E 83 J11
Gawthorpe Wakefd 90 H6
Gawthrop Cumb 95 P3
Gawthwaite Cumb 94 F4
Gay Bowers Essex 52 C11
Gaydon Warwks 48 C4
Gayhurst M Keyn 49 M5
Gayle N York 96 C3
Gayles N York 103 M9
Gay Street W Susx 24 C7
Gayton Nhants 49 K4
Gayton Norfk 75 P7
Gayton Staffs 70 H9
Gayton Wirral 81 K8
Gayton le Marsh Lincs 87 M4
Gayton Thorpe Norfk 75 P7
Gaywood Norfk 75 M6
Gazeley Suffk 63 M8
Gearraidh Bhaird W Isls 168 i6
Gearraidh na h-Aibhne W Isls 168 h4
Geary Highld 152 D5
Gedding Suffk 64 C10
Geddington Nhants 61 J4
Gedling Notts 72 G2
Gedney Lincs 74 H6
Gedney Broadgate Lincs 74 H6
Gedney Drove End Lincs 75 J5
Gedney Dyke Lincs 74 H5
Gedney Hill Lincs 74 F8
Gee Cross Tamesd 83 L6
Geeston Rutlnd 73 P10
Geldeston Norfk 65 M3
Gelli Rhondd 30 C6
Gelli Torfn 31 J4
Gellifor Denbgs 68 F2
Gelligaer Caerph 30 F5
Gelligroes Caerph 30 G6
Gelligron Neath 29 K4
Gellilydan Gwynd 67 M7
Gellinudd Neath 29 K4
Gelly Pembks 41 L7
Gellyburn P & K 141 Q10
Gellywen Carmth 41 Q6
Gelston D & G 108 G9
Gelston Lincs 86 B11
Gembling E R Yk 99 N9
Gentleshaw Staffs 58 G2
Georgefield D & G 110 F3
George Green Bucks 35 Q8
Georgeham Devon 16 H4
Georgemas Junction Station Highld 167 L5
George Nympton Devon 17 N7
Georgetown Blae G 30 G3
Georgia Cnwll 2 D7
Georth Ork 169 c4
Gerlan Gwynd 79 L11
Germansweek Devon 8 B6
Germoe Cnwll 2 F8
Gerrans Cnwll 3 M6
Gerrards Cross Bucks 36 B3
Gestingthorpe Essex 52 D4
Geuffordd Powys 56 C2
Gib Hill Ches W 82 D9
Gibraltar Lincs 87 Q9
Gibsmere Notts 85 M11
Giddeahall Wilts 32 G10
Giddy Green Dorset 12 D7
Gidea Park Gt Lon 37 M2
Gidleigh Devon 8 G7
Giffnock E Rens 125 P6
Gifford E Loth 128 E6
Giffordtown Fife 134 H5
Giggleswick N York 96 B8
Gigha Ag & B 123 K10
Gilberdyke E R Yk 92 D5
Gilbert's End Worcs 46 F6
Gilbert Street Hants 22 H8
Gilchriston E Loth 128 D6
Gilcrux Cumb 100 F3
Gildersome Leeds 90 H5
Gildingwells Rothm 85 J3
Gilesgate Moor Dur 103 Q2
Gileston V Glam 30 D11
Gilfach Caerph 30 G5
Gilfach Goch Brdgnd 30 C6
Gilfachrheda Cerdgn 42 H3
Gilgarran Cumb 100 D6
Gill Cumb 101 M5
Gillamoor N York 98 D2
Gillan Cnwll 3 K8
Gillen Highld 152 D6
Gillesbie D & G 110 C2
Gilling East N York 98 D5
Gillingham Dorset 20 F9
Gillingham Medway 38 C8
Gillingham Norfk 65 N3
Gilling West N York 103 N9
Gillock Highld 167 M5
Gillow Heath Staffs 70 F3
Gills Highld 167 P2
Gill's Green Kent 26 C5
Gilmanscleuch Border 117 J6
Gilmerton C Edin 127 P4
Gilmerton P & K 133 P3
Gilmonby Dur 103 J8
Gilmorton Leics 60 C3
Gilsland Nthumb 111 M7
Gilson Warwks 59 J7
Gilstead C Brad 90 E3
Gilston Border 128 C8
Gilston Herts 51 K8
Gilston Park Herts 51 K8
Giltbrook Notts 84 G11
Gilwern Mons 30 H2
Gimingham Norfk 77 K4
Ginclough Ches E 83 L9
Gingers Green E Susx 25 P8
Gipping Suffk 64 F9

Gipsey Bridge Lincs 87 J11
Girdle Toll N Ayrs 125 J9
Girlington C Brad 90 E4
Girlsta Shet 169 r8
Girsby N York 104 C9
Girtford C Beds 61 Q11
Girthon D & G 108 D10
Girton Cambs 62 F8
Girton Notts 85 P7
Girvan S Ayrs 114 C8
Gisburn Lancs 96 B11
Gisleham Suffk 65 Q4
Gislingham Suffk 64 F7
Gissing Norfk 64 G4
Gittisham Devon 10 C5
Gladestry Powys 45 J3
Gladsmuir E Loth 128 D5
Glais Swans 29 K4
Glaisdale N York 105 L9
Glamis Angus 142 F8
Glanaber Gwynd 67 L4
Glanaman Carmth 29 J2
Glandford Norfk 76 E3
Glan-Duar Carmth 43 K6
Glandwr Pembks 41 N5
Glan-Dwyfach Gwynd 66 H6
Glandyfi Cerdgn 54 F5
Glangrwyney Powys 45 J11
Glanllynfi Brdgnd 29 N6
Glanmule Powys 56 B6
Glanrhyd Pembks 41 M2
Glan-rhyd Powys 29 L3
Glanton Nthumb 119 L8
Glanton Pike Nthumb 119 L8
Glanvilles Wootton Dorset 11 P3
Glan-y-don Flints 80 H9
Glan-y-llyn Rhondd 30 F8
Glan-y-nant Powys 55 L8
Glan-yr-afon Gwynd 68 B6
Glan-yr-afon Gwynd 68 D6
Glan-yr-afon IoA 79 L8
Glan-yr-afon Swans 28 H3
Glan-y-wern Gwynd 67 L8
Glapthorn Nhants 61 M2
Glapwell Derbys 84 G7
Glasbury Powys 44 H7
Glascoed Denbgs 80 D10
Glascoed Mons 31 L3
Glascote Staffs 59 K4
Glascwm Powys 44 H4
Glasfryn Conwy 68 B4
Glasgow C Glas 125 P4
Glasgow Airport Rens 125 M4
Glasgow Prestwick Airport S Ayrs 114 G2
Glasgow Science Centre C Glas 125 P4
Glasinfryn Gwynd 79 K11
Glasnacardoch Bay Highld 145 L8
Glasnakille Highld 144 H5
Glasphein Highld 152 B8
Glaspwll Powys 54 G5
Glassenbury Kent 26 C4
Glassford S Lans 126 C8
Glass Houghton Wakefd 91 L6
Glasshouse Gloucs 46 D10
Glasshouse Hill Gloucs 46 D10
Glasshouses N York 97 J8
Glasslaw Abers 159 L6
Glasson Cumb 110 E8
Glasson Lancs 95 J9
Glassonby Cumb 101 Q3
Glasterlaw Angus 143 K7
Glaston Rutlnd 73 M10
Glastonbury Somset 19 P7
Glatton Cambs 61 Q3
Glazebrook Warrtn 82 E6
Glazebury Warrtn 82 E6
Glazeley Shrops 57 N7
Gleadless Sheff 84 E4
Gleadsmoss Ches E 82 H11
Gleaston Cumb 94 F6
Glebe Highld 147 N4
Gledhow Leeds 91 J3
Gledpark D & G 108 D10
Gledrid Shrops 69 K7
Glemsford Suffk 52 D2
Glenallachie Moray 157 P9
Glenancross Highld 145 L9
Glenaros House Ag & B 137 P7
Glen Auldyn IoM 80 f3
Glenbarr Ag & B 120 C4
Glenbarry Abers 158 E7
Glenbeg Highld 137 P3
Glenbervie Abers 151 K11
Glenboig N Lans 126 C4
Glenborrodale Ag & B 137 Q3
Glenbranter Ag & B 131 N8
Glenbreck Border 116 F6
Glenbrittle Highld 144 F3
Glenbuck E Ayrs 115 P2
Glencally Angus 142 F5
Glencaple D & G 109 L7
Glencarse P & K 134 F3
Glencoe Highld 139 L6
Glencothe Border 116 F5
Glencraig Fife 134 F9
Glencrosh D & G 115 Q10
Glendale Highld 152 B8
Glendaruel Ag & B 131 K11
Glendevon P & K 134 B7
Glendoe Lodge Highld 147 L6
Glendoick P & K 134 G3
Glenduckie Fife 134 H4
Glenegedale Ag & B 122 D9
Gleneig Highld 145 P4
Glenernie Moray 157 J8
Glenfarg P & K 134 E5
Glenfield Leics 72 E9
Glenfinnan Highld 145 R11
Glenfintaig Lodge Highld 146 G10
Glenfoot P & K 134 F4
Glenfyne Lodge Ag & B 131 Q4
Glengarnock N Ayrs 125 J7
Glengolly Highld 167 K3
Glengorm Castle Ag & B 137 L4
Glengrasco Highld 152 G9
Glenholm Border 116 G4
Glenhoul D & G 115 M10
Glenisla Angus 142 C5
Glenkin Ag & B 131 N11
Glenkindie Abers 150 C5
Glenlivet Moray 149 M2
Glenlochar D & G 108 G9
Glenlomond P & K 134 F6

Glenluce D & G......106 G6
Glenmassen Ag & B......131 N10
Glenmavis N Lans......126 D4
Glen Maye IoM......80 b6
Glen Mona IoM......80 g4
Glenmore Highld......152 G9
Glenmore Lodge Highld......148 H6
Glen Nevis House Highld......139 L3
Glenochil Clacks......133 P8
Glen Parva Leics......72 F11
Glenquiech Angus......142 G5
Glenralloch Ag & B......123 Q6
Glenridding Cumb......101 L7
Glenrothes Fife......134 H7
Glenshero Lodge Highld......147 P9
Glenstriven Ag & B......124 D2
Glentham Lincs......86 D2
Glentrool D & G......107 L2
Glen Trool Lodge D & G......114 H11
Glentruim Highld......148 B9
Glentworth Lincs......86 B3
Glenuig Highld......138 B2
Glenvarragill Highld......152 H10
Glen Vine IoM......80 d6
Glenwhilly D & G......106 G3
Glespin S Lans......115 R2
Glewstone Herefs......45 N10
Glinton C Pete......74 C9
Glooston Leics......73 K11
Glossop Derbys......83 M6
Gloster Hill Nthumb......119 Q10
Gloucester Gloucs......32 F11
Gloucester Services Gloucs..32 F2
Gloucestershire Airport
Gloucs......46 G10
Glusburn N York......96 F11
Glutt Lodge Highld......166 H9
Gluvian Cnwll......4 E9
Glympton Oxon......48 D10
Glynarthen Cerdgn......42 F5
Glyn Ceiriog Wrexhm......68 H7
Glyncoch Rhondd......30 E6
Glyncorrwg Neath......29 N5
Glynde E Susx......25 L9
Glyndebourne E Susx......25 L8
Glyndyfrdwy Denbgs......68 F6
Glynneath Neath......29 N3
Glyntaff Rhondd......30 E7
Glyntawe Powys......44 A11
Glynteg Carmth......42 G7
Gnosall Staffs......70 E10
Gnosall Heath Staffs......70 E10
Goadby Leics......73 K11
Goadby Marwood Leics......73 K5
Goatacre Wilts......33 K9
Goatham Green E Susx......26 D7
Goathill Dorset......20 C11
Goathland N York......105 M10
Goathurst Somset......19 J8
Goathurst Common Kent......37 L10
Goat Lees Kent......26 H2
Gobowen Shrops......69 K8
Godalming Surrey......23 Q6
Goddard's Corner Suffk......65 K8
Goddard's Green Kent......26 D5
Goddards Green W Susx......24 G6
Godden Green Kent......37 N9
Godford Cross Devon......10 C4
Godington Oxon......48 H9
Godley Tamesd......83 L5
Godmanchester Cambs......62 B6
Godmanstone Dorset......11 P5
Godmersham Kent......39 J11
Godney Somset......19 N6
Godolphin Cross Cnwll......2 G7
Godre'r-graig Neath......29 L3
Godshill Hants......21 N11
Godshill IoW......14 F10
Godstone Staffs......71 J8
Godstone Surrey......37 J10
Godsworthy Devon......8 D9
Godwinscroft Hants......13 L5
Goetre Mons......31 K3
Goff's Oak Herts......50 H10
Gogar C Edin......127 M3
Goginan Cerdgn......54 F8
Golan Gwynd......67 J6
Golant Cnwll......5 J11
Golberdon Cnwll......5 N7
Golborne Wigan......82 D5
Golcar Kirk......90 D7
Goldcliff Newpt......31 L8
Golden Cross E Susx......25 M8
Golden Green Kent......37 P11
Golden Grove Carmth......43 L11
Goldenhill C Stke......70 F4
Golden Hill Pembks......41 J10
Golden Pot Hants......23 K6
Golden Valley Derbys......84 F10
Golders Green Gt Lon......36 F3
Goldfinch Bottom W Berk......22 F2
Goldhanger Essex......52 F10
Gold Hill Cambs......62 H2
Gold Hill Dorset......12 D2
Golding Shrops......57 J4
Goldington Bed......61 N10
Goldsborough N York......97 N9
Goldsborough N York......105 M8
Golds Green Sandw......58 E6
Goldsithney Cnwll......2 E7
Goldstone Kent......39 N9
Goldstone Shrops......70 C9
Goldthorpe Barns......91 M10
Goldworthy Devon......16 F7
Golford Kent......26 C4
Golford Green Kent......26 C4
Gollanfield Highld......156 E7
Gollinglith Foot N York......96 H4
Golly Wrexhm......69 K3
Golsoncott Somset......18 E7
Golspie Highld......163 J6
Gomeldon Wilts......21 N7
Gomersal Kirk......90 G5
Gomshall Surrey......36 C11
Gonalston Notts......85 L11
Gonerby Hill Foot Lincs......73 N3
Gonfirth Shet......169 q7
Goodameavy Devon......6 D4
Good Easter Essex......51 P8
Gooderstone Norfk......75 Q10
Goodleigh Devon......17 L5
Goodmanham E R Yk......92 E2
Goodmayes Gt Lon......37 L3
Goodnestone Kent......38 H9
Goodnestone Kent......39 N11

Goodrich Herefs......45 R11
Goodrington Torbay......7 M7
Goodshaw Lancs......89 N5
Goodshaw Fold Lancs......89 N5
Goodstone Devon......7 K4
Goodwick Pembks......40 H3
Goodwood W Susx......15 N5
Goodworth Clatford Hants..22 C6
Goodyers End Warwks......59 M7
Goole E R Yk......92 B6
Goole Fields E R Yk......92 C6
Goonbell Cnwll......3 J4
Goonhavern Cnwll......3 K3
Goonvrea Cnwll......3 J4
Goosecruives Abers......151 K11
Gooseford Devon......8 G6
Goose Green Essex......53 K6
Goose Green Kent......26 D4
Goose Green Kent......37 P10
Goose Green S Glos......32 C10
Goose Green W Susx......24 D7
Goose Green Wigan......82 C4
Gooseham Cnwll......16 C8
Gooseham Mill Cnwll......16 C8
Goosehill Green Worcs......46 H2
Goose Pool Herefs......45 P7
Goosey Oxon......34 C6
Goosnargh Lancs......88 H3
Goostrey Ches E......82 G10
Gordano Services N Som......31 P9
Gorddinog Conwy......79 M10
Gordon Border......117 B2
Gordon Arms Hotel Border...117 L5
Gordonstown Abers......158 E6
Gordonstown Abers......158 H10
Gore Powys......45 K3
Gorebridge Mdloth......127 Q5
Gorefield Cambs......74 H8
Gore Pit Essex......52 E8
Gores Wilts......21 M3
Gore Street Kent......39 N8
Gorey Jersey......11 c2
Goring Oxon......34 H8
Goring-by-Sea W Susx......24 D10
Goring Heath Oxon......35 J9
Gorleston on Sea Norfk......77 Q11
Gorrachie Abers......158 H6
Gorran Churchtown Cnwll......3 P5
Gorran Haven Cnwll......3 Q5
Gorran High Lanes Cnwll......3 P5
Gorrig Cerdgn......42 H6
Gors Cerdgn......54 E9
Gorsedd Flints......80 H9
Gorse Hill Swindn......33 N7
Gorseinon Swans......28 G5
Gorseybank Derbys......71 P4
Gorsgoch Cerdgn......43 J4
Gorslas Carmth......28 G2
Gorsley Gloucs......46 C9
Gorsley Common Herefs......46 C9
Gorstage Ches W......82 D10
Gorstan Highld......155 L5
Gorstella Ches W......69 L2
Gorsten Ag & B......138 C11
Gorst Hill Worcs......57 N10
Gorsty Hill Staffs......71 L9
Gorthleck Highld......147 N3
Gorton Manch......83 J5
Gosbeck Suffk......64 H10
Gosberton Lincs......74 D4
Gosberton Clough Lincs......74 C5
Gosfield Essex......52 C6
Gosford Devon......10 C5
Gosford Oxon......34 E2
Gosforth Cumb......100 E10
Gosforth N u Ty......113 K7
Gosling Street Somset......19 P8
Gosmore Herts......50 E5
Gospel End Staffs......58 C6
Gospel Green W Susx......23 P8
Gosport Hants......14 H7
Gossard's Green C Beds......49 Q6
Gossington Gloucs......32 D4
Goswick Nthumb......119 L2
Gotham Notts......72 E4
Gotherington Gloucs......47 J9
Gotton Somset......18 H9
Goudhurst Kent......26 B4
Goulceby Lincs......87 J5
Gourdas Abers......159 J9
Gourdie C Dund......142 F11
Gourdon Abers......143 Q3
Gourock Inver......124 G2
Govan C Glas......125 N4
Goveton Devon......7 K9
Govilon Mons......31 J2
Gowdall E R Yk......91 Q6
Gower Highld......155 P6
Gowerton Swans......28 F6
Gowkhall Fife......134 D10
Gowthorpe E R Yk......98 F10
Goxhill E R Yk......93 L2
Goxhill N Linc......93 K6
Goytre Neath......29 L7
Grabhair W Isls......168 i6
Graby Lincs......74 A5
Grade Cnwll......3 J11
Gradeley Green Ches E......69 Q4
Graffham W Susx......23 P11
Grafham Cambs......61 Q7
Grafham Surrey......24 B2
Grafton Herefs......45 P7
Grafton N York......97 P8
Grafton Oxon......33 Q4
Grafton Shrops......69 M11
Grafton Worcs......46 A2
Grafton Worcs......47 J7
Grafton Flyford Worcs......47 J3
Grafton Regis Nhants......49 L5
Grafton Underwood Nhants...61 K4
Grafty Green Kent......26 E2
Graianrhyd Denbgs......68 H3
Graig Conwy......79 Q10
Graig Denbgs......80 F10
Graigfechan Denbgs......68 H4
Grain Medway......38 E6
Grains Bar Oldham......90 B9
Grainsby Lincs......93 N11
Grainthorpe Lincs......93 Q11
Grampound Cnwll......3 N4
Grampound Road Cnwll......3 N3
Gramsdal W Isls......168 d12
Gramsdale W Isls......168 d12

Granborough Bucks......49 L9
Granby Notts......73 K3
Grandborough Warwks......59 Q11
Grand Chemins Jersey......11 c2
Grandes Rocques Guern......10 b1
Grandtully P & K......141 M7
Grange Cumb......101 J7
Grange Medway......38 C8
Grange P & K......134 H7
Grange Wirral......81 J7
Grange Crossroads Moray...158 C7
Grange Hall Moray......157 K5
Grangehall S Lans......116 D2
Grange Hill Essex......37 K2
Grangemill Derbys......84 B9
Grange Moor Kirk......90 G7
Grangemouth Falk......133 Q11
Grange of Lindores Fife......134 H4
Grange-over-Sands Cumb...95 J3
Grangepans Falk......134 C11
Grange Park Gt Lon......60 G9
Grangetown R & Cl......104 F6
Grangetown Sundld......113 P10
Grange Villa Dur......113 K10
Gransmoor E R Yk......99 N9
Gransmore Green Essex......51 P6
Granston Pembks......40 G4
Grantchester Cambs......62 F9
Grantham Lincs......73 N3
Granton C Edin......127 N2
Grantown-on-Spey Highld...149 J2
Grantsfield Herefs......45 Q2
Grantshouse Border......129 L6
Grappenhall Warrtn......82 D7
Grasby Lincs......93 J10
Grasmere Cumb......101 K9
Grasscroft Oldham......83 L4
Grassendale Lpool......81 M7
Grassgarth Cumb......101 K2
Grass Green Essex......52 B4
Grassington N York......96 F8
Grassmoor Derbys......84 F7
Grassthorpe Notts......85 N7
Grateley Hants......21 Q6
Gratwich Staffs......71 J8
Graveley Cambs......62 C8
Graveley Herts......50 F5
Gravelly Hill Birm......58 H6
Gravelsbank Shrops......56 F4
Graveney Kent......39 J6
Gravesend Kent......37 Q6
Gravir W Isls......168 i6
Grayingham Lincs......92 F11
Grayrigg Cumb......101 Q11
Grays Thurr......37 P5
Grayshott Hants......23 N7
Grayson Green Cumb......100 C5
Grayswood Surrey......23 P8
Graythorpe Hartpl......104 F5
Grazeley Wokam......35 J11
Greasbrough Rothm......91 L11
Greasby Wirral......81 K7
Greasley Notts......84 G11
Great Abington Cambs......62 H11
Great Addington Nhants......61 L5
Great Alne Warwks......47 M3
Great Altcar Lancs......88 C9
Great Amwell Herts......51 J8
Great Asby Cumb......102 C8
Great Ashfield Suffk......64 D8
Great Ayton N York......104 G8
Great Baddow Essex......52 B11
Great Badminton S Glos......32 F8
Great Bardfield Essex......51 Q4
Great Barford Bed......61 P10
Great Barr Sandw......58 F5
Great Barrington Gloucs......33 P2
Great Barrow Ches W......81 P11
Great Barton Suffk......64 B8
Great Barugh N York......98 E5
Great Bavington Nthumb...112 E4
Great Bealings Suffk......53 M2
Great Bedwyn Wilts......21 Q2
Great Bentley Essex......53 K7
Great Billing Nhants......60 H8
Great Bircham Norfk......75 Q4
Great Blakenham Suffk......64 G11
Great Blencow Cumb......101 N4
Great Bolas Wrekin......70 A10
Great Bookham Surrey......36 D10
Great Bosullow Cnwll......2 C7
Great Bourton Oxon......48 E5
Great Bowden Leics......60 F3
Great Bradley Suffk......63 L10
Great Braxted Essex......52 E9
Great Bricett Suffk......64 E11
Great Brickhill Bucks......49 P8
Great Bridgeford Staffs......70 F9
Great Brington Nhants......60 E7
Great Bromley Essex......53 J6
Great Broughton Cumb......100 E4
Great Broughton N York......104 F9
Great Budworth Ches W......82 E9
Great Burdon Darltn......104 B7
Great Burstead Essex......37 Q2
Great Busby N York......104 F9
Great Canfield Essex......51 N7
Great Carlton Lincs......87 M3
Great Casterton Rutlnd......73 Q9
Great Chalfield Wilts......20 G2
Great Chart Kent......26 G3
Great Chatwell Staffs......57 P2
Great Chell C Stke......70 F4
Great Chesterford Essex......51 M2
Great Cheverell Wilts......21 J4
Great Chishill Cambs......51 K3
Great Clacton Essex......53 L8
Great Cliffe Wakefd......91 J7
Great Clifton Cumb......100 D5
Great Coates NE Lin......93 M9
Great Comberton Worcs......47 J6
Great Comp Kent......37 P9
Great Corby Cumb......111 J10
Great Cornard Suffk......52 E3
Great Cowden E R Yk......93 M2
Great Coxwell Oxon......33 Q6
Great Cransley Nhants......60 H5
Great Cressingham Norfk...76 B11
Great Crosthwaite Cumb...101 J6
Great Cubley Derbys......71 M7
Great Cumbrae Island
N Ayrs......124 F6
Great Dalby Leics......73 J8
Great Denham Bed......61 M11
Great Doddington Nhants...61 J8

Great Doward Herefs......45 Q11
Great Dunham Norfk......76 B9
Great Dunmow Essex......51 P6
Great Durnford Wilts......21 M7
Great Easton Essex......51 P5
Great Easton Leics......60 H2
Great Eccleston Lancs......88 E2
Great Edstone N York......98 E4
Great Ellingham Norfk......64 D2
Great Elm Somset......20 D5
Great Everdon Nhants......60 D9
Great Eversden Cambs......62 E10
Great Fencote N York......97 L9
Greatfield Wilts......33 L7
Great Finborough Suffk......64 E10
Great Fransham Norfk......76 B9
Great Gaddesden Herts......50 B8
Greatgate Staffs......71 K7
Great Gidding Cambs......61 P4
Great Givendale E R Yk......98 G10
Great Glemham Suffk......65 L9
Great Glen Leics......72 H11
Great Gonerby Lincs......73 M3
Great Gransden Cambs......62 C9
Great Green Cambs......50 G2
Great Green Norfk......65 K4
Great Green Suffk......64 C10
Great Green Suffk......64 C8
Great Habton N York......98 F5
Great Hale Lincs......74 B2
Great Hallingbury Essex......51 M7
Greatham Hants......23 L8
Greatham Hartpl......104 E5
Greatham W Susx......24 B7
Great Hampden Bucks......35 M4
Great Harrowden Nhants......61 J6
Great Harwood Lancs......89 L4
Great Haseley Oxon......34 H4
Great Hatfield E R Yk......93 L2
Great Haywood Staffs......70 H10
Great Heck N York......91 P6
Great Henny Essex......52 E4
Great Hinton Wilts......20 H3
Great Hockham Norfk......64 D2
Great Holland Essex......53 M8
Great Hollands Br For......35 N11
Great Horkesley Essex......52 G5
Great Hormead Herts......51 K5
Great Horton C Brad......90 E4
Great Horwood Bucks......49 L8
Great Houghton Barns......91 L9
Great Houghton Nhants......60 G9
Great Hucklow Derbys......83 Q9
Great Kelk E R Yk......99 N9
Great Kimble Bucks......35 M3
Great Kingshill Bucks......35 N5
Great Langdale Cumb......101 J9
Great Langton N York......103 Q11
Great Leighs Essex......52 B8
Great Limber Lincs......93 K9
Great Linford M Keyn......49 N6
Great Livermere Suffk......64 B7
Great Longstone Derbys......84 B6
Great Lumley Dur......113 L11
Great Lyth Shrops......56 H3
Great Malvern Worcs......46 E5
Great Maplestead Essex......52 D5
Great Marton Bpool......88 C3
Great Massingham Norfk...75 Q6
Great Melton Norfk......76 G10
Great Meols Wirral......81 J6
Great Milton Oxon......34 H4
Great Missenden Bucks......35 M3
Great Mitton Lancs......89 L3
Great Mongeham Kent......39 Q11
Great Moulton Norfk......64 H3
Great Munden Herts......51 J6
Great Musgrave Cumb......102 E8
Great Ness Shrops......69 L11
Great Notley Essex......52 B7
Great Oak Mons......31 L2
Great Oakley Essex......53 L6
Great Oakley Nhants......61 J3
Great Offley Herts......50 E5
Great Ormside Cumb......102 D7
Great Orton Cumb......110 F10
Great Ouseburn N York......97 P8
Great Oxendon Nhants......60 F4
Great Oxney Green Essex......51 Q9
Great Palgrave Norfk......76 A9
Great Park N u Ty......113 K6
Great Parndon Essex......51 K9
Great Pattenden Kent......26 B3
Great Paxton Cambs......62 B8
Great Plumpton Lancs......88 D4
Great Plumstead Norfk......77 L9
Great Ponton Lincs......73 N4
Great Potheridge Devon......17 J9
Great Preston Leeds......91 L5
Great Purston Nhants......48 F7
Great Raveley Cambs......62 C4
Great Rissington Gloucs......47 N11
Great Rollright Oxon......48 B8
Great Ryburgh Norfk......76 D6
Great Ryle Nthumb......119 K8
Great Ryton Shrops......56 H4
Great Saling Essex......52 Q5
Great Salkeld Cumb......101 Q3
Great Sampford Essex......51 P3
Great Saredon Staffs......58 E3
Great Saughall Ches W......81 M11
Great Saxham Suffk......63 N8
Great Shefford W Berk......34 C9
Great Shelford Cambs......62 G10
Great Smeaton N York......104 B10
Great Snoring Norfk......76 C5
Great Somerford Wilts......33 J8
Great Soudley Shrops......70 C9
Great Stainton Darltn......104 B6
Great Stambridge Essex......38 E3
Great Staughton Cambs......61 P8
Great Steeping Lincs......87 M8
Greatstone-on-Sea Kent......27 J7
Great Strickland Cumb......101 Q6
Great Stukeley Cambs......62 B6
Great Sturton Lincs......86 H5
Great Sutton Ches W......81 M9
Great Sutton Shrops......57 J7
Great Swinburne Nthumb...112 F5
Great Tew Oxon......48 D9
Great Tey Essex......52 E6
Great Thurlow Suffk......63 L10

Great Torrington Devon......16 H8
Great Tosson Nthumb......119 K10
Great Totham Essex......52 E9
Great Totham Essex......52 E9
Great Tows Lincs......86 H2
Great Urswick Cumb......94 F6
Great Wakering Essex......38 F4
Great Waldingfield Suffk......52 F3
Great Walsingham Norfk...76 C4
Great Waltham Essex......51 Q8
Great Warford Ches E......82 H9
Great Washbourne Gloucs...47 J8
Great Weeke Devon......8 H7
Great Welnetham Suffk......64 B10
Great Wenham Suffk......53 J4
Great Whittington Nthumb..112 H5
Great Wigborough Essex......52 G8
Great Wilbraham Cambs......63 J9
Great Wilne Derbys......72 C4
Great Wishford Wilts......21 L7
Great Witchingham Norfk...76 G7
Great Witcombe Gloucs......32 H2
Great Witley Worcs......57 P11
Great Wolford Warwks......47 Q8
Greatworth Nhants......48 E5
Great Wratting Suffk......63 L11
Great Wymondley Herts......50 F5
Great Wyrley Staffs......58 E3
Great Wytheford Shrops......69 Q11
Great Yarmouth Norfk......77 Q10
Great Yeldham Essex......52 C4
Grebby Lincs......87 M7
Greeba IoM......80 d5
Green Denbgs......80 F11
Green Bank Cumb......94 H4
Greenbottom Cnwll......3 K4
Greenburn W Loth......126 G5
Greencroft Hall Dur......113 J11
Green Cross Surrey......23 N7
Green Down Somset......19 Q4
Green End Bed......61 M11
Green End Bed......61 N8
Green End Bed......61 P10
Green End Bed......61 P8
Green End Cambs......61 Q4
Green End Cambs......62 B6
Green End Cambs......62 E9
Green End Cambs......62 G7
Green End Cambs......62 G8
Green End Herts......50 G4
Green End Herts......51 H4
Green End Herts......50 H4
Greenend Oxon......48 B10
Green End Warwks......59 L7
Greenfield Ag & B......131 Q9
Greenfield C Beds......50 C4
Greenfield Flints......80 H9
Greenfield Highld......146 G7
Greenfield Oldham......83 L4
Greenfield Oxon......35 K6
Greenford Gt Lon......36 D4
Greengairs N Lans......126 D3
Greengates C Brad......90 F3
Greengill Cumb......100 F3
Greenhalgh Lancs......88 E3
Greenham Somset......18 E10
Greenham W Berk......34 E11
Green Hammerton N York...97 N9
Greenhaugh Nthumb......111 Q3
Green Head Cumb......110 G11
Greenhead Nthumb......111 N7
Green Heath Staffs......58 E2
Greenheys Salfd......82 F4
Greenhill D & G......109 P3
Greenhill Falk......126 E2
Greenhill Herefs......46 D5
Greenhill Kent......39 L8
Greenhill S Lans......116 C4
Green Hill Wilts......33 L7
Greenhillocks Derbys......84 F11
Greenhills S Lans......125 Q7
Greenhithe Kent......37 N5
Greenholm E Ayrs......125 N10
Greenholme Cumb......101 Q9
Greenhouse Border......117 R6
Greenhow Hill N York......96 H8
Greenland Highld......167 M3
Greenland Sheff......84 E3
Greenlands Bucks......35 L7
Green Lane Devon......9 J3
Green Lane Worcs......47 L2
Greenlaw Border......129 J10
Greenlea D & G......109 M5
Greenloaning P & K......133 N6
Green Moor Barns......90 H11
Greenmount Bury......89 M8
Green Oak E R Yk......92 D5
Greenock Inver......124 H2
Greenodd Cumb......94 G4
Green Ore Somset......19 Q4
Green Quarter Cumb......101 N10
Greensgate Norfk......76 G8
Greenshields S Lans......116 E2
Greenside Gatesd......112 H8
Greenside Kirk......90 F7
Greens Norton Nhants......49 J5
Greenstead Green Essex......52 D6
Greensted Green Essex......51 M10
Green Street E Susx......26 C9
Green Street Gloucs......46 G11
Green Street Herts......50 E11
Green Street Herts......51 H4
Green Street Worcs......46 G5
Green Street Green Gt Lon...37 N6
Green Street Green Kent......37 N6
Greenstreet Green Suffk......52 H3
Green Tye Herts......51 K7
Greenway Somset......19 K10
Greenway V Glam......30 E10
Greenway Worcs......57 N10
Greenwich Gt Lon......37 J5
Greenwich Maritime Gt Lon..37 J5
Greet Gloucs......47 K8
Greete Shrops......57 K10
Greetham Lincs......87 K6
Greetham Rutlnd......73 N8
Greetland Calder......90 D6
Gregson Lane Lancs......88 H5
Greinton Somset......19 M7
Grenaby IoM......80 c7
Grendon Nhants......61 J8
Grendon Warwks......59 K4
Grendon Green Herefs......46 A3

Grendon Underwood Bucks...49 J10
Grenofen Devon...6 D4
Grenoside Sheff...84 D2
Greosabhagh W Isls...168 g8
Gresford Wrexhm...69 K4
Gresham Norfk...76 H4
Greshornish Highld...152 E7
Gressenhall Norfk...76 D8
Gressenhall Green Norfk...76 D8
Gressingham Lancs...95 M7
Gresty Green Ches E...70 C4
Greta Bridge Dur...103 L8
Gretna D & G...110 F7
Gretna Green D & G...110 F7
Gretna Services D & G...110 F7
Gretton Gloucs...47 K8
Gretton Nhants...61 J2
Gretton Shrops...57 J5
Grewelthorpe N York...97 K5
Grey Friars Suffk...65 P7
Greygarth N York...97 J6
Grey Green N Linc...92 C9
Greylake Somset...19 L8
Greylees Lincs...73 Q2
Greyrigg D & G...109 N3
Greys Green Oxon...35 K8
Greysouthen Cumb...100 E5
Greystoke Cumb...101 M4
Greystone Angus...143 J9
Greywell Hants...23 K4
Gribb Dorset...10 H4
Gribthorpe E R Yk...92 C3
Griff Warwks...59 N7
Griffithstown Torfn...31 J3
Griffydam Leics...72 C7
Griggs Green Hants...23 M8
Grimeford Village Lancs...89 J8
Grimesthorpe Sheff...84 E3
Grimethorpe Barns...91 L9
Grimley Worcs...46 F2
Grimmet S Ayrs...114 F5
Grimoldby Lincs...87 L3
Grimpo Shrops...69 L9
Grimsargh Lancs...88 H4
Grimsby NE Lin...93 N8
Grimscote Nhants...49 J4
Grimscott Cnwll...16 D10
Grimshader W Isls...168 j5
Grimshaw Bl w D...89 L6
Grimshaw Green Lancs...88 F8
Grimsthorpe Lincs...73 Q6
Grimston E R Yk...93 N3
Grimston Leics...72 H6
Grimston Norfk...75 P6
Grimstone Dorset...11 N6
Grimstone End Suffk...64 C8
Grinacombe Moor Devon...5 M3
Grindale E R Yk...99 N6
Grindle Shrops...57 N4
Grindleford Derbys...84 B5
Grindleton Lancs...95 R11
Grindley Brook Shrops...69 P6
Grindlow Derbys...83 Q9
Grindon Nthumb...118 H2
Grindon S on T...104 C5
Grindon Staffs...71 K4
Grindon Hill Nthumb...112 B7
Grindonrigg Nthumb...118 H2
Gringley on the Hill Notts...85 M2
Grinsdale Cumb...110 G9
Grinshill Shrops...69 P10
Grinton N York...103 K11
Griomaisiader W Isls...168 j5
Grishipoll Ag & B...136 F4
Grisling Common E Susx...25 K6
Gristhorpe N York...99 M4
Griston Norfk...64 C2
Gritley Ork...169 e6
Grittenham Wilts...33 K8
Grittleton Wilts...32 G8
Grizebeck Cumb...94 E4
Grizedale Cumb...94 G2
Groby Leics...72 E9
Groes Conwy...68 D2
Groes-faen Rhondd...30 E8
Groesffordd Gwynd...66 D7
Groesffordd Powys...44 F9
Groesffordd Marli Denbgs...80 E10
Groeslon Gwynd...66 H3
Groeslon Gwynd...67 J2
Groes-lwyd Powys...56 C2
Groes-Wen Caerph...30 F7
Grogarry W Isls...168 c14
Grogport Ag & B...120 F3
Groigearraidh W Isls...168 c14
Gromford Suffk...65 M10
Gronant Flints...80 F8
Groombridge E Susx...25 M3
Grosebay W Isls...168 g8
Grosmont Mons...45 N10
Grosmont N York...105 M9
Groton Suffk...52 G3
Grotton Oldham...83 L4
Grouville Jersey...11 c2
Grove Bucks...49 P10
Grove Dorset...11 P10
Grove Kent...39 M9
Grove Notts...85 M5
Grove Oxon...34 D6
Grove Pembks...41 J10
Grove Green Kent...38 C10
Grovenhurst Kent...26 B3
Grove Park Gt Lon...37 K6
Grovesend S Glos...32 C7
Grovesend Swans...28 G4
Grubb Street Kent...37 N7
Gruinard Highld...160 E9
Gruinart Ag & B...122 C6
Grula Highld...144 E2
Gruline Ag & B...137 N7
Grumbla Cnwll...2 C8
Grundisburgh Suffk...65 J11
Gruting Shet...169 p9
Grutness Shet...169 r12
Gualachulain Highld...139 L8
Guanockgate Lincs...74 G8
Guardbridge Fife...135 M4
Guarlford Worcs...46 F5
Guay P & K...141 P7
Guernsey Guern...10 b2
Guernsey Airport Guern...10 b2
Guestling Green E Susx...26 E9
Guestling Thorn E Susx...26 E9
Guestwick Norfk...76 F7
Guide Bridge Tamesd...83 K5

Guide Post Nthumb...113 L3
Guilden Morden Cambs...50 G2
Guilden Sutton Ches W...81 N11
Guildford Surrey...23 Q5
Guildstead Kent...38 D9
Guildtown P & K...142 A11
Guilsborough Nhants...60 E6
Guilsfield Powys...56 C2
Guilton Kent...39 N10
Guiltreehill S Ayrs...114 G5
Guineaford Devon...17 K4
Guisborough R & Cl...104 H7
Guiseley Leeds...90 F2
Guist Norfk...76 E6
Guiting Power Gloucs...47 L10
Gullane E Loth...128 D3
Gulling Green Suffk...64 A10
Gulval Cnwll...2 D7
Gulworthy Devon...6 D4
Gumfreston Pembks...41 M10
Gumley Leics...60 E3
Gummow's Shop Cnwll...4 D10
Gunby E R Yk...92 B3
Gunby Lincs...73 N6
Gunby Lincs...87 N7
Gundleton Hants...22 H8
Gun Green Kent...26 C5
Gun Hill E Susx...25 N8
Gun Hill Warwks...59 L7
Gunn Devon...17 L5
Gunnerside N York...103 J11
Gunnerton Nthumb...112 D6
Gunness N Linc...92 D8
Gunnislake Cnwll...6 C4
Gunnista Shet...169 s9
Gunthorpe C Pete...74 C10
Gunthorpe N Linc...92 D11
Gunthorpe Norfk...76 E5
Gunthorpe Notts...72 H2
Gunton Suffk...65 Q2
Gunwalloe Cnwll...2 H9
Gupworthy Somset...18 C8
Gurnard IoW...14 E7
Gurnett Ches E...83 K10
Gurney Slade Somset...20 B5
Gurnos Powys...29 L3
Gushmere Kent...38 H10
Gussage All Saints Dorset...12 H2
Gussage St Andrew Dorset...12 G2
Gussage St Michael Dorset...12 G2
Guston Kent...27 P3
Gutcher Shet...169 s4
Guthrie Angus...143 K7
Guyhirn Cambs...74 H10
Guyhirn Gull Cambs...74 G10
Guy's Marsh Dorset...20 F10
Guyzance Nthumb...119 P10
Gwaenysgor Flints...80 F8
Gwalchmai IoA...78 F9
Gwastadnant Gwynd...67 L3
Gwaun-Cae-Gurwen
Carmth...29 J2
Gwbert on Sea Cerdgn...42 C4
Gwealavellan Cnwll...2 G5
Gweek Cnwll...3 J8
Gwehelog Mons...31 L4
Gwenddwr Powys...44 F6
Gwennap Cnwll...3 J5
Gwennap Mining District
Cnwll...3 K5
Gwenter Cnwll...3 J10
Gwernaffield Flints...81 J11
Gwernesney Mons...31 M4
Gwernogle Carmth...43 K8
Gwernymynydd Flints...68 H2
Gwersyllt Wrexhm...69 K4
Gwespyr Flints...80 G8
Gwindra Cnwll...3 P3
Gwinear Cnwll...2 F6
Gwithian Cnwll...2 F5
Gwredog IoA...78 G7
Gwrhay Caerph...30 G5
Gwyddelwern Denbgs...68 E5
Gwyddgrug Carmth...43 J7
Gwynfryn Wrexhm...69 J4
Gwystre Powys...55 P11
Gwytherin Conwy...68 A2
Gyfelia Wrexhm...69 K5
Gyrn Goch Gwynd...66 G5

H

Habberley Shrops...56 F4
Habberley Worcs...57 Q9
Habergham Lancs...89 N4
Habertoft Lincs...87 P7
Habin W Susx...23 M10
Habrough NE Lin...93 K8
Hacconby Lincs...74 B5
Haceby Lincs...73 Q3
Hacheston Suffk...65 L10
Hackbridge Gt Lon...36 G7
Hackenthorpe Sheff...84 F4
Hackford Norfk...76 F11
Hackforth N York...97 K2
Hack Green Ches E...70 A5
Hackland Ork...169 c4
Hackleton Nhants...60 H9
Hacklinge Kent...39 P11
Hackman's Gate Worcs...58 C9
Hackness N York...99 K2
Hackness Somset...19 K5
Hackney Gt Lon...36 H4
Hackthorn Lincs...86 C4
Hackthorpe Cumb...101 P6
Hacton Gt Lon...37 N3
Hadden Border...118 E3
Haddenham Bucks...35 K3
Haddenham Cambs...62 G5
Haddington E Loth...128 E5
Haddington Lincs...86 B8
Haddiscoe Norfk...65 N2
Haddo Abers...159 K10
Haddon Cambs...61 P2
Hade Edge Kirk...83 P4
Hadfield Derbys...83 M5
Hadham Cross Herts...51 K7
Hadham Ford Herts...51 K6
Hadleigh Essex...38 D4
Hadleigh Suffk...52 H3
Hadleigh Heath Suffk...52 G3
Hadley Worcs...46 F2
Hadley Wrekin...57 M2

Hadley End Staffs...71 L10
Hadley Wood Gt Lon...50 G11
Hadlow Kent...37 P10
Hadlow Down E Susx...25 M6
Hadnall Shrops...69 P10
Hadrian's Wall...112 E7
Hadstock Essex...51 N2
Hadston Nthumb...119 Q11
Hadzor Worcs...46 H2
Haffenden Quarter Kent...26 E3
Hafod-y-bwch Wrexhm...69 K5
Hafod-y-coed Blae G...30 H4
Hafodyrynys Caerph...30 H5
Haggate Lancs...89 P3
Haggbeck Cumb...111 J6
Haggersta Shet...169 q9
Haggerston Nthumb...119 K2
Haggington Hill Devon...17 K2
Haggs Falk...126 D2
Hagley Herefs...45 R6
Hagley Worcs...58 D8
Hagmore Green Suffk...52 G4
Hagnaby Lincs...87 K8
Hagnaby Lincs...87 N5
Hagworthingham Lincs...87 K7
Haigh Wigan...89 J9
Haighton Green Lancs...88 H4
Haile Cumb...100 D9
Hailey Herts...51 J8
Hailey Oxon...34 C2
Hailey Oxon...34 H7
Hailsham E Susx...25 N9
Hail Weston Cambs...61 Q8
Hainault Gt Lon...37 L2
Haine Kent...39 Q8
Hainford Norfk...77 J8
Hainton Lincs...86 G4
Hainworth C Brad...90 D3
Haisthorpe E R Yk...99 N8
Hakin Pembks...40 G9
Halam Notts...85 L10
Halbeath Fife...134 E10
Halberton Devon...9 P2
Halcro Highld...167 M4
Hale Cumb...95 L5
Hale Halton...81 P8
Hale Hants...21 N11
Hale Somset...20 D9
Hale Surrey...23 M5
Hale Traffd...82 G7
Hale Bank Halton...81 P8
Hale Barns Traffd...82 G7
Hale Green E Susx...25 N8
Hale Nook Lancs...88 D2
Hales Norfk...65 M2
Hales Staffs...70 C8
Halesgate Lincs...74 F5
Hales Green Derbys...71 M6
Halesowen Dudley...58 E8
Hales Place Kent...39 K10
Hale Street Kent...37 Q11
Halesville Essex...38 F3
Halesworth Suffk...65 M6
Halewood Knows...81 P7
Halford Devon...7 L4
Halford Shrops...56 G8
Halford Warwks...47 Q5
Halfpenny Cumb...95 L3
Halfpenny Green Staffs...58 B6
Halfpenny Houses N York...97 K4
Halfway Carmth...43 M8
Halfway Carmth...44 A8
Halfway Sheff...84 F4
Halfway W Berk...34 D11
Halfway Bridge W Susx...23 P10
Halfway House Shrops...56 E2
Halfway Houses Kent...38 F7
Halifax Calder...90 D5
Halket E Ayrs...125 L7
Halkirk Highld...167 K5
Halkyn Flints...81 J10
Hall E Rens...125 L7
Hallam Fields Derbys...72 D3
Halland E Susx...25 L7
Hallaton Leics...73 K11
Hallatrow BaNES...20 B3
Hallbankgate Cumb...111 L9
Hallbeck Cumb...95 N3
Hall Cliffe Wakefd...90 H7
Hall Cross Lancs...88 E4
Hall Dunnerdale Cumb...100 H11
Hallen S Glos...31 Q8
Hall End Bed...61 M11
Hall End C Beds...50 C3
Hallfield Gate Derbys...84 E9
Hallgarth Dur...104 B2
Hallglen Falk...126 F2
Hall Green Birm...58 H8
Hallin Highld...152 D6
Halling Medway...38 B9
Hallington Lincs...87 K3
Hallington Nthumb...112 E5
Halliwell Bolton...89 K8
Halloughton Notts...85 L10
Hallow Worcs...46 F3
Hallow Heath Worcs...46 F3
Hallsands Devon...7 L11
Hall's Green Essex...51 K9
Hall's Green Herts...50 G5
Hallthwaites Cumb...94 D3
Hallworthy Cnwll...5 K4
Hallyne Border...116 H2
Halmer End Staffs...70 D5
Halmond's Frome Herefs...46 C5
Halmore Gloucs...32 D4
Halnaker W Susx...15 P5
Halsall Lancs...88 D8
Halse Nhants...48 G5
Halse Somset...18 F9
Halsetown Cnwll...2 E6
Halsham E R Yk...93 N5
Halsinger Devon...17 J4
Halstead Essex...52 D5
Halstead Kent...37 L8
Halstead Leics...73 K9
Halstock Dorset...11 L3
Halsway Somset...18 F7
Haltcliff Bridge Cumb...101 L3
Haltham Lincs...86 H8
Haltoft End Lincs...87 L11
Halton Bucks...35 N3
Halton Halton...81 R8
Halton Lancs...95 L8

Halton Leeds...91 K4
Halton Nthumb...112 E7
Halton Wrexhm...69 K7
Halton East N York...96 F10
Halton Fenside Lincs...87 M8
Halton Gill N York...96 C5
Halton Green Lancs...95 L7
Halton Holegate Lincs...87 M7
Halton Lea Gate Nthumb...111 M9
Halton Quay Cnwll...5 Q8
Halton Shields Nthumb...112 F7
Halton West N York...96 B10
Haltwhistle Nthumb...111 P8
Halvana Cnwll...5 L6
Halvergate Norfk...77 N10
Halwell Devon...7 K8
Halwill Devon...8 B5
Halwill Junction Devon...8 B4
Ham Devon...10 E4
Ham Gloucs...32 C5
Ham Gloucs...47 J10
Ham Gt Lon...36 E6
Ham Kent...39 P11
Ham Somset...19 J9
Ham Somset...20 C5
Ham Wilts...22 B2
Hambleden Bucks...35 L7
Hambledon Hants...14 H4
Hambledon Surrey...23 Q7
Hamble-le-Rice Hants...14 E5
Hambleton Lancs...88 D2
Hambleton N York...91 N4
Hambleton Moss Side Lancs...88 D2
Hambridge Somset...19 L10
Hambrook S Glos...32 B9
Hambrook W Susx...15 L5
Ham Common Dorset...20 F9
Hameringham Lincs...87 K7
Hamerton Cambs...61 P5
Ham Green Herefs...46 E6
Ham Green Kent...26 E6
Ham Green Kent...38 D8
Ham Green N Som...31 P9
Ham Green Worcs...47 K2
Ham Hill Kent...37 Q8
Hamilton S Lans...126 C6
Hamilton Services S Lans...126 C6
Hamlet Dorset...11 M3
Hamlins E Susx...25 N9
Hammerpot W Susx...24 C9
Hammersmith Gt Lon...36 F5
Hammerwich Staffs...58 G3
Hammerwood E Susx...25 K3
Hammond Street Herts...50 H10
Hammoon Dorset...12 D2
Hamnavoe Shet...169 q10
Hampden Park E Susx...25 P10
Hamperden End Essex...51 N4
Hampnett Gloucs...47 L11
Hampole Donc...91 N8
Hampreston Dorset...13 J5
Hampsfield Cumb...95 J4
Hampson Green Lancs...95 K10
Hampstead Gt Lon...36 G3
Hampstead Norreys W Berk...34 F9
Hampsthwaite N York...97 L9
Hampton C Pete...61 Q2
Hampton Devon...10 F5
Hampton Gt Lon...36 D7
Hampton Kent...39 L8
Hampton Shrops...57 N7
Hampton Swindn...33 N6
Hampton Worcs...47 K6
Hampton Bishop Herefs...45 R7
Hampton Court Palace
Gt Lon...36 E7
Hampton Fields Gloucs...32 G5
Hampton Green Ches W...69 P5
Hampton Heath Ches W...69 P5
Hampton-in-Arden Solhll...59 K8
Hampton Loade Shrops...57 N7
Hampton Lovett Worcs...58 C11
Hampton Lucy Warwks...47 Q3
Hampton Magna Warwks...59 L11
Hampton on the Hill
Warwks...47 Q2
Hampton Poyle Oxon...48 F11
Hampton Wick Gt Lon...36 E7
Hamptworth Wilts...21 P11
Hamrow Norfk...76 C7
Hamsey E Susx...25 K8
Hamsey Green Surrey...37 J9
Hamstall Ridware Staffs...71 L11
Hamstead Birm...58 G6
Hamstead IoW...14 D8
Hamstead Marshall W Berk...34 D11
Hamsterley Dur...103 M4
Hamsterley Dur...112 H9
Hamstreet Kent...26 H5
Ham Street Somset...19 Q8
Hamworthy BCP...12 G6
Hanbury Staffs...71 M9
Hanbury Worcs...47 J2
Hanby Lincs...73 Q4
Hanchurch Staffs...70 E6
Handa Island Highld...164 D7
Handale R & Cl...105 K7
Hand and Pen Devon...9 P5
Handbridge Ches W...81 N11
Handcross W Susx...24 G5
Handforth Ches E...83 J8
Hand Green Ches W...69 P2
Handley Ches W...69 N3
Handley Derbys...84 E8
Handley Green Essex...51 Q10
Handsacre Staffs...71 K11
Handsworth Birm...58 F7
Handsworth Sheff...84 F3
Handy Cross Bucks...35 N6
Hanford C Stke...70 F6
Hanford Dorset...12 D2
Hanging Heaton Kirk...90 H6
Hanging Houghton Nhants...60 G6
Hanging Langford Wilts...21 L7
Hangleton Br & H...24 G9
Hangleton W Susx...24 C10
Hanham S Glos...32 B10
Hankelow Ches E...70 B5
Hankerton Wilts...33 J6
Hankham E Susx...25 P9
Hanley C Stke...70 F5
Hanley Castle Worcs...46 F6
Hanley Child Worcs...57 M11

Hanley Swan Worcs...46 F6
Hanley William Worcs...57 M11
Hanlith N York...96 C8
Hanmer Wrexhm...69 N7
Hannaford Devon...17 L6
Hannah Lincs...87 N5
Hannington Hants...22 F3
Hannington Nhants...60 H6
Hannington Swindn...33 N6
Hannington Wick Swindn...33 N5
Hanscombe End C Beds...50 D4
Hanslope M Keyn...49 M5
Hanthorpe Lincs...74 A6
Hanwell Gt Lon...36 E5
Hanwell Oxon...48 D6
Hanwood Shrops...56 G3
Hanworth Gt Lon...36 D6
Hanworth Norfk...76 H4
Happendon Services S Lans...116 B4
Happisburgh Norfk...77 M5
Happisburgh Common
Norfk...77 M6
Hapsford Ches W...81 P10
Hapton Lancs...89 M4
Hapton Norfk...64 H2
Harberton Devon...7 K7
Harbertonford Devon...7 K7
Harbledown Kent...39 K10
Harborne Birm...58 F8
Harborough Magna Warwks...59 Q9
Harbottle Nthumb...118 H10
Harbourneford Devon...7 J6
Harbours Hill Worcs...58 E11
Harbridge Hants...13 K2
Harbridge Green Hants...13 K2
Harbury Warwks...48 C3
Harby Leics...73 J4
Harby Notts...85 Q6
Harcombe Devon...9 L8
Harcombe Devon...10 D6
Harcombe Bottom Devon...10 G5
Harden C Brad...90 D3
Harden Wsall...58 F4
Hardendale Cumb...101 Q8
Hardenhuish Wilts...32 H10
Hardgate Abers...151 K7
Hardgate D & G...108 H7
Hardgate N York...97 L8
Hardgate W Duns...125 N3
Hardham W Susx...24 B7
Hardhorn Lancs...88 D3
Hardingham Norfk...76 E11
Hardingstone Nhants...60 G9
Hardington Somset...20 D4
Hardington Mandeville
Somset...11 L2
Hardington Marsh Somset...11 L3
Hardington Moor Somset...11 L2
Hardisworthy Devon...16 C7
Hardley Hants...14 D6
Hardley Street Norfk...77 M11
Hardmead M Keyn...49 P5
Hardraw N York...96 C2
Hardsough Lancs...89 M6
Hardstoft Derbys...84 F8
Hardway Hants...14 H6
Hardway Somset...20 D8
Hardwick Bucks...49 M11
Hardwick Cambs...62 E9
Hardwick Nhants...60 H7
Hardwick Norfk...65 J4
Hardwick Oxon...34 C3
Hardwick Oxon...48 G9
Hardwick Rothm...84 G3
Hardwick Wsall...58 G5
Hardwicke Gloucs...32 E2
Hardwicke Gloucs...46 H9
Hardwick Hall Derbys...84 G8
Hardwick Village Notts...85 K5
Hardy's Green Essex...52 F7
Harebeating E Susx...25 N8
Hareby Lincs...87 K7
Hare Croft C Brad...90 D3
Harefield Gt Lon...36 C2
Hare Green Essex...53 K6
Hare Hatch Wokham...35 M9
Harehill Derbys...71 M7
Harehills Leeds...91 J4
Harehope Nthumb...119 L6
Harelaw Border...117 Q6
Harelaw D & G...110 H5
Harelaw Dur...113 J10
Hareplain Kent...26 D4
Haresceugh Cumb...102 B2
Harescombe Gloucs...32 F2
Haresfield Gloucs...32 F2
Harestock Hants...22 E8
Hare Street Essex...51 K9
Hare Street Essex...51 M10
Hare Street Herts...51 J5
Harewood Leeds...97 M11
Harewood End Herefs...45 Q9
Harford Devon...6 G7
Hargate Norfk...64 G3
Hargatewall Derbys...83 P9
Hargrave Ches W...69 N2
Hargrave Nhants...61 M6
Hargrave Suffk...63 N9
Harker Cumb...110 G8
Harkstead Suffk...53 L5
Harlaston Staffs...59 K2
Harlaxton Lincs...73 M4
Harlech Gwynd...67 K8
Harlech Castle Gwynd...67 K8
Harlescott Shrops...69 N11
Harlesden Gt Lon...36 F4
Harlesthorpe Derbys...84 G5
Harleston Devon...7 K9
Harleston Norfk...65 J5
Harleston Suffk...64 E9
Harlestone Nhants...60 F8
Harle Syke Lancs...89 P3
Harley Rothm...91 K11
Harley Shrops...57 K3
Harlington C Beds...50 B4
Harlington Donc...91 M10
Harlington Gt Lon...36 C5
Harlosh Highld...152 D9
Harlow Essex...51 K8
Harlow Carr RHS N York...97 L10
Harlow Hill Nthumb...112 G7
Harlthorpe E R Yk...92 B3
Harlton Cambs...62 E10
Harlyn Cnwll...4 D6

Harman's Cross Dorset 12 G8
Harmby N York 96 H3
Harmer Green Herts 50 G7
Harmer Hill Shrops 69 N10
Harmondsworth Gt Lon 36 C5
Harmston Lincs 86 C8
Harnage Shrops 57 K4
Harnham Nthumb 112 G4
Harnhill Gloucs 33 L4
Harold Hill Gt Lon 37 M2
Haroldston West Pembks 40 G7
Haroldswick Shet 169 t2
Harold Wood Gt Lon 37 N2
Harome N York 98 C4
Harpenden Herts 50 D8
Harpford Devon 10 B6
Harpham E R Yk 99 M8
Harpley Norfk 75 Q5
Harpley Worcs 46 C2
Harpole Nhants 60 E8
Harpsdale Highld 167 K5
Harpsden Oxon 35 L8
Harpswell Lincs 86 B3
Harpurhey Manch 83 J4
Harpur Hill Derbys 83 N10
Harraby Cumb 110 H10
Harracott Devon 17 K6
Harrapool Highld 145 L3
Harrietfield P & K 134 B2
Harrietsham Kent 38 E11
Harringay Gt Lon 36 H3
Harrington Cumb 100 C5
Harrington Lincs 87 L6
Harrington Nhants 60 G4
Harringworth Nhants 73 N11
Harris W Isls 168 f8
Harriseahead Staffs 70 F3
Harriston Cumb 100 G2
Harrogate N York 97 M9
Harrold Bed 61 K9
Harrop Dale Oldham 90 C9
Harrow Gt Lon 36 E3
Harrowbarrow Cnwll 5 Q7
Harrowden Bed 61 N11
Harrowgate Village Darltn 103 Q7
Harrow Green Suffk 64 E11
Harrow Hill Gloucs 46 C11
Harrow on the Hill Gt Lon 36 E3
Harrow Weald Gt Lon 36 E2
Harston Cambs 62 F10
Harston Leics 73 L4
Harswell E R Yk 92 D2
Hart Hartpl 104 E3
Hartburn Nthumb 112 G3
Hartburn S on T 104 D7
Hartest Suffk 64 A11
Hartfield E Susx 25 L3
Hartford Cambs 62 C6
Hartford Ches W 82 D10
Hartford Somset 18 C9
Hartfordbridge Hants 23 L3
Hartford End Essex 51 Q7
Hartforth N York 103 N9
Hartgrove Dorset 20 F11
Harthill Ches W 69 N3
Harthill N Lans 126 E5
Harthill Rothm 84 G4
Harthope D & G 116 E8
Hartington Derbys 71 L2
Hartington Nthumb 112 F3
Hartland Devon 16 D7
Hartland Quay Devon 16 C7
Hartlebury Worcs 58 B10
Hartlepool Hartpl 104 F4
Hartley Cumb 102 E9
Hartley Kent 26 C5
Hartley Kent 37 P7
Hartley Nthumb 113 M5
Hartley Green Kent 37 P7
Hartley Green Staffs 70 H9
Hartley Wespall Hants 23 J3
Hartley Wintney Hants 23 L3
Hartlip Kent 38 D9
Hartoft End N York 98 E2
Harton N York 98 E8
Harton S Tyne 113 N7
Harton Shrops 56 H7
Hartpury Gloucs 46 E10
Hartshead Kirk 90 F6
Hartshead Moor Services
  Calder 90 F6
Hartshill C Stke 70 F5
Hartshill Warwks 59 M6
Hartshorne Derbys 71 Q10
Hartside Nthumb 119 J7
Hartsop Cumb 101 M8
Hart Station Hartpl 104 E3
Hartswell Somset 18 E9
Hartwell Nhants 49 L4
Hartwith N York 97 K8
Hartwood N Lans 126 E6
Hartwoodmyres Border 117 N6
Harvel Kent 37 Q8
Harvington Worcs 47 L5
Harvington Worcs 58 C10
Harwell Notts 85 L2
Harwell Oxon 34 E7
Harwich Essex 53 N5
Harwood Bolton 89 L8
Harwood Dur 102 F4
Harwood Nthumb 112 F2
Harwood Dale N York 105 Q11
Harwood Lee Bolton 89 L8
Harworth Notts 85 K2
Hasbury Dudley 58 E8
Hascombe Surrey 24 B3
Haselbech Nhants 60 F5
Haselbury Plucknett Somset 11 K2
Haseley Warwks 59 K11
Haseley Green Warwks 59 K11
Haseley Knob Warwks 59 K10
Haselor Warwks 47 M3
Hasfield Gloucs 46 F9
Hasguard Pembks 40 G9
Hasholme E R Yk 92 D4
Haskayne Lancs 88 D9
Hasketon Suffk 65 J11
Hasland Derbys 84 E7
Haslemere Surrey 23 P8
Haslingden Lancs 89 M6
Haslingfield Cambs 62 F10
Haslington Ches E 70 C3
Hassall Ches E 70 D3
Hassall Green Ches E 70 D3
Hassell Street Kent 27 J2

Hassingham Norfk 77 M10
Hassness Cumb 100 G7
Hassocks W Susx 24 H7
Hassop Derbys 84 B6
Haste Hill Surrey 23 P8
Haster Highld 167 P6
Hasthorpe Lincs 87 N7
Hastigleigh Kent 27 J2
Hastings E Susx 26 D10
Hastings Somset 19 K11
Hastingwood Essex 51 L9
Hastoe Herts 35 P3
Haswell Dur 104 C2
Haswell Plough Dur 104 C2
Hatch C Beds 61 Q11
Hatch Beauchamp Somset 19 K10
Hatch End Bed 61 N8
Hatch End Gt Lon 36 D2
Hatchet Gate Hants 14 C6
Hatching Green Herts 50 D8
Hatcliffe NE Lin 93 M10
Hatfield Donc 91 R9
Hatfield Herefs 46 A3
Hatfield Herts 50 F9
Hatfield Worcs 46 G4
Hatfield Broad Oak Essex 51 M7
Hatfield Heath Essex 51 M7
Hatfield Peverel Essex 52 C9
Hatfield Woodhouse Donc 92 A9
Hatford Oxon 34 A6
Hatherden Hants 22 B4
Hatherleigh Devon 8 D4
Hathern Leics 72 E6
Hatherop Gloucs 33 N3
Hathersage Derbys 84 B4
Hathersage Booths Derbys 84 B4
Hatherton Ches E 70 B5
Hatherton Staffs 58 E2
Hatley St George Cambs 62 C10
Hatt Cnwll 5 Q9
Hattersley Tamesd 83 L6
Hattingley Hants 22 H7
Hatton Abers 159 Q10
Hatton Angus 142 H9
Hatton Derbys 71 N8
Hatton Gt Lon 36 C5
Hatton Lincs 86 G5
Hatton Shrops 56 H6
Hatton Warrtn 82 C8
Hatton Warwks 59 K11
Hatton Heath Ches W 69 N2
Hatton of Fintray Abers 151 L4
Haugh E Ayrs 115 J2
Haugh Lincs 87 M5
Haugh Rochdl 89 Q8
Haugham Lincs 87 K4
Haughhead E Duns 125 Q2
Haugh Head Nthumb 119 K5
Haughley Suffk 64 E9
Haughley Green Suffk 64 E9
Haugh of Glass Moray 158 B10
Haugh of Urr D & G 108 H7
Haughs of Kinnaird Angus 143 L6
Haughton Ches E 69 Q3
Haughton Notts 85 L6
Haughton Powys 69 K11
Haughton Shrops 57 M5
Haughton Shrops 57 N3
Haughton Shrops 69 Q11
Haughton Shrops 69 L9
Haughton Staffs 70 F10
Haughton Green Tamesd 83 K6
Haughton le Skerne Darltn 104 B7
Haultwick Herts 50 H6
Haunton Staffs 59 K2
Hautes Croix Jersey 11 b1
Hauxton Cambs 62 F10
Havannah Ches E 70 F2
Havant Hants 15 K5
Haven Herefs 45 N4
Haven Bank Lincs 86 H10
Haven Side E R Yk 93 L5
Havenstreet IoW 14 G8
Havercroft Wakefd 91 K8
Haverfordwest Pembks 41 J7
Haverhill Suffk 63 L11
Haverigg Cumb 94 D5
Havering-atte-Bower
  Gt Lon 37 M2
Haversham M Keyn 49 M6
Haverthwaite Cumb 94 G4
Haverton Hill S on T 104 E6
Havyatt N Som 19 N2
Havyatt Somset 19 P7
Hawarden Flints 81 L11
Hawbridge Worcs 46 H5
Hawbush Green Essex 52 C7
Hawcoat Cumb 94 E6
Hawen Cerdgn 42 F5
Hawes N York 96 C3
Hawe's Green Norfk 65 J2
Hawford Worcs 46 F2
Hawick Border 117 Q8
Hawkchurch Devon 10 G4
Hawkedon Suffk 63 N10
Hawkenbury Kent 26 D2
Hawkeridge Wilts 20 G4
Hawkerland Devon 9 Q7
Hawker's Cove Cnwll 4 E6
Hawkesbury S Glos 32 E7
Hawkesbury Warwks 59 N8
Hawkesbury Upton S Glos 32 E7
Hawkes End Covtry 59 L8
Hawk Green Stockp 83 L7
Hawkhill Nthumb 119 P8
Hawkhurst Kent 26 C5
Hawkhurst Common E Susx 25 M7
Hawkinge Kent 27 M4
Hawkley Hants 23 K9
Hawkley Wigan 82 C4
Hawkridge Somset 17 N5
Hawksdale Cumb 110 G11
Hawkshaw Bury 89 M7
Hawkshead Cumb 101 L11
Hawkshead Hill Cumb 101 K11
Hawksland S Lans 116 A3
Hawkspur Green Essex 51 Q4
Hawkstone Shrops 69 Q8
Hawkswick N York 96 E6
Hawksworth Leeds 90 F2
Hawksworth Notts 73 K2
Hawkwell Essex 38 E3
Hawkwell Nthumb 112 G6
Hawley Hants 23 N3

Hawley Kent 37 M6
Hawling Gloucs 47 L10
Hawnby N York 98 A3
Haworth C Brad 90 C3
Hawridge Bucks 35 P3
Hawstead Suffk 64 B10
Hawstead Green Suffk 64 B10
Hawthorn Dur 113 P11
Hawthorn Hants 23 J8
Hawthorn Rhondd 30 E7
Hawthorn Hill Br For 35 N10
Hawthorn Hill Lincs 86 H9
Hawthorpe Lincs 73 Q5
Hawton Notts 85 N10
Haxby C York 98 C9
Haxby Gates C York 98 C9
Haxey N Linc 92 C11
Haxey Carr N Linc 92 C10
Haxted Surrey 37 K11
Haxton Wilts 21 M5
Hay Cnwll 3 P3
Hay Cnwll 4 F7
Haydock St Hel 82 C5
Haydon BaNES 20 C4
Haydon Dorset 20 C11
Haydon Somset 19 J10
Haydon Bridge Nthumb 112 B8
Haydon Wick Swindn 33 M7
Haye Cnwll 5 P7
Hayes Gt Lon 36 C4
Hayes Gt Lon 37 K7
Hayes End Gt Lon 36 C4
Hayfield Ag & B 131 M3
Hayfield Derbys 83 M7
Hayfield Green Donc 91 R11
Haygate Wrekin 57 L2
Hay Green Norfk 75 K7
Hayhillock Angus 143 J9
Hayle Cnwll 2 F6
Hayle Port Cnwll 2 F6
Hayley Green Dudley 58 E8
Hayling Island Hants 15 K6
Haymoor Green Ches E 70 B4
Hayne Devon 9 J7
Hayne Devon 18 C11
Haynes C Beds 50 C2
Haynes Church End C Beds 50 C2
Haynes West End C Beds 50 C2
Hay-on-Wye Powys 45 J6
Hayscastle Pembks 40 G5
Hayscastle Cross Pembks 40 H5
Haysden Kent 37 N11
Hay Street Herts 51 J5
Hayton Cumb 100 F2
Hayton Cumb 111 K9
Hayton E R Yk 98 G11
Hayton Notts 85 M4
Hayton's Bent Shrops 57 J8
Haytor Vale Devon 9 J9
Haytown Devon 16 F9
Haywards Heath W Susx 24 H6
Haywood Donc 91 P8
Haywood Herefs 45 P8
Haywood Oaks Notts 85 K9
Hazards Green E Susx 25 Q8
Hazelbank S Lans 126 E8
Hazelbury Bryan Dorset 12 B3
Hazeleigh Essex 52 D11
Hazeley Hants 23 K3
Hazelford Notts 85 M11
Hazel Grove Stockp 83 K7
Hazelhurst Bury 89 L4
Hazelslade Staffs 58 F2
Hazel Street Kent 25 Q3
Hazel Stub Suffk 51 Q2
Hazelton Walls Fife 135 J2
Hazelwood Derbys 84 D11
Hazlemere Bucks 35 N5
Hazlerigg N u Ty 113 K6
Hazles Staffs 71 J5
Hazleton Gloucs 47 L11
Heacham Norfk 75 N3
Headbourne Worthy Hants 22 E8
Headbrook Herefs 45 K3
Headcorn Kent 26 D3
Headingley Leeds 90 H3
Headington Oxon 34 F3
Headlam Dur 103 N7
Headlesscross N Lans 126 G6
Headless Cross Worcs 58 F11
Headley Hants 22 F2
Headley Hants 23 M7
Headley Surrey 36 F10
Headley Down Hants 23 M7
Headley Heath Worcs 58 G9
Headon Devon 16 F11
Headon Notts 85 M5
Heads Nook Cumb 111 K10
Heage Derbys 84 E10
Healaugh N York 97 R11
Healaugh N York 103 K11
Heald Green Stockp 82 H7
Heale Devon 17 L2
Heale Somset 18 H10
Heale Somset 19 L9
Healey N York 97 J4
Healey Nthumb 112 F9
Healey Rochdl 89 P7
Healey Wakefd 90 H7
Healeyfield Dur 112 G11
Healing NE Lin 93 M8
Heamoor Cnwll 2 D7
Heanor Derbys 84 F11
Heanton Punchardon Devon 17 J4
Heapham Lincs 85 Q3
Hearn Hants 23 M7
Heart of Scotland Services
  N Lans 126 G5
Hearts Delight Kent 38 E9
Heasley Mill Devon 17 N5
Heaste Highld 145 K4
Heath Derbys 84 F7
Heath Wakefd 91 K6
Heath and Reach C Beds 49 P9
Heath Common W Susx 24 D7
Heathcote Derbys 71 L2
Heathcote Shrops 70 B9
Heath End Bucks 35 N5
Heath End Hants 22 D2
Heath End Leics 72 B6
Heath End Warwks 47 P2
Heather Leics 72 B8
Heathfield Cambs 62 G11
Heathfield Devon 9 K9
Heathfield E Susx 25 N6

Heathfield N York 96 H7
Heathfield Somset 18 E9
Heathfield Village Oxon 48 F11
Heath Green Worcs 58 G10
Heath Hall D & G 109 L5
Heath Hayes &
  Wimblebury Staffs 58 F2
Heath Hill Shrops 57 P2
Heath House Somset 19 M5
Heathrow Airport Gt Lon 36 C5
Heathstock Devon 10 E4
Heathton Shrops 57 Q6
Heath Town Wolves 58 D5
Heathwaite N York 104 E10
Heatley Staffs 71 K9
Heaton Bolton 89 K9
Heaton C Brad 90 E3
Heaton Lancs 95 J8
Heaton N u Ty 113 L7
Heaton Staffs 70 H2
Heaton Chapel Stockp 83 J6
Heaton Mersey Stockp 83 J6
Heaton Norris Stockp 83 J6
Heaton's Bridge Lancs 88 D8
Heaverham Kent 37 N9
Heaviley Stockp 83 K7
Heavitree Devon 9 M6
Hebburn S Tyne 113 M8
Hebden N York 96 F8
Hebden Bridge Calder 90 B5
Hebden Green Ches W 82 D11
Hebing End Herts 50 H6
Hebron Carmth 41 N5
Hebron IoA 78 H8
Hebron Nthumb 113 J3
Heckfield Hants 23 K2
Heckfield Green Suffk 64 H6
Heckfordbridge Essex 52 F7
Heckington Lincs 74 B2
Heckmondwike Kirk 90 G6
Heddington Wilts 33 J11
Heddon-on-the-Wall
  Nthumb 112 H7
Hedenham Norfk 65 L3
Hedge End Hants 14 E4
Hedgerley Bucks 35 Q7
Hedgerley Green Bucks 35 Q7
Hedging Somset 19 K9
Hedley on the Hill Nthumb 112 G9
Hednesford Staffs 58 E2
Hedon E R Yk 93 L5
Hedsor Bucks 35 P7
Heeley Sheff 84 E4
Hegdon Hill Herefs 46 A4
Heglibister Shet 169 q8
Heighington Darltn 103 P6
Heighington Lincs 86 D7
Heightington Worcs 57 P10
Heiton Border 118 D4
Hele Devon 7 J4
Hele Devon 9 N4
Hele Devon 17 J2
Hele Somset 18 G10
Helebridge Cnwll 16 C11
Hele Lane Devon 9 J2
Helensburgh Ag & B 132 B11
Helenton S Ayrs 125 K11
Helford Cnwll 3 K8
Helford Passage Cnwll 3 K8
Helhoughton Norfk 76 B6
Helions Bumpstead Essex 51 Q2
Hellaby Rothm 84 H2
Helland Cnwll 4 H7
Hellandbridge Cnwll 4 H7
Hell Corner W Berk 22 C2
Hellescott Cnwll 5 M4
Hellesdon Norfk 77 J9
Hellesveor Cnwll 2 E5
Hellidon Nhants 60 B9
Hellifield N York 96 C9
Hellingly E Susx 25 N8
Hellington Norfk 77 L11
Helm Nthumb 119 N11
Helmdon Nhants 48 G6
Helme Kirk 90 D8
Helmingham Suffk 64 H10
Helmington Row Dur 103 N3
Helmsdale Highld 163 N3
Helmshore Lancs 89 M6
Helmsley N York 98 C4
Helperby N York 97 P7
Helperthorpe N York 99 K6
Helpringham Lincs 74 B2
Helpston C Pete 74 B9
Helsby Ches W 81 P9
Helsey Lincs 87 P6
Helston Cnwll 2 H8
Helstone Cnwll 4 H5
Helton Cumb 101 P6
Helwith Bridge N York 96 B7
Hemblington Norfk 77 L9
Hembridge Somset 19 Q7
Hemel Hempstead Herts 50 C9
Hemerdon Devon 6 F7
Hemingbrough N York 91 R4
Hemingby Lincs 86 H6
Hemingfield Barns 91 K10
Hemingford Abbots Cambs 62 C6
Hemingford Grey Cambs 62 C6
Hemingstone Suffk 64 G11
Hemington Leics 72 D5
Hemington Nhants 61 N3
Hemington Somset 20 D4
Hemley Suffk 53 N3
Hemlington Middsb 104 F8
Hempholme E R Yk 99 M10
Hempnall Norfk 65 J3
Hempnall Green Norfk 65 J3
Hempriggs Moray 157 L5
Hempstead Essex 51 P3
Hempstead Medway 38 C9
Hempstead Norfk 76 G4
Hempstead Norfk 77 N6
Hempsted Gloucs 46 F11
Hempton Norfk 76 C6
Hempton Oxon 48 D8
Hemsby Norfk 77 P8
Hemswell Lincs 86 B2
Hemswell Cliff Lincs 86 B3
Hemsworth Wakefd 91 L8
Hemyock Devon 10 C2
Henbury Bristl 31 Q9
Henbury Ches E 83 J10

Hendham Devon 7 J8
Hendomen Powys 56 C5
Hendon Gt Lon 36 F3
Hendon Sundld 113 P9
Hendra Cnwll 3 J6
Hendra Cnwll 4 G6
Hendre Brdgnd 29 P8
Hendre Flints 80 H11
Hendy Carmth 28 G4
Heneglwys IoA 78 G9
Henfield W Susx 24 F7
Henford Devon 5 P3
Henfynw Cerdgn 43 J2
Henghurst Kent 26 G4
Hengoed Caerph 30 G6
Hengoed Powys 45 J4
Hengoed Shrops 69 J8
Hengrave Suffk 63 P7
Henham Essex 51 M5
Heniarth Powys 55 Q3
Henlade Somset 19 J10
Henley Dorset 11 P4
Henley Gloucs 46 H11
Henley Shrops 56 H7
Henley Shrops 57 J9
Henley Somset 19 M8
Henley Suffk 64 H11
Henley W Susx 23 N9
Henley Green Covtry 59 N8
Henley-in-Arden Warwks 59 J11
Henley-on-Thames Oxon 35 L8
Henley Park Surrey 23 P4
Henley's Down E Susx 26 B9
Henley Street Kent 37 Q7
Henllan Cerdgn 42 G6
Henllan Denbgs 80 E11
Henllan Amgoed Carmth 41 N7
Henllys Torfn 31 J6
Henlow C Beds 50 E3
Hennock Devon 9 K8
Henny Street Essex 52 E4
Henryd Conwy 79 P10
Henry's Moat (Castell
  Hendre) Pembks 41 K5
Hensall N York 91 P6
Henshaw Nthumb 111 Q8
Hensingham Cumb 100 C7
Henstead Suffk 65 P4
Hensting Hants 22 E10
Henstridge Somset 20 D11
Henstridge Ash Somset 20 D10
Henstridge Marsh Somset 20 D10
Henton Oxon 35 L4
Henton Somset 19 N5
Henwick Worcs 46 F3
Henwood Cnwll 5 M7
Henwood Cnwll 34 D3
Heolgerrig Myr Td 30 D3
Heol-las Swans 29 J5
Heol Senni Powys 44 C10
Heol-y-Cyw Brdgnd 29 P8
Hepburn Nthumb 119 L6
Hepple Nthumb 119 J10
Hepscott Nthumb 113 K4
Heptonstall Calder 90 B5
Hepworth Kirk 90 F9
Hepworth Suffk 64 D7
Herbrandston Pembks 40 G9
Hereford Herefs 45 Q7
Hereson Kent 39 Q8
Heribusta Highld 152 F3
Heriot Border 128 C9
Hermiston C Edin 127 M3
Hermitage Border 117 Q11
Hermitage Dorset 11 P3
Hermitage W Berk 34 F10
Hermitage W Susx 15 L5
Hermit Hill Barns 91 J10
Hermon Carmth 42 G8
Hermon IoA 78 F11
Hermon Pembks 41 P4
Herne Kent 39 L8
Herne Bay Kent 39 L8
Herne Common Kent 39 L8
Herne Hill Gt Lon 36 H6
Herne Pound Kent 37 Q10
Herner Devon 17 K6
Hernhill Kent 39 J9
Herodsfoot Cnwll 5 L9
Heronden Kent 39 N11
Herongate Essex 37 P2
Heronsford S Ayrs 114 E11
Heronsgate Herts 36 B2
Herriard Hants 23 J5
Herringfleet Suffk 65 P2
Herring's Green Bed 50 C2
Herringswell Suffk 63 M6
Herringthorpe Rothm 84 F2
Herrington Sundld 113 N10
Hersden Kent 39 M9
Hersham Cnwll 16 D10
Hersham Surrey 36 D8
Herstmonceux E Susx 25 P8
Herston Dorset 12 H9
Herston Ork 169 d7
Hertford Herts 50 H8
Hertford Heath Herts 51 J8
Hertingfordbury Herts 50 H8
Hesketh Bank Lancs 88 E6
Hesketh Lane Lancs 89 J2
Hesket Newmarket Cumb 101 K3
Heskin Green Lancs 88 G7
Hesleden Dur 104 D3
Hesleden N York 96 C6
Hesley Donc 85 K2
Hesleyside Nthumb 112 B4
Heslington C York 98 C10
Hessay C York 97 R10
Hessenford Cnwll 5 N10
Hessett Suffk 64 C9
Hessle E R Yk 92 H5
Hessle Wakefd 91 L7
Hest Bank Lancs 95 K7
Hestley Green Suffk 64 H8
Heston Gt Lon 36 D5
Heston Services Gt Lon 36 D5
Hestwall Ork 169 b5
Heswall Wirral 81 K8
Hethe Oxon 48 G9
Hethersett Norfk 76 G11
Hethersgill Cumb 111 J7
Hetherside Cumb 110 H7
Hetherson Green Ches W 69 P4
Hethpool Nthumb 118 G5
Hett Dur 103 Q3

Hetton N York....96 E9
Hetton-le-Hole Sundld...113 N11
Hetton Steads Nthumb...119 K3
Heugh Nthumb...112 G6
Heughhead Abers...150 B5
Heugh Head Border...129 M7
Heveningham Suffk...65 L7
Hever Kent...37 L11
Heversham Cumb...95 K4
Hevingham Norfk...76 H7
Hewas Water Cnwll...3 P4
Hewelsfield Gloucs...31 Q4
Hewenden C Brad...90 D3
Hewish N Som...19 M2
Hewish Somset...11 J3
Hewood Dorset...10 H4
Hexham Nthumb...112 D8
Hextable Kent...37 M6
Hexthorpe Donc...91 P10
Hexton Herts...50 D4
Hexworthy Cnwll...5 P7
Hexworthy Devon...6 H4
Hey Lancs...89 P2
Heybridge Essex...51 P11
Heybridge Essex...52 E10
Heybridge Basin Essex...52 E10
Heybrook Bay Devon...6 D9
Heydon Cambs...51 K3
Heydon Norfk...76 H6
Heydour Lincs...73 Q3
Hey Houses Lancs...88 C5
Heylipoll Ag & B...136 B7
Heylor Shet...169 p5
Heysham Lancs...95 J8
Heyshaw N York...97 J8
Heyshott W Susx...23 N11
Heyside Oldham...89 Q9
Heytesbury Wilts...20 H6
Heythrop Oxon...48 C9
Heywood Rochdl...89 P8
Heywood Wilts...20 G4
Hibaldstow N Linc...92 G10
Hickleton Donc...91 M9
Hickling Norfk...77 N7
Hickling Notts...72 H5
Hickling Green Norfk...77 N7
Hickling Heath Norfk...77 N7
Hickling Pastures Notts...72 H5
Hickmans Green Kent...39 J10
Hicks Forstal Kent...39 L9
Hickstead W Susx...24 G6
Hidcote Bartrim Gloucs...47 N6
Hidcote Boyce Gloucs...47 N6
High Ackworth Wakefd...91 L7
Higham Barns...91 J9
Higham Derbys...84 E9
Higham Kent...37 P11
Higham Kent...38 B7
Higham Lancs...89 N3
Higham Suffk...52 H4
Higham Suffk...63 M7
Higham Dykes Nthumb...112 H6
Higham Ferrers Nhants...61 L7
Higham Gobion C Beds...50 D4
Higham Hill Gt Lon...37 J2
Higham on the Hill Leics...72 B11
Highampton Devon...8 C4
Highams Park Gt Lon...37 J2
High Angerton Nthumb...112 G3
High Ardwell D & G...106 E8
High Auldgirth D & G...109 K3
High Bankhill Cumb...101 Q2
High Beach Essex...51 K11
High Bentham N York...95 P7
High Bewaldeth Cumb...100 H4
High Bickington Devon...17 L7
High Biggins Cumb...95 N5
High Birkwith N York...96 B5
High Blantyre S Lans...126 B6
High Bonnybridge Falk...126 E2
High Borrans Cumb...101 M10
High Bradley N York...96 F11
High Bray Devon...17 M5
Highbridge Hants...22 E10
Highbridge Somset...19 K5
Highbrook W Susx...25 J4
High Brooms Kent...25 N2
High Bullen Devon...17 J7
Highburton Kirk...90 F8
Highbury Gt Lon...36 H3
Highbury Somset...20 C5
High Buston Nthumb...119 P9
High Callerton Nthumb...113 J6
High Casterton Cumb...95 N5
High Catton E R Yk...98 E10
Highclere Hants...22 F3
Highcliffe BCP...13 M6
High Close Dur...103 N7
High Cogges Oxon...34 C3
High Common Norfk...76 D10
High Coniscliffe Darltn...103 P7
High Crosby Cumb...111 J9
High Cross Cnwll...3 J8
High Cross E Ayrs...125 L8
High Cross Hants...23 K9
High Cross Herts...51 J7
Highcross Lancs...88 C3
High Cross W Susx...24 F7
High Cross Warwks...59 K11
High Drummore D & G...106 F10
High Dubmire Sundld...113 M11
High Easter Essex...51 P8
High Eggborough N York...91 P6
High Ellington N York...97 J4
Higher Alham Somset...20 C6
Higher Ansty Dorset...12 C4
Higher Ballam Lancs...88 D4
Higher Bartle Lancs...88 G4
Higher Berry End C Beds...49 Q8
Higher Bockhampton Dorset...12 B6
Higher Brixham Torbay...7 N8
Higher Burrowton Devon...9 P5
Higher Burwardsley Ches W...69 P3
High Ercall Wrekin...69 Q11
Higher Chillington Somset...10 H2
Higher Clovelly Devon...16 E7
Highercombe Somset...18 B8
Higher Coombe Somset...11 L6
Higher Disley Ches E...83 L8
Higher Folds Wigan...82 E4
Higherford Lancs...89 P2
Higher Gabwell Devon...7 N5
Higher Halstock Leigh Dorset...11 L3

Higher Harpers Lancs...89 N3
Higher Heysham Lancs...95 J8
Higher Hurdsfield Ches E...83 K10
Higher Irlam Salfd...82 F5
Higher Kingcombe Dorset...11 L5
Higher Kinnerton Flints...69 K2
Higher Marston Ches W...82 E9
Higher Muddiford Devon...17 K4
Higher Nyland Dorset...20 D10
Higher Ogden Rochdl...90 B8
Higher Pentire Cnwll...2 H8
Higher Penwortham Lancs...88 G5
Higher Prestacott Devon...5 P2
Higher Studfold N York...96 B6
Higher Town Cnwll...3 L5
Higher Town Cnwll...4 G9
Higher Town IoS...2 c1
Higher Tregantle Cnwll...5 Q11
Higher Walton Lancs...88 H5
Higher Walton Warrtn...82 C7
Higher Wambrook Somset...10 F3
Higher Waterston Dorset...11 Q5
Higher Whatcombe Dorset...12 D4
Higher Wheelton Lancs...89 J6
Higher Whitley Ches W...82 D8
Higher Wincham Ches W...82 E9
Higher Wraxhall Dorset...11 M4
Higher Wych Ches W...69 N6
High Etherley Dur...103 N5
High Ferry Lincs...87 L11
Highfield E R Yk...92 B3
Highfield Gatesd...112 H9
Highfield N Ayrs...125 J7
Highfields Donc...91 N9
High Flats Kirk...90 G9
High Garrett Essex...52 C6
Highgate E Susx...25 K4
Highgate Gt Lon...36 G3
Highgate Kent...26 C5
High Grange Dur...103 N4
High Grantley N York...97 K7
High Green Cumb...101 M10
High Green Kirk...90 G8
High Green Norfk...64 H4
High Green Norfk...76 G10
High Green Sheff...91 J11
High Green Shrops...57 N8
High Green Suffk...64 B9
High Green Worcs...46 G5
Highgreen Manor Nthumb...112 B2
High Halden Kent...26 E4
High Halstow Medway...38 C6
High Ham Somset...19 M8
High Harrington Cumb...100 D5
High Harrogate N York...97 M9
High Haswell Dur...104 C2
High Hatton Shrops...69 R10
High Hauxley Nthumb...119 Q10
High Hawsker N York...105 P9
High Hesket Cumb...101 N2
High Hoyland Barns...90 H9
High Hunsley E R Yk...92 G3
High Hurstwood E Susx...25 L5
High Hutton N York...98 F7
High Ireby Cumb...100 H3
High Kelling Norfk...76 G3
High Kilburn N York...97 R5
High Killerby N York...99 M4
High Knipe Cumb...101 P7
High Lands Dur...103 M5
Highlane Ches E...83 J11
Highlane Derbys...84 F4
High Lane Stockp...83 L7
High Lanes Cnwll...2 F6
High Laver Essex...51 M9
Highlaws Cumb...109 P11
Highleadon Gloucs...46 E10
High Legh Ches E...82 F8
Highleigh W Susx...15 M7
High Leven S on T...104 E8
Highley Shrops...57 N8
High Littleton BaNES...20 B3
High Lorton Cumb...100 G5
High Marishes N York...98 G5
High Marnham Notts...85 P6
High Melton Donc...91 N10
High Mickley Nthumb...112 G8
Highmoor Cumb...110 E11
Highmoor Oxon...35 K8
Highmoor Cross Oxon...35 K8
Highmoor Hill Mons...31 N7
High Moorsley Sundld...113 M11
Highnam Gloucs...46 E11
Highnam Green Gloucs...46 E10
High Newport Sundld...113 N10
High Newton Cumb...95 J4
High Nibthwaite Cumb...94 F3
High Offley Staffs...70 D9
High Ongar Essex...51 N10
High Onn Staffs...70 E11
High Park Corner Essex...52 H7
High Pennyvenie E Ayrs...115 J6
High Post Wilts...21 N7
Highridge N Som...31 Q11
High Roding Essex...51 P7
High Row Cumb...101 L3
High Row Cumb...101 L6
High Salter Lancs...95 N8
High Salvington W Susx...24 D9
High Scales Cumb...110 C11
High Seaton Cumb...100 D4
High Shaw N York...96 C2
High Side Cumb...100 H4
High Spen Gatesd...112 H9
Highstead Kent...39 M8
Highsted Kent...38 F9
High Stoop Dur...103 M2
High Street Cnwll...3 P3
High Street Kent...26 B5
High Street Suffk...39 J9
High Street Suffk...65 N10
High Street Suffk...65 N7
Highstreet Green Essex...52 C5
Highstreet Green Surrey...23 Q7
Hightae D & G...109 N5
Highter's Heath Birm...58 G9
High Throston Hartpl...104 E4
Hightown Ches E...70 F2
Hightown Hants...13 L4
Hightown Sefton...81 L4
High Town Staffs...58 E2
Hightown Green Suffk...64 D10
High Toynton Lincs...87 J7
High Trewitt Nthumb...119 K9
High Urpeth Dur...113 K10

High Valleyfield Fife...134 C10
High Warden Nthumb...112 D7
Highway Herefs...45 P5
Highway Wilts...33 K10
Highweek Devon...7 L4
High Westwood Dur...112 H9
Highwood Essex...51 P10
Highwood Staffs...71 K8
Highwood Hill Gt Lon...36 F2
High Woolaston Gloucs...31 Q5
High Worsall N York...104 C9
Highworth Swindn...33 P6
High Wray Cumb...101 L11
High Wych Herts...51 L8
High Wycombe Bucks...35 N6
Hilborough Norfk...75 R10
Hilcote Derbys...84 G9
Hilcott Wilts...21 M3
Hildenborough Kent...37 N11
Hilden Park Kent...37 N11
Hildersham Cambs...62 H11
Hilderstone Staffs...70 H8
Hilderthorpe E R Yk...99 P7
Hilfield Dorset...11 N3
Hilgay Norfk...75 M11
Hill S Glos...32 B5
Hill Warwks...59 Q11
Hillam N York...91 N5
Hillbeck Cumb...102 E7
Hillborough Kent...39 M8
Hill Brow Hants...23 L9
Hillbutts Dorset...12 G4
Hill Chorlton Staffs...70 D7
Hillclifflane Derbys...71 P5
Hill Common Norfk...77 N7
Hill Common Somset...18 F9
Hill Deverill Wilts...20 G6
Hilldyke Lincs...87 K11
Hill End Dur...103 K3
Hill End Fife...134 C8
Hillend Fife...134 E11
Hill End Gloucs...46 H7
Hillend Mdloth...127 P4
Hillend N Lans...126 E4
Hillend Swans...28 D5
Hillersland Gloucs...31 Q2
Hillerton Devon...8 H5
Hillesden Bucks...49 J9
Hillesley Gloucs...32 E7
Hillfarrance Somset...18 G10
Hill Green Kent...38 D9
Hillgrove W Susx...23 P9
Hillhampton Herefs...46 A5
Hillhead Abers...158 E10
Hillhead Devon...7 N8
Hill Head Hants...14 F5
Hillhead S Lans...116 D11
Hillhead of Cocklaw Abers...159 Q9
Hilliard's Cross Staffs...59 J2
Hilliclay Highld...167 L4
Hillingdon Gt Lon...36 C4
Hillington C Glas...125 N5
Hillington Norfk...75 P5
Hillis Corner IoW...14 E8
Hillmorton Warwks...60 B6
Hillock Vale Lancs...89 M5
Hill of Beath Fife...134 F9
Hill of Fearn Highld...163 J11
Hillowton D & G...108 G9
Hillpool Worcs...58 C9
Hillpound Hants...22 G11
Hill Ridware Staffs...71 K11
Hillside Abers...151 N8
Hillside Angus...143 N5
Hillside Devon...7 J6
Hill Side Kirk...90 F7
Hill Side Worcs...46 E2
Hills Town Derbys...84 G7
Hillstreet Hants...22 B11
Hillswick Shet...169 p6
Hill Top Dur...103 J4
Hill Top Hants...14 D6
Hill Top Kirk...90 D8
Hill Top Rothm...84 E2
Hill Top Sandw...58 E6
Hill Top Wakefd...91 J7
Hillwell Shet...169 q12
Hilmarton Wilts...33 K9
Hilperton Wilts...20 G3
Hilperton Marsh Wilts...20 G3
Hilsea C Port...15 J6
Hilston E R Yk...93 N4
Hiltingbury Hants...22 D10
Hilton Border...129 M9
Hilton Cambs...62 C7
Hilton Cumb...102 D6
Hilton Derbys...71 N8
Hilton Dorset...12 C4
Hilton Dur...103 N6
Hilton Highld...156 D7
Hilton S on T...104 E8
Hilton Shrops...57 P5
Hilton Park Services Staffs...58 E4
Himbleton Worcs...46 H3
Himley Staffs...58 C6
Hincaster Cumb...95 L4
Hinchley Wood Surrey...36 E7
Hinckley Leics...59 P6
Hinderclay Suffk...64 E6
Hinderwell N York...105 K7
Hindford Shrops...69 K8
Hindhead Surrey...23 N7
Hindhead Tunnel Surrey...23 N7
Hindle Fold Lancs...89 L4
Hindley Nthumb...112 F9
Hindley Wigan...82 D4
Hindley Green Wigan...82 D4
Hindlip Worcs...46 G3
Hindolveston Norfk...76 E6
Hindon Wilts...20 H8
Hindringham Norfk...76 D4
Hindley Suffk...76 E11
Hinksford Staffs...58 C7
Hinstock Shrops...70 B9
Hintlesham Suffk...53 J3
Hinton Gloucs...32 C4
Hinton Hants...13 M5
Hinton Herefs...45 L7
Hinton S Glos...32 D9
Hinton Shrops...56 G3
Hinton Shrops...57 M8
Hinton Admiral Hants...13 M5
Hinton Ampner Hants...22 H9
Hinton Blewett BaNES...19 Q3
Hinton Charterhouse BaNES...20 E3

Hinton Cross Worcs...47 K6
Hinton-in-the-Hedges Nhants...48 G7
Hinton Marsh Hants...22 G9
Hinton Martell Dorset...12 H3
Hinton on the Green Worcs...47 K6
Hinton Parva Swindn...33 P8
Hinton St George Somset...11 J2
Hinton St Mary Dorset...20 E11
Hinton Waldrist Oxon...34 C5
Hints Shrops...57 L10
Hints Staffs...59 J4
Hinwick Bed...61 K8
Hinxhill Kent...26 H3
Hinxton Cambs...62 G11
Hinxworth Herts...50 F2
Hipperholme Calder...90 E5
Hipsburn Nthumb...119 P8
Hipswell N York...103 N11
Hirn Abers...151 J7
Hirnant Powys...68 D10
Hirst Nthumb...113 L3
Hirst Courtney N York...91 Q6
Hirwaen Denbgs...68 F2
Hirwaun Rhondd...30 C3
Hiscott Devon...17 J6
Histon Cambs...62 F8
Hitcham Suffk...64 D11
Hitcham Causeway Suffk...64 D11
Hitcham Street Suffk...64 D11
Hitchin Herts...50 E5
Hither Green Gt Lon...37 J6
Hittisleigh Devon...8 H5
Hive E R Yk...92 D4
Hixon Staffs...71 J9
Hoaden Kent...39 N10
Hoar Cross Staffs...71 L10
Hoarwithy Herefs...45 Q9
Hoath Kent...39 M9
Hoathly Kent...25 Q3
Hobarris Shrops...56 E9
Hobbles Green Suffk...63 M10
Hobbs Cross Essex...51 L11
Hobbs Cross Essex...51 L8
Hobkirk Border...118 A8
Hobsick Notts...84 G11
Hobson Dur...113 J9
Hoby Leics...72 H7
Hoccombe Somset...18 F9
Hockering Norfk...76 F9
Hockerton Notts...85 M9
Hockley Covtry...59 L9
Hockley Essex...38 D3
Hockley Staffs...59 K4
Hockley Heath Solhll...59 J10
Hockliffe C Beds...49 Q9
Hockwold cum Wilton Norfk...63 M3
Hockworthy Devon...18 D11
Hoddesdon Herts...51 J9
Hoddlesden Bl w D...89 L6
Hoddom Cross D & G...110 C6
Hoddom Mains D & G...110 C6
Hodgehill Ches E...82 H11
Hodgeston Pembks...41 K11
Hodnet Shrops...69 R9
Hodsock Notts...85 K3
Hodsoll Street Kent...37 P8
Hodson Swindn...33 N8
Hodthorpe Derbys...84 H5
Hoe Hants...22 G11
Hoe Norfk...76 D8
Hoe Benham W Berk...34 D11
Hoe Gate Hants...14 H4
Hoff Cumb...102 C7
Hogben's Hill Kent...38 H10
Hoggards Green Suffk...64 B10
Hoggeston Bucks...49 M10
Hoggrill's End Warwks...59 K6
Hog Hill E Susx...26 E8
Hoghton Lancs...89 J5
Hoghton Bottoms Lancs...89 J5
Hognaston Derbys...71 N4
Hogsthorpe Lincs...87 P6
Holbeach Lincs...74 G6
Holbeach Bank Lincs...74 G5
Holbeach Clough Lincs...74 G5
Holbeach Drove Lincs...74 F8
Holbeach Hurn Lincs...74 G5
Holbeach St Johns Lincs...74 G7
Holbeach St Mark's Lincs...74 G4
Holbeach St Matthew Lincs...74 H4
Holbeck Notts...84 H6
Holbeck Woodhouse Notts...84 H6
Holberrow Green Worcs...47 K3
Holbeton Devon...6 G8
Holborn Gt Lon...36 H4
Holborough Kent...37 Q8
Holbrook Derbys...72 B2
Holbrook Sheff...84 F4
Holbrook Suffk...53 L4
Holbrook Moor Derbys...84 E11
Holbrooks Covtry...59 M8
Holburn Nthumb...119 K3
Holbury Hants...14 D6
Holcombe Devon...7 P4
Holcombe Somset...20 C5
Holcombe Rogus Devon...18 E11
Holcot Nhants...60 G7
Holden Lancs...96 A11
Holdenby Nhants...60 E7
Holden Gate Calder...89 P6
Holder's Green Essex...51 P5
Holdgate Shrops...57 K7
Holdingham Lincs...86 E11
Holditch Dorset...10 G4
Holdsworth Calder...90 D5
Holehouse Derbys...83 M6
Hole-in-the-Wall Herefs...46 B9
Holemoor Devon...16 G10
Hole Street W Susx...24 D8
Holford Somset...18 F6
Holgate C York...98 B10
Holker Cumb...94 H4
Holkham Norfk...76 B3
Hollacombe Devon...16 F11
Holland Fen Lincs...86 H11
Holland Lees Lancs...88 G9
Holland-on-Sea Essex...53 L8
Hollandstoun Ork...169 g1
Hollee D & G...110 E7
Hollesley Suffk...53 P3
Hollicombe Torbay...7 M6
Hollingbourne Kent...38 D10

Hollingbury Br & H...24 H9
Hollingdon Bucks...49 N9
Hollingrove E Susx...25 Q6
Hollingthorpe Leeds...91 K4
Hollington Derbys...71 N7
Hollington Staffs...71 K7
Hollingworth Tamesd...83 M5
Hollins Bury...89 N9
Hollins Derbys...84 D6
Hollins Staffs...70 H5
Hollinsclough Staffs...83 N11
Hollins End Sheff...84 E4
Hollins Green Warrtn...82 E6
Hollins Lane Lancs...95 K10
Hollinswood Wrekin...57 N3
Hollinwood Shrops...69 P7
Hollocombe Devon...17 L9
Holloway Derbys...84 D9
Holloway Gt Lon...36 H3
Holloway Wilts...20 G8
Hollowell Nhants...60 E6
Hollowmoor Heath Ches W...81 P11
Hollows D & G...110 G5
Hollybush Caerph...30 G4
Hollybush E Ayrs...114 G4
Hollybush Herefs...46 E7
Holly End Norfk...75 J9
Holly Green Worcs...46 G6
Hollyhurst Ches E...69 Q6
Hollym E R Yk...93 P5
Hollywood Worcs...58 G9
Holmbridge Kirk...90 E9
Holmbury St Mary Surrey...24 D2
Holmbush Cnwll...3 Q3
Holmcroft Staffs...70 G10
Holme Cambs...61 Q3
Holme Cumb...95 L5
Holme Kirk...90 E9
Holme N Linc...92 F9
Holme N York...97 N4
Holme Notts...85 P9
Holme Chapel Lancs...89 P5
Holme Green N York...91 P2
Holme Hale Norfk...76 B10
Holme Lacy Herefs...45 R7
Holme Marsh Herefs...45 L4
Holme next the Sea Norfk...75 P2
Holme on the Wolds E R Yk...99 K11
Holme Pierrepont Notts...72 G3
Holmer Herefs...45 Q6
Holmer Green Bucks...35 P5
Holmes Chapel Ches E...82 G11
Holmesfield Derbys...84 D5
Holmes Hill E Susx...25 M8
Holmeswood Lancs...88 E7
Holmethorpe Surrey...36 G10
Holme upon Spalding Moor E R Yk...92 D3
Holmewood Derbys...84 F7
Holmfield Calder...90 D5
Holmfirth Kirk...90 E9
Holmhead E Ayrs...115 L3
Holmpton E R Yk...93 Q6
Holmrook Cumb...100 E11
Holmshurst E Susx...25 P5
Holmside Dur...113 K11
Holmwrangle Cumb...111 K11
Holne Devon...7 J5
Holnest Dorset...11 P3
Holnicote Somset...18 B5
Holsworthy Devon...16 E11
Holsworthy Beacon Devon...16 F10
Holt Dorset...12 H4
Holt Norfk...76 F4
Holt Wilts...20 G2
Holt Worcs...46 F2
Holt Wrexhm...69 M4
Holtby C York...98 D10
Holt End Worcs...58 G11
Holt Fleet Worcs...46 F2
Holt Green Lancs...88 D9
Holt Heath Dorset...13 J4
Holt Heath Worcs...46 F2
Holton Oxon...34 H3
Holton Somset...20 C9
Holton Suffk...65 N6
Holton cum Beckering Lincs...86 F4
Holton Heath Dorset...12 F6
Holton Hill E Susx...25 Q5
Holton le Clay Lincs...93 N10
Holton le Moor Lincs...93 J11
Holton St Mary Suffk...53 J4
Holt Street Kent...39 N11
Holtye E Susx...25 L3
Holwell Flints...80 H9
Holwell Dorset...11 P2
Holwell Herts...50 E4
Holwell Leics...73 J6
Holwell Oxon...33 P3
Holwick Dur...102 H5
Holworth Dorset...12 C8
Holybourne Hants...23 K6
Holy Cross Worcs...58 D9
Holyfield Essex...51 J10
Holyhead IoA...78 C8
Holy Island Nthumb...119 M2
Holy Island Nthumb...119 M2
Holymoorside Derbys...84 D7
Holyport W & M...35 N9
Holystone Nthumb...119 J10
Holytown N Lans...126 D5
Holywell C Beds...50 B7
Holywell Cambs...62 D6
Holywell Cnwll...2 B10
Holywell Dorset...11 M4
Holywell Flints...80 H9
Holywell Nthumb...113 M6
Holywell Warwks...59 K11
Holywell Green Calder...90 D7
Holywell Lake Somset...18 F10
Holywell Row Suffk...63 M5
Holywood D & G...109 L4
Holywood Village D & G...109 L5
Homer Shrops...57 L4
Homer Green Sefton...81 L4
Homersfield Suffk...65 K4
Homescales Cumb...95 M3
Hom Green Herefs...46 A10
Homington Wilts...21 M9
Honeyborough Pembks...40 H9
Honeybourne Worcs...47 M6
Honeychurch Devon...8 F4
Honey Hill Kent...39 L9

276 Honeystreet – Inverarnan

Honeystreet Wilts 21 M2
Honey Tye Suffk 52 G4
Honiley Warwks 59 K10
Honing Norfk 77 L6
Honingham Norfk 76 G9
Honington Lincs 73 N2
Honington Suffk 64 C7
Honington Warwks 47 Q6
Honiton Devon 10 D4
Honley Kirk 90 E8
Honnington Wrekin 70 C11
Hoo Kent 39 N9
Hoobrook Worcs 58 B10
Hood Green Barns 91 J10
Hood Hill Rothm 91 K11
Hooe C Plym 6 E8
Hooe E Susx 25 Q8
Hoo End Herts 50 E6
Hoo Green Ches E 82 F8
Hoohill Bpool 88 C3
Hook Cambs 62 F2
Hook Devon 10 G3
Hook E R Yk 92 C5
Hook Gt Lon 36 E8
Hook Hants 14 F5
Hook Hants 23 K4
Hook Pembks 41 J8
Hook Wilts 33 L8
Hook-a-Gate Shrops 56 H3
Hook Bank Worcs 46 F6
Hooke Dorset 11 L4
Hook End Essex 51 N10
Hookgate Staffs 70 C7
Hook Green Kent 25 Q3
Hook Green Kent 37 P6
Hook Norton Oxon 48 C8
Hook Street Gloucs 32 C5
Hook Street Wilts 33 L8
Hookway Devon 9 L5
Hookwood Surrey 24 G2
Hooley Surrey 36 G9
Hooley Bridge Rochdl 89 P8
Hoo Meavy Devon 6 E5
Hoo St Werburgh Medway 38 C7
Hooton Ches W 81 M9
Hooton Levitt Rothm 84 H2
Hooton Pagnell Donc 91 M9
Hooton Roberts Rothm 91 M11
Hopcrofts Holt Oxon 48 E9
Hope Derbys 83 Q8
Hope Devon 6 H10
Hope Flints 69 K3
Hope Powys 56 D3
Hope Shrops 56 E4
Hope Staffs 71 L4
Hope Bagot Shrops 57 K10
Hope Bowdler Shrops 56 H6
Hope End Green Essex 51 N6
Hopehouse Border 117 K7
Hopeman Moray 157 L4
Hope Mansell Herefs 46 B11
Hopesay Shrops 56 F8
Hopetown Wakefd 91 K6
Hope under Dinmore Herefs 45 Q4
Hopgrove C York 98 C10
Hopperton N York 97 P9
Hop Pole Lincs 74 C8
Hopsford Warwks 59 P8
Hopstone Shrops 57 P6
Hopton Derbys 71 P4
Hopton Shrops 69 L10
Hopton Staffs 70 G9
Hopton Suffk 64 D6
Hopton Cangeford Shrops 57 J8
Hopton Castle Shrops 56 F9
Hoptonheath Shrops 56 F9
Hopton on Sea Norfk 65 Q2
Hopton Wafers Shrops 57 L9
Hopwas Staffs 59 J4
Hopwood Rochdl 89 P9
Hopwood Worcs 58 F9
Hopwood Park Services Worcs 58 F10
Horam E Susx 25 N7
Horbling Lincs 74 B3
Horbury Wakefd 90 H7
Horcott Gloucs 33 N4
Horden Dur 104 D2
Horderley Shrops 56 G7
Hordle Hants 13 N5
Hordley Shrops 69 L8
Horeb Carmth 28 E3
Horeb Cerdgn 42 G6
Horfield Bristl 31 Q9
Horham Suffk 65 J7
Horkesley Heath Essex 52 G6
Horkstow N Linc 92 G7
Horley Oxon 48 D6
Horley Surrey 24 G2
Hornblotton Green Somset 19 Q8
Hornby Lancs 95 M7
Hornby N York 97 K2
Hornby N York 104 C9
Horncastle Lincs 87 J7
Hornchurch Gt Lon 37 M3
Horncliffe Nthumb 129 N10
Horndean Border 129 N10
Horndean Hants 15 K4
Horndon Devon 8 D8
Horndon on the Hill Thurr 37 Q4
Horne Surrey 24 H2
Horner Somset 18 B5
Horne Row Essex 52 C11
Horners Green Suffk 52 G3
Horney Common E Susx 25 L5
Horn Hill Bucks 36 B2
Horning Norfk 77 L8
Horninghold Leics 73 L11
Horninglow Staffs 71 N9
Horningsea Cambs 62 G8
Horningsham Wilts 20 F6
Horningtoft Norfk 76 C7
Horningtops Cnwll 5 M9
Hornsbury Somset 10 G2
Hornsby Cumb 111 K10
Hornsbygate Cumb 111 K10
Horns Cross Devon 16 F7
Horns Cross E Susx 26 D7
Hornsea E R Yk 99 P11
Hornsey Gt Lon 36 H3
Horn's Green Gt Lon 37 L9
Horn Street Kent 27 L4
Hornton Oxon 48 C5
Horpit Swindn 33 P8
Horra Shet 169 r4
Horrabridge Devon 6 E5
Horringer Suffk 64 A9
Horringford IoW 14 F9
Horrocks Fold Bolton 89 L8
Horrocksford Lancs 89 M2
Horsacott Devon 17 J5
Horsebridge Devon 5 Q6
Horsebridge E Susx 25 N8
Horsebridge Hants 22 B8
Horsebridge Shrops 56 F3
Horsebridge Staffs 70 H4
Horsebrook Staffs 58 C2
Horsecastle N Som 31 M11
Horsedown Cnwll 2 G7
Horsehay Wrekin 57 M3
Horseheath Cambs 63 K11
Horsehouse N York 96 F4
Horsell Surrey 23 Q3
Horseman's Green Wrexhm 69 M6
Horsenden Bucks 35 L4
Horsey Norfk 77 P7
Horsey Somset 19 K7
Horsey Corner Norfk 77 P7
Horsford Norfk 76 H8
Horsforth Leeds 90 G3
Horsham W Susx 24 E4
Horsham Worcs 46 D3
Horsham St Faith Norfk 77 J8
Horsington Lincs 86 G7
Horsington Somset 20 D10
Horsley Derbys 72 B2
Horsley Gloucs 32 F5
Horsley Nthumb 112 G7
Horsley Nthumb 118 F11
Horsley Cross Essex 53 K6
Horsleycross Street Essex 53 K6
Horsley-Gate Derbys 84 D5
Horsleyhill Border 117 Q7
Horsley's Green Bucks 35 L6
Horsley Woodhouse Derbys 72 B2
Horsmonden Kent 26 B3
Horspath Oxon 34 G3
Horstead Norfk 77 K8
Horsted Keynes W Susx 25 J5
Horton Bucks 49 P11
Horton Dorset 12 H3
Horton Lancs 96 C10
Horton Nhants 49 M4
Horton S Glos 32 E8
Horton Shrops 69 N9
Horton Somset 10 G2
Horton Staffs 70 G3
Horton Surrey 36 E8
Horton Swans 28 E7
Horton W & M 36 B5
Horton Wilts 21 K2
Horton Wrekin 57 M2
Horton Cross Somset 19 K11
Horton-cum-Studley Oxon 34 G2
Horton Green Ches W 69 N5
Horton Heath Hants 22 E11
Horton-in-Ribblesdale N York 96 B6
Horton Kirby Kent 37 N7
Horwich Bolton 89 J8
Horwich End Derbys 83 M8
Horwood Devon 17 J6
Hoscar Lancs 88 F8
Hoscote Border 117 M8
Hose Leics 73 J5
Hosey Hill Kent 37 L10
Hosh P & K 133 P3
Hoswick Shet 169 r11
Hotham E R Yk 92 E4
Hothfield Kent 26 G3
Hoton Leics 72 F6
Hott Nthumb 111 Q3
Hough Ches E 70 C4
Hough Ches E 83 J9
Hougham Lincs 73 M2
Hough End Leeds 90 G4
Hough Green Halton 81 P7
Hough-on-the-Hill Lincs 86 B11
Houghton Cambs 62 C6
Houghton Cumb 110 H9
Houghton Hants 22 B8
Houghton Nthumb 112 H7
Houghton Pembks 41 J9
Houghton W Susx 24 B8
Houghton Conquest C Beds 50 B2
Houghton Gate Dur 113 M10
Houghton Green E Susx 26 F7
Houghton Green Warrtn 82 D6
Houghton le Side Darltn 103 P6
Houghton-le-Spring Sundld 113 M11
Houghton on the Hill Leics 72 H10
Houghton Regis C Beds 50 B6
Houghton St Giles Norfk 76 C4
Hound Green Hants 23 K3
Houndslow Border 128 G10
Houndsmoor Somset 18 F9
Houndwood Border 129 L7
Hounslow Gt Lon 36 D5
Househill Highld 156 F6
Houses Hill Kirk 90 F7
Housieside Abers 151 M2
Houston Rens 125 L4
Houstry Highld 167 L10
Houton Ork 169 c6
Hove Br & H 24 G10
Hove Edge Calder 90 E6
Hoveringham Notts 85 L11
Hoveton Norfk 77 L8
Hovingham N York 98 D5
Howbrook Barns 91 J11
How Caple Herefs 46 B8
Howden E R Yk 92 B5
Howden-le-Wear Dur 103 N4
Howe Highld 167 P4
Howe IoM 80 a8
Howe N York 97 N4
Howe Norfk 65 K2
Howe Bridge Wigan 82 E4
Howe Green Essex 52 B11
Howegreen Essex 52 D11
Howell Lincs 86 F11
How End C Beds 50 B2
Howe of Teuchar Abers 159 J8
Howes D & G 110 C7
Howe Street Essex 51 Q4
Howe Street Essex 51 Q8
Howey Powys 44 F3
Howgate Cumb 100 C6
Howgate Mdloth 127 N6
Howgill Lancs 96 B11
Howick Nthumb 119 Q7
Howle Wrekin 70 B10
Howle Hill Herefs 46 B10
Howlett End Essex 51 N4
Howley Somset 10 F3
How Mill Cumb 111 K9
Howmore W Isls 168 c14
Hownam Border 118 E7
Howrigg Cumb 110 F11
Howsham N Linc 92 H10
Howsham N York 98 E8
Howtel Nthumb 118 G4
Howt Green Kent 38 E8
Howton Herefs 45 N9
Howtown Cumb 101 M7
How Wood Herts 50 D10
Howwood Rens 125 K5
Hoxa Ork 169 d7
Hoxne Suffk 64 H6
Hoy Ork 169 b7
Hoylake Wirral 81 J7
Hoyland Barns 91 K10
Hoyland Common Barns 91 K10
Hoylandswaine Barns 90 H10
Hoyle W Susx 23 P11
Hoyle Mill Barns 91 K9
Hubberholme N York 96 D5
Hubberston Pembks 40 G9
Hubbert's Bridge Lincs 74 E2
Huby N York 97 L11
Huby N York 98 B7
Huccaby Devon 6 H4
Hucclecote Gloucs 46 G11
Hucking Kent 38 D10
Hucknall Notts 84 H11
Huddersfield Kirk 90 E7
Huddington Worcs 46 H3
Hudnall Herts 50 B8
Hudswell N York 103 M10
Huggate E R Yk 98 H9
Hugglescote Leics 72 C8
Hughenden Valley Bucks 35 N5
Hughley Shrops 57 K5
Hugh Town IoS 2 c2
Huish Devon 17 J9
Huish Wilts 21 M2
Huish Champflower Somset 18 E9
Huish Episcopi Somset 19 M9
Hùisinis W Isls 168 e6
Huisinish W Isls 168 e6
Hulcote C Beds 49 P7
Hulcote Nhants 49 K5
Hulcott Bucks 49 N11
Hulham Devon 9 P8
Hulland Derbys 71 N5
Hulland Ward Derbys 71 P5
Hullavington Wilts 32 G8
Hull Bridge E R Yk 93 J2
Hullbridge Essex 38 D2
Hull, Kingston upon C KuH 93 J5
Hulme Manch 82 H5
Hulme Staffs 70 G5
Hulme Warrtn 82 D6
Hulme End Staffs 71 L3
Hulme Walfield Ches E 82 H11
Hulse Heath Ches E 82 F8
Hulton Lane Ends Bolton 89 K9
Hulverstone IoW 14 C10
Hulver Street Norfk 76 C9
Hulver Street Suffk 65 P4
Humber Devon 9 L9
Humber Herefs 45 Q3
Humber Bridge N Linc 92 H6
Humberside Airport N Linc 93 J8
Humberston NE Lin 93 P9
Humberstone C Leic 72 G9
Humberton N York 97 P7
Humbie E Loth 128 D7
Humbleton E R Yk 93 M4
Humbleton Nthumb 119 J5
Humby Lincs 73 Q4
Hume Border 118 D2
Humshaugh Nthumb 112 D6
Huna Highld 167 Q2
Huncoat Lancs 89 M4
Huncote Leics 72 E11
Hundalee Border 118 B7
Hundall Derbys 84 E5
Hunderthwaite Dur 103 J6
Hundleby Lincs 87 L7
Hundle Houses Lincs 86 H10
Hundleton Pembks 41 J10
Hundon Suffk 63 M11
Hundred End Lancs 88 E6
Hundred House Powys 44 G4
Hungarton Leics 72 H9
Hungerford Hants 13 L2
Hungerford Somset 18 D6
Hungerford W Berk 34 B11
Hungerford Newtown W Berk 34 C10
Hunger Hill Bolton 89 K9
Hunger Hill Lancs 88 G8
Hungerstone Herefs 45 N7
Hungerton Lincs 73 M5
Hungryhatton Shrops 70 B9
Hunmanby N York 99 M5
Hunningham Warwks 59 N11
Hunnington Worcs 58 E8
Hunsbury Hill Nhants 60 F9
Hunsdon Herts 51 K8
Hunsingore N York 97 P10
Hunslet Leeds 91 J4
Hunsonby Cumb 101 Q3
Hunstanton Norfk 75 N2
Hunstanworth Dur 112 D11
Hunsterson Ches E 70 B5
Hunston Suffk 64 D8
Hunston W Susx 15 N6
Hunston Green Suffk 64 D8
Hunstrete BaNES 20 B2
Hunsworth Kirk 90 F5
Hunt End Worcs 47 K2
Hunter's Inn Devon 17 M2
Hunter's Quay Ag & B 124 F2
Huntham Somset 19 K9
Hunthill Lodge Angus 142 H3
Huntingdon Cambs 62 B6
Huntingfield Suffk 65 L7
Huntingford Dorset 20 F9
Huntington C York 98 C9
Huntington Ches W 69 M2
Huntington E Loth 128 D5
Huntington Herefs 45 K4
Huntington Herefs 45 P6
Huntington Staffs 58 E2
Huntingtowerfield P & K 134 D2
Huntley Gloucs 46 D11
Huntly Abers 158 D10
Hunton Hants 22 E6
Hunton Kent 26 B2
Hunton N York 97 J2
Hunton Bridge Herts 50 C10
Hunt's Corner Norfk 64 F4
Huntscott Somset 18 B6
Hunt's Cross Lpool 81 N7
Hunts Green Bucks 35 N4
Hunts Green Warwks 59 J5
Huntsham Devon 18 D10
Huntshaw Devon 17 J7
Huntshaw Cross Devon 17 J7
Huntspill Somset 19 K5
Huntstile Somset 19 J8
Huntworth Somset 19 K8
Hunwick Dur 103 N4
Hunworth Norfk 76 F4
Hurcott Somset 19 L11
Hurdcott Wilts 21 N8
Hurdsfield Ches E 83 K10
Hurley W & M 35 M8
Hurley Warwks 59 K5
Hurley Bottom W & M 35 M8
Hurley Common Warwks 59 K5
Hurlford E Ayrs 125 M10
Hurlston Green Lancs 88 D8
Hurn BCP 13 K5
Hurn's End Lincs 87 M11
Hursley Hants 22 D9
Hurst Dorset 12 C6
Hurst N York 103 K10
Hurst Somset 19 N11
Hurst Wokham 35 L10
Hurstbourne Priors Hants 22 D5
Hurstbourne Tarrant Hants 22 C4
Hurst Green E Susx 26 B6
Hurst Green Essex 53 J8
Hurst Green Lancs 89 K3
Hurst Green Surrey 37 K10
Hurst Hill Dudley 58 D6
Hurstley Herefs 45 M5
Hurstpierpoint W Susx 24 G7
Hurst Wickham W Susx 24 G7
Hurstwood Lancs 89 P4
Hurtiso Ork 169 e6
Hurtmore Surrey 23 P5
Hurworth Burn Dur 104 D4
Hurworth-on-Tees Darltn 104 B9
Hurworth Place Darltn 103 Q9
Hury Dur 103 J7
Husbands Bosworth Leics 60 D4
Husborne Crawley C Beds 49 Q7
Husthwaite N York 97 R6
Hutcherleigh Devon 7 K8
Hut Green N York 91 P6
Huthwaite Notts 84 G9
Huttoft Lincs 87 P5
Hutton Border 129 N9
Hutton Cumb 101 M5
Hutton E R Yk 99 L10
Hutton Essex 37 P2
Hutton Lancs 88 F5
Hutton N Som 19 L3
Hutton Bonville N York 104 B10
Hutton Buscel N York 99 K4
Hutton Conyers N York 97 M6
Hutton Cranswick E R Yk 99 L10
Hutton End Cumb 101 N3
Hutton Hang N York 97 J3
Hutton Henry Dur 104 D3
Hutton-le-Hole N York 98 E2
Hutton Lowcross R & Cl 104 G8
Hutton Magna Dur 103 M8
Hutton Mulgrave N York 105 M9
Hutton Roof Cumb 95 M5
Hutton Roof Cumb 101 L4
Hutton Rudby N York 104 E9
Hutton Sessay N York 97 Q5
Hutton Wandesley N York 97 R10
Huxham Devon 9 M5
Huxham Green Somset 19 Q7
Huxley Ches W 69 P2
Huyton Knows 81 N6
Hycemoor Cumb 94 B3
Hyde Gloucs 32 G4
Hyde Hants 13 L2
Hyde Tamesd 83 K6
Hyde Heath Bucks 35 P4
Hyde Lea Staffs 70 G11
Hydestile Surrey 23 Q6
Hykeham Moor Lincs 86 B7
Hylands House & Park Essex 51 Q10
Hyndford Bridge S Lans 116 C2
Hynish Ag & B 136 B8
Hyssington Powys 56 E6
Hystfield Gloucs 32 C5
Hythe Essex 52 H6
Hythe Hants 14 D5
Hythe Kent 27 L5
Hythe Somset 19 M4
Hythe End W & M 36 B6
Hyton Cumb 94 B3

I

Ibberton Dorset 12 C3
Ible Derbys 84 B9
Ibsley Hants 13 L3
Ibstock Leics 72 C9
Ibstone Bucks 35 L6
Ibthorpe Hants 22 C4
Iburndale N York 105 N9
Ibworth Hants 22 G4
Icelton N Som 31 L11
Ichrachan Ag & B 139 J11
Ickburgh Norfk 75 R11
Ickenham Gt Lon 36 C3
Ickford Bucks 34 H3
Ickham Kent 39 M10
Ickleford Herts 50 E4
Icklesham E Susx 26 E8
Ickleton Cambs 51 L2
Icklingham Suffk 63 N6
Ickornshaw N York 90 B2
Ickwell Green C Beds 61 Q11
Icomb Gloucs 47 P10
Idbury Oxon 47 P11
Iddesleigh Devon 17 K10
Ide Devon 9 L6
Ideford Devon 9 L9
Ide Hill Kent 37 L10
Iden E Susx 26 F7
Iden Green Kent 26 B4
Iden Green Kent 26 D5
Idle C Brad 90 F3
Idless Cnwll 3 L4
Idlicote Warwks 47 Q6
Idmiston Wilts 21 N7
Idole Carmth 42 H11
Idridgehay Derbys 71 P5
Idrigill Highld 152 F5
Idstone Oxon 33 Q8
Iffley Oxon 34 F4
Ifield W Susx 24 G3
Ifold W Susx 24 B4
Iford BCP 13 K6
Iford E Susx 25 K9
Ifton Mons 31 N7
Ifton Heath Shrops 69 K7
Ightfield Shrops 69 Q7
Ightham Kent 37 N9
Iken Suffk 65 N10
Ilam Staffs 71 L4
Ilchester Somset 19 P10
Ilderton Nthumb 119 K6
Ilford Gt Lon 37 K3
Ilford Somset 19 L11
Ilfracombe Devon 17 J2
Ilkeston Derbys 72 D2
Ilketshall St Andrew Suffk 65 M4
Ilketshall St John Suffk 65 M4
Ilketshall St Lawrence Suffk 65 M5
Ilketshall St Margaret Suffk 65 L4
Ilkley C Brad 96 H11
Illand Cnwll 5 M6
Illey Dudley 58 E8
Illidge Green Ches E 70 D2
Illingworth Calder 90 D5
Illogan Cnwll 2 H5
Illston on the Hill Leics 73 J11
Ilmer Bucks 35 L3
Ilmington Warwks 47 P6
Ilminster Somset 10 H2
Ilsington Devon 9 J9
Ilsington Dorset 12 C6
Ilston Swans 28 G6
Ilton N York 97 J5
Ilton Somset 19 L11
Imachar N Ayrs 120 G3
Immingham NE Lin 93 L8
Immingham Dock NE Lin 93 L7
Impington Cambs 62 F8
Ince Ches W 81 P9
Ince Blundell Sefton 81 L4
Ince-in-Makerfield Wigan 82 C4
Inchbae Lodge Hotel Highld 155 M4
Inchbare Angus 143 L4
Inchberry Moray 157 Q6
Incheril Highld 154 D5
Inchinnan Rens 125 M4
Inchlaggan Highld 146 F7
Inchmichael P & K 134 G2
Inchmore Highld 155 Q8
Inchnadamph Highld 161 M2
Inchture P & K 134 H2
Inchvuilt Highld 154 H10
Inchyra P & K 134 F3
Indian Queens Cnwll 4 E10
Ingatestone Essex 51 P11
Ingbirchworth Barns 90 G9
Ingerthorpe N York 97 L7
Ingestre Staffs 70 H10
Ingham Lincs 86 B4
Ingham Norfk 77 M6
Ingham Suffk 64 B7
Ingham Corner Norfk 77 M6
Ingleborough Norfk 75 J7
Ingleby Derbys 72 A5
Ingleby Arncliffe N York 104 D10
Ingleby Barwick S on T 104 D8
Ingleby Cross N York 104 E10
Ingleby Greenhow N York 104 G9
Ingleigh Green Devon 8 F3
Inglesbatch BaNES 20 D2
Inglesham Swindn 33 P5
Ingleston D & G 109 L7
Ingleton Dur 103 N6
Ingleton N York 95 P6
Inglewhite Lancs 88 G3
Ingmanthorpe N York 97 P10
Ingoe Nthumb 112 F6
Ingol Lancs 88 G4
Ingoldisthorpe Norfk 75 N4
Ingoldmells Lincs 87 Q7
Ingoldsby Lincs 73 Q5
Ingram Nthumb 119 K7
Ingrave Essex 37 P2
Ingrow C Brad 90 D3
Ings Cumb 101 M11
Ingst S Glos 31 Q7
Ingthorpe Rutlnd 73 P9
Ingworth Norfk 76 H6
Inkberrow Worcs 47 K3
Inkerman Dur 103 M3
Inkhorn Abers 159 M10
Inkpen W Berk 22 C2
Inkstack Highld 167 N2
Inmarsh Wilts 20 H2
Innellan Ag & B 124 F3
Innerleithen Border 117 L3
Innerleven Fife 135 K7
Innermessan D & G 106 E5
Innerwick E Loth 129 J5
Innesmill Moray 157 P5
Innsworth Gloucs 46 G10
Insch Abers 150 G2
Insh Highld 148 E7
Inskip Lancs 88 F3
Inskip Moss Side Lancs 88 F3
Instow Devon 16 H5
Insworke Cnwll 6 C8
Intake Sheff 84 E4
Inver Abers 149 N9
Inver Highld 163 K10
Inver P & K 141 P9
Inverailort Highld 145 N11
Inveralligin Highld 153 Q6
Inverallochy Abers 159 P4
Inveran Highld 162 D7
Inveraray Ag & B 131 M6
Inverarish Highld 153 K10
Inverarity Angus 142 H9
Inverarnan Stirlg 132 C4

Inverasdale – King's Coughton 277

Inverasdale Highld 160 C10
Inverbeg Ag & B 132 C8
Inverbervie Abers 143 Q3
Inverboyndie Abers 158 G5
Invercreran House Hotel Ag & B 139 J8
Inverdruie Highld 148 F5
Inveresk E Loth 127 Q3
Inveresragan Ag & B 138 H10
Inverey Abers 149 K10
Inverfarigaig Highld 147 N3
Inverfolla Ag & B 138 H9
Invergarry Highld 147 J7
Invergeldie P & K 133 L2
Invergloy Highld 146 G10
Invergordon Highld 156 C4
Invergowrie P & K 142 E11
Inverguseran Highld 145 M6
Inverhadden P & K 140 G6
Inverie Highld 145 N7
Inverinan Ag & B 131 K4
Inverinate Highld 145 R3
Inverkeilor Angus 143 M8
Inverkeithing Fife 134 E11
Inverkeithny Abers 158 F8
Inverkip Inver 124 G3
Inverkirkaig Highld 160 H3
Inverlael Highld 161 K9
Inverlair Highld 139 Q2
Inverliever Lodge Ag & B 130 H6
Inverlochy Ag & B 131 P2
Invermark Angus 150 C11
Invermoriston Highld 147 L4
Invernaver Highld 166 B4
Inverneill Ag & B 123 P3
Inverness Highld 156 B8
Inverness Airport Highld 156 D7
Invernettie Abers 159 R9
Invernoaden Ag & B 131 N8
Inveroran Hotel Ag & B 139 P9
Inverquharity Angus 142 G6
Inverquhomery Abers 159 P8
Inverroy Highld 146 H11
Inversanda Highld 138 G6
Invershiel Highld 146 A4
Invershin Highld 162 D7
Invershore Highld 167 M9
Inversnaid Hotel Stirlg 132 C6
Inverugie Abers 159 Q8
Inveruglas Ag & B 132 C6
Inveruglass Highld 148 E7
Inverurie Abers 151 K3
Inwardleigh Devon 8 E5
Inworth Essex 52 E8
Iochdar W Isls 168 c13
Iona Ag & B 136 H10
Iping W Susx 23 N10
iPort Logistics Park Donc 91 Q11
Ipplepen Devon 7 L5
Ipsden Oxon 34 H7
Ipstones Staffs 71 J5
Ipswich Suffk 53 L3
Irby Wirral 81 K8
Irby in the Marsh Lincs 87 N8
Irby upon Humber NE Lin 93 L10
Irchester Nhants 61 K7
Ireby Cumb 100 H3
Ireby Lancs 95 P5
Ireland C Beds 50 D2
Ireleth Cumb 94 E5
Ireshopeburn Dur 102 G3
Ireton Wood Derbys 71 P5
Irlam Salfd 82 F6
Irnham Lincs 73 Q5
Iron Acton S Glos 32 C8
Iron Bridge Cambs 75 J11
Ironbridge Wrekin 57 M4
Ironbridge Gorge Wrekin 57 M4
Iron Cross Warwks 47 L4
Ironmacannie D & G 108 E5
Irons Bottom Surrey 36 F11
Ironville Derbys 84 F10
Irstead Norfk 77 M7
Irthington Cumb 111 J8
Irthlingborough Nhants 61 K6
Irton N York 99 L4
Irvine N Ayrs 125 J10
Isauld Highld 166 G3
Isbister Shet 169 q4
Isbister Shet 169 s7
Isfield E Susx 25 K7
Isham Nhants 61 J6
Isington Hants 23 L6
Islandpool Worcs 58 C8
Islay Ag & B 122 E4
Islay Airport Ag & B 122 D9
Isle Abbotts Somset 19 L10
Isle Brewers Somset 19 L10
Isleham Cambs 63 K6
Isle of Dogs Gt Lon 37 J5
Isle of Grain Medway 38 E6
Isle of Lewis W Isls 168 i4
Isle of Man IoM 80 e4
Isle of Man Ronaldsway Airport IoM 80 c8
Isle of Mull Ag & B 137 Q8
Isle of Purbeck Dorset 12 H8
Isle of Sheppey Kent 38 G8
Isle of Skye Highld 152 G10
Isle of Thanet Kent 39 P8
Isle of Walney Cumb 94 D7
Isle of Whithorn D & G 107 N10
Isle of Wight IoW 14 F9
Isleornsay Highld 145 M5
Isles of Scilly IoS 2 c2
Isles of Scilly St Mary's Airport IoS 2 c2
Islesteps D & G 109 L6
Islet Village Guern 10 c1
Isleworth Gt Lon 36 E5
Isley Walton Leics 72 C6
Islibhig W Isls 168 f5
Islington Gt Lon 36 H4
Islip Nhants 61 L5
Islip Oxon 34 F2
Islivig W Isls 168 f5
Isombridge Wrekin 57 L2
Istead Rise Kent 37 P6
Itchen Abbas Hants 22 F8
Itchen Stoke Hants 22 G8
Itchingfield W Susx 24 D5
Itchington S Glos 32 C7
Itteringham Norfk 76 G5
Itton Devon 8 G5
Itton Mons 31 N5
Itton Common Mons 31 N5
Ivegill Cumb 101 M2
Ivelet N York 102 H11
Iver Bucks 36 B4
Iver Heath Bucks 36 B4
Iveston Dur 112 H10
Ivinghoe Bucks 49 P11
Ivinghoe Aston Bucks 49 Q11
Ivington Herefs 45 P3
Ivington Green Herefs 45 P3
Ivybridge Devon 6 G7
Ivychurch Kent 26 H6
Ivy Cross Dorset 20 G10
Ivy Hatch Kent 37 N10
Ivy Todd Norfk 76 B10
Iwade Kent 38 F8
Iwerne Courtney Dorset 12 E2
Iwerne Minster Dorset 12 E2
Ixworth Suffk 64 C7
Ixworth Thorpe Suffk 64 C7

J

Jack Green Lancs 88 H5
Jack Hill N York 97 J10
Jack-in-the-Green Devon 9 P5
Jack's Bush Hants 21 Q7
Jacksdale Notts 84 F10
Jackson Bridge Kirk 90 F9
Jackton S Lans 125 P7
Jacobstow Cnwll 5 K2
Jacobstowe Devon 8 E4
Jacobs Well Surrey 23 Q4
Jameston Pembks 41 L11
Jamestown Highld 155 N6
Jamestown W Duns 132 D11
Janetstown Highld 167 L10
Janetstown Highld 167 Q6
Jardine Hall D & G 109 P3
Jarrow S Tyne 113 M8
Jarvis Brook E Susx 25 M5
Jasper's Green Essex 52 B6
Jawcraig Falk 126 E2
Jaywick Essex 53 L9
Jealott's Hill Br For 35 N10
Jeater Houses N York 97 P2
Jedburgh Border 118 B6
Jeffreyston Pembks 41 L9
Jemimaville Highld 156 C4
Jerbourg Guern 10 c2
Jersey Jersey 11 b1
Jersey Airport Jersey 11 a2
Jersey Marine Neath 29 K6
Jerusalem Lincs 86 B6
Jesmond N u Ty 113 L7
Jevington E Susx 25 N10
Jingle Street Mons 31 N2
Jockey End Herts 50 B8
Jodrell Bank Ches E 82 G10
Johnby Cumb 101 M4
John Lennon Airport Lpool 81 N8
John o' Groats Highld 167 Q2
Johns Cross E Susx 26 B7
Johnshaven Abers 143 P4
Johnson Street Norfk 77 M8
Johnston Pembks 40 H8
Johnstone D & G 117 J10
Johnstone Rens 125 L5
Johnstonebridge D & G 109 P2
Johnstown Carmth 42 G11
Johnstown Wrexhm 69 K5
Joppa C Edin 127 Q3
Joppa Cerdgn 54 D11
Joppa S Ayrs 114 H4
Jordans Bucks 35 Q6
Jordanston Pembks 40 H4
Jordanthorpe Sheff 84 E4
Joyden's Wood Kent 37 M6
Jubilee Corner Kent 26 D2
Jump Barns 91 K10
Jumper's Town E Susx 25 L4
Juniper Nthumb 112 D9
Juniper Green C Edin 127 M4
Jura Ag & B 122 H3
Jurassic Coast Devon 10 G7
Jurby IoM 80 e2
Jurston Devon 8 G8

K

Kaber Cumb 102 E8
Kaimend S Lans 126 H8
Kames Ag & B 124 B3
Kames E Ayrs 115 N2
Kea Cnwll 3 L5
Keadby N Linc 92 D8
Keal Cotes Lincs 87 L8
Kearby Town End N York 97 M11
Kearsley Bolton 82 G4
Kearsley Nthumb 112 F5
Kearsney Kent 27 N3
Kearstwick Cumb 95 N5
Kearton N York 103 J11
Keasden N York 95 Q7
Keaton Devon 6 G8
Keckwick Halton 82 C8
Keddington Lincs 87 K3
Keddington Corner Lincs 87 L3
Kedington Suffk 63 M11
Kedleston Derbys 71 Q6
Keelby Lincs 93 L8
Keele Staffs 70 E5
Keele Services Staffs 70 E6
Keele University Staffs 70 E5
Keeley Green Bed 61 M11
Keelham C Brad 90 D4
Keeres Green Essex 51 N8
Keeston Pembks 40 H7
Keevil Wilts 20 H3
Kegworth Leics 72 D5
Kehelland Cnwll 2 G5
Keig Abers 150 G4
Keighley C Brad 90 D2
Keilarsbrae Clacks 133 P9
Keillour P & K 134 B2
Keiloch Abers 149 M9
Keils Ag & B 122 H6
Keinton Mandeville Somset 19 P8
Keir Mill D & G 109 J2
Keirsleywell Row Nthumb 111 Q10
Keisby Lincs 73 Q5
Keisley Cumb 102 D6
Keiss Highld 167 P4
Keith Moray 158 B7
Keithick P & K 142 C10
Keithock Angus 143 L5
Keithtown Highld 155 P6
Kelbrook Lancs 89 Q2
Kelby Lincs 73 Q2
Keld Cumb 101 Q8
Keld N York 102 G10
Keld Head N York 98 F4
Keldholme N York 98 E3
Kelfield N Linc 92 D10
Kelfield N York 91 P3
Kelham Notts 85 N9
Kelhead D & G 109 P7
Kellacott Devon 5 Q4
Kellamergh Lancs 88 E5
Kellas Angus 142 H10
Kellas Moray 157 M7
Kellaton Devon 7 L11
Kelleth Cumb 102 C9
Kelling Norfk 76 F3
Kellington N York 91 P6
Kelloe Dur 104 B3
Kelloholm D & G 115 P5
Kells Cumb 100 C7
Kelly Devon 5 P5
Kelly Bray Cnwll 5 P7
Kelmarsh Nhants 60 F5
Kelmscott Oxon 33 P5
Kelsale Suffk 65 M8
Kelsall Ches W 81 Q11
Kelshall Herts 50 H3
Kelsick Cumb 110 C10
Kelso Border 118 D4
Kelstedge Derbys 84 D8
Kelstern Lincs 86 H3
Kelsterton Flints 81 K10
Kelston BaNES 32 D11
Keltneyburn P & K 141 J8
Kelton D & G 109 L6
Kelty Fife 134 E9
Kelvedon Essex 52 E8
Kelvedon Hatch Essex 51 N11
Kelynack Cnwll 2 B8
Kemacott Devon 17 M2
Kemback Fife 135 L5
Kemberton Shrops 57 N4
Kemble Gloucs 33 J5
Kemble Wick Gloucs 33 J5
Kemerton Worcs 47 J7
Kemeys Commander Mons 31 K4
Kemnay Abers 151 J4
Kempe's Corner Kent 26 H2
Kempley Gloucs 46 C9
Kempley Green Gloucs 46 C9
Kempsey Worcs 46 F5
Kempsford Gloucs 33 N5
Kemps Green Warwks 58 H10
Kempshott Hants 22 H4
Kempston Bed 61 M11
Kempston Hardwick Bed 50 B2
Kempton Shrops 56 F8
Kemp Town Br & H 24 H10
Kemsing Kent 37 N9
Kemsley Kent 38 F8
Kemsley Street Kent 38 D9
Kenardington Kent 26 G5
Kenchester Herefs 45 N6
Kencot Oxon 33 Q4
Kendal Cumb 95 L2
Kenderchurch Herefs 45 N9
Kendleshire S Glos 32 C9
Kenfig Brdgnd 29 M8
Kenfig Hill Brdgnd 29 M8
Kenilworth Warwks 59 L10
Kenley Gt Lon 36 H8
Kenley Shrops 57 K4
Kenmore Highld 153 P6
Kenmore P & K 141 J8
Kenn Devon 9 M7
Kenn N Som 31 M11
Kennacraig Ag & B 123 P7
Kennall Vale Cnwll 3 J6
Kennards House Cnwll 5 M5
Kenneggy Cnwll 2 F8
Kennerleigh Devon 9 K3
Kennet Clacks 133 Q9
Kennethmont Abers 150 E2
Kennett Cambs 63 L7
Kennford Devon 9 M7
Kenninghall Norfk 64 E4
Kennington Kent 26 H2
Kennington Oxon 34 F4
Kennoway Fife 135 K7
Kenny Somset 19 K11
Kenny Hill Suffk 63 L5
Kennythorpe N York 98 F7
Kenovay Ag & B 136 B6
Kensaleyre Highld 152 G7
Kensington Gt Lon 36 G5
Kensington Palace Gt Lon 36 G4
Kensworth Common C Beds 50 B7
Kentallen Highld 139 J6
Kentchurch Herefs 45 N9
Kentford Suffk 63 M7
Kent Green Ches E 70 E3
Kentisbeare Devon 9 Q3
Kentisbury Devon 17 L3
Kentisbury Ford Devon 17 L3
Kentish Town Gt Lon 36 G4
Kentmere Cumb 101 N10
Kenton Devon 9 N8
Kenton Gt Lon 36 E3
Kenton N u Ty 113 K7
Kenton Suffk 64 H8
Kenton Bankfoot N u Ty 113 K7
Kentra Highld 138 B4
Kents Bank Cumb 94 H5
Kent's Green Gloucs 46 D10
Kent's Oak Hants 22 B10
Kent Street E Susx 26 C8
Kent Street Kent 37 Q10
Kenwick Shrops 69 M8
Kenwyn Cnwll 3 L4
Kenyon Warrtn 82 D5
Keoldale Highld 165 J3
Keppoch Highld 145 Q3
Kepwick N York 97 Q2
Keresley Covtry 59 M8
Kermincham Ches E 82 H11
Kernborough Devon 7 K10
Kerne Bridge Herefs 46 A11
Kerrera Ag & B 130 G2
Kerridge Ches E 83 K9
Kerridge-end Ches E 83 K9
Kerris Cnwll 2 C8
Kerry Powys 55 Q6
Kerrycroy Ag & B 124 E5
Kersall Notts 85 M8
Kersbrook Devon 9 Q8
Kerscott Devon 17 L6
Kersey Suffk 52 H3
Kersey Tye Suffk 52 G3
Kersey Upland Suffk 52 G3
Kershader W Isls 168 i6
Kershopefoot Cumb 111 J4
Kersoe Worcs 47 J6
Kerswell Devon 10 B3
Kerswell Green Worcs 46 G5
Kerthen Wood Cnwll 2 F7
Kesgrave Suffk 53 M2
Kessingland Suffk 65 Q4
Kessingland Beach Suffk 65 Q4
Kestle Cnwll 3 P4
Kestle Mill Cnwll 4 C10
Keston Gt Lon 37 K8
Keswick Cumb 101 J6
Keswick Norfk 77 J11
Ketsby Lincs 87 L5
Kettering Nhants 61 J5
Ketteringham Norfk 76 H11
Kettins P & K 142 C10
Kettlebaston Suffk 64 D11
Kettlebridge Fife 135 J6
Kettlebrook Staffs 59 K4
Kettleburgh Suffk 65 K9
Kettle Green Herts 51 K7
Kettleholm D & G 109 P5
Kettleness N York 105 M7
Kettleshulme Ches E 83 L9
Kettlesing N York 97 K9
Kettlesing Bottom N York 97 K9
Kettlestone Norfk 76 D5
Kettlethorpe Lincs 85 P5
Kettletoft Ork 169 f3
Kettlewell N York 96 E6
Ketton Rutlnd 73 P10
Kew Gt Lon 36 E5
Kew Royal Botanic Gardens Gt Lon 36 E5
Kewstoke N Som 19 K2
Kexbrough Barns 91 J9
Kexby C York 98 E10
Kexby Lincs 85 Q3
Key Green Ches E 70 F2
Key Green N York 105 M10
Keyham Leics 72 H9
Keyhaven Hants 13 P6
Keyingham E R Yk 93 M5
Keymer W Susx 24 H7
Keynsham BaNES 32 C11
Keysoe Bed 61 N8
Keysoe Row Bed 61 N8
Keyston Cambs 61 M5
Key Street Kent 38 E9
Keyworth Notts 72 G4
Kibbear Somset 18 H10
Kibblesworth Gatesd 113 K9
Kibworth Beauchamp Leics 60 E2
Kibworth Harcourt Leics 60 E2
Kidbrooke Gt Lon 37 K5
Kidburngill Cumb 100 E6
Kiddemore Green Staffs 58 C3
Kidderminster Worcs 58 B9
Kiddington Oxon 48 D10
Kidd's Moor Norfk 76 G11
Kidlington Oxon 34 E2
Kidmore End Oxon 35 J9
Kidsdale D & G 107 M10
Kidsgrove Staffs 70 E4
Kidstones N York 96 E4
Kidwelly Carmth 28 D3
Kiel Crofts Ag & B 138 G10
Kielder Nthumb 111 M2
Kielder Forest 111 M3
Kiells Ag & B 122 F6
Kilbarchan Rens 125 L5
Kilbeg Highld 145 L6
Kilberry Ag & B 123 M7
Kilbirnie N Ayrs 125 J7
Kilbride Ag & B 123 M4
Kilbride Ag & B 124 C4
Kilbuiack Moray 157 K5
Kilburn Derbys 84 E11
Kilburn Gt Lon 36 F4
Kilburn N York 97 R5
Kilby Leics 72 G11
Kilchamaig Ag & B 123 P7
Kilchattan Ag & B 124 E7
Kilchattan Ag & B 136 b2
Kilcheran Ag & B 138 E10
Kilchoan Highld 137 M3
Kilchoman Ag & B 122 B7
Kilchrenan Ag & B 131 L3
Kilconquhar Fife 135 M7
Kilcot Gloucs 46 C9
Kilcoy Highld 155 Q7
Kilcreggan Ag & B 131 Q11
Kildale N York 104 H9
Kildalloig Ag & B 120 E8
Kildary Highld 156 D3
Kildavaig Ag & B 124 B4
Kildavanan Ag & B 124 C4
Kildonan Highld 163 L2
Kildonan N Ayrs 121 K7
Kildonan Lodge Highld 163 L2
Kildonnan Highld 144 G10
Kildrochet House D & G 106 E6
Kildrummy Abers 150 D4
Kildwick N York 96 F11
Kilfinan Ag & B 124 A2
Kilfinnan Highld 146 H8
Kilford Denbgs 80 F11
Kilgetty Pembks 41 M9
Kilgrammie S Ayrs 114 E7
Kilgwrrwg Common Mons 31 N5
Kilham E R Yk 99 M8
Kilham Nthumb 118 G4
Kilkenneth Ag & B 136 A7
Kilkenzie Ag & B 120 C7
Kilkerran Ag & B 120 D8
Kilkhampton Cnwll 16 D9
Killamarsh Derbys 84 G4
Killay Swans 28 H6
Killearn Stirlg 132 G10
Killen Highld 156 B6
Killerby Darltn 103 N7
Killerton Devon 9 N4
Killichonan P & K 140 D6
Killiechonate Highld 146 G11
Killiechronan Ag & B 137 N7
Killiecrankie P & K 141 M5
Killilan Highld 154 B11
Killimster Highld 167 P5
Killin Stirlg 140 E11
Killinghall N York 97 L9
Killington Cumb 95 N3
Killington Devon 17 M2
Killington Lake Services Cumb 95 M2
Killingworth N Tyne 113 L6
Killiow Cnwll 3 L5
Killochyett Border 128 D10
Kilmacolm Inver 125 K3
Kilmahog Stirlg 133 J6
Kilmahumaig Ag & B 130 F9
Kilmaluag Highld 152 G3
Kilmany Fife 135 K3
Kilmarnock E Ayrs 125 L10
Kilmartin Ag & B 130 G8
Kilmaurs E Ayrs 125 L9
Kilmelford Ag & B 130 H5
Kilmersdon Somset 20 C4
Kilmeston Hants 22 G9
Kilmichael Ag & B 120 C7
Kilmichael Glassary Ag & B 130 H9
Kilmichael of Inverlussa Ag & B 130 F10
Kilmington Devon 10 F5
Kilmington Wilts 20 E7
Kilmington Common Wilts 20 E7
Kilmington Street Wilts 20 E7
Kilmorack Highld 155 N9
Kilmore Ag & B 130 H2
Kilmore Highld 145 L6
Kilmory Ag & B 123 M5
Kilmory Highld 137 N2
Kilmory N Ayrs 121 J7
Kilmuir Highld 152 D8
Kilmuir Highld 152 F3
Kilmuir Highld 156 B8
Kilmuir Highld 156 D3
Kilmun Ag & B 131 P11
Kilnave Ag & B 122 C5
Kilncadzow S Lans 126 F8
Kilndown Kent 26 B4
Kiln Green Wokham 35 M9
Kilnhill Cumb 100 H4
Kilnhouses Ches W 82 D11
Kilnhurst Rothm 91 M11
Kilninver Ag & B 130 G3
Kiln Pit Hill Nthumb 112 F9
Kilnsea E R Yk 93 R7
Kilnsey N York 96 E7
Kilnwick E R Yk 99 K11
Kilnwick Percy E R Yk 98 G11
Kiloran Ag & B 136 b2
Kilpatrick N Ayrs 120 H6
Kilpeck Herefs 45 N8
Kilpin E R Yk 92 C5
Kilpin Pike E R Yk 92 C5
Kilrenny Fife 135 P7
Kilsby Nhants 60 C6
Kilspindie P & K 134 G2
Kilstay D & G 106 F10
Kilsyth N Lans 126 C2
Kiltarlity Highld 155 P9
Kilton R & Cl 105 K7
Kilton Somset 18 G6
Kilton Thorpe R & Cl 105 J7
Kilvaxter Highld 152 F4
Kilve Somset 18 F6
Kilvington Notts 73 L2
Kilwinning N Ayrs 125 J9
Kimberley Norfk 76 F11
Kimberley Notts 72 D2
Kimberworth Rothm 84 F2
Kimblesworth Dur 113 L11
Kimble Wick Bucks 35 M3
Kimbolton Cambs 61 P7
Kimbolton Herefs 45 Q2
Kimcote Leics 60 C3
Kimmeridge Dorset 12 F9
Kimmerston Nthumb 119 J3
Kimpton Hants 21 Q5
Kimpton Herts 50 E7
Kimworthy Devon 16 E9
Kinbrace Highld 166 E10
Kinbuck Stirlg 133 M6
Kincaple Fife 135 M4
Kincardine Fife 133 Q10
Kincardine Highld 162 E9
Kincardine Bridge Fife 133 Q10
Kincardine O'Neil Abers 150 F8
Kinclaven P & K 142 B10
Kincorth C Aber 151 N7
Kincorth House Moray 157 J5
Kincraig Highld 148 E6
Kincraigie P & K 141 N8
Kindallachan P & K 141 N8
Kinerarach Ag & B 123 L9
Kineton Gloucs 47 L9
Kineton Warwks 48 B4
Kinfauns P & K 134 F3
Kingarth Ag & B 124 D6
Kingcausie Abers 151 M8
Kingcoed Mons 31 M3
Kingerby Lincs 86 E2
Kingford Devon 16 D10
Kingham Oxon 47 Q10
Kingholm Quay D & G 109 L6
Kinghorn Fife 134 H10
Kinglassie Fife 134 G8
Kingoodie P & K 135 J2
King's Acre Herefs 45 P6
Kingsand Cnwll 6 C8
Kingsash Bucks 35 N3
Kingsbarns Fife 135 P5
Kingsbridge Devon 7 J10
Kingsbridge Somset 18 C7
Kings Bridge Swans 28 G5
King's Bromley Staffs 71 L11
Kingsburgh Highld 152 F6
Kingsbury Gt Lon 36 E3
Kingsbury Warwks 59 K5
Kingsbury Episcopi Somset 19 M10
King's Caple Herefs 45 R9
Kingsclere Hants 22 F3
King's Cliffe Nhants 73 Q11
Kings Clipstone Notts 85 K8
Kingscote Gloucs 32 F5
Kingscott Devon 17 J8
King's Coughton Warwks 47 L3

Kingscross N Ayrs 121 K6
Kingsdon Somset 19 P9
Kingsdown Kent 27 Q2
Kingsdown Swindn 33 N7
Kingsdown Wilts 32 F11
Kingseat Abers 151 N4
Kingseat Fife 134 E9
Kingsey Bucks 35 K3
Kingsfold W Susx 24 E3
Kingsford C Aber 151 M6
Kingsford E Ayrs 125 L8
Kingsford Worcs 57 Q8
Kingsgate Kent 39 Q7
Kings Green Gloucs 46 E8
Kingshall Street Suffk 64 C9
Kingsheanton Devon 17 K4
King's Heath Birm 58 G8
Kings Hill Kent 37 Q9
King's Hill Wsall 58 E5
Kings House Hotel Highld 139 P7
Kingshurst Solhll 59 J7
Kingside Hill Cumb 110 C10
Kingskerswell Devon 7 M5
Kingskettle Fife 135 J6
Kingsland Dorset 11 K5
Kingsland Herefs 45 N2
Kingsland IoA 78 D8
Kings Langley Herts 50 C10
Kingsley Ches W 82 C10
Kingsley Hants 23 L7
Kingsley Staffs 71 J5
Kingsley Green W Susx 23 N8
Kingsley Holt Staffs 71 J5
Kingsley Park Nhants 60 G8
Kingslow Shrops 57 P5
King's Lynn Norfk 75 M6
Kings Meaburn Cumb 102 B6
Kingsmead Hants 14 G4
King's Mills Guern 10 b2
King's Moss St Hel 81 Q4
Kingsmuir Angus 142 H8
Kings Muir Border 117 K3
Kingsmuir Fife 135 N6
Kings Newnham Warwks 59 Q9
King's Newton Derbys 72 B5
Kingsnorth Kent 26 H4
King's Norton Birm 58 G9
King's Norton Leics 72 H10
Kings Nympton Devon 17 M8
King's Pyon Herefs 45 N4
Kings Ripton Cambs 62 C5
King's Somborne Hants 22 C8
King's Stag Dorset 11 Q2
King's Stanley Gloucs 32 F4
King's Sutton Nhants 48 E7
Kingstanding Birm 58 G6
Kingsteignton Devon 7 M4
King Sterndale Derbys 83 N10
Kingsthorne Herefs 45 P8
Kingsthorpe Nhants 60 G8
Kingston Cambs 62 D9
Kingston Cnwll 5 P6
Kingston Devon 6 D9
Kingston Devon 9 Q7
Kingston Dorset 12 C3
Kingston Dorset 12 G9
Kingston E Loth 128 E3
Kingston Hants 13 K4
Kingston IoW 14 E10
Kingston Kent 39 L11
Kingston W Susx 24 C10
Kingston Bagpuize Oxon 34 D5
Kingston Blount Oxon 35 K5
Kingston Deverill Wilts 20 F7
Kingstone Herefs 45 N7
Kingstone Somset 10 H2
Kingstone Staffs 71 K9
Kingstone Winslow Oxon 33 Q7
Kingston Lacy House & Gardens Dorset 12 G4
Kingston Lisle Oxon 34 B7
Kingston near Lewes E Susx 25 J9
Kingston on Soar Notts 72 E5
Kingston on Spey Moray 157 Q4
Kingston Russell Dorset 11 M6
Kingston St Mary Somset 18 H9
Kingston Seymour N Som 31 M11
Kingston Stert Oxon 35 K4
Kingston upon Hull C KuH 93 J5
Kingston upon Thames Gt Lon 36 E7
King's Walden Herts 50 E6
Kingswear Devon 7 M8
Kingswells C Aber 151 M6
Kings Weston Bristl 31 P9
Kingswinford Dudley 58 C7
Kingswood Bucks 49 J11
Kingswood Gloucs 32 D6
Kingswood Kent 38 D11
Kingswood Powys 56 C4
Kingswood S Glos 32 B10
Kingswood Somset 18 F7
Kingswood Surrey 36 F9
Kingswood Warwks 59 J10
Kingswood Brook Warwks 59 J10
Kingswood Common Herefs 45 K4
Kingswood Common Staffs 58 B4
Kings Worthy Hants 22 E8
Kingthorpe Lincs 86 F5
Kington Herefs 45 K3
Kington S Glos 32 B6
Kington Worcs 47 J3
Kington Langley Wilts 32 H9
Kington Magna Dorset 20 E10
Kington St Michael Wilts 32 H9
Kingussie Highld 148 D7
Kingweston Somset 19 P8
Kinharrachie Abers 159 M11
Kinharvie D & G 109 K7
Kinkell Bridge P & K 133 Q4
Kinknockie Abers 159 P9
Kinlet Shrops 57 N8
Kinloch Highld 144 F8
Kinloch Highld 164 H10
Kinloch Highld 165 N6
Kinloch P & K 142 A9
Kinlochard Stirlg 132 F7
Kinlochbervie Highld 164 F5
Kinlocheil Highld 138 H2
Kinlochewe Highld 154 D5
Kinloch Hourn Highld 146 B6
Kinlochlaggan Highld 147 N10
Kinlochleven Highld 139 M5

Kinlochmoidart Highld 138 C3
Kinlochnanuagh Highld 145 M11
Kinloch Rannoch P & K 140 G6
Kinloss Moray 157 K5
Kinmel Bay Conwy 80 D8
Kinmuck Abers 151 L4
Kinmundy Abers 151 M4
Kinnabus Ag & B 122 C11
Kinnadie Abers 159 N9
Kinnaird P & K 141 N6
Kinneff Abers 143 Q2
Kinnelhead D & G 116 E10
Kinnell Angus 143 L7
Kinnerley Shrops 69 K10
Kinnersley Herefs 45 L5
Kinnersley Worcs 46 G6
Kinnerton Powys 45 J2
Kinnerton Shrops 56 F5
Kinnerton Green Flints 69 K2
Kinnesswood P & K 134 F7
Kinninvie Dur 103 L6
Kinnordy Angus 142 F6
Kinoulton Notts 72 H4
Kinross P & K 134 E7
Kinrossie P & K 142 B11
Kinross Services P & K 134 E7
Kinsbourne Green Herts 50 D7
Kinsey Heath Ches E 70 B6
Kinsham Herefs 56 F11
Kinsham Worcs 46 H7
Kinsley Wakefd 91 L8
Kinson BCP 13 J5
Kintail Highld 146 B4
Kintbury W Berk 34 C11
Kintessack Moray 157 J5
Kintillo P & K 134 E4
Kinton Herefs 56 G10
Kinton Shrops 69 L11
Kintore Abers 151 K4
Kintour Ag & B 122 G9
Kintra Ag & B 122 D10
Kintraw Ag & B 137 J10
Kintra Ag & B 130 G7
Kintyre Ag & B 120 D4
Kinveachy Highld 148 G4
Kinver Staffs 58 B8
Kiplin N York 103 Q11
Kippax Leeds 91 L4
Kippen Stirlg 133 J9
Kippford D & G 108 H10
Kipping's Cross Kent 25 P2
Kirbister Ork 169 c6
Kirby Bedon Norfk 77 K10
Kirby Bellars Leics 73 J7
Kirby Cane Norfk 65 M3
Kirby Corner Covtry 59 L9
Kirby Cross Essex 53 M7
Kirby Fields Leics 72 E10
Kirby Green Norfk 65 M3
Kirby Grindalythe N York 99 J7
Kirby Hill N York 97 N7
Kirby Hill N York 103 M9
Kirby Knowle N York 97 Q3
Kirby-le-Soken Essex 53 M7
Kirby Misperton N York 98 F5
Kirby Muxloe Leics 72 E10
Kirby Sigston N York 97 P2
Kirby Underdale E R Yk 98 G3
Kirby Wiske N York 97 N4
Kirdford W Susx 24 B5
Kirk Highld 167 N5
Kirkabister Shet 169 r10
Kirkandrews D & G 108 D11
Kirkandrews upon Eden Cumb 110 G9
Kirkbampton Cumb 110 F9
Kirkbean D & G 109 L9
Kirk Bramwith Donc 91 Q8
Kirkbride Cumb 110 D9
Kirkbridge N York 97 L2
Kirkbuddo Angus 143 J9
Kirkburn Border 117 K3
Kirkburn E R Yk 99 K9
Kirkburton Kirk 90 F8
Kirkby Knows 81 N5
Kirkby Lincs 86 E2
Kirkby N York 104 F9
Kirkby Fleetham N York 97 L2
Kirkby Green Lincs 86 E9
Kirkby-in-Ashfield Notts 84 H9
Kirkby-in-Furness Cumb 94 E4
Kirkby la Thorpe Lincs 86 E11
Kirkby Lonsdale Cumb 95 N5
Kirkby Malham N York 96 C8
Kirkby Mallory Leics 72 D10
Kirkby Malzeard N York 97 K6
Kirkby Mills N York 98 E3
Kirkbymoorside N York 98 D3
Kirkby on Bain Lincs 86 H8
Kirkby Overblow N York 97 M11
Kirkby Stephen Cumb 102 E9
Kirkby Thore Cumb 102 B5
Kirkby Underwood Lincs 73 R5
Kirkby Wharf N York 91 N2
Kirkby Woodhouse Notts 84 G10
Kirkcaldy Fife 134 H9
Kirkcambeck Cumb 111 K7
Kirkchrist D & G 108 E10
Kirkcolm D & G 106 D4
Kirkconnel D & G 115 P5
Kirkconnell D & G 109 L7
Kirkcowan D & G 107 K5
Kirkcudbright D & G 108 E10
Kirkdale Lpool 81 L6
Kirk Deighton N York 97 N10
Kirk Ella E R Yk 92 H5
Kirkfieldbank S Lans 116 B2
Kirkgunzeon D & G 109 J7
Kirk Hallam Derbys 72 D2
Kirkham Lancs 88 E4
Kirkham N York 98 E7
Kirkhamgate Wakefd 90 H6
Kirk Hammerton N York 97 N9
Kirkharle Nthumb 112 F4
Kirkhaugh Nthumb 111 N11
Kirkheaton Kirk 90 F7
Kirkheaton Nthumb 112 F5
Kirkhill Highld 155 Q8
Kirkhope S Lans 116 D9
Kirkhouse Cumb 111 L9
Kirkhouse Green Donc 91 Q8
Kirkibost Highld 145 J4
Kirkinch P & K 142 E9
Kirkinner D & G 107 M7
Kirkintilloch E Duns 126 B3

Kirk Ireton Derbys 71 P4
Kirkland Cumb 100 E7
Kirkland Cumb 102 B4
Kirkland D & G 109 M3
Kirkland D & G 115 P5
Kirkland D & G 115 R9
Kirkland Guards Cumb 100 G2
Kirkleatham R & Cl 104 G6
Kirk Langley Derbys 71 P7
Kirkleavington S on T 104 D9
Kirkley Suffk 65 Q3
Kirklington N York 97 M4
Kirklington Notts 85 L9
Kirklinton Cumb 110 H7
Kirkliston C Edin 127 L3
Kirkmabreck D & G 107 N6
Kirkmaiden D & G 106 F10
Kirk Merrington Dur 103 Q4
Kirk Michael IoM 80 d3
Kirkmichael P & K 141 Q6
Kirkmichael S Ayrs 114 F6
Kirkmuirhill S Lans 126 D9
Kirknewton Nthumb 118 H4
Kirknewton W Loth 127 L4
Kirkney Abers 158 D11
Kirk of Shotts N Lans 126 E5
Kirkoswald Cumb 101 Q2
Kirkoswald S Ayrs 114 D6
Kirkpatrick D & G 109 K2
Kirkpatrick Durham D & G 108 G6
Kirkpatrick-Fleming D & G 110 E6
Kirk Sandall Donc 91 Q9
Kirksanton Cumb 94 C4
Kirk Smeaton N York 91 N7
Kirkstall Leeds 90 H3
Kirkstead Lincs 86 G8
Kirkstile Abers 158 D10
Kirkstile D & G 110 G2
Kirkstone Pass Inn Cumb 101 M9
Kirkstyle Highld 167 P2
Kirkthorpe Wakefd 91 K6
Kirkton Abers 150 G2
Kirkton D & G 109 L4
Kirkton Fife 135 K2
Kirkton Highld 145 P2
Kirkton Highld 154 B9
Kirkton P & K 134 B4
Kirkton Manor Border 117 J3
Kirkton of Airlie Angus 142 E7
Kirkton of Auchterhouse Angus 142 E10
Kirkton of Barevan Highld 156 E8
Kirkton of Collace P & K 142 B11
Kirkton of Glenbuchat Abers 150 B4
Kirkton of Kingoldrum Angus 142 E6
Kirkton of Lethendy P & K 142 A9
Kirkton of Logie Buchan Abers 151 P2
Kirkton of Maryculter Abers 151 M8
Kirkton of Menmuir Angus 143 J5
Kirkton of Monikie Angus 143 J10
Kirkton of Rayne Abers 158 G11
Kirkton of Skene Abers 151 L6
Kirkton of Tealing Angus 142 G10
Kirkton of Tough Abers 150 G5
Kirktown Abers 159 N4
Kirktown Abers 159 Q7
Kirktown of Alvah Abers 158 G5
Kirktown of Bourtie Abers 151 L2
Kirktown of Fetteresso Abers 151 M10
Kirktown of Mortlach Moray 157 Q10
Kirktown of Slains Abers 151 Q2
Kirkurd Border 116 G2
Kirkwall Ork 169 d5
Kirkwall Airport Ork 169 d6
Kirkwhelpington Nthumb 112 E4
Kirk Yetholm Border 118 F5
Kirmington N Linc 93 K8
Kirmond le Mire Lincs 86 G2
Kirn Ag & B 124 F2
Kirriemuir Angus 142 F7
Kirstead Green Norfk 65 K2
Kirtlebridge D & G 110 D6
Kirtling Cambs 63 L9
Kirtling Green Cambs 63 L9
Kirtlington Oxon 48 E11
Kirtomy Highld 166 B4
Kirton Lincs 74 F3
Kirton Notts 85 L7
Kirton Suffk 53 N3
Kirton End Lincs 74 E2
Kirtonhill W Duns 125 K2
Kirton Holme Lincs 74 E2
Kirton in Lindsey N Linc 92 F11
Kirwaugh D & G 107 M7
Kishorn Highld 153 Q10
Kislingbury Nhants 60 E9
Kitebrook Warwks 47 P8
Kite Green Warwks 59 J11
Kites Hardwick Warwks 59 Q11
Kitleigh Cnwll 5 L2
Kitt Green Wigan 88 G9
Kittisford Somset 18 E10
Kittle Swans 28 G7
Kitts Green Birm 59 J7
Kittybrewster C Aber 151 N6
Kitwood Hants 23 J8
Kivernoll Herefs 45 P8
Kiveton Park Rothm 84 G4
Knaith Lincs 85 P4
Knaith Park Lincs 85 P3
Knap Corner Dorset 20 F10
Knaphill Surrey 23 Q3
Knapp Somset 19 K9
Knapp Hill Hants 22 D10
Knapthorpe Notts 85 M9
Knapton C York 98 B10
Knapton N York 98 H5
Knapton Norfk 77 L5
Knapton Green Herefs 45 N4
Knapwell Cambs 62 D8
Knaresborough N York 97 M9
Knarsdale Nthumb 111 N10
Knaven Abers 159 L9
Knayton N York 97 P3
Knebworth Herts 50 F6
Knedlington E R Yk 92 B5
Kneesall Notts 85 M8
Kneeton Notts 85 M11
Knelston Swans 28 E7
Knenhall Staffs 70 G6
Knettishall Suffk 64 D5

Knightacott Devon 17 M4
Knightcote Warwks 48 D4
Knightley Staffs 70 E9
Knightley Dale Staffs 70 E10
Knighton BCP 12 H5
Knighton C Leic 72 G10
Knighton Devon 6 E7
Knighton Dorset 11 N2
Knighton Powys 56 D10
Knighton Somset 18 G6
Knighton Staffs 70 C6
Knighton Staffs 70 D9
Knighton Wilts 33 Q10
Knighton on Teme Worcs 57 L11
Knightsbridge Gloucs 46 G9
Knightsmill Cnwll 4 H5
Knightwick Worcs 46 D3
Knill Herefs 45 K2
Knipoch Ag & B 130 G3
Knipton Leics 73 L4
Knitsley Dur 112 H11
Kniveton Derbys 71 N4
Knock Cumb 102 C5
Knock Highld 145 L6
Knock Moray 158 D7
Knock W Isls 168 j4
Knockally Highld 167 K11
Knockan Highld 161 L4
Knockando Moray 157 M9
Knockbain Highld 155 Q9
Knockbain Highld 156 A6
Knock Castle N Ayrs 124 F5
Knockdee Highld 167 L4
Knockdow Ag & B 124 E3
Knockdown Wilts 32 F7
Knockeen S Ayrs 114 F8
Knockenkelly N Ayrs 121 K6
Knockentiber E Ayrs 125 L10
Knockhall Kent 37 N6
Knockholt Kent 37 L9
Knockholt Pound Kent 37 L9
Knockin Shrops 69 K10
Knockinlaw E Ayrs 125 L10
Knockmill Kent 37 N8
Knocknain Highld 106 C5
Knockrome Ag & B 123 J5
Knocksharry IoM 80 c4
Knocksheen D & G 108 C4
Knockvennie Smithy D & G 108 G6
Knodishall Suffk 65 N9
Knodishall Common Suffk 65 N9
Knole Somset 19 N9
Knole Park S Glos 31 Q8
Knolls Green Ches E 82 H9
Knolton Wrexhm 69 L7
Knook Wilts 20 H6
Knossington Leics 73 L9
Knott End-on-Sea Lancs 94 H11
Knotting Bed 61 M8
Knotting Green Bed 61 M8
Knottingley Wakefd 91 N6
Knotty Ash Lpool 81 N6
Knotty Green Bucks 35 P6
Knowbury Shrops 57 K9
Knowe D & G 107 K3
Knowehead D & G 115 M9
Knoweside S Ayrs 114 E5
Knowl Hill W & M 35 M9
Knowle Bristl 32 B10
Knowle Devon 9 J4
Knowle Devon 9 P3
Knowle Devon 9 Q8
Knowle Devon 6 H4
Knowle Shrops 57 K10
Knowle Solhll 59 J9
Knowle Somset 18 C6
Knowle Cross Devon 9 P5
Knowlefield Cumb 110 H9
Knowle Green Lancs 89 J3
Knowle Hill Surrey 35 Q11
Knowle St Giles Somset 10 G2
Knowle Village Hants 14 G5
Knowle Wood Calder 89 Q6
Knowl Green Essex 52 C3
Knowl Hill W & M 35 M9
Knowlton Dorset 12 H3
Knowlton Kent 39 N11
Knowsley Knows 81 N5
Knowsley Safari Park Knows 81 P6
Knowstone Devon 17 Q7
Knox N York 97 L9
Knox Bridge Kent 26 C3
Knoydart Highld 145 P7
Knucklas Powys 56 D10
Knuston Nhants 61 K7
Knutsford Ches E 82 F9
Knutsford Services Ches E 82 F9
Knutton Staffs 70 E5
Krumlin Calder 90 D7
Kuggar Cnwll 3 J10
Kyleakin Highld 145 N2
Kyle of Lochalsh Highld 145 N2
Kylerhea Highld 145 N3
Kylesku Highld 164 F10
Kylesmorar Highld 145 P9
Kyles Scalpay W Isls 168 h8
Kylestrome Highld 164 F10
Kynaston Herefs 46 B7
Kynaston Shrops 69 L10
Kynnersley Wrekin 70 B11
Kyre Green Worcs 46 B2
Kyre Park Worcs 46 B2
Kyrewood Worcs 57 K11
Kyrle Somset 18 E10

L

La Bellieuse Guern 10 b2
Lacasaigh W Isls 168 i5
Lacasdal W Isls 168 j4
Laceby NE Lin 93 M9
Lacey Green Bucks 35 M4
Lach Dennis Ches W 82 F10
Lackford Suffk 63 N6
Lackford Green Suffk 63 N6
Lacock Wilts 32 H11
Ladbroke Warwks 48 D3
Ladderedge Staffs 70 H4
Laddingford Kent 37 Q11
Lade Bank Lincs 87 L10
Ladock Cnwll 3 M3
Lady Ork 169 f2
Ladybank Fife 135 J6

Ladycross Cnwll 5 N4
Ladygill S Lans 116 C5
Lady Hall Cumb 94 D3
Ladykirk Border 129 M10
Ladyridge Herefs 46 A8
Lady's Green Suffk 63 N9
Ladywood Birm 58 G7
Ladywood Worcs 46 G2
La Fontenelle Guern 10 c1
La Fosse Guern 10 b2
Lag D & G 109 J3
Laga Highld 138 A5
Lagavulin Ag & B 122 F10
Lagg N Ayrs 121 J7
Laggan Highld 146 H8
Laggan Highld 147 Q9
Lagganlia Highld 148 F7
La Greve Guern 10 c1
La Grève de Lecq Jersey 11 a1
La Hougue Bie Jersey 11 c2
La Houguette Guern 10 b2
Laid Highld 165 K5
Laide Highld 160 E8
Laig Highld 144 G10
Laigh Clunch E Ayrs 125 M8
Laigh Fenwick E Ayrs 125 M9
Laigh Glenmuir E Ayrs 115 M3
Laighstonehall S Lans 126 C7
Laindon Essex 37 Q3
Lairg Highld 162 D5
Laisterdyke C Brad 90 F4
Laithes Cumb 101 N4
Lake Devon 8 D7
Lake Devon 17 K5
Lake IoW 14 G10
Lake Wilts 21 M7
Lake District Cumb 100 H8
Lake District National Park Cumb 100 H8
Lakenheath Suffk 63 M4
Laker's Green Surrey 24 B3
Lakes End Norfk 75 K11
Lakeside Cumb 94 H3
Laleham Surrey 36 C7
Laleston Brdgnd 29 N9
Lamanva Cnwll 3 K7
Lamarsh Essex 52 E4
Lamas Norfk 77 J7
Lambden Border 118 D2
Lamberhurst Kent 25 Q3
Lamberhurst Down Kent 25 Q3
Lamberton Border 129 P8
Lambeth Gt Lon 36 H5
Lambfair Green Suffk 63 M10
Lambley Notts 85 K11
Lambley Nthumb 111 N9
Lambourn W Berk 34 B9
Lambourne End Essex 37 L2
Lambourn Woodlands W Berk 34 B9
Lamb Roe Lancs 89 L3
Lambs Green W Susx 24 F3
Lambston Pembks 40 H7
Lamellion Cnwll 5 L9
Lamerton Devon 8 C9
Lamesley Gatesd 113 L9
Lamington S Lans 116 D4
Lamlash N Ayrs 121 K6
Lamonby Cumb 101 M3
Lamorick Cnwll 4 G9
Lamorna Cnwll 2 C9
Lamorran Cnwll 3 M5
Lampen Cnwll 5 K8
Lampeter Cerdgn 43 L5
Lampeter Velfrey Pembks 41 N8
Lamphey Pembks 41 K10
Lamplugh Cumb 100 E6
Lamport Nhants 60 G6
Lamyatt Somset 20 C7
Lana Devon 5 N2
Lana Devon 16 E10
Lanark S Lans 116 B2
Lancaster Lancs 95 K8
Lancaster Services Lancs 95 L10
Lancaut Gloucs 31 P5
Lanchester Dur 113 J11
Lancing W Susx 24 E10
L'Ancresse Guern 10 c1
Landbeach Cambs 62 G7
Landcross Devon 16 H7
Landerberry Abers 151 J7
Landford Wilts 21 Q11
Land-hallow Highld 167 L10
Landimore Swans 28 E6
Landkey Devon 17 K5
Landore Swans 29 J5
Landrake Cnwll 5 P9
Landscove Devon 7 K5
Land's End Cnwll 2 A8
Land's End Airport Cnwll 2 B8
Landshipping Pembks 41 K8
Landue Cnwll 5 P6
Landulph Cnwll 6 C6
Landwade Suffk 63 K7
Lane Cnwll 4 C9
Laneast Cnwll 5 L5
Lane Bottom Lancs 89 P3
Lane End Bucks 35 M6
Lane End Cnwll 4 G8
Lane End Hants 22 G9
Lane End Kent 37 N6
Lane End Lancs 96 C11
Lane End Warrtn 82 E6
Lane End Wilts 20 F5
Lane Ends Derbys 71 N8
Lane Ends Lancs 89 M4
Lane Ends N York 90 B2
Lane Green Staffs 58 C4
Laneham Notts 85 P5
Lanehead Dur 102 F2
Lane Head Dur 103 M8
Lanehead Nthumb 111 Q3
Lane Head Wigan 82 D5
Lane Head Wsall 58 E4
Lane Heads Lancs 88 E3
Lanercost Cumb 111 L8
Laneshaw Bridge Lancs 89 Q2
Lane Side Lancs 89 M6
Langaford Devon 5 P2
Langal Highld 138 C4
Langaller Somset 19 J9
Langar Notts 73 J4
Langbank Rens 125 K3
Langbar N York 96 G10
Langbaurgh N York 104 G8

Langcliffe N York 96 B8
Langdale End N York 99 J2
Langdon Cnwll 5 N4
Langdon Beck Dur 102 G4
Langdown Hants 14 D5
Langdyke Fife 135 J7
Langenhoe Essex 52 H8
Langford C Beds 50 E2
Langford Devon 9 P4
Langford Essex 52 D10
Langford N Som 19 N2
Langford Notts 85 P9
Langford Oxon 33 P4
Langford Budville Somset 18 F10
Langham Dorset 20 E9
Langham Essex 52 H5
Langham Norfk 76 E3
Langham Rutlnd 73 L8
Langham Suffk 64 D8
Langho Lancs 89 L4
Langholm D & G 110 G4
Langland Swans 28 H7
Langlee Border 117 Q3
Langley Ches E 83 K10
Langley Derbys 84 F11
Langley Gloucs 47 K9
Langley Hants 14 D6
Langley Herts 50 F6
Langley Kent 38 D11
Langley Nthumb 112 B8
Langley Oxon 47 Q11
Langley Rochdl 89 P9
Langley Slough 36 B5
Langley Somset 18 E9
Langley W Susx 23 M9
Langley Warwks 47 N2
Langley Burrell Wilts 32 H9
Langley Castle Nthumb 112 B8
Langley Common Derbys 71 P7
Langley Green Derbys 71 P7
Langley Green Essex 52 E7
Langley Green Warwks 47 N2
Langley Heath Kent 38 D11
Langley Lower Green Essex 51 K4
Langley Marsh Somset 18 E9
Langley Mill Derbys 84 F11
Langley Moor Dur 103 Q2
Langley Park Dur 113 K11
Langley Street Norfk 77 M11
Langley Upper Green Essex 51 K4
Langley Vale Surrey 36 F9
Langney E Susx 25 P10
Langold Notts 85 J3
Langore Cnwll 5 M4
Langport Somset 19 M9
Langrick Lincs 87 J11
Langridge BaNES 32 D11
Langridgeford Devon 17 K7
Langrigg Cumb 110 C11
Langrish Hants 23 K10
Langsett Barns 90 G10
Langside P & K 133 M5
Langstone Hants 15 K6
Langstone Newpt 31 L7
Langthorne N York 97 K2
Langthorpe N York 97 N7
Langthwaite N York 103 K10
Langtoft E R Yk 99 L7
Langtoft Lincs 74 B8
Langton Dur 103 N7
Langton Lincs 86 H7
Langton Lincs 87 L6
Langton N York 98 F7
Langton by Wragby Lincs 86 F5
Langton Green Kent 25 M3
Langton Green Suffk 64 G7
Langton Herring Dorset 11 N8
Langton Long Blandford
Dorset 12 F3
Langton Matravers Dorset 12 H9
Langtree Devon 16 H8
Langtree Week Devon 16 H8
Langwathby Cumb 101 Q4
Langwell House Highld 163 Q2
Langwith Derbys 84 H7
Langwith Junction Derbys 84 H7
Langworth Lincs 86 E5
Lanhydrock House &
Gardens Cnwll 4 H9
Lanivet Cnwll 4 G9
Lanjeth Cnwll 3 P3
Lank Cnwll 4 H6
Lanlivery Cnwll 4 H10
Lanner Cnwll 3 J6
Lanoy Cnwll 5 N6
Lanreath Cnwll 5 K10
Lansallos Cnwll 5 K11
Lanteglos Cnwll 4 H5
Lanteglos Highway Cnwll 5 J11
Lanton Border 118 B6
Lanton Nthumb 118 H4
La Passee Guern 10 b1
Lapford Devon 8 H3
Laphroaig Ag & B 122 E10
Lapley Staffs 58 C2
La Pulente Jersey 11 a2
Lapworth Warwks 59 J10
Larachbeg Highld 138 B8
Larbert Falk 133 P11
Larbreck Lancs 88 E2
Largie Abers 158 F11
Largiemore Ag & B 131 J10
Largoward Fife 135 M6
Largs N Ayrs 124 G6
Largybeg N Ayrs 121 K7
Largymore N Ayrs 121 K7
Larkbeare Devon 9 Q5
Larkfield Inver 124 G2
Larkfield Kent 38 B10
Larkhall S Lans 126 D7
Larkhill Wilts 21 M6
Larling Norfk 64 D4
La Rocque Jersey 11 c2
La Rousaillerie Guern 10 b1
Lartington Dur 103 K7
Lasborough Gloucs 32 F6
Lasham Hants 23 J6
Lashbrook Devon 8 B3
Lashbrook Devon 16 G10
Lashenden Kent 26 D3
Lask Edge Staffs 70 G3
Lasswade Mdloth 127 Q4
Lastingham N York 98 E2
Latcham Somset 19 M5
Latchford Herts 51 J6

Latchford Oxon 35 J4
Latchford Warrtn 82 D7
Latchingdon Essex 52 E11
Latchley Cnwll 5 Q7
Lately Common Warrtn 82 E5
Lathbury M Keyn 49 N6
Latheron Highld 167 M10
Latheronwheel Highld 167 L10
Lathom Lancs 88 F8
Lathones Fife 135 M6
Latimer Bucks 50 B11
Latteridge S Glos 32 C8
Lattiford Somset 20 C9
Latton Wilts 33 L5
Lauder Border 128 E10
Laugharne Carmth 28 B2
Laughterton Lincs 85 P5
Laughton E Susx 25 L8
Laughton Leics 60 E3
Laughton Lincs 74 A4
Laughton Lincs 92 D11
Laughton-en-le-Morthen
Rothm 84 H3
Launcells Cnwll 16 C10
Launcells Cross Cnwll 16 D10
Launceston Cnwll 5 N5
Launton Oxon 48 H10
Laurencekirk Abers 143 N3
Laurieston D & G 108 E8
Laurieston Falk 126 G2
Lavendon M Keyn 49 P4
Lavenham Suffk 52 F2
Lavernock V Glam 30 G11
Laversdale Cumb 111 J8
Laverstock Wilts 21 N8
Laverstoke Hants 22 E5
Laverton Gloucs 47 L7
Laverton N York 97 K6
Laverton Somset 20 E4
La Villette Guern 10 b2
Lavister Wrexhm 69 L3
Law S Lans 126 E7
Lawers P & K 140 G10
Lawford Essex 53 J5
Lawford Somset 18 F7
Law Hill S Lans 126 E7
Lawhitton Cnwll 5 P5
Lawkland N York 95 R7
Lawkland Green N York 96 A7
Lawley Wrekin 57 M3
Lawnhead Staffs 70 E9
Lawrence Weston Bristl 31 P9
Lawrenny Pembks 41 K9
Lawshall Suffk 64 B11
Lawshall Green Suffk 64 B11
Lawton Herefs 45 N3
Laxay W Isls 168 i5
Laxdale W Isls 168 j4
Laxey IoM 80 f5
Laxfield Suffk 65 K7
Laxford Bridge Highld 164 F7
Laxo Shet 169 r7
Laxton E R Yk 92 C5
Laxton Nhants 73 P11
Laxton Notts 85 M7
Laycock C Brad 90 C2
Layer Breton Essex 52 F8
Layer-de-la-Haye Essex 52 G7
Layer Marney Essex 52 F8
Layham Suffk 52 H3
Layland's Green W Berk 34 C11
Laymore Dorset 10 H4
Layter's Green Bucks 35 Q6
Laytham E R Yk 92 B3
Laythes Cumb 110 D9
Lazenby R & Cl 104 E7
Lazonby Cumb 101 P3
Lea Derbys 84 D9
Lea Herefs 46 C10
Lea Lincs 85 P3
Lea Shrops 56 F7
Lea Shrops 56 G3
Lea Wilts 33 J7
Leachkin Highld 156 A8
Leadburn Border 127 N6
Leadenham Lincs 86 B10
Leaden Roding Essex 51 N8
Leadgate Cumb 102 D2
Leadgate Dur 112 H10
Leadgate Nthumb 112 H9
Leadhills S Lans 116 B7
Leadingcross Green Kent 38 C11
Leadmill Derbys 84 B4
Leafield Oxon 48 B11
Leagrave Luton 50 C6
Leahead Ches W 70 B2
Lea Heath Staffs 71 J9
Leake N York 97 P2
Leake Common Side Lincs 87 L10
Lealholm N York 105 L9
Lealholm Side N York 105 L9
Lealt Highld 153 J5
Leam Derbys 84 B5
Lea Marston Warwks 59 K6
Leamington Hastings
Warwks 59 P11
Leamington Spa Warwks 59 M11
Leamside Dur 113 M11
Leap Cross E Susx 25 N8
Leasgill Cumb 95 K4
Leasingham Lincs 86 E11
Leasingthorne Dur 103 Q4
Leatherhead Surrey 36 E9
Leathley N York 97 K11
Leaton Shrops 69 N11
Leaton Wrekin L2
Lea Town Lancs 88 F4
Leaveland Kent 38 H11
Leavenheath Suffk 52 G4
Leavening N York 98 F8
Leaves Green Gt Lon 37 K8
Lea Yeat Cumb 95 R3
Lebberston N York 99 M4
Le Bigard Guern 10 b2
Le Bourg Guern 10 b2
Le Bourg Jersey 11 c2
Lechlade on Thames Gloucs 33 P5
Lecht Gruinart Ag & B 122 C6
Leck Lancs 95 N5
Leckbuie P & K 140 H9
Leckford Hants 22 C7
Leckhampstead Bucks 49 K7
Leckhampstead W Berk 34 D9
Leckhampstead Thicket
W Berk 34 D9

Leckhampton Gloucs 46 H11
Leckmelm Highld 161 K9
Leckwith V Glam 30 G10
Leconfield E R Yk 92 H2
Ledaig Ag & B 138 G10
Ledburn Bucks 49 P10
Ledbury Herefs 46 D7
Leddington Gloucs 46 C8
Ledgemoor Herefs 45 N4
Ledicot Herefs 45 N2
Ledmore Highld 161 L4
Ledsham Ches W 81 M10
Ledsham Leeds 91 M5
Ledston Leeds 91 L5
Ledstone Devon 7 J9
Ledston Luck Leeds 91 L4
Ledwell Oxon 48 D9
Lee Devon 16 H2
Lee Gt Lon 37 J5
Lee Hants 22 C11
Lee Shrops 69 M8
Leebotwood Shrops 56 H5
Lee Brockhurst Shrops 69 P9
Leece Cumb 94 E7
Lee Chapel Essex 37 Q3
Lee Clump Bucks 35 P4
Lee Common Bucks 35 P4
Leeds Kent 38 D11
Leeds Leeds 90 H4
Leeds Bradford Airport
Leeds 90 G2
Leeds Castle Kent 38 D11
Leedstown Cnwll 2 G7
Lee Green Ches E 70 B2
Leek Staffs 70 H3
Leek Wootton Warwks 59 L11
Lee Mill Devon 6 F7
Leeming C Brad 90 C4
Leeming N York 97 L3
Leeming Bar N York 97 L3
Lee Moor Devon 6 F6
Lee-on-the-Solent Hants 14 G6
Lees C Brad 90 C3
Lees Derbys 71 P7
Lees Oldham 83 L4
Lees Green Derbys 71 P7
Leesthorpe Leics 73 K8
Leeswood Flints 69 J2
Leetown P & K 134 G3
Leftwich Ches W 82 E10
Legar Powys 45 J11
Legbourne Lincs 87 L4
Legburthwaite Cumb 101 K7
Legerwood Border 118 A2
Legoland W & M 35 P10
Le Gron Guern 10 b2
Legsby Lincs 86 F3
La Haguais Jersey 11 c2
Le Hocq Jersey 11 c2
Leicester C Leic 72 F10
Leicester Forest East Leics 72 E10
Leicester Forest East
Services Leics 72 E10
Leigh Devon 17 N9
Leigh Dorset 11 N3
Leigh Gloucs 46 G9
Leigh Kent 37 M3
Leigh Shrops 56 E4
Leigh Surrey 36 F11
Leigh Wigan 82 E5
Leigh Wilts 33 L4
Leigh Worcs 46 E4
Leigh Beck Essex 38 D5
Leigh Delamere Wilts 32 G9
Leigh Delamere Services
Wilts 32 G9
Leigh Green Kent 26 F5
Leigh Knoweglass S Lans 125 Q6
Leighland Chapel Somset 18 D7
Leigh-on-Sea Sthend 38 D4
Leigh Park Dorset 12 H5
Leigh Park Hants 15 K5
Leigh Sinton Worcs 46 E4
Leighswood Wsall 58 G4
Leighterton Gloucs 32 F6
Leighton N York 97 J5
Leighton Powys 56 C3
Leighton Shrops 57 L3
Leighton Somset 20 D6
Leighton Bromswold Cambs 61 P5
Leighton Buzzard C Beds 49 P9
Leigh upon Mendip Somset 20 C5
Leigh Woods N Som 31 Q10
Leinthall Earls Herefs 56 G11
Leinthall Starkes Herefs 56 G11
Leintwardine Herefs 56 G10
Leire Leics 60 B3
Leiston Suffk 65 N9
Leith C Edin 127 P2
Leitholm Border 118 E2
Lelant Cnwll 2 E6
Lelley E R Yk 93 M4
Lem Hill Worcs 57 N9
Lemreway W Isls 168 i6
Lemsford Herts 50 F8
Lenchwick Worcs 47 K5
Lendalfoot S Ayrs 114 B9
Lendrick Stirlg 132 H6
Lendrum Terrace Abers 159 R9
Lenham Kent 38 E11
Lenham Heath Kent 26 F2
Lenie Highld 147 N2
Lennel Border 118 G2
Lennox Plunton D & G 108 D10
Lennoxtown E Duns 125 Q3
Lent Bucks 35 P8
Lenton C Nott 72 F3
Lenton Lincs 73 Q4
Lenwade Norfk 76 F8
Lenzie E Duns 126 B3
Leochel-Cushnie Abers 150 G5
Leomansley Staffs 58 H3
Leominster Herefs 45 P3
Leonard Stanley Gloucs 32 F4
Leoville Jersey 11 a1
Lepe Hants 14 D7
Lephin Highld 152 B8
Leppington N York 98 F8
Lepton Kirk 90 G7
Lerags Ag & B 130 H2
L'Erée Guern 10 a2
Lerryn Cnwll 5 J10
Lerwick Shet 169 r9
Les Arquêts Guern 10 b2

Lesbury Nthumb 119 P8
Les Hubits Guern 10 c2
Leslie Abers 150 F3
Leslie Fife 134 H7
Les Lohiers Guern 10 b2
Les Murchez Guern 10 b2
Lesnewth Cnwll 5 J3
Les Nicolles Guern 10 b2
Les Quartiers Guern 10 c1
Les Quennevais Jersey 11 a2
Les Sages Guern 10 b2
Lessingham Norfk 77 M6
Lessonhall Cumb 110 D10
Lestowder Cnwll 3 K9
Les Villets Guern 10 b2
Leswalt D & G 106 C5
L'Etacq Jersey 11 a1
Letchmore Heath Herts 50 E11
Letchworth Garden City
Herts 50 F4
Letcombe Bassett Oxon 34 C8
Letcombe Regis Oxon 34 C7
Letham Angus 143 J8
Letham Border 118 C9
Letham Falk 133 P10
Letham Fife 135 J5
Letham Grange Angus 143 L8
Lethenty Abers 150 F3
Lethenty Abers 159 K9
Letheringham Suffk 65 K10
Letheringsett Norfk 76 F3
Lettaford Devon 8 H8
Letterewe Highld 154 C3
Letterfearn Highld 145 Q3
Letterfinlay Lodge Hotel
Highld 146 H9
Lettermorar Highld 145 M10
Letters Highld 161 K9
Lettershaw S Lans 116 B6
Letterston Pembks 40 H5
Lettoch Highld 149 J4
Lettoch Highld 157 L11
Letton Herefs 45 L5
Letton Herefs 56 F10
Lett's Green Kent 37 L9
Letty Green Herts 50 G8
Letwell Rothm 85 J3
Leuchars Fife 135 M3
Leumrabhagh W Isls 168 i6
Leurbost W Isls 168 i5
Levalsa Meor Cnwll 3 Q4
Levedale Staffs 70 F11
Level's Green Essex 51 L6
Leven E R Yk 99 N11
Leven Fife 135 K7
Levens Cumb 95 K3
Levens Green Herts 51 J6
Levenshulme Manch 83 J6
Levenwick Shet 169 r11
Leverburgh W Isls 168 f9
Leverington Cambs 74 H8
Leverstock Green Herts 50 C9
Leverton Lincs 87 M11
Le Villocq Guern 10 b1
Levington Suffk 53 M4
Levisham N York 98 G2
Lew Oxon 34 B3
Lewannick Cnwll 5 M5
Lewdown Devon 8 C7
Lewes E Susx 25 K8
Leweston Pembks 40 H6
Lewisham Gt Lon 37 J5
Lewiston Highld 147 N2
Lewistown Brdgnd 29 P7
Lewis Wych Herefs 45 L3
Lewknor Oxon 35 K5
Leworthy Devon 16 E11
Leworthy Devon 17 M4
Lewson Street Kent 38 G9
Lewth Lancs 88 F3
Lewtrenchard Devon 8 C7
Lexden Essex 52 G6
Lexworthy Somset 19 J7
Ley Cnwll 5 K8
Leybourne Kent 37 Q9
Leyburn N York 96 H2
Leycett Staffs 70 D5
Leygreen Herts 50 E6
Ley Hill Bucks 35 Q4
Leyland Lancs 88 G6
Leyland Green St Hel 82 C4
Leylodge Abers 151 K5
Leys Abers 159 P7
Leys P & K 142 D10
Leysdown-on-Sea Kent 38 H7
Leysmill Angus 143 L8
Leys of Cossans Angus 142 F8
Leysters Herefs 45 P2
Leyton Gt Lon 37 J3
Leytonstone Gt Lon 37 J3
Lezant Cnwll 5 N6
Lezerea Cnwll 2 H7
Lhanbryde Moray 157 P5
Libanus Powys 44 D9
Libberton S Lans 116 D2
Libbery Worcs 47 J3
Liberton C Edin 127 P4
Lichfield Staffs 58 H3
Lickey Worcs 58 E10
Lickey End Worcs 58 E10
Lickey Rock Worcs 58 E10
Lickfold W Susx 23 P9
Liddaton Green Devon 8 B8
Liddesdale Highld 138 D6
Liddington Swindn 33 P8
Lidgate Derbys 84 D5
Lidgate Suffk 63 M9
Lidget Donc 91 R10
Lidgett Notts 85 M7
Lidham Hill E Susx 26 D8
Lidlington C Beds 49 Q7
Lidsey W Susx 15 P6
Lidsing Kent 38 C9
Liff Angus 142 E11
Lifford Birm 58 G8
Lifton Devon 5 P5
Liftondown Devon 5 P5
Lighthorne Warwks 48 B3
Lighthorne Heath Warwks 48 C3
Lightwater Surrey 23 P2
Lightwater Valley Theme
Park N York 97 L5
Lightwood C Stke 70 G6
Lightwood Green Ches E 70 A6

Lightwood Green Wrexhm 69 L6
Lilbourne Nhants 60 C5
Lilburn Tower Nthumb 119 K6
Lilleshall Wrekin 70 C11
Lilley Herts 50 D5
Lilley W Berk 34 D9
Lilliesleaf Border 117 Q5
Lillingstone Dayrell Bucks 49 K7
Lillingstone Lovell Bucks 49 K6
Lillington Dorset 11 N2
Lilliput BCP 12 H7
Lilstock Somset 18 G5
Lilyhurst Shrops 57 N2
Limbrick Lancs 89 J7
Limbury Luton 50 C6
Limebrook Herefs 56 F11
Limefield Bury 89 N8
Limekilnburn S Lans 126 C7
Limekilns Fife 134 D11
Limerigg Falk 126 F3
Limerstone IoW 14 D10
Limestone Brae Nthumb 111 Q11
Lime Street Worcs 46 F8
Limington Somset 19 P10
Limmerhaugh E Ayrs 115 M2
Limpenhoe Norfk 77 M11
Limpley Stoke Wilts 20 E2
Limpsfield Surrey 37 K10
Limpsfield Chart Surrey 37 K10
Linby Notts 84 H10
Linchmere W Susx 23 N8
Lincluden D & G 109 L5
Lincoln Lincs 86 C6
Lincomb Worcs 57 Q11
Lincombe Devon 7 J10
Lincombe Devon 16 H2
Lindale Cumb 95 J4
Lindal in Furness Cumb 94 E5
Lindfield W Susx 24 H5
Lindford Hants 23 M7
Lindley Kirk 90 E7
Lindley N York 97 K11
Lindores Fife 134 H4
Lindow End Ches E 82 H9
Lindridge Worcs 57 M11
Lindsell Essex 51 P5
Lindsey Suffk 52 G2
Lindsey Tye Suffk 52 G2
Liney Somset 19 L7
Linford Hants 13 L3
Linford Thurr 37 Q5
Lingbob C Brad 90 D3
Lingdale R & Cl 105 J7
Lingen Herefs 56 F11
Lingfield Surrey 25 J2
Lingwood Norfk 77 M10
Liniclate W Isls 168 c13
Linicro Highld 152 F4
Linkend Worcs 46 F8
Linkenholt Hants 22 C4
Linkhill Kent 26 D6
Linkinhorne Cnwll 5 N7
Linktown Fife 134 H9
Linkwood Moray 157 N5
Linley Shrops 56 F6
Linley Green Herefs 46 C4
Linleygreen Shrops 57 M5
Linlithgow W Loth 126 H2
Linshiels Nthumb 118 G9
Linsidemore Highld 162 C4
Linslade C Beds 49 P9
Linstead Parva Suffk 65 L6
Linstock Cumb 110 H9
Linthurst Worcs 58 E10
Linthwaite Kirk 90 E8
Lintlaw Border 129 L8
Lintmill Moray 158 D4
Linton Border 118 E5
Linton Cambs 63 J11
Linton Derbys 71 P11
Linton Herefs 46 C9
Linton Kent 38 C11
Linton Leeds 97 N11
Linton N York 96 E8
Linton Nthumb 113 L2
Linton Heath Derbys 71 P11
Linton Hill Herefs 46 C10
Linton-on-Ouse N York 97 Q8
Linwood Hants 13 L3
Linwood Lincs 86 F3
Linwood Rens 125 L5
Lionacleit W Isls 168 c13
Lional W Isls 168 k1
Lions Green E Susx 25 N7
Liphook Hants 23 M8
Lipley Shrops 70 C8
Liscard Wirral 81 K6
Liscombe Somset 18 A8
Liskeard Cnwll 5 M9
Lismore Ag & B 138 G9
Liss Hants 23 L9
Lissett E R Yk 99 N9
Liss Forest Hants 23 L9
Lissington Lincs 86 F4
Liston Essex 52 E3
Lisvane Cardif 30 G8
Liswerry Newpt 31 K7
Litcham Norfk 76 B9
Litchborough Nhants 48 H4
Litchfield Hants 22 E4
Litherland Sefton 81 L5
Litlington Cambs 50 H2
Litlington E Susx 25 M10
Little Abington Cambs 62 H11
Little Addington Nhants 61 L6
Little Airies D & G 107 M8
Little Almshoe Herts 50 F5
Little Alne Warwks 47 M2
Little Altcar Sefton 88 C8
Little Amwell Herts 51 J8
Little Asby Cumb 102 C9
Little Aston Staffs 58 G5
Little Atherfield IoW 14 E11
Little Ayton N York 104 G8
Little Baddow Essex 52 C10
Little Badminton S Glos 32 F8
Little Bampton Cumb 110 D9
Little Bardfield Essex 51 Q4
Little Barford Bed 61 Q9
Little Barningham Norfk 76 G5
Little Barrington Gloucs 33 P2
Little Barrow Ches W 81 P11
Little Barugh N York 98 F5
Little Bavington Nthumb 112 E5
Little Bealings Suffk 53 M2

Place	County	Page	Grid
Littlebeck	N York	105	N10
Little Bedwyn	Wilts	33	Q11
Little Bentley	Essex	53	K6
Little Berkhamsted	Herts	50	G9
Little Billing	Nhants	60	H8
Little Billington	C Beds	49	P10
Little Birch	Herefs	45	Q8
Little Bispham	Bpool	88	C2
Little Blakenham	Suffk	53	K2
Little Blencow	Cumb	101	N4
Little Bloxwich	Wsall	58	F4
Little Bognor	W Susx	24	B6
Little Bolehill	Derbys	71	P4
Little Bollington	Ches E	82	F7
Little Bookham	Surrey	36	D10
Littleborough	Devon	9	K2
Littleborough	Notts	85	P4
Littleborough	Rochdl	89	Q7
Littlebourne	Kent	39	M10
Little Bourton	Oxon	48	E6
Little Bowden	Leics	60	F3
Little Bradley	Suffk	63	L10
Little Brampton	Herefs	45	L2
Little Brampton	Shrops	56	F8
Little Braxted	Essex	52	D9
Little Brechin	Angus	143	K5
Littlebredy	Dorset	11	M7
Little Brickhill	M Keyn	49	P8
Little Bridgeford	Staffs	70	F9
Little Brington	Nhants	60	E8
Little Bromley	Essex	53	J6
Little Broughton	Cumb	100	E4
Little Budworth	Ches W	82	C11
Littleburn	Highld	156	A7
Little Burstead	Essex	37	Q2
Littlebury	Essex	51	M3
Littlebury Green	Essex	51	L3
Little Bytham	Lincs	73	Q7
Little Canfield	Essex	51	N6
Little Carlton	Lincs	87	L3
Little Carlton	Notts	85	N9
Little Casterton	RutInd	73	Q9
Little Catwick	E R Yk	93	K2
Little Catworth	Cambs	61	P6
Little Cawthorpe	Lincs	87	L4
Little Chalfont	Bucks	35	Q5
Little Chart	Kent	26	F2
Little Chesterford	Essex	51	M2
Little Cheveney	Kent	26	B3
Little Cheverell	Wilts	21	J4
Little Chishill	Cambs	51	K3
Little Clacton	Essex	53	L8
Little Clanfield	Oxon	33	Q4
Little Clifton	Cumb	100	E5
Little Coates	NE Lin	93	M9
Little Comberton	Worcs	47	J6
Little Common	E Susx	26	B10
Little Comp	Kent	37	P9
Little Compton	Warwks	47	Q8
Little Corby	Cumb	111	J9
Little Cornard	Suffk	52	F4
Littlecott	Wilts	21	M4
Little Cowarne	Herefs	46	B4
Little Coxwell	Oxon	33	Q6
Little Crakehall	N York	97	K2
Little Cransley	Nhants	60	H5
Little Cressingham	Norfk	76	B11
Little Crosby	Sefton	81	L4
Little Crosthwaite	Cumb	100	H5
Little Cubley	Derbys	71	M7
Little Dalby	Leics	73	K8
Littledean	Gloucs	32	C2
Little Dewchurch	Herefs	45	Q8
Little Ditton	Cambs	63	L9
Little Doward	Herefs	45	Q11
Littledown	Hants	22	H3
Little Downham	Cambs	62	H4
Little Driffield	E R Yk	99	L9
Little Dunham	Norfk	76	B9
Little Dunkeld	P & K	141	P9
Little Dunmow	Essex	51	Q6
Little Durnford	Wilts	21	M8
Little Easton	Essex	51	P6
Little Eaton	Derbys	72	B2
Little Ellingham	Norfk	64	E2
Little Elm	Somset	20	D5
Little Everdon	Nhants	60	C9
Little Eversden	Cambs	62	E10
Little Faringdon	Oxon	33	P4
Little Fencote	N York	97	L2
Little Fenton	N York	91	N3
Littleferry	Highld	163	J7
Little Fransham	Norfk	76	C9
Little Gaddesden	Herts	35	Q2
Little Garway	Herefs	45	N10
Little Gidding	Cambs	61	P4
Little Glemham	Suffk	65	L10
Little Gorsley	Herefs	46	C10
Little Gransden	Cambs	62	C9
Little Green	Notts	73	J2
Little Green	Somset	20	D5
Little Grimsby	Lincs	87	K2
Little Gringley	Notts	85	M4
Little Habton	N York	98	E5
Little Hadham	Herts	51	K6
Little Hale	Lincs	74	B2
Little Hallam	Derbys	72	D2
Little Hallingbury	Essex	51	M7
Littleham	Devon	9	P8
Littleham	Devon	16	G7
Little Hampden	Bucks	35	N4
Littlehampton	W Susx	24	B10
Little Hanford	Dorset	12	D2
Little Harrowden	Nhants	61	J6
Little Haseley	Oxon	34	H4
Little Hatfield	E R Yk	93	K2
Little Hautbois	Norfk	77	K7
Little Haven	Pembks	40	G4
Littlehaven	W Susx	24	E4
Little Hay	Staffs	58	H4
Little Hayfield	Derbys	83	M7
Little Haywood	Staffs	71	J10
Little Heath	Staffs	70	F11
Little Heath	W Berk	35	J10
Littlehempston	Devon	7	L6
Little Hereford	Herefs	57	K11
Little Horkesley	Essex	52	G5
Little Hormead	Herts	51	K5
Little Horsted	E Susx	25	L7
Little Horton	C Brad	90	F4
Little Horton	Wilts	21	K2
Little Horwood	Bucks	49	L8
Little Houghton	Barns	91	L9
Little Houghton	Nhants	60	H9
Littlehoughton	Nthumb	119	P7
Little Hucklow	Derbys	83	Q9
Little Hulton	Salfd	82	F4
Little Hungerford	W Berk	34	F10
Little Hutton	N York	97	Q5
Little Irchester	Nhants	61	K7
Little Kelk	E R Yk	99	M9
Little Keyford	Somset	20	E5
Little Kimble	Bucks	35	M3
Little Kineton	Warwks	48	B4
Little Kingshill	Bucks	35	N5
Little Knox	D & G	108	D9
Little Langdale	Cumb	101	K10
Little Langford	Wilts	21	K7
Little Laver	Essex	51	M9
Little Leigh	Ches W	82	D9
Little Leighs	Essex	52	B8
Little Lever	Bolton	89	M9
Little Linford	M Keyn	49	M6
Little Load	Somset	19	N10
Little London	Bucks	34	H2
Little London	Cambs	74	H11
Little London	E Susx	25	N6
Little London	Essex	51	L5
Little London	Essex	51	Q3
Little London	Gloucs	46	D11
Little London	Hants	22	C5
Little London	Hants	22	H3
Little London	Leeds	90	G3
Little London	Lincs	74	D6
Little London	Lincs	74	H6
Little London	Lincs	87	K6
Little London	Norfk	75	L6
Little London	Powys	55	N7
Little Longstone	Derbys	83	Q10
Little Madeley	Staffs	70	D5
Little Malvern	Worcs	46	E6
Little Mancot	Flints	81	L11
Little Maplestead	Essex	52	D5
Little Marcle	Herefs	46	C7
Little Marland	Devon	17	J9
Little Marlow	Bucks	35	M7
Little Massingham	Norfk	75	Q6
Little Melton	Norfk	76	H10
Littlemill	Abers	149	Q8
Littlemill	Highld	156	G7
Little Mill	Mons	31	K4
Little Milton	Oxon	34	H4
Little Missenden	Bucks	35	P5
Little Mongeham	Kent	39	P11
Littlemoor	Derbys	84	E8
Little Moor	Somset	19	K8
Littlemore	Oxon	34	F4
Little Musgrave	Cumb	102	E8
Little Ness	Shrops	69	M11
Little Neston	Ches W	81	K9
Little Newcastle	Pembks	41	J5
Little Newsham	Dur	103	M7
Little Norton	Somset	19	N11
Little Oakley	Essex	53	M6
Little Oakley	Nhants	61	J3
Little Odell	Bed	61	L9
Little Offley	Herts	50	D5
Little Ormside	Cumb	102	D7
Little Orton	Cumb	110	G9
Little Ouse	Cambs	63	K3
Little Ouseburn	N York	97	P8
Littleover	C Derb	72	A4
Little Oxendon	Nhants	60	F4
Little Packington	Warwks	59	K8
Little Pattenden	Kent	26	B2
Little Paxton	Cambs	61	Q8
Little Petherick	Cnwll	4	E7
Little Plumpton	Lancs	88	D4
Little Plumstead	Norfk	77	L9
Little Ponton	Lincs	73	N4
Littleport	Cambs	63	J3
Littleport Bridge	Cambs	63	J3
Little Posbrook	Hants	14	F6
Little Potheridge	Devon	17	J9
Little Preston	Leeds	91	K4
Little Preston	Nhants	48	G4
Littler	Ches W	82	D11
Little Raveley	Cambs	62	C5
Little Reedness	E R Yk	92	D6
Little Ribston	N York	97	N10
Little Rissington	Gloucs	47	N11
Little Rollright	Oxon	47	Q8
Little Rowsley	Derbys	84	C7
Little Ryburgh	Norfk	76	D6
Little Ryle	Nthumb	119	K8
Little Ryton	Shrops	56	H4
Little Salkeld	Cumb	101	Q3
Little Sampford	Essex	51	Q4
Little Sandhurst	Br For	23	M2
Little Saredon	Staffs	58	D3
Little Saughall	Ches W	81	M11
Little Saxham	Suffk	63	P8
Little Scatwell	Highld	155	L6
Little Shelford	Cambs	62	G10
Little Shrewley	Warwks	59	K11
Little Silver	Devon	9	M3
Little Singleton	Lancs	88	D3
Little Skipwith	N York	91	R3
Little Smeaton	N York	91	N4
Little Snoring	Norfk	76	D5
Little Sodbury	S Glos	32	E8
Little Sodbury End	S Glos	32	D8
Little Somborne	Hants	22	C8
Little Somerford	Wilts	33	J8
Little Soudley	Shrops	70	C9
Little Stainforth	N York	96	B7
Little Stainton	Darltn	104	B6
Little Stanion	Nhants	61	J3
Little Stanney	Ches W	81	N10
Little Staughton	Bed	61	P8
Little Steeping	Lincs	87	M8
Little Stoke	Staffs	70	G7
Littlestone-on-Sea	Kent	27	J7
Little Stonham	Suffk	64	H9
Little Stretton	Leics	72	H10
Little Stretton	Shrops	56	H6
Little Strickland	Cumb	101	Q7
Little Stukeley	Cambs	62	B5
Little Sugnall	Staffs	70	E8
Little Sutton	Ches W	81	M9
Little Sutton	Shrops	57	J8
Little Swinburne	Nthumb	112	D5
Little Sypland	D & G	108	F10
Little Tew	Oxon	48	C9
Little Tey	Essex	52	F7
Little Thetford	Cambs	62	H5
Little Thirkleby	N York	97	Q5
Little Thornage	Norfk	76	F4
Little Thornton	Lancs	88	D3
Little Thorpe	Dur	104	D2
Littlethorpe	Leics	72	E11
Littlethorpe	N York	97	M7
Little Thurlow	Suffk	63	L10
Little Thurlow Green	Suffk	63	L10
Little Thurrock	Thurr	37	P5
Littleton	Angus	142	E7
Littleton	BaNES	19	Q2
Littleton	Ches W	81	N11
Littleton	D & G	108	D9
Littleton	Dorset	12	E4
Littleton	Hants	22	E8
Littleton	Somset	19	N8
Littleton	Surrey	23	Q5
Littleton	Surrey	36	C7
Littleton Drew	Wilts	32	F8
Littleton-on-Severn	S Glos	31	Q7
Littleton Pannell	Wilts	21	K4
Little Torrington	Devon	16	H8
Little Totham	Essex	52	E9
Little Town	Cumb	100	H7
Littletown	Dur	104	B2
Little Town	Lancs	89	K3
Little Town	Warrtn	82	D6
Little Twycross	Leics	72	A9
Little Urswick	Cumb	94	F6
Little Wakering	Essex	38	F4
Little Walden	Essex	51	M2
Little Waldingfield	Suffk	52	F2
Little Walsingham	Norfk	76	C4
Little Waltham	Essex	52	B9
Little Warley	Essex	37	P2
Little Washbourne	Gloucs	47	J8
Little Weighton	E R Yk	92	G4
Little Welnetham	Suffk	64	B10
Little Welton	Lincs	87	K3
Little Wenham	Suffk	53	J4
Little Wenlock	Wrekin	57	L3
Little Weston	Somset	20	B9
Little Whitefield	IoW	14	G9
Little Whittingham Green	Suffk	65	K6
Little Whittington	Nthumb	112	E7
Littlewick Green	W & M	35	M9
Little Wilbraham	Cambs	62	H9
Littlewindsor	Dorset	11	J4
Little Witcombe	Gloucs	46	H11
Little Witley	Worcs	46	E2
Little Wittenham	Oxon	34	G6
Little Wolford	Warwks	47	Q7
Littlewood	Staffs	58	E3
Little Woodcote	Gt Lon	36	G8
Littleworth	Bucks	49	N10
Littleworth	Oxon	34	B5
Littleworth	Staffs	58	F2
Littleworth	Staffs	70	G10
Littleworth	W Susx	24	E6
Littleworth	Worcs	46	G4
Littleworth	Worcs	47	J2
Littleworth Common	Bucks	35	P7
Little Wratting	Suffk	63	L11
Little Wymington	Bed	61	L8
Little Wymondley	Herts	50	F5
Little Wyrley	Staffs	58	F3
Little Wytheford	Shrops	69	Q11
Little Yeldham	Essex	52	C4
Littley Green	Essex	51	Q7
Litton	Derbys	83	Q9
Litton	N York	96	D6
Litton	Somset	19	Q4
Litton Cheney	Dorset	11	L6
Liurbost	W Isls	168	i5
Liverpool	L'pool	81	L6
Liverpool Maritime Mercantile City	L'pool	81	L7
Liversedge	Kirk	90	F6
Liverton	Devon	9	K9
Liverton	R & Cl	105	K7
Liverton Mines	R & Cl	105	K7
Liverton Street	Kent	38	E11
Livingston	W Loth	127	K4
Livingston Village	W Loth	127	J4
Lixwm	Flints	80	H10
Lizard	Cnwll	3	J11
Llaingoch	IoA	78	C8
Llaithddu	Powys	55	P8
Llan	Powys	55	K4
Llanaber	Gwynd	67	L11
Llanaelhaearn	Gwynd	66	F6
Llanafan	Cerdgn	54	F10
Llanafan-Fawr	Powys	44	D3
Llanafan-fechan	Powys	44	D4
Llanallgo	IoA	79	J7
Llanarmon	Gwynd	66	G7
Llanarmon Dyffryn Ceiriog	Wrexhm	68	G8
Llanarmon-yn-Ial	Denbgs	68	G3
Llanarth	Cerdgn	42	H3
Llanarth	Mons	31	L2
Llanarthne	Carmth	43	K11
Llanasa	Flints	80	G8
Llanbabo	IoA	78	F7
Llanbadarn Fawr	Cerdgn	54	E8
Llanbadarn Fynydd	Powys	55	P9
Llanbadarn-y-garreg	Powys	44	G5
Llanbadoc	Mons	31	L5
Llanbadrig	IoA	78	F6
Llanbeder	Newpt	31	L6
Llanbedr	Gwynd	67	K9
Llanbedr	Powys	44	G10
Llanbedr	Powys	45	J10
Llanbedr-Dyffryn-Clwyd	Denbgs	68	F3
Llanbedrgoch	IoA	79	J8
Llanbedrog	Gwynd	66	E8
Llanbedr-y-Cennin	Conwy	79	P11
Llanberis	Gwynd	67	K2
Llanbethêry	V Glam	30	D11
Llanbister	Powys	55	Q10
Llanblethian	V Glam	30	C10
Llanboidy	Carmth	41	P6
Llanbradach	Caerph	30	F6
Llanbrynmair	Powys	55	M3
Llancadle	V Glam	30	D11
Llancarfan	V Glam	30	D10
Llancayo	Mons	31	L4
Llancloudy	Herefs	45	P10
Llancynfelyn	Cerdgn	54	E6
Llandaff	Cardif	30	G9
Llandanwg	Gwynd	67	K9
Llandarcy	Neath	29	K5
Llandawke	Carmth	41	Q8
Llanddaniel Fab	IoA	78	H10
Llanddarog	Carmth	43	J10
Llanddeiniol	Cerdgn	54	D10
Llanddeiniolen	Gwynd	79	J11
Llandderfel	Gwynd	68	C7
Llanddeusant	Carmth	43	Q10
Llanddeusant	IoA	78	E7
Llanddew	Powys	44	F8
Llanddewi	Swans	28	E7
Llanddewi Brefi	Cerdgn	43	N3
Llanddewi'r Cwm	Powys	44	E5
Llanddewi Rhydderch	Mons	31	L3
Llanddewi Velfrey	Pembks	41	M7
Llanddewi Ystradenni	Powys	55	Q11
Llanddoged	Conwy	67	Q2
Llanddona	IoA	79	K9
Llanddowror	Carmth	41	Q8
Llanddulas	Conwy	80	C9
Llanddwywe	Gwynd	67	K10
Llanddyfnan	IoA	79	J9
Llandecwyn	Gwynd	67	L7
Llandefaelog-Tre'r-Graig	Powys	44	G9
Llandefalle	Powys	44	G7
Llandegfan	IoA	79	K10
Llandegla	Denbgs	68	G4
Llandegley	Powys	55	G2
Llandegveth	Mons	31	K5
Llandegwning	Gwynd	66	D9
Llandeilo	Carmth	43	M10
Llandeilo Graban	Powys	44	F6
Llandeilo'r Fan	Powys	44	B8
Llandeloy	Pembks	40	G5
Llandenny	Mons	31	M4
Llandevaud	Newpt	31	M6
Llandevenny	Mons	31	M7
Llandinabo	Herefs	45	Q9
Llandinam	Powys	55	N7
Llandissilio	Pembks	41	M6
Llandogo	Mons	31	P4
Llandough	V Glam	30	C10
Llandough	V Glam	30	G10
Llandovery	Carmth	43	Q8
Llandow	V Glam	29	P10
Llandre	Carmth	54	N6
Llandre	Carmth	54	E7
Llandre Isaf	Pembks	41	M5
Llandrillo	Denbgs	68	D7
Llandrillo-yn-Rhos	Conwy	79	Q8
Llandrindod Wells	Powys	44	F2
Llandrinio	Powys	69	J11
Llandudno	Conwy	79	P8
Llandudno Junction	Conwy	79	P9
Llandulas	Powys	44	B6
Llandwrog	Gwynd	66	H3
Llandybie	Carmth	43	M11
Llandyfaelog	Carmth	42	D2
Llandyfan	Carmth	43	M11
Llandyfriog	Cerdgn	42	F6
Llandyfrydog	IoA	78	G7
Llandygai	Gwynd	79	K10
Llandygwydd	Cerdgn	41	P2
Llandynan	Denbgs	68	G5
Llandyrnog	Denbgs	80	G11
Llandyssil	Powys	56	B5
Llandysul	Cerdgn	42	H6
Llanedeyrn	Cardif	30	H8
Llanedi	Carmth	28	G3
Llaneglwys	Powys	44	F7
Llanegryn	Gwynd	54	E3
Llanegwad	Carmth	43	K10
Llaneilian	IoA	78	H6
Llanelian-yn-Rhôs	Conwy	80	B9
Llanelidan	Denbgs	68	F4
Llanelieu	Powys	44	H8
Llanellen	Mons	31	K2
Llanelli	Carmth	28	F4
Llanelltyd	Gwynd	67	N11
Llanelly	Mons	30	H2
Llanelly Hill	Mons	30	H2
Llanelwedd	Powys	44	E4
Llanenddwyn	Gwynd	67	K10
Llanengan	Gwynd	66	D9
Llanerch	Gwynd	68	A11
Llanerch	Powys	56	E6
Llanerchymedd	IoA	78	G8
Llanerfyl	Powys	55	N3
Llanfachraeth	IoA	78	E8
Llanfachreth	Gwynd	67	P10
Llanfaelog	IoA	78	E10
Llanfaelrhys	Gwynd	66	C9
Llanfaenor	Mons	31	N11
Llanfaes	IoA	79	L9
Llanfaes	Powys	44	E9
Llanfaethlu	IoA	78	E7
Llanfair	Gwynd	67	K9
Llanfair Caereinion	Powys	55	Q3
Llanfair Clydogau	Cerdgn	43	M4
Llanfair Dyffryn Clwyd	Denbgs	68	F3
Llanfairfechan	Conwy	79	M10
Llanfair Kilgeddin	Mons	31	L3
Llanfair-Nant-Gwyn	Pembks	41	N3
Llanfairpwllgwyngyll	IoA	79	J10
Llanfair Talhaiarn	Conwy	80	C10
Llanfair Waterdine	Shrops	56	C9
Llanfairynghornwy	IoA	78	E6
Llanfair-yn-Neubwll	IoA	78	E9
Llanfallteg	Carmth	41	N6
Llanfallteg West	Carmth	41	M7
Llanfarian	Cerdgn	54	D9
Llanfechain	Powys	68	G10
Llanfechell	IoA	78	F6
Llanferres	Denbgs	68	G2
Llanfflewyn	IoA	78	F7
Llanfigael	IoA	78	E8
Llanfihangel-ar-arth	Carmth	43	J7
Llanfihangel Glyn Myfyr	Conwy	68	C5
Llanfihangel Nant Bran	Powys	44	C8
Llanfihangel-nant-Melan	Powys	44	H3
Llanfihangel Rhydithon	Powys	55	B11
Llanfihangel Rogiet	Mons	31	N7
Llanfihangel Tal-y-llyn	Powys	44	G9
Llanfihangel-uwch-Gwili	Carmth	43	J10
Llanfihangel-y-Creuddyn	Cerdgn	54	F9
Llanfihangel-yng-Ngwynfa	Powys	68	E11
Llanfihangel yn Nhowyn	IoA	78	E9
Llanfihangel-y-pennant	Gwynd	54	F3
Llanfihangel-y-pennant	Gwynd	67	J6
Llanfihangel-y-traethau	Gwynd	67	K8
Llanfilo	Powys	44	G8
Llanfoist	Mons	31	J2
Llanfor	Gwynd	68	B7
Llanfrechfa	Torfn	31	K6
Llanfrothen	Gwynd	67	L6
Llanfrynach	Powys	44	F9
Llanfwrog	Denbgs	68	F3
Llanfwrog	IoA	78	E8
Llanfyllin	Powys	68	F11
Llanfynydd	Carmth	43	L9
Llanfynydd	Flints	69	J3
Llanfyrnach	Pembks	41	P4
Llangadfan	Powys	55	N2
Llangadog	Carmth	28	D3
Llangadog	Carmth	43	P9
Llangadwaladr	IoA	78	F11
Llangadwaladr	Powys	68	G8
Llangaffo	IoA	78	G11
Llangain	Carmth	42	G11
Llangammarch Wells	Powys	44	C5
Llangan	V Glam	30	C9
Llangarron	Herefs	45	Q10
Llangasty-Talyllyn	Powys	44	G9
Llangathen	Carmth	43	L10
Llangattock	Powys	45	J11
Llangattock Lingoed	Mons	45	M10
Llangattock-Vibon-Avel	Mons	31	P11
Llangedwyn	Powys	68	G10
Llangefni	IoA	78	H9
Llangeinor	Brdgnd	29	P7
Llangeitho	Cerdgn	43	M3
Llangeler	Carmth	42	G7
Llangelynin	Gwynd	54	D3
Llangendeirne	Carmth	28	E2
Llangennech	Carmth	28	G4
Llangennith	Swans	28	D6
Llangenny	Powys	45	J11
Llangernyw	Conwy	80	B11
Llangian	Gwynd	66	D9
Llangiwg	Neath	29	K3
Llanglydwen	Pembks	40	H4
Llanglydwen	Carmth	41	N5
Llangoed	IoA	79	L9
Llangoedmor	Cerdgn	42	D5
Llangollen	Denbgs	68	H6
Llangolman	Pembks	41	M5
Llangors	Powys	44	G9
Llangorwen	Cerdgn	54	E8
Llangovan	Mons	31	N3
Llangower	Gwynd	68	B8
Llangrannog	Cerdgn	42	F4
Llangristiolus	IoA	78	G10
Llangrove	Herefs	45	Q11
Llangua	Mons	45	M9
Llangunllo	Powys	56	C10
Llangunnor	Carmth	42	H10
Llangurig	Powys	55	L9
Llangwm	Conwy	68	C6
Llangwm	Mons	31	M5
Llangwm	Pembks	41	J9
Llangwnnadl	Gwynd	66	C8
Llangwyfan	Denbgs	80	G11
Llangwyllog	IoA	78	G9
Llangwyryfon	Cerdgn	54	D10
Llangybi	Cerdgn	43	M4
Llangybi	Gwynd	66	G6
Llangybi	Mons	31	L5
Llangyfelach	Swans	28	H5
Llangynhafal	Denbgs	68	F2
Llangynidr	Powys	44	H11
Llangynin	Carmth	41	Q7
Llangynllo	Cerdgn	42	G6
Llangynog	Carmth	28	B2
Llangynog	Powys	68	E9
Llangynwyd	Brdgnd	29	N7
Llanhamlach	Powys	44	F9
Llanharan	Rhondd	30	D8
Llanharry	Rhondd	30	D8
Llanhennock	Mons	31	L6
Llanhilleth	Blae G	30	H4
Llanidan	IoA	78	H11
Llanidloes	Powys	55	M8
Llaniestyn	Gwynd	66	D8
Llanigon	Powys	45	J7
Llanilar	Cerdgn	54	E9
Llanilid	Rhondd	30	C8
Llanina	Cerdgn	42	H3
Llanio	Cerdgn	43	M3
Llanishen	Cardif	30	G8
Llanishen	Mons	31	N4
Llanllechid	Gwynd	79	L11
Llanlleonfel	Powys	44	C4
Llanllowell	Mons	31	L5
Llanllugan	Powys	55	N3
Llanllwch	Carmth	42	G11
Llanllwchaiarn	Powys	55	Q6
Llanllwni	Carmth	43	J7
Llanllyfni	Gwynd	66	H4
Llanmadoc	Swans	28	D6
Llanmaes	V Glam	30	C11
Llanmartin	Newpt	31	L7
Llanmerewig	Powys	56	B6
Llanmihangel	V Glam	30	C10
Llanmiloe	Carmth	41	P9
Llanmorlais	Swans	28	F6
Llannefydd	Conwy	80	D10
Llannon	Carmth	28	F3
Llannor	Gwynd	66	F7
Llanon	Cerdgn	54	C11
Llanover	Mons	31	K3
Llanpumsaint	Carmth	42	H9
Llanrhaeadr-ym-Mochnant	Powys	68	F9
Llanrhian	Pembks	40	F4
Llanrhidian	Swans	28	E6
Llanrhos	Conwy	79	P8
Llanrhyddlad	IoA	78	E7
Llanrhystud	Cerdgn	54	C11
Llanrothal	Herefs	45	P11
Llanrug	Gwynd	67	J2
Llanrumney	Cardif	30	H8
Llanrwst	Conwy	67	Q2
Llansadurnen	Carmth	41	Q8
Llansadwrn	Carmth	43	N8
Llansadwrn	IoA	79	K9
Llansaint	Carmth	28	C3
Llansamlet	Swans	29	J5

Llansanffraid Glan Conwy
Conwy 79 Q9
Llansannan Conwy 80 C11
Llansannor V Glam 30 C9
Llansantffraed Powys 44 G10
Llansantffraed-
Cwmdeuddwr Powys 55 M11
Llansantffraed-in-Elvel
Powys 44 F4
Llansantffraid Cerdgn 54 C11
Llansantffraid-ym-
Mechain Powys 68 H10
Llansawel Carmth 43 M7
Llansilin Powys 68 H9
Llansoy Mons 31 M4
Llanspyddid Powys 44 E9
Llanstadwell Pembks 40 H10
Llansteffan Carmth 28 C2
Llanstephan Powys 44 G6
Llantarnam Torfn 31 K6
Llanteg Pembks 41 N8
Llanthewy Skirrid Mons 45 L11
Llanthony Mons 45 K9
Llantilio-Crossenny Mons 31 L2
Llantilio Pertholey Mons 45 L11
Llantood Pembks 41 N2
Llantrisant IoA 78 F8
Llantrisant Mons 31 L5
Llantrisant Rhondd 30 D8
Llantrithyd V Glam 30 D10
Llantwit Fardre Rhondd 30 E7
Llantwit Major V Glam 30 C11
Llantysilio Denbgs 68 G6
Llanuwchllyn Gwynd 68 A8
Llanvaches Newpt 31 M6
Llanvair Discoed Mons 31 M6
Llanvapley Mons 31 L2
Llanvetherine Mons 45 M11
Llanveynoe Herefs 45 L8
Llanvihangel Crucorney
Mons 45 L10
Llanvihangel Gobion Mons 31 K3
Llanvihangel-Ystern-
Llewern Mons 31 M2
Llanwddyn Powys 68 D11
Llanwenarth Mons 31 J2
Llanwenog Cerdgn 43 J5
Llanwern Newpt 31 L7
Llanwinio Carmth 41 Q5
Llanwnda Gwynd 66 H3
Llanwnda Pembks 40 H3
Llanwnnen Cerdgn 43 K5
Llanwnog Powys 55 N6
Llanwonno Rhondd 30 D5
Llanwrda Carmth 43 P8
Llanwrin Powys 54 H4
Llanwrthwl Powys 44 D2
Llanwrtyd Powys 44 B5
Llanwrtyd Wells Powys 44 B5
Llanwyddelan Powys 55 P4
Llanyblodwel Shrops 68 H10
Llanybri Carmth 28 B2
Llanybydder Carmth 43 K6
Llanycefn Pembks 41 L6
Llanychaer Pembks 41 J3
Llanycil Gwynd 68 B8
Llanycrwys Carmth 43 M5
Llanymawddwy Gwynd 68 B11
Llanymynech Powys 69 J10
Llanynghenedl IoA 78 E8
Llanynys Denbgs 68 F2
Llan-y-pwll Wrexhm 69 L4
Llanyre Powys 44 E2
Llanystumdwy Gwynd 66 H7
Llanywern Powys 44 G9
Llawhaden Pembks 41 L7
Llawnt Shrops 68 H8
Llawryglyn Powys 55 L6
Llay Wrexhm 69 K3
Llechcynfarwy IoA 78 F8
Llechfaen Powys 44 F9
Llechrhyd Caerph 30 F3
Llechryd Cerdgn 41 P2
Llechylched IoA 78 E9
Lledrod Cerdgn 54 E10
Lleyn Peninsula Gwynd 66 E7
Llidiardau Gwynd 68 A7
Llidiartnenog Carmth 43 K7
Llidiart-y-parc Denbgs 68 F6
Llithfaen Gwynd 66 F6
Lloc Flints 80 G9
Llowes Powys 44 H6
Llwydcoed Rhondd 30 C4
Llwydiarth Powys 68 D11
Llwyn Powys 68 E2
Llwyncelyn Cerdgn 42 H3
Llwyndafydd Cerdgn 42 G3
Llwynderw Powys 56 C4
Llwyn-drain Pembks 41 Q4
Llwyn-du Mons 45 K11
Llwyndyrys Gwynd 66 F6
Llwyngwril Gwynd 54 D3
Llwynhendy Carmth 28 F5
Llwynmawr Wrexhm 68 H7
Llwyn-on Myr Td 30 D2
Llwyn-y-brain Carmth 41 N8
Llwyn-y-groes Cerdgn 43 L3
Llwynpia Rhondd 30 C6
Llynclys Shrops 69 J10
Llynfaes IoA 78 G9
Llyn-y-pandy Flints 81 J11
Llysfaen Conwy 80 B9
Llyswen Cerdgn 43 J2
Llyswen Powys 44 G7
Llysworney V Glam 30 C10
Llys-y-frân Pembks 41 K6
Llywel Powys 44 B8
Load Brook Sheff 84 C3
Loan Falk 126 H2
Loanend Nthumb 129 N9
Loanhead Mdloth 127 P4
Loaningfoot D & G 109 L9
Loans S Ayrs 125 J11
Lobb Devon 16 H4
Lobhillcross Devon 8 C7
Lochailort Highld 145 N11
Lochaline Highld 138 B9
Lochans D & G 106 E6
Locharbriggs D & G 109 L4
Lochavich Ag & B 131 J4
Lochawe Ag & B 131 N2
Loch Baghasdail W Isls 168 c16
Lochboisdale W Isls 168 c16
Lochbuie Ag & B 137 Q10

Lochcarron Highld 154 A10
Lochdon Ag & B 138 C11
Lochdonhead Ag & B 138 C11
Lochead Ag & B 123 N4
Lochearnhead Stirlg 132 H3
Lochee C Dund 142 F11
Locheilside Station Highld 138 H2
Lochend Highld 155 Q10
Locheport W Isls 168 d11
Loch Euphoirt W Isls 168 d11
Lochfoot D & G 109 J6
Lochgair Ag & B 131 J9
Lochgelly Fife 134 F9
Lochgilphead Ag & B 130 H10
Lochgoilhead Ag & B 131 Q7
Lochieheads Fife 134 H5
Lochill Moray 157 P5
Lochindorb Lodge Highld 156 H10
Lochinver Highld 160 H2
Loch Lomond and The
Trossachs National
Park 132 E5
Loch Loyal Lodge Highld........165 P7
Lochluichart Highld 155 K5
Lochmaben D & G 109 N4
Loch nam Madadh W Isls 168 e11
Lochmaddy W Isls 168 e11
Loch Ness Highld 147 N2
Lochore Fife 134 F8
Lochranza N Ayrs 124 A7
Loch Sgioport W Isls 168 d14
Lochside Abers 143 N5
Lochside D & G 109 L5
Lochside Highld 156 E7
Lochskipport W Isls 168 d14
Lochslin Highld 163 J10
Lochton S Ayrs 107 J2
Lochty Angus 143 J5
Lochty Fife 135 N6
Lochuisge Highld 138 D6
Lochwinnoch Rens 125 K6
Lochwood D & G 116 F11
Lockengate Cnwll 4 G9
Lockerbie D & G 109 P4
Lockeridge Wilts 33 M11
Lockerley Hants 22 B9
Locking N Som 19 L3
Locking Stumps Warrtn 82 D6
Lockington E R Yk 99 K11
Lockington Leics 72 D5
Lockleywood Shrops 70 B9
Locksbottom Gt Lon 37 K7
Locksgreen IoW 14 D8
Locks Heath Hants 14 F5
Lockton N York 98 G3
Loddington Leics 73 K10
Loddington Nhants 60 H5
Loddiswell Devon 7 J9
Loddon Norfk 65 M2
Lode Cambs 62 H8
Lode Heath Solhll 59 J8
Loders Dorset 11 K6
Lodsworth W Susx 23 P10
Lofthouse Leeds 91 J5
Lofthouse N York 96 H6
Lofthouse Gate Wakefd 91 J6
Loftus R & Cl 105 K7
Logan E Ayrs 115 L3
Loganbeck Cumb 94 D2
Loganlea W Loth 126 H5
Loggerheads Staffs 70 C7
Logie Angus 143 M5
Logie Fife 135 L3
Logie Moray 157 J7
Logie Coldstone Abers 150 C7
Logie Newton Abers 158 G10
Logie Pert Angus 143 M5
Logierait P & K 141 N7
Logierieve Abers 151 N2
Login Carmth 41 N6
Lolworth Cambs 62 E8
Lonbain Highld 153 M7
Londesborough E R Yk 98 H11
London Gt Lon 36 H4
London Apprentice Cnwll 3 Q4
London Beach Kent 26 E4
London Colney Herts 50 E10
Londonderry N York 97 M3
London End Nhants 61 K7
London Gateway Services
Gt Lon 36 E2
London Gatwick Airport
W Susx 24 G2
London Heathrow Airport
Gt Lon 36 C5
London Luton Airport Luton ...50 D6
London Oxford Airport
Oxon 48 E11
London Southend Airport
Essex 38 E4
London Stansted Airport
Essex 51 N6
Londonthorpe Lincs 73 P3
London Zoo ZSL Gt Lon 36 G4
Londubh Highld 160 D10
Lonemore Highld 153 P2
Long Ashton N Som 31 P10
Long Bank Worcs 57 P10
Long Bennington Lincs 73 L2
Longbenton N Tyne 113 L7
Longborough Gloucs 47 N9
Long Bredy Dorset 11 M6
Longbridge Birm 58 F9
Longbridge Warwks 47 Q2
Longbridge Deverill Wilts 20 G6
Long Buckby Nhants 60 D7
Longburgh Cumb 110 F9
Longburton Dorset 11 N2
Long Cause Devon 7 K5
Long Clawson Leics 73 J5
Longcliffe Derbys 84 B9
Longcombe Devon 7 K7
Long Common Hants 14 F4
Long Compton Staffs 70 F10
Long Compton Warwks 47 Q8
Longcot Oxon 33 Q6
Long Crendon Bucks 35 J3
Long Crichel Dorset 12 G2
Longcross Surrey 35 Q11
Longden Shrops 56 G3
Longden Common Shrops 56 G3
Long Ditton Surrey 36 E7
Longdon Staffs 58 G2
Longdon Worcs 46 F7

Longdon Green Staffs 58 G2
Longdon Heath Worcs 46 F7
Longdon upon Tern Wrekin 69 R11
Longdown Devon 9 L4
Longdowns Cnwll 3 J7
Long Drax N York 92 A5
Long Duckmanton Derbys 84 F6
Long Eaton Derbys 72 D4
Longfield Kent 37 P7
Longford Covtry 59 N8
Longford Derbys 71 N7
Longford Gloucs 46 F10
Longford Gt Lon 36 C5
Longford Kent 37 M9
Longford Shrops 70 A8
Longford Wrekin 70 C11
Longforgan P & K 134 H2
Longformacus Border 128 H8
Longframlington Nthumb 119 M10
Long Green Ches W 81 P10
Long Green Worcs 46 F8
Longham Dorset 13 J5
Longham Norfk 76 C8
Long Hanborough Oxon 34 D2
Longhaven Abers 159 R10
Long Hedges Lincs 87 L11
Longhirst Nthumb 113 K3
Longhope Gloucs 46 C11
Longhope Ork 169 c7
Longhorsley Nthumb 112 H4
Longhoughton Nthumb 119 P7
Long Itchington Warwks 59 P11
Longlands Cumb 101 J3
Longlane Derbys 71 N7
Longleat Safari &
Adventure Park Wilts 20 F6
Longlevens Gloucs 46 G11
Longley Calder 90 D6
Longley Kirk 90 E9
Longley Green Worcs 46 D4
Longleys P & K 142 D9
Long Load Somset 19 N10
Longmanhill Abers 158 H5
Long Marston Herts 49 N11
Long Marston N York 97 N10
Long Marston Warwks 47 N5
Long Marton Cumb 102 C6
Long Meadowend Shrops 56 G8
Long Melford Suffk 52 E2
Longmoor Camp Hants 23 L8
Longmorn Moray 157 N6
Longmoss Ches E 83 J10
Long Newnton Gloucs 32 H6
Longnewton Border 118 A5
Long Newton E Loth 128 C7
Longnewton S on T 104 C7
Longney Gloucs 32 E2
Longniddry E Loth 128 C4
Longnor Shrops 56 H4
Longnor Staffs 71 K2
Longparish Hants 22 D5
Longpark Cumb 110 H8
Long Preston N York 96 B9
Longridge Lancs 89 J3
Longridge Staffs 70 G11
Longridge W Loth 126 G5
Longriggend N Lans 126 E3
Long Riston E R Yk 93 K2
Longrock Cnwll 2 E7
Longsdon Staffs 70 H4
Longshaw Wigan 82 B4
Longside Abers 159 P8
Long Sight Oldham 89 Q9
Longslow Shrops 70 B7
Longstanton Cambs 62 E7
Longstock Hants 22 C7
Longstone Pembks 41 M9
Longstowe Cambs 62 D10
Long Stratton Norfk 65 H3
Long Street M Keyn 49 L5
Longstreet Wilts 21 M4
Long Sutton Hants 23 K5
Long Sutton Lincs 74 H6
Long Sutton Somset 19 N9
Longthorpe C Pete 74 C11
Long Thurlow Suffk 64 E8
Longthwaite Cumb 101 M6
Longton C Stke 70 G6
Longton Lancs 88 F5
Longtown Cumb 110 G7
Longtown Herefs 45 L9
Longueville Jersey 11 c2
Longville in the Dale Shrops 57 J6
Long Waste Wrekin 69 R11
Long Whatton Leics 72 D6
Longwick Bucks 35 L3
Long Wittenham Oxon 34 F6
Longwitton Nthumb 112 G3
Longwood D & G 108 F8
Longwood Shrops 57 L3
Longworth Oxon 34 C5
Longyester E Loth 128 E7
Lôn-las Swans 29 K5
Lonmay Abers 159 P6
Lonmore Highld 152 D8
Looe Cnwll 5 M11
Loose Kent 38 C11
Loosebeare Devon 8 H3
Loosegate Lincs 74 F5
Loosley Row Bucks 35 M4
Lootcherbrae Abers 158 F7
Lopcombe Corner Wilts 21 Q7
Lopen Somset 11 J2
Loppington Shrops 69 N9
Lorbottle Nthumb 119 K9
Lordington W Susx 15 L5
Lordsbridge Norfk 75 L8
Lordshill C Sotn 22 C11
Lords Wood Medway 38 C9
Lornty P & K 142 C8
Loscoe Derbys 84 F11
Loscombe Dorset 11 K5
Losgaintir W Isls 168 f8
Lossiemouth Moray 157 N3
Lostford Shrops 69 R8
Lostock Gralam Ches W 82 E10
Lostock Green Ches W 82 E10
Lostock Hall Lancs 88 G5
Lostock Hall Fold Bolton 89 K9
Lostock Junction Bolton 89 K9
Lostwithiel Cnwll 5 J10
Lothbeg Highld 163 L4
Lothersdale N York 96 E11
Lothmore Highld 163 M4

Loudwater Bucks 35 P6
Loughborough Leics 72 E7
Loughor Swans 28 G5
Loughton Essex 51 K11
Loughton M Keyn 49 M7
Loughton Shrops 57 L8
Lound Lincs 73 R7
Lound Notts 85 L3
Lound Suffk 65 Q2
Lounston Devon 9 J4
Lount Leics 72 B7
Louth Lincs 87 K3
Loveclough Lancs 89 N5
Lovedean Hants 15 J4
Lover Wilts 21 P10
Loversall Donc 91 P11
Loves Green Essex 51 P10
Lovesome Hill N York 104 C11
Loveston Pembks 41 L9
Lovington Somset 19 Q8
Low Ackworth Wakefd 91 M7
Low Angerton Nthumb 112 G4
Lowbands Gloucs 46 E8
Low Barbeth D & G 106 D4
Low Barlings Lincs 86 E6
Low Bell End N York 105 K11
Low Bentham N York 95 N7
Low Biggins Cumb 95 N5
Low Borrowbridge Cumb 102 B10
Low Bradfield Sheff 84 C2
Low Bradley N York 96 F11
Low Braithwaite Cumb 101 M2
Low Burnham N Linc 92 C10
Low Buston Nthumb 119 P9
Lowca Cumb 100 C6
Low Catton E R Yk 98 E10
Low Coniscliffe Darltn 103 P8
Low Crosby Cumb 110 H9
Lowdham Notts 85 L11
Low Dinsdale Darltn 104 B8
Lowe Shrops 69 N8
Lowe Hill Staffs 70 H3
Low Ellington N York 97 K4
Lower Aisholt Somset 18 H7
Lower Ansty Dorset 12 C4
Lower Apperley Gloucs 46 G9
Lower Arboll Highld 163 K10
Lower Arncott Oxon 48 H11
Lower Ashton Devon 9 K8
Lower Assendon Oxon 35 K8
Lower Badcall Highld 164 E8
Lower Ballam Lancs 88 D4
Lower Bartle Lancs 88 F4
Lower Basildon W Berk 34 H9
Lower Bearwood Herefs 45 M3
Lower Beeding W Susx 24 F5
Lower Benefield Nhants 61 L3
Lower Bentley Worcs 58 E11
Lower Beobridge Shrops 57 P6
Lower Birchwood Derbys 84 F10
Lower Boddington Nhants 48 E4
Lower Boscaswell Cnwll 2 B7
Lower Bourne Surrey 23 M6
Lower Brailes Warwks 48 B7
Lower Breakish Highld 145 L11
Lower Bredbury Stockp 83 K6
Lower Broadheath Worcs 46 F3
Lower Broxwood Herefs 45 M4
Lower Buckenhill Herefs 46 B8
Lower Bullingham Herefs 45 Q7
Lower Burgate Hants 21 N11
Lower Burrowton Devon 9 P5
Lower Burton Herefs 45 N3
Lower Caldecote C Beds 61 Q11
Lower Cam Gloucs 32 D4
Lower Canada N Som 19 L3
Lower Catesby Nhants 60 B9
Lower Chapel Powys 44 E7
Lower Chicksgrove Wilts 21 J9
Lower Chute Wilts 22 B4
Lower Clapton Gt Lon 36 H3
Lower Clent Worcs 58 D9
Lower Common Hants 23 L2
Lower Creedy Devon 9 K4
Lower Crossings Derbys 83 M8
Lower Cumberworth Kirk 90 G9
Lower Darwen Bl w D 89 K5
Lower Dean Bed 61 N7
Lower Denby Kirk 90 G9
Lower Diabaig Highld 153 P5
Lower Dicker E Susx 25 N8
Lower Dinchope Shrops 56 H8
Lower Down Shrops 56 E8
Lower Dunsforth N York 97 P8
Lower Egleton Herefs 46 B5
Lower Elkstone Staffs 71 K3
Lower Ellastone Staffs 71 L7
Lower End M Keyn 49 P7
Lower End Nhants 60 H9
Lower End Nhants 61 J8
Lower Everleigh Wilts 21 N4
Lower Exbury Hants 14 D7
Lower Eythorne Kent 27 N2
Lower Failand N Som 31 P10
Lower Farringdon Hants 23 K7
Lower Feltham Gt Lon 36 C6
Lower Fittleworth W Susx 24 B7
Lower Foxdale IoM 80 c6
Lower Frankton Shrops 69 L9
Lower Freystrop Pembks 41 J8
Lower Froyle Hants 23 L6
Lower Gabwell Devon 7 N5
Lower Gledfield Highld 162 D8
Lower Godney Somset 19 N6
Lower Gornal Dudley 58 D6
Lower Gravenhurst C Beds 50 D3
Lower Green Herts 50 E4
Lower Green Herts 51 K4
Lower Green Kent 25 N2
Lower Green Kent 25 P2
Lower Green Norfk 76 D4
Lower Green Staffs 58 D3
Lower Hacheston Suffk 65 L10
Lower Halstock Leigh
Dorset 11 L3
Lower Halstow Kent 38 E8
Lower Hamworthy BCP 12 G6
Lower Hardres Kent 39 L11
Lower Harpton Herefs 45 K2
Lower Hartlip Kent 38 D9
Lower Hartshay Derbys 84 E10
Lower Hartwell Bucks 35 L2
Lower Hatton Staffs 70 E7

Lower Hawthwaite Cumb 94 E3
Lower Hergest Herefs 45 K3
Lower Heyford Oxon 48 E10
Lower Heysham Lancs 95 J8
Lower Higham Kent 38 B7
Lower Holbrook Suffk 53 L4
Lower Hordley Shrops 69 L9
Lower Horncott W Susx 24 B7
Lowerhouse Lancs 89 N4
Lower Houses Kirk 90 F7
Lower Irlam Salfd 82 F6
Lower Kilburn Derbys 72 B2
Lower Kilcott Gloucs 32 E7
Lower Killeyan Ag & B 122 C11
Lower Kingcombe Dorset 11 M5
Lower Kingswood Surrey 36 F10
Lower Kinnerton Ches W 69 K2
Lower Langford N Som 19 N2
Lower Largo Fife 135 L7
Lower Leigh Staffs 71 J7
Lower Lemington Gloucs 47 P8
Lower Llanfadog Powys 55 M11
Lower Lovacott Devon 17 J6
Lower Loxhore Devon 17 L4
Lower Lydbrook Gloucs 46 A11
Lower Lye Herefs 56 G11
Lower Machen Newpt 30 H7
Lower Maes-coed Herefs 45 L8
Lower Mannington Dorset 13 J4
Lower Marston Somset 20 E6
Lower Meend Gloucs 31 Q4
Lower Merridge Somset 18 H8
Lower Middleton Cheney
Nhants 48 F6
Lower Milton Somset 19 P5
Lower Moor Worcs 47 J5
Lower Morton S Glos 32 B6
Lower Nazeing Essex 51 J9
Lower Norton Warwks 47 P2
Lower Nyland Dorset 20 E10
Lower Penarth V Glam 30 G11
Lower Penn Staffs 58 C5
Lower Pennington Hants 13 P6
Lower Penwortham Lancs 88 G5
Lower Peover Ches E 82 F10
Lower Place Rochdl 89 Q8
Lower Pollicott Bucks 35 K2
Lower Quinton Warwks 47 N5
Lower Rainham Medway 38 D8
Lower Raydon Suffk 52 H4
Lower Roadwater Somset 18 D7
Lower Salter Lancs 95 N8
Lower Seagry Wilts 33 J8
Lower Sheering Essex 51 L8
Lower Shelton C Beds 49 Q6
Lower Shiplake Oxon 35 L9
Lower Shuckburgh Warwks 48 E2
Lower Slaughter Gloucs 47 N10
Lower Soothill Kirk 90 H6
Lower Soudley Gloucs 32 C3
Lower Standen Kent 27 M3
Lower Stanton St Quintin
Wilts 32 H8
Lower Stoke Medway 38 D6
Lower Stondon C Beds 50 E3
Lower Stone Gloucs 32 C6
Lower Stonnall Staffs 58 G4
Lower Stow Bedon Norfk 64 D3
Lower Street Dorset 12 D5
Lower Street E Susx 26 B9
Lower Street Norfk 77 K4
Lower Street Suffk 63 N10
Lower Street Suffk 64 G11
Lower Stretton Warrtn 82 D8
Lower Stroud Dorset 11 K5
Lower Sundon C Beds 50 C5
Lower Swanwick Hants 14 E5
Lower Swell Gloucs 47 N9
Lower Tadmarton Oxon 48 D7
Lower Tale Devon 9 Q4
Lower Tasburgh Norfk 64 H2
Lower Tean Staffs 71 J7
Lower Thurlton Norfk 65 N2
Lower Town Cnwll 2 H8
Lower Town Devon 7 J4
Lower Town Herefs 46 B6
Lower Town Herefs 41 J3
Lower Trebullett Cnwll 5 N6
Lower Treluswell Cnwll 3 K6
Lower Tysoe Warwks 48 B5
Lower Ufford Suffk 65 K11
Lower Upcott Devon 9 L8
Lower Upham Hants 22 F11
Lower Upnor Medway 38 C7
Lower Vexford Somset 18 F7
Lower Walton Warrtn 82 D7
Lower Waterston Dorset 12 B5
Lower Weare Somset 19 M4
Lower Weedon Nhants 60 D9
Lower Welson Herefs 45 K4
Lower Westmancote Worcs 46 H7
Lower Whatcombe Dorset 12 D4
Lower Whatley Somset 20 D5
Lower Whitley Ches W 82 D9
Lower Wick Gloucs 32 D5
Lower Wick Worcs 46 F4
Lower Wield Hants 22 H6
Lower Willingdon E Susx 25 N10
Lower Withington Ches E 82 H11
Lower Woodend Bucks 35 M7
Lower Woodford Wilts 21 M7
Lower Wraxall Dorset 11 M4
Lower Wyche Worcs 46 E6
Lower Wyke C Brad 90 F5
Lowesby Leics 73 J9
Lowestoft Suffk 65 Q3
Loweswater Cumb 100 F6
Low Fell Gatesd 113 L9
Lowfield Heath W Susx 24 G3
Low Gartachorrans Stirlg 132 F10
Low Gate Nthumb 112 D8
Low Gettbridge Cumb 111 K9
Lowgill Cumb 102 B11
Lowgill Lancs 95 P8
Low Grantley N York 97 K6
Low Green N York 97 K9
Low Habberley Worcs 57 Q9
Low Ham Somset 19 M9
Low Harrogate N York 97 L9
Low Hawsker N York 105 P9
Low Hesket Cumb 111 J11
Low Hutton N York 98 F7
Lowick Cumb 94 F3
Lowick Nhants 61 L4

Lowick Nthumb 119 K3
Lowick Bridge Cumb 94 F3
Lowick Green Cumb 94 F3
Low Knipe Cumb 101 P7
Low Laithe N York 97 J8
Lowlands Dur 103 M5
Lowlands Torfn 31 J5
Low Langton Lincs 86 G5
Low Leighton Derbys 83 M7
Low Lorton Cumb 100 G5
Low Marishes N York 98 G5
Low Marnham Notts 85 P7
Low Middleton Nthumb 119 M3
Low Mill N York 105 H10
Low Moor C Brad 90 F5
Low Moorsley Sundld 113 M11
Low Moresby Cumb 100 C6
Low Newton Cumb 95 J4
Low Row Cumb 100 G2
Low Row Cumb 101 L3
Low Row Cumb 111 L8
Low Row N York 103 J11
Low Salchrie D & G 106 D4
Low Santon N Linc 92 F8
Lowsonford Warwks 59 J11
Low Street Norfk 77 L7
Low Street Thurr 37 Q5
Low Tharston Norfk 64 H2
Lowther Cumb 101 P6
Lowthorpe E R Yk 99 M8
Lowton Devon 8 G4
Lowton Somset 18 G11
Lowton Wigan 82 D5
Lowton Common Wigan 82 D5
Lowton St Mary's Wigan 82 D5
Low Torry Fife 134 C10
Low Toynton Lincs 87 J6
Low Valley Barns 91 L10
Low Wood Cumb 94 G4
Low Worsall N York 104 C9
Low Wray Cumb 101 L10
Loxbeare Devon 18 B11
Loxhill Surrey 24 B3
Loxhore Devon 17 L4
Loxhore Cott Devon 17 L4
Loxley Warwks 47 Q4
Loxley Green Staffs 71 K7
Loxter Herefs 46 D6
Loxton N Som 19 L3
Loxwood W Susx 24 B4
Lubenham Leics 60 F3
Lucasgate Lincs 87 M11
Luccombe Somset 18 B6
Luccombe Village IoW 14 G11
Lucker Nthumb 119 N4
Lucking Street Essex 52 D5
Luckington Wilts 32 F8
Lucklawhill Fife 135 L3
Lucknam Wilts 32 F10
Luckwell Bridge Somset 18 B7
Lucton Herefs 45 N2
Lucy Cross N York 103 P8
Ludag W Isls 168 c16
Ludborough Lincs 93 N11
Ludbrook Devon 6 H8
Ludchurch Pembks 41 M8
Luddenden Calder 90 C5
Luddenden Foot Calder 90 C5
Luddenham Court Kent 38 G9
Luddesdown Kent 37 Q7
Luddington N Linc 92 D7
Luddington Warwks 47 N4
Luddington in the Brook
 Nhants 61 P4
Ludford Lincs 86 G3
Ludford Shrops 57 J10
Ludgershall Bucks 49 J11
Ludgershall Wilts 21 Q4
Ludgvan Cnwll 2 E7
Ludham Norfk 77 M8
Ludlow Shrops 57 J9
Ludney Somset 10 H2
Ludwell Wilts 20 H10
Ludworth Dur 104 C2
Luffenhall Herts 50 G5
Luffincott Devon 5 N3
Luffness E Loth 128 D4
Lugar E Ayrs 115 L3
Luggate Burn E Loth 128 F5
Lugg Green Herefs 45 N2
Luggiebank N Lans 126 D3
Lugton E Ayrs 125 L7
Lugwardine Herefs 45 R6
Luib Highld 145 J2
Luing Ag & B 130 E5
Lulham Herefs 45 N6
Lullington Derbys 59 K2
Lullington E Susx 25 M10
Lullington Somset 20 E4
Lulsgate Bottom N Som 31 P11
Lulsley Worcs 46 D3
Lulworth Camp Dorset 12 D8
Lumb Calder 90 C6
Lumb Lancs 89 N6
Lumbutts Calder 90 B6
Lumby N York 91 M4
Lumphanan Abers 150 F7
Lumphinnans Fife 134 F9
Lumsden Abers 150 D3
Lunan Angus 143 M7
Lunanhead Angus 142 H7
Luncarty P & K 134 D2
Lund E R Yk 99 K11
Lund N York 91 R4
Lundie Angus 142 D10
Lundin Links Fife 135 L7
Lundin Mill Fife 135 L7
Lundy Devon 16 A2
Lundy Green Norfk 65 J3
Lunga Ag & B 130 E6
Lunna Shet 169 r7
Lunsford Kent 37 Q9
Lunsford's Cross E Susx 26 B9
Lunt Sefton 81 L4
Luntley Herefs 45 M3
Luppitt Devon 10 D3
Lupridge Devon 7 J7
Lupset Wakefd 91 J7
Lupton Cumb 95 M4
Lurgashall W Susx 23 P9
Lurley Devon 18 B11
Lusby Lincs 87 K7
Luscombe Devon 7 K7

Luson Devon 6 G8
Luss Ag & B 132 D9
Lussagiven Ag & B 130 C10
Lusta Highld 152 D6
Lustleigh Devon 9 J8
Luston Herefs 45 P2
Luthermuir Abers 143 M4
Luthrie Fife 135 J4
Lutley Dudley 58 D8
Luton Devon 9 M9
Luton Devon 10 B4
Luton Luton 50 C6
Luton Medway 38 C8
Luton Airport Luton 50 D6
Lutterworth Leics 60 B4
Lutton Devon 6 F7
Lutton Devon 6 H6
Lutton Lincs 74 H5
Lutton Nhants 61 P3
Luxborough Somset 18 C7
Luxulyan Cnwll 4 H10
Luxulyan Valley Cnwll 4 H10
Luzley Tamesd 83 L4
Lybster Highld 167 M9
Lydbury North Shrops 56 F7
Lydcott Devon 17 M4
Lydd Kent 26 H7
Lydd Airport Kent 27 J7
Lydden Kent 27 N2
Lydden Kent 39 Q8
Lyddington Rutlnd 73 M11
Lydd-on-Sea Kent 27 J8
Lydeard St Lawrence
 Somset 18 F8
Lyde Green Hants 23 K3
Lydford Devon 8 D7
Lydford on Fosse Somset 19 Q8
Lydgate Calder 89 Q5
Lydgate Rochdl 90 B7
Lydham Shrops 56 E6
Lydiard Green Wilts 33 L7
Lydiard Millicent Wilts 33 L7
Lydiard Tregoze Swindn 33 M8
Lydiate Sefton 81 M4
Lydiate Ash Worcs 58 E9
Lydlinch Dorset 12 B2
Lydney Gloucs 32 B4
Lydstep Pembks 41 L11
Lye Dudley 58 D8
Lye Cross N Som 19 N2
Lye Green Bucks 35 Q4
Lye Green E Susx 25 M4
Lye Green Warwks 59 J11
Lye Head Worcs 57 P10
Lyford Oxon 34 C6
Lymbridge Green Kent 27 K3
Lyme Regis Dorset 10 G6
Lyminge Kent 27 L3
Lymington Hants 13 P5
Lyminster W Susx 24 B10
Lymm Warrtn 82 E7
Lymm Services Warrtn 82 E8
Lympne Kent 27 K4
Lympsham Somset 19 K4
Lympstone Devon 9 N8
Lynbridge Devon 17 N2
Lynch Green Norfk 76 H10
Lyndhurst Hants 13 P3
Lyndon Rutlnd 73 N10
Lyndon Green Birm 58 H7
Lyne Border 117 J2
Lyne Surrey 36 B7
Lyneal Shrops 69 M8
Lyne Down Herefs 46 B8
Lyneham Devon 9 L9
Lyneham Oxon 47 Q10
Lyneham Wilts 33 K9
Lyneholmford Cumb 111 K6
Lynemouth Nthumb 113 L2
Lyne of Skene Abers 151 K5
Lynesack Dur 103 L5
Lyness Ork 169 c7
Lyng Norfk 76 F8
Lyng Somset 19 K9
Lynmouth Devon 17 N2
Lynn Staffs 58 G4
Lynn Wrekin 70 D11
Lynsted Kent 38 F9
Lynstone Cnwll 16 C10
Lynton Devon 17 N2
Lynton Cross Devon 17 J3
Lyon's Gate Dorset 11 P3
Lyonshall Herefs 45 L3
Lytchett Matravers Dorset 12 F5
Lytchett Minster Dorset 12 G6
Lyth Highld 167 N4
Lytham Lancs 88 D5
Lytham St Annes Lancs 88 C5
Lythbank Shrops 56 H3
Lythe N York 105 M8
Lythmore Highld 167 J3

M

Mabe Burnthouse Cnwll 3 K7
Mablethorpe Lincs 87 P4
Macclesfield Ches E 83 K10
Macduff Abers 158 H5
Macharioch Ag & B 120 D10
Machen Caerph 30 H7
Machrie Ag & B 120 G5
Machrihanish Ag & B 120 B7
Machrins Ag & B 136 b3
Machynlleth Powys 54 G4
Machynys Carmth 28 F5
Mackworth Derbys 71 Q7
Macmerry E Loth 128 C5
Maddaford Devon 8 D6
Madderty P & K 134 B3
Maddington Wilts 21 L6
Maddiston Falk 126 G2
Madehurst W Susx 15 Q4
Madeley Staffs 70 D6
Madeley Wrekin 57 M4
Madeley Heath Staffs 70 D5
Madford Devon 10 C2
Madingley Cambs 62 E8
Madley Herefs 45 N7
Madresfield Worcs 46 F5
Madron Cnwll 2 D7
Maenaddwyn IoA 78 H8

Maenan Conwy 79 P11
Maenclochog Pembks 41 L5
Maendy V Glam 30 D9
Maenporth Cnwll 3 K8
Maentwrog Gwynd 67 M6
Maen-y-groes Cerdgn 42 G3
Maer Cnwll 16 C10
Maer Staffs 70 D7
Maerdy Carmth 43 N9
Maerdy Conwy 68 D6
Maerdy Rhondd 30 C5
Maesbrook Shrops 69 K10
Maesbury Shrops 69 K9
Maesbury Marsh Shrops 69 K9
Maes-glas Newpt 31 J7
Maesgwynne Carmth 41 P6
Maeshafn Denbgs 68 H2
Maesllyn Cerdgn 42 G6
Maesmynis Powys 44 E5
Maesmynis Powys 44 E5
Maesteg Brdgnd 29 N6
Maesybont Carmth 43 L11
Maesycwmmer Caerph 30 G6
Magdalen Laver Essex 51 M9
Maggieknockater Moray 157 Q8
Maggots End Essex 51 L5
Magham Down E Susx 25 P8
Maghull Sefton 81 M4
Magna Park Leics 60 B4
Magor Mons 31 M7
Magor Services Mons 31 M7
Maidenbower W Susx 24 G3
Maiden Bradley Wilts 20 F7
Maidencombe Torbay 7 N5
Maidenhayne Devon 10 F5
Maiden Head N Som 31 Q11
Maidenhead W & M 35 N8
Maiden Law Dur 113 J11
Maiden Newton Dorset 11 M5
Maidens S Ayrs 114 D7
Maiden's Green Br For 35 P10
Maidenwell Lincs 87 K5
Maiden Wells Pembks 41 J11
Maidford Nhants 48 H4
Maids Moreton Bucks 49 K7
Maidstone Kent 38 C10
Maidstone Services Kent 38 D10
Maidwell Nhants 60 H5
Mail Shet 169 r9
Maindee Newpt 31 K7
Mainland Ork 169 d6
Mainland Shet 169 r8
Mainsforth Dur 104 B4
Mains of Balhall Angus 143 J5
Mains of Balnakettle Abers 143 L3
Mains of Dalvey Highld 157 L11
Mains of Haulkerton Abers 143 N3
Mains of Lesmoir Abers 150 D2
Mains of Melgunds Angus 143 J6
Mainsriddle D & G 109 K9
Mainstone Shrops 56 D7
Maisemore Gloucs 46 F10
Major's Green Worcs 58 H9
Makeney Derbys 72 B2
Malborough Devon 7 J11
Malcoff Derbys 83 N8
Malden Rushett Gt Lon 36 E8
Maldon Essex 52 E10
Malham N York 96 D8
Maligar Highld 152 H5
Mallaig Highld 145 L8
Mallaigvaig Highld 145 L8
Malleny Mills C Edin 127 M4
Mallows Green Essex 51 L5
Malltraeth IoA 78 G11
Mallwyd Gwynd 55 K2
Malmesbury Wilts 32 H7
Malmsmead Devon 17 P2
Malpas Ches W 69 N5
Malpas Cnwll 3 L5
Malpas Newpt 31 K6
Malshanger Hants 22 G4
Malswick Gloucs 46 D10
Maltby Lincs 87 K4
Maltby Rothm 84 H3
Maltby S on T 104 E8
Maltby le Marsh Lincs 87 N4
Malting Green Essex 52 G7
Maltman's Hill Kent 26 F3
Malton N York 98 F6
Malvern Worcs 46 E5
Malvern Hills 46 E5
Malvern Link Worcs 46 E5
Malvern Wells Worcs 46 E5
Mamble Worcs 57 M10
Mamhilad Mons 31 K4
Manaccan Cnwll 3 K9
Manafon Powys 55 Q4
Manais W Isls 168 g9
Manaton Devon 9 J8
Manby Lincs 87 L3
Mancetter Warwks 59 M5
Manchester Manch 82 H5
Manchester Airport Manch 82 H8
Mancot Flints 81 L11
Mandally Highld 146 H7
Manea Cambs 62 G3
Maney Birm 58 H5
Manfield N York 103 P8
Mangersta W Isls 168 f4
Mangerton Dorset 11 K5
Mangotsfield S Glos 32 C9
Mangrove Green Herts 50 D6
Mangurstadh W Isls 168 f4
Manhay Cnwll 2 H7
Manish W Isls 168 g9
Mankinholes Calder 90 B6
Manley Ches W 81 Q10
Manmoel Caerph 30 G4
Mannal Ag & B 136 B7
Manningford Bohune Wilts 21 M3
Manningford Bruce Wilts 21 M3
Manningham C Brad 90 E3
Mannings Heath W Susx 24 F5
Mannington Dorset 13 J3
Manningtree Essex 53 K5
Mannofield C Aber 151 N7
Manorbier Pembks 41 K10
Manorbier Newton Pembks 41 K10
Manordeilo Carmth 43 N9
Manorhill Border 118 C4
Manorowen Pembks 40 H3
Manor Park Gt Lon 37 K3
Mansell Gamage Herefs 45 M6
Mansell Lacy Herefs 45 N5

Mansergh Cumb 95 N4
Mansfield E Ayrs 115 M5
Mansfield Notts 84 H8
Mansfield Woodhouse Notts 84 H8
Mansriggs Cumb 94 F4
Manston Dorset 20 F11
Manston Kent 39 P8
Manston Leeds 91 K4
Manswood Dorset 12 G3
Manthorpe Lincs 73 N3
Manthorpe Lincs 73 R7
Manton N Linc 92 F10
Manton Notts 85 K5
Manton Rutlnd 73 M10
Manton Wilts 33 N11
Manuden Essex 51 L5
Manwood Green Essex 51 M8
Maperton Somset 20 C9
Maplebeck Notts 85 M8
Maple Cross Herts 36 B2
Mapledurham Oxon 35 J9
Mapledurwell Hants 23 J4
Maplehurst W Susx 24 E6
Maplescombe Kent 37 N8
Mapleton Derbys 71 M5
Mapleton Kent 37 L11
Mapperley Derbys 72 C2
Mapperley Park C Nott 72 F2
Mapperton Dorset 11 L5
Mappleborough Green
 Warwks 58 G11
Mappleton E R Yk 93 M2
Mapplewell Barns 91 J8
Mappowder Dorset 12 B3
Marazanvose Cnwll 3 K3
Marazion Cnwll 2 E7
Marbhig W Isls 168 j6
Marbury Ches E 69 Q5
March Cambs 74 H11
March S Lans 116 D8
Marcham Oxon 34 E5
Marchamley Shrops 69 Q9
Marchamley Wood Shrops 69 Q8
Marchington Staffs 71 L8
Marchington Woodlands
 Staffs 71 L9
Marchros Gwynd 66 E9
Marchwiel Wrexhm 69 L5
Marchwood Hants 14 C4
Marcross V Glam 29 P11
Marden Herefs 45 Q5
Marden Kent 26 B3
Marden Wilts 21 L3
Marden Ash Essex 51 N10
Marden Beech Kent 26 B3
Marden's Hill E Susx 25 M4
Marden Thorn Kent 26 C3
Mardlebury Herts 50 G7
Mardy Mons 45 L11
Marefield Leics 73 J9
Mareham le Fen Lincs 87 J8
Mareham on the Hill Lincs 87 J7
Marehay Derbys 84 E11
Marehill W Susx 24 C7
Maresfield E Susx 25 L6
Marfleet C KuH 93 K5
Marford Wrexhm 69 L3
Margam Neath 29 L7
Margaret Marsh Dorset 20 F11
Margaret Roding Essex 51 N8
Margaretting Essex 51 Q10
Margaretting Tye Essex 51 Q10
Margate Kent 39 Q7
Margnaheglish N Ayrs 121 K5
Margrie D & G 108 C10
Margrove Park R & Cl 105 J7
Marham Norfk 75 P9
Marhamchurch Cnwll 16 C11
Marholm C Pete 74 B10
Marian-glas IoA 79 J8
Mariansleigh Devon 17 N7
Marine Town Kent 38 F7
Marionburgh Abers 151 J6
Marishader Highld 152 H5
Maristow Devon 6 D6
Marjoriebanks D & G 109 N4
Mark Somset 19 L5
Markbeech Kent 25 L2
Markby Lincs 87 N5
Mark Causeway Somset 19 L5
Mark Cross E Susx 25 N4
Markeaton C Derb 72 A3
Market Bosworth Leics 72 C10
Market Deeping Lincs 74 B9
Market Drayton Shrops 70 B8
Market Harborough Leics 60 F3
Market Lavington Wilts 21 K4
Market Overton Rutlnd 73 M7
Market Rasen Lincs 86 G3
Market Stainton Lincs 86 H5
Market Warsop Notts 85 J7
Market Weighton E R Yk 92 E2
Market Weston Suffk 64 D6
Markfield Leics 72 D9
Markham Caerph 30 G4
Markham Moor Notts 85 M6
Markinch Fife 134 H7
Markington N York 97 L7
Markle E Loth 128 F4
Marksbury BaNES 20 C2
Mark's Corner IoW 14 E8
Marks Tey Essex 52 F7
Markwell Cnwll 5 P10
Markyate Herts 50 C7
Marlborough Wilts 33 N11
Marlbrook Herefs 45 Q4
Marlbrook Worcs 58 E10
Marlcliff Warwks 47 L4
Marldon Devon 7 M6
Marle Green E Susx 25 N7
Marlesford Suffk 65 L10
Marley Kent 39 L11
Marley Kent 39 P11
Marley Green Ches E 69 Q5
Marley Hill Gatesd 113 K9
Marlingford Norfk 76 G10
Marloes Pembks 40 E9
Marlow Bucks 35 M7
Marlow Herefs 56 G9
Marlow Bottom Bucks 35 M7
Marlpit Hill Kent 25 K11
Marlpits E Susx 25 L5
Marlpits E Susx 26 B9
Marlpool Derbys 84 F11
Marnhull Dorset 20 E11

Marple Stockp 83 L7
Marple Bridge Stockp 83 L7
Marr Donc 91 N9
Marrick N York 103 L11
Marros Carmth 41 P9
Marsden Kirk 90 C8
Marsden S Tyne 113 N8
Marsden Height Lancs 89 P3
Marsett N York 96 D3
Marsh Bucks 35 M3
Marsh C Brad 90 C3
Marsh Devon 10 F2
Marshall's Heath Herts 50 E8
Marshalswick Herts 50 E9
Marsham Norfk 76 H7
Marsh Baldon Oxon 34 G5
Marsh Benham W Berk 34 D11
Marshborough Kent 39 P10
Marshbrook Shrops 56 G7
Marshchapel Lincs 93 Q11
Marsh Farm Luton 50 C5
Marshfield Newpt 31 J8
Marshfield S Glos 32 E10
Marshgate Cnwll 5 K3
Marsh Gibbon Bucks 48 H10
Marsh Green Devon 9 P6
Marsh Green Kent 25 L2
Marsh Green Wrekin 57 L2
Marshland St James Norfk 75 M9
Marsh Lane Derbys 84 F5
Marsh Lane Gloucs 31 Q3
Marshside Sefton 88 D7
Marsh Street Somset 18 C6
Marshwood Dorset 10 H5
Marske N York 103 M10
Marske-by-the-Sea R & Cl 104 H6
Marsland Green Wigan 82 E5
Marston Ches W 82 E9
Marston Herefs 45 M3
Marston Lincs 73 M2
Marston Oxon 34 F3
Marston Staffs 58 B2
Marston Staffs 70 G9
Marston Warwks 59 K6
Marston Wilts 21 J3
Marston Green Solhll 59 J7
Marston Jabbet Warwks 59 N7
Marston Magna Somset 19 Q10
Marston Meysey Wilts 33 M5
Marston Montgomery
 Derbys 71 L7
Marston Moretaine C Beds 49 Q6
Marston on Dove Derbys 71 N9
Marston St Lawrence
 Nhants 48 F6
Marston Stannett Herefs 45 R3
Marston Trussell Nhants 60 E3
Marstow Herefs 45 R11
Marsworth Bucks 35 P2
Marten Wilts 21 Q2
Marthall Ches E 82 G9
Martham Norfk 77 P8
Martin Hants 21 L11
Martin Kent 27 P2
Martin Lincs 86 F9
Martin Lincs 86 H7
Martindale Cumb 101 M7
Martin Dales Lincs 86 G8
Martin Drove End Hants 21 L10
Martinhoe Devon 17 M2
Martin Hussingtree Worcs 46 G2
Martinscroft Warrtn 82 E7
Martinstown Dorset 11 N7
Martlesham Suffk 53 M2
Martlesham Heath Suffk 53 M2
Martletwy Pembks 41 K8
Martley Worcs 46 E2
Martock Somset 19 N11
Marton Ches E 83 J11
Marton Ches E 82 D11
Marton Cumb 94 E5
Marton E R Yk 93 L3
Marton E R Yk 99 Q7
Marton Lincs 85 P4
Marton Middsb 104 E7
Marton N York 97 P8
Marton N York 98 E4
Marton Shrops 56 D4
Marton Warwks 59 P11
Marton-le-Moor N York 97 N6
Martyr's Green Surrey 36 C9
Martyr Worthy Hants 22 F8
Marvig W Isls 168 j6
Marwell Wildlife Hants 22 F10
Marwick Ork 169 b4
Marwood Devon 17 J4
Marybank Highld 155 N7
Maryburgh Highld 155 P6
Marygold Border 129 L8
Maryhill C Glas 125 P4
Marykirk Abers 143 M4
Maryland Mons 31 P3
Marylebone Gt Lon 36 G4
Marylebone Wigan 88 H9
Marypark Moray 157 M10
Maryport Cumb 100 D3
Maryport D & G 106 F11
Marystow Devon 8 B8
Mary Tavy Devon 8 D7
Maryton Angus 143 M6
Marywell Abers 150 F8
Marywell Abers 151 N8
Marywell Angus 143 M9
Masham N York 97 K4
Mashbury Essex 51 Q8
Mason N u Ty 113 K6
Masongill N York 95 P5
Mastin Moor Derbys 84 G5
Matching Essex 51 M8
Matching Green Essex 51 M8
Matching Tye Essex 51 M8
Matfen Nthumb 112 F6
Matfield Kent 25 Q2
Mathern Mons 31 P6
Mathon Herefs 46 D5
Mathry Pembks 40 G4
Matlask Norfk 76 H5
Matlock Derbys 84 D8
Matlock Bank Derbys 84 D8
Matlock Bath Derbys 84 C8
Matlock Dale Derbys 84 C8
Matson Gloucs 46 G11
Matterdale End Cumb 101 L6
Mattersey Notts 85 L3
Mattersey Thorpe Notts 85 L3

Mattingley – Mockbeggar 283

Mattingley Hants 23 K3
Mattishall Norfk 76 F9
Mattishall Burgh Norfk 76 F9
Mauchline E Ayrs 115 J2
Maud Abers 159 M8
Maufant Jersey 11 c1
Maugersbury Gloucs 47 P9
Maughold IoM 80 g3
Mauld Highld 155 M10
Maulden C Beds 50 C3
Maulds Meaburn Cumb 102 B7
Maunby N York 97 N3
Maund Bryan Herefs 45 R4
Maundown Somset 18 E9
Mautby Norfk 77 P9
Mavesyn Ridware Staffs 71 K11
Mavis Enderby Lincs 87 L7
Mawbray Cumb 109 N11
Mawdesley Lancs 88 F8
Mawdlam Brdgnd 29 M8
Mawgan Cnwll 3 J8
Mawgan Porth Cnwll 4 D8
Maw Green Ches E 70 C3
Mawla Cnwll 3 J4
Mawnan Cnwll 3 K8
Mawnan Smith Cnwll 3 K8
Mawsley Nhants 60 H5
Mawthorpe Lincs 87 N6
Maxey C Pete 74 B9
Maxstoke Warwks 59 K7
Maxted Street Kent 27 K3
Maxton Border 118 B4
Maxton Kent 27 P3
Maxwelltown D & G 109 L5
Maxworthy Cnwll 5 M3
Mayals Swans 28 H7
May Bank Staffs 70 F5
Maybole S Ayrs 114 E6
Maybury Surrey 36 B9
Mayes Green Surrey 24 D3
Mayfield E Susx 25 N5
Mayfield Mdloth 128 B7
Mayfield Staffs 71 M5
Mayford Surrey 23 Q3
May Hill Gloucs 46 D10
Mayland Essex 52 F11
Maylandsea Essex 52 F11
Maynard's Green E Susx 25 N7
Maypole Birm 58 G9
Maypole Kent 39 M9
Maypole Mons 45 P11
Maypole Green Norfk 65 N2
Maypole Green Suffk 64 C10
Maypole Green Suffk 65 K8
May's Green Oxon 35 K8
May's Green Surrey 36 C9
Mead Devon 16 C8
Meadgate BaNES 20 C3
Meadle Bucks 35 M3
Meadowfield Dur 103 P3
Meadowtown Shrops 56 E4
Meadwell Devon 5 Q5
Meaford Staffs 70 F7
Mealabost W Isls 168 j4
Meal Bank Cumb 101 P11
Mealrigg Cumb 109 P11
Mealsgate Cumb 100 H2
Meanwood Leeds 90 H3
Mearbeck N York 96 B8
Meare Somset 19 N6
Meare Green Somset 19 J10
Meare Green Somset 19 K9
Mearns E Rens 125 N6
Mears Ashby Nhants 60 H7
Measham Leics 72 A8
Meath Green Surrey 24 G2
Meathop Cumb 95 J4
Meaux E R Yk 93 J3
Meavaig W Isls 168 f4
Meavy Devon 6 E5
Medbourne Leics 60 H2
Medburn Nthumb 112 H6
Meddon Devon 16 D8
Meden Vale Notts 85 J7
Medlam Lincs 87 K9
Medlar Lancs 88 E3
Medmenham Bucks 35 M8
Medomsley Dur 112 H10
Medstead Hants 23 J7
Medway Services Medway 38 D9
Meerbrook Staffs 70 H2
Meer Common Herefs 45 M4
Meesden Herts 51 K4
Meeson Wrekin 70 A10
Meeth Devon 17 J10
Meeting Green Suffk 63 M9
Meeting House Hill Norfk 77 L6
Meidrim Carmth 41 Q6
Meifod Powys 56 B2
Meigle P & K 142 D9
Meikle Carco D & G 115 Q5
Meikle Earnock S Lans 126 C7
Meikle Kilmory Ag & B 124 D5
Meikle Obney P & K 141 P10
Meikleour P & K 142 B10
Meikle Wartle Abers 158 H11
Meinciau Carmth 28 E2
Meir C Stke 70 G6
Meir Heath Staffs 70 G6
Melbost W Isls 168 j4
Melbourn Cambs 51 J2
Melbourne Derbys 72 B5
Melbourne E R Yk 92 C2
Melbur Cnwll 3 N3
Melbury Devon 16 F8
Melbury Abbas Dorset 20 G10
Melbury Bubb Dorset 11 M3
Melbury Osmond Dorset 11 M3
Melbury Sampford Dorset 11 M3
Melchbourne Bed 61 M7
Melcombe Bingham Dorset 12 C4
Meldon Devon 8 E6
Meldon Nthumb 112 H4
Meldon Park Nthumb 112 H3
Meldreth Cambs 62 E11
Meldrum Stirlg 133 L8
Melfort Ag & B 130 G5
Meliden Denbgs 80 F8
Melinau Pembks 41 N8
Melin-byrhedyn Powys 55 J5
Melincourt Neath 29 M4
Melin-y-coed Conwy 67 Q2
Melin-y-ddol Powys 55 P3
Melin-y-wig Denbgs 68 D5
Melkinthorpe Cumb 101 Q5
Melkridge Nthumb 111 P8
Melksham Wilts 20 H2
Mellangoose Cnwll 2 H8
Mell Green W Berk 34 E9
Mellguards Cumb 110 H11
Melling Lancs 95 M6
Melling Sefton 81 M4
Melling Mount Sefton 81 N4
Mellis Suffk 64 F7
Mellon Charles Highld 160 C8
Mellon Udrigle Highld 160 D7
Mellor Lancs 89 K4
Mellor Stockp 83 L7
Mellor Brook Lancs 89 J4
Mells Somset 20 D5
Mells Suffk 65 N6
Melmerby Cumb 102 B3
Melmerby N York 96 G3
Melmerby N York 97 M5
Melness Highld 165 N4
Melon Green Suffk 64 A10
Melplash Dorset 11 K5
Melrose Border 117 Q4
Melsetter Ork 169 b8
Melsonby N York 103 N9
Meltham Kirk 90 E8
Meltham Mills Kirk 90 E8
Melton E R Yk 92 G5
Melton Suffk 65 K11
Meltonby E R Yk 98 F10
Melton Constable Norfk 76 E5
Melton Mowbray Leics 73 K7
Melton Ross N Linc 93 J8
Melvaig Highld 160 A9
Melverley Shrops 69 K11
Melverley Green Shrops 69 K11
Melvich Highld 166 E4
Membury Devon 10 F4
Membury Services W Berk 34 B9
Memsie Abers 159 N5
Memus Angus 142 G6
Menabilly Cnwll 4 H11
Menagissey Cnwll 3 J4
Menai Bridge IoA 79 K10
Mendham Suffk 65 K5
Mendip Hills 19 P4
Mendlesham Suffk 64 G8
Mendlesham Green Suffk 64 F9
Menheniot Cnwll 5 M9
Menithwood Worcs 57 N11
Menna Cnwll 3 N3
Mennock D & G 115 R6
Menston C Brad 90 F2
Menstrie Clacks 133 P8
Menthorpe N York 92 B4
Mentmore Bucks 49 P11
Meoble Highld 145 N10
Meole Brace Shrops 56 H2
Meonstoke Hants 22 H11
Meopham Kent 37 P7
Meopham Green Kent 37 P7
Meopham Station Kent 37 P7
Mepal Cambs 62 F4
Meppershall C Beds 50 D3
Merbach Herefs 45 L5
Mere Ches E 82 F8
Mere Wilts 20 F8
Mere Brow Lancs 88 E7
Mereclough Lancs 89 P4
Mere Green Birm 58 H5
Mere Green Worcs 47 J2
Mere Heath Ches W 82 E10
Meresborough Medway 38 D9
Mereworth Kent 37 Q10
Meriden Solhll 59 K8
Merkadale Highld 152 F11
Merley BCP 12 H5
Merlin's Bridge Pembks 40 H8
Merrington Shrops 69 N10
Merrion Pembks 40 H11
Merriott Somset 11 J2
Merrivale Devon 8 D9
Merrow Surrey 36 B10
Merry Field Hill Dorset 12 H4
Merry Hill Herts 36 D2
Merryhill Wolves 58 C5
Merry Lees Leics 72 D9
Merrymeet Cnwll 5 M8
Mersea Island Essex 52 H8
Mersey Crossing Halton 81 Q8
Mersham Kent 27 J3
Merstham Surrey 36 G10
Merston W Susx 15 N6
Merstone IoW 14 F9
Merther Cnwll 3 M5
Merthyr Carmth 42 G10
Merthyr Cynog Powys 44 D7
Merthyr Dyfan V Glam 30 F11
Merthyr Mawr Brdgnd 29 N9
Merthyr Tydfil Myr Td 30 D3
Merthyr Vale Myr Td 30 E5
Merton Devon 17 J9
Merton Gt Lon 36 G6
Merton Norfk 64 C2
Merton Oxon 48 G11
Meshaw Devon 17 P8
Messing Essex 52 E8
Messingham N Linc 92 E10
Metfield Suffk 65 K5
Metherell Cnwll 5 Q8
Metheringham Lincs 86 E8
Methil Fife 135 K8
Methilhill Fife 135 K7
Methley Leeds 91 K5
Methley Junction Leeds 91 K5
Methlick Abers 159 L10
Methven P & K 134 C2
Methwold Norfk 63 M2
Methwold Hythe Norfk 63 M2
Mettingham Suffk 65 M4
Metton Norfk 76 J4
Mevagissey Cnwll 3 Q5
Mexborough Donc 91 M10
Mey Highld 167 N2
Meysey Hampton Gloucs 33 M4
Miabhaig W Isls 168 f4
Michaelchurch Herefs 45 Q9
Michaelchurch Escley Herefs 45 L8
Michaelchurch-on-Arrow Powys 45 J4
Michaelstone-y-Fedw Newpt 30 H8
Michaelston-le-Pit V Glam 30 G10
Michaelstow Cnwll 4 H6
Michaelwood Services Gloucs 32 D5
Michelcombe Devon 6 H5
Micheldever Hants 22 F7
Micheldever Station Hants 22 F6
Michelmersh Hants 22 B9
Mickfield Suffk 64 G9
Micklebring Donc 84 H2
Mickleby N York 105 M8
Micklefield Leeds 91 L4
Micklefield Green Herts 50 B11
Mickleham Surrey 36 E10
Mickleover C Derb 71 Q8
Micklethwaite C Brad 90 E2
Micklethwaite Cumb 110 E10
Mickleton Dur 103 J6
Mickleton Gloucs 47 N6
Mickletown Leeds 91 L5
Mickle Trafford Ches W 81 N11
Mickley Derbys 84 D5
Mickley N York 97 L5
Mickley Green Suffk 64 A10
Mickley Square Nthumb 112 G8
Mid Ardlaw Abers 159 M5
Midbea Ork 169 d2
Mid Beltie Abers 150 G7
Mid Bockhampton BCP 13 L5
Mid Calder W Loth 127 K4
Mid Clyth Highld 167 N9
Mid Culbeuchly Abers 158 G5
Middle Assendon Oxon 35 K7
Middle Aston Oxon 48 E9
Middle Barton Oxon 48 D9
Middlebie D & G 110 D5
Middlebridge P & K 141 L4
Middle Chinnock Somset 11 K2
Middle Claydon Bucks 49 K9
Middlecliffe Barns 91 L9
Middlecott Devon 8 H7
Middle Duntisbourne Gloucs 33 J3
Middleham N York 96 H3
Middle Handley Derbys 84 F5
Middle Harling Norfk 64 D4
Middlehill Cnwll 5 M8
Middlehill Wilts 32 F11
Middlehope Shrops 56 H7
Middle Kames Ag & B 131 J10
Middle Littleton Worcs 47 L5
Middle Madeley Staffs 70 D5
Middle Maes-coed Herefs 45 L8
Middlemarsh Dorset 11 P3
Middle Mayfield Staffs 71 L6
Middle Mill Pembks 40 F5
Middlemoor Devon 6 D4
Middle Quarter Kent 26 E4
Middle Rasen Lincs 86 E3
Middle Rocombe Devon 7 N5
Middle Salter Lancs 95 N8
Middlesbrough Middsb 104 E7
Middlesceugh Cumb 101 M2
Middleshaw Cumb 95 M3
Middlesmoor N York 96 G6
Middle Stoford Somset 18 G10
Middle Stoke Medway 38 D6
Middlestone Dur 103 Q4
Middlestone Moor Dur 103 P4
Middle Stoughton Somset 19 M5
Middlestown Wakefd 90 H7
Middle Street Gloucs 32 E4
Middle Taphouse Cnwll 5 K9
Middlethird Border 118 C2
Middleton Ag & B 136 A7
Middleton Cumb 95 N3
Middleton Derbys 71 M2
Middleton Derbys 84 C9
Middleton Essex 52 E4
Middleton Hants 22 D6
Middleton Herefs 57 J11
Middleton Lancs 95 J9
Middleton Leeds 91 J5
Middleton N York 96 H11
Middleton N York 98 F3
Middleton Nhants 60 H3
Middleton Norfk 75 N7
Middleton Nthumb 112 G4
Middleton Nthumb 119 M3
Middleton P & K 134 E6
Middleton Rochdl 89 P9
Middleton Shrops 57 J9
Middleton Shrops 69 K9
Middleton Suffk 65 N8
Middleton Swans 28 D7
Middleton Warwks 59 J5
Middleton Cheney Nhants 48 E6
Middleton Green Staffs 70 H7
Middleton Hall Nthumb 119 J5
Middleton-in-Teesdale Dur 102 H5
Middleton Moor Suffk 65 N8
Middleton One Row Darltn 104 C8
Middleton-on-Leven N York 104 E9
Middleton-on-Sea W Susx 15 Q6
Middleton on the Hill Herefs 45 Q2
Middleton on the Wolds E R Yk 99 J11
Middleton Park C Aber 151 N5
Middleton Priors Shrops 57 L6
Middleton Quernhow N York 97 M5
Middleton St George Darltn 104 B8
Middleton Scriven Shrops 57 M7
Middleton Stoney Oxon 48 F10
Middleton Tyas N York 103 P9
Middletown Cumb 100 C9
Middle Town IoS 2 b3
Middletown N Som 31 N10
Middletown Powys 56 E2
Middle Tysoe Warwks 48 B6
Middle Wallop Hants 21 Q7
Middlewich Ches E 82 F11
Middle Winterslow Wilts 21 P8
Middlewood Cnwll 5 M6
Middlewood Herefs 45 K6
Middle Woodford Wilts 21 M7
Middlewood Green Suffk 64 F9
Middle Yard Gloucs 32 F4
Middlezoy Somset 19 L8
Middridge Dur 103 P5
Midford BaNES 20 E2
Midge Hall Lancs 88 G6
Midgeholme Cumb 111 M9
Midgham W Berk 34 G11
Midgley Calder 90 C5
Midgley Wakefd 90 H8
Mid Holmwood Surrey 36 E11
Midhopestones Sheff 90 G11
Midhurst W Susx 23 N10
Mid Lavant W Susx 15 N5
Midlem Border 117 Q5
Mid Mains Highld 155 M10
Midney Somset 19 N9
Midpark Ag & B 124 C6
Midsomer Norton BaNES 20 C4
Midtown Highld 165 N4
Midville Lincs 87 L9
Midway Ches E 83 K8
Mid Yell Shet 169 s4
Migdale Highld 162 E8
Migvie Abers 150 C6
Milborne Port Somset 20 C11
Milborne St Andrew Dorset 12 D5
Milborne Wick Somset 20 C10
Milbourne Nthumb 112 H5
Milbourne Wilts 33 J7
Milburn Cumb 102 C5
Milbury Heath S Glos 32 C6
Milby N York 97 P7
Milcombe Oxon 48 D8
Milden Suffk 52 G2
Mildenhall Suffk 63 M6
Mildenhall Wilts 33 P11
Milebrook Powys 56 E10
Milebush Kent 26 C2
Mile Elm Wilts 33 J11
Mile End Essex 52 G6
Mile End Gloucs 31 Q2
Mile End Suffk 65 L4
Mileham Norfk 76 C8
Mile Oak Br & H 24 F9
Mile Oak Kent 25 Q2
Mile Oak Staffs 59 J4
Miles Hope Herefs 45 R2
Milesmark Fife 134 D10
Miles Platting Manch 83 J5
Mile Town Kent 38 F7
Milfield Nthumb 118 H4
Milford Derbys 84 E11
Milford Devon 16 C7
Milford Powys 55 P6
Milford Staffs 70 H10
Milford Surrey 23 P6
Milford Haven Pembks 40 H9
Milford on Sea Hants 13 N6
Milkwall Gloucs 31 Q3
Millais Jersey 11 a1
Milland W Susx 23 M9
Milland Marsh W Susx 23 M9
Mill Bank Calder 90 C6
Millbeck Cumb 101 J5
Millbreck Abers 159 P9
Millbridge Surrey 23 M6
Millbrook C Beds 50 B3
Millbrook C Sotn 14 C4
Millbrook Cnwll 6 C8
Millbrook Jersey 11 b2
Millbrook Tamesd 83 L5
Mill Brow Stockp 83 L7
Millbuie Abers 151 K6
Millbuie Highld 155 Q7
Millcombe Devon 7 L9
Mill Common Norfk 77 L11
Mill Common Suffk 65 N5
Millcorner E Susx 26 D7
Millcraig Highld 156 B3
Mill Cross Devon 7 J6
Milldale Staffs 71 L4
Mill End Bucks 35 L7
Millend Gloucs 32 D5
Mill End Herts 50 H4
Millerhill Mdloth 127 Q4
Miller's Dale Derbys 83 P10
Millers Green Derbys 71 P4
Miller's Green Essex 51 N9
Millerston C Glas 125 Q4
Millgate Lancs 89 P7
Mill Green Cambs 63 K11
Mill Green Essex 51 P10
Mill Green Herts 50 F8
Mill Green Lincs 74 D6
Mill Green Norfk 64 G5
Millgreen Shrops 70 B9
Mill Green Staffs 58 G4
Mill Green Staffs 71 K10
Mill Green Suffk 52 G3
Mill Green Suffk 64 D10
Mill Green Suffk 64 G9
Mill Green Suffk 65 L9
Millhalf Herefs 45 K5
Millhayes Devon 10 E4
Millhead Lancs 95 K6
Millheugh S Lans 126 C7
Mill Hill E Susx 25 P9
Mill Hill Gt Lon 36 F2
Millhouse Ag & B 124 B3
Millhouse Cumb 101 L3
Millhousebridge D & G 109 P3
Millhouse Green Barns 90 G10
Millhouses Barns 91 L10
Millhouses Sheff 84 D4
Milliken Park Rens 125 L5
Millin Cross Pembks 41 J8
Millington E R Yk 98 G10
Mill Lane Hants 23 L4
Millmeece Staffs 70 E8
Millness Cumb 95 L4
Mill of Drummond P & K 133 N4
Mill of Haldane W Duns 132 D11
Millom Cumb 94 D4
Millook Cnwll 5 K2
Millpool Cnwll 2 F7
Millpool Cnwll 5 J7
Millport N Ayrs 124 F7
Mill Side Cumb 95 J4
Mill Street Kent 37 Q9
Mill Street Norfk 76 F8
Mill Street Suffk 64 F7
Millthorpe Derbys 84 D5
Millthrop Cumb 95 P2
Milltimber C Aber 151 M7
Milltown Abers 149 P6
Milltown Abers 150 D4
Milltown Cnwll 5 J10
Milltown D & G 110 F5
Milltown Derbys 84 E8
Milltown Devon 17 K4
Milltown Highld 153 N9
Milltown of Auchindoun Moray 157 R9
Milltown of Campfield Abers 150 H7
Milltown of Edinvillie Moray 157 P9
Milltown of Learney Abers 150 G7
Milltown of Rothiemay Moray 158 E8
Milnathort P & K 134 E7
Milngavie E Duns 125 P3
Milnrow Rochdl 89 Q8
Milnthorpe Cumb 95 K4
Milnthorpe Wakefd 91 J7
Milovaig Highld 152 B8
Milson Shrops 57 L10
Milstead Kent 38 F10
Milston Wilts 21 N5
Milthorpe Lincs 74 B4
Milthorpe Nhants 48 G5
Milton C Stke 70 G4
Milton Cambs 62 G8
Milton Cumb 111 L8
Milton D & G 106 H7
Milton D & G 108 H6
Milton Derbys 71 Q9
Milton Highld 155 N11
Milton Highld 155 Q8
Milton Highld 156 D3
Milton Highld 167 P6
Milton Inver 125 K4
Milton Kent 37 Q6
Milton Moray 149 M4
Milton Moray 158 D5
Milton N Som 19 K2
Milton Newpt 31 L7
Milton Notts 85 M6
Milton Oxon 34 E6
Milton Oxon 48 E7
Milton P & K 141 Q5
Milton Pembks 41 K10
Milton Somset 19 N10
Milton Stirlg 132 G7
Milton W Duns 125 L3
Milton Abbas Dorset 12 D4
Milton Abbot Devon 5 Q6
Milton Bridge Mdloth 127 P5
Milton Bryan C Beds 49 Q8
Milton Clevedon Somset 20 C7
Milton Combe Devon 6 D5
Milton Common Oxon 35 J4
Milton Damerel Devon 16 F9
Milton End Gloucs 32 D2
Milton End Gloucs 33 M4
Milton Ernest Bed 61 M9
Milton Green Ches W 69 N3
Milton Hill Oxon 34 E6
Milton Keynes M Keyn 49 N7
Milton Lilbourne Wilts 21 N2
Milton Malsor Nhants 60 F9
Milton Morenish P & K 140 F10
Milton of Auchinhove Abers 150 F7
Milton of Balgonie Fife 135 J7
Milton of Buchanan Stirlg 132 E9
Milton of Campsie E Duns 126 B2
Milton of Finavon Angus 142 H6
Milton of Leys Highld 156 B9
Milton of Murtle C Aber 151 M7
Milton on Stour Dorset 20 E9
Milton Regis Kent 38 F9
Milton Street E Susx 25 M10
Milton-under-Wychwood Oxon 47 Q11
Milverton Somset 18 F9
Milverton Warwks 59 M11
Milwich Staffs 70 H8
Milwr Flints 80 H10
Minard Ag & B 131 K8
Minchington Dorset 12 G2
Minchinhampton Gloucs 32 G4
Mindrum Nthumb 118 F4
Minehead Somset 18 C5
Minera Wrexhm 69 J4
Minety Wilts 33 K6
Minffordd Gwynd 67 K7
Mingarrypark Highld 138 B4
Miningsby Lincs 87 K8
Minions Cnwll 5 M7
Minishant S Ayrs 114 F5
Minllyn Gwynd 55 K2
Minnigaff D & G 107 M4
Minnonie Abers 159 J5
Minshull Vernon Ches E 70 B2
Minskip N York 97 N8
Minstead Hants 13 N2
Minsted W Susx 23 N10
Minster Kent 39 P9
Minsterley Shrops 56 F3
Minster Lovell Oxon 34 B2
Minster-on-Sea Kent 38 G7
Minsterworth Gloucs 46 E11
Minterne Magna Dorset 11 P4
Minterne Parva Dorset 11 P4
Minting Lincs 86 G6
Mintlaw Abers 159 N8
Minto Border 117 R6
Minton Shrops 56 G6
Minwear Pembks 41 K8
Minworth Birm 59 J6
Mirehouse Cumb 100 C7
Mireland Highld 167 P4
Mirfield Kirk 90 G7
Miserden Gloucs 32 H3
Miskin Rhondd 30 D5
Miskin Rhondd 30 D8
Misson Notts 85 L2
Misterton Leics 60 C4
Misterton Notts 85 N2
Misterton Somset 11 K3
Mistley Essex 53 K5
Mistley Heath Essex 53 K5
Mitcham Gt Lon 36 G7
Mitcheldean Gloucs 46 C11
Mitchell Cnwll 3 M3
Mitchellslacks D & G 116 D11
Mitchel Troy Mons 31 N2
Mitford Nthumb 113 J3
Mithian Cnwll 3 J3
Mitton Staffs 70 F11
Mixbury Oxon 48 H8
Mixenden Calder 90 D5
Moats Tye Suffk 64 E10
Mobberley Ches E 82 G9
Mobberley Staffs 71 J6
Moccas Herefs 45 M6
Mochdre Conwy 79 Q9
Mochdre Powys 55 P7
Mochrum D & G 107 K8
Mockbeggar Hants 13 L3
Mockbeggar Kent 26 B2

284 Mockerkin – Netherton

Mockerkin Cumb 100 E6
Modbury Devon 6 H8
Moddershall Staffs 70 G7
Moelfre IoA 79 J7
Moelfre Powys 68 G9
Moel Tryfan Gwynd 67 J3
Moffat D & G 116 F9
Mogador Surrey 36 F10
Moggerhanger C Beds 61 P11
Moira Leics 71 Q11
Molash Kent 38 H11
Mol-chlach Highld 144 G5
Mold Flints 68 H2
Moldgreen Kirk 90 F7
Molehill Green Essex 51 N6
Molehill Green Essex 52 B7
Molescroft E R Yk 92 H2
Molesden Nthumb 112 H4
Molesworth Cambs 61 N5
Moll Highld 153 K11
Molland Devon 17 Q6
Mollington Ches W 81 M10
Mollington Oxon 48 D5
Mollinsburn N Lans 126 C3
Monachty Cerdgn 43 K2
Mondynes Abers 143 P2
Monewden Suffk 65 J10
Moneydie P & K 134 D2
Moneyrow Green W & M 35 N9
Moniaive D & G 115 Q9
Monifieth Angus 142 H11
Monikie Angus 142 H10
Monimail Fife 134 H5
Monington Pembks 41 M2
Monk Bretton Barns 91 K9
Monken Hadley Gt Lon 50 F11
Monk Fryston N York 91 N5
Monkhide Herefs 46 B6
Monkhill Cumb 110 F9
Monkhopton Shrops 57 L6
Monkland Herefs 45 P3
Monkleigh Devon 16 H7
Monknash V Glam 29 P10
Monkokehampton Devon 8 E3
Monkseaton N Tyne 113 M6
Monks Eleigh Suffk 52 G2
Monk's Gate W Susx 24 F5
Monks Heath Ches E 82 H10
Monk Sherborne Hants 22 H3
Monks Horton Kent 27 K3
Monksilver Somset 18 E7
Monks Kirby Warwks 59 Q8
Monk Soham Suffk 65 J8
Monkspath Solhll 58 H9
Monks Risborough Bucks 35 M4
Monksthorpe Lincs 87 M7
Monk Street Essex 51 P5
Monkswood Mons 31 K4
Monkton Devon 10 D4
Monkton Kent 39 N9
Monkton S Ayrs 114 G2
Monkton S Tyne 113 M8
Monkton V Glam 29 P10
Monkton Combe BaNES 20 E2
Monkton Deverill Wilts 20 G7
Monkton Farleigh Wilts 32 F11
Monkton Heathfield Somset 19 J9
Monkton Up Wimborne Dorset 12 H2
Monkton Wyld Dorset 10 G5
Monkwearmouth Sundld 113 N9
Monkwood Hants 23 J8
Monmore Green Wolves 58 D5
Monmouth Mons 31 P2
Monnington on Wye Herefs 45 M6
Monreith D & G 107 L9
Montacute Somset 19 N11
Montcliffe Bolton 89 K8
Montford Shrops 56 G2
Montford Bridge Shrops 69 M11
Montgarrie Abers 150 F4
Montgomery Powys 56 C5
Monton Salfd 82 G5
Montrose Angus 143 N6
Mont Saint Guern 10 b2
Monxton Hants 22 B6
Monyash Derbys 83 Q11
Monymusk Abers 150 H4
Monzie P & K 133 P2
Moodiesburn N Lans 126 B3
Moonzie Fife 135 J4
Moor Allerton Leeds 91 J3
Moorbath Dorset 11 J5
Moorby Lincs 87 J8
Moorcot Herefs 45 M3
Moor Crichel Dorset 12 G3
Moordown BCP 13 J6
Moore Halton 82 C8
Moor End C Beds 49 Q10
Moor End Calder 90 D5
Moor End Devon 17 M10
Moorend Gloucs 32 D4
Moor End Lancs 88 D2
Moor End N York 91 Q3
Moorends Donc 92 A7
Moorgreen Hants 22 E11
Moor Green Herts 50 H5
Moorgreen Notts 84 G11
Moorhall Derbys 84 D6
Moorhampton Herefs 45 M5
Moorhead C Brad 90 E3
Moor Head Leeds 90 G5
Moorhouse Cumb 110 E10
Moorhouse Cumb 110 F9
Moorhouse Donc 91 M8
Moorhouse Notts 85 N7
Moorhouse Bank Surrey 37 K10
Moorland Somset 19 K8
Moorlinch Somset 19 L7
Moor Monkton N York 97 R9
Moor Row Cumb 100 D8
Moor Row Cumb 110 D11
Moorsholm R & Cl 105 J8
Moorside Dorset 20 E11
Moorside Dur 112 G11
Moor Side Lancs 88 E4
Moor Side Lancs 88 F3
Moorside Leeds 90 G3
Moor Side Lincs 87 J9
Moorside Oldham 89 Q9
Moorstock Kent 27 K4
Moor Street Birm 58 E8
Moor Street Medway 38 D8
Moorswater Cnwll 5 L9
Moorthorpe Wakefd 91 M8
Moortown Devon 6 E4
Moortown Hants 13 L4
Moortown IoW 14 D10
Moortown Leeds 90 H3
Moortown Lincs 93 J11
Moortown Wrekin 69 R11
Morangie Highld 162 H10
Morar Highld 145 L9
Morborne Cambs 61 P2
Morchard Bishop Devon 9 J3
Morchard Road Devon 9 J3
Morcombelake Dorset 11 J6
Morcott Rutlnd 73 N10
Morda Shrops 69 J9
Morden Dorset 12 F5
Morden Gt Lon 36 G7
Mordiford Herefs 45 R7
Mordon Dur 104 B5
More Shrops 56 E6
Morebath Devon 18 C9
Morebattle Border 118 E6
Morecambe Lancs 95 J8
Moredon Swindn 33 M7
Morefield Highld 161 J7
Morehall Kent 27 M4
Moreleigh Devon 7 K8
Morenish P & K 140 F10
Moresby Parks Cumb 100 C7
Morestead Hants 22 F9
Moreton Dorset 12 D7
Moreton Essex 51 M9
Moreton Herefs 45 Q2
Moreton Oxon 35 J4
Moreton Staffs 70 D11
Moreton Staffs 71 L9
Moreton Wirral 81 K7
Moreton Corbet Shrops 69 Q10
Moretonhampstead Devon 9 J7
Moreton-in-Marsh Gloucs 47 P8
Moreton Jeffries Herefs 46 B5
Moretonmill Shrops 69 Q10
Moreton Morrell Warwks 48 B3
Moreton on Lugg Herefs 45 Q5
Moreton Paddox Warwks 48 B4
Moreton Pinkney Nhants 48 G5
Moreton Say Shrops 70 A8
Moreton Valence Gloucs 32 E3
Morfa Cerdgn 42 F4
Morfa Bychan Gwynd 67 J7
Morfa Dinlle Gwynd 66 G3
Morfa Glas Neath 29 N3
Morfa Nefyn Gwynd 66 D6
Morganstown Cardif 30 F8
Morgan's Vale Wilts 21 N10
Morham E Loth 128 F5
Moriah Cerdgn 54 E9
Morland Cumb 102 B6
Morley Ches E 82 H8
Morley Derbys 72 B2
Morley Dur 103 M5
Morley Leeds 90 H5
Morley Green Ches E 82 H8
Morley St Botolph Norfk 64 F2
Mornick Cnwll 5 N7
Morningside C Edin 127 N3
Morningside N Lans 126 E6
Morningthorpe Norfk 65 J3
Morpeth Nthumb 113 J3
Morphie Abers 143 N5
Morrey Staffs 71 L11
Morridge Side Staffs 71 J4
Morriston Swans 29 J5
Morston Norfk 76 E3
Mortehoe Devon 16 H2
Morthen Rothm 84 G3
Mortimer W Berk 23 J2
Mortimer Common W Berk 35 J11
Mortimer's Cross Herefs 45 N2
Mortimer West End Hants 22 H2
Mortlake Gt Lon 36 F5
Morton Cumb 101 N3
Morton Cumb 110 G10
Morton Derbys 84 F8
Morton IoW 14 H9
Morton Lincs 74 A6
Morton Lincs 85 P2
Morton Lincs 85 Q8
Morton Notts 85 M10
Morton Shrops 69 J10
Morton-on-Swale N York 97 M2
Morton on the Hill Norfk 76 G8
Morton Tinmouth Dur 103 N6
Morvah Cnwll 2 C6
Morval Cnwll 5 M10
Morvich Highld 146 B3
Morville Shrops 57 M6
Morville Heath Shrops 57 M6
Morwenstow Cnwll 16 C8
Mosborough Sheff 84 F4
Moscow E Ayrs 125 M9
Mose Shrops 57 P6
Mosedale Cumb 101 L4
Moseley Birm 58 G8
Moseley Wolves 58 D5
Moseley Worcs 46 F3
Moses Gate Bolton 89 L9
Moss Ag & B 136 B7
Moss Donc 91 P8
Moss Wrexhm 69 K4
Mossat Abers 150 D4
Mossbank Shet 169 r6
Moss Bank St Hel 81 Q5
Mossbay Cumb 100 C5
Mossblown S Ayrs 114 H3
Mossbrow Traffd 82 F7
Mossburnford Border 118 C7
Mossdale D & G 108 E6
Mossdale E Ayrs 115 J7
Moss Edge Lancs 88 E2
Moss End Ches E 82 E9
Mossend N Lans 126 C5
Mosser Mains Cumb 100 F5
Mossley Ches E 70 F2
Mossley Tamesd 83 L4
Mosspaul Hotel Border 117 M11
Moss Side Cumb 110 C10
Moss-side Highld 156 F6
Moss Side Lancs 88 D4
Moss Side Sefton 81 M4
Mosstodloch Moray 157 Q6
Mossyard D & G 107 P7
Mossy Lea Lancs 88 G8
Mosterton Dorset 11 K3
Moston Manch 83 J4
Moston Shrops 69 Q9
Moston Green Ches E 70 C2
Mostyn Flints 80 H8
Motcombe Dorset 20 G9
Mothecombe Devon 6 G9
Motherby Cumb 101 M5
Motherwell N Lans 126 C6
Motspur Park Gt Lon 36 F7
Mottingham Gt Lon 37 K6
Mottisfont Hants 22 B9
Mottisfont Hants 22 B9
Mottistone IoW 14 D10
Mottram in Longdendale Tamesd 83 L5
Mottram St Andrew Ches E 83 J9
Mouilpied Guern 10 b2
Mouldsworth Ches W 81 Q10
Moulin P & K 141 M6
Moulsecoomb Br & H 24 H9
Moulsford Oxon 34 G8
Moulsoe M Keyn 49 P6
Moultavie Highld 156 A3
Moulton Ches W 82 E11
Moulton Lincs 74 F6
Moulton N York 103 P10
Moulton Nhants 60 G7
Moulton Suffk 63 L8
Moulton V Glam 30 E11
Moulton Chapel Lincs 74 E7
Moulton St Mary Norfk 77 M10
Moulton Seas End Lincs 74 F5
Mount Cnwll 4 B10
Mount Cnwll 5 J8
Mount Kirk 90 D7
Mountain C Brad 90 D4
Mountain Ash Rhondd 30 D5
Mountain Cross Border 127 M8
Mountain Street Kent 39 J11
Mount Ambrose Cnwll 3 J5
Mount Bures Essex 52 F5
Mountfield E Susx 26 B7
Mountgerald Highld 155 Q5
Mount Hawke Cnwll 3 J4
Mount Hermon Cnwll 2 H10
Mountjoy Cnwll 4 D9
Mount Lothian Mdloth 127 P6
Mountnessing Essex 51 P11
Mounton Mons 31 P6
Mount Pleasant Ches E 70 E3
Mount Pleasant Derbys 71 P11
Mount Pleasant Derbys 84 D11
Mount Pleasant Dur 103 Q4
Mount Pleasant E R Yk 93 N3
Mount Pleasant E Susx 25 K7
Mount Pleasant Norfk 64 D3
Mount Pleasant Suffk 63 M11
Mount Pleasant Worcs 47 K2
Mountsorrel Leics 72 F8
Mount Sorrel Wilts 21 K10
Mount Tabor Calder 90 D5
Mousehole Cnwll 2 D8
Mouswald D & G 109 N6
Mow Cop Ches E 70 F3
Mowhaugh Border 118 F6
Mowmacre Hill C Leic 72 F9
Mowsley Leics 60 D3
Moy Highld 147 L11
Moy Highld 156 D11
Moyle Highld 145 Q4
Moylegrove Pembks 41 M2
Muasdale Ag & B 120 C3
Muchalls Abers 151 N9
Much Birch Herefs 45 Q8
Much Cowarne Herefs 46 B5
Much Dewchurch Herefs 45 P8
Muchelney Somset 19 M10
Muchelney Ham Somset 19 M10
Much Hadham Herts 51 K7
Much Hoole Lancs 88 F6
Much Hoole Town Lancs 88 F6
Muchlarnick Cnwll 5 L10
Much Marcle Herefs 46 C8
Much Wenlock Shrops 57 L5
Muck Highld 144 F12
Mucking Thurr 37 Q4
Muckleburgh Collection Norfk 76 G3
Muckleford Dorset 11 N6
Mucklestone Staffs 70 C7
Muckley Shrops 57 L5
Muckton Lincs 87 L4
Muddiford Devon 17 K4
Muddles Green E Susx 25 M8
Mudeford BCP 13 L6
Mudford Somset 19 Q11
Mudford Sock Somset 19 Q11
Mudgley Somset 19 N5
Mud Row Kent 38 H7
Mugdock Stirlg 125 P2
Mugeary Highld 152 G10
Mugginton Derbys 71 P6
Muggintonlane End Derbys 71 P6
Muggleswick Dur 112 F11
Muirden Abers 158 H7
Muirdrum Angus 143 K10
Muiresk Abers 158 G8
Muirhead Angus 142 E11
Muirhead Fife 134 H6
Muirhead N Lans 126 B4
Muirhouses Falk 134 C11
Muirkirk E Ayrs 115 N2
Muirmill Stirlg 133 L11
Muir of Fowlis Abers 150 F5
Muir of Miltonduff Moray 157 M6
Muir of Ord Highld 155 P7
Muirshearlich Highld 146 E11
Muirtack Abers 159 N10
Muirton P & K 133 Q5
Muirton Mains Highld 155 N7
Muirton of Ardblair P & K 142 B9
Muker N York 102 H11
Mulbarton Norfk 76 H11
Mulben Moray 157 R7
Mulfra Cnwll 2 D7
Mull Ag & B 137 Q9
Mullacott Cross Devon 17 J3
Mullion Cnwll 2 H10
Mullion Cove Cnwll 2 H10
Mumby Lincs 87 P6
Munderfield Row Herefs 46 B4
Munderfield Stocks Herefs 46 C4
Mundesley Norfk 77 L4
Mundford Norfk 63 P2
Mundham Norfk 65 L2
Mundon Hill Essex 52 E11
Mundy Bois Kent 26 F2
Mungrisdale Cumb 101 L4
Munlochy Highld 156 A7
Munnoch N Ayrs 124 H8
Munsley Herefs 46 C6
Munslow Shrops 57 J7
Murchington Devon 8 G7
Murcot Worcs 47 L6
Murcott Oxon 48 G11
Murcott Wilts 33 J6
Murkle Highld 167 L3
Murlaggan Highld 146 C9
Murrell Green Hants 23 K3
Murroes Angus 142 H10
Murrow Cambs 74 G9
Mursley Bucks 49 M9
Murston Kent 38 F9
Murthill Angus 142 H6
Murthly P & K 141 R10
Murton C York 98 C10
Murton Cumb 102 D6
Murton Dur 113 N11
Murton N Tyne 113 M6
Murton Nthumb 129 P10
Murton Swans 28 G7
Musbury Devon 10 F6
Muscoates N York 98 D5
Musselburgh E Loth 127 Q3
Muston Leics 73 L3
Muston N York 99 M5
Mustow Green Worcs 58 C10
Muswell Hill Gt Lon 36 G3
Mutehill D & G 108 E11
Mutford Suffk 65 P4
Muthill P & K 133 P4
Mutterton Devon 9 P3
Muxton Wrekin 57 N2
Mybster Highld 167 L6
Myddfai Carmth 43 Q8
Myddle Shrops 69 N10
Mydroilyn Cerdgn 43 J3
Myerscough Lancs 88 F3
Mylor Cnwll 3 L6
Mylor Bridge Cnwll 3 L6
Mynachlog ddu Pembks 41 M4
Myndd-llan Flints 80 H10
Myndtown Shrops 56 F7
Mynydd Bach Cerdgn 54 G9
Mynydd-bach Mons 31 N6
Mynydd-Bach Swans 29 J5
Mynyddgarreg Carmth 28 D3
Mynydd Isa Flints 69 J2
Mynydd Llandygai Gwynd 79 L11
Mynytho Gwynd 66 E8
Myrebird Abers 151 J8
Myredykes Border 118 A11
Mytchett Surrey 23 N3
Mytholm Calder 90 B5
Mytholmroyd Calder 90 C5
Mythop Lancs 88 D4
Myton-on-Swale N York 97 P7

N

Naast Highld 160 C10
Nab's Head Lancs 89 J5
Na Buirgh W Isls 168 f8
Naburn C York 98 B11
Naccolt Kent 27 J3
Nackington Kent 39 L11
Nacton Suffk 53 M3
Nafferton E R Yk 99 M9
Nag's Head Gloucs 32 G5
Nailbridge Gloucs 46 B11
Nailsbourne Somset 18 H9
Nailsea N Som 31 N10
Nailstone Leics 72 C9
Nailsworth Gloucs 32 F5
Nairn Highld 156 F6
Nalderswood Surrey 36 F11
Nancegollan Cnwll 2 G7
Nancledra Cnwll 2 D6
Nanhoron Gwynd 66 D8
Nannerch Flints 80 H11
Nanpantan Leics 72 E7
Nanpean Cnwll 4 F10
Nanquidno Cnwll 2 B8
Nanstallon Cnwll 4 G8
Nant-ddu Powys 30 D2
Nanternis Cerdgn 42 G3
Nantgaredig Carmth 43 J10
Nantgarw Rhondd 30 F7
Nant-glas Powys 55 M11
Nantglyn Denbgs 68 D2
Nantgwyn Powys 55 M9
Nant Gwynant Gwynd 67 L4
Nantlle Gwynd 67 J4
Nantmawr Shrops 69 J10
Nantmel Powys 55 N11
Nantmor Gwynd 67 L5
Nant Peris Gwynd 67 L3
Nantwich Ches E 70 B4
Nant-y-Bwch Blae G 30 F2
Nantycaws Carmth 43 J11
Nant-y-derry Mons 31 K3
Nantyffyllon Brdgnd 29 N6
Nantyglo Blae G 30 G2
Nant-y-gollen Shrops 68 H9
Nant-y-moel Brdgnd 29 P6
Nant-y-pandy Conwy 79 M10
Naphill Bucks 35 M5
Napleton Worcs 46 G5
Nappa N York 96 C10
Napton on the Hill Warwks 48 E2
Narberth Pembks 41 M8
Narborough Leics 72 E11
Narborough Norfk 75 P8
Narkurs Cnwll 5 N10
Nasareth Gwynd 66 H5
Naseby Nhants 60 E5
Nash Bucks 49 L8
Nash Gt Lon 37 K8
Nash Herefs 45 L2
Nash Newpt 31 K8
Nash Shrops 57 L10
Nash End Worcs 57 P8
Nashes Green Hants 23 J5
Nash Lee Bucks 35 M3
Nash Street Kent 37 P7
Nassington Nhants 73 R11
Nastend Gloucs 32 E3
Nasty Herts 51 J6
Nateby Cumb 102 E9
Nateby Lancs 88 F2
National Memorial Arboretum Staffs 59 J2
National Motor Museum (Beaulieu) Hants 14 C6
National Space Centre C Leic 72 F9
Natland Cumb 95 L3
Naughton Suffk 52 H2
Naunton Gloucs 47 M10
Naunton Worcs 46 G7
Naunton Beauchamp Worcs 47 J4
Navenby Lincs 86 C9
Navestock Essex 51 M11
Navestock Side Essex 51 N11
Navidale Highld 163 N3
Navity Highld 156 D5
Nawton N York 98 D4
Nayland Suffk 52 G5
Nazeing Essex 51 K9
Nazeing Gate Essex 51 K9
Neacroft Hants 13 L5
Neal's Green Warwks 59 M8
Neap Shet 169 s8
Near Cotton Staffs 71 K5
Near Sawrey Cumb 101 L11
Neasden Gt Lon 36 F3
Neasham Darltn 104 B8
Neath Neath 29 L5
Neatham Hants 23 K6
Neatishead Norfk 77 L7
Nebo Cerdgn 54 C11
Nebo Conwy 67 Q3
Nebo Gwynd 66 H4
Nebo IoA 78 H6
Necton Norfk 76 B10
Nedd Highld 164 D10
Nedderton Nthumb 113 K4
Nedging Suffk 52 G2
Nedging Tye Suffk 52 H2
Needham Norfk 65 J5
Needham Market Suffk 64 F10
Needham Street Suffk 63 M7
Needingworth Cambs 62 D6
Neen Savage Shrops 57 M9
Neen Sollars Shrops 57 M10
Neenton Shrops 57 L7
Nefyn Gwynd 66 E6
Neilston E Rens 125 M6
Nelson Caerph 30 F5
Nelson Lancs 89 P3
Nemphlar S Lans 116 B2
Nempnett Thrubwell BaNES 19 P2
Nenthall Cumb 111 Q11
Nenthead Cumb 102 E2
Nenthorn Border 118 C3
Neopardy Devon 9 J5
Nep Town W Susx 24 F7
Nerabus Ag & B 122 B8
Nercwys Flints 68 H2
Nerston S Lans 125 Q6
Nesbit Nthumb 119 J4
Nesfield N York 96 G11
Ness Ches W 81 L9
Nesscliffe Shrops 69 L11
Neston Ches W 81 K9
Neston Wilts 32 G11
Netchwood Shrops 57 L6
Nether Abington S Lans 116 C6
Nether Alderley Ches E 82 H9
Netheravon Wilts 21 M5
Nether Blainslie Border 117 Q2
Netherbrae Abers 159 J6
Nether Broughton Leics 72 H5
Netherburn S Lans 126 D8
Netherbury Dorset 11 K5
Netherby Cumb 110 G6
Netherby N York 97 M11
Nether Cerne Dorset 11 P5
Nethercleuch D & G 109 P3
Nether Compton Dorset 19 Q11
Nethercote Warwks 60 B8
Nethercott Devon 5 P2
Nethercott Devon 16 H4
Nether Crimond Abers 151 L3
Nether Dallachy Moray 157 R5
Netherend Gloucs 31 Q4
Nether Exe Devon 9 M4
Netherfield E Susx 26 B8
Netherfield Leics 72 F7
Netherfield Notts 72 G2
Nether Fingland S Lans 116 C8
Nethergate N Linc 92 C11
Nethergate Norfk 76 F6
Netherhampton Wilts 21 M9
Nether Handley Derbys 84 F5
Nether Handwick Angus 142 F9
Nether Haugh Rothm 91 L11
Netherhay Dorset 11 J3
Nether Headon Notts 85 M5
Nether Heage Derbys 84 E10
Nether Heyford Nhants 60 E9
Nether Kellet Lancs 95 L7
Nether Kinmundy Abers 159 Q9
Netherland Green Staffs 71 L8
Nether Langwith Notts 84 H6
Netherlaw D & G 108 F12
Netherley Abers 151 M9
Nethermill D & G 109 M3
Nethermuir Abers 159 M9
Netherne-on-the-Hill Surrey 36 G9
Netheroyd Hill Kirk 90 E7
Nether Padley Derbys 84 B5
Nether Poppleton C York 98 B10
Nether Row Cumb 101 K3
Netherseal Derbys 59 L2
Nether Silton N York 97 Q2
Nether Skyborry Shrops 56 D10
Nether Stowey Somset 18 G7
Nether Street Essex 51 N8
Netherstreet Wilts 21 J2
Netherthong Kirk 90 E9
Netherthorpe Derbys 84 F6
Netherton Angus 143 J6
Netherton Devon 7 M4
Netherton Dudley 58 D7
Netherton Hants 22 C3
Netherton Herefs 45 Q9
Netherton Kirk 90 E8
Netherton N Lans 126 D7
Netherton Nthumb 119 J9
Netherton Oxon 34 D5
Netherton P & K 142 A7
Netherton Sefton 81 M5
Netherton Shrops 57 N8

Netherton – North Corner 285

Netherton Stirlg 125 P2
Netherton Wakefd 90 H7
Netherton Worcs 47 J6
Nethertown Cumb 100 C9
Nethertown Highld 167 Q1
Nethertown Lancs 89 L3
Nethertown Staffs 71 L11
Netherurd Border 116 G2
Nether Wallop Hants 22 B7
Nether Wasdale Cumb 100 F10
Nether Welton Cumb 110 G11
Nether Westcote Gloucs 47 P10
Nether Whitacre Warwks 59 K6
Nether Whitecleuch S Lans 116 A7
Nether Winchendon Bucks 35 K2
Netherwitton Nthumb 112 G2
Nethy Bridge Highld 149 J3
Netley Hants 14 E5
Netley Marsh Hants 13 P2
Nettlebed Oxon 35 J7
Nettlebridge Somset 20 B5
Nettlecombe Dorset 11 L5
Nettlecombe IoW 14 F11
Nettleden Herts 50 B8
Nettleham Lincs 86 D5
Nettlestead Kent 37 Q10
Nettlestead Green Kent 37 Q10
Nettlestone IoW 14 H8
Nettlesworth Dur 113 L11
Nettleton Lincs 93 K10
Nettleton Wilts 32 F9
Nettleton Shrub Wilts 32 F9
Netton Devon 6 F9
Netton Wilts 21 M7
Neuadd Carmth 43 P10
Neuadd-ddu Powys 55 L9
Nevendon Essex 38 C3
Nevern Pembks 41 L2
Nevill Holt Leics 60 H2
New Abbey D & G 109 L7
New Aberdour Abers 159 L5
New Addington Gt Lon 37 J8
Newall Leeds 97 J11
New Alresford Hants 22 G8
New Alyth P & K 142 C8
Newark C Pete 74 D10
Newark Ork 169 g2
Newark-on-Trent Notts 85 N10
New Arram E R Yk 92 H2
Newarthill N Lans 126 D6
New Ash Green Kent 37 P7
New Balderton Notts 85 P10
Newbarn Kent 27 L3
New Barn Kent 37 P7
New Barnet Gt Lon 50 G11
New Barton Nhants 61 J8
Newbattle Mdloth 127 Q4
New Bewick Nthumb 119 L6
Newbie D & G 110 C7
Newbiggin Cumb 94 B2
Newbiggin Cumb 94 F7
Newbiggin Cumb 101 N5
Newbiggin Cumb 102 B5
Newbiggin Cumb 111 L11
Newbiggin Dur 102 H5
Newbiggin Dur 112 H11
Newbiggin N York 96 E2
Newbiggin N York 96 F3
Newbiggin-by-the-Sea Nthumb 113 M3
Newbigging Angus 142 D9
Newbigging Angus 142 G10
Newbigging Angus 142 H10
Newbigging S Lans 127 J8
Newbiggin-on-Lune Cumb 102 D10
New Bilton Warwks 59 Q9
Newbold Derbys 84 E6
Newbold Leics 72 C7
Newbold on Avon Warwks 59 Q9
Newbold on Stour Warwks 47 P5
Newbold Pacey Warwks 47 Q3
Newbold Revel Warwks 59 Q8
Newbold Verdon Leics 72 C10
New Bolingbroke Lincs 87 K9
Newborough C Pete 74 D9
Newborough IoA 78 G11
Newborough Staffs 71 L9
Newbottle Nhants 48 F7
Newbottle Sundld 113 M10
New Boultham Lincs 86 C6
Newbourne Suffk 53 N3
New Bradwell M Keyn 49 M6
New Brampton Derbys 84 E6
New Brancepeth Dur 103 P2
Newbridge C Edin 127 L3
Newbridge Caerph 30 H5
Newbridge Cerdgn 43 K3
Newbridge Cnwll 2 C7
Newbridge Cnwll 3 K5
Newbridge D & G 109 K5
Newbridge Hants 21 Q11
Newbridge IoW 14 D9
New Bridge N York 98 G3
Newbridge Oxon 34 D4
Newbridge Wrexhm 69 J6
Newbridge Green Worcs 46 F7
Newbridge-on-Usk Mons 31 L6
Newbridge-on-Wye Powys 44 E3
New Brighton Flints 81 K11
New Brighton Wirral 81 L6
New Brinsley Notts 84 G10
New Brotton R & Cl 105 J6
Newbrough Nthumb 112 C7
New Broughton Wrexhm 69 K4
New Buckenham Norfk 64 F3
Newbuildings Devon 9 J4
Newburgh Abers 151 P2
Newburgh Abers 159 N6
Newburgh Fife 134 G4
Newburgh Lancs 88 F8
Newburn N u Ty 113 J7
New Bury Bolton 82 F4
Newbury Somset 20 C5
Newbury W Berk 34 E11
Newbury Wilts 20 F6
Newbury Park Gt Lon 37 K3
Newby Cumb 101 Q6
Newby Lancs 96 B11
Newby N York 95 Q7
Newby N York 99 L2
Newby N York 104 F8
Newby Bridge Cumb 94 H3
Newby Cross Cumb 110 G10
Newby East Cumb 111 J9
Newby Head Cumb 101 Q6
New Byth Abers 159 K7
Newby West Cumb 110 G10
Newby Wiske N York 97 N3
Newcastle Mons 45 N11
Newcastle Shrops 56 D8
Newcastle Airport Nthumb 113 J6
Newcastle Emlyn Carmth 42 F6
Newcastleton Border 111 J3
Newcastle-under-Lyme Staffs 70 E5
Newcastle upon Tyne N u Ty 113 K8
Newchapel Pembks 41 P3
Newchapel Staffs 70 F4
Newchapel Surrey 25 J2
Newchurch Blae G 30 G2
Newchurch Herefs 45 M4
Newchurch IoW 14 G9
Newchurch Kent 27 J5
Newchurch Mons 31 N5
Newchurch Powys 45 J4
Newchurch Staffs 71 L10
Newchurch in Pendle Lancs 89 N3
New Costessey Norfk 76 H9
New Cowper Cumb 109 P11
Newcraighall C Edin 127 Q3
New Crofton Wakefd 91 K7
New Cross Cerdgn 54 E9
New Cross Gt Lon 37 J5
New Cross Somset 19 M11
New Cumnock E Ayrs 115 M5
New Cut E Susx 26 D8
New Deer Abers 159 L8
New Delaval Nthumb 113 L5
New Delph Oldham 90 B9
New Denham Bucks 36 B4
Newdigate Surrey 24 E2
New Duston Nhants 60 F8
New Earswick C York 98 C9
New Eastwood Notts 84 G11
New Edlington Donc 91 N11
New Elgin Moray 157 N5
New Ellerby E R Yk 93 L3
Newell Green Br For 35 N10
New Eltham Gt Lon 37 K6
New End Worcs 47 L2
Newenden Kent 26 D6
New England C Pete 74 C10
New England Essex 52 B3
Newent Gloucs 46 D9
New Farnley Leeds 90 H4
New Ferry Wirral 81 L7
Newfield Dur 103 P4
Newfield Dur 113 K10
Newfield Highld 156 D2
New Fletton C Pete 74 C11
New Forest National Park 13 N3
Newfound Hants 22 G4
New Fryston Wakefd 91 M5
Newgale Pembks 40 G6
New Galloway D & G 108 D5
Newgate Norfk 76 E3
Newgate Street Herts 50 H9
New Gilston Fife 135 L6
New Grimsby IoS 2 b1
Newhall Ches E 69 R5
Newhall Derbys 71 P10
Newham Nthumb 119 N5
New Hartley Nthumb 113 M5
Newhaven C Edin 127 P2
Newhaven Derbys 71 M2
Newhaven E Susx 25 K10
New Haw Surrey 36 C8
New Hedges Pembks 41 M10
New Herrington Sundld 113 M10
Newhey Rochdl 89 Q8
New Holkham Norfk 76 B4
New Holland N Linc 93 J6
Newholm N York 105 N8
New Houghton Derbys 84 G7
New Houghton Norfk 75 Q5
Newhouse N Lans 126 D5
New Houses N York 96 B6
New Houses Wigan 82 C4
New Hutton Cumb 95 M2
New Hythe Kent 38 B10
Newick E Susx 25 K6
Newingreen Kent 27 K4
Newington Kent 27 L4
Newington Kent 38 E9
Newington Oxon 34 H5
Newington Shrops 56 G8
Newington Bagpath Gloucs 32 F6
New Inn Carmth 43 J7
New Inn Torfn 31 K5
New Invention Shrops 56 D9
New Lakenham Norfk 77 J10
New Lanark S Lans 116 B2
New Lanark Village S Lans 116 B2
Newland C KuH 93 J4
Newland Cumb 94 G5
Newland E R Yk 92 D5
Newland Gloucs 31 Q3
Newland N York 92 A6
Newland Oxon 34 C3
Newland Somset 17 Q4
Newland Worcs 46 E5
Newlandrig Mdloth 128 B7
Newlands Border 111 K2
Newlands Cumb 101 K3
Newlands Nthumb 112 G9
Newlands of Dundurcas Moray 157 P7
New Lane Lancs 88 E8
New Lane End Warrtn 82 D6
New Langholm D & G 110 G4
New Leake Lincs 87 M9
New Leeds Abers 159 N7
New Lodge Barns 91 K9
New Longton Lancs 88 G5
New Luce D & G 106 G5
Newlyn Cnwll 2 D8
Newmachar Abers 151 M4
Newmains N Lans 126 E6
New Malden Gt Lon 36 F7
Newman's End Essex 51 M8
Newman's Green Suffk 52 E3
Newmarket Suffk 63 K8
Newmarket W Isls 168 j4
New Marske R & Cl 104 H6
New Marston Oxon 34 F3
New Marton Shrops 69 K8
New Mill Abers 151 K11
Newmill Border 117 P8
New Mill Cnwll 2 D7
New Mill Herts 35 P2
New Mill Kirk 90 F9
Newmill Moray 158 B7
Newmillerdam Wakefd 91 J7
Newmill of Inshewan Angus 142 G5
Newmills C Edin 127 M4
New Mills Cnwll 3 M3
New Mills Derbys 83 M7
Newmills Fife 134 C10
Newmills Mons 31 P3
New Mills Powys 55 P4
Newmiln P & K 142 A11
Newmilns E Ayrs 125 N10
New Milton Hants 13 M5
New Mistley Essex 53 K5
New Moat Pembks 41 L5
Newnes Shrops 69 L8
Newney Green Essex 51 Q9
Newnham Hants 23 K4
Newnham Herts 50 F3
Newnham Kent 38 G10
Newnham Nhants 60 C9
Newnham Bridge Worcs 57 L11
Newnham on Severn Gloucs 32 C2
New Ollerton Notts 85 L7
New Oscott Birm 58 G6
New Pitsligo Abers 159 L6
New Polzeath Cnwll 4 E6
Newport Cnwll 5 N4
Newport Dorset 12 E5
Newport E R Yk 92 E4
Newport Essex 51 M4
Newport Gloucs 32 D5
Newport Highld 163 Q2
Newport IoW 14 F9
Newport Newpt 31 K7
Newport Norfk 77 Q8
Newport Pembks 41 L3
Newport Wrekin 70 C11
Newport-on-Tay Fife 135 L2
Newport Pagnell M Keyn 49 N6
Newport Pagnell Services M Keyn 49 N6
Newpound Common W Susx 24 C5
New Prestwick S Ayrs 114 F3
New Quay Cerdgn 42 G3
Newquay Cnwll 4 C9
New Quay Essex 52 H7
Newquay Zoo Cnwll 4 C9
New Rackheath Norfk 77 K9
New Radnor Powys 45 J2
New Rent Cumb 101 N3
New Ridley Nthumb 112 G9
New Road Side N York 90 B2
New Romney Kent 27 J7
New Rossington Donc 91 Q11
New Row Cerdgn 54 G10
New Row Lancs 89 J3
New Sauchie Clacks 133 P9
Newsbank Ches E 82 H11
Newseat Abers 158 H11
Newsham Lancs 88 G3
Newsham N York 97 N4
Newsham N York 103 M8
Newsham Nthumb 113 M5
New Sharlston Wakefd 91 K7
Newsholme E R Yk 92 B5
Newsholme Lancs 96 B10
New Shoreston Nthumb 119 N4
New Silksworth Sundld 113 N10
New Skelton R & Cl 105 J7
Newsome Kirk 90 F8
New Somerby Lincs 73 N3
New Springs Wigan 88 H9
Newstead Border 117 R4
Newstead Notts 84 H10
Newstead Nthumb 119 N5
New Stevenston N Lans 126 D6
New Street Herefs 45 L3
New Swannington Leics 72 C7
Newthorpe N York 91 M4
Newthorpe Notts 84 G11
New Thundersley Essex 38 C4
Newtimber W Susx 24 G8
Newtoft Lincs 86 D3
Newton Ag & B 131 L8
Newton Border 118 B6
Newton Brdgnd 29 M9
Newton C Beds 50 F2
Newton Cambs 62 F11
Newton Cambs 74 H8
Newton Cardif 30 H9
Newton Ches W 69 P3
Newton Ches W 81 N11
Newton Ches W 82 B9
Newton Cumb 94 E6
Newton Derbys 84 F9
Newton Herefs 45 L8
Newton Herefs 45 Q4
Newton Herefs 56 F11
Newton Highld 155 Q7
Newton Highld 156 C8
Newton Highld 156 D4
Newton Highld 167 P7
Newton Lancs 88 C3
Newton Lancs 95 M6
Newton Lincs 73 Q3
Newton Mdloth 127 Q4
Newton Moray 157 M5
Newton Moray 157 Q5
Newton N York 98 H6
Newton Nhants 61 J4
Newton Norfk 76 A8
Newton Notts 72 H2
Newton Nthumb 112 F8
Newton Nthumb 118 H9
Newton S Lans 116 C4
Newton S Lans 126 B5
Newton Sandw 58 F6
Newton Shrops 69 M8
Newton Somset 18 F7
Newton Staffs 71 J9
Newton Suffk 52 F3
Newton W Loth 127 K2
Newton Warwks 60 B5
Newton Wilts 21 P10
Newton Abbot Devon 7 M4
Newton Arlosh Cumb 110 D9
Newton Aycliffe Dur 103 Q6
Newton Bewley Hartpl 104 E5
Newton Blossomville M Keyn 49 P4
Newton Bromswold Nhants 61 L7
Newton Burgoland Leics 72 B9
Newton-by-the-Sea Nthumb 119 P5
Newton by Toft Lincs 86 D3
Newton Ferrers Devon 6 F9
Newton Ferry W Isls 168 d10
Newton Flotman Norfk 65 J2
Newtongrange Mdloth 127 Q5
Newton Green Mons 31 P6
Newton Harcourt Leics 72 G11
Newton Heath Manch 83 J4
Newtonhill Abers 151 N9
Newton Hill Wakefd 91 J6
Newton-in-Bowland Lancs 95 P10
Newton Kyme N York 91 M2
Newton-le-Willows N York 97 K3
Newton-le-Willows St Hel 82 C5
Newtonloan Mdloth 127 Q5
Newton Longville Bucks 49 M8
Newton Mearns E Rens 125 N6
Newtonmill Angus 143 L5
Newtonmore Highld 148 C8
Newton Morrell N York 103 P9
Newton Mountain Pembks 41 J9
Newton Mulgrave N York 105 L7
Newton of Balcanquhal P & K 134 F5
Newton of Balcormo Fife 135 N7
Newton-on-Ouse N York 97 R9
Newton-on-Rawcliffe N York 98 G2
Newton on the Hill Shrops 69 N10
Newton-on-the-Moor Nthumb 119 N9
Newton on Trent Lincs 85 P6
Newton Poppleford Devon 10 B7
Newton Purcell Oxon 48 H8
Newton Regis Warwks 59 L3
Newton Reigny Cumb 101 N4
Newton St Cyres Devon 9 L5
Newton St Faith Norfk 77 J8
Newton St Loe BaNES 20 D2
Newton St Petrock Devon 16 G9
Newton Solney Derbys 71 P9
Newton Stacey Hants 22 D6
Newton Stewart D & G 107 M4
Newton Tony Wilts 21 P6
Newton Tracey Devon 17 J6
Newton under Roseberry R & Cl 104 G8
Newton Underwood Nthumb 112 H3
Newton upon Derwent E R Yk 98 E11
Newton Valence Hants 23 K8
Newton Wamphray D & G 109 P2
Newton with Scales Lancs 88 F4
Newtown BCP 12 H6
Newtown Blae G 30 G3
Newtown Ches W 82 B9
Newtown Cnwll 2 F8
Newtown Cnwll 5 M6
Newtown Cumb 101 P6
Newtown Cumb 109 P11
Newtown Cumb 110 G8
Newtown Cumb 111 K8
Newtown D & G 115 Q5
Newtown Derbys 83 L8
Newtown Devon 9 Q5
Newtown Devon 17 P6
Newtown Dorset 11 K4
New Town Dorset 12 G3
New Town Dorset 21 J11
New Town Dorset 21 J11
New Town E Susx 25 L6
Newtown Gloucs 32 C4
Newtown Hants 13 N2
Newtown Hants 14 H4
Newtown Hants 22 E2
Newtown Herefs 45 P3
Newtown Herefs 45 Q8
Newtown Herefs 46 B5
Newtown Highld 147 K7
Newtown IoW 14 D8
New Town Nhants 61 L5
Newtown Nthumb 119 J4
Newtown Nthumb 119 K10
Newtown Nthumb 119 K5
Newtown Powys 55 Q6
Newtown Rhondd 30 E5
Newtown Shrops 69 M10
Newtown Shrops 69 N8
Newtown Somset 10 F2
Newtown Staffs 58 E4
Newtown Staffs 70 G2
Newtown Wigan 82 C4
Newtown Wilts 20 H9
Newtown Wilts 21 Q2
New Town Wilts 33 Q10
Newtown Worcs 46 G3
Newtown Worcs 58 D9
Newtown-in-St Martin Cnwll 3 J9
Newtown Linford Leics 72 E9
Newtown of Beltrees Rens 125 K6
Newtown St Boswells Border 117 R4
Newtown Unthank Leics 72 D10
New Tredegar Caerph 30 F4
New Trows S Lans 126 E10
New Tupton Derbys 84 E7
Newtyle Angus 142 D9
New Walsoken Cambs 75 J9
New Waltham NE Lin 93 N10
New Whittington Derbys 84 E5
New Winton E Loth 128 C5
New Yatt Oxon 34 C2
Newyears Green Gt Lon 36 C3
Newyork Ag & B 131 K5
New York Lincs 86 H9
New York N Tyne 113 M6
New York N York 97 J8
Nextend Herefs 45 L3
Neyland Pembks 41 J9
Niarbyl IoM 80 b6
Nibley Gloucs 32 C3
Nibley S Glos 32 C8
Nibley Green Gloucs 32 D5
Nicholashayne Devon 18 F11
Nicholaston Swans 28 F7
Nickies Hill Cumb 111 K7
Nidd N York 97 M8
Nigg C Aber 151 N7
Nigg Highld 156 E3
Nigg Ferry Highld 156 D4
Nimlet BaNES 32 D10
Ninebanks Nthumb 111 Q10
Nine Elms Swindn 33 M7
Nine Wells Pembks 40 E6
Ninfield E Susx 26 B9
Ningwood IoW 14 C9
Nisbet Border 118 C5
Nisbet Hill Border 129 K9
Niton IoW 14 F11
Nitshill C Glas 125 N5
Noah's Ark Kent 37 N9
Noak Bridge Essex 37 Q2
Noak Hill Gt Lon 37 M2
Noblethorpe Barns 90 H9
Nobold Shrops 56 H2
Nobottle Nhants 60 E8
Nocton Lincs 86 E8
Nogdam End Norfk 77 M11
Noke Oxon 34 F2
Nolton Pembks 40 G7
Nolton Haven Pembks 40 G7
No Man's Heath Ches W 69 P5
No Man's Heath Warwks 59 L3
No Man's Land Cnwll 5 M10
Nomansland Devon 9 K2
Nomansland Wilts 21 Q11
Noneley Shrops 69 N9
Nonington Kent 39 N11
Nook Cumb 95 L4
Nook Cumb 111 J5
Norbiton Gt Lon 36 E7
Norbreck Bpool 88 C2
Norbridge Herefs 46 D6
Norbury Ches E 69 Q5
Norbury Derbys 71 L6
Norbury Gt Lon 36 H7
Norbury Shrops 56 F6
Norbury Staffs 70 D10
Norbury Common Ches E 69 Q5
Norbury Junction Staffs 70 D10
Norchard Worcs 58 B11
Norcott Brook Ches W 82 D8
Norcross Lancs 88 C2
Nordelph Norfk 75 L10
Norden Rochdl 89 P8
Nordley Shrops 57 M5
Norfolk Broads Norfk 77 P10
Norham Nthumb 129 N10
Norland Town Calder 90 D6
Norley Ches W 82 C10
Norleywood Hants 14 C7
Norlington E Susx 25 K8
Normanby Lincs 86 C3
Normanby N Linc 92 E7
Normanby N York 98 E4
Normanby R & Cl 104 F7
Normanby le Wold Lincs 93 K11
Norman Cross Cambs 61 Q2
Normandy Surrey 23 P4
Normans Bay E Susx 25 Q9
Norman's Green Devon 9 Q4
Normanton C Derb 72 A4
Normanton Leics 73 L2
Normanton Notts 85 M10
Normanton Rutlnd 73 N9
Normanton Wakefd 91 K6
Normanton Wilts 21 M6
Normanton le Heath Leics 72 B8
Normanton on Cliffe Lincs 86 B11
Normanton on Soar Notts 72 E6
Normanton on the Wolds Notts 72 G4
Normanton on Trent Notts 85 N7
Normoss Lancs 88 C3
Norney Surrey 23 P6
Norrington Common Wilts 20 G2
Norris Green Cnwll 5 Q8
Norris Green Lpool 81 M6
Norris Hill Leics 72 A7
Norristhorpe Kirk 90 G6
Northacre Norfk 64 D2
Northall Bucks 49 Q10
Northallerton N York 97 N2
Northall Green Norfk 76 D9
Northam C Sotn 14 D4
Northam Devon 16 H6
Northampton Nhants 60 G8
Northampton Worcs 58 B11
Northampton Services Nhants 60 F9
North Anston Rothm 84 H4
North Ascot Br For 35 P11
North Aston Oxon 48 E9
Northaw Herts 50 G10
Northay Somset 10 F2
North Baddesley Hants 22 C10
North Ballachulish Highld 139 K5
North Barrow Somset 20 B9
North Barsham Norfk 76 C4
Northbay W Isls 168 c17
North Benfleet Essex 38 C4
North Berwick E Loth 128 E3
North Bitchburn Dur 103 N4
North Blyth Nthumb 113 M4
North Boarhunt Hants 14 H4
North Bockhampton BCP 13 L5
Northborough C Pete 74 C9
Northbourne Kent 39 P11
North Bovey Devon 8 H8
North Bradley Wilts 20 G3
North Brentor Devon 8 C8
North Brewham Somset 20 D7
North Bridge Surrey 23 Q7
Northbridge Street E Susx 26 B7
Northbrook Hants 22 F7
Northbrook Oxon 48 E10
North Brook End Cambs 50 G2
North Buckland Devon 16 H3
North Burlingham Norfk 77 M10
North Cadbury Somset 20 B9
North Carlton Lincs 86 B5
North Carlton Notts 85 J4
North Cave E R Yk 92 E4
North Cerney Gloucs 33 K3
North Chailey E Susx 25 J6
Northchapel W Susx 23 Q9
North Charford Hants 21 N11
North Charlton Nthumb 119 N6
North Cheam Gt Lon 36 F7
North Cheriton Somset 20 C9
North Chideock Dorset 11 J6
Northchurch Herts 35 Q3
North Cliffe E R Yk 92 E3
North Clifton Notts 85 P6
North Close Dur 103 Q4
North Cockerington Lincs 87 L2
North Connel Ag & B 138 G11
North Cornelly Brdgnd 29 M8
North Corner Cnwll 3 K10

North Cotes Lincs 93 P10
Northcott Devon 5 N3
Northcott Devon 10 B2
Northcott Devon 10 C3
North Country Cnwll 2 H5
Northcourt Oxon 34 K3
North Cove Suffk 65 P4
North Cowton N York 103 N10
North Crawley M Keyn 49 P6
North Cray Gt Lon 37 L6
North Creake Norfk 76 B4
North Curry Somset 19 K9
North Dalton E R Yk 99 J10
North Deighton N York 97 N10
Northdown Kent 39 Q7
North Downs 38 F10
North Duffield N York 92 A3
Northedge Derbys 84 E7
North Elham Kent 27 L3
North Elkington Lincs 87 J2
North Elmham Norfk 76 D7
North Elmsall Wakefd 91 M8
Northend Bucks 35 K6
North End C Port 15 J6
North End Cumb 110 F9
North End Dorset 20 F9
North End E R Yk 93 L2
North End E R Yk 93 N4
North End Essex 51 Q7
North End Hants 21 M11
North End Hants 22 G9
North End Leics 72 F7
North End Lincs 74 D2
North End Lincs 87 M3
North End Lincs 92 H11
North End Lincs 93 P10
North End N Linc 93 K6
North End N Som 31 M11
North End Nhants 61 L7
North End Norfk 64 D3
North End Nthumb 119 M10
North End Sefton 81 L4
North End W Susx 15 Q6
North End W Susx 24 D9
Northend Warwks 48 C4
Northenden Manch 82 H7
Northend Woods Bucks 35 P7
North Erradale Highld 160 A10
North Evington C Leic 72 G10
North Fambridge Essex 38 E2
North Featherstone Wakefd 91 L6
North Ferriby E R Yk 92 G5
Northfield Birm 58 F9
Northfield C Aber 151 N6
Northfield E R Yk 92 H5
Northfields Lincs 73 Q9
Northfleet Kent 37 P6
North Frodingham E R Yk 99 N10
North Gorley Hants 13 L2
North Green Suffk 65 J4
North Green Suffk 65 L9
North Green Suffk 65 M8
North Greetwell Lincs 86 D6
North Grimston N York 98 G7
North Halling Medway 38 B8
North Haven Shet 169 t14
North Hayling Hants 15 K6
North Hazelrigg Nthumb 119 L4
North Heasley Devon 17 N5
North Heath W Susx 24 C6
North Hele Devon 18 D10
North Hill Cnwll 5 M6
North Hillingdon Gt Lon 36 C4
North Hinksey Village Oxon 34 E3
North Holmwood Surrey 36 E11
North Huish Devon 7 J7
North Hykeham Lincs 86 B7
Northiam E Susx 26 D7
Northill C Beds 61 P11
Northington Gloucs 32 D3
Northington Hants 22 G7
North Kelsey Lincs 92 H10
North Kessock Highld 156 B8
North Killingholme N Linc 93 K7
North Kilvington N York 97 P3
North Kilworth Leics 60 D4
North Kingston Hants 13 L4
North Kyme Lincs 86 G10
North Lancing W Susx 24 E9
North Landing E R Yk 99 Q6
Northlands Lincs 87 K10
Northleach Gloucs 33 M2
North Lee Bucks 35 M3
North Lees N York 97 L6
Northleigh Devon 10 D5
Northleigh Devon 17 L5
North Leigh Kent 27 K2
North Leigh Oxon 34 C2
North Leverton with Habblesthorpe Notts 85 N4
Northlew Devon 8 D5
North Littleton Worcs 47 L5
Northload Bridge Somset 19 N7
North Lopham Norfk 64 E5
North Luffenham Rutlnd 73 N10
North Marden W Susx 23 M11
North Marston Bucks 49 L10
North Middleton Mdloth 128 B8
North Middleton Nthumb 119 J6
North Millbrex Abers 159 K9
North Milmain D & G 106 E7
North Molton Devon 17 N6
Northmoor Oxon 34 D4
North Moreton Oxon 34 G7
Northmuir Angus 142 F6
North Mundham W Susx 15 N6
North Muskham Notts 85 N9
North Newbald E R Yk 92 F3
North Newington Oxon 48 D6
North Newnton Wilts 21 M3
North Newton Somset 19 K8
Northney Hants 15 K6
North Nibley Gloucs 32 D5
North Oakley Hants 22 F4
North Ockendon Gt Lon 37 N3
Northolt Gt Lon 36 D4
Northolt Airport Gt Lon 36 C3
Northop Flints 81 J11
Northop Hall Flints 81 K11
North Ormesby Middsb 104 E7
North Ormsby Lincs 87 J2
Northorpe Kirk 90 G6
Northorpe Lincs 74 A7
Northorpe Lincs 74 D3
Northorpe Lincs 92 E11

North Otterington N York 97 N3
Northover Somset 19 N7
Northover Somset 19 P10
North Owersby Lincs 86 E2
Northowram Calder 90 E5
North Perrott Somset 11 K3
North Petherton Somset 19 J8
North Petherwin Cnwll 5 M4
North Pickenham Norfk 76 B10
North Piddle Worcs 47 J4
North Poorton Dorset 11 L5
Northport Dorset 12 F7
North Poulner Hants 13 L3
North Queensferry Fife 134 E11
North Radworthy Devon 17 P5
North Rauceby Lincs 86 D11
Northrepps Norfk 77 J4
North Reston Lincs 87 L4
North Rigton N York 97 L11
North Ripley Hants 13 L5
North Rode Ches E 83 J11
North Ronaldsay Ork 169 g1
North Ronaldsay Airport Ork 169 g1
North Row Cumb 100 H4
North Runcton Norfk 75 M7
North Scale Cumb 94 D7
North Scarle Lincs 85 P7
North Seaton Nthumb 113 L3
North Seaton Colliery Nthumb 113 L3
North Shian Ag & B 138 G9
North Shields N Tyne 113 N7
North Shoebury Sthend 38 F4
North Shore Bpool 88 C3
North Side C Pete 74 E11
North Side Cumb 100 C5
North Skelton R & Cl 105 J7
North Somercotes Lincs 93 R11
North Stainley N York 97 L5
North Stainmore Cumb 102 F7
North Stifford Thurr 37 P4
North Stoke BaNES 32 D11
North Stoke Oxon 34 H7
North Stoke W Susx 24 B8
Northstowe Cambs 62 F7
North Street Cambs 63 J7
North Street Hants 21 N11
North Street Hants 22 H8
North Street Kent 38 H10
North Street Medway 38 D7
North Street W Berk 34 H10
North Sunderland Nthumb 119 P4
North Tamerton Cnwll 5 M4
North Tawton Devon 8 G4
North Third Stirlg 133 M10
North Thoresby Lincs 93 N11
North Togston Nthumb 119 P10
North Tolsta W Isls 168 k3
Northton W Isls 168 e9
North Town Devon 17 J10
North Town Somset 19 Q6
North Town W & M 35 N8
North Tuddenham Norfk 76 E9
North Uist W Isls 168 c10
Northumberland National Park Nthumb 111 Q4
North Walbottle N u Ty 113 J7
North Walsham Norfk 77 K5
North Waltham Hants 22 G5
North Warnborough Hants 23 K4
Northway Somset 18 F9
North Weald Bassett Essex 51 L10
North Wheatley Notts 85 N3
North Whilborough Devon 7 M5
Northwich Ches W 82 E10
North Wick BaNES 31 Q11
Northwick S Glos 31 Q7
Northwick Somset 19 L5
Northwick Worcs 46 F3
North Widcombe BaNES 19 Q3
North Willingham Lincs 86 G3
North Wingfield Derbys 84 F7
North Witham Lincs 73 N6
Northwold Norfk 75 Q11
Northwood C Stke 70 F5
Northwood Derbys 84 C8
Northwood Gt Lon 36 C2
Northwood IoW 14 E8
Northwood Shrops 69 N8
Northwood Green Gloucs 46 D11
North Wootton Dorset 11 P2
North Wootton Norfk 75 M6
North Wootton Somset 19 Q6
North Wraxall Wilts 32 F9
North Wroughton Swindn 33 M8
North York Moors National Park 105 K10
Norton Donc 91 N7
Norton E Susx 25 L10
Norton Gloucs 46 G10
Norton Halton 82 C8
Norton Hants 22 E6
Norton Herts 50 F4
Norton IoW 13 P7
Norton Mons 45 N10
Norton N Som 19 K2
Norton Nhants 60 C8
Norton Notts 85 J6
Norton Powys 56 E11
Norton S on T 104 D6
Norton Sheff 84 E4
Norton Shrops 56 H8
Norton Shrops 57 K3
Norton Shrops 57 L8
Norton Shrops 57 N4
Norton Suffk 64 D8
Norton Swans 28 H7
Norton W Susx 15 P5
Norton Wilts 32 G8
Norton Worcs 46 G4
Norton Worcs 47 K5
Norton Bavant Wilts 20 H6
Norton Bridge Staffs 70 F8
Norton Canes Staffs 58 F3
Norton Canes Services Staffs 58 F3
Norton Canon Herefs 45 M5
Norton Corner Norfk 76 F6
Norton Disney Lincs 85 Q9
Norton Ferris Wilts 20 E7
Norton Fitzwarren Somset 18 G9
Norton Green IoW 13 P7
Norton Hawkfield BaNES 31 Q2
Norton Heath Essex 51 P10

Norton in Hales Shrops 70 C7
Norton-Juxta-Twycross Leics 59 M3
Norton-le-Clay N York 97 P6
Norton-le-Moors C Stke 70 F4
Norton Lindsey Warwks 47 N2
Norton Little Green Suffk 64 D8
Norton Malreward BaNES 20 B2
Norton Mandeville Essex 51 N10
Norton-on-Derwent N York 98 F8
Norton St Philip Somset 20 E3
Norton Subcourse Norfk 65 N2
Norton sub Hamdon Somset 19 N11
Norton Wood Herefs 45 M5
Norwell Notts 85 N8
Norwell Woodhouse Notts 85 M8
Norwich Norfk 77 J10
Norwich Airport Norfk 77 J9
Norwick Shet 169 t2
Norwood Clacks 133 P9
Norwood Derbys 84 D5
Norwood Kent 27 J5
Norwood End Essex 51 N9
Norwood Green Calder 90 E5
Norwood Green Gt Lon 36 D5
Norwood Hill Surrey 24 F2
Norwoodside Cambs 74 H11
Noseley Leics 73 J11
Noss Mayo Devon 6 F7
Nosterfield N York 97 L4
Nosterfield End Cambs 51 P2
Nostie Highld 145 Q2
Notgrove Gloucs 47 M10
Nottage Brdgnd 29 M9
Notter Cnwll 5 P9
Nottingham C Nott 72 F3
Nottington Dorset 11 P8
Notton Wakefd 91 J8
Notton Wilts 32 H11
Nounsley Essex 52 C9
Noutard's Green Worcs 57 Q11
Nowton Suffk 64 B9
Nox Shrops 56 G2
Nuffield Oxon 35 J7
Nunburnholme E R Yk 98 G11
Nuncargate Notts 84 H10
Nunclose Cumb 111 J11
Nuneaton Warwks 59 N6
Nuneham Courtenay Oxon 34 G5
Nunhead Gt Lon 36 H5
Nunkeeling E R Yk 99 N11
Nun Monkton N York 97 R9
Nunney Somset 20 D5
Nunney Catch Somset 20 D6
Nunnington Herefs 45 R6
Nunnington N York 98 D5
Nunsthorpe NE Lin 93 N9
Nunthorpe C York 98 C10
Nunthorpe Middsb 104 F8
Nunthorpe Village Middsb 104 F8
Nunton Wilts 21 N9
Nunwick N York 97 M6
Nunwick Nthumb 112 C6
Nupdown S Glos 32 B5
Nup End Bucks 49 N11
Nupend Gloucs 32 E3
Nuptown Br For 35 N10
Nursling Hants 22 C11
Nursted Hants 23 L10
Nursteed Wilts 21 K2
Nurton Staffs 58 B5
Nutbourne W Susx 15 L5
Nutbourne W Susx 24 C7
Nutfield Surrey 36 H10
Nuthall Notts 72 E2
Nuthampstead Herts 51 K4
Nuthurst W Susx 24 E5
Nutley E Susx 25 K5
Nutley Hants 22 H6
Nuttall Bury 89 M7
Nutwell Donc 91 Q10
Nybster Highld 167 Q4
Nyetimber W Susx 15 N7
Nyewood W Susx 23 M10
Nymans W Susx 24 G5
Nymet Rowland Devon 17 N10
Nymet Tracey Devon 8 H4
Nympsfield Gloucs 32 F4
Nynehead Somset 18 F10
Nythe Somset 19 M8
Nyton W Susx 15 P5

O

Oadby Leics 72 G10
Oad Street Kent 38 E9
Oakall Green Worcs 46 F2
Oakamoor Staffs 71 J6
Oakbank W Loth 127 K4
Oak Cross Devon 8 D5
Oakdale Caerph 30 G5
Oake Somset 18 G9
Oaken Staffs 58 C4
Oakenclough Lancs 95 L11
Oakengates Wrekin 57 N2
Oakenholt Flints 81 K10
Oakenshaw Dur 103 N3
Oakenshaw Kirk 90 F5
Oakerthorpe Derbys 84 E10
Oakford Cerdgn 43 J3
Oakford Devon 18 B10
Oakfordbridge Devon 18 B10
Oakgrove Ches E 83 K11
Oakham Rutlnd 73 M9
Oakhanger Ches E 70 D4
Oakhanger Hants 23 L7
Oakhill Somset 20 B5
Oakington Cambs 62 F8
Oaklands Powys 44 E4
Oakle Street Gloucs 46 E11
Oakley Bed 61 M10
Oakley Bucks 34 H4
Oakley Fife 134 C10
Oakley Hants 22 G4
Oakley Oxon 35 L4
Oakley Suffk 64 H6
Oakley Green W & M 35 P9
Oakley Park Powys 55 M7
Oakridge Lynch Gloucs 32 H4
Oaks Lancs 89 K4
Oaks Shrops 56 G4

Oaksey Wilts 33 J6
Oaks Green Derbys 71 M8
Oakshaw Ford Cumb 111 K5
Oakshott Hants 23 K9
Oakthorpe Leics 59 M2
Oak Tree Darltn 104 C8
Oakwood C Derb 72 B3
Oakwood Nthumb 112 D7
Oakworth C Brad 90 C3
Oare Kent 38 H9
Oare Somset 17 P2
Oare Wilts 21 N2
Oasby Lincs 73 Q3
Oath Somset 19 L9
Oathlaw Angus 142 H6
Oatlands Park Surrey 36 C7
Oban Ag & B 130 H2
Oban Airport Ag & B 138 G10
Obley Shrops 56 E9
Obney P & K 141 P10
Oborne Dorset 20 C11
Obthorpe Lincs 74 A8
Occold Suffk 64 H7
Occumster Highld 167 N9
Ochiltree E Ayrs 115 K3
Ockbrook Derbys 72 C3
Ocker Hill Sandw 58 E6
Ockeridge Worcs 46 E2
Ockham Surrey 36 C9
Ockle Highld 137 P1
Ockley Surrey 24 D2
Ocle Pychard Herefs 46 A5
Octon E R Yk 99 L7
Odcombe Somset 19 P11
Odd Down BaNES 20 D2
Oddendale Cumb 101 Q8
Oddingley Worcs 46 H3
Oddington Gloucs 47 P9
Oddington Oxon 48 G11
Odell Bed 61 L9
Odham Devon 8 C4
Odiham Hants 23 K4
Odsal C Brad 90 F5
Odsey Cambs 50 G3
Odstock Wilts 21 M9
Odstone Leics 72 B9
Offchurch Warwks 59 N11
Offenham Worcs 47 L5
Offerton Stockp 83 K7
Offerton Sundld 113 M9
Offham E Susx 25 K8
Offham Kent 37 Q9
Offham W Susx 24 B9
Offleymarsh Staffs 70 D9
Offord Cluny Cambs 62 B7
Offord D'Arcy Cambs 62 B7
Offton Suffk 53 J2
Offwell Devon 10 D5
Ogbourne Maizey Wilts 33 N10
Ogbourne St Andrew Wilts 33 N10
Ogbourne St George Wilts 33 P10
Ogden Calder 90 D4
Ogle Nthumb 112 H5
Oglet Lpool 81 N8
Ogmore V Glam 29 N9
Ogmore-by-Sea V Glam 29 N9
Ogmore Vale Brdgnd 29 P6
Ogwen Bank Gwynd 79 L11
Okeford Fitzpaine Dorset 12 D2
Okehampton Devon 8 E5
Oker Side Derbys 84 C8
Okewood Hill Surrey 24 D3
Olchard Devon 9 L7
Old Nhants 60 G6
Old Aberdeen C Aber 151 N6
Old Alresford Hants 22 G8
Oldany Highld 164 C10
Old Auchenbrack D & G 115 Q8
Old Basford C Nott 72 F2
Old Basing Hants 23 J4
Old Beetley Norfk 76 D8
Old Bewick Nthumb 119 L6
Old Bolingbroke Lincs 87 L7
Old Bramhope Leeds 90 G2
Old Brampton Derbys 84 D6
Old Bridge of Urr D & G 108 G7
Old Buckenham Norfk 64 F3
Old Burghclere Hants 22 E3
Oldbury Kent 37 N9
Oldbury Sandw 58 E7
Oldbury Shrops 57 N6
Oldbury Warwks 59 M6
Oldbury Naite S Glos 32 B6
Oldbury-on-Severn S Glos 32 B6
Oldbury on the Hill Gloucs 32 F7
Old Byland N York 98 B3
Old Cantley Donc 91 Q10
Old Cassop Dur 104 B3
Oldcastle Mons 45 L10
Oldcastle Heath Ches W 69 N5
Old Catton Norfk 77 J9
Old Churchstoke Powys 56 D6
Old Clee NE Lin 93 N9
Old Cleeve Somset 18 D6
Old Colwyn Conwy 80 B9
Oldcotes Notts 85 J4
Old Coulsdon Gt Lon 36 H9
Old Dailly S Ayrs 114 D6
Old Dalby Leics 72 H6
Old Dam Derbys 83 P9
Old Deer Abers 159 N8
Old Ditch Somset 19 P5
Old Edlington Donc 91 N11
Old Eldon Dur 103 P5
Old Ellerby E R Yk 93 L3
Old Felixstowe Suffk 53 P4
Oldfield C Brad 90 C3
Oldfield Worcs 46 F2
Old Fletton C Pete 74 C11
Oldford Somset 20 E4
Old Forge Herefs 45 R11
Old Furnace Herefs 45 P10
Old Glossop Derbys 83 M6
Old Goole E R Yk 92 B6
Old Grimsby IoS 2 b1
Old Hall Green Herts 51 J6
Oldhall Green Suffk 64 B10
Old Hall Street Norfk 77 L5
Oldham Oldham 83 K4
Oldhamstocks E Loth 129 J5
Old Harlow Essex 51 L8
Old Heath Essex 52 H7
Old Hunstanton Norfk 75 N2
Old Hurst Cambs 62 D5

Old Hutton Cumb 95 M3
Old Inns Services N Lans 126 D2
Old Kea Cnwll 3 L5
Old Kilpatrick W Duns 125 M3
Old Knebworth Herts 50 F6
Old Lakenham Norfk 77 J10
Oldland S Glos 32 C10
Old Langho Lancs 89 L3
Old Laxey IoM 80 f5
Old Leake Lincs 87 M10
Old Malton N York 98 F6
Oldmeldrum Abers 151 L2
Oldmill Cnwll 5 P7
Old Milverton Warwks 59 L11
Oldmixon N Som 19 K3
Old Newton Suffk 64 F9
Old Oxted Surrey 37 J10
Old Portlethen Abers 151 N8
Old Quarrington Dur 104 B3
Old Radnor Powys 45 K3
Old Rayne Abers 150 H2
Old Romney Kent 26 H7
Old Shoreham W Susx 24 F9
Oldshoremore Highld 164 F5
Old Soar Kent 37 P10
Old Sodbury S Glos 32 E8
Old Somerby Lincs 73 P4
Oldstead N York 98 A5
Old Stratford Nhants 49 L6
Old Struan P & K 141 K4
Old Swarland Nthumb 119 N10
Old Swinford Dudley 58 D8
Old Tebay Cumb 102 B9
Old Thirsk N York 97 P4
Old Town Calder 90 C5
Old Town Cumb 95 M4
Old Town Cumb 101 N4
Old Town E Susx 25 N11
Old Town IoS 2 c2
Old Trafford Traffd 82 H5
Old Tupton Derbys 84 E7
Oldwall Cumb 111 J8
Oldwalls Swans 28 E6
Old Warden C Beds 50 D2
Oldways End Somset 17 R7
Old Weston Cambs 61 N5
Old Wick Highld 167 Q7
Old Windsor W & M 35 Q10
Old Wives Lees Kent 39 J11
Old Woking Surrey 36 B9
Old Wolverton M Keyn 49 M6
Old Woodhall Lincs 86 H7
Old Woods Shrops 69 N10
Olgrinmore Highld 167 J6
Olive Green Staffs 71 L11
Oliver's Battery Hants 22 E9
Ollaberry Shet 169 q5
Ollach Highld 153 J10
Ollerton Ches E 82 G9
Ollerton Notts 85 L7
Ollerton Shrops 70 A9
Olmarch Cerdgn 43 M3
Olmstead Green Cambs 51 P2
Olney M Keyn 49 N4
Olrig House Highld 167 L3
Olton Solhll 58 H8
Olveston S Glos 32 B7
Ombersley Worcs 46 F2
Ompton Notts 85 L7
Once Brewed Nthumb 111 P7
Onchan IoM 80 e6
Onecote Staffs 71 J3
Onehouse Suffk 64 D10
Onen Mons 31 M2
Ongar Street Herefs 56 F11
Onibury Shrops 56 H7
Onich Highld 139 J5
Onllwyn Neath 29 M2
Onneley Staffs 70 D6
Onslow Green Essex 51 Q7
Onslow Village Surrey 23 Q6
Onston Ches W 82 C10
Openwoodgate Derbys 84 E11
Opinan Highld 153 N3
Orbliston Moray 157 Q6
Orbost Highld 152 D9
Orby Lincs 87 N7
Orchard Portman Somset 18 H10
Orcheston Wilts 21 L5
Orcop Herefs 45 P9
Orcop Hill Herefs 45 P9
Ord Abers 158 F6
Ordhead Abers 150 H5
Ordie Abers 150 D7
Ordiequish Moray 157 Q6
Ordley Nthumb 112 D9
Ordsall Notts 85 M5
Ore E Susx 26 D9
Oreleton Common Herefs 56 H11
Oreton Shrops 57 M8
Orford Suffk 65 N11
Orford Warrtn 82 D6
Organford Dorset 12 F6
Orgreave Staffs 71 L11
Orkney Islands Ork 169 d4
Orkney Neolithic Ork 169 c5
Orlestone Kent 26 H5
Orleton Herefs 56 H11
Orleton Worcs 57 N11
Orlingbury Nhants 61 J6
Ormathwaite Cumb 101 J5
Ormesby R & Cl 104 F7
Ormesby St Margaret Norfk 77 P9
Ormesby St Michael Norfk 77 P9
Ormiscaig Highld 160 G6
Ormiston E Loth 128 C6
Ormsaigmore Highld 137 M3
Ormsary Ag & B 123 M5
Ormskirk Lancs 88 E9
Ornsby Hill Dur 113 J11
Oronsay Ag & B 136 b4
Orphir Ork 169 c6
Orpington Gt Lon 37 L7
Orrell Sefton 81 L5
Orrell Wigan 82 B4
Orrell Post Wigan 88 G9
Orrisdale IoM 80 d3
Orroland D & G 108 G11
Orsett Thurr 37 P4
Orsett Heath Thurr 37 P4
Orslow Staffs 70 E11
Orston Notts 73 K2
Orthwaite Cumb 101 J4
Ortner Lancs 95 L10

Orton Cumb 102 B9
Orton Nhants 60 H5
Orton Staffs 58 C5
Orton Longueville C Pete 74 C11
Orton-on-the-Hill Leics 59 M4
Orton Rigg Cumb 110 F10
Orton Waterville C Pete 74 C11
Orwell Cambs 62 E10
Osbaldeston Lancs 89 J4
Osbaldeston Green Lancs 89 J4
Osbaldwick C York 98 C10
Osbaston Leics 72 C10
Osbaston Shrops 69 K10
Osborne IoW 14 F8
Osborne House IoW 14 F8
Osbournby Lincs 73 R3
Oscroft Ches W 81 Q11
Ose Highld 152 E9
Osgathorpe Leics 72 C7
Osgodby Lincs 86 E2
Osgodby N York 91 Q4
Osgodby N York 99 M4
Oskaig Highld 153 J10
Oskamull Ag & B 137 M7
Osmaston Derbys 71 M6
Osmington Dorset 11 Q8
Osmington Mills Dorset 12 B8
Osmondthorpe Leeds 91 J4
Osmotherley N York 104 E11
Osney Oxon 34 E3
Ospringe Kent 38 H9
Ossett Wakefd 90 H6
Ossington Notts 85 N8
Ostend Essex 38 F2
Osterley Gt Lon 36 E5
Oswaldkirk N York 98 C5
Oswaldtwistle Lancs 89 L5
Oswestry Shrops 69 J9
Otford Kent 37 M9
Otham Kent 38 C11
Otham Hole Kent 38 D11
Othery Somset 19 L8
Otley Leeds 97 K11
Otley Suffk 65 J10
Otley Green Suffk 65 J10
Otterbourne Hants 22 E10
Otterburn N York 96 C9
Otterburn Nthumb 112 C2
Otter Ferry Ag & B 131 J11
Otterham Cnwll 5 K3
Otterhampton Somset 18 H6
Otterham Quay Kent 38 D8
Otterham Station Cnwll 5 K4
Otternish W Isls 168 e10
Ottershaw Surrey 36 B8
Otterswick Shet 169 s5
Otterton Devon 10 B7
Otterwood Hants 14 D6
Ottery St Mary Devon 10 C5
Ottinge Kent 27 L3
Ottringham E R Yk 93 N6
Oughterby Cumb 110 E9
Oughtershaw N York 96 C4
Oughterside Cumb 100 F2
Oughtibridge Sheff 84 D2
Oughtrington Warrtn 82 E7
Oulston N York 98 A6
Oulton Cumb 110 D10
Oulton Leeds 91 K5
Oulton Norfk 76 G6
Oulton Staffs 70 D10
Oulton Staffs 70 G7
Oulton Suffk 65 Q3
Oulton Broad Suffk 65 Q3
Oulton Street Norfk 76 H6
Oundle Nhants 61 M3
Ounsdale Staffs 58 C6
Our Dynamic Earth C Edin 127 P3
Ousby Cumb 102 B4
Ousden Suffk 63 M9
Ousefleet E R Yk 92 D6
Ouston Dur 113 L10
Outchester Nthumb 119 M4
Out Elmstead Kent 39 M11
Outgate Cumb 101 L11
Outhgill Cumb 102 E10
Outhill Warwks 58 H11
Outlands Staffs 70 D8
Outlane Kirk 90 D7
Out Newton E R Yk 93 Q6
Out Rawcliffe Lancs 88 E2
Out Skerries Shet 169 t6
Outwell Norfk 75 K10
Outwick Hants 21 M11
Outwood Surrey 36 H11
Outwood Wakefd 91 J6
Outwood Gate Bury 89 M9
Outwoods Leics 72 C7
Outwoods Staffs 70 D11
Ouzlewell Green Leeds 91 J5
Ovenden Calder 90 D5
Over Cambs 62 E6
Over Ches W 82 D11
Over Gloucs 46 F11
Over S Glos 31 Q8
Over Burrows Derbys 71 J7
Overbury Worcs 47 J7
Overcombe Dorset 11 P8
Over Compton Dorset 19 Q11
Over End Cambs 61 N2
Overgreen Derbys 84 D6
Over Green Warwks 59 J6
Over Haddon Derbys 84 B7
Over Kellet Lancs 95 L7
Over Kiddington Oxon 48 D10
Overleigh Somset 19 N7
Overley Staffs 71 M11
Over Monnow Mons 31 P2
Over Norton Oxon 48 B9
Over Peover Ches E 82 G10
Overpool Ches W 81 M9
Overscaig Highld 161 Q2
Overseal Derbys 71 P11
Over Silton N York 97 P2
Oversland Kent 39 J10
Oversley Green Warwks 47 L3
Overstone Nhants 60 G7
Over Stowey Somset 18 G7
Overstrand Norfk 77 J3
Over Stratton Somset 19 M11
Overstreet Wilts 21 L7
Over Tabley Ches E 82 F9
Overthorpe Nhants 48 E6
Overton C Aber 151 M4
Overton Ches W 81 Q9

Overton Hants 22 F5
Overton Lancs 95 J9
Overton N York 98 B9
Overton Shrops 57 J10
Overton Swans 28 E7
Overton Wakefd 90 H7
Overton Wrexhm 69 L6
Overton Bridge Wrexhm 69 L6
Overton Green Ches E 70 E2
Overtown Lancs 89 P5
Overtown N Lans 126 E7
Overtown Swindn 33 N9
Overtown Wakefd 91 K7
Over Wallop Hants 21 Q7
Over Whitacre Warwks 59 L6
Over Woodhouse Derbys 84 G6
Over Worton Oxon 48 D9
Overy Oxon 34 G6
Oving Bucks 49 L10
Oving W Susx 15 P6
Ovingdean Br & H 25 J10
Ovingham Nthumb 112 G8
Ovington Dur 103 M8
Ovington Essex 52 C3
Ovington Hants 22 G8
Ovington Norfk 76 C11
Ovington Nthumb 112 G8
Ower Hants 14 E6
Ower Hants 22 B11
Owermoigne Dorset 12 C7
Owlbury Shrops 56 E6
Owlerton Sheff 84 D3
Owlpen Gloucs 32 E5
Owl's Green Suffk 65 K8
Owlsmoor Br For 23 M2
Owlswick Bucks 35 L3
Owmby Lincs 86 D3
Owmby Lincs 93 J10
Owslebury Hants 22 F10
Owston Donc 91 P8
Owston Leics 73 K9
Owston Ferry N Linc 92 D10
Owstwick E R Yk 93 N4
Owthorne E R Yk 93 P5
Owthorpe Notts 72 H4
Owton Manor Hartpl 104 E5
Oxborough Norfk 75 P10
Oxbridge Dorset 11 K5
Oxcombe Lincs 87 K5
Oxcroft Derbys 84 G6
Oxen End Essex 51 Q5
Oxenholme Cumb 95 L3
Oxenhope C Brad 90 C4
Oxen Park Cumb 94 G3
Oxenpill Somset 19 M6
Oxenton Gloucs 47 J8
Oxenwood Wilts 22 B3
Oxford Oxon 34 F3
Oxford Airport Oxon 48 E11
Oxford Services Oxon 34 H4
Oxhey Herts 50 D11
Oxhill Dur 113 J10
Oxhill Warwks 48 B5
Oxley Wolves 58 D4
Oxley Green Essex 52 F9
Oxley's Green E Susx 25 Q6
Oxlode Cambs 62 G3
Oxnam Border 118 C7
Oxnead Norfk 77 J7
Oxshott Surrey 36 D8
Oxshott Heath Surrey 36 D8
Oxspring Barns 90 H10
Oxted Surrey 37 J10
Oxton Border 128 D9
Oxton N York 91 N2
Oxton Notts 85 K10
Oxton Wirral 81 L7
Oxwich Swans 28 E7
Oxwich Green Swans 28 E7
Oxwick Norfk 76 C6
Oykel Bridge Highld 161 P6
Oyne Abers 150 H2
Oystermouth Swans 28 H7
Ozleworth Gloucs 32 E6

P

Pabail W Isls 168 k4
Packers Hill Dorset 11 Q2
Packington Leics 72 B8
Packmoor C Stke 70 F4
Packmores Warwks 59 L11
Padanaram Angus 142 G7
Padbury Bucks 49 K8
Paddington Gt Lon 36 G4
Paddington Warrtn 82 D7
Paddlesworth Kent 27 L4
Paddlesworth Kent 37 Q8
Paddock Wood Kent 25 Q2
Paddolgreen Shrops 69 P8
Padfield Derbys 83 M3
Padgate Warrtn 82 D7
Padhams Green Essex 51 P7
Padiham Lancs 89 M4
Padside N York 97 J9
Padstow Cnwll 4 E6
Padworth W Berk 34 H11
Page Bank Dur 103 P3
Pagham W Susx 15 N7
Paglesham Essex 38 F3
Paignton Torbay 7 M6
Pailton Warwks 59 Q8
Paine's Cross E Susx 25 P6
Painleyhill Staffs 71 J8
Painscastle Powys 44 H5
Painshawfield Nthumb 112 G8
Painsthorpe E R Yk 98 G9
Painswick Gloucs 32 G3
Painter's Forstal Kent 38 G10
Paisley Rens 125 M5
Pakefield Suffk 65 Q3
Pakenham Suffk 64 C8
Pale Gwynd 68 C7
Pale Green Essex 51 Q2
Palestine Hants 21 Q6
Paley Street W & M 35 N9
Palfrey Wsall 58 F5
Palgrave Suffk 64 G6
Pallington Dorset 12 C6
Palmersbridge Cnwll 5 K6
Palmers Green Gt Lon 36 H2
Palmerston E Ayrs 115 K4

Palmerstown V Glam 30 F11
Palnackie D & G 108 H9
Palnure D & G 107 N5
Palterton Derbys 84 G7
Pamber End Hants 22 H3
Pamber Green Hants 22 H3
Pamber Heath Hants 22 H3
Pamington Gloucs 46 H8
Pamphill Dorset 12 G4
Pampisford Cambs 62 G11
Panborough Somset 19 N5
Panbride Angus 143 K10
Pancrasweek Devon 16 D10
Pancross V Glam 30 D11
Pandy Caerph 30 G7
Pandy Gwynd 54 E4
Pandy Gwynd 68 A9
Pandy Mons 45 L10
Pandy Powys 55 L4
Pandy Wrexhm 68 E7
Pandy'r Capel Denbgs 68 E4
Pandy Tudur Conwy 67 R2
Panfield Essex 52 B6
Pangbourne W Berk 34 H9
Pangdean W Susx 24 G8
Panks Bridge Herefs 46 B5
Pannal N York 97 M10
Pannal Ash N York 97 L10
Pant Shrops 69 J10
Pantasaph Flints 80 H9
Panteg Pembks 40 H4
Pantersbridge Cnwll 5 K8
Pant-ffrwyth Brdgnd 29 P8
Pant Glas Gwynd 66 H5
Pantglas Powys 54 H5
Pant-Gwyn Carmth 43 L9
Pant-lasau Swans 29 J4
Pant Mawr Powys 55 J8
Panton Lincs 86 G5
Pant-pastynog Denbgs 68 D2
Pantperthog Gwynd 54 G4
Pant-y-dwr Powys 55 M10
Pant-y-ffridd Powys 56 B3
Pantyffynnon Carmth 28 H2
Pantygaseg Torfn 31 J5
Pantygelli Mons 45 L11
Pant-y-gog Brdgnd 29 P7
Pantymenyn Carmth 41 M5
Pant-y-mwyn Flints 68 G2
Panxworth Norfk 77 M9
Papa Stour Shet 169 n7
Papa Stour Airport Shet 169 n8
Papa Westray Ork 169 d1
Papa Westray Airport Ork 169 d1
Papcastle Cumb 100 F4
Papigoe Highld 167 Q6
Papple E Loth 128 F5
Papplewick Notts 84 H10
Papworth Everard Cambs 62 C8
Papworth St Agnes Cambs 62 C8
Par Cnwll 3 R3
Paramour Street Kent 39 N9
Parbold Lancs 88 F8
Parbrook Somset 19 Q7
Parbrook W Susx 24 C5
Parc Gwynd 68 A8
Parcllyn Cerdgn 42 D4
Parc Seymour Newpt 31 M6
Pardshaw Cumb 100 E6
Parham Suffk 65 L9
Park D & G 109 K2
Park Nthumb 111 N8
Park Bottom Cnwll 2 H5
Park Bridge Tamesd 83 K4
Park Corner E Susx 25 M3
Park Corner Oxon 35 J7
Park Corner W & M 35 N8
Park End Bed 49 Q4
Parkend Gloucs 32 B3
Park End Nthumb 112 C5
Parker's Green Kent 37 P11
Parkeston Essex 53 M5
Parkeston Quay Essex 53 M5
Park Farm Kent 26 H4
Parkgate Ches W 81 K9
Parkgate Cumb 110 D11
Parkgate D & G 109 M3
Parkgate E Susx 26 B9
Parkgate Essex 51 Q5
Park Gate Hants 14 F5
Parkgate Kent 26 E5
Parkgate Kent 37 M8
Park Gate Leeds 90 F2
Parkgate Surrey 24 F2
Park Gate Worcs 58 D10
Park Green Essex 51 L5
Park Green Suffk 64 G9
Parkhall W Duns 125 M3
Parkham Devon 16 F7
Parkham Ash Devon 16 F7
Park Head Derbys 84 E10
Park Hill Gloucs 31 Q5
Parkhouse Mons 31 P4
Parkmill Swans 28 F7
Park Royal Gt Lon 36 E4
Parkside Dur 113 P11
Parkside N Lans 126 E6
Parkside Wrexhm 69 L3
Parkstone BCP 12 H6
Park Street Herts 50 D10
Park Street W Susx 24 D4
Parkway Herefs 46 D7
Parley Green BCP 13 K5
Parmoor Bucks 35 L7
Parracombe Devon 17 M2
Parrog Pembks 41 K2
Parsonby Cumb 100 F3
Parson Cross Sheff 84 D2
Parson Drove Cambs 74 G9
Parson's Heath Essex 52 H6
Parson's Hill Derbys 71 P9
Partick C Glas 125 N4
Partington Traffd 82 F6
Partney Lincs 87 M7
Parton Cumb 100 C6
Partridge Green W Susx 24 E7
Partrishow Powys 45 K10
Parwich Derbys 71 M4
Paslow Wood Common Essex 51 N10
Passenham Nhants 49 L7
Passfield Hants 23 M8
Passingford Bridge Essex 51 N11
Paston C Pete 74 C10
Paston Norfk 77 L5

Pasturefields Staffs 70 H10
Patchacott Devon 8 C5
Patcham Br & H 24 H9
Patchetts Green Herts 50 D11
Patching W Susx 24 C9
Patchole Devon 17 L3
Patchway S Glos 32 B8
Pateley Bridge N York 97 J7
Paternoster Heath Essex 52 F8
Pathe Somset 19 L8
Pathhead Fife 134 H9
Pathhead Mdloth 128 D11
Pathlow Warwks 47 N3
Path of Condie P & K 134 D5
Patmore Heath Herts 51 K5
Patna E Ayrs 114 H5
Patney Wilts 21 L3
Patrick IoM 80 b5
Patrick Brompton N York 97 K2
Patricroft Salfd 82 G5
Patrington E R Yk 93 P6
Patrington Haven E R Yk 93 P6
Patrixbourne Kent 39 L10
Patterdale Cumb 101 L7
Pattingham Staffs 57 Q5
Pattishall Nhants 49 J4
Pattiswick Green Essex 52 D7
Patton Shrops 57 K5
Patton Bridge Cumb 101 Q11
Paul Cnwll 2 D8
Paulerspury Nhants 49 K5
Paull E R Yk 93 L5
Paulton BaNES 20 C3
Paultons Park Hants 22 B11
Paunton Herefs 46 C4
Pauperhaugh Nthumb 119 M11
Pave Lane Wrekin 70 D11
Pavenham Bed 61 L9
Pawlett Somset 19 J6
Pawston Nthumb 118 G4
Paxford Gloucs 47 N7
Paxton Border 129 N9
Payden Street Kent 38 F11
Payhembury Devon 10 B4
Paynter's Lane End Cnwll 2 H6
Paythorne Lancs 96 B10
Paytoe Herefs 56 G10
Peacehaven E Susx 25 K10
Peak Dale Derbys 83 N9
Peak District National Park 83 Q6
Peak Forest Derbys 83 P9
Peak Hill Lincs 74 E7
Peakirk C Pete 74 C9
Pearson's Green Kent 25 Q2
Peartree Green Herefs 46 A8
Peasedown St John BaNES 20 D3
Peasehill Derbys 84 F11
Peaseland Green Norfk 76 F8
Peasemore W Berk 34 E9
Peasenhall Suffk 65 M8
Pease Pottage W Susx 24 G4
Pease Pottage Services W Susx 24 G4
Peaslake Surrey 24 C2
Peasley Cross St Hel 81 Q6
Peasmarsh E Susx 26 E7
Peasmarsh Somset 10 G2
Peasmarsh Surrey 23 Q5
Peathill Abers 159 M4
Peat Inn Fife 135 M6
Peatling Magna Leics 60 C2
Peatling Parva Leics 60 C3
Peaton Shrops 57 J7
Pebmarsh Essex 52 E5
Pebsham E Susx 26 C10
Pebworth Worcs 47 M5
Pecket Well Calder 90 B5
Peckforton Ches E 69 Q3
Peckham Gt Lon 36 H5
Peckleton Leics 72 D10
Pedairffordd Powys 68 F10
Pedlinge Kent 27 K4
Pedmore Dudley 58 D8
Pedwell Somset 19 M7
Peebles Border 117 K2
Peel IoM 80 b5
Peel Lancs 88 D4
Peel Common Hants 14 G6
Peene Kent 27 L4
Peening Quarter Kent 26 E6
Peggs Green Leics 72 C7
Pegsdon C Beds 50 E4
Pegswood Nthumb 113 K3
Pegwell Kent 39 Q9
Peinchorran Highld 153 J11
Peinlich Highld 152 G6
Pelcomb Pembks 40 H7
Pelcomb Bridge Pembks 40 H7
Pelcomb Cross Pembks 40 H7
Peldon Essex 52 G8
Pell Green E Susx 25 P4
Pelsall Wsall 58 F4
Pelsall Wood Wsall 58 F4
Pelton Dur 113 L10
Pelton Fell Dur 113 L10
Pelutho Cumb 109 P11
Pelynt Cnwll 5 L10
Pemberton Carmth 28 F4
Pemberton Wigan 82 C4
Pembles Cross Kent 26 E2
Pembrey Carmth 28 D4
Pembridge Herefs 45 M3
Pembroke Pembks 41 J10
Pembroke Dock Pembks 41 J10
Pembrokeshire Coast National Park Pembks 40 F6
Pembury Kent 25 P2
Pen-allt Herefs 45 R9
Penallt Mons 31 P2
Penally Pembks 41 M11
Penare Cnwll 3 P5
Penarth V Glam 30 G10
Penblewin Pembks 41 M7
Pen-bont Rhydybeddau Cerdgn 54 F8
Penbryn Cerdgn 42 E4
Pencader Carmth 42 H7
Pencaenewydd Gwynd 66 G6
Pencaitland E Loth 128 C6
Pencarnisiog IoA 78 F10
Pencarreg Carmth 43 K5
Pencarrow Cnwll 5 J5
Pencelli Powys 44 F9
Penclawdd Swans 28 F5

Pencoed Brdgnd 30 C8
Pencombe Herefs 46 A4
Pencoyd Herefs 45 Q9
Pencraig Herefs 45 R10
Pencraig Powys 68 D9
Pendeen Cnwll 2 B7
Penderyn Rhondd 29 P3
Pendine Carmth 41 P9
Pendlebury Salfd 82 G4
Pendleton Lancs 89 M3
Pendock Worcs 46 E8
Pendoggett Cnwll 4 G6
Pendomer Somset 11 L2
Pendoylan V Glam 30 E9
Penegoes Powys 54 H4
Penelewey Cnwll 3 L5
Pen-ffordd Pembks 41 L6
Pengam Caerph 30 G5
Pengam Cardif 30 H9
Penge Gt Lon 37 J6
Pengelly Cnwll 4 H5
Pengenffordd Powys 44 H9
Pengover Green Cnwll 5 M8
Pen-groes-oped Mons 31 K3
Pengwern Denbgs 80 E9
Penhale Cnwll 2 H10
Penhale Cnwll 4 E10
Penhale Cnwll 4 H9
Penhale Cnwll 5 Q11
Penhallow Cnwll 3 K3
Penhalurick Cnwll 3 J6
Penhalvean Cnwll 3 J6
Penhill Swindn 33 N7
Penhow Newpt 31 M6
Penhurst E Susx 25 Q7
Peniarth Gwynd 54 E3
Penicuik Mdloth 127 N6
Peniel Carmth 42 H10
Peniel Denbgs 68 D2
Penifiler Highld 152 H9
Peninver Ag & B 120 E7
Penisarwaun Gwynd 67 K2
Penistone Barns 90 G10
Penjerrick Cnwll 3 K7
Penketh Warrtn 82 C7
Penkill S Ayrs 114 D8
Penkridge Staffs 58 D2
Penlean Cnwll 5 L2
Penleigh Wilts 20 G4
Penley Wrexhm 69 M6
Penllergaer Swans 28 H5
Pen-llyn IoA 78 F8
Penllyn V Glam 30 C9
Pen-lôn IoA 78 G11
Penmachno Conwy 67 P4
Penmaen Caerph 30 G5
Penmaen Swans 28 F7
Penmaenan Conwy 79 N9
Penmaenmawr Conwy 79 N9
Penmaenpool Gwynd 67 M11
Penmark V Glam 30 E11
Penmon IoA 79 L8
Penmorfa Gwynd 67 J6
Penmynydd IoA 79 J10
Penn Bucks 35 P6
Penn Wolves 58 C5
Pennal Gwynd 54 F4
Pennan Abers 159 K4
Pennant Cerdgn 43 K2
Pennant Denbgs 68 D8
Pennant Powys 55 K5
Pennant-Melangell Powys 68 D9
Pennar Pembks 41 J10
Pennard Swans 28 G7
Pennerley Shrops 56 F5
Pennicott Devon 9 L4
Pennines 90 B3
Pennington Cumb 94 F5
Pennington Hants 13 P5
Pennington Green Wigan 89 J9
Pennorth Powys 44 G9
Penn Street Bucks 35 P5
Pennsylvania S Glos 32 D10
Penny Bridge Cumb 94 G4
Pennycross Ag & B 137 N10
Pennygate Norfk 77 L7
Pennyghael Ag & B 137 N10
Pennyglen S Ayrs 114 E5
Penny Green Derbys 84 H5
Penny Hill Lincs 74 G5
Pennymoor Devon 9 L2
Pennywell Sundld 113 N9
Penparc Cerdgn 42 D5
Penparcau Cerdgn 54 D8
Penpedairheol Caerph 30 F5
Penpedairheol Mons 31 K4
Penpergwm Mons 31 K4
Penperlleni Mons 31 K4
Penpethy Cnwll 4 H4
Penpillick Cnwll 3 H10
Penpol Cnwll 3 L6
Penpoll Cnwll 5 J11
Penponds Cnwll 2 G6
Penpont Cnwll 4 H7
Penpont D & G 108 B2
Penpont Powys 44 D9
Penquit Devon 6 H7
Penrest Cnwll 5 N6
Penrherber Carmth 41 Q3
Pen-rhiw Pembks 41 P2
Penrhiwceiber Rhondd 30 E5
Pen Rhiwfawr Neath 29 K2
Penrhiwllan Cerdgn 42 G4
Penrhiw-pal Cerdgn 42 F5
Penrhos Gwynd 66 E8
Penrhos IoA 78 D8
Penrhos Mons 31 M2
Penrhos Powys 29 M2
Penrhos garnedd Gwynd 79 K10
Penrhyn Bay Conwy 79 P8
Penrhyn-coch Cerdgn 54 E8
Penrhyndeudraeth Gwynd 67 K7
Penrhyn-side Conwy 79 Q8
Penrhys Rhondd 30 D6
Penrice Swans 28 E7
Penrioch N Ayrs 120 G3
Penrith Cumb 101 P4
Penrose Cnwll 4 D7
Penruddock Cumb 101 M5
Penryn Cnwll 3 K7
Pensarn Conwy 80 D9
Pensax Worcs 57 N11
Pensby Wirral 81 K8
Penselwood Somset 20 E8

288 Pensford – Port Nis

Pensford BaNES 20 B2
Pensham Worcs 46 H6
Penshaw Sundld 113 M10
Penshurst Kent 25 M2
Penshurst Station Kent 37 M11
Pensilva Cnwll 5 M7
Pensnett Dudley 58 D7
Penstone Devon 9 J4
Penstrowed Powys 55 P6
Pentewan Cnwll 3 Q4
Pentir Gwynd 79 K11
Pentire Cnwll 4 B9
Pentlepoir Pembks 41 M9
Pentlow Essex 63 P11
Pentlow Street Essex 63 P11
Pentney Norfk 75 P8
Pentonbridge Cumb 110 H5
Penton Grafton Hants 22 B5
Penton Mewsey Hants 22 B5
Pentraeth IoA 79 J9
Pentre Denbgs 68 E2
Pentre Flints 81 L11
Pentre Mons 31 K3
Pentre Mons 31 M4
Pentre Powys 55 P7
Pentre Powys 56 B7
Pentre Powys 56 D6
Pentre Rhondd 30 C5
Pentre Shrops 69 L11
Pentre Wrexhm 69 J6
Pentre-bâch Cerdgn 43 L5
Pentre Bach Flints 81 J9
Pentrebach Myr Td 30 E4
Pentre-bach Powys 44 C8
Pentrebeirdd Powys 56 B2
Pentre Berw IoA 78 H10
Pentre-bont Conwy 67 N4
Pentre-cagel Carmth 42 F6
Pentrecelyn Denbgs 68 F4
Pentre-celyn Powys 55 K3
Pentre-chwyth Swans 29 J6
Pentre-clawdd Shrops 69 J8
Pentre-cwrt Carmth 42 G7
Pentredwr Denbgs 68 G5
Pentrefelin Gwynd 67 J7
Pentrefelin IoA 78 G6
Pentre Ffwrndan Flints 81 K10
Pentrefoelas Conwy 67 R4
Pentregalar Pembks 41 N4
Pentregat Cerdgn 42 G4
Pentre-Gwenlais Carmth 43 M11
Pentre Gwynfryn Gwynd 67 K9
Pentre Halkyn Flints 81 J10
Pentre Hodrey Shrops 56 E9
Pentre Isaf Conwy 80 D10
Pentre Llanrhaeadr Denbgs 68 E2
Pentre Llifior Powys 56 B5
Pentre-llwyn-llwyd Powys 44 D4
Pentre-llyn Cerdgn 54 E9
Pentre-llyn-cymmer Conwy 68 C4
Pentre-Maw Powys 55 K4
Pentre Meyrick V Glam 30 C9
Pentre-piod Torfn 31 J4
Pentre-poeth Newpt 31 J7
Pentre'rbryn Cerdgn 42 G4
Pentre'r-felin Cerdgn 43 M5
Pentre'r Felin Conwy 79 Q11
Pentre'r-felin Powys 44 C8
Pentre Saron Denbgs 68 D2
Pentre-tafarn-y-fedw Conwy 67 Q2
Pentre ty gwyn Carmth 43 R7
Pentrich Derbys 84 E10
Pentridge Dorset 21 K11
Pen-twyn Caerph 30 H4
Pen-twyn Mons 31 P3
Pen-twyn Torfn 31 J4
Pentwynmaur Caerph 30 G5
Pentyrch Cardif 30 F8
Penwithick Cnwll 4 G10
Penwood Hants 22 D2
Penwyllt Powys 44 B11
Penybanc Carmth 43 M10
Penybont Powys 44 G2
Pen-y-bont Powys 68 H10
Penybontfawr Powys 68 E10
Pen-y-bryn Pembks 41 N2
Pen-y-cae Powys 29 M2
Penycae Wrexhm 69 J5
Pen-y-cae-mawr Mons 31 M5
Penycaerau Gwynd 66 B9
Pen-y-cefn Flints 80 G9
Pen-y-clawdd Mons 31 N3
Pen-y-coedcae Rhondd 30 E7
Penycwn Pembks 40 G6
Pen-y-fai Brdgnd 29 N8
Pen-y-felin Flints 80 H11
Penyffordd Flints 69 K2
Pen-y-ffordd Flints 80 G8
Penyffridd Gwynd 67 J3
Pen-y-garn Cerdgn 54 E7
Pen-y-Garnedd Powys 68 F10
Pen-y-graig Gwynd 66 C8
Penygraig Rhondd 30 D6
Penygroes Carmth 28 G2
Penygroes Gwynd 66 H4
Penygroeslon Gwynd 66 C8
Pen-y-Gwryd Gwynd 67 M3
Pen-y-lan V Glam 30 C9
Pen-y-Mynydd Carmth 28 E4
Penymynydd Flints 69 K2
Pen-y-pass Gwynd 67 L3
Pen-yr-Heol Mons 31 M2
Penysarn IoA 78 H6
Pen-y-stryt Denbgs 68 H4
Penywaun Rhondd 30 C4
Penzance Cnwll 2 D7
Peopleton Worcs 46 H4
Peover Heath Ches E 82 G10
Peper Harow Surrey 23 P6
Peplow Shrops 70 A10
Pepper's Green Essex 51 P8
Pepperstock C Beds 50 C7
Perceton N Ayrs 125 K9
Percyhorner Abers 159 N4
Perelle Guern 10 b2
Perham Down Wilts 21 Q5
Periton Somset 18 C5
Perivale Gt Lon 36 E4
Perkins Village Devon 9 P6
Perkinsville Dur 113 L10
Perlethorpe Notts 85 K6
Perranarworthal Cnwll 3 K6
Perranporth Cnwll 3 K3
Perranuthnoe Cnwll 2 E8
Perranwell Cnwll 3 K3
Perranwell Cnwll 3 K6
Perran Wharf Cnwll 3 K6
Perranzabuloe Cnwll 3 K3
Perrott's Brook Gloucs 33 K3
Perry Birm 58 G6
Perry Barr Birm 58 G6
Perry Green Essex 52 D7
Perry Green Herts 51 K7
Perry Green Wilts 33 J7
Perrystone Hill Herefs 46 B9
Perry Street Somset 10 G3
Pershall Staffs 70 E9
Pershore Worcs 46 H5
Pertenhall Bed 61 N7
Perth P & K 134 E3
Perthy Shrops 69 L8
Perton Herefs 46 A6
Perton Staffs 58 C5
Pertwood Wilts 20 G7
Peterborough C Pete 74 C11
Peterborough Services Cambs 61 P2
Peterchurch Herefs 45 L7
Peterculter C Aber 151 L7
Peterhead Abers 159 R8
Peterlee Dur 104 D2
Petersfield Hants 23 K10
Peter's Green Herts 50 D7
Petersham Gt Lon 36 E6
Peters Marland Devon 16 H9
Peterstone Wentlooge Newpt 31 J9
Peterston-super-Ely V Glam 30 E9
Peterstow Herefs 45 R10
Peters Village Kent 38 B9
Peter Tavy Devon 8 D9
Petham Kent 39 K11
Petherwin Gate Cnwll 5 M4
Petrockstow Devon 17 J10
Petsoe End M Keyn 49 N5
Pet Street Kent 27 J2
Pett E Susx 26 E9
Pettaugh Suffk 64 H10
Pett Bottom Kent 39 L11
Petterden Angus 142 G10
Pettinain S Lans 116 D2
Pettistree Suffk 65 L10
Petton Devon 18 D10
Petton Shrops 69 M9
Petts Wood Gt Lon 37 L7
Pettycur Fife 134 H10
Petty France S Glos 32 E7
Pettymuk Abers 151 N3
Petworth W Susx 23 Q10
Pevensey E Susx 25 P9
Pevensey Bay E Susx 25 Q10
Pewsey Wilts 21 N2
Pewsham Wilts 32 H10
Pheasant's Hill Bucks 35 L7
Phepson Worcs 46 H3
Philadelphia Sundld 113 M10
Philham Devon 16 D7
Philiphaugh Border 117 N5
Phillack Cnwll 2 F6
Philleigh Cnwll 3 M6
Philpot End Essex 51 P7
Philpstoun W Loth 127 K2
Phocle Green Herefs 46 B9
Phoenix Green Hants 23 L3
Pibsbury Somset 19 M9
Pica Cumb 100 D6
Piccadilly Warwks 59 K5
Piccotts End Herts 50 B9
Pickburn Donc 91 N9
Pickering N York 98 F4
Picket Piece Hants 22 C5
Picket Post Hants 13 L3
Picket Twenty Hants 22 C5
Pickford Covtry 59 L8
Pickford Green Covtry 59 L8
Pickhill N York 97 M4
Picklescott Shrops 56 G5
Pickmere Ches E 82 E9
Pickney Somset 18 G9
Pickstock Wrekin 70 C10
Pickup Bank Bl w D 89 L6
Pickwell Devon 16 H3
Pickwell Leics 73 K8
Pickwick Wilts 32 G10
Pickworth Lincs 73 Q4
Pickworth Rutlnd 73 P8
Picton Ches W 81 N10
Picton Flints 80 G8
Picton N York 104 D9
Piddinghoe E Susx 25 K10
Piddington Bucks 35 M6
Piddington Nhants 49 M4
Piddington Oxon 48 H11
Piddlehinton Dorset 11 Q5
Piddletrenthide Dorset 11 Q5
Pidley Cambs 62 D5
Piercebridge Darltn 103 P7
Pierowall Ork 169 d2
Piff's Elm Gloucs 46 H9
Pigdon Nthumb 113 J3
Pigeon Green Warwks 47 P2
Pig Oak Dorset 12 H4
Pig Street Herefs 45 M5
Pikehall Derbys 71 M3
Pilford Dorset 12 H4
Pilgrims Hatch Essex 51 N11
Pilham Lincs 85 Q2
Pill N Som 31 P9
Pillaton Cnwll 5 P9
Pillatonmill Cnwll 5 P9
Pillerton Hersey Warwks 47 Q5
Pillerton Priors Warwks 47 Q5
Pilleth Powys 56 D11
Pilley Barns 91 J10
Pilley Hants 13 P5
Pilley Bailey Hants 13 P5
Pillgwenlly Newpt 31 K7
Pillhead Devon 16 H6
Pilling Lancs 95 J11
Pilling Lane Lancs 94 H11
Pilning S Glos 31 Q7
Pilot Inn Kent 27 J8
Pilsbury Derbys 71 L2
Pilsdon Dorset 11 J5
Pilsgate C Pete 73 R9
Pilsley Derbys 84 B6
Pilsley Derbys 84 F8
Pilson Green Norfk 77 M9
Piltdown E Susx 25 K6
Pilton Devon 17 K5
Pilton Nhants 61 M4
Pilton Rutlnd 73 N10
Pilton Somset 19 Q6
Pilton Green Swans 28 D7
Pimbo Lancs 81 P4
Pimlico Herts 50 C9
Pimlico Lancs 89 L2
Pimlico Nhants 48 H6
Pimperne Dorset 12 F3
Pinchbeck Lincs 74 D5
Pinchbeck Bars Lincs 74 C5
Pincheon Green Donc 91 R7
Pinchinthorpe R & Cl 104 G8
Pincock Lancs 88 G7
Pinfold Lancs 88 D8
Pinford End Suffk 64 A10
Pinged Carmth 28 D4
Pingewood W Berk 35 J11
Pin Green Herts 50 G5
Pinhoe Devon 9 N6
Pinkett's Booth Covtry 59 L8
Pinkney Wilts 32 G7
Pinkneys Green W & M 35 N8
Pinley Covtry 59 N9
Pinley Green Warwks 59 K11
Pin Mill Suffk 53 M4
Pinminnoch S Ayrs 114 C9
Pinmore S Ayrs 114 D9
Pinn Devon 10 C7
Pinner Gt Lon 36 D3
Pinner Green Gt Lon 36 D2
Pinsley Green Ches E 69 Q5
Pinvin Worcs 47 J5
Pinwherry S Ayrs 114 D10
Pinxton Derbys 84 G10
Pipe and Lyde Herefs 45 Q6
Pipe Aston Herefs 56 H10
Pipe Gate Shrops 70 C6
Pipehill Staffs 58 G3
Piperdam Angus 142 D11
Piperhill Highld 156 F7
Pipers Pool Cnwll 5 M5
Pipewell Nhants 60 H3
Pippacott Devon 17 J4
Pippin Street Lancs 88 H6
Pipton Powys 44 H7
Pirbright Surrey 23 P3
Pirbright Camp Surrey 23 P3
Pirnie Border 118 C5
Pirnmill N Ayrs 120 G3
Pirton Herts 50 D4
Pirton Worcs 46 G5
Pisgah Cerdgn 54 F9
Pishill Oxon 35 K7
Pistyll Gwynd 66 E6
Pitblae Abers 159 N5
Pitcairngreen P & K 134 D2
Pitcalnie Highld 156 E3
Pitcaple Abers 151 J2
Pitcarity Angus 142 E4
Pitchcombe Gloucs 32 G3
Pitchcott Bucks 49 L10
Pitcher Row Lincs 74 E4
Pitchford Shrops 57 J4
Pitch Green Bucks 35 L4
Pitch Place Surrey 23 N7
Pitch Place Surrey 23 Q4
Pitchroy Moray 157 M10
Pitcombe Somset 20 C8
Pitcot V Glam 29 N10
Pitcox E Loth 128 G5
Pitfichie Abers 150 H4
Pitglassie Abers 158 G9
Pitgrudy Highld 162 H8
Pitlessie Fife 135 J6
Pitlochry P & K 141 M6
Pitmachie Abers 150 H2
Pitmain Highld 148 C7
Pitmedden Abers 151 M2
Pitmedden Garden Abers 151 M2
Pitminster Somset 18 H11
Pitmuies Angus 143 K8
Pitmunie Abers 150 H5
Pitney Somset 19 N9
Pitroddie P & K 134 G2
Pitscottie Fife 135 L5
Pitsea Essex 38 B4
Pitses Oldham 83 K4
Pitsford Nhants 60 G7
Pitstone Bucks 49 P11
Pitt Devon 18 D11
Pitt Hants 22 E9
Pittarrow Abers 143 N3
Pitt Court Gloucs 32 D5
Pittenweem Fife 135 P7
Pitteuchar Fife 134 H8
Pittington Dur 104 B2
Pittodrie House Hotel Abers 150 H3
Pitton Wilts 21 P8
Pitt's Wood Kent 37 P11
Pittulie Abers 159 N4
Pityme Cnwll 4 F6
Pity Me Dur 113 L11
Pivington Kent 26 F2
Pixey Green Suffk 65 J6
Pixham Surrey 36 E10
Plains N Lans 126 D4
Plain Street Cnwll 4 F6
Plaish Shrops 57 J5
Plaistow Gt Lon 37 K4
Plaistow W Susx 24 B4
Plaitford Hants 21 Q11
Plank Lane Wigan 82 D5
Plas Cymyran IoA 78 D9
Plastow Green Hants 22 F2
Platt Bridge Wigan 82 D4
Platt Lane Shrops 69 P7
Platts Heath Kent 38 E11
Plawsworth Dur 113 L11
Plaxtol Kent 37 P10
Playden E Susx 26 F7
Playford Suffk 53 M2
Play Hatch Oxon 35 K9
Playing Place Cnwll 3 L5
Playley Green Gloucs 46 E8
Plealey Shrops 56 G3
Plean Stirlg 133 N10
Pleasance Fife 134 G5
Pleasington Bl w D 89 J5
Pleasley Derbys 84 H8
Pleasleyhill Notts 84 H8
Pleasurewood Hills Suffk 65 Q2
Pleck Dorset 11 Q2
Pledgdon Green Essex 51 N5
Pledwick Wakefd 91 J7
Pleinheaume Guern 10 b1
Plemont Jersey 11 a1
Plemstall Ches W 81 P10
Plenmeller Nthumb 111 P8
Pleshey Essex 51 Q8
Plockton Highld 153 Q11
Plowden Shrops 56 F7
Plox Green Shrops 56 F4
Pluckley Kent 26 F2
Pluckley Station Kent 26 F3
Pluckley Thorne Kent 26 F3
Plucks Gutter Kent 39 N9
Plumbland Cumb 100 G3
Plumgarths Cumb 95 K2
Plumley Ches E 82 F10
Plump Hill Gloucs 46 C11
Plumpton Cumb 94 G5
Plumpton Cumb 101 N3
Plumpton E Susx 25 J8
Plumpton Nhants 48 G5
Plumpton End Nhants 49 K6
Plumpton Green E Susx 25 J7
Plumpton Head Cumb 101 P3
Plumstead Gt Lon 37 K5
Plumstead Norfk 76 G5
Plumstead Green Norfk 76 G4
Plumtree Notts 72 G4
Plumtree Green Kent 26 D2
Plungar Leics 73 K4
Plurenden Kent 26 F4
Plush Dorset 11 Q4
Plusha Cnwll 5 M5
Plushabridge Cnwll 5 N7
Plwmp Cerdgn 42 G4
Plymouth C Plym 6 D8
Plympton C Plym 6 E7
Plymstock C Plym 6 E8
Plymtree Devon 9 Q4
Pockley N York 98 C3
Pocklington E R Yk 98 G11
Pode Hole Lincs 74 D6
Podimore Somset 19 P10
Podington Bed 61 K8
Podmore Staffs 70 D7
Point Clear Essex 53 K9
Pointon Lincs 74 B4
Pokesdown BCP 13 K6
Polbain Highld 160 F4
Polbathic Cnwll 5 N10
Polbeth W Loth 127 J5
Polbrock Cnwll 4 G8
Poldark Mine Cnwll 2 H7
Polebrook Nhants 61 N3
Pole Elm Worcs 46 F4
Polegate E Susx 25 N10
Pole Moor Kirk 90 D7
Polesden Lacey Surrey 36 D10
Polesworth Warwks 59 L4
Polgigga Cnwll 2 B9
Polglass Highld 160 G5
Polgooth Cnwll 3 P3
Polgown D & G 115 P7
Poling W Susx 24 B10
Poling Corner W Susx 24 B9
Polkerris Cnwll 4 H11
Pollard Street Norfk 77 L5
Pollington E R Yk 91 Q7
Polloch Highld 138 D4
Pollokshaws C Glas 125 P5
Pollokshields C Glas 125 P5
Polmassick Cnwll 3 P4
Polmear Cnwll 4 H11
Polmont Falk 126 G2
Polnish Highld 145 N11
Polperro Cnwll 5 L11
Polruan Cnwll 5 J11
Polsham Somset 19 P6
Polstead Suffk 52 G4
Polstead Heath Suffk 52 G3
Poltalloch Ag & B 130 G8
Poltescoe Cnwll 3 J10
Poltimore Devon 9 N5
Polton Mdloth 127 P5
Polwarth Border 129 J9
Polyphant Cnwll 5 M5
Polzeath Cnwll 4 E6
Pomathorn Mdloth 127 N6
Pomeroy Derbys 83 P11
Ponde Powys 44 G7
Pondersbridge Cambs 62 C2
Ponders End Gt Lon 51 J11
Ponsanooth Cnwll 3 K6
Ponsonby Cumb 100 E9
Ponsongath Cnwll 3 K10
Ponsworthy Devon 8 J4
Pont Abraham Services Carmth 28 G3
Pontac Jersey 11 c2
Pontamman Carmth 28 H2
Pontantwn Carmth 28 D2
Pontardawe Neath 29 K4
Pontarddulais Swans 28 G4
Pont-ar-gothi Carmth 43 K10
Pont-ar-Hydfer Powys 44 B9
Pont-ar-llechau Carmth 43 P10
Pontarsais Carmth 42 H9
Pontblyddyn Flints 69 J2
Pont Cyfyng Conwy 67 N3
Pontcysyllte Aqueduct Wrexhm 69 J6
Pont Dolgarrog Conwy 79 P11
Pontdolgoch Powys 55 N6
Pont-Ebbw Newpt 31 J7
Pontefract Wakefd 91 M6
Ponteland Nthumb 113 J6
Ponterwyd Cerdgn 54 G8
Pontesbury Shrops 56 F3
Pontesbury Hill Shrops 56 F3
Pontesford Shrops 56 G3
Pontfadog Wrexhm 68 H7
Pontfaen Pembks 41 K4
Pont-faen Powys 44 D8
Pontgarreg Cerdgn 42 F4
Pontgarreg Pembks 41 M2
Ponthenri Carmth 28 E3
Ponthir Torfn 31 K6
Ponthirwaun Cerdgn 42 E5
Pontllanfraith Caerph 30 G5
Pontlliw Swans 28 H4
Pontllyfni Gwynd 66 G4
Pontlottyn Caerph 30 F3
Pont Morlais Carmth 28 F3
Pontnêddféchan Neath 29 P3
Pontnewydd Torfn 31 J5
Pontnewynydd Torfn 31 J4
Pont Pen-y-benglog Gwynd 67 M2
Pontrhydfendigaid Cerdgn 54 G11
Pont Rhyd-sarn Gwynd 67 R9
Pont Rhyd-y-cyff Brdgnd 29 N7
Pont-rhyd-y-fen Neath 29 L6
Pontrhydygroes Cerdgn 54 G10
Pontrhydyrun Torfn 31 J5
Pontrilas Herefs 45 M9
Pont Robert Powys 55 Q2
Pont-rug Gwynd 67 J2
Ponts Green E Susx 25 Q7
Pontshaen Cerdgn 42 H5
Pontshill Herefs 46 B10
Pontsticill Myr Td 30 E2
Pont Walby Neath 29 N3
Pontwelly Carmth 42 H6
Pontyates Carmth 28 E3
Pontyberem Carmth 28 F2
Pont-y-blew Wrexhm 69 K7
Pontybodkin Flints 69 J3
Pontyclun Rhondd 30 D8
Pontycymer Brdgnd 29 P6
Pontyglasier Pembks 41 M3
Pontygwaith Rhondd 30 D6
Pontygynon Pembks 41 M3
Pontymister Caerph 30 H6
Pont-y-pant Conwy 67 P4
Pontypool Torfn 31 J4
Pontypridd Rhondd 30 E7
Pont-yr-hafod Pembks 40 H5
Pont-yr-Rhyl Brdgnd 29 P7
Pontywaun Caerph 30 H6
Pool Cnwll 2 H5
Pool IoS 2 b2
Poole BCP 12 H6
Poole Keynes Gloucs 33 J5
Poolewe Highld 160 D10
Pooley Bridge Cumb 101 N6
Pooley Street Norfk 64 F5
Poolfold Staffs 70 F3
Pool Head Herefs 45 R4
Poolhill Gloucs 46 D9
Pool in Wharfedale Leeds 97 K11
Pool of Muckhart Clacks 134 C7
Pool Quay Powys 56 D2
Pool Street Essex 52 C4
Pooting's Kent 37 L11
Popham Hants 22 G6
Poplar Gt Lon 37 J4
Poplar Street Suffk 65 N8
Porchfield IoW 14 D8
Poringland Norfk 77 K11
Porkellis Cnwll 2 H7
Porlock Somset 18 A5
Porlock Weir Somset 17 R2
Portachoillan Ag & B 123 N8
Port-an-Eorna Highld 153 P11
Port Appin Ag & B 138 G8
Port Askaig Ag & B 122 F6
Portavadie Ag & B 124 A4
Port Bannatyne Ag & B 124 D4
Portbury N Som 31 P9
Port Carlisle Cumb 110 D8
Port Charlotte Ag & B 122 C8
Portchester Hants 14 H5
Port Clarence S on T 104 E6
Port Driseach Ag & B 124 B3
Port Ellen Ag & B 122 E10
Port Elphinstone Abers 151 K3
Portencalzie D & G 106 D3
Portencross N Ayrs 124 F8
Port Erin IoM 80 a8
Portesham Dorset 11 N7
Portessie Moray 158 B4
Port e Vullen IoM 80 g3
Port Eynon Swans 28 E7
Portfield Gate Pembks 40 H7
Portgate Devon 5 Q4
Port Gaverne Cnwll 4 G5
Port Glasgow Inver 125 J3
Portgordon Moray 158 A5
Portgower Highld 163 N4
Porth Cnwll 4 C9
Porth Rhondd 30 D6
Porthallow Cnwll 3 K9
Porthallow Cnwll 5 L11
Porthcawl Brdgnd 29 M9
Porthcothan Cnwll 4 D7
Porthcurno Cnwll 2 B9
Porthdinllaen Gwynd 66 D6
Port Henderson Highld 153 P3
Porthgain Pembks 40 F4
Porthgwarra Cnwll 2 B9
Porthill Staffs 70 E5
Porthkea Cnwll 3 L5
Porthkerry V Glam 30 E11
Porthleven Cnwll 2 G8
Porthmadog Gwynd 67 K7
Porthmeor Cnwll 2 C6
Porth Navas Cnwll 3 K8
Portholland Cnwll 3 P5
Porthoustock Cnwll 3 L9
Porthpean Cnwll 3 Q3
Porthtowan Cnwll 2 H4
Porthwgan Wrexhm 69 L5
Porthyrhyd Carmth 43 K11
Porth-y-Waen Shrops 69 J10
Portincaple Ag & B 131 Q9
Portinfer Jersey 11 a1
Portington E R Yk 92 C4
Portinnisherrich Ag & B 131 K5
Portinscale Cumb 101 J6
Port Isaac Cnwll 4 F5
Portishead N Som 31 N9
Portknockie Moray 158 C4
Portland Dorset 11 P10
Portlethen Abers 151 N8
Portling D & G 109 J10
Portloe Cnwll 3 N6
Port Logan D & G 106 E9
Portlooe Cnwll 5 L11
Portmahomack Highld 163 L10
Portmeirion Gwynd 67 K7
Portmellon Cnwll 3 Q5
Port Mòr Highld 144 F12
Portmore Hants 13 P5
Port Mulgrave N York 105 L7
Portnacroish Ag & B 138 G8
Portnaguran W Isls 168 k4
Portnahaven Ag & B 122 A9
Portnalong Highld 152 E11
Port nan Giuran W Isls 168 k4
Port nan Long W Isls 168 d10
Port Nis W Isls 168 k1

Portobello C Edin — 127 Q3
Portobello Gatesd — 113 L9
Portobello Wolves — 58 E5
Port of Menteith Stirlg — 132 H7
Port of Ness W Isls — 168 k1
Porton Wilts — 21 N7
Portontown Devon — 5 Q6
Portpatrick D & G — 106 C7
Port Quin Cnwll — 4 F5
Port Ramsay Ag & B — 138 F8
Portreath Cnwll — 2 H4
Portreath Harbour Cnwll — 2 H4
Portree Highld — 152 H9
Port Righ Ag & B — 120 F4
Port St Mary IoM — 80 b8
Portscatho Cnwll — 3 M6
Portsea C Port — 14 H6
Portskerra Highld — 166 E3
Portskewett Mons — 31 N7
Portslade Br & H — 24 G9
Portslade-by-Sea Br & H — 24 G9
Portslogan D & G — 106 C6
Portsmouth C Port — 14 H7
Portsmouth Calder — 89 Q5
Portsmouth Arms Devon — 17 L8
Portsmouth Dockyard C Port — 14 H6
Port Soderick IoM — 80 d7
Port Solent C Port — 14 H5
Portsonachan Hotel Ag & B — 131 L3
Portsoy Abers — 158 E4
Port Sunlight Wirral — 81 L8
Portswood C Sotn — 14 D4
Port Talbot Neath — 29 L7
Port Tennant Swans — 29 J6
Portuairk Highld — 137 L2
Portway Herefs — 45 P6
Portway Herefs — 45 P7
Portway Sandw — 58 E7
Portway Worcs — 58 G10
Port Wemyss Ag & B — 122 A9
Port William D & G — 107 L8
Portwrinkle Cnwll — 5 P11
Portyerrock D & G — 107 N10
Posbury Devon — 9 K5
Posenhall Shrops — 57 M4
Poslingford Suffk — 63 N11
Posso Border — 117 J3
Postbridge Devon — 8 G9
Postcombe Oxon — 35 K4
Post Green Dorset — 12 G6
Postling Kent — 27 K4
Postwick Norfk — 77 K10
Potarch Abers — 150 G8
Potsgrove C Beds — 49 Q8
Potten End Herts — 50 B9
Potten Street Kent — 39 N8
Potter Brompton N York — 99 K5
Pottergate Street Norfk — 64 H3
Potterhanworth Lincs — 86 E7
Potterhanworth Booths Lincs — 86 E7
Potter Heigham Norfk — 77 N8
Potterne Wilts — 21 J3
Potterne Wick Wilts — 21 J3
Potter Row Bucks — 35 P4
Potters Bar Herts — 50 F10
Potters Brook Lancs — 95 K10
Potter's Cross Staffs — 58 B8
Potter's Crouch Herts — 50 D9
Potter's Forstal Kent — 26 E2
Potter's Green Covtry — 59 N8
Potter's Green E Susx — 25 N6
Potter's Green Herts — 51 J6
Pottersheath Herts — 50 F7
Potters Marston Leics — 72 D11
Potter Somersal Derbys — 71 L7
Potterspury Nhants — 49 L6
Potter Street Essex — 51 L9
Potterton Abers — 151 N4
Potterton Leeds — 91 K4
Potthorpe Norfk — 76 C7
Pottle Street Wilts — 20 F6
Potto N York — 104 E10
Potton C Beds — 62 B11
Pott Row Norfk — 75 P6
Pott's Green Essex — 52 F7
Pott Shrigley Ches E — 83 K9
Poughill Cnwll — 16 C10
Poughill Devon — 9 L3
Poulner Hants — 13 L3
Poulshot Wilts — 21 J3
Poulton Gloucs — 33 L4
Poulton Wirral — 81 L6
Poulton-le-Fylde Lancs — 88 C3
Poulton Priory Gloucs — 33 L5
Pound Bank Worcs — 57 N10
Poundbury Dorset — 11 P6
Poundffald Swans — 28 G6
Poundgate E Susx — 25 L5
Pound Green E Susx — 25 M6
Pound Green Suffk — 63 M10
Pound Green Worcs — 57 P9
Pound Hill W Susx — 24 G3
Poundon Bucks — 48 H9
Poundsbridge Kent — 25 M2
Poundsgate Devon — 7 J4
Poundstock Cnwll — 5 L2
Pounsley E Susx — 25 M6
Pouton D & G — 107 N8
Pouy Street Suffk — 65 M7
Povey Cross Surrey — 24 G2
Powburn Nthumb — 119 L7
Powderham Devon — 9 N8
Powerstock Dorset — 11 L5
Powfoot D & G — 109 P7
Pow Green Herefs — 46 D6
Powhill Cumb — 110 D9
Powick Worcs — 46 F4
Powmill P & K — 134 C8
Poxwell Dorset — 12 B8
Poyle Slough — 36 B5
Poynings W Susx — 24 G8
Poyntington Dorset — 20 C10
Poynton Ches E — 83 K8
Poynton Wrekin — 69 Q11
Poynton Green Wrekin — 69 Q11
Poyston Cross Pembks — 41 J7
Poystreet Green Suffk — 64 D10
Praa Sands Cnwll — 2 F9
Pratt's Bottom Gt Lon — 37 L8
Praze-an-Beeble Cnwll — 2 G6
Predannack Wollas Cnwll — 2 H10

Prees Shrops — 69 Q8
Preesall Lancs — 94 H11
Prees Green Shrops — 69 Q8
Preesgweene Shrops — 69 J7
Prees Heath Shrops — 69 Q7
Prees Higher Heath Shrops — 69 Q7
Prees Lower Heath Shrops — 69 Q8
Prendwick Nthumb — 119 K8
Pren-gwyn Cerdgn — 42 H4
Prenteg Gwynd — 67 K6
Prenton Wirral — 81 L7
Prescot Knows — 81 P6
Prescott Devon — 10 B2
Prescott Shrops — 57 M8
Prescott Shrops — 69 M10
Presnerb Angus — 142 B4
Pressen Nthumb — 118 F3
Prestatyn Denbgs — 80 F8
Prestbury Ches E — 83 J9
Prestbury Gloucs — 47 J10
Presteigne Powys — 45 L2
Prestleigh Somset — 20 B6
Prestolee Bolton — 89 M9
Preston Border — 129 K8
Preston Br & H — 24 H9
Preston Devon — 7 M4
Preston Dorset — 11 Q8
Preston E R Yk — 93 L4
Preston Gloucs — 33 K4
Preston Herts — 50 E5
Preston Kent — 38 H9
Preston Kent — 39 M9
Preston Lancs — 88 G5
Preston Nthumb — 119 N5
Preston Rutlnd — 73 M10
Preston Shrops — 57 J2
Preston Somset — 18 E7
Preston Torbay — 7 M6
Preston Wilts — 33 K9
Preston Wilts — 33 Q10
Preston Bagot Warwks — 59 J11
Preston Bissett Bucks — 49 J9
Preston Bowyer Somset — 18 F9
Preston Brockhurst Shrops — 69 P10
Preston Brook Halton — 82 C8
Preston Candover Hants — 22 H6
Preston Capes Nhants — 48 G4
Preston Crowmarsh Oxon — 34 H6
Preston Deanery Nhants — 60 G9
Preston Green Warwks — 59 J11
Preston Gubbals Shrops — 69 N11
Preston Montford Shrops — 56 G2
Preston on Stour Warwks — 47 P5
Preston on Tees S on T — 104 D7
Preston on the Hill Halton — 82 C8
Preston on Wye Herefs — 45 M6
Prestonpans E Loth — 128 B5
Preston Patrick Cumb — 95 L4
Preston Plucknett Somset — 19 P11
Preston St Mary Suffk — 64 C11
Preston Street Kent — 39 N9
Preston-under-Scar N York — 96 G2
Preston upon the Weald Moors Wrekin — 70 B11
Preston Wynne Herefs — 45 R5
Prestwich Bury — 82 H4
Prestwick Nthumb — 113 J6
Prestwick S Ayrs — 114 G2
Prestwick Airport S Ayrs — 114 G2
Prestwood Bucks — 35 N4
Prestwood Staffs — 58 C7
Price Town Brdgnd — 29 P6
Prickwillow Cambs — 63 J4
Priddy Somset — 19 P4
Priestacott Devon — 8 B3
Priestcliffe Derbys — 83 P10
Priestcliffe Ditch Derbys — 83 P10
Priest Hutton Lancs — 95 L6
Priestland E Ayrs — 125 P10
Priestley Green Calder — 90 E5
Priest Weston Shrops — 56 D5
Priestwood Green Kent — 37 Q8
Primethorpe Leics — 60 B2
Primrose Green Norfk — 76 F8
Primrosehill Border — 129 K8
Primrose Hill Cambs — 62 E3
Primrose Hill Derbys — 84 F9
Primrose Hill Dudley — 58 D7
Primrose Hill Lancs — 88 D9
Primsidemill Border — 118 F5
Prince of Wales Bridge Mons — 31 P7
Princes Gate Pembks — 41 M8
Princes Risborough Bucks — 35 M4
Princethorpe Warwks — 59 P10
Princetown Devon — 6 F4
Prinsted W Susx — 15 L5
Prion Denbgs — 68 E2
Prior Rigg Cumb — 111 J7
Priors Halton Shrops — 56 H9
Priors Hardwick Warwks — 48 C4
Priorslee Wrekin — 57 N2
Priors Marston Warwks — 48 C4
Priors Norton Gloucs — 46 G10
Priory Wood Herefs — 45 K5
Prisk V Glam — 30 D9
Priston BaNES — 20 C2
Pristow Green Norfk — 64 G4
Prittlewell Sthend — 38 E4
Privett Hants — 23 J9
Prixford Devon — 17 K4
Probus Cnwll — 3 M4
Prora E Loth — 128 C4
Prospect Cumb — 100 F2
Prospidnick Cnwll — 2 G7
Protstonhill Abers — 159 K4
Prussia Cove Cnwll — 2 F8
Pubil P & K — 140 C9
Publow BaNES — 20 B2
Puckeridge Herts — 51 J6
Puckington Somset — 19 L11
Pucklechurch S Glos — 32 C9
Puckrup Gloucs — 46 G7
Puddinglake Ches W — 82 F11
Puddington Ches W — 81 L9
Puddington Devon — 9 K2
Puddledock Norfk — 64 F3
Puddletown Dorset — 12 C6
Pudleston Herefs — 45 R3
Pudsey Leeds — 90 G4
Pulborough W Susx — 24 B7
Puleston Wrekin — 70 C10
Pulford Ches W — 69 L3
Pulham Dorset — 11 Q4

Pulham Market Norfk — 64 H4
Pulham St Mary Norfk — 65 J4
Pullens Green S Glos — 32 B6
Pulloxhill C Beds — 50 C4
Pulverbatch Shrops — 56 G4
Pumpherston W Loth — 127 K4
Pumsaint Carmth — 43 N6
Puncheston Pembks — 41 K5
Puncknowle Dorset — 11 L7
Punnett's Town E Susx — 25 P6
Purbrook Hants — 15 J5
Purfleet Thurr — 37 N5
Puriton Somset — 19 K6
Purleigh Essex — 52 D11
Purley Gt Lon — 36 H8
Purley on Thames W Berk — 35 J9
Purlogue Shrops — 56 D9
Purlpit Wilts — 32 G11
Purls Bridge Cambs — 62 G3
Purse Caundle Dorset — 20 C11
Purshull Green Worcs — 58 C10
Purslow Shrops — 56 F8
Purston Jaglin Wakefd — 91 L7
Purtington Somset — 10 H3
Purton Gloucs — 32 C3
Purton Gloucs — 32 C4
Purton Wilts — 33 L7
Purton Stoke Wilts — 33 L6
Pury End Nhants — 49 K5
Pusey Oxon — 34 C5
Putley Herefs — 46 B7
Putley Green Herefs — 46 B7
Putloe Gloucs — 32 E3
Putney Gt Lon — 36 F6
Putsborough Devon — 16 G3
Puttenham Herts — 35 N2
Puttenham Surrey — 23 P5
Puttock End Essex — 52 D3
Putton Dorset — 11 N8
Putts Corner Devon — 10 C5
Puxley Nhants — 49 L6
Puxton N Som — 19 M2
Pwll Carmth — 28 E4
Pwllcrochan Pembks — 40 H10
Pwll-du Mons — 30 H2
Pwll-glâs Denbgs — 68 F4
Pwllgloyw Powys — 44 E8
Pwllheli Gwynd — 66 F7
Pwll-trap Carmth — 41 Q7
Pwll-y-glaw Neath — 29 L6
Pydew Conwy — 79 P9
Pye Bridge Derbys — 84 F10
Pyecombe W Susx — 24 G8
Pye Corner Newpt — 31 K7
Pye Green Staffs — 58 E2
Pyle Brdgnd — 29 M8
Pyleigh Somset — 18 F8
Pylle Somset — 20 B7
Pymoor Cambs — 62 G3
Pymore Dorset — 11 K6
Pyrford Surrey — 36 B9
Pyrton Oxon — 35 J5
Pytchley Nhants — 61 J6
Pyworthy Devon — 16 E11

Q

Quabbs Shrops — 56 C8
Quadring Lincs — 74 D4
Quadring Eaudike Lincs — 74 D4
Quainton Bucks — 49 K10
Quaker's Yard Myr Td — 30 E5
Quaking Houses Dur — 113 J10
Quantock Hills Somset — 18 G7
Quarff Shet — 169 r10
Quarley Hants — 21 Q6
Quarndon Derbys — 72 A2
Quarr Hill IoW — 14 G8
Quarrier's Village Inver — 125 K4
Quarrington Lincs — 73 R2
Quarrington Hill Dur — 104 B3
Quarrybank Ches W — 82 C11
Quarry Bank Dudley — 58 D7
Quarrywood Moray — 157 M5
Quarter N Ayrs — 124 F5
Quarter S Lans — 126 C7
Quatford Shrops — 57 N6
Quatt Shrops — 57 P7
Quebec Dur — 103 N2
Quedgeley Gloucs — 32 F2
Queen Adelaide Cambs — 63 J4
Queenborough Kent — 38 F7
Queen Camel Somset — 19 Q10
Queen Charlton BaNES — 32 B11
Queen Dart Devon — 17 Q8
Queen Elizabeth Forest Park Stirlg — 132 G7
Queenhill Worcs — 46 G7
Queen Oak Dorset — 20 E8
Queen's Bower IoW — 14 G9
Queensbury C Brad — 90 E4
Queensferry Flints — 81 L11
Queensferry Crossing Fife — 134 E11
Queen's Head Shrops — 69 K9
Queen's Hills Norfk — 76 H9
Queenslie C Glas — 126 B4
Queen's Park Bed — 61 M11
Queen's Park Nhants — 60 G8
Queen Street Kent — 37 Q11
Queen Street Wilts — 33 K7
Queenzieburn N Lans — 126 B2
Quendon Essex — 51 M4
Queniborough Leics — 72 G8
Quenington Gloucs — 33 M4
Quernmore Lancs — 95 L9
Queslett Birm — 58 G6
Quethiock Cnwll — 5 N9
Quick's Green W Berk — 34 G9
Quidenham Norfk — 64 F4
Quidhampton Hants — 22 F4
Quidhampton Wilts — 21 M8
Quina Brook Shrops — 69 P8
Quinbury End Nhants — 48 H4
Quinton Dudley — 58 E8
Quinton Nhants — 49 L4
Quinton Green Nhants — 49 L4
Quintrell Downs Cnwll — 4 C9
Quixhall Staffs — 71 L6
Quixwood Border — 129 K7
Quoditch Devon — 5 Q2
Quoig P & K — 133 N3
Quoisley Ches E — 69 P5
Quorn Leics — 72 E7

Quothquan S Lans — 116 D3
Quoyburray Ork — 169 e6
Quoyloo Ork — 169 b4

R

Raasay Highld — 153 K9
Rabbit's Cross Kent — 26 C2
Rableyheath Herts — 50 F7
Raby Cumb — 110 C10
Raby Wirral — 81 L9
Rachan Mill Border — 116 G4
Rachub Gwynd — 79 L11
Rackenford Devon — 17 R8
Rackham W Susx — 24 B8
Rackheath Norfk — 77 K9
Racks D & G — 109 M6
Rackwick Ork — 169 b7
Radbourne Derbys — 71 P7
Radcliffe Bury — 89 M9
Radcliffe Nthumb — 119 Q10
Radcliffe on Trent Notts — 72 G3
Radclive Bucks — 49 J8
Radcot Oxon — 33 Q5
Raddery Highld — 156 C6
Raddington Somset — 18 D9
Radernie Fife — 135 M6
Radford Covtry — 59 M8
Radford BaNES — 20 C4
Radford Semele Warwks — 48 B2
Radlet Somset — 18 H7
Radlett Herts — 50 E10
Radley Devon — 17 N7
Radley Oxon — 34 F5
Radley W Berk — 34 C11
Radley Green Essex — 51 P9
Radmore Green Ches E — 69 Q3
Radnage Bucks — 35 L5
Radstock BaNES — 20 C4
Radstone Nhants — 48 G6
Radway Warwks — 48 C5
Radwell Bed — 61 M9
Radwell Herts — 50 F3
Radwinter Essex — 51 P3
Radwinter End Essex — 51 P3
Radyr Cardif — 30 F8
RAF College (Cranwell) Lincs — 86 D11
Rafford Moray — 157 K6
RAF Museum Cosford Shrops — 57 P3
RAF Museum Hendon Gt Lon — 36 F2
Ragdale Leics — 72 H7
Ragdon Shrops — 56 H6
Raginnis Cnwll — 2 D8
Raglan Mons — 31 M3
Ragnall Notts — 85 P6
Raigbeg Highld — 148 E2
Rainbow Hill Worcs — 46 G3
Rainford St Hel — 81 P4
Rainham Gt Lon — 37 M4
Rainham Medway — 38 D8
Rainhill St Hel — 81 P6
Rainhill Stoops St Hel — 81 Q6
Rainow Ches E — 83 K9
Rainsough Bury — 82 H4
Rainton N York — 97 N5
Rainworth Notts — 85 J9
Raisbeck Cumb — 102 B9
Raise Cumb — 111 P11
Raisthorpe N York — 98 H8
Rait P & K — 134 G2
Raithby Lincs — 87 K4
Raithby Lincs — 87 L7
Raithwaite N York — 105 N8
Rake Hants — 23 M9
Rakewood Rochdl — 89 Q8
Ralia Highld — 148 C8
Ram Carmth — 43 L5
Ramasaig Highld — 152 B9
Rame Cnwll — 3 J7
Rame Cnwll — 5 C9
Ram Hill S Glos — 32 C9
Ram Lane Kent — 26 G2
Rampisham Dorset — 11 M4
Rampside Cumb — 94 E7
Rampton Cambs — 62 F7
Rampton Notts — 85 P5
Ramsbottom Bury — 89 M7
Ramsbury Wilts — 33 Q10
Ramscraigs Highld — 167 K11
Ramsdean Hants — 23 K10
Ramsdell Hants — 22 G3
Ramsden Oxon — 48 C11
Ramsden Worcs — 46 H5
Ramsden Bellhouse Essex — 38 B3
Ramsden Heath Essex — 38 B2
Ramsey Cambs — 62 C3
Ramsey Essex — 53 M5
Ramsey IoM — 80 g3
Ramsey Forty Foot Cambs — 62 D3
Ramsey Heights Cambs — 62 B4
Ramsey Island Essex — 52 F10
Ramsey Island Pembks — 40 D6
Ramsey Mereside Cambs — 62 C3
Ramsey St Mary's Cambs — 62 C3
Ramsgate Kent — 39 Q8
Ramsgill N York — 96 H6
Ramshaw Dur — 103 M5
Ramshaw Dur — 112 H5
Ramsholt Suffk — 53 P3
Ramshope Nthumb — 118 E9
Ramshorn Staffs — 71 K5
Ramsley Devon — 8 F6
Ramsnest Common Surrey — 23 P8
Ranby Lincs — 86 H5
Ranby Notts — 85 L4
Rand Lincs — 86 F5
Randwick Gloucs — 32 F3
Ranfurly Rens — 125 K4
Rangemore Staffs — 71 M10
Rangeworthy S Glos — 32 C7
Rankinston E Ayrs — 115 J3
Ranksborough Rutlnd — 73 L8
Rank's Green Essex — 52 B7
Rannoch Station P & K — 140 B6
Ranscombe Somset — 18 B6
Ranskill Notts — 85 L3
Ranton Staffs — 70 F10
Ranton Green Staffs — 70 E10
Ranworth Norfk — 77 M9
Raploch Stirlg — 133 M9
Rapness Ork — 169 e2

Rapps Somset — 19 K11
Rascarrel D & G — 108 G11
Rashfield Ag & B — 131 N11
Rashwood Worcs — 58 D11
Raskelf N York — 97 Q6
Rassau Blae G — 30 G2
Rastrick Calder — 90 E6
Ratagan Highld — 145 R4
Ratby Leics — 72 E9
Ratcliffe Culey Leics — 72 A11
Ratcliffe on Soar Notts — 72 D5
Ratcliffe on the Wreake Leics — 72 G8
Rathen Abers — 159 N5
Rathillet Fife — 135 K3
Rathmell N York — 96 B9
Ratho C Edin — 127 L3
Ratho Station C Edin — 127 L3
Rathven Moray — 158 B4
Ratlake Hants — 22 D10
Ratley Warwks — 48 C5
Ratling Kent — 39 M11
Ratlinghope Shrops — 56 G5
Rattar Highld — 167 N2
Ratten Row Cumb — 101 K2
Ratten Row Cumb — 110 G11
Ratten Row Lancs — 88 E2
Rattery Devon — 7 J6
Rattlesden Suffk — 64 D10
Ratton Village E Susx — 25 N10
Rattray P & K — 142 B8
Raughton Cumb — 110 G11
Raughton Head Cumb — 110 G11
Raunds Nhants — 61 L6
Ravenfield Rothm — 91 M11
Ravenglass Cumb — 100 E11
Ravenhills Green Worcs — 46 D4
Raveningham Norfk — 65 M2
Ravenscar N York — 105 Q10
Ravenscraig N Lans — 126 D6
Ravensdale IoM — 80 e3
Ravensden Bed — 61 N10
Ravenseat N York — 102 E10
Ravenshead Notts — 85 J10
Ravensmoor Ches E — 69 R4
Ravensthorpe Kirk — 90 G6
Ravensthorpe Nhants — 60 E6
Ravenstone Leics — 72 C8
Ravenstone M Keyn — 49 M4
Ravenstonedale Cumb — 102 D10
Ravenstruther S Lans — 126 G8
Ravensworth N York — 103 M9
Raw N York — 105 P9
Rawcliffe C York — 98 B10
Rawcliffe E R Yk — 92 A6
Rawcliffe Bridge E R Yk — 92 A6
Rawdon Leeds — 90 G3
Rawling Street Kent — 38 F10
Rawmarsh Rothm — 91 L11
Rawnsley Staffs — 58 F2
Rawreth Essex — 38 C3
Rawridge Devon — 10 E3
Rawtenstall Lancs — 89 N6
Raydon Suffk — 52 H4
Raylees Nthumb — 112 D2
Rayleigh Essex — 38 D3
Raymond's Hill Devon — 10 G5
Rayne Essex — 52 B7
Raynes Park Gt Lon — 36 F7
Reach Cambs — 63 J7
Read Lancs — 89 M4
Reading Readg — 35 K10
Reading Services W Berk — 35 J11
Reading Street Kent — 26 F5
Reading Street Kent — 39 Q8
Reagill Cumb — 102 B7
Realwa Cnwll — 2 G6
Rearquhar Highld — 162 G8
Rearsby Leics — 72 H8
Rease Heath Ches E — 70 A4
Reay Highld — 166 G4
Reculver Kent — 39 M8
Red Ball Devon — 18 E11
Redberth Pembks — 41 L10
Redbourn Herts — 50 D8
Redbourne N Linc — 92 G11
Redbrook Gloucs — 31 P3
Redbrook Wrexhm — 69 P6
Redbrook Street Kent — 26 F4
Redburn Highld — 156 G8
Redburn Nthumb — 111 Q8
Redcar R & Cl — 104 H6
Redcastle D & G — 108 H7
Redcastle Highld — 155 Q8
Red Dial Cumb — 110 E11
Redding Falk — 126 G2
Reddingmuirhead Falk — 126 G2
Reddish Stockp — 83 J6
Redditch Worcs — 58 F11
Rede Suffk — 63 P11
Redenhall Norfk — 65 K5
Redenham Hants — 22 B5
Redesmouth Nthumb — 112 C4
Redford Angus — 143 J9
Redford W Susx — 23 N9
Redfordgreen Border — 117 M7
Redgate Rhondd — 30 D7
Redgorton P & K — 134 D2
Redgrave Suffk — 64 E6
Redhill Abers — 151 K7
Red Hill BCP — 13 J5
Redhill Herts — 50 H4
Redhill N Som — 19 N2
Redhill Surrey — 36 G10
Red Hill Warwks — 47 M3
Redisham Suffk — 65 N5
Redland Bristl — 31 Q9
Redland Ork — 169 c4
Redlingfield Suffk — 64 H7
Redlingfield Green Suffk — 64 H7
Red Lodge Suffk — 63 L6
Red Lodge Rochdl — 89 N7
Redlynch Somset — 20 D8
Redlynch Wilts — 21 P10
Redmain Cumb — 100 F4
Redmarley Worcs — 57 P11
Redmarley D'Abitot Gloucs — 46 E8
Redmarshall S on T — 104 C6
Redmile Leics — 73 K3
Redmire N York — 96 G2
Redmyre Abers — 143 P2
Rednal Birm — 58 F9
Rednal Shrops — 69 L9
Redpath Border — 118 A3

Redpoint Highld 153 N4
Red Post Cnwll 16 D10
Red Rock Wigan 88 H9
Red Roses Carmth 41 P8
Red Row Nthumb 119 Q11
Redruth Cnwll 2 H5
Redstocks Wilts 20 H2
Redstone P & K 142 B11
Redstone Cross Pembks 41 M7
Red Street Staffs 70 E4
Redvales Bury 89 N9
Red Wharf Bay IoA 79 J8
Redwick Newpt 31 M8
Redwick S Glos 31 P7
Redworth Darltn 103 P6
Reed Herts 51 J3
Reedham Norfk 77 N11
Reedness E R Yk 92 C6
Reeds Beck Lincs 86 H7
Reeds Holme Lancs 89 N6
Reepham Lincs 86 D6
Reepham Norfk 76 G7
Reeth N York 103 K11
Reeves Green Solhll 59 L9
Regaby IoM 80 f2
Regil N Som 19 P2
Reiff Highld 160 F4
Reigate Surrey 36 G10
Reighton N York 99 N5
Reinigeadal W Isls 168 h7
Reisque Abers 151 M4
Reiss Highld 167 P6
Rejerrah Cnwll 4 B10
Releath Cnwll 2 H7
Relubbus Cnwll 2 F7
Relugas Moray 156 H8
Remenham Wokhm 35 L8
Remenham Hill Wokham 35 L8
Rempstone Notts 72 F6
Rendcomb Gloucs 33 K3
Rendham Suffk 65 L9
Rendlesham Suffk 65 L11
Renfrew Rens 125 N4
Renhold Bed 61 N10
Renishaw Derbys 84 G5
Rennington Nthumb 119 P7
Renton W Duns 125 K2
Renwick Cumb 101 Q2
Repps Norfk 77 N8
Repton Derbys 71 Q9
Reraig Highld 145 P2
Rescassa Cnwll 3 P5
Rescorla Cnwll 3 P4
Resipole Burn Highld 138 C5
Reskadinnick Cnwll 2 G5
Resolis Highld 156 B4
Resolven Neath 29 M4
Rest and be thankful Ag & B 131 Q6
Reston Border 129 M7
Restronguet Cnwll 3 L6
Reswallie Angus 143 J7
Reterth Cnwll 4 E9
Retford Notts 85 M4
Retire Cnwll 4 G9
Rettendon Essex 38 C2
Retyn Cnwll 4 D10
Revesby Lincs 87 J8
Rew Devon 7 J11
Rew Devon 7 K4
Rewe Devon 9 M5
Rew Street IoW 14 E8
Rexon Devon 5 Q4
Reydon Suffk 65 P6
Reymerston Norfk 76 E10
Reynalton Pembks 41 L9
Reynoldston Swans 28 E7
Rezare Cnwll 5 P6
Rhadyr Mons 31 L4
Rhandirmwyn Carmth 43 Q6
Rhayader Powys 55 M11
Rheindown Highld 155 P8
Rhenigidale W Isls 168 h7
Rhes-y-cae Flints 80 H10
Rhewl Denbgs 68 F2
Rhewl Denbgs 68 G6
Rhewl Mostyn Flints 80 H8
Rhicarn Highld 164 C11
Rhiconich Highld 164 G6
Rhicullen Highld 156 B3
Rhigos Rhondd 29 P3
Rhives Highld 163 J6
Rhiwbina Cardif 30 G8
Rhiwbryfdir Gwynd 67 M5
Rhiwderyn Newpt 31 J7
Rhiwen Gwynd 67 K2
Rhiwinder Rhondd 30 D7
Rhiwlas Gwynd 68 B7
Rhiwlas Gwynd 79 K11
Rhiwlas Gwynd 68 G8
Rhiwsaeson Rhondd 30 E8
Rhode Somset 19 J8
Rhoden Green Kent 37 Q11
Rhodesia Notts 85 J5
Rhodes Minnis Kent 27 L3
Rhodiad-y-brenin Pembks 40 E5
Rhonehouse D & G 108 F9
Rhoose V Glam 30 E11
Rhos Carmth 42 G7
Rhos Denbgs 68 F2
Rhos Neath 29 K4
Rhosaman Carmth 29 K2
Rhosbeirio IoA 78 F6
Rhoscefnhir IoA 79 J9
Rhoscolyn IoA 78 D9
Rhoscrowther Pembks 40 H10
Rhosesmor Flints 81 J11
Rhos-fawr Gwynd 66 F7
Rhosgadfan Gwynd 67 J3
Rhosgoch IoA 78 G7
Rhosgoch Powys 44 H5
Rhos Haminiog Cerdgn 43 K2
Rhoshill Pembks 41 N2
Rhoshirwaun Gwynd 66 C9
Rhoslan Gwynd 66 H6
Rhoslefain Gwynd 54 D3
Rhosllanerchrugog Wrexhm 69 J5
Rhôs Lligwy IoA 78 H7
Rhosmaen Carmth 43 M10
Rhosmeirch IoA 78 H9
Rhosneigr IoA 78 E10
Rhosnesni Wrexhm 69 L4
Rhôs-on-Sea Conwy 79 Q8
Rhosrobin Wrexhm 69 K4
Rhossili Swans 28 D7

Rhostrehwfa IoA 78 G10
Rhostryfan Gwynd 66 H3
Rhostyllen Wrexhm 69 K5
Rhosybol IoA 78 G7
Rhos-y-brithdir Powys 68 F10
Rhosygadfa Shrops 69 K8
Rhos-y-garth Cerdgn 54 E10
Rhos-y-gwaliau Gwynd 68 B8
Rhos-y-llan Gwynd 66 C7
Rhosymedre Wrexhm 69 J6
Rhos-y-meirch Powys 56 D11
Rhu Ag & B 132 B11
Rhuallt Denbgs 80 F9
Rhubodach Ag & B 124 C3
Rhuddall Heath Ches W 69 Q2
Rhuddlan Cerdgn 43 J6
Rhuddlan Denbgs 80 E9
Rhulen Powys 44 G5
Rhyd Gwynd 67 L6
Rhydargaeau Carmth 42 H9
Rhydcymerau Carmth 43 J7
Rhydd Worcs 46 F5
Rhyd-Ddu Gwynd 67 K4
Rhydding Neath 29 K5
Rhydgaled Conwy 68 C2
Rhydlanfair Conwy 67 Q4
Rhydlewis Cerdgn 42 F5
Rhydlios Gwynd 66 B9
Rhydlydan Conwy 68 A4
Rhydowen Cerdgn 42 H5
Rhydroser Cerdgn 54 D11
Rhydspence Herefs 45 J5
Rhydtalog Flints 68 H4
Rhyd-uchaf Gwynd 68 B7
Rhyd-y-clafdy Gwynd 66 E8
Rhydycroesau Shrops 68 H8
Rhydyfelin Cerdgn 54 D9
Rhydyfelin Rhondd 30 B2
Rhyd-y-foel Conwy 80 C9
Rhyd-y-groes Gwynd 79 K11
Rhydymain Gwynd 67 Q10
Rhyd-y-meirch Mons 31 K3
Rhydymwyn Flints 81 J11
Rhyd-y-pennau Cerdgn 54 E7
Rhyd-yr-onnen Gwynd 54 L4
Rhyd-y-sarn Gwynd 67 M6
Rhyl Denbgs 80 E8
Rhymney Caerph 30 F3
Rhynd P & K 134 F3
Rhynie Abers 150 D2
Rhynie Highld 163 J11
Ribbesford Worcs 57 P10
Ribbleton Lancs 88 H4
Ribby Lancs 88 E4
Ribchester Lancs 89 K3
Riber Derbys 84 D9
Riby Lincs 93 L9
Riccall N York 91 Q3
Riccarton Border 111 K2
Riccarton E Ayrs 125 L10
Richards Castle Herefs 56 H11
Richings Park Bucks 36 B5
Richmond Gt Lon 36 E6
Richmond N York 103 N10
Richmond Sheff 84 F3
Rich's Holford Somset 18 F8
Rickerscote Staffs 70 G10
Rickford N Som 19 N3
Rickham Devon 7 K11
Rickinghall Suffk 64 E6
Rickling Essex 51 L4
Rickling Green Essex 51 M4
Rickmansworth Herts 36 C2
Riddell Border 117 Q6
Riddings Derbys 84 F10
Riddlecombe Devon 17 L9
Riddlesden C Brad 90 D2
Ridge BaNES 19 Q3
Ridge Dorset 12 F7
Ridge Herts 50 F10
Ridge Wilts 21 J8
Ridgebourne Powys 44 F2
Ridge Green Surrey 36 H11
Ridge Lane Warwks 59 L6
Ridge Row Kent 27 M3
Ridgeway Derbys 84 F4
Ridgeway Worcs 47 K2
Ridgeway Cross Herefs 46 D5
Ridgewell Essex 52 B3
Ridgewood E Susx 25 L7
Ridgmont C Beds 49 Q7
Riding Mill Nthumb 112 F8
Ridley Kent 37 P8
Ridley Nthumb 111 Q8
Ridley Green Ches E 69 Q4
Ridlington Norfk 77 L5
Ridlington Rutlnd 73 L10
Ridlington Street Norfk 77 L5
Ridsdale Nthumb 112 D4
Rievaulx N York 98 B3
Rigg D & G 110 E7
Riggend N Lans 126 D3
Righoul Highld 156 F7
Rigmadon Park Cumb 95 N4
Rigsby Lincs 87 M5
Rigside S Lans 116 B3
Riley Green Lancs 89 J5
Rileyhill Staffs 58 H2
Rilla Mill Cnwll 5 M7
Rillaton Cnwll 5 M7
Rillington N York 98 H6
Rimington Lancs 96 B11
Rimpton Somset 20 B10
Rimswell E R Yk 93 P5
Rinaston Pembks 41 J5
Rindleford Shrops 57 N5
Ringford D & G 108 E9
Ringinglow Sheff 84 C4
Ringland Norfk 76 G9
Ringles Cross E Susx 25 L6
Ringlestone Kent 38 E10
Ringley Bolton 89 M9
Ringmer E Susx 25 K8
Ringmore Devon 6 H9
Ringmore Devon 7 N4
Ringorm Moray 157 P9
Ring's End Cambs 74 G10
Ringsfield Suffk 65 N4
Ringsfield Corner Suffk 65 N4
Ringshall Herts 35 Q2
Ringshall Suffk 64 E11
Ringshall Stocks Suffk 64 F11
Ringstead Nhants 61 L5

Ringstead Norfk 75 P2
Ringwood Hants 13 L3
Ringwould Kent 27 Q2
Rinmore Abers 150 C4
Rinsey Cnwll 2 F8
Rinsey Croft Cnwll 2 G8
Ripe E Susx 25 M8
Ripley Derbys 84 E10
Ripley Hants 13 L3
Ripley N York 97 L8
Ripley Surrey 36 C9
Riplingham E R Yk 92 G4
Riplington Hants 23 J10
Ripon N York 97 M6
Rippingale Lincs 74 A5
Ripple Kent 39 Q11
Ripple Worcs 46 G7
Ripponden Calder 90 C7
Risabus Ag & B 122 D11
Risbury Herefs 45 Q4
Risby N Linc 92 F8
Risby Suffk 63 P7
Risca Caerph 30 H6
Rise E R Yk 93 L2
Riseden E Susx 25 P4
Riseden Kent 26 B4
Risegate Lincs 74 D5
Riseholme Lincs 86 C5
Risehow Cumb 100 D4
Riseley Bed 61 M8
Riseley Wokham 23 K2
Rishangles Suffk 64 H8
Rishton Lancs 89 L4
Rishworth Calder 90 C7
Rising Bridge Lancs 89 M5
Risley Derbys 72 D3
Risley Warrtn 82 E6
Risplith N York 97 K7
Rivar Wilts 22 B2
Rivenhall End Essex 52 D8
River Kent 27 N3
River W Susx 23 P10
River Bank Cambs 62 H7
Riverford Highld 155 P7
Riverhead Kent 37 M9
Rivers Corner Dorset 12 C2
Rivington Lancs 89 J8
Rivington Services Lancs 89 J8
Roachill Devon 17 R7
Roade Nhants 49 L4
Road Green Norfk 65 K3
Roadhead Cumb 111 K6
Roadmeetings S Lans 126 F8
Roadside E Ayrs 115 L4
Roadside Highld 167 L4
Roadwater Somset 18 D7
Roag Highld 152 D9
Roa Island Cumb 94 E7
Roan of Craigoch S Ayrs 114 E7
Roast Green Essex 51 L4
Roath Cardif 30 G9
Roberton Border 117 N8
Roberton S Lans 116 C5
Robertsbridge E Susx 26 B7
Roberttown Kirk 90 F6
Robeston Wathen Pembks 41 L7
Robgill Tower D & G 110 D6
Robin Hill Staffs 70 G4
Robin Hood Lancs 88 G8
Robin Hood Leeds 91 J5
Robin Hood's Bay N York 105 P9
Roborough Devon 6 E6
Roborough Devon 17 K8
Robroyston C Glas 125 Q4
Roby Knows 81 N6
Roby Mill Lancs 88 G9
Rocester Staffs 71 L7
Roch Pembks 40 G5
Rochdale Rochdl 89 P8
Roche Cnwll 4 F9
Rochester Medway 38 B8
Rochester Nthumb 118 F11
Rochford Essex 38 E3
Rochford Worcs 57 M11
Roch Gate Pembks 40 G6
Rock Cnwll 4 E7
Rock Neath 29 L6
Rock Nthumb 119 P6
Rock W Susx 24 D8
Rock Worcs 57 N10
Rockbeare Devon 9 P6
Rockbourne Hants 21 M11
Rockcliffe Cumb 110 G8
Rockcliffe D & G 108 H10
Rockcliffe Cross Cumb 110 F8
Rock End Staffs 70 F3
Rockend Torbay 7 N6
Rockfield Highld 163 L10
Rockfield Mons 31 N2
Rockford Devon 17 P2
Rockford Hants 13 L3
Rockgreen Shrops 57 J9
Rockhampton S Glos 32 C6
Rockhead Cnwll 4 H5
Rockhill Shrops 56 D9
Rock Hill Worcs 58 F11
Rockingham Nhants 61 J2
Rockland All Saints Norfk 64 D11
Rockland St Mary Norfk 77 L11
Rockland St Peter Norfk 64 D11
Rockley Notts 85 M6
Rockley Wilts 33 N10
Rockliffe Lancs 89 P6
Rockwell End Bucks 35 L7
Rockwell Green Somset 18 F10
Rodborough Gloucs 32 F4
Rodbourne Swindn 33 M7
Rodbourne Wilts 32 H6
Rodd Herefs 45 L2
Roddam Nthumb 119 L6
Rodden Dorset 11 N8
Roddymoor Dur 103 N3
Rode Somset 20 F4
Rode Heath Ches E 70 E2
Rode Heath Ches E 83 J11
Rodel W Isls 168 f9
Roden Wrekin 69 Q11
Rodhuish Somset 18 D7
Rodington Wrekin 57 K2
Rodington Heath Wrekin 57 K2
Rodley Gloucs 32 D2
Rodley Leeds 90 G3

Rodmarton Gloucs 32 H5
Rodmell E Susx 25 K9
Rodmersham Kent 38 F9
Rodmersham Green Kent 38 F9
Rodney Stoke Somset 19 M4
Rodsley Derbys 71 N6
Rodway Somset 19 J6
Roecliffe N York 97 N7
Roe Cross Tamesd 83 L5
Roe Green Herts 50 H4
Roe Green Herts 50 H4
Roe Green Salfd 82 F4
Roehampton Gt Lon 36 F6
Roffey W Susx 24 E4
Rogart Highld 162 G6
Rogate W Susx 23 M10
Roger Ground Cumb 101 L11
Rogerstone Newpt 31 J7
Roghadal W Isls 168 f9
Rogiet Mons 31 N7
Roke Oxon 34 H7
Roker Sundld 113 P9
Rollesby Norfk 77 N8
Rolleston Leics 73 J10
Rolleston Notts 85 M10
Rolleston on Dove Staffs 71 N9
Rolston E R Yk 93 M2
Rolstone N Som 19 L2
Rolvenden Kent 26 D5
Rolvenden Layne Kent 26 E5
Romaldkirk Dur 103 J6
Romanby N York 97 N2
Romanno Bridge Border 127 M8
Romansleigh Devon 17 N7
Romden Castle Kent 26 E3
Romesdal Highld 152 G7
Romford Dorset 13 J3
Romford Gt Lon 37 M3
Romiley Stockp 83 K6
Romney Street Kent 37 N8
Romsey Cambs 62 G9
Romsey Hants 22 C10
Romsley Shrops 57 P8
Romsley Worcs 58 E8
Rona Highld 153 L6
Ronachan Ag & B 123 N9
Rood Ashton Wilts 20 G3
Rookhope Dur 102 H2
Rookley IoW 14 F10
Rookley Green IoW 14 F10
Rooks Bridge Somset 19 L4
Rooks Nest Somset 18 E8
Rookwith N York 97 K3
Roos E R Yk 93 N4
Roose Cumb 94 E7
Roosebeck Cumb 94 F7
Roothams Green Bed 61 N9
Ropley Hants 22 H8
Ropley Dean Hants 22 H8
Ropley Soke Hants 23 J8
Ropsley Lincs 73 P4
Rora Abers 159 Q7
Rorrington Shrops 56 F4
Rosarie Moray 158 A7
Rose Cnwll 3 K3
Roseacre Lancs 88 E4
Rose Ash Devon 17 P7
Rosebank S Lans 126 E8
Rosebush Pembks 41 L5
Rosecare Cnwll 5 K2
Rosecliston Cnwll 4 C10
Rosedale Abbey N York 105 K11
Rose Green Essex 52 F6
Rose Green Suffk 52 F4
Rose Green Suffk 52 G3
Rose Green W Susx 15 P7
Rosehall Highld 162 B6
Rosehearty Abers 159 M4
Rose Hill E Susx 25 L7
Rose Hill Lancs 89 N4
Rosehill Shrops 69 N11
Roseisle Moray 157 L4
Roselands E Susx 25 P10
Rosemarket Pembks 41 J9
Rosemarkie Highld 156 C6
Rosemary Lane Devon 10 D2
Rosemount P & K 142 B9
Rosenannon Cnwll 4 F8
Rosenithon Cnwll 3 L9
Roser's Cross E Susx 25 M6
Rosevean Cnwll 4 G10
Rosevine Cnwll 3 M6
Rosewarne Cnwll 2 G6
Rosewell Mdloth 127 P5
Roseworth S on T 104 E6
Roseworthy Cnwll 2 G6
Rosgill Cumb 101 P7
Roskestal Cnwll 2 B9
Roskhill Highld 152 D9
Roskorwell Cnwll 3 K9
Rosley Cumb 110 F11
Roslin Mdloth 127 P5
Rosliston Derbys 71 N11
Rosneath Ag & B 132 B11
Ross D & G 108 D12
Ross Nthumb 119 M3
Rossett Wrexhm 69 L3
Rossett Green N York 97 L10
Rossington Donc 91 Q11
Ross-on-Wye Herefs 46 A10
Roster Highld 167 N9
Rostherne Ches E 82 F8
Rosthwaite Cumb 101 J8
Roston Derbys 71 L6
Rosudgeon Cnwll 2 F8
Rosyth Fife 134 E11
Rothbury Nthumb 119 L10
Rotherby Leics 72 H7
Rotherfield E Susx 25 N5
Rotherfield Greys Oxon 35 K8
Rotherfield Peppard Oxon 35 K8
Rotherham Rothm 84 F3
Rothersthorpe Nhants 60 F9
Rotherwick Hants 23 J3
Rothes Moray 157 P7
Rothesay Ag & B 124 D5
Rothiebrisbane Abers 158 H10
Rothiemurchus Lodge Highld 148 H6
Rothienorman Abers 158 H10
Rothley Leics 72 F8
Rothley Nthumb 112 F3
Rothmaise Abers 158 G11
Rothwell Leeds 91 J5

Rothwell Lincs 93 K11
Rothwell Nhants 60 H4
Rotsea E R Yk 99 M10
Rottal Lodge Angus 142 F4
Rottingdean Br & H 25 J10
Rottington Cumb 100 C8
Roucan D & G 109 M5
Roud IoW 14 F10
Rougham Norfk 76 A7
Rougham Suffk 64 C9
Rough Close Staffs 70 G7
Rough Common Kent 39 K10
Roughlee Lancs 89 N2
Roughpark Abers 149 N5
Roughton Lincs 86 H8
Roughton Norfk 77 J4
Roughton Shrops 57 P6
Roughway Kent 37 P10
Roundbush Essex 52 E11
Round Bush Herts 50 D11
Roundbush Green Essex 51 N8
Round Green Luton 50 D6
Roundham Somset 11 J3
Roundhay Leeds 91 J3
Rounds Green Sandw 58 E7
Roundstreet Common W Susx 24 C5
Roundswell Devon 17 J5
Roundway Wilts 21 K2
Roundyhill Angus 142 F7
Rousay Ork 169 c3
Rousdon Devon 10 F6
Rousham Oxon 48 E10
Rous Lench Worcs 47 K4
Routenburn N Ayrs 124 F5
Routh E R Yk 93 J2
Rout's Green Bucks 35 L5
Row Cnwll 4 H6
Row Cumb 95 K3
Row Cumb 102 B4
Rowanburn D & G 110 H5
Rowardennan Stirlg 132 D8
Rowarth Derbys 83 M7
Row Ash Hants 14 F4
Rowberrow Somset 19 N3
Rowborough IoW 14 E10
Rowde Wilts 21 J2
Rowden Devon 8 F5
Rowen Conwy 79 P10
Rowfield Derbys 71 M5
Rowfoot Nthumb 111 N8
Rowford Somset 18 H9
Row Green Essex 52 B7
Rowhedge Essex 52 H7
Rowhook W Susx 24 D4
Rowington Warwks 59 K11
Rowland Derbys 84 B6
Rowland's Castle Hants 15 K4
Rowlands Gill Gatesd 113 J9
Rowledge Surrey 23 M7
Rowley Dur 112 G11
Rowley E R Yk 92 G4
Rowley Shrops 56 E3
Rowley Hill Kirk 90 F8
Rowley Regis Sandw 58 E7
Rowlstone Herefs 45 M9
Rowly Surrey 24 B2
Rowner Hants 14 G4
Rowney Green Worcs 58 F10
Rownhams Hants 22 C11
Rownhams Services Hants 22 C11
Rowrah Cumb 100 E7
Rowsham Bucks 49 M11
Rowsley Derbys 84 C7
Rowstock Oxon 34 E7
Rowston Lincs 86 E9
Rowthorne Derbys 84 G8
Rowton Ches W 69 M2
Rowton Shrops 56 F2
Rowton Shrops 56 G8
Rowton Wrekin 69 R11
Row Town Surrey 36 B8
Roxburgh Border 118 C4
Roxby N Linc 92 F7
Roxby N York 105 L7
Roxton Bed 61 Q10
Roxwell Essex 51 P9
Royal Leamington Spa Warwks 59 M11
Royal Oak Darltn 103 P6
Royal Oak Lancs 81 N4
Royal's Green Ches E 69 R6
Royal Sutton Coldfield Birm 58 H5
Royal Tunbridge Wells Kent 25 N3
Royal Wootton Bassett Wilts 33 L8
Royal Yacht Britannia C Edin 127 P2
Roy Bridge Highld 146 H11
Roydhouse Kirk 90 G8
Roydon Essex 51 K8
Roydon Norfk 64 G5
Roydon Norfk 75 P6
Roydon Hamlet Essex 51 K9
Royston Barns 91 K8
Royston Herts 51 J2
Royton Oldham 89 Q8
Rozel Jersey 11 c1
Ruabon Wrexhm 69 K6
Ruaig Ag & B 136 D6
Ruan High Lanes Cnwll 3 N6
Ruan Lanihorne Cnwll 3 M5
Ruan Major Cnwll 3 J10
Ruan Minor Cnwll 3 J10
Ruardean Gloucs 46 B11
Ruardean Hill Gloucs 46 B11
Ruardean Woodside Gloucs 46 B11
Rubery Birm 58 E8
Rubha Ban W Isls 168 c16
Ruckcroft Cumb 101 P2
Ruckhall Herefs 45 P7
Ruckinge Kent 26 H5
Ruckland Lincs 87 K5
Ruckley Shrops 57 K4
Rudbaxton Pembks 41 J6
Rudby N York 104 F9
Rudchester Nthumb 112 H7
Ruddington Notts 72 F4
Ruddle Gloucs 32 C2
Ruddlemoor Cnwll 3 Q3
Rudford Gloucs 46 E10
Rudge Somset 20 F4
Rudgeway S Glos 32 B7

Rudgwick W Susx ...24 C4
Rudhall Herefs ...46 B9
Rudheath Ches W ...82 E10
Rudheath Woods Ches E ...82 F10
Rudley Green Essex ...52 D11
Rudloe Wilts ...32 F10
Rudry Caerph ...30 H7
Rudston E R Yk ...99 M7
Rudyard Staffs ...70 H3
Ruecastle Border ...118 B6
Rufford Lancs ...88 F7
Rufford Abbey Notts ...85 K8
Rufforth C York ...98 A10
Rug Denbgs ...68 E6
Rugby Warwks ...60 B5
Rugeley Staffs ...71 J11
Ruigh'riabhach Highld ...160 G7
Ruisgarry W Isls ...168 e9
Ruishton Somset ...19 J9
Ruisigearraidh W Isls ...168 e9
Ruislip Gt Lon ...36 C3
Rùm Highld ...144 E8
Rumbach Moray ...158 A7
Rumbling Bridge P & K ...134 C8
Rumburgh Suffk ...65 L5
Rumby Hill Dur ...103 N4
Rumford Cnwll ...4 D7
Rumford Falk ...126 G2
Rumney Cardif ...30 H9
Rumwell Somset ...18 G10
Runcorn Halton ...81 Q8
Runcton W Susx ...15 N6
Runcton Holme Norfk ...75 M9
Runfold Surrey ...23 N5
Runhall Norfk ...76 F10
Runham Norfk ...77 P9
Runham Norfk ...77 Q10
Runnington Somset ...18 F10
Runsell Green Essex ...52 C10
Runshaw Moor Lancs ...88 G2
Runswick N York ...105 M7
Runtaleave Angus ...142 D4
Runwell Essex ...38 C3
Ruscombe Wokham ...35 L9
Rushall Herefs ...46 B7
Rushall Norfk ...64 H5
Rushall Wilts ...21 M3
Rushall Wsall ...58 F4
Rushbrooke Suffk ...64 B9
Rushbury Shrops ...57 J6
Rushden Herts ...50 H4
Rushden Nhants ...61 L7
Rushenden Kent ...38 F7
Rusher's Cross E Susx ...25 P5
Rushford Devon ...8 D7
Rushford Norfk ...64 C5
Rush Green Essex ...53 L8
Rush Green Gt Lon ...37 M3
Rush Green Herts ...50 F7
Rush Green Warrtn ...82 E7
Rushlake Green E Susx ...25 P7
Rushmere Suffk ...65 P4
Rushmere St Andrew Suffk ...53 L2
Rushmoor Surrey ...23 N6
Rushock Herefs ...45 L3
Rushock Worcs ...58 C10
Rusholme Manch ...83 J6
Rushton Ches W ...69 Q2
Rushton Nhants ...60 H4
Rushton Shrops ...57 L3
Rushton Spencer Staffs ...70 G2
Rushwick Worcs ...46 F4
Rushyford Dur ...103 Q5
Ruskie Stirlg ...133 J7
Ruskington Lincs ...86 E10
Rusland Cross Cumb ...94 G3
Rusper W Susx ...24 F3
Ruspidge Gloucs ...32 C2
Russell Green Essex ...52 B9
Russell's Water Oxon ...35 K7
Russel's Green Suffk ...65 K7
Russ Hill Surrey ...24 F2
Rusthall Kent ...25 N3
Rustington W Susx ...24 B10
Ruston N York ...99 K4
Ruston Parva E R Yk ...99 M8
Ruswarp N York ...105 N9
Ruthall Shrops ...57 K6
Rutherford Border ...118 B4
Rutherglen S Lans ...125 Q5
Ruthernbridge Cnwll ...4 G8
Ruthin Denbgs ...68 F3
Ruthrieston C Aber ...151 N7
Ruthven Abers ...158 D8
Ruthven Angus ...142 D8
Ruthven Highld ...148 D8
Ruthven Highld ...156 E11
Ruthvoes Cnwll ...4 E9
Ruthwaite Cumb ...100 H3
Ruthwell D & G ...109 N7
Ruxley Corner Gt Lon ...37 L6
Ruxton Green Herefs ...45 Q11
Ruyton-XI-Towns Shrops ...69 L10
Ryal Nthumb ...112 F6
Ryall Dorset ...11 J5
Ryall Worcs ...46 G6
Ryarsh Kent ...37 Q8
Rycote Oxon ...35 J3
Rydal Cumb ...101 L9
Ryde IoW ...14 G8
Rye E Susx ...26 F7
Ryebank Shrops ...69 P8
Ryeford Herefs ...46 B10
Rye Foreign E Susx ...26 E7
Rye Harbour E Susx ...26 F8
Ryehill E R Yk ...93 M5
Ryeish Green Wokham ...35 K11
Rye Street Worcs ...46 E7
Ryhall Rutlnd ...73 Q8
Ryhill Wakefd ...91 K8
Ryhope Sundld ...113 P10
Rylah Derbys ...84 G7
Ryland Lincs ...86 D5
Rylands Notts ...72 E3
Rylstone N York ...96 E9
Ryme Intrinseca Dorset ...11 M2
Ryther N York ...91 P3
Ryton Gatesd ...113 J8
Ryton N York ...98 F6
Ryton Shrops ...57 P4
Ryton Warwks ...59 P7
Ryton-on-Dunsmore Warwks ...59 N10
Ryton Woodside Gatesd ...112 H8
RZSS Edinburgh Zoo C Edin ...127 N3

S

Sabden Lancs ...89 M3
Sabine's Green Essex ...51 M11
Sacombe Herts ...50 H7
Sacombe Green Herts ...50 H7
Sacriston Dur ...113 K11
Sadberge Darltn ...104 B7
Saddell Ag & B ...120 E5
Saddington Leics ...60 E2
Saddle Bow Norfk ...75 M7
Saddlescombe W Susx ...24 G8
Sadgill Cumb ...101 N9
Saffron Walden Essex ...51 M3
Sageston Pembks ...41 L10
Saham Hills Norfk ...76 C11
Saham Toney Norfk ...76 B11
Saighton Ches W ...69 M2
St Abbs Border ...129 N6
St Agnes Border ...128 H7
St Agnes Cnwll ...3 J3
St Agnes IoS ...2 b3
St Agnes Mining District Cnwll ...3 J4
St Albans Herts ...50 D9
St Allen Cnwll ...3 L3
St Andrew Guern ...10 b2
St Andrews Fife ...135 N4
St Andrews Botanic Garden Fife ...135 N4
St Andrews Major V Glam ...30 F10
St Andrews Well Dorset ...11 K6
St Anne's Lancs ...88 C5
St Ann's D & G ...109 N2
St Ann's Chapel Cnwll ...5 Q8
St Ann's Chapel Devon ...6 H9
St Anthony-in-Meneage Cnwll ...3 K8
St Anthony's Hill E Susx ...25 P10
St Arvans Mons ...31 P5
St Asaph Denbgs ...80 E10
St Athan V Glam ...30 D11
St Aubin Jersey ...11 a2
St Austell Cnwll ...3 Q3
St Bees Cumb ...100 C8
St Blazey Cnwll ...3 R3
St Blazey Gate Cnwll ...3 R3
St Boswells Border ...118 A4
St Brelade Jersey ...11 a2
St Brelade's Bay Jersey ...11 a2
St Breock Cnwll ...4 F7
St Breward Cnwll ...4 H6
St Briavels Gloucs ...31 Q4
St Brides Pembks ...40 F8
St Bride's Major V Glam ...29 N10
St Brides Netherwent Mons ...31 M7
St Brides-super-Ely V Glam ...30 E9
St Brides Wentlooge Newpt ...31 J8
St Budeaux C Plym ...6 D7
Saintbury Gloucs ...47 M7
St Buryan Cnwll ...2 C8
St Catherine BaNES ...32 E11
St Catherines Ag & B ...131 N6
St Chloe Gloucs ...32 F4
St Clears Carmth ...41 Q7
St Cleer Cnwll ...5 L8
St Clement Cnwll ...3 M5
St Clement Jersey ...11 c2
St Clether Cnwll ...5 L5
St Colmac Ag & B ...124 C4
St Columb Major Cnwll ...4 E9
St Columb Minor Cnwll ...4 C9
St Columb Road Cnwll ...4 E9
St Combs Abers ...159 Q5
St Cross South Elmham Suffk ...65 K5
St Cyrus Abers ...143 N5
St David's P & K ...133 Q3
St Davids Pembks ...40 E5
St Davids Cathedral Pembks ...40 E5
St Day Cnwll ...3 J5
St Decumans Somset ...18 E6
St Dennis Cnwll ...4 F10
St Devereux Herefs ...45 N8
St Dogmaels Pembks ...42 C5
St Dogwells Pembks ...41 J5
St Dominick Cnwll ...5 Q8
St Donats V Glam ...29 P11
St Edith's Marsh Wilts ...21 J2
St Endellion Cnwll ...4 F6
St Enoder Cnwll ...4 D10
St Erme Cnwll ...3 L4
St Erney Cnwll ...5 P10
St Erth Cnwll ...2 F6
St Erth Praze Cnwll ...2 F6
St Ervan Cnwll ...4 D7
St Eval Cnwll ...4 D8
St Ewe Cnwll ...3 P4
St Fagans Cardif ...30 F9
St Fagans: National History Museum Cardif ...30 F9
St Fergus Abers ...159 Q7
St Fillans P & K ...133 K3
St Florence Pembks ...41 L10
St Gennys Cnwll ...5 J2
St George Conwy ...80 D9
St Georges N Som ...19 L2
St George's V Glam ...30 F9
St George's Hill Surrey ...36 C8
St Germans Cnwll ...5 P10
St Giles in the Wood Devon ...17 J8
St Giles-on-the-Heath Devon ...5 P3
St Gluvia's Cnwll ...3 K7
St Harmon Powys ...55 M10
St Helen Auckland Dur ...103 N5
St Helens Cumb ...100 D4
St Helen's E Susx ...26 D9
St Helens IoW ...14 H9
St Helens St Hel ...81 Q5
St Helier Gt Lon ...36 G7
St Helier Jersey ...11 b2
St Hilary Cnwll ...2 E7
St Hilary V Glam ...30 D10
Saint Hill Devon ...10 B3
Saint Hill W Susx ...25 J3
St Illtyd Blae G ...30 H4
St Ippolyts Herts ...50 E5
St Ishmael's Pembks ...40 F9
St Issey Cnwll ...4 E7
St Ive Cnwll ...5 N8
St Ive Cross Cnwll ...5 N8
St Ives Cambs ...62 D6
St Ives Cnwll ...2 E5

St Ives Dorset ...13 K4
St James Norfk ...77 K7
St James's End Nhants ...60 F8
St James South Elmham Suffk ...65 L5
St Jidgey Cnwll ...4 E8
St John Cnwll ...5 Q11
St John Jersey ...11 b1
St Johns Dur ...103 L4
St John's E Susx ...25 M4
St John's IoM ...80 c5
St John's Kent ...37 M9
St Johns Surrey ...23 Q3
St Johns Worcs ...46 F4
St John's Chapel Devon ...17 J6
St John's Chapel Dur ...102 G3
St John's Fen End Norfk ...75 K8
St John's Highway Norfk ...75 K8
St John's Kirk S Lans ...116 D3
St John's Town of Dalry D & G ...108 D4
St John's Wood Gt Lon ...36 G4
St Judes IoM ...80 e2
St Just Cnwll ...2 B7
St Just-in-Roseland Cnwll ...3 L6
St Just Mining District Cnwll ...2 B7
St Katherines Abers ...159 J11
St Keverne Cnwll ...3 K9
St Kew Cnwll ...4 G6
St Kew Highway Cnwll ...4 G6
St Keyne Cnwll ...5 L9
St Lawrence Cnwll ...4 G8
St Lawrence Essex ...52 G11
St Lawrence IoW ...14 F11
St Lawrence Jersey ...11 b1
St Lawrence Kent ...39 Q8
St Leonards Bucks ...35 P3
St Leonards Dorset ...13 K4
St Leonards E Susx ...26 D10
St Leonard's Street Kent ...37 Q9
St Levan Cnwll ...2 B9
St Lythans V Glam ...30 F10
St Madoes P & K ...134 F3
St Margarets Herefs ...45 M8
St Margarets Herts ...51 J8
St Margaret's at Cliffe Kent ...27 Q3
St Margaret's Hope Ork ...169 d7
St Margaret South Elmham Suffk ...65 L5
St Marks IoM ...80 c7
St Martin Cnwll ...3 J9
St Martin Cnwll ...5 M10
St Martin Guern ...10 b2
St Martin Jersey ...11 c1
St Martin's IoS ...2 c1
St Martin's P & K ...142 B11
St Martin's Shrops ...69 K7
St Martin's Moor Shrops ...69 K7
St Mary Jersey ...11 a1
St Mary Bourne Hants ...22 D4
St Marychurch Torbay ...7 N5
St Mary Church V Glam ...30 D10
St Mary Cray Gt Lon ...37 L7
St Mary Hill V Glam ...30 C9
St Mary in the Marsh Kent ...27 J6
St Mary's IoS ...2 c2
St Mary's Ork ...169 d6
St Mary's Bay Kent ...27 J6
St Mary's Hoo Medway ...38 D6
St Mary's Platt Kent ...37 P9
St Maughans Mons ...45 P11
St Maughans Green Mons ...45 P11
St Mawes Cnwll ...3 L7
St Mawgan Cnwll ...4 D8
St Mellion Cnwll ...5 P8
St Mellons Cardif ...30 H8
St Merryn Cnwll ...4 D7
St Mewan Cnwll ...3 P3
St Michael Caerhays Cnwll ...3 P5
St Michael Church Somset ...19 K9
St Michael Penkevil Cnwll ...3 M5
St Michaels Kent ...26 E4
St Michaels Worcs ...57 K11
St Michael's Mount Cnwll ...2 E8
St Michael's on Wyre Lancs ...88 F2
St Michael South Elmham Suffk ...65 L5
St Minver Cnwll ...4 F6
St Monans Fife ...135 N7
St Neot Cnwll ...5 K8
St Neots Cambs ...61 Q8
St Newlyn East Cnwll ...4 C10
St Nicholas Pembks ...40 H3
St Nicholas V Glam ...30 E10
St Nicholas-at-Wade Kent ...39 N8
St Ninians Stirlg ...133 M9
St Olaves Norfk ...77 P2
St Osyth Essex ...53 K8
St Owen's Cross Herefs ...45 Q10
St Paul's Cray Gt Lon ...37 L7
St Paul's Walden Herts ...50 E6
St Peter Jersey ...11 a1
St Peter Port Guern ...10 c2
St Peter's Guern ...10 b2
St Peter's Kent ...39 Q8
St Peter's Hill Cambs ...62 B6
St Petrox Pembks ...41 J11
St Pinnock Cnwll ...5 L9
St Quivox S Ayrs ...114 G3
St Ruan Cnwll ...3 J10
St Sampson Guern ...10 c1
St Saviour Guern ...10 b2
St Saviour Jersey ...11 b2
St Stephen Cnwll ...3 N3
St Stephens Cnwll ...5 N4
St Stephens Cnwll ...5 Q10
St Teath Cnwll ...4 H5
St Thomas Devon ...9 M6
St Margaret's Bay Kent ...27 Q3
St Tudy Cnwll ...4 H6
St Twynnells Pembks ...41 J11
St Veep Cnwll ...5 J10
St Vigeans Angus ...143 L9
St Wenn Cnwll ...4 F9
St Weonards Herefs ...45 P10
St y-Nyll V Glam ...30 E9
Salcombe Devon ...7 M10
Salcombe Regis Devon ...10 D7
Salcott-cum-Virley Essex ...52 F9
Sale Traffd ...82 G6
Saleby Lincs ...87 N6

Sale Green Worcs ...46 H3
Salehurst E Susx ...26 C7
Salem Carmth ...43 M9
Salem Cerdgn ...54 F8
Salen Ag & B ...137 P7
Salen Highld ...138 B5
Salesbury Lancs ...89 K4
Salford C Beds ...49 P7
Salford Oxon ...47 Q9
Salford Salfd ...82 H5
Salford Priors Warwks ...47 L4
Salfords Surrey ...36 G11
Salhouse Norfk ...77 L9
Saline Fife ...134 C9
Salisbury Wilts ...21 M8
Salisbury Plain Wilts ...21 L6
Salkeld Dykes Cumb ...101 P3
Salle Norfk ...76 G7
Salmonby Lincs ...87 K6
Salperton Gloucs ...47 L10
Salph End Bed ...61 N10
Salsburgh N Lans ...126 E5
Salt Staffs ...70 H9
Salta Cumb ...109 N11
Saltaire C Brad ...90 E3
Saltash Cnwll ...6 C7
Saltburn Highld ...156 C3
Saltburn-by-the-Sea R & Cl ...105 J6
Saltby Leics ...73 M5
Salt Coates Cumb ...110 C10
Saltcoats Cumb ...100 E11
Saltcoats N Ayrs ...124 G9
Saltcotes Lancs ...88 D5
Saltdean Br & H ...25 J10
Salterbeck Cumb ...100 C5
Salterforth Lancs ...96 C11
Salterswall Ches W ...82 D11
Salterton Wilts ...21 M7
Saltfleet Lincs ...87 N2
Saltfleetby All Saints Lincs ...87 N2
Saltfleetby St Clement Lincs ...87 N2
Saltfleetby St Peter Lincs ...87 M3
Saltford BaNES ...32 C11
Salthouse Norfk ...76 F3
Saltley Birm ...58 H7
Saltmarsh Newpt ...31 K8
Saltmarshe E R Yk ...92 C6
Saltney Flints ...69 L2
Salton N York ...98 E5
Saltrens Devon ...16 H7
Saltwick Nthumb ...113 J4
Saltwood Kent ...27 L4
Salvington W Susx ...24 D9
Salwarpe Worcs ...46 G2
Salway Ash Dorset ...11 K5
Sambourne Warwks ...47 L2
Sambrook Wrekin ...70 C10
Samlesbury Lancs ...88 H4
Samlesbury Bottoms Lancs ...89 J5
Sampford Arundel Somset ...18 F11
Sampford Brett Somset ...18 E6
Sampford Courtenay Devon ...8 F4
Sampford Moor Somset ...18 F11
Sampford Peverell Devon ...9 P11
Sampford Spiney Devon ...6 E4
Samsonlane Ork ...169 f4
Samson's Corner Essex ...53 J8
Samuelston E Loth ...128 C5
Sanaigmore Ag & B ...122 B5
Sancreed Cnwll ...2 C8
Sancton E R Yk ...92 E3
Sand Somset ...19 M5
Sandaig Highld ...145 M7
Sandale Cumb ...100 H2
Sandal Magna Wakefd ...91 J7
Sanday Ork ...169 f2
Sanday Airport Ork ...169 f2
Sandbach Ches E ...70 D2
Sandbach Services Ches E ...70 D2
Sandbank Ag & B ...131 P11
Sandbanks BCP ...12 H7
Sandend Abers ...158 E4
Sanderstead Gt Lon ...36 H8
Sandford Cumb ...102 D7
Sandford Devon ...9 K4
Sandford Dorset ...12 F7
Sandford Hants ...13 L4
Sandford IoW ...14 F10
Sandford N Som ...19 M3
Sandford N Lans ...126 C9
Sandford Shrops ...69 K10
Sandford Shrops ...69 P9
Sandford-on-Thames Oxon ...34 F4
Sandford Orcas Dorset ...20 B10
Sandford St Martin Oxon ...48 D9
Sandgate Kent ...27 M4
Sandhaven Abers ...159 N4
Sandhead D & G ...106 E8
Sandhill Rothm ...91 L11
Sandhills Dorset ...11 M4
Sandhills Dorset ...11 P2
Sandhills Leeds ...91 K3
Sandhills Oxon ...34 G3
Sandhills Surrey ...23 P7
Sandhoe Nthumb ...112 E7
Sandhole Ag & B ...131 L8
Sand Hole E R Yk ...92 D3
Sandholme E R Yk ...92 D4
Sandholme Lincs ...74 F3
Sandhurst Br For ...23 M2
Sandhurst Gloucs ...46 F10
Sandhurst Kent ...26 D6
Sandhurst Cross Kent ...26 C6
Sandhutton N York ...97 N4
Sand Hutton N York ...98 D9
Sandiacre Derbys ...72 D3
Sandilands Lincs ...87 P4
Sandiway Ches W ...82 D10
Sandleheath Hants ...21 M11
Sandleigh Oxon ...34 E4
Sandley Dorset ...20 D10
Sandling Kent ...38 C10
Sandlow Green Ches E ...82 G11
Sandness Shet ...169 n8
Sandon Essex ...52 B11
Sandon Herts ...51 H4
Sandon Staffs ...70 G9
Sandon Bank Staffs ...70 G9
Sandown IoW ...14 G10
Sandplace Cnwll ...5 M10
Sandridge Herts ...50 E8
Sandridge Wilts ...32 H11
Sandringham Norfk ...75 N5
Sands Bucks ...35 M6

Sandsend N York ...105 N8
Sand Side Cumb ...94 E4
Sandside Cumb ...95 K4
Sandtoft N Linc ...92 B9
Sandway Kent ...38 E11
Sandwich Kent ...39 P10
Sandwich Bay Kent ...39 Q10
Sandwick Cumb ...101 M7
Sandwick Shet ...169 r11
Sandwick W Isls ...168 j4
Sandwith Cumb ...100 C8
Sandwith Newtown Cumb ...100 C8
Sandy C Beds ...61 Q11
Sandy Bank Lincs ...87 J9
Sandycroft Flints ...81 L11
Sandy Cross E Susx ...25 N6
Sandy Cross Herefs ...46 C3
Sandyford D & G ...110 D2
Sandygate Devon ...7 M4
Sandygate IoM ...80 e2
Sandy Haven Pembks ...40 G9
Sandyhills D & G ...109 J9
Sandylands Lancs ...95 J8
Sandylane C Brad ...90 E3
Sandylane Staffs ...70 C7
Sandylane Swans ...28 G7
Sandy Lane Wilts ...33 J11
Sandy Lane Wrexhm ...69 M6
Sandy Park Devon ...8 H7
Sandysike Cumb ...110 G7
Sandyway Herefs ...45 P9
Sangobeg Highld ...165 K3
Sangomore Highld ...165 K3
Sankey Bridges Warrtn ...82 C7
Sankyn's Green Worcs ...57 P11
Sanna Highld ...137 L2
Sanndabhaig W Isls ...168 j4
Sannox N Ayrs ...124 C8
Sanquhar D & G ...115 Q6
Santon Cumb ...100 F10
Santon IoM ...80 d7
Santon Bridge Cumb ...100 F10
Santon Downham Suffk ...63 P3
Sapcote Leics ...59 Q6
Sapey Common Herefs ...46 D2
Sapiston Suffk ...64 C6
Sapley Cambs ...62 B6
Sapperton Derbys ...71 M8
Sapperton Gloucs ...32 H4
Sapperton Lincs ...73 Q4
Saracen's Head Lincs ...74 F5
Sarclet Highld ...167 P8
Sarisbury Hants ...14 F5
Sarn Brdgnd ...29 P8
Sarn Powys ...56 C6
Sarnau Carmth ...42 F11
Sarnau Cerdgn ...42 F4
Sarnau Gwynd ...68 C7
Sarnau Powys ...44 E8
Sarnau Powys ...68 H11
Sarn Bach Gwynd ...66 E9
Sarnesfield Herefs ...45 M4
Sarn Meilteyrn Gwynd ...66 C8
Sarn Park Services Brdgnd ...29 P8
Sarn-wen Powys ...69 J11
Saron Carmth ...28 H2
Saron Carmth ...42 G7
Saron Gwynd ...66 H3
Saron Gwynd ...79 J11
Sarratt Herts ...50 B11
Sarre Kent ...39 N8
Sarsden Oxon ...47 Q10
Sarson Hants ...22 B6
Satley Dur ...103 M2
Satmar Kent ...27 N4
Satron N York ...102 H11
Satterleigh Devon ...17 M7
Satterthwaite Cumb ...94 G2
Satwell Oxon ...35 K8
Sauchen Abers ...151 J5
Saucher P & K ...142 B11
Sauchieburn Abers ...143 M4
Saul Gloucs ...32 D3
Saundby Notts ...85 N3
Saundersfoot Pembks ...41 M10
Saunderton Bucks ...35 L4
Saunderton Station Bucks ...35 M5
Saunton Devon ...16 H4
Sausthorpe Lincs ...87 L7
Saverley Green Staffs ...70 H7
Savile Town Kirk ...90 G6
Sawbridge Warwks ...60 B7
Sawbridgeworth Herts ...51 L8
Sawdon N York ...99 J4
Sawley Derbys ...72 D4
Sawley Lancs ...96 A11
Sawley N York ...97 K7
Sawston Cambs ...62 G11
Sawtry Cambs ...61 Q4
Saxby Leics ...73 L7
Saxby Lincs ...86 D4
Saxby All Saints N Linc ...92 G7
Saxelbye Leics ...72 H6
Saxham Street Suffk ...64 E9
Saxilby Lincs ...85 Q5
Saxlingham Norfk ...76 E4
Saxlingham Green Norfk ...65 J2
Saxlingham Nethergate Norfk ...65 J2
Saxlingham Thorpe Norfk ...65 J2
Saxmundham Suffk ...65 M3
Saxondale Notts ...72 H3
Saxon Street Cambs ...63 L9
Saxtead Suffk ...65 K8
Saxtead Green Suffk ...65 K9
Saxtead Little Green Suffk ...65 J8
Saxthorpe Norfk ...76 G5
Saxton N York ...91 M3
Sayers Common W Susx ...24 G7
Scackleton N York ...98 C6
Scadabay W Isls ...168 g8
Scadabhagh W Isls ...168 g8
Scafell Pike Cumb ...100 H9
Scaftworth Notts ...85 L2
Scagglethorpe N York ...98 G6
Scalasaig Ag & B ...136 b3
Scalby E R Yk ...92 D5
Scalby N York ...99 L2
Scald End Bed ...61 M9
Scaldwell Nhants ...60 G6
Scaleby Cumb ...110 H8
Scalebyhill Cumb ...110 H8
Scale Houses Cumb ...111 L11
Scales Cumb ...94 F6
Scales Cumb ...101 K5

Scalesceugh Cumb 110 H11
Scalford Leics 73 K6
Scaling N York 105 K8
Scaling Dam R & Cl 105 K8
Salloway Shet 169 r10
Scalpay Highld 153 L11
Scalpay W Isls 168 h8
Scambleby Lincs 87 J5
Scammonden Kirk 90 D7
Scamodale Highld 138 E3
Scampston N York 98 H5
Scampton Lincs 86 C5
Scaniport Highld 156 A10
Scapegoat Hill Kirk 90 D7
Scarba A & B 130 D7
Scarborough N York 99 L3
Scarcewater Cnwll 3 N3
Scarcliffe Derbys 84 G7
Scarcroft Leeds 91 K2
Scarfskerry Highld 167 N2
Scargill Dur 103 L8
Scarinish Ag & B 136 C7
Scarisbrick Lancs 88 D8
Scarness Cumb 100 H4
Scarning Norfk 76 D9
Scarrington Notts 73 J2
Scarth Hill Lancs 88 E9
Scarthingwell N York 91 M3
Scartho NE Lin 93 N9
Scatsta Airport Shet 169 q6
Scaur D & G 108 H10
Scawby N Linc 92 G9
Scawsby Donc 91 N10
Scawthorpe Donc 91 P9
Scawton N York 98 A4
Scayne's Hill W Susx 25 J6
Scethrog Powys 44 G9
Scholar Green Ches E 70 E3
Scholes Kirk 90 F5
Scholes Kirk 90 F9
Scholes Leeds 91 K3
Scholes Rothm 91 K11
Scholes Wigan 88 H9
School Aycliffe Dur 103 Q6
School Green C Brad 90 E4
School Green Ches W 70 A2
Schoolgreen Wokham 35 K11
School House Dorset 10 H4
Scissett Kirk 90 G8
Scleddau Pembks 40 H4
Scofton Notts 85 K4
Scole Norfk 64 H6
Scone P & K 134 E2
Sconser Highld 153 J11
Scoonie Fife 135 K7
Scopwick Lincs 86 E9
Scoraig Highld 160 G7
Scorborough E R Yk 99 L11
Scorrier Cnwll 3 J5
Scorriton Devon 7 J5
Scorton Lancs 95 L11
Scorton N York 103 Q10
Sco Ruston Norfk 77 K7
Scotby Cumb 110 H9
Scotch Corner N York 103 P9
Scotch Corner Rest Area N York 103 P9
Scotforth Lancs 95 K9
Scot Hay Staffs 70 D5
Scothern Lincs 86 D5
Scotland Lincs 73 Q4
Scotland Gate Nthumb 113 L4
Scotlandwell P & K 134 F7
Scot Lane End Bolton 89 J9
Scotscalder Station Highld 167 J5
Scotsdike Cumb 110 G6
Scot's Gap Nthumb 112 F3
Scotsmill Abers 150 F4
Scotstoun C Glas 125 N4
Scotswood N u Ty 113 K8
Scotter Lincs 92 E10
Scotterthorpe Lincs 92 E10
Scottish Seabird Centre E Loth 128 F2
Scottish Wool Centre Stirlg 132 G7
Scottlethorpe Lincs 73 R6
Scotton Lincs 92 E11
Scotton N York 97 M9
Scotton N York 103 N11
Scottow Norfk 77 K7
Scott Willoughby Lincs 73 R3
Scoulton Norfk 76 D11
Scounslow Green Staffs 71 K9
Scourie Highld 164 E8
Scourie More Highld 164 D8
Scousburgh Shet 169 q12
Scouthead Oldham 90 B9
Scrabster Highld 167 K2
Scraesburgh Border 118 C7
Scrafield Lincs 87 K7
Scrainwood Nthumb 119 J9
Scrane End Lincs 74 G2
Scraptoft Leics 72 G9
Scratby Norfk 77 Q8
Scrayingham N York 98 E9
Scrays E Susx 26 C8
Scredington Lincs 74 A2
Scremby Lincs 87 M7
Scremerston Nthumb 129 Q10
Screveton Notts 73 J2
Scrivelsby Lincs 87 J7
Scriven N York 97 M9
Scrooby Notts 85 L2
Scropton Derbys 71 M8
Scrub Hill Lincs 86 H9
Scruton N York 97 L2
Scuggate Cumb 110 H6
Scullomie Highld 165 P4
Sculthorpe Norfk 76 B5
Scunthorpe N Linc 92 E8
Scurlage Swans 28 D7
Sea Somset 10 G2
Seaborough Dorset 11 J3
Seabridge Staffs 70 E6
Seabrook Kent 27 L4
Seaburn Sundld 113 P9
Seacombe Wirral 81 L6
Seacroft Leeds 91 K3
Seacroft Lincs 87 Q8
Seadyke Lincs 74 F3
Seafield W Loth 127 J4
Seaford E Susx 25 L11
Seaforth Sefton 81 L5
Seagrave Leics 72 G7
Seagry Heath Wilts 33 J8

Seaham Dur 113 P11
Seahouses Nthumb 119 P4
Seal Kent 37 N9
Sealand Flints 81 M11
Seale Surrey 23 N5
Seamer N York 99 L4
Seamer N York 104 E8
Seamill N Ayrs 124 G8
Sea Palling Norfk 77 N6
Searby Lincs 93 J9
Seasalter End Kent 39 J9
Seascale Cumb 100 D10
Seathwaite Cumb 100 H11
Seathwaite Cumb 100 H8
Seatle Cumb 94 H4
Seatoller Cumb 100 H8
Seaton Cnwll 5 N11
Seaton Cumb 100 D4
Seaton Devon 10 E6
Seaton Dur 113 N11
Seaton E R Yk 99 P11
Seaton Kent 39 M10
Seaton Nthumb 113 M5
Seaton Rutlnd 73 N11
Seaton Burn N Tyne 113 K6
Seaton Carew Hartpl 104 F5
Seaton Delaval Nthumb 113 M5
Seaton Ross E R Yk 92 C2
Seaton Sluice Nthumb 113 M5
Seatown Dorset 11 J6
Seave Green N York 104 G10
Seaview IoW 14 H8
Seaville Cumb 110 C10
Seavington St Mary Somset 11 J2
Seavington St Michael Somset 19 M11
Sebastopol Torfn 31 J5
Sebergham Cumb 101 L2
Seckington Warwks 59 L3
Second Severn Crossing Mons 31 P7
Sedbergh Cumb 95 P2
Sedbury Gloucs 31 P6
Sedbusk N York 96 C2
Sedgeberrow Worcs 47 K7
Sedgebrook Lincs 73 M3
Sedge Fen Suffk 63 L4
Sedgefield Dur 104 C5
Sedgeford Norfk 75 P3
Sedgehill Wilts 20 G9
Sedgemoor Services Somset 19 L4
Sedgley Dudley 58 D6
Sedgley Park Bury 82 H4
Sedgwick Cumb 95 L3
Sedlescombe E Susx 26 C8
Sedrup Bucks 35 M2
Seed Kent 38 F10
Seend Wilts 20 H2
Seend Cleeve Wilts 20 H2
Seer Green Bucks 35 Q6
Seething Norfk 65 L2
Sefton Sefton 81 M4
Seghill Nthumb 113 L6
Seighford Staffs 70 F9
Seion Gwynd 79 J11
Seisdon Staffs 58 B5
Selattyn Shrops 69 J8
Selborne Hants 23 K8
Selby N York 91 Q4
Selham W Susx 23 P10
Selhurst Gt Lon 36 H7
Sellack Herefs 45 R9
Sellafield Station Cumb 100 D10
Sellafirth Shet 169 s4
Sellan Cnwll 2 C7
Sellick's Green Somset 18 H11
Sellindge Kent 27 J4
Selling Kent 38 H10
Sells Green Wilts 20 H2
Selly Oak Birm 58 F8
Selmeston E Susx 25 M9
Selsdon Gt Lon 37 J8
Selsey W Susx 15 N8
Selsfield Common W Susx 24 H4
Selside Cumb 101 P11
Selside N York 96 A5
Selsley Gloucs 32 F4
Selsted Kent 27 M3
Selston Notts 84 G10
Selworthy Somset 18 B5
Semer Suffk 52 G2
Semington Wilts 20 G2
Semley Wilts 20 G9
Sempringham Lincs 74 B4
Send Surrey 36 B9
Send Marsh Surrey 36 B9
Senghenydd Caerph 30 F6
Sennen Cnwll 2 B8
Sennen Cove Cnwll 2 B8
Sennybridge Powys 44 C9
Serlby Notts 85 K3
Sessay N York 97 Q5
Setchey Norfk 75 M8
Setley Hants 13 P4
Seton Mains E Loth 128 C4
Settle N York 96 B8
Settrington N York 98 G8
Seven Ash Somset 18 G8
Sevenhampton Gloucs 47 K10
Sevenhampton Swindn 33 P6
Seven Kings Gt Lon 37 L3
Sevenoaks Kent 37 M9
Sevenoaks Weald Kent 37 M10
Seven Sisters Neath 29 M3
Seven Springs Gloucs 47 J11
Seven Star Green Essex 52 F6
Severn Beach S Glos 31 P8
Severn Bridge S Glos 31 Q6
Severn Stoke Worcs 46 G6
Severn View Services S Glos 31 Q7
Sevick End Bed 61 N10
Sevington Kent 26 H3
Sewards End Essex 51 N3
Sewardstonebury Essex 51 J11
Sewell C Beds 49 Q10
Sewerby E R Yk 99 P7
Seworgan Cnwll 3 J7
Sewstern Leics 73 M6
Sexhow N York 104 E9
Sgalpaigh W Isls 168 h8
Sgiogarstaigh W Isls 168 k1
Shabbington Bucks 35 J3
Shackerley Shrops 57 Q3

Shackerstone Leics 72 B9
Shacklecross Derbys 72 C4
Shackleford Surrey 23 P5
Shade Calder 89 Q6
Shader W Isls 168 i2
Shadforth Dur 104 B2
Shadingfield Suffk 65 N5
Shadoxhurst Kent 26 G4
Shadwell Leeds 91 J3
Shadwell Norfk 64 C5
Shaftenhoe End Herts 51 K3
Shaftesbury Dorset 20 G10
Shaftholme Donc 91 P9
Shafton Barns 91 K8
Shafton Two Gates Barns 91 K8
Shakerley Wigan 82 E4
Shalbourne Wilts 22 B2
Shalcombe IoW 14 C9
Shalden Hants 23 J4
Shalden Green Hants 23 K6
Shaldon Devon 7 M7
Shalfleet IoW 14 D9
Shalford Essex 52 B6
Shalford Surrey 36 B11
Shalford Green Essex 52 B6
Shallowford Staffs 70 F9
Shalmsford Street Kent 39 J11
Shalstone Bucks 48 H7
Shamley Green Surrey 24 B2
Shandford Angus 142 H5
Shandon Ag & B 132 B10
Shandwick Highld 156 F2
Shangton Leics 73 J11
Shankhouse Nthumb 113 L5
Shanklin IoW 14 G10
Shantron Ag & B 132 C10
Shap Cumb 101 Q7
Shapinsay Ork 169 e5
Shapwick Dorset 12 F4
Shapwick Somset 19 M7
Shard End Birm 59 J7
Shardlow Derbys 72 C4
Shareshill Staffs 58 D3
Sharlston Wakefd 91 K7
Sharlston Common Wakefd 91 K7
Sharman's Cross Solhll 58 H9
Sharnal Street Medway 38 C7
Sharnbrook Bed 61 L9
Sharneyford Lancs 89 P6
Sharnford Leics 59 Q6
Sharnhill Green Dorset 11 Q3
Sharoe Green Lancs 88 G4
Sharow N York 97 M6
Sharpenhoe C Beds 50 C4
Sharperton Nthumb 119 J10
Sharp Green Norfk 77 M7
Sharpness Gloucs 32 C4
Sharpthorne W Susx 25 J4
Sharptor Cnwll 5 M7
Sharpway Gate Worcs 58 E11
Sharrington Norfk 76 E4
Shatterford Worcs 57 P8
Shatterling Kent 39 N10
Shatton Derbys 84 B4
Shaugh Prior Devon 6 E4
Shave Cross Dorset 11 J5
Shavington Ches E 70 B4
Shaw C Brad 90 C3
Shaw Oldham 89 Q9
Shaw Swindn 33 M7
Shaw W Berk 34 E11
Shaw Wilts 32 G11
Shawbirch Wrekin 57 L2
Shawbost W Isls 168 h3
Shawbury Shrops 69 Q10
Shawclough Rochdl 89 P8
Shaw Common Gloucs 46 C9
Shawdon Hill Nthumb 119 L8
Shawell Leics 60 B4
Shawford Hants 22 E9
Shawforth Lancs 89 P6
Shaw Green Herts 50 H4
Shaw Green Lancs 88 G7
Shaw Green N York 97 L10
Shawhead D & G 109 J5
Shaw Mills N York 97 L8
Shawsburn S Lans 126 D7
Shear Cross Wilts 20 G6
Shearington D & G 109 M7
Shearsby Leics 60 D2
Shearston Somset 19 J8
Shebbear Devon 16 G10
Shebdon Staffs 70 D9
Shebster Highld 166 H4
Shedfield Hants 14 G4
Sheen Staffs 71 L2
Sheepbridge Derbys 84 E6
Sheep Hill Dur 113 J9
Sheepridge Kirk 90 F7
Sheepscar Leeds 91 J4
Sheepscombe Gloucs 32 G4
Sheepstor Devon 6 F5
Sheepwash Devon 8 G4
Sheepwash Nthumb 113 L3
Sheepway N Som 31 N9
Sheepy Magna Leics 72 A10
Sheepy Parva Leics 72 A10
Sheering Essex 51 M8
Sheerness Kent 38 F7
Sheerwater Surrey 36 B8
Sheet Hants 23 L10
Sheffield Cnwll 2 D8
Sheffield Sheff 84 E3
Sheffield Bottom W Berk 34 H11
Sheffield Green E Susx 25 K5
Sheffield Park E Susx 25 K6
Shefford C Beds 50 D3
Shefford Woodlands W Berk 34 C10
Sheigra Highld 164 E4
Sheinton Shrops 57 L4
Shelderton Shrops 57 L4
Sheldon Birm 58 J8
Sheldon Derbys 83 Q11
Sheldon Devon 10 C3
Sheldwich Kent 38 H10
Sheldwich Lees Kent 38 H10
Shelf Calder 90 E5
Shelfanger Norfk 64 G5
Shelfield Warwks 47 M2
Shelfield Wsall 58 F4
Shelfield Green Warwks 47 M2
Shelford Notts 72 H2
Shelford Warwks 59 P7
Shellacres Nthumb 118 G2
Shelley Essex 51 N9

Shelley Kirk 90 G8
Shelley Suffk 52 H4
Shelley Far Bank Kirk 90 G8
Shellingford Oxon 34 B6
Shellow Bowells Essex 51 P9
Shelsley Beauchamp Worcs 46 D2
Shelsley Walsh Worcs 46 D2
Shelton Bed 61 M7
Shelton Norfk 65 J3
Shelton Notts 73 J3
Shelton Shrops 56 H2
Shelton Green Norfk 65 J3
Shelton Lock C Derb 72 B4
Shelton Under Harley Staffs 70 E7
Shelve Shrops 56 F5
Shelwick Herefs 45 Q6
Shenfield Essex 51 P11
Shenington Oxon 48 C6
Shenley Herts 50 E10
Shenley Brook End M Keyn 49 M7
Shenleybury Herts 50 E10
Shenley Church End M Keyn 49 M7
Shenmore Herefs 45 M7
Shennanton D & G 107 K5
Shenstone Staffs 58 H4
Shenstone Worcs 58 C10
Shenstone Woodend Staffs 58 H4
Shenton Leics 72 B11
Shenval Moray 149 N2
Shepeau Stow Lincs 74 F8
Shephall Herts 50 G6
Shepherd's Bush Gt Lon 36 F4
Shepherd's Green Oxon 35 K8
Shepherds Patch Gloucs 32 C4
Shepherdswell Kent 27 N2
Shepley Kirk 90 F9
Shepperdine S Glos 32 B5
Shepperton Surrey 36 C7
Shepperton Green Surrey 36 C7
Shepreth Cambs 62 E11
Shepshed Leics 72 D7
Shepton Beauchamp Somset 19 M11
Shepton Mallet Somset 20 B6
Shepton Montague Somset 20 C8
Shepway Kent 38 C11
Sheraton Dur 104 D3
Sherborne Dorset 20 B11
Sherborne Gloucs 33 N2
Sherborne Somset 19 Q3
Sherborne St John Hants 22 H3
Sherbourne Warwks 47 Q2
Sherburn Dur 104 B2
Sherburn N York 99 K5
Sherburn Hill Dur 104 B2
Sherburn in Elmet N York 91 M4
Shere Surrey 36 C11
Shereford Norfk 76 B6
Sherfield English Hants 21 Q10
Sherfield on Loddon Hants 23 J3
Sherfin Lancs 89 M5
Sherford Devon 7 K10
Sherford Dorset 12 F6
Sheriffhales Shrops 57 P2
Sheriff Hutton N York 98 F7
Sheringham Norfk 76 H3
Sherington M Keyn 49 N5
Shermanbury W Susx 24 F7
Shernborne Norfk 75 P4
Sherrington Wilts 21 J7
Sherston Wilts 32 G7
Sherwood C Nott 72 F2
Sherwood Forest Notts 85 K8
Shetland Islands Shet 169 r8
Shettleston C Glas 125 Q5
Shevington Wigan 88 G9
Shevington Moor Wigan 88 G8
Shevington Vale Wigan 88 G9
Sheviock Cnwll 5 P10
Shibden Head C Brad 90 D5
Shide IoW 14 F9
Shidlaw Nthumb 118 F3
Shiel Bridge Highld 146 A4
Shieldaig Highld 153 Q4
Shieldhill D & G 109 M3
Shieldhill Falk 126 F2
Shieldhill House Hotel S Lans 116 E2
Shields N Lans 126 D6
Shielfoot Highld 138 B3
Shielhill Angus 142 G6
Shielhill Inver 124 G3
Shifford Oxon 34 C4
Shifnal Shrops 57 N3
Shilbottle Nthumb 119 N8
Shildon Dur 103 P5
Shillford E Rens 125 M6
Shillingford Devon 18 C10
Shillingford Oxon 34 G6
Shillingford Abbot Devon 9 M7
Shillingford St George Devon 9 M7
Shillingstone Dorset 12 D2
Shillington C Beds 50 D4
Shillmoor Nthumb 118 H8
Shilton Oxon 33 Q3
Shilton Warwks 59 P8
Shimpling Norfk 64 H5
Shimpling Suffk 64 B11
Shimpling Street Suffk 64 B11
Shincliffe Dur 103 Q2
Shiney Row Sundld 113 M10
Shinfield Wokham 35 K11
Shingay Cambs 62 D11
Shingle Street Suffk 53 Q3
Shinnersbridge Devon 7 K5
Shinness Highld 162 C4
Shipbourne Kent 37 N10
Shipdham Norfk 76 D10
Shipham Somset 19 M3
Shiphay Torbay 7 M5
Shiplake Oxon 35 K9
Shiplake Row Oxon 35 K9
Shiplate N Som 19 L3
Shipley C Brad 90 F3
Shipley Derbys 72 C2
Shipley Shrops 57 Q5
Shipley W Susx 24 D6
Shipley Bridge Surrey 24 H2
Shipley Hatch Kent 26 H4
Shipmeadow Suffk 65 M3
Shippea Hill Station Cambs 63 K4
Shippon Oxon 34 D5
Shipston-on-Stour Warwks 47 Q6
Shipton Bucks 49 L9

Shipton Gloucs 47 K11
Shipton N York 98 B9
Shipton Shrops 57 K6
Shipton Bellinger Hants 21 P5
Shipton Gorge Dorset 11 K6
Shipton Green W Susx 15 M7
Shipton Moyne Gloucs 32 G7
Shipton-on-Cherwell Oxon 48 E11
Shiptonthorpe E R Yk 92 E2
Shipton-under-Wychwood Oxon 47 Q11
Shirburn Oxon 35 J5
Shirdley Hill Lancs 88 D8
Shire Cumb 102 B3
Shirebrook Derbys 84 H7
Shiregreen Sheff 84 E2
Shirehampton Bristl 31 P9
Shiremoor N Tyne 113 M6
Shirenewton Mons 31 N6
Shire Oak Wsall 58 G4
Shireoaks Notts 85 J4
Shirkoak Kent 26 F4
Shirland Derbys 84 F9
Shirl Heath Herefs 45 N3
Shirley C Sotn 14 D4
Shirley Derbys 71 N6
Shirley Gt Lon 37 J7
Shirley Solhll 58 H9
Shirl Heath Herefs 45 N3
Shirrell Heath Hants 14 G4
Shirwell Devon 17 L4
Shiskine N Ayrs 120 H6
Shittlehope Dur 103 K3
Shobdon Herefs 45 N2
Shobley Hants 13 L3
Shobrooke Devon 9 L4
Shoby Leics 72 H6
Shocklach Ches W 69 M5
Shocklach Green Ches W 69 M5
Shoeburyness Sthend 38 F4
Sholden Kent 39 Q11
Sholing C Sotn 14 E4
Shoot Hill Shrops 56 G2
Shop Cnwll 4 D7
Shop Cnwll 16 C9
Shopwyke W Susx 15 N5
Shore Rochdl 89 Q7
Shoreditch Gt Lon 36 H4
Shoreditch Somset 18 H10
Shoreham Kent 37 M8
Shoreham-by-Sea W Susx 24 F9
Shoreswood Nthumb 129 N10
Shorley Hants 22 G9
Shorncote Gloucs 33 K5
Shorne Kent 37 Q6
Shortacross Cnwll 5 M10
Shortbridge E Susx 25 L6
Shortfield Common Surrey 23 M6
Shortgate E Susx 25 L7
Short Heath Birm 58 G6
Shortheath Hants 23 L7
Short Heath Wsall 58 E4
Shortlanesend Cnwll 3 L4
Shortlees E Ayrs 125 L10
Shortstown Bed 61 N11
Shorwell IoW 14 E10
Shoscombe BaNES 20 D3
Shotesham Norfk 65 J2
Shotgate Essex 38 C3
Shotley Suffk 53 M4
Shotley Bridge Dur 112 G10
Shotleyfield Nthumb 112 G10
Shotley Gate Suffk 53 M5
Shotley Street Suffk 53 M4
Shottenden Kent 38 H11
Shottermill Surrey 23 N8
Shottery Warwks 47 N4
Shotteswell Warwks 48 D5
Shottisham Suffk 53 P3
Shottle Derbys 71 Q5
Shottlegate Derbys 71 Q5
Shotton Dur 104 C5
Shotton Dur 104 D3
Shotton Flints 81 L11
Shotton Nthumb 113 K5
Shotton Nthumb 118 F4
Shotton Colliery Dur 104 C2
Shotts N Lans 126 F6
Shotwick Ches W 81 L10
Shougle Moray 157 N6
Shouldham Norfk 75 N9
Shouldham Thorpe Norfk 75 N9
Shoulton Worcs 46 F3
Shover's Green E Susx 25 Q4
Shraleybrook Staffs 70 D5
Shrawardine Shrops 69 L11
Shrawley Worcs 57 Q11
Shreding Green Bucks 36 B4
Shrewley Warwks 59 K11
Shrewsbury Shrops 56 H2
Shrewton Wilts 21 L6
Shripney W Susx 15 P6
Shrivenham Oxon 33 P7
Shropham Norfk 64 D3
Shroton Dorset 12 E2
Shrub End Essex 52 G7
Shucknall Herefs 46 A6
Shudy Camps Cambs 51 P2
Shuna Ag & B 130 F6
Shurdington Gloucs 46 H11
Shurlock Row W & M 35 M10
Shurnock Worcs 47 K2
Shurrery Highld 166 H5
Shurrery Lodge Highld 166 H5
Shurton Somset 18 H6
Shustoke Warwks 59 K6
Shute Devon 9 L4
Shute Devon 10 F5
Shutford Oxon 48 C5
Shut Heath Staffs 70 F10
Shuthonger Gloucs 46 G7
Shutlanger Nhants 49 K5
Shutterton Devon 9 N5
Shutt Green Staffs 58 C3
Shuttington Warwks 59 J3
Shuttlewood Derbys 84 G6
Shuttleworth Bury 89 N7
Siabost W Isls 168 h3
Siadar W Isls 168 i2
Sibbertoft Nhants 60 E4
Sibdon Carwood Shrops 56 G8
Sibford Ferris Oxon 48 C5
Sibford Gower Oxon 48 C5
Sible Hedingham Essex 52 C5
Sibley's Green Essex 51 P5

Siblyback – Southwold 293

Siblyback Cnwll	5	L7
Sibsey Lincs	87	L10
Sibsey Fenside Lincs	87	K10
Sibson Cambs	74	A11
Sibson Leics	72	B10
Sibster Highld	167	P6
Sibthorpe Notts	85	M6
Sibthorpe Notts	85	N11
Sibton Suffk	65	M8
Sicklesmere Suffk	64	B9
Sicklinghall N York	97	N11
Sidbrook Somset	19	J9
Sidbury Devon	10	C6
Sidbury Shrops	57	M7
Sid Cop Barns	91	K9
Sidcot N Som	19	M3
Sidcup Gt Lon	37	L6
Siddick Cumb	100	D4
Siddington Ches E	82	H10
Siddington Gloucs	33	K5
Sidemoor Worcs	58	E10
Sidestrand Norfk	77	K4
Sidford Devon	10	C6
Sidlesham W Susx	15	N7
Sidlesham Common W Susx	15	N7
Sidley E Susx	26	B10
Sidmouth Devon	10	C7
Siefton Shrops	56	H8
Sigford Devon	7	K4
Sigglesthorne E R Yk	99	P11
Sigingstone V Glam	30	C10
Signet Oxon	33	P2
Silchester Hants	22	H2
Sileby Leics	72	G7
Silecroft Cumb	94	C4
Silfield Norfk	64	G2
Silian Cerdgn	43	L4
Silkstead Hants	22	D10
Silkstone Barns	90	H9
Silkstone Common Barns	90	H10
Silk Willoughby Lincs	73	R2
Silloth Cumb	109	P10
Silpho N York	99	K2
Silsden C Brad	96	F11
Silsoe C Beds	50	C3
Silton Dorset	20	E9
Silverburn Mdloth	127	N5
Silverdale Lancs	95	K6
Silverdale Staffs	70	E5
Silver End Essex	52	D8
Silverford Abers	159	J5
Silvergate Norfk	76	H6
Silverlace Green Suffk	65	L9
Silverley's Green Suffk	65	K6
Silverstone Nhants	49	J6
Silver Street Kent	38	E9
Silver Street Somset	19	P8
Silverton Devon	9	N4
Silverwell Cnwll	3	J4
Silvington Shrops	57	L9
Simister Bury	89	N9
Simmondley Derbys	83	M6
Simonburn Nthumb	112	C6
Simonsbath Somset	17	P4
Simonsburrow Devon	18	F11
Simonstone Lancs	89	M4
Simonstone N York	96	C2
Simprim Border	129	L11
Simpson M Keyn	49	N7
Simpson Cross Pembks	40	G7
Sinclair's Hill Border	129	L9
Sinclairston E Ayrs	115	J4
Sinderby N York	97	M4
Sinderhope Nthumb	112	B10
Sinderland Green Traffd	82	F7
Sindlesham Wokham	35	L11
Sinfin C Derb	72	A4
Singleborough Bucks	49	L8
Single Street Gt Lon	37	K9
Singleton Kent	26	H3
Singleton Lancs	88	D3
Singleton W Susx	15	N4
Singlewell Kent	37	Q6
Sinkhurst Green Kent	26	D3
Sinnarhard Abers	150	D5
Sinnington N York	98	E3
Sinope Leics	72	C7
Sinton Worcs	46	F2
Sinton Worcs	46	F2
Sinton Green Worcs	46	F2
Sipson Gt Lon	36	C5
Sirhowy Blae G	30	F2
Sissinghurst Kent	26	C4
Siston S Glos	32	C9
Sitcott Devon	5	P3
Sithney Cnwll	2	G8
Sithney Common Cnwll	2	G8
Sithney Green Cnwll	2	G8
Sittingbourne Kent	38	F9
Six Ashes Shrops	57	P7
Six Bells Blae G	30	H4
Six Hills Leics	72	G6
Sixhills Lincs	86	G3
Six Mile Bottom Cambs	63	J9
Sixmile Cottages Kent	27	K3
Sixpenny Handley Dorset	21	J11
Six Rues Jersey	11	b1
Sizewell Suffk	65	P9
Skaill Ork	169	e6
Skara Brae Ork	169	b5
Skares E Ayrs	115	K4
Skateraw Abers	151	N9
Skateraw E Loth	129	J5
Skeabost Highld	152	G8
Skeeby N York	103	N10
Skeffington Leics	73	J10
Skeffling E R Yk	93	Q7
Skegby Notts	84	G8
Skegby Notts	85	N7
Skegness Lincs	87	Q8
Skelbo Highld	162	H7
Skelbo Street Highld	162	H8
Skelbrooke Donc	91	N8
Skeldyke Lincs	74	F3
Skellingthorpe Lincs	86	B6
Skellorn Green Ches E	83	K8
Skellow Donc	91	N8
Skelmanthorpe Kirk	90	G8
Skelmersdale Lancs	88	F9
Skelmorlie N Ayrs	124	F4
Skelpick Highld	166	B5
Skelston D & G	108	H3
Skelton C York	98	B9
Skelton Cumb	101	M3
Skelton E R Yk	92	C5
Skelton N York	103	L10
Skelton R & Cl	105	J7
Skelton on Ure N York	97	N7
Skelwith Bridge Cumb	101	K10
Skendleby Lincs	87	M7
Skene House Abers	151	K5
Skenfrith Mons	45	P10
Skerne E R Yk	99	L9
Skerray Highld	165	Q4
Skerricha Highld	164	F6
Skerton Lancs	95	K8
Sketchley Leics	59	P6
Sketty Swans	28	H6
Skewen Neath	29	K5
Skewsby N York	98	C6
Skeyton Norfk	77	J6
Skeyton Corner Norfk	77	K6
Skiall Highld	166	H3
Skidbrooke Lincs	87	M2
Skidbrooke North End Lincs	93	R11
Skidby E R Yk	92	H4
Skigersta W Isls	168	k1
Skilgate Somset	18	C9
Skillington Lincs	73	M5
Skinburness Cumb	109	P9
Skinflats Falk	133	Q11
Skinidin Highld	152	C8
Skinners Green W Berk	34	D11
Skinningrove R & Cl	105	K7
Skipness Ag & B	123	R8
Skipper's Bridge D & G	110	G4
Skiprigg Cumb	110	G11
Skipsea E R Yk	99	P10
Skipsea Brough E R Yk	99	P10
Skipton N York	96	E10
Skipton-on-Swale N York	97	N5
Skipwith N York	91	R3
Skirlaugh E R Yk	93	K3
Skirling Border	116	F3
Skirmett Bucks	35	L6
Skirpenbeck E R Yk	98	E9
Skirwith Cumb	102	B4
Skirwith N York	95	Q6
Skirza Highld	167	Q3
Skitby Cumb	110	H7
Skittle Green Bucks	35	L4
Skokholm Island Pembks	40	D10
Skomer Island Pembks	40	D9
Skulamus Highld	145	L3
Skyborry Green Shrops	56	D10
Skye Green Essex	52	E7
Skye of Curr Highld	148	H3
Skyreholme N York	96	G8
Slack Calder	90	B5
Slackcote Oldham	90	B9
Slack Head Cumb	95	K5
Slackholme End Lincs	87	P6
Slacks of Cairnbanno Abers	159	K8
Slad Gloucs	32	G3
Slade Devon	10	C3
Slade Devon	17	J2
Slade Devon	17	Q6
Slade End Oxon	34	G6
Slade Green Gt Lon	37	M5
Slade Heath Staffs	58	D3
Slade Hooton Rothm	84	H3
Sladesbridge Cnwll	4	G7
Slades Green Worcs	46	F8
Slaggyford Nthumb	111	N10
Slaidburn Lancs	95	Q10
Slaithwaite Kirk	90	D8
Slaley Derbys	84	C9
Slaley Nthumb	112	E9
Slamannan Falk	126	F3
Slapton Bucks	49	P10
Slapton Devon	7	L9
Slapton Nhants	48	H5
Slattocks Rochdl	89	P9
Slaugham W Susx	24	G5
Slaughterford Wilts	32	F10
Slawston Leics	60	G2
Sleaford Hants	23	M7
Sleaford Lincs	86	E11
Sleagill Cumb	101	Q7
Sleap Shrops	69	N9
Sleapford Wrekin	70	A11
Sleapshyde Herts	50	E9
Sleasdairidh Highld	162	E7
Slebech Pembks	41	K7
Sledge Green Worcs	46	F8
Sledmere E R Yk	99	J8
Sleetbeck Cumb	111	K5
Sleight Dorset	12	G5
Sleightholme Dur	103	J8
Sleights N York	105	N9
Slepe Dorset	12	F6
Slickly Highld	167	N3
Sliddery N Ayrs	120	H7
Sligachan Highld	144	G2
Sligrachan Ag & B	131	P9
Slimbridge Gloucs	32	D4
Slindon Staffs	70	E8
Slindon W Susx	15	Q5
Slinfold W Susx	24	D4
Sling Gloucs	31	Q3
Sling Gwynd	79	L11
Slingsby N York	98	D6
Slip End C Beds	50	C7
Slip End Herts	50	G3
Slipton Nhants	61	L5
Slitting Mill Staffs	71	J11
Slockavullin Ag & B	130	G8
Sloley Norfk	77	K7
Sloncombe Devon	8	H7
Sloothby Lincs	87	N6
Slough Slough	35	Q9
Slough Green Somset	19	J11
Slough Green W Susx	24	G5
Slumbay Highld	154	A10
Slyfield Green Surrey	23	Q4
Slyne Lancs	95	K7
Smailholm Border	118	B3
Smallbridge Rochdl	89	Q7
Smallbrook Devon	9	L5
Smallbrook Gloucs	31	Q4
Smallburgh Norfk	77	L7
Smallburn E Ayrs	115	N2
Smalldale Derbys	83	N9
Smalldale Derbys	83	Q8
Small Dole W Susx	24	F8
Smalley Derbys	72	C2
Smalley Common Derbys	72	C2
Smalley Green Derbys	72	C2
Smallfield Surrey	24	H2
Small Heath Birm	58	H7
Small Hythe Kent	26	E5
Smallridge Devon	10	G4
Smallthorne C Stke	70	F4
Smallways N York	103	M8
Smallwood Ches E	70	E2
Small Wood Hey Lancs	94	H11
Smallworth Norfk	64	E5
Smannell Hants	22	C5
Smardale Cumb	102	D9
Smarden Kent	26	E3
Smarden Bell Kent	26	E3
Smart's Hill Kent	25	M2
Smeafield Nthumb	119	L3
Smeatharpe Devon	10	D2
Smeeth Kent	27	J4
Smeeton Westerby Leics	60	E2
Smelthouses N York	97	J8
Smerral Highld	167	L10
Smestow Staffs	58	C6
Smethwick Sandw	58	F7
Smethwick Green Ches E	70	E2
Smirisary Highld	138	A2
Smisby Derbys	72	A7
Smith End Green Worcs	46	E4
Smithfield Cumb	110	H7
Smith Green Lancs	95	K9
Smithies Barns	91	J9
Smithincott Devon	9	Q2
Smith's End Herts	51	K3
Smith's Green Essex	51	N6
Smith's Green Essex	51	Q2
Smithstown Highld	160	B11
Smithton Highld	156	C8
Smithy Bridge Rochdl	89	Q7
Smithy Green Ches E	82	F10
Smithy Green Stockp	83	J7
Smithy Houses Derbys	84	E11
Smockington Leics	59	Q7
Smoo Highld	165	K3
Smythe's Green Essex	52	F8
Snade D & G	108	H3
Snailbeach Shrops	56	F4
Snailwell Cambs	63	K7
Snainton N York	99	J4
Snaith E R Yk	91	Q6
Snake Pass Inn Derbys	83	P6
Snape N York	97	L4
Snape Suffk	65	M10
Snape Green Lancs	88	D8
Snape Street Suffk	65	M10
Snaresbrook Gt Lon	37	K3
Snarestone Leics	72	A9
Snarford Lincs	86	D4
Snargate Kent	26	G6
Snave Kent	26	H6
Sneachill Worcs	46	H4
Snead Powys	56	E6
Sneath Common Norfk	64	H4
Sneaton N York	105	N9
Sneatonthorpe N York	105	P9
Snelland Lincs	86	E4
Snelson Ches E	82	H10
Snelston Derbys	71	M6
Snetterton Norfk	64	D3
Snettisham Norfk	75	N4
Snibston Leics	72	C8
Snig's End Gloucs	46	E9
Snitter Nthumb	119	K10
Snitterby Lincs	86	C2
Snitterfield Warwks	47	P3
Snitterton Derbys	84	C8
Snitton Shrops	57	K9
Snoadhill Kent	26	F3
Snodhill Herefs	45	L6
Snodland Kent	38	B9
Snoll Hatch Kent	37	Q11
Snowden Hill Barns	90	H10
Snowdon Gwynd	67	L4
Snowdon Kent	39	M11
Snowdonia National Park	67	Q9
Snow End Herts	51	K4
Snowshill Gloucs	47	L8
Snow Street Norfk	64	F5
Soake Hants	15	J4
Soar Cardif	30	E8
Soar Devon	7	J11
Soar Powys	44	D8
Soay Highld	144	F5
Soberton Hants	22	H11
Soberton Heath Hants	14	H4
Sockbridge Cumb	101	N5
Sockburn Darltn	104	B9
Sodom Denbgs	80	F10
Sodylt Bank Shrops	69	K7
Soham Cambs	63	J6
Soham Cotes Cambs	63	J5
Solas W Isls	168	d10
Solbury Pembks	40	G8
Soldon Devon	16	E9
Soldon Cross Devon	16	E9
Soldridge Hants	23	J7
Sole Street Kent	27	J2
Sole Street Kent	37	Q7
Solihull Solhll	59	J9
Sollers Dilwyn Herefs	45	N3
Sollers Hope Herefs	46	B8
Sollom Lancs	88	F7
Solva Pembks	40	F6
Solwaybank D & G	110	F5
Somerby Leics	73	K8
Somerby Lincs	93	J9
Somercotes Derbys	84	F10
Somerford BCP	13	L6
Somerford Keynes Gloucs	33	K5
Somerley W Susx	15	M7
Somerleyton Suffk	65	P2
Somersal Herbert Derbys	71	L7
Somersby Lincs	87	K6
Somersham Cambs	62	E5
Somersham Suffk	53	J2
Somerton Oxon	48	E9
Somerton Somset	19	N9
Somerton Suffk	63	P10
Somerwood Shrops	57	K2
Sompting W Susx	24	E9
Sompting Abbotts W Susx	24	E9
Sonning Wokham	35	L9
Sonning Common Oxon	35	K8
Sonning Eye Oxon	35	K9
Sontley Wrexhm	69	K5
Sopley Hants	13	L5
Sopwell Herts	50	E9
Sopworth Wilts	32	F7
Sorbie D & G	107	M8
Sordale Highld	167	K4
Sorisdale Ag & B	136	H3
Sorn E Ayrs	115	L2
Sornhill E Ayrs	125	N11
Sortat Highld	167	N4
Sotby Lincs	86	H5
Sots Hole Lincs	86	F8
Sotterley Suffk	65	N5
Soughton Flints	81	J11
Soulbury Bucks	49	N9
Soulby Cumb	101	N5
Soulby Cumb	102	D8
Souldern Oxon	48	F8
Souldrop Bed	61	L8
Sound Ches E	70	A5
Sound Muir Moray	157	R7
Soundwell S Glos	32	C9
Sourton Devon	8	D6
Soutergate Cumb	94	E4
South Acre Norfk	75	R8
South Alkham Kent	27	M3
Southall Gt Lon	36	D5
South Allington Devon	7	K11
South Alloa Falk	133	P9
Southam Gloucs	47	J9
Southam Warwks	48	D2
South Ambersham W Susx	23	P10
Southampton C Sotn	14	D4
Southampton Airport Hants	22	E11
South Anston Rothm	84	H4
South Ascot W & M	35	P11
South Ashford Kent	26	H3
South Baddesley Hants	14	C7
South Ballachulish Highld	139	K6
South Bank C York	98	B10
South Bank R & Cl	104	F6
South Barrow Somset	20	B9
South Beddington Gt Lon	36	G8
South Beer Cnwll	5	N3
South Benfleet Essex	38	C4
South Bockhampton BCP	13	L5
Southborough Gt Lon	37	K7
Southborough Kent	25	N2
Southbourne BCP	13	K6
Southbourne W Susx	15	L5
South Bowood Dorset	11	J5
South Bramwith Donc	91	Q8
South Brent Devon	6	H6
South Brewham Somset	20	D7
South Broomhill Nthumb	119	P11
Southburgh Norfk	76	E10
South Burlingham Norfk	77	M10
Southburn E R Yk	99	K10
South Cadbury Somset	20	B9
South Carlton Lincs	86	B5
South Carlton Notts	85	J4
South Cave E R Yk	92	F4
South Cerney Gloucs	33	K5
South Chailey E Susx	25	J7
South Chard Somset	10	G3
South Charlton Nthumb	119	N6
South Cheriton Somset	20	C10
South Church Dur	103	P5
Southchurch Sthend	38	F4
South Cleatlam Dur	103	M7
South Cliffe E R Yk	92	E3
South Clifton Notts	85	P6
South Cockerington Lincs	87	L3
South Cornelly Brdgnd	29	M8
Southcott Cnwll	5	K2
Southcott Devon	8	D5
Southcott Devon	9	J8
Southcott Devon	16	G8
Southcott Wilts	21	N3
Southcourt Bucks	35	M2
South Cove Suffk	65	P5
South Creake Norfk	76	B4
South Crosland Kirk	90	E8
South Croxton Leics	72	H8
South Dalton E R Yk	99	K11
South Darenth Kent	37	N7
South Dell W Isls	168	j1
South Downs National Park	25	J9
South Duffield N York	92	A4
South Earlswood Surrey	36	G11
Southease E Susx	25	K9
South Elkington Lincs	87	J3
South Elmsall Wakefd	91	M8
Southend Ag & B	120	C10
South End E R Yk	93	Q7
South End Hants	21	M11
South End Herefs	46	D6
South End N Linc	93	K6
South End Norfk	64	D3
Southend Wilts	33	N10
Southend Airport Essex	38	E4
Southend-on-Sea Sthend	38	E4
Southernby Cumb	101	L3
Southernden Kent	26	E2
Southerndown V Glam	29	N10
Southerness D & G	109	L10
South Erradale Highld	153	N3
Southerton Devon	10	B6
Southery Norfk	63	K2
South Fambridge Essex	38	E3
South Fawley W Berk	34	C8
South Ferriby N Linc	92	G6
South Field E R Yk	92	H5
Southfield Falk	126	E3
Southfleet Kent	37	P6
Southgate Gt Lon	36	G2
Southgate Norfk	75	N4
Southgate Norfk	76	B4
Southgate Norfk	76	G7
Southgate Swans	28	G7
South Godstone Surrey	37	J11
South Gorley Hants	13	L2
South Gosforth N u Ty	113	K7
South Green Essex	37	Q2
South Green Essex	52	H8
South Green Kent	38	E9
South Green Norfk	76	F9
South Green Suffk	64	H6
South Gyle C Edin	127	M3
South Hanningfield Essex	38	B2
South Harting W Susx	23	L11
South Hayling Hants	15	K7
South Hazelrigg Nthumb	119	L4
South Heath Bucks	35	P4
South Heighton E Susx	25	K10
South Hetton Dur	113	N11
South Hiendley Wakefd	91	K8
South Hill Cnwll	5	N7
South Hill Somset	19	N9
South Hinksey Oxon	34	F4
South Hole Devon	16	C7
South Holmwood Surrey	24	E2
South Hornchurch Gt Lon	37	M4
South Horrington Somset	19	Q5
South Huish Devon	6	H10
South Hykeham Lincs	86	B8
South Hylton Sundld	113	N9
Southill C Beds	50	E2
Southington Hants	22	F5
South Kelsey Lincs	92	H11
South Kessock Highld	156	B8
South Killingholme N Linc	93	K7
South Kilvington N York	97	P4
South Kilworth Leics	60	D4
South Kirkby Wakefd	91	L8
South Knighton Devon	7	L4
South Kyme Lincs	86	G11
Southleigh Devon	10	E6
South Leigh Oxon	34	C3
South Leverton Notts	85	N4
South Littleton Worcs	47	L5
South Lopham Norfk	64	E5
South Luffenham Rutlnd	73	N10
South Lynn Norfk	75	M7
South Malling E Susx	25	K8
South Marston Swindn	33	N7
South Merstham Surrey	36	G10
South Middleton Nthumb	119	J6
South Milford N York	91	M4
South Milton Devon	6	J10
South Mimms Herts	50	F10
South Mimms Services Herts	50	F10
Southminster Essex	38	G2
South Molton Devon	17	N6
South Moor Dur	113	J10
Southmoor Oxon	34	C5
South Moreton Oxon	34	G7
Southmuir Angus	142	F7
South Mundham W Susx	15	N6
South Muskham Notts	85	N9
South Newbald E R Yk	92	F3
South Newington Oxon	48	D8
South Newton Wilts	21	L8
South Normanton Derbys	84	F9
South Norwood Gt Lon	36	H7
South Nutfield Surrey	36	H11
South Ockendon Thurr	37	N4
Southoe Cambs	61	Q8
Southolt Suffk	64	H8
South Ormsby Lincs	87	L5
Southorpe C Pete	74	A10
South Ossett Wakefd	90	H7
South Otterington N York	97	N3
Southover Dorset	11	N6
Southover E Susx	25	Q5
South Owersby Lincs	86	E2
Southowram Calder	90	E6
South Park Surrey	36	F11
South Perrott Dorset	11	K3
South Petherton Somset	19	M11
South Petherwin Cnwll	5	N5
South Pickenham Norfk	76	B11
South Pill Cnwll	5	Q10
South Pool Devon	7	K10
South Poorton Dorset	11	L5
Southport Sefton	88	C7
South Queensferry C Edin	127	L2
South Radworthy Devon	17	N5
South Rauceby Lincs	86	D11
South Raynham Norfk	76	B7
South Reddish Stockp	83	J6
Southrepps Norfk	77	K4
South Reston Lincs	87	M4
Southrey Lincs	86	F7
South Ronaldsay Ork	169	d8
Southrop Gloucs	33	N4
Southrope Hants	23	J6
South Runcton Norfk	75	M9
South Scarle Notts	85	P8
Southsea C Port	15	J7
Southsea Wrexhm	69	K4
South Shian Ag & B	138	G9
South Shields S Tyne	113	N7
South Shore Bpool	88	C4
Southside Dur	103	M5
South Somercotes Lincs	87	M2
South Stainley N York	97	M8
South Stifford Thurr	37	N5
South Stoke BaNES	20	D2
South Stoke Oxon	34	G8
South Stoke W Susx	24	B9
South Stour Kent	26	H4
South Street Kent	37	P8
South Street Kent	39	J10
South Street Kent	39	K8
South Tarbrax S Lans	127	J7
South Tawton Devon	8	G6
South Tehidy Cnwll	2	H5
South Thoresby Lincs	87	M5
South Thorpe Dur	103	M8
South Town Hants	23	J7
Southtown Norfk	77	Q10
Southtown Somset	19	K11
South Uist W Isls	168	d14
Southwaite Cumb	110	H11
Southwaite Services Cumb	110	H11
South Walsham Norfk	77	M9
Southwark Gt Lon	36	H5
South Warnborough Hants	23	K5
Southwater W Susx	24	E5
Southwater Street W Susx	24	E5
Southway C Plym	6	D6
Southway Somset	19	P6
South Weald Essex	37	N2
Southwell Dorset	11	P10
Southwell Notts	85	L10
South Weston Oxon	35	K5
South Wheatley Cnwll	5	L3
South Wheatley Notts	85	N3
Southwick Hants	14	H5
Southwick Nhants	61	M2
Southwick Somset	19	L5
Southwick Sundld	113	N9
Southwick W Susx	24	F9
Southwick Wilts	20	F3
South Widcombe BaNES	19	Q3
South Wigston Leics	72	F11
South Willesborough Kent	26	H3
South Willingham Lincs	86	G4
South Wingate Dur	104	D4
South Wingfield Derbys	84	E9
South Witham Lincs	73	N7
Southwold Suffk	65	Q6

South Wonston Hants....22 E7
Southwood Norfk....77 M10
Southwood Somset....19 Q8
South Woodham Ferrers Essex....38 D2
South Wootton Norfk....75 M6
South Wraxall Wilts....20 F2
South Zeal Devon....8 G6
Sovereign Harbour E Susx....25 P10
Sowerby Calder....90 C6
Sowerby N York....97 P4
Sowerby Bridge Calder....90 D6
Sowerby Row Cumb....101 L2
Sower Carr Lancs....88 D2
Sowerhill Somset....18 A10
Sowhill Torfn....31 J4
Sowley Green Suffk....63 M10
Sowood Calder....90 D7
Sowton Devon....6 E5
Sowton Devon....9 N6
Soyland Town Calder....90 C6
Spa Common Norfk....77 K5
Spain's End Essex....51 Q3
Spalding Lincs....74 D6
Spaldington E R Yk....92 C4
Spaldwick Cambs....61 P6
Spalford Notts....85 P7
Spanby Lincs....74 A3
Spanish Green Hants....23 J3
Sparham Norfk....76 F8
Sparhamill Norfk....76 F8
Spark Bridge Cumb....94 G4
Sparket Cumb....101 M5
Sparkford Somset....20 B9
Sparkhill Birm....58 H8
Sparkwell Devon....6 F7
Sparrow Green Norfk....76 C9
Sparrowpit Derbys....83 N8
Sparrows Green E Susx....25 P4
Sparsholt Hants....22 D8
Sparsholt Oxon....34 B7
Spartylea Nthumb....112 C11
Spath Staffs....71 K7
Spaunton N York....98 E3
Spaxton Somset....18 H7
Spean Bridge Highld....146 G11
Spear Hill W Susx....24 D7
Spearywell Hants....22 B9
Speen Bucks....35 M5
Speen W Berk....34 E11
Speeton N York....99 P6
Speke Lpool....81 N8
Speldhurst Kent....25 N2
Spellbrook Herts....51 L7
Spelmonden Kent....26 B4
Spelsbury Oxon....48 B10
Spen Kirk....90 F5
Spencers Wood Wokham....35 K11
Spen Green Ches E....70 E2
Spennithorne N York....96 H3
Spennymoor Dur....103 Q4
Spernall Warwks....47 L2
Spetchley Worcs....46 G4
Spetisbury Dorset....12 F4
Spexhall Suffk....65 M5
Spey Bay Moray....157 R4
Speybridge Highld....149 J2
Speyview Moray....157 P9
Spilsby Lincs....87 M7
Spindlestone Nthumb....119 N4
Spinkhill Derbys....84 G5
Spinningdale Highld....162 F9
Spion Kop Notts....85 J7
Spirthill Wilts....33 J9
Spital Wirral....81 L8
Spital Hill Donc....85 K2
Spital in the Street Lincs....86 C2
Spithurst E Susx....25 K7
Spittal E Loth....128 D4
Spittal E R Yk....98 F10
Spittal Highld....167 L6
Spittal Nthumb....129 Q9
Spittal Pembks....41 J6
Spittalfield P & K....141 R9
Spittal of Glenmuick Abers....149 Q10
Spittal of Glenshee P & K....141 R4
Spittal-on-Rule Border....118 A7
Spixworth Norfk....77 J8
Splatt Cnwll....4 E6
Splatt Cnwll....5 L4
Splatt Cnwll....8 F3
Splayne's Green E Susx....25 K6
Splott Cardif....30 H9
Spofforth N York....97 N10
Spondon C Derb....72 C3
Spon Green Flints....69 J2
Spooner Row Norfk....64 F2
Sporle Norfk....76 A9
Spott E Loth....128 H4
Spottiswoode Border....128 G10
Spratton Nhants....60 F7
Spreakley Surrey....23 M6
Spreyton Devon....8 G5
Spriddlestone Devon....6 E8
Spridlington Lincs....86 D4
Springburn C Glas....125 Q4
Springfield D & G....110 F7
Springfield Essex....52 B10
Springfield Fife....135 J5
Springhill Staffs....58 E4
Springhill Staffs....58 G3
Springholm D & G....108 H6
Springside N Ayrs....125 K10
Springthorpe Lincs....85 Q3
Spring Vale Barns....90 H10
Springwell Sundld....113 L9
Sproatley E R Yk....93 L4
Sproston Green Ches W....82 F11
Sprotbrough Donc....91 N10
Sproughton Suffk....53 K3
Sprouston Border....118 E3
Sprowston Norfk....77 K9
Sproxton Leics....73 M6
Sproxton N York....98 C4
Spunhill Shrops....69 M8
Spurstow Ches E....69 Q3
Spyway Dorset....11 L6
Square and Compass Pembks....40 F4
Stableford Shrops....57 P5
Stableford Staffs....70 E7
Stacey Bank Sheff....84 C2
Stackhouse N York....96 B7
Stackpole Pembks....41 J11
Stackpole Elidor Pembks....41 J11

Stacksford Norfk....64 F3
Stacksteads Lancs....89 P6
Staddiscombe C Plym....6 E8
Staddlethorpe E R Yk....92 D5
Staden Derbys....83 N10
Stadhampton Oxon....34 H5
Stadhlaigearraidh W Isls....168 c14
Staffield Cumb....101 P2
Staffin Highld....152 H4
Stafford Staffs....70 G10
Stafford Services (northbound) Staffs....70 F8
Stafford Services (southbound) Staffs....70 F8
Stagsden Bed....49 Q5
Stainborough Barns....91 J10
Stainburn Cumb....100 D5
Stainburn N York....97 L11
Stainby Lincs....73 N6
Staincross Barns....91 J8
Staindrop Dur....103 M6
Staines-upon-Thames Surrey....36 B6
Stainfield Lincs....74 A6
Stainfield Lincs....86 F6
Stainforth Donc....91 Q8
Stainforth N York....96 B7
Staining Lancs....88 C3
Stainland Calder....90 D7
Stainsacre N York....105 P9
Stainsby Derbys....84 G7
Stainton Cumb....95 L3
Stainton Cumb....101 N5
Stainton Cumb....110 G9
Stainton Donc....85 J2
Stainton Dur....103 L7
Stainton Middsb....104 E8
Stainton N York....103 M11
Stainton by Langworth Lincs....86 E5
Staintondale N York....105 Q11
Stainton le Vale Lincs....86 G2
Stainton with Adgarley Cumb....94 E6
Stair Cumb....100 H6
Stair E Ayrs....114 H3
Stairfoot Barns....91 K9
Stairhaven D & G....106 H7
Staithes N York....105 L7
Stakeford Nthumb....113 L3
Stake Pool Lancs....95 J11
Stakes Hants....15 J5
Stalbridge Dorset....20 D11
Stalbridge Weston Dorset....20 D11
Stalham Norfk....77 M6
Stalham Green Norfk....77 M7
Stalisfield Green Kent....38 G11
Stalland Common Norfk....64 E2
Stallen Dorset....20 B11
Stallingborough NE Lin....93 L8
Stalling Busk N York....96 D3
Stallington Staffs....70 G7
Stalmine Lancs....94 H11
Stalmine Moss Side Lancs....94 H11
Stalybridge Tamesd....83 L5
Stambourne Essex....52 B4
Stambourne Green Essex....51 Q3
Stamford Lincs....73 Q9
Stamford Nthumb....119 P7
Stamford Bridge Ches W....81 P11
Stamford Bridge E R Yk....98 E9
Stamfordham Nthumb....112 G6
Stamford Hill Gt Lon....36 H3
Stanah Cumb....101 L7
Stanborough Herts....50 F8
Stanbridge C Beds....49 Q10
Stanbridge Dorset....12 H4
Stanbury C Brad....90 C3
Stand Bury....89 M9
Stand N Lans....126 D4
Standburn Falk....126 G3
Standeford Staffs....58 D3
Standen Kent....26 E3
Standen Street Kent....26 D5
Standerwick Somset....20 F4
Standford Hants....23 M8
Standingstone Cumb....100 E4
Standish Gloucs....32 E3
Standish Wigan....88 H8
Standish Lower Ground Wigan....88 H9
Standlake Oxon....34 C4
Standon Hants....22 D9
Standon Herts....51 J6
Standon Staffs....70 E7
Standon Green End Herts....51 J7
Standwell Green Suffk....64 G8
Stane N Lans....126 F6
Stanfield Norfk....76 C7
Stanford C Beds....50 E2
Stanford Kent....27 K4
Stanford Shrops....56 E11
Stanford Bishop Herefs....46 C4
Stanford Bridge Worcs....57 N11
Stanford Bridge Wrekin....70 C10
Stanford Dingley W Berk....34 G10
Stanford in the Vale Oxon....34 B6
Stanford le Hope Thurr....37 Q4
Stanford on Avon Nhants....60 C5
Stanford on Soar Notts....72 E6
Stanford on Teme Worcs....57 N11
Stanford Rivers Essex....51 N10
Stanfree Derbys....84 G6
Stanghow R & Cl....105 J7
Stanground C Pete....74 D11
Stanhill Lancs....89 L5
Stanhoe Norfk....75 R3
Stanhope Border....116 G5
Stanhope Dur....103 J3
Stanhope Kent....26 H3
Stanhope Bretby Derbys....71 P10
Stanion Nhants....61 K3
Stanklin Worcs....58 C10
Stanley Derbys....72 C2
Stanley Dur....113 J10
Stanley Notts....84 G8
Stanley P & K....141 R11
Stanley Shrops....57 N8
Stanley Staffs....70 G4
Stanley Staffs....71 J3
Stanley Wakefd....91 J6
Stanley Common Derbys....72 C2
Stanley Crook Dur....103 N3
Stanley Ferry Wakefd....91 K6
Stanley Gate Lancs....88 E9
Stanley Moor Staffs....70 G4

Stanley Pontlarge Gloucs....47 K8
Stanmer Br & H....24 H9
Stanmore Gt Lon....36 E2
Stanmore Hants....22 E9
Stanmore W Berk....34 E9
Stannersburn Nthumb....111 P3
Stanningfield Suffk....64 B10
Stanningley Leeds....90 G4
Stannington Nthumb....113 K5
Stannington Sheff....84 C3
Stannington Station Nthumb....113 K4
Stansbatch Herefs....45 L2
Stansfield Suffk....63 N10
Stanshope Staffs....71 L4
Stanstead Suffk....52 D2
Stanstead Abbotts Herts....51 J8
Stansted Kent....37 P8
Stansted Airport Essex....51 N6
Stansted Mountfitchet Essex....51 M5
Stanton Derbys....71 P11
Stanton Gloucs....47 L8
Stanton Mons....45 L10
Stanton Nthumb....112 H2
Stanton Staffs....71 L5
Stanton Suffk....64 D7
Stanton by Bridge Derbys....72 B5
Stanton by Dale Derbys....72 C3
Stanton Drew BaNES....19 Q2
Stanton Fitzwarren Swindn....33 N4
Stanton Harcourt Oxon....34 D3
Stanton Hill Notts....84 G8
Stanton in Peak Derbys....84 B8
Stanton Lacy Shrops....56 H9
Stanton Lees Derbys....84 C8
Stanton Long Shrops....57 K6
Stanton-on-the-Wolds Notts....72 G4
Stanton Prior BaNES....20 C2
Stanton St Bernard Wilts....21 L2
Stanton St John Oxon....34 G3
Stanton St Quintin Wilts....32 H9
Stanton Street Suffk....64 D8
Stanton under Bardon Leics....72 D8
Stanton upon Hine Heath Shrops....69 Q10
Stanton Wick BaNES....20 B2
Stantway Gloucs....32 D2
Stanwardine in the Field Shrops....69 M10
Stanwardine in the Wood Shrops....69 M9
Stanway Essex....52 F6
Stanway Gloucs....47 L8
Stanway Green Essex....52 G7
Stanway Green Suffk....65 J7
Stanwell Surrey....36 C6
Stanwell Moor Surrey....36 B6
Stanwick Nhants....61 L6
Stanwick St John N York....103 N8
Stanwix Cumb....110 H9
Staoinebrig W Isls....168 c14
Stape N York....98 F12
Stapehill Dorset....13 J4
Stapeley Ches E....70 B5
Stapenhill Staffs....71 P10
Staple Kent....39 N10
Staple Cross Devon....18 D10
Staplecross E Susx....26 C7
Staplefield W Susx....24 G5
Staple Fitzpaine Somset....19 J11
Stapleford Cambs....62 G10
Stapleford Herts....50 H7
Stapleford Leics....73 L7
Stapleford Lincs....85 Q9
Stapleford Notts....72 D3
Stapleford Wilts....21 L7
Stapleford Abbotts Essex....37 M2
Stapleford Tawney Essex....51 M11
Staplegrove Somset....18 H9
Staplehay Somset....18 H10
Staple Hill Worcs....58 D11
Staplehurst Kent....26 C3
Staplers IoW....14 F9
Staplestreet Kent....39 J9
Stapleton Cumb....111 K6
Stapleton Herefs....56 E11
Stapleton Leics....72 C11
Stapleton N York....103 Q8
Stapleton Shrops....56 H4
Stapleton Somset....19 N10
Stapley Somset....10 D2
Staploe Bed....61 Q8
Staplow Herefs....46 C6
Star Fife....135 J7
Star IoA....79 J10
Star Pembks....41 P4
Star Somset....19 M3
Starbeck N York....97 M9
Starbotton N York....96 E6
Starcross Devon....9 N4
Stareton Warwks....59 M10
Starkholmes Derbys....84 D9
Starlings Green Essex....51 L4
Starr's Green E Susx....26 C8
Starston Norfk....65 J5
Start Devon....7 L10
Startforth Dur....103 K7
Startley Wilts....32 H8
Statenborough Kent....39 P10
Statham Warrtn....82 E7
Stathe Somset....19 L9
Stathern Leics....73 K4
Station Town Dur....104 D3
Staughton Green Cambs....61 P7
Staughton Highway Cambs....61 P8
Staunton Gloucs....31 Q2
Staunton Gloucs....32 D2
Staunton in the Vale Notts....73 L2
Staunton on Arrow Herefs....45 M2
Staunton on Wye Herefs....45 M6
Staveley Cumb....101 N11
Staveley Derbys....84 F6
Staveley N York....97 M8
Staveley-in-Cartmel Cumb....94 H3
Staverton Devon....7 K6
Staverton Gloucs....46 G10
Staverton Nhants....60 B8
Staverton Wilts....20 G2
Staverton Bridge Gloucs....46 G10
Stawell Somset....19 L8
Stawley Somset....18 E10
Staxigoe Highld....167 Q6
Staxton N York....99 L5
Staylittle Cerdgn....54 E7

Staylittle Powys....55 K6
Staynall Lancs....88 D2
Staythorpe Notts....85 N10
Stead C Brad....96 H11
Stean N York....96 G6
Stearsby N York....98 C6
Steart Somset....19 J5
Stebbing Essex....51 Q6
Stebbing Green Essex....51 Q6
Stechford Birm....58 H7
Stede Quarter Kent....26 E4
Stedham W Susx....23 N10
Steel Nthumb....112 D9
Steel Cross E Susx....25 M4
Steelend Fife....134 C9
Steele Road Border....111 K2
Steel Green Cumb....94 D5
Steel Heath Shrops....69 P7
Steen's Bridge Herefs....45 Q3
Steep Hants....23 K9
Steephill IoW....14 F11
Steep Lane Calder....90 C6
Steeple Dorset....12 F8
Steeple Essex....52 F11
Steeple Ashton Wilts....20 H3
Steeple Aston Oxon....48 E9
Steeple Barton Oxon....48 D10
Steeple Bumpstead Essex....51 Q2
Steeple Claydon Bucks....49 K9
Steeple Gidding Cambs....61 P4
Steeple Langford Wilts....21 L7
Steeple Morden Cambs....50 G2
Steep Marsh Hants....23 L9
Steeton C Brad....90 C2
Stein Highld....152 D6
Stella Gatesd....113 J8
Stelling Minnis Kent....27 K2
Stembridge Somset....19 M10
Stenalees Cnwll....4 G10
Stenhouse D & G....115 R9
Stenhousemuir Falk....133 P11
Stenigot Lincs....86 H4
Stenson Fields Derbys....72 A4
Stenton E Loth....128 G5
Steornabhagh W Isls....168 j4
Stepaside Pembks....41 M9
Stepford D & G....109 J4
Stepney Gt Lon....37 J4
Stepping Hill Stockp....83 K7
Steppingley C Beds....50 B3
Stepps N Lans....126 B4
Sternfield Suffk....65 M9
Stert Wilts....21 K3
Stetchworth Cambs....63 K9
Stevenage Herts....50 F5
Steven's Crouch E Susx....26 B8
Steventon Hants....22 H5
Steventon Oxon....34 E6
Steventon End Essex....51 N2
Stevington Bed....49 Q4
Stewartby Bed....50 B2
Stewartfield S Lans....125 Q6
Stewarton Ag & B....120 C8
Stewarton E Ayrs....125 L8
Stewkley Bucks....49 N9
Stewley Somset....19 K11
Stewton Lincs....87 L3
Steyne Cross IoW....14 H9
Steyning W Susx....24 E8
Steynton Pembks....40 H9
Stibb Cnwll....16 C9
Stibbard Norfk....76 D6
Stibb Cross Devon....16 G9
Stibb Green Wilts....21 P2
Stibbington Cambs....74 A11
Stichill Border....118 D3
Sticker Cnwll....3 P3
Stickford Lincs....87 L8
Sticklepath Devon....8 F6
Sticklepath Somset....18 D7
Stickling Green Essex....51 L4
Stickney Lincs....87 K9
Stiffkey Norfk....76 D3
Stifford Clays Thurr....37 P4
Stifford's Bridge Herefs....46 D5
Stiff Street Kent....38 E9
Stile Bridge Kent....26 C2
Stileway Somset....19 N6
Stilligarry W Isls....168 c14
Stillingfleet N York....91 P2
Stillington N York....98 B7
Stillington S on T....104 C6
Stilton Cambs....61 Q3
Stinchcombe Gloucs....32 D5
Stinsford Dorset....11 Q6
Stiperstones Shrops....56 F4
Stirchley Birm....58 G8
Stirchley Wrekin....57 M3
Stirling Abers....159 R9
Stirling Stirlg....133 M9
Stirling Castle Stirlg....133 M9
Stirling Services Stirlg....133 N10
Stirtloe Cambs....61 Q7
Stirton N York....96 E10
Stisted Essex....52 D7
Stitchcombe Wilts....33 P11
Stithians Cnwll....3 J6
Stivichall Covtry....59 M9
Stixwould Lincs....86 G8
St Michaels Fife....135 L3
Stoak Ches W....81 N10
Stobo Border....116 H3
Stoborough Dorset....12 F7
Stoborough Green Dorset....12 F7
Stobs Castle Border....117 Q9
Stobswood Nthumb....119 P11
Stock Essex....51 Q11
Stock N Som....19 M3
Stockbridge Hants....22 C7
Stockbriggs S Lans....126 D10
Stockbury Kent....38 D9
Stockcross W Berk....34 D11
Stockdalewath Cumb....110 G11
Stocker's Hill Kent....38 G11
Stockerston Leics....73 L11
Stock Green Worcs....47 J3
Stocking Herefs....46 B8
Stockingford Warwks....59 M6
Stocking Pelham Herts....51 L5
Stockland Devon....10 D4
Stockland Bristol Somset....18 H6
Stockland Green Kent....25 N2
Stockleigh English Devon....9 L3

Stockleigh Pomeroy Devon....9 L4
Stockley Wilts....33 J11
Stockley Hill Herefs....45 M7
Stocklinch Somset....19 L11
Stockmoor Herefs....45 M4
Stockport Stockp....83 J6
Stocksbridge Sheff....90 H11
Stocksfield Nthumb....112 G8
Stockton Herefs....45 Q2
Stockton Norfk....65 M3
Stockton Shrops....56 D4
Stockton Shrops....57 N5
Stockton Warwks....48 D2
Stockton Wilts....21 J7
Stockton Wrekin....70 D11
Stockton Brook Staffs....70 G4
Stockton Heath Warrtn....82 D7
Stockton-on-Tees S on T....104 D7
Stockton on Teme Worcs....57 N11
Stockton on the Forest C York....98 D9
Stockwell Gloucs....32 H2
Stockwell End Wolves....58 C4
Stockwell Heath Staffs....71 K10
Stockwood Bristl....32 B11
Stockwood Dorset....11 M3
Stock Wood Worcs....47 K3
Stodday Lancs....95 K9
Stodmarsh Kent....39 M9
Stody Norfk....76 F4
Stoer Highld....164 B11
Stoford Somset....11 M2
Stoford Wilts....21 L7
Stogumber Somset....18 E7
Stogursey Somset....18 H6
Stoke Covtry....59 N9
Stoke Devon....16 C7
Stoke Hants....15 K6
Stoke Hants....22 D4
Stoke Medway....38 D7
Stoke Abbott Dorset....11 K4
Stoke Albany Nhants....60 H3
Stoke Ash Suffk....64 G7
Stoke Bardolph Notts....72 G2
Stoke Bliss Worcs....46 C2
Stoke Bruerne Nhants....49 K5
Stoke-by-Clare Suffk....52 B3
Stoke-by-Nayland Suffk....52 G4
Stoke Canon Devon....9 M5
Stoke Charity Hants....22 E7
Stoke Climsland Cnwll....5 P7
Stoke Cross Herefs....46 B4
Stoke D'Abernon Surrey....36 D9
Stoke Doyle Nhants....61 M3
Stoke Dry Rutlnd....73 M11
Stoke Edith Herefs....46 B6
Stoke End Warwks....59 J5
Stoke Farthing Wilts....21 L9
Stoke Ferry Norfk....75 P10
Stoke Fleming Devon....7 M9
Stokeford Dorset....12 E7
Stoke Gabriel Devon....7 M7
Stoke Gifford S Glos....32 B9
Stoke Golding Leics....72 B11
Stoke Goldington M Keyn....49 M5
Stoke Green Bucks....35 Q8
Stokeham Notts....85 N5
Stoke Hammond Bucks....49 N9
Stoke Heath Shrops....70 B9
Stoke Heath Worcs....58 D11
Stoke Holy Cross Norfk....77 J11
Stokeinteignhead Devon....7 N4
Stoke Lacy Herefs....46 B5
Stoke Lyne Oxon....48 G9
Stoke Mandeville Bucks....35 M2
Stokenchurch Bucks....35 L5
Stoke Newington Gt Lon....36 H3
Stokenham Devon....7 L10
Stoke-on-Trent C Stke....70 F5
Stoke Orchard Gloucs....46 H9
Stoke Poges Bucks....35 Q8
Stoke Pound Worcs....58 E11
Stoke Prior Herefs....45 Q3
Stoke Prior Worcs....58 D11
Stoke Rivers Devon....17 L4
Stoke Rochford Lincs....73 N5
Stoke Row Oxon....35 J8
Stoke St Gregory Somset....19 K9
Stoke St Mary Somset....19 J10
Stoke St Michael Somset....20 C5
Stoke St Milborough Shrops....57 K8
Stokesay Shrops....56 G8
Stokesby Norfk....77 N9
Stokesley N York....104 F9
Stoke sub Hamdon Somset....19 N11
Stoke Talmage Oxon....35 J5
Stoke Trister Somset....20 D9
Stoke upon Tern Shrops....70 A9
Stoke-upon-Trent C Stke....70 F5
Stoke Wake Dorset....12 C3
Stoke Wharf Worcs....58 E11
Stolford Somset....18 H5
Stondon Massey Essex....51 N10
Stone Bucks....35 L2
Stone Gloucs....32 C5
Stone Kent....37 N6
Stone Rothm....85 J3
Stone Somset....19 Q8
Stone Staffs....70 G8
Stone Worcs....58 C9
Stonea Cambs....62 G2
Stone Allerton Somset....19 L4
Ston Easton Somset....20 B4
Stonebridge N Som....19 L3
Stonebridge Norfk....64 C3
Stonebridge Warwks....59 K8
Stone Bridge Corner C Pete....74 E10
Stonebroom Derbys....84 F9
Stone Chair Calder....90 E5
Stone Cross E Susx....25 M5
Stone Cross E Susx....25 P10
Stone Cross E Susx....25 P4
Stone Cross Kent....25 M3
Stone Cross Kent....25 H4
Stone Cross Kent....39 P10
Stonecross Green Suffk....63 P9
Stonecrouch Kent....26 B5
Stone-edge-Batch N Som....31 N10
Stoneferry C KuH....93 K4
Stonefield Castle Hotel Ag & B....123 Q5
Stonegate E Susx....25 Q5
Stonegate N York....105 L9
Stonegrave N York....98 D5
Stonehall Worcs....46 G5

Stonehaugh – Tal-y-Cafn 295

Stonehaugh Nthumb 111 Q5
Stonehaven Abers 151 M10
Stonehenge Wilts 21 M6
Stone Hill Donc 92 A9
Stonehouse C Plym 6 D8
Stone House Cumb 95 R3
Stonehouse Gloucs 32 F3
Stonehouse Nthumb 111 N9
Stonehouse S Lans 126 D8
Stone in Oxney Kent 26 F6
Stoneleigh Warwks 59 M10
Stoneley Green Ches E 69 R4
Stonely Cambs 61 P7
Stoner Hill Hants 23 K9
Stonesby Leics 73 L6
Stonesfield Oxon 48 C11
Stones Green Essex 53 L6
Stone Street Kent 37 N10
Stone Street Suffk 52 G4
Stone Street Suffk 52 H3
Stone Street Suffk 65 M5
Stonestreet Green Kent 27 J4
Stonethwaite Cumb 101 J8
Stonewells Moray 157 P4
Stonewood Kent 37 N6
Stoneybridge W Isls 168 c14
Stoneybridge Worcs 58 D9
Stoneyburn W Loth 126 H5
Stoney Cross Hants 13 N2
Stoneygate C Leic 72 G10
Stoneyhills Essex 38 G2
Stoneykirk D & G 106 E7
Stoney Middleton Derbys 84 B5
Stoney Stanton Leics 59 Q6
Stoney Stoke Somset 20 D8
Stoney Stratton Somset 20 C7
Stoney Stretton Shrops 56 F3
Stoneywood C Aber 151 M5
Stoneywood Falk 133 M11
Stonham Aspal Suffk 64 G10
Stonnall Staffs 58 G4
Stonor Oxon 35 K7
Stonton Wyville Leics 73 J11
Stony Cross Herefs 46 D5
Stony Cross Herefs 57 J11
Stonyford Hants 22 B11
Stony Houghton Derbys 84 G7
Stony Stratford M Keyn 49 L6
Stonywell Staffs 58 G2
Stoodleigh Devon 17 M5
Stoodleigh Devon 18 B11
Stop 24 Services Kent 27 K4
Stopham W Susx 24 B7
Stopsley Luton 50 D6
Stoptide Cnwll 4 E6
Storeton Wirral 81 L8
Storeyard Green Herefs 46 D6
Storey Arms Powys 44 D10
Stornoway W Isls 168 j4
Stornoway Airport W Isls 168 j4
Storridge Herefs 46 E5
Storrington W Susx 24 C8
Storth Cumb 95 K5
Storwood E R Yk 92 B2
Stotfield Moray 157 N3
Stotfold C Beds 50 F3
Stottesdon Shrops 57 M8
Stoughton Leics 72 G10
Stoughton Surrey 23 Q4
Stoughton W Susx 15 M4
Stoulton Worcs 46 H5
Stourbridge Dudley 58 C8
Stourhead Wilts 20 E8
Stourpaine Dorset 12 E3
Stourport-on-Severn Worcs 57 Q10
Stour Provost Dorset 20 E10
Stour Row Dorset 20 F10
Stourton Leeds 91 J4
Stourton Staffs 58 C8
Stourton Warwks 47 Q7
Stourton Wilts 20 E8
Stourton Caundle Dorset 20 D11
Stout Somset 19 M8
Stove Shet 169 r11
Stoven Suffk 65 N5
Stow Border 117 P2
Stow Lincs 85 Q4
Stow Bardolph Norfk 75 M9
Stow Bedon Norfk 64 D2
Stowbridge Norfk 75 M9
Stow-cum-Quy Cambs 62 H8
Stowe Gloucs 31 Q3
Stowe Shrops 56 E10
Stowe by Chartley Staffs 71 J9
Stowehill Nhants 60 D9
Stowell Somset 20 C10
Stowey BaNES 19 Q3
Stowford Devon 8 B5
Stowford Devon 8 B7
Stowford Devon 10 C7
Stowford Devon 17 M3
Stowlangtoft Suffk 64 D8
Stow Longa Cambs 61 P6
Stow Maries Essex 38 D2
Stowmarket Suffk 64 E10
Stow-on-the-Wold Gloucs 47 N9
Stowting Kent 27 K3
Stowting Common Kent 27 K3
Stowupland Suffk 64 F9
Straanruie Highld 148 H4
Strachan Abers 150 H9
Strachur Ag & B 131 M7
Stradbroke Suffk 65 J7
Stradbrook Wilts 20 H4
Stradishall Suffk 63 N10
Stradsett Norfk 75 N9
Stragglethorpe Lincs 86 B10
Stragglethorpe Notts 72 H3
Straight Soley Wilts 34 B10
Straiton Mdloth 127 P4
Straiton S Ayrs 114 G7
Straloch Abers 151 M3
Straloch P & K 141 P5
Stramshall Staffs 71 K7
Strang IoM 80 e6
Strangeways Salfd 82 H5
Strangford Herefs 46 A9
Stranraer D & G 106 E5
Strata Florida Cerdgn 54 G11
Stratfield Mortimer W Berk 23 J2
Stratfield Saye Hants 23 J2
Stratfield Turgis Hants 23 J3
Stratford C Beds 61 Q11
Stratford Gt Lon 37 J4
Stratford St Andrew Suffk 65 M9
Stratford St Mary Suffk 52 H5
Stratford sub Castle Wilts 21 M8
Stratford Tony Wilts 21 L9
Stratford-upon-Avon Warwks 47 P3
Strath Highld 160 B11
Strathan Highld 160 H2
Strathan Highld 165 N4
Strathaven S Lans 126 C9
Strathblane Stirlg 125 P2
Strathcanaird Highld 161 K6
Strathcarron Highld 154 B9
Strathcoil Ag & B 138 B11
Strathdon Abers 150 B5
Strathkinness Fife 135 M4
Strathloanhead W Loth 126 G3
Strathmashie House Highld 147 P9
Strathmiglo Fife 134 G6
Strathpeffer Highld 155 N6
Strathtay P & K 141 M7
Strathwhillan N Ayrs 121 K4
Strathy Highld 166 D4
Strathy Inn Highld 166 D3
Strathyre Stirlg 132 H4
Stratton Cnwll 16 C10
Stratton Dorset 11 P6
Stratton Gloucs 33 K4
Stratton Audley Oxon 48 H9
Stratton-on-the-Fosse Somset 20 C4
Stratton St Margaret Swindn 33 N7
Stratton St Michael Norfk 65 J3
Stratton Strawless Norfk 77 J7
Stream Somset 18 E7
Streat E Susx 25 J7
Streatham Gt Lon 36 H6
Streatley C Beds 50 C5
Streatley W Berk 34 G8
Street Devon 10 D7
Street Lancs 95 L10
Street N York 105 K10
Street Somset 19 N7
Street Ashton Warwks 59 Q8
Street Dinas Shrops 69 K7
Street End E Susx 25 P6
Street End Kent 39 K11
Street End W Susx 15 N7
Street Gate Gatesd 113 K9
Streethay Staffs 58 H2
Street Houses N York 98 A11
Streetlam N York 104 B11
Street Lane Derbys 84 E11
Streetly Wsall 58 G5
Streetly End Cambs 63 K11
Street on the Fosse Somset 20 B7
Strefford Shrops 56 G7
Strelitz P & K 142 B10
Strelley Notts 72 E2
Strensall C York 98 C8
Strensham Worcs 46 H6
Strensham Services (northbound) Worcs 46 G6
Strensham Services (southbound) Worcs 46 H6
Stretcholt Somset 19 J6
Strete Devon 7 L9
Stretford Herefs 45 N3
Stretford Herefs 45 Q3
Stretford Traffd 82 G6
Strethall Essex 51 L3
Stretham Cambs 62 H6
Strettington W Susx 15 N5
Stretton Ches W 69 M4
Stretton Derbys 84 E8
Stretton Rutlnd 73 N7
Stretton Staffs 58 C2
Stretton Staffs 71 P9
Stretton Warrtn 82 D8
Stretton en le Field Leics 59 M2
Stretton Grandison Herefs 46 B6
Stretton-on-Dunsmore Warwks 59 P10
Stretton on Fosse Warwks 47 P7
Stretton Sugwas Herefs 45 P6
Stretton under Fosse Warwks 59 Q8
Stretton Westwood Shrops 57 K5
Strichen Abers 159 M6
Strines Stockp 83 L7
Stringston Somset 18 G6
Strixton Nhants 61 K8
Stroat Gloucs 31 Q5
Strollamus Highld 145 J2
Stroma Highld 167 Q1
Stromeferry Highld 153 R11
Stromness Ork 169 b6
Stronaba Highld 146 G11
Stronachlachar Stirlg 132 E5
Stronafian Ag & B 131 L11
Stronchrubie Highld 161 L3
Strone Ag & B 131 P11
Strone Highld 146 E11
Strone Highld 147 N2
Stronmilchan Ag & B 131 P2
Stronsay Ork 169 f4
Stronsay Airport Ork 169 f4
Strontian Highld 138 E5
Strood Kent 26 E5
Strood Medway 38 B8
Strood Green Surrey 36 F11
Strood Green W Susx 24 B6
Stroud Gloucs 32 G3
Stroud Hants 23 K10
Stroude Surrey 36 B7
Stroud Green Essex 38 E3
Stroud Green Gloucs 32 F3
Stroxton Lincs 73 N4
Struan Highld 152 E10
Struan P & K 141 K4
Strubby Lincs 87 N4
Strumpshaw Norfk 77 L10
Strutherhill S Lans 126 D8
Struthers Fife 135 K6
Struy Highld 155 M9
Stryd-y-Facsen IoA 78 E8
Stryt-issa Wrexhm 69 J5
Stuartfield Abers 159 N8
Stubbers Green Wsall 58 F4
Stubbington Hants 14 G6
Stubbins Lancs 89 M7
Stubbs Green Norfk 65 K2
Stubhampton Dorset 12 F2
Stubley Derbys 84 D5
Stubshaw Cross Wigan 82 C5
Stubton Lincs 85 Q11
Stuckton Hants 13 L2
Studfold N York 96 B7
Stud Green W & M 35 N9
Studham C Beds 50 B7
Studholme Cumb 110 E9
Studland Dorset 12 H8
Studley Warwks 47 L2
Studley Wilts 33 J10
Studley Common Warwks 47 L2
Studley Roger N York 97 L7
Studley Royal N York 97 L6
Studley Royal Park & Fountains Abbey N York 97 L7
Stuntney Cambs 63 J5
Stunts Green E Susx 25 P8
Sturbridge Staffs 70 E8
Sturgate Lincs 85 Q3
Sturmer Essex 51 Q2
Sturminster Common Dorset 12 C2
Sturminster Marshall Dorset 12 G4
Sturminster Newton Dorset 12 C2
Sturry Kent 39 L9
Sturton N Linc 92 G10
Sturton by Stow Lincs 85 Q4
Sturton le Steeple Notts 85 N4
Stuston Suffk 64 G6
Stutton N York 91 M2
Stutton Suffk 53 L5
Styal Ches E 82 H8
Stydd Lancs 89 K3
Stynie Moray 157 Q5
Styrrup Notts 85 K2
Succoth Ag & B 132 B6
Suckley Worcs 46 D4
Suckley Green Worcs 46 D4
Sudborough Nhants 61 L4
Sudbourne Suffk 65 N11
Sudbrook Lincs 73 P2
Sudbrook Mons 31 P7
Sudbrooke Lincs 86 D5
Sudbury Derbys 71 M8
Sudbury Gt Lon 36 E3
Sudbury Suffk 52 E3
Sudden Rochdl 89 P8
Sudgrove Gloucs 32 H3
Suffield N York 99 K2
Suffield Norfk 77 J5
Sugdon Wrekin 69 R11
Sugnall Staffs 70 D8
Sugwas Pool Herefs 45 P6
Suisnish Highld 145 J4
Sulby IoM 80 e3
Sulgrave Nhants 48 G6
Sulham W Berk 34 H10
Sulhamstead W Berk 34 H11
Sulhamstead Abbots W Berk 34 H11
Sulhamstead Bannister W Berk 34 H11
Sullington W Susx 24 C8
Sullom Shet 169 q6
Sullom Voe Shet 169 r6
Sully V Glam 30 G11
Sumburgh Airport Shet 169 q12
Summerbridge N York 97 K8
Summercourt Cnwll 4 D10
Summerfield Norfk 75 Q3
Summerfield Worcs 58 B10
Summer Heath Bucks 35 K6
Summerhill Pembks 41 N9
Summerhill Staffs 58 G3
Summer Hill Wrexhm 69 K4
Summerhouse Darltn 103 P7
Summerlands Cumb 95 L3
Summerley Derbys 84 E5
Summersdale W Susx 15 N5
Summerseat Bury 89 M8
Summertown Oxon 34 F3
Summit Oldham 89 Q9
Summit Rochdl 89 Q7
Sunbiggin Cumb 102 C9
Sunbury-on-Thames Surrey 36 D7
Sundaywell D & G 108 H4
Sunderland Ag & B 122 B7
Sunderland Cumb 100 G3
Sunderland Lancs 95 J9
Sunderland Sundld 113 N9
Sunderland Bridge Dur 103 Q3
Sundhope Border 117 L5
Sundon Park Luton 50 C5
Sundridge Kent 37 L9
Sunk Island E R Yk 93 N7
Sunningdale W & M 35 Q11
Sunninghill W & M 35 P11
Sunningwell Oxon 34 E4
Sunniside Dur 103 M3
Sunniside Gatesd 113 K9
Sunny Brow Dur 103 N4
Sunnyhill C Derb 72 A4
Sunnyhurst Bl w D 89 K6
Sunnylaw Stirlg 133 M8
Sunnymead Oxon 34 F3
Sunton Wilts 21 P4
Surbiton Gt Lon 36 E7
Surfleet Lincs 74 E5
Surfleet Seas End Lincs 74 E5
Surlingham Norfk 77 L10
Surrex Essex 52 E7
Sustead Norfk 76 H4
Susworth Lincs 92 D10
Sutcombe Devon 16 E9
Sutcombemill Devon 16 E9
Suton Norfk 64 F2
Sutterby Lincs 87 L6
Sutterton Lincs 74 E3
Sutton C Beds 62 B11
Sutton C Pete 74 A11
Sutton Cambs 62 F5
Sutton Devon 7 J10
Sutton Devon 8 H4
Sutton Donc 91 P8
Sutton E Susx 25 L11
Sutton Gt Lon 36 G8
Sutton Kent 27 P2
Sutton N York 91 M5
Sutton Norfk 77 M7
Sutton Notts 73 K3
Sutton Oxon 34 D3
Sutton Pembks 40 H7
Sutton Shrops 57 J2
Sutton Shrops 57 N7
Sutton Shrops 69 L9
Sutton Shrops 70 B8
Sutton St Hel 82 B6
Sutton Staffs 70 D10
Sutton Suffk 53 P2
Sutton W Susx 23 Q11
Sutton Abinger Surrey 36 D11
Sutton-at-Hone Kent 37 N7
Sutton Bassett Nhants 60 G2
Sutton Benger Wilts 32 H9
Sutton Bingham Somset 11 L2
Sutton Bonington Notts 72 E6
Sutton Bridge Lincs 75 J6
Sutton Cheney Leics 72 C10
Sutton Coldfield Birm 58 H5
Sutton Courtenay Oxon 34 F6
Sutton Crosses Lincs 74 H6
Sutton cum Lound Notts 85 L4
Sutton Fields Notts 72 D5
Sutton Green Surrey 36 B10
Sutton Green Wrexhm 69 M5
Sutton Howgrave N York 97 M5
Sutton-in-Ashfield Notts 84 G9
Sutton-in-Craven N York 90 C2
Sutton in the Elms Leics 60 B2
Sutton Lane Ends Ches E 83 K10
Sutton Maddock Shrops 57 N4
Sutton Mallet Somset 19 L7
Sutton Mandeville Wilts 21 J9
Sutton Manor St Hel 81 Q6
Sutton Marsh Herefs 45 R6
Sutton Montis Somset 20 B10
Sutton-on-Hull C KuH 93 K4
Sutton on Sea Lincs 87 P4
Sutton-on-the-Forest N York 98 B8
Sutton on the Hill Derbys 71 N8
Sutton on Trent Notts 85 N7
Sutton Poyntz Dorset 11 Q8
Sutton St Edmund Lincs 74 G8
Sutton St James Lincs 74 G7
Sutton St Nicholas Herefs 45 Q5
Sutton Scotney Hants 22 E7
Sutton Street Kent 38 D10
Sutton-under-Brailes Warwks 48 B7
Sutton-under-Whitestonecliffe N York 97 Q4
Sutton upon Derwent E R Yk 98 E11
Sutton Valence Kent 26 D2
Sutton Veny Wilts 20 H6
Sutton Waldron Dorset 20 G11
Sutton Weaver Ches W 82 B9
Sutton Wick BaNES 19 Q3
Sutton Wick Oxon 34 E6
Swaby Lincs 87 L5
Swadlincote Derbys 71 P11
Swaffham Norfk 75 R9
Swaffham Bulbeck Cambs 63 J8
Swaffham Prior Cambs 63 J8
Swafield Norfk 77 K5
Swainby N York 104 E10
Swainshill Herefs 45 P6
Swainsthorpe Norfk 77 J11
Swainswick BaNES 32 E11
Swalcliffe Oxon 48 C7
Swalecliffe Kent 39 K8
Swallow Lincs 93 L10
Swallow Beck Lincs 86 B7
Swallowcliffe Wilts 21 J9
Swallowfield Wokham 23 K2
Swallownest Rothm 84 G3
Swallows Cross Essex 51 P11
Swampton Hants 22 D4
Swanage Dorset 12 H9
Swanbourne Bucks 49 M9
Swanbridge V Glam 30 G11
Swancote Shrops 57 N6
Swan Green Ches W 82 F10
Swanland E R Yk 92 G5
Swanley Kent 37 M7
Swanley Village Kent 37 M7
Swanmore Hants 22 G11
Swannington Leics 72 C7
Swannington Norfk 76 G8
Swanpool Lincs 86 C7
Swanscombe Kent 37 P6
Swansea Swans 29 J6
Swansea Airport Swans 28 G6
Swansea West Services Swans 28 H5
Swan Street Essex 52 E6
Swanton Abbot Norfk 77 K6
Swanton Morley Norfk 76 E8
Swanton Novers Norfk 76 E5
Swanton Street Kent 38 E10
Swan Valley Nhants 60 F9
Swan Village Sandw 58 E6
Swanwick Derbys 84 F10
Swanwick Hants 14 F5
Swarby Lincs 73 Q2
Swardeston Norfk 77 J11
Swarkestone Derbys 72 B5
Swarland Nthumb 119 N10
Swarraton Hants 22 G7
Swartha C Brad 96 G11
Swarthmoor Cumb 94 F5
Swaton Lincs 74 B3
Swavesey Cambs 62 E7
Sway Hants 13 N5
Swayfield Lincs 73 P6
Swaythling C Sotn 22 D11
Sweet Green Worcs 46 B2
Sweetham Devon 9 L5
Sweethaws E Susx 25 M5
Sweetlands Corner Kent 26 C2
Sweets Cnwll 5 K2
Sweetshouse Cnwll 4 H9
Swefling Suffk 65 L9
Swepstone Leics 72 B8
Swerford Oxon 48 C8
Swettenham Ches E 82 H11
Swffryd Blae G 30 H5
Swift's Green Kent 26 E3
Swilland Suffk 64 H11
Swillbrook Lancs 88 F4
Swillington Leeds 91 K4
Swimbridge Devon 17 L5
Swimbridge Newland Devon 17 L5
Swinbrook Oxon 33 Q2
Swincliffe Kirk 90 G5
Swincliffe N York 97 K9
Swincombe Devon 17 M3
Swindale Cumb 101 P8
Swinden N York 96 C10
Swinderby Lincs 85 Q8
Swindon Gloucs 46 H9
Swindon Nthumb 119 J11
Swindon Staffs 58 C6
Swindon Swindn 33 M8
Swine E R Yk 93 K3
Swinefleet E R Yk 92 C6
Swineford S Glos 32 C11
Swineshead Bed 61 N7
Swineshead Lincs 74 D2
Swineshead Bridge Lincs 74 D2
Swiney Highld 167 M9
Swinford Leics 60 C5
Swinford Oxon 34 D3
Swingfield Minnis Kent 27 M3
Swingfield Street Kent 27 M3
Swingleton Green Suffk 52 G2
Swinhoe Nthumb 119 P5
Swinhope Lincs 93 M11
Swinithwaite N York 96 F3
Swinmore Common Herefs 46 C6
Swinscoe Staffs 71 L5
Swinside Cumb 100 H6
Swinstead Lincs 73 Q6
Swinthorpe Lincs 86 E4
Swinton Border 129 L10
Swinton N York 97 K5
Swinton N York 98 F6
Swinton Rothm 91 M11
Swinton Salfd 82 G4
Swithland Leics 72 F8
Swordale Highld 155 Q4
Swordland Highld 145 N9
Swordly Highld 166 B4
Sworton Heath Ches E 82 E8
Swyddffynnon Cerdgn 54 F11
Swyncombe Oxon 35 J6
Swynnerton Staffs 70 F7
Swyre Dorset 11 L7
Sycharth Powys 68 H9
Sychnant Powys 55 M9
Sychtyn Powys 55 M3
Sydallt Wrexhm 69 K3
Syde Gloucs 33 J2
Sydenham Gt Lon 37 J6
Sydenham Oxon 35 K4
Sydenham Damerel Devon 5 Q6
Sydenhurst Surrey 23 Q8
Syderstone Norfk 76 A5
Sydling St Nicholas Dorset 11 N5
Sydmonton Hants 22 E3
Sydnal Lane Shrops 57 Q3
Syerston Notts 85 M11
Syke Rochdl 89 P7
Sykehouse Donc 91 Q7
Syleham Suffk 65 J6
Sylen Carmth 28 F3
Symbister Shet 169 s7
Symington S Ayrs 125 K11
Symington S Lans 116 D3
Symondsbury Dorset 11 J6
Symonds Yat (East) Herefs 45 R11
Symonds Yat (West) Herefs 45 R11
Sympson Green C Brad 90 F3
Synderford Dorset 10 H4
Synod Inn Cerdgn 42 H4
Syre Highld 165 Q8
Syreford Gloucs 47 K10
Syresham Nhants 48 H6
Syston Leics 72 G8
Syston Lincs 73 N2
Sytchampton Worcs 58 B11
Sywell Nhants 60 H7

T

Tabley Hill Ches E 82 F9
Tackley Oxon 48 E11
Tacolneston Norfk 64 G2
Tadcaster N York 91 M2
Taddington Derbys 83 P10
Taddington Gloucs 47 L8
Taddiport Devon 16 H8
Tadley Hants 22 H2
Tadlow Cambs 62 C11
Tadmarton Oxon 48 C7
Tadwick BaNES 32 D10
Tadworth Surrey 36 F9
Tafarnaubach Blae G 30 F2
Tafarn-y-bwlch Pembks 41 L4
Tafarn-y-Gelyn Denbgs 68 G2
Taff's Well Rhondd 30 F8
Tafolwern Powys 55 K4
Taibach Neath 29 L7
Tain Highld 162 H10
Tain Highld 167 M3
Tai'n Lôn Gwynd 66 G4
Tairbeart W Isls 168 g7
Tai'r Bull Powys 44 D9
Tairgwaith Neath 29 K2
Takeley Essex 51 N6
Takeley Street Essex 51 M6
Talachddu Powys 44 F8
Talacre Flints 80 G8
Talaton Devon 9 Q5
Talbenny Pembks 40 F8
Talbot Green Rhondd 30 D8
Talbot Village BCP 13 J6
Taleford Devon 10 B5
Talerddig Powys 55 L4
Talgarreg Cerdgn 42 H4
Talgarth Powys 44 H8
Talisker Highld 152 E11
Talke Staffs 70 E4
Talke Pits Staffs 70 E4
Talkin Cumb 111 L9
Talladale Highld 154 B3
Talla Linnfoots Border 116 G6
Tallaminnock S Ayrs 114 H8
Tallarn Green Wrexhm 69 M6
Tallentire Cumb 100 F3
Talley Carmth 43 M8
Tallington Lincs 74 A9
Tallwrn Wrexhm 69 J5
Talmine Highld 165 N4
Talog Carmth 42 F9
Talsarn Cerdgn 43 K3
Talsarnau Gwynd 67 L7
Talskiddy Cnwll 4 E8
Talwrn IoA 78 H9
Talwrn Wrexhm 69 L5
Tal-y-bont Cerdgn 54 F7
Tal-y-Bont Conwy 79 P11
Tal-y-bont Gwynd 67 K10
Tal-y-bont Gwynd 79 L10
Talybont-on-Usk Powys 44 G10
Tal-y-Cafn Conwy 79 P10

Tal-y-coed Mons 45 N11
Tal-y-garn Rhondd 30 D9
Tal-y-llyn Gwynd 54 G3
Talysarn Gwynd 66 H4
Tal-y-Waun Torfn 31 J4
Talywern Powys 55 J4
Tamar Valley Mining District Devon 6 C5
Tamer Lane End Wigan 82 D4
Tamerton Foliot C Plym 6 D6
Tamworth Staffs 59 K4
Tamworth Green Lincs 74 G2
Tamworth Services Warwks 59 K4
Tancred N York 97 Q9
Tancredston Pembks 40 G5
Tandridge Surrey 37 J10
Tanfield Dur 113 J9
Tanfield Lea Dur 113 J10
Tangasdale W Isls 168 b17
Tangiers Pembks 41 J7
Tangley Hants 22 B4
Tangmere W Susx 15 P5
Tan Hill N York 102 G9
Tankerness Ork 169 e6
Tankersley Barns 91 J11
Tankerton Kent 39 K8
Tannach Highld 167 P7
Tannachie Abers 151 K11
Tannadice Angus 142 H6
Tanner's Green Worcs 58 G10
Tannington Suffk 65 J8
Tannochside N Lans 126 C5
Tansley Derbys 84 D9
Tansor Nhants 61 N12
Tantobie Dur 113 J10
Tanton N York 104 F8
Tanwood Worcs 58 D10
Tanworth in Arden Warwks 58 H10
Tan-y-Bwlch Gwynd 67 M6
Tan-y-fron Conwy 68 C2
Tan-y-fron Wrexhm 69 J4
Tan-y-grisiau Gwynd 67 M5
Tan-y-groes Cerdgn 42 E5
Taobh Tuath W Isls 168 e9
Taplow Bucks 35 P8
Tarbert Ag & B 123 L9
Tarbert Ag & B 123 Q6
Tarbert W Isls 168 g7
Tarbet Ag & B 132 C7
Tarbet Highld 145 N9
Tarbet Highld 164 E7
Tarbock Green Knows 81 P7
Tarbolton S Lans 114 H2
Tarbrax S Lans 127 J6
Tardebigge Worcs 58 E11
Tarfside Angus 142 H2
Tarland Abers 150 D7
Tarleton Lancs 88 F6
Tarlscough Lancs 88 K8
Tarlton Gloucs 33 J5
Tarnock Somset 19 L4
Tarns Cumb 109 P11
Tarnside Cumb 95 J2
Tarporley Ches W 69 Q2
Tarr Somset 17 R5
Tarrant Crawford Dorset 12 F4
Tarrant Gunville Dorset 12 F2
Tarrant Hinton Dorset 12 F2
Tarrant Keyneston Dorset 12 F4
Tarrant Launceston Dorset 12 F3
Tarrant Monkton Dorset 12 F3
Tarrant Rawston Dorset 12 F3
Tarrant Rushton Dorset 12 F3
Tarring Neville E Susx 25 K10
Tarrington Herefs 46 B6
Tarskavaig Highld 145 J5
Tarves Abers 159 L11
Tarvin Ches W 81 P11
Tarvin Sands Ches W 81 P11
Tasburgh Norfk 65 J2
Tasley Shrops 57 M6
Taston Oxon 48 C10
Tatenhill Staffs 71 N10
Tathall End M Keyn 49 M5
Tatham Lancs 95 N7
Tathwell Lincs 87 K4
Tatsfield Surrey 37 K9
Tattenhall Ches W 69 N3
Tatterford Norfk 76 B6
Tattersett Norfk 76 A6
Tattershall Lincs 86 H9
Tattershall Bridge Lincs 86 G9
Tattershall Thorpe Lincs 86 H9
Tattingstone Suffk 53 K4
Tattingstone White Horse Suffk 53 K4
Tatton Park Ches E 82 F8
Tatworth Somset 10 G3
Tauchers Moray 157 R8
Taunton Somset 18 H10
Taunton Deane Services Somset 18 G10
Taverham Norfk 76 H9
Taverners Green Essex 51 N7
Tavernspite Pembks 41 N8
Tavistock Devon 6 D4
Tavistock Devon 6 D4
Taw Green Devon 8 G5
Tawstock Devon 17 K6
Taxal Derbys 83 M9
Tay Bridge C Dund 135 L2
Taychreggan Hotel Ag & B 131 L3
Tay Forest Park P & K 141 J5
Tayinloan Ag & B 123 L10
Taynton Gloucs 46 D10
Taynton Oxon 33 P2
Taynuilt Ag & B 139 J11
Tayport Fife 135 M2
Tayvallich Ag & B 130 E10
Tealby Lincs 86 G2
Tealing Angus 142 G10
Team Valley Gatesd 113 K9
Teangue Highld 145 L6
Teanord Highld 155 Q5
Tebay Cumb 102 B10
Tebay Services Cumb 102 B9
Tebworth C Beds 49 Q9
Tedburn St Mary Devon 9 J6
Teddington Gloucs 47 J8
Teddington Gt Lon 36 E6
Tedstone Delamere Herefs 46 C3
Tedstone Wafer Herefs 46 C3
Teesport R & Cl 104 F6
Teesside Park S on T 104 E7
Teeton Nhants 60 E6

Teffont Evias Wilts 21 J8
Teffont Magna Wilts 21 J8
Tegryn Pembks 41 P4
Teigh Rutlnd 73 M7
Teigncombe Devon 8 G7
Teigngrace Devon 7 M4
Teignmouth Devon 7 N4
Teindside Border 117 N9
Telford Wrekin 57 M3
Telford Services Shrops 57 N3
Tellisford Somset 20 F3
Telscombe E Susx 25 K10
Telscombe Cliffs E Susx 25 K10
Tempar P & K 140 G6
Templand D & G 109 N3
Temple Cnwll 5 J7
Temple Mdloth 127 Q6
Temple Balsall Solhll 59 K9
Temple Bar Cerdgn 43 K4
Temple Cloud BaNES 20 B3
Templecombe Somset 20 D10
Temple End Suffk 63 L10
Temple Ewell Kent 27 N3
Temple Grafton Warwks 47 M3
Temple Guiting Gloucs 47 L9
Temple Herdewyke Warwks 48 C4
Temple Hirst N York 91 Q6
Temple Normanton Derbys 84 F7
Temple of Fiddes Abers 151 L11
Temple Sowerby Cumb 102 B5
Templeton Devon 9 L2
Templeton Pembks 41 M8
Templetown Dur 112 H10
Tempsford C Beds 61 Q10
Tenbury Wells Worcs 57 K11
Tenby Pembks 41 M10
Tendring Essex 53 K7
Tendring Green Essex 53 K6
Tendring Heath Essex 53 K6
Ten Mile Bank Norfk 75 L11
Tenpenny Heath Essex 53 J7
Tenterden Kent 26 E5
Terling Essex 52 C8
Tern Wrekin 69 R11
Ternhill Shrops 70 A8
Terregles D & G 109 K5
Terrington N York 98 D6
Terrington St Clement Norfk 75 L6
Terrington St John Norfk 75 K8
Terry's Green Warwks 58 H10
Teston Kent 38 B11
Testwood Hants 14 C4
Tetbury Gloucs 32 G6
Tetbury Upton Gloucs 32 G5
Tetchill Shrops 69 L8
Tetcott Devon 5 N2
Tetford Lincs 87 K6
Tetney Lincs 93 P10
Tetney Lock Lincs 93 P10
Tetsworth Oxon 35 J4
Tettenhall Wolves 58 C4
Tettenhall Wood Wolves 58 C5
Teversal Notts 84 G8
Teversham Cambs 62 G9
Teviothead Border 117 N9
Tewin Herts 50 G8
Tewin Wood Herts 50 G7
Tewkesbury Gloucs 46 G8
Teynham Kent 38 G9
Thackley C Brad 90 F3
Thackthwaite Cumb 100 F6
Thackthwaite Cumb 101 M5
Thainstone Abers 151 K4
Thakeham W Susx 24 D7
Thame Oxon 35 K3
Thames Ditton Surrey 36 E7
Thamesmead Gt Lon 37 L4
Thamesport Medway 38 E7
Thanington Kent 39 K10
Thankerton S Lans 116 D3
Tharston Norfk 64 H3
Thatcham W Berk 34 F11
Thatto Heath St Hel 81 Q6
Thaxted Essex 51 P4
Theakston N York 97 M3
Thealby N Linc 92 E7
Theale Somset 19 N5
Theale W Berk 34 H10
Thearne E R Yk 93 J3
The Bank Ches E 70 E3
The Beeches Gloucs 33 K4
Theberton Suffk 65 N8
The Blythe Staffs 71 J9
The Bog Shrops 56 F5
The Bourne Worcs 47 J3
The Braes Highld 153 J11
The Bratch Staffs 58 C6
The Broad Herefs 45 P2
The Broads 77 P10
The Brunt E Loth 128 H5
The Bryn Mons 31 K3
The Bungalow IoM 80 e4
The Burf Worcs 57 Q11
The Camp Gloucs 32 H3
The Chequer Wrexhm 69 N6
The City Bed 61 P9
The City Bucks 35 L5
The Common Oxon 47 Q9
The Common Wilts 21 P8
The Common Wilts 33 K7
The Corner Kent 26 B3
The Cronk IoM 80 d2
Theddingworth Leics 60 E3
Theddlethorpe All Saints Lincs 87 N3
Theddlethorpe St Helen Lincs 87 N3
The Deep C KuH 93 J5
The Den N Ayrs 125 J7
The Forge Herefs 45 L3
The Forstal Kent 26 H4
The Fouralls Shrops 70 B8
The Green Cumb 94 D4
The Green Essex 52 C8
The Green N York 105 L9
The Green Wilts 20 G8
The Grove Worcs 46 G6
The Haven W Susx 24 C4
The Haw Gloucs 46 F9
The Headland Hartpl 104 F4
The Hendre Mons 31 N2
The Hill Cumb 94 D4
The Holt Wokham 35 M9
The Hundred Herefs 45 Q2
Thelbridge Cross Devon 9 J2

The Leacon Kent 26 G5
The Lee Bucks 35 P4
The Lhen IoM 80 e1
Thelnetham Suffk 64 E6
The Lochs Moray 157 Q5
Thelveton Norfk 64 H5
Thelwall Warrtn 82 E7
The Marsh Powys 56 E5
Themelthorpe Norfk 76 F7
The Middles Dur 113 K10
The Moor Kent 26 C6
The Mumbles Swans 28 H7
The Murray S Lans 125 Q7
The Mythe Gloucs 46 G8
The Narth Mons 31 P3
The Neuk Abers 151 J8
Thenford Nhants 48 F6
Theobald's Green Wilts 33 K11
The Quarry Gloucs 32 D5
The Quarter Kent 26 E3
The Reddings Gloucs 46 H10
Therfield Herts 50 H3
The Rhôs Powys 44 H8
The Ross P & K 133 M3
The Sands Surrey 23 N5
The Shoe Wilts 32 F10
The Smithies Shrops 57 M5
The Spring Warwks 59 L10
The Square Torfn 31 J5
The Stair Kent 37 P11
The Stocks Kent 26 F6
The Straits Hants 23 L7
The Strand Wilts 20 H3
Thetford Norfk 64 B5
Thetford Forest Park 63 P3
Thethwaite Cumb 101 J3
The Towans Cnwll 2 F6
The Vauld Herefs 45 Q5
The Wyke Shrops 57 N3
Theydon Bois Essex 51 K11
Theydon Mount Essex 51 L11
Thicket Priory N York 97 A2
Thickwood Wilts 32 F10
Thimbleby Lincs 86 H6
Thimbleby N York 104 D11
Thingwall Wirral 81 K8
Thirkleby N York 97 Q5
Thirlby N York 97 Q4
Thirlestane Border 128 F10
Thirn N York 97 K3
Thirsk N York 97 P4
Thirtleby E R Yk 93 L4
Thistleton Lancs 88 E3
Thistleton Rutlnd 73 N7
Thistley Green Suffk 63 L5
Thixendale N York 98 G8
Thockrington Nthumb 112 F5
Tholomas Drove Cambs 74 H9
Tholthorpe N York 97 Q7
Thomas Chapel Pembks 41 M9
Thomas Close Cumb 101 M2
Thomastown Abers 158 E10
Thompson Norfk 64 C2
Thong Kent 37 Q6
Thongsbridge Kirk 90 F9
Thoralby N York 96 F3
Thoresby Notts 85 K6
Thoresthorpe Lincs 87 N5
Thoresway Lincs 93 L11
Thorganby Lincs 93 M11
Thorganby N York 92 A2
Thorgill N York 105 K11
Thorington Suffk 65 N7
Thorington Street Suffk 52 H4
Thorlby N York 96 E10
Thorley Herts 51 L7
Thorley IoW 14 C9
Thorley Houses Herts 51 L6
Thorley Street IoW 14 C9
Thormanby N York 97 Q6
Thornaby-on-Tees S on T 104 E7
Thornage Norfk 76 F4
Thornborough Bucks 49 K8
Thornborough N York 97 L5
Thornbury C Brad 90 F4
Thornbury Devon 16 G10
Thornbury Herefs 46 B3
Thornbury S Glos 32 B6
Thornby Cumb 110 E10
Thornby Nhants 60 E5
Thorncliff Staffs 71 J3
Thorncombe Dorset 10 H4
Thorncombe Street Surrey 23 Q6
Thorncott Green C Beds 61 Q11
Thorncross IoW 14 D10
Thorndon Suffk 64 G8
Thorndon Cross Devon 8 D6
Thorne Donc 92 A8
Thorne Coffin Somset 19 P11
Thornecroft Devon 7 K5
Thornehillhead Devon 16 G8
Thorner Leeds 91 K2
Thornes Staffs 58 G4
Thornes Wakefd 91 J4
Thorne St Margaret Somset 18 F10
Thorney Bucks 36 B5
Thorney C Pete 74 E10
Thorney Notts 85 Q6
Thorney Somset 19 M10
Thorney Hill Hants 13 M5
Thorney Island W Susx 15 L5
Thorney Toll Cambs 74 F10
Thornfalcon Somset 19 J10
Thorngrove Somset 19 L8
Thorngumbald E R Yk 93 M5
Thornham Norfk 75 P2
Thornham Magna Suffk 64 G7
Thornham Parva Suffk 64 G7
Thornhaugh C Pete 73 R10
Thornhill C Sotn 14 E4
Thornhill Caerph 30 G7
Thornhill Cumb 100 D9
Thornhill D & G 116 B11
Thornhill Derbys 83 Q8
Thornhill Kirk 90 H7
Thornhill Stirlg 133 K7
Thornhill Lees Kirk 90 G7
Thornhills Calder 90 F6
Thornicombe Dorset 12 D4
Thornington Nthumb 118 H3
Thornley Dur 103 M3
Thornley Dur 104 C3

Thornley Gate Nthumb 112 B9
Thornliebank E Rens 125 P6
Thorns Suffk 63 M9
Thorns Green Ches E 82 G8
Thornthwaite Cumb 100 H5
Thornthwaite N York 97 J9
Thornton Angus 142 F8
Thornton Bucks 49 L7
Thornton C Brad 90 D4
Thornton E R Yk 98 D3
Thornton Fife 134 H8
Thornton Lancs 88 C2
Thornton Leics 72 D9
Thornton Lincs 86 H7
Thornton Middsb 104 E8
Thornton Nthumb 129 P10
Thornton Pembks 40 H9
Thornton Sefton 81 L4
Thornton Curtis N Linc 93 J7
Thorntonhall S Lans 125 P6
Thornton Heath Gt Lon 36 H7
Thornton Hough Wirral 81 L8
Thornton-in-Craven N York 96 D11
Thornton in Lonsdale N York 95 P6
Thornton-le-Beans N York 97 N2
Thornton-le-Clay N York 98 D7
Thornton-le-Dale N York 98 G4
Thornton le Moor Lincs 92 H11
Thornton-le-Moor N York 97 N3
Thornton-le-Moors Ches W 81 N10
Thornton-le-Street N York 97 P3
Thorntonloch E Loth 129 K5
Thornton Rust N York 96 E3
Thornton Steward N York 97 J3
Thornton Watlass N York 97 K3
Thornwood Common Essex 51 L9
Thornydykes Border 128 G10
Thornythwaite Cumb 101 L6
Thoroton Notts 73 K2
Thorp Arch Leeds 97 P11
Thorpe Derbys 71 M4
Thorpe E R Yk 99 K11
Thorpe Lincs 87 N4
Thorpe N York 96 F8
Thorpe Norfk 65 N2
Thorpe Notts 85 N11
Thorpe Surrey 36 B7
Thorpe Abbotts Norfk 64 H6
Thorpe Acre Leics 72 E7
Thorpe Arnold Leics 73 K6
Thorpe Audlin Wakefd 91 M7
Thorpe Bassett N York 98 H6
Thorpe Bay Sthend 38 F4
Thorpe by Water Rutlnd 73 M11
Thorpe Common Rothm 91 J6
Thorpe Constantine Staffs 59 L3
Thorpe End Norfk 77 K9
Thorpe Green Essex 53 L7
Thorpe Green Lancs 88 G5
Thorpe Green Suffk 64 C11
Thorpe Hesley Rothm 91 K11
Thorpe in Balne Donc 91 P8
Thorpe Langton Leics 60 F2
Thorpe Larches Dur 104 C5
Thorpe Lea Surrey 36 B6
Thorpe le Fallows Lincs 86 B4
Thorpe-le-Soken Essex 53 L7
Thorpe le Street E R Yk 92 D2
Thorpe Malsor Nhants 60 H5
Thorpe Mandeville Nhants 48 E5
Thorpe Market Norfk 77 J4
Thorpe Marriot Norfk 76 H8
Thorpe Morieux Suffk 64 C11
Thorpeness Suffk 65 Q9
Thorpe on the Hill Leeds 91 J5
Thorpe on the Hill Lincs 86 B7
Thorpe Park Surrey 36 B7
Thorpe St Andrew Norfk 77 K10
Thorpe St Peter Lincs 87 N8
Thorpe Salvin Rothm 84 H4
Thorpe Satchville Leics 73 J8
Thorpe Thewles S on T 104 C6
Thorpe Tilney Lincs 86 F9
Thorpe Underwood N York 97 Q9
Thorpe Underwood Nhants 60 G4
Thorpe Waterville Nhants 61 M4
Thorpe Willoughby N York 91 P4
Thorpland Norfk 75 M9
Thorrington Essex 53 J8
Thorverton Devon 9 M4
Thrales End C Beds 50 D7
Thrandeston Suffk 64 G6
Thrapston Nhants 61 L5
Threapland Cumb 100 G3
Threapland N York 96 E8
Threapwood Ches W 69 M6
Threapwood Staffs 71 J6
Threapwood Head Staffs 71 J6
Threave S Ayrs 114 F6
Three Ashes Herefs 45 Q10
Three Bridges W Susx 24 G3
Three Burrows Cnwll 3 K4
Three Chimneys Kent 26 D4
Three Cocks Powys 44 H7
Three Crosses Swans 28 G6
Three Cups Corner E Susx 25 P6
Three Gates Worcs 46 C2
Threehammer Common Norfk 77 L8
Three Hammers Cnwll 5 L4
Three Holes Norfk 75 K10
Threekingham Lincs 74 A3
Three Leg Cross E Susx 25 Q4
Three Legged Cross Dorset 13 J3
Three Mile Cross Wokham 35 K11
Threemilestone Cnwll 3 K4
Threemiletown W Loth 127 K2
Three Oaks E Susx 26 D9
Threlkeld Cumb 101 K5
Threshers Bush Essex 51 L9
Thrigby Norfk 77 P9
Thringarth Dur 102 H6
Thringstone Leics 72 C7
Thriplow Cambs 62 F11
Throapham Rothm 84 H3
Throckenhalt Lincs 74 G9
Throcking Herts 50 H4
Throckley N u Ty 113 J7
Throckmorton Worcs 47 J5
Throop BCP 13 K5
Throop Dorset 12 D6

Throphill Nthumb 112 H3
Thropton Nthumb 119 K10
Throsk Stirlg 133 P9
Througham Gloucs 32 H3
Throughgate D & G 109 J4
Throwleigh Devon 8 G6
Throwley Kent 38 G10
Throwley Forstal Kent 38 G11
Thrumpton Notts 72 E4
Thrumpton Notts 85 M4
Thrumster Highld 167 P7
Thrunscoe NE Lin 93 P9
Thrunton Nthumb 119 L8
Thrup Oxon 33 Q5
Thrupp Gloucs 32 G4
Thrupp Oxon 48 E11
Thrushelton Devon 8 B7
Thrussington Leics 72 H7
Thruxton Hants 21 Q5
Thruxton Herefs 45 N8
Thrybergh Rothm 91 M11
Thulston Derbys 72 C4
Thundersley Essex 38 C4
Thurcaston Leics 72 F8
Thurcroft Rothm 84 G3
Thurdon Cnwll 16 D9
Thurgarton Norfk 76 H5
Thurgarton Notts 85 L11
Thurgoland Barns 90 H10
Thurlaston Leics 72 E11
Thurlaston Warwks 59 Q10
Thurlbear Somset 19 J10
Thurlby Lincs 74 A7
Thurlby Lincs 86 B8
Thurlby Lincs 87 N5
Thurleigh Bed 61 N9
Thurlestone Devon 6 H10
Thurloxton Somset 19 J8
Thurlstone Barns 90 H9
Thurlton Norfk 65 N2
Thurlwood Ches E 70 E3
Thurmaston Leics 72 G9
Thurnby Leics 72 G10
Thurne Norfk 77 N8
Thurnham Kent 38 D10
Thurning Nhants 61 N4
Thurning Norfk 76 F6
Thurnscoe Barns 91 M9
Thurrock Services Thurr 37 N5
Thursby Cumb 110 F10
Thursden Lancs 89 Q4
Thursford Norfk 76 D5
Thursley Surrey 23 P7
Thurso Highld 167 K3
Thurstaston Wirral 81 J8
Thurston Suffk 64 C8
Thurston Clough Oldham 90 B9
Thurstonfield Cumb 110 F9
Thurstonland Kirk 90 F8
Thurston Planch Suffk 64 C9
Thurton Norfk 77 L11
Thurvaston Derbys 71 N7
Thuxton Norfk 76 E10
Thwaite N York 102 G11
Thwaite Suffk 64 G8
Thwaite Head Cumb 94 G3
Thwaites C Brad 90 D2
Thwaite St Mary Norfk 65 L2
Thwaites Brow C Brad 90 D2
Thwing E R Yk 99 L6
Tibbermore P & K 134 C3
Tibbers D & G 116 B11
Tibberton Gloucs 46 E10
Tibberton Worcs 46 H3
Tibberton Wrekin 70 B10
Tibenham Norfk 64 G4
Tibshelf Derbys 84 F8
Tibshelf Services Derbys 84 F8
Tibthorpe E R Yk 99 K9
Ticehurst E Susx 25 Q4
Tichborne Hants 22 G8
Tickencote Rutlnd 73 P9
Tickenham N Som 31 N10
Tickford End M Keyn 49 N6
Tickhill Donc 85 J2
Ticklerton Shrops 56 H6
Ticknall Derbys 72 B6
Tickton E R Yk 93 J2
Tidbury Green Solhll 58 H9
Tidcombe Wilts 21 Q3
Tiddington Oxon 34 H4
Tiddington Warwks 47 P3
Tiddleywink Wilts 32 G9
Tidebrook E Susx 25 P4
Tideford Cnwll 5 P10
Tideford Cross Cnwll 5 N9
Tidenham Gloucs 31 Q5
Tideswell Derbys 83 Q9
Tidmarsh W Berk 34 H10
Tidmington Warwks 47 Q7
Tidpit Hants 21 L11
Tidworth Wilts 21 P5
Tiers Cross Pembks 40 H8
Tiffield Nhants 49 K4
Tigerton Angus 143 J5
Tigh a' Ghearraidh W Isls 168 c10
Tigharry W Isls 168 c10
Tighnabruaich Ag & B 124 B3
Tigley Devon 7 K6
Tilbrook Cambs 61 N7
Tilbury Thurr 37 P5
Tilbury Dock Thurr 37 P5
Tilbury Green Essex 52 B3
Tilbury Juxta Clare Essex 52 C3
Tile Cross Birm 59 J7
Tile Hill Covtry 59 L9
Tilehouse Green Solhll 59 J9
Tilehurst Readg 35 J10
Tilford Surrey 23 N6
Tilgate W Susx 24 G4
Tilgate Forest Row W Susx 24 G4
Tilham Street Somset 19 Q7
Tillers Green Gloucs 46 C8
Tillicoultry Clacks 133 Q8
Tillietudlem S Lans 126 E8
Tillingham Essex 52 G11
Tillington Herefs 45 P6
Tillington W Susx 23 Q10
Tillington Common Herefs 45 P5
Tillybirloch Abers 150 H6
Tillyfourie Abers 150 G5
Tillygreig Abers 151 M3
Tillyrie P & K 134 E6
Tilmanstone Kent 39 P11
Tilney All Saints Norfk 75 L8

Tilney High End Norfk ...75 L7
Tilney St Lawrence Norfk ...75 K8
Tilshead Wilts ...21 K5
Tilstock Shrops ...69 P7
Tilston Ches W ...69 N4
Tilstone Bank Ches W ...69 Q3
Tilstone Fearnall Ches W ...69 Q2
Tilsworth C Beds ...49 Q10
Tilton on the Hill Leics ...73 J9
Tiltups End Gloucs ...32 F5
Tilty Essex ...51 N5
Timberland Lincs ...86 F9
Timbersbrook Ches E ...70 F2
Timberscombe Somset ...18 C6
Timble N York ...97 J10
Timpanheck D & G ...110 F6
Timperley Traffd ...82 G7
Timsbury BaNES ...20 C3
Timsbury Hants ...22 B10
Timsgarry W Isls ...168 f4
Timsgearraidh W Isls ...168 f4
Timworth Suffk ...64 B8
Timworth Green Suffk ...64 B8
Tincleton Dorset ...12 C6
Tindale Cumb ...111 M9
Tingewick Bucks ...49 J8
Tingley Leeds ...90 H5
Tingrith C Beds ...50 B4
Tingwall Airport Shet ...169 r9
Tingwell Ork ...169 d4
Tinhay Devon ...5 P4
Tinker's Hill Hants ...22 D5
Tinkersley Derbys ...84 C8
Tinsley Sheff ...84 F2
Tinsley Green W Susx ...24 G3
Tintagel Cnwll ...4 H4
Tintern Mons ...31 P4
Tintinhull Somset ...19 N11
Tintwistle Derbys ...83 M5
Tinwald D & G ...109 M4
Tinwell Rutlnd ...73 Q9
Tippacott Devon ...17 P2
Tipp's End Norfk ...75 K11
Tiptoe Hants ...13 N5
Tipton Sandw ...58 E6
Tipton Green Sandw ...58 E6
Tipton St John Devon ...10 B6
Tiptree Essex ...52 E8
Tiptree Heath Essex ...52 E8
Tirabad Powys ...44 B6
Tircoed Swans ...28 H4
Tiree Ag & B ...136 C7
Tiree Airport Ag & B ...136 C7
Tiretigan Ag & B ...123 M7
Tirley Gloucs ...46 F9
Tiroran Ag & B ...137 M10
Tirphil Caerph ...30 F4
Tirril Cumb ...101 P5
Tir-y-fron Flints ...69 J3
Tisbury Wilts ...20 H9
Tisman's Common W Susx ...24 C4
Tissington Derbys ...71 M4
Titchberry Devon ...16 C6
Titchfield Hants ...14 F5
Titchfield Common Hants ...14 F5
Titchmarsh Nhants ...61 M5
Titchwell Norfk ...75 Q2
Tithby Notts ...72 H3
Titley Herefs ...45 L2
Titmore Green Herts ...50 F5
Titsey Surrey ...37 K10
Titson Cnwll ...16 C11
Tittensor Staffs ...70 F7
Tittleshall Norfk ...76 B7
Titton Worcs ...58 B11
Tiverton Ches W ...69 Q2
Tiverton Devon ...9 N2
Tivetshall St Margaret Norfk ...64 H4
Tivetshall St Mary Norfk ...64 H4
Tivington Somset ...18 B5
Tivy Dale Barns ...90 H9
Tixall Staffs ...70 H10
Tixover Rutlnd ...73 P10
Toab Shet ...169 q12
Toadhole Derbys ...84 E9
Toadmoor Derbys ...84 D10
Tobermory Ag & B ...137 N4
Toberonochy Ag & B ...130 E6
Tobha Mòr W Isls ...168 c14
Tocher Abers ...158 G11
Tochieneal Moray ...158 D4
Tockenham Wilts ...33 K9
Tockenham Wick Wilts ...33 K8
Tocketts R & Cl ...104 H7
Tockholes Bl w D ...89 K6
Tockington S Glos ...32 B7
Tockwith N York ...97 Q10
Todber Dorset ...20 E11
Todburn Nthumb ...119 M11
Toddington C Beds ...50 B5
Toddington Gloucs ...47 K8
Toddington Services C Beds ...50 B5
Todds Green Herts ...50 F5
Todenham Gloucs ...47 P7
Todhills Angus ...142 G10
Todhills Cumb ...110 G8
Todhills Dur ...103 P4
Todhills Rest Area Cumb ...110 G8
Todmorden Calder ...89 Q6
Todwick Rothm ...84 G4
Toft Cambs ...62 E9
Toft Ches E ...82 G9
Toft Lincs ...73 R7
Toft Shet ...169 r6
Toft Warwks ...59 Q10
Toft Hill Dur ...103 N5
Toft Hill Lincs ...86 H8
Toft Monks Norfk ...65 N3
Toft next Newton Lincs ...86 D3
Toftrees Norfk ...76 B6
Toftwood Norfk ...76 D9
Togston Nthumb ...119 P10
Tokavaig Highld ...145 K5
Tokers Green Oxon ...35 K9
Tolastadh bho Thuath W Isls ...168 k3
Toldish Cnwll ...4 E10
Tolland Somset ...18 F8
Tollard Farnham Dorset ...21 J11
Tollard Royal Wilts ...20 H11
Toll Bar Donc ...92 P9
Tollbar End Covtry ...59 N9
Toller Fratrum Dorset ...11 M5
Toller Porcorum Dorset ...11 M5
Tollerton N York ...97 R8

Tollerton Notts ...72 G4
Toller Whelme Dorset ...11 L4
Tollesbury Essex ...52 G9
Tolleshunt D'Arcy Essex ...52 F9
Tolleshunt Knights Essex ...52 F9
Tolleshunt Major Essex ...52 F9
Tollingham E R Yk ...92 D3
Toll of Birness Abers ...159 P11
Tolpuddle Dorset ...12 C6
Tolworth Gt Lon ...36 E7
Tomatin Highld ...148 E2
Tomchrasky Highld ...146 H5
Tomdoun Highld ...146 F7
Tomich Highld ...147 J2
Tomich Highld ...155 P8
Tomich Highld ...155 B3
Tomich Highld ...162 E5
Tomintoul Moray ...149 M4
Tomlow Warwks ...48 E2
Tomnacross Highld ...155 P9
Tomnavoulin Moray ...149 N2
Tompkin Staffs ...70 G4
Ton Mons ...31 K4
Ton Mons ...31 L5
Tonbridge Kent ...37 N11
Tondu Brdgnd ...29 N8
Tonedale Somset ...18 F10
Tonfanau Gwynd ...54 D4
Tong C Brad ...90 G4
Tong Kent ...38 G10
Tong Shrops ...57 P3
Tong W Isls ...168 j4
Tonge Leics ...72 C6
Tong Green Kent ...38 G11
Tongham Surrey ...23 N5
Tongland D & G ...108 G10
Tong Norton Shrops ...57 P3
Tongue Highld ...165 N5
Tongue End Lincs ...74 C7
Tongwynlais Cardif ...30 F8
Tonmawr Neath ...29 M5
Tonna Neath ...29 L5
Ton-teg Rhondd ...30 E7
Tonwell Herts ...50 H7
Tonypandy Rhondd ...30 C6
Tonyrefail Rhondd ...30 D7
Toot Baldon Oxon ...34 G4
Toot Hill Essex ...51 M10
Toothill Hants ...22 C11
Toothill Swindn ...33 M8
Tooting Gt Lon ...36 G6
Tooting Bec Gt Lon ...36 G6
Topcliffe N York ...97 N5
Topcroft Norfk ...65 K3
Topcroft Street Norfk ...65 K3
Top End Bed ...61 M8
Topham Donc ...91 Q7
Top of Hebers Rochdl ...89 P9
Toppesfield Essex ...52 B4
Toprow Norfk ...64 H2
Topsham Devon ...9 M7
Top-y-rhos Flints ...69 J3
Torbeg N Ayrs ...120 G6
Torboll Highld ...162 H7
Torbreck Highld ...156 A9
Torbryan Devon ...7 L5
Torcastle Highld ...139 L2
Torcross Devon ...7 L10
Tore Highld ...155 R7
Torfrey Cnwll ...5 J11
Torinturk Ag & B ...123 P7
Torksey Lincs ...85 P5
Torlundy Highld ...139 L2
Tormarton S Glos ...32 E9
Tormore N Ayrs ...120 G5
Tornagrain Highld ...156 D7
Tornaveen Abers ...150 G6
Torness Highld ...147 P2
Toronto Dur ...103 N4
Torpenhow Cumb ...100 H3
Torphichen W Loth ...126 H3
Torphins Abers ...150 G7
Torpoint Cnwll ...6 C7
Torquay Torbay ...7 N6
Torquhan Border ...128 C10
Torr Devon ...6 F8
Torran Highld ...153 K8
Torrance E Duns ...125 Q3
Torranyard N Ayrs ...125 K9
Torre Somset ...18 D7
Torridon Highld ...154 B6
Torridon House Highld ...153 R6
Torrin Highld ...145 J3
Torrisdale Ag & B ...120 E4
Torrisdale Highld ...165 Q4
Torrish Highld ...163 M3
Torrisholme Lancs ...95 K8
Torrobull Highld ...162 D6
Torry C Aber ...151 N6
Torryburn Fife ...134 C10
Torteval Guern ...10 a2
Torthorwald D & G ...109 M5
Tortington W Susx ...24 B10
Torton Worcs ...58 B10
Tortworth S Glos ...32 D6
Torvaig Highld ...152 H9
Torver Cumb ...94 F2
Torwood Falk ...133 N11
Torwoodlee Border ...117 P3
Torworth Notts ...85 L3
Tosberry Devon ...16 D7
Toscaig Highld ...153 N10
Toseland Cambs ...62 B8
Tosside Lancs ...95 R9
Tostock Suffk ...64 D9
Totaig Highld ...152 C7
Tote Highld ...152 G8
Tote Hill W Susx ...23 N10
Totford Hants ...22 G7
Tothill Lincs ...87 M4
Totland IoW ...13 P7
Totley Sheff ...84 D5
Totley Brook Sheff ...84 D4
Totnes Devon ...7 L6
Toton Notts ...72 E4
Totronald Ag & B ...136 F3
Totscore Highld ...152 F4
Tottenham Gt Lon ...36 H2
Tottenhill Norfk ...75 M8
Totteridge Gt Lon ...36 F2
Totternhoe C Beds ...49 Q10
Tottington Bury ...89 M8
Tottleworth Lancs ...89 L4
Totton Hants ...14 C4

Touchen End W & M ...35 N9
Toulston N York ...91 M2
Toulton Somset ...18 G8
Toulvaddie Highld ...163 K10
Tovil Kent ...38 C11
Towan Cnwll ...3 Q4
Towan Cnwll ...4 D7
Toward Ag & B ...124 E4
Toward Quay Ag & B ...124 E4
Towcester Nhants ...49 J5
Towednack Cnwll ...2 D8
Tower of London Gt Lon ...36 H4
Towersey Oxon ...35 K3
Towie Abers ...150 C5
Tow Law Dur ...103 M3
Town End Cambs ...74 H11
Town End Cumb ...95 J4
Town End Cumb ...101 K9
Town End Cumb ...102 B5
Townend W Duns ...125 K2
Towngate Cumb ...111 B8
Towngate Lincs ...74 B8
Town Green Lancs ...88 E4
Town Green Norfk ...77 M9
Townhead Barns ...83 Q4
Townhead Cumb ...100 E3
Town Head Cumb ...101 M10
Townhead Cumb ...102 B4
Townhead D & G ...109 M3
Town Head N York ...96 B9
Townhead of Greenlaw D & G ...108 F8
Townhill Fife ...134 E10
Town Kelloe Dur ...104 C3
Townlake Devon ...5 Q8
Town Lane Wigan ...82 E5
Town Littleworth E Susx ...25 K7
Town of Lowton Wigan ...82 D5
Town Row E Susx ...25 N4
Towns End Hants ...22 G3
Townsend Somset ...10 H2
Townshend Cnwll ...2 E8
Town Street Suffk ...63 N3
Townwell S Glos ...32 D6
Town Yetholm Border ...118 F5
Towthorpe C York ...98 C9
Towthorpe E R Yk ...98 H8
Towton N York ...91 M3
Towyn Conwy ...80 D9
Toxteth Lpool ...81 M7
Toynton All Saints Lincs ...87 L8
Toynton Fen Side Lincs ...87 L8
Toynton St Peter Lincs ...87 M8
Toy's Hill Kent ...37 L10
Trabboch E Ayrs ...114 H3
Trabbochburn E Ayrs ...115 J3
Traboe Cnwll ...3 J9
Tracebridge Somset ...18 E10
Tradespark Highld ...156 F6
Trafford Park Traffd ...82 G5
Trallong Powys ...44 D9
Tranent E Loth ...128 C5
Tranmere Wirral ...81 L7
Trantelbeg Highld ...166 E6
Trantlemore Highld ...166 E6
Tranwell Nthumb ...113 J4
Trap Carmth ...43 N11
Trapp Carmth ...43 N11
Traprain E Loth ...128 F4
Trap's Green Warwks ...58 H11
Trapshill W Berk ...22 C2
Traquair Border ...117 L4
Trash Green W Berk ...35 J11
Trawden Lancs ...89 Q3
Trawscoed Cerdgn ...54 F10
Trawsfynydd Gwynd ...67 N4
Trealaw Rhondd ...30 D6
Treales Lancs ...88 E4
Trearddur Bay IoA ...78 D9
Treator Cnwll ...4 E6
Tre Aubrey V Glam ...30 D10
Trebanog Rhondd ...30 D6
Trebanos Neath ...29 K4
Trebartha Cnwll ...5 M6
Trebarwith Cnwll ...4 H4
Trebeath Cnwll ...5 M4
Trebetherick Cnwll ...4 E6
Treborough Somset ...18 D7
Trebudannon Cnwll ...4 D9
Trebullett Cnwll ...5 N6
Treburgett Cnwll ...4 H6
Treburley Cnwll ...5 P6
Treburrick Cnwll ...4 D7
Trebyan Cnwll ...4 H9
Trecastle Powys ...44 B9
Trecogo Cnwll ...5 N5
Trecott Devon ...8 F4
Trecwn Pembks ...41 J4
Trecynon Rhondd ...30 C4
Tredaule Cnwll ...5 L5
Tredavoe Cnwll ...2 D8
Tredegar Blae G ...30 F3
Tredethy Cnwll ...4 H7
Tredington Gloucs ...46 H9
Tredington Warwks ...47 Q6
Tredinnick Cnwll ...4 E7
Tredinnick Cnwll ...4 G10
Tredinnick Cnwll ...5 K8
Tredinnick Cnwll ...5 L10
Tredinnick Cnwll ...5 M10
Tredomen Powys ...44 G8
Tredrissi Pembks ...41 L2
Tredrizzick Cnwll ...4 F6
Tredunnock Mons ...31 L6
Tredustan Powys ...44 G8
Treen Cnwll ...2 B9
Treen Cnwll ...2 C6
Treesmill Cnwll ...4 H3
Treeton Rothm ...84 F3
Trefasser Pembks ...40 G3
Trefdraeth IoA ...78 G10
Trefecca Powys ...44 G8
Trefeglwys Powys ...55 M6
Trefenter Cerdgn ...54 E11
Treffgarne Pembks ...41 J5
Treffgarne Owen Pembks ...40 G4
Treffynnon Pembks ...40 G5
Trefil Blae G ...30 F2
Trefilan Cerdgn ...43 K3
Trefin Pembks ...40 F4
Treflach Wood Shrops ...69 J9
Trefnannau Powys ...68 H11
Trefnant Denbgs ...80 E10
Trefonen Shrops ...69 J9
Trefor Gwynd ...66 F5
Trefor IoA ...78 F8
Treforest Rhondd ...30 E7

Trefrew Cnwll ...5 J5
Trefriw Conwy ...67 P2
Tregadillett Cnwll ...5 M5
Tre-gagle Mons ...31 P3
Tregaian IoA ...78 H8
Tregare Mons ...31 M2
Tregarne Cnwll ...3 K9
Tregaron Cerdgn ...43 N3
Tregarth Gwynd ...79 L11
Tregaswith Cnwll ...4 D9
Tregatta Cnwll ...4 G8
Tregawne Cnwll ...4 G8
Tregeare Cnwll ...5 L4
Tregeiriog Wrexhm ...68 G8
Tregele IoA ...78 F6
Tregellist Cnwll ...4 G6
Tregenna Cnwll ...4 M5
Tregeseal Cnwll ...2 B7
Tregew Cnwll ...3 L7
Tre-Gibbon Rhondd ...30 C3
Tregidden Cnwll ...3 K9
Tregiskey Cnwll ...3 Q4
Treglemais Pembks ...40 F5
Tregole Cnwll ...5 K2
Tregolls Cnwll ...3 J6
Tregonce Cnwll ...4 E7
Tregonetha Cnwll ...4 F9
Tregonning & Gwinear Mining District Cnwll ...2 F7
Tregony Cnwll ...3 N5
Tregoodwell Cnwll ...5 J5
Tregorrick Cnwll ...3 Q3
Tregoss Cnwll ...4 F9
Tregoyd Powys ...44 H7
Tregrehan Mills Cnwll ...3 Q3
Tre-groes Cerdgn ...42 H6
Tregullon Cnwll ...4 H9
Tregunna Cnwll ...4 F7
Tregunnon Cnwll ...5 L5
Tregurrian Cnwll ...4 D8
Tregynon Powys ...55 P5
Tre-gynwr Carmth ...42 H11
Trehafod Rhondd ...30 D6
Trehan Cnwll ...5 Q10
Treharris Myr Td ...30 E5
Treharrock Cnwll ...4 G6
Trehemborne Cnwll ...4 D7
Treherbert Carmth ...43 L5
Treherbert Rhondd ...29 P5
Trehunist Cnwll ...5 N9
Trekenner Cnwll ...5 N6
Treknow Cnwll ...4 H4
Trelan Cnwll ...3 J10
Trelash Cnwll ...5 K3
Trelassick Cnwll ...3 L4
Trelawne Cnwll ...5 L11
Trelawnyd Flints ...80 E9
Treleague Cnwll ...3 K9
Treleaver Cnwll ...3 K10
Trelech Carmth ...41 Q4
Trelech a'r Betws Carmth ...42 F9
Treleddyd-fawr Pembks ...40 E5
Trelew Cnwll ...3 L6
Trelewis Myr Td ...30 E5
Treligga Cnwll ...4 G5
Trelights Cnwll ...4 F6
Trelill Cnwll ...4 G6
Trelinnoe Cnwll ...5 N5
Trelion Cnwll ...3 N3
Trelissick Cnwll ...3 L6
Trellech Mons ...31 P3
Trelleck Grange Mons ...31 N4
Trelogan Flints ...80 G8
Trelow Cnwll ...4 E8
Trelowarren Cnwll ...3 J9
Trelowia Cnwll ...5 M10
Treluggan Cnwll ...3 M6
Trelystan Powys ...56 D4
Tremadog Gwynd ...67 K7
Tremail Cnwll ...5 K4
Tremain Cerdgn ...42 D5
Tremaine Cnwll ...5 L4
Tremar Cnwll ...5 M8
Trematon Cnwll ...5 P10
Trembraze Cnwll ...5 M8
Tremeirchion Denbgs ...80 F10
Tremethick Cross Cnwll ...2 C7
Tremore Cnwll ...4 G9
Tre-Mostyn Flints ...80 G9
Trenance Cnwll ...3 L9
Trenance Cnwll ...4 C9
Trenance Cnwll ...4 E7
Trenarren Cnwll ...3 Q4
Trench Wrekin ...57 M2
Trench Green Oxon ...35 J9
Trendeal Cnwll ...3 M3
Trendrine Cnwll ...2 D6
Treneague Cnwll ...4 F7
Trenear Cnwll ...2 H7
Treneglos Cnwll ...5 L4
Trenerth Cnwll ...2 F8
Trenewan Cnwll ...5 K11
Trenewth Cnwll ...4 H6
Trengune Cnwll ...5 K3
Treninnick Cnwll ...4 C9
Trenowah Cnwll ...4 B10
Trenoweth Cnwll ...3 K7
Trent Dorset ...19 Q11
Trentham C Stke ...70 F6
Trentishoe Devon ...17 L2
Trentlock Derbys ...72 D4
Trent Port Lincs ...85 P4
Trent Vale C Stke ...70 F6
Trenwheal Cnwll ...2 G7
Treoes V Glam ...29 P9
Treorchy Rhondd ...30 C5
Trequite Cnwll ...4 G6
Tre'r-ddol Cerdgn ...54 F6
Trerhyngyll V Glam ...30 D9
Trerulefoot Cnwll ...5 N10
Tresaith Cerdgn ...42 E4
Tresawle Cnwll ...3 M4
Tresco IoS ...2 b2
Trescott Staffs ...58 C5
Tresean Cnwll ...4 B10
Tresham Gloucs ...32 E6
Treshnish Isles Ag & B ...136 G7
Tresillian Cnwll ...3 M4
Tresinney Cnwll ...5 J5
Treskinnick Cross Cnwll ...5 L2
Tresmeer Cnwll ...5 L4
Tresparrett Cnwll ...5 J3
Tressait P & K ...141 K5
Tresta Shet ...169 q8

Tresta Shet ...169 t4
Treswell Notts ...85 N5
Treswithian Cnwll ...2 G5
Tre Taliesin Cerdgn ...54 F6
Trethevey Cnwll ...4 H4
Trethewey Cnwll ...2 B9
Trethomas Caerph ...30 G7
Trethosa Cnwll ...3 N3
Trethurgy Cnwll ...3 G10
Tretio Pembks ...40 E5
Tretire Herefs ...45 Q10
Tretower Powys ...44 H10
Treuddyn Flints ...69 J3
Trevadlock Cnwll ...5 M6
Trevalga Cnwll ...4 H3
Trevalyn Wrexhm ...69 L3
Trevanger Cnwll ...4 F6
Trevanson Cnwll ...4 F7
Trevarrack Cnwll ...2 D7
Trevarren Cnwll ...4 E9
Trevarrian Cnwll ...4 D8
Trevarrick Cnwll ...3 P5
Trevarth Cnwll ...3 J5
Trevaughan Carmth ...41 P7
Tre-vaughan Carmth ...42 G10
Treveal Cnwll ...2 D5
Treveal Cnwll ...3 B10
Treveighan Cnwll ...4 H6
Trevellas Downs Cnwll ...3 J3
Trevelmond Cnwll ...5 L9
Trevemper Cnwll ...4 C10
Treveor Cnwll ...3 P5
Treverbyn Cnwll ...3 M4
Treverbyn Cnwll ...4 G10
Treverva Cnwll ...3 K7
Trevescan Cnwll ...2 B9
Trevethin Torfn ...31 J4
Trevia Cnwll ...4 H5
Trevigro Cnwll ...5 N8
Trevilla Cnwll ...3 L6
Trevilson Cnwll ...4 C10
Treviscoe Cnwll ...4 E10
Treviskey Cnwll ...3 N5
Trevithick Cnwll ...3 P4
Trevithick Cnwll ...4 D9
Trevoll Cnwll ...4 C10
Trevone Cnwll ...4 D6
Trevor Wrexhm ...69 J6
Trevorgans Cnwll ...2 C8
Trevorrick Cnwll ...4 E7
Trevose Cnwll ...4 D6
Trew Cnwll ...2 G8
Trewalder Cnwll ...4 H5
Trewalkin Powys ...44 H8
Trewarmett Cnwll ...4 H4
Trewassa Cnwll ...5 J4
Trewavas Mining District Cnwll ...2 F8
Treween Cnwll ...5 L5
Trewellard Cnwll ...2 B7
Trewen Cnwll ...5 M5
Trewennack Cnwll ...2 H8
Trewent Pembks ...41 K11
Trewern Powys ...56 D2
Trewetha Cnwll ...4 G5
Trewethern Cnwll ...4 G6
Trewidland Cnwll ...5 M10
Trewillis Cnwll ...3 K10
Trewint Cnwll ...5 L5
Trewint Cnwll ...5 M9
Trewithian Cnwll ...3 M6
Trewoodloe Cnwll ...5 N7
Trewoon Cnwll ...5 H10
Trewoon Cnwll ...3 P3
Treworga Cnwll ...3 M5
Treworgan Cnwll ...4 L4
Treworlas Cnwll ...3 M6
Treworld Cnwll ...5 J3
Tre-wyn Mons ...45 L10
Treyarnon Cnwll ...4 D7
Treyford W Susx ...23 M11
Trickett's Cross Dorset ...13 J4
Triermain Cumb ...111 L7
Triffleton Pembks ...41 J6
Trillacott Cnwll ...5 M4
Trimdon Dur ...104 C4
Trimdon Colliery Dur ...104 C3
Trimdon Grange Dur ...104 C3
Trimingham Norfk ...77 K4
Trimley Lower Street Suffk ...53 N4
Trimley St Martin Suffk ...53 N4
Trimley St Mary Suffk ...53 N4
Trimpley Worcs ...57 P9
Trimsaran Carmth ...28 E4
Trims Green Herts ...51 L7
Trimstone Devon ...17 J3
Trinafour P & K ...140 H5
Trinant Caerph ...30 H5
Tring Herts ...35 P2
Tringford Herts ...35 P2
Tring Wharf Herts ...35 P2
Trinity Angus ...143 L5
Trinity Jersey ...11 b1
Trinity Gask P & K ...134 B4
Triscombe Somset ...18 G7
Trislaig Highld ...139 K3
Trispen Cnwll ...3 L3
Tritlington Nthumb ...113 L6
Troan Cnwll ...4 D10
Trochry P & K ...141 N9
Troedrhiwfuwch Caerph ...30 F4
Troedyraur Cerdgn ...42 F5
Troedyrhiw Myr Td ...30 E4
Trofarth Conwy ...80 B10
Trois Bois Jersey ...11 b1
Troon Cnwll ...2 G8
Troon S Ayrs ...125 J11
Tropical World Roundhay Park Leeds ...91 J3
Trossachs Stirlg ...132 G6
Trossachs Pier Stirlg ...132 F6
Troston Suffk ...64 B7
Troswell Cnwll ...5 M3
Trotshill Worcs ...46 G3
Trottiscliffe Kent ...37 P8
Trotton W Susx ...23 M10
Troughend Nthumb ...112 C2
Trough Gate Lancs ...89 P6
Troutbeck Cumb ...101 L5
Troutbeck Cumb ...101 M10
Troutbeck Bridge Cumb ...101 M10
Troway Derbys ...84 E5
Trowbridge Wilts ...20 G3

Trowell Notts 72 D3
Trowell Services Notts 72 D2
Trowle Common Wilts 20 F3
Trowley Bottom Herts 50 C8
Trowse Newton Norfk 77 J10
Troy Leeds 90 G3
Trudoxhill Somset 20 D6
Trull Somset 18 H10
Trumfleet Donc 91 Q8
Trumpan Highld 152 C5
Trumpet Herefs 46 C7
Trumpington Cambs 62 F10
Trumpsgreen Surrey 35 Q11
Trunch Norfk 77 K5
Trunnah Lancs 88 C2
Truro Cnwll 3 L5
Truscott Cnwll 5 M4
Trusham Devon 7 L8
Trusley Derbys 71 P7
Trusthorpe Lincs 87 P4
Trysull Staffs 58 C6
Tubney Oxon 34 D5
Tuckenhay Devon 7 L7
Tuckhill Shrops 57 P7
Tuckingmill Cnwll 2 H5
Tuckingmill Wilts 20 H9
Tuckton BCP 13 K6
Tucoyse Cnwll 3 P4
Tuddenham Suffk 53 L2
Tuddenham Suffk 63 M6
Tudeley Kent 37 P11
Tudhoe Dur 103 Q3
Tudorville Herefs 46 A10
Tudweiliog Gwynd 66 C7
Tuesley Surrey 23 Q6
Tuffley Gloucs 32 F2
Tufton Hants 22 E5
Tufton Pembks 41 K5
Tugby Leics 73 K10
Tugford Shrops 57 K7
Tughall Nthumb 119 P5
Tullibody Clacks 133 P8
Tullich Abers 150 B8
Tullich Highld 147 Q2
Tullich Highld 156 F2
Tulliemet P & K 141 P7
Tulloch Abers 159 K11
Tullochgorm Ag & B 131 K8
Tulloch Station Highld 147 K11
Tullymurdoch P & K 142 B7
Tullynessle Abers 150 F4
Tulse Hill Gt Lon 36 H6
Tumble Carmth 28 F2
Tumbler's Green Essex 52 D6
Tumby Lincs 86 H9
Tumby Woodside Lincs 87 J9
Tummel Bridge P & K 141 J4
Tunbridge Wells Kent 25 N3
Tundergarth D & G 110 C4
Tunga W Isls 168 j4
Tungate Norfk 77 K6
Tunley BaNES 20 C3
Tunstall C Stke 70 F4
Tunstall E R Yk 93 P4
Tunstall Kent 38 E9
Tunstall Lancs 95 N6
Tunstall N York 103 P11
Tunstall Norfk 77 N10
Tunstall Staffs 70 D9
Tunstall Suffk 65 M10
Tunstall Sundld 113 N10
Tunstead Derbys 83 P10
Tunstead Norfk 77 K7
Tunstead Milton Derbys 83 M8
Tunworth Hants 23 J5
Tupsley Herefs 45 Q6
Turgis Green Hants 23 J3
Turkdean Gloucs 47 M11
Tur Langton Leics 60 F2
Turleigh Wilts 20 F2
Turleygreen Shrops 57 P7
Turn Lancs 89 N7
Turnastone Herefs 45 M7
Turnberry S Ayrs 114 D6
Turnchapel C Plym 6 D8
Turnditch Derbys 71 P5
Turner Green Lancs 89 J4
Turner's Green E Susx 25 P7
Turner's Green Warwks 59 J11
Turners Hill W Susx 24 H3
Turners Puddle Dorset 12 D6
Turnford Herts 51 J10
Turnhouse C Edin 127 M3
Turnworth Dorset 12 D3
Turriff Abers 158 H7
Turton Bottoms Bl w D 89 L7
Turves Cambs 74 F11
Turvey Bed 49 P4
Turville Bucks 35 L6
Turville Heath Bucks 35 K6
Turweston Bucks 48 H7
Tushielaw Inn Border 117 L7
Tutbury Staffs 71 N9
Tutnall Worcs 58 E10
Tutshill Gloucs 31 P6
Tuttington Norfk 77 J6
Tutwell Cnwll 5 P6
Tuxford Notts 85 M6
Twatt Ork 169 b4
Twatt Shet 169 q8
Twechar E Duns 126 B2
Tweedmouth Nthumb 129 P9
Tweedsmuir Border 116 G3
Twelveheads Cnwll 3 K5
Twelve Oaks E Susx 25 Q6
Twemlow Green Ches E 82 G11
Twenty Lincs 74 C6
Twerton BaNES 20 D2
Twickenham Gt Lon 36 E6
Twigworth Gloucs 46 F10
Twineham W Susx 24 G7
Twineham Green W Susx 24 G6
Twinhoe BaNES 20 E3
Twinstead Essex 52 E4
Twitchen Devon 17 P5
Twitchen Shrops 56 F9
Twitham Kent 39 N10
Two Bridges Devon 6 G4
Two Dales Derbys 84 C8
Two Gates Staffs 59 K4
Two Mile Ash W Susx 24 D5
Two Mile Oak Cross Devon 7 L5
Two Pots Devon 17 J3
Two Waters Herts 50 C9

Twycross Leics 72 A10
Twycross Zoo Leics 59 M3
Twyford Bucks 49 J9
Twyford Hants 22 E10
Twyford Leics 73 J8
Twyford Lincs 73 N6
Twyford Norfk 76 E7
Twyford Wokham 35 L9
Twyford Common Herefs 45 Q7
Twyn-carno Caerph 30 F3
Twynholm D & G 108 E10
Twyning Green Gloucs 46 H7
Twynllanan Carmth 43 Q10
Twyn-yr-Odyn V Glam 30 F10
Twyn-y-Sheriff Mons 31 M3
Twywell Nhants 61 L5
Tyberton Herefs 45 M7
Tyburn Birm 58 H6
Tycroes Carmth 28 H7
Ty Croes IoA 78 E10
Tycrwyn Powys 68 F11
Tydd Gote Lincs 75 J7
Tydd St Giles Cambs 74 H7
Tydd St Mary Lincs 74 H7
Tye Hants 15 K6
Tye Green Essex 51 M8
Tye Green Essex 51 N3
Tye Green Essex 52 C7
Tyersal C Brad 90 F4
Tyldesley Wigan 82 E4
Tyler Hill Kent 39 K9
Tylers Green Bucks 35 P6
Tyler's Green Essex 51 M9
Tylers Green Surrey 37 J10
Tylorstown Rhondd 30 D5
Tylwch Powys 55 M8
Ty-nant Conwy 68 C6
Ty-nant Gwynd 68 B9
Tyndrum Stirlg 139 Q11
Ty'n-dwr Denbgs 68 H6
Tyneham Dorset 12 E8
Tynemouth N Tyne 113 N7
Tyne Tunnel S Tyne 113 M7
Tynewydd Rhondd 29 P5
Tyninghame E Loth 128 G4
Tynron D & G 115 R9
Ty'n-y-bryn Rhondd 30 D7
Ty'n-y-coedcae Caerph 30 G7
Tynygongl IoA 79 J8
Tyn-y-graig Cerdgn 54 F11
Ty'n-y-Groes Conwy 79 P10
Tyn-y-nant Rhondd 30 E7
Tyrie Abers 159 M5
Tyringham M Keyn 49 N5
Tyseley Birm 58 H8
Tythegston Brdgnd 29 N9
Tytherington Ches E 83 K9
Tytherington S Glos 32 C7
Tytherington Somset 20 E6
Tytherington Wilts 20 H6
Tytherleigh Devon 10 G4
Tytherton Lucas Wilts 32 H10
Tyttenhanger Herts 50 E9
Tywardreath Cnwll 4 H11
Tywardreath Highway Cnwll 4 H10
Tywyn Conwy 79 P9
Tywyn Gwynd 54 D4

U

Ubbeston Green Suffk 65 L7
Ubley BaNES 19 P3
Uckerby N York 103 P10
Uckfield E Susx 25 L6
Uckinghall Worcs 46 G7
Uckington Gloucs 46 H10
Uckington Shrops 57 K2
Uddingston S Lans 126 B5
Uddington S Lans 116 B4
Udimore E Susx 26 E8
Udny Green Abers 151 M2
Udny Station Abers 151 N3
Uffcott Wilts 33 M9
Uffculme Devon 9 Q2
Uffington Lincs 73 R9
Uffington Oxon 34 B7
Uffington Shrops 57 J2
Ufford C Pete 74 A10
Ufford Suffk 65 K11
Ufton Warwks 48 C2
Ufton Nervet W Berk 34 H11
Ugadale Ag & B 120 E6
Ugborough Devon 6 H7
Uggeshall Suffk 65 N5
Ugglebarnby N York 105 N9
Ughill Sheff 84 C2
Ugley Essex 51 M5
Ugley Green Essex 51 M5
Ugthorpe N York 105 L8
Uibhist A Deas W Isls 168 d14
Uibhist A Tuath W Isls 168 c10
Uig Ag & B 136 F5
Uig Highld 152 B7
Uig Highld 152 F5
Uig W Isls 168 f4
Uigshader Highld 152 G10
Uisken Ag & B 137 K12
Ulbster Highld 167 P8
Ulcat Row Cumb 101 M6
Ulceby Lincs 87 M6
Ulceby N Linc 93 K8
Ulceby Skitter N Linc 93 K7
Ulcombe Kent 26 D2
Uldale Cumb 100 H3
Uley Gloucs 32 E5
Ulgham Nthumb 113 L2
Ullapool Highld 161 J8
Ullenhall Warwks 58 H11
Ullenwood Gloucs 46 H11
Ulleskelf N York 91 N3
Ullesthorpe Leics 60 B3
Ulley Rothm 84 G3
Ullingswick Herefs 45 A5
Ullinish Lodge Hotel Highld 152 E10
Ullock Cumb 100 E6
Ullswater Cumb 101 M6
Ullswater Steamers Cumb 101 L7
Ulnes Walton Lancs 88 G7
Ulpha Cumb 94 D2
Ulpha Cumb 95 K4
Ulrome E R Yk 99 P9
Ulsta Shet 169 r5

Ulva Ag & B 137 K7
Ulverley Green Solhll 58 H8
Ulverston Cumb 94 F5
Ulwell Dorset 12 H8
Ulzieside D & G 115 Q6
Umberleigh Devon 17 L7
Unapool Highld 164 F10
Underbarrow Cumb 95 K2
Under Burnmouth Border 111 J4
Undercliffe C Brad 90 F4
Underdale Shrops 57 J2
Underling Green Kent 26 C2
Underriver Kent 37 N10
Underwood Newpt 31 L7
Underwood Notts 84 G10
Undley Suffk 63 L4
Undy Mons 31 M7
Union Mills IoM 80 e6
Union Street E Susx 26 B5
Unst Shet 169 s3
Unstone Derbys 84 E5
Unstone Green Derbys 84 E5
Unthank Cumb 101 N3
Unthank Cumb 102 B2
Unthank Cumb 110 G11
Unthank Derbys 84 D5
Unthank Nthumb 129 P10
Upavon Wilts 21 M4
Upchurch Kent 38 D8
Upcott Devon 17 P6
Upcott Herefs 45 L4
Upend Cambs 63 M9
Up Exe Devon 9 M4
Upgate Norfk 76 G8
Upgate Street Norfk 64 F3
Upgate Street Norfk 65 K3
Uphall Dorset 11 M4
Uphall W Loth 127 K3
Upham Devon 9 L3
Upham Hants 22 F10
Uphampton Herefs 45 M2
Uphampton Worcs 46 F2
Uphill N Som 19 K3
Up Holland Lancs 88 G9
Uplawmoor E Rens 125 L6
Upleadon Gloucs 46 E9
Upleatham R & Cl 104 H7
Uplees Kent 38 H9
Uploders Dorset 11 L6
Uplowman Devon 18 D11
Uplyme Devon 10 G6
Up Marden W Susx 15 L4
Upminster Gt Lon 37 N3
Up Mudford Somset 19 Q10
Up Nately Hants 23 J4
Upottery Devon 10 E3
Upper Affcot Shrops 56 G7
Upper Arley Worcs 57 P8
Upper Arncott Oxon 48 H11
Upper Astrop Nhants 48 F7
Upper Badcall Highld 164 E8
Upper Basildon W Berk 34 G9
Upper Batley Kirk 90 G5
Upper Beeding W Susx 24 E8
Upper Benefield Nhants 61 L3
Upper Bentley Worcs 58 E11
Upper Bighouse Highld 166 E5
Upper Birchwood Derbys 84 F9
Upper Boat Rhondd 30 F6
Upper Boddington Nhants 48 E4
Upper Borth Cerdgn 54 E7
Upper Brailes Warwks 48 B7
Upper Breinton Herefs 45 P6
Upper Broadheath Worcs 46 F3
Upper Broughton Notts 72 H5
Upper Bucklebury W Berk 34 F11
Upper Burgate Hants 21 N11
Upper Bush Medway 37 Q7
Upperby Cumb 110 H10
Upper Caldecote C Beds 61 Q11
Upper Canada N Som 19 L3
Upper Canterton Hants 13 N2
Upper Catesby Nhants 60 D9
Upper Catshill Worcs 58 E10
Upper Chapel Powys 44 E6
Upper Cheddon Somset 18 H9
Upper Chicksgrove Wilts 21 J9
Upper Chute Wilts 21 Q4
Upper Clapton Gt Lon 36 H3
Upper Clatford Hants 22 C5
Upper Coberley Gloucs 47 J11
Upper Cotton Staffs 71 K5
Upper Cound Shrops 57 K3
Upper Cudworth Barns 91 K9
Upper Cumberworth Kirk 90 G9
Upper Dallachy Moray 157 R5
Upper Deal Kent 39 Q11
Upper Dean Bed 61 M7
Upper Denby Kirk 90 G9
Upper Denton Cumb 111 M7
Upper Dicker E Susx 25 N9
Upper Dinchope Shrops 56 H8
Upper Dounreay Highld 166 H3
Upper Dovercourt Essex 53 M5
Upper Drumbane Stirlg 133 K6
Upper Dunsforth N York 97 P8
Upper Eashing Surrey 23 Q6
Upper Eathie Highld 156 D5
Upper Egleton Herefs 46 B6
Upper Elkstone Staffs 71 K3
Upper Ellastone Staffs 71 L6
Upper End Derbys 83 N9
Upper Enham Hants 22 C4
Upper Farmcote Shrops 57 P6
Upper Farringdon Hants 23 K7
Upper Framilode Gloucs 32 E2
Upper Froyle Hants 23 L4
Upperglen Highld 152 E7
Upper Godney Somset 19 N6
Upper Gravenhurst C Beds 50 D3
Upper Green Mons 45 M11
Upper Green Suffk 63 M8
Upper Green W Berk 22 C2
Upper Grove Common Herefs 45 R9
Upper Hackney Derbys 84 C8
Upper Hale Surrey 23 M5
Upper Halliford Surrey 36 C7
Upper Halling Medway 37 Q8
Upper Hambleton Rutlnd 73 M9
Upper Harbledown Kent 39 K10
Upper Hardres Court Kent 39 L11
Upper Hardwick Herefs 45 N3
Upper Hartfield E Susx 25 L4

Upper Hartshay Derbys 84 E10
Upper Hatherley Gloucs 46 H10
Upper Hatton Staffs 70 E7
Upper Haugh Rothm 91 L11
Upper Hayton Shrops 57 J8
Upper Heaton Kirk 90 F7
Upper Helmsley N York 98 D9
Upper Hergest Herefs 45 K4
Upper Heyford Nhants 60 E9
Upper Heyford Oxon 48 E9
Upper Hill Herefs 45 P4
Upper Hockenden Kent 37 M7
Upper Hopton Kirk 90 F7
Upper Howsell Worcs 46 E5
Upper Hulme Staffs 71 J2
Upper Ifold Surrey 24 B4
Upper Inglesham Swindn 33 P5
Upper Kilcott Gloucs 32 E7
Upper Killay Swans 28 G6
Upper Kinchrackine Ag & B 131 P2
Upper Knockando Moray 157 M9
Upper Lambourn W Berk 34 B8
Upper Landywood Staffs 58 E3
Upper Langford N Som 19 N3
Upper Langwith Derbys 84 H7
Upper Largo Fife 135 L7
Upper Leigh Staffs 71 J7
Upper Littleton N Som 19 Q2
Upper Lochton Abers 150 H8
Upper Longdon Staffs 58 G2
Upper Ludstone Shrops 57 Q5
Upper Lybster Highld 167 N9
Upper Lydbrook Gloucs 46 B11
Upper Lyde Herefs 45 P6
Upper Lye Herefs 56 F11
Upper Maes-coed Herefs 45 L8
Upper Midhope Sheff 90 G11
Uppermill Oldham 90 B9
Upper Milton Worcs 57 Q10
Upper Minety Wilts 33 K6
Upper Moor Worcs 47 J5
Upper Moor Side Leeds 90 G4
Upper Mulben Moray 157 R7
Upper Netchwood Shrops 57 L6
Upper Nobut Staffs 71 J7
Upper Norwood W Susx 23 P11
Upper Padley Derbys 84 B5
Upper Pennington Hants 13 P5
Upper Pollicott Bucks 35 K2
Upper Poppleton C York 98 B10
Upper Quinton Warwks 47 N5
Upper Ratley Hants 22 C7
Upper Rissington Gloucs 47 P11
Upper Rochford Worcs 57 L11
Upper Ruscoe D & G 108 C8
Upper Sapey Herefs 46 C2
Upper Saxondale Notts 72 H3
Upper Seagry Wilts 32 H8
Upper Shelton C Beds 49 Q6
Upper Sheringham Norfk 76 G3
Upper Skelmorlie N Ayrs 124 G4
Upper Slaughter Gloucs 47 N10
Upper Soudley Gloucs 32 C2
Upper Spond Herefs 45 L4
Upper Standen Kent 27 M3
Upper Staploe Bed 61 P9
Upper Stoke Norfk 77 K11
Upper Stondon C Beds 50 E3
Upper Stowe Nhants 60 D9
Upper Street Hants 21 N11
Upper Street Norfk 64 H6
Upper Street Norfk 77 L8
Upper Street Norfk 77 M8
Upper Street Suffk 53 K10
Upper Street Suffk 63 N10
Upper Street Suffk 64 G11
Upper Strensham Worcs 46 G7
Upper Sundon C Beds 50 B5
Upper Swell Gloucs 47 N9
Upper Tankersley Barns 91 J11
Upper Tean Staffs 71 J7
Upperthong Kirk 90 E9
Upperthorpe Derbys 84 G4
Upperthorpe N Linc 92 C10
Upper Threapwood Ches W 69 M5
Upperton W Susx 23 Q10
Upper Town Derbys 71 N4
Upper Town Dur 103 L3
Uppertown Derbys 84 D8
Upper Town Herefs 46 A5
Uppertown Highld 167 Q1
Upper Town N Som 31 P11
Upper Town Suffk 64 C8
Upper Tumble Carmth 28 F2
Upper Tysoe Warwks 48 B6
Upper Ufford Suffk 65 K11
Upperup Gloucs 33 K5
Upper Upham Wilts 33 P9
Upper Upnor Medway 38 C7
Upper Victoria Angus 143 J10
Upper Vobster Somset 20 D5
Upper Wardington Oxon 48 E5
Upper Weald M Keyn 49 M7
Upper Weedon Nhants 60 D9
Upper Welland Worcs 46 E6
Upper Wellingham E Susx 25 L8
Upper Weston BaNES 32 D11
Upper Weybread Suffk 65 J6
Upper Wick Worcs 46 F4
Upper Wield Hants 22 H7
Upper Winchendon Bucks 35 K2
Upperwood Derbys 84 C9
Upper Woodford Wilts 21 M7
Upper Wootton Hants 22 H4
Upper Wraxall Wilts 32 F10
Upper Wyche Worcs 46 E6
Uppincott Devon 9 M3
Uppingham RutInd 73 M11
Uppington Dorset 12 H3
Uppington Shrops 57 K3
Upsall N York 97 Q3
Upsettlington Border 129 M10
Upshire Essex 51 K10
Up Somborne Hants 22 C8
Up Sydling Dorset 11 N4
Upthorpe Suffk 64 D7
Upton Bucks 35 L2
Upton C Pete 61 Q9
Upton Ches W 81 N11
Upton Cnwll 5 M7
Upton Cnwll 16 C11
Upton Cumb 101 K3
Upton Devon 7 J10

Upton Devon 10 B4
Upton Dorset 12 B8
Upton Dorset 12 G6
Upton E R Yk 99 N10
Upton Halton 81 P7
Upton Hants 22 C11
Upton Hants 22 C3
Upton Leics 72 B11
Upton Lincs 85 Q3
Upton Nhants 60 F9
Upton Nhants 77 M8
Upton Notts 85 M10
Upton Notts 85 M5
Upton Oxon 33 P2
Upton Oxon 34 F7
Upton Pembks 41 K10
Upton R & Cl 105 K7
Upton Slough 35 Q9
Upton Somset 18 C9
Upton Somset 19 N9
Upton Wakefd 91 M8
Upton Warwks 47 M3
Upton Wilts 20 G8
Upton Wirral 81 K7
Upton Bishop Herefs 46 C9
Upton Cheyney S Glos 32 C10
Upton Cressett Shrops 57 M6
Upton Crews Herefs 46 B9
Upton Cross Cnwll 5 M7
Upton End C Beds 50 D4
Upton Grey Hants 23 J5
Upton Heath Ches W 81 N11
Upton Hellions Devon 9 K4
Upton Lovell Wilts 21 H6
Upton Magna Shrops 57 K2
Upton Noble Somset 20 D7
Upton Pyne Devon 9 M5
Upton St Leonards Gloucs 46 G11
Upton Scudamore Wilts 20 G5
Upton Snodsbury Worcs 46 H4
Upton Towans Cnwll 2 F5
Upton-upon-Severn Worcs 46 F6
Upton Warren Worcs 58 D11
Upwaltham W Susx 15 P4
Upware Cambs 62 H6
Upwell Norfk 75 J10
Upwey Dorset 11 P7
Upwick Green Herts 51 L6
Upwood Cambs 62 C4
Urchfont Wilts 21 K3
Urdimarsh Herefs 45 Q5
Ure Bank N York 97 M6
Urlay Nook S on T 104 D8
Urmston Traffd 82 G6
Urpeth Dur 113 L10
Urquhart Moray 157 P5
Urquhart Castle Highld 147 N2
Urra N York 104 G10
Urray Highld 155 P7
Usan Angus 143 N7
Ushaw Moor Dur 103 P2
Usk Mons 31 L4
Usselby Lincs 86 E2
Usworth Sundld 113 M9
Utkinton Ches W 82 B11
Utley C Brad 90 D2
Uton Devon 9 K5
Utterby Lincs 87 K2
Uttoxeter Staffs 71 K8
Uwchmynydd Gwynd 66 B9
Uxbridge Gt Lon 36 C4
Uyeasound Shet 169 s3
Uzmaston Pembks 41 J8

V

Vale Guern 10 c1
Valley IoA 78 D9
Valley End Surrey 23 Q2
Valley Truckle Cnwll 4 H5
Valtos Highld 153 J5
Valtos W Isls 168 f4
Vange Essex 38 B4
Varteg Torfn 31 J3
Vatsetter Shet 169 s5
Vatten Highld 152 D9
Vaynor Myr Td 30 D2
Vazon Bay Guern 10 b2
Veensgarth Shet 169 r9
Velindre Powys 44 H7
Vellow Somset 18 E7
Velly Devon 16 D7
Venngreen Devon 16 F9
Vennington Shrops 56 E3
Venn Ottery Devon 10 B6
Venny Tedburn Devon 9 K5
Venterdon Cnwll 5 P7
Ventnor IoW 14 G11
Venton Devon 6 F7
Vernham Dean Hants 22 B3
Vernham Street Hants 22 B3
Vernolds Common Shrops 56 H8
Verwood Dorset 13 J3
Veryan Cnwll 3 N6
Veryan Green Cnwll 3 N5
Vicarage Devon 10 E7
Vickerstown Cumb 94 D7
Victoria Barns 90 F9
Victoria Blae G 30 G3
Victoria Cnwll 4 F9
Vidlin Shet 169 r7
Viewfield Moray 157 P5
Viewpark N Lans 126 C5
Vigo Kent 37 P8
Village de Putron Guern 10 c2
Villa la Bas Jersey 11 a1
Villiaze Guern 10 b2
Vinehall Street E Susx 26 C7
Vines Cross E Susx 25 N7
Virginia Water Surrey 36 B7
Virginstow Devon 5 P3
Vobster Somset 20 D5
Voe Shet 169 r7
Vowchurch Herefs 45 M7
Vulcan Village St Hel 82 C6

W

Waberthwaite Cumb 94 C2
Wackerfield Dur 103 N6
Wacton Norfk 64 H3

Wadborough Worcs 46 H5
Waddesdon Bucks 49 K11
Waddesdon Manor Bucks 49 K11
Waddeton Devon 7 M7
Waddicar Sefton 81 H5
Waddingham Lincs 92 G11
Waddington Lancs 89 M4
Waddington Lincs 86 C8
Waddon Devon 9 L9
Waddon Dorset 11 N7
Waddon Gt Lon 36 H8
Wadebridge Cnwll 4 F7
Wadeford Somset 10 G2
Wadenhoe Nhants 61 M4
Wadesmill Herts 51 J7
Wadhurst E Susx 25 P4
Wadshelf Derbys 84 D6
Wadswick Wilts 32 F11
Wadworth Donc 91 P11
Waen Denbgs 68 C2
Waen Denbgs 80 G11
Waen Powys 68 H11
Waen Powys 68 H11
Waen Fach Powys 79 K11
Waen-pentir Gwynd 79 K11
Waen-wen Gwynd 79 K11
Wagbeach Shrops 56 F4
Wainfelin Torfn 31 J4
Wainfleet All Saints Lincs 87 N9
Wainfleet Bank Lincs 87 N9
Wainfleet St Mary Lincs 87 N9
Wainford Norfk 65 L3
Wainhouse Corner Cnwll 5 K2
Wainscott Medway 38 B7
Wain's Hill N Som 31 L10
Wainstalls Calder 90 C5
Waithe Lincs 93 N10
Waitby Cumb 102 E9
Wakefield Wakefd 91 J6
Wake Green Birm 58 G8
Wakerley Nhants 73 P11
Wakes Colne Essex 52 E6
Walberswick Suffk 65 P7
Walberton W Susx 15 Q5
Walbottle N u Ty 113 J7
Walbutt D & G 108 F7
Walby Cumb 110 H8
Walcombe Somset 19 Q5
Walcot Lincs 73 R3
Walcot N Linc 92 E6
Walcot Shrops 56 E7
Walcot Shrops 57 K2
Walcot Swindn 33 N8
Walcote Leics 60 C4
Walcote Warwks 47 M3
Walcot Green Norfk 64 G5
Walcott Lincs 86 F9
Walcott Norfk 77 M5
Walden N York 96 F4
Walden Head N York 96 F4
Walden Stubbs N York 91 P7
Walderslade Medway 38 C9
Walderton W Susx 15 L4
Walditch Dorset 11 K6
Waldley Derbys 71 L7
Waldridge Dur 113 L11
Waldringfield Suffk 53 N2
Waldron E Susx 25 M7
Wales Rothm 84 G4
Wales Somset 19 Q10
Walesby Lincs 86 F2
Walesby Notts 85 L6
Walford Herefs 46 A10
Walford Herefs 56 F10
Walford Shrops 69 M10
Walford Staffs 70 E8
Walford Shrops Herefs 69 M11
Walgherton Ches E 70 B5
Walgrave Nhants 60 H6
Walhampton Hants 13 P5
Walkden Salfd 82 F4
Walker N u Ty 113 L8
Walkerburn Border 117 M3
Walker Fold Lancs 89 K2
Walkeringham Notts 85 N2
Walkerith Lincs 85 N2
Walkern Herts 50 G5
Walker's Green Herefs 45 Q5
Walker's Heath Birm 58 G9
Walkerton Fife 134 G7
Walkford BCP 13 M6
Walkhampton Devon 6 E5
Walkington E R Yk 92 G3
Walkley Sheff 84 D3
Walk Mill Lancs 89 P5
Walkwood Worcs 47 K2
Wall Nthumb 112 D7
Wall Staffs 58 H3
Wallacetown S Ayrs 114 E7
Wallacetown S Ayrs 114 F3
Wallands Park E Susx 25 K8
Wallasey Wirral 81 K6
Wallasey (Kingsway)
Tunnel Wirral 81 L6
Wall End Cumb 94 E4
Wall End Herefs 45 N3
Wallend Medway 38 E6
Waller's Green Herefs 46 C7
Wallhead Cumb 111 J8
Wall Heath Dudley 58 C7
Wall Houses Nthumb 112 F7
Wallingford Oxon 34 H7
Wallington Gt Lon 36 G8
Wallington Hants 14 G5
Wallington Herts 50 G4
Wallington Heath Wsall 58 E4
Wallis Pembks 41 K5
Wallisdown BCP 13 J6
Walliswood Surrey 24 D3
Walls Shet 169 p9
Wallsend N Tyne 113 L7
Wallthwaite Cumb 101 L5
Wall under Haywood Shrops 57 J6
Wallyford E Loth 128 B5
Walmer Kent 39 Q11
Walmer Bridge Lancs 88 F6
Walmersley Bury 89 N8
Walmestone Kent 39 N10
Walmley Birm 58 H6
Walmley Ash Birm 58 H6
Walmsgate Lincs 87 L5
Walney Cumb 94 D7
Walpole Somset 19 K6
Walpole Suffk 65 M7
Walpole Cross Keys Norfk 75 K7

Walpole Highway Norfk 75 K8
Walpole St Andrew Norfk 75 K7
Walpole St Peter Norfk 75 K7
Walrow Somset 19 K5
Walsall Wsall 58 F5
Walsall Wood Wsall 58 F4
Walsden Calder 89 Q6
Walsgrave on Sowe Covtry 59 N8
Walsham le Willows Suffk 64 E7
Walshaw Bury 89 M8
Walshford N York 97 P10
Walsoken Norfk 75 J8
Walston S Lans 127 K8
Walsworth Herts 50 E4
Walter's Ash Bucks 35 M5
Walters Green Kent 25 M2
Walterston V Glam 30 E10
Walterstone Herefs 45 L9
Waltham Kent 27 K2
Waltham NE Lin 93 N10
Waltham Abbey Essex 51 J10
Waltham Chase Hants 14 G4
Waltham Cross Herts 51 J10
Waltham on the Wolds
Leics 73 L6
Waltham St Lawrence
W & M 35 M9
Waltham's Cross Essex 51 Q4
Walthamstow Gt Lon 37 J3
Walton C Pete 74 C10
Walton Cumb 111 K8
Walton Derbys 84 E7
Walton Leeds 97 P11
Walton Leics 60 C3
Walton M Keyn 49 N7
Walton Powys 45 K3
Walton Shrops 56 H9
Walton Somset 19 N7
Walton Staffs 70 F8
Walton Staffs 70 F9
Walton Suffk 53 N4
Walton W Susx 15 M6
Walton Wakefd 91 K7
Walton Warwks 47 Q4
Walton Wrekin 69 L11
Walton Cardiff Gloucs 46 H8
Walton East Pembks 41 K6
Walton Elm Dorset 20 E11
Walton Grounds Nhants 48 F8
Walton Highway Norfk 75 J8
Walton-in-Gordano N Som 31 M10
Walton-le-Dale Lancs 88 H5
Walton-on-the-Hill Staffs 70 H10
Walton-on-the-Hill Surrey 36 F9
Walton-on-the-Naze Essex 53 N7
Walton on the Wolds Leics 72 F7
Walton-on-Trent Derbys 71 N11
Walton Park N Som 31 M10
Walton West Pembks 40 G8
Walwen Flints 80 G9
Walwen Flints 80 H10
Walwen Flints 81 J9
Walwick Nthumb 112 D6
Walworth Darltn 103 P7
Walworth Gt Lon 36 H5
Walworth Gate Darltn 103 P6
Walwyn's Castle Pembks 40 G8
Wambrook Somset 10 F3
Wampool Cumb 110 D10
Wanborough Surrey 23 P5
Wanborough Swindn 33 P8
Wandon End Herts 50 D6
Wandsworth Gt Lon 36 G6
Wangford Suffk 65 P6
Wanlip Leics 72 F8
Wanlockhead D & G 116 B8
Wannock E Susx 25 N10
Wansford C Pete 73 R11
Wansford E R Yk 99 M9
Wanshurst Green Kent 26 C2
Wanstead Gt Lon 37 K3
Wanstrow Somset 20 D6
Wanswell Gloucs 32 C4
Wantage Oxon 34 C7
Wants Green Worcs 46 E3
Wapley S Glos 32 D9
Wappenbury Warwks 59 N11
Wappenham Nhants 48 H5
Warbleton E Susx 25 P7
Warborough Oxon 34 G6
Warboys Cambs 62 D4
Warbreck Bpool 88 C3
Warbstow Cnwll 5 K3
Warburton Traffd 82 F7
Warcop Cumb 102 D7
Warden Kent 38 H7
Warden Nthumb 112 D7
Ward End Birm 58 H7
Warden Street C Beds 50 D2
Ward Green Suffk 64 E9
Ward Green Cross Lancs 89 J3
Wardhedges C Beds 50 C3
Wardington Oxon 48 E5
Wardle Ches E 69 R3
Wardle Rochdl 89 Q7
Wardley Gatesd 113 M8
Wardley Rutlnd 73 L10
Wardley Salfd 82 G4
Wardlow Derbys 83 Q10
Wardsend Ches E 83 K8
Wardy Hill Cambs 62 G4
Ware Herts 51 J8
Wareham Dorset 12 F7
Warehorne Kent 26 G5
Warenford Nthumb 119 M5
Waren Mill Nthumb 119 M4
Warenton Nthumb 119 M4
Wareside Herts 51 J8
Waresley Cambs 62 C10
Waresley Worcs 58 B10
Ware Street Kent 38 C10
Warfield Br For 35 M10
Warfleet Devon 7 M8
Wargate Lincs 74 D4
Wargrave Wokham 35 L9
Warham Herefs 45 P7
Warham Norfk 76 C3
Wark Nthumb 112 C5
Wark Nthumb 118 F3
Warkleigh Devon 17 L7
Warkton Nhants 61 J6
Warkworth Nhants 48 E6
Warkworth Nthumb 119 P9
Warlaby N York 97 M2

Warland Calder 89 Q6
Warleggan Cnwll 5 K8
Warleigh BaNES 20 E2
Warley Town Calder 90 D6
Warlingham Surrey 37 J9
Warmbrook Derbys 71 P4
Warmingham Ches E 70 C2
Warmington Nhants 61 N2
Warmington Warwks 48 E5
Warminster Wilts 20 G5
Warmley S Glos 32 C10
Warmsworth Donc 91 N10
Warmwell Dorset 12 D7
Warndon Worcs 46 G3
Warner Bros. Studio Tour
Herts 50 C10
Warnford Hants 22 H10
Warnham W Susx 24 E4
Warnham Court W Susx 24 E4
Warningcamp W Susx 24 B9
Warninglid W Susx 24 F5
Warren Ches E 83 J10
Warren Pembks 40 H11
Warrenby R & Cl 104 G5
Warrenhill S Lans 116 C3
Warren Row W & M 35 M8
Warren's Green Herts 50 G5
Warren Street Kent 38 F11
Warrington M Keyn 49 N4
Warrington Warrtn 82 D7
Warriston C Edin 127 P2
Warsash Hants 14 E5
Warslow Staffs 71 K3
Warsop Vale Notts 84 H7
Warter E R Yk 98 H10
Warthermaske N York 97 K5
Warthill N York 98 D9
Wartling E Susx 25 Q9
Wartnaby Leics 73 J6
Warton Lancs 88 E5
Warton Lancs 95 K6
Warton Nthumb 119 K10
Warton Warwks 59 L4
Warwick Warwks 59 L11
Warwick Bridge Cumb 111 J9
Warwick Castle Warwks 47 Q2
Warwick-on-Eden Cumb 111 J9
Warwick Services Warwks 48 B3
Warwicksland Cumb 111 J5
Wasbister Ork 169 c3
Wasdale Head Cumb 100 G9
Wash Derbys 83 N8
Washall Green Herts 51 K4
Washaway Cnwll 4 G8
Washbourne Devon 7 K8
Washbrook Somset 19 M4
Washbrook Suffk 53 K3
Washfield Devon 18 B11
Washfold N York 103 L10
Washford Somset 18 E6
Washford Pyne Devon 9 K2
Washingborough Lincs 86 D6
Washington Sundld 113 M10
Washington W Susx 24 D8
Washington Services
Gatesd 113 L9
Washwood Heath Birm 58 H7
Wasing W Berk 22 G2
Waskerley Dur 112 H11
Wasperton Warwks 47 Q3
Wasps Nest Lincs 86 E8
Wass N York 98 B5
Wast Water Cumb 100 G9
Watchet Somset 18 E6
Watchfield Oxon 33 P6
Watchfield Somset 19 K5
Watchgate Cumb 101 P11
Watchill Cumb 100 G2
Watcombe Torbay 7 N5
Watendlath Cumb 101 J7
Water Devon 9 J8
Water Lancs 89 N5
Waterbeach Cambs 62 G7
Waterbeach W Susx 15 N5
Waterbeck D & G 110 D5
Waterden Norfk 76 B4
Water Eaton Oxon 34 F2
Water Eaton Staffs 58 D2
Water End Bed 61 P10
Water End Bed 61 P11
Water End C Beds 50 C3
Waterend Cumb 100 F6
Water End E R Yk 92 C3
Water End Essex 51 N2
Water End Herts 50 B8
Water End Herts 50 F10
Waterfall Staffs 71 K4
Waterfoot Ag & B 120 D2
Waterfoot E Rens 125 P6
Waterford Herts 50 H8
Water Fryston Wakefd 91 M5
Watergate Cnwll 5 J5
Waterhead Cumb 101 L10
Waterheads Border 127 N7
Waterhouses Dur 103 N2
Waterhouses Staffs 71 K4
Wateringbury Kent 37 Q10
Waterlane Gloucs 32 H4
Waterloo Cnwll 5 J7
Waterloo Derbys 84 F8
Waterloo Herefs 45 L5
Waterloo Highld 145 L3
Waterloo N Lans 126 E7
Waterloo Norfk 77 J8
Waterloo P & K 141 Q10
Waterloo Pembks 41 J10
Waterloo Sefton 81 L5
Waterloo Cross Devon 9 E2
Waterloo Port Gwynd 66 H2
Waterlooville Hants 15 J5
Watermead Bucks 49 M11
Watermillock Cumb 101 M6
Water Newton Cambs 74 B11
Water Orton Warwks 59 J6
Waterperry Oxon 34 H3
Waterrow Somset 18 E9
Watersfield W Susx 24 B7
Waterside Bl w D 89 L6
Waterside Bucks 35 M3
Waterside Cumb 110 D11
Waterside Donc 91 R8
Waterside E Ayrs 114 H6
Waterside E Ayrs 125 M9
Waterside E Duns 126 B3

Water's Nook Bolton 89 K9
Waterstein Highld 152 A8
Waterstock Oxon 34 H3
Waterston Pembks 40 H9
Water Stratford Bucks 49 J8
Water Street Neath 29 M8
Waters Upton Wrekin 70 A11
Water Yeat Cumb 94 F3
Watford Herts 50 D11
Watford Nhants 60 D7
Watford Gap Services 60 D7
Wath N York 96 H7
Wath N York 97 M5
Wath upon Dearne Rothm 91 L10
Watlington Norfk 75 M8
Watlington Oxon 35 J6
Watnall Notts 84 H11
Watten Highld 167 M6
Wattisfield Suffk 64 E7
Wattisham Suffk 64 E11
Watton Dorset 11 K6
Watton E R Yk 99 L10
Watton Norfk 76 C11
Watton-at-Stone Herts 50 H7
Watton Green Norfk 76 C11
Wattons Green Essex 51 M11
Wattston N Lans 126 D3
Wattstown Rhondd 30 D6
Wattsville Caerph 30 H6
Wauldby E R Yk 92 G5
Waulkmill Abers 150 G9
Waunarlwydd Swans 28 H5
Waunfawr Cerdgn 54 E8
Waunfawr Gwynd 67 J3
Waungron Swans 28 G4
Waunlwyd Blae G 30 G3
Wavendon M Keyn 49 P7
Waverbridge Cumb 110 D11
Waverton Ches W 69 N2
Waverton Cumb 110 D11
Wawne E R Yk 93 J3
Waxham Norfk 77 N6
Waxholme E R Yk 93 P5
Way Kent 39 P8
Waye Devon 7 K4
Wayford Somset 11 J3
Waytown Dorset 11 K5
Way Village Devon 9 L2
Way Wick N Som 19 L2
Weacombe Somset 18 F6
Weald Oxon 34 B4
Wealdstone Gt Lon 36 E3
Weardley Leeds 90 H2
Weare Somset 19 M4
Weare Giffard Devon 16 H7
Wearhead Dur 102 G3
Wearne Somset 19 M9
Weasdale Cumb 102 C10
Weasenham All Saints
Norfk 76 A7
Weasenham St Peter Norfk 76 B7
Weaste Salfd 82 H5
Weatheroak Hill Worcs 58 G10
Weaverham Ches W 82 D10
Weaverslake Staffs 71 L11
Weaverthorpe N York 99 K6
Webbington Somset 19 L3
Webb's Heath S Glos 32 C10
Webheath Worcs 58 F11
Webton Herefs 45 N7
Wedderlairs Abers 159 L11
Wedding Hall Fold N York 96 D11
Weddington Kent 39 N10
Weddington Warwks 59 N6
Wedhampton Wilts 21 L3
Wedmore Somset 19 M5
Wednesbury Sandw 58 E5
Wednesfield Wolves 58 D4
Weecar Notts 85 P7
Weedon Bucks 49 M11
Weedon Bec Nhants 60 D9
Weedon Lois Nhants 48 H5
Weeford Staffs 58 H4
Week Devon 7 K6
Week Devon 17 K6
Week Devon 17 N8
Weeke Devon 9 J3
Weeke Hants 22 E8
Weekley Nhants 61 J4
Week St Mary Cnwll 5 L2
Weel E R Yk 93 J3
Weeley Essex 53 K7
Weeley Heath Essex 53 L7
Weem P & K 141 K8
Weeping Cross Staffs 70 G10
Weethley Warwks 47 L3
Weeting Norfk 63 N3
Weeton E R Yk 93 P4
Weeton Lancs 88 D4
Weeton N York 97 L11
Weetwood Leeds 90 H3
Weir Lancs 89 P5
Weirbrook Shrops 69 K10
Weir Quay Devon 6 C5
Weisdale Shet 169 q8
Welborne Norfk 76 F9
Welbourn Lincs 86 C10
Welburn N York 98 D7
Welbury N York 104 C10
Welby Lincs 73 P3
Welches Dam Cambs 62 G4
Welcombe Devon 16 C8
Weldon Nhants 61 K3
Weldon Bridge Nthumb 119 M11
Welford Nhants 60 D10
Welford W Berk 34 D10
Welford-on-Avon Warwks 47 M4
Welham Leics 60 G2
Welham Notts 85 M4
Welham Bridge E R Yk 92 C4
Welham Green Herts 50 F9
Well Hants 23 J6
Well Lincs 87 M6
Well N York 97 L4
Welland Worcs 46 E6
Wellbank Angus 142 H10
Well End Bucks 35 N7
Well End Herts 50 F11
Wellesbourne Warwks 47 Q3
Wellesbourne Mountford
Warwks 47 Q3
Well Head Herts 50 D5
Well Hill Kent 37 L8
Wellhouse W Berk 34 F10

Welling Gt Lon 37 L5
Wellingborough Nhants 61 J7
Wellingham Norfk 76 B7
Wellingore Lincs 86 C9
Wellington Cumb 100 E10
Wellington Herefs 45 P5
Wellington Somset 18 F10
Wellington Wrekin 57 M2
Wellington Heath Herefs 46 D6
Wellington Marsh Herefs 45 P5
Wellow BaNES 20 D3
Wellow IoW 14 C9
Wellow Notts 85 L7
Wellpond Green Herts 51 K6
Wells Somset 19 P5
Wellsborough Leics 72 B10
Wells Green Ches E 70 B4
Wells Head C Brad 90 D4
Wells-next-the-Sea Norfk 76 C3
Wellstye Green Essex 51 P7
Well Town Devon 9 M3
Welltree P & K 134 B3
Wellwood Fife 134 D10
Welney Norfk 62 H2
Welshampton Shrops 69 M7
Welsh Bicknor Herefs 46 A11
Welsh End Shrops 69 P7
Welsh Frankton Shrops 69 L8
Welsh Hook Pembks 40 H5
Welsh Newton Herefs 45 Q11
Welshpool Powys 56 C3
Welsh St Donats V Glam 30 D9
Welton Cumb 101 L2
Welton E R Yk 92 G5
Welton Lincs 86 D5
Welton Nhants 60 C7
Welton le Marsh Lincs 87 N7
Welton le Wold Lincs 87 J3
Welwick E R Yk 93 P6
Welwyn Herts 50 F7
Welwyn Garden City Herts 50 F8
Wem Shrops 69 P9
Wembdon Somset 19 J7
Wembley Gt Lon 36 E3
Wembury Devon 6 E9
Wembworthy Devon 17 M10
Wemyss Bay Inver 124 F4
Wenallt Cerdgn 54 F10
Wendens Ambo Essex 51 M3
Wendlebury Oxon 48 G11
Wendling Norfk 76 C9
Wendover Bucks 35 N3
Wendron Cnwll 2 H7
Wendron Mining District
Cnwll 2 H7
Wendy Cambs 62 D11
Wenfordbridge Cnwll 4 H6
Wenhaston Suffk 65 N6
Wennington Cambs 62 B5
Wennington Gt Lon 37 M4
Wennington Lancs 95 N7
Wensley Derbys 84 C8
Wensley N York 96 G3
Wentbridge Wakefd 91 M7
Wentnor Shrops 56 F6
Wentworth Cambs 62 G5
Wentworth Rothm 91 K11
Wentworth Castle Barns 91 J10
Wenvoe V Glam 30 F10
Weobley Herefs 45 N4
Weobley Marsh Herefs 45 N4
Wepham W Susx 24 B9
Wereham Norfk 75 N10
Wergs Wolves 58 C4
Wern Gwynd 67 J7
Wern Powys 44 G11
Wern Powys 56 D2
Wern Shrops 69 J8
Werneth Low Tamesd 83 L6
Wernffrwd Swans 28 F6
Wern-y-gaer Flints 81 J11
Werrington C Pete 74 C10
Werrington Cnwll 5 N4
Werrington Staffs 70 G5
Wervin Ches W 81 N10
Wesham Lancs 88 E4
Wessington Derbys 84 E9
West Aberthaw V Glam 30 D11
West Acre Norfk 75 Q7
West Allerdean Nthumb 129 P10
West Alvington Devon 7 J10
West Amesbury Wilts 21 M6
West Anstey Devon 17 R6
West Appleton N York 97 K2
West Ashby Lincs 87 J6
West Ashling W Susx 15 M5
West Ashton Wilts 20 G3
West Auckland Dur 103 N5
West Ayton N York 99 K4
West Bagborough Somset 18 G8
West Bank Blae G 30 H3
West Bank Halton 81 Q8
West Barkwith Lincs 86 G4
West Barnby N York 105 M8
West Barns E Loth 128 H4
West Barsham Norfk 76 C5
West Bay Dorset 11 K6
West Beckham Norfk 76 G4
West Bedfont Surrey 36 C6
Westbere Kent 39 L9
West Bergholt Essex 52 G6
West Bexington Dorset 11 L7
West Bilney Norfk 75 P7
West Blatchington Br & H 24 G9
West Boldon S Tyne 113 N8
Westborough Lincs 73 M2
Westbourne BCP 13 J6
Westbourne W Susx 15 L5
West Bourton Dorset 20 E9
West Bowling C Brad 90 F4
West Brabourne Kent 27 J3
West Bradenham Norfk 76 C10
West Bradford Lancs 89 L2
West Bradley Somset 19 Q7
West Bretton Wakefd 90 H8
West Bridgford Notts 72 F3
West Briscoe Dur 103 J7
West Bromwich Sandw 58 F6
Westbrook Kent 39 P7
Westbrook W Berk 34 D10
Westbrook Wilts 33 J11
West Buckland Devon 17 M5
West Buckland Somset 18 G10
West Burrafirth Shet 169 p8
West Burton N York 96 F3

Place	County	Page	Grid
West Burton	W Susx	15	Q4
Westbury	Bucks	48	H7
Westbury	Shrops	56	F3
Westbury	Wilts	20	G4
Westbury Leigh	Wilts	20	G5
Westbury-on-Severn	Gloucs	32	D2
Westbury-on-Trym	Bristl	31	Q9
Westbury-sub-Mendip	Somset	19	P5
West Butsfield	Dur	103	M2
West Butterwick	N Linc	92	D9
Westby	Lancs	88	D4
West Byfleet	Surrey	36	B8
West Cairngaan	D & G	106	F11
West Caister	Norfk	77	Q9
West Calder	W Loth	127	J5
West Camel	Somset	19	Q10
West Chaldon	Dorset	12	C8
West Challow	Oxon	34	C7
West Charleton	Devon	7	K10
West Chelborough	Dorset	11	L3
West Chevington	Nthumb	119	P11
West Chiltington	W Susx	24	C7
West Chinnock	Somset	11	K2
West Chisenbury	Wilts	21	M4
West Clandon	Surrey	36	B10
West Cliffe	Kent	27	P3
Westcliff-on-Sea	Sthend	38	E4
West Coker	Somset	11	L2
West Combe	Devon	7	K6
Westcombe	Somset	20	C7
West Compton	Somset	19	Q6
West Compton Abbas	Dorset	11	M6
Westcote	Gloucs	47	P10
Westcote Barton	Oxon	48	D9
Westcott	Bucks	49	K11
Westcott	Devon	9	P4
Westcott	Surrey	36	D11
West Cottingwith	N York	92	A2
Westcourt	Wilts	21	P2
West Cowick	E R Yk	91	Q6
West Cross	Swans	28	H7
West Curry	Cnwll	5	M3
West Curthwaite	Cumb	110	F11
Westdean	E Susx	25	M11
West Dean	W Susx	15	N4
West Dean	Wilts	21	Q9
West Deeping	Lincs	74	B9
West Derby	Lpool	81	M6
West Dereham	Norfk	75	N10
West Ditchburn	Nthumb	119	M6
West Down	Devon	17	J3
Westdown Camp	Wilts	21	K5
Westdowns	Cnwll	4	H5
West Drayton	Gt Lon	36	C5
West Drayton	Notts	85	M6
West Dunnet	Highld	167	M2
Wested	Kent	37	M7
West Ella	E R Yk	92	H5
West End	Bed	49	Q4
West End	Br For	35	N10
West End	Caerph	30	H5
West End	Cambs	62	D7
West End	Cumb	110	F9
West End	E R Yk	92	F4
West End	E R Yk	93	L4
West End	E R Yk	93	N5
Westend	Gloucs	32	E3
West End	Hants	14	E4
West End	Hants	22	H7
West End	Herts	50	G9
West End	Herts	50	H9
West End	Lancs	89	L5
West End	Leeds	90	G3
West End	Lincs	93	Q11
West End	N Som	31	N11
West End	N York	91	N2
West End	Norfk	76	C10
West End	Norfk	77	Q9
West End	Oxon	34	G7
West End	S Glos	32	D7
West End	Somset	20	C8
West End	Surrey	23	P2
West End	Surrey	36	D8
West End	W & M	35	M9
West End	W Susx	24	F7
West End	Wilts	20	H10
West End	Wilts	21	J10
West End	Wilts	33	J9
West End Green	Hants	23	J2
Westend Town	Nthumb	111	Q7
Westenhanger	Kent	27	K4
Wester Aberchalder	Highld	147	P3
Westerdale	Highld	167	K6
Westerdale	N York	105	J9
Westerfield	Suffk	53	L2
Westergate	W Susx	15	P5
Westerham	Kent	37	K10
Westerhope	N u Ty	113	J7
Westerland	Devon	7	M6
Westerleigh	S Glos	32	C9
Western Isles	W Isls	168	f8
Wester Ochiltree	W Loth	127	J3
Wester Pitkierie	Fife	135	P6
Wester Ross	Highld	160	F11
Westerton	W Susx	15	N5
Westerton of Rossie	Angus	143	M7
Westerwick	Shet	169	p9
West Ewell	Surrey	36	F8
West Farleigh	Kent	38	B11
West Farndon	Nhants	48	F4
West Felton	Shrops	69	K9
Westfield	BaNES	20	C4
Westfield	Cumb	100	C5
Westfield	E Susx	26	D8
Westfield	Highld	167	J4
Westfield	N Lans	126	C3
Westfield	Norfk	76	D10
Westfield	W Loth	126	G3
Westfields	Dorset	12	B3
Westfields	Herefs	45	P6
Westfields of Rattray	P & K	142	B8
Westfield Sole	Kent	38	C9
West Flotmanby	N York	99	M5
Westford	Somset	18	F10
Westgate	Dur	102	H3
Westgate	N Linc	92	C9
Westgate	Norfk	76	D3
Westgate Hill	C Brad	90	G5
Westgate-on-Sea	Kent	39	P7
Westgate Street	Norfk	76	H7
West Ginge	Oxon	34	D7
West Grafton	Wilts	21	P2
West Green	Hants	23	K3
West Grimstead	Wilts	21	P9
West Grinstead	W Susx	24	E6
West Haddlesey	N York	91	P5
West Haddon	Nhants	60	D6
West Hagbourne	Oxon	34	F7
West Hagley	Worcs	58	D8
Westhall	Suffk	65	N5
West Hallam	Derbys	72	C2
West Hallam Common	Derbys	72	C2
West Halton	N Linc	92	F6
Westham	Dorset	11	P9
West Ham	Gt Lon	37	J4
Westham	E Susx	25	P10
Westham	Somset	19	M5
Westhampnett	W Susx	15	N5
West Handley	Derbys	84	E5
West Hanney	Oxon	34	D6
West Hanningfield	Essex	38	B2
West Harnham	Wilts	21	M9
West Harptree	BaNES	19	Q3
West Harting	W Susx	23	L10
West Hatch	Somset	19	J10
West Hatch	Wilts	20	H9
West Haven	Angus	143	K10
Westhay	Somset	19	M6
West Head	Norfk	75	L9
West Heath	Birm	58	F9
West Heath	Hants	22	G3
West Helmsdale	Highld	163	N10
West Hendred	Oxon	34	D7
West Heslerton	N York	99	J5
West Hewish	N Som	19	L2
Westhide	Herefs	46	A6
Westhill	Abers	151	L6
West Hill	Devon	9	Q6
Westhill	Highld	156	C9
West Hoathly	W Susx	25	J4
West Holme	Dorset	12	E7
Westholme	Somset	19	Q6
Westhope	Herefs	45	P4
Westhope	Shrops	56	H7
West Horndon	Essex	37	P3
Westhorp	Nhants	48	F4
Westhorpe	Lincs	74	D4
Westhorpe	Suffk	64	E8
West Horrington	Somset	19	Q5
West Horsley	Surrey	36	C10
West Horton	Nthumb	119	L4
West Hougham	Kent	27	N3
Westhoughton	Bolton	89	K9
Westhouse	N York	95	P6
Westhouses	Derbys	84	F9
West Howe	BCP	13	J5
West Howetown	Somset	18	B8
Westhumble	Surrey	36	E10
West Huntingtower	P & K	134	D2
West Huntspill	Somset	19	K6
West Hyde	C Beds	50	D7
West Hyde	Herts	36	B2
West Hythe	Kent	27	K5
West Ilkerton	Devon	17	N2
West Ilsley	W Berk	34	E8
West Itchenor	W Susx	15	L6
West Keal	Lincs	87	L8
West Kennett	Wilts	33	M11
West Kilbride	N Ayrs	124	G8
West Kingsdown	Kent	37	N8
West Kington	Wilts	32	F9
West Kirby	Wirral	81	J7
West Knapton	N York	98	H5
West Knighton	Dorset	12	B7
West Knoyle	Wilts	20	G8
West Kyloe	Nthumb	119	L2
Westlake	Devon	6	G8
West Lambrook	Somset	19	M11
Westland Green	Herts	51	K6
West Langdon	Kent	27	P2
West Lavington	W Susx	23	N10
West Lavington	Wilts	21	K4
West Layton	N York	103	M8
West Leake	Notts	72	E5
West Learmouth	Nthumb	118	F3
West Lees	N York	104	E10
West Leigh	Devon	8	G3
Westleigh	Devon	16	H6
Westleigh	Devon	18	E11
West Leigh	Somset	18	F8
Westleton	Suffk	65	N8
West Lexham	Norfk	76	A8
Westley	Shrops	56	F3
Westley	Suffk	63	P8
Westley Waterless	Cambs	63	K9
West Lilling	N York	98	C8
Westlington	Bucks	35	L2
West Linton	Border	127	M7
Westlinton	Cumb	110	G8
West Littleton	S Glos	32	E9
West Lockinge	Oxon	34	D7
West Lulworth	Dorset	12	D8
West Lutton	N York	99	J7
West Lydford	Somset	19	Q8
West Lyn	Devon	17	N2
West Lyng	Somset	19	K9
West Lynn	Norfk	75	M6
West Malling	Kent	37	Q9
West Malvern	Worcs	46	E5
West Marden	W Susx	15	L4
West Markham	Notts	85	M6
Westmarsh	Kent	39	N9
West Marsh	NE Lin	93	N9
West Marton	N York	96	C10
West Melbury	Dorset	20	G10
West Melton	Rothm	91	L10
West Meon	Hants	22	H10
West Meon Hut	Hants	23	J9
West Meon Woodlands	Hants	22	H9
West Mersea	Essex	52	H9
Westmeston	E Susx	24	H8
West Mickley	Nthumb	112	G8
West Midland Safari Park	Worcs	57	Q9
Westmill	Herts	50	H7
Westmill	Herts	51	J5
West Milton	Dorset	11	L5
West Minster	Kent	38	G5
Westminster Abbey & Palace	Gt Lon	36	G5
West Molesey	Surrey	36	D7
West Monkton	Somset	19	J9
West Moors	Dorset	13	J4
West Morden	Dorset	12	F5
West Morriston	Border	118	B2
West Morton	C Brad	90	D2
West Mudford	Somset	19	Q10
Westmuir	Angus	142	F7
West Ness	N York	98	D5
West Newbiggin	Darltn	104	C7
Westnewton	Cumb	100	F2
West Newton	E R Yk	93	M3
West Newton	Norfk	75	N5
West Newton	Somset	19	J9
West Norwood	Gt Lon	36	H6
Westoe	S Tyne	113	N7
West Ogwell	Devon	7	L4
Weston	BaNES	32	D11
Weston	Ches E	70	C4
Weston	Devon	10	C4
Weston	Devon	10	D7
Weston	Dorset	11	P10
Weston	Halton	81	Q8
Weston	Hants	23	K10
Weston	Herefs	45	M3
Weston	Herts	50	G4
Weston	Lincs	74	E6
Weston	N York	97	J11
Weston	Nhants	48	G5
Weston	Notts	85	N7
Weston	Shrops	56	E10
Weston	Shrops	57	L6
Weston	Shrops	69	J9
Weston	Staffs	70	H9
Weston	Suffk	65	N4
Weston	W Berk	34	C10
Weston Beggard	Herefs	46	A6
Westonbirt	Gloucs	32	G7
Weston by Welland	Nhants	60	G2
Weston Colley	Hants	22	F7
Weston Colville	Cambs	63	K10
Weston Corbett	Hants	23	J5
Weston Coyney	C Stke	70	G6
Weston Favell	Nhants	60	G8
Weston Green	Cambs	63	K10
Weston Heath	Shrops	57	P2
Weston Hills	Lincs	74	E6
Weston in Arden	Warwks	59	N7
Westoning	C Beds	50	B4
Weston-in-Gordano	N Som	31	M10
Westoning Woodend	C Beds	50	B4
Weston Jones	Staffs	70	D10
Weston Longville	Norfk	76	G8
Weston Lullingfields	Shrops	69	M10
Weston-on-Avon	Warwks	47	N4
Weston-on-the-Green	Oxon	48	F11
Weston Park	Staffs	57	Q2
Weston Patrick	Hants	23	J5
Weston Rhyn	Shrops	69	J7
Weston-sub-Edge	Gloucs	47	M6
Weston-super-Mare	N Som	19	K2
Weston Turville	Bucks	35	N3
Weston-under-Lizard	Staffs	57	Q2
Weston under Penyard	Herefs	46	B10
Weston-under-Redcastle	Shrops	69	Q9
Weston under Wetherley	Warwks	59	N11
Weston Underwood	Derbys	71	P6
Weston Underwood	M Keyn	49	N6
Weston-upon-Trent	Derbys	72	C5
Westonzoyland	Somset	19	L8
West Orchard	Dorset	20	F11
West Overton	Wilts	33	M11
Westow	N York	98	F7
West Panson	Devon	5	N3
West Park	Abers	151	K8
West Parley	Dorset	13	J5
West Peckham	Kent	37	P10
West Peeke	Devon	5	N3
West Pelton	Dur	113	K10
West Pennard	Somset	19	P7
West Pentire	Cnwll	4	B9
West Perry	Cambs	61	P7
West Pinchbeck	Lincs	74	D6
West Porlock	Somset	17	R2
Westport	Somset	19	L10
West Pulham	Dorset	11	Q3
West Putford	Devon	16	F8
West Quantoxhead	Somset	18	F6
Westquarter	Falk	126	G2
Westra	V Glam	30	F10
West Raddon	Devon	9	L4
West Rainton	Dur	113	M11
West Rasen	Lincs	86	E3
West Ravendale	NE Lin	93	M11
Westray	Ork	169	d2
Westray Airport	Ork	169	d1
West Raynham	Norfk	76	B7
West Retford	Notts	85	L4
Westridge Green	W Berk	34	G9
West Rigg	W Loth	126	G4
Westrop	Swindn	33	P6
West Rounton	N York	104	D10
West Row	Suffk	63	L5
West Rudham	Norfk	75	R5
West Runton	Norfk	76	H3
Westruther	Border	128	G3
Westry	Cambs	74	H11
West Saltoun	E Loth	128	C6
West Sandford	Devon	9	K4
West Sandwick	Shet	169	r5
West Scrafton	N York	96	G4
West Sleekburn	Nthumb	113	L4
West Somerton	Norfk	77	P7
West Stafford	Dorset	11	Q7
West Stockwith	Notts	92	C11
West Stoke	W Susx	15	M5
West Stonesdale	N York	102	G10
West Stoughton	Somset	19	M5
West Stour	Dorset	20	E10
West Stourmouth	Kent	39	N9
West Stow	Suffk	63	P6
West Stowell	Wilts	21	M2
West Stratton	Hants	22	F6
West Street	Kent	38	F11
West Street	Kent	39	P11
West Street	Medway	38	B6
West Street	Suffk	64	D7
West Tanfield	N York	97	L5
West Taphouse	Cnwll	5	K9
West Tarbert	Ag & B	123	Q6
West Tarring	W Susx	24	D10
West Thirston	Nthumb	119	N11
West Thorney	W Susx	15	L6
Westthorpe	Derbys	84	G5
West Thorpe	Notts	72	G5
West Thurrock	Thurr	37	N5
West Tilbury	Thurr	37	Q5
West Tisted	Hants	23	J9
West Torrington	Lincs	86	F4
West Town	BaNES	19	P2
West Town	Hants	15	K7
West Town	Herefs	45	N7
West Town	N Som	31	N11
West Town	Somset	19	P7
West Town	Somset	20	D6
West Tytherley	Hants	21	Q9
West Walton	Norfk	75	J8
Westward	Cumb	101	J2
Westward Ho!	Devon	16	G6
Westwell	Kent	26	G2
Westwell	Oxon	33	P3
Westwell Leacon	Kent	26	G2
West Wellow	Hants	21	Q11
West Wembury	Devon	6	E9
West Wemyss	Fife	135	J9
Westwick	Cambs	62	F7
Westwick	Dur	103	L7
West Wick	N Som	19	L2
Westwick	Norfk	77	K6
West Wickham	Cambs	63	K11
West Wickham	Gt Lon	37	J7
West Williamston	Pembks	41	K9
West Winch	Norfk	75	M7
West Winterslow	Wilts	21	P8
West Wittering	W Susx	15	L7
West Witton	N York	96	G3
Westwood	Devon	9	P5
Westwood	Kent	37	P6
Westwood	Kent	39	Q8
Westwood	Notts	84	G10
Westwood	Nthumb	111	Q7
Westwood	Wilts	20	F3
West Woodburn	Nthumb	112	C3
West Woodhay	W Berk	22	C2
Westwood Heath	Covtry	59	L9
West Woodlands	Somset	20	E6
Westwoodside	N Linc	92	B10
West Worldham	Hants	23	K7
West Worthing	W Susx	24	D10
West Wratting	Cambs	63	K10
West Wycombe	Bucks	35	M6
West Wylam	Nthumb	112	H8
West Yatton	Wilts	32	G9
West Yoke	Kent	37	P7
West Youlstone	Cnwll	16	D8
Wetham Green	Kent	38	D8
Wetheral	Cumb	111	J10
Wetherby	Leeds	97	P11
Wetherby Services	N York	97	P10
Wetherden	Suffk	64	E9
Wetheringsett	Suffk	64	G8
Wethersfield	Essex	52	B5
Wetherup Street	Suffk	64	G8
Wetley Rocks	Staffs	70	H5
Wettenhall	Ches E	69	R2
Wetton	Staffs	71	L3
Wetwang	E R Yk	99	J9
Wetwood	Staffs	70	D8
Wexcombe	Wilts	21	Q3
Wexham	Slough	35	Q8
Wexham Street	Bucks	35	Q8
Weybourne	Norfk	76	G3
Weybourne	Surrey	23	N5
Weybread	Suffk	65	J5
Weybread Street	Suffk	65	J5
Weybridge	Surrey	36	C8
Weycroft	Devon	10	G5
Weydale	Highld	167	L4
Weyhill	Hants	22	B5
Weymouth	Dorset	11	P9
Whaddon	Bucks	49	M8
Whaddon	Cambs	62	E11
Whaddon	Gloucs	32	F2
Whaddon	Wilts	20	G8
Whaddon	Wilts	21	N9
Whale	Cumb	101	P6
Whaley	Derbys	84	G6
Whaley Bridge	Derbys	83	M8
Whaley Thorns	Derbys	84	H6
Whaligoe	Highld	167	P8
Whalley	Lancs	89	L3
Whalley Banks	Lancs	89	L3
Whalsay	Shet	169	s7
Whalton	Nthumb	112	H4
Whaplode	Lincs	74	F6
Whaplode Drove	Lincs	74	F7
Wharf	Warwks	48	D4
Wharfe	N York	96	A7
Wharles	Lancs	88	E3
Wharley End	C Beds	49	P6
Wharncliffe Side	Sheff	84	C2
Wharram-le-Street	N York	98	H7
Wharton	Ches W	82	E11
Wharton	Herefs	45	Q3
Whashton	N York	103	N9
Whasset	Cumb	95	L4
Whatcote	Warwks	47	Q6
Whateley	Warwks	59	K5
Whatfield	Suffk	52	H2
Whatley	Somset	10	H3
Whatley	Somset	20	D5
Whatley's End	S Glos	32	C8
Whatlington	E Susx	26	C8
Whatsole Street	Kent	27	K3
Whatstandwell	Derbys	84	D10
Whatton-in-the-Vale	Notts	73	J3
Whauphill	D & G	107	M8
Whaw	N York	103	J10
Wheal Peevor	Cnwll	3	J5
Wheal Rose	Cnwll	3	J5
Wheatacre	Norfk	65	P3
Wheatfield	Oxon	35	J5
Wheathampstead	Herts	50	D7
Wheathill	Shrops	57	L8
Wheathill	Somset	19	Q8
Wheatley	Calder	90	D5
Wheatley	Hants	23	L6
Wheatley	Oxon	34	G3
Wheatley Hill	Dur	104	C3
Wheatley Hills	Donc	91	P10
Wheatley Lane	Lancs	89	N3
Wheaton Aston	Staffs	58	C2
Wheddon Cross	Somset	18	B7
Wheelbarrow Town	Kent	27	K2
Wheeler End	Bucks	35	M6
Wheeler's Green	Wokham	35	L10
Wheelerstreet	Surrey	23	P6
Wheelock	Ches E	70	D2
Wheelock Heath	Ches E	70	D3
Wheelton	Lancs	89	J6
Wheldale	Wakefd	91	M5
Wheldrake	C York	92	A2
Whelford	Gloucs	33	N5
Whelpley Hill	Bucks	35	Q4
Whelpo	Cumb	101	K3
Whelston	Flints	81	J9
Whempstead	Herts	50	H6
Whenby	N York	98	C7
Whepstead	Suffk	64	A10
Wherstead	Suffk	53	L3
Wherwell	Hants	22	C6
Wheston	Derbys	83	P9
Whetsted	Kent	37	Q11
Whetstone	Gt Lon	36	G4
Whetstone	Leics	72	F11
Wheyrigg	Cumb	110	C11
Whicham	Cumb	94	C4
Whichford	Warwks	48	B8
Whickham	Gatesd	113	K8
Whiddon	Devon	8	C5
Whiddon Down	Devon	8	G6
Whigstreet	Angus	142	H9
Whilton	Nhants	60	D8
Whimble	Devon	16	F11
Whimple	Devon	9	P5
Whimpwell Green	Norfk	77	M6
Whinburgh	Norfk	76	E10
Whin Lane End	Lancs	88	D2
Whinnieliggate	D & G	108	F10
Whinnow	Cumb	110	F10
Whinnyfold	Abers	159	Q11
Whinny Hill	S on T	104	C7
Whippingham	IoW	14	F8
Whipsnade	C Beds	50	B7
Whipsnade Zoo ZSL	C Beds	50	B7
Whipton	Devon	9	M6
Whirlow	Sheff	84	D4
Whisby	Lincs	86	B7
Whissendine	Rutlnd	73	L8
Whissonsett	Norfk	76	C7
Whistlefield	Ag & B	131	Q9
Whistlefield Inn	Ag & B	131	N9
Whistley Green	Wokham	35	L10
Whiston	Knows	81	P6
Whiston	Nhants	60	H8
Whiston	Rothm	84	F3
Whiston	Staffs	58	C2
Whiston	Staffs	71	J5
Whiston Cross	Shrops	57	P4
Whiston Eaves	Staffs	71	J5
Whitacre Fields	Warwks	59	L6
Whitbeck	Cumb	94	C4
Whitbourne	Herefs	46	D3
Whitbourne	S Tyne	113	P8
Whitburn	W Loth	126	G5
Whitby	Ches W	81	M9
Whitby	N York	105	M8
Whitbyheath	Ches W	81	M10
Whitchester	Border	129	J8
Whitchurch	BaNES	32	B11
Whitchurch	Bucks	49	M10
Whitchurch	Cardif	30	G9
Whitchurch	Devon	6	D4
Whitchurch	Hants	22	E5
Whitchurch	Herefs	45	R11
Whitchurch	Oxon	34	H9
Whitchurch	Pembks	40	F5
Whitchurch	Shrops	69	P6
Whitchurch Canonicorum	Dorset	10	H5
Whitchurch Hill	Oxon	34	H9
Whitcombe	Dorset	11	Q7
Whitcot	Shrops	56	F6
Whitcott Keysett	Shrops	56	D8
Whiteacre	Kent	27	K2
Whiteacre Heath	Warwks	59	K6
Whiteash Green	Essex	52	C5
White Ball	Somset	18	F11
Whitebridge	Highld	147	M4
Whitebrook	Mons	31	P3
Whitebushes	Surrey	36	G11
Whitecairns	Abers	151	N4
Whitechapel	Gt Lon	36	H4
White Chapel	Lancs	88	H2
Whitechurch	Pembks	41	N3
Whitecliff	Gloucs	31	Q3
White Colne	Essex	52	E6
White Coppice	Lancs	89	J7
Whitecraig	E Loth	127	Q3
Whitecroft	Gloucs	32	B3
Whitecrook	D & G	106	G6
Whitecross	Cnwll	2	E7
White Cross	Cnwll	2	H9
Whitecross	Cnwll	4	F7
Whitecross	Falk	126	H2
White End	Worcs	46	E8
Whiteface	Highld	162	G9
Whitefarland	N Ayrs	120	G3
Whitefaulds	S Ayrs	114	E6
Whitefield	Bury	89	N9
Whitefield	Devon	17	N4
Whitefield	Somset	18	E9
Whitefield Lane End	Knows	81	P7
Whitefield	Abers	151	J2
Whitegate	Ches W	82	D11
Whitehall	Hants	23	K4
Whitehall	Ork	169	f4
Whitehall	W Susx	24	D6
Whitehaven	Cumb	100	C7
Whitehill	Kent	38	H10
Whitehill	Leics	72	C8
Whitehill and Bordon	Hants	23	L8
Whitehills	Abers	158	G4
Whitehouse	Abers	150	G5
Whitehouse	Ag & B	123	Q5
Whitehouse Common	Birm	58	H5
Whitekirk	E Loth	128	F3
White Kirkley	Dur	103	K3
White Lackington	Dorset	11	Q5
Whitelackington	Somset	19	L11
White Ladies Aston	Worcs	46	H4
Whiteleaf	Bucks	35	M4
White-le-Head	Dur	113	J10
Whiteley Bank	IoW	14	F10
Whiteley Green	Ches E	83	K9
Whiteley Village	Surrey	36	C8
Whitemans Green	W Susx	24	H5
White Mill	Carmth	43	J10
Whitemire	Moray	156	H7
Whitemoor	C Nott	72	E2
Whitemoor	Cnwll	4	F10
Whitemoor	Derbys	84	E11
Whitemoor	Staffs	70	F2
Whiteness	Shet	169	q9
White Notley	Essex	52	C8

Whiteoak Green Oxon...34 B2
White Ox Mead BaNES...20 D3
Whiteparish Wilts...21 P10
White Pit Lincs...87 L5
Whiterashes Abers...151 M3
White Roding Essex...51 N8
Whiterow Highld...167 Q7
Whiterow Moray...157 J6
Whiteshill Gloucs...32 F3
Whitesmith E Susx...25 M8
White Stake Lancs...88 G5
Whitestaunton Somset...10 F2
White Stone Herefs...45 R6
Whitestone Devon...9 L6
Whitestone Cross Devon...9 L6
Whitestreet Green Suffk...52 G4
Whitewall Corner N York...98 F7
White Waltham W & M...35 M9
Whiteway BaNES...20 D2
Whiteway Gloucs...32 H2
Whitewell Lancs...95 P11
Whiteworks Devon...6 G4
Whitfield C Dund...142 G11
Whitfield Kent...27 P2
Whitfield Nhants...48 H7
Whitfield Nthumb...111 Q9
Whitfield S Glos...32 C6
Whitfield Hall Nthumb...111 Q9
Whitford Devon...10 F5
Whitford Flints...80 G9
Whitgift E R Yk...92 D6
Whitgreave Staffs...70 G9
Whithorn D & G...107 M9
Whiting Bay N Ayrs...121 K6
Whitkirk Leeds...91 K4
Whitland Carmth...41 N7
Whitlaw Border...117 Q8
Whitletts S Ayrs...114 G3
Whitley N York...91 P6
Whitley Readg...35 K10
Whitley Sheff...84 D2
Whitley Wilts...32 G11
Whitley Bay N Tyne...113 N6
Whitley Chapel Nthumb...112 D9
Whitley Heath Staffs...70 E9
Whitley Lower Kirk...90 G7
Whitley Row Kent...37 L10
Whitlock's End Solhll...58 H9
Whitminster Gloucs...32 E3
Whitmore Dorset...13 J3
Whitmore Staffs...70 E6
Whitnage Devon...18 D11
Whitnash Warwks...48 B2
Whitney-on-Wye Herefs...45 K5
Whitrigg Cumb...100 H3
Whitrigg Cumb...110 D9
Whitrigglees Cumb...110 D9
Whitsbury Hants...21 M11
Whitsome Border...129 M9
Whitson Newpt...31 L4
Whitstable Kent...39 K8
Whitstone Cnwll...5 M2
Whittingham Nthumb...119 L8
Whittingslow Shrops...56 G7
Whittington Derbys...84 E5
Whittington Gloucs...47 K10
Whittington Lancs...95 N5
Whittington Norfk...75 P11
Whittington Shrops...69 K8
Whittington Staffs...58 C8
Whittington Staffs...59 J3
Whittington Warwks...59 L5
Whittington Worcs...46 G4
Whittington Moor Derbys...84 E6
Whittlebury Nhants...49 J6
Whittle-le-Woods Lancs...88 H6
Whittlesey Cambs...74 E11
Whittlesford Cambs...62 G11
Whittlestone Head Bl w D...89 L7
Whitton N Linc...92 F6
Whitton Nthumb...119 L10
Whitton Powys...56 D11
Whitton S on T...104 C6
Whitton Shrops...57 K10
Whitton Suffk...53 K2
Whittonditch Wilts...33 Q10
Whittonstall Nthumb...112 G9
Whitway Hants...22 E4
Whitwell Derbys...84 H5
Whitwell Herts...50 E6
Whitwell IoW...14 F11
Whitwell N York...103 N10
Whitwell Rutlnd...73 N9
Whitwell-on-the-Hill N York...98 E7
Whitwell Street Norfk...76 H7
Whitwick Leics...72 C7
Whitwood Wakefd...91 L6
Whitworth Lancs...89 P7
Whixall Shrops...69 P8
Whixley N York...97 P9
Whorlton Dur...103 M8
Whorlton N York...104 E10
Whyle Herefs...45 R2
Whyteleafe Surrey...36 H9
Wibdon Gloucs...31 Q5
Wibsey C Brad...90 E4
Wibtoft Warwks...59 Q7
Wichenford Worcs...46 E2
Wichling Kent...38 F10
Wick BCP...13 L6
Wick Devon...10 D4
Wick Highld...167 Q6
Wick S Glos...32 D10
Wick Somset...18 H6
Wick Somset...19 M9
Wick V Glam...29 P10
Wick W Susx...24 B10
Wick Wilts...21 N10
Wick Worcs...47 J5
Wicken Cambs...63 J6
Wicken Nhants...49 K7
Wicken Bonhunt Essex...51 L4
Wickenby Lincs...86 E4
Wick End Bed...49 Q4
Wicken Green Village Norfk...76 A5
Wickersley Rothm...84 G2
Wicker Street Green Suffk...52 G4
Wickford Essex...38 B3
Wickham Hants...14 G4
Wickham W Berk...34 C10
Wickham Bishops Essex...52 D9
Wickhambreaux Kent...39 M10
Wickhambrook Suffk...63 N10
Wickhamford Worcs...47 L6

Wickham Green Suffk...64 F8
Wickham Green W Berk...34 D10
Wickham Heath W Berk...34 D11
Wickham Market Suffk...65 L10
Wickhampton Norfk...77 N10
Wickham St Paul Essex...52 D4
Wickham Skeith Suffk...64 F8
Wickham Street Suffk...63 N10
Wickham Street Suffk...64 F8
Wickhurst Green W Susx...24 D4
Wick John o' Groats Airport Highld...167 Q6
Wicklewood Norfk...76 F11
Wickmere Norfk...76 H5
Wick St Lawrence N Som...31 L11
Wicksteed Park Nhants...61 J5
Wickstreet E Susx...25 M9
Wickwar S Glos...32 D7
Widdington Essex...51 M4
Widdop Calder...89 Q4
Widdrington Nthumb...119 Q11
Widdrington Station Nthumb...113 K2
Widecombe in the Moor Devon...8 H9
Widegates Cnwll...5 M10
Widemouth Bay Cnwll...16 C11
Wide Open N Tyne...113 K6
Widford Essex...51 Q10
Widford Herts...51 K7
Widham Wilts...33 L7
Widley Hants...15 J5
Widmer End Bucks...35 N5
Widmerpool Notts...72 G5
Widmore Gt Lon...37 K7
Widnes Halton...81 Q7
Widworthy Devon...10 E5
Wigan Wigan...88 H9
Wigborough Somset...19 M11
Wiggaton Devon...10 C6
Wiggenhall St Germans Norfk...75 L8
Wiggenhall St Mary Magdalen Norfk...75 L8
Wiggenhall St Mary the Virgin Norfk...75 L8
Wiggens Green Essex...51 Q2
Wiggenstall Staffs...71 K2
Wigginton Shrops...69 K7
Wigginton C York...98 C9
Wigginton Herts...35 P2
Wigginton Oxon...48 C8
Wigginton Staffs...59 K3
Wigginton Bottom Herts...35 P3
Wigglesworth N York...96 B9
Wiggonby Cumb...110 E10
Wiggonholt W Susx...24 C7
Wighill N York...97 Q11
Wighton Norfk...76 C4
Wightwick Wolves...58 C5
Wigley Derbys...84 D6
Wigley Hants...22 B11
Wigmore Herefs...56 G11
Wigmore Medway...38 C9
Wigsley Notts...85 Q6
Wigsthorpe Nhants...61 M4
Wigston Leics...72 G11
Wigston Fields Leics...72 G10
Wigston Parva Leics...59 Q7
Wigthorpe Notts...85 J4
Wigtoft Lincs...74 E3
Wigton Cumb...110 E11
Wigtown D & G...107 M6
Wigtwizzle Sheff...90 G11
Wike Leeds...91 J2
Wilbarston Nhants...60 H3
Wilberfoss E R Yk...98 E10
Wilburton Cambs...62 G5
Wilby Nhants...61 J7
Wilby Norfk...64 E4
Wilby Suffk...65 J7
Wilcot Wilts...21 M2
Wilcott Shrops...69 L11
Wilcrick Newpt...31 M7
Wilday Green Derbys...84 D6
Wildboarclough Ches E...83 L11
Wilden Bed...61 N9
Wilden Worcs...58 B10
Wilde Street Suffk...63 N5
Wildhern Hants...22 C4
Wildhill Herts...50 G9
Wildmanbridge S Lans...126 E7
Wildmill Brdgnd...29 P8
Wildmoor Hants...23 J3
Wildmoor Worcs...58 E9
Wildsworth Lincs...92 D11
Wilford C Nott...72 F3
Wilkesley Ches E...70 A6
Wilkhaven Highld...163 L9
Wilkieston W Loth...127 L4
Wilkin's Green Herts...50 E9
Wilksby Lincs...87 J8
Willand Devon...9 P2
Willards Hill E Susx...26 B6
Willaston Ches E...70 B4
Willaston Ches W...81 L9
Willen M Keyn...49 N6
Willenhall Covtry...59 N9
Willenhall Wsall...58 E5
Willerby E R Yk...92 H4
Willerby N York...99 L5
Willersey Gloucs...47 M7
Willersley Herefs...45 L5
Willesborough Kent...26 H3
Willesborough Lees Kent...26 H3
Willesden Gt Lon...36 F4
Willesleigh Devon...17 L5
Willesley Wilts...32 G7
Willett Somset...18 F8
Willey Shrops...57 M5
Willey Warwks...59 Q8
Willey Green Surrey...23 P4
Williamscot Oxon...48 E5
Williamstown Rhondd...30 D6
Willian Herts...50 F4
Willicote Warwks...47 N4
Willingale Essex...51 N9
Willingdon E Susx...25 N10
Willingham Cambs...62 F6
Willingham by Stow Lincs...85 Q4
Willingham Green Cambs...63 K10
Willingham St Mary Suffk...65 N5
Willington Bed...61 P10
Willington Derbys...71 P9

Willington Dur...103 N3
Willington Kent...38 C11
Willington N Tyne...113 M7
Willington Warwks...47 Q7
Willington Corner Ches W...82 B11
Willitoft E R Yk...92 B4
Williton Somset...18 E6
Willoughby Lincs...87 N6
Willoughby Warwks...60 B7
Willoughby-on-the-Wolds Notts...72 G5
Willoughby Waterleys Leics...60 C2
Willoughton Lincs...86 B2
Willow Green Ches W...82 D9
Willows Green Essex...52 B8
Willsbridge S Glos...32 C10
Willsworthy Devon...8 D8
Willtown Somset...19 L10
Wilmcote Warwks...47 N3
Wilmington BaNES...20 C2
Wilmington Devon...10 E5
Wilmington E Susx...25 M10
Wilmington Kent...37 M6
Wilmslow Ches E...82 H8
Wilnecote Staffs...59 K4
Wilpshire Lancs...89 K4
Wilsden C Brad...90 D3
Wilsford Lincs...73 Q2
Wilsford Wilts...21 M3
Wilsford Wilts...21 M7
Wilsham Devon...17 P2
Wilshaw Kirk...90 E9
Wilsill N York...97 J8
Wilsley Green Kent...26 C4
Wilsley Pound Kent...26 C4
Wilson Herefs...45 R10
Wilson Leics...72 C6
Wilsontown S Lans...126 G6
Wilstead Bed...50 C2
Wilsthorpe Lincs...74 A8
Wilstone Herts...35 P2
Wilstone Green Herts...35 P2
Wilton Cumb...100 D8
Wilton Herefs...46 A10
Wilton N York...98 H4
Wilton R & Cl...104 G7
Wilton Wilts...21 L8
Wilton Wilts...21 Q2
Wilton Dean Border...117 P8
Wimbish Essex...51 N3
Wimbish Green Essex...51 P3
Wimbledon Gt Lon...36 F6
Wimblington Cambs...62 F2
Wimboldsley Ches W...70 B2
Wimborne Minster Dorset...12 H5
Wimborne St Giles Dorset...12 H2
Wimbotsham Norfk...75 M9
Wimpole Cambs...62 E11
Wimpstone Warwks...47 P5
Wincanton Somset...20 D9
Winceby Lincs...87 K7
Wincham Ches W...82 E9
Winchburgh W Loth...127 K3
Winchcombe Gloucs...47 K9
Winchelsea E Susx...26 F8
Winchelsea Beach E Susx...26 F8
Winchester Hants...22 E9
Winchester Services Hants...22 F7
Winchet Hill Kent...26 B3
Winchfield Hants...23 L4
Winchmore Hill Bucks...35 P5
Winchmore Hill Gt Lon...36 H2
Wincle Ches E...83 L11
Wincobank Sheff...84 E2
Winder Cumb...100 D7
Windermere Cumb...101 M11
Windermere Jetty Cumb...101 M11
Winderton Warwks...48 B6
Windhill Highld...155 P8
Windlehurst Stockp...83 L7
Windlesham Surrey...23 P2
Windmill Cnwll...4 D7
Windmill Derbys...83 Q9
Windmill Hill E Susx...25 P8
Windmill Hill Somset...19 K11
Windrush Gloucs...33 N2
Windsole Abers...158 E5
Windsor W & M...35 Q9
Windsor Castle W & M...35 Q9
Windsoredge Gloucs...32 F4
Windsor Green Suffk...64 B11
Windygates Fife...135 J7
Windyharbour Ches E...82 H10
Windy Hill Wrexhm...69 K4
Wineham W Susx...24 F6
Winestead E R Yk...93 N6
Winewall Lancs...89 Q2
Winfarthing Norfk...64 G4
Winford IoW...14 G10
Winford N Som...19 P2
Winforton Herefs...45 K5
Winfrith Newburgh Dorset...12 D8
Wing Bucks...49 N10
Wing Rutlnd...73 M10
Wingate Dur...104 D3
Wingates Bolton...89 K9
Wingates Nthumb...119 L11
Wingerworth Derbys...84 E7
Wingfield C Beds...50 B5
Wingfield Suffk...65 J6
Wingfield Wilts...20 G4
Wingfield Green Suffk...65 J6
Wingham Kent...39 M10
Wingland Lincs...75 J6
Wingmore Kent...27 L2
Wingrave Bucks...49 N11
Winkburn Notts...85 M9
Winkfield Br For...35 P10
Winkfield Row Br For...35 N10
Winkhill Staffs...71 K4
Winkhurst Green Kent...37 L11
Winkleigh Devon...17 L11
Winksley N York...97 L6
Winkton BCP...13 L5
Winlaton Gatesd...113 J8
Winlaton Mill Gatesd...113 J8
Winless Highld...167 Q6
Winllan Powys...68 H10
Winmarleigh Lancs...95 K11
Winnall Hants...22 E9
Winnersh Wokham...35 L11
Winnington Ches W...82 D10
Winscales Cumb...100 D5
Winscombe N Som...19 M3

Winsford Ches W...82 E11
Winsford Somset...18 B8
Winsham Devon...17 J4
Winsham Somset...10 H3
Winshill Staffs...71 P10
Winshwen Swans...29 J5
Winskill Cumb...101 Q4
Winslade Hants...23 J5
Winsley Wilts...20 E2
Winslow Bucks...49 L9
Winson Gloucs...33 L3
Winsor Hants...13 P2
Winster Cumb...95 J2
Winster Derbys...84 B8
Winston Dur...103 M7
Winston Suffk...64 H9
Winstone Gloucs...33 J3
Winswell Devon...16 H9
Winterborne Came Dorset...11 Q7
Winterborne Clenston Dorset...12 D4
Winterborne Herringston Dorset...11 P7
Winterborne Houghton Dorset...12 D4
Winterborne Kingston Dorset...12 E5
Winterborne Monkton Dorset...11 P7
Winterborne Stickland Dorset...12 D4
Winterborne Tomson Dorset...12 E5
Winterborne Whitechurch Dorset...12 D4
Winterborne Zelston Dorset...12 E5
Winterbourne S Glos...32 B8
Winterbourne W Berk...34 E10
Winterbourne Abbas Dorset...11 N6
Winterbourne Bassett Wilts...33 L10
Winterbourne Dauntsey Wilts...21 N8
Winterbourne Earls Wilts...21 N8
Winterbourne Gunner Wilts...21 N7
Winterbourne Monkton Wilts...33 L10
Winterbourne Steepleton Dorset...11 N7
Winterbourne Stoke Wilts...21 L6
Winterbrook Oxon...34 H7
Winterburn N York...96 D9
Winteringham N Linc...92 F6
Winterley Ches E...70 C3
Wintersett Wakefd...91 K7
Winterslow Wilts...21 P8
Winterton N Linc...92 F7
Winterton-on-Sea Norfk...77 P8
Winthorpe Lincs...87 Q7
Winthorpe Notts...85 P9
Winton BCP...13 J6
Winton Cumb...102 E8
Winton E Susx...25 M10
Winton N York...104 D11
Wintringham N York...98 H6
Winwick Cambs...61 P4
Winwick Nhants...60 D6
Winwick Warrtn...82 D6
Wirksworth Derbys...71 P4
Wirral...81 K7
Wirswall Ches E...69 P6
Wisbech Cambs...75 J9
Wisbech St Mary Cambs...74 H9
Wisborough Green W Susx...24 C5
Wiseman's Bridge Pembks...41 M9
Wiseton Notts...85 M3
Wishanger Gloucs...32 H3
Wishaw N Lans...126 D6
Wishaw Warwks...59 J6
Wisley Surrey...36 C9
Wisley Garden RHS Surrey...36 C9
Wispington Lincs...86 H6
Wissenden Kent...26 F3
Wissett Suffk...65 M6
Wissington Norfk...75 N11
Wistanstow Shrops...56 G7
Wistanswick Shrops...70 B9
Wistaston Ches E...70 B3
Wistaston Green Ches E...70 B4
Wisterfield Ches E...82 H10
Wiston Pembks...41 K7
Wiston S Lans...116 D4
Wiston W Susx...24 D8
Wistow Cambs...62 C4
Wistow Leics...72 G11
Wistow N York...91 P3
Wiswell Lancs...89 L3
Witcham Cambs...62 G4
Witchampton Dorset...12 G3
Witchford Cambs...62 H5
Witcombe Somset...19 N10
Witham Essex...52 D9
Witham Friary Somset...20 D6
Witham on the Hill Lincs...73 R7
Witham St Hughs Lincs...85 Q8
Withcall Lincs...87 J4
Withdean Br & H...24 H9
Witherenden Hill E Susx...25 P5
Witheridge Devon...9 K2
Witherley Leics...72 A11
Withern Lincs...87 M4
Withernsea E R Yk...93 P5
Withernwick E R Yk...93 L2
Withersdale Street Suffk...65 K5
Withersfield Suffk...63 L11
Witherslack Cumb...95 J4
Withiel Cnwll...4 F8
Withiel Florey Somset...18 C8
Withielgoose Cnwll...4 G8
Withington Gloucs...47 K11
Withington Herefs...45 R6
Withington Manch...82 H6
Withington Shrops...57 K2
Withington Staffs...71 J7
Withington Green Ches E...82 H10
Withington Marsh Herefs...45 R6
Withleigh Devon...9 M2
Withnell Lancs...89 J6
Withnell Fold Lancs...89 J6
Withybed Green Worcs...58 F10
Withybrook Warwks...59 P8
Withycombe Somset...18 D6
Withyham E Susx...25 L3
Withy Mills BaNES...20 C3
Withypool Somset...17 Q4
Withywood Bristl...31 Q11

Witley Surrey...23 P7
Witnesham Suffk...64 H11
Witney Oxon...34 C2
Wittering C Pete...73 R10
Wittersham Kent...26 F6
Witton Birm...58 G6
Witton Norfk...77 L10
Witton Norfk...77 L5
Witton Gilbert Dur...113 K11
Witton Green Norfk...77 M11
Witton le Wear Dur...103 M4
Witton Park Dur...103 M4
Wiveliscombe Somset...18 E9
Wivelrod Hants...23 J7
Wivelsfield E Susx...24 H6
Wivelsfield Green E Susx...25 J7
Wivelsfield Station W Susx...24 H7
Wivenhoe Essex...52 H7
Wivenhoe Cross Essex...52 H7
Wiveton Norfk...76 E3
Wix Essex...53 L6
Wixams Bed...50 C2
Wixford Warwks...47 L4
Wix Green Essex...53 L6
Wixhill Shrops...69 Q9
Wixoe Suffk...52 B3
Woburn C Beds...49 P8
Woburn Safari Park C Beds...49 Q8
Woburn Sands M Keyn...49 P7
Wokefield Park W Berk...35 J11
Woking Surrey...36 B9
Wokingham Wokham...35 M11
Wolborough Devon...7 M4
Woldingham Surrey...37 J9
Wold Newton E R Yk...99 L6
Wold Newton NE Lin...93 M11
Wolfclyde S Lans...116 E3
Wolferlow Herefs...46 C2
Wolferton Norfk...75 N5
Wolfhampcote Warwks...60 B7
Wolfhill P & K...142 B11
Wolf Hills Nthumb...111 P9
Wolf's Castle Pembks...41 J5
Wolfsdale Pembks...40 H6
Wollaston Dudley...58 C8
Wollaston Nhants...61 K8
Wollaston Shrops...56 E2
Wollaton C Nott...72 E3
Wollaton Hall & Park C Nott...72 E3
Wolleigh Devon...9 K8
Wollerton Shrops...69 R8
Wollescote Dudley...58 D8
Wolseley Bridge Staffs...71 J10
Wolsingham Dur...103 L3
Wolstanton Staffs...70 F5
Wolstenholme Rochdl...89 N8
Wolston Warwks...59 P9
Wolsty Cumb...109 P10
Wolvercote Oxon...34 E2
Wolverhampton Wolves...58 D5
Wolverhampton Halfpenny Green Airport Staffs...58 B6
Wolverley Shrops...69 N8
Wolverley Worcs...58 B9
Wolverton Hants...22 G3
Wolverton Kent...27 N3
Wolverton M Keyn...49 M6
Wolverton Warwks...47 P2
Wolverton Wilts...20 E8
Wolverton Common Hants...22 G3
Wolvesnewton Mons...31 N5
Wolvey Warwks...59 P7
Wolvey Heath Warwks...59 P7
Wolviston S on T...104 E5
Wombleton N York...98 D4
Wombourne Staffs...58 C6
Wombwell Barns...91 L10
Womenswold Kent...39 M11
Womersley N York...91 N7
Wonastow Mons...31 N2
Wonersh Surrey...36 B11
Wonford Devon...9 M6
Wonson Devon...8 G7
Wonston Dorset...12 B3
Wonston Hants...22 E7
Wooburn Bucks...35 P7
Wooburn Green Bucks...35 P7
Wooburn Moor Bucks...35 P7
Woodacott Devon...16 F10
Woodale N York...96 F5
Woodall Rothm...84 G4
Woodall Services Rothm...84 G4
Woodbank Ches W...81 M10
Woodbastwick Norfk...77 L8
Woodbeck Notts...85 N5
Wood Bevington Warwks...47 L4
Woodborough Notts...85 K11
Woodborough Wilts...21 M3
Woodbridge Devon...10 D5
Woodbridge Dorset...20 G11
Woodbridge Suffk...53 N2
Wood Burcote Nhants...49 J5
Woodbury Devon...9 P7
Woodbury Salterton Devon...9 P7
Woodchester Gloucs...32 F4
Woodchurch Kent...26 F5
Woodchurch Wirral...81 K7
Woodcombe Somset...18 C5
Woodcote Gt Lon...36 G8
Woodcote Oxon...34 H8
Woodcote Wrekin...70 D11
Woodcote Green Worcs...58 D10
Woodcott Hants...22 D4
Woodcroft Gloucs...31 P5
Woodcutts Dorset...21 J11
Wood Dalling Norfk...76 F6
Woodditton Cambs...63 L9
Woodeaton Oxon...34 F2
Wood Eaton Staffs...70 E11
Wooden Pembks...41 M9
Wood End Bed...61 M11
Wood End Bed...61 N7
Wood End C Beds...49 Q6
Wood End Cambs...62 C5
Wood End Gt Lon...36 D4
Wood End Herts...50 H5
Woodend Highld...138 D5
Woodend Nhants...48 H5
Woodend Staffs...71 M9
Woodend W Loth...126 G4
Wood End W Susx...15 M5
Wood End Warwks...58 H10
Wood End Warwks...59 K5
Wood End Warwks...59 L7
Wood End Wolves...58 D4

Wood Enderby Lincs....87 J8
Woodend Green Essex....51 N5
Woodfalls Wilts....21 N10
Woodford Cnwll....16 C9
Woodford Devon....7 K8
Woodford Gloucs....32 C5
Woodford Gt Lon....37 K2
Woodford Nhants....61 L5
Woodford Stockp....83 J8
Woodford Bridge Gt Lon....37 K2
Woodford Green Gt Lon....37 K2
Woodford Halse Nhants....48 F4
Woodford Wells Gt Lon....37 K2
Woodgate Birm....58 E8
Woodgate Devon....18 F11
Woodgate Norfk....76 B8
Woodgate Norfk....76 E8
Woodgate W Susx....15 P6
Woodgate Worcs....58 E11
Wood Green Gt Lon....36 H2
Woodgreen Hants....21 N11
Woodgreen Oxon....34 C2
Woodhall N York....96 E2
Woodhall Hill Leeds....90 G3
Woodhall Spa Lincs....86 G8
Woodham Bucks....49 K11
Woodham Dur....103 Q5
Woodham Surrey....36 B8
Woodham Ferrers Essex....38 C2
Woodham Mortimer Essex....52 D11
Woodham Walter Essex....52 D10
Wood Hayes Wolves....58 D4
Woodhead Abers....159 J10
Woodhill Shrops....57 N8
Woodhill Somset....19 L9
Woodhorn Nthumb....113 L3
Woodhorn Demesne Nthumb....113 M3
Woodhouse Leeds....90 H4
Woodhouse Leics....72 E8
Woodhouse Sheff....84 F4
Woodhouse Wakefd....91 K6
Woodhouse Eaves Leics....72 E8
Woodhouse Green Staffs....70 G2
Woodhouselee Mdloth....127 N5
Woodhouselees D & G....110 G6
Woodhouse Mill Sheff....84 F3
Woodhouses Cumb....110 F10
Woodhouses Oldham....83 K4
Woodhouses Staffs....58 G3
Woodhouses Staffs....71 M11
Woodhuish Devon....7 N8
Woodhurst Cambs....62 D5
Woodingdean Br & H....25 J9
Woodkirk Leeds....90 H5
Woodland Abers....151 M3
Woodland Devon....6 G7
Woodland Devon....7 K5
Woodland Dur....103 L5
Woodland Kent....27 K3
Woodland S Ayrs....114 C8
Woodland Head Devon....9 J5
Woodlands Abers....151 K8
Woodlands Donc....91 N9
Woodlands Dorset....13 J3
Woodlands Hants....13 P2
Woodlands Kent....37 N8
Woodlands N York....97 M10
Woodlands Somset....18 G6
Woodlands Park W & M....35 N9
Woodlands St Mary W Berk....34 B9
Woodland Street Somset....19 P7
Woodland View Sheff....84 D3
Wood Lane Shrops....69 M8
Wood Lane Staffs....70 E5
Woodleigh Devon....7 J9
Woodlesford Leeds....91 K5
Woodley Stockp....83 K6
Woodley Wokham....35 L10
Woodmancote Gloucs....32 E5
Woodmancote Gloucs....33 K3
Woodmancote Gloucs....47 J9
Woodmancote W Susx....15 L5
Woodmancote W Susx....24 F8
Woodmancote Worcs....46 H6
Woodmancott Hants....22 G6
Woodmansey E R Yk....93 J3
Woodmansgreen W Susx....23 N9
Woodmansterne Surrey....36 G9
Woodmanton Devon....9 P7
Woodmarsh Wilts....20 G3
Woodmill Staffs....71 L10
Woodminton Wilts....21 K10
Woodnesborough Kent....39 P10
Woodnewton Nhants....61 M2
Woodnook Notts....84 G10
Wood Norton Norfk....76 E6
Woodplumpton Lancs....88 F4
Woodrising Norfk....76 D11
Wood Row Leeds....91 K5
Woodrow Worcs....58 C9
Wood's Corner E Susx....25 Q7
Woods Eaves Herefs....45 K5
Woodseaves Shrops....70 B8
Woodseaves Staffs....70 D9
Woodsend Wilts....33 P9
Woodsetts Rothm....84 H4
Woodsford Dorset....12 C6
Wood's Green E Susx....25 P4
Woodside Br For....35 P10
Woodside Cumb....100 C4
Woodside Essex....51 L10
Woodside Fife....135 L6
Woodside Gt Lon....36 H7
Woodside Hants....13 P6
Woodside Herts....50 F9
Woodside P & K....142 C10
Woodside Green Kent....38 F11
Woodstock Oxon....48 D11
Woodstock Pembks....41 K5
Woodston C Pete....74 C11
Wood Street Norfk....77 M7
Wood Street Village Surrey....23 Q4
Woodthorpe Derbys....84 G6
Woodthorpe Leics....72 E7
Woodthorpe Lincs....87 M4
Woodton Norfk....65 K3
Woodtown Devon....16 G7
Woodvale Sefton....88 C8
Woodville Derbys....71 Q11
Wood Walton Cambs....62 B4
Woodyates Dorset....21 K11
Woody Bay Devon....17 M2
Woofferton Shrops....57 J11

Wookey Somset....19 P5
Wookey Hole Somset....19 P5
Wool Dorset....12 D7
Woolacombe Devon....16 H3
Woolage Green Kent....27 M2
Woolage Village Kent....39 M11
Woolaston Gloucs....31 Q5
Woolaston Common Gloucs....31 Q4
Woolavington Somset....19 K6
Woolbeding W Susx....23 N10
Woolbrook Devon....10 C7
Woolcotts Somset....18 C8
Wooldale Kirk....90 F9
Wooler Nthumb....119 J5
Woolfardisworthy Devon....9 K3
Woolfardisworthy Devon....16 E7
Woolfold Bury....89 M8
Woolfords S Lans....127 J6
Woolhampton W Berk....34 G11
Woolhope Herefs....46 B7
Woolland Dorset....12 C3
Woollard BaNES....20 B2
Woollensbrook Herts....51 J9
Woolley BaNES....32 D11
Woolley Cambs....61 Q6
Woolley Cnwll....16 D8
Woolley Derbys....84 E8
Woolley Wakefd....91 J8
Woolley Bridge Derbys....83 M6
Woolley Edge Services Wakefd....91 J8
Woolley Green W & M....35 M8
Woolmere Green Worcs....47 J2
Woolmer Green Herts....50 G7
Woolmerston Somset....19 J8
Woolminstone Somset....11 J3
Woolpack Kent....26 E4
Woolpit Suffk....64 D9
Woolpit Green Suffk....64 D9
Woolscott Warwks....60 B7
Woolsgrove Devon....9 J4
Woolsington N u Ty....113 J6
Woolstaston Shrops....56 H5
Woolsthorpe by Belvoir Lincs....73 L4
Woolsthorpe-by-Colsterworth Lincs....73 N6
Woolston C Soth....14 D4
Woolston Devon....7 J10
Woolston Devon....7 J8
Woolston Shrops....56 G7
Woolston Shrops....69 K10
Woolston Somset....18 E7
Woolston Somset....20 C9
Woolston Warrtn....82 D7
Woolstone Gloucs....47 J8
Woolstone M Keyn....49 N7
Woolstone Oxon....33 Q7
Woolston Green Devon....7 K5
Woolton Lpool....81 N7
Woolton Hill Hants....22 D2
Woolverstone Suffk....53 L4
Woolverton Somset....20 E4
Woolwich Gt Lon....37 K5
Woonton Herefs....45 M4
Woonton Herefs....45 R2
Wooperton Nthumb....119 J5
Woore Shrops....70 C6
Wootten Green Suffk....65 J7
Wootton Bed....50 B2
Wootton Hants....13 M5
Wootton Herefs....45 L4
Wootton IoW....14 F8
Wootton Kent....27 M2
Wootton N Linc....93 J7
Wootton Nhants....60 G9
Wootton Oxon....34 E4
Wootton Oxon....48 D11
Wootton Shrops....69 K9
Wootton Staffs....71 E9
Wootton Staffs....71 L6
Wootton Bassett Wilts....33 L8
Wootton Bridge IoW....14 F8
Wootton Broadmead Bed....50 B2
Wootton Common IoW....14 F8
Wootton Courtenay Somset....18 B6
Wootton Fitzpaine Dorset....10 H5
Wootton Rivers Wilts....21 N2
Wootton St Lawrence Hants....22 G4
Wootton Wawen Warwks....47 N2
Worcester Worcs....46 G4
Worcester Park Gt Lon....36 F7
Wordsley Dudley....58 C7
Worfield Shrops....57 P5
Worgret Dorset....12 F7
Workhouse End Bed....61 P10
Workhouse Green Suffk....52 F4
Workington Cumb....100 D5
Worksop Notts....85 J5
Worlaby Lincs....87 K5
Worlaby N Linc....92 H8
Worlds End Bucks....35 N3
Worlds End Hants....14 H4
World's End W Berk....34 E9
Worlds End W Susx....24 H6
Worle N Som....19 L2
Worleston Ches E....70 B3
Worlingham Suffk....65 N4
Worlington Devon....9 J2
Worlington Suffk....63 L6
Worlingworth Suffk....65 J8
Wormald Green N York....97 M7
Wormbridge Herefs....45 N7
Wormegay Norfk....75 N8
Wormelow Tump Herefs....45 P8
Wormhill Derbys....83 P10
Wormhill Herefs....45 N7
Wormingford Essex....52 F5
Worminghall Bucks....34 H3
Wormington Gloucs....47 K7
Worminster Somset....19 Q6
Wormit Fife....135 L2
Wormleighton Warwks....48 E4
Wormley Herts....51 J9
Wormley Surrey....23 P7
Wormley Hill Donc....91 R7
Wormshill Kent....38 E10
Wormsley Herefs....45 N5
Worplesdon Surrey....23 Q4
Worrall Sheff....84 D2
Worrall Hill Gloucs....32 B2
Worsbrough Barns....91 K10
Worsbrough Bridge Barns....91 K10
Worsbrough Dale Barns....91 K10

Worsley Salfd....82 G4
Worstead Norfk....77 L6
Worsthorne Lancs....89 P4
Worston Devon....6 F8
Worston Lancs....89 M2
Worth Kent....39 P10
Worth Somset....19 P5
Worth W Susx....24 H3
Wortham Suffk....64 F6
Worthen Shrops....56 E4
Worthenbury Wrexhm....69 M5
Worthing Norfk....76 D8
Worthing W Susx....24 D10
Worthington Leics....72 C6
Worth Matravers Dorset....12 G9
Worthybrook Mons....31 N3
Worting Hants....22 G4
Wortley Barns....91 J11
Wortley Gloucs....32 E6
Wortley Leeds....90 H4
Worton N York....96 E3
Worton Wilts....21 J3
Wortwell Norfk....65 K5
Wotherton Shrops....56 D4
Wothorpe C Pete....73 Q9
Wotter Devon....6 F6
Wotton Surrey....36 D11
Wotton-under-Edge Gloucs....32 E6
Wotton Underwood Bucks....49 J11
Woughton on the Green M Keyn....49 N7
Wouldham Kent....38 B9
Woundale Shrops....57 P6
Wrabness Essex....53 L5
Wrafton Devon....16 H4
Wragby Lincs....86 F5
Wragby Wakefd....91 L7
Wramplingham Norfk....76 G10
Wrangaton Devon....6 H7
Wrangbrook Wakefd....91 M8
Wrangle Lincs....87 M10
Wrangle Common Lincs....87 M10
Wrangle Lowgate Lincs....87 M10
Wrangway Somset....18 F11
Wrantage Somset....19 K10
Wrawby N Linc....92 H9
Wraxall N Som....31 N10
Wraxall Somset....20 B7
Wray Lancs....95 N7
Wray Castle Cumb....101 L10
Wraysbury W & M....36 B6
Wrayton Lancs....95 N6
Wrea Green Lancs....88 D4
Wreaks End Cumb....94 E3
Wreay Cumb....101 M6
Wreay Cumb....110 H11
Wrecclesham Surrey....23 M6
Wrekenton Gatesd....113 L9
Wrelton N York....98 F3
Wrenbury Ches E....69 Q5
Wrench Green N York....99 K3
Wreningham Norfk....64 H2
Wrentham Suffk....65 P5
Wrenthorpe Wakefd....91 J6
Wrentnall Shrops....56 G4
Wressle E R Yk....92 B4
Wressle N Linc....92 G9
Wrestlingworth C Beds....62 C11
Wretton Norfk....75 N10
Wrexham Wrexhm....69 K4
Wrexham Industrial Estate Wrexhm....69 L4
Wribbenhall Worcs....57 P9
Wrickton Shrops....57 L7
Wrightington Bar Lancs....88 G8
Wright's Green Essex....51 M7
Wrinehill Staffs....70 D5
Wrington N Som....19 N2
Writhlington BaNES....20 C4
Writtle Essex....51 Q9
Wrockwardine Wrekin....57 L2
Wroot N Linc....92 B10
Wrose C Brad....90 F3
Wrotham Kent....37 P9
Wrotham Heath Kent....37 P9
Wrottesley Staffs....58 B4
Wroughton Swindn....33 M8
Wroxall IoW....14 G11
Wroxall Warwks....59 K10
Wroxeter Shrops....57 K3
Wroxham Norfk....77 L8
Wroxton Oxon....48 D6
Wyaston Derbys....71 M6
Wyatt's Green Essex....51 N11
Wyberton Lincs....74 F2
Wyboston Bed....61 Q9
Wybunbury Ches E....70 B5
Wychbold Worcs....58 D11
Wych Cross E Susx....25 K4
Wychnor Staffs....71 M11
Wychwood Ches E....70 C4
Wyck Hants....23 L7
Wyck Rissington Gloucs....47 N10
Wycliffe Dur....103 M8
Wycoller Lancs....89 Q3
Wycomb Leics....73 K6
Wycombe Marsh Bucks....35 N6
Wyddial Herts....51 J4
Wye Kent....27 J2
Wyesham Mons....31 P2
Wyfordby Leics....73 K7
Wyke C Brad....90 F5
Wyke Devon....9 J5
Wyke Devon....10 F5
Wyke Dorset....20 E9
Wyke Shrops....57 L4
Wyke Surrey....23 P4
Wyke Champflower Somset....20 C8
Wykeham N York....99 K4
Wyken Covtry....59 N8
Wyken Shrops....57 P4
Wyke Regis Dorset....11 P9
Wykey Shrops....69 L10
Wykin Leics....72 C11
Wylam Nthumb....112 H8
Wylde Green Birm....58 H6
Wylye Wilts....21 K7
Wymeswold Leics....72 G6
Wymington Bed....61 L8
Wymondham Leics....73 L7
Wymondham Norfk....76 G11
Wyndham Brdgnd....29 P6
Wynford Eagle Dorset....11 M5
Wynyard Park S on T....104 D5
Wynyard Village S on T....104 D5

Wyre Piddle Worcs....47 J5
Wysall Notts....72 G5
Wyson Herefs....57 J11
Wythall Worcs....58 G9
Wytham Oxon....34 E3
Wythburn Cumb....101 K8
Wythenshawe Manch....82 H7
Wythop Mill Cumb....100 H3
Wyton Cambs....62 C6
Wyton E R Yk....93 L4
Wyverstone Suffk....64 E8
Wyverstone Street Suffk....64 E8
Wyville Lincs....73 M5

Y

Yaddlethorpe N Linc....92 E9
Yafford IoW....14 D10
Yafforth N York....97 M2
Yalberton Torbay....7 M7
Yalding Kent....37 Q10
Yanwath Cumb....101 P5
Yanworth Gloucs....33 L2
Yapham E R Yk....98 F10
Yapton W Susx....15 Q6
Yarborough N Som....19 L3
Yarbridge IoW....14 H9
Yarburgh Lincs....87 L2
Yarcombe Devon....10 E3
Yard Devon....17 P7
Yardley Birm....58 H7
Yardley Gobion Nhants....49 L5
Yardley Hastings Nhants....61 J9
Yardley Wood Birm....58 H9
Yardro Powys....45 J3
Yarford Somset....18 H9
Yarkhill Herefs....46 B6
Yarley Somset....19 P6
Yarlington Somset....20 C9
Yarm S on T....104 D8
Yarmouth IoW....14 C9
Yarnacott Devon....17 L3
Yarnbrook Wilts....20 G4
Yarner Devon....9 J8
Yarnfield Staffs....70 F8
Yarnscombe Devon....17 K7
Yarnton Oxon....34 E2
Yarpole Herefs....45 P2
Yarrow Border....117 M5
Yarrow Somset....19 L5
Yarrow Feus Border....117 L5
Yarrowford Border....117 N4
Yarsop Herefs....45 N5
Yarwell Nhants....73 R11
Yate S Glos....32 D8
Yateley Hants....23 M2
Yatesbury Wilts....33 L10
Yattendon W Berk....34 G10
Yatton Herefs....56 G11
Yatton N Som....31 M11
Yatton Keynell Wilts....32 G9
Yaverland IoW....14 H9
Yawl Devon....10 G6
Yawthorpe Lincs....85 Q2
Yaxham Norfk....76 E9
Yaxley Cambs....61 Q2
Yaxley Suffk....64 G7
Yazor Herefs....45 N5
Yeading Gt Lon....36 D4
Yeadon Leeds....90 G2
Yealand Conyers Lancs....95 L6
Yealand Redmayne Lancs....95 L5
Yealand Storrs Lancs....95 K5
Yealmbridge Devon....6 F8
Yealmpton Devon....6 F8
Yearby R & Cl....104 G6
Yearngill Cumb....100 F2
Yearsley N York....98 B6
Yeaton Shrops....69 M11
Yeaveley Derbys....71 M6
Yeavering Nthumb....118 H4
Yedingham N York....98 H5
Yelford Oxon....34 C4
Yell Shet....169 r5
Yelland Devon....16 H5
Yelling Cambs....62 C8
Yelvertoft Nhants....60 C5
Yelverton Devon....6 E5
Yelverton Norfk....77 K11
Yenston Somset....20 D10
Yeoford Devon....9 J5
Yeolmbridge Cnwll....5 N4
Yeo Mill Devon....17 Q6
Yeo Vale Devon....16 G7
Yeovil Somset....19 Q11
Yeovil Marsh Somset....19 P11
Yeovilton Somset....19 P10
Yerbeston Pembks....41 L9
Yesnaby Ork....169 b5
Yetlington Nthumb....119 K9
Yetminster Dorset....11 M2
Yetson Devon....7 L7
Yettington Devon....9 Q7
Yetts o'Muckhart Clacks....134 C7
Yews Green C Brad....90 D4
Yew Tree Sandw....58 F5
Y Felinheli Gwynd....79 J11
Y Ferwig Cerdgn....42 C5
Y Ffôr Gwynd....66 F7
Yielden Bed....61 M7
Yieldingtree Worcs....58 C9
Yieldshields S Lans....126 F7
Yiewsley Gt Lon....36 C4
Y Nant Wrexhm....69 J4
Ynysboeth Rhondd....30 E5
Ynysddu Caerph....30 G5
Ynysforgan Swans....29 J5
Ynyshir Rhondd....30 D6
Ynyslas Cerdgn....54 E6
Ynysmaerdy Rhondd....30 D8
Ynysmeudwy Neath....29 K3
Ynystawe Swans....29 J4
Ynyswen Powys....29 M2
Ynyswen Rhondd....30 C5
Ynysybwl Rhondd....30 E6
Ynysymaengwyn Gwynd....54 D4
Yockenthwaite N York....96 D5
Yockleton Shrops....56 F2
Yokefleet E R Yk....92 D6
Yoker C Glas....125 N4
York C York....98 C10
York Lancs....89 L4
Yorkletts Kent....39 J9

Yorkley Gloucs....32 B3
Yorkshire Dales National Park....96 C5
York Town Surrey....23 N2
Yorton Heath Shrops....69 P10
Youlgreave Derbys....84 B8
Youlthorpe E R Yk....98 F9
Youlton N York....97 Q8
Youngsbury Herts....51 J7
Young's End Essex....52 B8
Yoxall Staffs....71 L11
Yoxford Suffk....65 M8
Y Rhiw Gwynd....66 C9
Ysbyty Cynfyn Cerdgn....54 H9
Ysbyty Ifan Conwy....67 Q5
Ysbyty Ystwyth Cerdgn....54 G10
Ysceifiog Flints....80 H10
Ysgubor-y-Coed Cerdgn....54 F5
Ystalyfera Neath....29 L3
Ystrad Rhondd....30 C5
Ystrad Aeron Cerdgn....43 K3
Ystradfellte Powys....29 P2
Ystrad Ffin Carmth....43 Q5
Ystradgynlais Powys....29 L2
Ystrad Meurig Cerdgn....54 G11
Ystrad Mynach Caerph....30 F6
Ystradowen V Glam....30 D9
Ystumtuen Cerdgn....54 G9
Ythanbank Abers....159 M11
Ythanwells Abers....158 F10
Ythsie Abers....159 L11

Z

Zeal Monachorum Devon....8 H4
Zeals Wilts....20 E8
Zelah Cnwll....3 L3
Zennor Cnwll....2 D6
Zoar Cnwll....3 K10
Zouch Notts....72 E6
ZSL London Zoo Gt Lon....36 G4
ZSL Whipsnade Zoo C Beds....50 B7